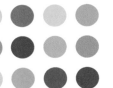

Take the
CESIM Global Challenge!

Students need more than theories alone to understand all the complexities of the international business world. With **CESIM: Global Challenge Simulation** (http://globalchallenge.cesim.com), students develop their decision-making skills when faced with choices on product differentiation, production sites, price options, and exchange rate fluctuations in three different world markets. Using the familiar personal digital assistant (PDA)

industry as a platform, students compete against each other on a global scale, learn how global business principles play out in the real world, and have fun in the process! CESIM creates a truly dynamic classroom environment where students learn to think and act like strategic global managers.

Discover more international business study tools, exercises, and resources online at the *International Business* Online Learning Center, **www.mhhe.com/ball11e**.

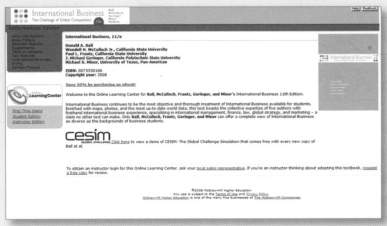

- Self-grading quizzes
- Chapter review material
- GlobalEDGE™/CIBER Research Tasks—use Web resources to solve international business problems
- Business Around the World Atlas—click on an area on the map to access regional data
- Concept Exercises—interactive exercises with dynamic graphic demonstrations of key concepts
- iGlobe—view "on-demand" PBS videos on breaking stories related to international business

Do Not Throw Away!

Welcome to the CESIM Global Challenge Simulation!

Experience the real world of truly interactive business simulation experience. During the simulation you will manage a global telecommunications company through fast-paced technological evolution and compete with your classmates on the simulated markets.

Your personal license code is:

YOS4QWJPLNGL

To access the CESIM Global Challenge:

- Use a Web browser to go to **http://globalchallenge.cesim.com** or follow the link on the text Web site **http://www.mhhe.com/ball11e**

- Choose "Play the Game as a Student" and the registration starts.

- Enter the course code given to you by your instructor.

- Enter your personal license code exactly as it appears on this card.

- Fill in the other required information and choose your personal password and login.
  NOTE: you need to give a valid e-mail address as your login. This e-mail address will be used during the game to inform you about important deadlines and other necessary information.

Later you can access the system and play the game by just entering your login and password on the main page. You can also view the CESIM Global Challenge demo by choosing Demo on the main page (recommended 56-kbps or faster connection).

After you have registered and filled in all of the required information, you are guided through the rest of the set-up procedure. During the set-up procedure you are asked to choose your team, view schedule notes and read the game intro. Just follow the instructions on the screen.

Fine tune your teamwork skills and get ready to use everything you know about international business management!

Good luck!
CESIM Team and McGraw-Hill/Irwin

ISBN-13: 978-0-07-334434-8
MHID: 0-07-334434-6

International Business
The Challenge of Global Competition

Donald A. Ball

Wendell H. McCulloch, Jr.

J. Michael Geringer

Michael S. Minor

Jeanne M. McNett

11e

McGraw-Hill
Irwin

Boston   Burr Ridge, IL   Dubuque, IA   Madison, WI   New York   San Francisco   St. Louis
Bangkok   Bogotá   Caracas   Kuala Lumpur   Lisbon   London   Madrid   Mexico City
Milan   Montreal   New Delhi   Santiago   Seoul   Singapore   Sydney   Taipei   Toronto

**McGraw-Hill
Irwin**

INTERNATIONAL BUSINESS: THE CHALLENGE OF GLOBAL COMPETITION

Published by McGraw-Hill/Irwin, a business unit of The McGraw-Hill Companies, Inc., 1221 Avenue of the Americas, New York, NY, 10020.

2 3 4 5 6 7 8 9 0 WCK/WCK 0 9 8 7

ISBN 978-0-07-353016-1
MHID 0-07-353016-6

Editorial director: *John E. Biernat*
Managing developmental editor: *Laura Hurst Spell*
Associate marketing manager: *Margaret A. Beamer*
Media producer: *Greg Bates*
Project manager: *Marlena Pechan*
Senior production supervisor: *Carol A. Bielski*
Senior designer: *Kami Carter*
Photo research coordinator: *Lori Kramer*
Media project manager: *Joyce J. Chappetto*
Typeface: *10.5/12 Times Roman*
Compositor: *Laserwords Private Limited, Chennai, India*
Printer: *Quebecor World Versailles Inc.*

Library of Congress Cataloging-in-Publication Data
International business : the challenge of global competition / Donald A. Ball . . . [et al.]. — 11th ed.
    p. cm.
  Includes index.
  ISBN 978-0-07-353016-1 (alk. paper)
  MHID 0-07-353016-6 (alk. paper)
  1. International business enterprises—Management. 2. International business enterprises.
  3. International economic relations. I. Ball, Donald A.
  HD62.4.B34 2008
  658'.049—dc22

                                                   2006100721

Mike dedicates this edition to his parents, Ray and JoAnn, and his partner, Barbara, who have provided continued support and encouragement for his writing and other life activities.

Michael dedicates this edition to his wife, Karen, and mother, Mary Ruth, both of whom passed away during the development of the eleventh edition.

Jeanne dedicates this edition to her finance professor, N. D. Quy, to her best friends, Nick Athanassiou and Raven McCrory, and to her research friends, ION.

About the Authors

Don A. Ball

Don A. Ball, a consultant to multinational corporations, was a professor of marketing and international business for several years after leaving industry. He has a degree in mechanical engineering from Ohio State and a doctorate in business administration from the University of Florida. Ball has published articles in the *Journal of International Business Studies* and other publications. Before obtaining his doctorate, he spent 15 years in various marketing and production management positions in Mexico, South America, and Europe.

Wendell H. McCulloch, Jr.

Wendell H. McCulloch, Jr., has been a professor of international business, finance, and law and is the former director of international business programs at California State University, Long Beach. He earned a bachelor's degree in economics at George Washington University and a JD from Yale University. He has published articles in *The Wall Street Journal,* the *Journal of International Business Studies,* and the *Collegiate Forum.* The results of McCulloch's research have appeared in publications by the Joint Economic Committee of the U.S. Congress and the Heritage Foundation. Before beginning his academic career, McCulloch spent 19 years as an executive for American and European multinationals that offered banking, insurance, and investment products in many countries. He was associate general counsel of International General Electric, headquartered in New York; member of the board of directors and general counsel of International General Electric, S.A., headquartered in Geneva; and cofounder and president of Trust of Properties, an investment fund, headquartered in London and Zurich.

J. Michael Geringer

J. Michael Geringer is a professor of strategy and international management at California Polytechnic University in San Luis Obispo. He earned a BS in business at Indiana University and MBA and PhD degrees at the University of Washington. He has authored or edited 14 books and monographs, over 110 published papers, and over 35 case studies; he serves on the editorial boards of several leading international academic journals; he served as the Saastamoinen Foundation Chair at the Helsinki School of Economics in Finland; he was the founding chair of the Strategic Alliances Committee of the Licensing Executives Society; he served as the chair of both the International Business and the Strategy and Policy divisions of the Administrative Sciences Association of Canada; and he is past chairperson of the Academy of Management's International Management division. His research has appeared in the *Strategic Management Journal, Academy of Management Journal, Journal of International Management, Columbia Journal of World Business, Management International Review, Journal of Management Studies, Human Resource Management Journal, Long Range Planning, Organisation Studies,* and *Journal of Applied Psychology,* among others. He has received 11 "best paper" awards for his research, including the Decade Award for most influential article from the *Journal of International Business Studies.* His teaching performance has earned numerous awards in the United States, Canada, Asia, Africa, Australia, and Europe, including the University Distinguished Teacher Award. He was the first recipient of the International Educator Award from Cal Poly, and he endowed a scholarship for students to work and study internationally. He has been active in a range of charitable and service activities, including spearheading the adoption of a school in Soweto, South Africa, and fundraising for public radio. In addition to working with universities around the world, Geringer is active in consulting and executive development for multinational corporations and executives from six continents. His clients have included Nokia; Lucent; Eastman Kodak; Sonera;

Northern Telecom; Rautaruukki; Eastman Chemical; UPM Kymmene; Industry, Science & Technology Canada; Jiangsu Telecom Industrial; California Highway Patrol; Economic Council of Canada; Perlos; YIT; California Department of Transportation; and Okobank, among others. For relaxation, he enjoys daily Stairmaster workouts, along with hiking, camping, gardening, cooking spicy vegetarian foods, and music.

Michael S. Minor

Michael S. Minor is a professor of marketing and international business at the University of Texas, Pan American. He was educated at the University of North Carolina, American University, and Cornell and holds a PhD from Vanderbilt University. His research focuses on comparative consumer behavior, international marketing strategy, political risk, and the consumption of high-technology experiential products. He has published in the *Journal of International Business Studies,* the *Journal of Consumer Marketing, International Studies of Management and Organization,* the *Journal of Services Marketing, International Business Review, Journal of Interactive Advertising,* and elsewhere. He has written for business and popular media from *PCWeek* to *Tennessee Business Magazine.* He is past chairperson of the Consumer Behavior Special Interest Group and past vice chair of the Technology and Marketing Special Interest Group of the American Marketing Association, as well as a former member of the Global Marketing SIG's board of directors. He is active in DOCNET, the association of business doctoral program administrators. He serves on multiple editorial advisory boards and is the coauthor with John C. Mowen of several consumer behavior books. He has won multiple master's-level teaching awards and was recently the doctoral program professor of the year. His consulting experience includes work for UNCTAD's Division on Investment, Technology and Enterprise Development and several U.S. and state government agencies. He has reviewed grant proposals for the Research Council of Norway as well as several U.S. agencies. He lived in Asia for a number of years and speaks Chinese. He relaxes by playing the mandolin and harmonica for the country/classic rock groups RiverRock and Coastlands.

Jeanne M. McNett

Jeanne M. McNett is a professor of management at Assumption College, in Worcester, Massachusetts. She earned a PhD at the University of Massachusetts, Amherst, and an MBA at the Cass School of Business, City University, London. She has had expatriate assignments in Germany, the United Kingdom, Saudi Arabia, Japan, and Korea. Her interests include the role of culture in international business and the pedagogy of international management. Her publications include the *Blackwell Encyclopedia of Management, Vol. VI: International Management,* second edition (Oxford, UK: Blackwell Publishing, 2005), and the *Blackwell Handbook of Global Management* (Oxford, UK: Blackwell Publishing, 2004). Her teaching, research, and presentations have received many awards, including the Roethlisberger Best Paper of the Year Award from the *Journal of Management Education* and the Alpha Phi Alpha Teacher of the Year Award. Her articles have been included in journals and collections focused on teaching in the area of international business. She is an avid master rower and enjoys running, reading, and gardening.

We are pleased to present the eleventh edition of *International Business: The Challenge of Global Competition.*

Purpose and Scope of This Text

Whether students are advanced undergraduates or are in MBA programs, an international business course is an ideal venue for a varied number of questions. Our hope is that this book will answer these questions about business in different cultures, the impact of geography, why products are the same (or different) across cultures, why people have different practices, the effect of the Internet on international business, and many, many more. There are always new questions, and sometimes there are new answers to old questions.

International Business 11/e is organized into four sections in order to maximize its utility to instructors and students alike. The opening section defines the nature of international business and the three environments in which it is conducted. Section Two is devoted to the continuing importance of international organizations and the international monetary system and how both affect business. Section Three focuses on the uncontrollable forces at work in all business environments and discusses their inevitable impact on business practice. We devote the final section of the book to a discussion of how managers deal with all the forces affecting international business. In the eleventh edition, we have continued section opening dialogues to help students better understand what they have learned and are about to learn.

Changes for the Eleventh Edition

With each new edition we have been blessed by an expanding network of those making helpful suggestions. Professors, reviewers, and business professionals who bought the book or received it at a conference and our own graduate and undergraduate students have made useful and constructive comments. We believe that *International Business 11/e* continues to offer you a solid and superior text infused with current topics relevant to current challenges. In this edition, we have extensively revised and updated the material in each chapter to reflect recent world events and new international business issues.

As with every new edition, tables, figures, and graphs have been updated to include the most current data available as of the publication of this text. Keeping an international business text topical and current is a challenge, and we have worked hard to provide you with the most recent information possible. We have also updated examples where relevant and replaced dated examples where appropriate. We have reorganized Chapter 4 to increase its focus on international institutions that influence international business. Chapter 12 ("Labor Forces") and Chapter 20 ("Human Resource Management") have been completely reorganized to avoid redundancies and better focus their respective content. The chapter on organizational design and control (Chapter 14) has been moved so that it follows directly after the discussion of strategy, reflecting suggestions of reviewers and users. As a result, the numbering and ordering of Chapters 15 through 21 have been modified slightly to improve the organization and flow of content. Chapter 21 has been renamed "Financial Management and Accounting" to emphasize an increased emphasis on issues of international accounting in addition to financial management.

Chapter 1   The Rapid Change of International Business

The opening case on the importance of international business experience has been updated and expanded; the popular Worldview box on buying American has been updated; new and updated examples have been added throughout the chapter to enhance understanding of key issues; the discussion of definitions and terminology has been refocused and is now more concise; discussion of the history of international business has been enhanced; the Worldview on the debate on globalization of trade and investment has been revised; and a new mini-case exercise has been added at the end of the chapter dealing with the ownership and nationality associated with many well-known companies and brands.

Chapter 2 International Trade and Foreign Direct Investment

This is a shorter, more focused chapter with an updated introduction and discussion of trade in goods and services. The data on international trade and investment have been updated throughout the chapter, to the most current figures available at the time of publication, and the presentation of these data has been improved to enhance the reader's ability to analyze and understand trends and traits of international trade and investment. Discussion of small and medium-size enterprises and their role in exporting has been updated and enhanced. There is a new Worldview box that examines how trade and investment impact economic and social development, as well as an enhanced Worldview examining why more investment does not flow to Africa. The discussion of maquiladoras has been fundamentally revised and made more concise, and the end-of-chapter minicase on a Mexican company trying to remain competitive in the face of emerging low-cost competition from China has been updated.

Chapter 3 Theories of International Trade and Investment

In Chapter 3 we have revised, reorganized, and clarified the discussion of theories of international trade and added new examples in order to facilitate student comprehension of these topics. Discussion has been added on imperfect competition as a theoretical explanation of trade; the Worldview on comparative advantage and offshoring of service jobs to India has been updated and enhanced; discussion of trade restrictions has been substantially updated, and new examples and discussion of sanctions have been added; and the Worldview on subsidies to the sugar industry has been updated. The discussion of theories of foreign investment has been substantially expanded and reorganized, including new discussion of theories such as financial factors and dynamic capabilities and expanded discussion of internalization and the eclectic theory. A new minicase added at the end of the chapter addresses issues associated with fair trade in cocoa and the use of child labor in Africa.

Chapter 4 International Institutions from an International Business Perspective

Chapter 4 has been renamed to reflect its more focused orientation, including an increased emphasis on the usefulness of international institutions for international business. The chapter's organization has been modified to reflect the political, economic, and shared purposes of the various international institutions. The United Nations' Millennium goals have been included, along with a progress report regarding their attainment. Cooperative military agreements (e.g., NATO) have been included as a type of political institution. Discussion of NAFTA, the World Trade Organization, the European Union, and OPEC has been expanded. A new Worldview has been added on the uneven benefits of trade.

Chapter 5 Understanding the International Monetary System

We have added more discussion on the historical background of the gold standard; added a section on the connection between monetary systems and terrorism; and modified the coverage of the IMF to focus on its contributions to trade growth. We have added an explanation of the Triffin paradox, and there is a new discussion of Jeffrey Sachs's challenges to the IMF. Other changes include additional discussion of the historical background of the emergence of the floating rate system; additional descriptions of the major currency arrangements and their users; and an expanded explanation of balance of payments.

Chapter 6 Sociocultural Forces

Chapter 6 emphasizes the critical area of culture as an uncontrolled force that influences international business. To enhance the chapter's focus, discussion of education has been moved to Chapter 12 ("Labor Forces"). We carefully reedited the section on religion and particularly the material dealing with Islam, after consulting with Muslims from several different national backgrounds. The Worldview on Disneyland has been updated. Information on changes in the South Korean workweek, as well as information on South Korea as an international leader in design, has been added. A new minicase has been added on the wine industry in India.

Chapter 7   Natural Resources and Environmental Sustainability

This chapter has been updated and expanded to better address the increasingly important areas of environmental sustainability and sustainable business. Changes include the use of Porter's diamond as a framework for discussing geographic factor conditions. China, Afghanistan, and Latin America have been added to the chapter's discussion, as well as an expanded section on natural resources. Further additions to the chapter include a consideration of the connection between innovation and factor conditions, a section on environmental sustainability, a review of the stakeholder model for sustainable business, and examples of sustainable businesses.

Chapter 8   Economic and Socioeconomic Forces

This chapter opens with an updated reflection of the reality of India's middle class—increasingly well-to-do and with a penchant for "getting ahead." A new section addresses levels of economic development, to help the reader understand how economic development is categorized by different institutions, and a new Worldview discusses characteristics of developing nations. The discussion of economic development indicators such as gross national income (GNI) and GNI/capita has been updated and expanded. There is a new discussion of the limitations of GNI-based measures, such as the underground economy and currency conversions. A new Worldview has been added that discusses new approaches to the assessment of economic development, such as the human-needs approach and the United Nations' Human Development Index, including a list of the top- and bottom-ranked nations on this index. Figures, tables, and examples have been updated throughout the chapter in order to provide current, relevant support for the concepts being discussed. There are two minicases at the end of the chapter to provide relevant opportunities to apply the concepts in a practical manner.

Chapter 9   Political Forces

In this chapter we examine the renationalization of Bolivia's natural gas industry and discuss the more general leftward turn in several Latin American countries. At the same time, we note the continued shrinkage of communism as, for example, China's millionaires continue to multiply. The section on terrorism reflects recent developments relevant to international business, and a new mini-MNE box discusses the resiliency of businesses and people in the face of hostilities. The material on international debt crises has been removed, and examples throughout the chapter have been updated to enhance comprehension of issues associated with political forces.

Chapter 10   Legal Forces

Chapter 10's discussion of legal forces has been revised to make the content more international and less U.S.-centric. We have eliminated the discussion of the dual court system of the United States. The section on taxation of expatriates has been updated and simplified, and the section on litigation has been made less U.S.-centric and shorter. New material has been introduced on the issue of a harmonized bankruptcy code. Examples in the chapter have been updated as well. A new section explores career prospects for those with a specialization in international law. The emerging issue of "patent trolls" is introduced.

Chapter 11   Financial Forces

Chapter 11 covers the rapidly changing and largely uncontrollable financial forces that are important to international businesspeople. The chapter has been reorganized to focus on exchange rates; their quotation, fluctuation, and forecasting; and then balance-of-payments accounts and other external financial forces. Euro-US$ relationships are used in many of the examples. The chapter contains an expanded discussion of why currencies fluctuate; a new discussion of the law of one price; an added discussion of parity relationships, the Fisher effect, and purchasing power parity; and an expanded section on exchange rate forecasting. We have added discussion of currency exchange controls, tariffs, and taxation and have expanded the discussion on inflation. There is a new Worldview on the effect of foreign aid in developing countries.

Chapter 12 Labor Forces

Labor is a critical element of all business. Labor's role in international business has become increasingly salient as a consequence of globalization and outsourcing. This chapter has been completely reorganized and refocused to avoid redundancies with the chapter on human resource management (Chapter 20) and to update and emphasize key labor issues relevant to international business. There are new examples, as well as new and updated data, throughout the chapter. We have included a new opening case example on differences in labor conditions in Japan and China. The discussion on labor conditions and trends has been revised and refocused, including discussion of the overall size and sector of a nation's work force, aging of populations, the shift of populations from rural to urban areas, unemployment considerations across nations and regions, the issue of immigrant labor and labor mobility, including brain drain, and considerations associated with child labor and forced labor. We have included a new mini-MNE box on the role of small business in generating jobs internationally. We have updated the Worldview on guest workers in Japan; updated and expanded the discussion of sexism in international business; and prepared a more concise and focused discussion of labor unions and their role internationally.

Chapter 13 International Competitive Strategy

Chapter 13 introduces Section Four, on the organizational environment. We have included a new opening case on the use of scenario planning to help manage the strategic uncertainties associated with international business activities. The discussion has been expanded on why firms need to engage in strategic planning if they want to compete successfully in international markets. Throughout the chapter, we have included new and updated examples to promote the reader's comprehension of international strategy concepts and tools. There is an expanded discussion, with examples, of mission, vision, and values statements and their role in international strategy. The use of quantitative and qualitative objectives in international strategic planning activities has been updated. There is an expanded discussion of the typology of multidomestic, global, and transnational strategies for international business, as well as a new section discussing home replication strategies. We have included a new Worldview on regional strategies for competing internationally. The discussion has been revised and expanded on the issue of managing standardization in international strategy, as well as on the use of scenarios in international strategy formulation. We have added a new section on performance measurement in international strategy and have updated the discussion on approaches and trends in the use of strategic planning for international business, including who is involved in the planning and what is incorporated in planning processes. There is an updated discussion of sources and techniques for competitor assessment. The minicase on Wal-Mart's internationalization efforts at the end of the chapter has been updated to include the company's failures in Korea and Germany, its efforts to dramatically expand operations in China through acquisitions and internal growth, and its strategic plans to enter India and other emerging markets.

Chapter 14 Organizational Design and Control

The discussion of organizational design and control in international business has been moved so that it now follows directly after the discussion of international strategy. The opening case on Kraft Foods has been updated to highlight the company's global reorganization of its structure in an effort to enhance Kraft's international competitiveness in a changing marketplace. There are new and updated examples throughout the chapter to help illustrate key concepts associated with the structure and design of international organizations. There are two new Worldviews, one on Accenture's "virtual" global structure and another on structural changes that can help enhance companies' global competitiveness. The minicase at the end of the chapter has been updated as well.

Chapter 15 Assessing and Analyzing Markets

This chapter's material, which addresses the assessment and analysis of markets, was in Chapter 14 in the previous edition. We begin this chapter with a vignette of a wealthy consultant who believes that we cannot consciously express our motivations for purchases but that these motivations can be uncovered in the "reptilian" part of the brain. Further, this insight should apply to national groups as well as individuals. We anticipate lively discussion of this issue in classrooms around the world! We continue to clarify the difference between country and segment screening. We continue our coverage—perhaps the most detailed anywhere—of the methods used in doing market research abroad. The chapter's appendix, "Sources of Information Used in Screenings," has been moved from the text to the book's Web site, www.mhhe.com/ball 11e, hosted by McGraw-Hill Higher Education.

Chapter 16 Entry Modes

This chapter provides an expanded treatment of the critical topic of how businesses make decisions about the best way to enter foreign markets. We have significantly reorganized the material in this chapter to improve coherency and flow and to promote improved student comprehension of this material. Data and examples have been updated throughout the chapter. There is new and expanded discussion of management contracts, contract manufacturing, and other nonequity forms of market entry.

Chapter 17 Export and Import Practices

In this chapter on exporting and importing we have continued to expand our emphasis on services as well as tangible products. We have added an update of export–import terminology and shortened the chapter slightly by reducing some detail on paperwork procedures. A discussion of changes in procedures as a result of security concerns has also been added.

Chapter 18 Marketing Internationally

The international marketing chapter continues to emphasize the standardization-adaptation dilemma. To reflect current trends in international marketing, we have included new and further developed examples, such as the opening case study on Procter & Gamble's path to globalization. All of the data in the chapter have been updated to maintain the currency of the topics being addressed. The discussion of international advertising has been expanded to include consideration of the pervasive impact of culture on advertising decisions at subtle levels. The chapter's Building Your Global Résumé box includes a wide variety of sources of information on career opportunities in international marketing, advertising, and sales. The discussion of international channels and the issue of disintermediation has been updated.

Chapter 19 Global Operations and Supply Chain Management

Chapter 19 focuses on global supply chain management, an increasingly critical part of global operations and a key to the international competitiveness of businesses. The presentation of material in this chapter has been made more concise. The updated opening case examines the Spanish company Zara and the use of operations management capabilities for achieving competitive advantage in the fashion industry. There are new and updated examples throughout the chapter. The mini-MNE box on Cognizant Technology Solutions of India and its global offshoring model has been updated. There is an expanded discussion on the use of mass-customization techniques. The Worldview on Johnson Controls has been updated to emphasize the company's use of design and manufacturing excellence to achieve competitive advantage in global markets for automobile interiors. We have included a new Worldview on Nestlé's GLOBE program for using global standardization of processes and systems to create strategic advantage within and across its worldwide network of food industry operations.

Chapter 20 Human Resource Management

Chapter 20's discussion of HRM issues in international business has been reorganized to reduce redundancies with Chapter 12's discussion of international labor forces. A new opening case addresses issues associated with expatriate positions. The section on the global mind-set of the international human resource management approach, and how that approach links strategy, selection, and training, has been revised. A new Worldview box examines the role of cultural backgrounds and nationality in selecting candidates for international positions. There is also a new Worldview on the appropriateness of women for international assignments, and the section on expatriates has been substantially revised. Another new Worldview considers culture shock and its effect on expatriate and repatriate personnel. The discussion of families of expatriates, including issues faced by trailing spouses and children, has been substantially revised. We have revised the discussion of challenges associated with repatriation, expatriate support services, and compensation and benefits for expatriates and other international personnel. A new minicase at the end of the chapter deals with considerations facing an employee who is deciding whether to accept an international position that has been offered to her.

Chapter 21   Financial Management and Accounting

This chapter has been renamed in order to highlight its increased emphasis on issues of international accounting in addition to financial management. The chapter has been reorganized to move from an emphasis on the capital structure of the firm to an emphasis on cash flow management and discussion of international exposure and hedging. Examples, including Chinese trends in initial public offerings, have been updated throughout the chapter. A new mini-MNE box examines the use of micro-lending in developing country environments. The discussion of multilateral netting has been expanded. Our discussion of financial risk management has been expanded with examples of transaction, translation, and economic exposure and their hedging. A new Worldview examines unintended consequences of U.S. law on repatriated cash flows. The discussion on swaps and derivatives has been expanded, and there is a new section that addresses the importance of networking for financial partners. Discussion of making sales without money has been expanded, and we have added sections on transfer pricing and taxation, international accounting, the role of foreign currency, accounting and culture, convergence of accounting standards, and triple-bottom-line accounting. There is a new Worldview on Sarbanes-Oxley as an unpopular export, and we have expanded the discussion of international finance centers.

Glossary

The Glossary is a very extensive collection of definitions of documents, institutions, concepts, and terms used in international business. The Glossary is an extremely valuable resource for students and instructors.

New Features

With the eleventh edition we introduce an innovative and unique set of Building Your Global Résumé boxes that appear in each of the chapters. Prepared by Bernard Yevin, dean of the Business Informational Technology Division of Forsyth Technical Community College, each box presents valuable tools and insights to help students build a foundation for entering and excelling in international business activities and careers. These boxes cover such topics as finding international job opportunities, building international skills and experience, gaining relevant knowledge and tools to increase success in finding and performing international business jobs, and learning from the practical experience and recommendations of global mentors who have successfully pursued careers involving international business activity.

The eleventh edition also continues to use the innovative globalEDGE™ Research Tasks, created by Tunga Kiyak and Tomas Hult of the CIBER Center at Michigan State. These end-of-chapter exercises challenge students to solve problems similar to those faced by practicing international business managers, and they acquaint students with the tools and data real managers use. The globalEDGE™ Research Tasks are ideal for Web-based courses. For example, in working on a product launch, students may be asked to compile a list of the top 10 countries in terms of their attractiveness for potential return of FDI. Students can access all the Internet resources needed to solve the problems at www.globaledge.msu.edu.

A new video collection features original business documentaries as well as NBC news footage. Featured titles include "Will Rallies Help Immigrants?" "Is China Cheating When It Comes to Trade?" "Cirque du Soleil: A Truly Global Workforce," and "J&J: Creating a Global Learning Organization." Videos correspond to the video cases (with discussion questions) at the end of the book.

Other Useful Elements

- Mini-MNE boxes discuss smaller-size businesses and how they function and compete in the global business world.
- Worldview boxes highlight real-world applications of key concepts to help students relate the material they are learning to their own business careers.
- An extensive set of maps throughout the text gives students important geographic perspectives.
- End-of-chapter tools include Summaries, Key Words, Questions, globalEDGE™ Research Tasks, and Minicases to further help students in their comprehension.

CESIM: Global Challenge Simulation

This online simulation involving international markets for mobile handsets is packaged with new copies of the text. There are three market areas (North America, Europe, and Asia). The simulation presents a range of features that could be offered (impacting product differentiation), a choice of production sites (in Asia or North America), price options, and exposure to exchange rate fluctuations. It can be used with 3 to 12 teams (6 to 50 students per simulation) and can involve teams from more than one class or university, if desired. There is an enhanced online support facility with the eleventh edition, as well as an improved user interface to enhance the performance and appearance of the simulation. The simulation can be used at no additional expense for either instructors or students who use new copies of the text.

Acknowledgments

The departure of Don Ball and Wendell McCulloch from active participation in this book leaves a gap in the field of international business. When Don and Wendell began this project, there were virtually no textbooks on international business. Few textbooks, and virtually none in international business, have reached an eleventh edition and maintained their market leadership as has been the case with this book. We will miss their guidance, and their personalities, as we attempt to fill their shoes. We also note the untimely passing of our colleague and coauthor, Paul Frantz, whose experience and friendship will also be missed. But we welcome the addition of Jeanne McNett, who has displayed abundant energy and valuable insight and contributions during the tenth and eleventh editions of this text.

To the long list of people to whom we are indebted, we want to add Professors Gary Anders, Arizona State University West; Gary Anderson, Bowling Green State University; John Anderson, University of Tennessee, Knoxville; Nicholas Athanassiou, Northeastern University; Robert T. Aubey, University of Wisconsin, Madison; Winston Awadzi, Delaware State University; Mark C. Baetz, Wilfred Laurier University; Bahman Bahrami, North Dakota State University; Rufus Barton, Murray State University; Lawrence Beer, Arizona State University; Joseph R. Biggs, California Polytechnic State University; S. A. Billon, University of Delaware; James R. Bradshaw, Brigham Young University; Sharon Browning, Northwest Missouri State University; Dennis Carter, University of North Carolina, Wilmington; Mark Chadwin, Old Dominion University; Aruna Chandras, Ashland University; John Cleek, University of Missouri, Kansas City; Gerald Crawford, University of North Alabama; Refik Culpan, Pennsylvania State University; Peter DeWill, University of Central Florida; Galpira Eshigi, Illinois State University; Christof Falli, Portland State University; Colette Frayne, California Polytechnic State University, San Luis Obispo; Prem Gandhi, State University of New York, Plattsburgh; Ellen Kaye Gerke, Alliant International University; Kenneth Gray, Florida Agricultural and Mechanical University; Robert Guffey, Elon College; Stanley D. Guzell, Youngstown State University; Gary Hankem, Mankato State University; Baban Hasnat, State University of New York, Brockport; Tom Hinthorne, Montana State University; Veronica Horton, University of Akron; Paul Jenner, Southwest Missouri State University; Bruce H. Johnson, Gustavus Adolphus College; Ahmad Karim, Indiana University–Purdue University, Ft. Wayne; Michael Kublin, University of New Haven; Eddie Lewis, University of Southern Mississippi; Carol Lopilato, California State University, Dominguez Hills; Mingfang Li, California State University Northridge; Lois Ann McElroy Lindell, Wartburg College; Dorinda Lynn, Pensacola Junior College; Lynette Mathur, Southern Illinois University, Carbondale; Hugh J. McCabe, Westchester Community College; Fraser McLeay, University of Montana; Les Mueller, Central Washington University; Gary Oddon, San Jose State University; Darrell Neron, Peirce College; Ebele Oriaku, Elizabeth City State University; Jaimie Ortiz, Florida Atlantic University; Mike Peng, Ohio State University; Susan A. Peterson, Maricopa College; Avin Raj, Assumption College; Jere Ramsey, California Polytechnic State University, San Luis Obispo; Tagi Sagafi-nejad, Loyola College, MD; Rakesh Sambharya, Rutgers University; Eugene Seeley, Utah Valley State College; John Setnicky, Mobile College; V. N. Subramanyam, Lancaster University; Angelo Tarallo, Ramapo College; Jesse S. Tarleton, William and Mary College; John Thanopoulos, University of Akron; Kenneth Tillery, Middle Tennessee State University; Hsin-Min Tong, Redford University; Dennis Vanden Bloomen, University of Wisconsin, Stout; Heidi Vernon, Northeastern University; George Westacott, State University of New York, Binghamton; Terry Witkowski, California State University; Habte Woldu, University of Texas, Dallas; and Bernard Yevin, Forsythe Technical Community College. Attorney Mary C. Tolton, Esq., of the law firm Parker, Poe, Adams & Bernstein of Raleigh, North Carolina, provided valuable supplementary readings for the legal forces chapter; and we acknowledge the help of Denalee Eaton and Kimberly Gainey, students at California State University, Long Beach; Handan Vicdan and Ebru Ulusoy, PhD students at the University of Texas–Pan American; Sandra de los Santos and Elizabeth Reyes, members of the PhD program staff at the University of Texas–Pan American; and Heidi Peterson, Bryan Esterly, Anna Byrd, and Kaley Phillips, students at California Polytechnic University, San Luis Obispo.

We are also indebted to the following reviewers for helping us fine-tune the eleventh edition to better meet market needs: Yeqing Bao, University of Alabama, Huntsville; Macgorine Cassell, Fairmont State University; Scott C. Hammond, Utah Valley State College; Mr. Haryanto, Monmouth College; Gregg Lattier, Lee College; Juan F. Ramirez, Nova Southeastern University; John C. Ruhnka, University of Colorado at Denver and Health Sciences Center; Linda C. Ueltschy, Bowling Green State University; and G. Bernard Yevin, Forsyth Tech Community College.

Hundreds of professors have reviewed this text over its eleven editions and have shaped it into the solid textbook it is. Their suggestions and feedback have been invaluable to us, and we very much appreciate their efforts and time.

We would like to offer our special thanks to Jeffrey Jones for contributing the Critical Thinking Exercises to the instructor's manual. And a special thanks is given to the outstanding editorial and production staff from McGraw-Hill/Irwin who have worked so hard and so well to make this project succeed and stay on schedule, particularly John Biernat, Ryan Blankenship, Laura Hurst Spell, Meg Beamer, Laura Griffin, and Marlena Pechan. We feel honored to work with such a talented and professional team.

A World of Resources . . .

International Business: The Challenge of Global Competition continues to be the most objective and thorough treatment of international business available for students. Enriched with maps, photos, and the most up-to-date world data, this text boasts the collective expertise of three current and three former authors with firsthand international business experience, specializing in international management, finance, law, global strategy, and marketing—a claim no other text can make. Only Ball, McCulloch, Geringer, Minor, and McNett can offer a complete view of international business as diverse as the backgrounds of your business students.

Worldview Examples

Worldview features in every chapter offer compelling examples of how international business is affected by legal, political, economic, and social issues, helping students understand how interrelated these business strategy and policy issues are.

WORLD view

Are You Really Buying American?

Consider the following scenario of a "typical" American family:

The Boltons, Mike and Barbara, live in New York City. Mike is a security consultant with the security services firm Wackenhut Corporation. Barbara is an advertising executive in the Global Head Office of J. Walter Thompson.

On her way home from work, Barbara listens to the new Dixie Chicks CD in her Chrysler van. She stops for gas at the Shell station, then drives to the grocery store. She fills her shopping cart with a variety of items, including Ortega taco shells and salsa, Hellmann's mayonnaise, ReaLemon lemon juice, Ragu spaghetti sauce, Carnation Instant Breakfast drink, a six-pack of Dr. Pepper, a quart of A&W Root Beer, a container of CoffeeMate nondairy coffee creamer, a can of Chicken-of-the-Sea tuna, Lipton tea, Mott's apple sauce, a half-dozen cans of Slim-Fast, frozen Bird's Eye vegetables, some Evian water, and several packages of Stouffer's Lean Cuisine frozen dinners. For a treat, she picks up a pint of Ben and Jerry's ice cream and a Baby Ruth candy bar. She also grabs several cans of Alpo for their dog, Sassy, and a box of Friskies and a bag of Tidy Cat cat litter for their cat, Millie. She selects a Philip Roth novel and a copy of *Elle* magazine, then goes down the toiletries aisle for some Dove soap and Jergen's moisturizing lotion. Before finishing, she calls Mike on her Samsung cellular phone from T-Mobile to see if there's anything else he needs. He asks her to pick up some PowerBars for him to take to the gym during his lunchtime workouts next week. On her way home, she stops at the bookstore and picks up a book—*The Da Vinci Code*.

After finishing up at work, Mike gets into his Jeep Cherokee and puts the new Ben Harper and the Innocent Criminals CD into the Clarion car stereo. He stops at the Amoco station to fill his gas tank and checks the air pressure in his Firestone tires. He makes a quick stop at Computerland to pick up the newest release of WordPerfect, signing the credit card slip with his Bic pen. Then he goes to the video store to pick up *The Pink Panther* on DVD, before heading to the package store for a bottle of Wild Turkey bourbon. He walks next door to the sporting goods store to pick up some Wilson racquetballs for his workouts next week and then heads home.

Barbara's favorite TV show, *Jeopardy!*, is just starting as Mike comes in the door, so she pours herself a glass of Beringer wine from Napa Valley and changes the Dish TV satellite channel on their Magnavox television so that she can watch her show. Before he prepares dinner, Mike opens a Miller beer and leafs through the day's mail, setting the most recent issue of *Road and Track* magazine aside to read later. Soon, dinner is ready and they sit down for their meal, while watching a show on the National Geographic Channel.

While this may sound like a very typical evening for many Americans, foreign-owned firms produced nearly every item that the Boltons purchased or consumed:

- Wackenhut is owned by Group 4 Falck of Denmark.
- J. Walter Thompson is owned by the WPP Group of the United Kingdom.
- Germany's DaimlerChrysler manufactures Chryslers and Jeeps.
- The British-Dutch company Royal Dutch Shell owns Shell.

mini MNE

>>A Little Guy Makes Global Business Easier for the Little Guys

DE Technologies, a tiny Virginia-based private company with only six employees and offices in the United States and Canada, has patented a technology for using the Internet/intranet to process sales globally. Intended for small and medium-size enterprises, development of the technology was stimulated by the frustrations that DE Technologies' founder encountered while attempting to arrange international trade deals in Russia for his own small company. Traditional systems for international trade, involving multiple, inefficient, and time-consuming layers of vertical service industries, can require 20 or more forms and 60 days to complete and cost 5 to 40 percent of the cost of the total transaction.

With DE's system, which is called the Electronic Commerce Backbone System (ECBS), small and medium-size firms can automatically export and import goods and services without previous international trade experience. The ECBS allows buyers and sellers to buy products in the currency of the destination country, view product descriptions in the language of the destination country, view digital still or motion video displays of the products for sale, and view the calculations and displays of prices for air, land, and sea transportation; it also ensures direct payment of goods via credit cards or documentary credit.

Procedures such as the preparation and filing of export–import documents, freight, insurance, titles, letters of credit, pro forma invoices, and bills of lading are done by the program. This eliminates the necessity of engaging foreign freight forwarders, export and import agents, and other international channels-of-distribution members. Thus, ECBS reduces the costs of ocean and air freight, banking, and human resources.

Small and medium-size enterprises (SMEs) can become members by paying a small membership fee, which gives them access to the ECBS. A transactional fee of 0.3 percent also is levied. According to the founder of DE Technologies, "the capability of the system will allow thousands of SMEs to compete effectively in the Import/Export business with 'The Big Guys' as the barriers to entry will be lowered tremendously."

The ECBS can be supplemented with the Borderless Order Entry System (BOES), a patented process for electronically managing international trade transactions in an integrated manner. It allows companies to create and file necessary electronic documents (in any currency or language), monitor and track steps in the transaction, calculate applicable freight costs as well as taxes and duties, and perform financial arrangements of a sophisticated nature. The result is a reduction of as much as 30 percent in the costs of conducting international trade transactions. SMEs can export and import products from any nation, using the Internet or Intranets, and thereby expand market share in international markets.

Source: "Cutting through a World of Red Tape," *BusinessWeek Online*, www.businesswe . . . m/smallbiz/0006/te000628.htm/script Framed (June 30, 2000); "Electronic Commerce Backbone System (ECBS)," *DE Technologies* Web site, www.detechnologies.com/ecbs.htm (July 1, 2004); "Information Technology and International Trade Position Paper," *DE Technologies* Web site, www .detechnologies.com/ecbs.htm (July 3, 2006); and "Borderless Order Entry Systems," *DETechnologiesWeb site*, www.detechnologies .com/boes.htm (July 3, 2006).

mini- MNE Examples

These boxed features in every chapter illustrate how small businesses compete for global markets. Students find these examples interesting as they learn that you don't have to be a multinational to sell overseas.

New! Building Your Global Résumé

Each box presents valuable tools and insights to help students build a foundation for entering and excelling in international business activities and careers. These boxes cover such topics as finding international job opportunities, building international skills and experience, gaining relevant knowledge and tools to increase success in finding and performing international business jobs, and learning from practical experience and recommendations from global mentors that have successfully pursued careers involving international business activity.

Visual Format

For the increasingly visual student population, the tables, figures, maps, and photos in the text bring international business to life. Students are better able to absorb ideas and compare and contrast information on different countries when it is presented in a visual format rather than long passages of text.

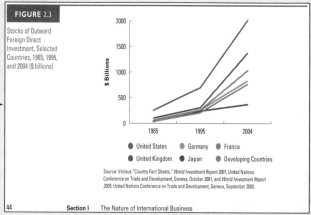

Instructive Maps

Numerous maps display valuable data and help students grasp geographic implications.

Summary

Explain the significance of culture for international business.

To be successful in their relationships overseas, international businesspeople must be students of culture. They must not only have factual knowledge; they must also become culturally sensitive. Culture affects all functional areas of the firm.

Identify the sociocultural components of culture.

Although experts differ about the components of culture, the following are representative of what numerous anthropologists believe exist: (1) aesthetics, (2) attitudes and beliefs, (3) religion, (4) material culture, (5) education, (6) language, (7) societal organization, (8) legal characteristics, and (9) political structures.

Discuss the significance of religion to businesspeople.

Knowing the basic tenets of other religions will contribute to a better understanding of their followers' attitudes. This may be a major factor in a given market.

Explain the cultural aspects of technology.

Material culture, especially technology, is important to managements contemplating overseas investment. Foreign governments have become increasingly involved in the sale and control of technical assistance. Technology may enable a firm to enter a new market successfully even if its competitors are already established there. It often enables the firm to obtain superior conditions for an overseas investment because the host government wants the technology.

Discuss the pervasiveness of the information technology era.

Businesspeople must keep abreast of the changes in information technology to avoid falling behind their competitors. The Internet enables small firms to compete in the global market, a fact that provides new opportunities for some firms and new

competition for others. Businesspeople who can capture information from transaction data have a significant advantage over those who cannot. The opinion in the retailing industry is that this capability is the primary reason for Wal-Mart's success, for example.

Explain the importance of the ability to speak the local language.

Language is the key to culture. A feel for a people and their attitudes naturally develops with a growing mastery of their language.

Discuss the importance of unspoken language in international business.

Because unspoken language can often tell businesspeople something that spoken language does not, they should know something about this form of cross-cultural communication.

Discuss the two classes of relationships within a society.

A knowledge of how a society is organized is useful because the arrangement of relationships within it defines and regulates the manner in which its members interface with one another. Anthropologists have broken down societal relationships into two classes: those based on kinship and those based on free association of individuals.

Discuss Hofstede's four cultural value dimensions.

Geert Hofstede analyzed IBM employees in 72 countries and found that the differences in their answers to 32 statements could be based on four value dimensions: (1) individualism versus collectivism, (2) large versus small power distance, (3) strong versus weak uncertainty, and (4) masculinity versus femininity. These dimensions help managers understand how cultural differences affect organizations and management methods.

End-of-Chapter Learning Tools

At the end of each chapter are a Summary, Key Words, and Questions. The Summary is tied to the Concept Previews that open the chapter. The Key Words list includes page references for easy reference. The Questions test students' ability to retain and apply what they've learned in the chapter.

Key Words

culture (p. 160)	Asian religions (p. 169)	lingua franca (p. 176)
ethnocentricity (p. 160)	caste system (p. 171)	unspoken language (p. 179)
aesthetics (p. 164)	material culture (p. 173)	bribes (p. 181)
demonstration effect (p. 168)	technological dualism (p. 175)	extortion (p. 181)
Protestant work ethic (p. 169)	appropriate technology (p. 175)	extended family (p. 183)
Confucian work ethic (p. 169)	boomerang effect (p. 175)	associations (p. 183)

Questions

1. Why is it helpful for international businesspeople to know that a national culture has two components?

2. A knowledge of culture has been responsible for Disney's success in Tokyo, and ignorance of culture was responsible for the company's large losses in Paris. Discuss.

3. Why do international businesspersons need to consider aesthetics when making marketing decisions?

4. How can the demonstration effect be used to improve productivity? To improve sales?

5. Some societies view change differently than do Americans. What impact does this have on the way American marketers operate in those markets? The way American production people operate?

6. Why must international businesspeople be acquainted with the beliefs of the major religions in the areas in which they work?

7. What Buddhist belief would cause American marketing and production managers to think carefully before transferring their marketing plans or bonus plans to an area where Buddhists are present in large numbers?

8. Why is technological superiority especially significant for international firms?

9. What is the significance of the extended family for international managers?

10. Use Hofstede's four dimensions to analyze this situation: John Adams, with 20 years of experience as general foreman in the United States, is sent as production superintendent to his firm's new plant in Colombia. He was chosen because of his outstanding success in handling workers. Adams uses the participative management style. Can you foresee his having any problems on this new job?

GlobalEDGE™ Research Tasks

Using the text and the globalEDGE™ Web site (www.globaledge.msu.edu), students solve realistic international business problems related to the types of tools and data sources international managers use to make informed decisions.

Research Task

globalEDGE.msu.edu 🌐 globalEDGE

Use the globalEDGE site (http://globalEDGE.msu.edu/) to complete the following exercises:

1. Assume you own an exporting company that specializes in consumer products. You have been selling your products in several different countries but have yet to enter the Asian market. You have chosen South Korea as the first Asian country to enter. Since you have not previously sold your products in any Asian market, you think it would be a good idea to form a strategic alliance with a local firm. You strongly believe that the first impression is important. Therefore, you have decided to collect some information regarding the business culture and local habits of South Korea from the *"Kwintessential"* Web site. Prepare a short report in terms of the most shocking characteristics that may influence business interactions in this country.

2. The cultural distance of countries in which your firm operates is one of the many explanations of significant differences that your U.S.-based employees face when travelling to different affiliates worldwide. Typically, an index of cultural distance can be determined by summing the differences of country-level scores such as those introduced by Hofstede's cultural dimensions. At the present time, your firm has operations in Austria, Guatemala, Iran, Malaysia, and South Africa. Using the *Hofstede Resource Center* based on studies involving cultural dimensions to assess all five countries, determine which affiliates are located in a culture that is least and most similar to the U.S. As there are four main components of each overall cultural distance score, which component(s) can be considered most influential for each country?

Minicase 13.1 Wal-Mart Takes On the World

Founded in the U.S. state of Arkansas by Sam Walton in 1962, Wal-Mart has developed into the largest retailer in the world and the largest company on the Fortune 500 list, with sales of $312.4 billion in fiscal 2006. Embodying high levels of service, strong inventory management, and purchasing economies, Wal-Mart overpowered competitors and became the dominant firm in the U.S. retail industry. After rapid expansion during the 1980s and 1990s, Wal-Mart faces limits to growth in its home market and has been forced to look internationally for opportunities.

Many skeptics claimed that Wal-Mart's business practices and culture could not be transferred internationally. Yet, in its first decade of operations outside the United States, the company's globalization efforts progressed at a rapid pace. As of 2006, over 40 percent of Wal-Mart's stores were located outside the United States. Its more than 2,700 international retail units employ over 450,000 associates in 13 international markets. In fiscal 2007, Wal-Mart planned to open at least 220 additional international units. Wal-Mart's sales from international operations are expected to reach $78 billion in 2007, a level that is expected to increase substantially over the next decade. If the international business were an independent chain, it would be the fourth-largest retailer in the world, behind Wal-Mart's U.S. operations, Home Depot, and Carrefour.

Globalizing Wal-Mart: Where and How to Begin?

When Wal-Mart began to expand internationally, it had to decide which countries to target. Although the European retail market was large, to succeed there Wal-Mart would have had to take market share from established competitors. Instead, Wal-Mart deliberately selected emerging markets as its starting point for international expansion. In Latin America, it targeted nations with large, growing populations—Mexico, Argentina, and Brazil—and in Asia it aimed at China. Because [m]any lacked the organizational, managerial, and fi[nancial] resources to simultaneously pursue all of these mar[kets, Wal]-Mart pursued a very deliberate entry strategy for [emer]ging markets, focusing first on the Americas rather [than the] more culturally and geographically distant Asian [marketpl]ace.

[Its] first international store, opened in 1991 in Mexico [City, the] company used a 50-50 joint venture. This entry mode [helped W]al-Mart manage the substantial differences in cul[ture and] income between the United States and Mexico. Its

Mexican partner, the retail conglomerate, Cifra, provided expertise in operating in the Mexican market and a base for learning about retailing in that country. When it entered Brazil in 1996, Wal-Mart was able to leverage its learning from the Mexican experience to take a majority position in a 60-40 venture with a local retailer, Lojas Americana. When the company subsequently entered Argentina, it did so on a wholly owned basis. After gaining experience with partners, in 1997 Wal-Mart expanded further in Mexico by acquiring a controlling interest in Cifra, which it renamed in 2000 to Wal-Mart de México S. A. de C. V. By 2006, Wal-Mart operated 808 units in Mexico in 30 states, achieving annual sales of $15.8 billion and employing over 130,000. It accounts for over half of all supermarket sales in Mexico.

Still, learning the dos and don'ts was a difficult process. "It wasn't such a good idea to stick so closely to the domestic Wal-Mart blueprint in Argentina, or in some of the other international markets we've entered, for that matter," said the president of Wal-Mart International. "In Mexico City we sold tennis balls that wouldn't bounce right in the high altitude. We built large parking lots at some of our Mexican stores, only to realize that many of our customers there rode the bus to the store, then trudged across those large parking lots with bags full of merchandise. We responded by creating bus shuttles to drop customers off at the door. These were all mistakes that were easy to address, but we're now working smarter internationally to avoid cultural and regional problems on the front end."[a] Wal-Mart's initial entry into Brazil used greenfield store sites and emphasized aggressive pricing to build market share, but the French retailer Carrefour and other Brazilian competitors retaliated, launching a costly price war. Wal-Mart's strength in international sourcing was initially of limited assistance in Brazil, since the leading sales category—food—was primarily sourced locally, where Carrefour and others already had strong relationships with local suppliers. Over time, Wal-Mart changed its competitive emphasis to customer service and a broader merchandise mix than smaller local companies could match. The company also pursued acquisitions to supplement internal growth, buying 118 Bompreço stores in 2004 and 140 Sonae stores in 2005. By 2006, Wal-Mart was the third-largest retailer in Brazil, operating 293 stores and employing 50,000 associates.

The Challenge of China

The lure of China, the world's most populous nation, proved too great to ignore. Wal-Mart was one of the first international

---

In 1984, Guy Laliberté left his home in Canada to make his way across Europe as a circus performer. There he and other artists performed in the street. The troupe was called Cirque du Soleil—"circus of the sun." It started with a simple dream: a group of young artists getting together to entertain audiences, see the world, and have fun doing it.[1] Laliberté and company quickly found that their entertainment form without words—stilt-walking, juggling, music, and fire breathing—transcended all barriers of language and culture. Though he understood that an entertainer could bring the exotic to every corner of the world, Laliberté did not envision the scope to which his Cirque du Soleil would succeed. Today Cirque performs nine permanent shows, such as *Algeria*, which is touring Japan, and *Mystere, O,* and *ZUMANITY,* all with permanent homes at the MGM Mirage resorts in Las Vegas. In 20 years of live performances, 44 million people have seen a Cirque show.[2] Despite a long-term decline in the circus industry, Cirque has increased revenue 22-fold over the last 10 years.[3]

Cirque du Soleil is a family of more than 600 individuals from 40 different countries. Each of Cirque's 3,000 employees is encouraged to make contributions to the group. This input has resulted in rich, deep performances and expansion into alternative media outlets such as music, books, television, Web sites, and merchandising. The company's diversity ensures that every show reflects many different cultural influences. Many different markets will have an exotic experience at a Cirque show, regardless of which show is playing where. Cirque does target specific markets with products designed to engage a particular audience. Yet Cirque has little need to adapt its product to new markets; the product is already a blend of global influences. The result is a presentation of acrobatic arts and traditional, live circus with an almost indescribable freshness and beauty.

Cirque du Soleil's commitment to excellence and innovation transcends cultural differences and the limits of many modern media. Its intense popularity has made Cirque both the global standard of live entertainment and the place for talented individuals from around the world to perfect their talents. The extent of the diversity, however, does pose a host of unique challenges. Every employee must be well versed in various forms and styles. To foster cultural enrichment, Cirque purchases and shares a large collection of art with employees and gives them tickets to different events and shows.

The performers work in the most grueling and intimate situations, with their lives depending on one another. The astounding spectacles they create on stage result from hours of planning, practice, and painstaking attention to detail among artists from diverse cultures who speak 25 different languages. Sensitivity, compromise, and hunger for new experiences are prerequisites for success at Cirque. The organization has learned the art of sensitivity and compromise in its recruiting. Cirque du Soleil has had a presence in the Olympics for a decade. It works closely with coaches and teams to help athletes consider a career with Cirque *after* their competitive years are over, rather than luring talent away from countries that have made huge investments in athletes. This practice has given Cirque a huge advantage in the athletic community, a source of great talent from all over the world.

Guy Laliberté has not forgotten his own humble beginnings as a Canadian street performer. Now that Cirque du Soleil has achieved an international presence and incredible success—the group expects to be doing $1 billion in annual gross revenue by 2007—it has chosen to help at-risk youth, especially street kids. Cirque allocates 1 percent of its revenues to outreach programs targeting youth in difficulty, regardless of location in the world.[4] Guy understands that to be successful in a world market, one must be a committed and sensitive neighbor. Cirque's headquarters in Montreal is the center of an urban revitalization project sponsored by Cirque. Community participation and outreach bring the company international goodwill and help Cirque du Soleil transcend many of the difficulties global brands often face when spanning cultures.

Questions for Discussion

1. Why is Cirque du Soleil successful throughout the world? How does the product transcend culture differences between countries?

2. How have the five major drivers of globalization influenced Cirque du Soleil?

3. Why is it important for Cirque du Soleil to be a good corporate citizen? How does the organization strive to fulfill this role?

Sources

1. "Founder's Message," www.cirquedusoleil.com.

2. Mario D'Amico, and Vincent Gagné, "Big Top Television," *Marketing* 109, no. 26 (August 9–August 16, 2004), p. 20.

3. Chan Kim and Renee Mauborgne, "Blue Ocean Strategy," *Harvard Business Review,* October 2004, p. 77.

4. "Social Action," www.cirquedusoleil.com.

Minicases

Minicases also appear at the end of each chapter. These brief scenarios challenge students to apply concepts discussed in the chapter to a real-world situation.

Video Cases

Video cases for most chapters are presented at the end of the book. Each video case illustrates applications of the relevant chapter concepts and has a corresponding video on the Instructor's Video DVD and/or online. These cases feature timely and thought-provoking topics affecting the international business environment—such as "Will Rallies Help Immigrants" and "Is China Cheating When It Comes to Trade"—as well as profiles of successful international businesses and managers—such as "J&J: Creating a Global Learning Organization" and "Starbucks: Building Relationships with Coffee Growers."

Supplements for Instructors

Online Learning Center, www.mhhe.com/ball11e

The Online Learning Center (OLC) with PowerWeb is a Web site that follows *International Business* chapter by chapter with digital supplementary content germane to the book. As students read the book, they can go online to take self-grading quizzes, review material, and work through interactive exercises. OLCs can be delivered multiple ways—through the textbook Web site, through PageOut, or within a course management system such as WebCT or Blackboard.

The following supplements are included on one convenient Instructor's Resource CD:

Instructor's Manual

Written by coauthor Jeanne McNett, the Instructor's Manual will help save you valuable time preparing for the course by providing suggestions for heightening your students' interest in the material. Each chapter-by-chapter section presents concept previews, an overview of the chapter, a detailed chapter outline, suggestions and comments, student involvement exercises, and solutions to end-of-chapter material. The manual also includes video case teaching notes. Special Critical Thinking Exercises, prepared by Jeffrey Jones, St. Louis Community College–ForestPark, are also provided for each chapter.

Test Bank

Written by coauthor Jeanne McNett, the Test Bank contains approximately 100 questions per chapter in multiple-choice, true/false, and short-answer format. Each question is ranked for difficulty level and includes page references to the text.

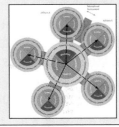

PowerPoint Slides

Created by coauthor Jeanne McNett, this PowerPoint presentation includes key points from each chapter, sample figures from the text, and supplemental exhibits that help illustrate the main points in a chapter. Over 600 images are included.

Explosive Growth

- Number of International Companies
  – UNCTAD-United Nations agency in charge of all matters relating to FDI and international corporations.
    - 1995–45,000 parent companies with 280,000 foreign affiliates ($7 trillion in sales)
    - 2004–70,000 parent companies with 690,000 foreign affiliates ($19 trillion in sales)

Videos

A new video collection features original business documentaries as well as NBC news footage. Featured titles include "Will Rallies Help Immigrants?" "Is China Cheating When It Comes to Trade?" "Cirque du Soleil: A Truly Global Workforce," and "J&J: Creating a Global Learning Organization." Videos correspond to the video cases (with discussion questions) at the end of the book.

Supplements for Students

CESIM: Global Challenge Simulation

This online simulation involving international markets for mobile handsets is packaged with new copies of the text. There are three market areas (North America, Europe, and Asia). The simulation presents a range of features that could be offered (impacting product differentiation), a choice of production sites (in Asia or North America), price options, and exposure to exchange rate fluctuations. It can be used with 3 to 12 teams (6 to 50 students per simulation and larger classes can readily be accommodated by using multiple simulations simultaneously) and can involve teams from more than one class or university, if desired. The simulation is also well-suited for many on-line courses. There is an enhanced online support facility with the eleventh edition, as well as an improved user interface to enhance the performance and appearance of the simulation. Use of this online simulation is free with new copies of this text.

Online Learning Center, www.mhhe.com/ball11e

The Online Learning Center (OLC) with PowerWeb is a Web site that follows *International Business* chapter by chapter with digital supplementary content germane to the book. As students read the book, they can go online to take self-grading quizzes, review material, and work through interactive exercises.

Financial Times

McGraw-Hill is pleased to be able to announce a partnership with *The Financial Times.* Order this package and students will receive a 15-week subscription at a specially discounted rate. Students enjoy the full benefits of a *Financial Times* subscription, including access to FT.com In-Depth, an online portal featuring breaking news, special reports, portfolio tools, and more. Free subscription for adopting instructors.

BusinessWeek Edition

Your students can subscribe to *BusinessWeek* for a specially priced rate of $8.25 in addition to the price of the text. Students will receive a pass code card shrink-wrapped with their new text. The card directs students to a Web site where they enter the code and then gain access to *BusinessWeek*'s registration page to enter address information and set up their subscription. Students can choose to receive their subscription in print copy or digital format.

Brief Table of Contents

Table of Contents

CHAPTER 6

Sociocultural Forces   158

CHAPTER 7

Natural Resources and Environmental Sustainability   190

CHAPTER 10

Legal Forces 278

CHAPTER 11

Financial Forces 302

CHAPTER 12

Labor Forces 322

CHAPTER 15

Assessing and Analyzing Markets   408

CHAPTER 16

Entry Modes   424

CHAPTER 17

Export and Import Practices   444

CHAPTER 21

Financial Management and Accounting   566

List of Maps

International Business
The Challenge of Global Competition

11e

The Nature of International Business

Section One describes the nature and scope of international business and introduces the three environments in which international business managers must operate. How well they perform in their undertakings will depend in great measure on their understanding of domestic, international, and foreign environments.

Chapter 1 presents the concepts of the three environments and their forces. From the history of international business, we learn that although the international firm existed before the Civil War, it differed markedly from the present-day global company, which is characterized by its explosive growth and closer central control of foreign operations.

In Chapter 2, information is presented to help you comprehend the dynamic growth and the magnitude of both international trade and foreign investment. We discuss why firms go abroad, and we examine the seven dimensions along which managers can globalize if they take their companies international.

An overview of the theories of international trade and investment is given in Chapter 3. A basic understanding of this material will help explain the actions already taken by managers and by government officials and provide insight into what they plan to do in the future.

1

The Rapid Change
of International Business

In the past, complex international transactions were the domain of diplomats and international policy and business experts. Today a converging set of powerful economic, technological, demographic and geopolitical trends will demand that all citizens, not just the elite, have that kind of global fluency. Knowledge of the world is no longer a luxury, it is a necessity.

—*Nicholas Platt, president emeritus of the Asia Society*

Why You Need International Business Experience and How to Get It

Gary Ellis, a young assistant controller for Medtronic, a Fortune 500 manufacturer of pacemakers and other medical equipment, was thought to be on the fast track for a top management position. However, company executives felt he first needed broader experience, so they sent him to head their European headquarters in Belgium. In his new job Gary was responsible for many top-level duties and worked with an array of officials (labor, government, production, and marketing, as well as financial).

Two years later, when the corporate controller's job in the company's home office in Minneapolis became vacant, Ellis was given the job. Bill George, Medtronic's CEO, summed up the company philosophy regarding necessary experience: "Successful executives of the future will have all lived in another country for several years."[a]

Medtronic is not the only firm with this policy. At FMC Corp., a heavy machinery and chemicals producer, the vice president for human resources says that his company believes that "no one will be in a general management job by the end of the decade who didn't have international exposure and experience."[b] Evidently, the boards of directors of many other American corporations have the same policy. Companies such as McDonald's, Coke, Kellogg, Alcoa, Altria, and Schering-Plough have all appointed leaders who had extensive experience as the heads of international operations. William Sullivan, the CEO of Agilent Technologies, commented on his three years in Singapore as an operations manager by saying, "It was a real career changer. In today's environment, having that overseas experience is a big deal."[c] As Carlos Gutierrez, who was the CEO of Kellogg before becoming the U.S. secretary of commerce, said, "Having a foreign perspective gives you an advantage not only for doing business outside the U.S. but domestically, where we have the most diverse society in the world. There's a built-in understanding that differences exist and are good."[d]

Although many American managers want their top executives at company headquarters to have years of foreign experience, do CEOs of the major firms recognize the value of internationalized business education for all employees in management? Surveying the CEOs of *Forbes*'s "100 Largest Multinational Firms" and *Fortune*'s "America's 50 Biggest Exporters," we found that (1) 79 percent believed that all business majors should take an introduction to international business course; (2) about 70 percent felt that business graduates' expertise in foreign languages, international aspects of functional areas (e.g., marketing, finance), and business, human, or political relations outside the United States is an important consideration in making hiring decisions; and (3) a majority of the respondents believed that a number of courses in the international business curriculum (e.g., international marketing, international finance, export–import, international management) are relevant to their companies.

It appears from our study, then, that the CEOs of major American firms doing business overseas are convinced that the business graduates they hire should have some education in the international aspects of business. Most seem to agree with the executive vice president of Texas Instruments, who said, "Managers must become familiar with other markets, cultures, and customs. That is because we operate under the notion that it is 'one world, one market,' and we must be able to compete with—and sell to—the best companies around the world."

CONCEPT PREVIEWS

After reading this chapter, you should be able to:

appreciate the dramatic internationalization of markets

understand the various names given to firms that have substantial operations in more than one country

understand the five kinds of drivers, all based on change, that are leading international firms to the globalization of their operations

comprehend why international business differs from domestic business

describe the three environments—domestic, foreign, and international—in which an international company operates

Clearly, the top executives from some of the largest corporations in the world are saying that they prefer business graduates who know something about markets, customs, and cultures in other countries. Companies that do business overseas have always needed some people who could work and live successfully outside their own countries, but now it seems that managers wanting to advance in their firms must have some foreign experience as well.

Did you note the reason for this emphasis on foreign experience for managers? It is increased involvement of the firm in international business. The top executives of many corporations want their employees to have a global business perspective. What about companies that have no foreign operations of any kind? Do their managers need this global perspective? They do indeed, because it will help them not only to be alert for both sales and sourcing opportunities in foreign markets but also to be watchful for new foreign competitors preparing to invade their domestic market. In addition, according to recruiters, foreign experience reflects independence, resourcefulness, and entrepreneurship. People who work and support themselves overseas tend to be inquisitive, adaptive, and flexible—qualities that are valuable in today's work environment.

The realization that overseas experience is important for career advancement has heightened the competition for foreign assignments. For example, nearly 500 mid-level engineering and technical managers in GE's aircraft engine unit applied for the 14 positions in the company's global marketing training program. The global human resource manager at another GE unit, GE Medical Systems, claims, "We have far more candidates than we have jobs offshore."[e] Kellogg's Gutierrez commented, "When you're working at one small international unit, you get to meet more key people" than would middle managers posted at headquarters, because the company's executives come to visit the international operations.[f] In the face of such competition, what can you do to improve your chances to obtain an overseas post?

It can be valuable to take classes in the area of international business, perhaps leading to a degree in an international business–related field. In addition, even while you are in school or shortly after graduation, consider going abroad to study, to work (whether as a business intern, as a teacher, or even in such positions as bartender or child care provider), or to volunteer in community development activities. The experience of living and working in another culture can be important in personal development, as well as being a career booster. As Lauren DiCioccio said of her international experience as a cook and farmworker, "When I went, I was hesitant because people looked at me and were surprised that I would graduate with a degree from Colgate and take time off to work and backpack around Australia. So when I came back and had it on my résumé, I couldn't believe all of the interviews were about my time in Australia." Brandon Steiner, a 24-year-old teaching in Japan, said, "Having international experience under your belt—employers are enthusiastic. It looks good and is not a bad step out of college. It shows you already are open-minded."[g] Upon your return, this experience may help you to land a job that involves international business activities. Although most positions are based in a person's home country, they may involve some international travel to see clients or perform other job-related activities, thus providing an opportunity for you to further broaden your international skills and experience.

If you already have a job, you can enhance your opportunities for international experience by making your boss and the human resource management department personnel aware of your interest and the fact that you have studied international business. Look for opportunities to remind them that you continue to be interested (performance review is a good time). Try to meet people in the home office who work with the company's foreign subsidiaries as well as visitors from overseas. As evidence of your strong interest in foreign employment, take additional international business courses and study foreign languages. Make sure that people in your company know what you are doing.

Throughout this book you will find examples of ways to develop, apply, and promote your international skills and experience, through features such as "Building Your Global Résumé" and "Your Global Mentor." Hopefully, through effective application of these suggestions, you will build a successful foundation for your own international experiences! ■

[a]"The Real Fast Track Is Overseas," *Fortune,* August 21, 1995, p. 129.

[b]"Path to Top Job Now Twists and Turns," *The Wall Street Journal,* March 15, 1993, p. B1.

[c]Erin White, "Future CEOs May Need to Have Broad Liberal-Arts Foundation," *The Wall Street Journal,* April 12, 2005, p. B4.

[d]Carol Hymowitz, "Why American Multinationals Have More Foreign-Born CEOs," *The Wall Street Journal Europe,* May 25, 2004, p. A10.

[e]"The Fast Track Leads Overseas," *BusinessWeek,* November 1993, pp. 64–68.

[f]Hymowitz, "Why American Multinationals Have More Foreign-Born CEOs."

[g]Hillary Chura, "A Year Abroad (or 3) as a Career Move," *New York Times,* February 25, 2006, www.nytimes.com/2006/02/25/business/worldbusiness/25abroad.html?ex=1298523600&en=6df6d07733a344ed&ei=5088&partner=rssnyt&emc=rss (July 5, 2006).

What about you? Are you involved in the global economy yet? Please read the nearby Worldview box, "Are You Really Buying American?" and then think back to how you began your own day. After you awoke, you may have looked at your Casio watch for the time, checked your Nokia cell phone for messages, and turned on your Samsung TV for the news and weather while you showered. After drying your hair with a Conair dryer, maybe you quickly swallowed some Dannon yogurt and a glass of Mott's apple juice, along with a cup of Taster's Choice coffee, brushed your teeth with Close-Up toothpaste, and drove off to class in your Honda with its Firestone tires and a tank full of Shell gasoline.

Meanwhile, on the other side of the world, a group of Japanese students dressed in Lacoste shirts, Levi's jeans, and Nike shoes may be turning off their Dell computers in the computer lab and debating whether they should stop for hamburgers and Cokes at McDonald's or coffee at Starbucks. They put on their Oakley sunglasses, get into their Ford Mustangs with Goodyear tires, and drive off.

What do you and the Japanese students have in common? You are all consuming products made by *foreign-owned companies.* This is international business.

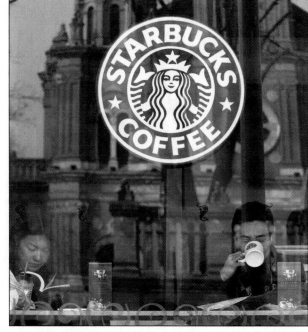

A Starbucks coffee store in Beijing China. Chairman Howard Schultz said China is the coffee chain's No.1 growth market.

All that you have read so far points to one salient fact: *All managers need to have a basic knowledge of international business to be able to meet the challenge of global competition.*

International Business Terminology

Acquiring this knowledge consists, in part, of learning the special terminology of international business, an important function, as you already know, of every introductory course. To assist you in learning the international business "language," we've included a glossary at the end of the book and listed the most important terms at the end of each chapter. They also appear in bold print where they are first used in the text, with their definitions in the margin.

MULTINATIONAL, GLOBAL, INTERNATIONAL, AND TRANSNATIONAL COMPANIES

Because international business is a relatively new discipline and is extremely dynamic, you will find that the definitions of a number of terms vary among users. For example, some people use the words *world* and *global* interchangeably and *multinational* to describe a business with widespread international operations. (The nearby Worldview, "Global Company—By Whose Definition?" has additional discussion of this issue.) Others define a *global firm* as one that attempts to standardize operations in all functional areas but that responds to national market differences when necessary. In contrast, a *multinational company* has been defined by some as a kind of holding company with a number of overseas operations, each of which is left to adapt its products and marketing strategy to what local managers perceive to be unique aspects of their individual markets. Some academic writers suggest using terms such as *multidomestic* and *multilocal* as synonyms for this definition of *multinational.*

You will also find those who consider *multinational corporation* to be synonymous with *multinational enterprise* and *transnational corporation.*[1] However, the United Nations and the governments of many developing nations have been using *transnational* instead of *multinational* to describe any firm doing business in more than one country. The specialized agency, the United Nations Conference on Trade and Development (UNCTAD), for example,

WORLD view

Are You Really Buying American?

Consider the following scenario of a "typical" American family:

The Boltons, Mike and Barbara, live in New York City. Mike is a security consultant with the security services firm Wackenhut Corporation. Barbara is an advertising executive in the Global Head Office of J. Walter Thompson.

On her way home from work, Barbara listens to the new Dixie Chicks CD in her Chrysler van. She stops for gas at the Shell station, then drives to the grocery store. She fills her shopping cart with a variety of items, including Ortega taco shells and salsa, Hellmann's mayonnaise, ReaLemon lemon juice, Ragu spaghetti sauce, Carnation Instant Breakfast drink, a six-pack of Dr. Pepper, a quart of A&W Root Beer, a container of CoffeeMate nondairy coffee creamer, a can of Chicken-of-the-Sea tuna, Lipton tea, Mott's apple sauce, a half-dozen cans of Slim-Fast, frozen Bird's Eye vegetables, some Evian water, and several packages of Stouffer's Lean Cuisine frozen dinners. For a treat, she picks up a pint of Ben and Jerry's ice cream and a Baby Ruth candy bar. She also grabs several cans of Alpo for their dog, Sassy, and a box of Friskies and a bag of Tidy Cat cat litter for their cat, Millie. She selects a Philip Roth novel and a copy of *Elle* magazine, then goes down the toiletries aisle for some Dove soap and Jergen's moisturizing lotion. Before finishing, she calls Mike on her Samsung cellular phone from T-Mobile to see if there's anything else he needs. He asks her to pick up some PowerBars for him to take to the gym during his lunchtime workouts next week. On her way home, she stops at the bookstore and picks up a book—*The Da Vinci Code*.

After finishing up at work, Mike gets into his Jeep Cherokee and puts the new Ben Harper and the Innocent Criminals CD into the Clarion car stereo. He stops at the Amoco station to fill his gas tank and checks the air pressure in his Firestone tires. He makes a quick stop at Computerland to pick up the newest release of WordPerfect, signing the credit card slip with his Bic pen. Then he goes to the video store to pick up *The Pink Panther* on DVD, before heading to the package store for a bottle of Wild Turkey bourbon. He walks next door to the sporting goods store to pick up some Wilson racquetballs for his workouts next week and then heads home.

Barbara's favorite TV show, *Jeopardy!*, is just starting as Mike comes in the door, so she pours herself a glass of Beringer wine from Napa Valley and changes the Dish TV satellite channel on their Magnavox television so that she can watch her show. Before he prepares dinner, Mike opens a Miller beer and leafs through the day's mail, setting the most recent issue of *Road and Track* magazine aside to read later. Soon, dinner is ready and they sit down for their meal, while watching a show on the National Geographic Channel.

While this may sound like a very typical evening for many Americans, foreign-owned firms produced nearly every item that the Boltons purchased or consumed:

- Wackenhut is owned by Group 4 Falck of Denmark.
- J. Walter Thompson is owned by the WPP Group of the United Kingdom.
- Germany's DaimlerChrysler manufactures Chryslers and Jeeps.
- The British-Dutch company Royal Dutch Shell owns Shell.

employs the following definition: "A transnational corporation is generally regarded as an enterprise comprising entities in more than one country which operate under a system of decision-making that permits coherent policies and a common strategy. The entities are so linked, by ownership or otherwise, that one or more of them may be able to exercise a significant influence over the others and, in particular, to share knowledge, resources and responsibilities with the others."[2] More recently, some academic writers have employed the term *transnational* for a company that combines the characteristics of global and multinational firms: (1) trying to achieve economies of scale through global integration of its functional areas and, at the same time, (2) being highly responsive to different local environments (a newer name is *multicultural multinational*).[3] Managers, though, sometimes define a transnational as a company formed by a merger of two firms of approximately the same size that are from two different countries. Examples of such companies include Unilever (Dutch-English, food), TeliaSonera (Swedish-Finnish, telecommunications), Shell (Dutch-English, oil), and ABB (Swedish-Swiss, electrotechnical, power generating).

- Nestlé of Switzerland produces Alpo, Baby Ruth, Carnation Instant Breakfast, CoffeeMate, Friskies, Ortega, PowerBar, Stouffer's Lean Cuisine, and Tidy Cat.
- Unilever, a Dutch-based company, makes Slim-Fast, Dove bars, Hellmann's, Ragu, Lipton, Bird's Eye, and Ben & Jerry's.
- Cadbury Schweppes of the United Kingdom owns Mott's, Dr. Pepper, A&W Root Beer, and ReaLemon.
- Groupe Danone of France produces Evian water.
- Chicken-of-the-Sea is made by Thai Union International of Thailand.
- Japan's Kao owns Jergen's.
- Samsung cell phones are made by Korea's Samsung.
- T-Mobile is owned by Deutsche Telekom of Germany.
- Bertelsmann AG of Germany owns Random House and Doubleday (which published *The Da Vinci Code*).
- EMI of the United Kingdom owns Virgin Records, which releases Ben Harper and the Innocent Criminals CDs.
- *Road and Track* and *Elle* are published by Hachette Filipacchi Médias, a wholly owned subsidiary of France's Lagardére.
- Japan's Clarion Co. Ltd. Produces Clarion car stereos.
- Britain's BP owns Amoco.
- Japan's Bridgestone owns Firestone.
- Computerland is owned by Synnex Information Technologies, Inc., which is 56 percent owned by MiTac International Corporation of Taiwan.
- Corel Corporation of Canada owns WordPerfect.
- Bic of France produces Bic pens.
- Columbia Pictures, owned by Sony of Japan, released *The Pink Panther,* and Sony Pictures Television distributes *Jeopardy!* The Dixie Chicks CDs are produced by Sony BMG Music Entertainment (a 50-50 joint venture of Sony and Bertelsmann of Germany).
- Pernod Ricard of France produces Wild Turkey bourbon.
- Amer Group of Finland owns Wilson Sporting Goods.
- Beringer Winery of Napa, California, is owned by Australia's Foster's Group.
- News Corporation of Australia owns DirectTV and the National Geographic Channel.
- Magnavox is owned by Philips of the Netherlands.
- SABMiller of the United Kingdom makes Miller beer.

This simple example reflects the impact of extensive foreign investments in the United States, especially in recent years. Even some of the best-known "American" products and brands are now produced by foreign firms. "Why invest in the U.S.A.? It's simple. It's a great economy, and it produces great returns. Beyond that, the U.S. is so competitive that we know the things we learn operating there will help us in all of our other markets around the world," said Sir Ian Prosser, former chairman of the U.K.-based Six Continents hotel group.

Investments have also flowed outward from the United States. American companies such as Coca-Cola, Starbucks, McDonald's, the Gap, Microsoft, and Levi's are found in Japan, South Korea, Australia, Singapore, and nearly every European nation. American companies have also purchased a range of foreign companies and brands. Ford Motor Company owns the Jaguar, Land Rover, Aston Martin, and Volvo automobile brands; General Motors has purchased all or part of such companies as Daewoo, Opel, Suzuki, Vauxhall, and Saab.

With the exception of a rather small number of deals such as the potential takeover of Unocal by China's CNOOC, there has been almost no negative backlash among Americans to the flood of foreign investment into their country. Perhaps Americans realize that the buying and selling of companies around the world is just part of globalization, or perhaps Americans just do not realize how much their daily lives are impacted by foreign-owned companies. In fact, the livelihood of many Americans may depend on foreign investment, and approximately one in six U.S. jobs is tied to international trade and investment.

Source: From T. R. Reid, "Buying American? Maybe Not; Many U.S. Brands European-Owned," *Washington Post*, May 18, 2002; Nicholas Platt, "Make Global Skills a Top Priority," *Financial Times*, July 2, 2004, p. 13; and company Web sites (accessed July 3, 2006).

DEFINITIONS USED IN THIS TEXT

To avoid confusion due to the range of different definitions of terms in international business, in this text we will employ the definitions listed below, which are generally accepted by managers:

1. *International business* is business whose activities are carried out across national borders. This definition includes not only international trade and foreign manufacturing but also the growing service industry in areas such as transportation, tourism, advertising, construction, retailing, wholesaling, and mass communications.

2. *Foreign business* denotes the operations of a company outside its home or domestic market; many refer to this as business conducted within a foreign country. This term sometimes is used interchangeably with *international business* by some writers.

3. A **multidomestic company (MDC)** is an organization with multicountry affiliates, each of which formulates its own business strategy based on perceived market differences.

multidomestic company (MDC)
An organization with multicountry affiliates, each of which formulates its own business strategy based on perceived market differences

global company (GC)
An organization that attempts to standardize and integrate operations worldwide in all functional areas

international company (IC)
Either a global or a multidomestic company

4. A **global company (GC)** is an organization that attempts to standardize and integrate operations worldwide in most or all functional areas.*

5. An **international company (IC)** is a global or multidomestic company.

Although we primarily use the terms *global, multidomestic,* and *international* firms or companies, at times we may use *multinational enterprise (MNE)* or *multinational company (MNC)* interchangeably with *international company (IC),* inasmuch as both terms are employed in the literature and in practice.

A Brief History of International Business

While international business as a discipline is relatively new, international business as a business practice is not. Well before the time of Christ, Phoenician and Greek merchants were sending representatives abroad to sell their goods. Subsequently, a vast expansion of agricultural and industrial production in China stimulated the emergence of an internationally integrated trading system. The saying that "all roads lead to China" had relevance within the international trade system of medieval times.

The impact of the emerging international trading system was extensive. Politics, the arts, agriculture, industry, and other sectors of human life were profoundly influenced by the goods and ideas that came with trade. Public health was also impacted. An interesting precursor to contemporary concerns about global health epidemics, such as severe acute respiratory syndrome (SARS) and avian flu, was international trade's association with the spread of the plague, one of the worst natural disasters in history. Believed to have originated in Asia, the plague moved west with traders and soldiers, carried by oriental rat fleas that lived on rodents that stowed away on ships and caravans. Called the Black Death in Europe and repeated in waves from the mid-1300s through the 1500s, the plague ravaged cities, caused widespread hysteria, and killed one-quarter of China's people and one-third of the population of Europe.[4]

The rise of the Ottoman Empire before 1300, ultimately spanning Europe, North Africa, and the Middle East, profoundly influenced the emerging trade routes for people, goods, money, animals, and microorganisms that spanned from England to China, across the Mediterranean and Northern Africa, and through Central Asia and the Indian Ocean region. The powerful central location of the Ottomans within this trading web had the effect of raising the cost of Asian trade for the Europeans. This spawned a search for sea routes to Asia, including expeditions that discovered the Americas.

In 1600, Great Britain's British East India Company, a newly formed trading firm, began to establish foreign branches throughout Asia, an action soon followed by many of the other European nations intent on exploiting trade opportunities for national advantage, including Portugal, the Netherlands, and France. In 1602, the Dutch East India Company was formed to carry out colonial activities in Asia and to open ocean trade routes to the East. The first company to issue stock, it is also frequently identified as the world's first multinational corporation.[5] By the end of the 1600s, ships commissioned by European trading companies regularly traveled to Asia via an interconnected Atlantic, Indian, and Pacific ocean system of government-protected trade routes. Their goal was to acquire goods for sale or resale within various Asian markets and ultimately to return to Europe with valuable cargoes of cloth, spices, and other goods that would yield significant profits for investors. The 17th and 18th centuries have frequently been termed the "age of mercantilism" because the power of nations depended directly on the sponsorship and control of merchant capital, which expanded under the direct subsidization and protection of national governments. The concept of mercantilism is discussed in Chapter 3.

Colonial traders in the Americas began operating in a similar fashion in the 1700s. Early examples of American foreign direct investment are the English plants set up by Colt Fire Arms and Ford[†] (vulcanized rubber), which were established before the Civil War. Both operations failed, however, after only a few years.

---

*Note that in this definition global ownership is not a requirement. However, you should be aware that some people do include this along with other criteria, such as the ratio of foreign to total employment or foreign to total assets.

[†]This Ford was no relation to Henry Ford.

Global Company—By Whose Definition?

After talking about having to be a multinational firm (a collection of national businesses) to gain a competitive advantage, consultants and managers turned to the buzzword *globalization* as a strategy to beat their competitors. Unfortunately, *globalization* and its root, *global,* are overused and misused in international business because of the prestige that managements believe these words bring to their companies. Here are elements of various definitions, which state that a global company is an organization that:

1. Searches the world for (*a*) market opportunities, (*b*) threats from competitors, (*c*) sources of products, raw materials, knowledge, innovation, and financing, and (*d*) personnel. In other words, it has global vision.

2. Maintains a presence in key markets around the world.

3. Looks for similarities, not differences, among markets.

4. Standardizes operations worldwide in one or more of the firm's functional areas.

5. Integrates its operations worldwide.

There are those who believe a global firm must possess all of these characteristics and have a worldwide locus of control and ownership. Critics of this definition claim there is no global firm by that definition. To see how firms define the term *global* to suit their purposes, compare the following two situations:

- Allen-Edmonds is a small, privately held shoe manufacturer in Port Washington, Wisconsin, whose sales rose from $9.5 million in 1978 to an estimated $70 million currently. The president explains that the firm accomplished this by "choosing a market niche—manufacturing high-quality dress shoes for men, and by viewing the whole globe as our marketplace. Today, although we produce all our shoes in [Wisconsin and Maine], Allen-Edmonds is a *global manufacturing company*."[a]

- Emerson's management describes its company this way: "Emerson is a *global company* that brings together technology and engineering to provide innovative solutions for our customers in a wide range of industrial, commercial, and consumer markets. . . . We have grown to become one of the world's leading manufacturing companies with operations around the globe. . . . Emerson has more than 60 divisions that operate approximately 275 manufacturing locations worldwide. . . . With a global presence spanning 150 countries, Emerson is advantageously positioned with the infrastructure, knowledge and experience to provide integrated product solutions around the world. . . . Over the past 100-plus years, Emerson has grown from a regional manufacturer into a global technology solutions powerhouse."[b]

Although the same term is used in both situations by both companies, the definitions are different. Allen-Edmonds' president claims the title *global* simply because his company exports to agents and distributors in 33 nations. Presumably, he calls his firm a global manufacturing company because Allen-Edmonds does its own manufacturing instead of subcontracting from China, Indonesia, and other Asian nations as Nike and Adidas do. For other firms, such as Emerson, attaining global company status requires meeting additional criteria, thereby reducing the number of companies able to reach that goal. Their definition is essentially based on marketing, production, supply chain, and technological globalization.

Recently, however, the definition of the term *global company* has taken on still more new criteria. A global company is now said to be more culturally diverse and to incorporate much more worldwide standardization in its marketing, technical, and production functions. To utilize its worldwide assets more efficiently against competitors, the new global company places production plants and other parts of its value chain in those places worldwide where the company can gain the benefits of lower-cost labor and better-educated workers. Improvements in communications technology such as electronic data interchange (EDI) data exchange (invoices, purchase orders) between computers of manufacturers and suppliers, international networking, and teleconferencing have made it possible for project teams around the world to meld ideas from different cultures for greater exploitation of geographically dispersed knowledge and to promote increased innovation.

Organizations are also removing the barriers within their companies to allow the free flow of people as well as ideas, suggesting a globalization in the corporate mind-set. Many firms are offering top management positions to citizens from countries other than the home country. Some are even calling this newly defined global company by a new name: *multicultural multinational.*

The aims of the "multicultural multinational" are (1) to be responsive to local markets, (2) to produce and market its products worldwide, and (3) to exploit its knowledge and technological capabilities on a global basis—elusive goals reached by few companies so far. Although it has become fashionable to speak of global corporations as being "stateless" or "borderless," measurement by any criterion shows that such firms don't exist. Each has a home government and tax authority and is owned by shareholders from primarily one nation, which essentially makes it a national firm with international operations.

[a] Allen Edmonds, "Corporate Fast Facts," www.allenedmonds.com/webapp/wcs/stores/servlet/AllenEdmonds/about/Allen-Edmonds_PressKit_2005_English.pdf (July 3, 2006).

[b] "Emerson's Global Reach," www.gotoemerson.com/global_reach/index.html (July 3, 2006); "About Emerson," www.gotoemerson.com/about_emerson/index.html (July 3, 2006); "Emerson Company History," www.gotoemerson.com/about_emerson/ae.ch.html (July 3, 2006).

Source: Vijay Govindarajan and Anil K. Gupta, *The Quest for Global Dominance* (San Francisco: Jossey-Bass, 2001); Yves Doz, Jose Santos, and Peter Williamson, *From Global to Metanational* (Boston, MA: Harvard Business School Press, 2001).

A number of multinational companies existed in the late 1800s. One of the first to own foreign production facilities, have worldwide distribution networks, and market its products under global brands was Singer Sewing Machine. In 1868, it built a factory in Scotland, the first successful American venture into foreign production. By 1880, the company had become a global organization with an outstanding international sales organization and several overseas manufacturing plants. Other firms, such as J&P Coats (United Kingdom) and Ford, soon followed, and by 1914, at least 37 American companies had production facilities in two or more overseas locations.[6] Interestingly, and quite a contrast to today's situation, in the 1920s *all* cars sold in Japan were made in the United States by Ford and General Motors and sent to Japan in knocked-down kits to be assembled locally. European companies were also moving overseas. For example, Friedrich Bayer purchased an interest in a New York plant in 1865, two years after setting up his plant in Germany. Then, because of high import duties in his overseas markets, he proceeded to establish plants in Russia (1876), France (1882), and Belgium (1908).[7]

As you have just read, multinational firms existed well before World War I, and the level of intracompany trade of multinationals in 1930, as a percentage of overall world trade, may have exceeded the proportion at the end of the 20th century.[8] Yet only in recent years have multinationals become the object of much discussion and investigation, especially concerning the increasing globalization of their operations. What is globalization? What are the reasons for globalization?

Globalization—What Is It?

Although globalization is discussed everywhere—television shows, Internet chat rooms, political demonstrations, parliaments, management boardrooms, and labor union meetings—so far it has no widely accepted definition. In fact, its definition continues to broaden. Now, for example, social scientists discuss the political, social, environmental, historical, geographic, and even cultural implications of globalization.[9] Some also speak of technological globalization, political globalization, and the like.

However, the most common definition and the one used in international business is that of *economic globalization*—the tendency toward an international integration of goods, technology, information, labor, and capital, or the process of making this integration happen. The term *globalization* was first coined by Theodore Levitt in a *Harvard Business Review* article in which he maintained that new technologies had "proletarianized" communication, transport, and travel, creating worldwide markets for standardized consumer products at lower prices. He maintained that the future belonged to global corporations that did not cater to local differences in taste but, instead, adopted strategies that operated "as if the entire world (or major regions of it) were a single entity; [such an organization] sells the same things in the same way everywhere."[10]

Interestingly, at the 1999 World Economic Forum (WEF) annual meeting in Davos, Switzerland, a new word, *globality*, was introduced as the meeting's theme. Daniel Yergin, coauthor of *The Commanding Heights*, decided that since globalization is a process, a different word was needed for "the results of this process—a place, a condition, the situation that comes afterward," something that is unhampered by time zones or national boundaries. Professor Klaus Schwab, founder of the WEF, explained, "We wanted to look beyond the economic dimensions of what is happening. It is a globality." Bill Gates announced at the meeting that Microsoft would add *globality* to Microsoft's dictionary.[11] German sociologist Ulrich Beck stated, "Globality means that from now on nothing that happens on our planet is only a limited local event; all inventions, victories, and catastrophes affect the whole world."[12] Although globalization forces may affect all nations, not all of them have achieved the same extent of globalization. Table 1.1 provides two alternative efforts to assess the degree of globalization of different nations. As you can see, the ranking of different countries is strongly impacted by the dimensions of globalization being evaluated, highlighting the difficulties associated with measuring this complex concept.

GLOBALIZATION FORCES

Five major kinds of drivers, all based on change, are leading international firms to the globalization of their operations: (1) political, (2) technological, (3) market, (4) cost, and (5) competitive:

1. Political   There is a trend toward the unification and socialization of the global community. Preferential trading arrangements, such as the North American Free Trade Agreement and the European Union, that group several nations into a single market have presented firms with significant marketing opportunities. Many have moved swiftly to gain access to the combined markets of these trading partners, either through exporting or by producing in the area.

Two other aspects of this trend are contributing to the globalization of business operations: (a) the progressive reduction of barriers to trade and foreign investment by most governments, which is hastening the opening of new markets by international firms that are both exporting to them and building production facilities in them, and (b) the privatization of much of the industry in formerly communist nations and the opening of their economies to global competition.

2. Technological   Advances in computers and communications technology are permitting an increased flow of ideas and information across borders, enabling customers to learn about foreign goods. Cable and satellite TV systems in Europe and Asia, for example, allow an advertiser to reach numerous countries simultaneously, thus creating regional and sometimes global demand. Global communications networks enable manufacturing personnel to coordinate production and design functions worldwide so that plants in many parts of the world may be working on the same product.

The Internet and network computing enable small companies to compete globally because they make possible the rapid flow of information regardless of the physical location of

TABLE 1.1 Globalization Rankings: The KOF Index of Globalization and the A. T. Kearney/Foreign Policy Globalization Index

KOF 2006 Index of Globalization					A. T. Kearney/Foreign Policy 2005 Globalization Index					
Overall Globalization Rank	Nation	Economic Globalization Rank	Social Globalization Rank	Political Globalization Rank	Overall Globalization Index Rank	Nation	Economic Integration Ranking	Personal Contact Ranking	Technological Connectivity Ranking	Political Engagement Ranking
1	United States	28	1	1	1	Singapore	1	3	11	32
2	Sweden	12	4	5	2	Ireland	2	2	13	19
3	Canada	18	2	8	3	Switzerland	9	1	7	29
4	United Kingdom	27	12	2	4	United States	60	40	1	43
5	Luxembourg	1	14	102	5	Netherlands	5	11	8	4
6	Austria	10	13	12	6	Canada	27	8	2	10
7	France	17	22	3	7	Denmark	29	7	5	13
8	Australia	38	3	36	8	Sweden	12	10	9	16
9	Switzerland	7	9	33	9	Austria	10	5	14	2
10	Hong Kong, China	2	6	123	10	Finland	15	20	6	15
11	Ireland	3	23	24	11	New Zealand	36	16	3	21
12	Singapore	5	7	65	12	United Kingdom	32	12	10	5
13	New Zealand	13	5	59	13	Australia	37	34	4	25
14	Finland	8	11	34	14	Norway	35	15	12	17
15	Japan	44	8	27	15	Czech Republic	11	4	24	35
16	Belgium	6	32	7	16	Croatia	7	6	28	26
17	Netherlands	4	18	44	17	Israel	19	9	16	46
18	Denmark	30	15	15	18	France	24	17	21	3
19	Norway	20	10	30	19	Malaysia	4	19	27	49
20	Germany	35	20	10	20	Slovenia	17	13	20	23

Source: Axel Dreher, "Does Globalization Affect Growth? Evidence from a New Index of Globalization." *Applied Economics* 38, no. 10 (2006), pp. 1091–1110: "Measuring Globalization: The Global Top 20," *Foreign Policy*, May–June 2005, pp. 52–60.

the buyer and seller. Internet videoconferencing allows sellers to demonstrate their products to prospective buyers all over the world without the need to travel. It also permits international companies to hold corporate meetings between managers from headquarters and overseas subsidiaries without expensive, time-consuming travel. In addition, communicating by e-mail on the Internet is faster and more reliable than using postal mail and much less expensive than using a fax machine. Both Internet uses have given home office managers greater confidence in their ability to direct overseas operations.

The Internet and network computing enable small companies to compete globally because they make possible the rapid flow of information regardless of the physical location of the buyer and seller.

The ease of obtaining information and making transactions on the Internet has started to have a profound effect on many firms and especially on business-to-business commerce. Whereas companies formerly used faxes, telephones, or regular mail to complete their transactions, they now use the cheaper and faster Internet. The emergence of third-generation (3G) broadband wireless telecommunications technologies and associated applications promises to further accelerate this trend.

3. Market

As companies globalize, they also become global customers. For years, advertising agencies established offices in foreign markets when their major clients entered those markets to avoid having a competitor steal the accounts. Likewise, when an automaker, about to set up a foreign plant where there was no tire factory, asked a tire company if it was interested in setting up a plant in this new market, the response was, "When do you want us there?" It is also quite common for a global supplier to make global supply contracts with a global customer.

Finding the home market saturated also sends companies into foreign markets. According to a recent Dow Jones survey of the world's largest companies, 84 percent of the respondents expect that international markets will generate most of their growth in the next five years.[13] Indeed, since the United States has only about 5 percent of the world's population, the vast proportion of most companies' potential customers are located abroad.

4. Cost

Economies of scale to reduce unit costs are always a management goal. One means of achieving them is to globalize product lines to reduce development, production, and inventory costs. The company can also move production or other parts of the company's value chain to countries where the costs are lower. Dramatic reductions in the cost of generating and transmitting information due to innovations in computing and telecommunications, as well as the decline in transportation costs, have facilitated this trend toward relocating activities worldwide.

5. Competitive

Competition continues to increase in intensity. New firms, many from newly industrialized and developing countries, have entered world markets in automobiles, computers, and electronics, for example. Another competitive driving force for globalization is the fact that companies are defending their home markets from competitors by entering the competitors' home markets to distract them. Many firms that would not have entered a single country because it lacked sufficient market size have established plants in the comparatively larger trading groups (European Union, ASEAN, Mercosur). It is one thing to be shut out of Belgium, but it is another to be excluded from all Europe.

The result of this rush to globalization has been an explosive growth in international business.

EXPLOSIVE GROWTH

Both the size and the number of U.S. and foreign international concerns have been increasing very rapidly.

Foreign Direct Investment and Exporting

One variable commonly used to measure where and how fast internationalization is taking place is the increase in total foreign direct investment (FDI). **Foreign direct investment** refers to direct investments in equipment,

foreign direct investment
Direct investments in equipment, structures, and organizations in a foreign country at a level that is sufficient to obtain significant management control; does not include mere foreign investment in stock markets

>>A Little Guy Makes Global Business Easier for the Little Guys

DE Technologies, a tiny Virginia-based private company with only six employees and offices in the United States and Canada, has patented a technology for using the Internet/intranet to process sales globally. Intended for small and medium-size enterprises, development of the technology was stimulated by the frustrations that DE Technologies' founder encountered while attempting to arrange international trade deals in Russia for his own small company. Traditional systems for international trade, involving multiple, inefficient, and time-consuming layers of vertical service industries, can require 20 or more forms and 60 days to complete and cost 5 to 40 percent of the cost of the total transaction.

With DE's system, which is called the Electronic Commerce Backbone System (ECBS), small and medium-size firms can automatically export and import goods and services without previous international trade experience. The ECBS allows buyers and sellers to buy products in the currency of the destination country, view product descriptions in the language of the destination country, view digital still or motion video displays of the products for sale, and view the calculations and displays of prices for air, land, and sea transportation; it also ensures direct payment of goods via credit cards or documentary credit.

Procedures such as the preparation and filing of export–import documents, freight, insurance, titles, letters of credit, pro forma invoices, and bills of lading are done by the program. This eliminates the necessity of engaging foreign freight forwarders, export and import agents, and other international channels-of-distribution members. Thus, ECBS reduces the costs of ocean and air freight, banking, and human resources.

Small and medium-size enterprises (SMEs) can become members by paying a small membership fee, which gives them access to the ECBS. A transactional fee of 0.3 percent also is levied. According to the founder of DE Technologies, "the capability of the system will allow thousands of SMEs to compete effectively in the Import/Export business with 'The Big Guys' as the barriers to entry will be lowered tremendously."

The ECBS can be supplemented with the Borderless Order Entry System (BOES), a patented process for electronically managing international trade transactions in an integrated manner. It allows companies to create and file necessary electronic documents (in any currency or language), monitor and track steps in the transaction, calculate applicable freight costs as well as taxes and duties, and perform financial arrangements of a sophisticated nature. The result is a reduction of as much as 30 percent in the costs of conducting international trade transactions. SMEs can export and import products from any nation, using the Internet or Intranets, and thereby expand market share in international markets.

Source: "Cutting through a World of Red Tape," *Business Week On-line*, www.businesswe . . . m/smallbiz/0006/te000628.htm?script Framed (June 30, 2000); "Electronic Commerce Backbone System (ECBS)," *DE Technologies Web site*, www.detechnologies.com/ecbs.htm (July 1, 2004); "Information Technology and International Trade Position Paper," *DE Technologies Web site*, www.detechnologies.com/ecbs.htm (July 3, 2006); and "Borderless Order Entry Systems," *DE Technologies Web site*, www.detechnologies.com/boes.htm (July 3, 2006).

structures, and organizations in a foreign country at a level that is sufficient to obtain significant management control. It does not include mere foreign investment in stock markets. In the United States, 10 percent ownership in a company is considered sufficient in order to be listed as FDI; in other countries, an investment is not considered FDI until a share of 20 or 25 percent is reached. The world stock of outward FDI was over $9.7 *trillion* in 2004, which was more than 17 times what it was 24 years earlier, in 1980 (see Table 1.2).

Note, in Table 1.2, that the total assets of multinational foreign affiliates were $26.5 trillion, generating $17.7 trillion in sales and 53.1 million jobs in 2002. The value of cross-border mergers and acquisitions (M&As) increased from $134 billion in 1995 to $1,144 billion in 2000, before declining to $594 billion in 2001 in response to economic recession in many nations and declining stock markets. The value of cross-border M&As then began increasing again, reaching an estimated $567 billion in 2006.

Of course, a substantial amount of international business involves exporting rather than FDI. **Exporting** is the transportation of any domestic good or service to a destination outside a country or region. It is the opposite of importing, which is the transportation of any good or service into a country or region, from a foreign origination point. Merchandise exports have grown faster than world output in nearly each of the past 55 years. Between 1980 and 2004, the level of world merchandise exports more than quadrupled, from $2,031 billion to $8,907

exporting

The transportation of any domestic good or service to a destination outside a country or region; the opposite of importing, which is the transportation of any good or service into a country or region, from a foreign origination point

TABLE 1.2 FDI Indicators and Multinational Company Statistics (billions of dollars and percentages)

FDI Data	Value ($ billions)				As % of Gross Domestic Product			
	1980	1990	2000	2004	1980	1990	2000	2004
Inflows	$ 55	$ 209	$1,393	$ 648				
Outflows	54	242	1,201	730				
Inward stock	699	1,954	6,147	8,895	6.1%	8.9%	20.0%	21.7%
Outward stock	564	1,763	5,992	9,732	5.4	8.4	19.6	24.0

	1990–1995 (annual average)	1996	1997	1998	1999	2000	2001	2002	2003	2004
Cross-border M&As	$118	$227	$305	$532	$766	$1,144	$594	$370	$297	$381

Foreign Affiliate Data	Value at Current Prices ($ billions)						
	1996	1997	2000	2002	1996–2000	2001	2002
Sales	$ 9,372	$ 9,728	$ 15,680	$ 17,685	10.9%	9.2%	7.4%
Total assets	11,246	12,211	21,102	26,543	19.2	4.5	8.3
Exports	1,841	2,035	3,572	2,613	9.6	−3.3	4.2
Employment (000s)	30,941	31,630	45,587	53,094	14.2	−1.5	5.7

Source: "Table 1. Selected Indicators of FDI and International Production, 1982–2000," *World Investment Report 2001*, UNCTAD; "Country Fact Sheet: United States," *World Investment Report 2005*, UNCTAD; "Foreign Direct Investment Flows," UNCTAD GlobStat database, http://globstat.unctad.org/html/index.html (July 4, 2004); and "Foreign Affiliates in Host Economies," UNCTAD GlobStat database, http://globstat.unctad.org/html/index.html (July 4, 2004).

billion. The level of service exports worldwide increased more than 5.5 times during the same period, growing from $385 billion to $2,125 billion.[14] Trends regarding FDI and exporting are discussed in Chapter 2, and theories for exporting and FDI are discussed in Chapter 3.

Number of International Companies We also have estimates of the number of global and multidomestic firms in the world. UNCTAD, the United Nations agency in charge of all matters relating to FDI and international corporations, estimated that there were 70,000 companies in 2004, with a total of 690,000 foreign affiliates, that accounted for approximately 25 percent of global output. They accounted for two-thirds of world trade. Foreign affiliates' sales (almost $19 trillion in 2004) were far in excess of global trade ($11 trillion).[15] In 1995, UNCTAD estimated that there were only 45,000 parent companies with 280,000 foreign affiliates, with total sales of US$7 trillion.[16]

As a result of this expansion, the subsidiaries of foreign companies have become increasingly important in the industrial and economic life of many nations, developed and developing. This situation is in sharp contrast to the one that existed when the dominant economic interests were in the hands of local citizens. The expanding importance of foreign-owned firms in local economies came to be viewed by a number of governments as a threat to their autonomy. However, there has been a marked liberalization of government policies and attitudes toward foreign investment in both developed and developing nations since the early 1980s. Leaders of these governments know that local firms must obtain modern commercial technology in the form of direct investment, purchase of capital goods, and the right to use the international company's expertise if they are to be competitive in world markets.*

Despite this change in attitude, there are still critics of large global firms who cite such statistics as the following to "prove" that host governments are powerless before them:

1. In 2004, only 19 nations had gross national incomes (GNIs) greater than the total annual sales of Wal-Mart, the company with the world's greatest sales.

2. Also in 2004, the total amount of money spent in Wal-Marts worldwide was greater than the combined GNIs of the 112 smallest economies of the 208 listed in the World Bank's World Development Indicators database.

As Table 1.3 indicates, these statements are true. In fact, when nations and industrial firms are ranked by GNI and total sales, respectively, 50 of the first 100 on the list are industrial firms. However, a nation's GNI and a company's sales are not directly comparable because GNI is a measure of value added, not sales. If a nation's total sales were computed, the result would be far greater than its GNI because there would be triple and quadruple counting. For example, suppose a steel manufacturer sells steel wire to a tire company, which uses it to build tires. Then the tire company sells the tires to automakers, which mount them on their automobiles, which they in turn sell to the public. Sales of the wire would be counted three times. However, in calculating GNI, governments merely sum the values added in each transaction, which is the difference between the sales of the company and the costs of materials bought outside the company. If company sales were measured by value added, Wal-Mart's sales of $288 billion would have been $65 billion. While Wal-Mart's sales are twice as large as Iceland's GNI, when the economy is measured by the value added, Iceland's economy is more than twice the size of Wal-Mart.

A firm's size may at times give it bargaining power, as in the case of a government that wants a firm to set up a subsidiary because of the employment it will offer and the purchases it will make from other firms in that country. Yet, regardless of the parent firm's size, each subsidiary is a local company that must comply with the laws in the country where it is located. If it does not, it can be subject to legal action or even government seizure.

THE GLOBALIZATION DEBATE AND YOU

Recently the merits of globalization have been the subject of many heated debates. When the World Trade Organization met in Seattle in 1999, there were extensive public protests about globalization and the liberalization of international trade. Further antiglobalization protests occurred when the WTO met in Davos, Switzerland, in early 2001, and at other gatherings of international organizations and leaders since that time. The debate is, in many respects, waged by diametrically opposed groups with extremely different views regarding the consequences of globalization. Sifting through the propaganda and hyperbole spouted by both sides is a challenge. However, it is important to recognize the various perspectives on globalization, as their arguments can generate appeal (or rejection) both intellectually and emotionally. The contributions of free trade and globalization to dramatic reductions in worldwide poverty are contrasted with anecdotal stories of people losing their livelihoods under the growing power of multinationals. Likewise, increases in service sector employment are contrasted against losses in high-paying manufacturing jobs.

We believe that a book such as this should acquaint you with the arguments from both sides, because how this debate is resolved will have a great effect on the international business activities you will one day manage, deal with, or be affected by. The evolution of the debate will

Protesters carry a banner linking free trade practices and sea turtle survival during the WTO meeting in Seattle in 1999. All seven species of sea turtles are currently endangered.

---

*Granting the right to use a firm's expertise for a fee is called *licensing*. See Chapter 16 for more details about licensing and other forms of international market entry.

Ranking	Nation or Company	GNI or Total Sales for 2004 ($ billion)	Ranking	Nation or Company	GNI or Total Sales for 2004 ($ billion)
1	United States	$12,168	51	Malaysia	113
2	Japan	4,734	52	Volkswagen (G)	111
3	Germany	2,532	53	Citigroup (U.S.)	108
4	United Kingdom	2,013	54	ING Group (N)	106
5	China	1,938	55	Venezuela, RB	105
6	France	1,888	56	Singapore	105
7	Italy	1,513	57	United Arab Emirates	103
8	Spain	919	58	Nippon Telegraph & Telephone (J)	101
9	Canada	905	59	American Int'l Group (U.S.)	98
10	Mexico	705	60	IBM (U.S.)	96
11	India	673	61	Philippines	95
12	Korea, Rep.	673	62	Czech Republic	93
13	Brazil	552	63	Siemens (G)	91
14	Australia	544	64	Colombia	91
15	Netherlands	523	65	Pakistan	91
16	Russian Federation	489	66	Egypt, Arab Rep.	91
17	Switzerland	366	67	Carrefour (F)	90
18	Belgium	326	68	Hungary	85
19	Sweden	322	69	Chile	84
20	Wal-Mart Stores (U.S.)	288	70	Hitachi (J)	84
21	BP (U.K.)	285	71	Assicurazioni Generali (It)	83
22	Exxon Mobil (U.S.)	271	72	New Zealand	81
23	Turkey	269	73	Matsushita Electric Industrial (J)	81
24	Royal Dutch Shell (U.K.-N)	269	74	McKesson (U.S.)	81
25	Austria	264	75	Honda (J)	80
26	Indonesia	248	76	Hewlett-Packard (U.S.)	80
27	Saudi Arabia	243	77	Nissan (J)	80
28	Norway	238	78	Fortis (B-N)	76
29	Poland	233	79	Sinopec (PRC)	75
30	Denmark	220	80	Berkshire Hathaway (U.S.)	74
31	General Motors (U.S.)	194	81	ENI (It)	74
32	Greece	185	82	Algeria	73
33	Hong Kong, China	184	83	Home Depot (U.S.)	73
34	DaimlerChrysler (G)	177	84	Aviva (U.K.)	73
35	Toyota (J)	173	85	HSBC Holdings (U.K.)	73
36	Finland	172	86	Deutsche Telekom (G)	72
37	Ford (U.S.)	172	87	Verizon Communications (U.S.)	72
38	South Africa	165	88	Samsung Electronics (K)	72
39	Thailand	158	89	State Grid (PRC)	71
40	Iran, Islamic Rep.	155	90	Peugeot (F)	71
41	General Electric (U.S.)	153	91	Metro (G)	70
42	Total (F)	153	92	Nestlé (S)	70
43	Portugal	149	93	U.S. Postal Service (U.S.)	69
44	Chevron Texaco (U.S.)	148	94	BNP Paribas (F)	69
45	Ireland	140	95	China National Petroleum (PRC)	68
46	Argentina	137	96	Sony (J)	67
47	ConocoPhillips (U.S.)	122	97	Cardinal Health (U.S.)	65
48	AXA (F)	122	98	Peru	65
49	Allianz (G)	119	99	Royal Ahold (N)	65
50	Israel	118	100	Altria Group (U.S.)	64

Note: Belgium (B), China (PRC), France (F), Germany (G), Italy (It), Netherlands (N), Switzerland (S), United Kingdom (U.K.), and United States (U.S.).

Source: *World Development Indicators* database, http://devdata.worldbank.org/data-query/ (July 4, 2006); and Fortune 2005 Global 500, http://money.cnn.com/magazines/fortune/global500/2005 (July 4, 2006).

affect all our lives. The nearby Worldview box, "The Debate on Globalization of Trade and Investment," briefly summarizes some of the arguments for and against the globalization process and its outcomes. Many of the issues associated with globalization are highly complex, and it is not possible to deal with them fully within an introductory text such as this. As was shown in Table 1.1, there is no single measure of globalization or of integration within the world economy. Each element of global integration can have different effects. However, the material presented in the various chapters of this book can help you, the reader, become more informed about globalization and the relative merits of various positions being taken regarding this important subject.

If the debate about globalization has been rancorous and divisive, the outcome of this debate is likely to change substantially the various aspects of the economic environment—both within and between various countries—and it will strongly affect your future as a participant in international business or a teacher of it. As you read the Worldview synopsis of the issues and arguments of supporters and opponents of globalization, and throughout your reading of this book, we hope that you will consider carefully the goals and process of globalization. Through informed education, perhaps the public debate can move beyond a simplistic argument for or against globalization and toward how best to strengthen the working of the global economy and thereby contribute to the enhancement of the welfare of the world and its inhabitants.

Why Is International Business Different?

International business differs from domestic business in that a firm operating across borders must deal with the forces of three kinds of environments—domestic, foreign, and international. In contrast, a firm whose business activities are carried out within the borders of one country needs to be concerned essentially with only the domestic environment. However, no domestic firm is entirely free from foreign or international environmental forces because the possibility of having to face competition from foreign imports or from foreign competitors that set up operations in its own market is always present. Let us first examine these forces and then see how they operate in the three environments.

FORCES IN THE ENVIRONMENTS

environment
All the forces surrounding and influencing the life and development of the firm

uncontrollable forces
External forces over which management has no direct control, although it can exert an influence

The term **environment** as used here means all the forces influencing the life and development of the firm. The forces themselves can be classified as *external* or *internal*. The external forces are commonly called **uncontrollable forces.** Management has no direct control over them, although it can exert influences such as lobbying for a change in a law and heavily promoting a new product that requires a change in a cultural attitude. External forces consist of the following:

1. *Competitive:* kinds and numbers of competitors, their locations, and their activities.

2. *Distributive:* national and international agencies available for distributing goods and services.

3. *Economic:* variables (such as GNP, unit labor cost, and personal consumption expenditure) that influence a firm's ability to do business.

4. *Socioeconomic:* characteristics and distribution of the human population.

5. *Financial:* variables such as interest rates, inflation rates, and taxation.

6. *Legal:* the many foreign and domestic laws governing how international firms must operate.

7. *Physical:* elements of nature such as topography, climate, and natural resources.

8. *Political:* elements of nations' political climates such as nationalism, forms of government, and international organizations.

9. *Sociocultural:* elements of culture (such as attitudes, beliefs, and opinions) important to international managers.

The Debate on Globalization of Trade and Investment

In recent years, the rapid pace of globalization of trade and investment has been accompanied by corresponding debate regarding globalization's implications. This Worldview provides a brief overview of some of the issues and arguments associated with the globalization debate; we hope it will whet your appetite for examining many of these issues in more depth in the chapters that follow.

Arguments supporting globalization

Expanding trade by collectively reducing barriers is the most powerful tool that countries, working together, can deploy to reduce poverty and raise living standards.

—Horst Kohler and James Wolfensohn

That free trade is the best strategy for advancing the world's economic development is one of the few propositions on which almost all economists agree, not only because it is theoretically compelling but also because it has been demonstrated in practice. On a wide range of measures—poverty, education, health, and life expectancy—more people have become better off at a faster pace in the past 60 years than at any other time in history. Evidence is strong regarding the dramatic decline in both the proportion and the absolute number of destitute people. The latest World Development Indicators from the World Bank show that the number of people in extreme poverty fell from 1.5 billion in 1981 to 1.1 billion in 2001. Measured as a proportion of the population in developing countries, the decline was from 39.5 percent in 1981 to 21.3 percent in 2001. Between 1981 and 1999, the proportion of people in the East Asia and Pacific region living on less than $1 a day fell from 56 to 16 percent. In China, it plummeted from 61 to 17 percent. In South Asia, it fell from 52 to 31 percent. The proportion of people living in nations with daily food supplies under 2,200 calories per capita has declined from 56 percent in the mid-1960s to less than 10 percent. Life expectancy in the developing world has nearly doubled since World War II, and infant mortality has decreased in all of the developing regions of the world. The proportion of children in the labor force fell from 24 percent in 1960 to 10 percent in 2000. Global literacy grew from 52 percent in 1950 to 81 percent in 1999, and on average the more globally integrated countries spend more on public education, especially in developing countries. Citizens from more globally integrated countries have greater levels of civil liberties and political rights. Within a generation's time, there has been an enormous improvement in the human condition, and every one of the development success stories was based on export-led growth facilitated by the liberalization of trade.

Of course, countries can reject globalization, and some have, including Myanmar, the Democratic Republic of Congo, Sierra Leone, Rwanda, Madagascar, Guinea-Bissau, Algeria, the Republic of Congo, Burundi, Albania, Syria, and Ukraine. They are among the most impoverished countries in the world.

As an article in the *Financial Times* puts it, "They are victims of their refusal to globalize."

Expanded trade is also linked with the creation of more and better jobs. Over the past two decades—a period of immense technological change and growth in trade—around 40 million more jobs were created than were destroyed in the United States. It is true that when a country opens to trade, just as when new technologies are developed, some of its sectors may not be competitive. Companies may go out of business, and some jobs will be lost. But trade creates new jobs, and these tend to be better than the old ones. The key is not to block change but, instead, to manage the costs of trade adjustment and to support the transition of workers to more competitive employment.

Concerns with globalization

We're not against trade; we want trade rules that allow Americans to compete fairly in the marketplace. The record is clear: Current trade policy isn't working. It has led to tremendous job loss and human rights abuses. The [proposed] FTAA [Free Trade Area of the Americas] will leave plant closings, trashed environments and sweatshops in its wake.

—Richard Trumka, secretary-treasurer, AFL-CIO

Broadly publicized demonstrations—such as the so-called Battle of Seattle that wrecked the Seattle World Trade Organization trade talks in 1999, as well as subsequent disruptions at venues such as the International Monetary Fund/World Bank meetings in Washington, D.C., and Prague—brought widespread public attention to the antiglobalization movement. Those expressing concern with globalization have come from a range of sectors of society, and they express a correspondingly diverse set of concerns. Some fundamentally oppose the very process and outcomes of globalization on ideological grounds, while others may merely be concerned about finding ways to better manage globalization processes and the resulting outcomes. Some of the opponents' concerns may be viewed as naïve or clearly inconsistent with the preponderance of evidence. Other challenges to globalization may have theoretic merit or other supporting evidence and certainly may be worthy of discussion and the fostering of substantive change.

Although perspectives on the globalization debate may in many respects depend on one's values and ideology, thus further compounding efforts to reach a mutually agreed-on resolution, let us first ask this question: What are some of the primary concerns of the opponents of globalization? While many of the antiglobalizers concede that globalization "increases the size of the pie," they also claim that it has been accompanied by a broad array of injurious social implications. Among their concerns, let us briefly examine three primary ones here: (1) that globalization has produced uneven results across nations and people, (2) that globalization has had deleterious effects on labor and labor standards, and (3) that globalization has contributed to a decline in environmental and health conditions.

(continued)

1. *Globalization has produced uneven results across nations and people.* In stark contrast to the positive picture presented by supporters of globalization, opponents describe the painful impact of foreign investment and trade liberalization on the people of the world. Far from everyone has been a winner, they say. The promise of export-led growth has failed to materialize in several places. For example, Latin America has failed to replicate Asia's success despite efforts to liberalize, privatize, and deregulate its economies, with results ranging from disappointment in Mexico to catastrophe in Argentina. Similarly, efforts in sub-Saharan Africa have failed to yield benefits, and the share of the population living in extreme poverty there rose from 42 to 47 percent between 1981 and 2001. Open world markets, it seems, may offer the possibility of economic development—but the recipe is neither easy in its implementation nor universal in its outcomes.

   Many opponents of globalization have claimed that there is a huge gap between the world's rich and poor and that globalization has caused that gap to increase. That there is a gap between rich and poor is unquestionable, but the evidence is perhaps not so clear regarding the charge that globalization has increased this inequality. Although Martin Wolf 's analysis shows that income inequality has not risen in most developing countries that have integrated with the world economy, it does show that inequality has increased in some places, most notably in China. Inequality has risen in some high-income countries as well, but he attributes that more to the nature of technological change than to globalization. When income data are adjusted to reflect relative purchasing power, the inequality in income between poor and rich nations diminishes. Wolf also notes that while globalization of trade and investment is an enabler to improved income and living standards, the results may vary if obstacles exist such as poor governance or excessive borrowing.

2. *Globalization has had deleterious effects on labor and labor standards.* The issue of the impact of globalization on labor standards has become an oft-mentioned concern of workers in the United States and other nations. With trade liberalization through the World Trade Organization and increased mobility of capital, measures to keep a country's industries within its borders have been reduced and companies have an easier time divesting their interests in one country and moving to another. Workers in developed countries frequently voice concerns that their jobs will migrate to developing nations where there are lower standards, and thus lower costs, leading to the infamous "race to the bottom," where developed nations with more rigorous labor standards become disadvantaged. Indeed, the Labor Secretariat for the North American Free Trade Agreement commissioned a report that found over half of firms surveyed used threats to close U.S. operations as a tool to fight union-organizing efforts. Since NAFTA's inception and the subsequent reduction in trade and investment barriers, these threats have become more plausible. As reported by Alan Tonelson, "In fact, more than 10 percent of employers studied . . . 'directly threatened to move to Mexico,' and 15 percent of firms, when forced to bargain with a union, actually closed part or all of a factory—triple the rate found in the late 1980s, before NAFTA."

   The concern can run both ways, however. Although labor standards in developing countries are usually lower than in industrialized countries, they are rising and evidence shows that multinationals investing in host nations pay higher wages, create new jobs at a faster rate, and spend more on R&D than do local firms. Developing countries may also view the imposition of more demanding labor standards within their borders as a barrier to free trade. They may feel that lower-cost labor constitutes their competitive advantage and that if they are forced to implement more stringent labor standards, then companies may no longer have an incentive to set up operations in their countries, damaging their prospects for improved economic development. As the authors of *Globaphobia* ask, "Is it humane for the United States to refuse to trade with these countries because their labor standards are not as high as we would prefer? The consequence of taking this position is that many third-world

10. *Labor:* composition, skills, and attitudes of labor.

11. *Technological:* the technical skills and equipment that affect how resources are converted to products.

controllable forces

Internal forces that management administers to adapt to changes in the uncontrollable forces

The elements over which management does have some control are the internal forces, such as the factors of production (capital, raw materials, and people) and the activities of the organization (personnel, finance, production, and marketing). These are the **controllable forces** management must administer in order to adapt to changes in the uncontrollable environmental variables. Look at how one change in the political forces—the expansion of the European Union in 2004—has affected all the controllable forces of firms worldwide that do business in or with the 25 member-nations. Suddenly these firms had to examine their business practices and change those affected by this new expansion. For example, some European concerns and foreign subsidiaries in the EU have relocated parts of their operations to other nations in the Union in order to exploit the lower wages there. Some American and Asian workers will have no jobs at all, or must take jobs that pay even lower wages and have even worse working conditions than those currently available in the export-oriented sector." A November 2003 study by the Carnegie Endowment for International Peace found that Mexico's agricultural sector, which provides most of the country's employment, had lost 1.3 million jobs since NAFTA was implemented in 1994. In addition, far from diminishing under NAFTA, the flow of impoverished Mexicans into the United States has risen dramatically, the study says.

3. *Globalization has contributed to a decline in environmental and health conditions.* Regarding concerns of antiglobalization forces that globalization contributes to declining environmental standards, former president Zedillo of Mexico stated, "Economic integration tends to favor, not worsen the environment. Since trade favors economic growth, it brings about at least part of the necessary means to preserve the environment. The better off people are, the more they demand a clean environment. Furthermore, it is not uncommon that employment opportunities in export activities encourage people to give up highly polluting marginal occupations." Yet a difficulty caused by the North American Free Trade Agreement and the maquiladora program that began before NAFTA has been the substantial increases in ground, water, and air pollution along the Mexico-U.S. border. Damage to the environment has been caused by the many new production facilities and the movement of thousands of Mexicans to that area to work in them. In addition, some health and environmental issues extend beyond the scope of trade agreements. Some of NAFTA's rules on trade in services may cause governments to weaken environmental standards for sometimes hazardous industries like logging, trucking, water supply, and real estate development. For example, to comply with NAFTA's rules on trade in services, the Bush administration recently waived U.S. clean air standards in order to allow trucks based in Mexico to haul freight on U.S. highways. Globalization opponents argue that this could increase air pollution and associated health concerns in border states, as the aging Mexican truck fleet pollutes more than similar U.S. trucks and these vehicles do not use the cleaner fuels required in the United States. Protesters have also claimed that, under liberalized rules regarding the globalization of trade and investment, businesses have an incentive to move their highly polluting activities to nations that have the least rigorous environmental regulations or a lower risk of liability associated with operations that can create environmental or health-related problems. On the other hand, the economic growth fostered by globalization can help generate and distribute additional resources for protecting the environment, and improved trade and investment can enhance the exchange of more environmentally friendly technologies and best practices, particularly within developing nations.

Source: Gary Burtless, Robert Z. Lawrence, Robert E. Litan, and Robert J. Shapiro, *Globaphobia: Confronting Fears about Open Trade* (Washington, DC: Brookings Institution Press, 1998); Alan Tonelson, *The Race to the Bottom: Why a Worldwide Worker Surplus and Uncontrolled Free Trade Are Sinking American Living Standards* (Boulder, CO: Westview Press, 2002); "Globalization," http://en.wikipedia.org/wiki/Globalization (July 5, 2006); "United States Rises, Russia Plummets in Annual Ranking of World's Most Globalized Nations," www.atkearney.com/main.taf?p=1,5,1,157 (July 5, 2006); "ICC Brief on Globalization," www.iccwbo.org/home/commercial_practice/case_for_the_global_economy/globalization%20brief/globalization_brief.asp (July 5, 2006); Daniel Seligman, "On NAFTA's Tenth Anniversary, Americans Demand Safe, Clean and Fair Trade," Sierra Club, San Francisco, www.sierraclub.org/pressroom/releases/pr2003-12-23a .asp (March 6, 2004); John-Thor Dahlburg, "Protesters Tell a Different Tale of Free Trade," *Los Angeles Times*, November 20, 2003, p. A3; Paul Krugman, "The Good News," *New York Times*, November 28, 2003, p. A31; Horst Kohler and James Wolfensohn, "We Can Trade Up to a Better World," *Financial Times*, December 12, 2003, p. 19; Martin Wolf, *Why Globalization Works* (New Haven, CT: Yale University Press, 2004); *Human Development Report 2003*, United Nations Development Program, New York, http://hdr.undp.org/reports/global/2003/pdf/hdr03_HDI.pdf (July 15, 2004); *World Development Indicators 2004*, World Bank, http://www .worldbank.org/data/countrydata/countrydata.html (July 15, 2004); and John Audley, Sandra Polaski, Demetrios G. Papademetriou, and Scott Vaughan, *NAFTA's Promise and Reality: Lessons from Mexico for the Hemisphere*, (Washington, DC: Carnegie Endowment for International Peace, 2003).

companies have set up production in one of the member-countries to supply this giant free trade area. By doing this, they avoid paying import duties on products coming from their home countries.

THE DOMESTIC ENVIRONMENT

The **domestic environment** is all the uncontrollable forces originating in the home country that influence the life and development of the firm. Obviously, these are the forces with which managers are most familiar. Being domestic forces does not preclude their affecting foreign operations, however. For example, if the home country is suffering from a shortage of foreign currency, the government may place restrictions on overseas investment to reduce its outflow. As a result, managements of multinationals find that they cannot expand overseas facilities as they would like to do. In another instance from real life, a labor union striking the home-based plants learned that management was supplying parts from its foreign

domestic environment
All the uncontrollable forces originating in the home country that surround and influence the firm's life and development

subsidiaries. The strikers contacted the foreign unions, which pledged not to work overtime to supply what the struck plants could not. The impact of this domestic environmental force was felt overseas as well as at home.

THE FOREIGN ENVIRONMENT

foreign environment
All the uncontrollable forces originating outside the home country that surround and influence the firm

The forces in the **foreign environment** are the same as those in the domestic environment except that they occur in foreign nations.* However, they operate differently for several reasons, including those below.

Forces Have Different Values
Even though the kinds of forces in the two environments are identical, their values often differ widely, and at times they are completely opposed to each other. A classic example of diametrically opposed political-force values and the bewilderment they create for multinational managers was the case of Dresser Industries and the gas pipeline in the former Soviet Union. When President Reagan extended the American embargo against shipments of equipment for the pipeline to include foreign companies manufacturing equipment under license from U.S. firms, the Dresser home office instructed its French subsidiary to stop work on an order for compressors. Meanwhile, the French government ordered Dresser-France to defy the embargo and begin scheduled deliveries under penalty of both civil and criminal sanctions. As a Dresser's vice president put it, "The order put Dresser between a rock and a hard place."

A similar case occurred when, because of the American export embargo on shipments to Cuba, that country could not buy buses from the U.S. manufacturer with which it had done business for years. To circumvent the embargo, the government ordered the buses from the firm's Argentine subsidiary. When word came from the firm's American headquarters that the order should not be filled because of the American embargo, the Argentine government ordered the Argentine subsidiary to fill the order, saying that Argentine companies, of which the subsidiary was one, did not answer to the demands of a foreign government. The Argentine management of the subsidiary was in a quandary. Finally, headquarters relented and permitted its Argentine subsidiary to fill the order.

Forces Can Be Difficult to Assess
Another problem with foreign forces is that they are frequently difficult to assess. This is especially true of legal and political forces. A highly nationalistic law may be passed to appease a section of the local population. To all outward appearances, the government may appear to be against foreign investment; yet pragmatic leaders may actually encourage it. A good example is Mexico, which until 1988 had a law prohibiting foreigners from owning a majority interest in a Mexican company. However, a clause permitted exceptions "if the investment contributes to the welfare of the nation." IBM, Eaton, and others were successful in obtaining permission to establish a wholly owned subsidiary under this clause.

The Forces Are Interrelated
In the chapters that follow, it will be evident that the forces are often interrelated. This in itself is not a novelty, because the same situation confronts a domestic manager. On the foreign scene, however, the kinds of interaction that occur and the outcomes may differ. For instance, the combination of high-cost capital and an abundance of unskilled labor in many developing countries may lead to the use of a lower level of technology than would be employed in the more industrialized nations. In other words, given a choice between installing costly, specialized machinery needing few workers and installing less expensive, general-purpose machinery requiring a larger labor force,

---

Foreign has multiple definitions according to the *American Heritage Dictionary,* including (1) originating from the outside—external, (2) originating from a country other than one's own, and (3) conducted or involved with other nations or governments. *Extrinsic* is a synonym. Note that we are not using another possible definition—unfamiliar or strange. Some writers have this last definition in mind when they state that overseas markets in which the firm does business are not foreign because their managers know them well. However, according to any of the first three definitions, the degree of familiarity has no bearing.

management will frequently choose the latter when faced with high interest rates and a large pool of available workers. Another example is the interaction between physical and sociocultural forces. Barriers to the free movement of a nation's people, such as mountain ranges and deserts, help maintain pockets of distinct cultures within a country, and this has an effect on decision making.

THE INTERNATIONAL ENVIRONMENT

The **international environment** consists of the interactions (1) between the domestic environmental forces and the foreign environmental forces and (2) between the foreign environmental forces of two countries when an affiliate in one country does business with customers in another. This agrees with the definition of international business: business that involves the crossing of national borders.

international environment
Interaction between domestic and foreign environmental forces or between sets of foreign environmental forces

For example, personnel at the headquarters of a multidomestic or global company work in the international environment if they are involved in any way with another nation, whereas those in a foreign subsidiary do not unless they too are engaged in international business through exporting or the management of other affiliates. In other words, a sales manager of Nokia's China operations does not work in the international environment if he or she sells cellular phones only in China. If Nokia's China operations export cell phones to Thailand, then the sales manager is affected by forces of both the domestic environment of China and the foreign environment of Thailand and therefore is working in the international environment. International organizations whose actions affect the international environment are also properly part of it. These organizations include (1) worldwide bodies (e.g., World Bank), (2) regional economic groupings of nations (e.g., North American Free Trade Agreement, European Union), and (3) organizations bound by industry agreements (e.g., Organization of Petroleum Exporting Countries).

Decision Making Is More Complex   Those who work in the international environment find that decision making is more complex than it is in a purely domestic environment. Consider managers in a home office who must make decisions affecting subsidiaries in just 10 different countries (many internationals are in 20 or more countries). They not only must take into account the domestic forces but also must evaluate the influence of 10 foreign national environments. Instead of having to consider the effects of a single set of 10 forces, as do their domestic counterparts, they have to contend with 10 sets of 10 forces, *both individually and collectively,* because there may be some interaction.

For example, if management agrees to labor's demands at one foreign subsidiary, chances are it will have to offer a similar settlement at another subsidiary because of the tendency of unions to exchange information across borders. Furthermore, as we shall observe throughout this text, not only are there many sets of forces, but there are also extreme differences among them.

Another common cause of the added complexity of foreign environments is managers' unfamiliarity with other cultures. To make matters worse, some managers will ascribe to others their own preferences and reactions. Thus, the foreign production manager, facing a backlog of orders, may offer the workers extra pay for overtime. When they fail to show up, the manager is perplexed: "Back home they always want to earn more money." This manager has failed to understand that the workers prefer time off to more money. This unconscious reference to the manager's own cultural values, called the **self-reference criterion**, is probably the biggest cause of international business blunders. Successful managers are careful to examine a problem in terms of the local cultural traits as well as their own.

self-reference criterion
Unconscious reference to one's own cultural values when judging behaviors of others in a new and different environment

International Business Model

The relationships of the forces in the three environments we have been discussing form the basis of our international business environments model, shown in Figure 1.1. The external or uncontrollable forces in both the domestic and the foreign environments surround the internal forces controlled by management. The domestic environment of the international firm's home country is surrounded by as many sets of foreign environments as there are countries in which the company does business. Solid lines connecting the internal forces at the home office to the internal forces in the foreign affiliates indicate the lines of control. The orange areas indicate the international environment in which personnel in the headquarters of the international firm work. If, for example, the affiliate in foreign environment A exports to or manages the affiliate in foreign environment B, then its personnel are also working in the international environment, as shown by the orange section.

Organization of This Book

We shall be using the international business environments model throughout the book. After describing the nature of international business in Section One, we examine the international institutions and the international monetary system in Section Two. In Section Three, we analyze the uncontrollable forces that make up the foreign and domestic environments and

---

FIGURE 1.1

International
Business
Environments

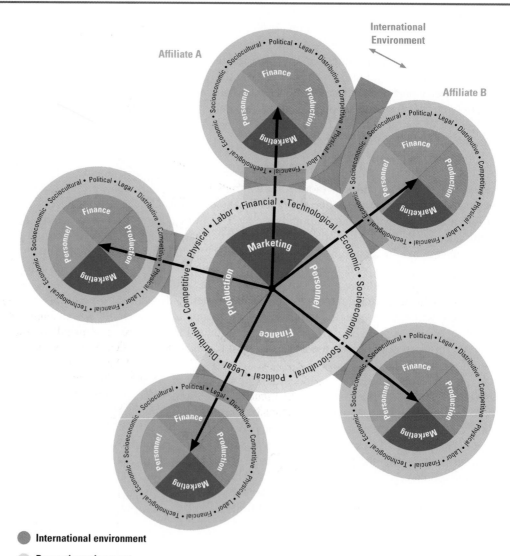

● **International environment**

○ **Domestic environment**
(Includes socioeconomic, sociocultural, political, legal, distributive, competitive, physical, labor, financial, technological, and economic environments)

● **Foreign environment**
(Includes socioeconomic, sociocultural, political, legal, distributive, competitive, physical, labor, financial, technological, and economic environments)

illustrate their effect on management functions. Finally, we reverse the procedure in Section Four and deal with the management functions, demonstrating how they are influenced by the uncontrollable forces.

A solid understanding of the business concepts and techniques employed in the United States and other advanced industrial nations is a requisite for success in international business. However, because transactions take place across national borders, three environments—domestic, foreign, and international—may be involved instead of just one. Thus, in international business, the international manager has three choices in deciding what to do with a concept or a technique employed in domestic operations: (1) transfer it intact, (2) adapt it to local conditions, or (3) not use it overseas. International managers who have discovered that there are differences in the environmental forces are better prepared to decide which option to follow. To be sure, no one can be an expert on all these forces for all nations, but just knowing that differences may exist will cause people to "work with their antennas extended." In other words, when they enter international business, they will know they must look out for important variations in many of the forces that they take as given in the domestic environment. It is to the study of the three environments that this text is directed.

Summary

Appreciate the dramatic internationalization of markets.

Global competition is mounting. The huge increase in import penetration, plus the massive amounts of overseas investment, means that firms of all sizes face competitors from everywhere in the world. This increasing internationalization of business is requiring managers to have a global business perspective gained through experience, education, or both.

Understand the various names given to firms that have substantial operations in more than one country.

The following definitions are used in this text: A *global company* is an organization that attempts to standardize operations worldwide in all functional areas. A *multidomestic company,* by contrast, is an organization with multicountry affiliates, each of which formulates its own business strategy based on perceived market differences. The term *international company* is often used to refer to both global and multidomestic firms.

Understand the five kinds of drivers, all based on change, that are leading international firms to the globalization of their operations.

Following are the five change-based drivers that are leading international firms to globalize their operations, with an example for each kind: (1) *political*—preferential trading agreements, (2) *technological*—advances in communications technology, (3) *market*—global firms become global customers, (4) *cost*—globalization of product lines and production helps reduce costs by achieving economies of scale, and (5) *competitive*—firms are defending their home markets from foreign competitors by entering the foreign competitors' markets.

Comprehend why international business differs from domestic business.

International business differs from its domestic counterpart in that it involves three environments—domestic, foreign, and international—instead of one. Although the kinds of forces are the same in the domestic and foreign environments, their values often differ, and changes in the values of foreign forces are at times more difficult to assess. The international environment is defined as the interactions (1) between the domestic environmental forces and the foreign environmental forces and (2) between the foreign environmental forces of two countries when an affiliate in one country does business with customers in another. An international business model helps explain this relationship.

Describe the three environments—domestic, foreign, and international—in which an international company operates.

The *domestic environment* is composed of all the uncontrollable forces originating in the home country that influence the firm's life and development. The *foreign environment* is composed of all the forces originating outside the home country that influence the firm. The *international environment* is the interaction between the domestic and foreign environment forces or between sets of foreign environmental forces.

Key Words

Questions

1. What are the differences between international, global, and multidomestic companies?

2. Give examples to show how an international business manager might manipulate one of the controllable forces in answer to a change in the uncontrollable forces.

3. "A nation whose GNI is smaller than the sales volume of a global firm is in no position to enforce its wishes on the local subsidiary of that firm." True or false? Explain.

4. Discuss the forces that are leading international firms to the globalization of their sourcing, production, and marketing.

5. Business is business, and every firm has to produce and market its goods. Why, then, might managers be unable to apply the techniques and concepts they have learned in their own country to other areas of the world?

6. What do you believe makes foreign business activities more complex than purely domestic ones?

7. Discuss some possible conflicts between host governments and foreign-owned companies.

8. Why, in your opinion, do the authors regard the use of the self-reference criterion as "probably the biggest cause of international business blunders"? Can you think of an example?

9. You have decided to take a job in your hometown after graduation. Why should you study international business?

10. Although forces in the foreign environment are the same as those in the domestic environment, they operate differently. Why is this so?

11. What examples of globalization can you identify within your community? How would you classify each of these examples (e.g., international investment, international trade)?

12. Why is there opposition to globalization of trade and integration of the world's economy? Please assess the major arguments for and against such globalization efforts.

Research Task

 globalEDGE.msu.edu

Use the globalEDGE site (http://globalEDGE.msu.edu/) to complete the following exercises:

1. Several classifications and rankings of multinational corporations (MNCs) are published to assess their relative size and success. One such set of rankings is the *Global 2000* published by Forbes. Which countries are represented in the top 25 of this list? You are required to analyze any industry patterns that may exist across the different countries represented in this list. Do you notice any differences in the industries represented? Is there a predominant industry that appears in the top

25 for the United States? What about the other countries represented in the top 25?

2. The WTO's *International Trade Statistics* is an annual report that provides comprehensive, comparable, and current statistics on trade in merchandise and commercial services. This report allows for an assessment of world trade flows by country and by main product or service categories. Using the most recent statistics available, identify the top five countries that lead in the export and import of merchandise, respectively.

Which of the following companies or brands are foreign-owned? Who are the owners and which country(ies) are the owners based in?

1. 7-Eleven Stores
2. Chesebrough-Pond (Vaseline)
3. Snapple
4. Coors beer
5. 7 Up
6. Baby Ruth (candy bar)
7. Holiday Inn
8. *Fast Company* magazine
9. TriStar Pictures
10. Arco (gasoline)
11. Scott Paper (Kleenex)
12. Elizabeth Arden
13. *Woman's Day* magazine
14. Ralston Purina
15. Motel 6
16. Pinkerton (security guards)
17. Ban deodorant
18. RCA Records
19. IBM Thinkpad (laptop computers)
20. Shaeffer pens

2

International Trade and Foreign Direct Investment

If you care about global poverty and, for that matter, about equality, your aim should be to raise the growth rates of poor countries. Successful countries have all exploited global market opportunities, predominantly international trade and, to a more variable extent, foreign direct investment, to accelerate their growth. Successful globalization has, in short, reduced both poverty and inequality.

—*Martin Wolf, global business analyst*

Large International Firms Invest Overseas, and They Also Export

Large American international firms, responding to such factors as (1) global competition, (2) liberalization by host governments in regard to foreign investment, and (3) advances in technology, were a major reason that American outward foreign direct investment (FDI) reached its highest level ever, $252 billion, in 2004. This represented nearly six times the U.S. average during the period from 1985 to 1995 and more than double the level of 2003.[a] Inasmuch as foreign direct investment generally is used to set up or acquire assets to produce goods and services abroad, have U.S. exports dropped as a result of the $1.26 trillion in U.S. FDI in the period 1996–2004?

Apparently not. Although some flows of goods and services from the United States to foreign markets have been replaced due to production from these investments abroad, the overall level of American exports of goods and services increased from $783 billion in 1995 to $1,272 billion in 2005, an increase of 62 percent in a decade.[b] Are small firms, large firms, or both kinds responsible for this growth? It is a common belief that small and medium-size companies, because they lack the financial and human resources, supply their foreign markets by exporting to them rather than producing in them and that large international companies do just the opposite. In fact, the U.S. Department of Commerce states that approximately two-thirds of U.S. exports of goods are by U.S.-owned multinational corporations, with over one-third of those exports being shipped by the U.S. parent to foreign affiliates.

We examined the largest multinationals in the 2006 Fortune Global 500 list of the largest multinationals. Among the companies examined, the ratio of foreign sales to total sales ranged from 86 percent for Daimler-Chrysler to 20 percent for Wal-Mart Stores, with an average of 50.0 percent (see Table 2.1). A similar examination of the world's 100 largest multinationals reported that foreign sales averaged 54 percent of these companies' total sales.[c] Many of the companies on these two lists sell to 100 countries or more. Even though large international companies such as these typically have numerous production facilities overseas, it is usually not feasible for them to have a factory in every market. The foreign investment would be too great for them to attempt to set up production facilities in each market. Also, many markets are too small to support local manufacturing; they must be served by exports.

To appreciate the importance of international trade and foreign investment for these companies, examine the last column in Table 2.1, which shows that the ratio of net income from foreign sales to total net income averaged 52 percent for these large multinationals. Overall, for the 500 members of the Standard & Poor's stock index, about 30 percent of their total worldwide profit came from overseas.[d] Without sales and profits generated from foreign operations, the competitiveness of many of these companies would be seriously damaged and some of them might be unable to remain in business. ■

[a]"Country Fact Sheet: United States," *World Investment Report 2005* (Geneva: UNCTAD, September 2005), and Finfacts Team, "US Foreign Direct Investment Outflow Hits Record; Ireland's Inflow Down in 20," www.finfacts.com/irelandbusinessnews/publish/article_10002361.shtml (July 14, 2006).

[b]*International Trade Statistics 2005* (Geneva: World Trade Organization, 2005), pp. 197 and 205, www.wto.org/english/res_e/statis_e/its2005_e/its2005_e.pdf (July 11, 2006), and "Table E.1, U.S. International Transactions in Goods and Services," *Survey of Current Business*, May 2006, p. D-58.

[c]"Table 1.4, Snapshot of the World's 100 Largest TNCs: Assets, Sales and Employment, 2002, 2003," *World Investment Report 2005* (Geneva: UNCTAD, 2005), p. 17.

[d]Based on figures for 2003, as presented in "Kerry Plan on Trade Irks Firms," *International Herald Tribune*, July 20, 2004, p. 17.

CONCEPT PREVIEWS

After reading this chapter, you should be able to:

appreciate the magnitude of international trade and how it has grown

identify the direction of trade, or who trades with whom

explain the size, growth, and direction of foreign direct investment, worldwide and in the United States

identify who invests and how much is invested in the United States

understand the reasons for entering foreign markets

comprehend that globalization of an international firm occurs over at least seven dimensions and that a company can be partially global in some dimensions and completely global in others

Rank in 2006 Fortune Global 500 list	Company	Total Sales ($ billions)	Total Net Income ($ billions)	Foreign Sales ($ billions)	Foreign Sales as % of Total Sales	Net Income from Foreign Operations ($ billions)	Income from Foreign Operations as % of Total Net Profit
1	ExxonMobil	$340	$36	—	—	$25	69%
2	Wal-Mart Stores	316	11	$ 63	20%	3	30
3	Royal Dutch/Shell	307	25	205	67	—	—
5	General Motors	193	−11	65	34	—	—
6	Chevron	190	14	112	59	9	66
7	DaimlerChrysler	186	4	160	86	–	—
8	Toyota Motor	186	12	99	57	3	26
9	Ford Motor	177	2	80	45	—	—
10	ConocoPhillips	167	14	49	29	6	42
11	General Electric	157	16	78	52	13	78
	Average				50		52

Note: Foreign sales refers to sales outside the home country of the company. All figures are based on 2005 fiscal year, as reported in 2006, except for Wal-Mart Stores, whose fiscal year ended January 31, 2006. This list excludes BP, which was ranked the 4th largest, because the company's annual report did not provide information on either foreign sales or net income from foreign operations.
— = information not provided in company annual report.

Source: Company annual reports, *Fortune* magazine's 2006 Global 500 listing of world's largest companies, http://money.cnn.com/magazines/fortune/global500/2006/full_list (July 14, 2006).

The opening section of this chapter illustrates the fact that both means of supplying overseas markets—*exporting* to and *production* in those markets—are essential to most major U.S. corporations. Moreover, these two international business activities are not confined to manufacturing concerns. Among the companies *Fortune* listed as the 500 largest multinationals, over 40 percent are classified as service companies with primary activities in banking, finance, insurance, business services, entertainment, computer software and services, transportation and travel, and retailing. However, smaller firms also have operations overseas. According to a division of the U.S. Department of Commerce, small and medium-size firms accounted for 97 percent of all U.S. exporters and over 27 percent of the value of American exports (see the nearby mini-MNE box).

In this chapter, we examine two topics directly related to exporting and production in foreign countries: (1) *international trade,* which includes exports and imports, and (2) *foreign direct investment,* which international companies must make to establish and expand their overseas operations.[1] Our focus in this chapter will be on trends and traits of international trade and investment across the globe. Chapter 3 will present an overview of theories that have been developed to explain the incidence and level of international trade and investment that we see in results presented in this chapter. Later, in the chapters on importing and global supply chain management (Chapters 17 and 19, respectively), we shall discuss the third activity of international business—**foreign sourcing**, the overseas procurement of raw materials, components, and products.

foreign sourcing

The overseas procurement of raw materials, components, and products

International Trade

The following discussion of international trade first examines the volume of trade, including which nations account for the largest volume of the world's exports and imports. We then discuss the direction of trade and the trend toward increased regionalization of international trade. We finish this section of the chapter by examining major trading partners and their relevance for managers.

>> How Important Are Small and Medium-Size Enterprises in Generating Export Sales?

The Exporter Data Base (a joint project of the International Trade Administration and the Census Bureau) provides some insight into the relative importance of small and medium-size enterprises (SMEs) in generating U.S. exports. If SMEs are categorized as companies with fewer than 500 employees, an analysis of the Exporter Data Base reveals the following:

- The total number of American companies exporting goods in 2003 was 225,190, nearly double the 112,854 companies that exported in 1992.[a] Of these exporters, 218,382 were SMEs (97 percent of all U.S. exporters). Nonmanufacturing companies, such as wholesalers, accounted for 68 percent of all SME exporters and 60 percent of the value of exports by SMEs.

- Very small companies, with fewer than 20 employees, accounted for 69 percent of all U.S. exporting firms. Firms with fewer than 100 employees generated 21 percent of the volume of U.S. merchandise exports.

- California has the largest number of SME exporters (53,700 companies), but 17 states have more than 5,000 SME exporters each.

- 61 percent of SME exporters sold goods to only one foreign market, and 5 percent sold to 10 or more countries.

- 93 percent of firms that exported advanced technology products were SMEs.

- 63 percent of all exports of wood products, 43 percent of textiles and fabric products, and 40 percent of apparel and accessories were made by SMEs.

- The proportion of U.S. merchandise exports generated by SMEs has been increasing, rising to over 27 percent of merchandise exports in 2003.

- The total export revenues of SMEs increased to $171.5 billion in 2003, a 67 percent increase in 11 years. Of all exports by SMEs, 28 percent ($48 billion) went to NAFTA countries (SMEs accounted for 95 percent of the American companies exporting to Canada, and 91 percent of those exporting to Mexico). The next-largest market in sales was Japan ($14 billion), followed by China and the United Kingdom ($9 billion each), South Korea ($7 billion), and Germany ($6 billion). The countries representing the largest growth in SME exports in the prior decade were China (increasing 416 percent), Malaysia (up 259 percent), Ireland (up 227 percent), and Brazil (increasing by 152 percent).

- California had the highest value of exports by SMEs, at $35.5 billion, followed by Texas ($19.5 billion), New York ($15.9 billion), Florida ($11.0 billion), and Illinois ($5.6 billion). SMEs accounted for 40 to 75 percent of all exports from nine states, including Alaska, California, Florida, Hawaii, Montana, New Hampshire, New York, Rhode Island, and Wyoming.

- In comparison to large companies, SMEs are highly dependent on initiatives undertaken by the U.S. government to open foreign markets to trade. Unlike large exporting companies, most SMEs lack offshore subsidiaries that can circumvent trade barriers and improve market access. Almost 90 percent of SME exporters operate from a single location in the United States, while only 11 percent of large exporting companies operate from a single location.

[a]The Exporter Data Base may slightly understate the total number of exporters. The database excludes exporters of services and includes only direct exporters. Only exporters with shipments exceeding $2,500 were included in the database.

Source: *Small and Medium-Sized Exporting Companies, Statistical Overview, 2003* (Washington, DC: International Trade Administration, Office of Trade and Economic Analysis, U.S. Department of Commerce), www.ita.doc.gov/td/industry/otea/sme_handbook/SME_index.htm (July 11, 2006).

VOLUME OF TRADE

In 1990, a milestone was reached when the volume of international trade in goods and services measured in current dollars surpassed $4 trillion. Fourteen years later, despite a global economic slowdown that began in 2000, international trade in goods and services had nearly tripled, exceeding $11 trillion (see Figure 2.1). The dollar value of total world exports in 2004 was greater than the gross national product of every nation in the world except the United States. One-fourth of everything grown or made in the world is now exported, another measure of the significance of international trade.

Of the $11 trillion in international trade in goods and services in 2004, exports of merchandise were $8.9 trillion, about 4.5 times what they had been 24 years earlier. While smaller in absolute terms, worldwide trade in services, at more than $2.1 trillion in 2004, has grown faster since 1980 than has trade in merchandise. Inflation was responsible for part of

FIGURE 2.1 — World Exports of Merchandise and Commercial Services, by Selected Region and Nation (FOB values; billions of current U.S. dollars)

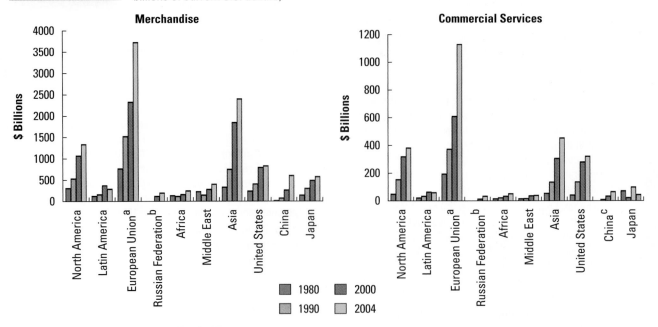

a Includes 15 members for 1980–2000, 25 members for 2004.

b Data not available for 1980 and 1990.

c Data not available for 1980.

Source: *Monthly Bulletin of Statistics* (New York: United Nations, June 1997), pp. 92–102 and 266–71; *Monthly Bulletin of Statistics* (New York: United Nations, August 2000), pp. 92–111 and 122; "World Merchandise Exports by Region and Selected Economy, 1980, 1985, 1990, 1995 and 1999–2001," World Trade Organization, Statistics Division, www.wto.org/english/res_e/statis_e/statis_e.htm (June 30, 2002); "World Exports of Commercial Services by Selected Region and Economy, 1980–2001," World Trade Organization, Statistics Division, www.wto.org/english/res_e/statis_e/statis_e.htm (June 5, 2002); "World Service Exports by Region and Selected Economy, 1992–02," *International Trade Statistics 2003* (Geneva: World Trade Organization, 2003), pp. 171–74, 179–81; and "Growth in the Value of World Merchandise Trade by Region, 2004," *International Trade Statistics 2005* (Geneva: World Trade Organization, 2005) pp. 20, 23.

this trade increase, but using a quantum index that eliminates the effects of inflation from the data shows that the volume of world trade in 2004 was approximately four times what it had been in 1970.

How even has this growth in trade been? Have some nations fared better than others? As Figure 2.1 shows, the proportion of world merchandise exports varied to some extent across regions during the time periods listed. Although the absolute value of their merchandise exports increased, the proportion of exports coming from the regions of Latin America, Africa, and the Middle East decreased between 1980 and 2004. For example, the level of exports from Africa grew by 92 percent from 1980 to 2004, yet the region's proportion of overall world merchandise exports declined by more than half. In contrast, the proportion of merchandise exports from Asia increased by about 70 percent between 1980 and 2004, with China accounting for just over half of that increase. The European Union and North America increased their proportion of world trade as well, although part of that increase is attributable to the expansion of the EU to 25 member-countries.

The results for services exports share some similarity with merchandise exports. The extensive growth in the level of overall worldwide trade in services means that all of the regions and essentially all of the primary nations have experienced an absolute increase in the dollar volume of services exports. The proportion of world exports of commercial services accounted for by Latin America, Africa, and the Middle East has evidenced an overall decline since 1980. However, the developed countries as a whole have been accounting for a large and rising proportion of services exports, particularly the United States. Asia has also been increasing its proportion of services exports, increasing from 13.7 to 21.2 percent between 1980 and 2004.

The rapid expansion of world exports since 1980 demonstrates that the opportunity to increase sales by exporting is a viable growth strategy. As you saw in Table 2.1, there are numerous large international firms that need these sales to survive. At the same time, however, the export growth of individual nations should be a warning to managers that they must be prepared to meet increased competition from exports to their own domestic markets. Figure 2.2 shows that the proportion of manufacturing value added that is located in developed countries has been roughly stable for the past 20 years, although Western Europe's share of this value-adding activity has slipped by over 20 percent since 1990. Developing countries' share of value added has been increasing during this time, although the location of value-adding activities has been changing substantially. For example, while Africa and Latin America have not added appreciably to their proportion of worldwide manufacturing value added, the proportion generated by the countries of Central and Eastern Europe declined dramatically in the years immediately before and after the demise of the Soviet Union. Further, South and East Asia's share of the world's manufacturing value added has nearly quadrupled since 1980. These trends have important implications for managers in terms of not merely where there may be new markets (e.g., for machine tools or other capital goods used by expanding manufacturing sectors) but also where competition in manufacturing may be intensifying or where new sources of export competition might emerge.

Which Nations Account for the Most Exports and Imports? Which nations are responsible for the large and growing levels of merchandise and services trade that we have seen worldwide? Table 2.2 presents the world's 20 largest nations in terms of exporters and importers of merchandise and of services. As you can see, the largest exporters and importers of merchandise are generally developed countries, although emerging economies such as China, Mexico, and Malaysia are also represented among the largest 20. These data also show that the largest exporters and importers account for a very high proportion of overall merchandise trade, approximately 75 percent of both exports and imports.

Trade in services evidences many similarities to trade in merchandise, in terms of the countries represented among the leaders. A notable difference is that the only emerging economies ranking among the leaders for both exports and imports of services are China and India. The concentration of worldwide services trade is approximately the same as that for merchandise trade, approximately 75 percent of both exports and imports.

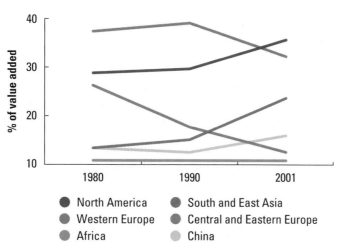

FIGURE 2.2

Manufacturing Value-Added for Developed and Developing Regions (percentage of value added at current prices)

Source: "Foreign Direct Investment: Foreign Direct Investment Flows," United Nations Conference on Trade and Development, http://globstat.unctad.org/html/index.html (July 14, 2006).

TABLE 2.2 20 Leading Exporters and Importers in World Merchandise and Service Trade (billions of dollars and percentage)

	Merchandise Exporters				Merchandise Importers				Service Exporters				Service Importers		
Rank	Nation	Value	Share	Rank	Nation	Value	Share	Rank	Nation	Value	Share	Rank	Nation	Value	Share
1	Germany	$912	10.0	1	United States	$1,526	16.1	1	United States	318	15.0	1	United States	260	12.4
2	United States	819	8.9	2	Germany	717	7.6	2	United Kingdom	172	8.1	2	Germany	193	9.2
3	China	593	6.5	3	China	561	5.9	3	Germany	134	6.3	3	United Kingdom	136	6.5
4	Japan	566	6.2	4	France	466	4.9	4	France	110	5.1	4	Japan	134	6.4
5	France	449	4.9	5	United Kingdom	464	4.9	5	Japan	95	4.5	5	France	96	4.6
6	Netherlands	358	3.9	6	Japan	455	4.8	6	Spain	85	4.0	6	Italy	81	3.8
7	Italy	349	3.8	7	Italy	351	3.7	7	Italy	82	3.9	7	Netherlands	72	3.5
8	United Kingdom	347	3.8	8	Netherlands	319	3.4	8	Netherlands	73	3.4	8	China	72	3.4
9	Canada	317	3.5	9	Belgium	286	3.0	9	China	62	2.9	9	Ireland	58	2.8
10	Belgium	307	3.3	10	Canada	280	2.9	10	Hong Kong	54	2.5	10	Canada	56	2.7
11	Hong Kong	266	2.9	11	Hong Kong	273	2.9	11	Belgium	49	2.3	11	Spain	54	2.6
12	S. Korea	254	2.7	12	Spain	249	2.6	12	Austria	48	2.3	12	S. Korea	50	2.4
13	Mexico	189	2.1	13	S. Korea	225	2.4	13	Ireland	47	2.2	13	Belgium	48	2.3
14	Russian Federation	184	2.0	14	Mexico	206	2.2	14	Canada	47	2.2	14	Austria	47	2.2
15	Taiwan, ROC	182	2.0	15	Taiwan, ROC	168	1.8	15	S. Korea	40	1.9	15	India	41	2.0
16	Singapore	180	2.0	16	Singapore	164	1.7	16	India	40	1.9	16	Singapore	36	1.7
17	Spain	179	2.0	17	Austria	118	1.2	17	Sweden	38	1.8	17	Denmark	33	1.6
18	Malaysia	127	1.4	18	Switzerland	112	1.2	18	Switzerland	37	1.7	18	Sweden	33	1.6
19	Saudi Arabia	126	1.4	19	Australia	109	1.2	19	Singapore	37	1.7	19	Russian Fed'n	33	1.6
20	Sweden	123	1.3	20	Malaysia	105	1.1	20	Denmark	36	1.7	20	Taiwan, ROC	30	1.4

Note: Rankings are based on trade data for 2004.

Source: World Trade Organization, *International Trade Statistics 2005* (Geneva: World Trade Organization, 2005), pp. 21, 23.

DIRECTION OF TRADE

What are the destinations of these merchandise exports? If you never have examined trade flows, you may think that international trade consists mainly of manufactured goods exported by the industrialized nations to the developing nations in return for raw materials. However, Table 2.3 shows that this is only partially correct. While more than half the exports from developing nations do go to developed countries, this proportion has been declining over the past 35 years, from 72 percent in 1970 to under 53 percent in 2004. Also, over 70 percent of exports from developed economies go to other industrialized nations, not to developing countries. As shown in the table, Japan and the United States are exceptions, with each sending a larger portion of its exports to developing nations than is the case for developed economies as a whole.

One reason Japan sells more to developing nations than most developed nations do is that it has had an extensive distribution system in those markets since the early 1900s. Because the country has no local sources for many raw materials, it has used general trading companies (*sogo shosha* in Japanese) to import many of the raw materials and components necessary for Japanese industry. The trading companies' offices in developing nations—where these raw materials and components are obtained—also market Japanese manufactured products to those nations (including components for industrial and consumer markets, such as electronic equipment and parts, as well as capital goods, such as machine tools). Many Japanese companies in consumer electronics, computers, and other areas have moved manufacturing operations to lower-cost nations such as China and various Southeast Asian countries, producing substantial "reverse imports" to Japan as these goods replace products traditionally manufactured in Japan. Overall, the percentage of Japanese imports coming from the "Asia-9" nations (China, Hong Kong, Indonesia, Korea, Malaysia, Philippines, Singapore, Taiwan, and Thailand) increased approximately 50 percent between 1990 and 2004. About 50 percent of Japan's imports come from developing countries in Asia, and about 50 percent of Japan's exports go to developing nations in Asia.[2]

The United States also exports a smaller proportion to other developed countries (DCs) and more to the developing nations than do developed countries generally, but for reasons somewhat different from those of Japan. American firms have significantly more subsidiaries in developing nations than Japanese companies do; these subsidiaries are captive customers for their American owners. In addition, some buyers in Southeast Asian countries, remembering that Japan was an aggressor nation in World War II and before, have preferred to buy from American firms. Notice also the high percentage of American exports that go to Latin America; this indicates the relative importance of this market to American firms. American exports to developing nations in the Americas were 21 percent of all American exports in 2004, and the dollar value of U.S. exports to that region is more than twice the value of these developing nations' exports to each other.

The Increasing Regionalization of Trade   The data in Table 2.3 illustrate how the direction of trade frequently changes over time among nations or regions of the world. The development of expanded regional trade agreements (discussed in Chapter 4), such as the Association of Southeast Asian Nations (ASEAN) and the EU, can substantially alter the level and proportion of trade flows within and across regions. For example, in Table 2.3, you see that most of Canada's exports go to the United States, mainly as a result, after 1989, of the U.S.-Canada Free Trade Agreement and the subsequent North American Free Trade Agreement. Over 20 percent of total American exports went to Canada in 2004, and their 2003 dollar value of $169 billion was more than double that in 1991. The $111 billion value of U.S. exports to Mexico in 2004 was over three times the level in 1991. The proportion of their total exports that Mexico, Canada, and the United States sent to one of their two partners in NAFTA increased from 46 percent in 1995 to over 55 percent in 2004. Overall, the share of world trade accounted for by members of regional trade agreements increased from 37 percent in 1980 to 60 percent in 1990 and to over 70 percent by 2005.

It appears that the American exporters have made major inroads in developing country markets, which in turn are selling more to the United States. This is due in part to their increasing ability to export manufactured goods and the growing intracompany trade among

TABLE 2.3

Direction of Trade for Selected Regions and Countries (percentage of region's or country's total merchandise exports to regions or countries in columns)

Exports from	Year	DE	U.S.	Can.	Jap.	EU	Dev.	DA	D. Am	East Eur.
					Exports to:					
Developed	1970	77	13	5	7	40	18	4	6	n.a.
economies (DE)	1980	71	19	4	10	43	25	5	6	3
	1990	71	20	5	8	46	20	2	4	2
	2000	72	16	5	3	44	23	2	6	3
	2004	70	14	4	3	48	23	2	5	2
United States	1970	70	—	21	11	27	29	2	15	n.a.
(U.S.)	1980	60	—	16	10	27	36	2	18	2
	1990	65	—	21	12	25	34	2	14	1
	2000	58	—	23	9	22	41	1	21	1
	2004	55	—	21	7	22	44	1	21	1
Canada (Can.)	1970	91	65	—	5	16	7	1	4	n.a.
	1980	85	63	—	6	13	12	1	5	3
	1990	91	75	—	6	8	8	1	2	1
	2000	95	87	—	2	5	5	<1	1	<1
	2004	93	85	—	2	6	6	<1	2	<1
Japan (Jap.)	1970	55	31	3	—	11	39	6	6	n.a.
	1980	48	25	2	—	14	50	5	7	3
	1990	59	32	2	—	19	40	1	3	1
	2000	51	30	2	—	16	48	1	4	1
	2004	46	25	1	—	16	53	1	3	<1
European	1970	81	8	1	1	51	14	5	4	n.a.
Union (EU)	1980	77	6	1	1	56	19	7	3	4
	1990	83	7	1	2	61	13	3	2	3
	2000	79	9	1	2	66	14	2	2	5
	2004	77	9	1	2	64	14	2	2	2
Developing	1970	72	18	2	11	34	20	3	7	n.a.
economies (Dev.)	1980	68	20	1	14	29	27	3	8	4
	1990	61	21	1	12	22	33	3	4	3
	2000	57	26	1	9	18	38	2	5	1
	2004	53	22	1	8	19	45	2	5	1
Developing	1970	81	7	1	4	61	11	6	2	n.a.
Africa (DA)	1980	83	26	<1	2	46	14	3	6	3
	1990	83	18	1	2	59	13	6	2	3
	2000	70	18	1	2	44	25	8	4	2
	2004	73	17	2	1	49	25	9	3	<1
Developing	1970	74	32	3	5	26	19	1	17	n.a.
America (D. Am.)	1980	64	32	3	4	22	28	2	21	7
	1990	63	33	1	5	21	21	1	14	3
	2000	74	56	2	2	12	24	1	18	1
	2004	71	52	2	2	14	27	1	18	1
Former USSR	1980	28	1	<1	1	19	21	3	3	51
and Eastern	1990	38	1	<1	2	28	23	2	5	40
Europe	2000	46	4	<1	2	34	23	2	4	31
(East Eur.)	2004	37	3	<1	1	33	23	2	2	19

Source: *Monthly Bulletin of Statistics* (New York: United Nations), July 2001, pp. 266–71, July 2000, pp. 258–61, June 1997, pp. 255–62, June 1993, pp. 266–71; *Statistical Yearbook* (New York: United Nations, 1969), pp. 376–83; and "International Trade—World Exports by Provenance and Destination," http://unstats.un.org/unsd/mbs/t41-July05-online.pdf (July 14, 2006).

international companies' affiliates. The fact that members of trade groups are increasingly selling more to each other is a development that will influence international companies' choices of locations for their plants and other operations. Note too that the United States and Japan, but not Europe, are fast approaching a 50-50 split in their exports to developing and developed nations.

MAJOR TRADING PARTNERS: THEIR RELEVANCE FOR MANAGERS

An analysis of the major trading partners of a firm's home country and those of the nations where it has affiliates that export can provide valuable insights to management.

Why Focus on Major Trading Partners?   There are a number of advantages to focusing attention on a nation that is already a sizable purchaser of goods coming from the would-be exporter's country:

1. The business climate in the importing nation is relatively favorable.

2. Export and import regulations are not insurmountable.

3. There should be no strong cultural objections to buying that nation's goods.

4. Satisfactory transportation facilities have already been established.

5. Import channel members (merchants, banks, and customs brokers) are experienced in handling import shipments from the exporter's area.

6. Foreign exchange to pay for the exports is available.

7. The government of a trading partner may be applying pressure on importers to buy from countries that are good customers for that nation's exports. We have seen the efforts of the Japanese, Korean, and Taiwanese governments to persuade their citizens to buy more American goods. They have also sent buying missions to the United States.

Major Trading Partners of the United States   Table 2.4 shows the major trading partners of the United States. The data indicate that the United States, an industrialized nation, generally follows the tendency we found in Table 2.3; that is, developed nations trade with one another. Mexico and Canada are major trading partners in great part because they share a common border with the United States. Freight charges are lower, delivery times are shorter, and contacts between buyers and sellers are easier and less expensive. Being joined with the United States in the North American Free Trade Agreement helps ensure that the three nations' mutual importance as trading partners will remain strong.

Note the changes in the rankings of America's trading partners in four decades. Of the top 15 nations, 8 have remained on the list over the years listed, including Canada, Mexico, Japan, Germany, the United Kingdom, France, Italy, and Brazil. However, each nation's ranking has changed over time, and some new nations have been added to replace other nations that have become relatively less important as trade partners. Nations from East and Southeast Asia, besides long-term trade partner Japan, have become increasingly important trade partners in recent years. China, South Korea, Taiwan, and Malaysia are supplying the United States with huge quantities of electronic products and components as well as a variety of largely labor-intensive manufactured goods, many of which are produced by affiliates of American international companies. Between 1991 and 2004, China rose from sixth to second place in exports to the United States (from $19 to $197 billion, a more than 900 percent increase in 13 years), and it also moved up to fifth place as an importer of U.S. goods in 2004 (although the $35 billion level of Chinese imports is less than 18 percent of the level of exports it sends to the United States).

Many of the same Asian countries appear as importers of American goods as well because (1) their rising standards of living enable their people to afford more imported products, and the countries' export earnings provide the foreign exchange to pay for them, (2) they

TABLE 2.4 Major Trading Partners of the United States, 1965, 1991, and 2004 ($ billions)

1965		1991		2004	
Imports from	**Amount**	**Imports from**	**Amount**	**Imports from**	**Amount**
1. Canada	$4.8	1. Japan	$92	1. Canada	$256
2. Japan	2.4	2. Canada	91	2. China	197
3. United Kingdom	1.4	3. Mexico	31	3. Mexico	156
4. W. Germany	1.3	4. Germany	26	4. Japan	130
5. Venezuela	1.0	5. Taiwan	23	5. Germany	77
6. Mexico	0.6	6. China	19	6. United Kingdom	46
7. Italy	0.6	7. United Kingdom	18	7. S. Korea	46
8. France	0.6	8. S. Korea	17	8. Taiwan	35
9. Brazil	0.5	9. France	13	9. France	32
10. Belgium & Luxembourg	0.5	10. Italy	12	10. Malaysia	28
11. Philippines	0.4	11. Saudi Arabia	11	11. Italy	28
12. India	0.4	12. Singapore	10	12. Ireland	27
13. Hong Kong	0.3	13. Hong Kong	9	13. Venezuela	25
14. Netherlands Antilles	0.3	14. Venezuela	8	14. Brazil	21
15. Australia	0.3	15. Brazil	7	15. Saudi Arabia	21

1965		1991		2004	
Exports to	**Amount**	**Exports to**	**Amount**	**Exports to**	**Amount**
1. Canada	$5.6	1. Canada	$85	1. Canada	$190
2. Japan	2.1	2. Japan	48	2. Mexico	111
3. W. Germany	1.7	3. Mexico	33	3. Japan	54
4. United Kingdom	1.6	4. United Kingdom	22	4. United Kingdom	36
5. Mexico	1.1	5. Germany	21	5. China	35
6. Netherlands	1.1	6. S. Korea	16	6. Germany	31
7. France	1.0	7. France	15	7. S. Korea	26
8. India	0.9	8. Netherlands	14	8. Netherlands	24
9. Italy	0.9	9. Taiwan	13	9. Taiwan	22
10. Australia	0.8	10. Belgium & Luxembourg	11	10. France	21
11. Belgium & Luxembourg	0.7	11. Singapore	9	11. Singapore	20
12. Venezuela	0.6	12. Italy	9	12. Belgium	17
13. Spain	0.5	13. Australia	8	13. Hong Kong	16
14. S. Africa	0.4	14. Hong Kong	8	14. Australia	14
15. Switzerland	0.4	15. Saudi Arabia	7	15. Brazil	14

Source: "U.S. Aggregate Foreign Trade Data, 1999 and Prior Years," *U.S. Foreign Trade Highlights,* tables 10 and 11, U.S. Department of Commerce International Trade Administration, www.ita.doc.gov/td/industry/otea/usfth/aggregate/H99t10.txt, www.ita.doc.gov/td/industry/otea/usfth/aggregate/H99t.11.txt; "Table 11: Top 50 Suppliers of U.S. Imports in 2004," U.S. Department of Commerce International Trade Administration, www.ita.doc.gov/td/industry/otea/usfth/tabcon.html (July 14, 2006); "Table 10: Top 50 Purchasers of U.S. Exports in 2004," U.S. Department of Commerce International Trade Administration, www.ita.doc.gov/td/industry/otea/usfth/tabcon.html (July 14, 2006).

are purchasing large amounts of capital goods to further their industrial expansion, (3) they are importing raw materials and components that will be assembled into subassemblies or finished goods that will subsequently be exported, often to the United States, and (4) their governments, pressured by the American government to lower their trade surpluses with the United States, have sent buying missions to this country to look for products to import.

The analysis of foreign trade that we have described would be helpful to anyone just starting to search outside the home market for new business opportunities. The preliminary steps of (1) studying the general growth and direction of trade (Table 2.3) and (2) analyzing major trading partners (Table 2.4) would provide an idea of where the trading activity is. What kinds of products do these countries import from the United States? The Department of Commerce's Office of Trade and Economic Analysis maintains a site on the Internet with downloadable files of trade statistics. One entry, "U.S. Foreign Trade Highlights," contains over 100 tables of goods and services, including one that reports on the top U.S. exports to and imports from its 80 largest trading partners. There are also tables from the Commerce Department's annual publication *U.S. Industry and Trade Outlook,* which replace the tables from *U.S. Industrial Outlook.* These tables compare the imports and exports of more than 100 industries for the last four years, providing an idea of their competitiveness in world markets.[3] Foreign trade reports are no longer available in hard copy. Trade data with much more information are available on CD-ROMs that are sent monthly to government depositories, such as many college and university libraries, or at online databases. The new reports have been expanded to contain additional data on units that permit analysts to make price comparisons by calculating average prices on exports and imports on a country basis.

The topic we have been examining—international trade—exists because firms export. As you know, however, exporting is only one aspect of international business. Another—overseas production—requires foreign investment, the topic of the next section.

Foreign Investment

Foreign investment can be divided into two components: **portfolio investment,** which is the purchase of stocks and bonds solely for the purpose of obtaining a return on the funds invested, and **direct investment,** by which the investors participate in the management of the firm in addition to receiving a return on their money. The distinction between these two components has begun to blur, particularly with the growing size and number of international mergers, acquisitions, and alliances in recent years. For example, investments by a foreign investor in the stock of a domestic company generally are treated as direct investment when the investor's equity participation ratio is 10 percent or more. In contrast, deals that do not result in the foreign investor's obtaining at least 10 percent of the shareholdings are classified as portfolio investments. With the increasing pace of business globalization, it is not uncommon for companies to form strategic relationships with firms from other nations in order to pool resources (such as manufacturing, marketing, and technology and other know-how) while still keeping their equity participation below 10 percent. Financing from foreign venture capitalists also tends to be treated as a portfolio investment, although these investors frequently become actively involved in the target company's business operations, with the goal of ultimately realizing substantial capital gains when the target company goes public.

portfolio investment
The purchase of stocks and bonds to obtain a return on the funds invested

direct investment
The purchase of sufficient stock in a firm to obtain significant management control

PORTFOLIO INVESTMENT

Although portfolio investors are not directly concerned with the control of a firm, they invest immense amounts in stocks and bonds from other countries. For example, data from the Department of Commerce show that persons residing outside the United States owned American stocks and bonds other than U.S. Treasury securities with a value of $4,391 billion in 2005 (including $2,115 billion in corporate stocks).[4] This represents a 190 percent increase over 1997. The very substantial proportion of the increase in the valuation of American stock held by persons residing outside this country is associated with the large number and scale of acquisitions of U.S. companies by foreign companies.

How Do Trade and Investment Impact Economic and Social Development?

All economies are increasingly open in today's economic environment of globalization. Trade plays a vital role in shaping economic and social performance and prospects of countries around the world, especially those of developing countries. No country has grown without trade. However, the contribution of trade to development depends a great deal on the context in which it works and the objectives it serves.

The above quote is the way the United Nations Conference on Trade and Development (UNCTAD) begins its groundbreaking report examining international trade and developing countries. International trade clearly has an important role in influencing nations' economic and social performance in a world of globalization. This role is even more fundamental in the case of developing countries. Yet the mere expansion of trade does not guarantee improvement for a country and its people. Rather, it is essential that trade performance be viewed in the context of its effects on employment levels, economic growth, development, and an improvement in the overall human condition.

To assist in efforts to ensure that trade plays a full and constructive role in enhancing growth and development, UNCTAD has launched an ambitious new initiative. Part of this initiative is the construction of the Trade and Development Index (TDI), a tool whose goal is to assist efforts "to systematically monitor the trade and development performance of developing countries with a view to facilitating national and international policies and strategies that would ensure that trade serves as a key instrument of development." By capturing the interactions among a range of factors underlying trade and development, the TDI attempts to provide a quantitative indication of a nation's trade and development performance. Although UNCTAD created the TDI primarily for assessing performance in developing nations, to facilitate comparisons and insight it also constructed the TDI for developed countries and for newly industrializing countries. Overall, 110 countries are evaluated. The 20 top- and bottom-ranked countries are listed in the accompanying table.

The average score for developed countries was 783, versus 408 for developing countries and 244 for the least developed countries. However, the top 10 performers from the developing countries had an average of 601, which was very close to the 637 average for the 10 nations that joined the European Union since May 2004, indicating that the gap in development can be shrunk—and has been in the case of several nations.

Results of the initial TDI evaluation reveal that the 30 highest-ranked nations are all developed countries, except for Singapore, South Korea, and Malaysia. This result is interpreted as evidence that few developing nations have been able to come close to the developed countries in terms of their trade and development performance. All of the bottom 10 nations are African, accentuating the severity of the trade and development problems confronting sub-Saharan Africa and least developed nations in general. The best regional performance among developing nations was that of the countries of the East Asia and Pacific region, followed by the Latin America and Caribbean region and the Middle East and North Africa region. The regions of South Asia and of sub-Saharan Africa significantly lagged behind the other three regional groups in terms of their TDI scores.

The most important factor contributing to high TDI scores is trade liberalization. The importance of this factor is highest for countries with lower TDI scores, and vice versa. This suggests that the extent of trade liberalization has much greater importance for developing countries, and especially the least developed countries, than for developed nations. In general, over the longer term and in the absence of externalities or market failures, trade liberalization is an effective policy promoting development. However, efforts to liberalize too rapidly can also result in short-term adjustment problems.

Both external and internal factors were found to influence a nation's export performance. External factors include market access conditions (e.g., transportation costs, geography, physical infrastructure, trade barriers, competition) and other factors that influence demand for imports. Internal factors include supply-side conditions within a nation (e.g., raw materials, labor and capital costs, access to technology, economic policy, institutional environment). A country's extent of market access is particularly important, since limitations on access for foreign markets is a major cause of poor export performance.

Americans, by contrast, owned $4,073 billion in foreign securities in 2005, of which $3,086 billion was in corporate stocks. This represents an increase of 145 percent over the corresponding level for 1997.[5] This increase reflects net U.S. purchases of foreign stocks, acquisitions of foreign companies by U.S. companies, and price appreciation in many foreign stocks. As you can see, foreign portfolio investment is sizable and will continue to grow as more international firms list their bonds and equities on foreign exchanges.

FOREIGN DIRECT INVESTMENT

The following discussion examines the volume, level, and direction of foreign direct investment, and the influence of international trade on foreign direct investment.

Top-Ranked Countries			Bottom-Ranked Countries		
Rank	Country	TDI Score	Rank	Country	TDI Score
1	Denmark	874	91	Madagascar	295
2	United States	854	92	Yemen	295
3	United Kingdom	825	93	Bangladesh	294
4	Sweden	811	94	Papua New Guinea	290
5	Norway	806	95	Pakistan	275
6	Japan	806	96	Malawi	272
7	Switzerland	805	97	Zambia	262
8	Germany	804	98	Nepal	255
9	Austria	791	99	Ivory Coast	254
10	Canada	790	100	Cameroon	248
11	France	774	101	Mozambique	238
12	Belgium-Luxembourg	773	102	Togo	230
13	Australia	772	103	Tanzania	229
14	New Zealand	770	104	Benin	225
15	Singapore	762	105	Sudan	206
16	Finland	761	106	Burkina Faso	195
17	Ireland	758	107	Ethiopia	186
18	Portugal	756	108	Nigeria	172
19	Spain	744	109	Mali	161
20	Italy	729	110	Niger	136

Foreign direct investment (FDI) was found to have a significant and positive impact on export performance across all of the nations studied and for every time period studied. FDI has a key role in influencing the composition of exports, including the technological content and the development of export supply capacity, and especially in knowledge-based industries. The impact of FDI is strongest for the two poorest-performing groups of exporters and at their early stages of export development.

UNCTAD emphasizes that merely improving trade factors, such as liberalizing the trade environment, will yield only marginal benefits for a nation unless these efforts are done in conjunction with a focus on other factors associated with development and poverty reduction. There is a strong need for integration and consistency between trade policy and other social, political, and economic undertakings. For example, nations must act simultaneously both on domestic capacity to supply goods and services and on access to foreign markets in order to produce strong performance. At early stages of development, important factors influencing domestic supply capacity include transportation infrastructure and macroeconomic stability.

Source: UNCTAD, *Developing Countries in International Trade 2005: Trade and Development Index* (New York: United Nations, 2005).

Volume   This section discusses the overall level of foreign direct investment, as well as annual outflows and inflows of FDI.

The Outstanding Stock of FDI   The *book value*—or the value of the total outstanding stock—of all foreign direct investment (FDI) worldwide was nearly $10 trillion at the end of 2004. Figure 2.3 shows how this total is divided among the largest investor nations. Individuals and corporations from the United States had over $2 billion invested abroad, which was 1.46 times the FDI of the next-largest investor, the United Kingdom, and 2.4 times that of the third-largest investor, Germany. The proportion of FDI accounted for by the United States declined by over 40 percent between 1985 and 2004, however, from 36 to 21 percent. During the same time period, the proportion of FDI accounted for by the European Union increased by over 25 percent, from 41 to 53 percent, although a portion of that increase was due to the inclusion of additional member-countries in the EU calculations. Japan's proportion of FDI declined from 12 percent in 1990 to 4 percent in 2004. Reflecting their continued economic development, developing countries have more than doubled their proportion of FDI, from 5 percent in 1985 to 11 percent in 2004.

Annual Outflows of FDI   Annual FDI outflows (the amount invested each year into other nations) hit a historical high in 2000—$1,201 billion, more than 250 percent of the level in 1997 (see Table 2.5). However, the slowdown that began to hit most of the world's economies in late 2000 resulted in a subsequent decline in the overall level of annual FDI flows. By 2002, the total was only $647 billion, only about 54 percent of the 2000 figure but still the fifth-highest annual level of FDI to that point in history. Outflows subsequently increased to $730 billion by 2004.

Although the United States had been the leading source of FDI outflows through most of the 1990s, in 2000 both the United Kingdom and France passed the United States. Indeed, the proportion of worldwide outward FDI accounted for by the United States declined from an average of 21 percent in 1985–1996 to 12 percent by 2000. However, the U.S. proportion rebounded, and the United States regained leadership on outward FDI from 2001 through 2004; American FDI outflows of $229 billion in 2004 exceeded by over 350 percent the outflows of the second-largest source of FDI, the United Kingdom (with $65 billion). The European Union's proportion of outward FDI grew from an average of around 47 percent in 1985–1997 to a peak of 75 percent by 2000, before subsequently declining to 61 percent of global outward FDI in 2002 and 38 percent in 2004. Japan declined from being the world's largest source of total global annual outflows of FDI in 1990, accounting for 22 percent of the total, to a position as the twelfth-largest in 2000, before rebounding by 2004 to being the sixth-largest source of outward FDI.

Although the overall volume of outward FDI from developing nations nearly quadrupled by 2004 compared to its average from 1985 to 1995, the proportion of worldwide outward FDI that comes from developing nations declined from 14 percent in 1997 to 11 percent by 2004. As a result, Table 2.5 shows that the vast proportion of outward FDI, over 87 percent, originates from the developed countries. The United States and the EU have been accounting for an increasing share, with their proportion of worldwide FDI increasing from an average of 68 percent in 1985–1995 to 87 percent by 2000, before falling back to 80 percent in 2002 and 70 percent in 2004. Much of this increase in outward FDI has been associated with mergers,

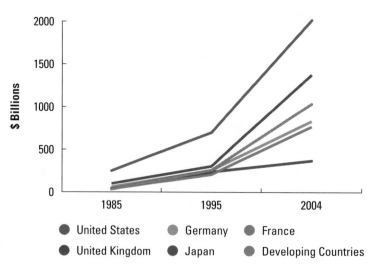

FIGURE 2.3

Stocks of Outward Foreign Direct Investment, Selected Countries, 1985, 1995, and 2004 ($ billions)

● United States   ● Germany   ● France
● United Kingdom   ● Japan   ● Developing Countries

Source: Various "Country Fact Sheets," *World Investment Report 2001*, United Nations Conference on Trade and Development, Geneva, October 2001, and *World Investment Report 2005*, United Nations Conference on Trade and Development, Geneva, September 2005.

TABLE 2.5

Direction of Foreign Direct Investment (Annual Flows) for Selected Regions and Countries, 1985–2004 ($ billions)

Where Funds Originate (net investment)	1985–1995 (annual average)	1996	2000	2004
World	$203	$391	$1,201	$730
Developed countries	182	332	1,098	637
Developing countries	22	58	99	83
North America	49	98	190	279
United States	43	84	143	229
Canada	6	13	47	48
Mexico	<1	<1	1	2
European Union	96	182	819	280
United Kingdom	26	34	250	65
Germany	18	51	57	−7
France	18	30	177	48
Italy	5	9	12	19
Russian Federation	<1	n.a.	3	10
Africa	1	<1	1	3
South, East, & Southeast Asia	17	50	81	67
India	<1	n.a.	<1	2
Japan	25	23	32	31
Hong Kong, China	8	27	59	40
China	2	2	1	2
Latin America & Caribbean	3	6	14	11

Where Funds Go (net investment)				
World	181	278	1,393	648
Developed countries	128	220	1,121	380
Developing countries	50	145	246	233
North America	54	103	396	119
United States	44	85	314	96
Canada	6	10	67	6
Mexico	4	9	16	17
European Union	66	109	684	216
United Kingdom	17	24	130	78
Germany	3	7	203	−39
France	12	22	43	24
Italy	3	4	13	17
Russian Federation	<1	n.a.	3	12
Africa	4	6	9	18
South, East, & Southeast Asia	30	88	139	126
India	<1	n.a.	2	5
Japan	1	<1	8	8
Hong Kong, China	4	11	62	34
China	12	40	41	61
Latin America & Caribbean	14	46	95	68

Note: Because of rounding, values may not equal 100%.

Source: Various "Country Fact Sheets," *World Investment Report 2001,* United Nations Conference on Trade and Development, Geneva, October 2001, and *World Investment Report 2005,* United Nations Conference on Trade and Development, Geneva, September 2005.

acquisitions, and other international investments made by companies in industries that are facing increased competition and consolidation globally. In fact, the developed countries accounted for 92 percent of the value of all cross-border purchases of foreign companies from 1995 to 2004, investing over $4.4 trillion into such acquisitions. Over 70 percent of the total amount of outward FDI by developed countries from 1997 to 2004 was used for the purchase of companies in other nations.

Annual Inflows of FDI   In which countries are investments being made, and where do the investments come from? Table 2.5 indicates that the industrialized nations invest primarily in one another, just as they trade more with one another. An average of over 70 percent of annual FDI investments have been going into developed countries. The United States and the EU accounted for an average of over 60 percent of all inward FDI from 1985 to 2004, exceeding 80 percent in 1999 and 2000. As noted above, much of this inward investment has gone to mergers and acquisitions made by companies whose businesses are confronting competition and consolidation globally. Japan has not been a significant recipient of inward FDI, averaging less than 1 percent of worldwide FDI from 1985 to 2004.

Worldwide, the developing countries as a whole obtained a 70 percent increase in the level of FDI between 1996 and 2000, before falling back by about one-third during the worldwide economic slowdown of the next two years. Although the overall dollar value of FDI going to developing countries increased, the proportion of FDI funds going to these nations declined from 15 percent in 1996 to 8 percent in 2000, before increasing again to over 11 percent by 2004. African nations participated relatively little in the growing flow of inward FDI, accounting for an average of less than 2 percent of all inflows from 1985 to 2004. The small nation of Singapore (population 3 million) received approximately as much foreign investment as the entire African continent did during this time. In Latin America, annual FDI inflows between 1997 and 2004 were 300 percent to more than 750 percent above the average of 1985–1995, although the annual flows fluctuated substantially. The proportion of worldwide inward FDI flows that have gone to Latin America declined from 15 percent in 1997 to 8.6 percent in 2002 before rising again to 10.5 percent in 2004. For Asia as a whole, total inflows to the region rose to a record $139 billion in 2000, more than 400 percent of the average inward investments during 1985 to 1995, yet the proportion of worldwide FDI inflows declined steadily from 1996 to 1999, at least partly due to the Asian financial crisis that hit in 1997. The proportion of investment going to Asia has increased since 1999, reaching over 19 percent by 2004. Asia as a whole moved up to being the second most popular region for inward FDI by 2004, behind the EU. Asia accounted for over one-third of all investments not directed to the United States and the European Union from 1985 to 2004. A particularly important trend is the proportion of Asian FDI that has been directed to China and its territories. Their combined proportion of Asian FDI grew from 52.4 percent during 1985–1995 to 75 percent in 2004, and it appears that some of the FDI previously directed toward other Asian nations might have been redirected toward these Chinese investments.

At a country level, the United States was the leader in terms of FDI inflows in 2000, which at $314 billion was the highest level of annual inward FDI ever recorded for a single nation. However, factors such as a declining stock market, slowed economy, and depreciating currency caused the level of inward FDI going to the United States to decline by over 90 percent in the next two years, to $30 billion in 2002, before subsequently rebounding. Still, from 2001 through 2004, the nation with the largest annual FDI inflows was China/Hong Kong, representing the first time that a developing economy has achieved such a distinction.

Level and Direction of FDI   Even though it is impossible to make an accurate determination of the present value of foreign investments, we can get an idea of the rate and amounts of such investments and of the places in which they are being made. This is the kind of information that interests managers and government leaders. It is analogous to what is sought in the analysis of international trade. If a nation is continuing to receive appreciable amounts of foreign investment, its investment climate must be favorable. This means that the political forces of the foreign environment are relatively attractive and that the opportunity to earn a profit is greater there than elsewhere. Other reasons for investing exist, to be sure; however, if the above factors are absent, foreign investment is not likely to occur.

Trade Leads to FDI Historically, foreign direct investment has followed foreign trade. One reason is that engaging in foreign trade is typically less costly and less risky than making a direct investment into foreign markets. Also, management can expand the business in small increments rather than through the considerably greater amounts of investment and market size that a foreign production facility requires. Typically, a firm would use domestic or foreign agents to export. As the export business increased, the firm would set up an export department and perhaps hire sales representatives to live in overseas markets. The firm might even establish its own sales company to import in its own name.

Meanwhile, managers would watch the total market size closely because they would know that their competitors were making similar studies. Generally, because the local market would not be large enough to support local production by all the firms exporting to it, the situation would become one of seeing who could begin manufacturing there first. Experienced managers know that governments often limit the number of local firms making a given product so that those that do set up local operations will be assured of having a profitable and continuing business. This is especially important to developing countries that are dependent on foreign investment to provide jobs and tax revenue.

Does Trade Lead FDI or Does FDI Lead Trade? The previous section described the linear path to market expansion that many international firms have taken and still take today. However, the new business environment of fewer government barriers to trade, increased competition from globalizing firms, and new production and communications technology is causing many international firms to disperse the activities of their production systems to locations close to available resources. They then integrate the entire production process either regionally or globally. As a result, the decision about where to locate may be either an FDI or a trade decision, illustrating just how closely FDI and trade are interlinked.

U.S. FOREIGN DIRECT INVESTMENT ABROAD

You saw in Figure 2.3 that the United States is by far the largest foreign investor (21 percent of the total outstanding stock of outward FDI stock in 2004), and American firms have invested much more in the developed nations (approximately 70 percent of the total, as of 2004) than they have in the developing nations. As Figure 2.4a indicates, during the two decades from 1985 to 2004, the proportion of total U.S. investment that went to Europe increased by nearly 14 percent (from 46 to 52 percent), while the proportion to Canada declined by approximately 50 percent. In 2004, the United Kingdom (15 percent) and the Netherlands (10 percent) represented the largest recipients of U.S. FDI among the European nations. Latin America's proportion of American FDI increased by over 30 percent, from 12 percent in 1985 to 16 percent in 2004. The proportion of American FDI in Asia and the Pacific increased over 25 percent during this time, from 15 to 19 percent. Although American firms had more FDI invested in Africa and the Middle East in 2004 than in 1985, the percentages of these two regions among total U.S. FDI abroad were less than half of what they had been in 1985.

Japan provides an interesting contrast to the United States in terms of recent FDI experience. During the early and middle 1990s, the focus of Japan's FDI outflows shifted from developed nations (down from 83 percent in 1989–1991 to 58 percent in 1994–1995) to Southeast Asia (up from 17 to 42 percent). However, the level of Japanese FDI going to Asian locations declined substantially at the end of the decade, falling from 22.6 percent in 1997 to 16 percent in 1998 and 12.2 percent in 2000. The proportion of Japanese FDI going to the United States and Europe was over 70 percent in 2003.[6]

FIGURE 2.4

U.S. Direct Investment Position Abroad and Foreign Direct Investment in the U.S., on a Historical-Cost Basis, 1985 and 2004 ($ billions)

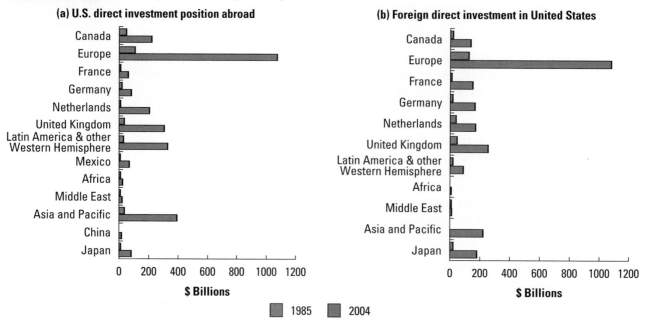

(a) U.S. direct investment position abroad

(b) Foreign direct investment in United States

1985   2004

Source: Maria Borga and Daniel R. Yorgason, "Direct Investment Positions for 2001: Country and Industry Detail," *Survey of Current Business,* July 2002, pp. 32–35; Jennifer L. Konez and Daniel R. Yorgason, "Direct Investment Positions for 2004: Country and Industry Detail," Survey of Current Business, July 2005, pp.50–53; and *Survey of Current Business, June 1986, pp. 31, 34.*

FOREIGN DIRECT INVESTMENT IN THE UNITED STATES

Foreign direct investment in the United States rose rapidly from $185 billion in 1985 to $1,874 billion in 2005 (see Figure 2.4b). This is an average annual increase of nearly 13 percent. Observe how concentrated FDI is in the United States. Approximately 85 percent of the total stock was owned by firms or individuals from just eight nations: (1) United Kingdom (17 percent), (2) Japan (12 percent), (3) Germany (11 percent), (4) Netherlands (11 percent), (5) France (10 percent), (6) Canada (9 percent), (7) Switzerland (8 percent), and (8) Luxembourg (7 percent). The proportion of FDI in the United States owned by Europeans increased from 66 percent in 1985 to 71 percent in 2004. The proportion owned by Latin Americans declined from 9 percent in 1985 to 6 percent in 2004.

Comparing the level of U.S. FDI abroad with the level of FDI in the United States reveals an important trend. Figure 2.5 examines this trend annually from 1976 through 2005. As this figure shows, the level of U.S. investment abroad exceeded the amount of foreign investment in the United States until 1986. Since that time, there has been an almost continuous increase in the excess of the value of foreign investment in the United States versus the value of the level of American FDI abroad. By 2005, FDI in the United States was nearly $2.4 trillion more than U.S. FDI abroad, an amount approximately three times larger than six years earlier, in 1999. Implications of this imbalance in foreign direct investment, as well as the imbalance between American exports and imports of goods and services, will be discussed in later chapters, particularly in Sections Two and Three.

Acquire Going Companies or Build New Ones?   As seen in Figure 2.5, foreign firms invested $1.5 trillion in the United States from 1999 to 2005. Approximately two-thirds of the value of their investments have been spent to acquire going companies rather than to establish new ones (similarly, the majority of American investments into foreign markets have gone to the acquisition of going companies). A number of reasons are responsible for this fact: (1) Corporate restructuring in the United States caused management to put on the market businesses or other assets that either did not meet management's profit standards or were considered to be unrelated to the company's main business; (2) foreign companies wanted to gain

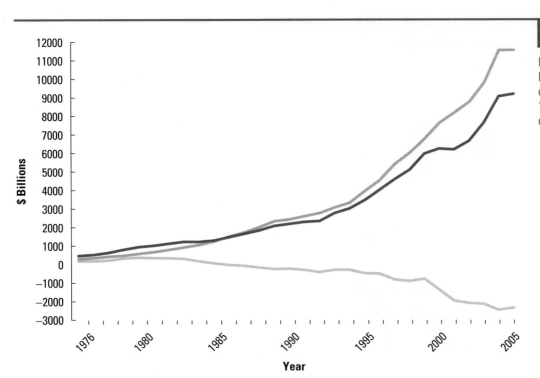

FIGURE 2.5

International Investment Position of the United States, 1976–2005 (billions of dollars)

● U.S.-owned assets abroad
● Foreign-owned assets in United States
● Net international investment position of the United States

Note: Figures are based on current cost.

Source: Elena L. Nguyen, "The International Investment Position of the United States at Year-End 2002," *Survey of Current Business*, July 2003, pp. 20–21;

rapid access in the United States to advanced technology, especially in computers and communications; (3) management of foreign firms felt that entrance into the large and prosperous American market could be more successful if they acquired known brand names rather than spending the time and money to promote new, unknown ones; and (4) increased international competitive pressures, including the pursuit of improved economies of scale, has led to restructuring and consolidation in many industries, and the acquisition of companies in major markets such as the United States has been a by-product of these industrial trends.

Why Enter Foreign Markets?

In the previous section, we mentioned briefly some of the reasons why foreign investors acquire companies more often than they establish them in the United States. Now let us examine the reasons why international firms enter foreign markets, which are all linked to the desire to increase profits and sales or protect them from being eroded by competitors.

INCREASE PROFITS AND SALES

Enter New Markets Managers are always under pressure to increase the sales and profits of their firms, and when they face a mature, saturated market at home, they begin to search for new markets outside the home country. They find that (1) markets with a rising GDP per capita and population growth appear to be viable candidates for their operations and (2) the economies of some nations where they are not doing business are growing at a considerably faster rate than is the economy of their own market.

New Market Creation As we will discuss in Chapter 15, there are many ways in which potential new markets can be identified and assessed. Sources of potential market size and overall market growth rate can be found in publications such as the annual *Human Development*

Why Doesn't More FDI Flow to Africa?

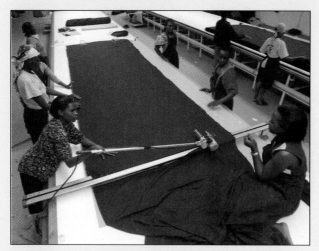

Factory workers cut material in July of 2003 at the Tristar clothing factory in Kampala, Uganda.

Despite the dramatic increases in international flows of foreign direct investment over the past two decades, the countries of sub-Saharan Africa have largely missed out on this trend. As a result, the problem of extensive and increasing levels of poverty among the populations of the sub-Saharan nations has been exacerbated. Taken as a whole, the 700 million residents of this region are experiencing declining per capita incomes, reduced life expectancy, increasing poverty, and social devastation resulting from epidemics such as HIV/AIDS and malaria.

Why hasn't more FDI flowed into the nations of Africa? Historically, many of these nations have suffered from glaring inadequacies of their regulatory and administrative practices with respect to the treatment of foreign investors and the protection of their investments, which sharply diminished the attractiveness of these nations for receiving incoming FDI. Combined with a range of additional social, political, economic, and other challenges on the continent, this has hindered Africa's ability to compete, when compared to investment opportunities within developed countries and in many of the other developing countries of the world.

There is some reason for hope, however, as the past decade has seen changes in attitudes toward FDI. The majority of African nations have introduced FDI liberalizing legislation as well as entered into trade agreements with other nations from Africa and other continents. State-owned enterprises are being privatized, often in conjunction with investment by foreign firms, although the pace of privatization lags behind that of other parts of the world. Regulatory conditions in many African nations are comparable with those in most other developing nations.

The introduction of sound standards for FDI is a positive step forward for attracting foreign investment. However, much work remains. According to the United Nations Conference on Trade and Development, the following problems still need to be addressed in order for sub-Saharan Africa to improve its attractiveness as a destination for foreign investment:

Report of the United Nations Development Program (www.sd.undp.org/HDR/HDR05e. pdf). Reviewing data in such reports will reveal great variety in growth rates among countries when ranked by variables such as GDP per capita.

Although nearly everyone looks to GDP per capita (or the counterpart statistic of GNI per capita) as a basis for making comparisons of nations' economies, extreme care must be exercised to avoid drawing unwarranted conclusions. First, because the statistical systems in many developing nations are deficient, the reliability of the data provided by such nations is questionable.

Second, to arrive at a common base of U.S. dollars, the World Bank and other international agencies convert local currencies to dollars. The Bank uses an average of the exchange rates for that year and the previous two years after adjusting for differences in relative inflation between the particular country and the United States.[7] World Bank economists admit that official exchange rates do not reflect the relative domestic purchasing powers of currencies. "However," they say, "exchange rates remain the only generally available means of converting GDP from national currencies to U.S. dollars."[8]

Third, you must remember that GDP per capita is merely an arithmetic mean obtained by dividing GDP by the total population. However, a nation with a lower GDP but more evenly distributed income may be a more desirable market than one with a higher GDP. On the other hand, as you will note in the chapter on economic forces (Chapter 8), a skewed distribution of income in a nation with a low GDP per capita may indicate that there is a viable market, especially for luxury goods.

1. Most countries have fiscal regimes that lack international competitiveness in terms of FDI for export-oriented activities. Many of the processes for providing investment incentives are slow, arbitrary, and lacking in integration.

2. Many countries lack good regulations with regard to the management of labor relations and dispute resolutions, an essential factor in a nation's attractiveness for investment in labor-intensive export manufacturing sectors.

3. Many countries lack updated systems for providing work and residence permits for expatriate personnel, who are often critical resources for the foreign investor during the early stages of an investment project due to the managerial and technical expertise they provide.

4. Potential investors frequently discount Africa as a destination for FDI because of a negative image of the continent as a whole, rather than understanding the diversity of economic performance among the various African countries and the existence of attractive investment opportunities in individual nations.

Despite these and other problems that continue to hinder FDI inflows, there are promising signs that political and economic changes currently under way may be able to be sustained. Economic performance of the region has substantially improved from the mid-1990s, exceeding a real growth rate of 5 percent per year in 2004 and 2005. There has been progress in unifying foreign exchange markets, achieving high levels of macroeconomic stability in many nations, and improving management of financial resources and public expenditures. Improved prices for oil and other nonfuel export commodities have contributed to growth in exports and GDP. Signs of momentum on economic and political reforms are evidenced by the 23 African nations that joined the African Peer Review Mechanism (APRM). The goal of the APRM is to encourage improved transparency and integrity in economic and political governance of the member-countries and thereby increase confidence of foreign investors in the sustainability of reform efforts in Africa.

Combined with the rich resource base found in many of the nations, these developments could provide a stronger foundation for future improvements in international investment and trade by African nations and improvements in the human condition on this vast continent. Recently, there have been increases in FDI into some of the African countries, which some observers have seen as a sign that Africa may be on the cusp of an "economic renaissance." Yet FDI can have costs as well as benefits for a host nation, and the receipt of FDI alone will not be sufficient to cure the ills of this region. Properly balanced and integrated with a range of other social, economic, and governance initiatives, however, FDI could indeed help to transform Africa and help its people to experience some of the prosperity that has characterized Asia and other developing regions in the past 30 years.

Source: United Nations Conference on Trade and Development, *World Investment Report 2003* (New York: United Nations, 2003), pp. 33–40; International Chamber of Commerce, "Business and UN Promote Foreign Investment in Africa," Press Release, Geneva, July 5, 1999, www.iccwbo.org/home/news_archives/1999/ business_and_un_for_african_fdi.asp (July 20, 2004); UNCTAD, "For Five African Least Developed Countries, 2002 a Bad Year for FDI," February 13, 2004, www.globalpolicy.org/socecon/ffd/fdi/2004/0213africa.htm (July 20, 2004); United Nations, *Foreign Direct Investment in Africa: Performance and Potential*, (New York: United Nations, 1999); UNCTAD, *Economic Development in Africa: Rethinking the Role of Foreign Direct Investment* (New York: United Nations, September 2005); and UNCTAD, *World Economic Situation and Prospects 2006* (New York: United Nations, 2006).

Data from sources such as the *Human Development Report* indicate that from a macro perspective, markets around the world are growing. However, this does not mean that equally good opportunities exist for all kinds of business. Perhaps surprisingly, economic growth in a nation causes markets for some products to be lost forever while, simultaneously, markets for other products are being created. Take the case of a country in the initial stage of development. With little local manufacturing, it is a good market for exporters of consumer goods. As economic development continues, however, managers see profit-making opportunities in (1) producing locally the kinds of consumer goods that require simple technology or (2) assembling from imported parts the products that demand a more advanced technology. Given the tendency of governments to protect local industry, the importation of goods being produced in that country will normally be prohibited or discouraged through taxes, tariffs, or other means once local production of those goods has been established. Thus, exporters of easy-to-manufacture consumer goods, such as paint, adhesives, toilet articles, clothing, and almost anything made of plastic, will begin to lose this market, which now becomes a new market for producers of the inputs to these "infant industries."

Preferential Trading Arrangements   The fact that most nations have experienced growth in population and GDP per capita does not necessarily mean they have attained sufficient size to warrant investment by an international firm in either (1) an organization for marketing exports from the home country or (2) a local manufacturing plant. For many products, a number of these nations still lack sufficient market potential. When such nations make some kind

preferential trading arrangement
An agreement by a small group of nations to establish free trade among themselves while maintaining trade restrictions with all other nations

of **preferential trading arrangement** (for example, the EU or the North American Free Trade Agreement), the resultant market is much larger. As a result, firms frequently bypass what is often the first step of exporting and make their initial market entry with local manufacturing facilities.

Faster-Growing Markets   Not only are new foreign markets appearing, but many of them are growing at a faster rate than is the home market. A firm looking for a market large enough to support the local production of appliances or machinery, for example, would be attracted by the wealth, growth, and population size of Japan and Spain. When you examine the low GDP per capita and negative growth rates of so many of the African nations, you realize why foreign direct investment in that entire continent is so low. Clearly, market analysts will investigate other factors, such as the legal and political situations (discussed in Chapters 9 and 10), but an examination of variables such as those contained in the *Human Development Report* mentioned above is a good place to start. Interestingly, 70 of the 177 countries in the World Bank database (40 percent) referenced in this report had average annual GDP per capita growth rates that were higher than or equal to the U.S. growth rate for the period 1990–2003.[9]

Faster growth in the markets of developing nations frequently occurs for another reason. When a firm that has supplied the market by exporting builds a factory for local production, the host government often prohibits imports or erects barriers that make it difficult for imports to be competitive. The firm, which may have had to share the market with 10 or 20 competitors during its exporting days, now might essentially have the local market all to itself or share it with only a small number of other local producers. That is a situation that allows for growth.

Improved Communications   This might be considered a supportive reason for opening up new markets overseas, because certainly the ability to communicate rapidly and less expensively with customers and subordinates by electronic mail, wireless and wired telephones, and videoconferencing, as we discussed in Chapter 1, has given managers confidence in their ability to control foreign operations. Advances in computer-based communications are allowing virtual integration, which permits firms to become more physically fragmented as their managements search the world for lower-cost inputs. For example, anyone in the home office or in a subsidiary anywhere in the world can instantly access databases and computer-generated drawings.

Good, relatively inexpensive international communication enables large insurance, banking, software, and other firms to "body shop," that is, transmit computer-oriented tasks worldwide to a cheap but skilled labor force. The clients of numerous Indian software companies are in the United States. A few years ago, software teams were required to fly back and forth between the two countries. Now, at the end of the day, customers in the United States e-mail their problems to India, and while they are sleeping, the Indians work on the solutions and have them back in the United States before the Americans have had breakfast. For their work, Indian software engineers receive only 15 to 20 percent as much as do their American counterparts. This "offshoring" of work has become increasingly common, as we will see in later chapters, including Chapters 3 and 20.

Obtain Greater Profits   As you know, greater profits may be obtained by either increasing total revenue or decreasing the cost of goods sold, and often conditions are such that a firm can do both.

Greater Revenue   Rarely will all of a firm's domestic competitors be in every foreign market in which it is located. Where there is less competition, the firm may be able to obtain a better price for its goods or services.

Increasingly, firms are obtaining greater revenue by simultaneously introducing products in foreign markets and in their domestic markets as they move toward greater globalization of their operations. This results in greater sales volume while lowering the cost of the goods sold.

Lower Cost of Goods Sold Going abroad, whether by exporting or by producing overseas, can frequently lower the cost of goods sold. Increasing total sales by exporting not only will reduce research and development (R&D) costs per unit but also will make other economies of scale possible.

Another factor that can positively affect the cost of goods sold is the inducements that some governments offer to attract new investment. For example, Turkey offers a range of incentives for new investors, including the following: (1) exemptions from customs fees, taxes, and duties, as well as value-added taxes (VAT), for imported machinery and equipment, (2) investment allowances of 20 to 70 percent of total fixed investment, (3) subsidized investment for research and development projects and environment investments, (4) exemption from building and construction taxes, (5) allocation of public land for company operations in priority development regions and industrial belts, (6) exemption from corporate taxes, and (7) export incentives such as exemptions on VAT, export taxes and duties, and export credits.[10] Incentives such as these are designed to attract prospective investors but generally are not a sufficient motive for foreign investment. Nevertheless, they do have a positive influence on the cost of goods sold.

Higher Overseas Profits as an Investment Motive There is no question that greater profits on overseas investments were a strong motive for going abroad in the early 1970s and 1980s. *Business International* reported that 90 percent of 140 Fortune 500 companies surveyed had achieved higher profitability on foreign than domestic assets in 1974, for example.[11] This trend continued into the 1990s. As an example, in 1993, only 18 of the 100 largest multinationals earned more than 50 percent of their revenue overseas, but 33 earned more than 50 percent of their profits from foreign operations.[12] Profits from foreign markets remain critical for U.S. multinationals. In 2004, for example, earnings from overseas operations accounted for 40 percent of the total profit growth achieved by U.S. companies, including those without international operations. The $315 billion in profits from overseas operations was up 26 percent from 2003 and 78 percent since 2000. The consulting firm McKinsey estimates that profits from overseas operations account for $2.7 trillion in stock market capitalization for American companies.[13]

Test Market Occasionally, an international firm will test-market a product in a foreign location that is less important to the company than its home market and major overseas markets. This provides an opportunity to make changes, if necessary, to any part of the marketing mix (product, promotion, price, channels of distribution) or drop the entire venture if the test indicates that this should be done. Management's thinking is that any mistakes made in the test market should not adversely affect the firm in any of its major markets. Since companies usually monitor their competitors' actions in all markets, there is always the danger that a market test will give those competitors an early warning. We shall examine this point again in Chapter 15, "Assessing and Analyzing Markets." Let's now look at some reasons for going abroad that are more related to the protection of present markets, profits, and sales.

PROTECT MARKETS, PROFITS, AND SALES

Protect Domestic Market Frequently, a firm will go abroad to protect its home market.

Follow Customers Overseas Service companies (for example, accounting, advertising, marketing research, banking, law) will establish foreign operations in markets where their principal accounts are to prevent competitors from gaining access to those accounts. They know that once a competitor has been able to demonstrate to top management what it can do by servicing a foreign subsidiary, it may be able to take over the entire account. Similarly, suppliers to original equipment manufacturers (for example, battery manufacturers supplying automobile producers) often follow their large customers. These suppliers have an added advantage in that they are moving into new markets with a guaranteed customer base.

Attack in Competitor's Home Market Occasionally, a firm will set up an operation in the home country of a major competitor with the idea of keeping the competitor so occupied defending that market that it will have less energy to compete in the firm's home country.

Using Foreign Production to Lower Costs   A company may also go abroad to protect its domestic market when it faces competition from lower-priced foreign imports. By moving part or all of its production facilities to the countries from which its competition is coming, it can enjoy such advantages as less costly labor, raw materials, and energy. Management may decide to produce certain components abroad and assemble them in the home country, or, if the final product requires considerable labor in the final assembly, it may send the components overseas for this operation. Many nations, especially developing countries, offer **export processing zones** in which firms, mostly foreign manufacturers, enjoy almost complete absence of taxation and regulation of materials brought into the zones for processing and subsequent re-export. This can also be accomplished by using in-bond plants.

In-Bond (Maquiladora) Plants.   **In-bond plants,** often called **maquiladoras,** came into existence because of an arrangement between Mexico and the United States. The Mexican government permitted duty-free importation of parts and materials from the United States for assembly, processing, and packaging within the in-bond plant, provided that the finished products were re-exported. The American government permitted the finished product containing the American-made parts and materials to be imported, with import duty paid only on the value added in Mexico.

Over 80 percent of Mexican trade with the United States, and more than 40 percent of all exports from Mexico, are from the maquiladora industry.[14] Maquiladoras employ nearly 1.2 million workers, or about one in five Mexican manufacturing jobs.[15] Their production, led by electronics, electronic machinery, transportation equipment, and textiles and apparel, was projected to exceed $115 billion in 2006. Although the number of in-bond plants has declined by 23 percent since 2001, partly due to the emergence of China as a competitor, there were over 2,800 in-bond plants in 2006.

The maquiladora sector is undergoing a major shift from so-called first-generation activities (those that are highly labor-intensive and entail limited technology) and toward higher-value-added work. This transformation is being hastened by rising Mexican wage rates, which increased more than 50 percent between 1998 and 2006, compounded by competition from China and other nations with labor cost advantages. China's labor costs are one-fourth the level of Mexico's, making the latter country uncompetitive in many low-skill, labor-intensive products. Minicase 2.1, on Jabil Circuit Inc., provides an example of one company that is attempting to navigate this changing competitive environment.

Protect Foreign Markets

Changing the method of going abroad from exporting to overseas production is often necessary to protect foreign markets. The management of a firm supplying a profitable overseas market by exporting may begin to note some ominous signs that this market is being threatened.

Lack of Foreign Exchange   One of the first signs is a delay in payment by the importers. The importers may have sufficient local currency but may be facing delays in buying foreign exchange (currency) from the government's central bank. The credit manager in the exporting firm, by checking with his or her bank and other exporters, learns that this condition is becoming endemic—a reliable sign that the country is facing a lack of foreign exchange. In examining the country's balance of payments, the financial manager may find that its export revenue has declined while the import volume remains high. Experienced exporters know that import and foreign exchange controls are in the offing and that there is a good chance of losing the market, especially if they sell consumer products. In times of foreign exchange scarcity, governments will invariably give priority to the importation of raw materials and capital goods.

If the advantages of making the investment outweigh the disadvantages, the company may decide to protect this market by producing locally. Managers know that once the company has a plant in the country, the government will do its utmost to provide foreign exchange for raw materials to keep the plant, a source of employment, in operation. Because imports of competing products are prohibited, the only competition, if any, will have to come from other local manufacturers.

Local Production by Competitors   Lack of foreign exchange is not the only reason a company might change from exporting to manufacturing in a market. For instance, while a firm may enjoy a growing export business and prompt payments, it still may be forced to set up a plant in the market. It may be that its competitors have also noticed their export volumes will support local production.

Should a competing firm move to put up a factory in the market, management must decide rapidly whether to follow suit or risk losing the market forever. Managers know that many governments, especially those in developing nations, not only will prohibit further imports once the product is produced in the country but also will permit only two or three other companies to enter so as to maintain a sufficient market for these local firms. For example, many foreign companies from sectors such as banking, insurance, securities underwriting, telecommunications, legal, and distribution services tried for years to enter the People's Republic of China. The Chinese government, however, prohibited or sharply restricted the options available to foreign firms for entering these sectors and competing with local companies, most of which were owned by local governmental organizations. Only as a result of negotiations associated with China's entry into the World Trade Organization were regulations liberalized to allow substantially increased participation of foreign firms within the Chinese market for these services.[16] As a result of these changes, numerous foreign firms have established operations in China for serving the local market.

Downstream Markets   A number of Organization of Petroleum Exporting Countries (OPEC) nations have invested in refining and marketing outlets, such as filling stations and heating-oil distributors, to guarantee a market for their crude oil at more favorable prices. Petróleos de Venezuela, owner of Citgo, is one of the largest foreign investors in the United States. Kuwait bought Gulf Oil's refining and marketing network in three European countries and also owns a substantial portion of BP Amoco, which has one of the largest foreign investments in the United States. Lukoil, Russia's largest oil company, bought the Getty Oil chain of gasoline retailers in the eastern United States. These are just three examples.

Protectionism   When a government sees that local industry is threatened by imports, it may erect import barriers to stop or reduce them.* Even threats to do this can be sufficient to induce the exporter to invest in production facilities in the importing country. This and a strong yen, which makes it more difficult for Japanese exports to compete with American products, are important reasons for Japanese investment in the United States.

Guarantee Supply of Raw Materials

Few developed nations possess sufficient domestic supplies of raw materials. Japan and Europe are almost totally dependent on foreign sources for many important materials, and even the United States depends on imports for more than half of its aluminum, chromium, manganese, nickel, tin, and zinc. Furthermore, the Department of the Interior estimates that iron, lead, tungsten, copper, potassium, and sulfur will be added soon to the critical list.†

To ensure a continuous supply, manufacturers in the industrialized countries are being forced to invest primarily in the developing nations, where most new deposits are being discovered. Interestingly, although Japan does this as well, for years it has also looked to the United States as a source of raw materials. A Japanese deputy general consul once stated,

> *The United States offers an abundance of many raw materials. Because Japan has long depended on the United States for various materials, such as grain, coking coal, and lumber, it is entirely logical for Japanese firms to establish facilities close to the sources of these essential raw materials.*

---

*See Chapter 3 for a discussion of import barriers.
†See Chapter 7 for a discussion of scarce industrial minerals.

Some analysts claim that the Japanese-American trade flows approximate those between an industrialized country and a developing country: The industrialized nation sends manufactured goods to the developing nation in return for raw materials. This is somewhat exaggerated, but practically all of Japan's exports to the United States consist of manufactured goods and services, while approximately one-third of American exports to Japan consist of foodstuffs, raw materials, and mineral fuels.

Acquire Technology and Management Know-How

A reason often cited by foreign firms for investing in the United States is the acquisition of technology and management know-how. Nippon Mining, for example, a Japanese copper mining company, came to Illinois and paid $1 billion for Gould Inc. to acquire technology leadership and market share in producing the copper foil used in printed circuit boards for electronics products.

Geographic Diversification

Many companies have chosen geographic diversification as a means of maintaining stable sales and earnings when the domestic economy or their industry goes into a slump. Often, in other parts of the world, the industry or the other economies are at their peak. Remember that the firms in Table 2.1 obtained an average of 50 percent of their revenues overseas and that an even higher proportion of their profits came from abroad.

Satisfy Management's Desire for Expansion

The faster growth mentioned previously helps fulfill management's desire for expansion. Stockholders and financial analysts also expect firms to continue to grow, and those companies operating only in the domestic market have found it increasingly difficult to sustain that expectation. As a result, many firms have expanded into foreign markets. This, of course, is what companies based in small countries, such as Nestlé (Switzerland), SKF Bearing (Sweden), and Nokia (Finland), discovered decades ago.

Another aspect of this reason sometimes motivates a company's top managers to begin searching for overseas markets. Being able to claim that the firm is a "multinational" creates the impression of importance, which can influence the firm's customers. Sun Microsystems, a manufacturer of computer workstations, opened a technical center in Germany and built a factory in Scotland. "To be a major player in the marketplace, you have to be internationally recognized," said the head of Sun's European operations.[17]

We also know of instances in which a company has examined and then entered a market because its president brought it to the attention of the market planners after enjoying a pleasant vacation there.

How to Enter Foreign Markets

Once a company has determined from an analysis such as the preceding that it needs or wants to enter into international markets, it must then address what means to use in order to enter these markets. As you learned in Chapter 1, all of the means for supplying foreign markets may be subsumed in just two activities: (1) exporting to a foreign market and (2) manufacturing in it. Chapter 16 provides a discussion of the various options available to a firm under each of these two activities.

Multidomestic or Global Strategy?

Many large global and multidomestic firms with numerous manufacturing subsidiaries all over the world began their foreign operations by exporting. Once they succeeded at this stage, they often established sales companies overseas to market their exports. Where sales companies were able to develop sufficiently large markets, their firms set up plants to assemble imported parts. Finally, complete products were produced locally. However, this sequence of foreign trade to foreign direct investment does not represent the only way firms have entered.

More than likely, your first job in international business will *not* come with a business class airline ticket to Tokyo, London, or Rio de Janeiro and a "sky's the limit" expense account. More realistically, it will come with a desk, phone, FAX machine, e-mail, and a computer. Many entry-level jobs in international business involve handling import–export documentation to move shipments across international boarders; tracking shipments by boat, plane, train, and truck; following sales to make sure orders and payments are received; and dealing with foreign customers by phone, FAX, and e-mail. Is this the glamour of international business? Probably not. But it is business, and it is international, and it does put your career track in the international arena, which is where you need to be to start your international business career. In addition to your willingness to take that all-important entry-level international job and work to be successful at it, here are several other suggestions:

- Let your boss and your company's human resource department know you are interested in a career in international business.

- Join several international business trade associations in your city, and regularly attend their meetings. For example:

  International Chamber of Commerce, www.iccwbo.org

  International Association of Business Communicators (IABC), www.iabc.com

  International Trade Association of the U.S. Department of Commerce (offers seminars and workshops), http://trade.gov/index.asp

  Federation of International Trade Associations (FITA) (offers a directory of international trade associations by specialty, with locations), www.fita.org

  Your state's Department of Commerce or Economic Development (offers workshops and seminars on international trade)

  By attending these meetings, you get to know the association's members, so they get to know you and learn about your interest in a career in international business.

- Read international business publications so that you are current with issues, trends, and practices in international trade. Here are several:

  World Trade (this is free), www.worldtrademag.com

  International Trade Update (published monthly by the International Trade Association of the U.S. Department of Commerce), http://trade.gov/press/publications/newsletters/ita_0506/index_0506.asp

  International Herald Tribune, www.iht.com

  Financial Times, www.ft.com

  The Economist, www.economist.com

- Find a mentor to teach, guide, and assist you in building your international business career.

- Be ready to travel internationally at a moment's notice—hold a valid passport.

- Not all international jobs are in business. Explore the possibilities.

World Fact: Brazil has the largest ethnic Japanese population outside Japan, approximately 1.5 million.

Culture Cue: In the United States, "business casual" dress and informality when addressing superiors and subordinates by their first name may be accepted, but in many parts of the world this behavior is considered rude, offensive, and disrespectful. Learn the business norms of the country you will be working in before you start. If you are not sure, it is safer to be conservative and formal in your dress and behavior.

World Wide Resource:

- www.transitionsabroad.com/listings/work/careers/keywebsitesprofessionspecific.shtml

THE WORLD ENVIRONMENT IS CHANGING

While this linear relationship still holds, changes in the world environment that affect trade and foreign investment are occurring: (1) Governments generally have liberalized the flows of capital, technology, people, and goods, and (2) improvements in information technology enable managers to direct company activities in diverse areas over long distances. As a result, global competition has increased, forcing companies to strive for better-quality and lower-cost products. To reduce costs, they have moved some production activities to lower-cost countries and, through acquisitions and mergers, have increased company size to achieve economies of scale. Increasing sales by opening up new markets also will provide more economies of scale for the manufacturing system, especially if the firm sells the same products in all markets.

The aforementioned increased global competition will drive companies to open up new markets either to take market share from their competitors or to go to markets where there is less competition. It is evident that numerous conditions are forcing companies to enter foreign markets. Which strategy will management follow—multidomestic or global? In other words, what can the company standardize worldwide?

SEVEN GLOBAL DIMENSIONS

There are at least seven dimensions along which management can globalize (standardize): (1) product, (2) markets, (3) promotion, (4) where value is added to the product, (5) competitive strategy, (6) use of non-home-country personnel, and (7) extent of global ownership in the firm. The possibilities range from zero standardization (multidomestic) to standardization along all seven dimensions (completely global). The challenge for company managers is to determine how far the firm should go with each one. Usually the amount of globalization will vary among the dimensions. For example, the promotion for washing machines might be standardized to a great extent: People use them to get their clothes clean, but for economic reasons, in poorer countries the machines must be simpler and less costly. Therefore, the product is not standardized worldwide. We shall return to this topic in various parts of the text, particularly in Chapter 13.

Summary

Appreciate the magnitude of international trade and how it has grown.

The volume of international trade in goods and services measured in current dollars exceeded $11 trillion in 2004. Merchandise exports, at $8.9 trillion, were about 4.5 times what they were in 1980. Services exports were only $2.1 trillion in 2004, but their rate of growth since 1980 has been faster than that of merchandise exports.

Identify the direction of trade, or who trades with whom.

Developed countries tend to trade with developed countries, with such trade accounting for more than 70 percent of their total trade, and they account for a majority of the exports worldwide. More than half of the exports from developed countries also go to developed countries, though this proportion has been declining for the past 35 years. The results for services exports are similar in many ways to those found for merchandise exports. The rise of regional trade agreements, as well as other factors, is transforming the volume and direction of world trade in merchandise and services. Over 70 percent of world trade now occurs between members of regional trade agreements.

Explain the size, growth, and direction of foreign direct investment, worldwide and in the United States.

The book value of foreign direct investment was nearly $10 trillion at the end of 2004. The United States is the largest source of this FDI, with a total value of outstanding investments 1.46 times that of the United Kingdom, the next-largest investor, and 2.4 times that of Germany, the third-largest investor. The proportion of global foreign direct investment accounted for by the United States has been declining, falling from 36 percent in 1985 to 21 percent in 2004, while the proportion accounted for by the European Union has risen to 53 percent. The proportion of FDI originating in the developing nations has also been increasing, reaching 11 percent in 2004. On an annual basis, the United States was the largest source of FDI flows in 2004, with $229 billion in outflows, over 350 percent of the level of the second-largest FDI source, the

United Kingdom. Overall, over 70 percent of annual FDI investments flow into developed countries, with a majority of this investment occurring in the form of acquisitions of existing companies. The leader in FDI inflows at a national level was China for each of the years 2001 through 2004, the first time an emerging market has held such a distinction as the target for worldwide FDI investments. The direction of FDI follows the direction of foreign trade; that is, developed nations invest in each other just as they trade with each other. Note that because of the new business environment, many international firms are dispersing the activities of their manufacturing systems to locations closer to available resources. Deciding where to locate may be either an FDI or a trade decision.

Identify who invests and how much is invested in the United States.

Foreign direct investment in the United States rose from $185 billion in 1985 to $1,874 billion in 2005. Firms from just eight nations—United Kingdom, Japan, Germany, Netherlands, France, Canada, Switzerland, and Luxembourg—own about 85 percent of the total stock of foreign direct investment in the United States.

Understand the reasons for entering foreign markets.

Companies enter foreign markets (exporting to and manufacturing in) to increase sales and profits and to protect markets, sales, and profits. Foreign firms often buy American firms to acquire technology and marketing know-how. Foreign investment also enables a company to diversify geographically.

Comprehend that globalization of an international firm occurs over at least seven dimensions and that a company can be partially global in some dimensions and completely global in others.

A firm can have, and usually does have, an international strategy that is partially multidomestic in some dimensions and partially global in others. Management must decide the extent to which the firm should globalize along each dimension.

Questions

1. How large and important a role do small and medium-size enterprises play in generating export sales?

2. How has trade in merchandise and services changed over the past decade? What have been the major trends? How might this information be of value to a manager?

3. "The greater part of international trade consists of an exchange of raw materials from developing nations for manufactured goods from developed nations." True or false? Explain.

4. "The volume of exports has increased, but the ranking of U.S. trading partners in order of importance remains the same year after year." True or false? Of what use is this information to a manager?

5. What is the value of analyzing foreign trade data? For example, what should the quadrupling in real terms of exports in less than 35 years indicate to managers?

6. Knowing that a nation is a major trading partner of another signifies what to a marketing analyst?

7. What are the different components of foreign investment? Why has the distinction between them begun to blur in recent years?

8. How has the level and direction of FDI changed over the past decade, both overall and in terms of annual outflows and inflows? Why would this information be of relevance to managers?

9. Why has FDI historically followed foreign trade? What is it about the new international business environment that is causing this path to market expansion to change?

10. Why has most foreign direct investment gone into acquiring existing companies rather than establishing new ones?

11. What are the main reasons that a firm might enter into foreign markets?

12. What are in-bond plants? Why might they be an attractive alternative for a manufacturing company?

13. How can a firm protect its domestic market by investing overseas?

14. What are the seven dimensions along which management can globalize? How is it possible for a firm to be multidomestic on one dimension of globalization and global on another?

Research Task

globalEDGE globalEDGE.msu.edu

Use the globalEDGE site (http://globalEDGE.msu.edu/) to complete the following exercises:

1. An important element of understanding the nature of international trade is identifying the breadth of non-financial transnational corporations (TNCs). Using the *Largest Transnational Corporations*, a series of rankings published by UNCTAD, locate a ranking of the world's largest 100 non-financial TNCs by foreign assets. Then, identify the ten TNCs with the highest Transnationality Index (TNI). What are the home economies and industries of these TNCs? Also, where do they rank in the overall survey?

2. The number of member-nations of the World Trade Organization (WTO) has increased recently. In addition to nations with full member status, some non–member countries have observer status that requires accession negotiations to begin within five years of attaining this preliminary position. Identify the current total number of WTO members. Also, prepare a list of observer countries.

Jabil Circuit Inc. is a St. Petersburg, Florida–based company involved in providing electronic manufacturing services for international electronics companies in the electronics and technology industries. Established in 1966, Jabil now has 55,000 employees in over 40 facilities located in 20 nations worldwide, and it generated $7.5 billion in revenues in 2005.

One of Jabil's facilities is a factory for electronics manufacturing located in Guadalajara, Mexico. It was set up to make electronics products for export to companies such as Dell Inc. and Nokia Corporation, taking advantage of lower wage costs and the proximity to the U.S. market.

The initial 150,000-square-foot facility was opened in November 1997, with subsequent expansions increasing it to 363,000 square feet. In announcing the expansion, Wesley "Butch" Edwards, senior vice president of operations, said, "We are seeing a strong demand for additional North American capacity, especially in areas that provide access to low-cost manufacturing. [Increasing] the size of our Mexico facility is an indication of the strength of both current and new business opportunities in Mexico." Edwards said the expansion of the Guadalajara plant would allow both current and new customers to take advantage of Mexico's lower production costs. The factory would continue to offer cost levels that would allow delivery of products to North American markets at globally competitive prices.

The electronics industry in Guadalajara had experienced great success after the North American Free Trade Agreement was signed in 1993. Between 1994 and 2000, Guadalajara's electronics exports increased from $2 billion to $10 billion. Jabil's Mexican facility shared in this success. Jabil's plant in Guadalajara was one of the electronics facilities being heralded as a model for the successful industrialization of Mexico. By August 2000, employment at the plant had expanded to 3,500 people, and in February 2001, the company was busy scaling up its business to the highest volume of production in its history. Its future looked bright.

Within three months, by May 2001, output at the Guadalajara facility had declined by 40 percent. Economic recession in the United States, a stronger peso, and a doubling of average wage rates helped to trigger a rapid movement of production activities out of Mexico as companies attempted to find and exploit lower costs in other nations. Much of this business ended up being transferred to low-cost suppliers in China. Within a year, almost every product being produced in the Guadalajara plant had been transferred to one of seven plants that the parent Jabil company had established in China. By the summer of 2002, Jabil's Guadalajara workforce had been cut in half, to 1,750 employees.

Jabil's experience was not unique. Between 2001 and 2004, an estimated 400,000 jobs were moved to China from Mexico as companies attempted to maintain their competitiveness by finding lower-cost production sites. China's rapid export growth catapulted it into the position of second-largest exporter to the United States—behind Canada but ahead of Mexico, the previous number-two exporter.

Struggling for survival, Jabil's managers had to decide how to proceed. One option was to try to compete against the Chinese, despite Mexican labor costs approximately four times higher than those in China. However, the futility of trying to compete in such a scenario was apparent. "We realized we couldn't compete with China's labor cost. We needed to compete as a North American factory. After all, that's where we are," said Ernesto Sanchez, the general director of the Guadalajara factory.

Its proximity to the U.S. marketplace gave the Guadalajara facility an opportunity to leverage logistical factors to its advantage. Product development and support activities between companies operating in the United States and China can be particularly challenging, requiring off-hour calls or lengthy and expensive travel, which was a factor in the Guadalajara site's advantage. Although workers in Mexican manufacturing plants earned an average of three to four times more than their counterparts in China, logistics costs for Mexican products tend to be a small fraction of the costs required to ship products from Asia. Many U.S. customers were trying to manage inventory costs, while simultaneously being able to respond quickly to market developments, and being located near the U.S. market meant that factories like Jabil's in Guadalajara could achieve delivery times that were several weeks quicker than shipping times from a plant in Asia. The supply chain between Mexico and the United States was also better understood and was supported by prompt and reliable truck and rail transport. As a result of such factors, Jabil's Mexican plant had the potential to create value that could not be achieved by its Chinese competitors, helping to negate the difference in labor costs. "The one advantage we have is our geographic position. We are close to one of the biggest markets in the world, plus our labor force is still less expensive than either the U.S. or Canada," said Sanchez.

One example of the benefits of location is the case of cell phones. One company discovered that a model of its cell phone cost 50 cents less to build in China, but the cost of transportation was 14 cents if shipped by sea and 71 cents if shipped by air versus only 5 cents if shipped from Mexico by truck. The added shipping time associated with sea transport from China—typically 21 to 23 days, as opposed to less than 8 hours from Mexico—as well as tightened customs procedures imposed on shipping from Asia to manage risks from terrorism, also required that the company carry a higher level of buffer inventory, another significant cost.

As a result of factors such as these, the managers in the Guadalajara plant decided to move away from their traditional low-end manufacturing orientation, where their competitiveness on labor costs had eroded quickly as opposed to the rapidly emerging Chinese market. Instead, they focused on the production of more complex and higher-value-added products, such as computer routers and handheld credit card machines used by restaurants. They particularly emphasized goods made by smaller U.S. manufacturers, against whom the Mexican facility still had a strong edge in labor costs.

In order to produce more complex products, many of which required a significant level of customization, the plant's managers had to make a number of changes. The production lines were reengineered to allow employees to quickly switch components, software, and engineering diagrams among different products or models of a product. The plant's inventory system was restructured to allow the effective management of the more extensive range of parts being used in the new product lines. Workers were trained to perform a broader range of tasks. High levels of absenteeism and turnover have been an endemic problem in many Mexican companies, so the company remodeled the cafeteria and broadened the range of food offerings in order to enhance worker satisfaction. Management also established quarterly meetings with line employees to listen to complaints and solicit suggestions. Despite these efforts, the transformation of the company and its production and inventory processes still encountered a range of problems, and it took months to identify and overcome the myriad difficulties that arose.

In the end, though, the plant achieved a remarkable turnaround. Many of the plant's initial new orders were taken from a Jabil factory in Boise, Idaho, a modern 500-employee facility that had opened in 2000. Within four months of the changeover, the Guadalajara facility had surpassed the performance of the Boise plant on such measures as quality, cost, and on-time delivery. The spare-parts tracking software that it developed ended up being adopted as the standard for the company's worldwide operations. Jabil's efforts in Mexico ultimately led to the closure of the Idaho plant. The Guadalajara plant has expanded to nearly 4,000 employees and produces over 600 different types of products for its customers, including communications switches, specialized handheld credit card processing machines, Internet firewalls, and electronic controls for washing machines.

Despite this success, Jabil's managers in Guadalajara cannot become complacent. As Ernesto Sanchez said, "Right now we're able to do more complex products than China, although you may be sure they are coming up very quickly."

Source: David Luhnow, "As Jobs Move East, Plants in Mexico Retool to Compete," *The Wall Street Journal,* March 5, 2004, pp. A1, A8; Joel Millman, "The Outlook," *The Wall Street Journal,* February 23, 2004, p. A2; Andrew MacLellan, "Mexico Hangs Tough as Alternative to China," *EBN*, September 15, 2003, p. 1; William Atkinson, "Mexico or China? Lower Costs Tip Scales toward Far East," *Purchasing,* April 17, 2003, pp. 15–16; "Jabil Announces Plans for Mexico Expansion," December 4, 1998, www.jabil.com/390_601.asp (July 21, 2004); Jabil Circuit Inc., 2005 Annual Report, http://jbl.client.shareholder.com/downloads/2005Annual.pdf (July 12, 2006); and "Company Profile," www.jabil.com/about.asp (July 12, 2006).

3

Theories of International Trade and Investment

Santiago, Chile, skyline at dusk.

If a foreign country can supply us with a commodity cheaper than we ourselves can make it, better buy it of them with some part of our own industry, employed in a way in which we have some advantage.

—*Adam Smith, The Wealth of Nations*

Free-Market Reforms Revive Chile's Economy

Business managers must have a good knowledge of economic theory to be able to understand a nation's economic development strategy, which depends greatly on the beliefs and education of the government's economic planners. By closely following the actions and speeches of government leaders, managers often can discover the economic theories on which those actions and speeches are based. If they know the underlying theories, they can anticipate changes in government strategy and use that knowledge to their advantage. As an example, look at what happened in Chile after the changeover from the Marxist regime of Salvador Allende.

The economy was in a shambles after Allende's regime. Inflation was running over 1,000 percent annually, and the nation's debt load was totally unmanageable. The Allende government had been following the policy of many developing nations at that time—heavy involvement in the economy. This included placing high duties on imports to protect local industry, levying high income taxes on the private sector to obtain funds for government-directed investment, and granting huge subsidies to selected industries.

Realizing that drastic changes had to be made, the post-Allende government appointed a group of conservative Chilean economists to design a new program. Known as the "Chicago Boys" for having graduated from the University of Chicago, they were followers of the free-market teachings of its economics professor and Nobel Prize winner Milton Friedman.

The contents of the Chicago Boys' program and its impact on Chilean business did not surprise anyone with knowledge of economic theory. In fact, much of what they proposed was based on the theory of comparative advantage. Managers who understood the significance of the proposals knew that Chile soon would have a free-market economy that would require a massive restructuring of Chilean manufacturing plants.

One of the most important reforms recommended by the economists and put into effect by the government was the reduction of import duties from a high of 1,000 percent to a basic level of 10 percent. Moreover, all other import barriers were removed so that virtually anyone was free to import anything. As a result, manufacturers and growers were forced to compete in world markets to stay in business. In addition, the lower import duties reduced the cost of imported capital equipment, which encouraged business investment. What was the reaction of the managers who were prepared to change to the new system?

The president of Chile's largest appliance maker, whose industry had been protected from foreign competition by a 1,000 percent import duty, gave his opinion of the new program: "We used to have 5,000 workers and an annual productivity of only $9,000 per worker. Now we have 1,860 workers and a productivity of $43,000 per worker, and we are finally showing a profit."

It was no surprise to those with knowledge of economics that there would be a contraction of local industry when companies lost their protection from imports. Although the leading appliance maker mentioned above was able to compete after losing its import protection, a number of other local appliance makers were forced to go out of business or contract their operations. "We're going to lose a large part of our appliance industry," conceded Alvaro Bardon, a 37-year-old Chicago Boy who was then the head of the central bank of Chile, "and also our electronics industry

CONCEPT PREVIEWS

After reading this chapter, you should be able to:

explain the theories that attempt to explain why certain goods are traded internationally

discuss the arguments for imposing trade restrictions

explain the two basic kinds of import restrictions: tariff and nontariff trade barriers

appreciate the relevance of the changing status of tariff and nontariff barriers to managers

explain some of the theories of foreign direct investment

and our automobile assembly plants." Bardon was hardly disappointed, however. "Those are products we should be importing," he said. "We have other things based on our farm products, our timberlands, our fisheries, and our mineral resources that we should be making because they give us a natural advantage over other countries."

How successful were these free-market policies adopted by Chile's government? Growth in real GDP averaged 8 percent during 1991–1997. Although tight monetary policies associated with a global financial crisis, accompanied by a severe drought, caused growth to decline in 1998 and 1999, Chile maintained its free-market policies and the confidence of the international markets. Recovery began by the end of 1999, and growth had accelerated to over 6 percent by 2006, while still maintaining a low inflation rate. Chile has subsequently signed free trade agreements with several nations or regions, including the European Union, Mercosur, the United States, Canada, Korea, Peru, Venezuela, Bolivia,

Columbia, Ecuador, China, and Mexico. The total stock of foreign direct investment in Chile exceeds $55 billion. The *Country Commercial Guide (CCG)* prepared by the combined efforts of various U.S. government agencies reported, "Chile is one of the Latin American region's most dynamic and promising markets. . . . Market-led reforms adopted close to 30 years ago and an increasingly diversified economy with strong ties to buyers and suppliers in the Americas, Europe, and Asia have given Chile a wide range of options for further growth. Prudent economic policy-making has secured long-term stability unknown elsewhere in Latin America." ■

Source: *World Development Indicators 2006* (Washington, DC: World Bank, 2006); *2006 CIA World Factbook*, www.cia.gov/cia/publications/factbook/geos/ci.html (July 7, 2006); UNCTAD, "Chile," *World Investment Report 2005*, www.unctad .org/templates/Page.asp?intItemID=2441&lang=1 (July 7, 2006); Dennis R. Appleyard, Alfred J. Field, Jr., and Steven L. Cobb, *International Economics*, 5th ed. (New York: McGraw-Hill Irwin, 2006); "Why Chile's Economy Roared While the World's Slumbered," *The Wall Street Journal*, January 22, 1993, p. A11; and *Doing Business in Chile—Country Commercial Guide* (Santiago, Chile: U.S. Commercial Service, 2004), www.buyusa.gov/chile/en/doing_business_in_chile.html (July 7, 2006).

The economic program that the Chilean economists put into effect is a practical application of the keystone of international trade theory—the law of comparative advantage. Note the education of the head of Chile's central bank. Economists are commonly found in governments as policy makers and advisers to government leaders worldwide. When they have a particularly strong influence in government affairs, they are frequently dubbed with such pejorative names as the "Chicago Boys" in Chile, "tecnicos" in Mexico, and the "Berkeley Mafia" (economists educated at the University of California–Berkeley) in Indonesia.

What is the significance for international managers? For one thing, since they frequently will be dealing with government officials trained in economics, managers must be prepared to speak their language. When presenting plans requiring governmental approval, managers must take care that the plans are economically sound, for they are almost certain to be studied by economists and will often need to be approved by them. Marketers proposing large projects to government planners must be aware that the key determinant now is economic efficiency rather than mere financial soundness.[1] Moreover, as you have seen in the case of Chile, knowledge of economic concepts, especially in the areas of (1) international trade, (2) economic development, and (3) foreign direct investment, frequently provide insights into future government action.

mercantilism

An economic philosophy based on the belief that (1) a nation's wealth depends on accumulated treasure, usually gold, and (2) to increase wealth, government policies should promote exports and discourage imports

International Trade Theory

Why do nations trade? This question and the equally important proposition of predicting the direction, composition, and volume of goods traded are what international trade theory attempts to address. Interestingly, as is the case with numerous economic writings, the first formulation of international trade theory was politically motivated. Adam Smith, incensed by government intervention and control over both domestic and foreign trade, published *An Inquiry into the Nature and Causes of the Wealth of Nations* (1776), in which he tried to destroy the mercantilist philosophy.

MERCANTILISM

Mercantilism, the economic philosophy Smith attacked, evolved in Europe between the 16th and 18th centuries. A complex political and economic arrangement, mercantilism traditionally has been interpreted as viewing the accumulation of precious metals as an activity essential to a nation's welfare. These metals were, in the mercantilists' view, the only source of wealth. Because England had no mines, the mercantilists looked to international trade to supply gold and silver. The government established economic policies that promoted exports and stifled imports, resulting in a trade surplus to be paid for in gold and silver. Import restrictions such as import duties reduced imports, while government subsidies to exporters increased exports. Those acts created a trade surplus, in addition to protecting jobs within the mercantilist nation. Of course, another outcome of mercantilism was the generation of benefits for certain economic groups, such as domestic merchants, artisans, and shippers, albeit at a cost to other groups such as consumers and emerging industrialists.

Although the mercantilist era ended in the late 1700s, its arguments live on. Many people still argue that exports are "good" for a person's country since they create jobs, while imports are "bad" because they transfer jobs from a person's country to other nations. This view essentially sees trade as a zero-sum activity, where one party must lose in order for another to gain. Similarly, a "favorable" trade balance still means that a nation exports more goods and services than it imports. In balance-of-payments accounting, an export that brings dollars to the country is called *positive*, but imports that cause dollar outflow are labeled *negative*.

In the United States, many managers believe that Japan, because of its protectionism, remains largely a nearly impenetrable market—a present-day "fortress of mercantilism." American managers are concerned that Japan's barriers to their imports are the result of Japanese insularity, traditional preoccupation with self-sufficiency, and "us against them" mentality. A U.S. secretary of commerce once said, "They tell us they have to protect their markets because of their culture. They haven't joined the world yet." Comments from the Japanese seem to confirm what some Americans are saying. "The public is not in favor of perfect markets," says a Japanese bank manager. "We would like to preserve the substance of our culture. If we move to free trade, we may lose Japanese virtue in the process."[2] One part of this mercantilist effort is Japan's continuing effort to maintain a cheap yen in order to capture attractive export markets while reducing the threat of imports. For example, the Bank of Japan spent 15 trillion yen in the first three months of 2004 to push the yen down against the U.S. dollar. As G. Richard Wagoner, Jr., chairman of General Motors, said, the Japanese "are keeping their currency artificially weak against the dollar and euro and really reducing the competitive position" of U.S. and European companies.[3] A similar neo-mercantilist argument has recently been made regarding China's approach to valuing their currency.

Despite impressive economic growth and burgeoning trade surpluses, Chinese authorities have resisted efforts to revalue their currency, instead continuing to hold their currency, the yuan, within a tight trading range relative to the U.S. dollar. By not allowing the yuan to appreciate in value relative to the dollar, the Chinese authorities were accused of engaging in mercantilist behavior because they were helping the international cost-competitiveness of Chinese companies relative to companies from the U.S. and other nations.

THEORY OF ABSOLUTE ADVANTAGE

absolute advantage
Theory that a nation has absolute advantage when it can produce a larger amount of a good or service for the same amount of inputs as can another country or when it can produce the same amount of a good or service using fewer inputs than could another country

Adam Smith argued against mercantilism by claiming that market forces, not government controls, should determine the direction, volume, and composition of international trade. He argued that under free, unregulated trade, each nation should specialize in producing those goods it could produce most efficiently (for which it had an **absolute advantage,** either natural or acquired). Some of these goods would be exported to pay for imports of goods that could be produced more efficiently elsewhere. Smith showed by his example of absolute advantage that both nations would gain from trade.

An Example   Assume that a world of two countries and two products has perfect competition and no transportation costs. Suppose that in the United States and China (1) one unit of input (combination of land, labor, and capital) can produce the quantities of soybeans and cloth listed below, (2) each nation has two input units it can use to produce either soybeans or cloth, and (3) each country uses one unit of input to produce each product. If

Successful international business professionals look beyond their home country borders and continually explore and learn more about the world in which they live and work. Can you answer these questions?

- Where is East Timor?
- What do you do with souvlaki and tzaziki? Where do they come from?
- How many time zones are in the world?
- On the globe, where does East become West?
- What is the International Date Line? Where is it?
- What is the largest country in the world? The smallest country?

To become a successful international business professional, you must become a "citizen of the world." To be a citizen of the world requires that you know about the world. The international business professional knows world facts and data and keeps current with world events that will impact his or her ability to successfully engage in global business transactions.

World Fact: The U.S. State Department recognizes 192 independent nations in the world. If Taiwan were recognized, the number would be 193. However, numerous territories and colonies under the governmental control of other countries are thought to be independent countries. Some of these are Bermuda, Greenland, Puerto Rico, and Western Sahara. England, Scotland, Wales, and Northern Ireland are part of the United Kingdom.

Culture Cue: In dealing with your foreign counterparts, listen as much as you speak. Feel free to talk about your home country, but also ask the people you are meeting to tell you about their country, their customs, and their way of life. This type of conversation helps you to learn more about their part of the world and it builds rapport. In many parts of the world, rapport and friendship must first be established before business will ever be discussed. This is a critical first step to doing business in much of Latin America, the Middle East, and Asia, for example.

World Wide Resources:

www.cia.gov/cia/publications/factbook

A link to English language newspapers from around the world listed by country:

www.unc.edu/world/Global%20Updates%202006/May_June/May06.htm

neither country imports or exports, the quantities shown in the table are also those that are available for local consumption. The total output of both nations is 4 tons of soybeans and 6 bolts of cloth.

Commodity	United States	China	Total
Tons of soybeans	3	1	4
Bolts of cloth	2	4	6

In the United States, 3 tons of soybeans or 2 bolts of cloth can be produced with one unit of output. Therefore, 3 tons of soybeans should have the same price as 2 bolts of cloth. In China, however, since only 1 ton of soybeans can be produced with the input unit that can produce 4 bolts of cloth, 1 ton of soybeans should cost as much as 4 bolts of cloth.

The United States has an absolute advantage in soybean production (3 to 1). China's absolute advantage is in cloth making (4 to 2). Will anyone anywhere give the Chinese cloth maker more than 1 ton of soybeans for 4 bolts of cloth? According to the example, all American soybean producers should because they can get only 2 bolts of cloth for 3 tons of soybeans at home. Similarly, Chinese cloth makers, once they learn that they can obtain more than 1 ton of soybeans for every 4 bolts of cloth in the United States, will be eager to trade Chinese cloth for American soybeans.

Each Country Specializes   Suppose each nation decides to use its resources to produce only the product at which it is more efficient. The following table shows each nation's output. Note that with the same quantity of input units, the total output is now greater.

Commodity	United States	China	Total
Tons of soybeans	6	0	6
Bolts of cloth	0	8	8

Terms of Trade (Ratio of International Prices) With specialization, now the total production of both goods is greater, but to consume both products, the two countries must trade some of their surplus. What are the limits within which both countries are willing to trade? Clearly, the Chinese cloth makers will trade some of their cloth for soybeans if they can get more than the 1 ton of soybeans that they get for 4 bolts of cloth in China. Likewise, the American soybean growers will trade their soybeans for Chinese cloth if they get a bolt of cloth for less than the 1.5 tons of soybeans it costs them in the United States.

If the two nations take the midpoint of the two trading limits so that each shares equally in the benefits of trade, they will agree to swap 1.33 bolts of cloth for 1 ton of soybeans. Both will gain from specialization because each now has the following quantities:

Commodity	United States	China	Total
Tons of soybeans	3	3	6
Bolts of cloth	4	4	8

Gains from Specialization and Trade Because each nation specialized in producing the product at which it was more efficient and then traded its surplus for goods that it could not produce as efficiently, both gained the following:

Commodity	United States	China
Tons of soybeans		2
Bolts of cloth	2	

Certainly, both nations have gained by trading.

Although Adam Smith's logic helped to convince many governments to dismantle trade barriers and encourage increased international trade, it failed to calm concerns of those whose countries lacked any absolute advantage. What if one country has an absolute advantage in the production of both soybeans and cloth? Will there still be a basis for trade?

THEORY OF COMPARATIVE ADVANTAGE

David Ricardo demonstrated in 1817 that even though one nation held an absolute advantage over another in the production of each of two different goods, international trade could still create benefit for each country (thus representing a positive-sum game, or one in which both countries "win" from engaging in trade). The only limitation to such benefit-creating trade is that the less efficient nation cannot be *equally* less efficient in the production of both goods.[4] To illustrate how this can occur, let us slightly change our first example so that now China has an absolute advantage in producing *both* soybeans and cloth. Note that compared to China, the United States is less inefficient in producing soybeans than in manufacturing cloth. Therefore, it has a relative advantage, or **comparative advantage,** according to Ricardo, in producing soybeans.

Commodity	United States	China	Total
Tons of soybeans	4	5	9
Bolts of cloth	2	5	7

Each Country Specializes If each country specializes in what it does best, its output will be as follows:

Commodity	United States	China	Total
Tons of soybeans	8	0	8
Bolts of cloth	0	10	10

Terms of Trade   In this case, the terms of trade will be somewhere between the 1 ton of soybeans for 1 bolt of cloth that Chinese soybean growers must pay in China and the $\frac{1}{2}$ bolt of cloth that American cloth makers must pay for 1 ton of American soybeans. Although the theory of comparative advantage did not address the ratios of exchange, it did state that the range of advantageous trade for both parties lies between the pre-trade price ratios.

Let us assume that the traders agree on an exchange rate of $\frac{3}{4}$ bolt of cloth for 1 ton of soybeans. Both will gain from this exchange and specialization, as the following table shows:

Commodity	United States	China
Tons of soybeans	4	4
Bolts of cloth	3	7

Note that this trade left China with 2 surplus bolts of cloth and 1 less ton of soybeans than it had before. America has the same quantity of soybeans and 1 more bolt of cloth. However, the Chinese cloth manufacturers should be able to trade 1 bolt of surplus cloth for at least 1 ton of soybeans elsewhere. Then the final result will be as follows:

Commodity	United States	China
Tons of soybeans	4	5
Bolts of cloth	3	6

Gains from Specialization and Trade   Gains from specialization and trade in this case are the following:

Commodity	United States	China
Tons of soybeans		
Bolts of cloth	1	1

Production Possibility Frontiers   We can also illustrate the gains from trade graphically, using production possibility frontiers. Figure 3.1 graphs the Chinese and U.S. production possibility frontiers using constant costs for simplicity. These curves, in the absence of trade, also illustrate the possible combinations of goods for consumption. Before trade, China might be producing and consuming 5 tons of soybeans and 5 bolts of cloth (point A), while the United States is producing and consuming 4 tons of soybeans and 2 bolts of cloth (point A).

FIGURE 3.1

Production and Consumption Possibility Frontiers before and after Trade

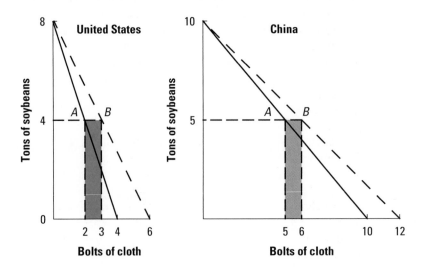

With each nation specializing in the production of the goods in which it has a comparative advantage and trading its surplus with the other, both nations are able to consume at point *B*. The shaded areas under each curve indicate the gains from trade.

This simple concept of comparative advantage serves as a basis for international trade, even when one nation has an advantage over another in the production of each of the goods being traded.

Note that in our examples we mentioned a unit of input. This is a more modern version of the examples of Ricardo and Smith, who used only labor input. They did so because at that time only labor was considered important in calculating production costs.[5] Also, no consideration was given to the possibility of producing the same goods with different combinations of factors, and no explanation was given as to why production costs differed. Not until 1933 did Bertil Ohlin, a Swedish economist building on work presented in 1919 by his Swedish economics professor, Eli Heckscher, develop the theory of factor endowment.[6]

HECKSCHER-OHLIN THEORY OF FACTOR ENDOWMENT

The Heckscher-Ohlin theory of **factor endowment** states that international and interregional differences in production costs occur because of differences in the supply of production factors. The goods that require a large amount of a nation's abundant—thus less costly—factor will have lower production costs, enabling those goods to be sold for less in international markets. For example, India, relatively well endowed with labor compared to Germany, ought to concentrate on producing labor-intensive goods; Germany, with relatively more capital than labor, should specialize in capital-intensive products. When these countries trade, each will obtain at a lower price those goods that require large amounts of the production factor that is relatively scarce in their own country, and both will benefit from the transaction.

How useful is this theory for explaining present-day trading patterns? In general, trade patterns correspond fairly well with the Heckscher-Ohlin theory. Countries with relatively large amounts of land (such as Australia) do export land-intensive products (such as grain and cattle), whereas countries with relatively large populations (such as Indonesia and Bangladesh) export labor-intensive goods.[7] There are exceptions, however, due in part to Ohlin's assumptions. One assumption was that the prices of the factors depend only on the factor endowment. We know this is untrue. Factor prices are not set in a perfect market. For example, legislated minimum wages and benefits can force the cost of labor to rise to a point greater than the value of the product that many workers can produce. Investment tax credits can reduce the cost of capital below market cost, and so forth. As a result, factor prices do not fully reflect factor supply.

Ohlin also assumed that a given technology is universally available, but this is not so. There is always a lag between the introduction of a new production method and its application worldwide. As a result, superior technology often permits a nation to produce goods at a cost lower than that of a country better endowed with the required factor. A closely related assumption was that a given product is either labor- or capital-intensive. Yet observation of construction methods in, for example, a less developed nation would show that wet concrete can be poured either by a gang of laborers with buckets or by a crane and its operator.

Leontief Paradox   A study made in 1953 by the economist Wassily Leontief disputed the usefulness of the Heckscher-Ohlin theory as a predictor of the direction of trade. The study, known as the *Leontief paradox*, found that the United States, one of the most capital-intensive countries in the world, was exporting relatively labor-intensive products in exchange for relatively capital-intensive products. Economists have speculated that this occurred because the United States exports technology-intensive products produced by highly skilled labor requiring a large capital investment to educate and train and at the same time imports goods made with mature technology requiring capital-intensive mass-production processes operated by unskilled labor. A study by the Harvard economists Sachs and Shatz did in fact show that the United States has increased its exports of skill-intensive goods to developing nations while reducing its production of unskilled goods.[8] Another possible explanation

factor endowment
Heckscher-Ohlin theory that countries export products requiring large amounts of their abundant production factors and import products requiring large amounts of their scarce production factors

Comparative Advantage and Offshoring of Service Jobs to India

Wipro employees in Bangalore, India, undergo training in the use of specialized software to provide services to overseas clients.

India, a nation with approximately 1 billion people, has relatively few other resources compared to developed nations. Therefore, it should have a comparative advantage in production of goods or services that require large amounts of labor and relatively little capital. However, India has an additional comparative advantage since many of its citizens speak English (which is taught in many Indian schools and universities rather than using

one of the other 18 major languages and 844 dialects spoken in the country). Thus labor has a relatively low price due to the large Indian work force (about 450 million, with nearly 10 million additional people entering the work force each year) and high levels of unemployment or underemployment (officially an unemployment rate of 8 percent, but a poverty rate that exceeds 20 percent). As Internet and cellular telephone communications continue to become less expensive, India increasingly is using its English-speaking pool of labor to export services—such as software engineering, customer service, telemarketing, reviews of credit or mortgage applications, analysis of blood tests and other medical services, and claims processing—to foreign companies and their customers, a process known as *offshoring*.

In 2005, the Indian IT industry generated revenues of $36 billion, nearly 5 percent of India's GDP, and exports of $60 billion are projected by 2010. Fortune 500 companies such as Amazon.com, International Business Machines, and American Express, as well as a range of more moderate-size firms, have already offshored millions of jobs. Gartner, the IT consultancy, estimated that up to 25 percent of traditional IT jobs will be offshored to developing countries by 2010. By 2015, it has been estimated that 3.4 million U.S. jobs, representing $136 billion in wages, will have been offshored, and India is well positioned to capture much of this business. According to Noshir Kaka of the consulting firm McKinsey, "This industry can do for India what automobiles did for Japan and oil for Saudi Arabia."

For example, over 250,000 U.S. individual and corporate tax returns were prepared in India in 2005, an increase from only about 20,000 in 2002, and these numbers are predicted to surge dramatically in subsequent years. Documents obtained from taxpayers are scanned and shipped electronically to India, where forms are completed and sent back to the United States to be examined, approved, and signed by an American accountant. While a U.S. tax preparer might cost $3,000 per month during the peak tax season, a comparable Indian worker might cost less than $300. There is no requirement that the taxpayer be informed that the tax work is done abroad, and most accounting firms charge the same fees as those charged if the job is done by accountants in the United States, thus helping to boost profitability.

Companies in financial services and insurance have also been actively pursuing offshoring. Over 80 percent of global financial services companies have an offshore facility. The international insurance giant Aviva, for example, expects to have 7,800 of its 59,000-person work force offshored by late 2007, primarily to India, and the range of services being

for this apparent paradox in trade patterns is that many products may be produced by either capital- or labor-intensive processes, as was noted in the previous paragraph. The international structure of barriers to trade could also partially explain Leontief's result. An important outcome of Leontief's work was recognizing the potential for differences in, for example, the kinds of labor (e.g., some labor is skilled, other labor is largely unskilled, and the potential productivity of these two groups can be quite different), as well as differences in natural and capital resources, and these factors can help to explain the level and direction of trade.[9]

offshored is rapidly being broadened, including IT, accounting, and claims processing. "Offshoring has released a new competitive dynamic. Larger firms are driving change across the financial services industry and using offshoring to open up a competitive advantage over their smaller rivals," said Chris Gentle of the professional services firm Deloitte. "Offshoring is fundamentally changing the way financial institutions do business, creating a global division of labor that demands new operating models, new structures and new management skills."

"This is a global industry in the throes of flux. It is a sector where [Indian companies] are rewriting the rules of the game. That is the difference that has become apparent and increasingly accepted," says Nandan Nilekani, CEO of the rapidly expanding Indian company Infosys Technologies. The basis for this change, he says, is the "global delivery model" being pioneered in India and replicated in other low-cost nations. In the IT sector, for example, a plentiful supply of Indian software engineers can work on projects "offshore," delivering the finished product to clients "on-site" in the United States. "Our business innovation is forcing rivals to redesign the way they do things."

This disruptive change is threatening to transform the business models in operation across a broad range of industries. Although many people think of low-skill jobs like telemarketing and call centers when they think of outsourcing to India, the sophistication and skill levels associated with processes being outsourced are rising rapidly. A big driver for this trend is the wealth of qualified personnel in India. A NASSCOM-McKinsey study found that India has 28 percent of the overall supply of skilled services personnel in low-cost nations, and these potential employees remain amazingly inexpensive. According to the Boston Consulting Group, an Indian IT engineer earns a typical annual salary of $5,000 and one with a master's degree in business earns $7,500 —about one-tenth the level of their American counterparts.

Services represent 60 percent of the U.S. economy and employ about two-thirds of American workers, so it is not surprising that the offshoring of service jobs has generated concerns across a broad spectrum of society. John Steadman, president of the Institute of Electrical and Electronics Engineers, cautioned, "If we continue to offshore high-skilled professional jobs, the U.S. risks surrendering its leading role in innovation." Andrew Grove, CEO of Intel Corp., warned that "it's a very valid question" whether the United States could lose its dominance in information technology as a result of this trend, as it did in electronics manufacturing. Responding to the outsourcing to an Indian firm of calls from New Jersey welfare recipients about their benefits, state senator Shirley Turner said, "I was outraged. Here we are in New Jersey, as we are in every state, requiring welfare recipients to go to work. And yet, we were

sending these jobs overseas … so that corporations can make more money." She noted that unemployed people do not pay taxes, and the loss of these tax revenues exacerbates budget deficits. Ironically, widespread publicity regarding concerns about offshoring may have hastened the trend by making more companies aware of the possible cost savings from such undertakings.

On the other hand, some have argued that offshoring will help to strengthen American industry and the economy as a whole. Outsourcing is not necessarily a zero-sum game, where one Indian worker substitutes for one American worker. When American firms hire lower-cost labor abroad, they often must hire other workers to complement the increased level of foreign labor. Overseas expansion can also cause companies to modify the scope of activities undertaken in the United States, placing increasing emphasis on higher-value-added activities rather than the lower-skill positions that have been offshored. Shifting work to lower-cost locations abroad has the potential to lower prices in the United States, thus raising the purchasing power of American consumers, enhancing consumer spending and economic activity, and thereby creating more jobs. As *The Wall Street Journal* editorialized, "The world economy is a dynamic enterprise. Jobs created overseas generate jobs at home. Not just more jobs for Americans, but higher-skilled and better paying ones. At the same time, trade offers consumers a greater quantity and variety of goods and services for lower prices. David Ricardo lives."

By companies' exploiting India's comparative advantage in providing English-speaking personnel for labor-intensive service activities, you may increasingly discover that you are discussing your charge card billing statement or online purchase with, or receiving assistance to fix your malfunctioning computer from, a service person who is located in India, not your own country.

Sources: Meg Fletcher, "Moving Services Offshore," *Business Insurance*, June 2006, pp. 16–17; Joanna Slater, "In India, a Job Paradox," *The Wall Street Journal*, May 5, 2004, p. A12; Julie Gallagher, "Redefining the Business Case for Offshore Outsourcing," *Insurance & Technology*, April 2002, pp. A5, A8–A9; Khozem Merchant, "The Future on India's Shores," *Financial Times*, April 21, 2004, p. 8; "Outsourcing 101," *The Wall Street Journal*, May 27, 2004, p. A20; Rebecca Paley, "Fighting for the Down and Out(sourced)," *Mother Jones*, May/June 2004, pp. 20–21; Paul Taylor, "Outsourcing of IT Jobs Predicted to Continue," *Financial Times*, March 17, 2004, p. 6; Manjeet Kripalani and Pete Engardio, "The Rise of India," *Business Week*, December 8, 2003, pp. 66–76; Robert Orr, "Offshoring Opens Gap in Financial Services Race," *Financial Times*, June 29, 2004, p. 9; and Richard D. Brody, Mary J. Miller, and Michael J. Rolleri, "Outsourcing Income Tax Returns to India: Legal, Ethical, and Professional Issues," *CPA Journal*, www.nysscpa.org/cpajournal/2004/1204/perspectives/p12.htm (July 10, 2006).

Differences in Taste Heckscher-Ohlin also ignored transportation costs, but there are goods for which freight charges are so high that the landed cost (export sales price plus transportation charges) is greater than the cost of a locally made product. In that case, there will be little trade. Why not say there will be no trade? It is because of a demand-side construct that is always difficult to deal with in economic theory and that we have so far neglected—*differences in taste*. Managers, however, cannot neglect this difference, which enables trade to flow in a direction completely contrary to that predicted by the theory of comparative advantage—from high- to low-cost nations. France sells wine, cosmetics, clothing, and even drinking water to the United States, all of which are produced in America and generally sold at lower prices. Germany and Italy send Porsches and Maseratis to America, even though the United States is one of the largest automobile producers in the world. Americans buy these goods not only on the basis of price, the implied independent variable in the trade theory we have been examining, but also because of taste preferences. Differences in cultures, climates, income levels, and population structures can produce diversity in preferences, and thus influence trade patterns.

We have presented the theory of comparative advantage without mentioning money; however, a nation's comparative advantage can be affected by differences between the costs of production factors in that country's currency and their costs in other currencies. As we shall see in the next section, money can change the direction of trade.

HOW MONEY CAN CHANGE THE DIRECTION OF TRADE

Suppose the total cost of land, labor, and capital to produce the daily output of soybeans or cloth in the example on absolute advantage is $10,000 in the United States and 80,000 yuan in China. The cost per unit is as follows:

Commodity	Price per Unit	
	United States	China
Ton of soybeans	$10,000/3 = $3,333/ton	80,000 yuan/1 = 80,000 yuan/ton
Bolt of cloth	$10,000/2 = $5,000/bolt	80,000 yuan/4 = 20,000 yuan/bolt

To determine whether it is more advantageous to buy locally or to import, the traders need to know the prices in their own currencies. To convert from foreign to domestic currency, they use the *exchange rate*.

exchange rate
The price of one currency stated in terms of another currency

Exchange Rate   The **exchange rate** is the price of one currency stated in terms of the other. If the prevailing rate is $1 = 8 yuan, then 1 yuan must be worth 0.125 dollar.* Using the exchange rate of $1 = 8 yuan, the prices in the preceding example appear to the U.S. trader as follows:

Commodity	Price per Unit (dollars)	
	United States	China
Ton of soybeans	$3,333	$10,000
Bolt of cloth	$5,000	$2,500

The American soybean producers can earn $6,667 more per ton by exporting soybeans to China than they can by selling locally,† but can the Chinese cloth makers gain by exporting to the United States? To find out, they must convert the American prices to Chinese yuan.

Commodity	Price per Unit (yuan)	
	United States	China
Ton of soybeans	26,664 yuan	80,000 yuan
Bolt of cloth	40,000 yuan	20,000 yuan

*If $1 = 8 yuan, to find the value of 1 yuan in dollars, divide both sides of the equation by 8. Then 1 yuan = 1/8 = $0.125.
†For example, to calculate this figure, you would multiply the American price of $3,333 per ton of soybeans times 8 yuan per dollar, yielding a price of 26,664 yuan per ton.

It is apparent that the Chinese cloth makers will export cloth to the United States because they can sell at the higher price of 40,000 yuan per bolt. The American cloth makers, however, will need some very strong sales arguments to sell in the United States if they are to overcome the $2,500 price differential. Ricardo did not consider this possibility; in his time, products were considered homogeneous and therefore were sold primarily on the basis of price.

Influence of Exchange Rate   Soybeans to China and cloth to the United States will be the direction of trade as long as the exchange rate remains around $1 = 8 yuan. But if the dollar strengthens to $1 = 24 yuan, American soybeans will cost as much in yuan as do Chinese soybeans, and importation will cease. On the other hand, should the dollar weaken to $1 = 4 yuan, then 1 bolt of Chinese cloth will cost $5,000 to American traders, and they will have little reason to import.

On December 4, 2005, the euro traded at a rate of 1.1720 per U.S. dollar. By June 6, 2006, the euro had decreased in value by more than 10 percent, reaching a rate of 1.2923 per dollar. American companies were pressured to decrease the dollar prices of their exports to Europe in order to maintain their market share. The following example demonstrates the impact of the euro's depreciation on the euro prices of American imports into Europe.

Suppose Boeing wanted $150 million for one of its 787 Dreamliner jet aircraft in December 2006. At an exchange rate of 1.1720 euros = $1, the company would have had to charge 175.8 million euros for its aircraft. To get $150 million for the aircraft in June 2006, with the exchange rate of 1.2923 euros = $1, Boeing would have had to charge over 193.8 million euros, or an additional 18 million euros. This change could place Boeing at some disadvantage versus a Europe-based competitor such as Airbus when trying to sell aircraft to price-sensitive airline companies in Europe.

Another way a nation can attempt to regain competitiveness in world markets is through **currency devaluation** (lowering its price in terms of other currencies). Note that in many but by no means all cases, this action can leave domestic prices largely unchanged.

To fight rampant inflation, the government of Argentina decided to set a fixed exchange rate of 1 peso to 1 U.S. dollar. Although the dollar peg succeeded in bringing financial stability to the country, it also made Argentina one of the world's most expensive economies for doing business. Many also blamed the peg for a recession that had dragged on since 1998 and had resulted in high unemployment. Although average wages were $600 per month, many prices were similar to those in Europe. Popular unrest led to widespread rioting, and the Argentine president resigned from office. In January 2002, three days after taking office, Argentina's interim government abandoned the decade-old fixed exchange rate policy. Almost immediately, the peso experienced a dramatic and sudden devaluation, declining from $1 to only 27 cents within five months. Imports became expensive, and exporting became attractive. Within a year of devaluation, exports had grown from 2 to 7 percent of national output. Increased domestic investment and production replaced imports. Unemployment was cut in half, to 13 percent. Gross domestic product increased 38 percent in three years.

currency devaluation
The lowering of a currency's price in terms of other currencies

SOME NEWER EXPLANATIONS FOR THE DIRECTION OF TRADE

The international trade theory we have been discussing was essentially the only theoretical explanation of trade available to us until the second half of the 20th century. Since that time, however, several other possible explanations for international trade have been developed.

The Linder Theory of Overlapping Demand   Another Swedish economist, Stefan Linder, recognized that the supply-oriented Heckscher-Ohlin theory, which depended on factor endowments, was adequate to explain international trade in primary products. However, he believed that another explanation was needed for trade in manufactured goods. In its purest form, the Heckscher-Ohlin theory would expect developed countries to be more likely to trade with developing countries, which have very different factor endowments, rather than with other developed countries that would have similar factor endowments. In contrast,

Linder's demand-oriented theory stated that customers' tastes are strongly affected by income levels, and therefore a nation's income per capita level determines the kinds of goods they will demand. Because an entrepreneur will produce goods to meet this demand, the kinds of products manufactured reflect the country's level of income per capita. Goods produced for domestic consumption will eventually be exported, due to similarity of income levels and therefore demand in other countries.

The Linder theory thus deduces that international trade in manufactured goods will be greater between nations with similar levels of per capita income than between those with dissimilar levels of per capita income, the very situation observed in Chapter 2 during our review of trade data. Even though two developed countries may have similar factor endowments, which under the Heckscher-Ohlin theory would result in limited trade between them, these nations still can have a large volume of trade with each other. The goods that will be traded are those for which there is an *overlapping demand* (consumers in both countries are demanding the same good).[10] For example, if a Finnish company such as Nokia invents a sophisticated cell phone with advanced features for its home market, the best export opportunities for this phone will be in other advanced nations such as the United States, Japan, and Western European countries, even if these countries have their own domestic producers of cell phones. Note that the Linder model differs from the model of comparative advantage in that it does not specify in which direction a given good will go. In fact, Linder specified that a good may go in either direction. You recognize, of course, that this intraindustry trade occurs because of *product differentiation*; for example, Motorola exports its cell phones to Sweden and Japan and Sony-Ericsson exports its cell phones to the United States, because consumers in both countries perceive a difference in the brands.

International Product Life Cycle   The hypothesis of an *international product life cycle* was formulated by Raymond Vernon in the 1960s.[11] This concept, which concerns the role of innovation in trade patterns, views a product as going through a full life cycle from the internationalization stage to standardization. The initial innovation stage of the cycle borrows from the Linder theory in terms of the motivations and response of entrepreneurs to perceived market opportunities. The subsequent three stages through which a product is said to pass are illustrated in Figure 3.2 and described below. This concept can be applied to new product introduction by firms in any of the industrialized nations, but because more new products have been successfully introduced on a commercial scale in the United States, let us examine the **international product life cycle (IPLC)** as it applies to this country.

international product life cycle (IPLC)

A theory explaining why a product that begins as a nation's export eventually becomes its import

---

FIGURE 3.2

International Product Life Cycle

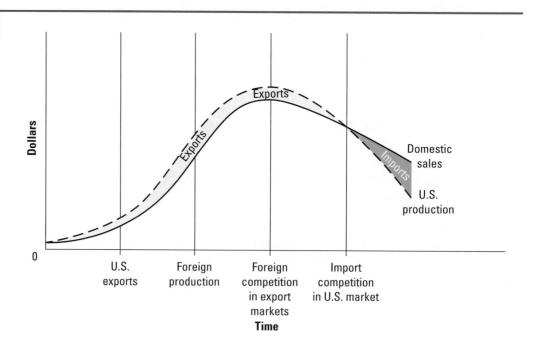

1. *U.S. exports:* Because the United States possesses the largest population of high-income consumers of any country in the world, competition for their patronage is intense. Manufacturers are therefore forced to search constantly for better ways to satisfy their customers' needs. To provide new products, companies maintain large research and development laboratories, which must be in constant contact with suppliers of the materials they need for product development. The fact that their suppliers are also in this country facilitates the contact.[12] In the early stages of the product life cycle, the design and the production methods are changing. By being close to the market, management can react quickly to customer feedback and more easily provide local repair services. These factors combine to make the United States a leader in new product introduction. For a while, American firms will be the only manufacturers of the product; overseas customers, as they learn of the product, will therefore have to buy from American firms. The export market develops.

2. *Foreign production begins:* Overseas consumers, especially those in developed nations, have similar needs and the ability to purchase the product. Export volume grows and becomes large enough to support local production. The technology for producing the good has become fairly stable, and if the innovator is a multinational firm, it will be sending its subsidiaries new product information with complete details on how to produce it. Where there are no affiliates, foreign managers, as they learn of the product, will obtain licenses for its production. Foreign production will begin, which also provides advantages of reduced costs for transportation and local communication. The American firm will still be exporting to those markets where there is no production, but its export growth will diminish as licensing and foreign direct investment substitutes for exports as a source of supply to various international markets.

3. *Foreign competition in export markets:* Later, as early foreign manufacturers gain experience in marketing and production, their costs will fall. Saturation of their local markets will cause them to look for buyers elsewhere. They may even be able to undersell the American producers if they enjoy an advantage such as lower labor or raw material costs. In this stage, foreign firms are competing in export markets, and as a result, American export sales will continue to decline. By this stage, the innovating American firms may have developed newer versions of the product and begun scaling back production of the original product in order to begin focusing instead on the newer innovations.

4. *Import competition in the United States:* If domestic and export sales enable foreign producers to attain the economies of scale enjoyed by the American firm, they may reach a point where they can compete in quality and undersell American firms in the American market. From that point on, the U.S. market will be served exclusively (or nearly so) by imports. Televisions, footwear, and DRAM (dynamic random access memory) semiconductor chips are examples of such products.

Authors discussing the IPLC concept have claimed that this cycle may be repeated as the less developed countries (LDCs) with still lower labor costs obtain the technology and thus acquire a cost advantage over the more industrialized nations. Although little research has been done to substantiate the IPLC concept, a World Bank study seems to provide a plausible reason for these changes in production locations, as suggested in the following excerpt:

> *With countries progressing on the comparative advantage scale, their exports can supplement the exports of countries that graduate to a higher level. . . . A case in point is Japan, whose comparative advantage has shifted towards highly capital-intensive exports. In turn, developing countries with a relatively high human capital endowment . . . can take Japan's place in exporting relatively human capital–intensive products, and countries with a relatively high physical capital endowment, such as Brazil and Mexico, can take Japan's place in exporting relatively physical capital–intensive products. Finally, countries at lower levels of development can supplant the middle-level countries in exporting unskilled labor–intensive commodities.*[13]

Technology Life Cycle   It is useful to distinguish between new products and new technologies used in the production of products (such as improved casting processes in steelmaking or robotic painting equipment in automobile manufacturing). While the IPLC concept discussed above focuses primarily on final goods for consumption, there seems to be a closely related phenomenon regarding production technology, which might be termed the *international technology life cycle*. Production techniques and equipment seem to have a cycle from initial development and use in industrially advanced countries to eventual adoption in developing nations. This cycle is important because production technologies and equipment can be important exports from industrialized countries.

The concept of a technology life cycle emanates from the tendency of industrialized countries to have high incomes—and high wages. There is an incentive to invest in new, labor-reducing technology in order to reduce the costs associated with high-cost labor. Industrialized countries therefore tend to be innovators in developing new production technology that increases labor productivity. Increased productivity tends to produce further increases in wages, contributing to continued efforts to develop new technology.

The result of these developments can be a technology cycle that resembles the IPLC. The initial stage involves the development of new technology (e.g., a machine for automating the welding of panels on an automobile) in an industrialized country. This technology is used in the innovating country and subsequently exported to other developed countries with high-cost labor. This technology would not be as quickly exported to developing nations, because the existence of abundant low-cost labor in such countries would make the use of the new technology too capital-intensive. Over time, the increasing cost of labor in the industrialized country reaches a point where it is no longer profitable to use the technology in that nation. At the same time, labor costs in some developing nations rise to the stage where the technology can be profitably employed. The technology becomes an export from the industrialized nation to the developing nation. Later in the cycle, the technology (e.g., a machine) might be produced abroad for domestic consumption in that developing nation or even for export to other international markets.

Of course, the industrialized nations have an incentive to continuously develop improved technology in order to maintain high incomes and economic prosperity. This pressure is particularly acute in situations where the developing countries are rapidly advancing up a technology "ladder," from production of simpler, more standardized goods to innovation of technologies and products. This process appears to be well under way in countries such as Korea, Taiwan, and Singapore, while nations such as China, Thailand, and India are at an earlier stage of advancement but have aspirations to also move quickly toward technological competence on an international scale. The quickening of this technology cycle, through developments such as improved capability and lower costs of telecommunications, greater freedom in the movement of capital and goods across borders, and increasing internationalization of markets and competition, is exacerbating the challenge for wealthy nations to maintain their positions as technological leaders.

Technology evolution need not always follow the cycle suggested above. Initial application of the technical innovation could even begin in a foreign, developing country market, as the following example suggests.

> *Automakers have recently begun applying a new technological approach called "modularity" within their manufacturing operations. Rather than supplying individual parts, suppliers instead provide modules of assembled parts to the automaker, such as complete suspension systems or dashboards. American labor unions have resisted modularization, viewing it as a form of outsourcing that would reduce the number of jobs in the automaker's operations. Consequently, Chrysler initiated the modularization concept within its Brazilian operations. As a result, for example, a local supplier is responsible for just-in-time delivery of the entire frame for the Chrysler Dakota pickup truck. It is expected that this production process innovation could reduce per-vehicle manufacturing costs by thousands of dollars.[14]*

Economies of Scale and the Experience Curve   In the 1920s, economists began to consider the fact that most industries benefit from economies of scale; that is, as a plant gets larger and output increases, the average cost of producing each unit of output decreases.

This occurs because larger and more efficient equipment can be employed, companies can obtain volume discounts on their larger-volume purchases, and fixed costs such as those of research and design and administrative overheads can be allocated over a larger quantity of output. Most manufacturing is subject to economies of scale, and mining and transportation industries also tend to benefit from increasing returns to scale. Production costs also drop because of the *learning curve*. As firms produce more products, they learn ways to improve production efficiency, causing production costs to decline by a predictable amount.[15]

Economies of scale and the experience curve affect international trade because they can permit a nation's industries to become low-cost producers without requiring that the nation have an abundance of a certain class of production factors. Then, just as in the case of comparative advantage, nations specialize in the production of a few products and trade with others to supply the rest of their needs. International trade is promoted because a nation's companies may not be able to fully achieve the potential scale economies through serving only the domestic market, even within countries as large as the United States. Examples include semiconductors, computers, and commercial aircraft. American consumers can benefit from higher quality and lower prices for these products because companies like Intel, Hewlett-Packard, and Boeing can spread very high fixed costs over sales within foreign as well as home markets.

Imperfect Competition By combining the concept of economies of scale with the existence of differentiated products, Paul Krugman developed a model that helps to explain the observed levels of intraindustry (within-industry) trade between nations.[16] Krugman reasoned that production of goods is concentrated geographically, due to economies of scale. He also reasoned that factors associated with resource constraints and imperfect competition cause companies in otherwise identical nations to produce some unique varieties of products in order to avoid direct competition. The existence of this *product differentiation*—the creation of a separate identity for a product, through actual (styling) or perceived (image) differences that are typically supported with advertising in order to encourage brand loyalty—is an important element in Krugman's model. Because products are differentiated, each company may act like a monopolist with respect to its own unique product, and more firms and more variety of goods will be present in the market. Because firms from different nations each produce unique varieties, but consumers in each nation buy some volume of each variety (as predicted by Linder), we see intraindustry trade between similar or even otherwise-identical nations. The existence of international trade can create a larger market, which allows for better utilization of internal (company-specific) economies of scale by the trading firms. Empirical support for Krugman's model has been shown in many studies, including such industries as automobiles, specialty chemicals, and wine, and this model helps to explain the high proportion (roughly one-quarter) of intraindustry trade in overall international trade.

First-Mover Theory As suggested in the preceding section, countries typically specialize when there are increasing returns to scale and experience. However, the observed pattern of trade in goods subject to scale economies may be determined by historical factors, such as which country entered an industry first. Some management theorists argue that firms that enter the market first (first movers) will be able to gain large market share, permitting them to obtain the benefits of reduced costs and improved technical expertise early. This can discourage foreign entrants that might have to enter at a higher cost, at least initially. One study across a broad range of industries revealed that first movers held a 30 percent market share compared to just 13 percent for late entries. Another found that 70 percent of the leaders in present-day markets were first movers.

New research, however, indicates that previous studies were flawed because they were based on surveys of surviving firms and did not include a large number of the true pioneers. As an example, it was an American firm, Ampex, that made the first VCRs, but because it charged so much ($50,000), it sold only a few. Sony and Matsushita saw the market potential and worked for 20 years to make a VCR they could sell for $500. They reached that goal and cornered the market. The researchers argue that the early success has gone to the companies that entered the market on average 13 years after the "first movers."[17]

national
competitiveness

A nation's relative
ability to design,
produce, distribute, or
service products within
an international
trading context while
earning increasing
returns on its
resources

National Competitive Advantage from Regional Clusters **National competitiveness** involves a nation's ability to design, produce, distribute, or service products within an international trading context while earning increasing returns on its resources. A nation's ability to achieve sustained international success within a particular industry may be explained by variables other than the factors of production on which the theories of comparative advantage and Heckscher-Ohlin are based. For example, Alfred Marshall's seminal work on economic theory helped to explain why, in many industries, firms tend to cluster together on a geographic basis.[18] He suggested that geographic clusters appeared for three reasons: (1) advantages associated with pooling of a common labor force so that staffing requirements can be met quickly, even with unexpected fluctuations in demand; (2) gains from the development of specialized local suppliers whose operations and skills can be coordinated with the needs of the buyers; and (3) benefits that result within the geographic region from the sharing of technological information and corresponding enhancement of the rate of innovation.

Michael Porter, an economics professor at Harvard, extended the work of Marshall.[19] His Diamond Model of national advantage claims that four kinds of variables will have an impact on the ability of the local firms in a country to utilize the country's resources to gain a competitive advantage:

1. *Demand conditions:* the nature, rather than merely the size, of the domestic demand. If a firm's customers are sophisticated and demanding, it will strive to produce high-quality and innovative products and, in doing so, will obtain a global competitive advantage over companies located where domestic pressure is less. This might have been the case in the past, when international firms introduced their new products in home markets first (a condition of the international product life cycle theory), but as more firms introduce new products globally, this variable will lose importance.

2. *Factor conditions:* level and composition of factors of production. Porter distinguishes between the basic factors (Heckscher-Ohlin theory) and the advanced factors (a nation's infrastructure, such as telecommunications and transportation systems, or university research institutes). He also distinguishes between created factors (e.g., from investments made by individuals, companies, or governments) and inherited factors (e.g., natural resources, location). Lack of natural endowments has caused nations to invest in the creation of the advanced factors, such as education of its work force, free ports, and advanced communications systems, to enable their industries to be competitive globally. Various Caribbean nations have upgraded their communications systems to attract banking and other service companies that have little dependence on the basic factors of production.

3. *Related and supporting industries:* suppliers and industry support services. For decades, firms in an industry with their suppliers, the suppliers' suppliers, and so forth, have tended to form a cluster in a given location, often without any apparent initial reason. Yet these related and supporting industries serve as an important foundation for competitive success by providing a network of suppliers, subcontractors, and a commercial infrastructure. For example, the San Francisco Bay Area has a range of related and supporting industries for the personal computer industry. These include research, design, production, or service operations of such suppliers as semiconductor designers, semiconductor manufacturers, technologically savvy venture capitalists, and intellectual property rights lawyers, as well as related industries such as scientific equipment, electronics (e.g., MP3 players, personal digital assistants), telecommunications equipment, software developers, and a wide range of Internet-related companies.[20]

4. *Firm strategy, structure, and rivalry:* the extent of domestic competition, the existence of barriers to entry, and the firms' management style and organization. Porter states that companies subject to heavy competition in their domestic markets are constantly striving to improve their efficiency and innovativeness, which makes them more competitive internationally. For decades, firms in oligopolistic industries have carefully watched their competitors' every move and have even entered foreign markets because their competitors had gone there. For example, Japanese automakers such as Toyota,

Honda, Nissan, and Mitsubishi, have competed vigorously with each other for decades in their domestic marketplace, constantly pressuring each other to improve the quality and performance of their products or else risk the loss of market share. This vigorous competition has enabled these firms to develop world-leading capabilities in auto design and manufacturing. As soon as one of these companies ventures forth into a new international market such as the United States, Europe, or Southeast Asia for the sale or manufacturing of autos, the competitors tend to be close behind in order to avoid a decline in their relative international competitiveness.

Porter argues that these four factors are fundamentally interrelated, creating a "virtuous circle" of resource generation and application, as well as responsiveness in meeting the demands of customers, as depicted in Figure 3.3.

Porter's work complements the theories of Ricardo and Heckscher-Ohlin. However, as the noted economist John Dunning stated, there is nothing new in Porter's analysis, but Porter does set out a model in which the determinants of national competitiveness may be identified.[21] Another problem is that Porter's evidence is anecdotal, rather than based on rigorous empirical research.[22] Furthermore, competitiveness generally applies to companies, rather than nations, although nation-specific factors can provide a critical foundation for creating and enhancing the competitiveness of a company, or industry, on an international level.

SUMMARY OF INTERNATIONAL TRADE THEORY

International trade occurs primarily because of relative price differences among nations. These differences stem from differences in production costs, which result from:

1. Differences in the endowments of the factors of production.

2. Differences in the levels of technology that determine the factor intensities used.

3. Differences in the efficiencies with which these factor intensities are utilized.

4. Foreign exchange rates.

However, taste differences, a demand variable, can reverse the direction of trade predicted by the theory.

International trade theory shows that nations will attain a higher level of living by specializing in goods for which they possess a comparative advantage and importing those for which they have a comparative disadvantage. Generally, trade restrictions that stop this free flow of goods will harm a nation's welfare. If this is true, why is every nation in the world surrounded by trade restrictions?

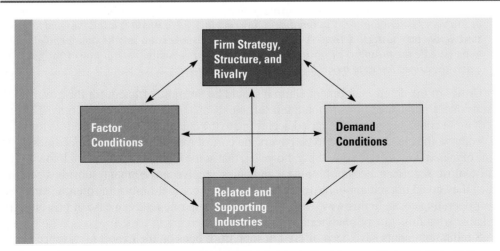

FIGURE 3.3

Variables Impacting Competitive Advantage: Porter's Diamond

Source: Reprinted by permission of the *Harvard Business Review.* "The Competitive Advantage of Nations" by Michael E. Porter, March–April 1990, p. 77. Copyright © 1990 by The President and Fellows of Harvard College; all rights reserved.

Trade Restrictions

This apparent contradiction occurs because the government officials who make decisions about import restrictions are particularly sensitive to the interest groups that will be hurt by the international competition. These groups consist of a small, easily identified body of people or organizations—as contrasted to the large, widespread number of consumers who typically benefit from free trade. In political debates over a proposed import restriction, the protectionist group will usually be united in exerting pressure on government officials, whereas pro-trade consumers rarely mount an organized effort. For example, for the past couple of decades, steel companies and steelworker unions have repeatedly initiated vehement protests to Congress and various government officials about the threat posed by lower-priced imported steel, yet consumer organizations have largely been silent about the potential negative impact of trade barriers on consumers' welfare. In other words, if you are employed by a chemical manufacturer or a hospital, you probably are not going to fight for unrestricted steel imports even though you may believe they contribute to a lower price for your automobile. As you read through the next section, note the importance of special-interest groups.

ARGUMENTS FOR TRADE RESTRICTIONS AND THEIR REBUTTAL

A number of arguments have traditionally been presented in support of efforts to restrict trade. In this section, we will address several of the most common such arguments, as well as associated rebuttal arguments.

National Defense   The argument supporting trade restrictions due to national defense factors suggests that certain industries need protection from imports because they are vital to the defense or security of a nation and must be kept operating even though they are at a comparative disadvantage with respect to foreign competitors. If competition from foreign firms drives these companies out of business and leaves the country dependent on imports, those imports may not be available in a time of war or some other threat to national security.

One problem with this argument is that the armed forces require hundreds of products, ranging from panty hose to bombs, and it is difficult to argue that any particular product is more critical to national security than another.

> The U.S. shoe industry, after failing to obtain relief from imports with arguments about loss of jobs, requested Congress to impose restrictions based on the fact that growing reliance on imported footwear was "jeopardizing the national security of the United States." Speaking to the Armed Services Committee of the U.S. Congress, the president of the Footwear Industry of America stated: "In the event of war or other national emergency, it is unlikely that the domestic footwear industry could provide sufficient footwear for the military and civilian population. . . . We won't be able to wait for ships to deliver shoes from Taiwan, or Korea or Brazil or Eastern Europe. . . . Improper footwear can lead to needless casualties and turn sure victory into possible defeat." A Defense Department spokesman said he knew of no plan to investigate the prospects of a wartime shoe crisis. Furthermore, federal law already requires the armed forces to buy U.S.-made footwear exclusively.[23]

Critics of the defense argument claim it would be far more efficient for the government to subsidize a number of firms to maintain sufficient capacity for wartime use only. The output of these companies could be varied according to the calculated defense needs. Moreover, a subsidy would clearly indicate to taxpayers the cost of maintaining these companies in the name of national security—something, however, that some interests do not want known. Currently, most American ocean shipping companies receive government subsidies without which they could not remain in business because of the competition from foreign firms with lower operating costs. In this way, we have a merchant marine ready in case of hostility, and we know what this state of readiness costs us.

Similar arguments have been offered in support of bans on the export of advanced technologies. Such bans, proponents argue, prevent valuable technologies from being used to strengthen competitors, especially militarily. However, these bans can reduce export revenues for the country's manufacturers by closing off potential markets. The bans can also impede efforts to sustain international market share and fund continued innovation, enabling competitors from other nations to improve their competitiveness.

Sanctions to Punish Offending Nations
A related argument for imposing trade restrictions is to inflict economic damage on other nations in order to punish them or otherwise encourage them to modify behavior. A common approach is to pass legislation that prohibits trade with the "offending" nation. A 2002 study found that the United States, for example, had some form of sanctions against over 75 countries.[24] Targeted nations have included Cuba, Iraq, Libya, North Korea, Iran, Syria, Sudan, and Myanmar.

What is typically ignored when imposing sanctions is that not only do they seldom achieve their goal of forcing change in the targeted country but they also tend to produce collateral economic damage in the nations applying them.[25] It was estimated that economic sanctions during the 1990s cost the United States approximately $15 billion to $23 billion annually in exports, in addition to losses resulting from restrictions on foreign direct investment, capital flows, tourism, and other sources of income or output.[26] During the time that the United States was imposing sanctions on Iraq that prohibited American firms from doing business there, it was reported that companies from France, Russia, and other nations were generating billions of dollars from business contracts that American firms were excluded from bidding for. It was also reported that the Iraqi trade sanctions unintentionally imposed substantial economic damage on Turkey, Jordan, and Greece, nations that had historically engaged in extensive trade with Iraq. In addition, limitations on exporting Iraqi oil resulted in substantial economic gains by Libya and Iran, nations whose behavior had also subjected them to U.S. trade sanctions.[27] Prior to the 2003 invasion and overthrow of Saddam Hussein's government, sanctions on Iraq tended to fall disproportionately on the poor and on Kurds and Shiite Muslims, rather than on the Sunni Muslim–dominated ruling Baath Party.

Protect Infant (or Dying) Industry
Advocates for the protection of an infant industry may claim that in the long run the industry will have a comparative advantage but that its firms need protection from imports until the required investment capital is obtained, the labor force is trained, production techniques are mastered, and economies of scale are achieved. When these objectives are met, import protection will no longer be necessary. Without the protection, advocates argue, a firm will not be able to survive because lower-cost imports from more mature foreign competitors will underprice it in its local market. Although the logic that a government will be able to predict future comparative advantage is questionable, international managers will find that the infant-industry argument is readily accepted by the governments of most developing nations. "There is a respectable historical case for tariff protection for industries that are not yet profitable, especially in developing countries," asserted Ha Joon Chang, writing for the South Centre, an intergovernmental forum for developing countries. "In the same way that we protect our children until they grow up and are able to compete with adults in the labor market, developing country governments need to protect their newly emerging industries until they go through a period of learning and become able to compete with the producers from more advanced countries."[28]

China's 10th five-year plan calls for an increase in semiconductor production from $2 billion in 2000 to $24 billion in 2010, and the country has encouraged the development of a domestic semiconductor manufacturing industry. In March 2004, the United States initiated proceedings for a World Trade Organization complaint, charging that China's policies offered its semiconductor industry unfair protection by refunding 82 percent of the 17 percent value-added tax imposed on semiconductors. Foreign companies argued that this tax break, which was not available for imported semiconductors unless designed in China, was part of a concerted effort to force foreign companies to establish joint venture production activities in China and to transfer their technology. "The rebate is to protect our infant industry," commented Li Ke of the China Semiconductor Industry Association. "You cannot say this is a discriminatory tax policy." After negotiations, the offending tax policy was changed and the WTO complaint resolved in July 2004.[29]

Efforts to protect emerging industries are not limited to developing nations, of course. For example, in early 2006, Representative Ken Salazar of Colorado argued for the maintenance of a protective 54-cents-a-gallon import duty on foreign-produced ethanol, including imports from low-cost producer Brazil, in order to give "our infant industries a greater chance to grow." The United States produced more gallons of ethanol in 2005 than any other nation, although the cost of subsidizing the American ethanol industry is estimated at $1 billion to $4 billion annually.[30]

Protection is meant to be temporary for the emerging industry, but realistically a protected firm will rarely admit it has matured and no longer needs this assistance. Protected from foreign competition by high import duties, the company's managers have little reason to improve efficiency or product quality.

A related argument concerns the protection of a "dying" industry, one threatened by a rapid onslaught of imports that endangers the survival of domestic companies and the jobs they provide. Under this argument, it takes time to make the necessary adjustments to move labor and capital out of the industry and into other sectors. Protecting the industry from imports can therefore facilitate a smoother transition. This sort of logic has been used in justifying protection for such sectors as textiles and footwear in the United States and Europe, in response to the rapid expansion of imports from China after the end of the Multifiber Agreement in 2005. Other assistance, such as subsidies for relocating to different geographic or industrial areas and for providing assistance to displaced workers, may also be part of the proposed solution.

Current international trade rules of the World Trade Organization prohibit import protection or government subsidies whose intent is primarily to help domestic industry to compete and gain international market share.

Protect Domestic Jobs from Cheap Foreign Labor   Protectionists who use this argument usually compare lower foreign hourly wage rates to those paid in their home country. They conclude that foreign exporters can flood the home country's market with low-priced goods, and thus simultaneously eliminate jobs of home country workers. The first fallacy of this argument is that wage costs are neither all of the production costs nor all of the labor costs, so a comparison merely based on relative hourly wages would be misleading. As discussed in Chapter 12, "Labor Forces," in many LDCs, legislated fringe benefits are a much higher percentage of direct wages than they are in industrialized countries.

Furthermore, the productivity per worker is frequently much greater in developed countries because of more capital per worker, superior management, and advanced technology. As a result, the labor cost component of the goods being produced is lower even though wages are higher.

The second fallacy results from failure to consider the costs of the other factors of production. Where wage rates are low, the capital costs are usually high, and thus production costs may actually be higher in a low-wage nation. Ironically, one of the arguments for protection used by manufacturers in developing nations is that they cannot compete against the low-cost, highly productive firms in the industrialized countries.

Those who might be persuaded by this argument to stop imports to save domestic jobs should remember that exports create jobs. For example, every $1 billion in American exports creates an average of 25,000 new jobs in the United States. If a nation imposes barriers on imports from a second country, that second country's government may retaliate with greater import duties on exports from the first nation. The result could be a net loss of jobs rather than the gain that was anticipated.

Scientific Tariff or Fair Competition   Supporters of this argument say they believe in fair competition. They simply want an import duty that will bring the cost of the imported goods up to the cost of the domestically produced article. This will eliminate any "unfair" advantage that a foreign competitor might have because of superior technology, lower raw material costs, lower taxes, or lower labor costs. It is not their intent to ban exports; they wish only to equalize the process for "fair" competition. If this were law, no doubt the rate of duty would be set to protect the least efficient American producer, thereby enabling the more efficient domestic manufacturers to earn large profits. The efficient foreign producers would be penalized, and, of course, their comparative advantage would be nullified. The impact on consumers might also be viewed as unfair, since the import duty would most assuredly result in an increase in the prices that they pay.

Retaliation   Representatives of an industry whose exports have had import restrictions placed on them by another country may ask their government to retaliate with similar restrictions. An example of how retaliation begins is the ban by the European Union (EU) on imports of hormone-treated beef from the United States.

> *Because the use of hormones in animal production is considered a health hazard in the EU, the European Union closed its market to $100 million worth of beef (12 percent of total U.S. meat exports) in 1988. American beef producers complained that no scientific evidence supported the claim, and the United States promptly retaliated by putting import duties on about $100 million worth of EU products, including boneless beef and pork, fruit juices, wine coolers, tomatoes, French cheese, and instant coffee. The EU then threatened to ban U.S. shipments of honey, canned soybeans, walnuts, and dried fruit worth $140 million. In reply, the United States announced that it would follow the EU ban with a ban on all European meat. If that had happened, about $500 million in U.S.-EU trade would have been affected.*
>
> *Generally, disputes like these go to the World Trade Organization (WTO). After having its beef banned by the EU for eight years, the United States launched a formal dispute settlement procedure with the WTO in May 1996, challenging the ban. When the WTO Appellate Body announced that the EU ban had been imposed without reason, the EU declared in March 1998 that it would implement the Appellate Body ruling, but it did not comply by May 1999, the date set by the WTO. When the United States asked the WTO for permission to retaliate, the EU requested arbitration to settle the amount. On July 26, 1999, the WTO authorized the United States to retaliate, resulting in the imposition of a 100 percent import duty on a list of EU products with an annual trade value of $116.8 million. In September 2003, the EU announced a new directive that it asserted was in compliance with the WTO's ruling, although it still banned most American and Canadian beef. The United States claimed that the new EU guidelines still violated WTO requirements. As of 2006, about 18 years after the imposition of EU barriers on hormone-treated beef from the United States, the full import duty penalty valued at $116.8 million was being applied to designated imports from the EU.*[31]

Dumping   Retaliation also occurs for **dumping.** According to WTO guidelines, dumping is the selling of a product abroad for less than (1) the average cost of production in the exporting nation, (2) the market price in the exporting nation, or (3) the price to third countries. A manufacturer may engage in dumping as a means of selling excess production without disrupting prices in its domestic market or as a response to cyclical or seasonal factors (e.g., during an economic downturn or at the end of a fashion season). A manufacturer may also lower its export price to force the importing nation's domestic producers out of business, expecting to raise prices once that objective is accomplished. This is called *predatory dumping*.

dumping
Selling a product abroad for less than the cost of production, the price in the home market, or the price to third countries

The United States became the first country to prohibit dumping of foreign goods into its own market, in 1916 (there is no U.S. law prohibiting American firms from dumping their goods abroad, though). Dumping is now within the domain of the WTO, which is the recipient of many related complaints through appeals by countries opposing the imposition of antidumping protections against their companies. In the United States, when a manufacturer believes a foreign producer is dumping a product, it can ask the Office of Investigation in the Department of Commerce to make a preliminary investigation. If Commerce finds that products have been dumped, the case goes to the International Trade Commission to determine whether the imports are injuring U.S. producers.* If the commission finds that they are, then the case is referred to the U.S. president, who decides whether antidumping tariffs should be assessed. Unlike most trade restrictions, which are applied to all exporters of a product, antidumping measures are applied to specific producers in selected nations.

Most governments retaliate when dumping is perceived to be harming local industry. For example:

---

* The International Trade Commission is a government agency that provides technical assistance and advice to the president and Congress on matters of international trade and tariffs.

In 2005, the average price of shoes imported into the European Union from China fell by about one-quarter, and the volume of imported shoes rose by nearly 700 percent in the first seven months after quotas were abolished. This resulted in complaints from European shoe-makers that they were being harmed by dumping from Chinese and Vietnamese shoe manu-facturers. Critics warned that unfair foreign competition in shoes and textiles was undermining national labor and social standards and causing job losses. Stating that there was "compelling evidence" that imported leather shoes were being illegally sold below cost and fearing that domestic EU footwear manufacturers could be forced out of business, in July 2006 the European Commission's trade department proposed antidumping tariffs on shoe imports from those two countries. The proposal would allow importation—without any "dumping duty"—of 140 million pairs of leather shoes from China and 95 million pairs from Vietnam. These volumes were about half the level of imports in 2005. Chinese imports above those quotas would face a 23 percent duty, while excess shoes from Vietnam would face a 29.5 percent duty. A spokesperson for EU trade commissioner Peter Mandelson said, "This is a fair and balanced system. While correcting the effects of unfair trade, the proposed allowance before dumping duties apply will allow substantial trade." Wang Shichun, director-general of the Bureau of Fair Trade of China's Commerce Ministry, said, "The European Union's ac-cusations lack basis. European products did not suffer actual harm." Said the general man-ager of one Chinese manufacturer, "It's no good limiting [the export of] Chinese goods. Nobody benefits—neither retailers nor consumers."[32]

New Types of Dumping   There are at least five new kinds of dumping for which fair-trade lobbies consider sanctions to be justified in order to level the playing field for international trade. In reality, these special-interest groups calling for level playing fields are seeking to raise the production costs of their overseas competitors to protect their local high-cost man-ufacturers. The classes of dumping include:

1. *Social dumping:* unfair competition caused by firms, usually from developing nations that have lower labor costs and poorer working conditions, which undermines social support systems, including worker benefits.

2. *Environmental dumping:* unfair competition caused by a country's lax environmental standards. It has been argued that globalization provides incentives to national govern-ments to set weak environmental policies, particularly regarding industries whose plants can be relocated internationally.

   The United States' refusal to commit to standards of the Kyoto treaty was criticized because American exporters would not bear the same costs as firms in signatory countries. A state-ment issued by Friends of the Earth (Europe) said, "The U.S. rejection of the Kyoto Protocol is unfair and puts European business at a disadvantage. With Bush's increasing rejection of international agreements that are essential to protect the environment, Europe should have the right to penalize U.S. goods for the pollution they cause."[33]

3. *Financial services dumping:* unfair competition caused by a nation's low requirements for bank capital-asset ratios.

4. *Cultural dumping:* unfair competition caused by cultural barriers aiding local firms.

5. *Tax dumping:* unfair competition caused by differences in corporate tax rates or related special breaks.

   In 2006 Slovakia was accused of tax dumping because its low (19 percent) corporate tax rate and generous incentive policies were perceived to give it an advantage over other European nations in attracting investment from multinationals.[34]

subsidies
Financial contributions, provided directly or indirectly by a govern-ment, which confer a benefit; include grants, preferential tax treatment, and govern-ment assumption of normal business expenses

Subsidies   Another cause of retaliation may be **subsidies** that a government makes to a domestic firm either to encourage exports or to help protect it from imports. Some examples are cash payments, government participation in ownership, low-cost loans to foreign buyers and exporters, and preferential tax treatment.

As shown in Figure 3.4, OECD nations provide $280 billion per year in subsidies to their farmers, including $133 billion in the EU, $49 billion in Japan, and $47 billion in the United

FIGURE 3.4   Value of OECD Member Farm Subsidies

Percent of value of production

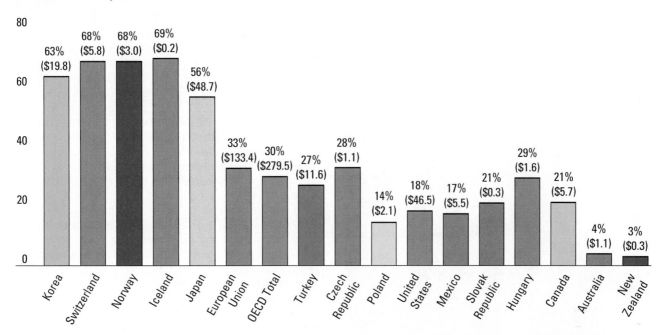

Source: "Agriculture: Support Estimates, 2004," *OECD in Figures: Statistics on the Member Countries.* Accessed 7/2005. Link: http://dx.doi.org/10.1787/758034618756.

States.[35] *In the case of rice, Japan imposes a tariff of nearly 500 percent in an effort to protect its farmers from international competition, while the maximum tariff on dairy products in the EU is over 200 percent. Perhaps the greatest damage caused by this assistance is its effect on the millions of farmers in the world's poorest nations. High customs duties restrict access to wealthy countries' markets, while subsidized overproduction in developed countries artificially depresses prices in world markets, harming the income of farmers in poorer nations. Most of the agricultural subsidies in developed countries go to a small percentage of recipients, usually large enterprises. For example, 72 percent of U.S. farm subsidies from 1995 to 2003 were distributed among only 10 percent of U.S. farmers, and the top 15 percent of French farmers received 60 percent of that country's direct subsidies.*[36] *Substantial reduction in agricultural subsidies has been a major focus of the Doha Round of world trade negotiations and reportedly a major factor leading to breakdown in negotiations.*

Competitors in importing nations frequently ask their governments to impose **countervailing duties** to offset the effects of a subsidy. In the United States, when the Department of Commerce receives a petition from an American firm claiming that imports from a particular country are subsidized, it first determines whether a subsidy actually was given. If the findings are positive, Commerce proceeds to impose countervailing duties equal to the subsidy's amount. In most cases involving members of the WTO, another independent government agency, the U.S. International Trade Commission, must determine whether the firm has been injured by the subsidy before Commerce assesses the duty.

countervailing duties
Additional import taxes levied on imports that have benefited from export subsidies

Other Arguments   The arguments we have examined are probably the ones most frequently given in support of trade restrictions. Others include the use of protection from imports to (1) permit diversification of the domestic economy or (2) improve the balance of trade. You should have gathered from this discussion that protection from imports generally serves the narrow interests of a special-interest group at the expense of many. Although the application of trade restrictions can sometimes buy time for the protected industry to modernize and become more competitive in the world market, a real danger exists that a nation's

Sugar Subsidies: Sweet for Producers, Not for Consumers

Nicaraguan Jackson Riveras carries a load of freshly cut sugarcane on a plantation near Turrucares of Alajuela, Costa Rica. Like many Nicaraguan immigrants, Ramirez came to Costa Rica to work the harvest season in order to earn higher wages and send money back to his family.

Although they lack comparative advantage in sugar production, the United States, Japan, and the EU, among others, have maintained strong protection for their domestic sugar industries. A World Bank report called sugar the "most policy-distorted of all commodities." Protectionism by developed countries harms foreign sugar producers, many of which are poor farmers in developing countries, by reducing demand and prices for their product. Brazil loses $500 million per year due to American sugar subsidies, and Oxfam estimated in 2004 that EU sugar supports had cost Ethiopia, Mozambique, and Malawi $238 million since 2001. Malawi's losses exceeded its total budget for primary health care. Before being forced by the WTO into making changes in November 2005, the EU maintained domestic sugar prices that were triple world market prices, and the EU spent 3.30 in subsidies for every 1 of the 5 million tons of sugar that it exported. Even after reducing its guaranteed prices by 36 percent over the subsequent four years, the EU still sharply restricted imports from least developed countries, delaying full access until as late as 2020.

In the United States, sugar tariffs have been in place since 1789. Imports are allocated through tariff-rate quotas among 41 nations and limited to about 15 percent of the U.S. market, except in years when there is a shortfall in the U.S. domestic supply, as in 2005 after Hurricane Katrina. High price supports have resulted in overproduction of sugar domestically. As a result, the price of raw sugar in the United States has averaged more than double the world price during the past decade, costing American consumers an estimated $2 billion annually. Excess sugar production also contributes to environmental problems. In Florida, for example, pollution and disruption of water flows from sugar production have been cited as a major contributor to environmental degradation of the Everglades.

Although sugar protection costs each American an average of only an additional $8 per year, the benefits are highly concen-

trading partners will retaliate with restrictions of their own, causing injury to industries that have received no protection. Let's examine these restrictions.

TARIFF BARRIERS

tariffs
Taxes on imported goods for the purpose of raising their price to reduce competition for local producers or stimulate local production

Tariffs, or import duties, are taxes levied on imported goods primarily for the purpose of raising their selling price in the importing nation's market to reduce competition for domestic producers. A few smaller nations also use them to raise revenue on both imports and exports. Exports of commodities such as coffee and copper are commonly taxed in developing nations. However, imposition of tariffs can result in retaliation that is harmful rather than helpful for a country and its well-being.

In the late 1920s, declining economic fortunes caused American farmers to lobby Congress for tariff protection on agricultural products. There were few supporters for this proposal, and only the Republican party publicly supported the protectionist effort. Over time, more domestic producers joined with agricultural interests, seeking their own protection from foreign competitors. The resulting legislative proposal increased tariffs for more than 20,000 items across a broad range of industries. The broad industrial support for the legislation

trated among a small number of companies. One family that owns a leading Florida sugar company is estimated to gain an extra $65 million in annual profits due to protectionist U.S. sugar policies.

Mechanization has eliminated the labor intensity of producing sugar from sugar beets or sugarcane in the United States. Only about 60,000 people now work in the production or refining of sugar, about 0.04 percent of the American labor force. Movement to free trade in sugar is estimated to eliminate less than 2,300 workers in the sugar industry, meaning that the cost for each protected job is over $825,000. In addition, protection of the U.S. sugar industry has cost thousands of jobs in other sectors, such as food and beverage manufacturing. For example, sugar accounts for 32.7 percent of the total costs in the production of breakfast cereals. A 2006 study by the U.S. Department of Commerce estimated that high sugar prices led to the loss of over 10,000 jobs at sugar-consuming companies between 1997 and 2002. High sugar prices were also a major factor in companies' decisions to relocate operations to non-U.S. sites, contributing to an increase in imports of sugar-containing products from $10.2 billion in 1997 to $18.7 billion in 2004. Undersecretary for Trade Franklin Lavin said, "We are seeing U.S. jobs move to countries that don't have the competitive disadvantage of high sugar prices that we face in the United States."

Despite this situation, efforts to reform protection of the sugar industry have made minimal progress in recent decades, at least partly due to the strength of the sugar lobby. Sugar accounts for less than 1 percent of U.S. agricultural sales, but 17 percent of all agricultural political contributions since 1990. "It's a very effective lobby," commented Claude Barfield of the American Enterprise Institute, a conservative think tank. "They've traditionally given a lot of money to both parties." Sugar lobbying helped disrupt the trade liberalization agenda of President George W. Bush, causing the administration to succumb to pressure and exclude sugar completely from the U.S.-Australia free trade agreement. This was the first bilateral trade treaty in which the United States required that a product be entirely excluded, "a dangerous precedent" according to Republican senator Charles Grassley. The Australian prime minister, John Howard, considered terminating the entire trade deal with the United States because of American insistence on excluding sugar from the agreement, saying that Australian sugar producers were "the victims of a corrupted world trading system."

However, perhaps change may yet occur. In 2006, the United States and Mexico finally ended their decade-long battle over access to the U.S. sugar market under NAFTA, and in 2008 all barriers to the trade in sugar are to be removed between the two countries.

Source: U.S. Department of Commerce, *Employment Changes in U.S. Food Manufacturing: The Impact of Sugar Prices*, February 2006, http://ita.doc.gov/media/Publications/pdf/sugar06.pdf (July 9, 2006); "Who Is to Blame for Loss of Candy Production Industry?" *Manufacturing & Technology News*, February 17, 2006, www.allbusiness.com/periodicals/article/869916-1.html (July 9, 2006); Foodproductiondaily-USA.com, "US Confectionery Jobs Threatened by High Sugar Prices," www.foodproductiondaily-usa.com/news/printNewsBis.asp?id=65871 (July 9, 2006); Edward Alden and Neil Buckley, "Sweet Deals: 'Big Sugar' Fights Threats from Free Trade and a Global Drive to Limit Consumption," *Financial Times*, February 27, 2004, p. 11; Michael Schroeder, "Sugar Growers Hold Up Push for Free Trade," *The Wall Street Journal*, February 3, 2004, p. A13; "The Fruits of Free Trade: Protection's Price," *2002 Annual Report—Federal Reserve Bank of Dallas* (Dallas: Federal Reserve Bank of Dallas, 2002); Oxfam International, "Dumping on the World: How EU Sugar Policies Hurt Poor Countries," March 2004, www.oxfam.org.uk/what_we_do/issues/trade/bp61_sugar_dumping.htm (July 9, 2006); and "Trade Scene: An Unsweet Debate on Sugar," *Journal of Commerce*, March 29, 2004, p. 1.

caused the Democratic and Progressive political parties to join the Republicans on October 28, 1929, in supporting the Smoot-Hawley Tariff Act to establish some of the highest levels of tariffs ever imposed by what was already a protectionist United States. That day the stock market crashed, falling 12 percent. In the following months, 34 foreign governments filed protests against Smoot-Hawley, and over 1,000 economists urged President Herbert Hoover not to sign the bill. Nevertheless, on June 17, 1930, Hoover signed the bill. The result was a retaliatory trade war, characterized by tit-for-tat tariffs and protectionism between trading nations, which soon engulfed most of the world's economies. The outcome was predictable: world trade plummeted from $5.7 billion in 1929 to $1.9 billion in 1932, industrial efficiency and the effects of comparative advantage were sharply reduced, unemployment increased dramatically, and the world was pushed into a decade-long economic depression.[37]

Ad Valorem, Specific, and Compound Duties

Import duties are (1) *ad valorem*, (2) *specific*, or (3) a combination of the two called *compound*. An **ad valorem duty** is stated as a percentage of the invoice value of the product. For example, the U.S. tariff schedule states that flavoring extracts and fruit flavors not containing alcohol are subject to a 6 percent ad valorem duty. Therefore, when a shipment of flavoring extract invoiced at $10,000 arrives in the United States, the importer is required to pay $600 to U.S. Customs before

ad valorem duty
An import duty levied as a percentage of the invoice value of imported goods

specific duty
A fixed sum levied on a physical unit of an imported good

compound duty
A combination of specific and ad valorem duties

taking possession of the goods. A **specific duty** is a fixed sum of money charged for a specified physical unit of the product. A company importing dynamite in cartridges or sticks suitable for blasting would have to pay $0.37 per pound irrespective of the invoice value. When the flavoring extracts and fruit flavors mentioned above contain over 50 percent alcohol by weight, they are subject to a specific duty of $0.12 per pound plus a 3 percent ad valorem. Thus, on a $10,000 shipment weighing 5,000 pounds, the importer would have to pay a **compound duty** of $900 [($0.12 × 5,000 pounds) + (0.03 × $10,000) = $600 + $300]. Note that in an inflationary period, a specific duty soon loses its importance unless changed frequently, whereas the amount collected from an ad valorem duty increases as the invoice price rises. Sometimes, however, an exporter may charge prices so much lower than domestic prices that the ad valorem duty fails to close the gap. Some governments set *official prices* or use *variable levies* to correct this deficiency.

Official Prices   Official prices are included in the customs tariff of some nations and are the basis for ad valorem duty calculations whenever the actual invoice price is lower. The official price guarantees that a certain minimum import duty will be paid irrespective of the actual invoice price. It thwarts a fairly common arrangement that numerous importers living in high-duty nations have with their foreign suppliers whereby a false low invoice price is issued to reduce the amount of duty to be paid. The importer sends the difference between the false invoice price and the true price separately.

variable levy
An import duty set at the difference between world market prices and local government-supported prices

Variable Levy   One form of **variable levy,** which guarantees that the market price of the import will be the same as that of domestically produced goods, has been used by the EU for imported grains. Calculated daily, the duty level is set at the difference between world market prices and the support price for domestic producers.

Lower Duty for More Local Input   Import duties are set by many nations in such a way that they encourage local input. For example, the finished product ready for sale to the consumer may have a 70 percent ad valorem duty. However, if the product is imported in bulk so that it must be packaged in the importing nation, the duty level may be 30 percent. To encourage some local production, the government may charge only a 10 percent duty on the semifinished inputs. These situations can provide opportunities for foreign manufacturers of low-technology products, such as paint articles and toiletries, to get behind a high-tariff wall with very modest investments.

When tariffs are assessed at very low rates, they are sometimes referred to as *nuisance tariffs*. That is because importers are still required to go through the frequently lengthy process of paying these tariffs, even though their low levels may no longer serve their original intention, such as protecting domestic producers.

NONTARIFF BARRIERS

nontariff barriers (NTBs)
All forms of discrimination against imports other than import duties

Nontariff barriers (NTBs) are all forms of discrimination against imports other than the import duties we have been examining. As nations progressively reduced import duties, nontariff barriers assumed greater relative importance and their use has been increasing rapidly, according to the United Nations.[38] For example, government-required testing and certification requirements increased 600 percent between 1994 and 2004. NTBs can take many forms, including the quantitative and nonquantitative ones discussed below, and the additional costs they impose on producers and exporters help to discourage trade.

quotas
Numerical limits placed on specific classes of imports

Quantitative   One type of quantitative barrier is **quotas,** which are numerical limits for a specific kind of good that a country will permit to be imported without restriction during a specified period. If the quota is *absolute*, once the specified amount has been imported, further importation for the rest of the period (usually a year) is prohibited. Quotas are generally *global*; that is, a total amount is fixed without regard to source. They may also be *allocated*, in which case the government of the importing nation assigns quantities to specific countries. The United States allocates quotas for specific tonnages of sugar to 41 nations. Because of

Section I   The Nature of International Business

their nature, allocated quotas are sometimes called *discriminatory quotas,* as exemplified by the example below on EU banana imports.

Some producers have used transshipping to fraudulently evade allocated quotas. In such cases, the finished goods are first shipped to a country with an unfilled quota, where the goods are labeled as products of that country, and then shipped to the quota-imposing nation. Prior to the ending of the Multi-Fiber Agreement in 2004 that limited textile imports from other nations, this deceptive labeling scheme was estimated to have brought $2 billion in illegal clothing imports from China into the United States annually. Gitano, for example, pled guilty to charges of fraud for importing Chinese blouses labeled "Made in the Maldives Islands."

Some goods are subject to *tariff-rate quotas,* which permit a stipulated amount to enter duty-free or at a low rate, but when that amount is reached, a much higher duty is charged for subsequent importations. For example, as of January 2006, the EU allows tariff-free importation of 775,000 tons of bananas annually from Caribbean and African countries. Imports beyond that level from Caribbean and African nations, as well as all imports from Central and South American producers, are subject to a tariff of 176 per ton. In effect, European consumers are subsidizing African and Caribbean banana producers (many of which are former colonies of European nations) to the detriment of Central and South American producers.[39]

For many years there has been an agreement among nations against imposing quotas unilaterally on goods (except agricultural products). Therefore, governments have negotiated **voluntary export restraints (VERs)** with other countries (e.g., the Japanese government established a VER to restrict the number of automobiles that its manufacturers could export to the United States annually, and the Canadian government agreed to a VER to limit the amount of Canadian lumber to be exported to the United States). Although *VER* is a generic term for all bilaterally agreed measures to restrict exports, it has a stricter legal definition in the United States: "an action unilaterally taken to restrict the volume or number of items to be exported during a given period and administered by the exporting country. It is 'voluntary' in the sense that the country has a formal right to eliminate or modify it." It is also voluntary in that the exporting nation may prefer its consequences to any trade barriers the importing nation might impose.

voluntary export restraints (VERs)
Export quotas imposed by the exporting nation

Orderly Marketing Arrangements

Orderly marketing arrangements are VERs consisting of formal agreements between the governments of exporting and importing countries to restrict international competition and preserve some of the national market for local producers. Usually, they stipulate the size of the export or import quotas that each nation will have for a particular good. The largest and oldest such arrangement was the Multi-Fiber Arrangement (MFA), which began in 1973 and regulated about 80 percent of the world's textile and clothing exports to the industrialized nations.

orderly marketing arrangements
Formal agreements between exporting and importing countries that stipulate the import or export quotas each nation will have for a good

Most nontariff barriers such as quotas, VERs, and orderly marketing arrangements are scheduled to be eliminated as a result of the 1994 GATT negotiations (Uruguay Round). For example, textile quotas under the MFA were phased out as of January 1, 2005.[40]

Nonquantitative Nontariff Barriers

Many international trade specialists claim that the most significant nontariff barriers are the nonquantitative type. Governments have tended to establish nontariff barriers to obtain the protection formerly afforded by import duties. A study of nonquantitative barriers revealed over 800 distinct forms, which may be classified under three major headings: (1) direct government participation in trade, (2) customs and other administrative procedures, and (3) standards.

1. *Direct government participation in trade:* The most common form of direct government participation is the subsidy. Besides protecting industries through subsidies, as was mentioned earlier, nearly all governments subsidize agriculture (see, for example, the earlier Worldview, "Sugar Subsidies: Sweet for Producers, Not for Consumers"). Agricultural support programs are often promoted as being targeted toward protecting smaller farms and traditional rural economies. However, the largest 25 percent of farms receive 90 percent of the total level of agricultural support in the United States, 75 percent in Canada, 70 percent in the EU, and 68 percent in Japan.[41]

Government procurement policies also are trade barriers because they usually favor domestic producers and severely restrict purchases of imported goods by government agencies. Policies may also require that products purchased by government agencies have a stipulated minimum *local content.* Since the WTO Government Procurement Agreement went into effect, most nations have opened their government business to foreign bidders to comply with its requirements. However, as noted by the EU, the American government still has policies in place that may substantially interfere with international trade. For example, similar to practices in Canada and elsewhere in the world, the Buy America Act has a range of measures that either prohibit public sector organizations from purchasing from foreign suppliers of goods or services or hinder such purchases through mechanisms such as requirements for local content or the provision of advantageous pricing terms for American suppliers. The Department of Defense, which is the U.S. government's largest public procurement agency, excludes foreign suppliers from many contracts, including but not restricted to "national security" issues that were discussed earlier in this chapter. During the reconstruction efforts in Iraq after the 2003 invasion, for example, many of the major contracts were permitted to be granted only to American firms.[42] The 1920 Jones Act requires that cargo being moved between U.S. ports travel only on ships built, owned, and crewed by Americans. The United States is one of only five nations that require ships for domestic use to be built in domestic shipyards.

2. *Customs and other administrative procedures:* These barriers cover a large variety of government policies and procedures that either discriminate against imports or favor exports. For example, in China, a product being imported may be subject to different rates of duty, depending on the port of entry and an arbitrary determination of the customs value. Because of this flexibility, customs charges often depend on negotiations between Chinese customs officials and managers. It is alleged that corruption is often involved.[43]

   Governments have also found ways to discriminate against the exportation of services. When serving international markets, airlines face a number of situations in which the national airline receives preferential treatment, such as in the provision of airport services, airport counter locations, and number of landing slots. Other examples of discrimination are the Canadian government's giving tax deductions to local businesses that advertise on Canadian TV, but not doing so when they use American stations across the border, and Australia's requiring that television commercials be shot in Australia.

3. *Standards:* Both governmental and private standards to protect the health and safety of a nation's citizens certainly are desirable, but for years exporting firms have been plagued by many standards that are complex and discriminatory. For example, Canadian regulations treat products such as calcium-enriched orange juice as drugs and thus subject to special production and marketing requirements.[44] Japan prohibits the importation of creamy mustard, light mayonnaise, or figs containing potassium sorbate, a food additive approved by numerous international food bodies and allowed by the Japanese in 36 other foods, primarily traditional Japanese products that are typically made only in Japan.[45] Kellogg Company must make four different versions of corn flakes at its European plants, because different nations have different standards regarding the vitamins that can be added to the cereal. Caterpillar discovered that requirements for the size and location of yield signs and license plate holders on the backs of vehicles differ, sometimes only by centimeters, from nation to nation.[46]

   The European Parliament passed biotech food labeling requirements that impose mandatory traceability of genetically modified (GM) organisms and stringent labeling of foods that contain GM ingredients. The rationale was ostensibly to protect consumers from potential harm associated with consumption of GMs, although the United States and other countries have protested that no scientific evidence exists of such harm. The requirements include labels stating "This product is produced from GM organisms" and strict limits on mixing GM and non-GM ingredients in food exported to the EU. The United States is one of the world's leading producers and exporters of GM crops, with 75 percent of soybeans, 71 percent of cotton, and 34 percent of corn being GM. "The new law will further restrict access for U.S. soybeans and soybean products while negatively impacting consumers in the EU," stated Ron Heck of the American Soybean Association. "Because there is a strong likelihood that the new labeling and traceability regime will simply serve as a 'replacement' nontariff barrier to trade with the EU, we are not particularly hopeful that the market will be open any time soon," stated Barbara Isman of the Canola Council of Canada. In response to U.S. threats to file a WTO complaint against the EU, the environmental group Friends of the Earth issued a press release that stated, "It is clear that this U.S. Administration, backed by some of the richest and most powerful lobbyists in U.S. politics, is determined to use the secretive, biased and undemocratic procedures of the WTO to bulldoze through attempts by other states to set minimum environmental, social and health standards. If this attempt succeeds, the U.S. will force GM foods onto European markets regardless of the wishes of consumers."[47]

These few examples give an idea of the complexity involved in trying to eliminate nontariff barriers. As a consequence of the Uruguay Round,* considerable progress has been made, but there is still much more work to be done before nontariff barriers and their trade-distorting effects are eliminated.

Exporting companies need to be informed about the changing status of tariff and nontariff barriers in the countries where they are doing business or would like to do business. Those that have stayed away from markets with extremely high import duties or nontariff barriers, such as product standards or customs procedures designed to keep out foreign products, may find these barriers no longer exist.

FROM MULTINATIONAL TO GLOBALLY INTEGRATED MANUFACTURING SYSTEMS

The lowering of import duties and the elimination or weakening of nontariff barriers are making it easier and less costly for companies to locate their production activities in lower-cost countries. Paying lower import duties on components manufactured elsewhere reduces their landed cost, and not having to overcome nontariff barriers makes the international dispersion of production activities possible and more economical. Also, a multidomestic company with numerous manufacturing plants, each of which has a complete manufacturing system to supply the country where it is located, may find that with lower barriers to importation, it has two possibilities for improving operational efficiency:

1. Close the least efficient plants, and supply their markets with imports from other subsidiaries.

2. Change the multidomestic manufacturing system to a globally integrated system in which each plant performs the activities at which it is most efficient.

COSTS OF BARRIERS TO TRADE

Trade restraints in the United States and other countries cost consumers tens of billions of dollars per year, while benefiting a relatively small number of companies in the protected sectors of the economy. The sugar industry provides an interesting example of this situation, as discussed in the earlier Worldview, "Sugar Subsidies: Sweet for Producers, Not for Consumers."

Sugar is not an isolated example of the costs associated with trade barriers. A recent study of just 20 product groups in protected industries showed that the average consumer cost per job saved was $231,289 per year. This means that consumers paid over seven times the average annual compensation of manufacturing workers to preserve jobs through import constraints. Many of these sectors have been shielded from imports for 45 years or more. Studies done in other countries show similar results.[48]

---

*The Uruguay Round is discussed in Chapter 4.

mini MNE

>>A Small Business Fights the Standards Barrier

If you sell in one EU member-country, you can sell in them all, right? Wrong. EU rules allow member-countries to prohibit imports that threaten public safety, and there is no agreement on what constitutes such a threat. Dermont Manufacturing Co., a small firm ($25 million in sales), makes hoses that connect gas appliances to gas outlets. It had been selling them throughout Europe when, suddenly, one day a U.S. manufacturer of deep-fat fryers who was supplying McDonald's told Dermont's president, Evan Seagal, that McDonald's could no longer use his hoses in its British restaurants. Similar situations began occurring elsewhere: French health inspectors ordered Euro Disney to replace Dermont hoses. The reason for the different national standards was that the gas hoses were considered essential to the safe operation of the gas appliances and therefore fell under product safety rules, thus permitting each nation to establish its own standards.

Seagal studied the various rules and realized that his product could not meet them. As is often the case, the rules were written by committees composed of a nation's experts. Who were they? The producers of the hoses who were Dermont's competitors. Designs varied from country to country, and all were different from Dermont's

hose. Seagal argues that there were no reasons for the differences in design except to keep his product out of the local market. They had no bearing on either safety or performance. The president of the American National Standards Institute, the U.S. standards organization, claimed that the Dermont case is "clearly a case of European standards being used as a barrier to trade."

Meanwhile, Dermont has begun obtaining product approval from individual EU countries. The U.S. government has been urging the European Committee for Standardization to begin developing a harmonized European standard for gas connector hoses for years. The initial draft of such a harmonized European standard impedes access to the EU by Dermont due to its design specifications, and the company has experienced extensive difficulties in gaining access to the process for standard setting. Both the U.S. government and U.S. industry have continued to argue in favor of performance-based standards as well as increased transparency in the standard-setting process.

Sources: "Europe's 'Unity' Undoes a U.S. Exporter," *The Wall Street Journal*, April 1, 1996, p. B1; Office of the Foreign Trade Representative, "The 2000 Estimate Report on Foreign Trade Barriers," www.ustr.gov/reports/nte/2000//contents.html (August 28, 2000); and Office of the Foreign Trade Representative, *2006 National Trade Estimate Report on Foreign Trade Barriers* (Washington, DC: United States Trade Representative, 2006), pp. 236–37.

The International Monetary Fund estimated that removal of tariff and subsidy supports for agriculture would increase global economic welfare by $128 billion per year, with nearly one-quarter of that benefit going to developing countries, including food-exporting nations in sub-Saharan Africa that have many of the world's poorest people.[49] The secretary-general of the United Nations, Kofi Annan, commented on the effects of barriers to trade by saying:

> *Rich countries' average tariffs on manufactured products imported from developing countries are now four times higher than those they levy on products which come mainly from other industrialized countries. Quotas and "antidumping" penalties are also used to keep Third World imports out of First World markets, especially in sectors where poorer countries have a competitive edge, such as agriculture, textiles and clothing.*[50]

International Investment Theories

Contemporary international investment theory has been expanded considerably from the classical theory, which postulated that differences in interest rates for investments of equal risk were the reason international capital moved from one nation to another. For this to happen, there had to be perfect competition, but as Kindleberger, a noted economist, stated, "Under perfect competition, foreign direct investment would not occur, nor would it be likely to occur in a world wherein the conditions were even approximately competitive."[51] This section focuses specifically on theories of foreign direct investment, which comprises both ownership and control of international investments involving real or physical assets such as plants and other facilities, rather than theories regarding other types of international investment such as portfolios of stocks, bonds, or other forms of debt. Foreign direct investment involves the establishment of production or other facilities abroad, either through greenfield investment (the establishment of new facilities from the ground up) or cross-border acquisition (the purchase of an existing business in another nation). It is usually assumed that strategic motives will be the driving force for decisions to invest abroad, driven by desire to find new markets, access raw materials, achieve production efficiencies, gain access to new technologies or managerial expertise, enhance political safety of the firm's operations, or respond to competitive or other pressures in the external environment.[52]

MONOPOLISTIC ADVANTAGE THEORY

The modern **monopolistic advantage theory** stems from Stephen Hymer's dissertation in the 1960s, in which he demonstrated that foreign direct investment occurs largely in oligopolistic industries rather than in industries operating under near-perfect competition. This means that the firms in these industries must possess advantages not available to local firms in order to overcome liabilities associated with being a foreigner—such as lack of knowledge about local market conditions, increased costs of operating at a distance, or differences in culture, language, laws and regulations, or institutions—that cause a foreign company to be at a disadvantage against local firms. Hymer reasoned that the advantages must be economies of scale, superior technology, or superior knowledge in marketing, management, or finance. Foreign direct investment takes place because of these product and factor market imperfections, which enable the multinational enterprise to operate more profitably in foreign markets than can local competitors.[53]

monopolistic advantage theory
Theory that foreign direct investment is made by firms in oligopolistic industries possessing technical and other advantages over indigenous firms

PRODUCT AND FACTOR MARKET IMPERFECTIONS

Caves, a Harvard economist, expanded Hymer's work to show that superior knowledge permitted the investing firm to produce differentiated products that consumers would prefer to similar locally made goods and this would give the firm some control over the selling price and an advantage over indigenous firms. To support these contentions, he noted that companies investing overseas were in industries that typically engaged in heavy product research and marketing efforts.[54]

FINANCIAL FACTORS

Other theories relate to financial factors. Aliber believes that the imperfections in the foreign exchange markets may be responsible for foreign investment. Companies in nations with overvalued currencies are attracted to invest in countries whose currencies are undervalued.[55] Another financially based theory, portfolio theory, suggests that international operations allow for a diversification of risk and therefore tend to maximize the expected return on investment.[56]

INTERNATIONAL PRODUCT LIFE CYCLE

We have already examined this theory to help explain international trade flows, but as we said, there is a close relationship between international trade and international investment. As you saw, the IPLC concept also explains that foreign direct investment is a natural stage in the life of a product. To avoid losing a market that it serves by exporting, a company is often forced to invest in overseas production facilities when other companies begin to offer similar products. This move overseas will be heightened during the third and fourth stages as the company that introduced the product strives to remain competitive, first in its export markets (stage 3) and later in its home market (stage 4), by locating in countries where the factors of production are less expensive.

FOLLOW THE LEADER

Another theory was developed by Knickerbocker, who noted that when one firm, especially the leader in an oligopolistic industry, entered a market, other firms in the industry followed. The follow-the-leader theory is considered defensive because competitors invest to avoid losing the markets served by exports when the initial investor begins local production. They may also fear that the initiator will achieve some advantage of risk diversification that they will not have unless they also enter the market.[57] In addition, suspecting that the initiator knows something they do not, they may feel it is better to be safe than sorry.

CROSS INVESTMENT

Graham noted a tendency for **cross investment** by European and American firms in certain oligopolistic industries; that is, European firms tended to invest in the United States when American companies had gone to Europe. He postulated that such investments would permit the American subsidiaries of European firms to retaliate in the home market of U.S. companies if the European subsidiaries of these companies initiated some aggressive tactic, such as price cutting, in the European market.[58] Of course, as we noted in Chapter 2, there are a number of other reasons investment by multinationals takes place in a foreign country, such as *following the customer* (Japanese parts manufacturers following Japanese auto manufacturers into the United States, Canada, or Europe), *seeking knowledge* (Japanese and European investment in Silicon Valley), and *benefiting from political and economic stability of the host country.*

INTERNALIZATION THEORY

The **internalization theory** is an extension of the market imperfection theory. A firm has superior knowledge, but due to inefficiency in external markets, the firm may obtain a higher price for that knowledge by using the knowledge itself rather than by selling it in the open market. By investing in foreign subsidiaries for activities such as supply, production, or distribution, rather than licensing, the company is able to send the knowledge across borders while maintaining it within the firm. The expected result is the firm's ability to realize a superior return on the investment made to produce this knowledge, particularly as the knowledge is embodied in various products or services that are sold to customers.[59]

DYNAMIC CAPABILITIES

The **dynamic capability** perspective, which is linked to resource-based views of the firm, argues that ownership of specific knowledge or resources is necessary, but not sufficient, for achieving success in international FDI. The firm must also be able to effectively create and exploit dynamic capabilities for quality and/or quantity-based deployment, and these capabilities must be transferable to international environments in order to produce competitive advantage. Companies typically develop centers of excellence in order to develop distinctive competencies that will be subsequently applied to their investments within the host countries.

DUNNING'S ECLECTIC THEORY OF INTERNATIONAL PRODUCTION

The eclectic theory, which combines elements of some of those we have discussed, is the most widely cited and accepted theory of FDI currently. Developed by Dunning, the **eclectic theory of international production** attempts to provide an overall framework for explaining why firms choose to engage in FDI rather than serve foreign markets through alternatives such as exporting, licensing, management contracts, joint ventures, or strategic alliances. This theory maintains that if a firm is going to invest in production facilities overseas, it must have three kinds of advantages:

1. *Ownership-specific:* This is the extent to which a firm has or can develop a firm-specific advantage through ownership of tangible and intangible assets that are not available to other firms and can be transferred abroad. The three basic types of ownership-specific advantages include knowledge or technology, economies of scale or scope, and monopolistic advantages associated with unique access to critical inputs or outputs. The advantage generates lower costs and/or higher revenues that will offset the added costs of operating at a distance within a foreign location.

2. *Location-specific:* A foreign market must have specific characteristics, of an economic, social, or political nature, that will permit the firm to profitably exploit its firm-specific advantages by locating to that market.

3. *Internalization:* Firms have various alternatives for entering foreign markets, ranging from arm's-length market transactions to the use of hierarchy via a wholly owned subsidiary, as we will discuss in Chapter 16. It is in the firm's best interests to exploit its ownership-specific advantages through internalization in those situations where either the market does not exist or it functions inefficiently, causing the transaction costs of using market-based (arm's-length) options to be too high.

Because of the names of these three types of advantages that a firm must have, the eclectic theory of international production is sometimes referred to as the *OLI model*. This theory provides an explanation for an international firm's choice of its overseas production facilities. The firm must have both location and ownership advantages to invest in a foreign plant. It will invest where it is most profitable to internalize its monopolistic advantage.[60] These investments can be proactive, being strategically anticipated and controlled in advance by the firm's management team, or reactive, in response to the discovery of market imperfections.

There is one commonality to nearly all of these theories that is supported by empirical tests—the major part of direct foreign investment is made by large, research-intensive firms in oligopolistic industries. Also, all these theories offer reasons companies find it *profitable* to invest overseas. However, as we stated in Chapter 2, all motives can be linked in some way to the desire to increase or protect not only profits but also *sales* and *markets*.

Summary

Explain the theories that attempt to explain why certain goods are traded internationally.

Why do nations trade? Mercantilists did so to build up storehouses of gold. Later, Adam Smith showed that a nation will export goods that it can produce with less labor than can other nations. Ricardo then proved that even though a country is less efficient than other nations, that country can still profit by exporting goods if it holds a comparative advantage in the production of those goods.

The idea that a nation tends to export products requiring a large amount of a relatively abundant factor was offered by Heckscher and Ohlin in their theory of factor endowment. In the 1920s, economists realized that economies of scale affect international trade because they permit the industries of a nation to become low-cost producers without having an abundance of a class of production factors. As in the case of comparative advantage, nations specialize in the production of a few products and trade to supply the rest. The Linder theory of overlapping demand states that because customers' tastes are strongly affected by income levels, a nation's income level per capita determines the kind of goods they will demand. The kinds of goods produced to meet this demand reflect the country's income per capita level. International trade in manufactured goods will be greater between nations with similar levels of per capita income.

The international product life cycle theory states that many products first produced in the United States or other developed countries are eventually produced in less developed nations and become imports to the very countries in which their production began. Krugman showed how economies of scale and imperfect competition can explain high levels of intraindustry trade. Marshall and Porter helped to explain how nations can achieve competitive advantage through the emergence of regional clusters, with Porter claiming that four classes of variables are critical in this regard: demand conditions, factor conditions, related and supporting industries, and firm strategy, structure, and rivalry.

Discuss the arguments for imposing trade restrictions.

Special-interest groups demand protection for defense industries so that their country will have these industries' output in wartime and will not depend on imports, which might not be available. Critics say that it would be far more efficient to subsidize some firms, that is, pay them to be ready. New industries in developing nations frequently request barriers to imports of competing products from developed countries. The argument is that the infant industry must have time to gain experience before having to confront world competition. Protectionists argue for protection from cheap imports by claiming that other countries with lower hourly labor rates than those in the protectionist's nation can flood the protectionist's nation with low-priced goods and take away domestic jobs. However, hourly labor rates are just a small part of production costs for many industries. There may be legislated fringe benefits that are a much higher percentage of the direct wages than is the case in developed nations. Productivity per worker may be considerably lower in developing nations, so less is produced for a given hourly rate. Commonly, also, the costs of the other factors of production that must be included in the cost of production often are higher in developing nations. Others want "fair" competition, that is, an import duty to raise the cost of the imported good to the price of the imported article to eliminate any "unfair" advantage that the foreign competitor may have. This, of course, nullifies the comparative advantage. Companies will also demand that their government retaliate against dumping and subsidies offered by their competitors in other countries.

Explain the two basic kinds of import restrictions: tariff and nontariff trade barriers.

In response to demands for protection, governments impose import duties (tariff barriers); nontariff barriers, such as quotas, voluntary export restraints, and orderly marketing arrangements; and nonquantitative nontariff barriers, such as direct government participation in trade, customs, and other administrative procedures and standards for health, safety, and product quality.

Appreciate the relevance of the changing status of tariff and nontariff barriers to managers.

Exporting firms may find that because tariff and nontariff barriers have been eliminated or lowered, they can now enter markets that were previously closed to them. It also is easier for firms to locate production activities in lower-cost nations to improve the efficiency of their manufacturing systems. Multidomestic firms may be able to close less efficient plants and supply those markets by exporting from more efficient ones.

Explain some of the theories of foreign direct investment.

International investment theory attempts to explain why foreign direct investment (FDI) takes place. Product and factor market imperfections provide firms, primarily in oligopolistic industries, with advantages not open to indigenous companies. The international product life cycle theory explains international investment as well as international trade. Some firms follow the industry leader, and the tendency of European firms to invest in the United States and vice versa seems to indicate that cross investment is done for defensive reasons. There are two financially based explanations of foreign direct investment. One holds that foreign exchange market imperfections attract firms from nations with overvalued currencies to invest in nations with undervalued currencies. The second theory postulates that FDI is made to diversify risk. Empirical tests reveal that most FDI is made by large, research-intensive firms in oligopolistic industries. The internalization theory states that firms will seek to invest in foreign subsidiaries, rather than license their superior knowledge, to receive a better return on the investment used to develop that knowledge. The dynamic capabilities perspective suggests that firms must have not only ownership of specific knowledge or resources but also the ability to dynamically create and exploit capabilities in order to achieve success in international FDI. The eclectic theory of international production explains an international firm's choice of its overseas production facilities. The firm must have location and ownership advantages to invest in a foreign plant. It will invest where it is most profitable to internalize its monopolistic advantage.

Key Words

mercantilism (p. 64)

absolute advantage (p. 65)

comparative advantage (p. 67)

factor endowment (p. 69)

exchange rate (p. 72)

currency devaluation (p. 73)

international product life cycle (IPLC) (p. 74)

national competitiveness (p. 78)

dumping (p. 83)

subsidies (p. 84)

countervailing duties (p. 85)

tariffs (p. 86)

ad valorem duty (p. 87)

specific duty (p. 88)

compound duty (p. 88)

variable levy (p. 88)

nontariff barriers (NTBs) (p. 88)

quotas (p. 88)

voluntary export restraints (VERs) (p. 89)

orderly marketing arrangements (p. 89)

monopolistic advantage theory (p. 93)

cross investment (p. 94)

internalization theory (p. 94)

dynamic capability (p. 94)

eclectic theory of international production (p. 94)

1. Describe mercantilism, and explain why mercantilism has been argued to be a poor approach to use in order to promote economic development and prosperity.

2. a. Explain Adam Smith's theory of absolute advantage.
   b. How does Ricardo's theory of comparative advantage differ from the theory of absolute advantage?
   c. Using the example from the chapter, explain why no gains from specialization exist (and thus why two countries could not trade in a manner that benefits each) if there is no pattern of comparative advantage (if the ratios of soybeans to cloth production are the same in the two countries).

3. Consider the case in which a country does not have a comparative advantage in the production of a product, such as apples, because its soils or climate are not appropriate. Explain who would be likely to favor free trade, and who would be likely to oppose free trade, in this product.

4. What is the relationship between the Heckscher-Ohlin factor endowment theory and the theories in question 2?

5. Why were Leontief's empirical results considered to be paradoxical?

6. Why does most of the world's international trade take place between economies that are similar in their level of economic development?

7. Name some products that you believe have passed through the four stages of the international product life cycle.

8. What factors increase the cost of trading goods and services across borders? Can these costs be reduced? How?

9. It seems that free, unrestricted international trade, in which each nation produces and exports products for which it has a comparative advantage, will enable everyone to have a higher level of living. Why, then, does every country have import duty restrictions?

10. "We certainly need defense industries, and we must protect them from import competition by placing restrictions on competitive imports." True or false? Is there an alternative to trade restrictions that might make more economic sense?

11. Suppose that a country negotiates an agreement with its trade partners to restrict its imports through voluntary export restrictions (VERs). What impacts might be expected from implementing such VERs?

12. "Workers are paid $20 an hour in the United States but only $4 in Taiwan. Of course we can't compete. We need to protect our jobs from cheap foreign labor." What are some possible problems with this statement?

13. There are two general classifications of import duties: tariff and nontariff barriers.
    a. Describe the various types of tariff barriers.
    b. What are some of the nontariff barriers?

14. "A firm entering the market first will soon dominate it, and the large market share it acquires will enable it to obtain the benefits of economies of scale." True or false? Remember that there are at least two studies showing that first movers held large market shares.

15. According to theories presented in this chapter, why do companies engage in foreign direct investment?

---

globalEDGE globalEDGE.msu.edu

Research Task

Use the globalEDGE site (http://globalEDGE.msu.edu/) to complete the following exercises:

1. Just as the worldwide export of manufactured products and commercial services varies across regions of the world, so does the difference between non-financial and financial transnational corporations (TNCs). The *World Investment Report* provides electronic access to comprehensive statistics on the top financial TNCs worldwide. So you can compare the top 10 nonfinancial TNCs from the previous chapter with the current exercise, locate the list of the 50 largest financial TNCs. Which countries are represented in the top 10 on each list (nonfinancial and financial TNCs)? Is there any difference in the countries represented in the two rankings? Which three TNCs score highest on this survey's Internationalization Index (II)? How does this compare to the top three nonfinancial institutions? What is the difference between this survey's II and the previous chapter's ranking based on the TNI? Why would the United Nations use two different methods to measure internationalization?

2. Your company is considering opening a new factory in Latin America. As such, the strategic management division is in the process of evaluating the specific locations for such an operation. The pool of candidate countries has been narrowed to Argentina, Mexico, and Brazil. By using the *country fact sheets* available through a resource provided by the United Nations at the globalEDGE Web site, prepare a short report comparing the foreign direct investment (*FDI*) environment and other relevant regulations in these three countries.

Minicase 3.1 Is Your Chocolate the Result of Unfair Exploitation of Child Labor?

When you last savored a bar of rich chocolate, a cup of hot cocoa, or a piece of chocolate cake or scoop of chocolate ice cream, did you know that you may have unwittingly been consuming a product made with child slaves?

Chocolate, made from the fruit (cocoa bean) of the Theobroma cacao tree, is one of the most-traded agricultural products in the world. The top 10 chocolate-consuming nations are all developed countries in Europe or the United States. In the United States, two-thirds of the $13 billion chocolate industry is dominated by two firms: M&M Mars and Hershey.

About 70 percent of the world's cocoa is produced in West Africa. In practice, beans from different nations are usually mixed together during their exportation and transport to processing plants in the importing nations. So Hershey bars, Snickers, M&Ms, KitKats, Nestlé chocolates, fudge, hot chocolate—essentially all of these delicacies that are regularly enjoyed by hundreds of millions of consumers—will include cocoa from West Africa, especially the Côte d'Ivoire (Ivory Coast). With about 43 percent of the world's total cocoa production, Côte d'Ivoire produces more than three times the level of the second-largest cocoa producer.

Results of a survey on child labor in West Africa, released in 2002, found that 284,000 children were working in hazardous conditions on West African cocoa farms, with the majority (200,000) working in Côte d'Ivoire. Nearly two-thirds of the child laborers were under the age of 14. Working conditions were described as slavelike, with 29 percent of the surveyed child workers in the Côte d'Ivoire indicating that "they were not free to leave their place of employment should they so wish." Many of these children had been brought into the cocoa-growing areas from distant regions of the Côte d'Ivoire or from poverty stricken countries such as Burkina Faso, Mali, and Togo, often after being kidnapped. Some of the child laborers had been sold by their parents in the expectation that the child's earnings would be sent home. Although paid less than 60 percent of the rate of adult workers, children frequently worked for over 12 hours per day, 6 days a week, and were regularly beaten. Over half of the children applied pesticides without protective gear. Only 34 percent of the children working on cocoa farms went to school, which was about half the level for children who were not working on cocoa farms. The rate of school enrollment was even lower for girls.

These child laborers seemed to be trapped in a vicious cycle: They were forced into work due to kidnapping or economic circumstances faced by themselves and/or their families, they earned subsistence wages, and because most had not been to school and had minimal skills, their prospects for seeking other employment options were limited.

In the late 1990s, exploitation of child labor in the cocoa industry began to receive publicity, primarily by nongovernmental organizations. Efforts to raise awareness of the situation faced great challenges, and even today a majority of consumers seem unaware of the circumstances behind the production of their favorite chocolate treats. Yet the atrocious nature of the child labor situation in the cocoa industry compelled the media, public interest groups, and others to continue their efforts. Hard-hitting news stories began to appear on television and radio and in magazines and newspapers across North America and Europe. Pressure grew for intervention, such as international trade sanctions. The Harkin-Engel bill, passed by the U.S. House of Representatives, proposed a federal system of certification and labeling requirements that would state whether a cocoa-based product had been made in a "slave-free" manner.

Fearing the implications of boycotts, trade sanctions, or certification and labeling requirements in key markets such as the United States and Europe, representatives from the chocolate industry attempted to develop a strategy for dealing with the problem. After the Chocolate Manufacturers Association hired former senators George Mitchell and Bob Dole to lobby against the Harkin-Engel bill and prevent its passage in the U.S. Senate, the industry agreed to self-regulate and attempt to change the child labor practices. A protocol for the industry was developed that established a timetable for eliminating child labor and forced labor in the production of cocoa. A self-imposed deadline was set for establishing a viable monitoring and certification system: July 1, 2005.

Industry representatives have complained that progress toward eliminating child labor in cocoa production has been hindered by traditional culture in the agriculturally based producing nations, compounded by civil war and other complications. Yet the important cocoa-producing nations of Nigeria and Ghana, with the assistance of the International Labor Organization and the International Programme on the Elimination of Child Labour (IPEC), have subsequently established national programs to eliminate child labor in their countries. So far, the Côte d'Ivoire has made only limited effort to initiate such programs.

In February 2005, several U.S. congressmen held a news conference in which they declared that they would not be buying chocolate for their wives for Valentine's Day, because the candy had probably been made from cocoa produced in the Côte d'Ivoire with child slaves. Subsequently, after charging that the industry had failed to meet its self-imposed July 2005 deadline, the International Labor Rights Fund filed a lawsuit in federal court in Los Angeles against several international manufacturers of chocolate. The suit claimed that the manufacturers had ignored repeated, well-documented warnings about the exploitative use of child labor on cocoa farms in the Côte d'Ivoire.

In the absence of prompt and effective action by the chocolate and cocoa industry, a number of companies have begun producing fair-trade-certified chocolate. Through observing a strict set of guidelines associated with fair-trade certification, these companies guarantee that a consumer of one of their chocolate products is "not an unwitting participant in this very inhumane situation." Fairtrade Labeling Organizations International, a consortium of fair-trade organizations from Canada, the United States, Japan, and 17 European nations, establishes certification standards. In the United States, Transfair USA is the sole independent, third-party body for certifying fair-trade practices (www.transfairusa.org).

Fair-trade practices essentially involve international subsidies to farmers in developing countries, ensuring that farmers who are certified as engaging in fair-trade practices will receive a price for their produce that will at least cover their costs of production. By providing a price floor, fair-trade practices protect Third World farmers from the ruinous fluctuations in commodity prices that result from free trade practices. At the same time, fair-trade certification requires that farmers engage in appropriate social, labor, and environmental practices, such as paying livable wages and not using child or slave labor. In addition the cocoa program, fair-trade certification programs have been implemented for a range of other products, such as coffee, bananas, and crafts.

Although still a nascent movement, sales of fair-trade-certified products are growing. For example, Dunkin' Donuts sells only fair-trade coffee in its stores. Will there be a similar result for chocolate? Already, about two dozen companies make fair-trade chocolate in the United States, including Clif-Bar, Cloud Nine, Newman's Own Organics, Kailua Candy Company, and Sweet Earth Organic Chocolates.

Discussion Questions

1. Should labor practices in another country be a relevant consideration in international trade? Why or why not?

2. With regard to trade in products such as cocoa, what options are available to governments, businesses, and consumers for dealing with practices such as child labor or slave labor in other countries? What are the implications associated with each of these options?

3. How would international trade theorists view the fair-trade movement?

Source: "Child Labor in the Cocoa Sector of West Africa," International Institute of Tropical Agriculture, August 2002, www.iita.org/news/cocoa.pdf (August 2, 2006); "Combating Child Labour in Cocoa Growing," International Programme on the Elimination of Child Labour, Geneva, February 2005; "Cal Poly Professor Heading to Africa to Investigate Chocolate–Slave Labor Ties," www.calstate.edu/newsline/2005/n20050819slo1.shtml (August 2, 2006); Sweet Earth Organic Chocolates, "Our Philosophy," www.sweetearthchocolates.com/level.itml/icOid/68 (August 2, 2006); Tom Neuhaus, "A Luscious Exploration of 3 Fair-Trade-Certified Cocoa Cooperatives," *HopeDance Magazine*, www.hopedance.org/new/issues/47/article6.html (August 2, 2006); "Fair Trade Q&A," www.globalexchange.org/campaigns/fairtrade/fairtradeqa.html (August 2, 2006); and Samlanchith Chanthavong, "Chocolate and Slavery: Child Labor in Côte d'Ivoire," www.american.edu/TED/chocolate-slave.htm (August 2, 2006).

Παγοσμιο Business Negócios Internacionai

التجارة العالمية Gli Affari Internazionali

Los negocios internacionales Internationales Geschäft

Affaires Internationales

International Business Los negocios internacionales 國際商務

Internationales Παγοσμιο Business

國際商務 Gli Affari Internazionali Intern

Negócios Internacionais

Gli Affari Internazionali التجارة العالمية

Cooperation among Nations

The world we share is becoming increasingly interconnected in complex and interesting ways. This complexity calls on international institutions and national governments to increase their cooperation to help ensure peace and lead to conditions that support international trade. Business students and business executives need to be aware of the significantly increasing role of intergovernmental and nongovernmental cooperation.

This section includes chapters on international institutions and the international monetary system. These institutions are important to the business student and business executive; they are becoming increasingly important in the daily news, as well, because our awareness of their impact and its potential is increasing. Years ago, a meeting of the IMF or the G8 (G4, G6 or G7) would draw little media attention, being of interest mainly to policy makers and academics. Today, such meetings draw huge numbers of people, many of whom appear to disagree with their objectives.

International institutions can be both a help and a hindrance to businesses. The UN, the World Bank, the IMF, the EU, and the Organization for Economic Cooperation and Development provide forums for coordination and are excellent sources of information for business executives and students. In addition, the World Bank and the regional development banks provide large amounts of financing for projects. On the other hand, businesses may be required to contact such organizations to secure licensing, merger approval, and a host of other items that national governments once provided.

The international institutions and agreements discussed in Chapter 4 are organizations of governments, along with some private organizations, whose main purpose is political, economic, or a combination of the two. Some of these organizations have large amounts of power (such as the EU), and others have less power, but all are important to business. The EU, for example, is especially important in its relationship to the U.S. Now the EU speaks for its 25 European member-countries in matters such as trade policy, antitrust issues, and monetary policy.

The international monetary system, discussed in Chapter 5, is developing and changing constantly, and the international business student and business executive do well to know the past in order to understand the system under which we operate today. Much like international institutions, the international monetary system is based on cooperation among governments, on multilateral cooperation. Chapter 5 reviews the history of our monetary system, moving from the gold standard to a fixed rate system, and on to the floating rate system that allows for today's huge growth in international trade. It concludes with a review of the balance of payments system.

4

International Institutions from an International Business Perspective

I believe that globalization—the removal of barriers to free trade and the closer integration of national economies—can be a force for good and that it has the potential to enrich everyone in the world, particularly the poor. But I also believe that if this is to be the case, the way globalization has been managed, including the international trade agreements that have played such a large role in removing those barriers and the policies that have been imposed on the developing countries in the process of globalization, need to be radically rethought.

—Joseph E. Stiglitz, former Chief Economist of the World Bank

In a world of interconnected threats and challenges, it is in each country's self-interest that all of them are addressed effectively. Hence, the cause of larger freedom can only be advanced by broad, deep and sustained global cooperation among States. Such cooperation is possible if every country's policies take into account not only the needs of its own citizens but also the needs of others. This kind of cooperation not only advances everyone's interests but also recognizes our common humanity.

—Kofi A. Annan, former Secretary-General, United Nations, In Larger Freedom, *2005*

The United Nations Millennium Goals: A Call for Change

Six billion human beings. Rapid globalization. Intractable conflicts. Genocide and ethnic cleansing. Promoting development. Combating poverty and AIDS. Controlling climate change. As humanity reflects on the challenges we face at this millennial milestone, it is a chance also to reflect on the only global organization to which we can turn: the United Nations.

—We the Peoples, the Millennium Assembly of the United Nations

These are facts about how others live on our shared globe: More than 1 billion people in the world live on less than one dollar a day. In total, 2.7 billion struggle to survive on less than two dollars per day. In some deeply impoverished nations less than half of the children are in primary school and under 20 percent go to secondary school. Around the world, a total of 114 million children do not get even a basic education, and 584 million women are illiterate. Overall illiteracy is 18 percent, 13 percent among males, and 23 percent among females.[a] To change these facts, at the beginning of the 21st century, at the largest meeting of world leaders in history, the United Nations established eight ambitious Millennium Development Goals, with a target date of 2015. These goals are to eradicate poverty and hunger, to achieve universal primary education, to promote gender equality and empower women, to reduce child mortality, to improve maternal health, to combat HIV/AIDS, malaria, and other diseases, to ensure environmental sustainability, and to develop a global partnership for development. The role of business organizations in these efforts is great, just as the achievement of these efforts is important to business. In addition to indicating the basic humanitarian obligation recognized by many businesses, these statistics represent potential markets and potential workers. The efforts themselves help to build a more stable world in which business can prosper.

The 2005 Millennium Development Goals Report indicates solid progress in some areas, with much greater work to be done in others. The progress chart on page 109 summarizes where the world stood as of September 2005 on the first seven goals. ∎

[a]UNESCO Institute for Statistics, 2004 literacy assessment, http://portal.unesco.org/education/en/ev.php-URL_ID=35964&URL_DO=DO_TOPIC&URL_SECTION=201.html (accessed May 22, 2006).

CONCEPT PREVIEWS

After reading this chapter, you should be able to:

describe the influence the mainly political international institutions have on international businesses and their relevance to international business

identify the major organs of the United Nations, their general purpose, and their significance to international business

discuss the World Trade Organization and its predecessor, GATT

appreciate the resources of the Organisation for Economic Cooperation and Development

describe the major purpose and effectiveness of OPEC

identify economic integration agreements and the effectiveness of the major ones

explain the North American Free Trade Agreement and its impact on business

discuss the impact of the EU and its future challenges

Gli Affari Internazionali
icionales
onales Geschäft Παγοσμιο Business
Negócios Internacionais   Los Negócios Internacionais
internacionales   Affaires Internationales 国際商務 Παγοσμιο Business

Within any given country, the national government takes responsibility for providing the economic, political, legal, and monetary stability that businesses in that country require in order to prosper. For example, in the United States, the federal government seeks to ensure that the financial and money markets are orderly and that inflation is constrained. The federal government also provides an orderly, predictable legal and political environment so that business decision makers can assess the risks their activities might face and then develop ways to control these risks as part of their long-term investment plans. When business activities cross national borders, they need the same sort of stability and predictability. To meet this need, a variety of international political, legal, military, and economic institutions have been developed through cooperative agreements among nations. Knowledge of these institutions is important for several reasons. First, they exist to foster peace and stability among nations—conditions that matter greatly to the conduct of international business. Second, they often are valuable resources for commercial data and important information about market conditions, demographics, and trade relationships. Third, they also may have regulatory functions.

To illustrate the importance of strong international institutions, think about the roles of the United States as the sole superpower on the global stage and of China as an upcoming nation preparing for a major global role. Martin Wolfe, chief economist at the *Financial Times*, notes in a recent article that both nations are fated to cooperate.[1] Yet look at their differences: As Wolfe points out, one is a democracy, the other an autocracy; one is "a child of the enlightenment," the other an agrarian empire. Although working together will not be easy for either, international institutions facilitate such endeavors by developing multilateral solutions, in which all nations cooperate. For individual nations, agreeing to a mutually negotiated UN resolution or a World Trade Organization rule is easier than agreeing to a bilateral negotiation, where there is a winner and a loser and where power and prestige are at stake. There is no humiliation at stake with a negotiated UN resolution that applies to all nations' behavior.

Note, too, that these institutions provide opportunities for interesting careers. The United Nations and the Organisation for Economic Cooperation and Development routinely have career positions to fill in such fields as economics, languages, law, project management, and information technology. For more information, contact the specific organization through its Web site (e.g., the UN's main portal is www.un.org; the Organisation for Economic Cooperation and Development is www.oecd.org; and the World Trade Organization's is www.wto.org).

In this chapter, we examine a number of these institutions. Some of them are worldwide, while others operate in specific regions of the world. Some have memberships composed of many countries, while others have relatively few member-nations. Most are groupings of governments, but a few are private. Our review of them is organized according to the institution's primary purpose—political or economic. *Political* means related to administration and governance, while *economic* suggests a focus on money, trade, and commerce. Institutions are dynamic; they continuously evolve, and as they do, their purposes tend to shift because the world itself is changing. Complex international institutions, such as those discussed in this chapter, frequently have purposes that are neither all political nor all economic. The European Union (EU), for example, illustrates well the growing overlap of the political and the economic arenas. The EU began with a primarily economic purpose and has grown to have a strong political purpose as well. Figure 4.1 illustrates international institutions based on their primary organizational purpose: political, economic, or both.

Our review begins with a look at the political institutions: the United Nations; two smaller, cooperative military alliances; and the Association of Southeast Asian Nations. Next, we explore the economic institutions: the World Trade Organization (WTO); the Organisation for Economic Cooperation and Development (OECD); and two smaller economic alliances, the Organization for Petroleum Exporting Countries (OPEC) and the Group of 8. We then examine agreements for economic integration, from low levels of integration, such as free trade areas, to progressively higher levels, such as customs unions and common markets. Finally, we explore an institution that has accomplished both extensive economic and extensive political integration, the European Union.

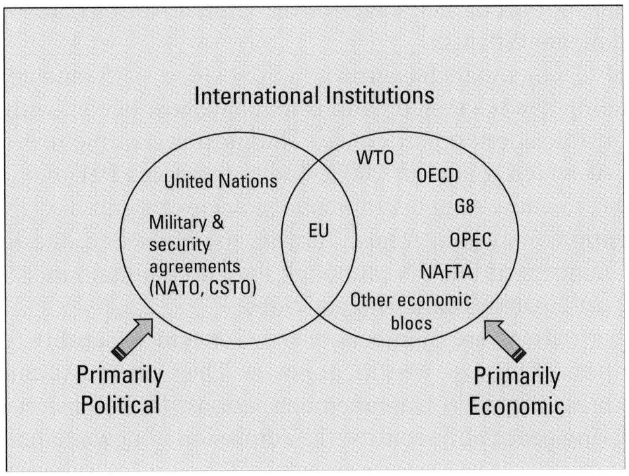

FIGURE 4.1

International
Institutions by
Purpose

International Institutions

International Political Institutions

THE UNITED NATIONS

UN Background   In 1944, representatives of China, the Soviet Union, the United Kingdom, and the United States, meeting at Dumbarton Oaks, in Washington, D.C., drew up draft proposals for an international political organization. On the basis of their plans, and in the optimism and hope that came with the close of World War II, representatives of 50 countries met in San Francisco in 1945 to develop the United Nations charter. The charter was signed by delegates of all 50 countries and later of Poland, for a total of 51 original member-states. Today the **United Nations (UN)** is probably the best-known worldwide organization. (For detailed information about the UN, including its organizational structure, see www.un.org.)

The UN has been responsible for many international agreements and much of the body of international law since 1945. For example, the Universal Declaration of Human Rights, which the General Assembly adopted in 1948, seeks to ensure basic human rights for all people worldwide. As a stabilizing force in the world economy, the UN contributes greatly to the conditions under which international business is conducted. Here are some general ways in which the UN plays a significant role:

United Nations (UN)
International organization of 191 member-nations dedicated to the promotion of peace and global stability; has many functions related to business

- Provides the "soft infrastructure" for the global economy by setting technical standards and norms.

- Prepares the ground for investment in emerging economies (health, governance, political stability, etc.).

- Addresses the downside of globalization (crime, drugs, and arms traffic).

- Seeks solutions to global environmental problems.

- Addresses education and health issues that require global-level solutions.

- Promotes social justice and human and labor rights.

- Builds the cornerstones of an interdependent world: trust and shared values.[2]

UN Organization   The work of the United Nations is carried out through five main bodies or organs: the General Assembly, the Security Council, the Economic and Social Council, the International Court of Justice, and the Secretariat. The UN conducts its work throughout the world and has offices in most major capitals. The International Court of Justice is located in The Hague, Netherlands. The other main bodies are at the United Nations headquarters in New York City. The six official languages of the United Nations are Arabic, Chinese, English, French, Russian, and Spanish.

The number of UN members has grown rapidly since 1945, and additional nations continue to join, including newly created nations that have just become eligible and established nations that have just decided to participate. The most recent members are East Timor and Switzerland, both of which joined in 2002. Today there are 191 members. Although there have been proposals to allow nongovernmental agencies to join the UN, at the current time only recognized nations may join. Thus, Taiwan, the Holy See, the European Union, and Palestine are not members of the UN, although they do maintain missions or offices at UN headquarters and participate in some UN activities.

All UN member-nations are members of the **General Assembly,** in which each nation has one vote regardless of its size, wealth, or power. The General Assembly acts by adopting resolutions that express the will of the member-nations. Decisions on important questions, such as those involving peace and security, the admission of new member-nations, and budgetary matters, require a two-thirds majority, while decisions on other matters require a simple majority. Although these decisions have no legally binding force for governments or citizens in the member-nations, they carry the heavy weight of world opinion.

The second major organ of the UN is the **Security Council,** whose goal is to maintain international peace and security. It is composed of 15 members—5 permanent members and 10 nonpermanent members. Each of the permanent members—China, France, Russia, the United Kingdom, and the United States—has the power to veto any measure. The 10 nonpermanent members are chosen by the General Assembly for two-year terms. Five of the nonpermanent members always come from Africa and Asia, one from Eastern Europe, two from Latin America, and the remaining two from Western Europe and other areas. The Security Council's peacekeeping functions are probably what the UN is best known for. UN peacekeeping efforts have taken place in many areas throughout the world. Presently, UN peacekeeping forces are in Africa (Sudan, Burundi, Cote d'Ivoire, Liberia, Democratic Republic of the Congo, Ethiopia and Eritrea, and the Western Sahara); the Americas (Haiti); Asia (on the Pakistani and Indian border in the state of Jammu and Kashmir); Europe (Cyprus, Kosovo, and Georgia); and the Middle East (Golan and Lebanon).

The **Economic and Social Council (ECOSOC),** the third UN organ, is concerned with economic issues, such as trade, transport, industrialization, and economic development, and social issues, including population growth, children, housing, women's rights, racial discrimination, illegal drugs, crime, social welfare, youth, the human environment, and food.

General Assembly
Deliberative body of the UN made up of all member-nations, each with one vote regardless of size, wealth, or power

Security Council
Main policy-setting body of the UN, composed of 15 members including 5 permanent members

Economic and Social Council (ECOSOC)
UN body concerned with economic and social issues such as trade, development, education, and human rights

Members of the UN Security Council in session.

Section 2   Cooperation among Nations

>>Significance of the UN for International Businesspeople

Given the complexities that face international business transactions, which are due to conducting business across national borders at geographic and cultural distances from the managers' home environment, global rules of the road are quite helpful. The UN provides such "soft infrastructure" (as former Secretary-General Kofi Annan called it) to facilitate the international exchange of goods, services, money, and information. Here are some examples of the UN's contributions to international business:

- The rules that protect freely sailing ships are legitimized in UN conferences.

- The International Civil Aviation Organization, part of the UN, negotiates the web of agreements that allow commercial airlines to fly across borders and land in case of emergencies.

- The World Health Organization sets standards for pharmaceutical quality and standardizes the names of drugs.

- Protocols of the universal Postal Union prevent losses and allow the mail to move across borders.

- The International Telecommunication Union allots airwave frequencies.

- The International Labor Organization promotes labor rights, work safety conditions, and training.

- The World Meteorological Organization collects and distributes data used in weather forecasting.

- The UN Sales Convention and the UN Convention on the Carriage of Goods by Sea contribute to establishing rights and obligations for buyers and sellers in international transactions.

Within the UN there are 28 major organizations, and each one contributes to commercial order and openness. The UN Commission on International Trade Law and the UN's International Labour Organization are noteworthy bodies from an international business perspective because they set conditions and protocols for international transactions and for labor standards.

Source: www.un.org/partners/business/index.asp (accessed May 19, 2006).

ECOSOC makes recommendations on how to improve education and health conditions and promotes respect for and observation of the human rights and freedom of people everywhere.

The **International Court of Justice (ICJ),** also known as the *World Court*, renders legal decisions involving disputes between national governments. Since only nations litigate before the court, governments often intervene on behalf of corporations and individuals in their countries. Even though the court has worldwide jurisdiction to hear disputes between governments, it hears relatively few cases, usually less than 10 a year. The ICJ has 15 judges, who must come from 15 different countries and serve nine-year terms. Majorities of the General Assembly and the Security Council must agree on the appointment of judges to the ICJ. The activities of the ICJ are explored more fully in Chapter 10.

International Court of Justice (ICJ)
UN body that renders legal decisions involving disputes between national governments

The **Secretariat,** headed by the secretary-general of the United Nations, is the staff of the UN. It carries out administrative functions and administers the UN's programs and policies. The secretary-general, who is appointed by the General Assembly on the recommendation of the Security Council for a five-year renewable term, supervises the Secretariat. The seventh secretary-general, Kofi A. Annan of Ghana, was the first to be elected from the ranks of United Nations staff. In December 2001, Kofi Annan and the United Nations received the Nobel Peace Prize for their efforts in bringing nations together to work for peace. In this recognition, the Nobel Committee said that it wished "to proclaim that the only negotiable road to global peace and cooperation goes by way of the United Nations."[3]

Secretariat
The staff of the UN, headed by the secretary-general

About 8,600 people from 170 countries make up the UN Secretariat staff. As international civil servants, they and the secretary-general take an oath not to seek or receive instructions from any governmental or outside authority. Worldwide, over 52,000 people work for the UN and its related organizations.

The United Nations has been responsible for the development of many international efforts that facilitate business transactions around the world. One example is the International Telecommunication Union (ITU), a UN agency headquartered in Geneva, Switzerland, that assists governments and the private sector in coordination of global telecommunication networks and services. Another example is the International Trade Center of the UN, which provides trade information to assist developing countries in their business efforts. A third example is the International Civil Aviation Organization (ICAO), which is headquartered in Montreal, Canada, and works with civil aviation agencies throughout the world.

The Future of the UN   As it becomes evident that many of today's problems require a global or regional solution, the UN faces formidable challenges: AIDS/HIV, terrorism and related issues of ethnicity that have led to genocide, environmental issues, humanitarian crises, military conflicts, and drug and human trafficking, to name but a few. Yet, for the first time in history, large groups of people throughout the world are connected in new ways. Much of the world's population reads and speaks English, so many people in diverse nations share a means of communication. Through technological advances, we can communicate almost everywhere, directly and immediately. We are also more informed than we were in the past, based on education levels, travel, and access to media, and we have access to the best minds in the world.[4] As we make efforts to meet many of the challenges that face our world, the UN is positioned to make a difference in leadership and coordination. There is no other body that brings together the world's citizens and addresses global needs. As mentioned at the start of the chapter, the UN's Millennium Development Goals aim to eliminate or reduce major social and environmental world problems. Figure 4.2 summarizes the progress made as of September 2005 on seven of the eight goals.

COOPERATIVE MILITARY AND SECURITY AGREEMENTS

Initially you might wonder why we include military and security alliances in our review of institutions whose goals are mainly political, since they are quite different from governance and trade alliances. Yet military alliances have a significant impact on international business because, when successful, they stabilize international conditions, and thus cross-border economic environments, just by their existence and not necessarily by their use. For example, the first NATO invocation of its Article 5 (any attack on one member is an attack on all members) did not occur until 42 years after its establishment, in 2001, just after 9/11. Military and security ties also complement and promote trade among partners. In considering the relationship between military alliances and international trade, Michael D. Kennedy, professor of sociology at the University of Michigan, argues that military alliances are a critical aspect of energy security.[5]

We briefly review below two current major military agreements, the North Atlantic Treaty Organization (NATO) and the Collective Security Treaty Organization (CSTO). This section concludes with a look at the Association of Southeast Asian Nations (ASEAN), an institution that began as a security agreement and has moved toward economic cooperation.

North Atlantic Treaty Organization (NATO)

Security alliance of 26 North American and European nations

North Atlantic Treaty Organization   The **North Atlantic Treaty Organization (NATO)** is a security alliance of 26 North American and European nations governed by the North Atlantic Treaty of 1949. (See Figure 4.3.) The main provision of the treaty is the agreement "that an armed attack against one or more of them in Europe or North America shall be considered an attack against them all."[6] NATO was established after World War II in response to a perceived growing threat from the Soviet Union. The first NATO secretary-general, Lord Ismay, gave a more colloquial appraisal of the NATO purpose when he claimed it was for "keeping the Russians out, the Germans down, and the Americans in." The only time NATO has invoked the collective response that is at its core was after the September 11, 2001, terrorist attacks in the United States. Among NATO's members today are several former Soviet bloc countries, Estonia, Latvia, Lithuania, Bulgaria, Slovakia, and Slovenia, which became members in 2004. NATO also has a partnership agreement with Russia that gives Russia a voice in certain NATO decisions.[7]

Collective Security Treaty Organization (CSTO)

Security alliance of six members of the Commonwealth of Independent States (former Union of Soviet Socialist Republics)

Collective Security Treaty Organization   The Commonwealth of Independent States (CIS), formerly the Union of Soviet Socialist Republics (U.S.S.R.), formed a security alliance under the Collective Security Treaty (CST) in 1992. This original group of nine member-nations was reduced to six, which formed the present **Collective Security Treaty Organization (CSTO)** in 2002. Current members are Russia, Belarus, Kazakhstan, Kyrgyzstan, Tajikistan, and Armenia. The nations that left are Azerbaijan, Georgia and Uzbekistan.

FIGURE 4.2

Goals and Targets	Africa		Asia				Oceania	Latin America & Caribbean	Commonwealth of Independent States	
	Northern	Sub-Saharan	Eastern	Sub-Eastern	Southern	Western			Europe	Asia
GOAL 1 | Eradicate extreme poverty and hunger										
Reduce extreme poverty by half	low poverty	very high poverty	moderate poverty	moderate poverty	high poverty	low poverty	–	moderate poverty	low poverty	low poverty
Reduce hunger by half	very low hunger	very high hunger	moderate hunger	moderate hunger	high hunger	moderate hunger	moderate hunger	moderate hunger	very low hunger	high hunger
GOAL 2 | Achieve universal primary education										
Universal primary schooling	high enrolment	low enrolment	high enrolment	high enrolment	moderate enrolment	moderate enrolment	moderate enrolment	high enrolment	moderate enrolment	high enrolment
GOAL 3 | Promote gender equality and empower women										
Equal girls' enrolment in primary school	close to parity	far from parity	parity	parity	far from parity	nearly close to parity	close to parity	parity	parity	parity
Women's share of paid employment	low share	medium share	high share	medium share	low share	low share	medium share	high share	high share	high share
Women's equal representation in national parliaments	low representation	low representation	moderate representation	low representation	low representation	very low representation	very low representation	moderate representation	low representation	low representation
GOAL 4 | Reduce child mortality										
Reduce mortality of under-five-year-olds by two thirds	moderate mortality	very high mortality	moderate mortality	moderate mortality	high mortality	moderate mortality	high mortality	moderate mortality	low mortality	high mortality
Measles immunization	high coverage	very low coverage	moderate coverage	moderate coverage	low coverage	moderate coverage	very low coverage	high coverage	high coverage	high coverage
GOAL 5 | Improve maternal health										
Reduce maternal mortality by three quarters*	moderate mortality	very high mortality	low mortality	high mortality	very high mortality	moderate mortality	high mortality	moderate mortality	low mortality	low mortality
GOAL 6 | Combat HIV/AIDS, malaria and other diseases										
Halt and reverse spread of HIV/AIDS	–	very high prevalence	low prevalence	moderate prevalence	moderate prevalence	–	moderate prevalence	moderate prevalence	high prevalence	low prevalence
Halt and reverse spread of malaria*	low risk	high risk	moderate risk	moderate risk	moderate risk	low risk	low risk	moderate risk	low risk	low risk
Halt and reverse spread of tuberculosis	low mortality	high mortality	moderate mortality	moderate mortality	moderate mortality	low mortality	moderate mortality	low mortality	moderate mortality	moderate mortality
GOAL 7 | Ensure environmental sustainability										
Reverse loss of forests	small area	medium area	medium area	large area	medium area	small area	large area	large area	large area	small area
Halve proportion without improved drinking water	high coverage	low coverage	moderate coverage	moderate coverage	high coverage	high coverage	low coverage	high coverage	high coverage	moderate coverage
Halve proportion without sanitation	high coverage	very low coverage	low coverage	moderate coverage	very low coverage	high coverage	moderate coverage	high coverage	high coverage	moderate coverage
Improve the lives of slum-dwellers	moderate proportion of slum-dwellers	very high proportion of slum-dwellers	high proportion of slum-dwellers	moderate proportion of slum-dwellers	very high proportion of slum-dwellers	high proportion of slum-dwellers	–	high proportion of slum-dwellers	low proportion of slum-dwellers	moderate proportion of slum-dwellers

Country experiences in each region may differ significantly from the regional average.
For the regional groupings and country data, see http://millennmumindicators.un.org.

Sources: United Nations, based on data and estimates provided by: Food and Agriculture Organization; Inter-Parliamentary Union; International Labour Organization; UNESCO; UNICEF; World Health Organization; UNAIDS; UN-Habitat, World Bank—based on statistics available September 2005. Compiled by: Statistics Division, UN DESA

The progress chart operates on two levels. The words in each box tell what the current rate of compliance with each target is. The colours show the trend, toward meeting the target by 2015 or not. See legend below:

- Target already met or very close to being met.
- Target is expected to be met by 2015 if prevailing trends persist, or the problem that this target is designed to address is not a serious concern in the region.
- Target is not expected to be met by 2015, if prevailing trends persist.
- No progress, or a deterioration or reversal.
- Insufficient data.

*The available data for maternal mortality and malaria do not allow a trend analysis. Progress in the chart has been assessed by the responsible agencies on the basis of proxy indicators.

FIGURE 4.3 NATO Member Countries

NATO Countries

☐ Member countries	20. Romania	38. Moldova
1. Belgium	21. Slovakia	39. Russia
2. Bulgaria	22. Slovenia	40. Sweden
3. Canada	23. Spain	41. Switzerland
4. Czech Republic	24. Turkey	42. Tajikistan
5. Denmark	25. United Kingdom	43. the former Yugoslov
6. Estonia	26. United States	Republic of Macedonia*
7. France		44. Turkmenistan
8. Germany	**☐ Partner countries**	45. Ukraine
9. Greece	27. Albania	46. Uzbekistan
10. Hungary	28. Armenia	
11. Iceland	29. Austria	**☐ Mediterranean**
12. Italy	30. Azerbaijan	**Dialogue countries**
13. Latvia	31. Belarus	47. Algeria
14. Lithuania	32. Croatia	48. Egypt
15. Luxembourg	33. Finland	49. Israel
16. Netherlands	34. Georgia	50. Jordan
17. Norway	35. Ireland	51. Mauritania
18. Poland	36. Kazakhstan	52. Morroco
19. Portugal	37. Kyrghyz Republic	53. Tunisia

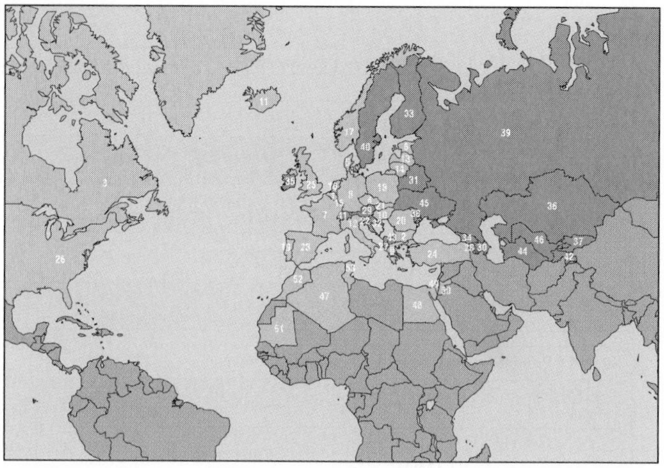

Source: www.nato.int/education/maps.htm.

Association of Southeast Asian Nations (ASEAN)
Ten-member body formed to promote peace and cooperation in the Southeast Asian region

Association of Southeast Asian Nations

Created in 1967, the **Association of Southeast Asian Nations (ASEAN)** was formed for political reasons, to foster peaceful relations among members and offer mutual protection against the growth of communism in their region. Political cooperation has led to some economic cooperation. The fundamental principles of ASEAN are:[8]

- Mutual respect for the independence, sovereignty, equality, territorial integrity, and national identity of all nations.

- The right of every state to lead its national existence free from external interference, subversion, or coercion.

- Noninterference by members in the internal affairs of one another.

- Settlement of differences or disputes in a peaceful manner.

- Renunciation of the threat or use of force.

- Effective cooperation among members.

Now that we are beyond the 1997 financial crisis, Southeast Asia is one of the most dynamic and fastest-developing economic regions in the world. Taken together, its members—Brunei, Cambodia, Indonesia, Laos, Malaysia, Myanmar (formerly Burma), the Philippines, Singapore, Thailand, and Vietnam—are major trading partners of the United States. Papua New Guinea has observer status. Figure 4.4 presents a map of ASEAN members. An ancillary institution, ASEAN +3, has recently been created to include China, Japan, and South Korea in some of the ASEAN discussions.

International Economic Institutions

The international institutions that result from economic agreements among countries are our focus in this section. They include the World Trade Organization (WTO), the Organisation for Economic Cooperation and Development (OECD), and economic agreements such as OPEC and the G8. Because of their unique nature, we devote a separate section, after this one, to institutions that are established by economic integration agreements among nations. The final section reviews the European Union (EU), an organization that began with an economic purpose and has evolved to include a political purpose as well.

World Trade Organization (WTO)
A multinational body of 149 members that deals with rules of trade between nations

WORLD TRADE ORGANIZATION

The **World Trade Organization (WTO)** is a multinational organization designed to establish and help implement rules of trade between nations. It currently has 149 members, including China (2001), Cambodia (2004), and Nepal (2004), and is headquartered in Geneva,

FIGURE 4.4

ASEAN Members

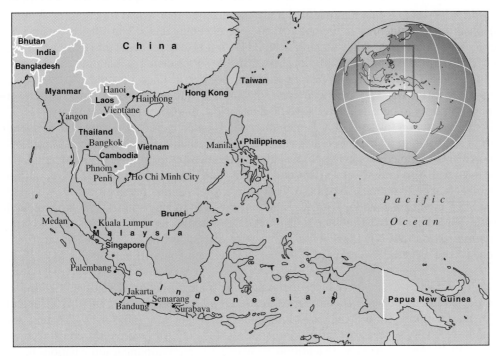

● Members of Association of Southeast Asian Nations (ASEAN).

Source: Association of Southeast Asian Nations.

Switzerland. The WTO functions according to its core agreements, which have been negotiated, signed, and ratified by all of its members. Because it is a rules-based, member-driven organization, all WTO decisions are made by the member governments, and the rules are the outcome of negotiations among members. The WTO's goal is to reduce or eliminate trade barriers and restrictions worldwide. Such reductions help producers of goods and services, exporters, and importers conduct their business by reducing costs. The history of the WTO helps to explain its present contributions to trade liberalization.

The WTO Trade Negotiation Committee meets in Geneva. Note the interesting seating arrangements in which the negotiators face each other in a series of face-to-face rows, fronted by a dais where the administrative leaders sit.

The Early Years of Global Trade Cooperation

After World War II, Western leaders shared a desire for an international trade organization that would function for commerce much as the UN functions in the political and peacekeeping areas. The allies drew up a charter for the International Trade Organization (ITO), but ITO never came into existence because the U.S. government did not ratify its charter. In 1947 President Truman did not even submit the ITO charter treaty to the Senate for ratification because he knew it would not have the votes to pass. After the war, U.S. politicians and some business interests feared that ceding any control or authority to outside interests would mean a loss of government sovereignty.

In preparation for an ITO, U.S. negotiators presented a draft of a general agreement on tariffs and trade to their ITO colleagues from 55 other nations at a meeting in Havana. The participants accepted this agreement as an interim measure pending ITO ratification. Thus the **General Agreement on Tariffs and Trade (GATT)** was born in 1947 with an initial membership of 23 nations.[9] The basic GATT principle was that member nations would treat all GATT members equally. So if two nations agreed to reduce a tariff, that tariff reduction was extended to all GATT members. This antidiscrimination agreement is known as the **most favored nation (MFN) clause.** GATT was extremely successful in the area of tariff reduction, as well as in the reduction of subsidies, quotas, and nontariff barriers.

GATT, 1947–1995

To reduce tariffs and other trade obstacles, GATT negotiations were conducted in eight extended conferences, called *rounds,* from the first in 1947 through the last, the **Uruguay Round,** which was launched in 1986 (see Table 4.1). The first seven rounds were very successful. Tariffs among developed countries were reduced from an average of 40 percent to 5 percent. In addition, 9 out of 10 disputes among trading nations brought to GATT were settled satisfactorily, discreetly, and without publicity. From 1947 through 2001, the volume of trade in manufactured goods multiplied 20-fold. Trade growth in manufactured goods grew at an average rate of 8 percent through the 1950s and 1960s, and throughout the GATT years trade growth consistently exceeded production growth.[10]

The Uruguay Round was a hugely ambitious undertaking. The seven preceding rounds had significantly reduced industrial product tariffs, and the Uruguay negotiators succeeded in lowering them by more than their target of an additional one-third. Uruguay also broke new GATT ground by writing international rules for trade in services and agriculture and for the protection of intellectual properties. Agreement was reached to phase out the multifiber arrangement, an agreement that covered textiles and clothing and was perhaps the oldest managed-trade system. Procedures to speed settlements of trade disputes were agreed on, as were means to reduce trade subsidies.

General Agreement on Tariffs and Trade (GATT)
International agreement that functioned to encourage trade liberalization from 1947 to 1995

most favored nation (MFN) clause
Agreement that GATT member-nations would treat all members equally in trade matters

Uruguay Round
The last extended conference of GATT negotiations

TABLE 4.1	GATT Rounds		
Year	**Place/Name**	**Subjects Covered**	**Countries**
1947	Geneva	Tariffs	23
1949	Annecy	Tariffs	13
1951	Torquay	Tariffs	38
1956	Geneva	Tariffs	26
1960–1961	Geneva, Dillon Round	Tariffs	26
1964–1967	Geneva, Kennedy Round	Tariffs and antidumping measures	62
1973–1979	Geneva, Tokyo Round	Tariffs, nontariff measures, framework agreements	102
1986–1994	Geneva, Uruguay Round	Tariffs, nontariff measures, rules, services, intellectual property, dispute settlement, textiles, agriculture, creation of WTO	123

Source: *OPEC Annual Statistical Bulletin, 2004.* Table 22. See http://www.ilo.org/public/english/fairglobalization/index.htm

Trade Benefits Uneven

The opening of borders, new trade agreements, and the World Trade Organization have not, so far, resulted in what trade theory (Chapter 3) suggests would be benefits for poorer nations. Instead, according to "A Fair Globalization," a UN study, the uneven benefits of globalization are building a growing divide between rich and poor countries, as well as within countries.* Globalization, it suggests, "is at a turning point and international institutions need to address social inequities as well as other consequences of open borders."[†]

The authors of the study, including the 2001 Nobel economist Joseph Stiglitz, were asked to describe the aspects of globalization that have given rise to growing protests about trade, the WTO, the World Bank, and other international institutions and agreements. The cochairs of the study, Tarja Halonen, president of Finland, and Benjamin William Mkapa, president of Tanzania, observe: "Currently, globalization is a divisive subject. It verges on a dialogue of the deaf, both nationally and internationally. Yet the future of our countries, and the destiny of our globe, demands that we all rethink globalization."

According to the report, 188 million people are unemployed worldwide, or 6.2 percent of the global labor force. Countries representing 14 percent of the world's population (largely the OECD countries) account for half the world's trade and foreign investment. The report also suggests that women's traditional livelihoods as small agricultural producers have been undermined by agricultural subsidies in the developed nations. In addition, when these women seek alternative occupations, they face discrimination. Two bright spots in the report are China and India, which together account for one-third of the global population. In both of these countries absolute poverty has declined. The future growth of world trade and the economic health of developed nations depend on getting globalization right so that all participants benefit from trade, just as a rising tide lifts all boats. New markets, an educated work force, economic growth, and political stability in emerging nations are all important for international business.

*The report can be found at www.ilo.org/public/english/fairglobalization/index.htm.

[†]Elizabeth Becker, "U.N. Study Finds Global Trade Benefits Are Uneven," *New York Times*, February 24, 2004, p. C5.

Many regarded a successful conclusion of the Uruguay Round as overambitious, but the negotiators met a GATT-imposed deadline by initialing a working agreement late on the last day of the deadline. There was disappointment with the final Uruguay Round agreement, though. Antidumping laws were not limited, and the United States entertainment industry wanted greater access to the European markets than the agreement allowed.[11] The Uruguay Round negotiators also recognized some of the weaknesses of GATT, and they created the World Trade Organization to take its place.

Creation of the World Trade Organization   At the start of the Uruguay Round, the economic environment was not positive, despite GATT's success at reducing tariffs. A series of economic recessions in the 1970s and 1980s led to initiatives by governments to create nontariff barriers to trade for sectors in their economies facing increased foreign competition. High levels of unemployment and increased subsidies, especially in the agricultural sector, led trade negotiators to seek a more solid platform for trade liberalization than GATT had provided. GATT had been, as commentators had suggested, a slender reed on which to hang an entire world trade system. Its dispute mechanisms were convoluted; there were many loopholes in agriculture, textiles, and clothing; and services were not covered at all by GATT. The world trading system had evolved since 1947, and the slender reed no longer could provide a sufficient framework to support the evolving world trade system. The Uruguay Round GATT negotiations established the World Trade Organization, and as of January 1, 1995, this new organization began to administer international trade agreements with a broader mandate than had GATT. For example, a trade policy review mechanism raises issues for discussion on a regular agenda, replacing the previous GATT practice of periodic rounds of negotiation. The WTO established a permanent process for revising the trade rules. The final GATT round, the Uruguay Round, included 123 participants. As of August 2006, the WTO had 149 members.

WTO Principles   In WTO negotiations, members have established five basic principles on which the global trade system can rest. These principles are the foundations of the multilateral trading system whose individual agreements are lengthy legal documents that address trade activities in areas as varied as agriculture, textiles and clothing, banking, telecommunications, government purchases, industrial standards and product safety, food sanitation regulations, and intellectual property. The WTO principles of the trading system are:

1. *Trade will be without discrimination.* This is the most favored nation (MFN) principle, and it requires that nations treat all WTO members equally. If one nation grants another nation a special trade deal, that deal has to be extended to all WTO members. Another aspect of nondiscrimination is that foreigners and locals should be treated equally. This means that imported goods, once they are in the market, should not face discrimination.

2. *Trade should be freer, with trade barriers negotiated downward.* Lower trade barriers, both visible ones such as import tariffs and less visible ones such as red tape, encourage trade growth.

3. *Trade should be predictable.* Predictability helps businesses know what the real costs will be. The WTO operates with tariff "bindings," or agreements to not raise a specific tariff over a given time. Such promises are as good as lowering a tariff because they give businesspeople realistic data. Transparency, making trade rules as clear and accessible as possible, also helps businesspeople anticipate a stable future.

4. *Trade should be more competitive.* Although many describe the WTO as a "free trade" organization, and it certainly does work toward trade liberalization, the WTO also realizes that trade relationships among nations can be exceedingly complex. Many WTO agreements support fair competition in agriculture, services, and intellectual property, discouraging subsidies and the dumping of products at prices below the cost of their manufacture. These agreements connect directly to the fifth principle.

5. *Trade should be more beneficial for less developed countries, encouraging development and economic reform.* Three-quarters of the WTO's members are developing economies and those transitioning to market economies. These economies were quite active in the Uruguay Round and have been active in the WTO's current **Doha Development Agenda,** informally called the *Doha Round*. A ministerial decision adopted at the end of the Uruguay Round suggests that developed nations should give market access to goods from the very least developed countries and increase technical assistance for them. Developed countries have started to allow duty-free and quota-free imports for almost all products from the least developed countries. The current Doha Development Agenda includes developing countries' concerns about the difficulties they face in implementing the Uruguay Round agreements. The importance of this issue for the WTO, for developing countries, and for poverty reduction cannot be overstated.

Doha Development Agenda
WTO extended conference on trade; also called *Doha Round*

The WTO and Developing Nations   The WTO's present director general is Pascal Lamy, the former EU trade commissioner, who began his four-year term in 2005. He succeeded the first WTO director general to come from a developing nation, Dr. Supachai Panitchipakdi, of Thailand, who pushed an agenda for the present Doha Round that is especially important for developing countries. In an address in Sao Paulo, Brazil, on June 14, 2004, he recognized that if developing nations lose faith in the Doha Development agreements presently being negotiated, many of which address special needs of developing countries, "the world's poorest and most vulnerable countries would be the biggest losers from a focus on other deals at the expense of multilateralism."[12]

The Doha Agenda has seen discord on many issues connected to the trading needs of developing nations, and when agreement on how to proceed on these issues was not reached by the original deadline of January 2005, the Doha Agenda was extended. Earlier talks that were part of the Doha Round held in Cancun, Mexico, in September 2003 had collapsed when delegates from developing nations in Africa, the Caribbean, and Asia walked out because they felt that many of the developed nations were unwilling to compromise on agricultural issues. That was the first time that developing nations had established themselves as a force in the talks, challenging the leadership of the United States and the EU. Twenty-one nations banded together to make the case that the agricultural subsidies wealthy nations pay to their own farmers undermine the poor farmers around the world. In particular, African farmers asked that the subsidies given to U.S. and EU cotton farmers be reduced and that they be paid $300 million in compensation for the losses they suffered because of this unfair competition. In response, the United States and the EU proposed that the question be studied and that the Africans grow other crops.[13] In June 2004, the WTO delegates once again agreed to debate a proposal from the developing nations calling for the reduction and elimination of agricultural tariffs. In the ensuing year, Brazil successfully sued the United States in the WTO over cotton subsidies. Brazil, India, and South Africa are leading the group of developing countries. The United States and the EU have each agreed to reduce subsidies if the other does. After the disappointment in Cancun in 2003, there is some hope, albeit slim, that the WTO can reach agreement on agricultural subsidies and tariffs soon and go on to address industrial tariffs and issues of services. Industrialized countries have a way to go in reducing agricultural subsidies. WTO Director General Lamy, who is French, says he doesn't understand his own country's position on agricultural subsidies. "As an efficient farm producer, the strategy should be to reduce subsidies and prices, because others won't be able to compete with you," he remarked to a *Wall Street Journal* reporter.[14]

In Spring 2006, Lamy advised WTO members that "genuine and important progress has been made but not fast enough." The WTO did not meet the April 30, 2006, deadline, set at the Doha Agenda's Hong Kong Ministerial Conference in December 2005, for agreement on a framework for tariff and subsidy cuts in agriculture and for nonagricultural market access. The discussions are ongoing, and their progress can be monitored at the WTO site at www.wto.org.[15]

WTO Challenges Trade negotiations are complex, especially among 149 countries—with differently developed economies, different cultures, and different priorities—that have committed to attempting consensus decisions. The progress of the GATT and the WTO has been impressive, with global trade up 14-fold and world gross product up sixfold.[16] As a result of the Uruguay Round and the early meetings on the Doha Agenda (Seattle, Cancun), developing nations have become more integrated into the WTO. Many of the current challenges relate to their increased role and their commitment to free trade. Economics professor Jagdish Bhagwati says that we should expect trade talks to be like a roller-coaster ride,[17] and so far the Doha Round has not disappointed. The Seattle meetings collapsed with violent demonstrations in 1999, so the round was re-launched in Doha in 2001 and continued in Cancun two years later and in Hong Kong, two years later still, in 2005. Protests, the core of which addressed the WTO's insensitivity toward environmental issues, human rights, working conditions, and labor protection, have died down since 9/11. The hurdles still facing the Doha Round include agricultural subsidies of the rich nations and manufactures subsidies of developing nations.

Regional trade agreements such as the European Union (EU) and the North American Free Trade Agreement (NAFTA) may weaken the WTO because such agreements could disrupt trade at the expense of countries that are not party to the agreements.[18] Since most of these trade agreements are among developed nations, the impact on developing nations could be substantial.

Another problem for the WTO is the question of whether its member-nations will abide by its decisions. For example, during the banana wars between the United States and the EU over the EU's failure to open its markets to U.S. banana imports, the WTO had twice ruled that the EU's policy was illegal.[19] Agreeing with Washington that the EU's preferential banana import rules were discriminatory, the WTO allowed the United States to impose $191.4 million in trade sanctions against EU goods. A cease-fire in the "banana war" has been reached. However, although initial EU lack of compliance with the ruling has changed, the underlying issue remains: The WTO relies on the goodwill of its members to implement its decisions. Recently both the EU and the United States have agreed to reduce agricultural subsidies as a result of WTO rulings.

Among the areas of negotiation at the WTO, one of the most difficult is **trade-related intellectual property rights (TRIPS).** The WTO agreement is that countries grant patents for 20-year periods and copyrights for 50 years. Intellectual property rights violations are endemic in several industries, such as music, software, and pharmaceuticals. These violations tend to occur in a small group of developing countries, with music and software piracy rampant in China and pharmaceutical patent violation legendary in India, China, and Brazil. The pharmaceutical patent infringement issue, however, also involves the ability of developing countries to provide health care. For example, Indian pharmaceutical companies can produce generic equivalents of

trade-related intellectual property rights (TRIPS) the acronym TRIPS refers to the WTO agreement that protects copyrights, trademarks, trade secrets, and other intellectual property matters.

Lin (Jimmy) Chiang is the international marketing manager at the Photonics Division of Universal Microelectronics Co. (UMEC), Ltd., headquartered in Taichung, Taiwan, R.O.C. UMEC is an ISO-9001/140001-, QS-9000-certified company and one of the world's leading manufacturers of Photonics Products, including fiber-

Lin (Jimmy) Chiang.

optic active and passive components, CATV integrated systems, magnetic components, power supplies, telecommunication products, and OEM assemblies. Over 80 percent of UMEC's production is exported to world markets. UMEC has branch offices in Taiwan, China, Hong Kong, the United States, Germany, and Italy. UMEC factories are located in Taichung, Taiwan, and in ShenZeng and Ningbo, China. Professionally, Lin travels to Japan, China, Thailand, Sweden, Denmark, Holland, Germany, Italy, France, the United Kingdom, and 23 U.S. cities.

Here's Lin's advice on how to get a job in international business:

- It is not difficult to get a job in international business. You only have to get a degree in international business or a related degree or related knowledge. (Lin holds undergraduate degrees in accounting, statistics, and business administration from colleges in Taiwan and an American MBA in international business.)
- Have language skills. English is the most popular language and Chinese is getting important. If you can understand both English and Chinese you can communicate with almost 2/3 of the people in the world.

- Be willing to work hard. Sometimes you have to work at night because your night is your customer's morning on the other side of the world.
- Be logical. Logic is a universal language. It can help you communicate and understand other parts of the world.

Here's Lin's advice on succeeding in international business:

- Develop good sales and marketing skills . . . international business is about selling your product globally.
- Do a Culture Analysis of your market—understand their culture before you do anything. You have to think and act locally. You even need to dress locally.
- Know about sports, music, and art. Doing business is not always talking business. If you can find out about your customer's hobbies and interests when you first meet, you increase the chance of business success.
- Show confidence. It will let your customer trust you are the best in the field.
- Have a humble attitude. This works in Asia, especially Taiwan, China, and Japan. Our ancestors always taught us that the more you know the more humble you act, so Asian people believe that humble people are the best.
- Give your customers quick responses and explanations. Cultures might be different, but the customer always thinks their own business is the most important, so prompt response is always necessary.
- On drinking: In all of Asia and some parts of South America, business is often settled at the dinner table, so it is quite important to reach your goal before you have too much to drink.

Source: www.umec-web.com.

drugs that are patent-protected in the West and sell these drugs in markets in developing countries at levels those countries can afford. The Doha meetings in 2001 stated that intellectual property should not take precedence over public health. Any country that adopts TRIPS will have the right to copy drugs patented before 1995. The WTO has also established a system of compulsory licensing which mandates that copyright holders license producers in developing countries.

The WTO has taken the GATT achievements, added a more stable framework to them, and continued progress in the development of a fair trading system for the world. How far forward the WTO can go remains to be seen, but it certainly is off to a good start in its efforts to stabilize the trading environment in which international business grows.

Organisation for Economic Cooperation and Development (OECD)
Group of developed countries dedicated to promoting economic expansion in its member-nations

ORGANISATION FOR ECONOMIC COOPERATION AND DEVELOPMENT

Headquartered in Paris, the **Organisation for Economic Cooperation and Development (OECD)** is often called the "rich man's club" because today it is composed of 30 of the wealthiest nations in the world (see Table 4.2).* Membership, though, is open to all nations committed to a market economy and a pluralistic democracy.

*Note that OECD uses the British spelling of *organisation* in its name.

TABLE 4.2	OECD Member Countries		
Country	**Date Joined**	**Country**	**Date Joined**
Australia	June 7, 1971	Korea	December 12, 1996
Austria	September 29, 1961	Luxembourg	December 7, 1961
Belgium	September 13, 1961	Mexico	May 18, 1994
Canada	April 10, 1961	Netherlands	November 13, 1961
Czech Republic	December 21, 1995	New Zealand	May 29, 1973
Denmark	May 30, 1961	Norway	July 4, 1961
Finland	January 28, 1969	Poland	November 22, 1996
France	August 7, 1961	Portugal	August 4, 1961
Germany	September 27, 1961	Slovak Republic	December 14, 2000
Greece	September 27, 1961	Spain	August 3, 1961
Hungary	May 7, 1996	Sweden	September 28, 1961
Iceland	June 5, 1961	Switzerland	September 28, 1961
Ireland	August 17, 1961	Turkey	August 2, 1961
Italy	March 29, 1962	United Kingdom	May 2, 1961
Japan	April 28, 1964	United States	April 12, 1961

The OECD developed from an earlier collaboration, the Organisation for European Economic Cooperation (OEEC), that was established to administer the Marshall Plan aid distribution in Europe after World War II and to begin to build economic cooperation within Europe. The OECD provides information on economic and other activities within its member-nations and gives them a setting in which to discuss economic and social policy. It publishes extensive research on a wide variety of international business and economic subjects, including highly regarded individual country surveys (see www.oecd.org). These publications and resource materials are valuable to researchers and businesspeople. Member-nations of OECD seek answers to common problems and work to coordinate domestic and international policies.

The OECD has been instrumental in many areas, including encouraging member-nations to eliminate bribery, to establish a code of conduct for multinational companies, and to propose the adoption of specific legislation. The Business and Industry Advisory Committee (BIAC) of OECD, created in 1962 to represent business and industry, works in various areas that concern business, such as trade liberalization, sustainable development, e-commerce, taxation, and biotechnology. Information about the BIAC can be found at www.biac.org.

OTHER ECONOMIC INSTITUTIONS

There are many other international institutions whose basic purpose is an economic one. Here we look at two of them that have considerable influence on international business, the Organization of Petroleum Exporting Countries (OPEC) and the Group of Eight (G8).

Organization of Petroleum Exporting Countries
Realizing that if the oil-exporting countries were united they could bargain more effectively with the large oil companies, Iran and Venezuela in 1959 joined the existing Arab Petroleum Congress at a meeting in Cairo. Discussions and secret agreements at that meeting became the seeds for OPEC.[20]

Early in 1960, the Venezuelan minister of mines and hydrocarbons and the Saudi oil minister wrote to the oil companies operating in Venezuela and the Middle East, requesting that they consult with the host governments before making any price changes. In August 1960, the oil companies reduced oil prices, and the host governments reported that they learned of this price reduction only when they read about it in the newspapers. That they had not been consulted angered them and increased their anxiety about their control and conservation of their country's natural resources. In that atmosphere, they called a meeting in Baghdad. Attending the meeting were representatives of Iran, Iraq, Kuwait, Saudi Arabia, and Venezuela. The

Organization of Petroleum Exporting Countries (OPEC) was formed, and the OPEC members took charge of pricing in order to control their valuable domestic natural resource.

Of the 11 OPEC member-nations today, all are developing economies. Most are in the Middle East (Iran, Iraq, Kuwait, Qatar, Saudi Arabia, and United Arab Emirates), but three are in Africa (Algeria, Libya, and Nigeria) and two are elsewhere in the world (Indonesia and Venezuela). There are other large oil-exporting countries (such as Mexico, Norway, Russia, and the United Kingdom) that are not members of OPEC.

OPEC's economic strength became evident to the oil-importing world in late 1973 and early 1974 through an oil embargo by its Arab members against the Netherlands and the United States, accompanied by very large price increases to all customers. Its strength stemmed from the comparative cohesiveness of the members and from its control of 68 percent of the world's known petroleum reserves.[21] OPEC supplied 84 percent of Europe's oil needs and over 90 percent of Japan's.[22]

Using its strength, OPEC drove up petroleum prices from about $3 a barrel (42 gallons) in 1973 to close to $35 in 1980. Such a drastic increase in energy prices caused recession and unemployment in oil-importing countries. It also sparked conservation measures and increased oil exploration in non-OPEC countries, along with research into alternative energy sources. Thanks to those initiatives, OPEC's market weakened, but its members refused to cut their production and an oversupply developed. OPEC had control of pricing in the mid-1970s, but by the early 1980s the free markets were setting prices, with major markets in Rotterdam, New York, and Chicago.[23] OPEC's control of the market has been diluted by the huge oil and gas projects being developed in Kazakhstan, Azerbaijan, and Russia.

The OPEC share of the world supply of oil in 2004 was 40 percent, compared with just over 20 percent in 1984. In addition, sustained low oil prices through the first half of 2005 weakened conservation efforts and made exploration, investment, and extraction less attractive. Oil sold at $42.32 a barrel in June 2004, but by August 2005 the price had jumped to over $60 a barrel, and in April 2006 it hit $75.35. Contributing to these high prices are the political instability in the Middle East, including the war in Iraq; Iran's nuclear crisis; hurricane disruptions to refining capability and oil platforms; Venezuelan political instability; political crises in West Africa; and increasing demand in developing countries such as China, India, and Indonesia.[24] At the same time, terrorism being exported from some of the oil-producing nations adds to the general instability. There is also the possibility that prices are reflecting a peak in the supply of this nonrenewable fossil fuel. Table 4.3 shows refined petroleum product consumption by region or country from 1960 through 2004. Consumption in developing countries continues to increase.

The Group of Eight (G8)   The **Group of Eight (G8)** developed from a small group of industrial countries whose economies were profoundly affected by the 1973 oil crisis and the recession to which it led. Financial officials from the United States, Europe, and Japan

TABLE 4.3	World Refined Petroleum Products Consumption by Region, 1960–2004 (1000 b/d)					
	1960	**1970**	**1980**	**1990**	**2000**	**2004**
North America	10,035.0	15,204.2	18,839.4	18,369.0	21,407.9	22,857.8
Latin America	1,424.7	2,699.8	4,267.2	4,944.6	6,435.0	6,452.4
Eastern Europe	2,167.4	6,028.5	10,350.2	9,739.4	4,862.9	4,932.3
Western Europe	3,690.9	11,695.4	13,435.4	12,632.9	13,865.9	14,189.8
Middle East	231.5	510.7	1,694.5	2,582.4	3,873.3	4,603.6
Africa	323.3	631.0	1,339.0	1,778.3	2,219.8	2,506.1
Asia and Pacific	1,453.1	6,623.0	10,000.0	12,935.9	19,667.8	22,400.0
Total World	**19,775.9**	**43,392.6**	**59,925.6**	**62,982.5**	**72,332.5**	**77,942.1**
OPEC	317.7	651.6	2,480.4	3,808.3	5,102.4	6,000.2
OPEC percentage	1.6	1.5	4.1	6.0	7.1	7.7

met to discuss global financial issues. The French then proposed a regular meeting of such a group, forming the G6—France, West Germany, the United Kingdom, Italy, Japan, and the United States—in 1975. Canada joined these meetings the following year, forming the G7. After the end of the cold war, Russia joined the meetings, first provisionally (G7+1) and then as a regular member (G8). An extension to the G8 includes discussions held after the G8 meetings by finance ministers of the G8+5 (South Africa, Brazil, China, Mexico, and India). In addition, a G8 summit is held annually for heads of state. There are some meetings in which Russia does not participate, though, due to its economic and democratic instability. At these meetings, the group consists of finance ministers and is still known as the G7.[25] Neither the G7 nor the G8 has a permanent staff or budget. The government of the country that is hosting the summit in a given year also provides facilities for other G7 and G8 meetings during that year.

Discussion areas in the G8 meetings have also expanded. They now include topics of global concern and involve government officials concerned with health, the environment, safety, law enforcement, development, and other areas that present issues of mutual concern. For example, in June 2005, the G8 interior and justice ministers agreed at a meeting to create an international database on pedophiles. Cooperation on terrorism is also a focus area for various ministers of the G8 countries.

The G8 meetings have been the focus of substantial antiglobalization protest, especially those in Genoa, Italy, in 2001. One of the main points of criticism is the impact that trade among G8 nations has on developing nations. The United Nations Development Program's *Human Development Report 2005* illustrates that the OECD countries, a larger group closely aligned with the G8, represent over two-thirds of the total world economy.[26] Because the OECD nations tend to trade with each other, developing nations lose potential development opportunities. Seen from a developing nation perspective, the G8 can appear to be a relatively closed trade alliance among the wealthy countries. Other points of criticism concern carbon emissions and global warming, poverty, and the developed nations' lack of adequate response to the AIDS crisis.[27] The G8 is responsive to the underlying issues of global poverty, trade, health, and environmental issues but not responsive enough to satisfy its critics, who may have grouped reasonable criticisms with more general—and emotional—criticisms of globalization.

As with international political institutions, the activities of international institutions whose purpose is primarily economic have significant impacts on international business. In the next section, we examine another type of institution whose activities influence the conduct of international business. Basically economic in nature, it is formed by nations that agree to move toward unified economic integration.

FIGURE 4.5

The G8 Members
(www.undp.org)

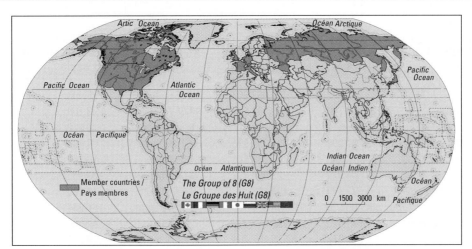

Source: Original map data provided by The Atlas of Canada. Produced under licence from Her Majesty the Queen in Right of Canada, with permission of Natural Resources Canada. http://atlas.nrcan.gc.ca/site/english/maps/reference/international/g8/map.jpg.

Economic Integration

Since the end of World War II, cooperation among nations has increased substantially. Often, the cooperation begins with a free trade area, develops into a customs union, and then evolves into a common market, and eventually the group may move toward complete economic integration. Such trading blocs are important for international businesspeople because they can greatly reduce costs to those inside the integrated area— through reduced tariffs, quotas, and other trade barriers—and increase costs to those outside it. Figure 4.6 compares the relative sizes of the major trading blocs and trading nations.

free trade area (FTA)
Area in which tariffs among members have been eliminated, but members keep their external tariffs

In a **free trade area (FTA)** tariffs are abolished among the members of the FTA, but each member-nation maintains its own external tariffs, those to countries in the rest of the world. So members have free trade among themselves but have their own trade restrictions with non-member nations. Within the FTA, restrictions generally remain on the movement of services (such as accounting, insurance, and legal services), people (labor), and capital. The North American Free Trade Agreement (NAFTA) and the European Free Trade Association (EFTA) are examples of FTAs.

customs Union
Collaboration that adds common external tariffs to an FTA

A **customs union** adds common external tariffs to the FTA. This is a logical extension of the FTA: There are no tariffs between countries in the customs union, and the tariffs charged by member-nations to the rest of the world are consistent among the member-nations. Examples are the South African Customs Union (South Africa, Lesotho, Namibia, Swaziland, and Botswana); Mercosur, the Common Market of the South (Argentina, Brazil, Paraguay, and Uruguay); and the Andean Community (Peru, Venezuela, Equador, Bolivia, and Colombia).

common Market
Customs union that includes mobility of services, people, and capital within the union

A **common market** is a customs union that has no restrictions on the mobility of services, people, and capital among the member-nations. Mercosur hopes to develop in this direction. The EU has developed beyond a common market and is moving toward **complete economic integration.** Such integration involves a high degree of political integration as well, as member-nations surrender certain important elements of their sovereignty. A central bureaucracy at the EU is responsible for coordinating and harmonizing tax rates, labor systems, education systems, and other social and legal systems for all EU members, while monetary policy is developed by the European Central Bank. A single currency, the euro, has been established to replace member-nations' currencies. Let's take a closer look at some of these efforts toward economic integration.

complete economic integration
Integration on both economic and political levels

NORTH AMERICAN FREE TRADE AGREEMENT

The **North American Free Trade Agreement (NAFTA)** created a free trade area among Canada, Mexico, and the United States that came into existence on January 1, 1994. NAFTA is intended to provide a framework to promote free trade among the three North American

FIGURE 4.6

Regional Trading Blocs and Major Trading Nations

Regional bloc	Area (sq km)	Population	GDP (US$)	GDP per capita	Members
EU	3,976,372	456,953,258	12.18 trillion	28,100	25
NAFTA	21,609,740	438,992,672	14.56 trillion	33,166	3
China	9,596,960	1,313,973,713	8.18 trillion	6,300	—
India	3,287,590	1,095,351,995	3.7 trillion	3,400	—
Russia	17,075,200	142,893,540	1.54 trillion	10,700	—
Canada	9,984,670	33,098,932	1.08 trillion	32,900	—
Mexico	1,972,550	107,449,525	1.07 trillion	10,100	—
ASEAN	4,400,000	553,900,000	2.172 trillion	4,044	10
United States	9,631,420	298,444,215	12.41 trillion	42,000	—
World	510.072 million	6,525,107,264	59.6 trillion GWP	9,300	

Source: CIA Factbook, www.cia.gov/cia/publications/factbook/, 2006.

signatories. Unlike the UN, the EU, and the WTO, NAFTA operates as part of the national law of each member-country.

The original 1988 debate in Canada over whether that country should join the United States in a bilateral agreement to promote trade was contentious. Proponents, including Prime Minister Brian Mulroney, argued that the agreement would be good for Canada and that free trade would open up large markets to the south to Canadian businesses. Opponents argued that Canadians would lose jobs and Canada would lose its national identity by approving the agreement. Some feared that the agreement would lead to the elimination of the border between Canada and the United States. Prime Minister Mulroney's party won the election, and the Canadian Parliament approved the agreement. The United States–Canada Free Trade Agreement proved so successful that both nations wanted to expand it to include Mexico and possibly other nations at a later date. Many also believed that opening markets in Mexico to U.S. interests would raise the standard of living and the wage rate of the citizens of Mexico. An improvement in the economy would increase Mexico's ability to retain valuable members of the work force who otherwise would be attracted by a higher wage rate in the United States. Discussions among the three nations were successful, and the agreement was presented to the elected officials in each country for approval. Despite fierce opposition from organized labor and some politicians, the negotiations succeeded and the national legislatures of Canada, Mexico, and the United States approved the NAFTA treaty. NAFTA was the first major trade agreement to include labor and environmental side agreements, topics that are now routinely included in trade deals.

Over the past 12 years, NAFTA has paved the way for strong economic growth and prosperity based on liberalized trade among the three nations. The U.S. trade representative, who participates on the NAFTA Trade Commission along with the Mexican secretary of the economy and the Canadian minister of international Trade, claims that NAFTA has delivered important benefits to consumers, businesses, workers, and farmers throughout North America.[28] Through NAFTA, the three countries have created the world's largest free trade zone—one of the most powerful productive forces in the global economy. NAFTA is expected to enourage continued growth in trade and investment flows, which lead to increased competitiveness and prosperity. In 2008, tariff liberalization is scheduled to be completed, and trade in North America will be virtually tariff-free.

The U.S. Department of Commerce reports substantial evidence across the United States, Canada, and Mexico that NAFTA has allowed firms to maximize efficiencies, remain globally competitive, and, as a result, increase sales and exports:[29]

- From 1993 to 2005, trade among NAFTA nations climbed 173 percent, from $297 billion to $810 billion. That's $2.2 billion in trilateral trade every day.

- U.S. merchandise exports to NAFTA grew at 133 percent, compared to growth in exports to the rest of the world, at 77 percent.

- Canada and Mexico are the largest export markets for the United States, totaling 36 percent of the U.S. export growth.

- In agriculture, Canada and Mexico account for 55 percent of the U.S. export growth since 1993.

- In real GDP, NAFTA nations have moved forward briskly, with growth from 1993 to 2005 for the United States at 48 percent, for Mexico at 40 percent, and for Canada at 49 percent.

Despite such positive results, the three nations have had serious and long-term trade disputes within NAFTA. One of the longest-standing ones is between the United States and Canada. The softwood lumber dispute actually predates NAFTA, but Canada brought its charge against the United States to a bi-national NAFTA review panel, a mechanism established for dispute settlement, in 2005 and again, to another panel, in 2006, as well as to the World Trade Organization. In May 2002 the United States had imposed tariffs of 27 percent on Canadian softwood exports to the United States, claiming that the Canadian lumber producers were unfairly subsidized by their government. The allegation was that

North American Free Trade Agreement (NAFTA)
Agreement creating a free trade area among Canada, Mexico, and the United States

While NAFTA has had some positive results, controversy among member nations has continued. One of the longest debates was the softwood lumber dispute between the United States and Canada. After the United States imposed 27 percent tariffs on Canadian softwood lumber exports, Canada brought its complaint to both NAFTA and the WTO. When both panels ruled in favor of Canada, in 2006 the United States finally agreed to return most of the duties it had collected.

the fee Canadian producers pay the government to log public land, called a *stumpage fee*, was low and amounted to a subsidy when compared to what logging public land costs U.S. producers. In the United States, logging rights are auctioned at market values. In 2005 and again in 2006, NAFTA panels and the WTO ruled in favor of Canada, concluding that the figures supporting the U.S. claim were based on U.S. market realities, not Canadian. Finally, in 2006, the United States agreed to return to Canada 80 percent of the $5 billion in duties that U.S. Customs had collected.[30]

There are some serious noneconomic concerns about NAFTA, but many of them have abated as, over the past 12 years, the agreement's economic benefits have become clearer. One concern is that Mexico meet the NAFTA mandate to raise environmental standards to the level of those in the United States. To address these issues, two side agreements to NAFTA established the North American Commission for Environmental Cooperation and the North American Development Bank. They work together to develop and fund projects to support Mexican environmental protection and the development of infrastructure.[31]

Another area of concern is the increase in illegal immigration from Mexico to the United States since the implementation of NAFTA. Commercial farming in Mexico has been successful under NAFTA, and this development has forced up to 2.5 million peasant farmers off the land they were farming. In a sense, NAFTA actually may mean the end of peasant agriculture in Mexico, which was organized as subsistence collectives.[32] Many of the illegal immigrants are peasants who are economic exiles to the United States. The noneconomic cost of such land redistribution splits families and creates severe pressures for traditional rural agriculture.

Many in the United States, the Caribbean, and throughout Latin America want to extend NAFTA to include other countries in the free trade area. Chile was mentioned as a possible candidate for initial expansion and the parties started discussions, but enthusiasm for these efforts has faded. Presently Colombia is taking the initiative for consultations among 34 nations of the Americas that have expressed interest in the Free Trade Agreement of the Americas (FTAA). The many areas in which to build agreements among the potential members include market access, government agricultural policy, competition policy, intellectual property rights, investment policy, trade in services, subsidies, and antidumping policies. There also needs to be agreement on how to monitor compliance and how to adjudicate noncompliance.

EUROPEAN FREE TRADE AGREEMENT

European Free Trade Agreement (EFTA)
Four-nation non-EU FTA in Europe

The **European Free Trade Agreement (EFTA)** was founded in 1960 by seven European countries: Austria, Denmark, Norway, Portugal, Sweden, Switzerland, and the United Kingdom. Finland joined in 1961, Iceland in 1970, and Liechtenstein in 1991. In 1973, the UK and Denmark moved to the European Community, an earlier version of the European Union. They were followed by Portugal, Austria, Finland, and Sweden. The four EFTA members today are Iceland, Lichtenstein, Norway, and Switzerland. Their free trade agreement focuses on goods rather than services or labor. EFTA has also negotiated a series of trade agreements with other countries and trading blocs, including Eastern European and Mediterranean countries and Mexico, Chile, and Singapore, and has established bilateral trade agreements with the EU. In that sense, it is evolving toward a customs union, with common external trade policies. Increasingly, though, EFTA's internal agreements have addressed services, the movement of persons, transportation, and technical barriers to trade.

AFRICAN TRADE AGREEMENTS

To promote economic growth throughout the continent, African countries have formed regional trade groups. Many of them are in the negotiation stages. Most African countries, though, have their main trade relationships with developed countries, in many cases with former colonial powers. Except for South Africa, African economies are small and underdeveloped, and governments face daunting challenges: infrastructure development; public health needs connected to HIV/AIDS, tuberculosis, and malaria; corruption; and insurgencies and civil wars. The unstable environment is not conducive to economic growth, yet the collaborations persevere. Three of these groups are the *Economic Community of West African States (ECOWAS)*, the *Common Market for Eastern and Southern Africa (COMESA)*, and the *Southern African Development Community (SADC)*. Figure 4.7 includes their locations and member-nations. A new group has recently formed that may be able to build an institution that would provide solid trade benefits to its members. The *African Union (AU)* was established in 1999 to replace the Organization of African Unity (OAU), whose goals had focused on moving forward from colonization and apartheid. AU has 53 members and is modeled on the European Union. Its long-term goals, outlined on its Web site (www.au.org), include social and political initiatives as well as economic integration.

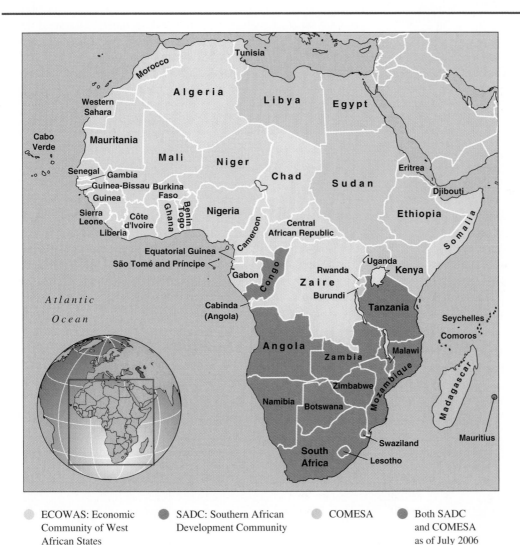

FIGURE 4.7

African Trade Agreements

ECOWAS: Economic Community of West African States

SADC: Southern African Development Community

COMESA

Both SADC and COMESA as of July 2006

MERCOSUR (MERCOSUL)

Mercosur (Mercosul)

Economic free trade area in South America modeled on the EU

Mercosur (Spanish) or *Mercosul* (Portuguese) is an acronym for Mercado Commun del Sur, or Common Market of the South. **Mercosur** was created in 1991 by the Treaty of Asunción, which united Argentina, Brazil, Paraguay, and Uruguay in an effort to create a common market. Venezuela has been accepted as a new member, to take effect in late 2006, and Bolivia has been invited to join. (See Figure 4.8.) Mercosur's purpose is to develop a common market; the alliance has made progress, and it is growing. Most trade within Mercosur is tariff-free. A common external tariff has been adopted on most products, but Mercosur has not yet become a customs union.

Since its inception, trade within Mercosur has grown rapidly, at an average of 27 percent a year, while trade with the rest of the world has expanded at an annual rate of 7.5 percent. Yet there is poor infrastructure (e.g., inadequate roads and bridges) in the member-nations, and the case has been made that by setting high external tariffs and thus insulating themselves from external markets, Mercosur members are allowing inefficiencies that make their production costly, especially for export outside Mercosur. At one point fairly recently, both Brazil and Argentina were believed to be able to lead Latin America out of its economic problems, but both major countries have undergone several years of severe economic challenges.

FIGURE 4.8

Regional Trade Agreements in Central America and South America

Andean Community • Central American Free Trade Zone • Mercosur • None

These problems will hinder Mercosur's future. In addition, Argentina and Uruguay have a serious border dispute. At issue is the construction of two cellulose factories, one Spanish and the other Finnish, on the river that forms their border. Argentina closed bridge access to Uruguay so that delivery of construction materials was hampered.[33] Late in the spring of 2006, Bolivia's socialist president nationalized the oil and gas industry in his country, encouraged by Venezuela's leader, Hugo Chavez. Brazil, as the largest consumer of Bolivian gas, is the main victim of Bolivia's decision to nationalize. Brazilians may pay up to 60 percent more for gas.[34] Relationships among the nations of Mercosur appear to be in considerable disarray.

CENTRAL AMERICAN FREE TRADE AGREEMENT

The United States and Guatemala, Honduras, Nicaragua, and El Salvador concluded an agreement in late 2003 establishing the **Central American Free Trade Agreement (CAFTA)**, which Costa Rica and the Dominican Republic later joined. (See Figure 4.8.) CAFTA opens all public services to private investment, grants guarantees to foreign investment, and opens government procurement to transnational bids. It also provides market access as a result of government pledges to reduce and eventually eliminate tariffs and other measures, including protectionist barriers in all sectors, that protect domestic products. CAFTA has agreed to duty-free imports and elimination of subsidies on agricultural products, the protection of intellectual property rights, antidumping rules, and the right of transnationals to sue countries in private international courts.

> **Central American Free Trade Agreement (CAFTA)**
> FTA among the United States and several Central American nations

CAFTA has created the second-largest U.S. export market in Latin America. In 2004, the United States exported more to these six countries ($16 billion) than to Russia, India, and Indonesia combined.[35] U.S. export growth to the CAFTA region has outperformed overall U.S. exports. From 2000 to 2004, export shipments to CAFTA destinations grew by almost 16 percent, compared with less than 5 percent for overall U.S. exports.

OTHER CENTRAL AND SOUTH AMERICAN TRADE AGREEMENTS

The **Andean Community (CAN)**, whose members are Colombia, Peru, Ecuador, Bolivia, and Venezuela (see Figure 4.8), is presently in a crisis over Venezuela's decision to withdraw from the community. Venezuela's President, Hugo Chavez, announced his country's withdrawal in the spring of 2006 because other Andean Community members, Colombia and Peru, had signed trade deals with the United States and are, in his view, "overly aligned with the U.S."[36]

> **Andean Community (CAN)**
> South American five-nation trading bloc

The *Organization of American States (OAS)*, headquartered in Washington, D.C., is an organization of countries in the Western Hemisphere dedicated to promoting democracy and cooperation in the region. The OAS was formed in 1948 with the United States as one of the original 21 countries, but its origins date back to 1890, when the First International Conference of American States, held in Washington, D.C., established the International Union of American Republics. Today all 35 independent countries of the Americas have ratified the charter and are members of OAS. Even though Cuba is a member of the OAS, in 1962 the organization excluded the Cuban government from participation in its activities. The OAS focus has been on fostering democracy, protecting human rights, strengthening security, fostering free trade, combating illegal drugs, and fighting corruption.[37]

ASIA-PACIFIC ECONOMIC COOPERATION

In response to the growing importance of the economies of the Pacific Rim countries, the *Asia-Pacific Economic Cooperation (APEC)* was established in 1989 to serve as a regional vehicle for promoting open trade and practical economic cooperation. The United States is one of the 21 current members. APEC is a nontreaty organization whose decisions are reached by consensus and are nonbinding. Information about APEC can be found at its Web site, www.apec.org.

The European Union, our next focus, has developed from an institution with an economic purpose, a common market, to one with an added political purpose.

The European Union

European Union (EU)
A body of 25 European countries dedicated to economic and political integration

The **European Union** is an institution of 25 independent countries that have committed to develop close economic and political cooperation. The EU began as a customs union; developed into a common market, known as the European Community (EC) or European Economic Community (EEC); and now is substantially integrated economically and is well on the way to political integration. The EU's movement toward monetary integration is a huge step forward for both economic and political cooperation. So far 12 EU members use the EU currency, the euro (€), forming the euro zone. Slovenia was granted entry into the euro zone in 2007. Of the 15 EU countries that were members at the time the euro was introduced, only the United Kingdom, Denmark, and Sweden have not joined the euro zone.

EU BACKGROUND

World War II left Europe in shambles, with damage not only to physical structures from direct fighting but also to the economic, political, and social infrastructure from the necessity of devoting almost all resources and investments to the war effort. The war devastated people's lives along with buildings, railroads, highways, and businesses. Europeans found themselves with the enormous task of rebuilding European society—economically, politically, and culturally—and as they began, there was concern throughout the continent that the previous economic and political systems had failed. Out of this concern slowly developed a willingness to relinquish certain aspects of national sovereignty for the greater economic and political good.

While most Europeans understood the need to establish national democracies and free-market economies, many argued for greater continentwide cooperation as the way to peace. Much of the support for European unity came from resistance movements formed during the war. Resistance fighters had put aside their devotion to a political ideology to join others fighting for a common objective. One of the most ardent proponents of a united Europe was the Italian resistance fighter Altiero Spinelli. In 1944, Spinelli argued for "a federal Europe with a written constitution, a supranational government directly responsible to the people of Europe and not national governments, along with an army under its control, with no other military forces being permitted."[38] The end of the war, though, brought many changes in Europe, and with those changes, support for a "United States of Europe" waned. Exiled or imprisoned political leaders reemerged in their respective countries. Ideological and traditional divisions between socialists, communists, and conservatives that had been put aside during the resistance movement resurfaced. The emergence of the cold war and the resulting division of Europe helped blur the vision of a united Europe. Many of the proponents of greater European unity, including Britain's Winston Churchill, lost political power in their own nations. In addition to these factors, as a practical matter, many Europeans were concerned not with debates about politics and economics but with basic problems such as food supplies, fuel, shelter, and physical reconstruction. Thinking in terms of grand European unification was difficult when there was little food.

In 1950, Robert Schuman, the French foreign minister, proposed a united Europe, beginning with the integration of the coal and steel industries. The European Coal and Steel Community (ECSC) initially had six members—Belgium, West Germany, France, Italy, Luxembourg, and the Netherlands—held together by the Treaty of Paris. Continued integration led to the Treaty of Rome in 1957, which established a common market among the six members. By 1967, this core group had established the European Community (EC), with a European Parliament, a European Commission, and a Council of Ministers.

Early EU history shows that European integration was largely a continental European movement. Even though Winston Churchill in 1945 called for the building of a kind of United States of Europe, the United Kingdom did not join the European integration process until 1973. The United Kingdom had delayed because of its concerns about associating with its longtime adversary, France, and about losing its status as a world power by becoming an equal with other European nations.

FIGURE 4.9   European Union: Current Member-Nations and Candidate Nations

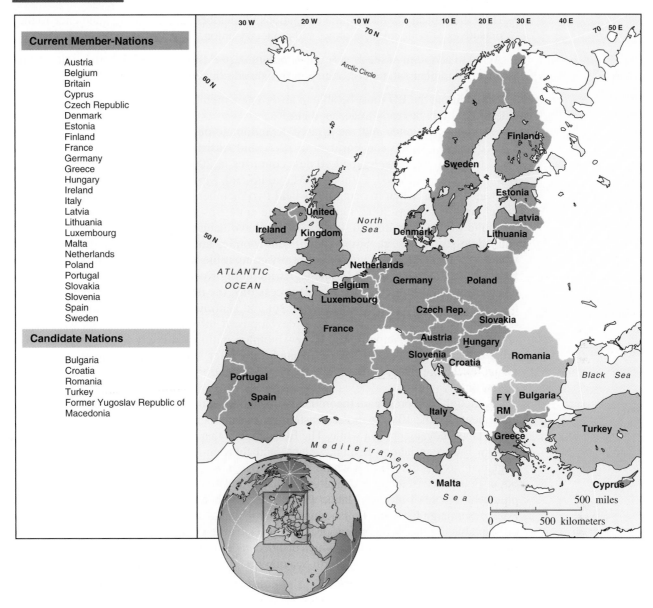

Current Member-Nations

Austria
Belgium
Britain
Cyprus
Czech Republic
Denmark
Estonia
Finland
France
Germany
Greece
Hungary
Ireland
Italy
Latvia
Lithuania
Luxembourg
Malta
Netherlands
Poland
Portugal
Slovakia
Slovenia
Spain
Sweden

Candidate Nations

Bulgaria
Croatia
Romania
Turkey
Former Yugoslav Republic of Macedonia

Source: European Union, http://europa.eu.int/abc/maps/print_index_en.htm, August 2, 2004 © European Communities, 1995–2004.

EU GROWTH

The EU has grown in size, with successive waves of accessions, to 25 member-countries, creating one body that includes most of the economic, industrial, and population strengths of Europe. Its highly educated population is presently 457 million people, far larger than the United States' population of 298.5 million, and it accounts for 42 percent of world merchandise trade.[39]

Any European country may apply for EU membership if it respects the principles of liberty, democracy, respect for human rights and fundamental freedoms, and the rule of law, principles that are common to the member-states. Accession, however, can follow only if the given country fulfills all the required criteria . Specifically, the country must:

- Have stable political institutions guaranteeing democracy, the rule of law, human rights, and respect for protection of minorities.

- Have a functioning market economy and the capacity to cope with competition and market forces in the EU.

- Have the capacity to take on the obligations of membership, including adherence to the objectives of political, economic, and monetary union.

- Agree to adoption of the *acquis communautaire* (the entire European legislation) and its effective implementation through appropriate administrative and judicial structures.

In addition, the EU must be able to absorb new members, so it reserves the right to decide when it will be ready to accept them.[40]

Denmark, Ireland, and the United Kingdom joined the EU in 1973, followed by Greece in 1981, Spain and Portugal in 1986, and Austria, Finland, and Sweden in 1995. The European Union welcomed 10 new countries in 2004: Cyprus, the Czech Republic, Estonia, Hungary, Latvia, Lithuania, Malta, Poland, Slovakia, and Slovenia. In 2006, the EU was debating when to bring in its next two members, Bulgaria and Romania, whose initial target date was 2007. Other candidate countries are Croatia, the former Yugoslav Republic of Macedonia, and Turkey, which have been approved for accession with an entry date still to be set. Some EU citizens wonder how far the EU should extend and whether a Muslim country will be culturally compatible with the EU. Albania, Bosnia and Herzegovina, and Serbia and Montenegro, including Kosovo, are potential candidates for EU membership. In the 2004 round of accessions, the new members, except Cyprus and Malta, were recent converts from socialism and centrally planned economies. The EU's enlargement process has guided their development into market economies with democratic governments. Actually, the 10 new member-nations add only 5 percent to the EU's gross domestic product. On the other hand, they offer low wages, low taxes, and undervalued exchange rates, which make them good locations for manufacturing and service operations.[41]

Although EU borders are theoretically open to the movement of labor, the EU accession agreements for the 10 new, mostly Eastern European, members included provisions to hold off on labor movement for a while. The EU members that have opened their borders fully to Eastern European labor—Britain, Ireland, and Sweden—have benefited greatly from enlargement, as has the EU as a whole.[42] A French campaign to keep Eastern European labor out of France focused on the dangers of Polish plumbers taking French jobs, making Polish plumbers a symbol of cheap labor. Poland's tourist board countered with a playful visit-Poland campaign featuring Polish plumbers who plan to stay in Poland.

Notable are the Western European countries that have rejected membership in the EU, Switzerland and Norway, both of which decided not to join on the basis of national elections. Norway's economy is based on North Sea oil reserves, and Switzerland has valued its role as a neutral country for a long time.

EVOLVING PURPOSE OF THE EU

The EU is a supranational body in that its governance transcends *(supra)* the national level; it is a regional government. In order to join the EU, member-nations cede some of their sovereignty to this larger body. The supranational status of the EU makes the EU different from other international organizations, such as the United Nations, and from treaties, such as the North American Free Trade Agreement (NAFTA). Because of its supranational status, the EU has certain powers that the UN and NAFTA lack. For example, it can tax member-nations directly and implement legislation directly in each of the member-nations, much as in the United States, where Congress has the power to enact legislation that has a direct effect in each of the states. The EU also has a court, the European Court of Justice, with the power to impose fines and other sanctions on individuals, companies, and even member-nations that violate the Treaty of Rome.

As originally established in the 1950s, European integration was limited to economic issues. In the 1957 Treaty of Rome, which still serves as the fundamental law of the EU, members sought to achieve four fundamental freedoms: movement of goods, services, capital, and people across national borders. Today, goods, services, capital, and people are able to move freely among most member-nations of the EU, with few negotiated limitations. For example, a citizen of the United Kingdom has the right to work in Greece without any additional approval from the Greek government. A dentist in Madrid can move to Berlin without any additional licensing or exams. This freedom of movement is in sharp contrast to the same situation under NAFTA: a citizen of Mexico must obtain the proper visa in order to work legally in the United States.

As the EU developed, it began to include monetary and political integration as well as economic. The development of a common foreign policy, security policy, approach to justice, and monetary union was initiated by the Maastricht Treaty of 1992. This treaty calls for the EU "to assert its identity on the international scene, in particular through the implementation of a common foreign and security policy including the eventual framing of a common defense policy, which might in time lead to a common defense." A common agricultural policy has developed to support food production and protection of the environment throughout the EU. Passport and customs checks have been abolished at most EU country internal borders.[43] The euro currency has been adopted in 12 of the original 15 EU member-countries, with the 10 new accession nations trying hard to meet the economic criteria to join this currency union. The Maastricht Treaty also established the European Central Bank to develop and implement monetary policy for the euro area.

Another step forward in political integration for the EU is a proposed EU constitution that establishes the EU as subsidiary to the member-states and describes the division of responsibilities, the decision-making process, the foreign and defense policy, the reform process, and a charter of individual rights. This constitution, designed to strengthen the institutional basis of the EU, was agreed to by the European Commission in 2004 but must be ratified by all EU members. (See Figure 4.10.) Spain, Luxembourg, Estonia, Latvia and Lithuania, Slovakia, Slovenia, Hungary, Austria, Italy, Greece, Malta, and Cyprus have ratified it. France and the Netherlands rejected the constitution in 2005. Presently it is on hold while the 25 EU members engage in a period of reflection, but European Commission president Jose Manuel Barroso of Spain describes the situation with some optimism: "We are going into extra time. We are not yet at the stage of penalty shoot-outs."[44]

FIGURE 4.10

EU Constitution: State of the Debate

Source: EU Constitution: Where Member States Stand, http://news.bbe.co.uk/1/hi/world/europe/3954327.stm. Posted 9 May 2006. Accessed 13 May 2006.

Flag of the European Union.

INSTITUTIONS OF THE EU

There are nine main institutions of the EU that perform functions similar to those performed by a national government:[45] the European Parliament, the Council of the European Union, the European Commission, the Court of Justice, the Court of Auditors, the European Economic and Social Committee, the Committee of the Regions, the European Central Banks, and the European Investment Bank. Here we will examine the first four bodies in detail, because they are the most critical, and then briefly describe the roles of the remaining five.

European Parliament
EU legislative body whose members are popularly elected from member-nations

European Parliament The **European Parliament** was first elected in 1979 and is now elected by popular vote throughout Europe every five years. The present EU Parliament was elected in June 2004 and has 732 members from all 25 EU countries. Parliament members are seated by political party affiliation rather than by their country. This party identification underscores the nature of the EU as a European rather than a national institution. Seven parties are presently represented, the largest representation going to the center-right European People's Party (Christian Democrats), followed by the Socialist Party, the Liberal Party, and the Green Party. The European Parliament holds its sessions in Strasbourg, France. The main function of the Parliament is to pass European laws, and it is widely seen as the voice of the European people in the EU. Parliamentary sessions are available live at www.europarl.europa.eu.

Council of the European Union
Group that is the EU's primary policy-setting institution

Council of the European Union The **Council of the European Union** is the primary policy-setting institution of the EU and is the voice of the member-states. This is where important decisions are made on common foreign policy and security issues. The ministers who make up the Council are members of their respective national governments. Generally, when the Council meets, the minister who represents the area being discussed serves as the representative of that country. When financial matters are discussed, for example, the finance ministers of all countries are present. When agricultural matters are discussed, agricultural ministers are present. The presidency of the Council rotates among the member-nations, with each one holding the presidency for six months. So when the United Kingdom holds the presidency, the United Kingdom's prime minister is effectively the head of government of the EU. Each country has votes based on population, although the weighting favors the smaller countries. Sensitive issues before the Council such as immigration policy, security and defense policy, and foreign policy require unanimous votes to pass, and most other issues require majority vote. Here is the vote distribution:[46]

Germany, France, Italy, United Kingdom	29
Spain, Poland	27
Netherlands	13
Belgium, Czech Republic, Greece, Hungary, Portugal	12
Austria, Sweden	10
Denmark, Ireland, Lithuania, Slovakia, Finland	7
Cyprus, Estonia, Latvia, Luxembourg, Slovenia	4
Malta	3
Total	321

The Council presidency rotates among members in a predetermined sequence, with each holding the position for a six-month term. From 2007 through 2011, the rotation is Germany, Portugal, Slovenia, France, Czech Republic, Sweden, Spain, Belgium, Hungary, and Poland.

The president sets the agenda and the location of any meetings, so holding the presidency is quite important and the president has great power to influence EU policy decisions.

The Council's decisions are set forth in regulations and directives. Recent directives deal with foreign policy issues (support for elections in the Congo, declarations on Darfur, relations with other trading blocs such as Mercosur), issues of health and safety (bird flu precautions, disaster planning, workplace safety equipment, computer use rules, and environmental safety for workers), and issues related to terrorism. The Council has come under some criticism for its power relative to the other EU institutions and even to the national parliaments.[47] One frequently voiced concern is that the Council's decisions are not reviewed or evaluated through any democratic process.

European Commission   The **European Commission** is the executive institution and represents the interests of Europe as a whole. It administers the daily operations of the EU and ensures implementation of the provisions of the Treaty of Rome. In addition, the European Commission drafts laws that it presents to the European Parliament and the Council. The Commission consists of 25 commissioners, one from each member-nation. Commission members are nominated by their countries, appointed by the Commission president-elect, and then approved by a vote of the European Parliament. The present commissioners serve with Commission president Jose Manuel Barroso from 2004 to 2009, when his term expires.

European Commission
Institution that runs the EU's day-to-day operations

European Court of Justice   The **European Court of Justice (ECJ)** decides cases arising under the Treaty of Rome. On EU matters, its authority supersedes that of the member-nations' national courts. The influence of the ECJ is growing steadily as it is deciding an increasing number of cases. In addition, many decisions in the EU are now made by the EU Court of First Instance in the various member-nations, which has more limited jurisdiction than the ECJ. The responsibilities of the Court of First Instance include claims made in several areas of interest to businesspeople: competition, commercial policy, regional policy, social policy, institutional law, trademark law, and transport.

European Court of Justice (ECJ)
Court that rules on issues related to EU policies

Other EU Institutions   The remaining five EU institutions focus on financial and social issues. The *Court of Auditors* is the financial conscience of the EU. It reviews the spending of EU funds to make sure they are spent legally and for the intended purpose. EU funding is tax-based and includes the value-added tax (VAT), customs duties, and other fees paid by member-states. The 2005 EU budget amounted to $0.64 per day per citizen of the EU.[48] The *European Economic and Social Committee (EESC)* is an advisory and consultative body of specialists in areas of occupational and social interest groups. The 317 members are divided by member population size and represent employers, employees, and other social interests. Members are nominated by national governments to serve four-year terms. The *Committee of the Regions (CoR)* is a consultative group that represents local viewpoints on issues such as transportation, education, and health. Its 317 members are often local government leaders. The CoR ensures that the EU continues its commitment to four levels of participation: local, regional, national, and European. The **European Central Bank (ECB)** manages the euro to ensure the price stability of European markets. Its primary concern is to manage inflation, and it makes decisions independent of member governments. The *European Investment Bank (EIB)* supports lending programs for projects of interest to the EU, both internal and external. Activities of the EIB include developing infrastructure, such as transportation systems and buildings, especially in less developed regions; supporting small businesses; and lending to member governments.

European Central Bank (ECB)
Institution that sets and implements EU monetary policy

The term "Fortress Europe" has been used by outsiders, including Americans, Japanese, and others, to express their fear that the EU would deny its privileges to them, their companies, and their products.[49] Although such fears persist, with the recent accession of eight former Soviet bloc countries that had centrally planned economies, they are not as compelling.

THE EU GOING FORWARD

EU members cannot agree at present on whether they want to have a centralized federal system with most of the power held by the EU institutions (that is, the Parliament, Council, and Commission). Several members have shown reluctance to surrender their national currencies, central banks, and other powers to a distant authority, particularly an unelected one. Such decisions, represented in a constitution, will take time. After all, there are 25 sovereign nations in the EU—and more want to join—with long, proud histories and national loyalties, cultures, and languages. There have been bitter, bloody wars among them.

But one subject about which there is unhappy agreement is the concern about fraud that plagued the EU through 2004, especially in the area of the agriculture budget, the largest item in the EU budget. The Commission's public image was tarnished by revelation of fraudulently claimed agricultural subsidies by many EU members. The EU response has been impressive. It quickly established the Fraud Prevention Expert Group to investigate and deter fraudulent practices and function as a control group. As a result, the Court of Auditors, which reviews all expenditures, has been able to approve an increased number of payments in farm subsidies and regional development categories, the two largest spending areas. The Court of Auditors approved one-third of all payments in 2005, which is a huge step forward from 2004, when only 6 percent of the spending was approved.[50] The trend toward timely and effective monitoring appears to be in the right direction.

In the June 2004 EU elections, record low voter turnout was recorded across Europe, even in the newly acceded nations. The overall turnout was 44.2 percent, with 20 percent in Slovakia, 21 percent in Poland, and 27 percent in Estonia. (Even so, the election marked the largest democratic election in history, with almost 350 million voters.)[51] This poor voter turnout suggests that the EU is struggling to maintain credibility with its electorate; yet, at the same time, the EU has increased its own power.

EU ACHIEVEMENTS

The countries in the EU have made great strides toward union, and the EU is now a major world political and economic force. EU directives have superseded 25 sets of national rules. They have harmonized 100,000 national standards, labeling laws, testing procedures, and consumer protection measures covering everything from toys to food, stock brokering to teaching. The 25 nations have scrapped as many as 60 million customs and tax formalities at their shared borders. These successes are impressive, and many, Europeans and others, expect even more progress with continued European integration.

European Monetary Union (EMU)

Group that established use of euro (€) in the 12-country euro zone

The **European Monetary Union (EMU)** is one of the most significant agreements to come out of the EU. The euro, in both notes and coins, went into general usage in 12 of the original 15 EU countries on January 1, 2002, with Denmark, Sweden, and the United Kingdom standing outside the EMU. This single currency reduces the cost of doing business across EMU country borders, both because there are no currency exchange costs and because there is now no risk of currency exchange fluctuations among these 12 countries. The Web site for the European Central Bank, which sets monetary policy for the EMU, contains a discussion of the history of the EMU and the adoption of the euro. See www.ecb.int.

THE EU'S IMPACT

The EU increasingly is making its presence known in the world business community. It accounts for roughly 20 percent of world exports and imports and 30 percent of the world's foreign direct investment (FDI). It is the world's largest trading economy and the world's prime source of FDI outflows.

A significant number of EU regulations have an impact in the United States, Japan, China, and elsewhere because of the size of the EU and the importance of the EU as a trading partner. EU rules forced changes by Microsoft in its contracts with software makers and even forced McDonald's to stop serving soft-plastic toys with its Happy Meals. "Twenty years ago, if you designed something to U.S. standards you could pretty much sell it all over the world. Now the shoe's on the other foot," said Maja Wessels, a Brussels-based lobbyist for United Technologies Corporation.[52] For example, in an effort to prevent electrical and electronic equipment waste, the EU requires recycling of at least 50 percent of all such equipment, including cell phones, computers, household appliances, and televisions. It requires 80 percent recovery by weight for larger appliances, 75 percent for IT and telecommunications equipment, and 70 percent for small appliances.[53] In addition, the manufacturers are required to provide collection for the waste that is not from private households.

In fact, today the EU has built the economic force necessary to make many of the rules that influence world trade. Most notably, in 2001 the European Commission voted to veto a proposed merger between two U.S. companies, General Electric and Honeywell, that had been approved by the U.S. Justice Department. "The merger between GE and Honeywell, as it was notified, would have severely reduced competition in the aerospace industry and resulted ultimately in higher prices for customers, particularly airlines," observed EU Competition Commissioner Mario Monti. If the merger had taken place, the $42 billion giant would not have been able to operate in the EU, the largest single market in the world.

Microsoft's practices have also been influenced by the EU. In 2004, the European Commission ordered the company to pay €497 million, share its software code with competitors, and offer an unbundled version of the Windows operating system. Microsoft complied. Then, in 2005, the EU ruled that Microsoft would be fined $2.37 million per day if the software code it provided competitors didn't have better documentation. The point is clear: If foreign companies want access to the EU market, they must conduct business by the European Union's rules.

The three most important trading relationships the EU has, based on the value of trade flows, are those with China, Japan, and the United States. EU trade relations with China have changed dramatically over the last 20 years, going from a sizable trade surplus in the 1980s to a widening deficit with China in the 2000s (around €78.5 billion in 2004); this is the EU's biggest bilateral trade deficit. Overall, China is now the EU's second-largest trading partner after the United States, and the EU became China's largest trading partner in 2004. In recent years, EU companies have invested considerably in China, with total EU FDI at over $35 billion.

The EU trade deficit with China reflects, at least in part, the effect of trade barriers or market access obstacles in China. The EU list of trade barriers its merchants have encountered in China includes barriers in the pharmaceutical, automotive, agricultural and fisheries, chemical, and electronic sectors. EU policy in this area aims at the liberalization of markets, as does the policy of the World Trade Organization. Key objectives include the removal of barriers to imports of specific goods (price controls, discriminatory registration requirements, arbitrary sanitary standards); the removal of obstacles to investment (geographic restrictions, joint venture requirements, discriminatory licensing procedures, outright closure of certain sectors to foreigners, restrictive foreign exchange regulations); and the improvement of the business environment (protection of intellectual property rights).[54]

The EU trade relationship with Japan is one of the central trade relationships in the world. Along with the United States, the EU and Japan are the main pillars of the world economy.[55] Japan and the EU are responsible for 40 percent of world trade, with Japan accounting for 14 percent of that total. The Japanese economy is the largest economy in Asia and the EU's fifth-largest export market and import source. Europe is also an important export market for Japan. What is unusual about Japan is its high savings rate and large foreign currency reserves. Japanese savings total 250 percent of GDP, the highest rate in the world.

The United States and Europe have always enjoyed a well-established commercial relationship, and the increase in European prosperity as a result of the EU's success has made this relationship even stronger. The European Union and the United States are the world's largest economies and each other's largest trading partner. Their combined GDP accounts for approximately 57 percent of world GDP and 40 percent of world trade. In addition, these two economies greatly influence world trade patterns, since either the European Union or the United States is the largest trading partner for most other economies. Many businesses in the United States are realizing the EU's vast potential for trade opportunities. The cross-Atlantic trade flows are running at over €1.7 billion per day. Total foreign direct investment is over €1.5 trillion per year, with the EU being the largest source of FDI for the United States. This is not to say that no disputes occur. They do, but they affect only about 2 percent of the EU-U.S. trade.[56] The trade disputes have been over products as diverse as bananas, beef, and steel.

The EU Web site has a wealth of information in the 11 EU official languages (Danish, Dutch, English, Finnish, French, German, Greek, Italian, Portuguese, Spanish, and Swedish). See www.europa.eu. The EU has a special Web site that focuses on matters of interest concerning EU-U.S. relations and includes information about the EU's trade activities with individual states. See www.eurunion.org.

Summary

Describe the influence the mainly political international institutions have on international businesses and their relevance to international business.

International organizations such as the United Nations, military alliances, and ASEAN can have profound influence on international businesses. By providing a forum for governments to talk to each other, they contribute toward peace and stability, conditions that stimulate international business. Such dialogue also results in collaborative efforts that support multilateral cooperation in areas of immediate concern to business, such as maritime agreements, communication accords, and other rules and standards. In addition, many of these institutions support development projects, which stimulate business directly, through their contracts, and also through their support of the development of markets.

Identify the major organs of the United Nations, their general purpose, and their significance to international business.

The work of the United Nations is carried out through five main bodies or organs: the General Assembly, the Security Council, the Economic and Social Council, the International Court of Justice, and the Secretariat. The General Assembly is a forum where every nation has one vote; the Security Council focuses on peace and security and has permanent members and elected members; the Economic and Social Council addresses issues related to trade, education, health, and other economic and social issues; the International Court of Justice hears cases between nations; and the Secretariat, headed by the secretary-general,

is the administrative arm of the UN. The UN has a variety of agencies throughout the world that work to promote peace and stability and to facilitate trade and economic activity.

Discuss the World Trade Organization and its predecessor, GATT.

The WTO attempts to remove trade barriers worldwide. Its membership is composed of the major trading countries in the world, so it has the potential to significantly influence world trade. The WTO routinely issues decisions on trade disputes between countries. GATT, the predecessor of the WTO, greatly contributed to the growth of trade through trade liberalization.

Appreciate the resources of the Organisation for Economic Cooperation and Development.

OECD conducts extensive research on a wide variety of international business and economic subjects, and it produces highly regarded individual country surveys. These resource materials are valuable to researchers and businesspeople as they develop an understanding of markets.

Describe the major purpose and effectiveness of OPEC.

The major purpose of OPEC is to allow developing nations to increase their price control over the oil they are selling on international markets. OPEC has had periods of marked effectiveness. Today, despite unrest in the Middle East and the ability of OPEC to influence oil prices in the short term, the number of non-OPEC nations that produce or soon will be producing oil has increased significantly. Adding to the OPEC dilemma is the possibility that price gouging will lead to the development of fuel alternatives and increased conservation and, eventually, to a reduction in demand. Admittedly, the popularity of SUVs in the U.S. market suggests that the price of oil would have to escalate considerably to trigger this possibility.

Identify economic integration agreements and the effectiveness of the major ones.

The four major forms of economic integration are the free trade area (tariffs abolished among members), the customs union (a free trade agreement plus a common external tariff), the common market (a customs union plus mobility of services, people, and capital), and complete economic integration (a common market plus a common currency). NAFTA has been quite effective, while Mercosur, whose goal is a common market, has faced difficulties recently, as has the Andean Community. The EU has been markedly successful.

Explain the North American Free Trade Agreement and its impact on business.

NAFTA was ratified by Canada, Mexico, and the United States. Its purpose is to facilitate trade among the three countries. NAFTA lowers tariffs on goods moving from one NAFTA country to another and makes it easier for businesses to sell goods and operate in other NAFTA countries.

Discuss the impact of the EU and its future challenges.

The EU is a supranational entity with 25 European membernations. Its purpose is to integrate the economies of its membernations, creating a trading region where goods, services, people, and capital move freely. In recent years, the EU has made major steps toward political union as well. The EU is a regional government and as such has regulatory power over social and environmental matters, including mergers and business operations, in Europe. The EU adopted a common currency, the euro, which is being used in 12 EU countries. The EU's success at monetary integration reduces the risk for businesses within the EMU. The EU can be seen as one large market with fewer restrictions than existed among the 25 nations before integration.

Key Words

United Nations (UN) (p. 105)

General Assembly (p. 106)

Security Council (p. 106)

Economic and Social Council (ECOSOC) (p. 106)

International Court of Justice (ICJ) (p. 107)

Secretariat (p. 107)

North Atlantic Treaty Organization (NATO) (p. 108)

Collective Security Treaty Organization (CSTO) (p. 108)

Association of Southeast Asian Nations (ASEAN) (p. 110)

World Trade Organization (WTO) (p. 110)

General Agreement on Tariffs and Trade (GATT) (p. 112)

most favored nation (MFN) clause (p. 112)

Uruguay Round (p. 112)

Doha Development Agenda (p. 114)

trade-related intellectual property rights (TRIPS) (p. 115)

Organisation for Economic Cooperation and Development (OECD) (p. 116)

Organization of Petroleum Exporting Countries (p. 118)

Group of 8 (G8) (p. 118)

free trade area (FTA) (p. 120)

customs union (p. 120)

common market (p. 120)

complete economic integration (p. 120)

North American Free Trade Agreement (NAFTA) (p. 121)

European Free Trade Agreement (EFTA) (p. 122)

Mercosur (Mercosul) (p. 124)

Central American Free Trade Agreement (CAFTA) (p. 125)

Andean Community (CAN) (p. 125)

European Union (EU) (p. 126)

European Parliament (p. 130)

Council of the European Union (p. 130)

European Commission (p. 131)

European Court of Justice (ECJ) (p. 131)

European Central Bank (ECB) (p. 131)

European Monetary Union (EMU) (p. 132)

Questions

1. What are some reasons that businesspeople should be aware of important international institutions?

2. Even though the UN is best known for peacekeeping missions, it has many agencies involved in activities affecting businesses. In your judgment, do these activities justify support for the UN? Would it be better if the activities of these agencies were done by private entities such as trade groups?

3. How did the WTO come into existence? What purpose does it serve? Would bilateral trading agreements work better than the multilateral WTO approach?

4. What are the four main organs of the EU, and what is the purpose of each?

5. What is the impact of the EU on business?

6. The U.S. Congress approved the North American Free Trade Agreement despite strong opposition from organized labor. Why would labor have opposed NAFTA?

7. What is the importance of the OECD for business?

8. Mercosur's major trading partner is the EU rather than the United States. Why might this be the case?

9. How might a small businessperson in Des Moines, Iowa, who is exporting agricultural products find useful the international institutions and agreements that this chapter describes?

Research Task

globalEDGE.msu.edu globalEDGE

Use the globalEDGE site (http://globalEDGE.msu.edu/) to complete the following exercises:

1. You are currently making a decision concerning which landlocked and lesser developed country you will visit for your next overseas trip so you can better understand the dynamics of international institutions among developing countries. To assist in this process, *InfoNation* is an easy-to-use, two-step database that allows one to view and compare the most current statistical data for United Nations member states. Select the following six countries to facilitate your decision: Afghanistan, Bhutan, Chad, Lao People's Democratic Republic, Lesotho, and Rwanda. Then, to gain additional insight into the conditions in each country, select data for the following categories: Population-Population in 2003; Population-Largest Urban Agglomeration; Economy-Tourist Arrivals; Technology-Telephone Lines; Technology-

Television Receivers; and Environment-Water Resources per Capita. Which countries rank highest and lowest in each category? Which country would you choose for your next trip? Given the international regional organizations discussed in the text, which regional grouping of nations will you be visiting? What are your reasons for choosing this country? Were there other factors that influenced your decision? If so, what were they?

2. The *World Development Indicators* (WDI) is the World Bank's premier data compilation on development. Utilize the WDI for the Czech Republic to gather information on this country. Considering that your company currently produces an emerging video game system technology and is planning to enter this country soon, prepare a short report on the infrastructure of this country as it applies to your company's product.

You are an international business consultant in the United States. Your specialty is exporting to and investing, licensing, or franchising in developing countries.

One of your clients is a hotel company that wants to build, operate, and 100 percent own a hotel in a Latin American country.

To which organizations discussed in this chapter might you look for assistance in developing a list of country-selection criteria and then a list of possible sites for the investment?

5

Understanding the International Monetary System

The function of money is not to make money but to move goods. Money is only one part of our transportation system. It moves goods from man to man. A dollar bill is like a postage stamp: it is no good unless it will move commodities between persons. If a postage stamp will not carry a letter, or money will not move goods, it is just the same as an engine that will not run. Someone will have to get out and fix it.

—widely attributed to Henry Ford in a speech at the Ford Motor Company

All truth passes through three phases: First, it is ridiculed. Second, it is violently opposed, and Third, it is accepted as self-evident.

—Schopenhauer

Money Laundering, Terrorism, and International Monetary Institutions

One of the critical requirements for international terrorism is funding. Much of international terrorism's funding involves an ability to launder money, that is, disguise its sources, and move it unmonitored across international borders. If the money flow can be stopped, the terrorism will stop.

In the effort to combat money laundering connected to terrorist financing, international monetary institutions have taken a lead role, through the international Financial Action Task Force on Money Laundering (FATF). Established by the G7 countries (now G8), FATF develops and promotes policies, both national and international, that make money laundering more difficult and more risky. FATF works closely with the IMF, the World Bank, the United Nations, FATF-style regional bodies (FSRBs), and national bodies such as the U.S. Department of the Treasury.

FATF monitors what countries do to control the financing of terrorism and regularly publishes a list of countries that are not cooperating with international standards established to prevent money laundering. As of June 2006, the noncooperative countries and territories on the list are Myanmar and Nigeria. The list is markedly reduced from 2005, when it included the Cook Islands, Indonesia, Myanmar, Nauru, Nigeria, and the Philippines. Appearance on this list means that the international financial monitors sent in by FATF found serious problems: loopholes in financial regulations that allowed for money laundering, other domestic obstacles such as no requirements to register businesses, systemic obstacles to international cooperation, and/or inadequate resources for preventing and detecting money laundering activities.[1] Appearing on this list is *not* a goal of governments. It means that other governments have been notified to advise their banks and other financial institutions to give special attention to any transactions in the listed countries by exercising appropriate due diligence and caution. The financial world is watching you closely if you are on this list.

What suggestions does FATF offer to help safeguard against terrorism, from the finance side? Its recommendations include criminalizing the financing of terrorism, freezing and confiscating terrorist assets, reporting suspicious transactions related to terrorism, tracking parallel or alternative remittance systems, such as hawala (which avoids the banking system and relies on trust and family or religious connections),[2] and monitoring wire transfers, nonprofit organizations, and cash couriers. In the United States, the Department of the Treasury lists assets of suspected terrorist organizations and individuals that have been frozen by the government. You can see this list, which is updated regularly, at www.treasury.gov/offices/enforcement/key-issues/freezing. ∎

CONCEPT PREVIEWS

After reading this chapter, you should be able to:

explain the functioning of the gold standard

describe the purposes of the IMF

appreciate the accomplishments of the Bretton Woods system and the developments shaping the world monetary system from the end of World War II to the present

describe the purpose of the World Bank

discuss the purpose of the Bank for International Settlements

discuss the floating exchange rate system

describe the development of the common currency area for the euro

explain the role of the balance of payments (BOP)

discuss the major BOP accounts

explain the uses of special drawing rights (SDRs)

The international monetary system consists of institutions, agreements, rules, and processes that allow for the payments, currency exchange, and movements of capital required by international transactions.[3] To gain a sense of where we are now in the arrangements of the international monetary system, it's useful to look first at where we've been with these arrangements. This will build an understanding of how the institutions and arrangements that facilitate payments across national borders have evolved. Thus we begin this chapter with a review of the gold standard and the Bretton Woods system. Next, we examine the institutions established at Bretton Woods—the International Monetary Fund (IMF) and the World Bank—and take a brief look at another institution that plays a central role in the international monetary system, the Bank for International Settlements. Then we consider the emergence of the floating exchange rate system and current exchange rate arrangements, including the newest currency development, the euro. Moving from the institutions that participate in the international monetary process to how the process is recorded, we conclude the chapter with an overview of the balance-of-payments accounts and special drawing rights (SDR).

This chapter addresses the cooperation among nations that makes possible and supports our international monetary system. How the foreign exchange market works is covered in Chapter 11, "Financial Forces."

The Gold Standard: A Brief History

Since ancient times, based on its scarcity and easily assessed level of purity, gold has been trusted as a way for people to store value, exchange value, and measure value. Actually, from about A.D. 1200 to the present, the price of gold has generally been going up.[4] In ancient trading, international traders used used both gold and silver coins until 1875. However, as trade grew, carrying large amounts of gold became impractical. Gold is heavy, has transportation and storage costs, and does not earn interest, plus its bulk made it an obvious target for thieves. These drawbacks led to the evolution of paper script that was backed by governments with a pledge to exchange the script for gold at a fixed rate.

In 1717, Sir Isaac Newton, the great mathematician who held a sinecure as master of the English mint, established the price of gold at 3 pounds, 17 shillings, 10.5 pence per ounce, putting England de facto on the gold standard. Except during the Napoleonic Wars, England stood willing to convert gold to currency, or vice versa, until World War I. During those two centuries, London was the dominant center of international finance. Estimates hold that more than 90 percent of world trade was financed in London.[5]

gold standard
The use of gold at an established number of units per currency

Most trading or industrial countries followed England's move and adopted the **gold standard.** Each country set a certain number of units of its currency per ounce of gold, and the ratios of their gold equivalence established the exchange rate between any two currencies on the gold standard. In essence, currencies were pegged to gold. So suppose the British pound was pegged to gold at 5 pounds per ounce and the French franc was pegged at 10 pounds per ounce. The exchange rate between the pound and the franc would have been 2 francs per pound, or .5 pound per franc.

The simplicity of the gold standard was a large part of its appeal. When there were trade imbalances, they would be corrected by a flow of gold in the direction of the surplus. The money supply would rise or fall in direct relation to the gold flows. This automatic adjustment is known as the *price-specie-flow mechanism* (*specie* is another word for "coined money"), a concept developed by the Scottish philosopher David Hume. As early as 1758, Hume was making impressive attempts to illustrate that trade is not a zero-sum game but, rather, that all participants can benefit from trade. Until his arguments and those of his friend Adam Smith gained acceptance, mercantilism held sway, a belief that a nation's wealth is best measured by its money stocks and that richer nations are those that have trade surpluses. Hume argued in *Of the Jealousy of Trade* that the wealth of all nations is directly related to the total volume of trade, that a rising tide lifts all boats.[6]

Modern monetary arrangements assign no special role to gold. The Federal Reserve, the central bank of the United States, is not required to tie the dollar to anything. This gives the Federal Reserve flexibility that is helpful during economic crises. For example, the Fed can print money to pump into a recession. Economist Paul Krugman points out that this flexibility is why the 1987 stock market crash did not cause a depression similar to that of 1929.[7]

The international gold standard ended when the financial burdens of World War I forced Britain to sell a substantial portion of its gold. Other countries involved in the war, including Germany, France, and Russia, suspended the exchange of paper money for gold and stopped exports of gold. Between World War I and World War II there was a short-lived flirtation with a renewal of the gold standard, but it was not successfully reestablished.

Although the gold standard has not been the international monetary system for many years, it continues to have some ardent and influential advocates—most economists not among them[8]—who call for a return to the gold

An Iranian currency trader counts gold coins. One expert called gold coins "Iranians' political hedge fund."

standard and fixed exchange rates. Among its advocates are the publisher of *Forbes* and twice presidential candidate Steve Forbes, politician and vice-presidential candidate Jack Kemp, and *The Wall Street Journal* editor and Pulitzer Prize editorialist Robert Bartley. One of the staunchest supporters of a return to the gold standard was the French economist Jacques Rueff, a member of the French Academy and an adviser to the French government. The heart of Rueff's argument is expressed in one word: *discipline*. Under the gold standard, a government cannot create money that is not backed by gold. Therefore, no matter how great the temptation to create more money for political advantage, a government cannot do so without the required amount of gold.[9] Unfortunately, this discipline sacrifices the flexibility of a freely floating monetary system.

Yet gold remains a refuge for people who fear inflation. For example, in Iran, with tension escalating over its nuclear program and the economy stalling, the demand for gold has risen dramatically. "Gold coins are Iranians' political hedge fund. We keep them at home and they make us feel secure," observes Heydar Pourian, editor of *Iqtisad Iran* (Iran Economics).[10] With official reports of inflation at 14 percent in Iran, gold's value has gained 21 percent. Refugees, from Hitler's Germany of World War II to today's terror-based regimes, can attest that the small bars of bullion they managed to smuggle out can be credited with their survival. There is no question that the world's interest in gold remains high, especially when considering its other applications in industrial uses and jewelry. Figure 5.1 is an advertisement in the *Financial Times* (of London) of gold bullion, coins, and bars for sale.

BRETTON WOODS

During World War II, the countries of the world were much too involved with the hostilities to consider the gold standard or any other monetary system. However, many officials realized some system had to be established to operate when peace returned. In 1944, representatives of the 44 allied nations met at the Mount Washington Hotel in **Bretton Woods,** New Hampshire, to plan for the future. This was a historic undertaking: It resulted in the first negotiated agreement to support trade through the establishment of monetary institutions among independent nations.

There was a consensus among the Bretton Woods representatives that (1) stable exchange rates were desirable but experience might dictate adjustments, (2) floating or fluctuating exchange rates had proved unsatisfactory, though the reasons for this opinion were little discussed, and (3) the government controls of trade, exchange, production, and so forth, that had developed from 1931 through World War II were wasteful, discriminatory, and detrimental to expansion of world trade and investment. To achieve its goals, the Bretton Woods Conference established two international monetary institutions, the International Monetary Fund (IMF) and the International Bank for Reconstruction and Development (IBRD), also called the World Bank. The IMF Articles of Agreement contained the rules for international monetary policies and their enforcement. The agreement went into effect in December 1945

Bretton Woods
The New Hampshire town where treasury and central bank representatives met near the end of World War II; they established the IMF, the World Bank, and the gold exchange standard

and served as the basis of the international monetary system until 1971. The World Bank's function was to lend money for development projects.

International Monetary Fund

International Monetary Fund (IMF) Institution that coordinates multilateral monetary rules and their enforcement

The premise of the **International Monetary Fund (IMF)** is that the common interest of all nations in a workable international monetary system far transcends conflicting national interests.[11] The first article of the IMF Articles of Agreement outlines the institution's purpose in six points:[12]

- To promote international monetary cooperation.

- To facilitate the expansion and balanced growth of international trade.

- To promote exchange stability and orderly exchange arrangements among members.

- To assist in the establishment of a multilateral system of payments.

- To make the fund's resources available for balance-of-payments corrections.

- To shorten the duration and lessen the disequilibrium of members' balances of payments.

Although the International Monetary Fund deals solely with governments, its policies and actions have a profound impact on businesses and people worldwide because they set the framework for trade. The IMF has become much more visible in recent years as its policies and actions routinely make world headlines.

The IMF Articles of Agreement, the center of the Bretton Woods system, set up fixed exchange rates among member-nations' currencies, with **par value** based on gold and the U.S. dollar, which was valued at $35 per ounce of gold. For example, the British pound's par value was US$2.40, the French franc's was US$0.18, and the German mark's was US$0.2732. There was an understanding that the U.S. government would redeem dollars for gold and that the dollar was the only currency to be redeemable for gold. The Bretton Woods meetings resulted in a dollar-based gold exchange standard, and thus the U.S. dollar became both a means of international payment and a reserve currency.

This system supported substantial international trade growth during the 1950s and 1960s. Other countries changed their currency's value against the dollar and gold, but the U.S. dollar remained fixed. This meant that the United States, in order to satisfy the growing demand for reserves, since countries would hold dollars as a proxy for gold, had to run a balance-of-payments deficit. That is, in the United States the flow of dollars out was greater than the flow in; the demand on dollars for holding outside the country was greater than the dollars that they were making through exports. From 1958 through 1971, the United States ran up a cumulative deficit of $56 billion. The deficit was financed partly by use of the U.S. gold reserves, which shrank from $24.8 billion to $12.2 billion,[13] and partly by incurring liabilities to foreign central banks. During this period, those liabilities increased from $13.6 billion to $62.2 billion.[14] By 1971, the Treasury held only 22 cents' worth of gold for each US$ held by those banks.

Such a deficit would eventually inspire a lack of confidence in the reserve currency and lead to a financial crisis. Known as the **Triffin paradox,**[15] that is exactly what happened when, after trade deficits in the late 1960s, President Charles De Gaulle pushed the Bank of France to redeem its dollar holdings for gold. Eventually, in 1971, President Nixon suspended the dollar's convertibility into gold. Bretton Woods had tried to make adjustments by creating Special Drawing Rights (SDRs) in 1969, an international reserve asset we'll review later in this chapter, whose value was based on a basket of currencies, to save the fixed rate system. The Smithsonian Agreement was a further attempt to restructure the monetary system, but by 1973, Japan and Europe had allowed their currencies to float, bringing an end to the Bretton Woods system.

The IMF operates as a collaboration of nations. Each of the 184 members contributes funds, known as its quota, which is determined based on relative size in the world economy. The aggregate quotas, which as of March 2006 totaled $308 billion, form a pool of money from which the IMF can lend to countries. As of 2006, the IMF's outstanding loans totaled $34 billion to 65 countries. Of that total, $6 billion was loaned on special concessions to 56 heavily indebted poor countries.[16] The quota also is used as a basis to determine how much a nation can borrow from the IMF, how much its SDR allocation is, and how many votes it has.[17] For example, the United States has 17.08 percent of the total votes and its quota is 17.1, while the United Kingdom has 4.95 percent of the total, China 2.94, and Japan 6.13.[18]

The IMF was begun before the United Nations, and when the UN was formed, the IMF was brought into relationship with the UN. This relationship preserved the IMF's independence, which was justified by the need for independent control of monetary management. Presently the IMF is addressing economic and exchange rate policies of countries with the largest trade imbalances. Causes of these imbalances include low levels of savings in the United States, high levels of savings in China, inflexibility of the Chinese currency, and continued balance of payment surpluses in Japan, Germany, and oil-producing countries. From a U.S. perspective, this is a welcome development because it suggests a recognition that the increasing U.S. trade deficit is caused by global forces in addition to its own budget deficit. The focus on trade issues by the IMF is welcomed because it comes at a time when the World Trade Organization's latest attempts in the Doha Round seem to have failed.[19]

The economist Jeffrey Sachs, director of the Earth Institute, observes that the IMF has been able to reinvent itself as challenges have evolved on the economic, monetary, and

par value
Stated value

Triffin paradox
The concept that a national currency that is also a reserve currency will eventually run a deficit, which eventually inspires a lack of confidence in the reserve currency and leads to a financial crisis

financial levels. He sees five major challenges facing today's IMF and the international monetary system. The first is that the rise of Asian economies will make the U.S.-centric approach of the IMF obsolete. As he puts it, "The U.S. will no longer be conductor of the global monetary orchestra."[20] The IMF needs to play a valuable role in convincing the rising economies to accept multilateral responsibilities that reach beyond their own economies. Second, as Asia rises, so will the temptation toward protectionism in the United States and Europe. These countries will exert pressure on China to manipulate its currency to meet their objectives, and the IMF can help to make certain that China's monetary policy is managed both for China and for long-term multilateral stability.

The third challenge Sachs foresees for the IMF is that financial crises will become more global and more intricate. That suggests that the IMF will have to become more action-prone. The African debt cancellation came 20 years after the African debt crisis. Such time lags won't work in a fast-paced, global, evolving economy. Debtor liquidity will need to be maintained, and the IMF can ensure that it is by developing institutional debtor-creditor workout schemes. Meanwhile, as global trade continues to increase, Sachs sees fewer currencies in circulation, both because smaller economies will adopt major currencies such as the dollar or the euro and because regional trading groups will develop regional currencies on the euro model. The IMF can support this process, its fourth challenge, in political, economic, and technical ways.

The fifth challenge has to do with an increasing number of ecological shocks, such as the recent Southeast Asian tsunami, earthquakes in Pakistan and Indonesia, and hurricanes in the United States. Such shocks also include an increasing number of diseases, such as HIV/AIDS and the bird flu. The IMF challenge here is to develop a way for global financial markets to spread these risks through insurance against such ecological disasters for governments.

The IMF has had many successes. It has developed and maintained a system of currency exchange that makes global trade possible. It has supported governments in their noninflationary monetary management, and it has helped the world trading system avoid financial disasters. The five challenges Sachs outlines for the IMF represent possible next steps in its evolution as a global monetary institution and are a result of its past successes. That is not to suggest that the IMF has not had enormous failures, because it certainly has. Most of these failures involve the mismanagement of crises in developing countries.

In early 2006, Brazil and Argentina surprised the IMF by paying off their loans ahead of schedule. Brazil, Argentina, Turkey, and Indonesia account for 70 percent of the IMF loans, so these early repayments raised some concerns.[21] Does the IMF need a new business model? In addition to the early repayments, the number of new loans is the lowest it has been since 1970. Reduced demand for loans from the IMF is due to the solid economic performance of the economies of emerging markets, so this can be seen as a positive development. Yet IMF interest rates cover the fund's operating costs, close to $1 billion in 2005, so when the IMF books fewer loans, their income falls. They do have a reserve, though. More information about the IMF can be found at its Web site, www.imf.org.

The World Bank

World Bank

Institution that focuses on funding of development projects

The **World Bank**, also known as the International Bank for Reconstruction and Development (IBRD), was established along with the IMF at Bretton Woods with the purpose of addressing development issues in a postwar world. Today the World Bank Group, made up of five institutions, is the world's largest source of development assistance, providing nearly $16 billion in loans a year to its client countries.[22] The World Bank itself focuses on projects in middle-income and creditworthy poor countries, while the International Development Association (IDA) loans to the poorest countries. Together they provide low-interest loans and grants for projects designed to help countries develop infrastructure, health and education, and other areas connected to development. The World Bank Group is owned by its 184 member nations.

The International Finance Corporation (IFC), the private sector arm of the World Bank, invests in companies and financial institutions in developing countries. IFC is the World Bank's investment banker, arranging private risk ventures in developing countries.

>>IFC Supports Small Loans to Entrepreneurs

IFC is helping to build domestic capital markets so that local entrepreneurs in developing countries will have access to funding. Such funding is especially important

to entrepreneurs in segments traditionally excluded from the formal economy—women, indigenous groups, and people in rural areas. In 2005, IFC invested $15 million in a Mexican microfinance institution, Financiera Compartamos, in the form of a structured bond. The proceeds of the transaction are being used to fund some 400,000 Mexican small businesses, of which more than 99 percent are owned by women in rural areas. Compartamos provides microloans through village banking, solidarity group loans, and individual loans. Loans provide working capital for the company's clients to build small businesses.

Emma Acosta Salazar is a manufacturer of straw hats who is financed by Compartamos. She started her business because she needed a fixed job and so that her husband would not have to emigrate to the United States. Emma began by buying a machine and subcontracting to people who bought hats. As she made money, she bought more machines. She has been with Compartamos for two years, and has used her loans to purchase material and close good business deals. Emma is teaching the trade to her children while making a way for them to continue their studies and one day go to college.

Source: www.ifc.org (accessed June 23, 2006).

The last two organizations that constitute the World Bank Group are the Multilateral Investment Guarantee Agency (MIGA) and the International Centre for the Settlement of Investment Disputes (ICSID). MIGA guarantees private sector investment in developing countries through political risk insurance, technical assistance, and dispute mediation. ICSID helps to resolve disputes between governments and foreign investors and, in that way, helps build direct foreign investment. As of 2006, 155 nations had signed the dispute resolution convention established by ICSID.

In addition to the World Bank Group, there are several other multilateral development banks that provide support and advice for investment activities in the developing world. They include the African Development Bank, the Asian Development Bank, the European Bank for Reconstruction and Development, and the Inter-American Development Bank. The Bank for International Settlements also merits a brief focus here, because it offers central bankers a forum for their discussions on the global financial system. Its role has become increasingly important in a floating exchange environment.

Bank for International Settlements

The **Bank for International Settlements (BIS)** is an international organization of central banks that exists to "foster cooperation among central banks and other agencies in pursuit of monetary and financial stability."[23] Central bankers of major industrial countries meet at least seven times a year at the BIS to discuss the global financial system. Its clients are governments and international agencies, not private individuals or corporations. BIS is the oldest international financial institution in the world, having been founded in 1930 to address war reparations imposed on Germany by the Treaty of Versailles. Today the BIS has four main functions. It serves as a banker for central banks, as a forum for international monetary

Bank for International Settlements
Institution for central bankers; operates as their bank

BIS is known as the most discreet financial institution in the world. Although its round tower stands out as a distinctive landmark in Basel, Switzerland, there is no sign identifying the building.

cooperation, as a center for research, and as an agent or trustee for governments in various international financial arrangements.

BIS is known as the most discreet financial institution in the world. In fact, although the round tower of the bank is the first landmark in Basel, Switzerland, for anyone leaving the main railway station and heading toward the city center, there is no sign identifying the building.

Now that we have reviewed the role of Bretton Woods in establishing two of the major international monetary institutions, the IMF and the World Bank, and briefly looked at the Bank for International Settlements, our attention can move on to what happened after the gold exchange system of Bretton Woods ceased to function.

The Emergence of a Floating Currency Exchange Rate System

When, in response to De Gaulle's push for France to redeem its dollar holdings for gold, President Nixon announced in 1971 that the United States would no longer exchange gold for the paper dollars held by foreign central banks, he was said to have "closed the gold window." The shock caused currency exchange markets to remain closed for several days, and when they reopened, they began developing a new system for which few rules existed. Currencies were floating, and the stated US$ value of 35 dollars per ounce of gold was now meaningless because the United States would no longer exchange any of its gold for dollars.

Two attempts were made to agree on durable, new sets

fixed currency exchange rates
Rates that governments agree on and undertake to maintain

floating currency exchange rates
Rates that are allowed to float against other currencies and are determined by market forces

Jamaica Agreement
The 1976 IMF agreement that allows flexible exchange rates among members

of **fixed currency exchange rates,** one in December 1971 and the other in February 1973. Both times, however, banks, businesses, and individuals felt that the central banks had pegged the rates incorrectly, and the speculators were correct each time. In March 1973 the major currencies began to float in the foreign exchange markets, and the system of **floating currency exchange rates** still prevails. The agreement that established the rules for the floating system was accepted by IMF members after the fact, at a meeting in Jamaica in 1976. Known as the **Jamaica Agreement**, it allows for flexible exchange rates among IMF members, while condoning central bank operations in the money markets to smooth out volatile periods. Gold was demonetized, as well; it was abandoned as a reserve currency. The Jamaica Agreement also gives less developed countries greater access to IMF funds, while quotas for developed countries were increased.

CURRENT CURRENCY ARRANGEMENTS

Initially the IMF recognized three types of currency exchange arrangements, but it later extended the categories to eight. First, we'll look at the three original categories—a free float, a managed float, and a fixed peg—and then we'll look more closely at the variations that have developed. The *free (clean) float* is one of the world's closest approaches to perfect competition, because there is no government intervention and large amounts of various monies are being traded by thousands of buyers and sellers. Buyers and sellers may change sides on short notice as information, rumors, or moods change or as their clients' needs differ. In the *managed (dirty) float,* governments intervene in the currency markets as they perceive their national interests to be served. Nations may explain their interventions in the currency market in terms of "smoothing market irregularities" or "ensuring orderly markets." In a *fixed peg,* a country pegs the value of its currency at a fixed rate to another currency.

BUILDING YOUR GLOBAL RÉSUMÉ | **Knowing How to Follow the International Money Trail**

Money is central to business, international or domestic. Currencies, currency fluctuations, exchange rates, and the mechanics of buying and selling foreign currency are fundamental tools of the international business professional and are used daily in the practice of international trade. In fact, foreign currency trading is growing into an increasingly profitable commodity market in banks and financial institutions worldwide. The information in this box will help you understand how to follow the international money trail.

How to Designate Currencies

Almost every country in the world has its own currency, and the euro is the now the single currency of most EU countries. Some countries like Japan, with the yen (¥), and Great Britain, with the pound sterling (£), use symbols to identify their currencies. Most world currencies use the first letter of the currency name, such as *P*, but globally this can be confusing. Does "P20" mean 20 pesetas, pesos, pounds, pataca, or pa'anga or 20 of another currency? And if it means 20 pesos, are they pesos from Mexico, Bolivia, Argentina, Chile, Colombia, or some other country? To address this confusion, the international banking community developed the ISO 4217 set of currency abbreviations, which standardizes how currencies are identified.

ISO 4217 uses three-letter abbreviations, such as *USD* for "United States dollar." When currencies are defined by supra-national entities, the ISO system assigns two-letter entity codes starting with *X* to be used instead of country codes, as in the case of *XCD* for "Central Caribbean dollar."

Depending on whether you are using e-mail, news or the Web, some currency symbols may be used but many others should *not* be used. In e-mail and news, the only currency symbol that may be used safely is the dollar symbol ($). To express a value in any other currency, you should use the ISO 4217 abbreviation. For "£10," *GBP 10* should be used. In HTML, the only currency symbols that may be used safely are $ for "dollar," ¢ for "cent," £ for "pound," ¥ for "yen," and ¤ for a generic currency. To show the value of any other currency, the ISO 4217 abbreviation should be used.

World Fact: According to the *CIA World Factbook,* there were 178 currencies in the world until February 28, 2002, when European national bank notes and currencies were taken out of circulation and replaced by the euro, which added one new currency and eliminated 12.

Culture Cue: Bosque Real is the world's largest country club and is located near Mexico City. See www.bosquereal.com.

World Wide Resource:

- www.oanda.com/convert/classic
- www.x-rates.com/
- www.banknotes.com/images.htm
- http://fx.sauder.ubc.ca/currency_table.html

Source: www.jhall.demon.co.uk/currency (accessed July 13, 2006).

The eight categories of exchange rate arrangements that the IMF now uses to describe how countries position their currencies in relation to other currencies are explained below, from not having any legal tender to having fixed and then freely floating exchange rate arrangements:

- *Exchange arrangements with no separate legal tender* describe one country's adopting the currency of another or a group of countries adopting a common currency. An example of the first is the U.S. dollar's use in Panama, El Salvador, and Ecuador. An example of the second is the European Union's euro being used as shared currency in 12 of the EU countries (soon to be joined by the 13th, Slovenia).

- *Currency board arrangements* describe a legislated commitment to exchange domestic currency for a specific foreign currency at a fixed rate. The currency board arrangement commits the government to hold foreign reserves equal to its domestic currency supply. In Estonia, for example, the rise and fall of the kroon (EEK) is tied to the euro. In Hong Kong, the Hong Kong dollar (HKD) is tied to the U.S. dollar.

- *Other conventional fixed peg arrangements* describe a peg in which there is a fixed rate relationship and exchange rate fluctuations are allowed within a narrow band of less than 1 percent. The peg could be to one currency or to a basket of currencies. The Saudi Riyal is pegged in this way to the U.S. dollar.

- *Pegged exchange rates within horizontal bands* describe pegged arrangements in which the exchange rate fluctuations are allowed to be greater than 1 percent around a central rate. Denmark's krone is pegged in this way to the euro.

- *Crawling pegs* describe arrangements in which the currency is readjusted periodically at a fixed, preannounced rate or in response to changes in indicators. Bolivia, Costa Rica, and Tunisia operate crawling peg arrangements.

- *Exchange rates within crawling bands* describe fluctuating margins around a central rate within which the currency is maintained and adjusted periodically. Romania is an example of this arrangement.

- *Managed floating with no preannounced path for the exchange rate* describes a monetary authority that actively intervenes on the exchange market without specifying or making public its goals and targets. Algeria, India, Malaysia, and Singapore are examples of this approach.

- *Independently floating exchange rates* is an approach that relies on the market. There may be interventions, yet they are conducted to moderate the rate of change rather than to establish the currency's level. Examples of countries following this approach are the United States, Mexico, Canada, and the United Kingdom.

Below is a summary of the number of countries that presently follow each approach:[24]

Exchange arrangements with no separate legal tender	41 countries
Currency board arrangements	7 countries
Other conventional fixed peg arrangements	40 countries
Pegged exchange within horizontal bands	5 countries
Crawling pegs	6 countries
Exchange rates within crawling bands	2 countries
Managed floating with no preannounced path	50 countries
Independently floating	36 countries

The floating exchange rate system, with its various approaches, seems to be meeting its challenges. Admittedly, economic policy coordination as practiced by the G7 and, with the recent addition of Russia, the G8, has emerged as a key factor in the foreign exchange (Fx) markets. And although there is little doubt the G8 central banks have become more adept at influencing currency movements, another development challenges their efforts. That is the explosive growth in the volume of currencies being traded in the world's foreign exchange markets. From an annual volume of roughly $18 billion in 1979, foreign exchange transactions are now estimated at $1.9 trillion daily.[25] Even the richest countries have government reserves of "only" a few billion dollars available to influence exchange rates. For example, if the foreign exchange market players believe the Japanese yen should be stronger in US$ terms, the yen will strengthen in spite of any government market intervention. The floating system seems to be able to respond to market movements with flexibility and relative order.

Floating currencies can move against one another quickly and in large swings. Such changes have many causes, including political events, expectations, and government economic policies, such as allowing trade imbalances and deficits. Relative inflation becomes a significant issue for international businesspeople. One means of measuring relative inflation is *purchasing power parity (PPP),* the theory of which is that an exchange rate between the currencies of two countries is in equilibrium when it equates the prices of a basket of goods and services in both countries.

The review of floating currency arrangements is important for international business managers as it brings attention to the fact that currencies can change value in terms of each other in large amounts. These changes create major uncertainties. Managers protect their organizations and themselves through a process called *hedging,* which is explained in Chapter 21.

THE EURO

euro (€)
Currency of the European Monetary Union

In January 1999, a new major currency, the **euro** (€), joined the world markets. It began trading at 1 euro for US$1.14. Despite forecasts that the euro would be a strong currency, it fell to as low as $0.8455 in 2001, but by May 31, 2002, it had rebounded to $0.93.[26] In the fall of 2002, the euro and the U.S. dollar were trading at par, and by January 2004 the euro had strengthened to a record high of $1.3625. In late May 2006, the rate was at $1.2739. [27]

The agreement to move to a common currency, the Maastricht Treaty, was signed by the European Union members in 1991, with a target date of 1999. To prepare for such cooperation, EU members had to first coordinate their monetary policies to achieve a harmonization of their economies. Budget deficits, public debt, and exchange rates all had to be carefully controlled. Then these countries had to cede monetary control of their economies to a central EU institution, the European Central Bank. On January 1, 1999, for the first time since the Roman Empire, 11 of the original 15 EU countries shared a common currency, the Euro. Those countries were Austria, Belgium, Finland, France, Germany, Ireland, Italy, Luxembourg, the Netherlands, Portugal, and Spain. Greece joined in 2001, to make 12 EU countries committed to European Monetary Union (EMU). Sweden, Denmark, and the United Kingdom chose to remain outside the euro zone. The euro was used for pricing in local markets, along with the traditional script, until January 1, 2002, when the euro script was introduced and, gradually, the local currency withdrawn. Although there were many forecasts of doom, such as ATM chaos, loss of savings, and counterfeiting, in actuality, the conversion from local currencies to the euro went smoothly. Slovenia will be joining the euro zone in 2007.

"May I have my allowance in euros, Dad?"

Source: From the *Wall Street Journal* — Permission, Cartoon Features Syndicate.

The effect of the euro on business has been largely positive, both for members of the euro zone and for those trading into the euro zone. There are two main benefits: The euro's use reduces transaction costs for conducting business within the zone and eliminates exchange rate fluctuation risk. No longer does a business need to take the time and pay banking fees to change Greek drachma into French francs. In addition, corporate finance managers no longer need to hedge their exposure across the 12 replaced currencies. Establishment of the euro is also one step closer to an integrated, single market, which will allow greater efficiencies. For European business, the euro also has encouraged a transition from a local or national market focus to a European focus. That means a rethinking of production and distribution systems. In terms of financing business ventures, the capital markets are now more extensive, as well.

We began our discussion of the international monetary system with a focus on its development, the gold standard, the Bretton Woods system, the transition from fixed to floating exchange rates, and the establishment of a new currency, the euro. These monetary institutions and arrangements are important to the conduct of international business for they establish the rules and processes that give shape to the way international business is conducted. Now we adjust our focus to the methods governments use to track and record their and their citizens' participation in international trade, the balance-of-payments accounts. These accounts are also used by economists and businesspeople to analyze a country's level of participation in international trade.

Balance of Payments

The **balance of payments (BOP)** is a record of a country's transactions with the rest of the world. BOP data are of interest to international businesspeople for several reasons. First, the balance of payments reveals demand for the country's currency. If a country is exporting more than it imports, there will be a high demand for the currency in other countries in order to pay for the exported goods. This demand may well create pressure on the exporter's currency, in which case it might be expected to strengthen. Another value of the BOP is that its trend helps managers predict what sort of economic environment may develop in the country. This impacts their choice of strategic risks to take in specific countries. For example, if there are BOP difficulties, a country may not be able to increase its imports. It may well

balance of payments (BOP)
Record of a country's transactions with the rest of the world

institute measures to decrease imports and to limit repatriation of funds. Businesses active in such markets would want to develop strategies to address such possible constraints.

BOP ACCOUNTS

Each international transaction is an exchange of assets with a debit and a credit side. Payments *to* other countries, funds flowing out, are tracked as debits (–), while transactions that are payments *from* other countries, funds flowing in, are tracked as credits (+). The BOP is presented as a double-entry accounting statement in which total credits and debits are always equal. The statement of a country's BOP is divided into several accounts and many subaccounts. A sample of these subaccounts is included in Table 5.1, and the more significant ones are reviewed below.

Current Account

The **current account** tracks the net changes in exports and imports of goods and services, sometimes called *tangibles* and *intangibles*. Three subaccounts are included in the current account: (*a*) goods or merchandise, (*b*) services, and (*c*) unilateral transfers. The first two subaccounts are sometimes treated together, and they include the real (as opposed to the financial) international transactions, that is, exports and imports.

a. The **goods or merchandise account** deals with tangibles, such as autos, grain, clothing, and machinery, which can be seen and felt as they are exported or imported. The net balance on merchandise transactions is referred to as the **trade balance**.

b. The **services account** deals with intangibles that are exchanged internationally. Examples include insurance, banking, dividends or interest on foreign investments, royalties on patents or trademarks held abroad, travel, and transportation.

c. **Unilateral transfers** are transactions with no reciprocity, that is, no return flow. Some of these transfers are made by private persons or institutions and some by governments. Some private unilateral transfers are for charitable, educational, or missionary purposes; others are gifts from migrant workers to their families in their home countries and bequests or the transfer of capital by people migrating from one country to another. The largest government unilateral transfers are aid—which may be in money or in kind—from developed countries to developing countries. Pension payments to nonresidents and tax receipts from nonresidents are two other government-related unilateral transfers. To satisfy the needs of double-entry recording, an entry is made that treats the aid or gift as if it were a purchase of goodwill.

Capital Account

The **capital account** records the net changes in a nation's international financial assets and liabilities over the BOP period, usually one year, with quarterly reports. A capital inflow—a credit entry—occurs when a resident sells stock, bonds, or other financial assets to nonresidents. Money flows to the resident, while at the same time the resident's long-term international liabilities (debit entry) are increased, because dividends (profit) may be paid on the stock, rent will be paid on other assets, and interest must be paid on the bonds. And at maturity the bonds' face amounts must be repaid.

Subaccounts under the capital account are (*a*) direct investment, (*b*) portfolio investment, and (*c*) international movements of short-term capital:

a. **Direct investments** are investments in enterprises or properties located in one country that are effectively controlled by residents of another country. Effective control is assumed for BOP purposes (1) when residents of one country own 50 percent or more of the voting stock of a company in another country or (2) when one resident or an organized group of residents of one country own 25 percent or more of the voting stock of a company in another country.

b. **Portfolio investments** include all long-term—more than one year—investments that do not give the investors effective control over the object of the investment. Such transactions typically involve the purchase of stocks or bonds of foreign issuers for investment—not control—purposes, and they also include long-term commercial credits to finance trade.

---

current account
Record of a country's exports and imports in goods and services

goods or merchandise account
Record of tangible exports and imports

trade balance
The balance on the merchandise account

services account
Record of intangibles that are exchanged internationally

unilateral transfer
A transfer with no matched return flow, no reciprocity

capital account
Record of the net changes in a nation's international financial assets and liabilities

direct investments
Investments located in one country that are effectively controlled by residents of another country

portfolio investments
Long-term investments that do not give the investors control over the investment

TABLE 5.I U.S. International Transactions (millions of dollars)

	2004	2005
Current account		
Exports of goods and services and income receipts	**1,530,975**	**1,740,897**
Exports of goods and services	1,151,448	1,272,223
Goods, balance-of-payments basis	807,536	892,619
Services	343,912	379,604
Income receipts	379,527	468,674
Income receipts on U.S.-owned assets abroad	376,489	465,631
Compensation of employees	3,038	3,043
Imports of goods and services and income payments	**−2,118,119**	**−2,462,946**
Imports of goods and services	−1,769,031	−1,995,839
Income payments	−349,088	−467,107
Income payments on foreign-owned assets in the United States	−340,255	−458,225
Compensation of employees	−8,833	−8,882
Unilateral current transfers, net	**−80,930**	**−82,896**
U.S. government grants	−23,317	−30,362
U.S. government pensions and other transfers	−6,264	−6,312
Private remittances and other transfers	−51,349	−46,222
Capital account		
Capital account transactions, net	**−1,648**	**−5,647**
Financial account		
U.S.-owned assets abroad, net [increase/financial outflow (−)]	**−855,509**	**−491,729**
U.S. official reserve assets, net	2,805	14,096
Gold	. . . .	. . . .
Special drawing rights	−398	4,511
Reserve position in the International Monetary Fund	3,826	10,200
Foreign currencies	−623	−615
U.S. government assets, other than official reserve assets, net	1,215	7,580
U.S. credits and other long-term assets	−3,044	−2,217
Repayments on U.S. credits and other long-term assets	4,221	5,720
U.S. foreign currency holdings and U.S. short-term assets, net	38	4,077
U.S. private assets, net	−859,529	−513,405
Direct investment	−252,012	−21,481
Foreign securities	−102,383	−155,244
U.S. claims on unaffiliated foreigners reported by U.S. nonbanking concerns	−149,001	−118,522
U.S. claims reported by U.S. banks, not included elsewhere	−356,133	−218,158
Foreign-owned assets in the United States, net [increase/financial inflow (+)]	**1,440,105**	**1,292,695**
Foreign official assets in the United States, net	394,710	220,676
U.S. government securities	311,133	177,179
Other U.S. government liabilities	488	−134
U.S. liabilities reported by U.S. banks, not included elsewhere	70,329	24,272
Other foreign official assets	12,760	19,359
Other foreign assets in the United States, net	1,045,395	1,072,019
Statistical discrepancy (sum of above items with sign reversed)	**85,126**	**9,626**
Memoranda:		
Balance on goods	−665,390	−781,642
Balance on services	47,807	58,026
Balance on goods and services	−617,583	−723,616
Balance on income	30,439	1,567
Unilateral current transfers, net	−80,930	−82,896
Balance on current account	−668,074	−804,945

Source: U.S. Dept. of Commerce Bureau of Economic Analysis, International Economic Accounts, http://www.bea.gov/bea/international/bp_web/simple.cfm?anon = 71& table_id = 1 & area_id = 3.

short-term capital flows

Changes in international assets and liabilities with an original maturity of one year or less

c. **Short-term capital flows** involve changes in international assets and liabilities with an original maturity of one year or less. Some of the fastest-growing types of short-term flows are for currency exchange rate and interest rate hedging in the forward, futures, option, and swap markets. (These subjects have to do with risk coverage and will be addressed in Chapter 20, "Financial Management.") Among the more traditional types of short-term capital flows are payments and receipts for international finance and trade, short-term borrowings from foreign banks, exchanges of foreign notes or coins, and purchases of foreign commercial paper or foreign government bills or notes. The volatility, private nature, and wide varieties of short-term capital flows make them the most difficult BOP items to measure and, therefore, predictably the least reliable measurement in the BOP. Wide fluctuations of currency exchange rates and interest rates from the 1980s forward due to the floating exchange system have led to the surge in hedging activities.

official reserves account

Record of the assets held by the government, gold, foreign currencies, and accounts in foreign banks; a balance of the country's foreign currency

Official Reserves Account   The **official reserves account** deals with (a) gold imports and exports, (b) increases or decreases in foreign exchange (foreign currencies) held by the government, and (c) decreases or increases in liabilities to foreign central banks. Because some BOP figures are inaccurate and incomplete (for example, the short-term capital flows item or time lags), the statistical discrepancy item is used to bring total credits and debits into accounting balance.

DEFICITS AND SURPLUSES IN BOP ACCOUNTS

The BOP current account and capital account add up to the total account, which, given the double-entry approach, is balanced. So a deficit in the current account is always accompanied by an equal surplus in the capital account, and vice versa. Let's see how this works. If you purchase a case of French wine in the United States for $200, your payment, as it heads out of the United States and to the French winery, will be recorded as a debit in the U.S. current account. Once the winery receives your dollars, it has to do something with them. If the treasurer of the winery decides to deposit your payment in a dollar account at a U.S. bank, the amount will show up as a credit in the U.S. capital account. If the winery exchanges your dollar payment for euros, then the bank receiving the dollars will have to make a decision about how to spend or invest the dollars. Sooner or later, these dollars will show up as a credit on the U.S. account.

Contrary to the commonly held belief, a current account deficit is not, in itself, a sign of bad economic conditions. What it means is that the country is importing capital. This is no more unnatural or dangerous than importing wine or cheese. The deficit is a response to conditions in the country. Among these conditions could be excessive inflation, low productivity, or inadequate saving. In the case of the United States, a current account deficit could occur because investments in the United States are secure and profitable. If there is a problem, it is in the underlying conditions and not in the deficit per se.[28] Countries with relatively high price levels, gross national products, interest rates, and exchange rates, as well as relatively low barriers to imports and attractive investment opportunities, are more likely to have current account deficits than are other countries.[29]

Right now the United States has a substantial deficit in its current account, $804.9 billion in 2005.[30] Citizens of the United States are importing more goods and services than they are exporting. At the same time, there is a surplus in the U.S. capital account. Those dollars that leave the United States to pay for imported goods come back into the United States in the form of foreign-owned investments, for example, Treasury bills and investment property in New York City. So let's remember that a deficit or surplus in the current account cannot be explained or evaluated without simultaneously examining an equal surplus or deficit in the capital account.[31]

When the U.S. current account balance shifted from a surplus of $8 billion in 1981 to a deficit of $147 billion in 1987, there was much concern. The shift was cited as the cause of unemployment in the United States. Herbert Stein points out, though, that "between 1981 and 1987, the number of people employed rose by over 12 million, and employment as a percent of population rose from 60 percent to 62.5 percent."[32]

As is to be expected, the capital accounts showed a parallel surplus, which was interpreted as a danger to the country. The popular fear was that the United States was becoming owned by foreigners. In particular, Arab investment in commercial agriculture and Japanese trophy real estate investments such as Rockefeller Center (now owned by a wealthy Chicago

WORLD view

Central Reserve/National Currency Conflict

Every member of the IMF keeps a *reserve account,* a bit like a savings account, with holdings the country can draw on when needed to finance trade or investments or to intervene in currency markets. As of March 2006, the countries with the largest reserve accounts are China ($875 billion), Japan ($852 billion), Taiwan (Republic of China, $257 billion), Russia ($231 billion), Korea ($223 billion), India ($148 billion), and Hong Kong ($125 billion). The reserve assets are gold, foreign exchange, SDRs, and reserve positions in the IMF. The U.S. dollar has been the most used central reserve asset in the world since the end of World War II, and at the end of the first quarter of 2005, roughly 60 percent of the world's $3.8 trillion reserve assets were held in dollars and 25 percent in euros. The dollars, held in the form of U.S. Treasury bonds, earn interest, so the more dollars held in the central reserve account, the better. But the countries holding those U.S. dollars in their foreign reserve accounts don't want their central reserve asset to lose value, and therein lies a contradiction: At some point, holding large numbers of U.S. dollars (or any other product) in supply causes them to lose value—the law of supply and demand.

At the same time, the U.S. dollar is the national currency of the United States of America, whose government must deal with inflation, recession, interest rates, unemployment, and other national, internal problems. The U.S. government uses fiscal and monetary policies to meet those problems—higher or lower taxes, decisions on how to spend available revenue, growth or contraction of the money supply, and rate of its growth or contraction.

It would be only accidental if the national interests of the United States in dealing with its internal problems were to coincide with the interests of the multitude of countries holding U.S. dollars in their central reserve asset accounts. For example, the United States may be slowing money supply growth and raising taxes to combat U.S. inflation, while the world needs more liquidity, in the form of U.S. dollars, to finance growth, trade, or investment. Or the United States may be stimulating its economy through faster money supply growth and lower taxes at a time when so many U.S. dollars are already outstanding that their value is dropping—not a happy state of affairs for countries holding U.S. dollars.

It was a quirk of history that thrust the currency of the United States into this conflicting role. The IMF hoped that a nonnational asset, the SDR, would rescue the US$ and the world from this conflict.

Source: Remarks by Chairman Alan Greenspan, November 14, 2005. See www.federalreserve.gov/BOARDDOCS/Speeches/2005/20051114/default.htm.

---

family and a New York real estate developer) scared many Americans. The fact is, though, that the foreign capital did not reduce the assets owned by Americans. Instead, it added to the capital stock within the country.[33]

SPECIAL DRAWING RIGHT (SDR)

The IMF created the **special drawing right (SDR)** in 1969 as a reserve asset, in an attempt to support the Bretton Woods fixed exchange rate system. We have seen already that Bretton Woods' fixed exchange rate regime did not hold. A country participating in this system had to have official government reserves that could be used to purchase its currency in world foreign exchange markets in order to maintain the exchange rate. As trade and international finance volumes expanded, the two main reserve assets, the U.S. dollar and gold, could no longer meet the need. Therefore, the IMF created this new international reserve asset—not a currency but, rather, an accounting transaction, a ledger entry. The objective was to make the SDR the principal reserve asset in the international monetary system.[34] The SDR also may be a step toward a truly international currency, albeit a small step.

The SDR's value is based on a basket of the following four currencies (with the percentage of each currency in parentheses): U.S. dollar (44), euro (34), Japanese yen (11), and British pound sterling (11). The weights broadly reflect the relative importance of the currencies in trade and payments, based on the value of the exports of goods and services by the member-countries issuing these currencies, reevaluated every five years. The dollar value of the SDR is posted daily on the IMF site at www.imf.org/external/np/fin/rates/rms_sdrv.cfm. Actually, because four currencies are involved in determining its value, the SDR remains more stable than any of the single currencies. That stability has made the SDR increasingly attractive as a unit for denominating international transactions. Future payment under a contract, for example, may be negotiated to be in a specified national currency at its rate in terms

special drawing right (SDR)
An international reserve asset established by the IMF; the unit of account for the IMF and other international organizations

of the SDR on the payment date, and some Swiss and British banks now accept accounts denominated in SDRs. The Bank for International Settlements also uses the SDR as its unit of account, as does the IMF, its 184 members, and 15 other official international institutions.

Yet today the SDR has limited use as a reserve asset. When the Bretton Woods system collapsed, the major currencies shifted to a floating exchange rate regime. In addition, the growth in international capital markets facilitated borrowing by creditworthy governments. Both of these developments lessened the need for SDRs. The ability of the SDR to serve as a safety net should the international monetary system run into serious difficulty has yet to be tested.

Summary

Explain the functioning of the gold standard.

Since ancient times, gold has been trusted as a way for people to store value, to exchange value, and to measure value. Under a gold standard, each country set a certain number of units of its currency per ounce of gold, and the ratios of their gold equivalence would establish the exchange rate between any two currencies. In essence, currencies were pegged to gold.

Describe the purposes of the IMF.

The basic idea of the IMF is that a workable international monetary system is in the interests of all nations. Its Articles of Agreement outline the purpose of the fund in six points: to promote international monetary cooperation, to facilitate the expansion and balanced growth of international trade, to promote exchange stability and orderly exchange arrangements among members, to assist in the establishment of a multilateral system of payments, to make the fund's resources available for balance-of-payments corrections, and to shorten the duration and lessen the disequilibrium of members' balance of payments.[35]

Appreciate the accomplishments of the Bretton Woods system and the developments shaping the world monetary system from the end of World War II to the present.

The gold exchange standard, established at Bretton Woods after World War II, worked until the 1970s, when it collapsed due to inflation and the surplus of U.S. dollars held outside the United States. Until then, the Bretton Woods system provided monetary stability that supported the growth of international trade.

Describe the purpose of the World Bank.

The World Bank lends money for development projects in middle-income and creditworthy poor countries. It provides low-interest loans and grants for projects designed to help countries develop infrastructure, health and education, and other areas connected to development.

Discuss the purpose of the Bank for International Settlements.

The Bank for International Settlements operates as a central bankers' bank. In addition, it serves as a forum for central bankers' discussions, leading to international monetary cooperation; as a center for research; and as an agent or trustee for governments in various international financial arrangements.

Discuss the floating exchange rate system.

There are three basic arrangements found in the floating exchange rate system: a free float, a managed float, and a fixed peg. Under a free (clean) float, market demand and supply regulate the exchange rate. In the managed (dirty) float, governments may intervene in the currency markets as they perceive their national interests to be served. In a fixed peg, the value of a currency is set at a fixed rate to another currency. There are other modifications of these three basic approaches, including having no currency and using that of another country; using different approaches to the peg, including operating it within a band or allowing it to crawl; having a currency board; and managing a floating exchange.

Describe the development of the common currency area for the euro.

The euro zone, established by the Maastricht treaty, began trading only in euros in 2002. There are presently 12 members in the euro zone, and many of the newly acceding countries want to join. Slovenia will be joining in 2007.

Explain the role of the balance of payments (BOP).

The balance of payments is a statistical record of a country's transactions with the rest of the world. From a business perspective, the BOP helps businesspeople predict what sort of economic environment might develop in the country.

Discuss the major BOP accounts.

The major BOP accounts are the current account, which tracks the net changes in exports and imports of goods and services; the capital account, which records the net changes in a nation's international financial assets and liabilities; and the official reserves account, which deals with the government's holdings of foreign currency, gold, and, possibly, SDRs.

Explain the uses of special drawing rights (SDRs).

SDRs were established by the IMF to replace the U.S. dollar as the main central reserve asset. They have not yet done so. SDRs do not circulate; they are an accounting entry.

gold standard (p. 140)
Bretton Woods (p. 141)
Interntional Monetary Fund (p. 142)
par value (p. 143)
Triffin paradox (p. 143)
World Bank (p. 144)
Bank for International Settlements
   (p. 145)

fixed currency exchange rates (p. 146)
floating currency exchange rates (p. 146)
Jamaica Agreement (p. 146)
euro (p. 148)
balance of payments (BOP) (p. 149)
current account (p. 150)
goods or merchandise account (p. 150)
trade balance (p. 150)

services account (p. 150)
unilateral transfer (p. 150)
capital account (p. 150)
direct investment (p. 150)
portfolio investment (p. 150)
short term capital flows (p. 152)
official reserves account (p. 152)
special drawing right (SDR) (p. 153)

Questions

1. Explain the appeal gold holds for people. Discuss the pros and cons of a gold standard.

2. What is the Bretton Woods system?

3. Explain the role of the IMF.

4. Given the purpose of the IMF and World Bank, why do you think they are the target of considerable criticism? In your opinion, is this criticism justified?

5. Explain the current exchange rate arrangements.

6. The euro has now replaced 12 national currencies. What are some of the resulting advantages and savings for EU members?

7. What advantages does the euro zone offer to businesses outside the EU?

8. The European Central Bank now sets monetary policy for 12 European countries. What sorts of difficulties might that cause?

9. Why should managers monitor the BOP of the country in which their business operates?

10. Why were SDRs created? Discuss their success in their original mission and their current uses.

Research Task

globalEDGE globalEDGE.msu.edu

Use the globalEDGE site (http://globalEDGE.msu.edu/) to complete the following exercises:

1. The international reserves set aside is one way that countries attempt to maintain financial stability in times of economic turbulence. As such, the United Nations Conference on Trade and Development (UNCTAD) maintains international finance statistics on many developing countries. Using the *UNCTAD Handbook*, determine the international reserves for Costa Rica, Indonesia, Lebanon, Nigeria, and South Africa for 2004. Which country has the highest reserves? Which country has the lowest reserves? Do you think

these statistics provide any indication as to the level of protection each economy may have in light of unforeseen economic turbulence? Why or why not?

2. The Biz/ed Web site presents a "Trade Balance and Exchange Rate Simulation" which helps one understand how a change in exchange rates influences a country's trade balance. Locate the online simulator (check under the Academy section of globalEDGE) and identify what the trade balance is assumed to be a function of. Run the simulation to identify how exchange rate changes affect the exports, imports, and trade balance.

SDR Exchange Risk Minicase 5.1

The Asian Development Bank has made loans denominated in SDRs to several of its MNE customers in Southeast Asia. It has built up a portfolio to the amount of SDR 8 million.

Management decides to hedge by selling in the forward market the currencies that make up the SDR basket. How much of each currency must be hedged?

section three

International Environmental Forces

In Chapter 1, we stated that many practices followed at home can be transferred intact to other countries. However, we also mentioned that because of the differences in environmental forces, some ways of doing business must be adapted to local conditions or changed completely.

In Section Three, we shall examine these forces to see how they differ from those we encounter at home.

We begin Section Three with Chapter 6, which discusses cultural forces and points out that the variety of attitudes and values among cultures affects managers of all the business functions.

Next we look at the physical forces—location, topography, and climate (Chapter 7). The importance of natural resources and environmental sustainability is emphasized.

In Chapter 8, we explore economic and socioeconomic forces, including the underground economy. Management must know how land, labor, and capital are allocated to production and distribution.

In Chapter 9, we investigate the political forces that affect the success or failure of a foreign venture. Some of these are nationalism, terrorism, unstable governments, international organizations, and government-owned businesses.

Legal forces, the subject of Chapter 10, set the constraints within which managers must operate.

We continue with a discussion of the financial forces in Chapter 11. Some of these forces are currency exchange risks, taxation, tariffs, monetary and fiscal policies, inflation, and national accounting rules.

Finally, the composition, skills, and attitudes of an area's labor pool must be investigated because these forces affect productivity and, ultimately, the firm's profitability. Chapter 12 discusses these forces.

6

Sociocultural Forces

Speaking about cultural differences among Europeans . . . it is no good focusing on similarities and common interests and hoping things will work out. We have to recognize the differences and work with them.

—*Dr. Allan Hjorth, Copenhagen Business School, trainer in cross-cultural behavior*

Six Rules of Thumb for Doing Business across Cultures

Knowing your customer is just as important anywhere in the world as it is at home, whether one is aiming to sell computers in Abidjan or soft drinks in Kuala Lumpur. Each culture has its logic, and within that logic are real, sensible reasons for the way foreigners do things. If the businessperson can figure out the basic pattern of the culture, he or she will be more effective interacting with foreign clients and colleagues. The following six rules of thumb are helpful:

1. *Be prepared.* Whether traveling abroad or selling from home, no one should approach a foreign market without doing his or her homework. A mentor is most desirable, complemented by lots of reading on social and business etiquette, history and folklore, current affairs (including relations between your two countries), the culture's values, geography, sources of pride (artists, musicians, sports), religion, political structure, and practical matters such as currency and hours of business. Mimi Murphy, an exporter who trades primarily in Indonesia, says, "Whenever I travel, the first thing I do in any town is read the newspaper. Then when I meet my customer, I can talk about the sports or the news of the day. He knows that I am interested in the things he is interested in, and he will want to do business with me." The Internet can be helpful here as a source of information.

2. *Slow down.* Americans are clock watchers. In many countries, Americans are seen to be in a rush—in other words, unfriendly, arrogant, and untrustworthy. In other countries, the Japanese and Germans are considered to be somewhat time-obsessed. As current "mobile culture" teenagers become businesspeople, however, we may more and more tend to self-organize "on the fly."

3. *Establish trust.* Often American-style crisp business relationships will get you nowhere. Product quality, pricing, and clear contracts compete with the personal *relationship and trust* that are developed carefully and sincerely over time. The marketer must be established as *simpatico,* worthy of the business, and dependable in the long run.

4. *Understand the importance of language.* Obviously, translations must be done by a professional who speaks both languages fluently, who has a vocabulary sensitive to nuance and connotation, and who has talent with the idioms and imagery of each culture. An interpreter is often critical and may be helpful even when one of the parties speaks the other's language.

5. *Respect the culture.* Manners are important. The traveling representative is a guest in the country and must respect the host's rules. As a Saudi Arabian official states in one of the *Going International* films, "Americans in foreign countries have a tendency to treat the natives as foreigners, and they forget that actually it is *they* who are the foreigners themselves!"

6. *Understand components of culture.* Any region is a sort of cultural iceberg with two components: *surface culture* (fads, styles, food, etc.) and *deep culture* (attitudes, beliefs, values). Less than 15 percent of a region's culture is visible, and strangers to the culture must look below the surface. Consider the British habit of automatically lining up on the sidewalk when

CONCEPT PREVIEWS

After reading this chapter, you should be able to:

explain the significance of culture for international business

identify the sociocultural components of culture

discuss the significance of religion to businesspeople

explain the cultural aspects of technology

discuss the pervasiveness of the information technology era

explain the importance of the ability to speak the local language

discuss the importance of unspoken language in international business

discuss the two classes of relationships within a society

discuss Hofstede's four cultural value dimensions

waiting for a bus. This surface cultural trait seems to reflect a deep cultural desire to lead neat and controlled lives. Knowledge about other cultures and how they affect the way people do business may show businesspeople working in a culture different from their own that their solutions are not always the appropriate ones for a given task. Understanding this is the first step in learning to use cultural differences to gain a strategic advantage. Mishandling or ignoring cultural differences can cause numerous problems, such as lost sales, the departure of competent employees, and low morale that contributes to low productivity. When these differences are blended successfully, however, they can result in innovative business practices superior to those that either culture could produce by itself. ■

Source: Lisa Hoecklin, "Managing Cultural Differences," www .latinsynergy.org/strategicjointventure.htm#CHILE (December 27, 2000); "How to Negotiate European Style," *Journal of European Business,* July–August 1993, p. 46; and "Japanese Punctuality," http://joi.ito.com/ archives/2005/04/28/japanese_punctuality.html (August 4, 2006).

The national characteristics you encounter in this chapter and elsewhere are generalizations. They are broadly true, but there are always exceptions. Furthermore, characteristics change over time. The Scandinavians were considered by a 10th-century writer to be "the filthiest race God ever created," and a noted 18th-century writer was amazed at the lack of German military spirit and how easygoing Germans were compared to the French.[1] Before we examine the significance of culture for international businesspeople, let us first define culture.

What Is Culture?

culture

Sum total of beliefs, rules, techniques, institutions, and artifacts that characterize human populations

Although there are countless definitions of culture, most anthropologists view **culture** as the *sum total of the beliefs, rules, techniques, institutions, and artifacts that characterize human populations.*[2] In other words, culture consists of the "individual worldviews, social rules, and interpersonal dynamics characterizing a group of people set in a particular time and place."[3] Most anthropologists also agree that:

1. Culture is *learned,* not innate.

2. The various aspects of culture are *interrelated.*

3. Culture is *shared.*

4. Culture *defines the boundaries* of different groups.[4]

Because society is composed of people and their culture, it is virtually impossible to speak of one without referring to the other. Anthropologists often use the terms interchangeably or combine them into one word—*sociocultural.*[5] This is the term we shall use, because the variables in which businesspeople are interested are both social and cultural.

When people work in societies and cultures different from their own, the problems they encounter in dealing with a single set of cultures are multiplied by the number of cultural sets they find in each of their foreign markets. All too often, unfortunately, people who are familiar with only one cultural pattern may believe they have an awareness of cultural differences elsewhere, when in reality they do not. Unless they have had occasion to make comparisons with other cultures, they are probably not even aware of the important features of their own. They are probably also oblivious to the fact that many societies consider their culture superior to all others (**ethnocentricity**) and that their attempts to introduce the "German way" or the "American way" may be met with stubborn resistance.

ethnocentricity

Belief in the superiority of one's own ethnic group (see the *self-reference criterion* in Chapter 1)

How do international businesspeople learn to live with other cultures? The first step is to realize that there are cultures different from their own. Then they must go on to learn the characteristics of those cultures so that they may adapt to them. E. T. Hall, a famous anthropologist, claims this can be accomplished in only two ways: (1) Spend a lifetime in a country, or (2) undergo an extensive, highly sophisticated training program that covers the main characteristics of a culture, including the language. The program he mentions must be more than a briefing on a country's customs. It should be a study of what culture is and what it does, imparting some knowledge of the various ways in which human behavior has been institutionalized in a country.[6]

Culture Affects All Business Functions

MARKETING

In marketing, the wide variation in attitudes and values requires that many firms use diffferent marketing mixes in different markets.

> In Japan, Procter & Gamble (P&G) used an advertisement for Camay soap in which a man meeting a woman for the first time compared her skin to that of a fine porcelain doll. Although the ad had worked well in South America and Europe, it insulted the Japanese. "For a Japanese man to say something like that to a Japanese woman means he's either unsophisticated or rude," said an advertising man who worked on the account. Interestingly, P&G used the ad despite the warning from the advertising agency.
>
> Another Camay ad that failed in Japan showed a Japanese woman bathing when her husband walks into the bathroom. She begins to tell him about her new beauty soap, but the husband, stroking her shoulder, hints that suds are not what are on his mind. Although it was well received in Europe, it failed badly in Japan, where it is considered bad manners for a husband to intrude on his wife.
>
> P&G also erred because it lacked knowledge about the business culture. The company introduced Cheer detergent by discounting its price, but this lowered the soap's reputation. Said a competitor, "Unlike in Europe and the United States, once you discount your product here, it's hard to raise the price again." Wholesalers were alienated because they made less money due to lower margins. Moreover, apparently P&G didn't realize that Japanese housewives shop in the 50,000 or more neighborhood convenience stores close to home. These small retailers, who sell 30 percent of all the detergent bought in Japan, have limited shelf space and thus do not like to carry discounted products because of the lower profit earned.[7]

Although acquiring knowledge about Japanese culture was both time-consuming and expensive, evidently P&G was a good learner. Eight years after its difficulties with Cheer detergent, the company reentered the soap market, which was then controlled by two powerful Japanese consumer products concerns, Kao and Lion Corporation. Just two years later P&G held 20 percent of the market. What did it do differently this time?

When the home office told the Japanese affiliate to find new markets for products in which the firm was strong elsewhere in the world, P&G–Japan sent researchers to study Japanese dishwashing habits. They found that Japanese homemakers used much more detergent than was needed. This indicated that consumers wanted a more powerful soap, which P&G's laboratory created. The marketing message was simple: A little bit of Joy cleans better yet is easier on the hands. This message hit home. Said a Japanese homemaker who, after seeing the pilot commercials, rushed to buy a bottle, "Grease on Tupperware, that's the toughest thing to wash off. I had to try it."

Retailers wanted the product because P&G did the things it hadn't done with Cheer. For example, this time the profit margins for the retailers were high. P&G also exploited a weakness in the competing Japanese products: Their long-necked bottles wasted space, but Joy bottles were compact cylinders that took up less space in stores, warehouses, and delivery trucks. A buyer for a large Japanese store chain estimated that the bottle improved the efficiency of the store's distribution by 40 percent.

The P&G ad campaign also delighted Japanese retailers. Its agency designed a TV commercial in which a famous comedian dropped in on homemakers unannounced with a camera crew to test Joy on dirty dishes in the home. The camera focused on a patch of oil in a pan full of water. After a drop of Joy, the oil dramatically disappeared. Japanese soapmakers found that over 70 percent of Joy users had begun using it after seeing the commercial. "We mistakenly assumed Japanese didn't care much about grease-fighting power in dish soaps," the Kao dish-soap brand manager said. P&G, which had studied this part of Japanese culture, did know.[8]

Cultural Success and Failure in Disneyland

Why is it that Disneyland Paris had problems with falling attendance and losses while Tokyo Disneyland had steadily increasing attendance and is the most profitable Disney park? The experts who predicted that Tokyo Disneyland attendance would peak in the first year and then taper off were wrong; it has increased steadily. The park owes some of its success to its location in a metropolitan area of 30 million people, but a cultural change is believed to be a major reason for its success. Some say that Walt Disney Productions has written a new chapter in Japanese social history by popularizing the idea that family outings can be fun. Families now account for half of the park's visitors. An executive of Disney states, "Leisure was not always a part of the Japanese lifestyle. Fathers used to see family outings as a duty."

The early staggering losses at Disneyland Paris stemmed from the high interest costs and high overheads, many of which were caused by cultural errors. To cover the project's $4 billion cost, Disney put up just $170 million for 49 percent of the operation and public shareholders paid $1 billion for the 51 percent they own. The $2.9 billion balance was borrowed at interest rates of up to 11 percent. Disney management expected to reduce the debt by selling the six big hotels it had built, but the $340-per-night price it charged had kept them about half full. Moreover, the guests weren't staying as long or spending as much as Disney had planned.

Disney executives believed, incorrectly, that they could change the French attitude of not wanting to take their children from school during the school year, as Americans do, or not wanting to take more short breaks during the year, instead of one long vacation during the month of August. This would have given Euro Disney steady, high attendance all year rather than for just one month. One reason the visitors didn't spend more was the extremely high prices. Almost two years passed before Disney lowered them. Another reason the guests didn't spend

more, even though in this case they wanted to, was also due to a cultural problem: the breakfast debacle. Apparently, a decision involving millions of dollars in revenue was based not on research but only on what someone told Disney. One executive said, "We were told that Europeans don't take breakfast, so we downsized the restaurants." However, when the park opened, everyone wanted breakfast and wouldn't settle for just croissants and coffee; they wanted bacon and eggs. Disney tried to serve 2,500 breakfasts in hotel restaurants seating 350 people. The Disney solution for the French public, known worldwide as connoisseurs of good eating: prepackaged breakfasts delivered to hotel rooms.

After 1995, Disneyland Paris worked to correct the cultural and financial errors that kept attendance down and losses up. The park cut admission prices by 22 percent and hotel rates by one-third. In addition to the original expensive, sit-down restaurants that Disney mistakenly believed all Europeans would demand, cheaper fast food is now available in self-service restaurants. Instead of marketing the park to Europe as if it were a single country, Disneyland Paris has offices in all the main European capitals, and each office tailors tour packages to fit its own market. By 1998 Disneyland Paris was France's biggest tourist attraction.

Disney is also continuing to build in Asia. A second park near Tokyo—DisneySea—opened in late 2001. In China, Disney has opened Hong Kong Disneyland. Again, Disney stumbled early, with low attendance and confusion among guests as to what to expect. Disney responded with a new marketing campaign and dozens of changes inside the park, including more seats because Chinese guests take an average of 10 minutes longer to eat than Americans. Management has also taken steps to see that Mandarin speakers don't accidentally get in the lines to hear English-speaking guides. Disney has a second Chinese Disney site planned for Shanghai, to open in 2010, which will be four times larger than the Hong Kong attraction.

Source: "Euro Disney's Fortunes Turn as Number of Visitors Rises," *Financial Times*, November 14, 1997, p. 13; "The Kingdom inside a Republic," *The Economist*, April 13, 1996, pp. 66–67; "Tokyo Disney Shifts Japanese Ideas on Leisure," *The Columbian*, May 1, 1994, p. F7; "Mickey n'est pas fini," *Forbes*, February 14, 1994, p. 42; "Euro Disney's Wish Comes True," *The Economist*, March 19, 1994, p. 83; http://hongkongdisneyland.com/eng (Sept. 22, 2004); and Merissa Marr and Geoffrey A. Fowler, "Chinese Lessons for Disney," *The Wall Street Journal*, June 12, 2006, pp. A1, A5.

It's important that each element of marketing be considered for its cultural relevance. For example, studies show that background music in ads that isn't consistent with the rest of the ad—say, traditional Chinese music in an ad for a modern shampoo product featuring blond models—will increase recall of the ad but will probably produce an overall negative response.[9]

Unlike P&G, Disney seemed to have an ideal global product and global promotion. According to the *Tokyo Disneyland Guidebook,* the Tokyo theme park is the same as those in California and Florida. Disneyland Paris is also similar, although, because of the French insistence on protecting their language and culture, Mickey and Donald developed French accents, and the Sleeping Beauty castle is called *Le Chateau de la Belle au Bois Dormant.* The Worldview box illustrates the problems a global firm can have when its management makes culturally insensitive decisions.

HUMAN RESOURCE MANAGEMENT

The national culture is also a key determinant for the evaluation of managers. In Great Britain, an American general manager complained, people were promoted because of the school they had attended and their family background but not for their accomplishments. School ties are important in France, too. In fact, this phenomenon extends elsewhere—an example is the elite Bishop Cotton Boys School in India.

PRODUCTION AND FINANCE

Personnel problems can result from differences in attitudes toward authority, another sociocultural variable. Latin Americans have traditionally regarded the manager as the *patron,* an authoritarian figure responsible for their welfare. When American managers accustomed to a participative leadership style are transferred to Latin America, they must become more authoritarian, or their employees will consider them weak and incompetent.

> *A production manager who had been sent to Peru from the United States was convinced that he could motivate the workers to achieve higher productivity by instituting a more democratic decision-making style. He brought in trainers from the home office to teach the supervisors how to solicit suggestions and feedback from the workers. Shortly after the new management style was introduced, the workers began quitting their jobs. When asked why, they replied that the new production manager and his supervisors apparently didn't know what to do and were therefore asking the workers for advice. The workers thought the company wouldn't last long with that kind of management, and they wanted to quit before the collapse, because then everyone would be hunting for a job at the same time.*

Production managers have found that attitudes toward change can seriously influence the acceptance of new production methods; even treasurers realize the strength of the sociocultural forces when, armed with excellent balance sheets, they approach local banks, only to find that the banks attach far more importance to who they are than to how strong their companies are.[10] One reason for Disney's financial problems in Paris was the insensitive attitude of Disney executives toward European business culture. A top French banker involved in the negotiations to restructure the park's debt claimed, "The Walt Disney group is making a major error in thinking it can impose its will once more."[11] These are just a few examples to show that sociocultural differences do affect all the business functions. As we examine the components of the sociocultural forces, we shall mention others.

Sociocultural Components

It should be apparent that to be successful in their relationships with people in other countries, international businesspeople must be students of culture. They must have factual knowledge, which is relatively easy to obtain, but they must also become sensitive to cultural differences, and this is more difficult. Hall, as we saw, recommended spending a lifetime in a country or, in lieu of this, undergoing an extensive program to study what the culture is and what it does. But most newcomers to international business do not even have the opportunity for area orientation. They can, however, take the important first step of realizing that there *are* other cultures. In this chapter we cannot do more than point out some of the important sociocultural differences as they concern businesspeople in the hope that you will become more aware of the need to be culturally sensitive—to know that there are cultural differences for which you must look. Remember that the more you know about another person's culture, the better your predictions of that person's behavior will be.

The concept of culture is so broad that even ethnologists (cultural anthropologists) have to break it down into topics to facilitate its study. A listing of such topics will give us a better understanding of what culture is and may also serve as a guide for international managers when they are analyzing a particular problem from the sociocultural viewpoint.

Experts' opinions on the components of culture vary, but the following list is representative of their thinking. Culture is:

1. Aesthetics
2. Attitudes and beliefs
3. Religion
4. Material culture
5. Language
6. Societal organization
7. Education
8. Legal characteristics
9. Political structures[12]

We shall examine the first six components in this chapter and leave educational issues, legal characteristics, and political structures for later chapters.

Aesthetics

aesthetics
A culture's sense of beauty and good taste

Aesthetics pertains to a culture's sense of beauty and good taste and is expressed in its art, drama, music, folklore, and dances.

ART

Of particular interest to international businesspeople are the formal aspects of art, color, and form because of the symbolic meanings they convey. Colors, especially, can be deceptive because they mean different things to different cultures. The color of mourning is black in the United States and Mexico, black and white in the Far East, and purple in Brazil. Green is a propitious color in the Islamic world, and any ad or package featuring green is looked at favorably there. While in the United States mints are packaged in blue or green paper, in Africa the wrapper is red. So marketers must be careful to check whether colors have any special meanings before using them for products, packages, or advertisements.

Be careful of symbols, too. The number seven signifies good luck in the United States but the opposite in Singapore, Ghana, and Kenya. In Japan, the number four is unlucky. If you are giving a Japanese client golf balls, make sure there are more or less than four in the package. Also, in general, avoid using a nation's flag or any symbols connected with religion.

Nike, the athletic shoe marketer, recalled 38,000 pairs of shoes carrying the word air *written in flaming letters because, according to Muslims, it resembles the word* Allah *in Arabic. Another 30,000 pairs were diverted from Arabian countries to less sensitive countries. Recently, protests in Europe followed the publication in Denmark of cartoons showing Mohammed wearing a turban shaped like a bomb.[13]*

It is also important to learn whether there are local aesthetic preferences for form that could affect the design of products, packaging, or even the building in which the firm is located. The American style of steel and glass in the midst of oriental architecture will be a constant reminder to the local population of the outsider's presence.

Feng Shui   In Asia, it is often believed that if buildings, furniture, roads, and other human-made objects are placed in harmony with nature, they can bring good fortune. If they are not, they will cause a disaster. Before building a house, scheduling a funeral, or making an investment, a master of *feng shui* (pronounced "fung shway") is called in to give a seal of approval.

Occupancy in a five-star hotel in Shanghai was down to just 5 percent. Desperate to find a remedy, the management called in a master of feng shui *to examine the hotel. His analysis—very bad*

BUILDING YOUR GLOBAL RÉSUMÉ Tips from Your Personal Global Mentor

Kelty McRae is a human resources business partner and vice president at Wachovia Securities in Charlotte, North Carolina, where she consults with senior leaders in the Corporate and Investment Banking Division to develop and drive the planning and execution of the human capital business plan. She partners with business leaders to build a culture that minimizes risk, maximizes diversity, and enhances business performance, resulting in improved efficiency, employee retention and utilization, and human capital ROI. Kelty serves as a coach to leaders on both personal development and the development of leaders' direct reports, as well as practices that reinforce a high-performance culture. Kelty works with clients who conduct business in India, China, Korea, Taiwan, Singapore, Germany, France, England, and Ireland. For her first international business experience, Kelty traveled to India in the spring of 2006. Here are Kelty's comments about the impacts of a foreign culture as experienced on her first-time international business trip:

My most memorable first-time international business experience occurred while delivering stand-up training to newly hired Genpact employees in Gurgaon, India. Wachovia partners with Genpact Corporation in support of its offshoring and outsourcing efforts. Learning about social norms prior to my arrival prepared me for how to interact with business leaders from another culture and what to expect in the classroom. For example, many of the students initially avoided direct eye contact, which is a sign of respect in India for one's elders. In America, a teacher might assume lack of eye contact as a lack of interest in learning; however, in the Genpact training room this proved to be far from reality. The seemingly "shy" Genpact employees absorbed and conquered knowledge aggressively. Initially, there were many times throughout the course of training that we felt compelled to check for understanding of the material, as there didn't seem to be an uninhibited openness of the students to ask questions as you might see in an American training class. We determined after a period of time that silence to "Are you familiar with XXX" definitely meant that we needed to provide more information. The culture calls for "saving face," and although Indians are voracious learners with a strong achievement orientation, the norm seemed to be to not cause embarrassment to any individual for lack of knowledge.

I found India to differ dramatically from any other place I have been, and the experience invigorating while at times energy zapping. The sheer increase in the number of people around you, social norms about personal space, and various styles of interpersonal communication absorb your attention. There is extreme poverty and what may appear to an American as a lack of residential vs. commercial zoning. Migrant workers line all streets with tent villages. Cars and trucks, mopeds and bikes, donkeys and an occasional camel or elephant share the road with sacred cows. Orderly chaos is the best description. The system seems crazy, ineffective, and light years behind America, but amazingly it works!

You cannot pick up a Newsweek, Time, or other business magazine without hearing about "Incredible India." India's advancement and economical potential is and will increasingly be a powerful worldly force. It is clear that India has infrastructure issues to address; however, a magical underlying energy waits to slowly make its mark on society. In my view, regardless of political party alignments associated with outsourcing/offshoring efforts, Americans should seek to learn about the impact India is having on the world's economy and how their culture offers a unique and important lesson for us all.

Kelty's advice on how to get a job in international business:

- "Target positions in multinational organizations and or organizations involved in the offshoring and outsourcing of work to foreign countries."

- "Choose internship opportunities that will allow you to work with a diverse population."

Kelty's advice on succeeding in international business:

- "Cultural awareness, exceptional interpersonal/communication skills, ability to be nimble, flexible in approach to problem solving."

- "Openness to new experiences/change and foreign language skills."

- "Assume nothing, be open to learning. Seek to understand the source of difference. Do your homework—proactively learn about other countries' cultural values."

World Wide Resources:

www.wachoviasecurities.com

www.eweek.com/article2/0,1895,1853721,00.asp

www.kwintessential.co.uk/etiquette/doing-business-in.html

feng shui *because the building was at the end of a very long street, "like a river rushing toward the hotel." To overcome this, he had them change the color of the roof, put reflective material over the main entrance, and dig up the flagpoles outside and put them at an angle to the street instead of being parallel to it. This, he claimed, was done "to diversify the energy flow." He also asked management to put a fountain in front of the hotel, nine dragons and nine turtles in the fountain, and a pair of lions in the front garden. The hotel's occupancy rate shot up to 80 percent.*[14]

MUSIC AND FOLKLORE

Musical commercials are generally popular worldwide, but tastes vary and the marketer must know what kind of music each market prefers. Thus, a commercial that used a ballad in the United States might be better received to the tune of a bolero in Mexico or a samba in Brazil. However, if the advertiser is looking to the youth market with a product that is patently American, then American music will help reinforce its image. And singers like Shakira appeal to both markets.

Those who wish to steep themselves in a culture find it useful to study its folklore, which can disclose much about a society's way of life. The incorrect use of folklore can sometimes cost the firm a share of the market. For example, associating a product with the cowboy would not obtain the same results in Chile or Argentina as in the United States, because in those countries the cowboy is a far less romantic figure—it's just a job. On the other hand, Smirnoff's use of an image of late revolutionary leader Ernesto "Che" Guevara in an advertisement for spicy vodka sparked controversy in Cuba, where Guevara is a national hero.[15] As another instance, a U.S. company might be paying handsome royalties to use American cartoon characters in its promotion, only to find they are considerably less important in foreign markets. In Mexico, songs of the "Singing Cricket" are known to all youngsters and their mothers, and a commercial tie-in with that character would be as advantageous to the firm as its use of Peanuts or Mickey Mouse. In many areas, especially where nationalistic feeling is strong, local firms have been able to compete successfully with foreign affiliates by making use of indigenous folklore in the form of slogans and proverbs. Tales and folklore are valuable in maintaining a sense of group unity.[16] Knowing them is an indication that one belongs to the group, which recognizes that an outsider is unfamiliar with its folklore.

Attitudes and Beliefs

Every culture has a set of attitudes and beliefs that influence nearly all aspects of human behavior and help bring order to a society and its individuals. The more managers can learn about certain key attitudes, the better prepared they will be to understand why people behave as they do, especially when their reactions differ from those that the managers have learned to expect in dealing with their own people.

Among the wide variety of cultural attitudes and beliefs, some are of prime importance to the businessperson, especially attitudes toward time, toward achievement and work, and toward change.

ATTITUDES TOWARD TIME

The attitudes-toward-time cultural characteristic may present more adaptation problems for Americans overseas than does any other. Time is important in the United States, and if we must wait past the appointed hour to see an individual, we may assume this person is not giving our meeting the importance it deserves. Yet the wait could mean just the opposite elsewhere. Latin American or Middle Eastern executives may be taking care of the minor details of their business so that they can attend to their important visitor without interruption.

> An American who has worked in the Middle East for 20 years explains the Middle Eastern concept of time this way: "At worst, there is no concept at all of time in the Middle East. At best, there is a sort of open-ended concept." The head of Egypt's Industrial Design Center, an Egyptian, states, "The simple wristwatch is, in some respects, much too sophisticated an instrument for the Middle East. One of the first things a foreigner should learn in Egypt is to ignore the second hand. The minute hand can also be an obstacle if he expects Egyptians to be as conscious as he of time ticking away."[17]

Probably even more critical than short-term patience is long-term patience. American preoccupation with monthly profit and loss is a formidable barrier to the establishment of successful business relationships with Asian and Middle Eastern executives, especially during the development of joint ventures and other business relationships that have good potential in the long run—precisely the factors in which these people are most interested.[18]

>>Cultural Habits Spread: In Vino, India?

The next big Indian export may be not computer chips but something a bit stronger. More precisely, wine in Maharashtra. In parts of this west Indian state, conditions for grape growing mimic those of other grape-growing regions of the world, so a domestic wine industry has sprung up. Well, conditions aren't exactly right—it is too hot for the best conditions—so the grape-growing season is in the winter. Sula Vineyards, started by a software engineer with Oracle in Silicon Valley, has brought in eight harvests and is producing over a million bottles of wine. Sula wines are already being exported, mainly to Indian restaurants abroad. But so far it and most other Indian wines are mostly for domestic consumption because there is an Indian tariff of 264 percent on foreign wine imports. Thus, foreign wine-makers are coming to the area—Seagram started producing wine in the same area in 2005.

Will other cultures be making incursions against French winemakers? Mexico is better known for tequila, but seven states already make wine, and the first official winery in the Western Hemisphere was in Mexico. Mexican wineries tend to take their inspiration more from European than Californian wines. And the Chilean reputation for wine is actually quite solid. Australia is also a large producer. So the answer is yes.

Source: Higo Restall, "Indo Vino Nouveau," *The Wall Street Journal*, May 17, 2006, p. D14: "Vino Mex," http://mexicanwines.homestead.com (June 27, 2006).

Americans, Be Prompt   If an appointment is made to see a group of Germans at 12 noon, we can be sure they will be there, but to get the same response from Brazilians, we must say "noon English hour." If not, the Brazilians may show up anytime between noon and 2 o'clock.

Should Americans follow the local custom or be prompt? It depends. In Spain, a general rule is to never be punctual. If you are, you will be considered early. However, in the Middle East, the American penchant for punctuality is well known and lateness by Americans is considered impolite. The Arabian executives, nonetheless, usually will not arrive at the appointed hour; why should they change their lifetime habits for a stranger?

Mañana   Some visitors to Latin American are puzzled by the term *mañana*. The literal translation is "tomorrow," but it really means "in the near future." This example illustrates that the ability to speak the local language is only half the task of communicating. A manager of an American subsidiary in Saudi Arabia says, "You can be talking the same language with someone, but are you talking on the same wavelength?" He states that he has met few Japanese or Koreans fluent in Arabic, yet they are able to understand and adapt to local conditions much better than Westerners can because they seem to be more sensitive to the Middle Easterner's mentality.[19]

Adios, Siesta   The revered three-hour siesta has disappeared from Mexico. In 1999 the federal government began requiring that most public employees, from clerks to cabinet ministers, begin work at 9 A.M. and leave work at 6 P.M., and instead of three hours for lunch, they now have only one hour. To be sure that people leave at 6 P.M. and not at 8 P.M., the lights and air-conditioning are turned off at 6 P.M. sharp. One result of this change is that people are finding that much work is being done before noon, a rarity under the old schedule. Since people are no longer drowsy in the afternoon as a result of the banquet they used to eat at lunchtime, they now tend to make decisions in the afternoon instead of waiting until the evening.[20]

In Spain the three-hour siesta is less common in the big cities. Spain's growing economy has allowed young people to move to the suburbs, but this has created longer commutes, making it more difficult to dash home for a siesta. A survey taken by a Spanish mattress company found that only 25 percent of all Spaniards surveyed still take a siesta and few people actually get into bed anymore. The company's marketing director claimed, "The siesta is nothing more than a cliché for most working people in Spain. They don't have time for it."[21] But this may not be true for areas outside the larger cities.

Directness   American directness and drive are interpreted by many foreigners as brash and rude. Americans want to get to the point in a discussion, and this attitude often irritates others. Formalities help establish amicable relations, which are considered in many countries to be a necessary prerequisite to business discussions. Any attempt to move the negotiations along by ignoring the accepted courtesies invites disaster.

Deadlines   Western emphasis on speed and deadlines may also be a liability abroad. In Far Eastern countries such as Japan, an American may be asked how long he or she plans to stay at the first meeting. Then negotiations are purposely not finalized until a few hours before the American's departure, when the Japanese know they can wring extra concessions from the foreigner because of his or her haste to finish and return home on schedule.

> *Three Americans, none of whom had ever been to Japan, went to sell tractors to Japanese buyers. They thought the discussions had gone well and prepared to wrap up the deal. However, there was no reaction from the Japanese. The silence became disquieting, and so the Americans lowered the price. Because there was still no reaction, they again lowered the price. This went on until their price was far lower than they had planned. What they didn't know was that the Japanese had become silent not to indicate rejection of the proposition but merely to think it over, a customary Japanese negotiating practice.[22]*

ATTITUDES TOWARD ACHIEVEMENT AND WORK

"Germans put leisure first and work second," says a German-born woman now living in the United States. "In America, it's the other way around."

> *Angela Clark was born in Germany but now works for JCPenney as a merchandising manager in Washington, D.C. Andreas Drauschke has a comparable job for comparable pay in Berlin. There is no comparison, however, in the hours each works. Drauschke works a 37-hour week, with a six-week annual vacation. Clark works a minimum of 44 hours a week, including evenings and often Saturdays and Sundays. She brings work home and never takes more than one week's vacation at a time. "If I took any more, I'd feel like I was losing control," she says.[23]*

To the consternation of expatriate managers, the promise of overtime may fail to keep workers on the job. In fact, raising employees' salaries can actually result in their working less (economists call this effect the "backward-bending" labor supply curve). But it is important to note that another change has occurred repeatedly in developing countries as more consumer goods have become available. The **demonstration effect** (seeing others with these goods) and improvements in infrastructure (roads to bring the products to consumers and electric power to operate the products) cause workers to realize they can have greater prestige and pleasure by owning more goods. Thus, their attitude toward work changes not because of any alteration of their moral or religious values but because they now want what only money can buy.

demonstration effect
Result of having seen others with desirable goods

> *A Mexican distributor once complained that many of his salesmen were producing well for the first week or two of the month but were then slacking off. Investigation showed that the commissions plus salary earned during the periods of high production were about the same each time. It was apparent that the salesmen had earned what they required to live, so they could loaf the rest of the month. By instituting contests and informing the salesmen's wives about the prizes to be won, the company obtained considerable improvement.*

In the industrialized nations, trends are generally downward. After peaking at 43.3 hours per week in 1994, the U.S. weekly average for production workers had already dropped to 42.6 hours by 1996. The 1996 averages for Germany and France were 39.0 and 38.3 hours, respectively (France and Germany officially have a 35-hour workweek). Even in Japan the weekly average, which reached 43 hours in 1988, fell to 39.5 hours in 1996. In fact, by 2001 Japanese workers were putting in nearly 25 hours less per month than their counterparts in 1988.[24]

Job Prestige   Another aspect of the attitude toward work is the prestige associated with certain kinds of employment. The distinction between blue-collar workers and office employees is especially great, as typified by the use of two words in Spanish for the worker—*obrero* (one who labors) signifies a blue-collar worker, whereas an office worker is an *empleado* (employee).[25]

Religion

Religion, an important component of culture, is responsible for many of the attitudes and beliefs affecting human behavior. A knowledge of the basic tenets of some of the more popular religions will contribute to a better understanding of why people's attitudes vary so greatly from country to country. Figure 6.1 presents a map of the major religions of the world.

WORK ETHIC

We have already mentioned differences in attitudes toward work. Europeans and Americans are believed to view work as a moral virtue and look unfavorably on the idle. This view may stem in part from the **Protestant work ethic** as expressed by Luther and Calvin, who believed it was one's duty to glorify God by hard work and the practice of thrift.

In Asian countries where Confucianism is strong, the same attitude toward work is called the **Confucian work ethic**. As mentioned, because of other factors—such as a growing feeling of prosperity and a shift to a five-day workweek (with two days off, workers develop new interests)—Japanese employers are finding that younger workers may not have the same dedication to their jobs as their predecessors had. Workers rarely show up early to warm the oil in their machines before work starts, and some management trainees are actually taking all of their vacation time. A recent college graduate claims, "Students ski in the winter and play tennis in the summer. What the companies sometimes find out is that some new employees like skiing better than working."[26]

Protestant work ethic
Duty to glorify God by hard work and the practice of thrift

Confucian work ethic
Drive toward hard work and thrift; similar to Protestant work ethic

ASIAN RELIGIONS

People from the Western world will encounter some very different notions about God, people, and reality in **Asian religions.** In the Judeo-Christian tradition, this world is real and significant because it was created by God. Human beings are likewise significant; so is time, because it began with God's creation and will end when His will has been fulfilled. Each human being has only one lifetime to heed God's word and achieve everlasting life.

In the religions of India, there is a notion that this world is an illusion because nothing is permanent. Time is cyclical, and so all living things, including humans, are in a constant process of birth, death, and reincarnation. The goal of salvation is to escape from the cycle and move into a state of eternal bliss *(nirvana).* The notion of *karma* (moral retribution) holds

Asian religions
Primary ones: Hinduism, Buddhism, Jainism, and Sikhism (India); Confucianism and Taoism (China); and Shintoism (Japan)

"The Protestant work ethic isn't cutting it, so we're switching to Shinto."

Source: From *The Wall Street Journal*—Permission, Cartoon Features Syndicate.

FIGURE 6.1 World Religions

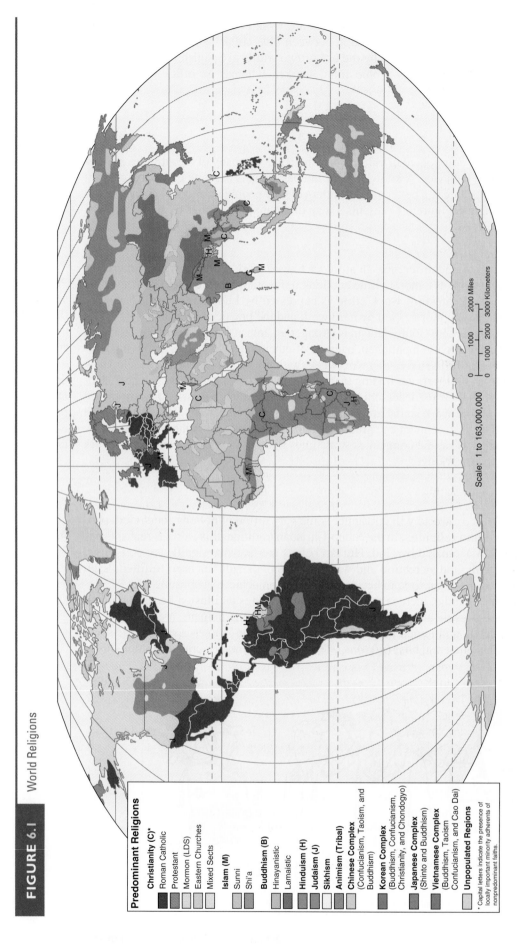

Predominant Religions

Christianity (C)*
- Roman Catholic
- Protestant
- Mormon (LDS)
- Eastern Churches
- Mixed Sects

Islam (M)
- Sunni
- Shi'a

Buddhism (B)
- Hinayanistic
- Lamaistic

Hinduism (H)
Judaism (J)
Sikhism
Animism (Tribal)
Chinese Complex
(Confucianism, Taoism, and Buddhism)

Korean Complex
(Buddhism, Confucianism, Christianity, and Chondogyo)

Japanese Complex
(Shinto and Buddhism)

Vietnamese Complex
(Buddhism, Taoism Confucianism, and Cao Dai)

Unpopulated Regions

* Capital letters indicate the presence of locally important minority adherents of nonpredominant faiths.

Scale: 1 to 163,000,000

| 0 | 1000 | 2000 Miles |
| 0 | 1000 | 2000 | 3000 Kilometers |

Source: Map 18, "World Religions," *Student Atlas of World Geography*, 3rd ed., by John L. Allen. Copyright 2003: The McGraw-Hill Companies, Inc.

that evil committed in one lifetime will be punished in the next. Thus, *karma* is a powerful impetus to do good so as to achieve a higher spiritual status in the next life. Asians who hold these views cannot imagine that they have not had past lives in which they may have been plants, animals, or human beings. Of the seven best-known religions that originated in Asia, four came from India (Hinduism, Buddhism, Jainism, and Sikhism), two from China (Confucianism and Taoism), and one from Japan (Shintoism).

Hinduism   Hinduism does not have a single founder or a central authority but is practiced by more than 80 percent of India's population. Although there is great diversity among regions and social classes, Hinduism has certain characteristic features. Most Hindus believe that everything in the world is subject to an eternal process of death and rebirth *(samsura)* and that individual souls *(atmans)* migrate from one body to another. They believe one can be liberated from the samsura cycle and achieve eternal bliss *(nirvana)* through (1) yoga (purification of mind and body), (2) devout worship of the gods, or (3) good works and obedience to the laws and customs *(dharmas)* of one's caste.

A knowledge of the **caste system** is important to managers because the castes are the basis of the social division of labor. The highest caste, the Brahmins or priesthood, is followed by the warriors (politicians, landowners), the merchants, the peasants, and the *dalits,* a Hindi word meaning "downtrodden" or "oppressed" that has replaced *untouchables.*[27] An individual's position in a caste is inherited, as is that person's job within the caste, and movement to a higher caste can be made only in subsequent lives. Although the government of India has outlawed discrimination based on the caste system and has worked to improve the situation of those in the lower castes, such discrimination still exists. Indian newspapers usually carry a classified section for those seeking marriage partners, and ads are often explicit about the caste of the ad buyer and the caste requirement of the marriage partner.

In Japan a somewhat similar system exists, as a holdover from the 17th century, when the feudal Tokugawa regime imposed a rigid social pecking order. The warrior-administrator samurai were at the top. Below them were farmers and artisans, then merchants, and, at the bottom, those with occupations considered dirty and distasteful, such as slaughterers, butchers, and tanners. As in India, where discrimination against untouchables is illegal, all natives of Japan who are of Japanese descent are legally equal. However, the descendants of the lowest Japanese class remain trapped in their ghettos, working in small family firms that produce knitted garments, bamboo wares, fur and leather goods, shoes, and sandals. They call themselves *burakumin* ("ghetto people") and claim they number about 3 million people living in some 6,000 ghettos. Their average income is far below that of other Japanese.

Buddhism   Buddhism began in India as a reform of Hinduism. At the age of 29, Prince Gautama rejected his wife, son, and wealth and set out to solve the mysteries of misery, old age, and death. After six years of experimenting with yoga, he suddenly understood how to break the laws of *karma* and the cycle of rebirth *(samsura)*. Gautama emerged as the Buddha (the Enlightened One). He renounced the austere self-discipline of the Hindus as well as the extremes of self-indulgence, both of which depended on a craving that locked people into the cycle of rebirth. Gautama taught that by extinguishing desire, his followers could attain enlightenment and escape the cycle of existence into nirvana. By opening his teaching to everyone, he opposed the caste system.

Jainism   The Jain religion was founded by Mahavira, a contemporary of Buddha. Jain doctrine teaches that there is no creator, no god, and no absolute principle. Through right faith, correct conduct, and knowledge of the soul, Jains can purify themselves, become free of samsura, and achieve nirvana. Although relatively few in number, Jains are influential leaders in commerce and scholarship. Their greatest impact on Indian culture is manifested in the widespread acceptance of their doctrine of nonviolence, which prohibits animal slaughter, war, and even violent thoughts.

caste system
An aspect of Hinduism by which the entire society is divided into four groups (plus the outcasts) and each is assigned a certain class of work

Sikhism   Sikhism is the religion of an Indian ethnic group, a military brotherhood,* and a political movement that was founded by Nanak, who sought a bridge between Hinduism and Islam. Sikhs believe there is a single god, but they also accept the Hindu concepts of samsura, karma, and spiritual liberation. More than 80 percent of Sikhs live in the state of Punjab.[28]

Confucianism   The name of Confucius is inseparable from Chinese culture and civilization, which were already well developed when he set out to transform ancient traditions into a system capable of guiding personal and social behavior. Confucianism may be considered a religion since Confucius built his philosophy on the notion that all reality is subject to an eternal mandate from heaven. Confucius taught that each person bears within himself or herself the principle of unselfish love for others, *jen,* the cultivation of which is its own reward. A second principle, *li,* prescribes a gentle decorum in all actions and may account for the Chinese emphasis on politeness and deference to elders.

Taoism   Taoism is a mystical philosophy founded by Lao-tzu, a contemporary of Confucius. It is just as likely that he never existed, and that the *Lao Tzu* is an anthology. Taoism, which means "philosophy of the way," holds that each of us mirrors the male and the female energies (yin and yang) that govern the cosmos. The aim of Taoist meditation and rituals is to free the self from distractions and become empty to allow the cosmic forces to act.[29]

Shintoism   Shintoism is the indigenous religion of Japan. Shinto legends define the founding of the Japanese empire as a cosmic act, and the emperor was believed to have divine status. As a part of the World War II settlement, the emperor was forced to renounce such a claim. Shintoism has no elaborate theology or weekly worship. Many homes contain a small Shinto shrine.

ISLAM

About 1.3 billion followers make this faith the second largest after Christianity, which has 2 billion adherents. Islam accepts as God's eternal word the Koran, a collection of Allah's

The Dome of the Rock mosque in Jerusalem is a historic center of worship for Muslims, followers of Islam. With 1.3 billion followers, Islam is the second-largest faith after Christianity.

*Baptism into the Sikh brotherhood requires that all members take *Singh* as a second name.

(God's) revelations to Muhammad, who is viewed by Muslims as the messenger of God. Muhammad was not only the prophet of God, but also led the Islamic state.

The basic spiritual duties of all Muslims consist of the five pillars of faith: (1) accepting the confession of faith ("There is no God but God, and Muhammad is the Messenger of God"), (2) making the five daily prayers while facing Mecca (Muhammad's birthplace), (3) giving charity, (4) fasting during the daylight hours of Ramadan, a 29- or 30-day month in Islam's lunar calendar, and (5) making a pilgrimage to Mecca at least once in a person's lifetime. Some Muslims claim there is another duty, *jihad,* which refers to the various forms of striving for the faith, such as the inner struggle for purification. However, this term is often translated as "holy war." We discuss other aspects of jihad in Chapter 9.

A dispute over the succession to leadership after Muhammad died led to the formation of two major divisions, the Sunnis and the Shiites (Shia). The Sunnis may be less authoritarian and more pragmatic than the Shiites. In their view, as long as Muslims accept Allah, they are free to interpret their religion as they like. The Shiites, in contrast, insist that those claiming to be Muslim must put themselves under the authority of a holy man *(ayatollah).*[30] This has created a clergy that wields enormous temporal and spiritual power, with the result that religious leaders affect business as well as religion.

Sunni-Shia Conflict   Businesspeople doing business with Muslim countries should understand the Sunni-Shia conflict. Although most Muslim countries are Sunni-governed, many of them, such as Kuwait, the emirates, Bahrain, and other small states in the Gulf, have substantial Shia populations. Furthermore, small Shia minorities can cause trouble for the government. For example, Saudi Arabia's Shia population is very small—only 250,000—and is concentrated in the eastern oil fields. Iran's Shia government continually broadcasts appeals to the Saudi Shiites to overthrow the regime. The group Hamas is Sunni; Hezbollah is Shiite.

Two of the five pillars of faith can be bothersome to foreign managers. Dawn-to-dusk fasting during the month of Ramadan causes workers' output to drop sharply, and the requirement to pray five times daily also affects output, because when Muslim workers hear the call to prayer they stop whatever they are doing and pray where they are.

ANIMISM

In a number of African and Latin American countries, animism, a kind of spirit worship that includes magic and witchcraft, is a major religion. It is often combined with other religions to present a mixture of mysticism, taboos, and fatalism. According to historians, animism is perhaps one of humanity's oldest beliefs, with its origin probably dating back to the Paleolithic age. The term *animism* derives from the Latin word *anima,* meaning "breath" or "soul." Animism is the belief that everything in nature—including living things like trees and plants and even nonliving rocks or streams—has its own spirit or divinity. Japanese shintoism is equated by some to animism.

Religions have a pervasive influence on business. Religious holidays and rituals can affect employee performance and work scheduling. When members of different religious groups work together, there may even be strife within the work force. Managers must respect the religious beliefs of others and adapt business practices to the religious constraints present in other cultures. Of course, to be able to do this, they must first know what those beliefs and constraints are.

material culture
All human-made objects; concerned with *how* people make things (technology) and *who* makes *what* and *why* (economics)

Material Culture

Material culture refers to all human-made objects and is concerned with *how* people make things (technology) and *who* makes *what* and *why* (economics).

TECHNOLOGY

The *technology* of a society is the mix of the usable knowledge that the society applies and directs toward the attainment of cultural and economic objectives; it exists in some form in every cultural organization. It is significant in the improvement of living standards and a vital factor in the competitive strategies of multinational firms. Technological superiority is the goal of most companies, of course, but it is especially important to international companies for a number of reasons:

1. It enables a firm to be competitive or even attain leadership in world markets.

   The Korean firm Samsung was once known for cheap and unappealing electronics. But its skills in the design of sleek, attractive products have made it a leader in cell phones, and it tops global markets for color televisions, flash memory, and LCD panels. Samsung's elegant Experience showroom in New York City draws 1,500 visitors on a typical Saturday.

2. It can be sold (via licensing or management contract), or it can be embodied in the company's products.

3. It can give a firm confidence to enter a foreign market even when other companies are already established there.

4. It can enable the firm to obtain better-than-usual conditions for a foreign market invest-ment because the host government wants the technology that only the firm has (for example, permission for a wholly owned subsidiary in a country where the government normally insists on joint ventures with a local majority).

   IBM, confident of its superior technology, insisted on and obtained permission from the Mex-ican government to set up a wholly owned subsidiary when other computer manufacturers were forced to accept local partners.

5. It can enable a company with only a minority equity position to control a joint venture and preserve it as a captive market for semiprocessed inputs that it—but not the joint venture—produces.

6. It can change the international division of labor. Some firms that moved production overseas where labor was cheaper have returned to their home countries because production methods based on new technology have reduced the direct labor content of their products. With labor costs as low as 5 percent of total production costs, going overseas to save 30 to 40 percent in labor costs, for example, produces only about a 2 percent cost saving. This may be more than offset by the transportation costs to bring the finished merchandise to the United States. Fender Musical Instruments Co. makes Fender guitars in both Ensenada, Mexico, and Corona, California, and sales of guitars from both locations are about even.

7. It is causing major firms to form competitive alliances in which each partner shares technology and the high costs of research and development. This is known as *strategic technology leveraging,* which is the concept of using external technology to comple-ment rather than substitute for internal technology.

Cultural Aspects of Technology

Technology's cultural aspects are certainly impor-tant to international managers, because new production methods and new products often re-quire that people change their beliefs and ways of living. A self-employed farmer may find that factory work is unappealing. If workers have been accustomed to the conditions of cot-tage industries in which each individual performs all the operations, they find it difficult to adjust to the monotony of tightening a single bolt. The "throw away instead of repair" phi-losophy behind the design of many new products necessitates a change in the use habits of people who have been accustomed to repairing something to keep it operating until it is thor-oughly worn out. Generally, the greater the difference is between the old and the new method or product, the more difficult it is for the firm to institute a change.

Technological Dualism

Technological dualism is a prominent feature of many developing nations. In the same country, one industry sector may be technologically advanced, with high productivity, while the production techniques of another sector may be old and labor-intensive. This condition may be the result of the host government's insistence that foreign investors import only the most modern machinery rather than used but serviceable equipment that would be less costly and could create more employment.

Sometimes the preferences are reversed. A host government beset by high unemployment may argue for labor-intensive processes, while the foreign firm prefers automated production both because it is the kind the home office is most familiar with and because its use lessens the need for skilled labor. To understand which policy the host government is following, management must study its laws and regulations and talk with host country officials.

Appropriate Technology

Rather than choosing between labor-intensive and capital-intensive processes, many experts in economic development recommend **appropriate technology,** which can be labor-intensive, intermediate, or capital-intensive. The idea is to choose the technology that most closely fits the society using it.

Appropriate technology may be embodied in product delivery. For example, the development of single chips that will handle many cell phone functions has vastly expanded the cell phone market in India because the physical phone cost has dropped.

Boomerang Effect

One reason firms sometimes fear to sell their technology abroad is the **boomerang effect.** For example, Japanese firms have been less willing to sell their technology to industrialized economies such as Korea. Interestingly, fear of the boomerang effect caused some American firms to restrict the sale of their technology to the Japanese. However, a study of the flat-panel-display industry suggested that there was no difference between U.S. and Japanese firms' tendency to share, or appropriate, knowledge from the rest of the world.

THE INFORMATION TECHNOLOGY ERA

The information technology industry is changing at a pace that is bewildering to many business executives. Managing the flood of data available electronically is a challenge, but capturing information from transaction data, for example, offers profitable opportunities to mine the data for trend spotting. The Internet's worldwide reach has enabled firms to enter global markets with a minimal investment. It also, of course, has brought new competition to these companies in their own home markets. Apparently, the investment in new information technology is worth it. As early as 2000 the Internet economy had already reached $850 billion, exceeding the size of the life insurance and real estate industries.[31]

MATERIAL CULTURE AND CONSUMPTION

One of the unique expressions of Japanese material culture is the wide use of automation—not only in robots for manufacturing but in vending machines for a variety of items, including hot meals and (until recently) alcohol. Until a ban was enacted in 2000, Japan had nearly 170,000 alcohol vending machines. Teenage males were buying beer that they were too young to buy in a store (Japan's official age for alcohol purchase is 20). Of course, it is feared that the vacuum will be filled by convenience stores that won't bother to check the age of patrons.[32]

Language

Probably the most apparent cultural distinction that the newcomer to international business perceives is in the means of communication. Differences in the spoken language are readily discernible, and after a short period in the new culture it becomes apparent that there are variations in the unspoken language (manners and customs) as well.

SPOKEN LANGUAGE

Language is the key to culture, and without it, people find themselves locked out of all but a culture's perimeter. At the same time, in learning a language, people can't understand the nuances, double meanings of words, and slang unless they also learn the other aspects of the culture. Fortunately, the learning of both goes hand in hand; a certain feel for a people and their attitudes naturally develops with a growing mastery of their language.

Languages Delineate Cultures
Spoken languages demarcate cultures just as physical barriers do. In fact, nothing equals the spoken language for distinguishing one culture from another. If two languages are spoken in a country, there will be two separate cultures (Belgium); if four languages are spoken, there will be four cultures (Switzerland); and so forth.

The sharp divisions in Canada between the English- and French-speaking regions is ample evidence of the force of languages in delineating cultures. The differences among the Basques, Catalans, and Spaniards and the differences between the French and Flemish in Belgium are other notable examples of the sharp cultural and often political differences between language groups. However, it does not follow from this generalization that cultures are the same wherever the same language is spoken. As a result of Spain's colonization, Spanish is the principal language of 21 Latin American nations, but no one should believe that they are culturally similar. Moreover, generally because of cultural differences, many words in both the written and the spoken languages of these countries are completely different. A Chilean told one of the authors of her surprise at seeing Puerto Rican coffee selling under the "El Pico" brand. In Chile, she said, *el pico* is a reference to the male sex organ.

lingua franca
A foreign language used to communicate among a nation's diverse cultures that have diverse languages

Foreign Language
When many spoken languages exist in a single country (India and many African nations), one language usually serves as the principal vehicle for communication across cultures. Nations that were formerly colonies often use the language of their ex-rulers; thus, French is the **lingua franca,** or "link" language, of the former French and Belgian colonies in Africa; English, in India; and Portuguese, in Angola. These are the only languages many speak in some previously colonized African countries. Thus they may be more, or less, effective than the native tongues for reaching mass markets or for day-to-day conversations between managers and workers. Even in countries with only one principal language, such as Germany and France, problems of communication arise because of the large numbers of "guest workers" who were recruited to ease labor shortages. A German supervisor may have workers from three or four countries and be unable to speak directly with any of them. To ameliorate this situation, some managers try to separate the work force according to origin; for instance, all Turks are placed in the paint shop, all Greeks on the assembly line, and so on. But the preferred solution is to teach managers the language of their workers. Invariably, such training has resulted in an increase in production, fewer product defects, and higher worker morale.

English, the Link Language of Business
When a Swedish businessperson talks with a Japanese businessperson, the conversation generally will be in English. English as a business *lingua franca* has spread so rapidly in Europe that well over half of EU adults can speak English. Over 40 percent of people in the EU speak it as a second language. An even larger percentage—69 percent—agree that "everyone should speak English."[33]

At the same time, other languages are not being abandoned. For example, EU headquarters in Brussels estimated that, after the EU was enlarged, interpreters would be needed for all possible combinations of about 22 languages—a total of 462 combinations![34]

Must Speak the Local Language
Even though more and more businesspeople are speaking English, when they buy, they often insist on doing business in their own language. The seller who speaks the local language has a competitive edge. Moreover, knowing the language of the area indicates respect for its culture and people. Figure 6.2 shows a map of the major languages of the world. As we have said, usually it is a social blunder to begin a business conversation by talking business. Most foreigners expect to establish a social relationship

first, and the casual, exploratory conversation that precedes business talks may require several meetings. Obviously, people can establish a better rapport in a one-on-one conversation than through an interpreter. Consider the trouble this person would have avoided if he had spoken Spanish:

> *A German engineer, in Colombia to work on a pipeline, arrived at a hotel in the interior, where he tried to explain to the desk clerk that he had a suitcase full of cash that he wanted the hotel to keep. Because he knew no Spanish, he was having difficulty making himself understood. During the conversation, the desk clerk opened the suitcase in front of everyone in the lobby. A week later, the engineer was kidnapped by a guerrilla group and held for a month.*[35]

Translation   The ability to speak the language well does not eliminate the need for translators. The smallest of markets requires technical manuals, catalogs, and good advertising ideas, and a lack of local talent to do the work does not mean that the organization must do without these valuable sales aids. The solution is to obtain this material from headquarters and have it translated if the costs are not prohibitive and suitable reproduction facilities are available locally. Remember, though, a French or Spanish translation will be up to 25 percent longer than its English equivalent.

Allowing headquarters to translate can be extremely risky because words from the same language frequently vary in meaning from one country to another or even from one region to another, as was mentioned earlier. A famous example that illustrated how only a single word incorrectly translated can ruin an otherwise good translation occurred in Mexico. The American headquarters of a deodorant manufacturer sent a Spanish translation of the manufacturer's international theme, "If you use our deodorant, you won't be embarrassed in public." Unfortunately, the translator used the word *embarazada* for "embarrassed," which in Mexican Spanish means "pregnant." Imagine the time that the Mexican subsidiary had with that one.[36]

Back Translations   To avoid translation errors, the experienced marketer will prefer what are really two translations. The first will be made by a bilingual native, whose work will then be translated back by a bilingual foreigner to see how it compares with the original. This work preferably should be done in the market where the material is to be used. No method is foolproof, but the back-translation approach is the safest way devised so far.

Some problems with translations:

- A sign in a Paris hotel that sought to discourage Americans from wearing slacks in the plush dining room: "A sports jacket may be worn to dinner, but no trousers." The menu advised patrons that they could enjoy "tea in a bag just like mother."

- In a Copenhagen airline ticket office: "We take your bags and send them in all directions."

- In a Japanese hotel: "You are invited to take advantage of the chambermaid."

- A Bangkok dry cleaner's boast: "Drop your trousers here for best results."

- An Acapulco hotel that wanted to reassure guests about the drinking water: "The manager has personally passed all the water served here."

- Sign in a Czech tourist office: "Take one of our horse-driven city tours—we guarantee no miscarriages."

- Infoscope, a prototype PDA-type translator, translated a Bank of America sign in Chinese as "Great Wall of Money Bin."

Technical Words   Translators have difficulty with technical terms that do not exist in a language and with common words that have a special meaning for a certain industry. Portuguese, for example, is rich in fishing and marine terms, but it is limited with respect to technical terms for the newer industries. The only solution is to employ the English word or fabricate a new word in Portuguese. Unless translators have a special knowledge of the industry, they will go to the dictionary for a literal translation that frequently makes no sense

FIGURE 6.2 Major Languages of the World

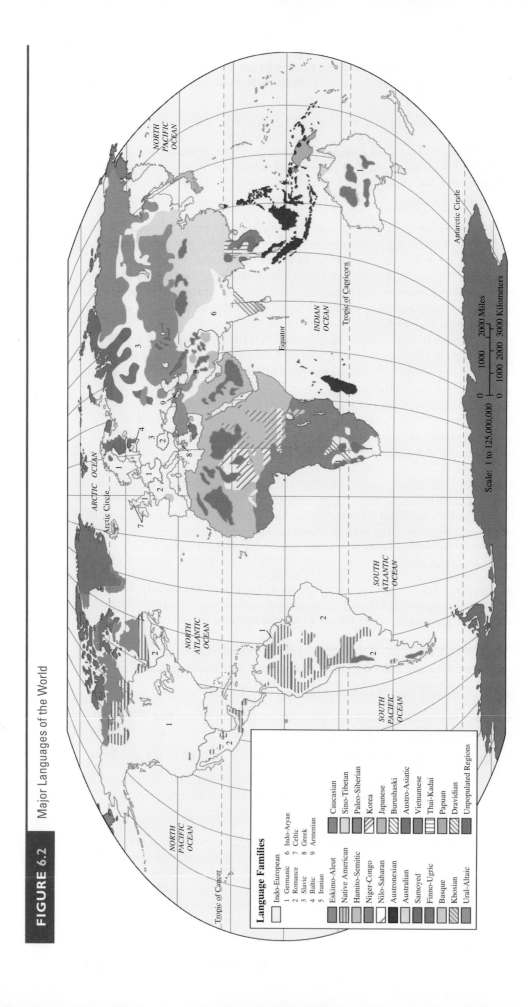

Language Families

Indo-European
1 Germanic   6 Indo-Aryan
2 Romance   7 Celtic
3 Slavic   8 Greek
4 Baltic   9 Armenian
5 Iranian

Eskimo-Aleut
Native American
Hamito-Semitic
Niger-Congo
Nilo-Saharan
Austronesian
Australian
Samoyed
Finno-Ugric
Basque
Khosian
Ural-Altaic

Caucasian
Sino-Tibetan
Paleo-Siberian
Korea
Japanese
Burushaski
Austro-Asiatic
Vietnamese
Thai-Kadai
Papuan
Dravidian
Unpopulated Regions

Scale: 1 to 125,000,000

0   1000   2000 Miles
0   1000 2000 3000 Kilometers

or is erroneous. Resolving such problems by using English words may not be a satisfactory solution even if the public understands them, especially in France and Spain, which have national academies to keep the language "pure." The French, in their effort to keep their language free of English words, prohibit the use of foreign words and phrases in all business and government communications and advertising when there are suitable French equivalents. Two out of five songs broadcast on French radio must be in French. In Spain, the Royal Spanish Academy attempts to perform much the same function for Spanish.

French Crackdown on English   In a continuing effort to protect the French language against the encroachment of other languages, various French watchdog groups, partially funded by the Culture Ministry, regularly sue those who in their opinion have violated the law. In 1997, they filed suits against the French campus of Georgia Tech for writing its Internet site in English, the Body Shop for selling products in France without French labels, and an electronics chain for selling computer games with English-only instructions.[37]

Although the French government and other defenders of the French language are struggling to maintain a French presence on the Internet, they are losing. An estimated 75 percent of the world's Internet sites are in English.[38] Adding insult to injury, France is McDonald's most profitable subsidiary in Europe. It adapts to both French language and tastes ("Croque McDo" is a version of the *croque monsieur,* a ham-and-cheese French favorite).[39] More than pride is involved here. One scientific rule of thumb is to "publish in English, or perish in French."

Note the economic reason for keeping the language pure and separate from other languages. Those learning a foreign language not only are potential tourists but are likely to be empathetic toward anything that comes from that country. An Argentine fashion buyer who speaks German and not Bulgarian may feel more comfortable attending fashion shows in Germany than in Budapest.

In Japan, the reverse situation exists, probably because for decades the country coveted foreign products while it struggled to overtake the West. Even now, most Japanese cars sold in the domestic market have almost nothing but English on them. A Nissan official explains that English is thought to be more attractive to the eye. Perhaps this is why people quench their thirst with a best-selling soft drink called "Pocari Sweat" and order from menus announcing "sand witches" and "miss Gorilla" (mixed grill). They also puff away on a cigarette called "Hope."[40]

No Unpleasantness   One last aspect of the spoken language worthy of mention is the reluctance in many areas to say anything disagreeable to the listener. The politeness of the Japanese makes *no* a little-used word even when there are disagreements. An American executive, pleased that her Japanese counterpart is nodding and saying yes to all of her proposals, may be shaken later to learn that all the time the listener was saying yes ("I hear you") and not yes ("I agree"). Western managers who ask Brazilians whether something can be done may receive the answer *meio deficil* ("somewhat difficult"). If managers take this answer literally, they will probably ask that it be done anyway. The Brazilians will then elaborate on the difficulties until, they hope, it will dawn on the executives that what they ask is impossible but the Brazilians don't want to give them the bad news.

UNSPOKEN LANGUAGE

Nonverbal communication, or the **unspoken language,** can often tell businesspeople something that the spoken language does not—if they understand it. Unfortunately, the differences in customs among cultures may cause misinterpretations of the communication.

unspoken language
Nonverbal communication, such as gestures and body language

Gestures   Although gestures are a common form of cross-cultural communication, gestures vary from one region to another. For instance, Americans and most Europeans understand the thumbs-up gesture to mean "all right," but in southern Italy and Greece, it transmits

" First, le coca cola. Now peanut butter. Who will save La Belle Langue Française? "

Source: *Pearson/Knickerbocker News,* NY/Rothco. Reprinted with permission.

Department store greeter in Tokyo bows politely to a customer.

the message for which we reserve the middle finger. Making a circle with the thumb and the forefinger is friendly in the United States, but it means "you're worth nothing" in France and Belgium and is a vulgar sexual invitation in Greece and Turkey.[41]

Former Japanese prime minister Yoshiro Mori paid his respects to his predecessor, Keizo Obuchi, by bowing *twice* before an urn containing Obuchi's ashes. Unfortunately, Japanese etiquette requires bowing *three* times to show respect for the deceased. Mori's gaffe was obvious to the 6,000 mourners in the hall and to millions watching on TV.[42]

Closed Doors   Americans know that one of the perquisites of an important executive is a large office with a door that can be closed. Normally, the door is open as a signal that the occupant is ready to receive others, but when it is closed, something of importance is going on. Contrary to the American open-door policy, Germans regularly keep their doors closed. Hall, the anthropologist mentioned earlier in this chapter, says that the closed door does not mean that the person behind it wants no visitors but only that he or she considers open doors sloppy and disorderly.[43]

Office Size   Although office size is an indicator of a person's importance, it means different things in different cultures. In the United States, the higher the status of the executive, the larger and more secluded the office, but in the Arab world, the president may be in a small, crowded office. In Japan, the top floor of a department store is reserved for the "bargain basement" (bargain penthouse?), not for top management. The French prefer to locate important department heads in the center of activities, with their assistants located outward on radii from this center. To be safe, never gauge people's importance by the size and location of their offices.

Conversational Distance   Cultural experts report that conversational distances are smaller in the Middle East, and possibly larger in Asia, than the Western average. Conversational distances vary by gender as well as culture, and comfortable distance may also vary by the degree of familiarity of the parties involved: We have an intimate distance for embracing or whispering (6 to 18 inches), a personal distance for conversations among good friends (1.5 to 4 feet), a social distance for conversations among acquaintances (4 to 12 feet), and a public distance for public speaking (12 feet or more).[44]

THE LANGUAGE OF GIFT GIVING

Gift giving is an important aspect of every businessperson's life both here and overseas. Entertainment outside office hours and the exchange of gifts are part of the process of getting better acquainted. However, the etiquette or language of gift giving varies among cultures, just as the spoken language does, and although foreigners will usually be forgiven for not knowing the language, certainly they and their gifts will be better received if they follow local customs.

Acceptable Gifts In Japan, for example, one never gives an unwrapped gift or visits a Japanese home empty-handed. A gift is presented with the comment that it is only a trifle, which implies that the humble social position of the giver does not permit giving a gift in keeping with the high status of the recipient. The recipient, in turn, will not open the gift in front of the giver because the recipient knows better than to embarrass the giver by exposing the trifle in the giver's presence.

The Japanese use gift giving to convey thoughtfulness and consideration for the receiver, who over time builds up trust and confidence in the giver. White and yellow flowers are not good choices for gifts because in many areas they connote death. In Germany, red roses given to a woman indicate strong feelings for her, and if you give cutlery, always ask for a coin in payment so that the gift will not cut your friendship. Cutlery is a "friendship cutter" for the Russians and French also. Traditions vary greatly throughout the world, but generally safe gifts everywhere are chocolates, red roses, and a good Scotch whiskey (not in the Arab world, however—instead, bring a good book or something useful for the office).[45]

Gifts or Bribes? Occasional bribery scandals have exposed the practice of giving very expensive gifts and money to well-placed government officials in return for special favors, large orders, and protection. Some payments were **bribes;** that is, payments were made to induce the payee to do something for the payer that is illegal. But others were the result of **extortion,** the demand for payment to keep the payee from harming the payer in some way. Still others were tips to induce government officials to do their jobs.[46]

Welcome to the murky world of payments for services Some other examples (from the U.S. perspective): If you tip the head waiter to get a good table, that is a bribe, but if you tip him because you know that without it he'll put you near the kitchen, that's extortion. If you tip him for good service after eating, that is a tip. Gifts or payments are sometimes needed to obtain favorable action from government officials, whether to obtain a large order, avoid having a plant shut down, or receive faster service from customs agents. Their pervasiveness worldwide is illustrated by the variety of names for these payments—*mordida* ("bite"—Latin America), *dash* (West Africa, where it might also mean "tip"), *pot de vin* ("jug of wine"—France), *la bustarella* (envelope left on Italian bureaucrat's desk), and *grease* (United States).

Questionable Payments These come in all forms and sizes, from the small "expediting" payments necessary to get poorly paid government officials to do their normal duties to huge sums to win large orders.

> *One of the writers was able to reduce by one-half the average age of receivables from a major Mexican governmental customer through the payment of $4 a month to a clerk whose sole job was to arrange suppliers' invoices according to their dates, so that the oldest were on top and would be paid first. The invoices of the writer's company were placed on top regardless of their date and were paid promptly.*

Transparency International (TI) has a mission to "create change toward a world free of corruption."[47] Its Corruption Perception Index (CPI) draws on surveys of businesspeople and political analysts. The CPI is designed so that countries perceived to be the *least corrupt* are given the highest score, 10. TI urges analysts to look at scores, not rankings, to understand how business perceives corruption in individual countries. Frequently, a country will have a higher score from one year to the next but will still fall in the ranking. See Figure 6.3 for 2003 CPI scores and rankings.

bribes
Gifts or payments to induce the receiver to do something illegal for the giver

extortion
Demand for payment to keep the receiver from causing harm to the payer

FIGURE 6.3   2003 Corruption Perception Index Scores and Ranking

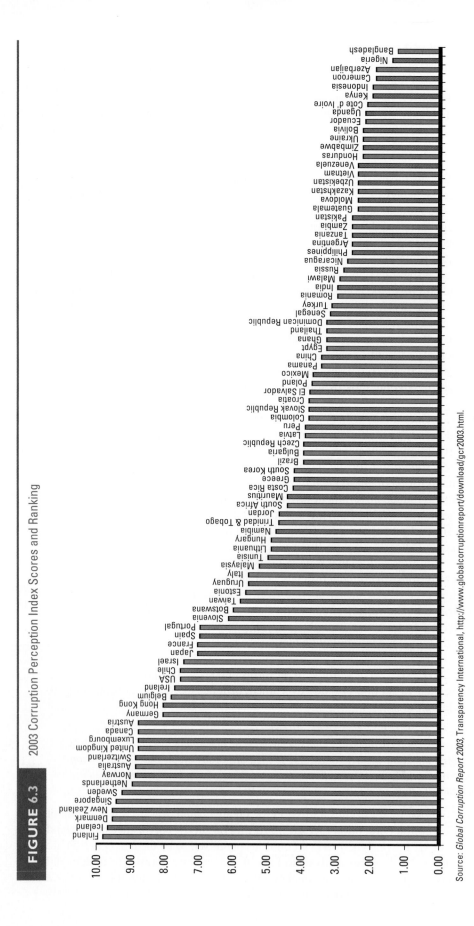

Source: *Global Corruption Report 2003*, Transparency International, http://www.globalcorruptionreport/download/gcr2003.html.

Societal Organization

Every society has a structure or an organization that is the patterned arrangement of relationships defining and regulating the manner by which its members interface with one another. Anthropologists generally study this important aspect of culture by breaking down its parts into two classes of institutions: those based on *kinship* and those based on the *free association* of individuals.

KINSHIP

The family is the basic unit of institutions based on kinship. Unlike the American family, which is generally composed of the parents and their children, families in many nations—especially the developing ones—are extended to include all relatives by blood and by marriage.

Extended Family   For the foreign firm, the **extended family** is a source of employees and business connections. The trust that people place in their relatives, however distant, may motivate them to buy from a supplier owned by their cousin's cousin, even though the price is higher. Local personnel managers are prone to fill the best jobs with family members, regardless of their qualifications.

extended family
Family that includes blood relatives and relatives by marriage

Member's Responsibility   Although the extended family is large, each member's feeling of responsibility to it is strong. An individual's initiative to work is discouraged if he or she is asked to share personal earnings with unemployed extended-family members no matter what the kinship is. Responsibility to the family is frequently a cause of high absenteeism in developing countries, where the worker is often called home to help with the harvest. Managements have spent large sums to provide comfortable housing for workers and their immediate families, only to find them living in crowded conditions after members of their extended families have moved in.

PEDRO DIAZ MARIN

In Latin America, where the extended-family form is common, individuals use the maternal family surname (e.g., Marin) as well as the paternal (e.g., Diaz) to indicate both branches of the family. It is common to see two people, when meeting for the first time, exploring each other's family tree to see whether they have common relatives. If they find any kinship at all, the meeting goes much more smoothly, since they're relatives. By the way, in Korea, China, and Japan, the paternal family name appears first of all.

ASSOCIATIONS

Social units not based on kinship, known as **associations** by anthropologists, may be formed by age, gender, or common interest.[48]

associations
Social units based on age, gender, or common interest, not on kinship

Age   Manufacturers of consumer goods are well aware of the importance of segmenting a market by age groups, which often cut across cultures. This fact has enabled marketers to succeed in selling such products as clothing and records to the youth market in both developed and developing nations. However, international marketers may go too far if they assume that young people everywhere exert the same buying influence on their parents as they do here. Kellogg's attempt to sell cereals in Great Britain through children was not successful because English mothers are less influenced by their children with respect to product choice than are American mothers. Senior citizens form an important segment in the United States, where older people live apart from their children, but where the extended-family concept is prevalent, older people continue to live with and exert a powerful influence on younger members of the family.

Gender   As nations industrialize, more women enter the job market and thus assume greater importance in the economy. This trend is receiving further impetus as the women's movement for equality of the sexes spreads to the traditionally male-dominated societies of less developed countries. Whatever the workplace status of women in a particular market, consumer purchasing in virtually any country is likely to reflect a strong female influence.

While the Chinese husband is sometimes referred to as the "minister of defense," the wife is the "minister of the interior."

Free Association   *Free-association groups* are composed of people joined together by a common bond, which can be political, occupational, recreational, or religious. Even before entering a country, management should identify such groups and assess their political and economic power. As we will see in later chapters, consumer organizations have forced firms to change their products, promotion, and prices, and investments have been supported or opposed by labor unions, which are often a powerful political force. The increasing popularity of social networks pioneered by myspace.com and others may have an influence on firms in the future.

ENTREPRENEURIAL SPIRIT

One common interest that may be unexpected by many people is the desire to be an entrepreneur. We may assume that some countries may have a more intrinsically entrepreneurial culture than others, and this turns out to be true, but the countries with more would-be entrepreneurs may be unexpected. In a straightforward study where researchers asked whether citizens would prefer to be an employee or to be self-employed, Blanchflower and Oswald found that the percentage of the would-be self-employed is high. And even in countries at the bottom of their sample, a quarter of the working-age population wanted to be self-employed. Figure 6.4 shows the results of their survey.

Understanding National Cultures

Geert Hofstede, a Dutch social psychologist, analyzed an employee survey database, collected by the IBM World Trade Corporation, that contained over 116,000 questionnaires from 72 countries. He found that the differences in respondents' answers to 32 statements could be based on four value dimensions: (1) individualism versus collectivism, (2) large versus small power distance, (3) strong versus weak uncertainty avoidance, and (4) masculinity versus femininity.[49] (Hofstede later added a fifth dimension, long- versus short-term orientation.)

FIGURE 6.4

Pecent Preferring to Be Self-Employed

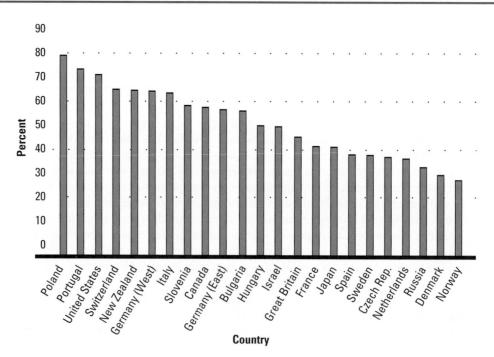

Source: David Blanchflower and Andrew Oswald, "Countries with the Spirit of Enterprise, *The Financial Times,* February 17, 2000, p. 27. Reprinted with permission.

INDIVIDUALISM VERSUS COLLECTIVISM

According to Hofstede, people in *collectivistic* cultures belong to groups that are supposed to look after them in exchange for loyalty, whereas people in *individualistic* cultures are supposed to look after only themselves and the immediate family.[50] Therefore, organizations operating in collectivistic cultures are more likely to rely on group decision making than are those in individualistic cultures, where the emphasis is on individual decision making.

LARGE VERSUS SMALL POWER DISTANCE

Power distance is the extent to which members of a society accept the unequal distribution of power among individuals. In large-power-distance societies, employees believe their supervisors are right even when they are wrong, and thus employees do not take any initiative in making nonroutine decisions. On the other hand, a participative management style of leadership is likely to be productive for an organization in a low-power-distance country.[51]

STRONG VERSUS WEAK UNCERTAINTY AVOIDANCE

Uncertainty avoidance is the degree to which the members of a society feel threatened by ambiguity and are rule-oriented. Employees in high-uncertainty-avoidance cultures, such as Japan, Greece, and Portugal, tend to stay with their organizations for a long time. In contrast, those from low-uncertainty-avoidance nations, such as the United States, Singapore, and Denmark, are much more mobile.

It should be apparent that organizational change in high-uncertainty-avoidance nations is likely to receive strong resistance from employees, which makes the implementation of change difficult to administer.[52]

MASCULINITY VERSUS FEMININITY

The *masculinity-femininity* dimension is the degree to which the dominant values in a society emphasize assertiveness, acquisition of money and status, and achievement of visible and symbolic organizational rewards (masculinity) compared to the degree to which they emphasize relationships, concern for others, and the overall quality of life (femininity).[53]

THE FOUR DIMENSIONS AND MANAGEMENT IMPLICATIONS

Table 6.1 presents the scores for Hofstede's four dimensions for about one-third of the countries in his sample.

TABLE 6.1	Scores for Hofstede's Value Dimensions			
Country	**Power Distance**	**Uncertainty Avoidance**	**Individualism**	**Masculinity**
Mexico	81	82	30	69
Venezuela	81	76	12	73
Colombia	64	80	13	64
Peru	90	87	16	42
Chile	63	86	23	28
Portugal	63	104	27	31
United States	50	46	91	62
Australia	49	51	90	61
South Africa (SAF)	49	49	65	63
New Zealand	45	49	79	58
Canada	39	48	80	52
Great Britain	35	35	89	66
Ireland	28	35	70	68

Source: Geert Hofstede, "Cultural Dimensions in Management and Planning," *Asia Pacific Journal of Management*, January 1984, p. 83.

FIGURE 6.5

Plot of Selected
Nations on Power
Distance and
Uncertainty
Avoidance

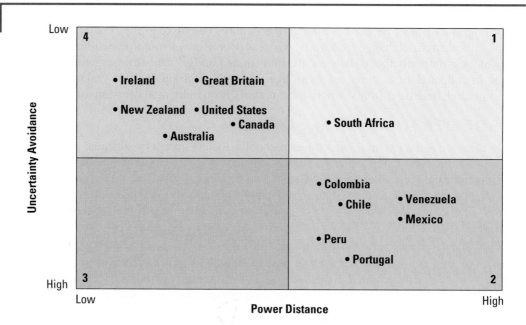

Figure 6.5 plots the scores for selected Anglo and Latin American (Hofstede's terms) nations on the power-distance and uncertainty-avoidance dimensions. The Latin American countries in the second quadrant scored relatively high on power distance and uncertainty avoidance. The lines of communication in organizations in these countries are vertical, and employees know who reports to whom. By clearly defining roles and procedures, the organizations are very predictable. The Anglo nations in the fourth quadrant scored low on both dimensions. Organizations in these countries are characterized by less formal controls and fewer layers of management. More informal communication is used.[54]

The scores for individualism and power distance are plotted in Figure 6.6. The Latin countries (first quadrant) scored relatively high on power distance and low on individualism. Employees tend to expect their organizations to look after them and defend their interests. They expect close supervision and managers who act paternally. On the other hand, people in the Anglo countries (third quadrant), which scored low on power distance and high on individualism, prefer to do things for themselves and do not expect organizations to look after them.

FIGURE 6.6

Plot of Selected
Nations on
Individualism and
Power Distance

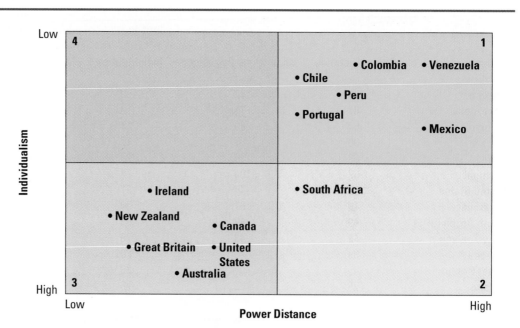

Hofstede's four dimensions have given managers a basis for understanding how cultural differences affect organizations and management methods. They assist in showing that management skills are culturally specific; that is, "a management technique or philosophy that is appropriate in one national culture is not necessarily appropriate in another." Clearly, managing in different Western countries requires different activities, and thus generalizations are not justified. However, other researchers, using other data, have found the same or closely similar dimensions, leading Hofstede to conclude that "there is solid evidence that the four dimensions are, indeed, universal."[55]

Summary

Explain the significance of culture for international business.

To be successful in their relationships overseas, international businesspeople must be students of culture. They must not only have factual knowledge; they must also become culturally sensitive. Culture affects all functional areas of the firm.

Identify the sociocultural components of culture.

Although experts differ about the components of culture, the following are representative of what numerous anthropologists believe exist: (1) aesthetics, (2) attitudes and beliefs, (3) religion, (4) material culture, (5) language, (6) societal organization, (7) education, (8) legal characteristics, and (9) political structures.

Discuss the significance of religion to businesspeople.

Knowing the basic tenets of other religions will contribute to a better understanding of their followers' attitudes. This may be a major factor in a given market.

Explain the cultural aspects of technology.

Material culture, especially technology, is important to managements contemplating overseas investment. Foreign governments have become increasingly involved in the sale and control of technical assistance. Technology may enable a firm to enter a new market successfully even if its competitors are already established there. It often enables the firm to obtain superior conditions for an overseas investment because the host government wants the technology.

Discuss the pervasiveness of the information technology era.

Businesspeople must keep abreast of the changes in information technology to avoid falling behind their competitors. The Internet enables small firms to compete in the global market, a fact that provides new opportunities for some firms and new competition for others. Businesspeople who can capture information from transaction data have a significant advantage over those who cannot. The opinion in the retailing industry is that this capability is the primary reason for Wal-Mart's success, for example.

Explain the importance of the ability to speak the local language.

Language is the key to culture. A feel for a people and their attitudes naturally develops with a growing mastery of their language.

Discuss the importance of unspoken language in international business.

Because unspoken language can often tell businesspeople something that spoken language does not, they should know something about this form of cross-cultural communication.

Discuss the two classes of relationships within a society.

A knowledge of how a society is organized is useful because the arrangement of relationships within it defines and regulates the manner in which its members interface with one another. Anthropologists have broken down societal relationships into two classes: those based on kinship and those based on free association of individuals.

Discuss Hofstede's four cultural value dimensions.

Geert Hofstede analyzed IBM employees in 72 countries and found that the differences in their answers to 32 statements could be based on four value dimensions: (1) individualism versus collectivism, (2) large versus small power distance, (3) strong versus weak uncertainty avoidance, and (4) masculinity versus femininity. These dimensions help managers understand how cultural differences affect organizations and management methods.

Key Words

culture (p. 160)
ethnocentricity (p. 160)
aesthetics (p. 164)
demonstration effect (p. 168)
Protestant work ethic (p. 169)
Confucian work ethic (p. 169)

Asian religions (p. 169)
caste system (p. 171)
material culture (p. 173)
technological dualism (p. 175)
appropriate technology (p. 175)
boomerang effect (p. 175)

lingua franca (p. 176)
unspoken language (p. 179)
bribes (p. 181)
extortion (p. 181)
extended family (p. 183)
associations (p. 183)

Questions

1. Why is it helpful for international businesspeople to know that a national culture has two components?

2. A knowledge of culture has been responsible for Disney's success in Tokyo, and ignorance of culture was responsible for the company's large losses in Paris. Discuss.

3. Why do international businesspersons need to consider aesthetics when making marketing decisions?

4. How can the demonstration effect be used to improve productivity? To improve sales?

5. Some societies view change differently than do Americans. What impact does this have on the way American marketers operate in those markets? The way American production people operate?

6. Why must international businesspeople be acquainted with the beliefs of the major religions in the areas in which they work?

7. What Buddhist belief would cause American marketing and production managers to think carefully before transferring their marketing plans or bonus plans to an area where Buddhists are present in large numbers?

8. Why is technological superiority especially significant for international firms?

9. What is the significance of the extended family for international managers?

10. Use Hofstede's four dimensions to analyze this situation: John Adams, with 20 years of experience as general foreman in the United States, is sent as production superintendent to his firm's new plant in Colombia. He was chosen because of his outstanding success in handling workers. Adams uses the participative management style. Can you foresee his having any problems on this new job?

Research Task

globalEDGE.msu.edu globalEDGE

Use the globalEDGE site (http://globalEDGE.msu.edu/) to complete the following exercises:

1. Assume you own an exporting company that specializes in consumer products. You have been selling your products in several different countries but have yet to enter the Asian market. You have chosen South Korea as the first Asian country to enter. Since you have not previously sold your products in any Asian market, you think it would be a good idea to form a strategic alliance with a local firm. You strongly believe that the first impression is important. Therefore, you have decided to collect some information regarding the business culture and local habits of South Korea from the *"Kwintessential"* Web site. Prepare a short report in terms of the most shocking characteristics that may influence business interactions in this country.

2. The cultural distance of countries in which your firm operates is one of the many explanations of significant differences that your U.S.-based employees face when travelling to different affiliates worldwide. Typically, an index of cultural distance can be determined by summing the differences of country-level scores such as those introduced by Hofstede's cultural dimensions. At the present time, your firm has operations in Austria, Guatemala, Iran, Malaysia, and South Africa. Using the *Hofstede Resource Center* based on studies involving cultural dimensions to assess all five countries, determine which affiliates are located in a culture that is least and most similar to the U.S. As there are four main components of each overall cultural distance score, which component(s) can be considered most influential for each country?

The proverb "When in Rome, do as the Romans do" applies to business representatives as well as tourists. Being attuned to a country's business etiquette can make or break a sale, particularly in countries where 1,000-year-old traditions can dictate the rules for proper behavior. Anyone interested in being a successful marketer should be aware of the following considerations:

- *Local customer, etiquette, and protocol:* An exporter's behavior in a foreign country can reflect favorably or unfavorably on the exporter, the company, and even the sales potential for the product.

- *Body language and facial expressions:* Often, actions do speak louder than words.

- *Expressions of appreciation:* Giving and receiving gifts can be a touchy subject in many countries. Doing it badly may be worse than not doing it at all.

- *Choices of words:* Knowing when and whether to use slang, tell a joke, or just keep silent is important.

The following informal test will help exporters rate their business etiquette. See how many of the following you can answer correctly. (Answers follow the last question.)

1. You are in a business meeting in an Arabian Gulf country. You are offered a small cup of bitter cardamom coffee. After your cup has been refilled several times, you decide you would rather not have any more. How do you decline the next cup offered to you?
   a. Place your palm over the top of the cup when the coffeepot is passed.
   b. Turn your empty cup upside down on the table.
   c. Hold the cup and twist your wrist from side to side.

2. In which of the following countries are you expected to be punctual for business meetings?
   a. Peru.   c. Japan.   e. Morocco.
   b. Hong Kong.   d. China.

3. Gift giving is prevalent in Japanese society. A business acquaintance presents you with a small wrapped package. Do you:
   a. Open the present immediately and thank the giver?
   b. Thank the giver and open the present later?
   c. Suggest that the giver open the present for you?

4. In which of the following countries is tipping considered an insult?
   a. Great Britain.   b. Iceland.   c. Canada.

5. What is the normal workweek in Saudi Arabia?
   a. Monday through Friday.
   b. Friday through Tuesday.
   c. Saturday through Wednesday.

6. You are in a business meeting in Seoul. Your Korean business associate hands you his calling card, which states his name in the traditional Korean order: Park Chul Su. How do you address him?
   a. Mr. Park.   b. Mr. Chul.   c. Mr. Su.

7. In general, which of the following would be good topics of conversation in Latin American countries?
   a. Sports.   c. Local politics.   e. Travel.
   b. Religion.   d. The weather.

8. In many countries, visitors often are entertained in the homes of clients. Taking flowers as a gift to the hostess is usually a safe way to express thanks for the hospitality. However, both the type and the color of the flower can have amorous, negative, or even ominous implications. Match the country where presenting them would be a social faux pas.
   a. Brazil.   1. Red roses.
   b. France.   2. Purple flowers.
   c. Switzerland.   3. Chrysanthemums.

9. In Middle Eastern countries, which hand does one use to accept or pass food?
   a. Right hand.   b. Left hand.   c. Either hand.

10. Body language is just as important as the spoken word in many countries. For example, in most countries, the thumbs-up sign means "OK." But in which of the following countries is the sign considered a rude gesture?
    a. Germany.   b. Italy.   c. Australia.

Answers: 1—*c*. It is also appropriate to leave the cup full. 2—*a, b, c, d,* and *e.* Even in countries where local custom does not stress promptness, overseas visitors should be prompt. 3—*b.* 4—*b.* 5—*c.* 6—*a.* The traditional Korean pattern is surname, followed by two given names. 7—*a, d,* and *e.* 8—*a* and 2 (purple flowers are a sign of death in Brazil), *b* and 3 (the same is true of chrysanthemums in France), *c* and 1 (in Switzerland, as well as in many other north European countries, red roses suggest romantic intentions). 9—*a.* Using the left hand would be a social gaffe. 10—*b, c.*

How's Your Business Etiquette?
Add up your correct answers:

8–10: Congratulations, you have obviously done your homework when it comes to doing business overseas.

5–7: Although you have some sensitivity to the nuances of other cultures, you still might make some social errors that could cost you sales abroad.

1–4: Look out, you could be headed for trouble if you leave home without consulting the experts.

Where to Turn for Help
Whether you struck out completely in the business etiquette department or just want to polish your skills, there are several sources you can turn to for help:

- *Books:* Most good bookstores today carry a variety of resource materials to help the traveling business representative.

- *Workshops and seminars:* Many private business organizations and universities sponsor training sessions for the exporter interested in unraveling the mysteries of doing business abroad.

- *State marketing specialists:* In some states, your first contact should be your state commerce or agriculture department, where international specialists can pass on their expertise or put you in touch with someone who can.

Source: *Foreign Agriculture,* U.S. Department of Agriculture, February 1987, pp. 18–19.

7

Natural Resources and Environmental Sustainability

Swiss Mountain Valley

Climate change may prove to be the most important business issue of the 21st century. Managers who wish to be responsible to shareholders and the broader community must be prepared to face the challenges and opportunities presented by our shifting climate. Trillions of dollars, millions of lives, thousands of species-infinite solutions.

—*Stanford University's Graduate School of Business,* The MBA's Climate Change Primer

If an economy is to sustain progress, it must satisfy the basic principles of ecology. If it does not, it will decline and eventually collapse. There is no middle ground.

—*Lester Brown, President, Earth Policy Institute*

Switzerland, Where Geography Drives Competitive Advantage: Geography, Watches, Chocolate, and Cheese

Watches, lace, carvings, chocolate, cheese, precision machinery, pharmaceuticals—what do they have in common? All are produced in Switzerland; all have a high value per kilo; the Swiss versions are known for their quality; and Switzerland's natural resources, or lack of them, are partially responsible for their being produced in Switzerland.

To appreciate why this is so, consider the following: (1) Switzerland is mostly mountainous, with little level land; (2) it is close to the heavily populated lowlands of Western Europe; (3) transportation across the mountains to these markets is relatively expensive; and (4) Switzerland has practically no mineral resources.

One way to overcome these endowment disadvantages—lack of local sources of raw materials and high transportation costs—is to import small amounts of raw materials, add high value to them, and export a lightweight finished product. The Swiss have done precisely this with the manufacture of watches. They import small volumes of high-quality Swedish steel costing 40 cents per ounce that they then convert to watch movements selling for $60 per ounce. Because of their light weight, the cost of transporting these movements to market is minimal. Precision machinery and pharmaceuticals are other products that minimize the need for importing bulky raw materials. For all of these products, emphasis is placed on the value added by manufacturing, a process that is based on skill, care, and tradition.

Now think about the highly protected Swiss agricultural sector. Although the mountain slopes do not support much agriculture, they are adequate for raising cattle and goats. Production of milk is no problem, but getting it to its major markets outside Switzerland is. Fluid milk is bulky in relation to its value and expensive to transport. The dairymen do to the milk what the watchmakers do to the steel—convert it to a concentrated, high-value product: cheese. Because Swiss cheesemakers have no advantage over their counterparts in the lowland dairying areas nearer to the important markets, they have to compete on the basis of high quality and reputation, which they have carefully promoted.

The plentiful supply of milk is responsible for another product: milk chocolate. The Swiss import the raw chocolate and convert the milk into another high-value-per-kilo product. Certainly the Swiss manufacturer pays higher transportation costs to bring sugar and chocolate in and ship the finished product out than does Hershey in Pennsylvania. Again, the Swiss product must be perceived to be superior so that it will bring a higher price to offset the greater costs.

What about the Swiss lace and carvings? Here, too, is evidence of adjustment to geography—this time, climate. The heavy snowfall and cold temperatures of the Swiss winter leave the farmers with little to do. About the only work necessary is feeding the animals with stored hay. To help pass the time and earn some money, Swiss women make lace and embroidery while the men carve wooden figures. ■

Source: Adapted from Rhoads Murphey, *The Scope of Geography*, 2nd ed. (Skokie, IL: Rand McNally, 1973), pp. 65–67.

CONCEPT PREVIEWS

After reading this chapter, you should be able to:

describe the role of location, topography, climate, and natural resources as factor conditions in Porter's diamond model

explain how surface features contribute to economic, cultural, political, and social differences among nations and among regions of a single country

comprehend the importance of inland waterways and outlets to the sea

recognize that climate exerts a broad influence on business

understand the options available for nonrenewable and renewable energy sources

explain how factor conditions can impact innovation

describe environmental sustainability and its characteristics

draw on the stakeholder theory as a framework for environmental sustainability

As the Swiss example illustrates, geography—location, topography, climate, and natural resources—can have a profound impact on the way people organize their activities, because the physical environment provides the basic context in which we conduct our economic lives. Other basic factors that influence us include the cultural, political, legal, and economic characteristics of a country. They determine what decisions we make about resource use and the nature of the economy.

We consider the physical elements as largely uncontrollable forces because, much like the foreign environmental forces we discussed in Chapter 1, they are givens around which managers must adjust their strategies to compensate for differences in these forces among markets. Still another way to explain the importance of the environment and natural resources is to examine Michael Porter's diamond, a model he developed to explain differing levels of success among the many national players in world markets.[1] Please see Figure 3.3 on page 79.

Porter's diamond model considers four aspects of a country's economic environment that impact its competitive position: factor conditions, related and supporting industries, demand conditions and firm strategy, and structure and rivalry. His theory suggests that competitively successful countries are the ones that have the most favorable "diamonds." It is the box on the left, **factor conditions,** that we are considering when we examine the natural environment. Porter actually breaks factor conditions into *basic factors,* which are those a country inherits, such as the mountains for the Swiss, and *advanced factors,* those a country readily can mold, such as the labor force and infrastructure.

In this chapter, we address the basic factors, the ones over whose existence we have either no or quite limited control, such as the topography, climate, and natural resources. Earlier economists called these inherited factors "land" (as part of the trio of land, capital, and labor factors of production that Marx refers to as "the holy trinity"). Porter makes the point that local disadvantages in factor conditions can be recognized as advantages and become a force for innovation. Adverse conditions such as local terrain and climate or scarce raw materials, at the basic-factor level, or labor shortages, at the advanced-factor level, force firms to develop new methods, and this innovation often leads to a national comparative advantage. Hence, understanding these attributes is important.

Going back to the Swiss example of high-value-added concentrated goods, the Swiss have developed expertise areas that take into account their geography, in this case, mostly constraints (basic factors), by intentionally developing advanced-factor conditions that recognize and incorporate these basic, inherited conditions. The Swiss have built an educated, skilled, and specialized workforce; they protect agriculture against foreign competition; they pursue neutrality, thus keeping trade relationships open; they have established a reliable transportation system that overcomes their topographical challenges; and they have encouraged high levels of savings, so they can draw on both domestic and foreign savings in Switzerland. Switzerland has taken a strategic approach to developing its resources by drawing on its basic endowments and building its advanced endowments. This approach has led to the Swiss competitive advantage in the areas of watches, chocolate, and cheese, among others.

The scope of the topic *natural resources* by its very nature is quite broad. We begin with a consideration of the basics, location, topography, and climate, and then continue with a focus on the major natural resources of energy and nonfuel minerals. The consideration of natural resources leads directly to concerns about their stewardship. The final section addresses those issues through a focus on environmental sustainability.

Location

Where a country is located, who its neighbors are, and how its capital and major cities are situated are basic-factor conditions (Porter's diamond). These factors, as well as how they contribute to the way a country builds its competitive advantage, should be part of the general knowledge of all international businesspeople. Location helps to explain a number of a country's political and trade relationships, many of which directly affect a company's

---

factor conditions
Attributes that a country inherits, such as climate and natural resources, and those a country can mold, such as the labor force and infrastructure

---

operations. We look first at the connection between location and political relationships and then at that between location and trade relationships.

POLITICAL RELATIONSHIPS

At the height of the cold war, the location of Austria enabled that country to be a political bridge between the noncommunist nations of the West and the communist nations of the East (see Figure 7.1). It was bounded on the west by Germany and Switzerland, on the northeast by Czechoslovakia, on the east by Hungary, and on the south by Italy and Yugoslavia (Slovenia). In addition, Austria's political neutrality made it a popular location for the offices of international firms servicing Eastern European operations. Furthermore, since Austria had led the Austro-Hungarian Empire until 1918, the Austrians were completely familiar with the cultures and practices of those neighboring countries that they had once been joined to. Finally, Vienna, Austria's capital, is only 40 kilometers (24 miles) from the Czech Republic and 60 kilometers (36 miles) from Hungary.

Because of the political and economic changes in both Western and Eastern Europe, Austria took advantage of its location to (1) increase trade with the East, (2) become the principal financial intermediary between the two regions, and (3) strengthen its role as the regional headquarters for international businesses operating in Eastern Europe.

The collapse of the Soviet bloc (COMECON, consisting of Bulgaria, Czechoslovakia, East Germany, Hungary, Romania, Poland, the Soviet Union, Cuba, Mongolia, and Vietnam) in 1991 forced Eastern European enterprises to reorient their trade toward the West. Because of their location—sharing borders with the Czech Republic, Slovakia, Hungary, and Slovenia—and their location-based relationships, Austrian entrepreneurs have captured an important share of the Western nations' exports to the East. Because of low wage costs in the East and low transport costs due to Austria's proximity to its Eastern neighbors, Austrian producers send textiles, furniture, and machinery components to Eastern countries for further processing and assembly and then bring them back to Austria. Called **passive processing,** this is similar to what foreign firms do in the Mexican maquiladoras. In addition, Austria has been active in bridge building to the east, increasing contacts at all levels with Eastern Europe and the states of the former Soviet Union. Austrians maintain a constant exchange of business representatives, political leaders, students, cultural groups, and tourists with the countries of Central and Eastern Europe. The Austrian government and other organizations provide assistance to former Eastern bloc countries to help them adjust to the changes under way in the region.[2]

passive processing
The finishing or refining in Eastern European countries of semifinished goods from the West, which are then returned to the West after finishing; similar to Mexican maquiladora operations

FIGURE 7.1

Austria and Her Neighbors

Finland is another country whose location has contributed to shaping its political relationships. The Finns had been part of the Swedish kingdom from the 12th century until they became part of the Russian Empire in the 19th century. Finland achieved its independence from Russia in 1917, before the Bolshevik Revolution. Then Finland, which shared a 780-mile border with the Soviet Union, thrived on a balancing act it did between that country and Western Europe while maintaining a policy of neutrality. It was the only nation in the world that was at the same time a member of the Soviet trading bloc (COMECON) and the European Free Trade Association (EFTA). However, with the Soviet collapse, Finland lost an important market in the East and turned more fully toward the West. As a result of its active participation in the earlier EC/EFTA negotiations, Finland had already established a high level of integration with the European Union (EU). Finland became a full member of the EU in 1995.

TRADE RELATIONSHIPS

Geographical proximity is often the major reason for trade between nations. As we saw in Chapter 2, the two largest trading partners of the United States—Canada and Mexico—lie on its borders. In 2005, Canada and Mexico represented 27.3 percent of U.S. imports and 36.6 percent of U.S. exports.[3] With proximity, delivery is likely to be faster, freight costs are lower, and service costs for sellers to their clients are likely to be lower, too. Geographic proximity has always been a major factor in the formation of trading groups such as the EU, EFTA, and NAFTA.

Proximity to the market also helps to explain why Japan is one of the Association of Southeast Asian Nations' (ASEAN's) major trading partners, along with the United States, and usually its top source for foreign direct investment. (For membership of ASEAN, see Figure 7.2) Because of Japan's proximity to China, and because Japan needs to maintain good political relationships with its fast-growing neighbor, Japan has also increased its agricultural imports from China, including fresh vegetables. China has been able to take over part of the soybean and wheat imports that were formerly supplied by the United States.

Chile's location in the southern hemisphere accounts, in part, for its exports of grapes, peaches, and raspberries that we eat in North America November through March, when there are few domestically grown supplies. Chile's export of fruit to the United States, which represents more than 20 percent of all Chilean fruit exports and averages over $1 billion in sales annually, is possible because the nation is located where the growing seasons are the opposite of those of the northern hemisphere (Europe and the United States).[4]

FIGURE 7.2

ASEAN Members

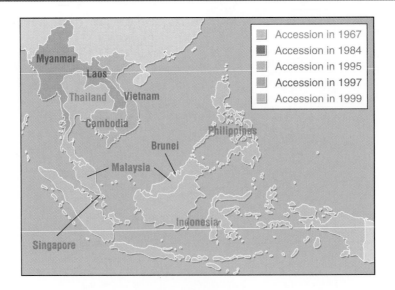

	Accession in 1967
	Accession in 1984
	Accession in 1995
	Accession in 1997
	Accession in 1999

Topography

We now examine some of the principal surface features to establish an idea of which of these physical features may impact business and how. Surface features such as mountains, plains, deserts, and bodies of water contribute to differences in economies, cultures, politics, and social structures both among nations and among regions of a single country. Physical distribution is aided by some features and hindered by others. Differences in **topography,** the features on the surface of the land, may require that products be altered. For example, the effects of altitude on food products begin to be seen at heights above 3,000 feet, so producers of cake mixes must change their baking instructions. Internal combustion engines begin to lose power noticeably at 5,000 feet, which may require the manufacturer of gasoline-powered machinery to use larger engines.

topography
The surface features of a region

MOUNTAINS AND PLAINS

Mountains are barriers that tend to separate and impede exchange and interaction, whereas level areas (plains and plateaus) facilitate them, unless climate makes exchange unlikely, as in the Sahara and Gobi deserts. The extent to which mountains serve as barriers depends on their height, breadth, and length; the ruggedness of the terrain; and whether there are any transecting valleys.

One example of such a barrier is the Himalaya Mountains. Travel across them is so difficult that transportation between India and China is by air or sea rather than overland. The contrast between the cultures of the Indo-Malayan people living to the south of the mountains and those of the Chinese living to the north is evidence of the Himalayas' effectiveness as a barrier. Another example of the influence of mountain barriers is found in Afghanistan, where mountains dominate the landscape, running northeast to southwest through the center of the country, including the Hindukush ("Hindu Killer") area. Over 40 percent of Afghanistan lies above 6,000 feet.[5] For comparison, there are two peaks east of the Mississippi in the United States that hit 6,000 feet, Mt. Mitchell in North Carolina and Mt. Washington in New Hampshire. In Afghanistan, high passes transect the mountains, creating a network for caravans. There are at least 10 major ethnic groups and 33 languages spoken in Afghanistan itself.[6] Figure 7.3. illustrates Afghanistan's topography. In similar fashion, the Alps, Carpathians, Balkans, and Pyrenees have long separated the Mediterranean cultures from those of northern Europe.

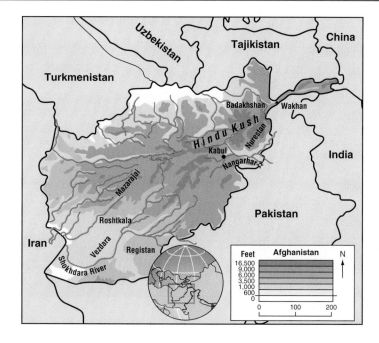

FIGURE 7.3

Afghanistan Mountains

Nations whose mountain ranges divide them into smaller regional areas, as in Afghanistan, pose a serious challenge to businesspeople because each regional market will have its own distinctive industries, climate, culture, dialect, and sometimes even language. We now look more closely at four such market examples, Spain, Switzerland, China, and Colombia.

Spain   Spain's 17 provinces are often divided into five regions, whose cultural differences are great. Two of them, Catalonia and the Basque country (see Figure 7.4), have separate languages, Catalan and Euskara. Each also has sizable minorities that wish to secede from Spain to form a separate nation. Although the Basques and the Catalans can speak Spanish, when they are among themselves they use their own languages, which are completely unintelligible to other Spaniards. This creates the same kinds of problems as those found wherever there are language differences: Spanish-speaking managers do not attain the empathy with their local employees that they do in other parts of Spain, and sales representatives who speak the local language are more effective. Moreover, the language differences increase promotional costs if, to be more effective, Spanish companies choose to prepare their material in Euskara, Catalan, and Spanish.[7]

You may be aware of the Basques due to the political unrest that is prevalent among them (similar unrest is present, to a lesser extent, among the Catalans). Since 1968 an armed terrorist group called ETA, the Basque-language acronym for Basque Homeland and Liberty (Euskadita Askatasuni), has killed over 800 people, mostly members of the security forces, in its campaign for Basque independence. ETA financed its attacks by charging local businesses

FIGURE 7.4

Spain

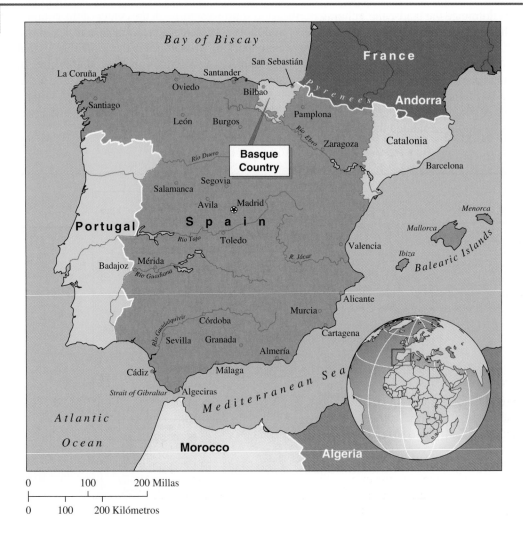

FIGURE 7.5 The Cantons and Major Language Areas of Switzerland

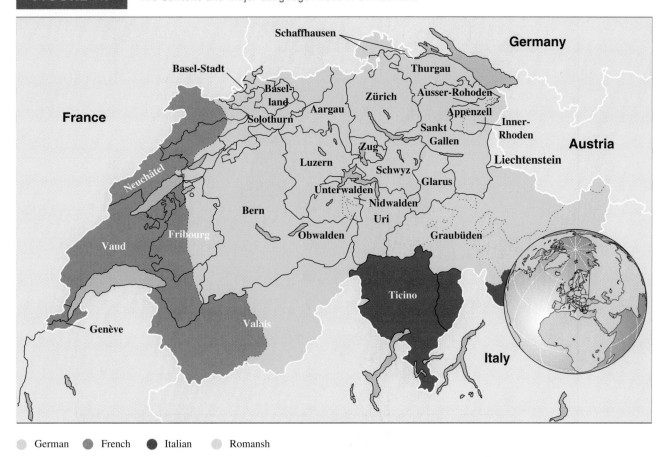

● German ● French ● Italian ● Romansh

a "revolutionary tax" or by holding wealthy businesspeople for ransom. In March 2006, ETA declared a permanent cease-fire.[8] The Spanish and French governments had arrested many Basque activists, and the Madrid train bombings in March 2004, thought to be the work of Islamic terrorists, has made the public unsympathetic to violence as a political tool.

Switzerland Switzerland is another country separated into distinctive cultural regions by mountains. In a country one-half the size of Maine, four different languages—Italian, French, German, and Romansh (related to Latin)—are spoken, along with over 35 dialect variations among them (see Figure 7.5). To the consternation of advertising managers attempting to reach all the regions of the country, each of the three major language groups—German (75 percent), French (20 percent), and Italian (4 percent)—has its own radio and television network, and the German stations broadcast in Romansh, too.

China In China, dozens of languages, each having many dialects, developed in villages separated by mountains. This caused a communication problem that hindered economic development until the government decreed Mandarin to be the official language, known as *Putonghua*, in 1956. Today, though, many dialects persist. The written language is shared among the many language groups, but spoken language is virtually incomprehensible across language borders. Look at the map on the right in Figure 7.6 and compare it to the topographical map beside it. Note that the language areas correspond to topographical features such as mountains and plains.

Colombia Colombia is similar to Switzerland in that mountains divide its markets. Three ranges of the Andes run like spines from north to south and divide Colombia into four separate markets, each with its own culture and dialects (see Figure 7.7). Depending on the product, marketers may need to create four distinctive promotional mixes.

FIGURE 7.6 Topographical and Language Maps of China

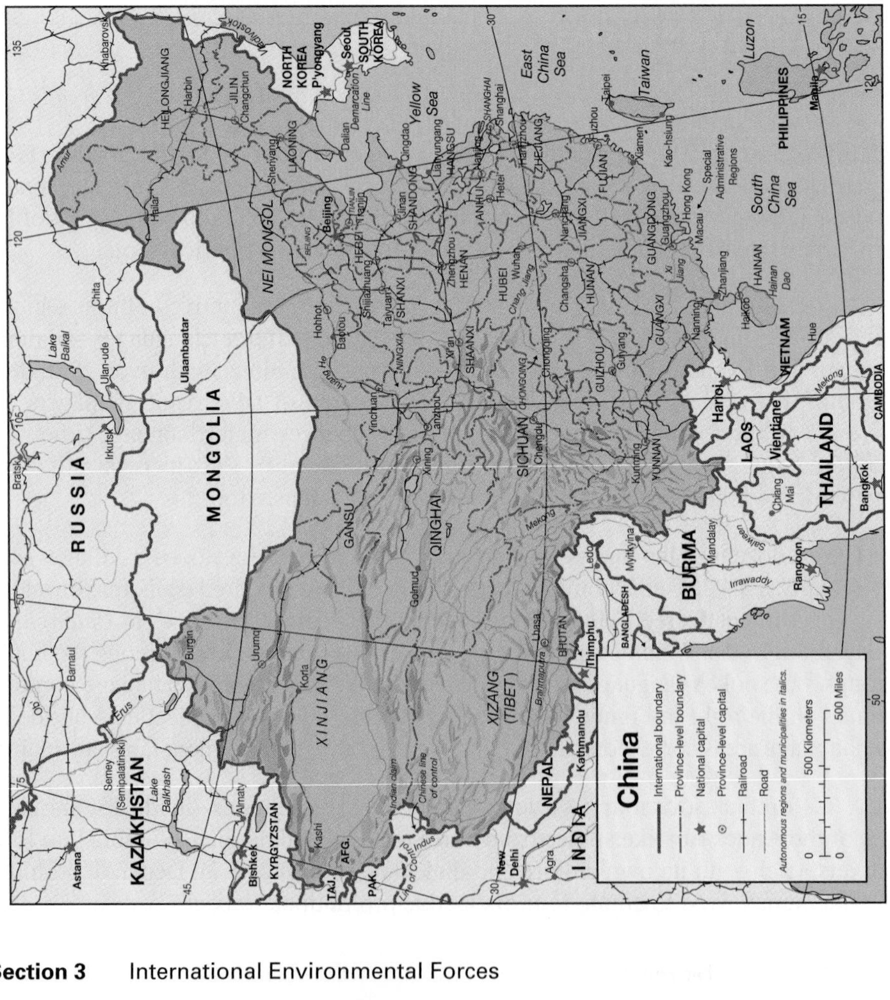

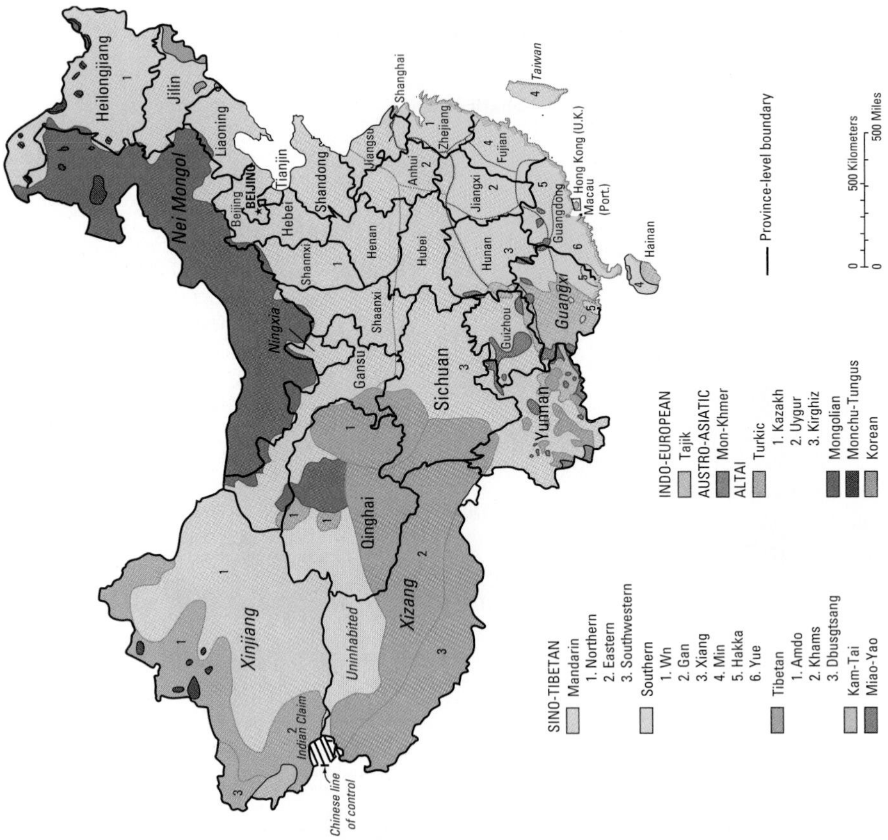

FIGURE 7.7

Colombia

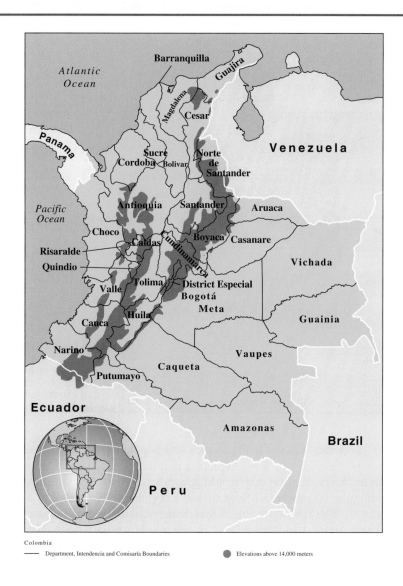

Colombia

—— Department, Intendencia and Comisaría Boundaries   ● Elevations above 14,000 meters

Colombia differs from Switzerland, however, in that besides containing distinct cultures within its borders, it experiences a range of distinct climates. Because of its location near the equator, Colombia has no seasons, but the great differences in altitude throughout habitable parts of the country result in a variety of climates. These range from hot and humid at sea level (mean average temperature of 82 degrees in Barranquilla) to cold and dry in the 10,000-foot-high snowcapped mountains (57 degrees in Bogotá). Such variation creates production and inventory challenges for a manufacturer that must produce a distinct product and package for each zone. A product with adequate cooling and lubrication for the temperate zone would function well in Bogotá but might be woefully deficient in tropical Barranquilla. Similarly, a machine powered with an internal combustion engine might perform well in Barranquilla but be severely underpowered in the 10,000-foot altitude of Bogotá.

Such climatic conditions are not peculiar to Colombia, so international businesspeople should examine topographical maps to see which tropical countries possess this combination of lowlands and mountains. If the firm's products will not function properly in such climate extremes, the firm must either redesign the products or bypass at least part of the market.

We also see in Colombia another effect of mountains. Because they function as barriers and causes of climate variations, they create concentrations of population. These concentrations occur either because the climate is more pleasant at higher altitudes or because the mountains are barriers to population movement. For example, nearly 80 percent of Colombia's population is located in the western highlands (only one-third of the nation's area) because the

FIGURE 7.8

Australia

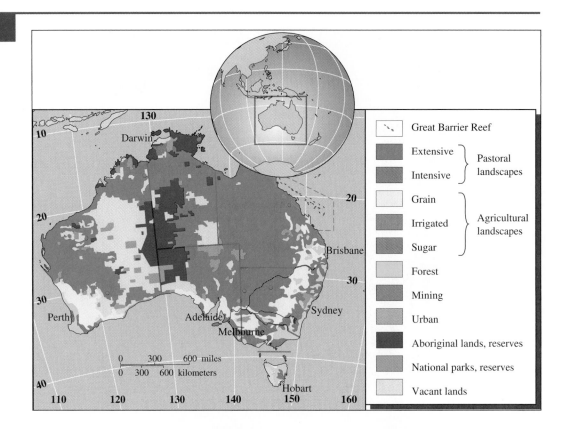

climate there is moderate. Except in the tropics, the population density generally decreases as the elevation increases. If you were to place a population map over a topographical map, the blank areas on the population map would generally coincide with the areas of higher elevation. For example, 90 percent of Switzerland's population is located in a narrow belt at the base of the Alps. The reason for this is that dense population requires commerce, manufacturing, and agriculture, which all depend on the good transportation and ease of communication afforded by the plains.

DESERTS AND TROPICAL FORESTS

Deserts and tropical forests, like mountains, separate markets, increase the cost of transportation, and create concentrations of population.

Deserts   Over one-third of the earth's surface consists of arid and semiarid regions located either on the coasts, where the winds blow away from the land, or in the interior, where mountains or long distances cause the winds to lose their moisture before reaching these regions. Every continent has them, and every west coast between 20 and 30 degrees north or south of the equator is dry. Since people, plants, and animals must have water to exist, the climate and vegetation deserts are also human deserts. Only where there is a major source of water, as in Egypt, is there a concentration of population.

Nowhere is the relationship between water supply and population concentration better illustrated than in Australia, a continent the size of the continental United States but with only 20.1 million inhabitants. This compares with a U.S. population of 295.7 million. Australia's surrounding coastline is humid and fertile, whereas the huge center of the country is mainly a desert closely resembling the Sahara. Figure 7.8 illustrates this. Because of its geography, Australia's population has tended to concentrate along the coastal areas in and around the state capitals, which are also major seaports, and in the southeastern fifth of the nation, where more than one-half of the population lives. This gives Australia one of the highest percentages of urban population in the world, 85 percent.

FIGURE 7.9

Canadian Shield

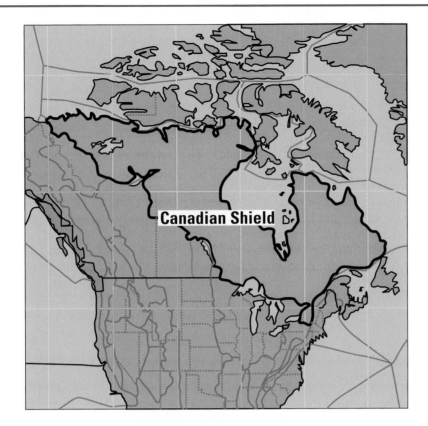

The distances between Australian cities and the fact that they are seaports make coastal shipping preferred over road and rail transportation. However, the long distances between major markets result in transportation accounting for as much as 30 percent of the final cost of the product, compared with the more usual 10 percent in the United States and Europe.

The population distribution in Australia also has a profound impact on the media. Most TV and print media are concentrated in capital city areas and are not national. This requires that advertisers buy space or time on a state-by-state or city-by-city basis. Although most capital city areas have three commercial TV channels, there is little networking.

Even though 70 percent of the country is arid or semiarid, some areas in the northern rim of Australia receive up to 100 inches of rainfall annually, much like the monsoon areas of India. Thus, firms entering the Australian market face the same extreme differences of temperature and humidity as encountered in Colombia.

Australia has little land above 3,000 feet in altitude. Were it not for this uniform topography, the temperature differences there would be great, as they are in countries with large, hot desert areas and irregular surfaces. Iran is such a nation. In the summer, temperatures may reach 130°F, whereas winter temperatures in high altitudes may drop to –18°F. From December to March, it is possible to ski just an hour and a half's drive from Teheran, the capital. Like Australia, Iran's population distribution is heavily influenced by climate and topography. More than 70 percent of the country—consisting mostly of mountains and deserts—is uninhabited, and one-half of the population lives in urban areas.

Tropical Forests   At the other extreme from deserts, tropical rain forests also are a barrier to economic development and human settlement, especially when they are combined with a harsh climate and poor soil. This occurs in the tropical rain forests located in the Amazon basin, Southeast Asia, and the Congo. Except in parts of West Africa and Java, rain forests are thinly populated and little developed economically. For example, the greatest rain forest of them all—in the Brazilian Amazon basin—has been called one of the world's greatest deserts because of its low population density. Although it covers more than 1 million square miles (one-fourth of the U.S. land area) and occupies one-half of Brazil, the Brazilian rain forest is inhabited by just 4 percent of the country's population. Only true deserts have a population density lower than the Amazon's one person per square mile.

Canadian Shield

A massive area of bedrock covering one-half of Canada's landmass

The Canadian Shield Although the **Canadian Shield** is neither a desert nor a tropical forest, this massive area of bedrock covering one-half of Canada's landmass merits mention because it has most of their characteristics—forbidding topography, poor soil, and harsh climate (see Figure 7.9 on the previous page). The Shield is swept by polar air, which permits a frost-free growing season of only four months. During that time, residents are joined by swarms of black flies and mosquitoes. Like deserts and tropical forests, its population density is very low: Only 10 percent of Canada's population inhabits this region of 3,000,000 square miles.[9]

Managers know that in more densely populated nations, marketing and distributing their products costs less because population centers are closer, communication systems are better, and more people are available for employment. Therefore, when they compare population densities such as Canada's 3 inhabitants per square kilometer, Australia's 2, Brazil's 21, and the United States' 30 with the Netherlands' 395 or Japan's 337, they may draw the wrong conclusions.[10] However, if they are aware that the population in Canada, Australia, or Brazil is highly concentrated in a relatively small area, for the reasons we have been examining, then a very different situation prevails.

The next section explores how bodies of water also are responsible for concentrations of population.

BODIES OF WATER

Bodies of water, unlike mountains, deserts, and tropical forests, attract people and facilitate transportation. A world population map clearly shows that bodies of water have attracted more people than have areas remote from water (see Figure 7.10). Densely populated regions that do not coincide with rivers or lakes are generally close to the sea. As you can see from the population map, people cluster around the Amazon, the Congo, the Mississippi, the St. Lawrence, and the Great Lakes. In Europe, the plains of the Po River in Italy and the Rhine, running from the glaciers in Switzerland, past Liechtenstein, Austria, and France, into

FIGURE 7.10

World Population Map

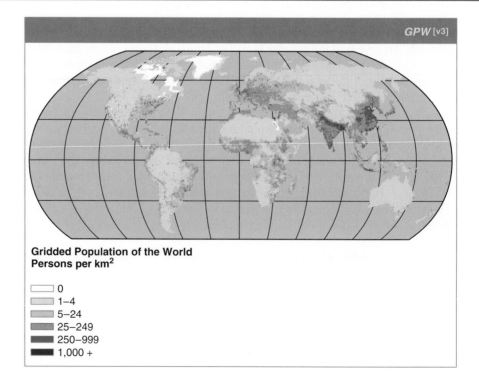

GPW [v3]

**Gridded Population of the World
Persons per km²**

- 0
- 1–4
- 5–24
- 25–249
- 250–999
- 1,000 +

Germany and on to the Netherlands on its way to the North Sea, are easily recognizable. So are rivers that cross deserts, such as the Nile, the Indus (Pakistan), the Tigris-Euphrates (Iraq), and the Amu Darya (central Asia), although these rivers are more important for the irrigation water and fertile soil they bring than for transportation.

Inland Waterways   Bodies of water that are significant because they provide inexpensive access to markets in the interior of various nations are called **inland waterways.** Before the construction of railways, water transport was the only economically practical carrier for bulk goods moving over long distances. Water transport increased even after the building of railroads; and today, in every continent except Australia, which has no inland waterways, extensive use is still made of water transportation. The importance of waterways relative to railroads, however, has diminished everywhere with one exception—the Rhine waterway, the world's most important inland waterway system.

inland waterways
Waterways that provide access to interior regions

Europe   The **Rhine waterway,** the main transportation artery of Europe, carries a greater volume of goods than do the combined railways that run parallel to it. To illustrate the Rhine's significance, one-half of Switzerland's exports and nearly three-fourths of its imports pass through the city of Basel, the Swiss inland port. This cargo is carried on the country's own 31-vessel oceangoing fleet via the Rhine waterway to Rotterdam, 500 miles to the north. (See Figure 7.11.) From ancient times, shipments have moved between the Netherlands, Belgium, Germany, France, Austria, Liechtenstein, and Switzerland by means of the Rhine and its connecting waterways. The Rhine-Main-Danube Canal, completed in 1992, creates access from the Netherlands and the North Sea through 15 countries to the Black Sea. From there, shipments can continue to Moscow over the interconnected system of the Volga and Don rivers. Not many ships undertake the entire 30-day voyage from Rotterdam to the Black Sea (3,500 kilometers), but this waterway has stimulated shipping over shorter east-west

Rhine waterway
A system of rivers and canals that is the main transportation artery of Europe

FIGURE 7.11   Rhine-Main-Danube Canal

Source: Center for International Earth Science Information Network (CIESIN), Columbia University; and Centro Internacional de Agricultura Tropical (CIAT). Used by permission. http://ciesin.columbia/edu/gpw

WORLD view

U.S. Inland Ports Offer Global Shippers a New Advantage

Congestion, security, and environmental concerns have continued to play major roles in U.S. coastal ports, both on the East and West coasts. (They have also become increasingly burdensome in other modes of transportation, air, rail, and road, as anyone who has traveled recently can testify.) At the coastal ports, huge cargo ships arrive from Asia, Latin America, and Europe and find themselves beginning the slowest part of their journey, waiting in a queue for dock space, unloading, and reloading. Inland ports offer global shippers to the United States a solution. They can be quick, efficient, and reliable and can cut the costs of reaching the middle of the nation.

At inland ports, large global shipments can be unloaded, warehoused, sorted for further movement in the delivery process (called *break bulk services*), and sent on their ways. The availability of rail, road, and air routes and major trade corridors make intermodal transport attractive, as well.

One example of a new inland port that has been thriving is in Kansas City. *Kansas City SmartPort* was created as a nonprofit entity in 2001 to unify a number of efforts by several area organizations concerned with trade and commerce. The area is on the Missouri River, which connects to the Mississippi, forming the largest inland waterway in the United States. Three major interstate highways connect at its center, as does the second-busiest U.S. rail yard.

International businesspeople see the advantages of operations such as SmartPort. Chris Gutierrez, SmartPort's president, notes that a number of business distribution centers have located in Kansas City. Case New Holland, the agricultural and industrials equipment designer and manufacturer, has built a 500,000-square-foot facility, and Musician's Friend, the largest music equipment company in the nation, has built a 700,000-square-foot facility. Take a look at SmartPort's operations at www.kcsmartport.com.

Roger Morton, "Logistics Today," June 2006, www.logisticstoday.com/showStoryBody.asp?SID={C8B678CB-4698-447F-BC76-DEB2F199AA7E}&nID=7961 (accessed June 6, 2006).

routes, such as Nuremburg to Budapest and Vienna to Rotterdam. Increasingly, firms have been turning to the Rhine waterway as an environmentally friendly alternative to road transportation.

The EU recently announced a new program to shift transportation toward inland waterways. Called Navigation and Inland Waterway Action and Development in Europe (NAIADES),[11] the program will run from 2006 to 2013. Naiads are the mythological nymphs who preside over bodies of fresh water. The NAIADES fleet of 11,000 vessels has a capacity equivalent to 10,000 trains or 440,000 trucks. Inland waterways can make transport in Europe more efficient, reliable, and environmentally friendly. According to the commissioner in charge of transport, inland waterways in the Benelux countries and France have captured significant shares of the transport business, The Netherlands uses inland waterways the most intensively of any European country, with approximately 40 percent of its transport traffic on these important arteries. In comparison, in Central and Eastern Europe, only 7 to 10 percent of the Danube's capacity is being tapped. (Because water transport tends to be inexpensive and create little pollution, recently many governments have developed programs to increase the use of inland waterways. The Worldview box describes such a program in Kansas City, aimed at more fully developing use of the Missouri River.)

South America In South America, the Amazon and its tributaries offer some 57,000 kilometers of navigable waterways during the flood season (see Figure 7.12). Oceangoing vessels can reach Manaus, Brazil (1,600 kilometers upstream), and smaller river steamers can go all the way to Iquitos, Peru (3,600 kilometers from the Atlantic).

Farther south, the Mercosur governments of Argentina, Brazil, Paraguay, and Uruguay are working to develop the Paraná and Paraguay rivers as a trade corridor connecting the vast landlocked interior of South America with seaports at the River Plate estuary near Montevideo (see Figure 7.13 on page 206). Although at present the rivers are only partly navigable, Argentina uses river ports on the Paraná to handle 25 percent of its exports and Paraguay imports most of its fuel on the Paraguay River. The Mercosur governments embarked on a $1 billion project called Hidrovia to dredge the 3,400-kilometer river system to permit reliable barge transport from the heart of South America's farmland in northern Argentina, eastern Bolivia, and western Brazil to the port of Rosario, near Buenos Aires. However, the project was suspended in 2001 due to environmental concerns. The original plans would not have spared the Pantanal, the world's largest tropical wetlands. More environmental studies are under way, and the shape that the Hidrovia project will take is still uncertain.

FIGURE 7.12 Amazon River

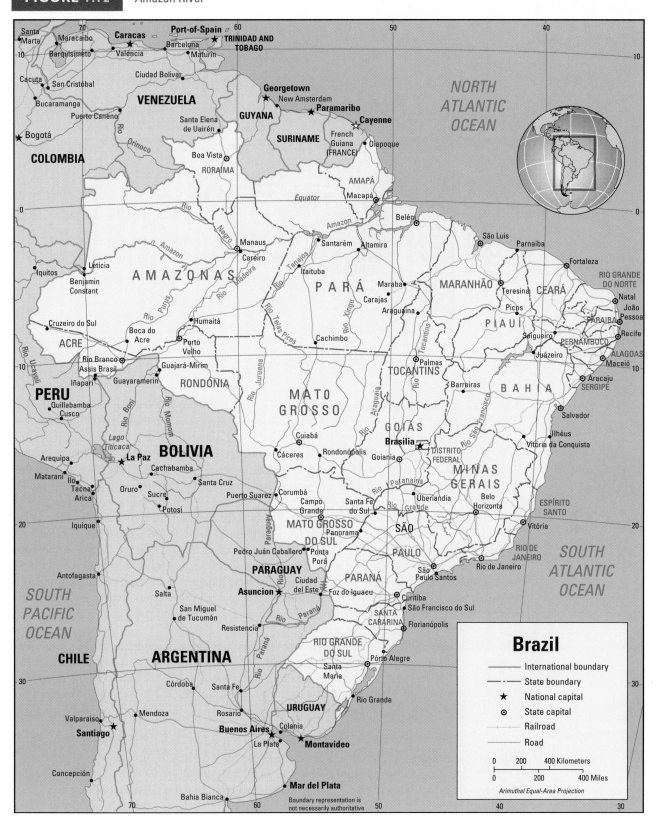

Asia In Asia, the major waterways are the Yangtze (China), the Ganges (India), and the Indus (Pakistan). Rivers are especially important in China because water is the least expensive, and often the only, means of moving industrial raw materials to the manufacturing centers.

FIGURE 7.13

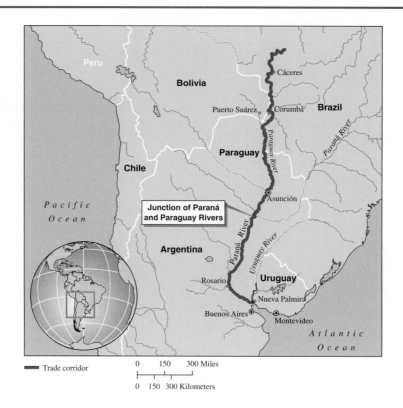

Oceangoing vessels can travel up the Yangtze as far as Wuhan, 1,000 kilometers from the sea. When the massive Three Gorges dam hydroelectric project is finished in 2009, oceangoing vessels will be able to continue past Wuhan to Chongquing, which will become an inland seaport 2,400 kilometers from the ocean. The dam itself, the largest concrete dam ever constructed, was completed in May 2006,[12] but the project has other construction to complete before it begins to operate. The reservoir the dam creates is 650 kilometers long. An estimated 1.9 million persons have lost their homes along the river's densely populated shores as a result. Because of environmental issues (the project is flooding an area comparable to the Grand Canyon in the United States, but with three gorges) as well as the human rights issues, the World Bank refused to fund the dam. Multinational construction companies and some commercial banks have participated in the project. The Chinese government estimates that the total cost of the dam will reach $24.5 billion by the time it is finished. At the International Rivers network site,[13] you can view a video of the clearing of a village area connected to the Three Gorges project and travel on a boat on the Yangtze. See www.irn.org/programs/threeg.

United States The United States depends heavily on two waterways. One, the Great Lakes–St. Lawrence, enables ocean freighters to travel 3,700 kilometers inland, thus transforming lake ports into ocean ports. The other waterway, the Mississippi, connects the Great Lakes to the Gulf of Mexico and is especially important for carrying bulky commodities, such as wheat, cotton, coal, timber, and iron ore.

Outlets to the Sea   Outlets to the sea are another notable aspect of waterways. Historically, navigable waterways with connections to the ocean have permitted the low-cost transportation of goods and people from a country's coast to its interior, and even now they are the only means of access from the coasts of numerous developing nations. In Africa, where 14 of the world's 20 landlocked developing countries are located, access to the coast is a major issue. Governments must construct costly, long truck routes and extensive feeder networks for relatively low volumes of traffic. Furthermore, governments in countries with coastlines through which the imports and exports of the landlocked nations must pass are in a position to exert considerable political influence. Struggles for outlets to the sea still exist as important political and economic factors.

Cargo ships passing through Germany on Europe's main transportation artery, the Rhine waterway.
Hans Wolf

Bolivia offers a good example of this struggle. It lost an outlet to the Pacific Ocean in the 1879–83 War of the Pacific with Chile. Many decades of discussions followed with no workable agreement. Bolivia must ship through Arica, the free port in northern Chile, and inland waterways. In 1996, Bolivia opened its first paved road link to the Pacific, a 192-kilometer highway to the Bolivian-Chilean border, the last section of Bolivia's 1,000-kilometer Export Corridor, which has opened Asian markets to Bolivian and Brazilian farmers (see Figure 7.14). Although Bolivia uses a Chilean port as an outlet to the sea, the country still does not maintain full diplomatic relations with Chile, having severed them in 1978 over this very issue. This dispute affects business relations beyond transportation. Neither country is inclined to buy from its neighbor.[14]

FIGURE 7.14

Bolivia's Export Corridor

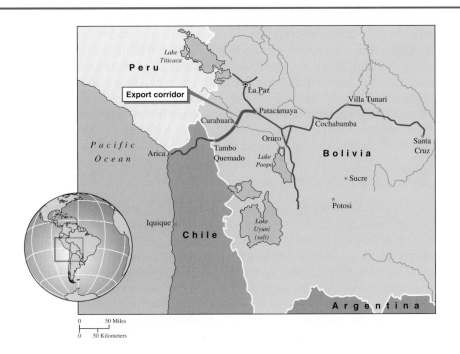

Climate

Climate (temperature, precipitation, and wind) is the most important element of the physical forces because it, more than any other factor, sets the limits on what people can do, physically and economically. Where the climate is harsh, there are few human settlements, but where it is permissive, there tends to be population density. However, climate is not deterministic—it allows certain developments to occur, but it does not cause them. Nonclimatic factors, such as mineral deposits, accessibility to an area, economic and political organizations, cultural tradition, availability of capital, and the growth of technology, are more important than climate in the development of trade and manufacturing. That is, in terms of Porter's diamond, although climate is an inherited asset as a factor condition, technology can be applied to modify its impact.

Similar climates occur in similar latitudes and continental positions, and the more water-dominated an area, the more moderate its climate. Thus, the northwest United States and northwest Europe, which are at similar latitudes and are both influenced by the sea, have mild, moist climates. Southeast Australia, New Zealand, and part of South Africa are at the same latitude and close to the sea, and they too have mild, moist climates. At the other extreme, Kansas and Central Asia, which are at the same latitude but far from the sea, are dry and have cold winters and hot summers.

CLIMATE AND DEVELOPMENT

For centuries, writers have used climatic differences to explain differences in human and economic development. They have suggested that the greatest economic and intellectual development has occurred in the temperate climates of northern Europe and the United States because the less temperate climates limit human energy and mental powers.[15] However, businesspeople must not be taken in by this ethnocentric reasoning, which fails to explain the difference in the level of technology employed in the 1600s by the inhabitants of northeastern North America and the inhabitants of northern Europe. Clearly there were other factors involved, such as the Industrial Revolution, population size, and location. The Pulitzer Prize–winning *Guns, Germs, and Steel: The Fates of Human Societies,* by Jared Diamond, explores the basis of these factors.[16] Diamond argues that the gaps in technology among human societies are caused by environmental differences amplified by feedback loops and that these differences do not lead to intellectual or moral superiority.

Climate has had some influence on economic development. Studies by the World Bank have shown that many of the factors responsible for the underdeveloped state of most tropical nations are present because of the tropical climate. Continuous heat and the lack of winter temperatures to constrain the reproduction and growth of weeds, insects, viruses, birds, and parasites result in destroyed crops, dead cattle, and people infected with debilitating diseases.[17] As grim as this may sound, there is hope. The World Bank points out that techniques are becoming available to control pests and parasites. Once this is accomplished, the very characteristics that are now detrimental to tropical Africa will give it sizable advantages over the temperate zones in agriculture. The resulting income would create a market in tropical Africa that could easily surpass that of the Middle East. In a similar way, the huge development shift from the northern to the southern U.S. states was supported by two technological innovations, DDT for malaria and air-conditioning.[18]

CLIMATE IMPLICATIONS

The differences in climate conditions among a firm's manufacturing locations and markets can have a significant impact on its manufacturing and its product mix. For example, internal combustion engines designed for temperate climates generally require extra cooling capacity and special lubrication to withstand the higher temperatures of the tropics. Goods that deteriorate in high humidity require special, more expensive packaging; machinery operating in dusty conditions needs special dust protection; and so forth.

When climatic extremes exist in a single market and the product is temperature- or humidity-sensitive, the company may have to produce and stock two distinct versions to satisfy the entire market. Severe winters, such as those in Canada, or the heavy monsoon rains that fall in northern Australia and India can impede distribution. This may require that the firm carry extraordinarily large inventories in its major markets to compensate for delays in delivery from the factory. All these conditions may have an adverse effect on profitability.

Location, topography, and climate form the basic, inherited context for business ventures; they are some of the givens. Try as the Swiss might to alter things, Switzerland is likely to continue to be a mountainous country with a heavily populated plain at the foot of the Alps. Of course, people may undertake massive modifications: Holland, situated below the North Sea level, has protected itself through a system of dykes. Singapore has greatly increased its landmass by reclaiming land from the surrounding sea, as have the Japanese in their expansion into Tokyo Harbor through extensive landfill. In a sense, these countries have affected their natural resources through human action. Such modification of an inherited factor illustrates Porter's idea of changing a disadvantage to an advantage.

Yet for the most part, location, topography, and climate are permanent facts. Often, attempts to change these natural characteristics can backfire. Right now in central China, the Badain Jaran desert is fast swallowing entire villages and leaving lakebeds near the provincial city of Minqin dry and dusty.[19] As Chia Erlong, an environmentalist who lives in Minqin, explains, "We must find ways to live with nature in some kind of balance. The government mainly wants to control nature, which is what did all the harm in the first place." In contrast, natural resources, our next focus, present businesspeople with sources of raw materials that, unlike location, topography and climate, are extractable and malleable.

Natural Resources

What are **natural resources**? For our purposes, we define them as anything supplied by nature on which people depend. Some of the principal types of natural resources important to business are energy and nonfuel minerals. In this section, we look first at energy sources, both nonrenewable and renewable. These two types of important natural resources are central to productive capacity. Then we direct our attention to nonfuel minerals. The final section of this chapter addresses sustainability.

natural resources
Anything supplied by nature on which people depend

ENERGY

Natural resources related to energy can be categorized as nonrenewable and renewable. The fossil fuels, which are the source of much of our energy, include petroleum, coal, and natural gas and are *nonrenewable*—once we use them, their supplies are depleted. Among renewable energy sources are hydroelectric, wind, solar, geothermal, waves, tides, biomass, and ocean thermal energy conversion. Figure 7.15 illustrates the world's energy supply by fuel. We look first at the major nonrenewable energy sources, and then at the burgeoning area of renewable energy sources.

Nonrenewable Energy Sources   The principal nonrenewable energy sources are the fossil fuels and nuclear power.

Petroleum   Petroleum has been a cheap source of energy and a raw material for plastics, fertilizers, and other industrial applications. According to some analysts, the world is running out of oil, but according to other sources, there are reserves sufficient to last for 50 years at the present rate of consumption.[20] Estimates of reserves change for a number of reasons:[21]

- New discoveries continue to be made in proven fields with the aid of improved prospecting equipment.

- Governments open up their countries to exploration and production. For example, the countries of the former Soviet Union have allowed commercial exploitation of the reserves under the Caspian Sea.

FIGURE 7.15

Total Primary Energy
Supply

The World

Evolution from 1971 to 2004 of World Total Primary Energy Supply*
by Fuel (Mtoe)

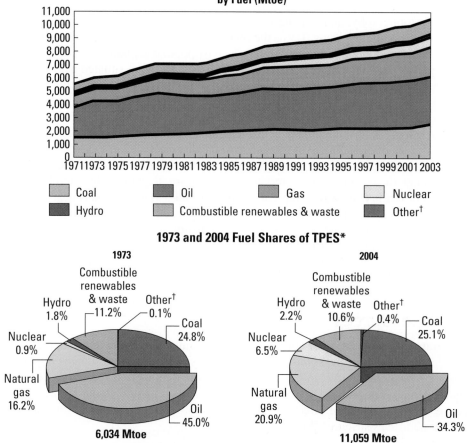

1973 and 2004 Fuel Shares of TPES*

*Excludes international marine bunkers and electricity trade.
†Includes geothertmal, solar, wind heat, etc.
Source: International Energy Agency, Key World Energy Statistics, 2005.

- New techniques, such as steam and hot water injection, enable producers to obtain greater output from wells already in operation, thus increasing the recoverable amount in an oil field.

- Automated, less expensive equipment lowers drilling costs; for instance, wellheads located on the ocean floor can replace expensive offshore platforms. This allows a company to profitably work smaller-sized discoveries that otherwise it would not touch.

Nevertheless, there is no doubt that we face a dependency issue with oil. A group of oil industry professionals, the Association for the Study of Peak Oil and Gas, points out that we are probably in the peak production time period right now.[22] The question is, How long do we have to make adjustments before the price of oil becomes prohibitive? This association of scientists interested in the impact of resource constraints notes that running out of oil is not the issue: rather, it is affording the price of this depleting resource once there are signs that we have reached the production peak.

The U.S. Energy Information Administration projects that world energy consumption will continue to increase through 2025, with dramatic increases in developing countries such as China and India as they industrialize.[23] Oil is projected to remain the world's dominant

TABLE 7.1	Greatest Oil Reserves, by Country	

Rank	Country	Proved Reserves (billion barrels)
1	Saudi Arabia	261.9
2	Canada	178.8
3	Iran	125.8
4	Iraq	115.0
5	Kuwait	101.5
6	United Arab Emirates	97.8
7	Venezuela	77.2
8	Russia	60.0
9	Libya	39.0
10	Nigeria	35.3

Source: *Oil & Gas Journal* 102, no. 47 (December 10, 2004). From U.S. Energy Information Administration, www.eia.doe.gov/emeu/international/petroleu.html.

energy source in this period. Present production is around 84 million barrels per day. Conservative analysts suggest that at 90 million barrels per day, the peak may come 30 years out.[24] Whether 30 years or 50 years, we know that such a day is coming. Table 7.1 shows the greatest oil reserves by country.

There are unconventional sources of synthetic petroleum whose usefulness, as conventional sources are depleted, increases. Among them are oil sands, oil-bearing shale, coal, and natural gas. The last two are also used to generate energy on their own.

The *oil sands* are located primarily in Canada (Athabasca, in Alberta) and in Venezuela. The sands, which contain bitumin, a tarlike crude oil, account for about 39 percent (1 million barrels per day) of Canada's crude oil production. However, production capacities are increasing, and the latest estimates are that oil-sands production will reach 2.7 million barrels per day by the year 2012.[25] At the June 2006 rate of US$75 per barrel, the cost of extracting bitumen, the source material for the oil, is competitive with that of conventional crude. The oil that can be recovered economically from the Canadian oil sands with present extraction techniques is estimated to be in the range of 180 billion barrels, exceeding the proven oil reserves of every oil-producing country except Saudi Arabia. At present consumption rates, 180 billion barrels would supply the planet for about five years.[26] A new technology, steam-assisted gravity drainage (SAGD), enables producers to exploit additional resources that are too deep to mine from the surface.

Oil-bearing **shale** is fine-grained sedimentary rocks that yield 25 liters or more of liquid hydrocarbons per ton of rock when heated to 500°C. The largest source of this material is the three-state area of Utah, Colorado, and Wyoming, in the U.S. This source has remained undeveloped because of the availability of less expensive conventional oil, the environmental problems of waste rock disposal, and the great quantities of water needed for processing. Recent technological advances have increased the likelihood that such recovery can be done with minimal environmental impact. A March 2004 Department of Energy report describes the increasing significance of the oil shale resource in the United States and calls for cooperation among federal and state agencies to shepherd oil shale projects through the permitting process, which can present a considerable hurdle.[27] An Australian oil shale project was cancelled after Greenpeace campaigned against it. The major Greenpeace argument was that extracting the oil from shale created four times the greenhouse impact as did extracting conventionally drilled oil. The project also received considerable government funding. The Greenpeace position was that putting money and effort into developing more nonrenewable energy sources, when we know that we will have to switch to renewable energy sources, doesn't make sense. "We face a switch either to clean energy sources or to fuels even dirtier than today's, such as shale oil. It beggars belief that anyone would choose the latter."[28]

shale
A fissile rock (capable of being split) composed of laminated layers of claylike, fine-grained sediment

As conventional sources of oil become depleted, synthetic petroleum sources, such as oil sands, oil-bearing shale, coal, and natural gas, are becoming more useful.

Coal and natural gas can also be converted to oil through a complex chemical process. During the South Africa apartheid boycotts, when oil exporters refused to sell oil to that nation, the South African government commercialized a process developed in Germany, the Fischer-Tropsch process, to obtain oil from coal through a catalyzed chemical reaction. Coal, under pressure and at high temperature, is converted to crude gas. After cooling and purification, the gas passes through a conversion process in which high-value chemical components and synthetic oil are produced.[29] A similar process can be used for natural gas. Oil companies have long had a problem disposing of large, isolated gas reserves that are too far from markets to be profitable. However, converting the gas to a liquid enables it to be produced profitably and moved to world markets less expensively than is possible with the gaseous form. Through this process, the oil companies use gas that otherwise would be burned off and also produce cleaner fuels than are produced with other refining methods. Chevron has a joint venture with Sasol, the innovative South African petrochemical company, for worldwide use of its gas-to-liquid (GTL) technology. One of its successful projects is a GTL plant for the Nigerian National Petroleum Company.

Nuclear Power　Nuclear power was predicted to be on its way out, largely because, although the process does not create greenhouse gasses, its waste material's storage is problematic and accidents at the plants themselves can be dangerous far beyond the local surroundings, as we learned from Chernobyl, the 1986 Ukrainian nuclear disaster.[30] Yet because nuclear power plants generate little pollution in their normal operation, because the price of oil has increased, and because new, passive designs are available, nuclear power has not declined. Fewer nuclear plants are being retired, and those in service have a higher-capacity utilization.

Higher nuclear growth is expected in developing countries, where most of the reactors under construction worldwide are being built: India (8 reactors), Russia (6), Japan (3), Ukraine (2), Iran (1), Canada (1), and Romania (1). China has committed to two per year over the next 20 years, which is good for the rest of the world, since China's main source of energy is heavy-polluting coal.[31] In addition, France has made a concerted effort to curb fossil fuel consumption and, in doing so, has turned heavily to nuclear generation. France produces 78 percent of its electricity by nuclear power, and it has one of the lowest rates of greenhouse gas emissions in the industrialized world.[32] If the price of oil stays high, nuclear power is likely to continue to grow from its present 18 percent share of the world's energy grid. It's almost certain that nuclear is back on the horizon.

Coal　Coal, much like nuclear power, was predicted to be on its decline as an energy source, largely because it pollutes heavily, but this anticipated reduction is not occurring. However, because other fuel sources are developing at a faster pace than is coal, it will continue to account for a shrinking share of world primary energy consumption. Its share of world energy consumption declined from 27 percent to 22 percent in 2002 and since then has flattened out.[33] It is projected to fall to 20 percent of world primary energy consumption by 2020. This decline in share would be even greater if it were not for the consumption by China and India. Together they account for 97 percent of the expected annual increase in the use of coal of 1.7 percent through 2020.[34] The United States has coal reserves to last 200 years at current consumption rates,[35] which, as Figure 7.16 illustrates, puts the United States at the top of countries with substantial recoverable coal reserves.

Unfortunately, burning coal creates emissions that are directly responsible for global warming. Presently the United States has no regulations on carbon dioxide emission reductions, but the issue has become a political one, with vocal supporters for emissions control from both major parties. The United States has signed the United Nations Framework Convention on Climate Change, known as the **Kyoto Protocol,** which calls for nations to work together to reduce global warming by reducing their emissions of the gasses that contribute

Kyoto Protocol
United Nations Framework Convention on Climate Change, which calls for nations to reduce global warming by reducing their emissions of the gasses that contribute to it

FIGURE 7.16

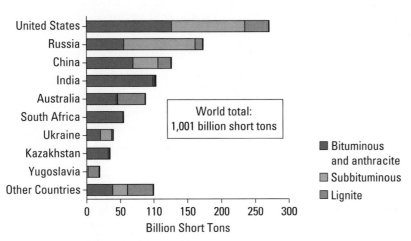

Note: Data for the United States represent recoverable coal estimates as of January 1, 2004. Data for other countries are as of January 1, 1003.

Source: Energy Information Administration, *International energy Annual 2003,* DOE/EIA-0219 (2003) (Washington, DC, June 2005), table 8.2; Web site: www.eia.doe.gov/iea.

to it, carbon dioxide first among them. To date, only the U.S. and Australian governments have declined to ratify the Kyoto Protocol. The United States and China are the two largest producers of coal-generated carbon dioxide, the principal global-warming gas. Together they produce more than half of the world's carbon dioxide emissions.[36]

Under development are several new technologies that promise to reduce emissions from coal-fired plants, one that vents the emissions deep into the ground, another that pulverizes the coal before it is burned, and another that uses the Fischer-Tropsch process to change the coal to a gas before it is burned. Given the coal reserves in the United States and in the developing countries of China and India, the total global use of coal may increase in the 21st century.

Natural Gas   Natural gas has been the fastest-growing source of energy, whose use is projected to almost double between 1999 and 2020. As a percentage of total energy consumption, natural gas should rise from 23 percent in 1999 to 28 percent in 2030. Its use surpassed that of coal (BTU basis) for the first time in 1999 and is expected to exceed the use of coal by 38 percent in 2020.[37]

Renewable Energy Sources

Most people in the energy industry believe that one day renewable energy sources will replace fossil fuels, either because the price of nonrenewable energy sources will become too high or the sources themselves will be depleted. There are at least eight alternative energy sources: hydroelectric, solar, wind, geothermal, waves, tides, biomass fuels such as ethanol, and ocean thermal energy conversion. None is available everywhere, but all appear to have applications under appropriate conditions. Of the eight, hydroelectric has had an extensive use—7 percent of the total energy consumed in the world comes from hydroelectric installations. Over 48 countries have programs to support the development and use of renewable energy.

Improved technology has resulted in new support for solar energy and wind power in many parts of the world. The fastest-growing energy technology right now is solar, in the form of grid-connected solar photovoltaic (PV) cells, whose capacity grew by 60 percent per year from 2000 to 2004, notably in Japan, Germany, and the United States. Developing nations such as India, Kenya, and Indonesia are using solar-powered PV cells for rural electrification in isolated communities that are far from power lines and have small electricity requirements. In developed countries, on the other hand, their primary use is for water and space heating.[38] Second is wind power, which grew by 43.4 percent last year.[39] The United States led in the percentage increase in wind power generating capacity, with an increase of 21.1 percent. Figure 7.17 shows wind power capacities by world region.

Ethanol is a **biomass** fuel and, coincidentally, the source of alcohol in alcoholic beverages. *Biomass* means that the energy source is photosynthesis, through which plants

biomass

A category of fuels whose energy source is photosynthesis, through which plants transform the sun's energy into chemical energy; sources include corn, sugarcane, wheat

A wind turbine farm in Palm Springs, California.

transform the sun's energy into chemical energy. Thus the plant sources of this energy are collectively known as "biomass" sources. Ethanol has risen in use since the cost of oil has increased beyond ethanol's production cost, $41 a barrel.[40] The sources of ethanol are diverse, with corn, wheat, and sugarcane among the popular ones. Brazil meets 40 percent of its gasoline demand with ethanol produced from sugarcane. Brazil has also pioneered the concept of flexible-fuel vehicles and has added 25 percent ethanol to fuel sold there. Technology to generate ethanol from agricultural waste such as corncobs is under development.

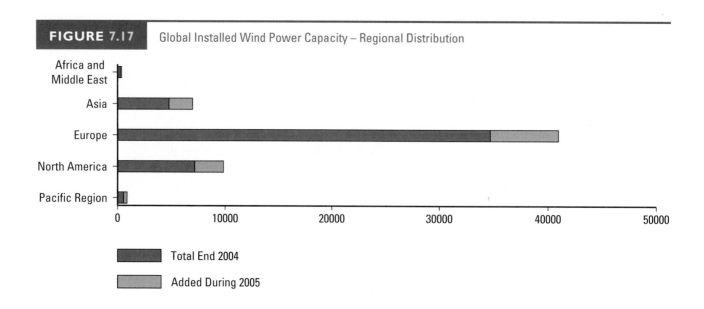

FIGURE 7.17 Global Installed Wind Power Capacity – Regional Distribution

Total End 2004

Added During 2005

>>Small Business: Ocean Mining and Environmental Impact

Nautilus Minerals, a mining company in Vancouver, Canada, has been scouring the ocean floor for dormant hydrothermal vents and has found them off the coast of Papua New Guinea. [Note that Papua New Guinea has the same place name as Papua (formerly Irian Jaya), Indonesia.] These vents are known to contain metal sulphides, rich sources of gold and copper. Nautilus is now working on environmental studies to allow it to apply for a mining lease from the Papua New Guinea government.

The world's two largest diamond-mining companies, De Beers and Namibian Mining, are mining diamonds off the coast of Namibia by using truck-size remote-controlled crawlers to excavate seabed sediment with a powerful pump and transport the sediment to a surface ship, where the diamonds are sorted and classified. A new daily production record was set on July 23, 2002, when a crawler produced 16,418 carats. The day's production consisted of 54,240 diamonds at an average size of 0.30 carat.[a]

Yet not everyone is thrilled by plans to mine the ocean floor. Craig Cary, a marine biologist at the University of Delaware in Newark, says the prospect is unthinkable because of the potential effects on marine life. "If I was in charge of reviewing permit requests there would be some serious questions to answer. Metal sulphides are nasty substances—how are they going to deal with that?"[b] In addition, what happens to the sand that is brought to the surface? Natural habitats of fish and bottom creatures are destroyed in the process.

There are already major problems in this area. The Chinese-owned Ramu Mine on the other half of the Papua island, in Papua New Guinea, has been the subject of considerable controversy both there and in Australia, in particular due to concerns that its ocean dumping affects the ocean ecology. Local people in Papua New Guinea, depend on the ecological health of the region, and river communities downstream from the mine are worried, too. For these reasons, the New Guinean National Fisheries Authority wrote in a report, "The Ramu Nickel Mine Project is an unsustainable project socially, economically, and environmentally; and cannot be allowed to proceed."[c]

Ocean mining is one of the new frontiers whose environmental regulation is developing while the projects move forward.

[a] "Underwater Gold," www.questacon.edu.au/innovaus/c4s4_004 .html (September 21, 2000); "Namibian Minerals Corporation Announces a New Daily Production Record," *MBendi Profile*, July 26, 2002, www.mbendi.co.za/a_sndmsg/news_view.asp?P=O+PG= 11+1=38744+M=O (September 3, 2002); "Namibian Minerals Corporation," *MBendi Profile*, www.mbendi.co.za/orgs/cbi7 .htm (September 21, 2000); and "NAMCO—Exploiting Profitable Diamond Niche," *Bull and Bear Financial Reporter*, www.thebulland bear.com/bb-reporter/bbfr-archive/nameco-1.html (September 21, 2000).

[b] "The Ocean Floor—Can They Dig It?" NewScientist.com News Service, June 4, 2006, www.newscientist.com/article/dn9266-the-ocean-floor--can-they-dig-it.html (accessed June 9, 2006).

[c] Oceanlink, http://oceanlink.island.net/oceanmatters/undersea% 20mining.html (accessed June 9, 2006).

As Figure 7.15 illustrates, renewable energy is still a small portion of the world's energy supply, yet it is a growing part.

NONFUEL MINERALS

Although much of the world's attention to natural resources has centered on the discovery of new energy sources, there are other mineral resources about which governments and industry need to think strategically. Nonfuel minerals are used in all areas of modern living, from house construction to the manufacture of computers and motor vehicles. Nearly all of the world's chrome, manganese, platinum, and vanadium are produced by South Africa and the former Soviet Union. Chrome and manganese are indispensable for hardening steel; platinum is a vital catalytic agent in the oil-refining process and is used in automotive catalytic converters; and vanadium is used in forming aerospace titanium alloys and in producing sulphuric acid. China produces most of the world's tin, barite and tungsten.

INNOVATION AND FACTOR CONDITIONS

Returning to Porter's diamond, we can see that innovation has a large role to play in the way natural resources, both energy resources and nonfuel minerals, contribute to a country's factor conditions. For example, with energy, there are alternative sources, some of which are

LOST May Not Be Lost

After six years of negotiations over the provisions of the United Nations Law of the Sea Treaty (LOST), representatives of 127 nations agreed on rules governing deep-seabed mining to be administered by the UN's International Seabed Authority (ISA). This is the first time regulations have been made to govern deep-seabed resources beyond national jurisdiction.

The ISA's code regulates the exploration and mining of potato-size polymetallic nodules lying outside the 200-mile economic zone of any country, as well as the metal deposits found in the crust of 100-foot-high chimneylike structures formed when hot water rushes up from volcanic vents in the seafloor. The recovery of hydrocarbons is also regulated. The new regulations empower the ISA to sign exploration contracts with registered pioneer investors (the first firms to make large investments in the survey of nodules). They include five companies, one each from Japan, France, Russia, and China and one jointly owned by Poland, Cuba, Bulgaria, Slovakia, and the Czech Republic.

American firms are not yet involved because the U.S. Senate has yet to approve the treaty, although the government has voiced support for it. Still to be worked out are sticking points for some members of the House of Representatives Committee on Foreign Relations, who play an advisory role in this matter to the Senate. These points are the treaty's stipulations requiring the transfer of mining technology to less developed countries (LDCs); the lack of weighted voting (the United States would be responsible for about 25 percent of the Seabed Authority's budget and have one vote along with each of the other members); and the treaty's attempt to regulate military intelligence gathering, such as submarine activity.

Source: Marjorie Ann Browne, "The Law of the Sea Convention and U.S. Policy," CRS Issue Brief for Congress, June 16, 2000, www.cnei.org/nle/mar-16.html (September 22, 2000); "Mines at Bottom of the Sea Move a Step Closer," *Financial Times*, August 15, 2000, p. 22; and International Seabed Authority, www.isa.org (June 11, 2006).

renewable such as wind and solar. These sources can be developed for broader use when the production of nonrenewable fossil fuels has peaked. In addition, synthetic fuels are being developed, as well as new processes, such as satellite mapping, for the acquisition of traditional fuels and and new methods for their processing. Then there are new technologies, such as fuel cells that use electrochemical processes to release energy. Interest in fuel cell technology has grown rapidly because of its increased fuel economy potential.[41]

Although to many the natural resource situation may appear bleak due to the threat of depletion, remember that innovation combined with sustainability can play a crucial role and also that we are discussing only known reserves. Other energy sources, attainable both through new technology and through traditional approaches, await our development. Alternative, renewable energy sources have great potential. Then, too, only relatively small areas, mostly in the traditional mining countries, have been adequately explored for the traditional fuel sources. Recent new discoveries have been reported in Brazil, Malaysia, and Libya. From a country perspective, energy and nonfuel minerals are factor conditions that can be modified through innovation as well as through import.

Environmental Sustainability

The concept of sustainability has broad scope. *Sustainability* is about maintaining something, and that something might be the environment, society, the economy, people within the economy, or the organization.[42] By its very nature, sustainability is a systems concept. The thing we are trying to sustain (a business, a way of life, the natural world) exists within a larger system, and if that larger system is not sustained, the subsystem is unlikely to survive. For example, the language of the Kamoro and Amungme peoples of Papua—will it be sustained if their communal way of life shifts to a settlement way of life and their children travel to cities in East Asia to become teachers, international bankers and marketing managers? Or let's take an ecological example. The Everglades—is it likely to be sustained if temperature and precipitation change significantly? The point here is that, given a specific, local geography, the likelihood of its being sustained if the larger environment is not sustained is quite slim. All sustainability is actually local and global, or international, in its very nature because it involves systems that are global.[43] The survival and maintenance or possible improvement of our quality

Why Europe Leads the Way: The Environment and Business

While the United States has been lowering environmental standards and stepping away from cooperation on environmental treaties (Kyoto Protocol, International Seabed Authority), the new Europe, the 25-member European Union, has made a concerted effort to raise environmental standards. Many of the European environmental regulations address the waste and toxic pollution that are by-products of manufacturing. Among EU initiatives are required vehicle recycling, elaborate tracing and checks on genetically modified crops, electronics recycling, bans on the most toxic chemicals used in electronics, chemical testing, and green design.[a] The EU has come to accept an approach to environmentalism known as the *precautionary principle*. This approach suggests regulation at the first sign of a possible danger rather than waiting for research to establish the facts. The precautionary principle puts the onus on the industry to prove that its products are not dangerous. In marked contrast, the U.S. approach tends toward, "If it ain't broke, don't fix it."

In the late 1960s, soon after publication of environmentalist Rachel Carson's book *Silent Spring* (1962), the United States led the world in environmental awareness, legislation, and responsibility. Congress established the Environmental Protection Agency (EPA) and passed the National Environmental Policy Act, the Clean Air Act, the Endangered Species Act, and the Clean Water Act. Yet recently the EU has far outpaced the United States in this area. Why? There is no one simple explanation for such a shift, but commentators point to cultural and demographic differences as a part of it. Most Europeans live in densely populated cities, so that environmental problems such as air and water pollution have a stronger, more directly observed impact on them than they do on the more spread-out rural and suburban American population.

Another reason for the shift may be attributable to culture. The United States was founded to protect individual citizens from a meddlesome, intrusive state. Business practices in the United States are thought of as acts of individual freedom. In Europe, business is thought to have quite a different purpose, one that includes obligations to society and higher levels of social responsibility. Such obligations reflect the demographic and cultural differences between the EU and the United States.

One example of the contrast in approach is the recent EU chemical industry restrictions: Registration, Evaluation and Authorization of Chemicals (REACH). In an address to the EU-U.S. Chemicals Conference, EU environment commissioner Margot Wallström observed that the success of chemicals as a key industrial sector could also be the Achilles' heel of our society: "We have developed a very high dependence on chemicals. Yet this is not matched by sufficient knowledge about their potential risks and long-term effects, for which we are paying a high price." The purpose of the EU regulations, which require that chemical companies show that their materials are not harmful, is to close this knowledge gap.

[a]http://ec.europa.eu/environment/policy_en.htm (accessed June 11, 2006).

Source: Samuel Lowenberg, "Old Europe's New Ideas," *Sierra*, January–February 2004; address by Margot Wallström, April 27, 2004, Charlottesville, VA, www.europa.eu.int/comm/environment/chemicals/reach.htm (accessed August 6, 2004).

---

of life is local in our experience of it and global in its larger context, from a system's perspective. Figure 7.18 illustrates this "act locally, think globally" truth of sustainability.

Environmental sustainability rests on the commitment of business to operate without reducing the capacity of the environment to provide for future generations.[44] An approach to the environment that commits to sustainability involves actions that have a positive, long-term social and/or environmental benefit and meet the needs of the present without compromising the ability of future generations to meet their own needs.[45] The challenges of such an approach are great, as the world has seen with the Three Gorges Dam project in China. The purpose of the dam is hydroelectric power generation to fuel China's development with a clean and low-environmental-impact energy source whose day-to-day operations are not costly. The initial project is very costly, both in money and human terms—$25 billion and displacement of 1.9 million people; once the dam is operating, however, the water that is the power source has little cost, unlike the cost of petroleum products for a conventional power plant. At the same time, the decision made by today's Chinese to sacrifice their future children's access to one of the major natural wonders of the world seems a costly one. The developed world moved forward by degrading natural resources, and, as many leaders of developing nations have pointed out, such degradation might be thought of as a given in development. An environmentally sustainable approach searches for alternatives. In doing so, it usually takes into account three areas, ecological, social, and economic, representing the contexts of participating systems—the natural world; the social world; and the world of value-added activities, the economic world. In this section, we look at characteristics of

environmental sustainability
Economic state in which the demands placed upon the environment by people and commerce can be met without reducing the capacity of the environment to provide for future generations

FIGURE 7.18

Sustainability Is Local
and International

Ecological	Social	Economic	
Survival Sustainability			Global ↕ Local
Production of life support systems Prevention of species extinction	Capacity to solve serious problems	Subsistence	
Maintaining Quality of Life			Global ↕ Local
Maintenance of decent environmental quality	Maintenance of decent social quality (e.g., vibrant community life)	Maintenance of decent standard of living	
Improving Quality of Life			Global ↕ Local
Improving environmental quality	Improving social quality	Improving standard of living	

Source: Philip Sutton, www.green-innovations.asn.au/sustblty.htm#local-global.

sustainable business practices, examine the stakeholder model for sustainability, and review two examples of businesses that promote sustainability.

CHARACTERISTICS OF ENVIRONMENTALLY SUSTAINABLE BUSINESS

There are three characteristics of evolving sustainable business practices that are widely agreed upon: limits, which apply to the ecological system; interdependence, which applies to the social system as well as to the other two; and equity in distribution, which applies to the economic system.[46] *Limits* have to do with the recognition that environmental resources are exhaustible. Water, soil, and air can become toxic, and their use needs to be informed by awareness of that danger. The current focus on greenhouse gasses and their contribution to global warming offers one example of limits. Control of emissions would be an ecologically responsible decision.

If such standards are inevitable in order to maintain survival sustainability, given the serious effects of global warming, a business that learns how to operate within the limits of emissions control early on in the adoption process would accrue advantages because they would be ahead of their competition by having learned how to do so.

Interdependence describes the relationship among ecological, social, and economic systems. Action in one system affects the others. This interdependence can be seen in stark dimensions in the extractive industries. Mining operations in Papua (formerly Irian Jaya), Indonesia, have settled areas that had previously been the hunting grounds of indigenous hunter-gatherer tribes, among them the Kamoro and Amungme, causing considerable social stress in those groups. The mining operations involve some river and stream pollution from tailings, which can be and in many cases have been abated. The mining company, Freeport McMoRan, provides health care and

An aerial view of a giant mine run by the U.S. firm Freeport-McMoran Cooper & Gold Inc. at the Grassberg mining operation. Indonesia will not hesitate to sue U.S. mining giant Freeport-McMoran if it fails to follow through on recommendations to stop pollution from its Papua operations, Environment Minister Rachmat Witoelar said.

Understanding the world in which you live and will work will set you apart and help to make you a "citizen of the world." But there is more to understanding the world than just reading an international paper, listening to *BBC World Service,* or appreciating world music. Do you really understand your world? What do you know about world geography? Do you understand global population distributions? What do you know about natural resources of the world? Can you answer the questions below?

- Which country produces more than 90 percent of the world's commercial and industrial diamonds?

- Bauxite is the primary mineral in aluminum. Where are the largest deposits of bauxite located?

- What is the longest river in the world?

- Which country has the largest landmass? Which ones are the next four in rank order?

- Which country has approximately 94 percent of its population living within 100 miles of its closest foreign neighbor's border?

- Which country is made up of over 17,000 islands?

- Which country produces the largest amount of natural rubber in the world?

If you are committed to a career in international business, your library, either digital or hardcopy, should have a comprehensive, detailed, up-to-date world atlas, one that contains statistics about natural resources, population, and climatic conditions, as well as topographical maps with the names of cities, mountains, rivers, seas, and oceans.

Aside from being "geo-savvy," you should be aware of many less-than-pleasant but important issues regarding our natural resources. Consider these facts from the Global Policy Forum:

- Illegal diamond sales in Angola, Liberia, Sierra Leone, and the Democratic Republic of Congo have been used to buy weapons, escalating local conflicts.

- Scarce water in some areas has caused conflict between neighboring countries due to perceived ownership rights of common waterways. "Water wars" are real in the Middle East and India and between Israel and the areas of Egypt, Syria and Jordan known as Palestine.

- Massive deforestation by loggers has displaced indigenous populations in Indonesia and Ecuador, to name just a few countries.

- Oil and natural gas extraction has caused military repression and human rights abuse in Sudan, Nigeria, Cameroon, Chad, and Sao Tome.

World Wide Resources:

http://geography.about.com

www.mywonderfulworld.org

www.globalpolicy.org/security/docs/minindx.htm

www.globalpolicy.org/visitctr/about.htm

Career Option: Global resource management or natural resource management are alternative international careers you might consider. Companies whose business involves the geosciences (petroleum, natural gas, coal and mineral mining, marine geology, forestry, environmental cleanup from biohazards, and waste and pollution management) also need professionals with business skills to manage the business side of their enterprise. Governments also take a leading role in resource management and offer many career opportunities for people with diverse skills.

World Wide Resources:

www.earthscienceworld.org/careers/brochure.html

http://edis.ifas.ufl.edu/FR127

education for the indigenous peoples in the area and appears to have made efforts to be a good citizen and a helpful, socially responsible neighbor. Yet the advancement the company brings is threatening the continued existence of the indigenous people, through development and education. Imagine the strains on a social system in which parents, wearing loincloths and using poisoned blow arrows to kill game, are living as traditional hunter-gatherers, while their children are being educated using Internet technologies and eating Western-style food. The interrelatedness of mining operations in a remote area and good corporate citizenship issues go beyond pollution and infringement of hunting grounds to complicated ethical and social issues related to development. The social, economic, and ecological systems are all players whose sustainability is threatened in this situation. In less stark dimensions, examples of interdependence among ecological, social, and economic systems cluster around decisions related to manufacturing and waste disposal. Filmmaker Michael Moore's eulogy to Flint, Michigan, *Roger and Me*, addresses one of those issues, location. It explores the economic, social, and ecological implications of GM's decision to move production out of Flint.

Equity in distribution suggests that for interdependence to work, there cannot be vast differences in the distribution of gains. Especially in a globalizing world, where relationships among populations are increasingly closer, or at least information about them is, vast inequities may lead to unrest and violence. Examples of corporate challenges presented by lack of equity in distribution include Shell Oil's operations in southern Nigeria, which have been forced to shut down after raids by groups claiming to speak for the local Ijaw tribe. The tribe claims they have been "cheated of oil wealth pumped from their land by the central government and oil companies."[47] Political tensions related to equity in distribution have also informed Venezuela's and Bolivia's oil businesses. These issues raise interesting questions about sustainability from a social perspective. Shell Oil has built a positive relationship with the president of Nigeria, whose southern populations, near the oil deposits, are close to insurrection because they see no gain from the oil that is in their territory. Shell needs to make decisions about sustainability that satisfy the president of Nigeria and that also satisfy the local population. It appears Shell has fallen short in the latter.

Increasingly, companies will need to make decisions about setting limits on how their operations affect the environment. They will also encounter increased signs of the interdependence that exists among the social, economic, and ecological systems that form the context for their business. Equity in distribution is one of the ways that such interdependence can work. It requires a business model that allocates gain from the business's value creation to all actors in the context. It's the notion that a rising tide raises all boats. Sam Palisano, CEO of IBM, recently spoke about this new way of understanding business when he said that IBM wanted to end its colonial company model and move on to a truly globally integrated model where high levels of trust persist among all stakeholders.[48]

THE STAKEHOLDER MODEL FOR SUSTAINABLE BUSINESS

The concept of sustainability is a complex one because it impacts all aspects of business decisions. Some of the areas that are most commonly involved are:

Alternative fuels	Office maintenance
Brownfield (contaminated-site) remediation	Pollution prevention
Corporate accountability	Social investing
Ecological development	Sustainable technology
Ecotourism	Transportation alternatives
Energy conservation	Waste reduction
Green building design	Water conservation

stakeholder theory
An understanding of how business operates that takes into account all identifiable interest holders

One model that offers a helpful framework for thinking about environmental sustainability as it relates to business is **stakeholder theory.**[49] Developed by R. Edward Freeman, this approach differs from the traditional input-process-output economic business model because it involves identification and consideration of the network of tensions caused by competing demands that any business exists within. The traditional economic model of business considers a far narrower scope of influences (employees, owners, and suppliers) that are driven by the single goal of creating profits. Stakeholder theory forces a business to address *underlying values and principles*. It "pushes managers to be clear about how they want to do business, specifically, what kind of relationships they want and need to create with their stakeholders to deliver on their purpose."[50] The theory also posits that the tensions among the varying interests in a business environment can be balanced. Business then becomes about relationships in the larger context and the responsibilities that develop from them. In stakeholder theory, profits are a *result* of value creation rather than the primary driver in the process, as in the economic model. Freeman points out that there are many companies whose operations are consistent with stakeholder theory, including J&J, eBay, Google, and Lincoln Electric.

To achieve this balance among competing tensions, the company sees itself in relation to its stakeholders, as illustrated in Figure 7.19. The company then views itself in a social context to identify its purpose, principles, and responsibilities clearly. Figure 7.20 illustrates this important step. It is at this point that limits, interdependence, and equity of distribution are addressed. One way to measure the company's activities in this larger context is the

FIGURE 7.19

Source: "The Stakeholder Based View, Who Are My Stakeholders?" Courtesy of Novo Nordisk A/S; World Resources Institute.

process of triple-bottom-line accounting. Here the company measures, in addition to its traditional economic performance, its social and environmental performance. For an example of triple-bottom-line reporting, see Freeport McMoRan's accounting of its mining operations in Indonesia (www.fcx.com, especially the Sustainable Development Report and the videos). The company's public materials suggest it is using a stakeholder approach, increasing value and contributing to the quality of life for its constituencies, including locals, while operating low-impact mining.

Culture matters in the process of moving toward environmentally sustainable business. Here are two examples of its potential impact: First, relationships matter more to collectivist

FIGURE 7.20

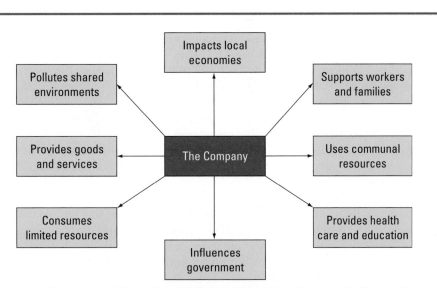

Source: "Your Company in a Societal Context," Slide 7 from Pathways PowerPoint presentation "Sustainability and Business," World Resources Institute, http://pathways.wri.org/index.asp?Topic1/,2004.

cultures than to individualist ones. This concept, explained in Chapter 3, suggests that in relationship-rich cultures, the transition to sustainable ways of operating might be more in line with traditional attitudes. For example, European cultures tend to focus more on relationships than does the U.S. culture, which has a more individualist orientation. That Europe is well on its way in the practice of sustainable business and that green approaches are demanded by European consumers may be explained partially by Europeans' assumptions about what business is and how it should be conducted. Traditionally, relationships and their obligations for Europeans suggest that the underlying purpose of business includes a level of social responsibility far beyond what American assumptions would suggest.

Second, another cultural dimension that may come into play as we move toward sustainability is found in the set of basic values, unarticulated and, unless challenged, usually invisible to their holders, that members of a culture hold about the role of the individual in connection to nature. In their values orientation theory, anthropologists Kluckhohn and Strodtbeck posit three value dimensions to describe an individual's relationship to the natural environment: mastery, submission, and harmony.[51] The mastery value posits an understanding of the natural world as a source of inputs; the relationship to nature is to control it. Submission involves understanding humans as objects of nature's forces. Harmony suggests that nature and humans can coexist without the destruction of one by the other. A strong orientation toward mastery may need to move toward the harmony dimension for sustainability to become a strong business value. That process has begun, as the following examples show.

EXAMPLES OF SUSTAINABILITY IN BUSINESS

Patagonia   Patagonia, Inc., the international outdoor gear and apparel company, has awareness of sustainability at the core of its business. In the 1970s, the climber Yvon Chouinard, from French-speaking Maine, founded Patagonia with the goal of providing equipment for "clean climbing," that is, climbing that minimizes environmental impact. Its purpose statement is, "Patagonia exists as a business to inspire and implement solutions to the environmental crisis." Michael Crooke, president and CEO, holds that the traditional approach to doing business, focusing on quarterly earnings and generally accepted accounting principles (GAAP), is not sustainable. He points out that such accounting does not account for negative externalities, such as environmental degradation and social ills, creates an unrealistic view of economic performance, and is bound to lead to an environmental crisis if something does not change. Crooke proposes an alternative "ecosystem model" for sustainability. Just as the elements of an ecosystem must work in harmony, a sustainable business model relies on the synergies between the environmental, social, and financial elements of a business. This synchronization creates a virtuous cycle: The company's environmental and social commitment attracts loyal customers and employees, which improves the financial performance of the firm, which facilitates further commitment, and so on.[52]

Patagonia has a series of social and production-related efforts to move the issues of sustainability forward. On the production side, it uses recycled materials, both in its building construction and in its products. In its fiber use, plastic soda cans are the source of much of the fleece, and organic cotton is used exclusively. Patagonia supports environmental causes, both indirectly through grant programs and directly through its sourcing decisions. Through its commitment to sustainability, Patagonia is developing a model for doing business in a sustainable way that may be of use to other companies as we move forward. As Chouinard observed several years ago, "No business can be done on a dead planet. A company that is taking the long view must accept that it has an obligation to minimize its impact on the natural environment."[53]

Dow Jones Sustainability Index   Dow Jones launched the Sustainability Index in 1999 as a global index to track the financial performance of sustainability-driven companies. Dow Jones reviews candidates for the index by conducting a thorough examination of the company's environmental, economic, and social performance. In 2005, 57 companies were added to the index and 54 deleted. Qualifying for the index and being accepted are two separate challenges, since the index members are limited to 20 percent per sector, with nationality not being considered. There are actually two versions of the Sustainability World index, one that excludes companies in the alcohol, armaments, firearms, tobacco, and gambling businesses. As of June 2006, the indexes listed 318 businesses. Among the U.S. businesses are General Electric, CitiGroup, Intel, Johnson & Johnson, Procter and Gamble, and Hewlett-Packard. Such is the demand for sustainable indexes that in January 2006, in addition to the Sustainability World indexes, Dow Jones launched more limited sustainability indexes that focus on specific sectors: European Blue Chip companies, American, North American, and Islamic companies. These can be explored at www.sustainability-indexes.com.

Summary

Describe the role of location, topography, climate, and natural resources as factor conditions in Porter's diamond model.

Location, topography, climate, and natural resources are inherited factors that underlie inputs that companies draw on. Local disadvantages in factor conditions can be recognized as advantages and become a force for innovation. Adverse conditions such as local terrain and climate or scarce raw materials, at the basic-factor level, or labor shortages, at the advanced-factor level, force firms to develop new methods, and this innovation often leads to a national comparative advantage. Hence, understanding these factors is important.

Explain how surface features contribute to economic, cultural, political, and social differences among nations and among regions of a single country.

Mountains divide nations into smaller regional markets that often have distinct cultures, industries, and climates. Sometimes even the languages are different. Deserts and tropical forests act as barriers to people, goods, and ideas.

Comprehend the importance of inland waterways and outlets to the sea.

Bodies of water attract people and facilitate transportation. Water transportation has increased even after the building of railroads and highways. Various European firms are shipping goods in barges on the Rhine waterway instead of using highways.

Recognize that climate exerts a broad influence on business.

The differences in climate conditions among a firm's markets and manufacturing sites can significantly affect its operations. In the case of the marketing mix, a product sold for use in northern Canada may need protection against cold weather, while the same product used in the tropics may require extra cooling to resist the heat. Heavy seasonal rains or long, very cold or dry spells can require that the firm carry large inventories because of the difficulty of replenishing stock in inclement weather. Other distribution challenges related to climate include protection from the cold, heat, and humidity.

Understand the options available for nonrenewable and renewable energy sources.

Nonrenewable energy sources include petroleum, both from conventional sources and nonconventional sources such as shale, oil sands, coal, and natural gas. Other nonrenewable sources are coal, nuclear power, and natural gas. Renewable energy sources include hydroelectric, wind, solar, geothermal, waves, tides, biomass, and ocean thermal energy conversion. Each of these energy sources has a cost that impacts its use. As nonrenewable sources approach depletion, renewable sources will become more widely applied as their relative cost decreases.

Explain how factor conditions can impact innovation.

Porter makes the point that local disadvantages in factor conditions can, if recognized, become a force for innovation. Adverse conditions such as local terrain and climate or scarce raw materials, at the basic-factor level, or labor shortages, at the advanced-factor level, may force firms to develop new approaches. This innovation often may lead to a national comparative advantage. Understanding these attributes is important.

Describe environmental sustainability and its characteristics.

Environmental sustainability rests on the commitment of business to operate without reducing the capacity of the environment to provide for future generations. There are three characteristics of evolving sustainable business practices that are widely agreed upon: limits, which apply to the ecological system; interdependence, which applies to the social system as well as to the other two; and equity in distribution, which applies to the economic system

Draw on the stakeholder theory as a framework for environmental sustainability.

Stakeholder theory forces a business to address its underlying values and principles. Stakeholder theory encourages managers to articulate clearly how they want to do business. What kind of relationships do they want and need to create with their stakeholders to deliver on their purpose? In this way, operating with stakeholder theory leads to a public discussion about responsibility of the business among all stakeholders.

Key Words

Questions

1. Of the 30 nations listed by the UN as the least developed nations, 16 are landlocked. Is this a coincidence, or might the lack of a seacoast contribute to their slower development?

2. Analyze the potential of oil shale and oil sands as future energy sources.

3. a. Why do you suppose the blank areas on a population map generally coincide with the areas of higher elevation on a topographical map?

   b. Why are the tropics an exception to this rule?

4. "International businesspeople, unless they are in the business of refining minerals or petroleum, have no need to concern themselves with world developments in natural resources." Agree or disagree with this assertion, and explain your reasoning.

5. Mountains, deserts, and tropical rain forests are generally culture barriers. Explain.

6. In 2005, Switzerland, a landlocked country, won the America's Cup sailing competition. How might this be explained using Porter's factor conditions?

7. From a multinational businessperson's point of view, how would you apply what you have learned about factor conditions as you explore locations for manufacturing?

8. Explain how the stakeholder model applies to an example of sustainable business. This example can be from your community.

9. How is the concept of sustainable business practice both local and global?

Research Task

globalEDGE.msu.edu

Use the globalEDGE site (http://globalEDGE.msu.edu/) to complete the following exercises:

1. Your small firm is an energy provider to a variety of markets in the United States and Canada. As such, you have been assigned to determine the general climate of the energy industry for the coming decades. By combining population data with energy consumption estimations, one can analyze trends in energy use per capita and differences in per capita energy use between countries. BP, one of the world's largest energy companies, provides an annual report with statistical data on energy trends worldwide. Using the *BP Statistical Review of World Energy* as reference, find which country consumes the most energy per person. How has energy consumption varied with a growing world population? What does this mean for your firm's future as an energy provider?

2. You are working for a pontoon manufacturer that is considering expansion to South America. An important determinant of the firm's market strategy to date, upper management strongly believes that bodies of water are an essential element for a pontoon market to develop. Therefore, by analyzing data on each Latin American country's ecosystem, your firm should invest in the country with abundant bodies of water. On the basis of management's single criterion, use the *EarthTrends* resource published by the World Resources Institute to suggest a South American country that best satisfies top management's ambition. What are other factors that may encourage the expansion of a private boat market?

United Steelworkers and the Sierra Club: A Case in Point

The largest manufacturing union in the United States, the United Steelworkers (USW), and the largest environmental action group in the nation, the Sierra Club, have joined forces in a collaboration called the "Blue/Green Alliance." This is an unexpected partnership that crosses geography and economic class. The environmentalists have opposed drilling for oil in the Alaskan Arctic National Wildlife Refuge, which the unions supported. The unions have often opposed environmentalism because their belief was that it cost jobs.

Now these two large groups (USW with 850,000 members and Sierra Club with 750,000) have joined forces to push for stronger environmental and worker protections in trade agreements, for ratification of the Kyoto Protocol to limit greenhouse gasses, and for higher fuel efficiency standards. "Good Jobs, a Clean Environment, and a Safer World" is their banner.

David Foster, the executive director of the alliance and the Steelworkers' regional director for the Northwest, explained: "The companies that embrace the soundest environmental principles, that move to alternative and renewable forms of energy, those will be the companies that survive. We're seeing a lot of that played out in the auto industry today."[a]

W. Leo Gerard, international president of USW, agrees: "Good jobs and a clean environment are important to American workers—we cannot have one without the other. . . . . In fact, secure 21st century jobs are those that will help solve the problem of global warming with energy efficiency and renewable energy."[b]

The executive director of the Sierra Club suggests that we are at a point globally where we can use resources for sustainability or "to create an ever more dangerous polarization of wealth and poverty."

[a]Steven Greenhouse, "Steelworkers and Sierra Club Unite," *New York Times,* June 8, 2006, www.nyt.com (accessed June 10, 2006).

[b]"Sierra Club, United Steelworkers Announce Blue/Green Alliance," June 7, 2006, www.uswa.org/uswa/program/content/3035.php (accessed June 12, 2006).

8

Economic and Socioeconomic Forces

There are well over one billion people in seventeen developing nations and three transition nations with enough income to rank as thoroughly middle class. They enjoy a collective spending power, measured in local purchasing capacity, of $6.3 trillion per year. They could well increase their numbers by half as soon as 2010, and their spending power by still more. This is the biggest consumption boom ever known in such a short time.

—*Norman Myers, author of* The New Consumers: The Influence of Affluence on the Environment

Of Zippies and the China-India Development Race

Newspapers in India refer to young people with good jobs as "zippies"—walking with confidence (zip in their step) and with plenty of money in their pockets. And there are plenty of these relative youngsters—by 2006, India's 20- to 34-year-old population was over 281 million. They are the young consumerist edge of a population of 1.11 billion and the fourth-largest economy in the world (based on purchasing power parity). The country's middle-income population in 2006 was estimated at nearly 600 million people.

But is India or China likely to "hit it rich" first? The current assumption is that China will be rich faster. China has a larger population as well as a larger economy. China has a higher savings rate. India attracted only 7 percent as much as the more than $600 billion in foreign direct investment that poured into China from 1990 to 2006. China's manufacturing productivity is higher: One source says that a Chinese worker makes 35 shirts in the time it takes an Indian to make 20.

China also has more high-net-worth individuals, with approximately 250,000 millionaires versus only 83,000 in India as of 2005. China is ranked third in the world in sales of luxury goods, accounting for more than 5 percent of the total world luxury market.

Looking further down the road, however, India has advantages for the long run. Not only do more Indians speak English—one estimate is that 150 million to 200 million Indians are completely fluent in English, and perhaps 20 million speak it as their primary language—but many are watching "Friends" reruns at employer expense to become accentless. And there may be more Indians in college, although the numbers are disputed. India's strength so far has been in services; China is the manufacturing powerhouse.

In fact, many observers feel that both India and China will have larger economies than that of the United States by mid-century. ∎

Source: U.S. Census Bureau, *International Data Base*, www.census.gov/ipc/www/idbpyr.html (October 8, 2006); "What's behind the Overseas Forays of U.S. Online Giants?" Knowledge@Wharton, July 14–27, 2004, knowledge.wharton.upenn.edu/article/1013.cfm; Om Malik, "The New Land of Opportunity," *Business 2.0,* July 2004, pp. 74–79; Jeffrey D. Sachs, "Welcome to the Asian Century," *Fortune,* January 2004, pp. 53–54; Anand Krishnamoorthy, "India Eases into the Lap of Luxury," *International Herald Tribune,* July 28, 2004, p. B4; S Rajagopalan, "Millionaires in India Grew by 19.3% in 2005: Survey," *Hindustan Times,* June 21, 2006, www.hindustantimes.com/news/181_1725069,00020008.htm (October 8, 2006); and "Millionaire Boom Favors Banks," *The Standard,* September 20, 2006, www.thestandard.com.hk/news_detail.asp?pp_cat=22&art_id=27647&sid=9992379&con_type=1 (October 8, 2006).

CONCEPT PREVIEWS

After reading this chapter, you should be able to:

state the purpose of economic analyses

identify different categories based on levels of national economic development and the common characteristics of developing nations

recognize the economic and socioeconomic dimensions of the economy and different indicators used to assess them

discuss the importance of a nation's consumption patterns and the significance of purchasing power parity

discuss the new definition of economic development, which includes more than economic growth

explain the degree to which labor costs can vary from country to country

discuss the significance for businesspeople of the large foreign debts of some nations

Gli Affari Internazionali

ionales

nales Geschäft Παγοσμιο Business

Negócios Internacionais   Los Negócios Internacionais

ternacionales   Affaires Internationales   国際商務 Παγοσμιο Business

227

Economic forces are among the most significant uncontrollable forces for managers. To keep abreast of the latest developments and also to plan for the future, firms for many years have been assessing and forecasting economic conditions at the national and international levels.

To do so, analysts use data published by governments and international organizations such as the World Bank and the International Monetary Fund (IMF). The data published by these organizations may not be as timely or as accurate as business analysts would like, but there is a large amount available.

Analysts do not work solely with government-published data. Private economic consultants—such as Data Resources, Inc., Chase Econometric Associates, Business International, the Economist Intelligence Unit, and Wharton Economic Forecasting Associates—provide economic forecasts (some do industry forecasts as well) to which many multinationals subscribe. Other sources are various industry associations, which generally provide industry-specific forecasts to their members.

In addition, economists and marketers use certain economic indicators that predict trends in their industry. We discuss the use of market indicators further in Chapter 15, "Assessing and Analyzing Markets."

The purpose of economic analyses is first to appraise the overall outlook of the economy and then to assess the impact of economic changes on the firm. An examination of Figure 8.1 will illustrate how a change in just one factor in the economy can affect all the major functions of the company.

A forecast of an increase in employment in a particular market would cause most marketing managers to revise their sales forecasts upward, which in turn would require that production managers augment production. This might be accomplished by adding an additional work shift, but if the plant is already operating 24 hours a day, new machinery will be needed. Either situation may require more workers and raw materials, which will result in an extra workload for the personnel and purchasing managers. Should both the raw materials and labor markets be tight, the firm will probably have to pay higher-than-normal prices and wage rates.

The financial manager may then have to negotiate with the banks for a loan to enable the firm to handle the greater cash outflow until additional revenue is received from increased sales. Note that this cascade of effects occurs because of a change in only one factor. Actually, of course, many economic factors are involved, and their relationships are complex. The object of an economic analysis is to isolate and assess the impact of those factors believed to affect the firm's operations.

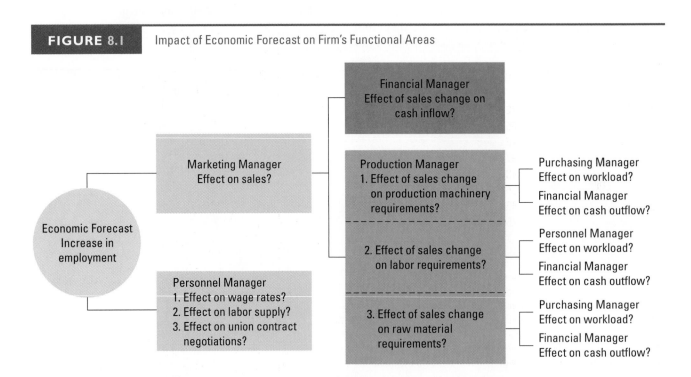

FIGURE 8.1   Impact of Economic Forecast on Firm's Functional Areas

International Economic Analyses

When a firm enters overseas markets, economic analyses become more complex because now managers must operate in two new environments: foreign and international. In the foreign environment, there are many economies instead of one, and they are highly divergent.

Because of these differences, policies designed for economic conditions in one market may be unsuitable for conditions in another market. For example, headquarters may require that its subsidiaries maintain the lowest inventories possible, and the chief financial officer may decree that they make only foreign currency–denominated loans because of more favorable interest rates. For nations whose annual inflation rates are low (0 to 15 percent), these policies usually work well. But what about countries such as Angola, with a 1995 inflation rate of 2,672 percent, and Zimbabwe, with an estimated 1,216 percent in 2006?

The least desirable scenario is for the subsidiaries in these countries to have cash or foreign currency–denominated loans, and so the policy for markets with high inflation rates will be just the reverse of what it is for countries with low inflation rates (see Table 8.1). Besides monitoring the foreign environments, analysts must stay informed of the actions taken by components of the international environment, such as regional groupings [European Union (EU), Central American Free Trade Agreement (CAFTA)] and international organizations [United Nations (UN), International Monetary Fund (IMF), World Trade Organization (WTO)]. American firms are very attentive to the EU's progress in reaching its goals and to the impact this will have on EU-U.S. trade relations. They are also following closely the UN's progress in developing world pollution standards, health standards, and so forth. Any of these actions can seriously affect firms.[1]

International economic analyses should provide economic data on both actual and prospective markets. As part of the competitive forces assessment, many companies monitor the economic conditions of nations in which their major competitors are located, because changing conditions may strengthen or weaken their competitors' ability to compete in world markets. Because of the importance of economic information to the control and planning functions at headquarters, the collection of data and the preparation of reports are usually the responsibility of the home office. However, foreign subsidiaries and field representatives are expected to contribute heavily to studies concerning their markets. Data from areas where the firm has no local representation can usually be somewhat less detailed and are generally available from national and international agencies.[2] The reports from central or international

TABLE 8.1	Annual Rates of Inflation for Selected Countries			
Country	1995	2001	2003	2006[e]
Angola	2,672%	325%[a]	106%[b]	13%
Turkmenistan	1,005	35	11[c]	9
Ukraine	376	15	8[c]	9
Russia	197	14	12[c]	10
Georgia	163	8	5[c]	10
Brazil	66	5	9[c]	5
Uruguay	42	5	10[c]	6
Zimbabwe	26	100	700[d]	1,216
Argentina	3	1	4[c]	4

[a] 2000 estimate, from www.cia.gov/cia/publications/factbook/index.html.

[b] 2002 estimate, from www.cia.gov/cia/publications/factbook/geos/ao.html#Econ.

[c] 2003 estimate, from www.odci.gov/cia/publications/factbook/rankorder/2092rank.html.

[d] 2004 estimate, from www.odci.gov/cia/publications/factbook/geos/zi.html#Econ (July 20, 2004).

[e] 2006 estimate, from International Monetary Fund, *World Economic Outlook 2006,* table 11, www.imf.org/external/pubs/ft/weo/2006/02/index.htm (October 7, 2006).

Source: www.imf.org/external/pubs/ft/weo/2000/02/index.htm (October 7, 2006).

banks are especially good sources for economic information on single countries. Other possible sources are the chambers of commerce located in most of the world's capitals, the commercial officers in embassies, the United Nations, the World Bank, the International Monetary Fund, and the Organization for Economic Cooperation and Development.[3]

Levels of Economic Development

When managers move from domestic to international business, they encounter markets with far greater differences in levels of economic development than those in which they have been working. It is important to understand this because a nation's level of economic development affects all aspects of business, including marketing, production, and finance. Although nations vary greatly with respect to economic development levels, we commonly group them into categories based on their level of economic development.

CATEGORIES BASED ON LEVELS OF ECONOMIC DEVELOPMENT

developed
A classification for all industrialized nations, which are the most technically developed

Developed is the name given to the industrialized, or postindustrial, service-based nations that have achieved high income per capita. Countries identified as being economically developed include the Western European nations, Japan, Australia, New Zealand, Canada, Israel, South Korea, and the United States. The term **developing** is a classification for the world's lower-income nations, which are less technically developed. Characteristics of developing countries are included in the nearby Worldview box, "Characteristics of Developing

Nations." At one time, **newly industrializing countries (NICs)** was a category that included only the four Asian tigers (Taiwan, Hong Kong, Singapore, and South Korea). These countries (1) had what the World Bank considers to be fast-growing, middle-income or higher economies, (2) possessed a heavy concentration of foreign investment, and (3) exported large quantities of manufactured goods, including high-tech products. Subsequently, other nations have achieved sufficient progress in their industrialization process to also be classified as NICs by various organizations. Depending on the criteria employed, more recent listings of NICS include some or all of the following countries: Brazil, Mexico, Argentina, Malaysia, Thailand, Chile, Venezuela, Hungary, South Africa, Indonesia, Pakistan, and China.

Because the economies of the four tigers have grown faster than those of other NICs and are approximating the size of developed nations' economies, the IMF and other organizations have begun to use the term **newly industrialized economies (NIEs)** to refer to the tigers.

You will also find that various different classification systems are employed by international agencies such as the United Nations, International Monetary Fund, and World Bank for reporting statistics.* For example, the IMF combines the NIEs with the industrialized nations to form a category termed *advanced economies.*

The rest of the noncommunist nations are in the category *developing countries,* which has a subcategory, *emerging market economies,* that includes Chile, Malaysia, China, Thailand, and Indonesia. The third category, called *transition countries,* includes the former communist countries. The UN uses simply *developed* and *developing economies* and refers to the former communist nations as *Eastern Europe* and the *former USSR.* When speaking of developed and developing nations as a bloc, UN economists frequently use the terms *North* and *South,* respectively.

The World Bank, by contrast, uses a classification based on 2004 gross national income per capita:

1. Low income ($745 or less).

2. Lower middle income ($746–$2,975).

3. Upper middle income ($2,976–$9,205).

4. High income ($9,206 or more).

The World Bank formerly employed a classification system based on gross national product (GNP) per capita, but in 2002 it changed to **gross national income (GNI)** per capita, which follows the current statistical practice of most countries. GNI measures the income generated by a nation's residents from international and domestic activity and is preferred by international organizations to gross domestic product (GDP), which measures income generated from domestic activity by residents of the country as well as nonresidents. Every economy is classified as low income, lower middle income, upper middle income, and high income, classes which are based on the World Bank's operational lending categories. The Bank also employs the term *developing countries* to refer to low- and middle-income countries.[4]

developing
A classification for the world's lower-income nations, which are less technically developed

newly industrializing countries (NICs)
The four Asian tigers and the middle-income economies such as Brazil, Mexico, Malaysia, Chile, and Thailand

newly industrialized economies (NIEs)
The fast-growing upper-middle-income and high-income economies of South Korea, Taiwan, Hong Kong, and Singapore

gross national income (GNI)
The total value of all income generated by a nation's residents from international and domestic activity

Dimensions of the Economy and Their Relevance for International Business

To estimate market potentials as well as to provide input to the other functional areas of the firm, managers require data on the sizes and the rates of change of a number of economic and socioeconomic factors. In order to be a potential market, an area must have sufficient people with the means to buy a firm's products. Socioeconomic data provide information on the number of people, and the economic dimensions tell us if they have purchasing power.

ECONOMIC DIMENSIONS

Among the more important economic indicators are gross domestic product, gross national income, distribution of income, private consumption expenditures, personal ownership of goods, private investment, unit labor costs, exchange rates, inflation rates, and interest rates.

*These agencies are discussed in Chapters 4 and 5.

WORLD view

Characteristics of Developing Nations

Although there is great diversity among the many developing nations, most share the following common characteristics:

1. GNI/capita of less than $9,206 (World Bank criterion).

2. Unequal distribution of income, with a very small middle class.

3. *Technological dualism*—a mix of firms employing the latest technology and companies using very primitive methods.

4. *Regional dualism*—high productivity and incomes in some regions and little economic development in others.

5. A majority of the population earning its living in a relatively unproductive agricultural sector.

6. Disguised unemployment or underemployment—two people doing a job that one person could do.

7. High population growth (2.5 to 4 percent annually).

8. High rate of illiteracy and insufficient educational facilities.

9. Widespread malnutrition and a wide range of health problems.

10. Political instability.

11. High dependence on a few products for export, generally agricultural products or minerals.

12. Inhospitable topography, such as deserts, mountains, and tropical forests.

13. Low savings rates and inadequate banking facilities.

You can see from these characteristics that a tremendous gap exists between the levels of living of the inhabitants of developing nations and those of developed nations. Although economists have studied and theorized about the various aspects of economic development for over two centuries, their preoccupation with the poorer nations of the world really began only after World War II. Among the developing nations, the United Nations lists the following as the 50 least developed countries in the world:

Afghanistan	Madagascar
Angola	Malawi
Bangladesh	Maldives
Benin	Mali
Bhutan	Mauritania
Burkina Faso	Mozambique
Burundi	Myanmar
Cambodia	Nepal
Cape Verde	Niger
Central African Republic	Rwanda
Chad	Samoa
Comoros	São Tomé and Principe
Democratic Republic of the Congo	Senegal
Djibouti	Sierra Leone
Equatorial Guinea	Solomon Islands
Eritrea	Somalia
Ethiopia	Sudan
Gambia	Timor-Lesté
Guinea	Togo
Guinea-Bissau	Tuvalu
Haiti	Uganda
Kiribati	United Republic of Tanzania
Lao People's Democratic Republic	Vanuatu
Lesotho	Yemen
Liberia	Zambia

Source: "Country Classification," World Bank, http://web.worldbank.org/WBSITE/EXTERNAL/DATASTATISTICS/0,contentMDK:20420458~menuPK:64133156~pagePK:64133150~piPK:64133175~theSitePK:239419,00.html (October 6, 2006); "List of Least Developed Countries," United Nations Office of the High Representative for the Least Developed Countries, Landlocked Developing Countries and Small Island Developing States, www.un.org/special-rep/ohrlls/ldc/list.htm (October 7, 2006); "Glossary," United Nations, www.un.org/cyberschoolbus/infonation3/menu/advanced.asp (October 7, 2006); and "The World's Economies," www.infoplease.com/cig/economics/world-economies.html (October 7, 2006).

Gross National Income   As mentioned earlier in this chapter, GNI is a measure of the income generated by a nation's residents from international and domestic activity. Most international organizations prefer GNI to GDP as a measure of economic size, since GDP measures income generated from domestic activity by residents of the country as well as nonresidents. GNIs range from $13.0 trillion for the United States to $0.2 billion for Guinea-Bissau.[5] What is the relevance of GNI for the international businessperson? Is India, with a 2005 GNI of $793 billion, a more attractive market than Denmark, whose $257 billion GNI is less than one-third the size? To compare the purchasing power of nations, managers need to know how many people GNI is divided among.

GNI/Capita   Employing GNI per capita from the tables of the World Bank to compare purchasing power reveals that Denmark is far richer than India: GNI/capita is $47,390 in Denmark versus $720 in India. Although India's economic pie is more than three times as big as Denmark's, there are almost 220 times as many people to eat it.

What can we learn from GNI/capita? We can generally assume that the higher its value, the more advanced the economy. Generally, however, the rate of growth is more important to marketers because a high growth rate indicates a fast-growing market—for which they are always searching. Frequently, given the choice between investing in a nation with a higher GNI/capita but a low growth rate and a nation in which the conditions are reversed, management will choose the latter.

Although GNI per capita is widely used to compare countries with respect to the well-being of their citizens and to assess market or investment potential, managers must use it with caution. For example, to arrive at GNI, government economists must impute monetary values to various goods and services not sold in the marketplace, such as food grown for personal consumption. Moreover, many goods and services are bartered in both low-income nations (because people have little cash) and high-income countries (because people wish to reduce reported income and thus pay less income tax). Transactions of this type are said to be part of the *underground economy*.

Underground Economy Much has been written about the part of the national income that is not measured by official statistics because it is either underreported or unreported. Included in this **underground economy** (also referred to as *black, parallel, informal, submerged, or shadow economy)* are undeclared legal production, production of illegal goods and services, and concealed income in kind (barter). As a general rule, the higher the level of taxation and the more oppressive the government red tape, the bigger the underground economy will be. Figure 8.2 shows estimates of some underground economies. The underground economy in the United States increased from 4 percent of GDP in 1970 to nearly 9 percent in 2003. On average for the 1999–2000 time period, it is estimated that the underground economy accounted for 18 percent of GDP in OECD countries, 38 percent of GDP in transition economies, and 41 percent of GDP in developing countries.[6] During the 1999–2000 time period, the underground economy in several nations exceeded 50 percent of GDP, including over 67 percent in Bolivia and Georgia. Estimates of the underground economy vary widely because of the different methodologies used to compile them; also, people who have undeclared income are not likely to admit it and be liable to prosecution for tax evasion. In addition to reducing the total taxes paid to government, the underground economy can result in distortions of economic data, which managers must take into account when using these data for business decisions.

underground economy

The part of a nation's income that, because of unreporting or underreporting, is not measured by official statistics

---

FIGURE 8.2   Underground Economies in Selected Nations (percentage of GNP, 2002–2003)

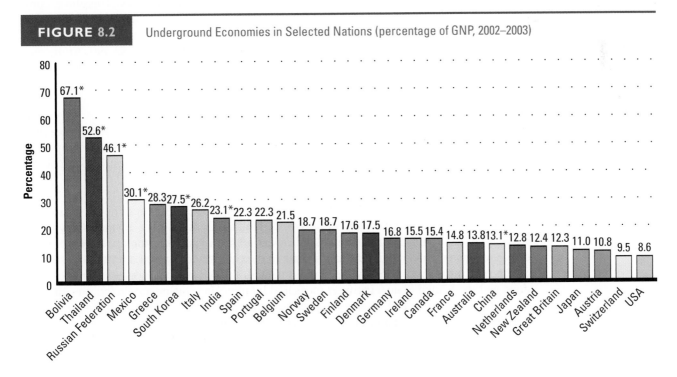

* Refers to Figures for 2002.

Source: Friedrich Schneider and Robert Klinglmair, "Shadow Economies around the World: What Do We Know?" March 2004, http://papers.ssrn.com/so13/papers.cfm? abstract_id=518526 (October 8, 2006).

Currency Conversion   Another problem with GNI estimates is that to compare them, the GNIs in local currency must be converted to a common currency—conventionally the dollar—by using an exchange rate. If the relative values of the two currencies accurately reflected consumer purchasing power, this conversion would be acceptable. However, the World Bank recognizes that "the use of official exchange rates to convert national currency figures to U.S. dollars does not reflect domestic purchasing powers of currencies."[7]

purchasing power parity (PPP)

The number of units of a currency required to buy the same amounts of goods and services in the domestic market that one dollar would buy in the United States

To overcome this deficiency, the UN International Comparison Program (ICP) has developed a method of comparing GNIs that is based on **purchasing power parity (PPP)** rather than on the international demand for currency (exchange rates). Here is how purchasing power parity rates are calculated.

Suppose Thailand reports to the World Bank that its GNI/capita for last year is 93,624 baht/capita. The Bank must translate this value to U.S. dollars. If the current exchange rate is 37.6 baht = $1, then using this rate would convert 93,624 baht to $2,490 (93,624 /37.6). How well does this measure Thailand's welfare? What can a Thai citizen consume with the 93,624 baht compared with what an American can consume with the $41,440 per capita income of the United States? Suppose that the following table reflects local prices in both countries of the same basket of goods:

Goods	Thailand (baht)	U.S. ($)
Soap (bar)	40	0.50
Rice (lb.)	25	0.35
Shoes (pair)	495	60.00
Dress	580	450.00
Socks (pair)	95	2.00
Total	1,235	$107.85

In Thailand 1,235 baht buys what $107.85 buys in the United States. Therefore, comparing the purchasing power of the currencies, 1,235 baht/$107.85 = 11.45 baht per $1. Using the exchange rate of 11.45 baht per dollar, Thailand's GNI/capita is now 93,624/11.45 = $8,177. At the official exchange rate of 37.6 baht/$1, Thailand's GNI is $2,490. At the purchasing power parity rate of 11.45 baht/$1, Thailand's GNI is $8,177.

Table 8.2 illustrates that comparisons based on purchasing power parity result in GNI/capita values that are considerably higher than those regularly given for developing nations and lower for many developed nations; that is, in considering purchasing power, the differences between the GNIs of developing and developed nations are smaller than those generally published. You will note how the smaller buying power of the Japanese yen compared to that of the U.S. dollar affects the GNI/capita based on purchasing power parity.

The Atlas Conversion Factor   Dissatisfaction with both the PPP and the conversion by using official exchange rates caused the World Bank to adopt the Atlas methodology to derive per capita GNI estimates. The *Atlas conversion factor* is the arithmetic average of the current exchange rate and the exchange rates in the two previous years adjusted by the ratio of domestic inflation to the combined inflation rates of the euro zone, Japan, the United Kingdom, and the United States. Incomes measured by the Atlas conversion factor are generally more stable over time and changes in income rankings are more likely to be due to relative economic performance than fluctuations in the exchange rate.

Although differences in GNI/capita do tell us something about the relative wealth of a nation's inhabitants, the information is somewhat misleading because wealth is usually not evenly spread. This first crude estimate of purchasing power must be refined by incorporating data on how national income is actually distributed.

Country	GNI/Capita in US$ Converted at World Bank–Adjusted Exchange Rates	Adjusted Exchange Rates Ranking	GNI/Capita in US$ Based on Purchasing Power Parity	Purchasing Power Parity Ranking
United States	$41,440	5	$39,820	3
Japan	37,050	9	29,810	18
Sweden	35,840	10	29,880	17
Canada	28,310	21	30,760	16
Mexico	6,790	70	9,640	80
Argentina	3,580	93	12,530	66
Russian Federation	3,400	94	9,680	79
Thailand	2,490	104	7,930	88
China	1,500	129	5,890	108
India	620	159	3,120	144
Nigeria	430	175	970	190

Source: *World Development Indicators 2006* (Washington, DC: World Bank, 2006), table 1.6.

Income Distribution   Data on **income distribution** are gathered by the World Bank from a number of sources and published yearly in the *World Development Indicators* (see Table 8.3). Despite the difficulties associated with income distribution studies, such as inconsistent measuring practices and wide variations in the representativeness of samples, the data provide useful insights for business.

1. They confirm the belief that, generally, income is more evenly distributed in the richer nations, although there are important variations among both developed and developing nations.

2. Comparisons over time demonstrate that income redistribution proceeds very slowly, so that older data are still useful.

3. The same comparisons indicate that income inequality increases in the early stages of development, with a reversal of this tendency in the later stages. For example, even as China's economy skyrockets, the number of truly destitute grew by 800,000 to nearly 85 million in 2004.[8] The fact that the middle quintiles in some nations are growing at the expense of the top and bottom 20 percent signifies an increase in middle-income families, which are especially significant to marketers.

     Depending on the type of product and the total population, either situation (relatively even or uneven income distribution) may represent market opportunities. For example, although Costa Rica's GNI was $42 billion in PPP terms in 2005, the fact that just 20 percent of the population receives nearly 55 percent of that income indicates that a sizable group of people are potential customers for low-volume, high-priced luxury products. On the other hand, the market is rather small (4 million population) for low-priced goods requiring a high sales volume. This simple calculation based on GNI, total population, and income distribution may be all that is required to indicate that a particular country is not a good market; however, if the results look promising, the analyst will proceed to gather data on private consumption.

Private Consumption   One area of interest to marketers is the manner in which consumers allocate their disposable income (after-tax personal income) between purchases of essential and nonessential goods. Manufacturers of household durables, for instance, will want to know the amounts spent in that category, whereas producers of nonessentials will be interested in the

income distribution
A measure of how a nation's income is apportioned among its people, commonly reported as the percentage of income received by population quintiles

TABLE 8.3	Percentage Share of Income or Consumption					
Country	Lowest 20 Percent	20–40 Percent	40–60 Percent	60–80 Percent	Highest 20 Percent	Highest 10 Percent
Argentina (2003)	3.2%	7.0%	12.1%	20.7%	56.8%	39.6%
Brazil (2003)	2.6	6.2	10.7	18.4	62.1	45.8
Bulgaria (2003)	8.7	13.7	17.2	22.1	38.3	23.9
Canada (2000)	7.2	12.7	17.2	23.0	39.9	24.8
Chile (2000)	3.3	6.6	10.5	17.4	62.2	47.0
China (2001)	4.7	9.0	14.2	22.1	50.0	33.1
Colombia (2003)	2.5	6.2	10.6	18.0	62.7	46.9
Costa Rica (2001)	3.9	8.1	12.8	20.4	54.8	38.4
Czech Rep. (96)	10.3	14.5	17.7	21.7	35.9	22.4
El Salvador (2002)	2.7	7.5	12.8	21.2	55.9	38.8
Finland (2000)	9.6	14.1	17.5	22.1	36.7	22.6
Germany (2000)	8.5	13.7	17.8	23.1	36.9	22.1
Ghana (99)	5.6	10.1	14.9	22.9	46.6	30.0
Hungary (2002)	9.5	13.9	17.6	22.4	36.5	22.2
India (2000)	8.9	12.3	16.0	21.2	43.3	28.5
Indonesia (2002)	8.4	11.9	15.4	21.0	43.3	28.5
Israel (2001)	5.7	10.5	15.9	23.0	44.9	28.8
Italy (2000)	6.5	12.0	16.8	22.8	42.0	26.8
Jamaica (2000)	6.7	10.7	15.0	21.7	46.0	30.3
Japan (1993)	10.6	14.2	17.6	22.0	35.7	21.7
Kazakhstan (2003)	7.4	11.9	16.4	22.8	41.5	25.9
Latvia (2003)	6.6	11.2	15.5	22.0	44.7	29.1
Malaysia (1997)	4.4	8.1	12.9	20.3	54.3	38.4
Mexico (2002)	4.3	8.3	12.6	19.7	55.1	39.4
Nepal (2003–2004)	6.0	9.0	12.4	18.0	54.6	40.6
Netherlands (1999)	7.6	13.2	17.2	23.3	38.7	22.9
Nigeria (2003)	5.0	9.6	14.5	21.7	49.2	33.2
Norway (2000)	9.6	14.0	17.2	22.0	37.2	23.4
Pakistan (2002)	9.3	13.0	16.3	21.1	40.3	26.3
Peru (2002)	3.2	7.1	11.8	19.3	58.7	43.2
Philippines (2000)	5.4	8.8	13.1	20.5	52.3	36.3
Poland (2002)	7.5	11.9	16.1	22.2	42.2	27.0
Russian Fed. (2002)	6.1	10.5	14.9	21.8	46.6	30.6
Senegal (1995)	6.4	10.3	14.5	20.6	48.2	33.5
South Africa (2000)	3.5	6.3	10.0	18.0	62.2	44.7
Sri Lanka (1999–2000)	8.3	12.5	16.0	21.0	42.2	27.8
Sweden (2000)	9.1	14.0	17.6	22.7	36.6	22.2
Thailand (2002)	6.3	9.9	14.0	20.8	49.0	33.4
United Kingdom (1999)	6.1	11.4	16.0	22.5	44.0	28.5
United States (2000)	5.4	10.7	15.7	22.4	45.8	29.9
Venezuela (2000)	4.7	9.4	14.5	22.1	49.3	32.8
Vietnam (2002)	7.5	11.2	14.8	21.1	45.4	29.9
Zambia (2002–2003)	6.1	10.2	14.2	20.7	48.8	33.7

Note: Numbers in parentheses indicate year of study.

Source: From *World Development Indicators 2006* by World Bank. Copyright © 2006 by World Bank. Reproduced with permission of World Bank via Copyright Clearance Center.

magnitude of **discretionary income** (disposable income less essential purchases), for this is the money available to be spent on their products. Fortunately, disposable incomes and the amounts spent on essential purchases are available from the *UN Statistical Yearbook,* and discretionary income may be obtained by subtracting the total of these items from disposable income. More detailed expenditure patterns can be found in the *World Development Indicators* published by the World Bank. Data from that publication are reproduced in Table 8.4, which includes data on private consumption expenditures for 10 high-income and 10 low-income economies, using PPP equivalents.

Because PPP-based consumer expenditures eliminate differences in relative prices, marketers use these data to analyze how the composition of consumption changes with the level of development. For example, the percentages of household expenditures spent on food and clothing by residents of developing nations are double the percentages consumers in industrialized nations spend. On the other hand, the percentages spent on (1) transport and communication, (2) consumer durables, (3) health care, and (4) other consumption (beverages, tobacco, and services, including meals eaten in restaurants or taken out) by households of developed nations are twice the percentages of those in developing nations. Note that the percentage differences within a consumption category do not vary with the consumption expenditures per capita. An example is clothing and footwear. Interestingly, in spite of the allure of French haute-couture, the percentage spent on clothing in France is less than half that spent by the residents of Hong Kong and only 78 percent of U.S. expenditures.

discretionary income
The amount of income left after paying taxes and making essential purchases

TABLE 8.4	Private Consumption Based on Purchasing Power Parity

				Percentage of Household Consumption					
Country	GNI/ Capita Based on Exchange Rates, 2005	GNI/ Capita Based on PPP, 2005	Household Consumption Expenditure % of GDP, 2005	Food	Clothing and Footwear	Education	Health Care	Transportation and Communication	Other Consumption
Austria	36,980	33,140	56	20	10	9	4	9	48
Canada	32,600	32,220	56	14	5	21	4	9	47
Belgium	35,700	32,640	54	17	6	1	3	7	66
Denmark	47,390	33,570	48	16	6	17	3	5	53
France	34,810	30,570	56	22	7	8	3	12	48
Germany	43,580	29,210	59	14	6	10	2	7	61
Hong Kong China	27,670	34,670	59	10	17	8	2	6	57
Japan	38,980	31,410	57	12	7	22	2	13	44
Kenya	530	1,170	70	31	9	8	2	3	47
Madagascar	290	880	84	61	8	2	2	5	22
Malawi	160	650	95	50	13	6	2	9	20
Mali	380	1,000	79	53	15	5	4	2	21
Nigeria	560	1,040	41	51	5	8	2	2	22
Sierra Leone	220	780	90	47	9	13	3	8	20
Switzerland	54,930	37,080	61	19	6	18	3	8	46
Tajikistan	330	1,260	95	48	7	14	0	5	26
Tanzania	340	730	77	67	6	12	4	6	5
United States	43,740	41,950	71	13	9	6	4	8	5
Yemen	600	920	80	25	5	5	3	5	57
Zambia	490	950	70	52	10	11	2	3	22

Source: *World Development Indicators 2004,* www.worldbank.org/data/wdi2004/tables/table1-1.pdf (July 2, 2004); *World Development Report 2003,* pp. 238–39 and pp. 234–35; and *World Development Report 2007,* pp. 288–89.

Telephones: An Economic Indicator?

Cellular phone vendor Wilfred Perera (right) shows handsets to a customer in Colombo, Sri Lanka, in February 2004. Sri Lanka was the first South Asian nation to introduce cellular phones in the late 1980s and there are now more than a million mobile phone users in a country of 18.6 million people.

Sena Vidanagama/AFP/Getty Images

What is the best gauge for measuring a country's level of development? Is it (1) per capita income, (2) state of the construction industry, (3) density of pollution, or (4) number of telephones? If you selected number 4, you are right, according to the International Telecommunications Union (ITU), a specialized agency of the United Nations. The ITU published an article in which the author claimed that the total number of telephone lines installed in a country is often a better indicator of a nation's level of development than is even per capita income.

Generally, the wealthier a country is, the more telephone lines it has. In 2005, the richest countries already had more than one phone line for every two people. The increase in mobile phone use has also been extremely rapid. China's mobile phone subscribers went from 1.6 million to 300 million between 1995 and 2005, making that country the largest mobile phone market in the world. In Finland the density of mobile phones approaches twice that of fixed phones (it has reached a multiple of three or four in other nations, such as Kuwait and Saudi Arabia). In fact, mobile phone use has increased across countries at all income levels. In Cambodia and Sri Lanka, for example, the number of cell phones per 1,000 people was already greater than that for mainlines by the late 1990s. For poor countries, it is faster and less expensive to add cell phone networks than to put in a mainline infrastructure.

ITU statistics show that about 34 percent of the world's inhabitants have a cell phone subscription and almost 20 percent have a fixed line. Allowing for duplication, that is considerable penetration. Admittedly, in countries such as Chad, there are only about 15 phones per 1,000 persons. However, that represents a tenfold increase for Chad in the last few years. It is evident that developing nations therefore are beginning to get a grip on their communications problem.

Source: *World Development Indicators 2000, 2001, 2006,* www.china-embassy.org/eng/xw/t140234.htm (August 6, 2004); ITU sources from Table 8.5.

International business managers know better than to underestimate the importance of small percentage differences among nations. They are aware that each percentage point is worth a large sum of money. To appreciate its value, try multiplying the total per capita consumption expenditure by 1 percent of the population. French designers might want to note that if American consumers had spent 1 percent more on clothing, for example, this would have amounted to $43,740 × 0.01 × 296 million inhabitants, or $129.5 billion in additional sales for the clothing industry.

Other indicators that add to our knowledge of personal consumption are those concerned with (1) the ownership of goods and (2) the consumption of key materials. For example, commercial energy use per capita is related to the size of the modern sectors—*urban areas, industry,* and *motorized transport.* The World Bank has found that the populations living in high-income economies use nearly seven times as much commercial energy per capita as do people in developing economies, and the quantity and mix of energy constitute a rough indicator of a country's level of development. As Table 8.5 illustrates, the more industrialized nations have considerably higher values for these indicators than do the developing nations. See the nearby Worldview box for an Asian Development Bank expert's opinion about the most significant indicator.

unit labor costs

Total direct labor costs divided by units produced

Unit Labor Costs   One factor that contributes to a favorable investment opportunity is the ability to obtain **unit labor costs** (total direct labor costs/units produced) lower than those currently available to the firm. Foreign trends in these costs are closely monitored because each country experiences a different rate of increase.

Countries with slower-rising unit labor costs attract management's attention for two reasons. First, they are investment prospects for companies striving to lower production costs, as discussed in Chapter 2; second, they may become sources of new competition in world markets if other firms in the same industry are already located there.

Changes in wage rates may also cause a multinational firm that obtains products or components from a number of subsidiaries to change its sources of supply.

Region/Country	Telephone Main Lines per 100 Inhabitants, 2005	Mobile Subscribers per 100 Inhabitants, 2005	Electricity Consumption/ Capita (1,000 kWh), 2003	Internet Users per 100 Inhabitants 2005
Europe				
Switzerland	69	92	8,191	50
Germany	67	96	6,896	45
France	59	79	—	43
Sweden	72	93	15,403	75
United Kingdom	56	102	6,209	63
Italy	43	124	5,620	48
Middle East				
Israel	43	112	6,599	47
Kuwait	19	89	14,808	26
Saudi Arabia	15	54	6,259	7
Egypt	14	18	1,127	7
Africa				
Mauritius	29	57	—	15
South Africa	10	72	4,399	11
Cameroon	1	14	178	1
Ghana	1	13	248	2
Ethiopia	1	1	28	0.2
Asia				
Japan	46	74	7,818	50
South Korea	49	79	7,018	68
China	27	30	1,379	8
India	5	8	435	5
Bangladesh	1	6	128	0.2
South America				
Uruguay	31	19	1,781	21
Chile	22	68	2,880	62
Brazil	23	46	1,883	12
Colombia	17	48	834	10
Bolivia	7	26	422	5
Eastern Europe				
Hungary	33	92	3,637	30
Czech Republic	31	115	6,070	50
Poland	31	76	3,329	26
Russia	28	84	5,480	15
Kazakhstan	17	33	3,510	3
North America and Caribbean				
United States	61	68	13,078	63
Canada	57	51	17,290	62
Trinidad and Tobago	25	61	4,721	12
Mexico	18	44	1,801	17
Haiti	2	5	31	6

Source: Electricity consumption—*World Development Indicators 2006,* table 5.9, http://devdata.worldbank.org/wdi2006/contents/Section5.htm (October 6, 2006); telephone mainlines, mobile phones, and Internet hosts—International Telecommunication Union, www.itu.int/ITU-D/icteye/Indicators/Indicators.aspx# (October 6, 2006).

Nike, which produces none of the shoes it sells in the United States, began using Japanese plants in 1964. When labor costs rose there in the mid-1970s, the company changed to factories in South Korea and Taiwan. Later, Nike added Thailand. But as labor costs rose in those countries, Nike began buying in over 50 Indonesian factories and in China. Alarmed because its $75 to $100 (retail) shoes were costing as much as $10 to produce and ship to the United States, Nike contracted for production in Vietnam and is also the largest seller of athletic shoes in China.[9]

What are the reasons for the relative changes in labor costs? Three factors are responsible: (1) compensation, (2) productivity, and (3) exchange rates. Hourly compensation tends to vary more widely than wages because of the differences in the size of fringe benefits. Unit labor costs will not rise in unison with compensation rates if gains in productivity outstrip increases in hourly compensation. In fact, if productivity increases fast enough, the unit costs of labor will decrease even though the firm is required to pay more to the workers.

Table 8.6 reveals why international firms keep a close watch on labor compensation rates around the world. For example, in 1975 Sweden had the highest hourly rate, with the United States and Germany tied for fifth place. Note that Japan's average hourly rate was less than half the American rate. However, by 1985, the U.S. rate was the world's highest, and American

TABLE 8.6	Labor Compensation Costs, 1975–2004*							
	Average Hourly Rate Including Fringe Benefits (US$ and local currencies)							
	2004		**1995**		**1985**		**1975**	
Country	**US$**	**Local**	**US$**	**Local**	**US$**	**Local**	**US$**	**Local**
Americas								
Canada	21.42	27.89	16.04	22.02	10.94	14.94	5.96	6.07
United States	23.17	23.17	17.19	17.19	13.01	13.01	6.36	6.36
Mexico	2.50	28.22	1.51	9.66	1.59	409.00	1.47	18.00
Asia and Oceania								
Hong Kong	5.51	42.90	4.82	37.30	1.73	13.46	0.76	3.73
Japan	21.90	2,370.00	23.66	2,223.00	6.34	1,512.00	3.00	889.00
Taiwan	5.97	199.1	5.82	154.26	1.50	59.60	0.40	15.17
Europe								
Austria	28.29	22.75	25.38	255.87	7.58	156.75	4.51	78.46
Belgium	29.98	24.11	26.88	792.10	8.97	532.39	6.41	235.10
Denmark	33.75	202.1	24.26	135.86	8.13	86.18	6.28	36.00
Finland	30.67	24.66	24.83	108.64	8.16	50.56	4.61	16.88
France	23.89	19.21	19.34	96.45	7.52	67.49	4.52	19.34
Germany[†]	34.05	26.15	31.85	45.61	9.60	28.23	6.35	15.59
Italy	20.48	16.46	16.52	26,911.00	7.63	14,563.00	4.67	3,048.00
Netherlands	30.76	24.73	24.18	38.79	8.75	29.04	6.58	16.59
Norway	34.64	233.5	24.38	154.46	10.37	89.11	6.77	35.29
Spain	17.10	13.75	12.70	1,582.00	4.66	792.00	2.53	145.00
Sweden	28.42	208.8	21.64	154.51	9.66	83.12	7.18	29.73
Switzerland	30.26	37.61	29.30	34.61	9.66	23.71	6.09	15.72
United Kingdom	24.71	13.49	13.73	8.70	6.27	4.84	3.37	1.52

*Dollar conversions are at average annual exchange rates.

[†]Former West Germany.

Source: Bureau of Labor Statistics, "International Comparisons of Hourly Compensation Costs for Production Workers in Manufacturing, Supplementary Tables," www.bls.gov/fls/hcompsupptabtoc.htm (October 6, 2004).

managers were searching for overseas production sites. Yet just 10 years later, the United States had fallen to 13th place in the hourly compensation cost ranking. Every European nation but the United Kingdom and Spain had higher costs. In 1995, American costs were still in 11th place, but there was one important change in the rankings: Japan's labor compensation rate, which was less than half of the U.S. rate in 1985, had jumped to 138 percent of the U.S. compensation rate. By that point many Japanese firms had moved significant parts of their production to other Asian countries with lower labor costs, such as Thailand, China, and Indonesia. (This movement abroad was also influenced by the retirement of many skilled machinists and other artisans in Japan, which made foreign labor more attractive.) By 2004, 11 European nations had higher labor costs than the United States, led by Norway's premium of 50 percent, while Japan's relative labor costs had declined to only 95 percent of those in the United States.

Other Economic Dimensions   We have mentioned only a few of the many economic indicators that analysts study, and you will learn about the importance to businesspeople of interest rates, balances of payments, and inflation rates in Chapter 11, "Financial Forces." The analyst will choose which economic measures to study depending on the industry and the purpose of the study.

The large international debts of a number of middle- and low-income nations are causing multiple problems not only for their governments but also for multinational firms. Just look at the situation of the countries with the highest debts that are listed in Table 8.7.

Is this a problem for international bankers only, or should it concern multinational managements as well? Is it significant to global and multidomestic firms with subsidiaries in these countries that high-indebtedness indicators such as debt to GDI and debt service to exports are a cause for concern? The World Bank claims that an empirical analysis of developing countries' experience shows that "debt service difficulties become increasingly likely when the ratio of the present value of debt to exports reaches 200–250 percent and the debt service ratio exceeds 20–25 percent."[10] If management agrees, then it will expect periodic reports on this situation from its analysts. Let's examine the ramifications of these large foreign debts for an international firm.

If a major part of the foreign exchange a nation earns cannot be used to import components used in local products, then either local industries must manufacture them or the companies that import them must stop production. Either alternative can cause the multinational

TABLE 8.7	Major International Debtors			
	Total External Debt ($ billion)			2004 Debt as Percentage of 1980 Debt
Country	2004	1990	1980	Percent
Brazil	$222	$120	$72	308%
Mexico	139	104	57	244
Argentina	169	62	27	626
China	249	55	5	4,980
Russia	197	6	—	3,283*
Indonesia	141	70	21	671
Turkey	162	49	19	853
India	123	84	21	586

* Comparison is to 1990 debt

Source: www.oecd.org/dac/debt/htm/data_index.htm, various country files; *World Bank Indicators 1999;* http://siteresources.worldbank.org/GDFINT2004/summary-tables/20179304/reg-external-debt.PDF (July 20, 2004); and *World Development Indicators 2006* (October 7, 2006).

vertically integrated
Descriptive term for a firm that produces inputs for its subsequent manufacturing processes

to lose sales if it has been selling the parts made in one of its home country plants to its subsidiary, a common occurrence because the home plant is usually more **vertically integrated** than its subsidiaries. A scarcity of foreign exchange can also make it difficult for the subsidiary to import raw materials and spare parts for its production equipment. If headquarters wants its affiliate to continue production, it may have to lend the foreign exchange and wait for repayment.

Campbell Soup, Revlon, and Gerber closed their operations in Brazil because of this problem. Other multinationals have resorted to barter or have begun to export their subsidiaries' products even though these actions have reduced exports or even local sales of their domestic plants.

Governments may impose price controls (which make it difficult for a subsidiary to earn a profit), cut government spending (which reduces company sales), and impose wage controls (which limit consumer purchasing power). The economic turmoil that follows can turn into a political crisis, as occurred in Argentina and Peru when rioting resulted after their presidents tried to impose austerity measures. During the Asian financial crisis, South Korea experienced nationwide strikes in response to laws passed to ease that country's economic problems.

Scarcity of foreign exchange can affect even firms that merely export to nations with high foreign debt because the governments will surely impose import restrictions. When Latin American debt increased rapidly from 1981 to 1983, that region's share of U.S. exports dropped by one-third. To protect these export markets, firms had to extend long-term credit. From this you can see that managements will expect to receive information on the status of the foreign debt in nations where it is high in addition to the other economic data we have been examining. This is especially important now that the same American banks that were involved in the developing-country debt crisis in the 1980s are once again lending huge sums to developing nations.

SOCIOECONOMIC DIMENSIONS

A complete definition of market potential must also include detailed information about the population's physical attributes as measured by the socioeconomic dimensions. We shall begin this section with an analysis of total population.

Total Population   Total population, the most general indicator of potential market size, is the first characteristic of the population that analysts examine. Population sizes vary immensely, from more than a billion inhabitants in China and India to 2,701 for Svalbard and the uninhabited Bassas da India. The fact that many developed nations have fewer than 10 million inhabitants makes it apparent that population size alone is a poor indicator of economic strength and market potential. Only for a few low-priced products, such as soft drinks, cigarettes, and soap, might population size alone provide a basis for estimating consumption.

For products not in this category, large populations and populations that are increasing rapidly may not signify an immediate enlargement of the market, but if incomes grow over time, eventually some part of the population will become customers. Insight into the speed at which this is occurring may be obtained by comparing population and economic growth rates. Where GNI increases faster than the population, there is probably an expanding market, whereas the converse situation not only indicates possible market contraction but may even point out a country as a potential area of political unrest. This possibility is strengthened if an analysis of the educational system discloses an accumulation of technical and university graduates. These groups expect to be employed as and receive the wages of professionals, and when enough new jobs are not being created to absorb them, the government can be in serious trouble. Various nations already face this difficulty; Egypt is an example.

human-needs approach
View that defines economic development as a reduction of poverty and unemployment as well as an increase in income

Age Distribution   Because few products are purchased by everyone, marketers must identify the segments of the population that are more apt to buy their goods. For some firms, age is a salient determinant of market size, but the distribution of age groups within populations varies widely. Generally, because of higher birth rates, developing countries have more youthful populations than do industrial countries.

WORLD view

New Approaches to Economic Development

Until the 1970s, economists generally considered *economic growth* to be synonymous with *economic development*. A nation was considered to be developing economically if its real output per capita as measured by GNI/capita was increasing over time. However, the realization that economic growth does not necessarily imply development—because the benefits of this growth so often have applied to only a few—has led to the widespread adoption of a new, more comprehensive definition of economic development.

The **human-needs approach** defines economic development as the reduction of poverty, unemployment, and inequality in the distribution of income. The definition of poverty also has been broadened. Instead of being defined in terms of income, as is common in developed countries, a reduction in poverty has come to mean less illiteracy, less malnutrition, less disease and early death, and a shift from agricultural to industrial production or service-based economic activity.

Because of the increased emphasis on human welfare and the lack of a clear link between income growth and human progress, the United Nations Development Program has devised a Human Development Index (HDI) based on three essential elements of human life: (1) a long and healthy life, (2) the ability to acquire knowledge, and (3) access to resources needed for a decent standard of living. These elements are measured by (1) life expectancy, (2) adult literacy, and (3) GDP/capita, adjusted for differences in purchasing power. In its latest report, as shown in the table below, the program ranked Norway as the most developed with respect to the HDI, followed by Iceland, Australia, Luxembourg, Canada, Sweden, Switzerland, Ireland, Belgium, and the United States. The 24 lowest-ranked countries are all located in Africa, a fact that further highlights the significant development challenges that confront that continent and its residents.

(continued)

HDI Rank	Country	Life Expectancy at Birth (years), 2003	Adult Literacy Rate (% ages 15 and above), 2003	GDP per Capita (PPP, US$), 2003
1	Norway	79.4	99%	$37,670
2	Iceland	80.7	99	31,243
3	Australia	80.3	99	29,632
4	Luxembourg	78.5	99	62,298
5	Canada	80.0	99	30,677
6	Sweden	80.2	99	26,750
7	Switzerland	80.5	99	30,552
8	Ireland	77.7	99	37,738
9	Belgium	78.9	99	28,335
10	United States	77.4	99	37,562
168	Mozambique	41.9	47	1,117
169	Burundi	43.6	59	648
170	Ethiopia	47.6	42	711
171	Central African Republic	39.3	49	1,089
172	Guinea-Bissau	44.7	40	711
173	Chad	43.6	26	1,210
174	Mali	47.9	19	994
175	Burkina Faso	47.5	13	1,174
176	Sierra Leone	40.8	30	548
177	Niger	44.4	14	835
High income		78.8	99	29,898
Middle income		70.3	90	6,104
Low income		58.4	61	2,168
High human development		78.0	99	25,665
Medium human development		67.2	79	4,474
Low human development		46.0	58	1,046
World		67.1	—	8,229

No accepted general theory of development

The inclusion of noneconomic variables has made it impossible to formulate a widely accepted general theory of development. Instead of pursuing a general theory, development economists are concentrating on specific problem areas, such as population growth, income distribution, unemployment, transfer of technology, the role of government in the process, and investment in human versus physical capital.

What is the relevance of a lack of consensus among specialists about development theory? If a particular theory has fallen into disfavor among the experts, can managers neglect it when dealing with government officials? That depends. Perhaps those officials still subscribe to it. In that case, managers should emphasize the parts of their proposals that are germane to the theory, which is generally not too difficult because nearly every proposal will provide not only investment in physical capital but also training of employees, employment, and the transfer of technology. There will even be some redistribution of income through the creation of a middle class composed of managers and highly skilled technicians. As an example, let's look at how managers might emphasize investment in human capital when making a proposal.

Investment in human capital

This development theory recognizes that more than just capital accumulation is needed for growth. There must also be investment in the education of people so that there will be managers to ensure that the capital is productive and skilled workers to operate and maintain the capital equipment. For developed countries, research suggests that investment in human capital has a return estimated at 4 to 12 percent per year of education. If basic labor has an income level of 100, then the return for 12 years of educational investments would yield an increased return ranging from 160 to 390 percent of that generated by basic labor.*

If managers know that this theory has strong acceptance in the country where they have an operation or are seeking permission to establish one, they should emphasize this aspect of their investment. A multinational or global firm that does not have training programs for workers is rare, and nearly all send local managers to the home office to update their skills.

Import substitution versus export promotion

Another strategy followed by some developing nations has been **import substitution.** Although developing nations have long considered the exporting of primary products (agricultural and raw materials) to be an important facet of their development strategy, many of these countries have not aggressively promoted the exporting of manufactured goods. Instead, they have concentrated on substituting these domestically manufactured products for imports as a way to lessen their dependence on developed countries.

Unfortunately, import substitution has not reduced their dependence on developed nations as much as it has changed the composition of imports from finished products to capital and semiprocessed inputs. Often, however, developing nations are unable to obtain these inputs because of a lack of foreign exchange, which can stop entire industries and throw thousands of people out of work, further increasing dependence on developed nations. This situation happened in several Asian nations as a result of the Asian economic crisis that began in 1997 and of subsequent events such as tightening of money supplies in conjunction with IMF assistance.

Another serious problem with the import substitution strategy stems from the protection to local industry that governments grant by levying high import duties on goods that also are made domestically. Under this umbrella, local manufacturers may not feel pressured to either lower their costs or improve their quality. Without such pressure, they rarely become competitive in world markets and thus cannot export. Furthermore, other domestic firms that must buy inputs from these protected industries cannot export either because their costs are excessive or their quality is inadequate.

Problems such as these have caused numerous governments to change from a strategy of import substitution to one of promoting exports of manufactured goods. Spurring them on to this decision has been the rapid export growth of the newly industrializing nations and the general opening of world markets to international trade and investment.

This change in strategy affects international firms in a variety of ways. First, local affiliate managers must be prepared for demands to export by government officials. They may even be given ultimatums, as some foreign manufacturers operating in China have reported: "If you need to import parts for your output, you must earn the foreign exchange to pay for them by exporting part of your production." Foreign companies seeking permission to set up a manufacturing facility are commonly asked by government administrators about plans for exporting. This is a new phenomenon to longtime managers accustomed to restricting an affiliate's sales to its internal market to save the export market for home country production. Second, managers can no longer count on having permanent protection from competing imports, as they once could. In some countries, they are likely to be told that after a certain date they will lose their protection and will be expected to compete internationally. Last, in a situation where two firms are competing for permission to establish a plant, the deciding factor may be that one offers its multinational channels of distribution to the affiliate's exports.

*If basic labor has an income level of 100, and if each year of education yields a return of 4 to 12 percent, then a worker with 12 years of education would produce returns from $100 \times (1.04)^{12} = 160$ to $100 \times (1.12)^{12} = 390$.

Source: *Human Development Report 2005* (New York: United Nations Development Program), pp. 219–22, http://hdr.undp.org/reports/global/2005 (October 6, 2006); Charles Kindleberger and Bruce Herrick, *Economic Development* (New York: McGraw-Hill, 1977), p. 1; George Psacharopoulos, "Returns to Investment in Education: A Global Update," *World Development* 22 (1994), p. 9; and Jean-Philippe Cotis, "Economic Growth and Productivity," www.oecd.org/dataoecd/49/34/37179645.pdf (October 6, 2006).

import substitution

The local production of goods to replace imports

The population of developing countries is over three-quarters of the world's total population. Figure 8.3 shows that of the 10 nations predicted to have the largest populations by the year 2050, only one is a high-income country (the United States); the rest are primarily low-income countries.

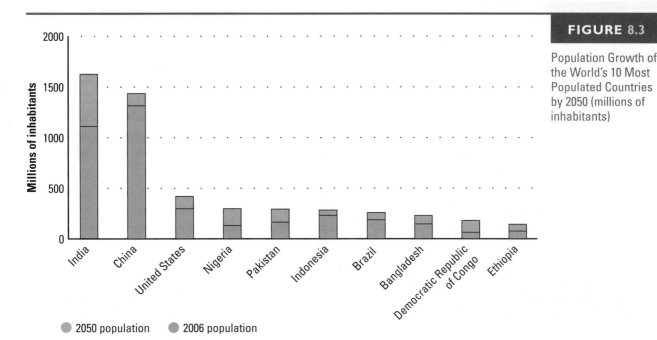

FIGURE 8.3

Population Growth of the World's 10 Most Populated Countries by 2050 (millions of inhabitants)

● 2050 population   ● 2006 population

Source: U.S. Census Bureau, *International Data Base*, www.census.gov/ipc/www/idbpyr.html (October 8, 2006); and Population Reference Bureau, *2006 World Population Data Sheet*, p. 2, www.prb.org/pdf06/06WorldDataSheet.pdf (October 8, 2006).

What does this mean for business managers? For the developed nations, there will be a decrease in the demand for products used in schools and for products bought by and for children, a smaller market for furniture and clothing, but an increased demand for medical care and related products, tourism, and financial services. Firms confronted by a decreasing demand for their products will have to look for sales increases in the developing economies, where the age distribution is reversed.

Many forces are responsible for reductions in birthrates. Governments are supporting family planning programs, to be sure, but there is ample evidence that improved levels of health and education along with an enhanced status for women, a more even distribution of income, and a greater degree of urbanization are all acting to reduce the traditional family size. In fact, experts have been claiming for some time that the combined effect of an effective family planning program and female education beyond the primary level is extremely powerful in reducing family size.

Concern in Developed Nations   The decrease in family size is welcomed by some countries in Africa and the Middle East, where fertility rates are as high as seven children per woman. But declining birthrates are causing concern in industrialized nations. The World Bank reports that the fertility rates in these countries are considerably below the *replacement number* of 2.1 children.* India, Mexico, and China have also experienced declines in their birthrates.

An increasing number of young Europeans are not marrying, and those who do marry are doing so later and having fewer children. Italy's population will fall by 15 million by midcentury, and the birthrate in Spain and Russia is even lower. By the year 2025 the present 9 percent unemployment rate in the European Union will be replaced by a shortage of workers. European governments will have to provide medical care and pensions for the 22 percent of their population that will be over 65 years old, and there will be fewer working taxpayers (see Figure 8.4).

*Number of children that will be born to a woman if she lives to the end of her childbearing years and bears children according to present age-specific fertility rates.

FIGURE 8.4 Percentages of Elderly (over 65) in Population, Selected Countries, 2006 and 2025

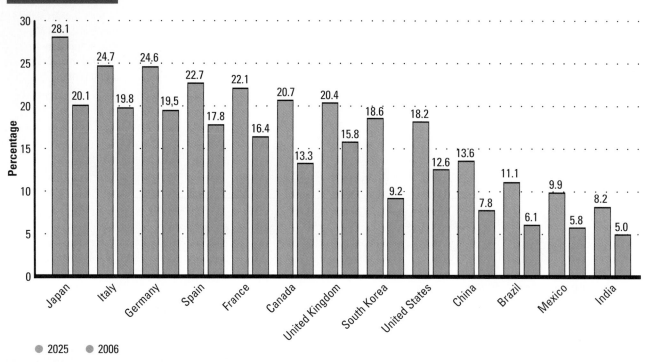

Source: U.S. Census Bureau, *International Data Base,* www.census.gov/ipc/www/idbpyr.html (October 8, 2006).

Japan's situation seems to be even more serious. Its fertility rate is only 1.5 children per woman, well below the 2.1 population replacement value, and in the year 2025 Japan's population age 65 and older will make up 26.8 percent of its total population, whereas the same age group in the United States will amount to only 18.5 percent of the total population. By the year 2025 Japan, which is the fastest-graying nation in the industrial world, will have twice as many old people as it has children. The government's reserve of social security funds will have run dry because retirement and health costs for the elderly are forecast to consume 73 percent of national income.

Early retirements and the fact that retirees are living longer are also straining the social security systems of many other countries. In the industrialized nations, not only are the costs of social security systems rising because of the growing number of retirees, but there are fewer people working and paying into the system to support them. However, in developing nations, just the opposite is occurring. The higher birthrates result in a younger population, and this reduces the dependency ratios and the costs to the workers supporting the system.

population density
A measure of the number of inhabitants per area unit (inhabitants per square kilometer or square mile)

population distribution
A measure of how the inhabitants are distributed over a nation's area

Population Density and Distribution Other aspects of population that concern business managers are **population density** and **population distribution.** Densely populated areas tend to make product distribution and communications simpler and less costly than they are in areas where population density is low; thus you might expect Pakistan, with 192 inhabitants per square kilometer, to be an easier market to serve than Canada (3 inhabitants/square kilometer) or Brazil (22 inhabitants/square kilometer).[11] The expectation, though, is another of those based on an arithmetic mean. We must know how these populations are distributed. One needs only to compare the urban percentages of total population to learn that Canada and Brazil possess population concentrations that facilitate the marketing process. While only 34 percent of Pakistan's population is urban, the percentages for Brazil and Canada are 83 and 80 percent, respectively.[12] The physical forces, as we saw in Chapter 7, contribute heavily to the formation of these concentrations.

An important phenomenon that is changing the population distribution is the **rural-to-urban shift,** which is occurring everywhere, especially in developing countries, as people move to cities in search of higher wages and more conveniences. An indicator of the extent of this movement is the change in the percentages of urban population. As Table 8.8 indicates,

| TABLE 8.8 | Rural-to-Urban Shift |

	Percentage of Population in Urban Areas					Percentage Change,
	1950	1970	1990	2005	2015 (estimated)	1950–2015
World	29%	36%	43%	49%	53%	82.8%
More developed regions	52	65	71	74	76	46.2
Less developed regions	18	25	35	43	48	166.7
Least developed countries	7	13	21	27	32	357.1
Less developed regions excluding least developed countries	20	27	37	46	51	155.0

Source: United Nations, *World Urbanization Prospects: The 2005 Revision Population Database,* http://esa.un.org/unup/index.asp?panel=1 (October 7, 2006).

the greatest urban shifts are occurring in the low- and middle-income countries. This shift is significant to marketers because city dwellers, being less self-sufficient than persons living in rural areas, must enter the market economy.

City governments also become customers for equipment that will expand municipal services to handle the population influx. Figure 8.5 contains some good sales prospects. Note that most of the fast-growing cities projected to be megacities by the year 2015 are in developing nations.

rural-to-urban shift
The movement of a nation's population from rural areas to cities

Other Socioeconomic Dimensions   Other socioeconomic dimensions can provide useful information to management. The increase in the number of working women, for example, is highly significant to marketers because it may result in larger family incomes, a greater market for convenience goods, and a need to alter the **promotional mix.** Personnel managers are interested in this increase because it results in a larger labor supply. It also signifies that changes may be required in production processes, employee facilities, and personnel management policies.

Data on a country's divorce rate will alert the marketer to the formation of single-parent families and single-person households, whose product needs and buying habits differ in many respects from those of a two-parent family. In many countries, important ethnic groups require special consideration by both marketing and personnel managers.

promotional mix
A blend of the promotional methods a firm uses to sell its products

> *Wal-Mart has had language problems on both sides of the border. In a country where labels and communications are made in English and French, the retailer mailed English-only circulars to residents of Quebec, where 83 percent of the population are French speakers. After apologizing for this mistake, Wal-Mart officials had to apologize a week later when the company was criticized severely for ordering Canadian employees to work 12 hours a week extra without pay by means of memos that also were in English only.*
>
> *One month later, the company had language-law problems on the other border when Mexican trade inspectors temporarily closed its Mexico City superstore, claiming that the firm had violated a 40-year-old law that requires the seller to place Spanish-language labels on all products on display.*[13]

INDUSTRY DIMENSIONS

Every firm is concerned about the general economic news because of its impact on consumer purchases, prices of raw materials, and investment decisions, but certain factors are more significant than others to a given industry or to a specific functional area of a firm. The size and growth trend of the automobile industry are of paramount importance to a tire manufacturer,

FIGURE 8.5   25 Megacities 1970–2015 (millions)

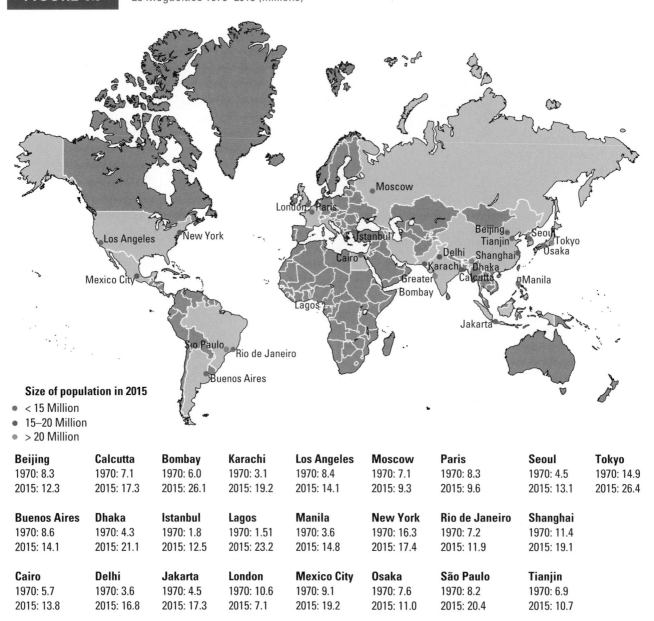

Size of population in 2015
- < 15 Million
- 15–20 Million
- > 20 Million

Beijing	Calcutta	Bombay	Karachi	Los Angeles	Moscow	Paris	Seoul	Tokyo
1970: 8.3	1970: 7.1	1970: 6.0	1970: 3.1	1970: 8.4	1970: 7.1	1970: 8.3	1970: 4.5	1970: 14.9
2015: 12.3	2015: 17.3	2015: 26.1	2015: 19.2	2015: 14.1	2015: 9.3	2015: 9.6	2015: 13.1	2015: 26.4

Buenos Aires	Dhaka	Istanbul	Lagos	Manila	New York	Rio de Janeiro	Shanghai
1970: 8.6	1970: 4.3	1970: 1.8	1970: 1.51	1970: 3.6	1970: 16.3	1970: 7.2	1970: 11.4
2015: 14.1	2015: 21.1	2015: 12.5	2015: 23.2	2015: 14.8	2015: 17.4	2015: 11.9	2015: 19.1

Cairo	Delhi	Jakarta	London	Mexico City	Osaka	São Paulo	Tianjin
1970: 5.7	1970: 3.6	1970: 4.5	1970: 10.6	1970: 9.1	1970: 7.6	1970: 8.2	1970: 6.9
2015: 13.8	2015: 16.8	2015: 17.3	2015: 7.1	2015: 19.2	2015: 11.0	2015: 20.4	2015: 10.7

Source: United Nations, 1995, www.megacities.nl/top 15/topworld/.html; *The Economist,* April 29, 1995, p. 122; *World Development Report 1994,* pp. 222–23; and www.jhuccp.org/pr/urbanpre.stm.

for example, but are of no interest to an appliance manufacturer. Nor would the quantity of machine operators graduated by technical schools be useful to financial officers, although these data are of vital interest to human resources managers of manufacturing plants. Managers want data not only about the firm's industry but also about industries that supply and purchase from the company. Minicase 8.2 at the end of this chapter illustrates the use of both macroeconomic and industry-specific data.

Industry studies are generally made by the firm's economists or its trade association, but they can also be purchased from independent research organizations, such as Fantus (New York) and the Economist Intelligence Unit (London). Government agencies, chambers of commerce, and trade publications such as *Advertising Age* publish them as well. Many international banks publish free newsletters containing useful economic data.

>>Using the Internet for Economic Research

You own a small business, and you don't have the money to hire an economic analyst. Yet you need economic and socioeconomic data to help you plan for market expansion just as the big multinationals do. What can you do? Do you have a personal computer with an Internet connection? Use it to get the information free of charge that the analyst you were going to hire would have gotten and then charged you for.

Suppose that up to now you have confined yourself to the U.S. market, but you are curious about the possibilities of expanding into the Canadian and Mexican markets. They are both nearby and relatively easy to get to. Can you find information about doing business with these countries on the Internet?

A quick search using an Internet search engine should uncover many sources of information for you. For example, you can obtain a free online report on "Doing Business in Canada," including key economic trends, trade regulations, and standards, by visiting the U.S. Department of Commerce's Commercial Services Web site at www.buyusa.gov/canada/en/ccg.html. This site also offers such services as assistance for American exporters in finding agents and

distributors, mailing products, and establishing a Canadian office. For trade statistics, geography, and culture, you can go to the Government of Canada's official Web site at http://canada.gc.ca/main_e.html.

To get data on Mexico, go to www.latinworld.com/norte/mexico/index.html for economic forecasts and an extensive Mexican financial commentary.

Michigan State University supports Global-EDGE, an excellent site for information on Mexico, Canada, or other countries. You can access this site at http://globaledge.msu.edu/ibrd/ibrd.asp. Using the Country Guide and typing in "Mexico" will bring you to an extensive list of resources, including the "Mexico: Country Commercial Guide" and "Mexico: Economist Country Briefing." You can also go to the Commercial Section of the U.S. embassy in Mexico City, which offers services to companies that want to do business in Mexico. Go directly from the GlobalEDGE site, or go directly to http://mexico.usembassy.gov/mexico/eeconomic.html. Another site, www.zonalatina.com, will provide even more information.

With the information you obtain from these sites, you should be able to decide whether you want to move into these new international markets.

Summary

State the purpose of economic analyses.

To keep abreast of the latest economic developments and also to plan for the future, firms regularly assess and forecast economic conditions at the local, state, and national levels. When they enter international operations, the economic analysis increases in complexity because managers are operating in two new environments: foreign and international. There are more economies to study, and these economies are frequently highly divergent.

Identify different categories based on levels of national economic development and the common characteristics of developing nations.

Managers involved in international business encounter markets with far greater differences in levels of economic development than those in which they have been working in domestic business settings. A nation's level of economic development affects all aspects of business, and we commonly group them into categories based on their level of economic development, such as developed, developing, newly industrializing, and newly industrialized economies. Developing nations have certain common characteristics, including unequal

distribution of income, technological and regional dualism, a large percentage of the population in agriculture, high population growth, high illiteracy rate, insufficient education, and low savings rates.

Recognize the economic and socioeconomic dimensions of the economy and different indicators used to assess them.

The various functional areas of a firm require data on the size and rates of change of a number of economic and socioeconomic factors. Among the more important economic dimensions are GDP, GNI, distribution of income, personal consumption expenditures, private investment, unit labor costs, and financial data, such as exchange rates, inflation rates, interest rates, and the amount of a nation's foreign debt. The principal socioeconomic dimensions are total population, rates of growth, age distribution, population density, and population distribution.

Discuss the importance of a nation's consumption patterns and the significance of purchasing power parity.

Marketers must know how consumers allocate their discretionary incomes, since this is money spent on their products.

They must also use purchasing power parity (PPP) to understand what the true purchasing power of a nation is. Consumers in a nation whose GNI appears to be too low to be a viable market may have some discretionary buying power when the GNI based on market exchange rates is converted to a GNI based on PPP.

Discuss the new definition of economic development, which includes more than economic growth.

The human-needs approach defines economic development as the reduction of poverty, unemployment, and inequality in the distribution of income.

Explain the degree to which labor costs can vary from country to country.

Hourly labor rates, especially when stated in U.S. dollars, change rather rapidly. There are three factors that are responsible:

(1) real changes in compensation, (2) changes in productivity, and (3) changes in exchange rates.

Discuss the significance for businesspeople of the large foreign debts of some nations.

Large foreign debts may indicate that the government will impose exchange controls on its country's businesses. If a large part of the country's export earnings go to service its external debt, there will be little remaining for use by firms in the country to pay for imports of raw materials, components used in their products, and production machinery. The government could impose price and wage controls. There is also the possibility that firms can buy some of the discounted debt to obtain local currency at a favorable exchange rate.

Key Words

developed (p. 230)

developing (p. 231)

newly industrializing countries (NICs) (p. 231)

newly industrialized economies (NIEs) (p. 231)

gross national income (GNI) (p. 231)

underground economy (p. 233)

purchasing power parity (PPP) (p. 234)

income distribution (p. 235)

discretionary income (p. 237)

unit labor costs (p. 238)

vertically integrated (p. 242)

human-needs approach (p. 243)

import substitution (p. 244)

population density (p. 246)

population distribution (p. 246)

rural-to-urban shift (p. 246)

promotional mix (p. 247)

Questions

1. Management learns from the economic analysis of Country A that wage rates are expected to increase by 10 percent next year. Which functional areas of the firm will be concerned? Why is management concerned?

2. What are "international dollars"? What is their significance to international businesspeople?

3. What common problem does the use of GNI per capita and population density values present?

4. If the clothing industry association to which your firm's Swiss subsidiary belongs could mount a successful promotional program to cause the Swiss to increase their clothing expenditures by 1 percent annually, what would be the total increase in sales for the clothing industry?

5. In 2004, Italy's average labor compensation costs stated in U.S. dollars were $20.48 compared to $16.52 in 1995, and they were 16.46 euros compared to 26,911 lira.

   a. What was the percentage increase or decrease in dollars?

   b. What accounts for the huge difference in local rates between 1995 and 2004 (hint: euros versus lira)?

6. The staff economist of a large multinational with an Argentine subsidiary has given to the firm's chief financial officer a report on Argentina's foreign debt situation, as shown in Table 8.7. What concerns might the chief financial officer have?

7. What would be the concerns of the chief financial officer in question 6 if he or she were to receive the information on annual inflation rates from Table 8.1?

8. Of what importance to marketers is a nation's level of economic development?

9. What problems with the import substitution strategy have caused some governments to increase their emphasis on export promotion?

10. What problems is the reduction in birthrates causing for European and Japanese governments?

11. Choose a country and a product and estimate the market potential of the product based on the economic and socioeconomic dimensions. What other environmental forces should you investigate?

Use the globalEDGE site (http://globalEDGE.msu.edu) to complete the following exercises:

1. The *Foreign Labor Statistics (FLS)* program provides international comparisons of hourly compensation costs; productivity and unit labor costs; labor force, employment and unemployment rates; and consumer prices. Using this resource, your firm is interested in comparing the real gross national income (GNI) per capita of five countries in which it has facilities: Australia, Belgium, Denmark, Japan, and Norway. From this list, which country has the highest GNI per capita? Which has the lowest?

2. You are working for a company that is planning to invest in Italy. Your company's executives have requested a report from you regarding Italy's current economic situation. One of your colleagues mentioned a useful Web site called *Country Briefings,* published by the *Economist* magazine. This site contains comprehensive information on 60 countries, including country profiles, recent news, political and economic forecasts, statistics, and more. Using this site, prepare a short executive report outlining Italy's current economic situation.

The Impact of Galawi's Development Policy Minicase 8.1

Armando Suarez, CEO of Industrias Globales, and Pedro Garcia, the firm's director of international operations, are discussing a statement made today by the secretary of treasury in Galawi.

Suarez: Pedro, did you listen to the secretary's comments today about the proposed change in development strategy?

Garcia: Yes, I did, and I'm concerned. We have spent considerable time and money planning our entry into the Galawi market, and if the government proceeds with the new economic strategy, we've got to change our plant design, plan to produce different product lines, and completely change our marketing plans.

Suarez: This apparently is more serious than I thought. How can a change in their development strategy from import substitution to export promotion affect us?

Garcia: Hang on to your chair, Chief, and I'll explain each strategy and how the change will affect our entire start-up program in Galawi. Oh, and by the way, our Galawi competitors are going to have to make changes, too.

Imagine you are Pedro Garcia.

1. Describe the two strategies for the CEO.

2. Explain how the change in development strategy will affect the firm in many ways.

3. What changes in its entry plans will the firm have to make?

World Laboratories Minicase 8.2

World Laboratories (WL) is a large multinational pharmaceutical manufacturer specializing in the production of ethical pharmaceuticals (available to the public only by prescription). These products are characterized by a high degree of research, and because of the limited protection offered by patents, they have a relatively short product life. WL does make some over-the-counter products, but these products account for only about 20 percent of total company sales.

The South American division manager must make a sales forecast for ethical drugs, which he will use to set quotas for the six countries in his division that have manufacturing plants. These products produce about 75 percent of the total sales in each market. At present, WL's market share and sales

by category of drug (pediatric, general, geriatric) in each country are as shown in the accompanying table.

Total health care has grown faster than world population and world income since 1970. A conservative average of the total amount per capita spent on health care, both private and public, for pharmaceuticals in South America is 20 percent. This is lower than in the United States and Europe, but in government clinics, medicine is generally offered without charge or at a substantial discount from the price charged in pharmacies. According to WL's subsidiaries, the patients at clinics pay, on average, 40 percent of the drugs' listed prices when the drugs given at no charge are included. Obviously, private drugstores that get only 40 percent off list (60 percent of list price is their cost) cannot compete. WL, however, still earns a 12 percent profit based on its selling prices when it sells to governments at list less 50 percent because of the low marketing costs on such large volumes, compared to an average 20 percent of selling price on sales to private pharmacies.

Here are the data that the staff economist has just given to the South American division manager. Help him do the fore-cast. If you have to make any assumptions, please make a note of them. If marketing costs for government sales average 6 percent of WL's selling price while they average 11.5 percent to private pharmacies, should the division manager try to change the present government–private pharmacy sales ratio that now prevails in any of the six markets? Should he have any other concerns based on these data?

	Market Share (percent)	Pediatric (0–14 years)	General (15–64 years)	Geriatric (65 and older)
Argentina	30%	32.0%	58.0%	10.0%
Brazil	24	29.3	65.7	5.0
Chile	55	32.1	65.8	5.1
Paraguay	65	41.2	55.4	3.4
Peru	45	42.0	56.5	1.5
Uruguay	38	27.0	63.9	9.1

	GDP (billions of dollars)					Foreign Debt (billions of dollars)			
	1989	1992	1999	2003		1989	1992	2000	2004
Argentina	$67.8	$200.3	$283.2	$129.6		$64.7	$49.1	$146.4	$157.7
Brazil	375.1	425.4	751.5	492.3		111.3	99.2	201.3	171.7
Chile	22.9	37.1	67.5	72.4		18.2	14.9	31.0	36.4
Paraguay	4.3	6.0	7.7	6.0		2.5	1.5	1.5	2.8
Peru	23.0	21.3	51.9	60.6		19.9	15.6	30.5	28.7
Uruguay	8.1	10.4	20.8	11.2		3.8	3.4	3.4	7.7

	Total Debt Service as Percentage of Export Receipts				Total Government Expenditures as Percentage of GNP				Percentage of Government Expenditures on Health Care			
	1989	1992	2000	2004	1989	1992	1998	2003	1989	1992	1998	2002
Argentina	36.1%	34.4%	85.5%	28.1%	15.5%	13.1%	20.4%	19.8%	2.0%	3.0%	4.9%	4.5%
Brazil	31.3	23.1	77.7	47.4	30.6	25.6	38.8	36.7	6.1	6.9	2.9	3.6
Chile	27.5	20.9	15.8	24.2	32.5	22.1	25.9	24.5	5.9	11.1	2.7	2.6
Paraguay	11.9	40.3	8.0	13.3	8.9	9.4	9.4	9.2	3.0	4.3	1.7	3.2
Peru	6.8	23.0	44.9	17.1	11.6	12.5	18.0	19.1	5.5	5.6	2.4	2.2
Uruguay	29.4	23.2	30.2	35.4	25.8	28.7	28.7	27.5	4.5	5.0	1.9	2.9

	Population per Physician				Annual Inflation Rate				Population (millions)				Population Distribution, 2003		
													0–14 Years	15–64 Years	65 + Years
	1984	1990	1993	2004	1989	1992	2001	2005	1989	1992	1999	2003			
Argentina	370	n.a.	373	332	3,081%	25%	1%	9%	31.9	33.1	36.6	38.0	27.1	64.2	8.7
Brazil	1,080	n.a.	746	485	1,431	1,022	1	7	147.8	153.9	168.2	181.4	28.4	66.7	4.9
Chile	1,230	2,150	926	917	17	15	4	7	13.0	13.6	15.0	16.0	26.1	67.3	6.6
Paraguay	1,460	1,250	1,493	854	3,127	15	n.a.	9	4.2	4.5	5.4	5.9	38.4	58.6	3.0
Peru	1,040	960	1,370	855	399	74	4	3	21.2	22.4	25.2	27.2	33.2	62.7	4.1
Uruguay	510	n.a.	324	275	81	68	5	2	3.1	3.1	3.3	3.4	24.5	64.0	11.5

	Percentage of GNP for Private Consumption Expenditure			Percentage of Private Consumption Expenditure for Health Care	
	1989	1992	2004	1998	2002
Argentina	54.8%	73.3%	67.3%	5.4%	4.4%
Brazil	55.3	60.0	59.7	3.7	4.3
Chile	72.7	65.8	68.4	3.1	3.2
Paraguay	75.9	69.3	70.2	3.6	5.2
Peru	84.6	72.6	71.5	3.7	2.2
Uruguay	64.0	65.8	67.3	7.2	7.1

9 Political Forces

Enthusiastic Poles celebrate their country's admission to the EU.

©Sean Gallup/Getty Images

Politics have no relation to morals.
—*Niccolò Machiavelli*

There Are Two Polands—Which One Joined the EU?

Poles are entrepreneurial. Over 1.5 million small and mid-size companies have been created since 1989. An example is Kross Bicycles, which has become the second-largest bike maker in Europe. Another is Delphia Yachts, which exports more that 90 percent of its output to Europe and elsewhere. Still another is Comarch, a software systems provider. Its 2nd quarter 2006 operating profit was 3 times higher than for the same period in 2005.

Foreign investors are arriving. Among them are Whirlpool Corp., which has been in Poland since 1993 and made significant new investments in 2005. It has been joined by the Spanish appliance maker Fagor and by the white-goods producer Merloni Electrodomestici from Italy.

Poland's GDP growth of some 3.2 percent is faster than the old EU countries' rates. In addition, Poland's productivity increase of over 3.7 percent in 2004 was over twice the EU average. Its labor costs are less than a sixth of the German costs.

Those facts present a picture of one of the Polands. But there is a second one.

This one is a dysfunctional political system sitting astride a communist-era welfare state. The bureaucracy is one of the worst in Europe. For example, the delay in securing permits to begin a business is commonly 8 to 10 months. Many Poles are concerned at the prospect of combining the Polish paper pushers with the substantial bureaucracy already operating on the EU payroll in Brussels.

Bureaucrats in Poland are blamed for the loss by Poland of investments by three of the largest automobile makers in Eastern Europe in the past several years. Another one, MG Rover of Britain, complained that negotiations for an auto plant near Warsaw were frustrated by the glacially slow decision making by Polish bureaucrats. It threatened to take its investment to China (and in fact is now owned by Nanjing Automobile).

Matters are made worse by the requirement to file tax returns every month. Naturally, they are quite complicated.

Two present EU members demonstrate the good and bad possible roads Poland may travel as a member. After joining, Spain boomed. It spent EU funds wisely and productively. It liberated and deregulated the economy and successfully restructured state finances. The bad road was followed by Greece. It squandered billions of EU funds on inefficient, government-owned companies.

The way Poland goes is important. It is far and away the largest of the 10 countries that joined the EU in 2004. It accounts for 41 percent of their total GDP, and more than half their population. ∎

Source: David Fairlamb and Bogdan Turek, *BusinessWeek,* May 10, 2004, pp. 54–56. Reprinted by special permission. Copyright © 2004 by the McGraw-Hill Companies, Inc. Other information from corporate Web sites.

CONCEPT PREVIEWS

After reading this chapter, you should be able to:

identify the ideological forces that affect business and understand the terminology used in discussing them

discuss the fact that although most governments own businesses, they are privatizing them in growing numbers

explain the changing sources and reasons for terrorism and the methods and growing power of terrorists

explain steps that traveling international business executives should take to protect themselves from terrorists

evaluate the importance to business of government stability and policy continuity

explain country risk assessment by international business

In a number of ways, the political climate of a country in which a business operates is as important as the country's topography, its natural resources, and its meteorological climate. Indeed, we shall see examples in which a hospitable, stable government can encourage business investment and growth despite geographic or weather obstacles and a scarcity of natural resources. The opposite is equally true. Some areas of the world that are relatively blessed with natural resources and manageable topography and weather have been very little developed because of government instability. Occasionally, a country's government is hostile to investment in its territory by foreign companies even though they might provide capital, technology, and training for development of the country's resources and people.

Many of the political forces with which business must cope have ideological sources, but there are a large number of other sources. These sources include nationalism, terrorism, traditional hostilities, unstable governments, international organizations, and government-owned business.

The international company itself can also be a political force. Some firms have budgets or sales larger than the gross national product (GNP) of some of the countries with which they negotiate. Although budgets and GNPs do not translate directly into power, it should be clear that companies with bigger budgets and countries with bigger GNPs possess more assets and facilities with which to negotiate. Refer back to Table 1.3 in Chapter 1 for some examples.

This chapter will provide an indication of the types of risks political forces pose to private business. As we shall see, some of the risks can stem from more than one political force.

Ideological Forces

Such names as communism, socialism, capitalism, liberal, conservative, left wing, and right wing are used to describe governments, political parties, and people. These names indicate ideological beliefs.

COMMUNISM

It is communist doctrine that the government should own all the major factors of production. With exceptions, all production in communist countries is done by state-owned factories and farms. Labor unions are government-controlled.

communism

Marx's theory of a classless society, developed by his successors into control of society by the Communist Party and the attempted worldwide spread of communism

Communism as conceived by Karl Marx was a theory of social change directed toward the ideal of a classless society. As developed by Lenin and others, communism typically involves the seizure of power by a conspiratorial political party, the maintenance of power by stern suppression of internal opposition, and commitment to the ultimate goal of a worldwide communist state.

Communist Government Takeover of a Previously Noncommunist Country

One of communism's basic tenets is state ownership of all the productive factors. This occurred in Russia after the 1917 Bolshevik Revolution, and it has been repeated after each communist takeover of a country.

Compensation for Expropriated Property   To date, none of the communist governments has compensated the foreign former owners directly. A few of the owners have gotten some reimbursement indirectly, from assets of the communist government seized abroad. For example, the U.S. government seized assets of the Soviet Union in the United States after American property in the Soviet Union was confiscated. American firms or individuals whose property had been confiscated in the U.S.S.R. could file claims with a U.S. government agency, and if they could substantiate their loss, a percentage of it was paid.

Expropriation and Confiscation   The rules of traditional international law recognize a country's right to expropriate the property of foreigners within its jurisdiction. But those rules require that the country compensate the foreign owners, and *in the absence of compensation,* **expropriation** *becomes* **confiscation.**[1]

Communism Collapses

We have insufficient space to detail the reasons for communism's failure as an economic and social system. We shall present a couple of basic reasons and a few anecdotes that illustrate the results. See the endnotes for more.

The U.S.S.R. concentrated its best scientists, engineers, managers, and raw materials in production for the military and neglected production of consumer goods. Gross production was the goal, and managers would go to ridiculous extremes to meet the production targets set by government central planners. For example, central planning allowed only one condom factory and birth control pills were very expensive, so the two products were not easily available. Abortion was the most common form of birth control. The abortions were then counted as part of doctors' gross production and therefore swelled the reported national income.

Factories under construction got a certificate putting them into commission on the scheduled completion date even though they were almost never actually completed on schedule. Because of the certificate, the factory had to report production coming from it even though it had not yet produced anything.

Some enterprises used other deceptions. For instance, a factory reaching only 50 percent of its targeted output could have made a small change in its next shipped machine and doubled the price, say, from \$10,000 to \$20,000—presto, doubled output.[2]

Tale of Two Cities

A spectacular result of communism's collapse was the reunification of East Germany with West Germany, accompanied by the revival of Berlin as the capital. The capital of West Germany had been Bonn, while East Germany's capital had been in its part of the divided Berlin. As reunited Berlin was renovated in the east and as hundreds of new buildings were constructed throughout the city, it resembled and was called a high-construction site. The picture on this page illustrates a small part of that.

CAPITALISM

The capitalist, free enterprise ideal is that all the factors of production should be privately owned. Under perfect **capitalism,** government is restricted to those functions that the private

expropriation
Government seizure of the property within its borders owned by foreigners, followed by prompt, adequate, and effective compensation paid to the former owners

confiscation
Government seizure of the property within its borders owned by foreigners without payment to them

capitalism
An economic system in which the means of production and distribution are for the most part privately owned and operated for private profit

Berlin under reconstruction after being restored as the capital of the new Germany in 1990. Formerly, the city and country had been divided, with East Berlin belonging to communist East Germany and West Berlin belonging to democratic West Germany.

sector cannot perform. These include national defense; police, fire, and other public services; and government-to-government international relations.

No such government exists. The reality in so-called capitalist countries is quite complex. The governments of such countries typically regulate privately owned businesses quite closely, and these governments also own businesses.

Regulations and Red Tape

All businesses are subject to countless government laws, regulations, and red tape in their activities in all capitalist countries. Special government approval is required to practice such professions as law and medicine. Tailored sets of laws and regulations govern banking, insurance, transportation, and utilities. States and local governments require business licenses and impose use restrictions on buildings and areas.

Complying with all the laws and regulations and coping with the red tape require expertise, time, and, of course, expense. A business found in noncompliance may incur fines or even the imprisonment of its managers.

SOCIALISM

socialism
Public, collective ownership of the basic means of production and distribution, operating for use rather than profit

Socialism advocates government ownership or control of the basic means of production, distribution, and exchange. Profit is not an aim.

In practice, so-called socialist governments have frequently performed in ways not consistent with the doctrine. One of the most startling examples of this is Singapore, which professes to be a socialist state but in reality is aggressively capitalistic.[3]

European Socialism

In Europe, socialist parties have been in power in several countries, including Great Britain, France, Spain, Greece, and Germany. In Britain, the Labour Party—as the socialists there call their political party—in the past nationalized some basic industries, such as steel, shipbuilding, coal mining, and the railroads, but did not go much further in that direction. A vocal left wing of the Labour Party advocates nationalizing all major British businesses, banks, and insurance companies.

The Germans use the term Social Democrats for their socialist political party. The Social Democrats are currently in a coalition government with the Christian Democrats. The socialist governments of France and Spain have embarked on programs to privatize government-owned businesses; such programs do not conform to socialist doctrine. In fact, since neither capitalism nor socialism seems to fit well, the words "corporatism" or "co-determination" are used to describe this Western European blend of capitalism and socialism.

Socialism in Developing Countries

The developing countries often profess some degree of socialism. The government typically owns and controls many of the factors of production. Shortages of capital, technology, and skilled management and labor are characteristic of developing countries, and developed countries or international organizations often provide aid through a developing country's government. Also, many of the educated citizens of a developing country tend to be in or connected with the government. It follows that the government would own or control major factories and farms.

Whatever a government's political label, most will permit and often seek capital investment. This happens when the developing country perceives advantages that would not be possible without the private capital, such as more jobs for its people, new technology, skilled managers or technicians, and export opportunities.

CONSERVATIVE OR LIBERAL

conservative
A person, group, or party that wishes to minimize government activities and maximize private ownership and business

We should not leave the subject of ideology without mention of the words *conservative* and *liberal* as they are currently used. Politically, in the United States, the word **conservative** connotes a person, group, or party that wishes to minimize government activity and maximize the activities of private businesses and individuals. *Conservative* is used to mean something similar to **right wing,** but in the United States and the United Kingdom, the latter term is more extreme. For instance, the Conservative Party, one of the major political parties in the United Kingdom, is said to have a right-wing minority.

Also, connotations of *conservative* can differ depending on the application. For example, as China and the countries of Eastern Europe and the former Soviet Union move from centrally planned economies to market economies and from dictatorships toward democracies, the people and groups trying to impede, stop, or reverse such movements are called *conservatives.* These people, often members of communist (usually renamed) parties or the armed forces, long for "the good old days" when the governments owned and ran everything. That is the opposite of the wishes of conservatives in the United States and the United Kingdom, who want the least possible government involvement.

In the United States the word **liberal** now means the opposite of what it meant in the 19th century. It now connotes a person, group, or party that urges greater government participation in the economy and regulation or ownership of business. Liberal and **left wing** are similar, but the latter may indicate a more extreme position closer to socialism.

Unique to the United States
This usage has not spread outside the United States. For example,

> A conversation one of the authors had with an Italian lawyer at lunch in Rome turned to politics. The Italian identified himself as a liberal, and the author understood it in the American sense. As the conversation proceeded, the author learned that he had been wrong. The lawyer was a member of the Liberal Party, a political party near the right end of the Italian political spectrum.

We do not want to overemphasize the importance of the labels *conservative, liberal, right wing,* and *left wing.* For one thing, individuals and organizations may change over time or as they perceive shifts in the moods of voters. These labels are simplistic or even naive, and reality is more complex. Nevertheless, we wanted to bring them to your attention because they are used in discussions of international events and because different political forces flow from, for example, a right-wing government than from a left-wing one. Businesspeople must do their best to influence those political forces and then forecast and react to them.

Examples of "left" and "right" terminology in current international political reporting are widespread. Excerpts from news articles illustrate this, for example, "Right wing coalition confident of French poll win," and "Mr. Jospin's sudden exit created a vacuum in the leadership of the left."[4] Political advocacy organizations, both left and right, grow in size and power every year. In the United States, one list shows about 60 of these groups beginning with the letter "A" alone. They are equally influential and powerful in the corridors of power of the European Union and other countries. Less well known but just as important, these organizations litigate precedent-setting lawsuits that affect judicial decisions for years to come. These court decisions, as well as the laws that result from such organizations' lobbying, powerfully affect business at every level.[5]

Government Ownership of Business

One might assume that government ownership of the factors of production is found only in communist or socialist countries, but that assumption is not correct. Businesses are owned by the governments of countries that do not consider themselves either communist or socialist. From country to country, there are wide differences in the industries that are government-owned and in the extent of government ownership.

WHY FIRMS ARE NATIONALIZED

A number of reasons, sometimes overlapping, explain why governments put their hands on firms. Some of them are (1) to extract more money from the firms—the government suspects that the firms are concealing profits; (2) profitability—the government believes it could run

right wing
A more extreme conservative position

liberal
In the contemporary United States, a person, group, or party that urges greater government involvement in business and other aspects of human activities

left wing
A more extreme liberal position

Getting Nationalization Right

Bolivia's president Evo Morales nationalized its oil and gas industry in 2006 by sending in troops. But he has had difficulty in doing more. State energy company YPFB (Yacimientos Petroliferos Fiscales Bolivianos) has asked the central bank for a $180 million credit line to finish the takeover. Fellow South American nations Venezuela and Ecuador have also turned to state intervention, but Bolivia's situation is perhaps the most dire. The current impass in some ways reflects Bolivia's earlier attempts—this is the third nationalization of Bolivia's energy industry in the past 100 years. Nor is the nationalization target "Big Oil" from North America. Rather, Bolivia's single largest client is Brazil,

and the Brazilian state oil company is the largest investor in Bolivia's energy. And although Bolivia may be able to increase revenue by charging Brazil higher prices, Brazil is itself developing natural-gas reserves which could allow it to walk away from Bolivian suppliers in a few years. Says one commentator, "[Venezuelan President] Chavez and Morales are both playing a game of chicken with foreign oil companies."

Source: David Luhnow, "Bolivia Renationalization Hits Snag," *The Wall Street Journal*, August 15, 2006, p. A5; and David Luchow and Jose de Cordoba,"Bolivia's President Morales Orders Nationalization of Natural Gas," *The Wall Street Journal*, May 2, 2006, pp. A1, A15.

the firms more efficiently and make more money; (3) ideology—governments sometimes nationalize industries, as has occurred in Britain, France, and Canada; (4) job preservation—to save jobs by putting dying industries on life-support systems; (5) because the government has pumped money into a firm or an industry, and control usually follows money; or (6) happenstance, as with the nationalization after World War II of German-owned firms in Europe.

UNFAIR COMPETITION?

Where government-owned companies compete with privately owned companies, the private companies sometimes complain that the government companies have unfair advantages. Some of the complaints are that (1) government-owned companies can cut prices unfairly because they do not have to make profits, (2) they get cheaper financing, (3) they get government contracts, (4) they get export assistance, and (5) they can hold down wages with government assistance.

Another advantage state-owned companies enjoy over privately owned business comes in the form of direct subsidies: payments by the government to those companies. The EU Commission has been trying to discourage such subsidy payments. For years it has required annual financial reports from state-controlled companies as part of a crackdown on the subsidies that can distort competition.[6]

GOVERNMENT–PRIVATE FIRM COLLABORATION DIFFICULT

The objectives of private firms and those of government agencies and operations usually differ. Figure 9.1 illustrates some of the differences.

Privatization

privatization
The transfer of public sector assets to the private sector, the transfer of management of state activities through contracts and leases, and the contracting out of activities previously conducted by the state

Britain's former prime minister, Margaret Thatcher, was the acknowledged leader of the **privatization** movement. During her 11 years in office, Thatcher decreased state-owned companies from a 10 percent share of Britain's GNP to 3.9 percent. She sold over 30 companies, raising some $65 billion.[7] Thatcher pioneered in what has become a worldwide movement to privatize all sorts of government activities.

AIRPORTS, GARBAGE, POSTAL SERVICES, AND...?

For example, the Lockheed Company began by running Burbank Airport in California for decades and then expanded abroad. As owner or manager, Lockheed has operated or bid to operate airports in Canada, Russia, Turkmenistan, Australia, Turkey, Hungary, Argentina,

FIGURE 9.1

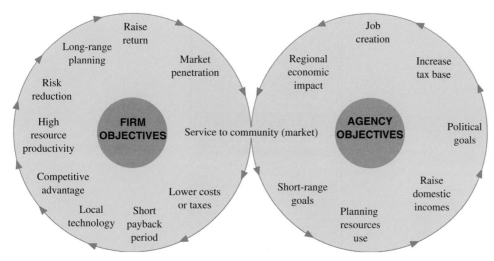

Source: Reprinted from *Long Range Planning,* Vol. 3, No. 1, Vichas et al., "Public Planners and Business Investors," p. 83. Copyright © 1981, with permission of Elsevier Science.

and Venezuela. Hughes Aircraft Company is in that business with Trinidad and Tobago and has completed studies for Ukraine on ways to upgrade that country's airports.[8]

Similarly, the management of Amsterdam's Schiphol Airport found that managing foreign airports was an excellent business. Schiphol Airport Group manages terminals in New York and Brisbane, Australia.[9]

One study found that it cost the New York Department of Sanitation $40, of which $32 was for labor, to deal with a ton of rubbish. It cost private collectors only $17 (of which $10 was for labor).[10]

Several countries are privatizing their postal services. Germany's Deutsche Post was privatized and is often counted as a privatization success story. Japan's postal system is scheduled to be privatized in 2007. Japan Post holds over $3 trillion in private savings accounts and insurance, so it is not just a mail service.

In 1997, the government of Mozambique brought in the British company Crown Agents to run its customs service. Given the low levels of public sector pay, bribery was endemic from top to bottom. Crown Agents set up antismuggling teams, and successes came quickly, stopping the smuggling of cigarettes, alcohol, electrical goods, meat, condensed milk, and even yogurt.[11]

Even the formerly rigid People's Republic of China now encourages state-run enterprises to diversify ownership. Private and even foreign investors may acquire stakes.[12] In 2006, Initial Public Offering (IPO), M&A, and privatization indices were begun to track China's super-hot economy.

Africa is not being left out of the privatization parade. Mozambique we mentioned above, and as illustrated by the advertisement shown in Figure 9.2, Nigeria, the most populous central African country, is cooperating with *Business in Africa International Magazine* to encourage privatization.[13]

The solvency and stability of the banking sector were found to be improved by the privatization of industrial and commercial companies. Privatized companies have improved their profitability more rapidly, which has led to notable improvements in the banks' loan portfolios.[14]

The list of government-owned businesses and activities being sold to private owners or turned over to private companies to manage and operate goes on and on. The space available here is too limited to treat the subject thoroughly; instead, we refer you to the chapter endnotes and to articles on privatization that frequently appear in newspapers and periodicals and on Web sites.

FIGURE 9.2

Privatization in Africa

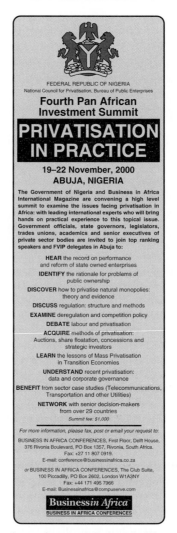

FEDERAL REPUBLIC OF NIGERIA
National Council for Privatisation, Bureau of Public Enterprises

**Fourth Pan African
Investment Summit**

**PRIVATISATION
IN PRACTICE**

**19–22 November, 2000
ABUJA, NIGERIA**

The Government of Nigeria and Business in Africa International Magazine are convening a high level summit to examine the issues facing privatisation in Africa: with leading international experts who will bring hands on practical experience to this topical issue. Government officials, state governors, legislators, trades unions, academics and senior executives of private sector bodies are invited to join top ranking speakers and FVIP delegates in Abuja to:

HEAR the record on performance
and reform of state owned enterprises

IDENTIFY the rationale for problems of
public ownership

DISCOVER how to privatise natural monopolies:
theory and evidence

DISCUSS regulation: structure and methods

EXAMINE deregulation and competition policy

DEBATE labour and privatisation

ACQUIRE methods of privatisation:
Auctions, share floatation, concessions and
strategic investors

LEARN the lessons of Mass Privatisation
in Transition Economies

UNDERSTAND recent privatisation:
data and corporate governance

BENEFIT from sector case studies (Telecommunications,
Transportation and other Utilities)

NETWORK with senior decision-makers
from over 29 countries

Summit fee: $1,000

For more information, please fax, post or email your request to:

BUSINESS IN AFRICA CONFERENCES, First Floor, Delft House,
376 Rivonia Boulevard, PO Box 1357, Rivonia, South Africa.
Fax: +27 11 807 0919.
E-mail: conference@businessinafrica.co.za

or BUSINESS IN AFRICA CONFERENCES, The Club Suite,
100 Piccadilly, PO Box 2602, London W1A3NY
Fax: +44 171 495 7966
E-mail: Businessinafrica@compuserve.com

Business*in Africa*

BUSINESS IN AFRICA CONFERENCES

Source: Courtesy of *Business in Africa Magazine.*

PRIVATE BUYERS DO WELL, BUT AN AMERICAN NEEDS A PASSPORT

Although privatization is a sizzling political trend all over the world, the activity is not as great in the United States.

Fortunately, American investors can partake in the trend by buying mutual funds that hold shares of the world's newly privatized companies.[15]

PRIVATIZATION ANYWHERE AND ANY WAY

Privatization does not always involve ownership transfer from government to private entities. Activities previously conducted by the state may be contracted out, as Mozambique has contracted a British firm to run its customs administration and Thailand has private companies operating some of the passenger trains of its state-owned railroad.

Governments may lease state-owned plants to private entities, as Togo has done. They may combine a joint venture with a management contract with a private group to run a previously government-operated business. Rwanda did this with its match factory.

Even unemployment services are being privatized. Australia is a leader in this field, and it has found church groups to be the most successful employment agency operators. Those groups have secured lucrative government contracts, and community-based and charitable agencies have been about 25 percent better than the average in helping the long-term unemployed.[16]

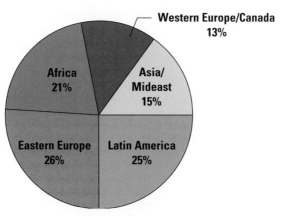

Western Europe/Canada
13%

Africa
21%

Asia/
Mideast
15%

Eastern Europe
26%

Latin America
25%

FIGURE 9.3

Privatizations by
Region

Source: "Privatization Worldwide Summary," prepared for the Transnational Corporations and Management Division of the United Nations. Used
here by permission of the author, Michael S. Minor.

Figure 9.3 shows privatization by geographic region. The percentages in the figure total
100 without reference to the United States; this illustrates that neither the U.S. government
nor the individual state governments are participating substantially in the privatization trend.

THE SUPER BOWL: GOVERNMENT VERSUS PRIVATE

A direct comparison is available. In England the Conservative government privatized the
water industry in 1989. From 1989 to the present, the water industry in England has been in
private company hands, while next door in Scotland it has been government-owned and
-operated.

Over that period Scottish household water bills have increased 94 percent, while English
bills have gone up 22 percent. A medium-size office in Scotland pays 16 times more than its
English counterpart. And not only have Scottish water prices soared above those in England,
but water quality and service have deteriorated. Scots get poorer drinking water and more
pollution from their sewers, and their pipes are more than twice as leaky.

Scotland is now moving toward privatization, but water bills won't start coming down
before 2007. Before they come down, Scottish Water must find some £2 billion to upgrade
the machinery, pipes, and sewers.[17]

Government Protection

A historical function of government, whatever its ideology, has been the protection of the
economic activities—farming, mining, manufacturing, and so forth—within its geographic
area of control. These activities must be protected from attacks and destruction or robbery by
bandits, revolutionaries, foreign invaders or terrorists. In 1990, the Iraqi armed forces in-
vaded Kuwait, quickly overwhelming the defenders of that much smaller country. Although
Kuwait is small, it is oil-rich. If Iraq held Kuwait, the combined petroleum reserves of the
two countries would make Iraq a major player in petroleum politics.

An even greater prize was lying next door: Saudi Arabia, with the world's largest proved
petroleum reserves. With armed forces no match for those of Iraq, Saudi Arabia might easily have fallen. That would have made Iraq the world's mightiest petroleum power and permitted it to influence the policies and actions of Europe, Japan, North America, and most of
the rest of the world.

A UN-sanctioned international coalition mobilized and transported armed forces to the
Middle East. A short war, code-named Desert Storm, in early 1991 forced Iraqi forces out of
Kuwait, although they set fire to hundreds of Kuwaiti oil wells as they retreated.

The aftermath of this war demonstrates the influence of politics on business. In grati-
tude for American leadership of Desert Storm, Kuwait and other Gulf Cooperation Council

Every international business transaction is impacted by two governments, that of the home country and that of the host country. You must abide by the laws, rules, and regulations of each country. You must also understand the political orientation of each country and geographic region in which you do business because the government and its political structure will determine your ability to do business in that country. Geopolitics goes well beyond government and politics. It includes, but is not limited to, such issues as:

- Country and regional economics.

- Terrorism and its support or condemnation.

- Military alliances.

- Human rights.

- Religion and the degree of separation between "church and state."

- Public policy.

- Natural resources.

- Government stability.

- Attitudes toward dumping and counterfeiting products.

- Arms control, chemical and biological warfare, and nuclear threat.

Political risk assessment is a major component of doing a potential market-entry analysis to determine the feasibility and risks of entering into a specific foreign market. Keeping current with the ever-changing global political scene and doing political risk assessment in market-entry planning are two critical tools of the successful international business professional.

World Fact: The U.S. government maintains comprehensive economic embargoes on the countries of Cuba, Iran, North Korea, and Sudan; arms embargoes on Liberia, Rwanda, Somalia, and the Federal Republic of Yugoslavia (Serbia and Montenegro); and an arms and commodity embargo on UNITA in Angola.

Culture Cue: In dealing with your foreign counterparts, socially or in business settings, it is extremely wise *not* to get into heated discussions or arguments about the importance or correctness of one political system over another. This also applies to any discussions of religion. In many parts of the world, the political and religious systems may be closely aligned or even one and the same.

World Wide Resources:

www.stratfor.com

www.sipri.org/contents/it/db/db3

countries—Saudi Arabia, Qatar, Bahrain, the United Arab Emirates, and Oman—bought some $36 billion of American arms. But in a 1997 competition to sell Kuwait 72 self-propelled howitzers, a Chinese company beat out an American company's widely considered superior versions. In private conversations, Kuwaiti officials said their reasons for buying Chinese had nothing to do with range, price, or accuracy and everything to do with politics. It seems China suggested it would withhold its support at the United Nations for extending trade sanctions against Iraq unless Kuwait gave the estimated $300 million order to the Chinese company. "Sometimes you get to a state when you feel you're being blackmailed," a senior Kuwaiti official said. "We lean toward the U.S. equipment, but we have to find a way to please the Chinese and not upset them in the Security Council."[18]

TERRORISM

terrorism

Unlawful acts of violence committed for a wide variety of reasons, including for ransom, to overthrow a government, to gain release of imprisoned colleagues, to exact revenge for real or imagined wrongs, and to punish nonbelievers of the terrorists' religion

Since the 1970s, the world has been plagued by **terrorism.** Various groups have hijacked airplanes, shot and kidnapped individuals, and bombed people and objects. During the 1970s and 1980s, Italy was particularly hard hit by terrorist violence directed against businesses and politicians. Between 1975 and 1982, terrorist groups almost shattered Italy's ability to govern itself. However, the Italian government struck back successfully by creating a special 25,000-strong antiterrorist squad. Once caught, terrorists were tried, convicted, and sentenced to prison by the Italian courts.

Coinciding with those events, the attraction of terrorist groups lessened for educated, idealistic young Italians, the original source of the groups' recruits. And with their cachet fading, the groups had many defectors. As these young Italians became disenchanted, terrorist leaders turned to more conventional crime. They began cooperating with the Mafia, which is growing and becoming more feared by Italian authorities. The Bank of Italy warned that the Mafia threatened to contaminate Italy's financial system.

September 11, 2001 On September 11, 2001, terrorists struck New York massively and lethally. They hijacked four civilian American airliners just after they took off from airports in Boston, Washington, D.C., and Newark, New Jersey, the planes fully loaded with jet fuel. They flew two of them into the two World Trade Center towers in New York and crashed one into the Pentagon in a Virginia suburb of Washington, D.C. The hijackers of the fourth plane were overwhelmed by the passengers, and the plane crashed in Pennsylvania. All told, thousands of lives were lost.

The United States immediately considered itself at war although there was no formal declaration of war by the U.S. Congress. There was no national government to declare war against as responsible for the attacks, which had been planned and executed by an Islamic fundamentalist organization calling itself al Qaeda, with headquarters and training camps at that time in Afghanistan and cells in many countries.

A main objective of the United States and its allies is to prevent Afghanistan from again becoming a base and hiding place for al Qaeda. Whether the West has the staying power to achieve this remains to be seen. At the same time, the campaign is ongoing to eradicate al Qaeda cells in countries around the world, even in the United States. There is a concern that al Qaeda will establish camps and headquarters in countries such as Somalia or Yemen. This struggle promises to be long, costly, and complex.

In the United States there have been widespread changes in airport and border security, immigration policy, student visas, and security of sensitive areas such as nuclear power plants and government installations. President George W. Bush called for and Congress approved a new cabinet-level government agency, the Homeland Security Department, to combine activities of many agencies protecting in many ways against terrorism. There are about 184,000 employees in the department, and housing them has been a challenge. For an idea of the size of that challenge, consider that the Pentagon, a 3.7-million-square-foot structure that boasts the largest roof in the world, accommodates a mere 23,000 workers.

Terrorism Worldwide
Al Qaeda is by no means the only terrorist organization in the world. Among the better-known groups are the Irish Republican Army (IRA), Hamas and other Islamic fundamentalist groups, the Basque separatist movement (ETA), the Japanese Red Army, the German Red Army Faction, and various terrorist organizations in Latin America.

Government-Sponsored Terrorism: An Act of War
A number of countries have financed, trained, and protected terrorists. In 1986, a British court convicted a Palestinian of trying to smuggle explosives (concealed in the baggage of his pregnant girlfriend) aboard an Israeli El Al 747 aircraft. The flight from London to Tel Aviv would have been blown up over Austria. It was revealed at the trial that the material for the explosives had been brought into London in Syrian diplomatic pouches aboard the Syrian government airline; the Syrian ambassador had sanctioned or even directed the operation. In international law, government action to damage or kill in another country is an act of war. The U.S. State Department has identified several countries that finance, sponsor, and train terrorists and/or provide sanctuaries for them. The current list includes Cuba, Iran, North Korea, Sudan, and Syria.[19]

Kidnapping for Ransom
Kidnapping is another weapon used by terrorists. The victims are held for ransom, frequently very large amounts, which provides an important source of funds for the terrorists. Estimates are that there are 8,000 to 10,000 ransom and kidnapping situations per year and that kidnappers take home up to $500 million. A list of FAQs from one firm engaged in corporate risk consulting notes that large ransoms can be physically daunting—$1 million in mixed $20 and $100 bills weighs about 66 pounds.

Colombia and Peru have become dangerous places for American executives, and a long stay by a high-ranking executive in either country is risky. Brief visits are usually fairly safe because kidnappings take a while to plan, and so top executives practice what is called "commando management." They arrive in Bogotá or Lima as secretly as possible, meet for a few days with local employees, and fly off before kidnappers learn of their presence.

Paying Ransom Becomes Counterproductive The hostage business is booming. A remarkable deal concluded in the Philippines in 2000 explains why.

Libya's Colonel Muammar Qaddafi, trying to shake off that country's pariah status, bought the release of several Western hostages held by a band of Islamist bandits in the Philippines. The price was about $1 million each. The kidnappers evidently have learned two lessons: Holding a few hostages keeps the army away, and grabbing more keeps the money rolling in. Within weeks after receiving the ransom money, the Philippine kidnappers had bought new weapons and a new speedboat with which to capture more people to sell.[20] As an illustration of the global reach of terrorism, the Philippine group is thought to have links with al Qaeda. It calls itself Abu Sayyaf.[21]

A Successful Counterterrorist Operation
A terrorist organization not named above, the Tupac-Amaru Revolutionary Movement (MRTA), seized the residence of the Japanese ambassador to Peru in Lima. It was just before Christmas in 1996, and the ambassador was hosting a large party; 104 hostages were taken, including high-level business, church, diplomatic, and government officials.

The terrorists demanded the release of 400 MRTA members being held in Peruvian prisons, money, and safe passage out of Peru to Cuba. Peru refused their demands, and there was much argument about whether they should be more accommodating to the terrorists to secure the hostages' release without endangering lives or should use troops to storm the building. Those advocating the use of force pointed out that giving in to terrorists' demands encourages more terrorism, and not only in Peru; indeed, the Lima hostage story was being carried by the media worldwide. For example, part of the information presented in these paragraphs comes from an article in a Bangkok, Thailand, newspaper.

The Peruvians carried out spirited negotiations with the terrorists and tunneled under the residence, covering the digging sounds by bombarding it with loud music. The tunnel went under a ground-floor room where several of the terrorists played a game of indoor soccer each afternoon, and during a game one afternoon in April 1997, the government detonated a bomb. It caught 8 to 10 of the terrorists, and about half of them were killed.

The blast was the signal for assault troops to pour in from all sides. It was a short battle with remarkably few casualties. Although all the terrorists were killed, only two Peruvian troopers and one hostage died. Michael Radis, an expert on guerrilla groups at the Foreign Policy Research Institute in Philadelphia, says that "it will go down in the books among the great counterterrorist operations in history."

Countermeasures by Industry
Insurance to cover ransom payments, antiterrorist schools, and companies to handle negotiations with kidnappers have come into being. The insurance is called KRE (kidnap, ransom and extortion), and it can pay for the ransom, the fees of specialist negotiators, the salary of the hostage, and counseling for the victim and the family. Unfortunately, the effects of the terrorist attacks on September 11, 2001, may mean that executives are less likely to be insured because there have been big premium increases for KRE insurance.[22]

As kidnapping and extortion directed against businesses and governments have become common fund-raising and political techniques for terrorists, insurance against such acts has grown into a multimillion-dollar business. The world's largest kidnapping and extortion underwriting firm is located in London. The firm, Cassidy and Davis, underwriter for Lloyd's of London, says that it covers some 9,000 companies. Cassidy and Davis does not sit back and wait for claims to be filed. It runs antiterrorism training courses for executives, with subjects ranging from defensive driving techniques—escape tactics and battering through blockades—to crisis management. Country-by-country risk analyses are instantly available on international computer hookups.

Cassidy and Davis works closely with Control Risk, Ltd., a London-based security service company that advises firms and families in negotiations with kidnappers. Cassidy and Davis encourages its clients to use Control Risk services. Of course, it is vastly preferable to stay out of such situations. Malcolm Nance of Real World Rescue says that while KRE insurance is highly desirable, what employers really should be doing is training employees to avoid being kidnapped in the first place.

FIGURE 9.4   Before Leaving

- Your personal and legal affairs should be in order.
- Except on a need-to-know basis, tell no one about your travel plans. This is not hysterical paranoia; it's good discipline. A business executive on a fishing boat out of Miami who discusses an upcoming business trip to Central America in the presence of Cuban deckhands may find that future stay in Central America considerably longer than planned.
- Sanitize all documents and business identity. All company logos and identification should be removed from briefcases and luggage. A last name, or a fictitious name you've created, is sufficient identification on these items. If you use business cards, acronyms such as CIA for certified internal auditor should be eliminated. Whatever documents you need to conduct your business can be mailed or wired ahead so that they are waiting for you. If the trip comes up

very suddenly or there are no company offices to receive the documents, carry them in your luggage. Never carry any business identification or documents on your person. In addition to a passport with visas, a jewelry bracelet or pendant-type ID with name, Social Security number, and blood type is the only identification you would need while in transit.

- Check with your company and other companies to find someone who has conducted business in the country you are going to. Contact that person and ask questions about cultural mores and the political climate in that country. Then look in an encyclopedia or go to the library and read all you can on the subject.
- If your company doesn't already have an individual designated to coordinate and monitor foreign trips, contact the appropriate management and see that someone

knows the where, when, and how of your trip. Your family should be given that person's name and phone numbers.

- The company should have an established code for use by all its personnel who are engaged in foreign business. If not, a simple code system should be devised so that communication can be made under extraordinary circumstances (like on a video made by terrorists who have kidnapped you). The code should be provided to the company and your family.
- Have your company acquire a telephone directory for the State Department from the Government Printing Office. It can be used to contact the appropriate departmental sections for pretrip inquiries (operational intelligence). And, in the unfortunate event of a company employee kidnapping, it would be an absolute necessity in crisis management.

Source: Reprinted with permission from the October 1986 issue of *Internal Auditor,* published by the Institute of Internal Auditors, Inc.

Figures 9.4 and 9.5 are checklists for executives traveling to and in countries where they are at risk of being kidnapped. Figure 9.4 indicates what should be done before leaving the home country; Figure 9.5 discusses what to do once in the host country.

In the United States, antiterrorist surveillance detection and evasive driving training are available. They are offered by International Training, Inc. (ITI), which teaches some 5,000 students each year how to frustrate would-be assassins and kidnappers. The students are company executives and high-wealth individuals.

To enhance your chances of success with your ITI training, you can harden your automobile. O'Gara Security Associates' car-armoring business for business executives and government officials is growing rapidly. It now has manufacturing facilities in Cincinnati in the United States and in Brazil, France, Italy, Mexico, and Russia.[23]

Ethnoterrorism   In the former Yugoslavia Croats, Muslims, and Serbs perpetrated "ethnic cleansing" against each other. In Africa, the Tutsis and Hutus have done the same. Violence of tribe against tribe, race against race, religion against religion is prevalent in the world, as witnessed in Ireland and the Middle East.

Nuclear Terrorism   Failing security standards at former Soviet nuclear installations are permitting uranium to be stolen, which is then smuggled for sale to unauthorized buyers such as terrorists. NATO describes this as the greatest threat to international security since the end of the cold war.

Interpol, the international police agency, has set up a specialized group involving police forces in 24 European nations, but the smuggling continues. Interpol is treating 30 cases as

FIGURE 9.5   After Arriving

- First, slow down. Leave yourself time to think and evaluate. You're not in America. The rush and rat-race pace of hyperactivity typical of American businesspeople will only get you in trouble here.
- Take nothing for granted. Locate where elevators and stairways are so you can find them, even in the dark.
- Learn your rooms. Locate windows and doors and check to see if they are locked or if they can be locked. If you are not satisfied with your room, either change rooms or change hotels. Remember, if you change hotels, let the company and your family know.
- Do not conduct any business in your room or over the phone. The reasons are obvious.
- Whenever possible, you schedule business meetings and the locations. If this is not possible, check with your contacts and determine whether the location of scheduled meetings is safe. Remember, it's not the people you're conducting business with that present the threat (unless

you're a major corporate executive and that fact is well known in advance); the danger is in becoming an object of surveillance.
- You are most vulnerable when you're moving, particularly if that movement is predictable. Vary times and methods of movement. Whether you're using a company-provided car and driver or taxis, use different entrances and exits when you enter and leave the hotel. If you are using company or rented transportation, change cars whenever the mood strikes you. Always follow your instincts.
- Always be aware of your surroundings and alert for surveillance. If terrorists are following you and they realize you recognize that fact, you've just made yourself a higher risk for them to consider. Terrorists will not just be lurking in the streets waiting for someone they can attack. They will spend many hours and much effort to observe potential targets. Then they will select the target that's going to

cost them the least. Being alert makes you a more difficult target and raises the possibility, from the terrorist's point of view, that you have notified or will notify the authorities.
- Avoid being photographed.
- Do not respond to telephone inquiries or apparent spontaneous interest by people you meet to know more about you, however innocent or sincere either may seem. Handle it diplomatically.
- Avoid night movements, but if you must go, never walk. Not walking anywhere, anytime, is the best rule; but if it can't be avoided, be particularly sensitive to surveillance and try to stay in crowded areas.
- Read newspapers and stay in touch with your in-country contacts on a daily basis to keep informed on political climate indicators.
- Try to fit in with the native people as much as possible regarding dress and manners. This not only ingratiates you with the locals but also makes you more difficult to see.

Source: Reprinted with permission from the October 1986 issue of *Internal Auditor,* published by the Institute of Internal Auditors, Inc.

extremely serious, but this could be just the tip of the iceberg. Some cases involve as much as 250 kilograms of weapons-grade uranium; others may involve more. It takes only 7 kilograms of such uranium to make a nuclear bomb.[24]

Chemical and Biological Terrorism   In 1995, the Aum Shin Rikyo cult launched a nerve gas attack in the Tokyo subway that killed 12 people and injured 5,500, many of whom suffered severe nerve damage. A malfunction in the bomb delivery system is believed to have prevented thousands of additional casualties. Sarin was the nerve gas used in the Tokyo subway attack. Chemical information about sarin is available on the Internet, making threats possible from self-taught terrorists anywhere.

stability

Characteristic of a government that maintains itself in power and whose fiscal, monetary, and political policies are predictable and not subject to sudden, radical changes

SECURITY IN THE FUTURE

For a recent global terrorism index, see Figure 9.6. It was prepared by the World Market Research Centre.

Government Stability

Government **stability** can be approached from two directions. One can speak of either a government's simple ability to maintain itself in power, or the stability or permanence of a

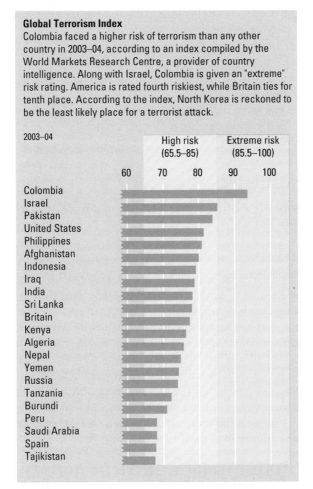

Global Terrorism Index

Colombia faced a higher risk of terrorism than any other country in 2003–04, according to an index compiled by the World Markets Research Centre, a provider of country intelligence. Along with Israel, Colombia is given an "extreme" risk rating. America is rated fourth riskiest, while Britain ties for tenth place. According to the index, North Korea is reckoned to be the least likely place for a terrorist attack.

Source: *The Economist,* August 30, 2003, p. 74. © 2003 The Economist Newspaper Group, Inc. Reprinted with permission. Further reproduction prohibited. www.economist.com.

FIGURE 9.6

Global Terrorism Index

government's policies. It is safe to generalize that business (indeed almost all agricultural, commercial, and financial activities) prospers most when there is a stable government with permanent—or at most gradually changing—policies. Instability can be caused by revolution, invasion from abroad, or racial conflict.

STABILITY AND INSTABILITY: EXAMPLES AND RESULTS

Instability in Lebanon   Here is a classic example of the impact of a change from order to chaos—from stability to **instability**—on the business and finances of a prosperous country. Until 1974, Lebanon prospered as the trading, banking, international company regional headquarters, business services (that is, accounting, legal, and financial services), transportation, and tourist center of the Middle East.

    Then civil war broke out in Lebanon. Offices, banks, stores, transportation, communications, and hospitals were destroyed. The people fled the country or fought and survived as best they could. Almost all of the previous commercial activities ended. The fighting between Israel and Lebanon in 2006 had much the same effect—tourists from other Arab countries fled to Egypt or Europe instead.

Instability in Zimbabwe   Zimbabwe was a relatively rich African country that was a net exporter of food. The Zimbabweans elected resistance leader Robert Mugabe as prime

instability
Characteristic of a government that cannot maintain itself in power or that makes sudden, unpredictable, or radical policy changes

minister. In the 1990s he decided to seize much land and equipment from big farms and to redistribute it to small holders. People close to Mugabe were able to get the best of the land, but they have failed to work it and produce food.

As a result, there is severe food shortage, and the country now depends on foreign aid. But the aid-donating countries have grown impatient with corruption in the government, army, courts, and police and are cutting back their aid. It is also generally conceded that Mugabe stole the last presidential election in 2003.

The resulting instability has caused a loss of confidence by potential foreign investors, so money, expertise, and technology are no longer coming in. Poverty and starvation are the lot of many Zimbabweans now.

Traditional Hostilities

traditional hostilities

Long-standing enmities between tribes, races, religions, ideologies, or countries

We need mention only a few of the world's **traditional hostilities** to illustrate their powerful impact on business and trade.

ARAB COUNTRIES AND ISRAEL

Israel is surrounded on three sides by Arab countries, but until the peace efforts initiated by former Egyptian President Anwar Sadat, the Arab countries would not trade or have other peaceful dealings with Israel. Indeed, some Arab countries still boycott companies that trade with Israel, and because some of the Arab countries are extremely rich Organization of Petroleum Exporting Countries (OPEC) members, the boycott can be financially painful.*

Israel then made peace with its neighbor Jordan and made progress in negotiations with the Palestine Liberation Organization (PLO). However, those ongoing and complex negotiations had not been successful as of the writing of the current edition of this book. This is a long and painful story beyond the scope of this text. Several issues remain, but the most difficult seems to be sovereignty over parts of Jerusalem.

HUTUS AND TUTSIS IN BURUNDI AND RWANDA

The majority Hutus and the Tutsis have been at each other's throats for many years. But hostilities were kept at low levels until the 1990s, first in Burundi, where they were quelled, and then in 1993 and 1994 in Rwanda. The Hutus ran the government and army in Rwanda, and at least part of the army embarked on a campaign to exterminate the Tutsis. Some million people were massacred, and a Tutsi-led army coming in from Uganda retaliated. The Tutsi army defeated the Hutus, whose subsequent retreat led to the worst refugee situation in the world's history. Over a million Hutus fled into the Congo, where they were held in camps at the border. Cholera and dysentery took thousands of lives.

Fighting among Hutus, Tutsis, and other tribal groups continued into 2005. At least some of the expense of the fighting, such as buying arms and ammunition, is met by mining and selling diamonds. Some of the part of Central Africa where the fighting is occurring is rich in diamond mines, and whichever tribe controls the mines takes out their riches. Such commandeering of diamond profits for misuse in civil wars has spread to other West African countries, jeopardizing the reputation of the diamond industry itself.

This has led to efforts by the mining company De Beers and by several countries where diamonds are cut and prepared for market to refuse to buy "dirty diamonds" that are being used to finance the fighting. That is proving difficult because rough diamonds are nearly identical and could have come from any mine.

TAMILS AND SINHALESE IN SRI LANKA

The Tamils form a substantial minority of the Sri Lankan population. An armed group calling itself the Tamil Tigers has been fighting with the Sri Lankan army.

*See Chapter 10 for a discussion of U.S. law dealing with this boycott.

>>Businesses—and People—
Are Resilient

It's business as usual in Bombay, India,
where these commuters are making their
way to work.

In mid-July 2006 bomb blasts killed 200 and wounded over
700 in Mumbai, India. Three years earlier, 60 people had
died in the same city. In fact, India has suffered a number
of terrorist attacks over the past few years.

Has this repeated terrorism slowed India down? The
evidence seems to be that any effect is small and
temporary. One key indicator is that the Bombay stock
market index went up 3 percent the next day after the
Mumbai attack. One study found that a sample of Indian
firms actually had abnormally high returns for foreign
investors who had bought their stock for the period after
terrorist attacks. Similarly, Indians themselves quickly
returned to "life as normal" after a Sikh separatist
movement in the early 1990s resulted in thousands of
deaths.

Source: Akash Dania, "Country Risk and ADR Volatility—Diversi-
fication in the Indian Subcontinent," working paper, 2005; and
Peter Wonacott and Eric Bellman, "India Is Resilient in Wake of
Deadly Blasts," *The Wall Street Journal*, July 13, 2006, p. A5.

The Tamils want a separate state, and a large Tamil population in India has given them
support. The late Indian president Rajiv Ghandi sent troops to Sri Lanka in an attempt to suppress the Tamil uprising. They failed, and the troops were withdrawn, but Ghandi reaped
Tamil hatred for his attempt. His murder—by a bomb hidden in a flower arrangement offered
to him by a woman when he was campaigning for election in the Indian Tamil state—was
blamed on the Tigers or their allies.

The Sinhalese-Tamil battles continued into 2006. As with other conflicts, business is adversely affected; businesspeople are afraid to enter combat areas even to attempt short-term
sales, and companies are even less apt to risk people on longer-term investment bases. These
areas are thus deprived not only of qualified people but also of the capital and technology that
would come with them.

International Companies

International business is not merely a passive victim of political forces. It can be a powerful
force in the world political arena. As noted in Chapter 1, about half of the world's 100 biggest
economic units are firms, not nations.

International companies (ICs) repeatedly make decisions about where to invest, where
to conduct research and development, and where to manufacture products. The country or
area in which an investment is made or a laboratory, research facility, or manufacturing plant
is located can benefit as jobs are created, new or improved technology becomes available, or
products are produced that can be exported or substituted for imports.

Of course the IC will seek the country and area where it can operate most beneficially
and profitably. It will negotiate with the national and local areas in which it is considering an
investment or location in efforts to maximize benefits such as tax breaks, infrastructure improvements, and worker training programs.

The financial size of many ICs provides them with a strong negotiating position. And an
IC's power need not rest solely on size. It can come from the possession of capital, technology, and management skills, plus the capability to deploy those resources around the world.
An IC may have the processing, productive, distributive, and marketing abilities necessary
for the successful utilization of raw materials or for the manufacture, distribution, and

marketing of certain products. Those abilities are frequently not available in developing countries. Recognition of the desirability of IC investments is growing.[25]

Country Risk Assessment

country risk assessment (CRA) An evaluation, conducted by a bank or business having an asset in or payable from a foreign country or considering a loan or an investment there, that assesses the country's economic situation and policies and its politics to determine how much risk exists of losing the asset or not being paid

Country risk assessment (CRA) involves many risks other than political risks. So we shall only introduce you to CRA here; if your interest runs deeper, you can find material in the growing literature on the topic.

The political events of recent years have caused firms to concentrate much more on CRA. Firms that had already done CRA updated and strengthened the function, and many other companies began to engage in the practice.

TYPES OF COUNTRY RISKS

Country risks are increasingly political in nature. Among them are wars, revolutions, and coups. Less dramatic, but nevertheless important for businesses, are government changes caused by election of a socialist or nationalist government, which may be hostile to private business and particularly to foreign-owned business.

The risks may be economic or financial. Countries may have persistent balance-of-payments deficits or high inflation rates. Repayment of loans may be questionable. Labor conditions may cause investors to pause. Labor productivity may be low, or labor unions may be militant.

Laws may be changed in regard to such subjects as taxes, currency convertibility, tariffs, quotas, and labor permits. The chances for a fair trial in local courts must be assessed.

Terrorism may be present. If it is, can the company protect its personnel and property?

INFORMATION CONTENT FOR CRA

The types of information a firm will need to judge country risks vary according to the nature of its business and the length of time required for the investment, loan, or other involvement to yield a satisfactory return.

Nature of Business   Consider, for example, the needs of a hotel company compared with those of heavy-equipment manufacturers, manufacturers of personal hygiene products, or mining companies. Banks have their own sets of problems and information needs. Sometimes variations exist between firms in the same industry or on a project-to-project basis. The nationality—home country—of the company may be a factor; does the host country bear a particular animus or friendly attitude toward the home country?

Length of Time Required   Export financing usually involves the shortest period of risk exposure. Typically, payments are made within 180 days—usually less—and exporters can get insurance or bank protection.

Bank loans can be short-, medium-, or long-term. However, when the business includes host country assembly, mixing, manufacture, or extraction of oil or minerals, long-term commitments are necessary.

With long-term investment or loan commitments, risk analysis entails inherent problems that cannot be resolved. Most such investment opportunities require 5, 10, or more years to pay off. But the utility of risk analyses of social, political, and economic factors decreases precipitously over longer time spans.

WHO DOES COUNTRY RISK ASSESSING?

General or specific analyses, macro or micro analyses, and political, social, and economic analyses have been conducted—perhaps under different names—for years. The Conference Board located bits and pieces of CRA being performed in various company

FIGURE 9.7   Assistance in Country Risk Assessment

WARNING: ONE OF THESE COUNTRIES COULD DAMAGE YOUR FINANCIAL HEALTH

You can now limit the risks to your business in 97 emerging and highly-indebted countries by subscribing to just one publication—the **Risk Ratings Review** from the Economist Intelligence Unit.

Every three months you receive ratings of the political, economic and financial risks for 97 emerging markets–providing early warnings of economies in trouble, and a spotlight on countries where conditions for trade, investment and lending are becoming more favourable.

The Risk Ratings Review–a one stop shop for reducing your risks around the world

The **Risk Ratings Review** offers you the highlights of the **Country Risk Service**, the Economist Intelligence Unit's international country credit rating service. It is an ideal introduction to the service and gives you access to all its ratings at a cost effective price.

Every three months the **Country Risk Service** publishes risk assessment reports for each of the 97 countries it covers. These project up to 180 economic and financial variables over a two year forecast horizon and include detailed ratings of political, economic and financial risk around the globe.

Identify deteriorating and improving economies–at a glance

The Risk Ratings Review summarises these findings, helping you to spot global trends and identify countries whose risk profile is changing. Each issue includes:

- **Comparative risk ratings tables–** listings of the current risk ratings scores produced by the Country Risk Service for all 97 countries;

- **Global and regional analysis**–what this quarter's rankings reveal about international and region-wide patterns of risk;

- **Up-to-date ratings focus**–an analytical summary of each country whose risk rating has changed in the previous quarter;

- **Watchlist**–early warnings of countries likely to deteriorate or improve over the next three-to-six months, and the factors that need to be monitored most carefully. The **Risk Ratings Review**: the first place to turn for country-by-country assessments of financial solvency, political stability and economic health.

Monitor these risks for all 97 countries:

- Overall country risk
- Political risk
- Economic structure risk
- Economic policy risk
- Liquidity risk
- Currency risk
- Sovereign debt risk
- Banking risk

Countries covered in the Risk Ratings Review

Western Europe	New Zealand	Czech Republic
Cyprus	Pakistan	Hungary
Greece	Papua New	Kazakstan
Italy	Guinea	Poland
Portugal	Philippines	Romania
Spain	Singapore	Russia
Turkey	South Korea	Slovakia
	Sri Lanka	Slovenia
Middle East &	Taiwan	Ukraine
North Africa	Thailand	Uzbekistan
Algeria	Vietnam	Yugoslavia
Bahrain		(Serbia-
Egypt	**Sub-Saharan**	Montenegro),
Iran	**Africa**	Macedonia
Iraq	Angola	
Israel	Botswana	**Latin America &**
Jordan	Cameroon	**the Caribbean**
Kuwait	Côte d'Ivoire	Argentina
Lebanon	Gabon	Bolivia
Libya	Ghana	Brazil
Morocco	Kenya	Chile
Oman	Malawi	Colombia
Qatar	Nigeria	Costa Rica
Saudi Arabia	Namibia	Cuba
Sudan	Senegal	Dominican
Syria	South Africa	Republic
Tunisia	Tanzania	Ecuador
UAE	Zambia	El Salvador
Yemen	Zimbabwe	Guatemala
		Honduras
Asia		Jamaica
Australia	**Eastern Europe**	Mexico
Bangladesh	**& the former**	Nicaragua
China	**Soviet Union**	Panama
Hong Kong	Azerbaijan	Paraguay
India	Baltic Republics:	Peru
Indonesia	Estonia, Latvia,	Trinidad &
Malaysia	Lithuania	Tobago
Myanmar	Bulgaria	Uruguay
	Croatia	Venezuela

Keep alert to worldwide patterns of risk— subscribe to the Risk Ratings Review today

Order form

How to order your **Risk Ratings Review** subscriptions. Complete your personal details, choose your payment method and post to: The Economist Intelligence Unit, NA, Incorporated. The Economist Building, 111 West 57th Street, New York, NY 10019, USA. Alternatively, you can order by telephone on: (1.212) 554 0600, by fax on (1.212) 586 11813 or by E-mail: newyork@eiu.com

Personal details

Name (Mr/Mrs/Ms/Dr) _____

Job title _____

Company name _____

Department _____

Address _____

_____

City _____ State _____

Zip + 4 _____ Country _____
Please add zip+4 to ensure fastest possible delivery

Nature of business _____

Tel _____ Fax _____

E-Mail _____

	Quantity	Price	Sub-total
Risk Ratings Review		US $795*	

Postage is included *Add applicable sales tax in Florida and Massachusetts.
In Canada add 7% GST #R 132 494 238.

Tax	
Total	

❑ Please send me details of the full **Country Risk Service.**

Payment details

❑ I enclose a check for US$ _____ payable to
  The Economist Intelligence Unit, NA, Incorporated

❑ Please charge US$_____ to my ❑ Visa ❑ Mastercard ❑ Amex ❑ Diners Club

Account Number _____

Signed _____ Expiry date _____

❑ Please proforma invoice me (Report will be sent on receipt of payment)

Billing address if different from above _____

_____

❑ I do not wish to receive promotional material from other companies

E·I·U

**The Economist
Intelligence Unit**

1ABLWA

Source: *The Economist,* December 6, 1997; p. 94. Reproduced by permission of the Economist Intelligence Unit.

departments—for example, the international division and the public affairs, finance, legal, economics, planning, and product-producing departments. Sometimes the efforts were duplicative, and the people in one department were unaware that others in the company were similarly involved.

Outside consulting and publishing firms are another source of country risk analysis. As CRA has mushroomed in perceived importance, a number of such firms have been formed or have expanded. Some of the better-known outside consulting and publishing firms for CRA include:

- Business Environment Risk Intelligence (BERI) S.A.

- Control Risks Information Services.

- Economist Intelligence Unit (EIU). Figure 9.7 on the previous page is an EIU advertisement for its *Risk Ratings Review* publication, and Figure 9.8 below is a chart showing EIU's country risk ratings.

- Euromoney.

- StratFor, Inc.

- *Harvard Business Review*'s Global Risk Navigator.

- Standard and Poor's Rating Group.

- Moody's Investor Services.[26]

Instead of or in addition to using outside consultants, a number of firms have supplemented their internal risk analysis staffs by hiring such experts as international business or political science professors or retired State Department, CIA, or military people.

| **FIGURE 9.8** | Country Risk |

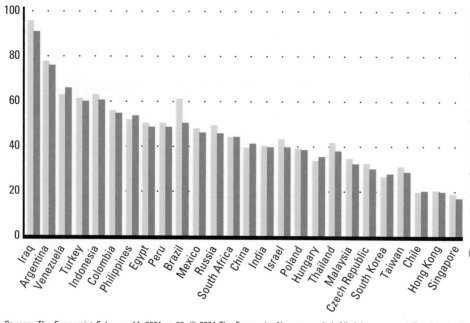

Country risk
0 = minimum risk, 100 = maximum risk

■ JAN 2003   ▨ JAN 2004

According to the Economist Intelligence Unit (a sister firm of *The Economist*), Iraq is a riskier destination for foreign investment than any of the emerging markets regularly tracked on this page. The EIU's country-risk ratings, which take account of 77 indicators of political stability and other measures of credit quality, show that Brazil has become less risky in the past year, thanks in part to better-than-expected economic policies. However Brazil's heavily indebted neighbour, Argentina, remains almost as risky as Iraq. Singapore and Hong Kong, by contrast, continue to be the safest places for foreign investment.

Identify the ideological forces that affect business and understand the terminology used in discussing them.

Ideological forces include capitalism, communism, and socialism. The chapter discusses terminology (conservative, liberal, right wing, and left wing) used to describe various political positions.

Discuss the fact that although most governments own businesses, they are privatizing them in growing numbers.

Even governments that consider themselves capitalist and conservative own some businesses. But almost all governments—with the United States lagging behind—are privatizing and getting out of business.

Explain the changing sources and reasons for terrorism and the methods and growing power of terrorists.

The former Soviet Union and Eastern European satellites no longer finance, train, and shelter terrorists, but they have been replaced by countries such as Iran and North Korea. Radical Islamic fundamentalists represent a growing threat. They are infuriated by the peace moves between Israel and its Arab neighbors. Nuclear terrorism is a new fear, as security has failed at nuclear sites in the former Soviet Union and enriched uranium is being stolen and smuggled around the world.

Explain steps that traveling international business executives should take to protect themselves from terrorists.

Figures 9.4 and 9.5 offer several suggestions. For example, Figure 9.4 suggests keeping travel plans confidential. At the same time, it is important to keep the firm aware of where business travelers are. This is true in case of natural disasters as well. One recent problem is that, with the presence of discounted tickets, some travelers stop using a travel management service. When a plot to blow up planes at London's Gatwick Airport was uncovered in August 2006, travel managers put in extra time helping traveling employees to rebook flights or avoid London entirely.

Evaluate the importance to business of government stability and policy continuity.

Business can rarely thrive in a country with an unstable government or rapid, drastic policy changes. The situation in Bolivia illustrates the problems.

Explain country risk assessment by international business.

Country risk assessment is now considered a necessity by most international businesses before they commit people, money, or technology to a foreign country. CRA involves evaluating a country's economic situation and policies as well as its politics.

Key Words

communism (p. 256)

expropriation (p. 257)

confiscation (p. 257)

capitalism (p. 257)

socialism (p. 258)

conservative (p. 258)

right wing (p. 259)

liberal (p. 259)

left wing (p. 259)

privatization (p. 260)

terrorism (p. 264)

stability (p. 268)

instability (p. 269)

traditional hostilities (p. 270)

country risk assessment (CRA) (p. 272)

Questions

1. a. What is ideology?

    b. Why is it important to international business?

2. a. What is the capitalist, free enterprise ideal?

    b. What is the actual situation in capitalist countries?

3. What impact can terrorism have on business?

4. Why does business fear sudden changes in government policies?

5. How can traditional hostilities affect business?

6. How can ICs use their strengths to influence government policies?

7. Is country risk assessment (CRA) an exact science? Explain.

8. a. In terms of exposure to political risk (for example, expropriation), which of the following businesses would you consider the most and least vulnerable? Explain.

banks	cosmetics
mines	manufactures
oil fields	manufactures of
oil refineries	personal hygiene
heavy-equipment	products
manufacturers	automobile
hotels	manufactures

    b. Are the most vulnerable businesses high-profile or low-profile? What are some ways to change the profile of a company in a foreign country?

9. Discuss the lessons CRA analysts should have learned from the world debt crises.

10. Islamic fundamentalism is a growing terrorist threat. Why?

Research Task

 globalEDGE.msu.edu globalEDGE

Use the globalEDGE site (http://globalEDGE.msu.edu) to complete the following exercises:

1. The *Enterprise Surveys* conducted by the World Bank examine the investment climate in a wide range of countries undergoing social transformation. You have been asked to develop a report that analyzes corruption and black-market practices in different countries. A coworker recently indicated that one proxy for this is the level of informality that firms use in reporting sales amounts for tax purposes. Identify the top three transition economies in which reported sales are most similar to actual sales amounts. Which three countries have the lowest reporting of sales amounts for tax purposes?

2. Financial stability is an important component of economic development. In fact, your colleagues indicate that the amount of capital a country exports can be an indication of its financial stability. As such, you have since discovered a "Global Financial Stability" report to assist in your assessment of international financial markets. Which three countries are the largest exporters of capital? Which three countries import the largest amount of capital?

You are the chief executive officer of a company that the government has just denationalized by selling the company's stock to the company's employees. In the past, any major decision about company policy required approval by a government agency, which was time-consuming. Wages and salaries had been established by reference to civil service "equivalents,"

and incentive payments were unheard of. Maintenance of the plant and equipment was lax, breakdowns were frequent and expensive, and utility expenses were high.

You want the newly privatized company to be a success. Suggest some programs that you would institute to improve its chances of success.

10 Legal Forces

The Peace Palace in The Hague, the Netherlands, is home to the International Court of Justice.

The role which the Court [International Court of Justice] plays, through the power of justice and international law . . . is widely recognized and evidenced by the number of cases on the Court's docket. . . . It is not uncommon that these cases deal with issues concerning international peace and security. In performing its dispute resolution function, the Court, which embodies the principle of equality of all before the law, acts as a guardian of international law, and assures the maintenance of a coherent international legal order.

—Judge Shi Jiuyong, former president of the International Court of Justice, to the General Assembly of the United Nations, October 31, 2003

When a Local Issue Can Have International Ramifications

The world has become increasingly interrelated, and the law reflects this trend. What may appear to be a local issue may take on national and often worldwide importance. In June 1996, the Commonwealth of Massachusetts decided to take a position against Myanmar (formerly Burma) for repressive actions the Myanmar government had taken. The Massachusetts legislature passed an act barring Massachusetts state entities from buying goods or services from businesses doing business with Myanmar. This included businesses having operations or franchises in Myanmar or providing any goods or services to the government of that country. Massachusetts exempted business entities providing medical supplies or international telecommunication goods or services or reporting the news. Three months after Massachusetts passed that law, the U.S. Congress passed the Foreign Operations, Export Financing, and Related Programs Appropriations Act, which banned aid to the Myanmar government with the exception of funds for certain forms of humanitarian assistance, funds used to fight drugs, and funds used to promote human rights and democracy. Congress also directed the U.S. president to develop a strategy to bring democracy to Myanmar and improve human rights practices there. The president was further empowered to waive any sanction if it was determined that the application of that sanction would be contrary to U.S. national security interests.

The National Foreign Trade Council, a private trade group, brought suit in the federal court in Massachusetts against Massachusetts state officials, seeking to prevent them from administering the state law. The federal district court agreed with the National Foreign Trade Council and blocked enforcement of the Massachusetts law. This decision was upheld by the federal court of appeals. The matter finally reached the U.S. Supreme Court, which agreed that enforcement of the Massachusetts law should be prevented. The Supreme Court found that the Massachusetts law was unconstitutional because Congress had intended to give the president flexibility and effective authority over economic sanctions against Myanmar. The Supreme Court held that it was "simply implausible" that Congress would have gone to such lengths if it had intended to permit state statutes to "blunt the consequences of discretionary Presidential action." On the basis of the Constitution's Supremacy Clause, the Supreme Court struck down the Massachusetts law because it conflicted with federal law. Massachusetts attempted to do something that was under the exclusive province of the federal government. Under the Constitution, the president and Congress have the power to set foreign policy. State laws that violate constitutional mandates will be struck down. ■

Source: U.S. Supreme Court, *Crosby v. National Foreign Trade Council*, No. 99–474, 530 U.S. 363 (2000).

CONCEPT PREVIEWS

After reading this chapter, you should be able to:

discuss the complexity of the legal forces that confront international business

recognize the importance of foreign law

explain contract devices and institutions that assist in interpreting or enforcing international contracts

recognize the need and methods to protect your intellectual property

recognize that many taxes have purposes other than to raise revenue

discuss enforcement of antitrust laws

explain the risk of product liability legal actions, which can result in imprisonment for employees or fines for them and the company

discuss some of the U.S. laws that affect international business operations

It is important for participants in international business to understand the enormous breadth and depth of laws in various jurisdictions worldwide. Unlike some other forces around which businesses must operate, legal forces cannot be ignored. Anyone studying legal forces affecting international business soon realizes that the immensity and variety of these forces complicate the task of understanding the laws. Laws too numerous to count enacted by governments at all levels on virtually every subject affect international business.

While on the one hand businesses must be aware of laws in order to comply, on the other hand businesses also expect that laws will assist them when necessary. An issue of great concern to businesses that operate internationally is the stability of a host government and its legal system. When a business enters a country, the business needs to know whether the country's host government will be able to protect the foreign business with an adequate legal system. The legal system must be able to enforce contracts and protect the basic rights of employees. In examining international legal forces, one must keep in mind that a stable government and an adequate court system are necessary to ensure a welcome environment for foreign businesses.

This chapter examines international law and looks at specific national laws that influence international business.

International Legal Forces

RULE OF LAW

When examining countries around the world, it is important to determine whether the country is governed by the rule of law. It is desirable that a country base its functions on the rule of law, instead of rule by political dictatorship or rule by a powerful elite. Basing a country's legal system on the rule of law makes encouraging foreign investment easier because foreign businesses will know that their interests will be protected. Following the rule of law also makes ensuring protection of human rights of local people easier.

In China, for example, Hong Kong has an advantage over Shanghai in attracting foreign investors because Hong Kong has a tradition of law adopted from British colonial days while Shanghai courts tend to favor Chinese litigants. "It is absolutely impossible for a foreign party to win a case against a Chinese party in a Chinese court," says Cao Siyuan, a Chinese commentator. This disparity in legal systems between the two cities is seen to give Hong Kong an advantage as a location for foreign firms.[1]

public international law
Legal relations between governments

private international law
Laws governing transactions of individuals and companies that cross international borders

treaties
Agreements between countries, which may be bilateral (between two countries) or multilateral (involving more than two countries); also called *conventions, covenants, compacts,* or *protocols*

WHAT IS INTERNATIONAL LAW?

Each sovereign nation is responsible for creating and enforcing laws within its jurisdiction. Once laws cross international borders, the matter of enforcement is complicated by the necessity of agreement between nations. The same concepts that apply to domestic laws do not always apply to international law.

What is called *international law* can be divided into public international law and private international law. **Public international law** includes legal relations between governments, including laws concerning diplomatic relations between nations and all matters involving the rights and obligations of sovereign nations. **Private international law** includes laws governing the transactions of individuals and companies crossing international borders. For example, private international law would cover matters involved in a contract between businesses in two different countries.

SOURCES OF INTERNATIONAL LAW

International law comes from several sources, the most important of which are bilateral and multilateral **treaties** between nations. Treaties are agreements between countries and may also be called *conventions, covenants, compacts,* or *protocols*. International organizations such as the United Nations have provided a forum for creation of many treaties. The UN has sponsored many conferences that have led to agreements among nations on a large range of matters, including postal delivery and use of driver's licenses in other countries. In addition, the International Court of Justice, one of the organs of the UN, creates international law when it decides disputes brought before it by member-nations.

Another source of international law is customary international law, which consists of international rules derived from customs and usage over centuries. An example of customary international law is the prohibition against genocide (there is also a specific international statute against genocide).

EXTRATERRITORIALITY

Many countries, including the United States and member-countries of the European Union, often attempt to enforce their laws outside their borders. This is referred to as **extraterritorial application of laws.** This attempt to enforce laws abroad is done not by force but through traditional legal means. For example, the U.S. government imposes taxes on U.S. citizens and U.S. permanent residents regardless of either the source of income or the residence of the taxpayer. If a U.S. citizen is living in Madrid and receives all of her income from Spanish sources, the United States will still expect the taxpayer to comply with U.S. tax laws. Likewise, when U.S. companies operate in other countries with U.S.-based personnel, the U.S. companies must comply with U.S. laws, including employment laws. Of course, these companies must also comply with the laws of the host country. Extraterritorial application of U.S. laws has been extended in many other areas including antitrust and environmental laws.

extraterritorial application of laws A country's attempt to apply its laws to foreigners or nonresidents and to acts and activities that take place outside its borders

International Dispute Settlement

LITIGATION

Litigation can be extremely complicated and expensive. In addition to involving the trial itself, most lawsuits entail lengthy pretrial activities, including a process called *discovery*. Discovery is the means of finding facts relevant to the litigation that are known to the other side, including obtaining documents in the other side's possession. Some discovery methods can seem quite intrusive since courts grant parties great latitude in obtaining information in the possession of the opposing side. Discovery is one reason many people outside the United States dislike litigation in the United States.

Litigation involving disputes that cross international lines can arise in both state and federal courts. Special rules exist for obtaining discovery in other countries, and they vary from country to country. Some countries freely allow U.S. litigators to obtain discovery. Others have restrictions. For example, if discovery is to occur in Switzerland even in a case involving only U.S. parties, permission must be obtained from Swiss authorities. Failure to obtain permission may result in penalties, including possible criminal sanctions.

One of the major problems usually involved in cross-border litigation is the question of which jurisdiction's law should apply and in which location the litigation should occur. Each country (and each state in the United States) has elaborate laws for determining which law should apply and where litigation should occur. As with any other disputed matter, the final decision on these issues rests with the court. Occasionally, courts in two countries (or two states) will attempt to resolve the same dispute. Again, this is resolved by reference to the particular choice of law provisions and can be quite complicated. For this reason, it is prudent to include in contracts a choice-of-law clause and a choice-of-forum clause in the event of a dispute. A *choice-of-law clause* is a paragraph in a contract that specifies which law will govern in the event of a dispute. For example, if there is a U.S. seller and an Australian buyer, the parties may agree that U.S. law would govern any dispute. A *choice-of-forum clause* is a paragraph in a contract that specifies where the dispute will be settled. For example, the parties in the above example may agree to have the dispute decided in California state courts in Los Angeles County, California.

PERFORMANCE OF CONTRACTS

Whenever businesses enter into agreements with other businesses, the possibility exists that there may be problems getting the other side to perform its obligations. No worldwide court has the power to enforce its decrees. The worldwide courts that do exist, such as the UN's

International Court of Justice (see Chapter 4), rely on the voluntary compliance of the parties before it. Each nation in the world is a sovereign nation and has its own rules for recognizing decrees and judgments from other nations.

When contracting parties are residents of a single country, the laws of that country govern contract performance and any disputes that arise between the parties. That country's courts have jurisdiction over the parties, and the courts' judgments are enforced in accordance with the country's procedures. When residents of two or more countries contract, those relatively easy solutions to dispute resolution are not available. Enforcing contracts that cross international lines is often quite complicated.

United Nations Solutions

When contract disputes arise between parties from two or more countries, which country's law is applicable? Many countries, including the United States, have ratified the UN Convention on Contracts for the International Sale of Goods (CISG) to solve such problems.

The CISG established uniform legal rules to govern the formation of international sales contracts and the rights and obligations of the buyer and seller. The CISG applies automatically to all contracts for the sale of goods between traders from different countries that have ratified the CISG. This automatic application will take place unless the parties to the contract expressly exclude—opt out of—the CISG.[2]

Private Solutions—Arbitration

As mentioned before, many people outside the United States dislike the U.S. court system. Likewise, many U.S. businesspeople dislike or at least fear litigation in other countries. For these reasons, international businesspeople often agree that any disputes will be resolved by arbitration, rather than by going to court in any country. **Arbitration** is a dispute resolution mechanism that is an alternative to litigation. Arbitration is usually quicker, less expensive, and more private than litigation, and it is usually binding on all parties. At least 30 organizations now administer international arbitrations, the best known of which is probably the International Court of Arbitration of the International Chamber of Commerce in Paris. In addition, London and New York are centers of arbitration. Some organizations specialize in the type of arbitration cases they will consider. For example, the World Intellectual Property Organization Arbitration and Mediation Center handles technological, entertainment, and intellectual property disputes. The International Centre for the Settlement of Investment Disputes specializes, logically, in investment disputes.

In summary, people and businesses may prefer arbitration for several reasons. They may be suspicious of foreign courts. Arbitration is generally faster than law courts, where cases are usually backlogged. Arbitration procedures are usually more informal than court procedures. Arbitration may be confidential, avoiding the perhaps unwelcome publicity accompanying an open court case. And generally it may be less expensive.

Enforcement of Foreign Arbitration Awards

Courts in countries around the world usually enforce arbitration awards, but occasionally enforcement can pose problems. One solution is the UN Convention on the Recognition and Enforcement of Foreign Arbitral Awards. The United States and many UN member-countries have ratified this convention. It binds ratifying countries to compel arbitration, when the parties have so agreed in their contract, and to enforce the resulting awards.

Other organizations are working toward a worldwide business law. The Incoterms of the International Chamber of Commerce and its Uniform Rules and Practice on Documentary Credits now receive almost universal acceptance. The UN Commission on International Trade Law and the International Institute for the Unification of Private Law are doing much useful work. The Hague-Vishy Rules on Bills of Lading sponsored by the International Law Association have been adopted by a number of countries.[3]

DESPITE LEGAL UNCERTAINTIES, INTERNATIONAL BUSINESS GROWS

Despite legal uncertainties of doing business in other countries, the trend indicates that international business activities will increase in the future. For this reason, international

---

arbitration
A process, agreed to by parties to a dispute in lieu of going to court, by which a neutral person or body makes a binding decision

Every business transaction involves a contract. Developing, writing, and executing contracts in international business transactions is very complex because there are typically:

- Two sets of expectations as to what the contract represents.
- Two languages.
- Two currencies.
- Two legal systems.
- Two political systems backing the two legal systems.
- At least two legal views and opinions on how each of the issues must be dealt with.

Earning a law degree with a specialization in international law can place you in a high corporate position dealing directly with the legal issues companies face daily in global commerce. You will also be in an extremely small group of legal professionals. The International Legal Committee of the American Bar Association's Section on International Law and Practice determined in a 1997 study that only 37 percent of law school students took any class in foreign law. A review of the current literature indicates that this has not changed to any significant degree. Yet, according to a study presented in the *American Journal of Comparative Law,* well over 10 percent of the revenue generated by the 100 largest American law firms comes from foreign clients. If the study's data are indicative of a trend, there could be a growing need for attorneys with expertise in international law. If you apply the law of supply and demand to the international law profession, you can only imagine what the rewards might be . . . and you'll also see the world on someone else's expense account. A growing area of corporate concern impacting international law is dealing with patent, copyright, and brand infringement that occurs when counterfeit products are sold in global markets.

World Fact: Counterfeiting of products and brands is a major legal problem, and it is growing. The World Trade Organization estimates that 7 percent of annual global trade involves the sale of counterfeit products. This translates to a $456 billion industry worldwide.

Culture Cue: The laws of many countries are steeped in the country's religious heritage. This means that breaking a law in such a country may also be seen as an act of huge disrespect for a population's religious beliefs. World religions such as Islam, Hinduism, and Buddhism clearly define accepted behavior and serve as a basis for the laws in countries where these religions are dominant. Become sensitive to and respectful of the religious influence in the countries with which you trade.

World Wide Resources:

www.eisil.org

www.smu.edu/ilra/til.htm

businesspeople must be aware of the legal environment in which they find themselves. Legal systems vary significantly from country to country, and it is important to understand the differences. The assumptions one makes on the basis of the U.S. legal system may not apply in other countries.

Intellectual Property: Patents, Trademarks, Trade Names, Copyrights, and Trade Secrets

A *patent* is a government grant giving the inventor of a product or process the exclusive right to manufacture, exploit, use, and sell that invention or process. *Trademarks* and *trade names* are designs and names, often officially registered, by which merchants or manufacturers designate and differentiate their products. *Copyrights* are exclusive legal rights of authors, composers, creators of software, playwrights, artists, and publishers to publish and dispose of their works. *Trade secrets* are any information that a business wishes to hold confidential. All are referred to as **intellectual property.**

Trade secrets can be of great value, but each country deals with and protects them in its own fashion. The duration of protection differs, as do the products that may or may not be protected. Some countries permit the production process to be protected but not the product. International companies must study and comply with the laws of each country where they may want to manufacture, create, or sell products.

intellectual property
Patents, trademarks, trade names, copyrights, and trade secrets, all of which result from the exercise of someone's intellect

PATENTS

In the field of patents, the International Convention for the Protection of Industrial Property, sometimes referred to as the Paris Union, provides some degree of standardization. Some 168 countries adhere to this convention—even North Korea is a contracting party. Most Latin American nations and the United States are members of the Inter-American Convention, which provides protection similar to that afforded by the Paris Union.

A major step toward the harmonization of patent treatment is the European Patent Organization (EPO). Through EPO, an applicant for a patent need file only one application in English, French, or German to be granted patent protection in all 24 member-countries. Before the EPO, an applicant had to file in each country in the language of that country.

The World Intellectual Property Organization (WIPO) is a UN agency that administers 16 international intellectual property treaties. WIPO advises developing countries on such matters as running patent offices and drafting intellectual property legislation. Interest in intellectual property matters has been growing in developing countries.[4] There is also another organization called TRIPS, "trade-related aspects of intellectual property," that operates under the aegis of the World Trade Organization.

At the UN, representatives of developing nations have been mounting attacks on the exclusivity and length of patent protection. They want to shorten the protection periods from the current 15 to 20 years down to 5 years or even 30 months. But companies in industrialized countries are resisting the changes. They point out that the only incentives they have to spend the huge amounts required to develop new technology are periods of patent protection long enough to recoup their costs and make profits.

An added problem is the growth of so called "patent trolls," who can be likened to modern-day highway robbers cashing in on the problem. These are lawyers and investors who buy patents that were mistakenly granted, mostly to failed companies. In one case a patent troll claimed that a patent bought for about $50,000 was infringed by Intel's microprocessors and threatened to sue Intel for $7 billlion in damages.

TRADEMARKS

Trademark protection varies from country to country, as does its duration, which may be from 10 to 20 years. Such protection is covered by the Madrid Agreement of 1891 for most of the world, though there is also the General American Convention for Trademark and Commercial Protection for the Western Hemisphere. In addition, protection may be provided on a bilateral basis in friendship, commerce, and navigation treaties.

An important step in harmonizing the rules on trademarks was taken in 1988 when regulations for a European Union trademark were drafted. A single European Trademark Office known as the Office of Harmonization in the Internal Market (OHIM) is responsible for the recognition and protection of proprietary marks in all EU countries, including trademarks belonging to companies based in non-EU member-countries.

Many companies such as Coca-Cola market their products throughout the world and understand the importance of protecting trademarks worldwide.

TRADE NAMES

Trade names are protected in all countries that adhere to the International Convention for the Protection of Industrial Property, which was mentioned earlier in connection with patents. Goods bearing illegal trademarks or trade names or false statements about their origin are subject to seizure upon importation into these countries.

COPYRIGHTS

Copyrights are protected under the Berne Convention of 1886, which is adhered to by 77 countries, and the Universal Copyright Convention of 1954, which has been adopted by some 92 countries. The United States did not ratify the Berne Convention until 1988. At that point, it was driven to do so by the need for greater protection against pirating of computer software. We discuss software piracy in Chapter 14.

mini MNE

>>A New Understanding of Patent Theory

Economist Petra Moser's recent work reveals that economic theory might be wrong on the purpose of patents. Until recently, the common wisdom among economists was that patents existed to stimulate innovation. Her historical research uncovered an interesting detail: "Many of the best innovators in what was the high technology of the day [19th century Denmark, the Netherlands, and Switzerland] came from some of the smallest countries in Europe, and these nations did not have patent laws." Further, at that time less than one in five inventors actually relied on patents, rather than secrecy.

Source: Teresa Riordan, "Patents," *New York Times*, September 19, 2003, p. C10. Copyright 2003 The New York Times Co. Reprinted with permission See also web.mit.edu/moser/www/Research .html (June 21, 2006).

TRADE SECRETS

Laws in most nations protect trade secrets. Employers everywhere use employee secrecy agreements, which are rigorously enforced in some countries.

Common Law or Civil Law?

Historically, there has been a clear distinction between the common law, which developed in England and spread to the English colonies, and civil law, which originated on the continent of Europe. Courts made common law as they decided individual cases; kings, princes, or legislatures issuing decrees or passing bills made civil law. Judges in a common law jurisdiction have the power to *interpret* the law, while judges in a civil law jurisdiction have the power only to *apply* the law. The difference can be quite significant. Judges in common law jurisdictions have more power to expand rules to fit particular cases. The civil law, by contrast, is more rigid in its application. A judge in a civil law jurisdiction is bound by the words in the code. This strict adherence to the language of the code, though, makes the civil law system much more predictable than the common law system. As time has passed, legislatures and government agencies in the United States have made more and more laws and regulations. The courts in turn have interpreted these laws and regulations as parties have argued about what they mean.

EUROPEAN PRACTICE

Europe has a history of thousands of years of tyranny, recently evolving to democracy. Such a long history gives people in Europe greater reason to fear their governments, compared with people in the United States. Before a new law is presented to the legislature (which, unlike legislatures in the United States, is always controlled by the same political party that controls the executive branch), consensus is achieved among most of the people, businesses, and government agencies that will be affected. In contrast to U.S. practices, European legislation is rarely amended, and regulations are rarely revised. Courts are not as often asked to give their interpretations, and if they are, the decisions are rarely appealed. Once a consensus has been reached, it is considered very bad form to open the subject again, and those who do may find themselves left out of the consultations the next time around.

The EU is a grouping of sovereign nations. As explained in Chapter 4, even though all EU member-countries have yielded a certain amount of sovereignty to the EU, the EU still has limited power to implement comprehensive legislation throughout the EU. That power is increasing, though. It is important to remember that the EU establishes laws in a manner very different than does the United States. The main policy-setting institution in the EU remains the Council of Ministers, which is controlled by the national governments. The EU may some day resemble the United States in terms of lawmaking, but not yet.

UNITED STATES PRACTICE

In contrast to European custom, people and businesses in the United States have a weaker tradition of obeying governments and have had very little fear of them. U.S. citizens are much more likely than Europeans to challenge laws in the courts, in the streets, or by disobedience. Legislation in the United States is a product of an ongoing adversarial proceeding, not of consensus; law is written by one independent branch of government for execution by a second and interpretation by a third. Different political parties or people with conflicting philosophies frequently control the three different branches of government.

In the United States, laws and regulations are constantly being amended or revised by the legislatures and the agencies. Courts interpret laws in ways that are sometimes surprising; the courts may strike laws down as being unconstitutional. Legislative power is vested by the U.S. Constitution in Congress, which has the authority to write laws for the whole country, subject to veto by the president.

DIFFERENCES BETWEEN THE UNITED STATES AND ENGLAND

As this chapter shows, it is important to be aware of differences between laws in different parts of the world. Even countries such as the United States and the United Kingdom, which share many legal traditions, including the common law, have significant differences in the modern practice of law. Here are five differences between the legal systems in the United States and England:

1. *England has a split legal profession with barristers and solicitors.* In the United States, there is no distinction in the legal profession. Once admitted to practice, a lawyer in the United States can represent clients in court. In England, by contrast, clients hire solicitors to advise them on legal matters. If an appearance is necessary in court, though, in most cases the solicitor must hire a barrister. Thus, in England, each party in a court case usually must retain at least two lawyers: the solicitor and the barrister.

2. *England has no jury for civil court actions.* Pursuant to the Constitution of the United States, parties in civil actions in the United States who are seeking monetary damages generally are entitled to have their cases heard by a jury. This is not the case in England. Parties in civil cases in England can have their cases heard by a jury only in certain specific cases, which are very unusual. Criminal defendants in both countries are entitled to a jury.

3. *Payment to lawyers differs.* It is common in the United States for a lawyer to take a case on a contingency fee basis, which means the lawyer will recover a fee only when the client receives money through settlement or a trial. Usually, the fee is a percentage, such as one-third, of the amount recovered. England also has contingency fees but this arrangement is less common.

4. *Award of costs to the winner in civil litigation differs.* In litigation in the United States, attorneys' fees are awarded only in very limited cases, when a contract or statute provides for an award of those fees. In England, the losing party must pay most (usually 60 to 70 percent) of the costs, including the attorneys' fees of the winning party.

5. *Pretrial discovery differs.* There is a significant difference between the United States and England in pretrial discovery. Pretrial discovery is the opportunity for the parties to learn facts known by or to obtain documents in the possession of the other party. Even though some U.S. courts are limiting discovery, compared to England the United States allows discovery with few restrictions. In the United States, parties are able to examine witnesses before trial at what is called a *deposition*. Discovery in the United States is much more far-reaching than it is in England. In England, parties generally are entitled to receive a list of witnesses with a brief explanation of the expected testimony.

Standardizing Laws around the World

Many attempts have been made to standardize laws among various countries. To international business, the advantage of standardization is that business flows much better when there is a uniform set of rules. Worldwide harmonization is progressing slowly, though, in most areas. For now, businesspeople must confront the reality of differing standards.

In the tax area, there are tax conventions, or treaties, among nations. Each country tries to make each such treaty as similar as possible to the others, and so patterns and common provisions may be found among them.

In antitrust, the EU member-nations operate under Articles 81 and 82 of the Treaty of Rome, which are similar to the antitrust laws in the United States. In an unusual bilateral move, Germany and the United States signed an executive agreement on antitrust cooperation. This was the first attempt by national governments to cooperate on antitrust matters concerning firms operating in both countries. There have been proposals to create worldwide agreements on antitrust.

Some agreement exists in the field of international commercial arbitration, including enforcement of arbitral awards. If the disputed contract involves investment from one country into another, it can be submitted for arbitration by the International Center for Settlement of Investment Disputes at the World Bank. Chapter 4 covered a number of other UN-related organizations and other worldwide associations. Each of them has some harmonizing or standardizing effect on laws in the member-countries. The same can be said of the regional international organizations dealt with in Chapter 4.

The UN Convention on the International Sale of Goods (CISG) provides uniformity in international sales agreements for those parties who elect to use it.

There have been attempts to make accounting and bankruptcy standards uniform worldwide. A Model Law on Cross-Border Insolvencies from UNCITRAL served as the basis for Chapter 15 of the U.S. Bankruptcy Code, for example.

Two standardizing organizations are the International Organization for Standardization (ISO) and the International Electrotechnical Commission (IEC). The IEC promotes standardization of measurement, materials, and equipment in almost every sphere of electrotechnology. The ISO recommends standards in other fields of technology. Most government and private purchasing around the world demands products that meet IEC or ISO specifications. All IEC and ISO measurements are in the metric system, so there is a cost of conversion for U.S. firms exporting products without metric measurements. The number of other nations which haven't gone metric is very small.

Some Specific National Legal Forces

TAXATION

Purposes   The primary purpose of certain taxes is not necessarily to raise revenue for the government, which may surprise those who have not studied taxation. Some of the many **nonrevenue tax purposes** are to redistribute income from one group to another in a country, to discourage consumption of such products as alcohol and tobacco, to encourage consumption of domestic rather than imported goods, to discourage investment abroad, to achieve equality of taxes paid by taxpayers earning comparable amounts, and to grant reciprocity to resident foreigners. Even this short list of purposes suggests the economic and political pressures influencing government officials responsible for tax legislation and collection. Powerful groups in every country push for tax policies that favor their interests. These groups and interests differ from country to country and frequently conflict, accounting in part for the complexity of the tax practices that affect multinationals.

nonrevenue tax purposes
Purposes such as redistributing income, discouraging consumption of products such as tobacco and alcohol, and encouraging purchase of domestic rather than imported products

National Differences of Approach   Among the many nations of the world, there are numerous differences in tax systems.

Tax Levels   Tax levels range from relatively high in some Western European countries to zero in tax havens, where income of defined types incurs no tax liability. Some countries impose capital gains taxes,* and some do not. Those countries that have them tax at different levels. The capital gains tax is controversial. Those favoring a higher capital gains tax argue that the tax rate should remain high because any reduction would reward the rich. Those who oppose a higher capital gains tax argue that the capital gains tax locks in money that would be better invested elsewhere. (A capital gains tax is imposed every time assets are sold. Thus, a high capital gains tax tends to cause money to stay put.) Some maintain that the United States should levy no capital gains tax,[5] following the example of several other countries.

Tax Types   Although the United States levies a relatively high capital gains tax, it relies for most of its revenue on the income tax. As indicated by the name, this tax is levied on the income of individuals and businesses. Income taxes are common in industrialized countries. Figure 10.1 shows tax rates on wage income in the member-countries of the Organization for Economic Cooperation and Development (OECD). Among the OECD members, the United States has a fairly low income tax rate. A generality, subject to exceptions, is that the higher the income, the higher the income tax. In the 1970s and 1980s, much discontent developed among Americans over the impact of the income tax and other taxes. Possibly as a result, support for a value-added tax (VAT) has been growing in the U.S. Congress and Treasury.

Many suggest that the United States should use a VAT similar to the VATs in effect in the EU, where are main sources of revenue. (A VAT is similar to a sales tax in that it is a tax based on the value of goods and services.) A simplified example of how a VAT works on a loaf of bread can be seen in Table 10.1. We will assume a VAT of 10 percent. The wheat farmer sells to the miller for 30 cents the part of the wheat that eventually becomes the loaf. So far, the farmer has added 30 cents of value by planting, growing, and harvesting the wheat. The farmer sets aside 3 cents (10 percent of 30 cents) to pay the VAT. The miller makes loaves of bread out of the wheat and sells them to the wholesaler for 50 cents each. Thus, the miller has added

FIGURE 10.1   Highest Statutory Personal Income Tax Rates in OECD Countries, 2003 (central government)

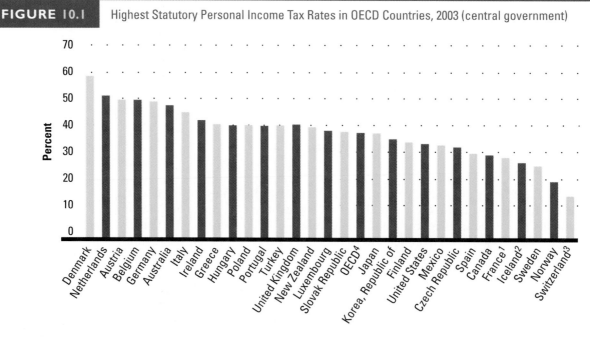

[1] Estimated rate for married taxpayers. Estimated top rate for single taxpayers is 35.7%.

[2] 2001 Rate from OECD Tax Database.

[3] The top marginal rate is 13% for spouses living together and 13.2% for other taxpayers. For incomes over CHF 788,400 and CHF 664,300, respectively, the tax rate is 11.5%.

[4] Midpoint tax rate used for countries with multiple tax rates.

Source: PricewaterhouseCoopers, *Individual Taxes 2003–2004: Worldwide Summaries* (2004).

*A capital gain is realized when an asset is sold for an amount greater than its cost.

| TABLE 10.1 | Value-Added Tax on a Loaf of Bread |

Stage of Production	Selling Price	Value Added	VAT at 10%	Cumulative VAT
Farmer	30¢	30¢	3¢	3¢
Miller	50¢	20¢	2¢	5¢
Wholesaler	70¢	20¢	2¢	7¢
Retailer	$1.10	40¢	4¢	11¢

20 cents of value (50 cents minus 30 cents) and must pay a VAT of 2 cents (10 percent of 20 cents). The wholesaler now advertises and distributes the loaves, selling them to retailers for 70 cents. The wholesaler has added 20 cents of value and owes 2 cents of VAT. Finally, the retailer adds 40 cents through its display, advertising, and sales efforts and owes 4 cents of VAT. The loaf of bread is sold for $1.10 retail and has borne a cumulative VAT of 11 cents, 10 percent of $1.10.

The VAT has proponents and opponents. The proponents say the VAT is relatively simple and can be raised or lowered easily to collect the amount of income desired by the government. The opponents argue that it is a consumption-type tax that bears most heavily on the poor.

In addition, some U.S. VAT proponents argue that the present situation, in which the major European countries rely heavily on the value-added tax while the United States does not, is unfair to the United States because of World Trade Organization (WTO)* regulations, which permit a rebate of VAT when a product is exported from a country but does not permit a rebate of income taxes. The rebates enable exporting countries to offer lower-priced, more competitive goods. VAT proponents want the United States to institute the VAT and lower income taxes to take advantage of these WTO rules.

Another tax on international companies that has been controversial for several decades is the unitary tax imposed by several U.S. states. Most states have since repealed such tax laws under threats of retaliation by foreign governments. International tax treaties are almost universally built on the "arm's length" or "water's edge" principle: Taxable profits for a subsidiary in a country will be assessed as though the subsidiary were conducting its business independently. The unitary tax system, by contrast, calculates the worldwide income of an international company and then assesses the tax due in proportion to the percentage of the group's property, payroll, and sales in the state.

Complexity of Tax Laws and Regulations   From country to country, the complexity of tax systems differs. By anyone's standards, the United States has a very complex tax code. The U.S. Department of the Treasury's Internal Revenue Service administrates the tax code. The tax law is part of U.S. federal law and includes thousands of pages. In addition, the Department of the Treasury also writes thousands of pages of tax *regulations* explaining or expanding the tax laws.

Many provisions of the IRC refer to other provisions of the IRC, making interpretation difficult. In addition, Congress frequently changes provisions of the IRC. Congress typically debates major tax legislation in every session. Once Congress approves provisions of the IRC, it often leaves it up to the Department of the Treasury to issue regulations. The Department of the Treasury has large numbers of staff members who write these regulations. As with the IRC, the regulations issued by the Department of the Treasury run thousands of pages. In addition to the IRC and the regulations, there are numerous court decisions interpreting the tax laws.

Who Obeys the Law?   Compliance with tax laws and their enforcement vary widely. Some countries, such as Germany and the United States, are strict. Others are relatively lax. Costa Rica estimates a tax evasion rate of 70%. The Italian practice allows a taxpayer to declare a very low taxable income to which the government counters with a very high amount. They then negotiate a compromise figure. It has been said that in Italy 83 percent of the people report an income of less than 4,000 Euros (about $5,110). In addition to paying

*See Chapter 4 for a discussion of the World Trade Organization.

corporate income tax, businesses in Italy may find themselves paying a chamber of commerce tax, a license tax, a trade association tax, a stamp tax, the local tax, a rental-agreement tax, a tax for registering with the office that collects the VAT, a tax for health inspection, a tax for the accounting books, a tax for the welfare system, a tax for water, and even a tax for an awning outside. By one estimate, businesses are expected to pay 300 separate taxes in Italy.[6]

Other Differences   There are many other differences in taxation, too numerous to list fully here. They include tax incentives to invest in certain areas, exemptions, costs, depreciation allowances, foreign tax credits, timing, and double corporate taxation (taxation of the profits of a corporation and then of dividends paid to its stockholders). U.S. tax laws give U.S. taxpayers relief from possible double taxation by more than one jurisdiction. For example, if a U.S. taxpayer is living and working in Sweden, that taxpayer is subject to tax laws both of the United States and of Sweden. Without some form of tax relief, that taxpayer could end up paying more than 100 percent of her or his income in taxes. This tax relief comes in the form of **foreign tax credits** and provisions of various tax treaties. U.S. tax laws allow U.S. taxpayers to take a credit against their U.S. taxes for taxes paid to another country. This relief is especially important because U.S. citizens and U.S. permanent residents (green card holders) are taxed on their worldwide income regardless of the source of the income and regardless of the residence of the taxpayer.

Tax Treaties or Conventions
Because of the innumerable differences between nations' tax practices, many of them have signed **tax treaties** or tax conventions with each other. Typically, tax treaties define such things as income, source, residency, and what constitutes taxable activities in each country. They address how much each country can tax the income earned by a national of one country living or working in the other. All these treaties contain provisions for the exchange of information between the tax authorities of the two countries. The United States has tax treaties with over 50 countries. Table 10.2 lists the countries with which the United States currently has tax treaties.

foreign tax credits
Allowances by which U.S. taxpayers who reside and pay income taxes in another country can credit those taxes against U.S. income tax

tax treaties
Treaties between countries that bind the governments to share information about taxpayers and cooperate in tax law enforcement; often called *tax conventions*

TABLE 10.2	U.S. Network of Tax Treaties

The United States Has Tax Treaties with the Following Countries

Argentina	India	Philippines
Australia	Indonesia	Poland
Austria	Ireland	Portugal
Barbados	Israel	Romania
Belgium	Italy	Russian Federation
Canada	Jamaica	Singapore
Chile	Japan	Slovak Republic
China, People's Republic of	Kazakstan	South Africa
Cyprus	Korea, Republic of	Spain
Czech Republic	Latvia	Sweden
Denmark	Lithuania	Switzerland
Egypt	Luxembourg	Thailand
Estonia	Mexico	Trinidad and Tobago
Finland	Morocco	Tunisia
France	Netherlands	Turkey
Germany	New Zealand	Ukraine
Greece	Norway	United Kingdom
Hungary	Pakistan	Uruguay
Iceland	Panama	Venezuela

Note: Some small states and territories have been omitted for purposes of brevity.
Source: "U.S. Tax Treaties," www.undefed.com/ForTaxProfs/Treaaties (November 9, 2006).

The presence or absence of a tax treaty is often a factor in international business and investment location decisions. Tax treaties make business operations much more predictable because they facilitate international flows of goods, capital, services, and technology. Countries, however, sign treaties for different motives. Most OECD countries regard treaties as providing a standard framework for all countries in allocating taxing jurisdiction. Tax treaties often determine which country will tax which income. In emerging-market countries, tax treaties may be viewed by foreign investors as a key sign of stability.[7]

The Disappearing Taxpayer

Electronic commerce—combined with the growing ease with which firms and people can shift their operations and residences from one country to another—make it easier for people to leave countries where taxes are high or to avoid taxes altogether by doing their business on the Internet, where it is often difficult to trace transactions.

Not all firms, workers, and products are equally mobile. Entrepreneurs, scientists, tennis players, and film stars may be able to uproot themselves in search of lower taxes, but the average worker is still unlikely to become a tax refugee. Thus, governments may have to cut taxes on the most mobile factors of production, notably skilled workers, while taxes on less mobile unskilled workers may rise. Other tax law changes being considered are to shift the tax base from income toward consumption and property.[8]

Taxing Americans Who Work Abroad

Observing a **national tax jurisdiction** rather than a **territorial tax jurisdiction,** the United States is almost alone among countries in taxing citizens according to nationality rather than on the basis of where they live and work. As was mentioned before, U.S. citizens and permanent residents (green card holders) are taxed on their worldwide income regardless of its source and regardless of the residence of the taxpayer. As a result, U.S. citizens and permanent residents living or working in another country must pay taxes to that country and to the United States. In addition to facing higher tax payments, these people are burdened by the time and expense of completing two sets of complicated tax returns. In 1981, the sections of the IRC dealing with this subject were again amended. Although the burden of completing two tax returns was not lifted, the new law gave relief, starting in 1982, in the amount of U.S. taxes to be paid by exempting the first $85,000 of earned income.* This exemption has been changed several times and is currently $82,400, with changes due to inflation after 2007. However, the 2006 version of the law reduces the amount of housing costs that the expat may deduct, so for most the total tax bill will increase.

national tax jurisdiction
A tax system for expatriate citizens of a country whereby the country taxes them on the basis of nationality even though they live and work abroad

territorial tax jurisdiction
A tax system in which expatriate citizens who neither live nor work in the country—and therefore receive none of the services for which taxes pay—are exempt from the country's taxes

Effect of U.S. Taxes

Suppose a U.S.-based multinational wants to open a new factory, store, warehouse, or office building in the United States. That expansion would create new jobs in the United States, along with all the benefits that flow from new jobs. But when the company's executives look at U.S. tax laws, they may hesitate because of the section dealing with allocation of interest expense. When a U.S. company with subsidiaries in many countries borrows money to finance a U.S. business, the interest is treated as if it were paid in part to finance foreign operations. That results in a partial loss of the interest tax deduction and thus a higher after-tax interest cost.

Foreign companies—including foreign-based multinationals—have no such requirement and can deduct 100 percent of interest on borrowings to finance a U.S. operation. Therefore, they have lower after-tax interest costs and, to that extent, can be more competitive in the United States than many U.S. companies.[9] Certainly, the tax code complicates the lives of U.S. businesspeople operating in other countries.

*Earned income includes salaries, bonuses, and commissions. Interest, dividend, and royalty income is called *unearned income.*

ANTITRUST LAWS

Antitrust laws are intended to prevent inappropriately large concentrations of economic power, such as monopolies. Actions brought to enforce antitrust laws usually involve government actions brought against business, but also may involve business actions against other businesses.

U.S. Laws and Attitudes Are Different—but the Differences Are Narrowing

antitrust laws
Laws to prevent price fixing, market sharing, and business monopolies

competition policy
The European Union equivalent of antitrust laws

The U.S. **antitrust laws** are strict and vigorously enforced. The U.S. Department of Justice is charged with enforcing U.S. antitrust laws. Other countries, as well as the European Union, are becoming more active in the antitrust field. In the EU, these laws sometimes are referred to as **competition policy.** The EU Commission is responsible for enforcing EU competition policy. In addition to enforcing competition policy against businesses, the EU Commission also has the power to force EU member-governments to dismantle state monopolies that block progress toward an open, communitywide market.[10]

A number of important differences in antitrust laws, regulations, and practices exist between the United States, other nations, and the EU. One difference is the per se concept of the U.S. law. Under the U.S. laws, certain activities, such as price fixing, are said to be illegal per se. This means that they are illegal even though no injury or damage results from them. The EU Treaty of Rome articles dealing with restrictive trade practices do not contain the per se illegality concept of U.S. antitrust law. For example, a cartel that allows consumers a fair share of the benefits is legally acceptable in the EU. Also, the treaty is not violated by market dominance—only by misuse of that dominance to damage competitors or consumers.

The U.S. focus on antitrust legislation is concerned with the impact of the business deal on the consumer, while the EU is more concerned about the industry's competitive structure and thus pays attention to rivals' objections.[11] In Japan, antitrust legislation was introduced by the United States during its occupation of Japan after World War II. This legislation, the Japanese Anti-Monopoly Law, was modeled on U.S. antitrust law and did not harmonize well with the existing cooperative *zaibatsu* (conglomerates) the Japanese government had established. In fact, the Japanese approach to a rational development of the economy regarded antitrust measures as an impediment. However, with increasing foreign presence, especially in the United States and in Europe, given the EU competition law, Japanese companies have incorporated antitrust thinking into their strategies. Since the Japanese culture so values cooperation, this is a challenge, especially when it comes to cartels.[12]

Worldwide Application of U.S. Antitrust Laws

The U.S. government often attempts to enforce its antitrust laws extraterritorially. For example, in 1979, a grand jury in Washington, D.C., indicted three foreign-owned ocean shipping groups on charges of fixing prices without getting approval from the U.S. Federal Maritime Commission. The other governments, European and Japanese, protested bitterly, arguing (1) that shipping is international by definition, so the United States has no right to act unilaterally, and (2) that the alleged offenses were both legal and ethical practices outside the United States.[13] The U.S. Supreme Court on several occasions has permitted overseas application of U.S. antitrust laws.[14]

EU Extraterritorial Application of Its Competition Policy

The EU Commission is charged with enforcement of EU competition policy. Like the U.S. Department of Justice, the EU Commission has increasingly sought enforcement of its competition policy abroad when there is an effect on commerce within the EU. For example, the EU Commission had to give its approval before merger talks between America Online and Time Warner could proceed. Before its approval was given to the merger, AOL–Time Warner had to agree to sever all ties with the German media group Bertelsmann. The EU has also viewed Microsoft as anticompetitive and in 2006 fined the firm €280 million ($358.3 million).[15]

Criminal Cases

U.S. antitrust laws contain both civil and criminal penalties.* A decision by the U.S. federal court of appeals held that criminal antitrust laws apply to foreign

*Civil liability calls for payment of money damages. Criminal liability may result in fines or imprisonment.

companies even if the conspiracy took place outside the United States. While earlier decisions had permitted U.S. antitrust laws to be used against foreign companies in civil cases, this decision, which was against Nippon Paper Industries, set the precedent that antitrust laws could be used also to get criminal convictions.[16]

Japan's "Toothless Tiger"

Japan's Fair Trade Commission (FTC), whose responsibility is to enforce antitrust laws, has been nicknamed the "toothless tiger." It is viewed as one of the weakest bodies in Japanese government, easily bullied by the powerful ministries of finance and international trade and industry (MITI), which have vested interests in ensuring that Japan's traditional, collaborative ways of doing business prevail. Most of the FTC's targets are small, foreign, or weak; when it has investigated powerful industries such as domestic cars, car parts, and construction, it has punished them at worst with "recommendations." The recommendations are usually accepted by the targeted company. If not, hearings follow, and then directives.

A major difference between American and Japanese trust busting is that around 90 percent of U.S. complaints are initiated by private parties, while in Japan a private antitrust action can be brought only if the FTC has investigated the case first. Because of Japan's limited discovery laws, the only way the FTC can obtain information on a firm is to raid it. As a result, the FTC won't make a move unless it is sure the laws are being broken. It is almost impossible to be sure of that without information. Given all this, it is easy to understand why the FTC is considered to be a toothless tiger.[17]

Proposal for Global Antitrust Approval

It is often difficult for international businesses to comply with the variety of antitrust laws worldwide. A good example is Microsoft. In the 1990s, the U.S. government and several U.S. states brought antitrust actions against Microsoft. The actions continued well into the early 21st century, with Japan's FTC issuing a recommendation to Microsoft in July 2004. The EU also brought an action against Microsoft. The Microsoft case is a good example of how one company can get bogged down with antitrust laws in multiple jurisdictions. In light of the numerous countries that impose antitrust rules worldwide, many argue that greater worldwide cooperation in antitrust enforcement is needed. Some think that the WTO is the proper avenue for such worldwide cooperation. Others believe an international antitrust authority would be appropriate. Reaching such an agreement would be difficult because of the differing interests involved.[18] The U.S. government has proposed a world organization for the clearance of antitrust issues. If approved, the organization would probably take the form of a clearinghouse for merger filings. Calls for such an entity are increasing because of the multinational nature of most large mergers.[19]

BANKRUPTCY

In a similar vein to proposed antitrust cooperation, the World Bank has also called for a global bankruptcy agreement in light of the large number of multinational companies that have problems with creditors worldwide. It is thought that a worldwide bankruptcy agreement would make it easier for creditors and others involved in bankruptcy proceedings. Now creditors must comply with rules in various countries before receiving relief from companies in bankruptcy.[20]

TARIFFS, QUOTAS, AND OTHER TRADE OBSTACLES

Although we introduced trade obstacles in Chapter 3, they are also legal forces. For that reason, we mention them again here. Every country has laws on these subjects. The stated purpose of a tariff is to raise revenue for the government, but it may serve the additional objective of keeping certain goods out of a country. Quotas limit the number or amount of imports.

There are many other forms of protection or obstacles to trade in national laws. Some are health or packaging requirements. Others deal with language, such as the mandatory use

TABLE 10.3   Worldwide Examples of Tariffs and Other Trade Obstacles

Product	Destination	Barrier
U.S. apples	Japan	Orchard inspection, buffer zones
U.S. beverages and syrups	Mexico	20% duty on non–cane sugar sweeteners
Integrated computer circuits	China	Tax rebates for locally produced circuits give them unfair price advantage against imports
Japanese carbon steel	United States	Charges of dumping
U.S. grains	EU	EU moratorium on biotech products (genetically modified grains)
U.S. computer technology	Brazil	30% tariffs
U.S. poultry	Russia	Import restrictions (quotas)

Source: Office of U.S. Trade Representative, Monitoring and Enforcement Press Releases, www.ustra.gov (August 1, 2004).

of French on labels and in advertising, manuals, warranties, and so forth, for goods sold in France, including Web sites located on servers physically in France. Table 10.3 is a sampling of trade barriers.

In many countries, U.S. and EU exports may encounter weak patent or trademark protection, high tariffs, quarantine periods, and a variety of other obstacles.

The United States has many options in dealing with trade obstacles abroad. It can impose retaliatory barriers on products from countries imposing barriers against U.S. goods. It sometimes uses tariffs and quotas. It also uses a form of quota called by some "voluntary" restraint agreements (VRAs) and by others "voluntary" export restraints (VERs). Voluntary is in quote marks because these barriers are imposed by the U.S. government on the exporting countries. The inevitable result is higher costs to American consumers, as exporters send only the higher-priced top of their lines and importers charge more for scarcer products.[21] The United States is not the only country that imposes VRAs and VERs on its trading partners—far from it. Japan, Canada, the EU countries, and many others require that countries exporting to them "voluntarily" limit the number or value of goods exported.

Other countries have found other ways to deal with trade barriers. The French came up with a novel protectionist device. Japanese videotape recorders were one of the French imports causing a large balance-of-payments deficit with Japan. The recorders normally entered France through the major port of Le Havre, which had a large detachment of customs officers to process imports. Then the French government issued a decree requiring that all the recorders enter France through the inland city of Poitiers, which had a tiny customs post. The result was long delays that reduced the number of recorders entering France. Japan then "voluntarily" agreed to limit the number of recorders it exported to France.

TORTS

Torts are injuries inflicted on other people, either intentionally or negligently. Tort cases in the United States often result in awards of very large sums of money. Other countries have tort laws that restrict the amount of money that can be obtained in tort actions.

product liability
Standard that holds a company and its officers and directors liable and possibly subject to fines or imprisonment when their product causes death, injury, or damage

Product Liability—Civil and Criminal   One important area of torts, especially in the international arena, is **product liability.** Product liability laws hold a company and its officers and directors liable and possibly subject to fines or imprisonment when its product causes death, injury, or damage. Such liability for faulty or dangerous products was a growth area for the U.S. legal profession beginning in the 1960s. Liability insurance premiums soared, and there were concerns that smaller, weaker manufacturing companies could not survive. In the 1980s that boom spread to Europe and elsewhere. In a Conference Board survey of more than 500 chief executives, more than one-fifth believed strict U.S. product liability laws had caused their companies to lose business to foreign competitors.[22] But as foreign firms buy or build U.S. plants, they are being hit by the same liability and insurance problems long faced by U.S. companies.

Manufacturers of products are often held to a standard of **strict liability,** which holds the designer/manufacturer liable for damages caused by a product without the need for a plaintiff to prove negligence in the product's design or manufacture. There are several reasons to believe that the impact of strict liability on product designers and manufacturers in Europe and Japan will not be as heavy or severe as it is in the United States. The EU allows companies to use "state-of-the-art" or "developmental risks" defenses, which allow the designer/manufacturer to show that at the time of design or manufacture, the most modern, latest-known technology was used. They also are permitted to cap damages. By comparison, damages awarded by American juries have been in the hundreds of millions of dollars.

strict liability
Standard that holds the designer/manufacturer liable for damages caused by a product without the need for a plaintiff to prove negligence in the product's design or manufacture

Other differences in legal procedures in the United States compared with those in Europe and Japan will limit or prevent product liability awards by European and Japanese courts. As mentioned, in the United States, but not elsewhere, lawyers take many cases on a contingency fee basis whereby the lawyer charges the plaintiff no fee to begin representation and action in a product liability case. The lawyer is paid only when the defendant settles or loses in a trial, but then the fee is relatively large, running between one-third and one-half of the settlement or award. In addition, outside the United States, when the defendant wins a lawsuit, the plaintiff is often called upon to pay all the defendant's legal fees and other costs caused by the plaintiff's action.[23]

In the United States, product liability cases are heard by juries that can award plaintiffs actual damages plus punitive damages. As the name indicates, punitive damages have the purpose of punishing the defendant, and if the plaintiff has been seriously injured or the jury's sympathy can be otherwise aroused, it may award millions of dollars to "teach the defendant a lesson." Outside the United States, judges, not juries, hear product liability cases. Judges are less prone to emotional reactions than juries are, and even if the judge is sympathetic toward a plaintiff, punitive damages are not awarded by non-U.S. courts.[24]

Punitive Damage Effects on Medicine

Multimillion-dollar punitive damage awards by U.S. courts have caused foreign firms to keep their products out of the United States. For instance, Axminster Electronics, a British firm whose devices help prevent crib death by monitoring a baby's breathing, does not sell in the United States because it cannot secure product liability insurance. Within the United States, every drug company knows that if a person uses a drug and subsequently gets ill, there is a chance that a jury somewhere in the United States may impose liability on the manufacturer and order it to pay damages.[25] Merck's recent judgments in the case of Vioxx is an example.

Buyer Beware in Japan

The Japanese law on product liability requires that the plaintiff prove design or manufacturing negligence, which is difficult with complex, high-tech devices. The plaintiffs' difficulties are exacerbated by the unique Japanese legal procedures to provide discovery, the process by which plaintiffs can seek defendants' documents relevant to their cases. Discovery is available to plaintiffs in U.S. courts but is limited in Japan.[26]

MISCELLANEOUS LAWS

Individuals working abroad must be alert to avoid falling afoul of local laws and police, army, or government officials. Some examples make the point.

A Plessey employee, a British subject, is serving a life sentence in Libya for "jeopardizing the revolution by giving information to a foreign company." Two Australians were executed in Malaysia for possession of 15 grams or more of hard drugs. Saudi Arabia and other Muslim countries strictly enforce sanctions against importing or drinking alcohol and wearing revealing clothing. Foreigners in Japan who walk out of their homes without their alien registration cards *(gaikakujin Toroku)* can be arrested, as happened to one man while he was carrying out the garbage. In Thailand, people can be jailed for mutilating paper money or for

Americans Accused in Film Piracy in China

In summer 2004, two American men were arrested in China and charged with intellectual piracy of motion picture DVDs. The men, Randolph Hobson Guthrie III (37) and Cody Abram Thrush (34), were taken into custody on July 1. Under Chinese law, a suspect can be held for 30 days without a formal arrest, and their arrests were announced July 29. They were tried and convicted. Both served prison sentences and paid fines. Upon their extradition to the United States, they were arrested and face trials here.

Their arrest was a result of cooperation between American and Chinese investigators and grew out of a federal operation in Gulfport, Mississippi, that spread to Houston, Washington, Beijing, and Shanghai. Chinese and American authorities seized more than 210,000 counterfeit movie DVDs and close to $1,000 in cash. In addition, authorities destroyed three warehouses used to store DVDs. The Chinese news agency Xinhua reported that the Americans had sold 1 million of the DVDs worldwide.

A *New York Times* report described a Web-based profile of Guthrie, which mentioned his MBA from Columbia University and his move to China in 1995. The site also described his claim to $25,000 monthly income from a DVD sales Web site.

The theft of intellectual property is a major problem for American filmmakers, estimated to cost them $3.5 billion a year. The Chinese government says it is committed to eliminating piracy. Vice Premier Wu Yi promised exactly this when she visited Washington. The irony of this public enforcement case involving two American businessmen whose alleged actions contribute to Chinese intellectual piracy is a good example of globalization.

Source: Michael Janofsky, "Two Americans Held in China on Charges of Film Piracy," *New York Times*, July 31, 2004, p. A12; and "The Cornerstone Report: Two Americans Convicted in China for DVD Piracy," www.ice .gov/pi/cornerstone/reports/CornerstoneReports_122805_Web3.htm (September 1, 2006).

damaging coins that bear the picture or image of the royal prince, as was one foreigner who stopped a rolling coin with his foot. Jaywalking, littering, and spitting are taken seriously in Singapore, and caning is permitted for some offenses. In China, unmarried couples—foreigners included—face a possible 10 days in jail if they stay overnight in the same room. In Greece, travelers who exceed their credit card limits may be sentenced to prison for as long as 12 years.

A Philadelphia law firm, International Legal Defense Counsel (ILDC), has made a reputation dealing with countries where American embassies and consulates are of little legal help and where prison conditions are so squalid that survival is the first concern. One of its cases involved a Virginia photographer named Conan Owen, who agreed to transport a package of cocaine from Colombia to Spain, where he was arrested and slapped with a stiff prison sentence. The U.S. attorney general personally interceded with no success, and Owen languished in prison for nearly two years. Then ILDC obtained his freedom through the use of a bilateral prisoner transfer treaty that permits American inmates in foreign jails to do their time in a facility back home. Once in the United States, Owen was quickly freed.

U.S. Laws That Affect the International Business of U.S. Firms

Although every law relating to business arguably has some effect on international activities, some laws warrant special notice. We will look briefly at several U.S. laws. Although many U.S. laws affect activities of international firms, there has not been a successful effort to coordinate them. Some are even at cross-purposes, and some diminish the ability of U.S. businesses to compete with foreign companies.

FEDERAL EMPLOYMENT LAWS

Numerous federal laws attempt in some manner to prevent unwarranted discrimination in employment. Even though there is no single federal law prohibiting illegal discrimination in employment, Title VII of the federal Civil Rights Act of 1964 is largely recognized as the focal point of federal employment discrimination law. Title VII prohibits discrimination in employment based on race, color, religion, sex, or national origin. Other major pieces of federal employment discrimination law include the Age Discrimination in Employment Act of 1967 (ADEA) and the Americans with Disabilities Act of 1990 (ADA).

Congress specifically intended these federal employment laws to apply extraterritorially. Title VII, ADEA, and ADA generally cover U.S. citizens working for U.S. companies abroad. For example, if a woman who is a U.S. citizen is denied a promotion because of her gender while working in Germany for an American company, she may bring an action in the United States under Title VII against her employer for unlawful discrimination in employment. Congress enacted one exception to the extraterritorial application of federal employment laws, though, and that is an exception for local foreign laws. It is not a violation of U.S. law for an employer to engage in conduct that ordinarily would constitute illegal behavior if such behavior is required by local law in the country where the conduct takes place. For example, certain countries prohibit women from engaging in certain activities, such as driving. If a U.S. company is required to discriminate in order to comply with the laws in such a nation, the U.S. company will be protected from suits in the United States for discrimination. Exceptions to Title VII's prohibitions, however, are extremely unusual.

FOREIGN CORRUPT PRACTICES ACT

During the 1970s, revelations of **questionable or dubious payments** by American companies to foreign officials rocked governments in the Netherlands and Japan. Congress considered corporate bribery "bad business" and "unnecessary." As a result, in 1977, Congress passed the **Foreign Corrupt Practices Act (FCPA)** and the president signed it into law.

Uncertainties   There are a number of uncertainties about terms used in the FCPA. An interesting one involves "grease." According to the FCPA's drafters, the act does not outlaw *grease,* facilitating payments made solely to expedite nondiscretionary official actions. Such actions as customs clearance and telephone calls have been cited. There is no clear distinction between supposedly legal grease payments and illegal bribes. To confuse matters further, U.S. Justice Department officials have suggested that they may prosecute some grease payments anyway under earlier antibribery laws written to get at corruption in the United States.

Other doubts raised by the FCPA concern the accounting standards it requires for compliance. That matter is connected to questions about how far management must go to learn whether any employees, subsidiaries, or agents may have violated the act; even if management were unaware of an illegal payment, it could be in violation if it "had reason to know" that some portion of a payment abroad might be used as a bribe.* [27]

The FCPA makes it unlawful to bribe foreign government officials to obtain or retain business. Facilitating payments for routine government actions such as visa issuance, import approvals, and the processing of government papers are permissible under the FCPA.

Critics at the time believed that the FCPA would harm American companies' competitiveness abroad because it would demand of American companies a higher standard of behavior than was common in the competitive environment. Congress decided that the potential economic damage to exports would be minimal and that the only companies that would be hurt would be those whose only means of competing was through the payment of bribes. The United States actively lobbied the international community to introduce similar legislation,

questionable or dubious payments
Bribes paid to government officials by companies seeking purchase contracts from those governments

Foreign Corrupt Practices Act (FCPA)
U.S. law against making payments to foreign government officials for special treatment

*Other words with similar connotations are *dash, squeeze, mordida, piston, cumshaw,* and *baksheesh.*

which it did in 1997, with the OECD Convention on Bribery. Thirty-five countries have signed the convention. There is also a UN Convention against Corruption, whose signing began in December 2003.

You may wonder if because of U.S. laws on bribery, U.S. businesses may be at a disadvantage in international competition. What seems to have happened on the bribery front is interesting. The FCPA, along with the OECD convention and the UN initiative, have brought a discussion of bribery and transparency out into the open. Such discussions were further stimulated by the Asian financial crisis of 1997, one of whose causes was widely attributed to lack of transparency in financial dealings. Having an international reputation for transparency and being perceived as "aboveboard" have become increasingly important for global companies. There appears to be a strong move for company values that support integrity in the belief that integrity is better for business than are corrupt activities.

In addition, the organization Transparency International (www.transparency.org) publishes a bribe payers index. Its data for 2006 are based on a survey of 11,232 respondents from 125 countries. The position of U.S. businesses, 10th on the list, suggests that businesspeople in the 9 nations that rank higher on the index than does the United States have found ways to conduct more transparent international business. These countries, such as Switzerland, Sweden, Canada, the Netherlands, Belgium, the United Kingdom and Germany, are headquarters for many major, competitive international companies (see Table 10.4).

ACCOUNTING LAW

Investor confidence in the integrity of financial reporting and corporate governance has been shaken by U.S. financial scandals including Enron, WorldCom, and Tyco. This crisis of confidence has substantially damaged the economic prospects of numerous companies, employees, retirees, customers, suppliers, and other stakeholders.

In the face of these concerns, the U.S. Congress passed the Sarbanes-Oxley Act in July 2002. It brings major changes to the regulation of corporate governance and financial practice. Sarbanes-Oxley addresses issues of auditor independence and attorney conduct. The act generally applies to any company, including non-U.S. companies, that has securities registered or is

TABLE 10.4	Bribe Payers Index							
	Rank				**Rank**			
Country	**2002**	**1999**	**2006**	**Country**	**2002**	**1999**	**2006**	
Australia	1	2	3	France	12	13	15	
Sweden	2	1	2	Japan	13	14	11	
Switzerland	2	5	1	United States	13	9	10	
Austria	4	4	4	Malaysia	15	15	25	
Canada	5	2	5	Hong Kong	15	n.a.	18	
Netherlands	6	6	8	Italy	17	16	20	
Belgium	6	8	9	South Korea	18	18	21	
United Kingdom	8	7	6	Taiwan	19	17	26	
Germany	9	9	7	China	20	19	29	
Singapore	9	11	12	Russia	21	n.a.	28	
Spain	11	12	13					

Source: Transparency International, "Bribe Payers Index 2002," www.transparency.org/cpi/2002/bpi2002.en.html; www. transparency.org/news_room/in_focus/bpi_2006.

required to file reports under the Securities Exchange Act of 1934. The provisions of the act affect the operation of public companies in several dimensions, including corporate governance, financial disclosure, officer and director activities and responsibilities, and auditor independence. The act also creates and regulates the Public Company Accounting Oversight Board to oversee public company audits and establishes conflict-of-interest rules for securities analysts. Most notably, the act bars a company's outside auditors from consulting and advising roles with the company; it requires CEO and CFO sign-off on financial statements; it requires the reporting of any off–balance sheet transactions; and it requires the independence of security analysts.

U.S. accounting practice is guided by the Securities and Exchange Commission (SEC) and the Financial Accounting Standards Board (FASB) and follows standards known as Generally Accepted Accounting Principles (GAAP), while many other countries, including those in the EU, follow standards issued by the International Accounting Standards Board (IAS) and the International Financial Reporting Standards (IFRS) issued by the European Federation of Accountants. These various standards differ in many aspects. The reporting requirements of Sarbanes-Oxley may lead to some harmonization of accounting standards across international markets, yet the trend outside the United States appears to be toward IAS.

Summary

Discuss the complexity of the legal forces that confront international business.

International business is affected by many thousands of laws and regulations issued by states, nations, and international organizations. Some are at cross-purposes, and some diminish the ability of firms to compete with foreign companies.

Recognize the importance of foreign law.

Miscellaneous laws in host countries can trip up foreign businesspeople or tourists. Charges can range from not carrying an alien registration card to narcotics possession.

Explain contract devices and institutions that assist in interpreting or enforcing international contracts.

International contracts should specify which country's law and courts should apply when disputes arise. The UN's CISG and the EU's Rome Convention have established rules for solving contract disputes. Arbitration is an increasingly popular solution.

Recognize the need and methods to protect your intellectual property.

Patents, trademarks, trade names, copyrights, and trade secrets are referred to as intellectual properties. Pirating of those properties is common and is expensive for their owners. The UN's World Intellectual Property Organization (WIPO) was created to administer international property treaties, as was TRIPS, a WTO agency with a similar purpose.

Recognize that many taxes have purposes other than to raise revenue.

Certain taxes have purposes other than to raise revenues. For example, some aim to redistribute income, discourage consumption of certain products, encourage use of domestic goods, or discourage investment abroad. In addition, taxes differ from country to country. Tax treaties, or conventions, between countries can affect decisions on investment and location.

Discuss enforcement of antitrust laws.

The United States and the European Union enforce antitrust laws extraterritorially. This is a concern for companies operating in many countries because of the complexity of dealing with so many laws in different jurisdictions.

Explain the risk of product liability legal actions, which can result in imprisonment for employees or fines for them and the company.

Product liability refers to the civil or criminal liability of the designer or manufacturer of a product for injury or damages it causes. In several ways, product liability is treated differently in the U.S. legal system than it is in other countries. For example, only in the United States does one find lawyers' contingency fees, jury trials of these cases, and punitive damages. Although the principle of strict liability has been adopted in Europe, defendants are permitted to use state-of-the-art defenses and countries can put a cap on damages. Product liability is virtually unknown in Japan.

Discuss some of the U.S. laws that affect international business operations.

Many U.S. laws affect international business operations, both of U.S. and of foreign companies. The United States applies federal employment laws to any U.S. company operating anywhere. This extraterritoriality means that U.S. companies operating in foreign countries are required to follow U.S. employment law as it applies to U.S. nationals. The Foreign Corrupt Practices Act and the Sarbanes-Oxley Act also apply to U.S. businesses in their foreign operations and to foreign businesses that conduct operations in the United States.

Key Words

public international law (p. 280)

private international law (p. 280)

treaties (p. 280)

extraterritorial application of laws (p. 281)

arbitration (p. 282)

intellectual property (p. 283)

nonrevenue tax purposes (p. 287)

foreign tax credits (p. 290)

tax treaties (p. 290)

national tax jurisdiction (p. 291)

territorial tax jurisdiction (p. 291)

antitrust laws (p. 292)

competition policy (p. 292)

product liability (p. 294)

strict liability (p. 295)

questionable or dubious payments (p. 297)

Foreign Corrupt Practices Act (FCPA) (p. 297)

Questions

1. What is the significance of determining whether a country follows the rule of law?

2. How does international law differ from national law? What are the sources of international law?

3. What objections do other countries have to extraterritorial application by the United States of its laws?

4. What are advantages of submitting contract disputes to arbitration instead of to litigation in courts?

5. Why do companies concern themselves with intellectual property issues?

6. Often taxes are used for reasons other than raising revenues. What are the other purposes for which taxes are used?

7. Why do some people feel that a VAT should replace some or all of the U.S. income tax?

8. Are tariffs the only type of obstacle to international trade? If not, name some others.

9. Can product liability be criminal? If so, in what sorts of situations would product liability become criminal behavior?

10. a. What are the differences in practices between the legal systems in the United States and England?
    b. What are the reasons for those differences?

Research Task

 globalEDGE.msu.edu globalEDGE

Use the globalEDGE site (http://globalEDGE.msu.edu) to complete the following exercises:

1. Prior to internationalizing your corporate legal representation firm, management is hoping to better understand which countries efficiently enforce legal contracts. The *Doing Business Indicators* follow statistics on many countries and regions of the world to provide users with an indication of the economic and legal conditions worldwide. Locate the three measures used by the resource to measure how different countries are enforcing contracts. Which countries rank as the five most and least efficient legal systems for each measure? Do any countries appear multiple times across these rankings? If so, list the countries

that would be most and least appealing for your firm to enter. If not, are there specific regions that are represented in your analysis? From this information, develop a brief report for management that outlines your recommendation for an internationalization strategy.

2. The *Corruption Perceptions Index (CPI)* is a comparative assessment of a country's integrity performance. Provide a description of this index and its ranking. Identify the five countries with the lowest and the five with the highest CPI scores according to this index. Do you see any trends between CPI scores and the level of economic and social development of a country?

A California-based company is expanding very well and has just made its first export sale. All of its sales and procurement contracts up to now have contained a clause providing that if any disputes arise under the contract, they will be settled under California law and that any litigation will be in California courts.

The new foreign customer, who is Italian, objects to these all-California solutions. She says she is buying and paying for the products, so the California company should compromise and allow Italian law and courts to govern and handle any disputes.

You are the CEO of the California company, and you very much want this order. You are pleased with the service your law firm has given, but you know it has no international experience.

What are the various forms of dispute resolution available to your California company? What are the advantages and disadvantages of each for your company?

11

Financial Forces

Money makes the world go round
The world go round, the world go round
Money makes the world go round
It makes the world go round
A mark, a yen, a buck or a pound
A buck or a pound, a buck or a pound
Is all that makes the world go round
That clinking, clanking sound
Can make the world go round

—*Kander and Ebb, "Money, Money, Money," Cabaret*

U.S. Consumers Credited with Saving the World from Recession: Heavy Lifting May Be Over

The U.S. consumers have been like Atlas recently, carrying the world on their shoulders. Larry Summers, former Treasury secretary under President Clinton and former president of Harvard University, likens the world economy to a plane flying on one engine, the U.S. economy.[a] The spending of Americans has been relentless, compared to that of Europeans and Asians, despite serious stock market dips, the Katrina natural disaster, terrorism, and war. A wide range of economists suggests that this spending has been an important factor in averting a deep world recession. This Atlas-like role has come at a cost to the United States: a huge current account deficit in the balance of payments. It looks, though, as if economic growth is evening out at last. Japan, the EU, and many emerging economies seem poised for increased growth.

Although U.S. consumers have been the main engine of their own economy and, Atlas-like, of the whole world's, the global economy may now be less vulnerable. This judgment is based on a view presented at the World Economic Forum in Davos in February 2006 by the chief economist at Goldman Sachs, Jim O'Neill. He argued that any slowdown in the United States would not lead to a global slowdown.

In Japan, industrial output jumped by an annual rate of 11 percent in the fourth quarter of 2005. Japan's labor market is also strengthening. In December the ratio of vacancies to job applicants rose to its highest since 1992. It is easier to find a job now than at any time since the Japanese bubble burst in the early 1990s. Stronger hiring by firms is also pushing up wages after years of decline. Workers are enjoying the biggest rise in bonuses for over a decade. That means that people are shopping again in Japan, 3.2 percent more in December 2005 than a year earlier. Domestic consumption growth in Japan suggests that exports will play a less significant role in Japan's economic health. Retail sales are reported to have risen in 2005 for the first time since 1996.

In Europe, the European Commission's surveys of business sentiment are showing positive results. They indicate that domestic demand has also been the main source of growth in Europe. *The Economist* reports that Germany's domestic demand is expected to contribute more to growth in 2006 than its net exports will.

According to Morgan Stanley, since 1999 Germany has been the source of 95 percent of the EU's GDP growth.

In addition to stronger domestic demand in Japan and the EU, emerging economies appear to be building domestic demand. Goldman Sachs' calculations indicate that Brazil, Russia, India and China combined have in recent years contributed more to the world's domestic demand than to its GDP growth.

This growth suggests that a slowdown in the United States need not halt the economies of the rest of the world. Ten years ago it would have. The increase in domestic consumption suggests that the economies will be more stable and resistant to external shocks than they would be if they were export-dependent. Today, Europe and Japan combined account for a larger portion of global GDP than does the United States. Increased growth there will help to keep the global economy flying.

One of the outcomes of huge rates of U.S. consumption is the huge deficit in the U.S. current account. A rebalancing of demand away from the United States to the rest of the world might also shrink this deficit. ■

[a]"The World Economy: Testing All Engines," *The Economist*, February 2, 2006, www.economist.com/displaystory.cfm?story_id=5474963 (accessed June 25, 2006).

Source: Christopher Swann, "Carefree Spenders Take Care of World Economy," *Financial Times*, February 10, 2004, p. 7.

CONCEPT PREVIEWS

After reading this chapter, you should be able to:

explain how money can be made—and lost—in the foreign exchange (FX) markets

understand FX quotations, including cross rates

describe currency exchange controls

explain how financial forces such as tariffs, taxes, inflation, and the balance of payments affect international management

In this chapter, we discuss the uncontrollable financial forces that confront international managers. These forces include currency exchange rate fluctuation and its related exchange risk, as well as other financial forces that are external to the firm but have a great impact on the firm's management, such as currency exchange controls, tariffs, taxation, inflation, and national-level balance-of-payments account balances. *Uncontrollable* means that these financial forces originate outside the business and are beyond its influence. However, financial managers of a company are not helpless in the face of these forces. Possible ways to manage around them are discussed in Chapter 21, where we consider financial management.

In the sections below, we look at exchange rate quotations, the causes of exchange rate fluctuations, and exchange rate forecasting. We also look at currency exchange controls, tariffs, taxation, inflation, and balance-of-payments accounts as the sources of other, external financial forces in whose context international managers need to operate.

Fluctuating Currency Values

In a post–Bretton Woods monetary system, freely floating currencies fluctuate against each other. At times, central banks occasionally intervene in the foreign exchange markets by buying and selling large amounts of a currency, yet, for the most part, the major currencies (the U.S. dollar, the British pound sterling, the Japanese yen, and the European Union euro) are allowed by their central banks to fluctuate freely against each other. As we discussed in Chapter 5, these fluctuations may be quite large. For example, in January 1999, the euro rate was established at US$1.1667. In May 2000, the euro had sunk to US$0.8895, a 23.75 percent drop. Then the trend reversed, as Figure 11.1 indicates, and by June 2006, the euro was trading at US$1.2644, an increase of 42.14 percent over its May 2000 rate. The euro had strengthened considerably against the dollar.

Such fluctuations have considerable impact on financial transactions. Imagine that you are operating with U.S. dollar earnings and that in May 2000 you signed a purchase agreement for the amount of $100,000, payable in euro when you receive your purchase. At that time, the cost of each euro was $0.8895. Now your purchase arrives, but the cost of each euro has risen to $1. So every euro costs you $0.1105 more than it did when you committed to the purchase. Your $100,000 purchase will cost you $11,050 more in U.S. dollars. That's a substantial difference. Why these currency fluctuations occur, that is, what forces determine exchange rates, is our focus below. We begin with an explanation of foreign exchange (FX) quotations and then move on to their causes.

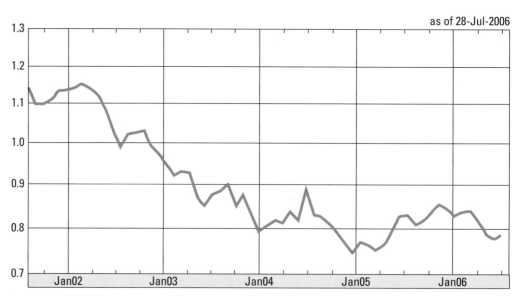

FIGURE 11.1

U.S. Dollar to Euro
Exchange Rate

as of 28-Jul-2006

Source: Copyright 2006 Yahoo Inc.

Other Countries Use the $ Symbol Too

In the United States, the symbol "$" generally refers to U.S. dollars. One must be careful, as the $ symbol is also used elsewhere in the world to denote local currencies. For example, Australia, Canada, and New Zealand call the local currency the dollar and use the $ symbol to refer to the local currency, as do Singapore, Taiwan, and Zimbabwe. The same is true in Hong Kong. And Mexico, which calls its currency the peso, uses the $ symbol to denote the Mexican peso. Argentina's peso, Brazil's real, and Chile's peso also use the dollar sign to indicate their currency.

Foreign Exchange

Foreign exchange quotations—the price of one currency expressed in terms of another—usually are reported in the world's currency exchange markets in terms of the U.S. dollar. Recent research shows that from 1998 to 2001, the U.S. dollar was on one side of around 90 percent of the foreign exchange transactions.[1] Even if a holder of Japanese yen wants British pounds, the trade, particularly if it involves a large amount, usually will be to buy U.S. dollars with the yen and then to buy pounds with the U.S. dollars. The reasons for this procedure are both historical and practical. On the historical side, the procedure goes back to Bretton Woods and the fixed rate exchange system with the dollar pegged to gold. The practical reasons for the continuing central position of the US$ in the foreign exchange process involve the functions it performs in the world. It is a main **central reserve asset** of many countries. It is the most used **vehicle currency** and **intervention currency.**

EXCHANGE RATE QUOTATIONS

Figure 11.2 is the listing of currency trading from *The Wall Street Journal* for the two business days preceding Tuesday, June 20, 2006. Figure 11.2 is divided into two main sections, "Key Currency Cross Rates" and "Exchange Rates." We will look at exchange rates first.

The Exchange Rates part of Figure 11.2 shows the US$ equivalent rate and the currency per US$ rate. The *US$ equivalent rate* is the cost in U.S. dollars of one unit of another currency. For example, the price (indicated as the US$ equivalent rate) of Switzerland's currency, the franc, on Monday, June 19, 2006, was .8058. This means that 1 Swiss franc cost US$0.8058, or about 80.5 cents. For another example, look at the Japanese yen, which is quoted at .008664. Each yen costs that fraction of a dollar, less than but approaching 1 cent. An example of a currency that costs more than a U.S. dollar is the British pound, listed under "U.K." at $1.8412, meaning 1 pound can be purchased for about $1.84.

We have looked at the cost of foreign currency in U.S. dollars. The *currency per US$ rate,* on the other hand, is the price of 1 U.S. dollar in the other currency, or how much of the foreign currency 1 U.S. dollar will buy. The currency per US$ rate of the Australian dollar for Monday, June 19, 2006, was 1.3574. That means 1 U.S. dollar costs about 1.36 Australian dollars.

Depending on the transaction, you may want to convert from the US$ equivalent rate to the currency per US$ rate. By using the reciprocal of the US$ equivalent rate, you can reach the currency per US$ rate, and vice versa:

$$\frac{1}{\text{US\$ equivalent rate}} = \text{currency per US\$ rate}$$

$$\frac{1}{\text{currency per US\$ rate}} = \text{US\$ equivalent rate}$$

central reserve asset
Asset, usually currency, held by a government's central bank

vehicle currency
A currency used as a vehicle for international trade or investment

intervention currency
A currency used by a country to intervene in the foreign currency exchange markets, often to buy (strengthen) its own currency

FIGURE 11.2

Exchange Rates for June 19 and June 16, 2006

Key Currency Cross Rates

Late New York Trading Monday, June 19, 2006

	Dollar	Euro	Pound	SFranc	Peso	Yen	CdnDir
Canada	1.1197	1.4082	2.0616	0.9023	.09753	.00970	...
Japan	115.42	145.16	212.51	93.006	10.053	...	103.082
Mexico	11.4811	14.4397	21.139	9.2514	...	.09947	10.2537
Switzerland	1.241	1.5608	2.2849	...	.10809	.01075	1.1083
U.K.	.54310	.6831	...	.4376	.04731	.00471	.48506
Euro	.79510	...	1.4639	.64069	.06925	.00689	.71011
U.S.	...	1.2577	1.8412	.80580	.08710	.00866	.89310

Source: Reuters   06.20.06   PA-16   WSJ.

Exchange Rates

June 19, 2006

The foreign exchange mid-range rates below apply to trading among banks in amounts of $1 million and more, as quoted at 4 p.m. Eastern time by Reuters and other sources. Retail transactions provide fewer units of foreign currency per dollar.

	U.S. $ EQUIVALENT		CURRENCY PER U.S. $	
Country	Mon	Fri	Mon	Fri
Argentina (Peso)-y	.3248	.3248	3.0788	3.0788
Australia (Dollar)	.7367	.7389	1.3574	1.3534
Bahrain (Dinar)	2.6525	2.6524	.3770	.3770
Brazil (Real)	.4440	.4456	2.2523	2.2442
Canada (Dollar)	.8931	.8909	1.1197	1.1225
1-month forward	.8938	.8916	1.1188	1.1216
3-months forward	.8955	.8933	1.1167	1.1194
6-months forward	.8980	.8958	1.1136	1.1163
Chile (Peso)	.001824	.001835	548.25	544.96
China (Renminbi)	.1249	.1250	8.0077	7.9983
Colombia (Peso)	.0003909	.0003909	2558.20	2558.20
Czech. Rep.(Koruna)				
Commercial rate	.04414	.04433	22.655	22.558
Denmark (Krone)	.1687	.1695	5.9277	5.8997
Ecuador (US Dollar)	1.0000	1.0000	1.0000	1.0000
Egypt (Pound)-y	.1738	.1737	5.7551	5.7574
Hong Kong (Dollar)	.1288	.1288	7.7663	7.7639
Hungary (Forint)	.004545	.004621	220.02	216.40
India (Rupee)	.02185	.02188	45.767	45.704
Indonesia (Rupiah)	.0001066	.0001076	9381	9294
Israel (Shekel)	.2248	.2252	4.4484	4.4405
Japan (Yen)	.008664	.008686	115.42	115.13
1-month forward	.008701	.008723	114.93	114.64
3-months forward	.008777	.008800	113.93	113.64
6-months forward	.008890	.008913	112.49	112.20
Jordan (Dinar)	1.4114	1.4112	.7085	.7086
Kuwait (Dinar)	3.4577	3.4583	.2892	.2892
Lebanon (Pound)	.0006634	.0006634	1507.39	1507.39
Malaysia (Ringgit)-b	.2726	.2746	3.6684	3.6417
Malta (Ura)	2.9297	2.9454	.3413	.3395
Mexico (Peso)				
Floating rate	.0871	.0874	11.4811	11.4390

	U.S. $ EQUIVALENT		CURRENCY PER U.S. $	
Country	Mon	Fri	Mon	Fri
New Zealand (Dollar)	.6166	.6177	1.6218	1.6189
Norway (Krone)	.1601	.1610	6.2461	6.2112
Pakistan (Rupee)	.01655	.01656	60.423	60.387
Peru (new Sol)	.3063	.3064	3.2648	3.2637
Philippines (Peso)	.01878	.01882	53.248	53.135
Poland (Zloty)	.3087	.3116	3.2394	3.2092
Russia (Ruble)-a	.03697	.03715	27.049	26.918
Saudi Arabia (Riyal)	.2666	.2666	3.7509	3.7509
Singapore (Dollar)	.6258	.6272	1.5980	1.5944
Solvak Rep. (Koruna)	.03299	.03327	30.312	30.057
South Africa (Rand)	.1427	.1451	7.0077	6.8918
South Korea (Won)	.0010404	.0010463	961.17	955.75
Sweden (Krona)	.1354	.1362	7.3855	7.3421
Switzerland (Franc)	.8058	.8124	1.2410	1.2309
1-month forward	.8084	.8150	1.2370	1.2270
3-months forward	.8139	.8206	1.2287	1.2186
6-months forward	.8218	.8285	1.2168	1.2070
Taiwan (Dollar)	.03069	.03080	32.584	32.468
Thailand (Baht)	.02599	.02601	38.476	38.447
Turkey (New Lira)-d	.6248	.6307	1.6005	1.5855
U.K. (Pound)	1.8412	1.8498	.5431	.5406
1-month forward	1.8422	1.8508	.5428	.5403
3-months forward	1.8448	1.8534	.5421	.5395
6-months forward	1.8483	1.8571	.5410	.5385
United Arab (Dirham)	.2724	.2724	3.6711	3.6711
Uraguay (Peso)				
Financial	.04200	.04200	23.810	23.810
Venezuela (Bollvar)	.000466	.000466	2145.92	2145.92
SDR	1.4737	1.4734	.6786	.6764
Euro	1.2577	1.2639	.7951	.7912

Special Drawing Rights (SDR) are based on exchange rates for the U.S., British, and Japanese currencies. Source: International Monetary Fund.

a-Russian Central Bank rate. b-Government rate. d-Rebased as of Jan. 1, 2005. y-Floating rate.

Source: *The Wall Street Journal.*

spot rate
The exchange rate between two currencies for delivery within two business days

forward currency market
Trading market for currency contracts deliverable 30, 60, 90, or 180 days in the future

forward rate
The exchange rate between two currencies for delivery in the future, usually 30, 60, 90, or 180 days

There is more to be learned from reading the exchange rate quotes. The Exchange Rates part of Figure 11.2 includes rates for the preceding Friday. Comparing the two prices tells you whether the currency is weakening or strengthening in the short term. For example, on Friday, June 16, 1 dollar would buy 115.13 Japanese yen. After the weekend, on Monday, that dollar would buy 115.42 yen. The dollar can buy more yen, so we describe it as strengthening against the yen; that is, the yen is weakening against the dollar. From Friday to Monday, the yen became cheaper or less expensive in dollar terms. Such rates are called the **spot rate,** the exchange rate for a trade today for delivery within two days. The spot rate for the euro on Friday, June 16, was $0.7912. By the way, the spot rate on Monday, after the weekend, was $0.7951, so the dollar was weakening against the euro. The euro was trading *at a premium* to the dollar.

You'll note, too, that *The Wall Street Journal* quotes a 1-, 3-, and 6-month price for several currencies, the yen, the Canadian dollar, the Swiss franc, and the British pound sterling. Those forward prices in dollar terms (U.S. equivalent) show what the market expects of the currency in these time periods. The **forward currency market** allows managers to lock in purchases of other currencies at known rates. The **forward rate** is the cost today for a commitment to buy or sell an agreed amount of a currency at a fixed, future date. The commitment is a forward contract, and for frequently traded currencies such as those listed in *The Wall Street Journal,* contracts are usually available on a 30-, 60-, 90-, or 180-day basis. You also may be able to negotiate with banks for different time periods or for contracts in other currencies.

In the Exchange Rates part of Figure 11.2, look under "Switzerland" and refer to the Swiss franc (CHF) one-month forward US$ equivalent quotation. For Monday, June 19, 2006, CHF 1 bought US$0.8084. Compare that rate with the spot rate of US$0.8058, and you will see that 1 Swiss franc will buy more dollars for delivery in one month than for delivery today. And the trend continues in the forward market quotes. The Swiss franc is **trading at a premium** in the forward market. If a currency's forward rate quotes are weaker than the spot rate, the currency is said to be **trading at a discount** in the forward market.

Whether there is a premium or a discount and what its size is depend on the expectations of the world financial community, businesses, individuals, and governments about what the future will bring. These expectations factor in such considerations as supply and demand forecasts for the two currencies, relative inflation in the two countries, relative productivity and unit labor cost changes, expected election results or other political developments, expected government fiscal, monetary, and currency exchange market actions, balance-of-payments accounts, and a psychological aspect.[2]

Look again, in Figure 11.2, at the "Currency per U.S. $" column for Monday, and you will see that it took not quite 115.5 yen to buy 1 U.S. dollar, whereas in the United Kingdom, a little over half a pound (.5431) was enough for a dollar. Glancing up and down the column, you find that an Indonesian rupiah holder would need over 9381 rupiahs for US$1 and that holders of each of the other currencies quoted require a different number. It might seem that the fewer units of a currency required to buy a dollar, the "harder" or better that currency is compared to the others, but that is not the case. Look at Japan, for example, an expensive market for dollar-based consumers. Note that currency prices alone tell us nothing about the relative purchasing power of the foreign currency.

Now turn to the "Key Currency Cross Rates" section of Figure 11.2. In addition to the U.S. dollar, currencies of other developed countries are also important in world transactions and are becoming more important. This is particularly true of the Japanese yen and the EU euro. Many expect the euro to become as frequently used as the dollar, both for transactions and as a reserve currency. Although most large currency exchanges go through the US$, it is possible to find exchange rates for trading directly between non-U.S. dollar currencies. These rates are called **cross rates.**

Until now, we have not discussed the way the foreign exchange market actually operates. Most of the transactions in the foreign exchange market are *over the counter (OTC)*, meaning that there is no actual trading floor; trades are done electronically. Most of the market is composed of banks and other large financial institutions such as pension funds and mutual funds. Prices consist of a **bid price** and an **ask price,** with the bid lower than the ask. "Buy low, sell high" is the general approach to currency trading. The difference between the two prices, known as the *bid-ask spread,* provides a margin for the bank or agency. The rates listed in financial publications, such as those we are using from *The Wall Street Journal,* are interbank rates, for customers buying large quantities, usually US$1 million or more. The rates charged to small customers are much less favorable to the customer. Banks intend to make a profit in currency transactions.

As you can imagine, the FX markets are large, liquid, and quite competitive, with 24-hour trading through international banks. The Bank for International Settlements reported daily turnover averages in the foreign exchange markets at $1.9 billion for 2004.[3] The FX markets are largely unregulated, as well. A *Wall Street Journal* article described them as "a Wild West of global capitalism where more than $1.2 trillion [2002] changes hands each day. Unlike major stock and commodities markets, the foreign-exchange market, or FX, operates with virtually no government or regulatory oversight."[4] In a world where many would say we are overregulated, this sector stands out.

CAUSES OF EXCHANGE RATE FLUCTUATION

Since 1973, the relative values of floating currencies and the ease of their convertibility have been set by market forces, which are influenced by many factors, including basic supply and demand of the currency, interest rates, inflation rates, and expectations of the future. Monetary

trading at a premium
Situation in which a currency's forward rate quotes are stronger than spot

trading at a discount
Situation in which a currency's forward rate quotes are weaker than spot

cross rates
Currency exchange rates for trading directly between non-US$ currencies

bid price
Price offered to buy

ask price
Sales price

monetary policies
Government policies that control the amount of money in circulation and its growth rate

fiscal policies
Policies that address the collecting and spending of money by the government

law of one price
Concept that in an efficient market, like products will have like prices

arbitrage
The process of buying and selling instantaneously to make profit with no risk

Fisher effect
The relationship between real and nominal interest rates: The real interest rate will be the nominal interest rate minus the expected rate of inflation

international Fisher effect
Concept that the interest rate differentials for any two currencies will reflect the expected change in their exchange rates

purchasing power parity (PPP)
Theory that predicts that currency exchange rates between two countries should equal the ratio of the price levels of their commodity baskets

and fiscal policies of the government, such as decisions on taxation, interest rates, and trade policies, and other forces external to the business, such as world events, all may play significant roles in this process. **Monetary policies** of a government control the amount of money in circulation, whether it is growing, and, if so, at what pace. **Fiscal policies** address the collecting and spending of money by the government.

What determines exchange rates is a wide and complex variety of factors, such that economists have not yet developed a widely accepted theory that explains them. However, most economists would agree that inflation, interest rates, and market expectations play central roles in exchange rate determination. Economists have determined several *parity relationships,* that is, relationships of equivalence, among some of the various complex factors involved in exchange rate movements. We look now at two of these relationships, interest rate parity and purchasing power parity, because they are fundamental to our further consideration of exchange rates. They both rest on the **law of one price,** which states that in an efficient market, like products will have like prices. If there are differences, the process of **arbitrage** (buying and selling to make a profit with no risk) will quickly close any gaps and the markets will be at equilibrium.

When the law of one price is applied to interest rates, it suggests that interest rates vary to take account of different anticipated levels of inflation. An investor would want to earn more in a high-inflation environment to compensate for the effect of inflation on the investment. The economic explanation of this relationship, which results in interest rate parity, is the **Fisher effect.** It states that the real interest rate will be the nominal interest rate minus the expected rate of inflation. Where the real rate of interest (r_r) is equal to the nominal interest rate (r_n) minus the expected rate of inflation (I):

$$r_r = (r_n) - I$$

So an increase in the expected inflation rate will lead to an increase in the interest rate. A decrease in the expected inflation rate will lead to a decrease in the interest rate.

The difference between the nominal interest rates in two countries reflects the expected change in exchange rates. For example, if the nominal interest rate in the United States is 5 percent per year and in the EU it is 3 percent, we would expect the dollar to decrease against the euro by 2 percent over the year. This is known as the **international Fisher effect:** The interest rate differentials for any two currencies reflect the expected change in their exchange rates.[5]

A second parity relationship is **purchasing power parity (PPP).** PPP is the result of the law of one price applied to a basket of commodity goods. PPP suggests that for a dollar to buy as much in the United Kingdom as in the United States, the cost of the goods in the UK should equal their U.S. cost times the exchange rate between the dollar and pound. This relationship is expressed in the following equation, where P is the price of a basket of commodity goods,

$$£P(\$/£) = \$P$$

Another way to think about what the PPP theory states is that currency exchange rates between two countries should equal the ratio of the price levels of their commodity baskets. That is, for the British pound sterling (£) and the U.S. dollar, where P is the price of a basket of commodity goods,

$$(\$/£) = \$P/£P$$

For example if a basket of goods costs \$1,500 in the United States and £1,000 in the United Kingdom, the PPP exchange rate would be \$1.50/£. If, in the trading market, the actual spot exchange rate was \$2/£, the pound would be overvalued by 33 percent, or, equivalently, the dollar undervalued by 25 percent.

The Economist, a British weekly focused on, as its name suggests, economic news, presents a playful application of PPP theory twice a year. It compiles a "Big Mac index," using PPP theory and substituting a Big Mac for a basket of goods. This index, whose May 2006 figures are displayed in Table 11.1, suggests that, in the long term, many of the developing countries' currencies are undervalued and the euro and many European currencies are overvalued. The Big Mac PPP is the exchange rate that would have burgers in other countries costing what

TABLE 11.1   The Big Mac Index

	Big Mac Prices		Implied PPP* of the Dollar	Actual Dollar Exchange Rate May 22	Under (−)/ Over (+) Valuation Against the Dollar, %
	In Local Currency	In Dollars			
United States[†]	$3.10	3.10	–	–	–
Argentina	Peso 7.00	2.29	2.26	3.06	−26
Australia	A$3.25	2.44	1.05	1.33	−21
Brazil	Real 6.40	2.78	2.06	2.30	−10
Britain	£1.94	3.65	1.60[‡]	1.88[‡]	+18
Canada	C$3.52	3.14	1.14	1.12	+1
Chile	Peso 1,560	2.94	503	530	−5
China	Yuan 10.5	1.31	3.39	8.03	−58
Czech Republic	Koruna 59.05	2.67	19.0	22.1	−14
Denmark	DKr27.75	4.77	8.95	5.82	+54
Egypt	Pound 9.50	1.65	3.06	5.77	−47
Euro area[β]	€2.94	3.77	1.05[∂]	1.28[∂]	+22
Hong Kong	HK$12	1.55	3.87	7.75	−50
Hungary	Forint 560	2.71	181	206	−12
Indonesia	Rupiah 14,600	1.57	4,710	9,325	−49
Japan	¥250	2.23	80.6	112	−28
Malaysia	Ringgit 5.50	1.52	1.77	3.63	−51
Mexico	Peso 29.00	2.57	9.35	11.3	−17
New Zealand	NZ$4.45	2.75	1.44	1.62	−11
Peru	New Sol 9.50	2.91	3.06	3.26	−6
Philippines	Peso 85.00	1.62	27.4	52.6	−48
Poland	Zloty 6.50	2.10	2.10	3.10	−32
Russia	Rouble 48.00	1.77	15.5	27.1	−43
Singapore	S$3.60	2.27	1.16	1.59	−27
South Africa	Rand 13.95	2.11	4.50	6.60	−32
South Korea	Won 2,500	2.62	806	952	−15
Sweden	SKr33.00	4.53	10.6	7.28	+46
Switzerland	SFr6.30	5.21	2.03	1.21	+63
Taiwan	NT$75.00	2.33	24.2	32.1	−25
Thailand	Baht 60.00	1.56	19.4	38.4	−50
Turkey	Lire 4.20	2.72	1.35	1.54	−12
Venezuela	Bolivar 5,701	2.17	1,839	2,630	−30
Aruba	Florin 4.95	2.77	1.60	1.79	−11
Bulgaria	Lev 2.99	1.94	0.96	1.54	−37
Colombia	Peso 6,500	2.60	2,097	2,504	−16
Costa Rica	Colon 1,130	2.22	365	510	−28
Croatia	Kuna 15.0	2.62	4.84	5.72	−15
Dominican Rep	Peso 60.0	1.84	19.4	32.6	−41
Estonia	Kroon 29.5	2.40	9.52	12.3	−23
Fiji	Fiji $4.65	2.69	1.50	1.73	−13
Georgia	Lari 4.15	2.31	1.34	1.80	−26
Guatemala	Quetzal 17.25	2.27	5.56	7.59	−27
Honduras	Lempira 35.95	1.90	11.6	18.9	−39
Iceland	Kronur 459	6.37	148	72.0	+106
Latvia	Lats 1.35	2.47	0.44	0.55	−20
Lithuania	Litas 6.50	2.41	2.10	2.69	−22
Macau	Pataca 11.1	1.39	3.59	7.99	−55

(continued)

TABLE 11.1   The Big Mac Index *Continued*

	Big Mac Prices		Implied PPP* of the Dollar	Actual Dollar Exchange Rate May 22	Under (-)/ over (+) Valuation Against the Dollar, %
	In Local Currency	In Dollars			
Moldova	Leu 23.0	1.75	7.42	13.2	−44
Morocco	Dirham 24.5	2.82	7.92	8.71	−9
Norway	Kroner 43.0	7.05	13.9	6.10	+127
Pakistan	Rupee 130	2.16	41.9	60.1	−30
Paraguay	Guarani 9,000	1.63	2,903	5,505	−47
Saudi Arabia	Riyal 9.00	2.40	2.90	3.75	−23
Slovakia	Koruna 58.0	1.97	18.7	29.5	−37
Slovenia	Totar 520	2.76	168	189	−11
Sri Lanka	Rupee 190	1.85	61.3	103	−40
Ukraine	Hryvna 8.50	1.68	2.74	5.05	−46
UAE	Dirham 9.00	2.45	2.90	3.67	−21
Uruguay	Peso 42.3	1.77	13.6	23.9	−43

*Purchasing-power parity: local price divided by price in United States.

†Average of New York, Chicago, Atlanta, and San Francisco.

‡Dollars per pound.

§Weighted average of prices in euro area.

ᵃDollars per euro.

they do in the United States. So, for example, in China the Big Mac costs 10.5 yuan, whereas in the United States a three-city average price is $3.10. To make the prices equal, the exchange rate would have to be 3.39 yuan for 1 dollar. The market rate is actually 8.03 yuan to the dollar. So the yuan is 56 percent below the implied PPP exchange rate. That's a pretty inexpensive burger. *The Economist* claims that in the long run its Big Mac index performs pretty well, with many of the discounted and premium-fetching currencies correcting. Remember, too, that the price of a Big Mac represents more than a basket of tradable goods, the situation PPP theory describes. The McDonald's service we may receive with our Big Mac can't be traded, nor can the rent McDonald's pays for its building, for example. Nevertheless, the Big Mac index is a helpful and playful way to get a quick sense of relative currency values and where they may be heading.

Now that we have looked at two parity relationships, interest rate parity and purchasing power parity, we can look more closely at exchange rate prediction.

EXCHANGE RATE FORECASTING

Because exchange rate movements are so important to all aspects of international business—production, sourcing, marketing, and finance—many business decisions take the risk of exchange rate movement into consideration. There are several approaches to forecasting, and three of the main ones are the efficient market approach, the fundamental approach, and the technical approach. We briefly examine each of them.

efficient market approach
Assumption that current market prices fully reflect all available relevant information

In the **efficient market approach,** the assumption is that current prices fully reflect all available relevant information. That suggests that we look at the forward exchange rates and assume that they are the best possible predictor of future spot rates because they will have taken into account all the available information. If interest rates are different between two countries, for example, the forward rate will reflect this (international Fisher effect). The efficient market approach does not suggest that the forward rates will be the future spot rates with perfect accuracy. Rather, the divergences will be random. A related approach is called the **random walk hypothesis,** and it holds that the short-term unpredictability of factors suggests that the best predictor of tomorrow's prices is today's prices.[6]

The **fundamental approach** to exchange rate prediction looks at the underlying forces that play a role in determining exchange rates and develops various econometric models that attempt to capture the variables and their correct relationships. The variables might include those mentioned above, such as the inflation rate, the interest rate, and the economic growth rate. Fundamental analysis builds on this set of independent variables, to which values or weighting is assigned. So, for a forecaster to predict an exchange rate two years forward, the first step would be to select a model. Then the predictor would estimate the values of the independent variables two years ahead. Already we have two major issues to consider: Is the formula correct? And then, are the variables predicted correctly? Cheol Eun and David Resnick, two noted international finance scholars, have surveyed the research on the various fundamental models and conclude that "the fundamental models failed to more accurately forecast exchange rates than either the forward rate model [what we have termed the efficient market model] or the random walk model."[7] OECD's Web site provides a good source of macroeconomic data used in fundamental analysis (www.oecd.org).

Technical analysis looks at history and then projects it forward. It analyzes historic data for trends and then, assuming that what was past will be future, projects these trends forward. Technical analysts think in terms of waves and trends. Since there is no theoretical underpinning to the technical approach, scholarly academic studies tend to dismiss it. Yet a review of currency-trading marketing materials suggests that traders often use it.

As for the performance of these various approaches, recent research by Eun and Sabherwalon the exchange rate forecasts of major commercial banks indicates that the 10 banks in the study could not outperform the random walk model.[8] Their findings also suggest that the forward exchange rate and the spot rate were both about equal in value for predicting future exchange rates. In another study, Richard Levich evaluated the forecasting of 13 professional forecasting services, whose approaches to forecasting varied. In only 24 percent of the cases did forecasters outperform the forward exchange rate as a predictor.[9] The evidence available indicates that neither the technical nor the fundamental approach outperforms the efficient market approach.

Other Financial Forces

We have examined a major financial force that international managers have to address, foreign exchange fluctuations, their causes and their prediction. How managers actually address the risk that such exposure creates is a topic we address in Chapter 21, "Financial Management," in our discussion of swaps and hedging. There are many other financial forces that international managers have to address, and presently we look at some of the more significant ones, beginning with currency exchange controls, tariffs, and taxation and then moving on to inflation and balance-of-payments effects.

CURRENCY EXCHANGE CONTROLS

Controls differ greatly from country to country and even within a country, depending on the type of transaction. In general, the developed countries have few or no currency exchange controls, but these nations are a minority of the world's countries. The majority of countries do impose some form of exchange control. Many developing countries, though, such as Mexico, have reduced or eliminated such controls in order to encourage foreign investment. The international business manager must be aware of whether currency exchange controls exist both before and while doing business in any country, because the situation can change quickly.

Currency exchange controls limit or prohibit the legal use of a country's currency in international transactions. When a currency is not freely convertible, its value is arbitrarily fixed, typically at a rate higher than its value in the free market, and the government decrees that all purchases or sales of other currencies be made through a government agency. The limitations might apply to residents of the country, while the currency is still externally convertible, or the limitations could be for both residents and nonresidents, resulting in a nonconvertible currency.

random walk hypothesis
Assumption that the unpredictability of factors suggests that the best predictor of tomorrow's prices is today's prices

fundamental approach
Exchange rate prediction based on econometric models that attempt to capture the variables and their correct relationships

technical analysis
An approach that analyzes data for trends and then projects these trends forward

Employees wait for customers at a currency exchange, licensed by the Bank of Bangladesh, in Dhaka. Some countries set "official rates" for currency and decree that all purchases or sales of other currencies be made through a government agency.

Limitations might also restrict the amount of domestic currency transferred into foreign currency. A black market inevitably springs up alongside such restrictions, but it is of little use to the international manager who wants to abide by the laws of a country in which the company is operating. In addition, the black market is rarely able to accommodate transactions of the size involved in international business.

Countries put limitations on the convertibility of their currency when they are concerned that their foreign reserves could be depleted. Foreign reserves are a source of currency for foreign debt service, import purchases, and other demands for foreign currency that domestic banks might encounter. In the banking world, these countries are known as "Article 14 countries," after the International Monetary Fund's provision for exchange controls for transitional economies. An example of a country with exchange controls is China, whose renmimbi (RMB) is convertible in current accounts (accounts for day-to-day banking) but not capital accounts (longer-term accounts). China is in the process of reducing the restrictions on foreign exchange controls of domestic company activities, allowing them to engage in direct foreign investment. Cuba operates with two currencies: One, the national peso, is not convertible and is the domestic currency, having no value outside Cuba. The other, the convertible peso, is the currency of tourism and is pegged to the dollar at $1.08. Neither currency is traded outside Cuba. The Iranian rial had an official exchange rate for imports and another for exports until 2002. The import rate was used for imports of essential goods and for oil exports, and often it was much lower than the export rate, by almost 50 percent. The export rate was used for nonoil exports and luxury imports. The Tunisian dinar is not allowed outside Tunisia; the Algerian dinar is not exportable by foreigners, but Algerian citizens are allowed to export small amounts.

Often when a government requires permission to purchase foreign currency, the international business must pay more than the free-market rate. If permission is not granted or if the cost of foreign currency is uneconomically high, the blocked currency can be used only within the country. Such repatriation limitations usually present the problem of finding suitable products and investments within the country.

People will go to remarkable extremes to get blocked money out of exchange-controlled countries. When faced with blocked currency in the former Soviet Union, Pepsi once bought an oil tanker in Russia and filled it with vodka, all paid for with blocked currency and all for export. Pepsi also bought decommissioned Soviet submarines, paying for them in rubles, and sold them for scrap in the West. In New Delhi, the local manager of a major international airline gave a case of Scotch to a government official. Shortly thereafter, the agency for which that official worked granted the airline permission to use blocked rupees to buy almost US$20 million and transfer them to the airline's home country. This was an extreme method of converting a blocked currency to a convertible currency. It was also illegal. Most financial managers would be hesitant to accept the vulnerability that accompanies such approaches. They can take legal steps to protect their firms from the adverse effects of currency exchange controls, as you will see in Chapter 21.

TARIFFS

In addition to currency exchange rates and restrictions, tariffs or duties (the terms often are used interchangeably) present international managers with challenges because they represent increased costs. Tariffs, as you remember from Chapter 3, are taxes, usually on imported goods. They may be ad valorem, specific, compound, or variable. There are two ways to cover increased costs: to increase price or to decrease profit margins. In a sector where there is price competition, neither of these options seems attractive.

BUILDING YOUR GLOBAL RÉSUMÉ
A Career in International Finance—Where Do You Look for a Job?

The allure and the rewards of a career in international finance—such as being a power broker who deals in stocks and bonds, commodities, or currency on a 24/7 basis across the time zones of the world—can be quite dramatic. So where are the jobs in international finance located? Where are the major financial markets of the world? The top 14 banking centers of the world are:

1. New York
2. London
3. Hong Kong
4. Singapore
5. Tokyo
6. Zurich/Geneva
7. Frankfurt/Hamburg
8. Paris
9. Los Angeles/San Francisco
10. Milan/Rome
11. Brussels
12. Toronto/Montreal
13. Amsterdam
14. Panama

Major commodities exchanges (not in rank order) are located in:

- Chicago
- Kansas City
- Minnesota
- New York
- Hong Kong
- Paris
- Singapore
- Sidney
- Winnipeg
- Montreal
- Tokyo
- London
- Madrid

World Fact and Culture Cue: Considering the monetary rewards that can be earned in a career in international finance, where are the best places to live in order to pursue such a career? In 2006, *WealthBriefing* announced that the two top wealth management centers in the world are Geneva and Zurich. In the same year, Mercer Human Resources Consulting ranked 215 of the world's cities on their quality of living: Zurich and Geneva ranked 1st and 2nd, respectively, with Düsseldorf in 5th place, Frankfurt in 7th, Munich in 8th, and Bern and Sydney, tied, in 9th. London ranked 39th and New York 46th. Baghdad came in at 215.

World Wide Resources:

www.fincareer.com

www.finix.at/fin/selinks.html

www.tdd.lt/slnews/Stock_Exchanges/Stock.Exchanges.htm

www.libraries.rutgers.edu/rul/rr_gateway/research_guides/busi/stocks.shtml

www.xpresstrade.com/more_futures.html

www.unctad.org/infocomm/exchanges/ex_overview.htm

The European Union and other groups of nations that have moved toward economic integration (discussed in Chapter 4) have lowered or abolished tariffs on trade among member-countries. (Lower tariffs are a significant factor that a country would consider when deciding whether to join a group of nations, but they are not the only factor.) Such developments add new dimensions to the decision-making processes of companies located outside the groupings. From a company point of view, an existing tariff in a large market might be a factor in the decision to produce in that foreign market. For example, at Toyota's 11, soon to be 14, foreign production facilities in the United States, the Toyota cars, vans, and trucks produced are not subject to tariffs or any other trade-restrictive agreement such as quotas. Presently the United States levies a 25 percent tariff on imported trucks. This tariff was initially imposed by President Lyndon Johnson in 1963 to object to unfair trade practices by Germany in regard to U.S. frozen-chicken exports, so it is known as the "chicken tax." In 1963, trucks were a good target in Germany because major truck manufacturers were there, including Volkswagen, which were pushed out of the U.S. sector by the tariff. Almost all of the trucks in the United States today are manufactured domestically because an imported $20,000 truck would have to sell for $25,000 to recoup the cost of the tariff. In effect, the tariff, gives domestic producers the OK for a $5,000 price increase, which represents a significant advantage for them.

You can see the present U.S. tariff schedule at the U.S. International Trade Commission Web site (www.usitc.gov/tata/hts/bychapter/index.htm). One interesting aspect of the tariff schedule is how specific it is. For example, in Harmonized Tariff Schedule (HTS) category 0704.10.20, cauliflower, the tariff rate is 2.5 percent between June 5 and October 25, when the U.S. crop is being harvested. If the cauliflower is cut or sliced, the rate is 14 percent at any time. The tariff for HTS 8703.2x.00, motor cars, is 2.5 percent, but for trucks (HTS 8704.22.50), it is 25 percent. The financial force of a tariff can be significant. (Tariffs as a legal force are discussed in Chapter 10.)

TAXATION

In Chapter 10, the legal aspects of taxation were covered. Taxation is also a financial force. Governments around the world widely use three types of taxation to generate revenue: income tax, value-added tax (VAT), and withholding tax.[10] The *income tax* is a direct tax on personal and corporate income. Table 11.2 compares corporate taxation rates in selected countries. The impact of taxes is a significant one, and if a corporation can achieve a lower tax burden than that of its competitors, it can lower prices to its customers or generate higher revenue with which to pay higher wages and dividends.

A *value-added tax (VAT)* is a tax charged on the value added to a good as it moves through production from raw materials to final purchaser. It is really a sales tax whose payment documentation from one stage to another in the production process becomes important for tax credits, since the seller collects the tax for the goods sold and then receives credits for VAT already paid earlier in the production process. Within the EU, VAT rates are still to be harmonized, so the process of moving goods across borders can have a VAT impact. For example, in Cyprus the rate is 15 percent, while in both Sweden and Denmark it is 25 percent. From a VAT perspective, sourcing in Sweden or Denmark would be 10 percent more costly, all else being equal. Countries that levy value-added taxes are permitted by World Trade Organization (WTO) rules to rebate the value-added taxes to exporters, an incentive that makes the exports less expensive and thus more competitive.

The third general tax category is the *withholding tax.* This is an indirect tax levied on passive income (income such as dividends, royalties, interest) that the corporation would pay out to nonresidents, people or companies in another tax jurisdiction. Countries establish bilateral tax treaties to categorize the various passive-income withholding rates. For example,

TABLE 11.2	Corporate Tax Rates	

Country	Percent
Ireland	12.50
Singapore	20.00
Switzerland[1]	24.10
Austria	25.00
Finland	26.00
Denmark	28.00
Netherlands	29.60
Australia	30.00
Japan	30.00
United Kingdom	30.00
France	33.33
United States[2]	35.00
Germany[3]	41.60

[1]This rate includes federal and canton taxes, which vary. The rate given is typical and would be for a company in Zurich.

[2]This is the federal tax rate. State and local tax rates range from 0 to 20%.

[3]This includes a professional tax, which is around 18% but varies by city from 12% to 20%.

Source: PricewaterhouseCoopers, "Corporate Taxes Worldwide Summaries, 2006." See www.taxsummaries.pwc.com.

on interest, the United States withholds 30 percent from residents of non-tax treaty countries. From UK residents it withholds nothing, while from residents of Pakistan it withholds 30 percent.

At the international level, taxes become important as a complex financial force about which companies have to be concerned. International companies need to understand tax laws in all countries in which they operate and how those tax laws relate to tax laws in other countries. This additional tax burden can create financial risk, but it can also be an opportunity for savings, given good tax planning. We will look at tax planning in Chapter 21, when we examine financial management.

INFLATION

Inflation is a trend of rising prices. Economists disagree on the underlying cause of inflation. Some hold that it is caused by demand exceeding supply, while others view the cause as an increase in the money supply. All, however, agree that in an inflated economy, prices increase. Figure 11.3 maps the world by inflation levels. Japan, the EU, and the United States have had relatively good records in keeping inflation down in recent years. Many Latin American countries have inflation troubles. From 1970 into the 1990s, the worst inflation in Latin America occurred in Bolivia, where the inflation rate reached 11,750 percent in 1985. That far outstripped Brazil, in second place with 3,118 percent in 1990. In a dramatic turnaround, Bolivia slashed its inflation to only 7.9 percent in 1996 and further pushed it down to 4.9 percent in 2005. Similarly, Brazil decreased its inflation to 5.7 percent in 2005. Chile is another Latin American economic success story, decreasing inflation from 505 percent in 1974 to 7.4 percent in 1996 and 3.2 percent in 2005. Argentina reduced inflation from 3,080 percent in 1989 to 12.3 percent in 2005. Mexico brought down inflation from 132 percent in 1988 to 3.3 percent in 2005. The United States is now in a period of relatively low inflation. In the 1970s and early 1980s, the United States had relatively high inflation, with the rate reaching around 20 percent.

Most inflation is measured by a *consumer price index (CPI)*, the price changes in a basket of consumer goods. OECD measures inflation by a broader indicator, the *gross domestic*

FIGURE 11.3   Inflation Map

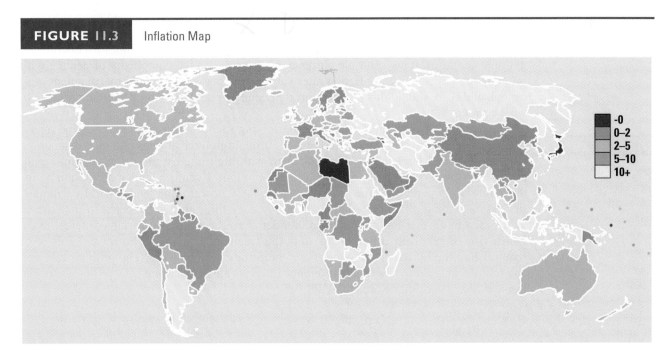

-0
0–2
2–5
5–10
10+

Source: CIA Factbook, 2006. Data reflects 2005 measures.

FIGURE 11.4 GDP Deflator: Average Annual Growth in Percentage, 1991–2004

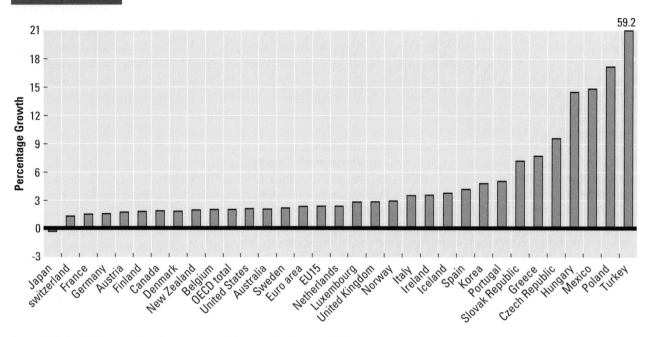

Source: OECD Factbook 2006, http://hermia.sourceoecd.org/vl=9709825/cl=11/nw=1/rpsv/factbook/02-02-04-g01.htm (accessed 22 June 2006).

product (GDP) deflator, which takes into account the prices of intermediate goods and services, not just those in a consumer basket, and the prices of capital assets. Figure 11.4 shows the inflation rates of OECD countries using the GDP deflator measure.

Inflation is a financial force, external to companies, that impacts international business in several major ways. Almost every company must borrow money occasionally, and the inflation rate determines the real cost of borrowing in capital markets.* You'll recall the Fisher effect, in our discussion of exchange rates. Even within a single country, inflation is of concern to management. High inflation rates make capital expenditure planning more risky. For example, management may allocate US$1 million for a plant and be forced to pay much more to complete construction because of the effects of inflation. When a firm operates in multiple countries, it has multiple currency exposures, and the complexity of dealing with inflation increases because inflation rates vary among countries. Should management raise capital, and if so, should this be done through equity or debt? In which capital markets? In what currency?

Increasing inflation rates encourage borrowing (debt) because the loan will be repaid with cheaper money. But high inflation rates bring high interest rates and may discourage lending. Potential lenders may fear that even with high interest rates, the amount repaid plus interest would be worth less than the amount lent. Even if a lender can obtain an interest rate of 25 percent, if the rate of inflation is 30 percent, the lender will lose money. Instead of lending, the money holder may buy something that is expected to increase in value, thereby further fueling inflation. Lenders have begun to use variable interest rates, which rise or fall with inflation, to shift the financial risk to the borrower. This shift requires that the borrower be much more careful about borrowing. The original rate and any future changes are based on a reference interest rate, such as the U.S. prime rate or the London Interbank Offer Rate (LIBOR).

---

*Real interest rates are found by subtracting inflation from the nominal interest rates.

FIGURE 11.5

Evolution of Long-Term Interest Rates

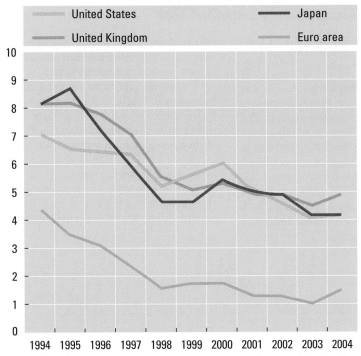

Source: Evolution of long-term interest rates, Main Economic Indicators, © OECD 2005. Used by permission.

As Figure 11.5 suggests, the long-term trend of interest rates has been toward conversion. They averaged 10 percent in 1991 but 4 percent by 2004. This trend may be explained by the globalization of financial markets as they become more integrated.[11]

As we have reviewed in our discussion on exchange rates, comparative inflation rates also will affect the comparative currency values (international Fisher effect), as the currencies of high-inflation countries weaken against the currencies of countries with lower inflation rates. Management usually will try to minimize holdings of the weaker currencies. Thus, relatively higher rates of inflation tend to discourage new investment.

Higher inflation rates cause the cost of the goods and services produced in a country to rise, and thus the goods and services become less competitive globally. The company's affiliate in the high-inflation country finds export sales more difficult, as do all other producers there. Such conditions may lead to balance-of-payments (BOP) deficits in the trade account, so under these conditions management must be alert to government policy changes that attempt to correct these deficits. Such changes could include more restrictive fiscal or monetary policies, currency controls, export incentives, and import obstacles.

BALANCE OF PAYMENTS

The balance-of-payments (BOP) account was discussed in some detail in Chapter 5, but we mention it here as it is a potential financial force. The state of a nation's BOP tells observant management much about the state of that country's economy. If the BOP is slipping into deficit, the government may be considering possible measures to correct or suppress that deficit. Management should be alert for either currency devaluation or restrictive monetary or fiscal policies to induce deflation. Another possibility is that currency or trade controls may be coming.

With foresight, the firm's management can adjust to the changing government policies or at least soften their impact. On the export side, the company may start shopping for export incentives—government incentives to make exporting easier or more profitable.

The Financial Force of Foreign Aid for Developing Countries

Promises aside, which rich countries actually have policies that bring important foreign aid into a developing country in order to help the poor? Such foreign aid is the traditional gauge of a country's commitment to development. The United States is the biggest donor in absolute terms, but it is the stingiest relative to the size of its economy, spending only 0.14 percent of its GDP on foreign aid. Of this aid, 72 percent is tied to the purchase of U.S. exports. Denmark's aid is .92 percent of GDP, while Norway's is .94 percent of GDP. However, aid is not the only, or even the best, measure of help. Trade policy is crucial: Shutting out developing

countries' exports is a sure way of condemning the poor to remain poor. Liberal immigration policies can also help, because migrant workers' remittances support their home economies.

A three-year-old index dawn up by the Center for Global Development (CGD), a Washington think tank, with *Foreign Policy* magazine, ranks 21 rich countries by averaging their scores in six development-related policies: aid, trade, the environment, migration, investment, and peacekeeping. In 2005, Denmark scored the highest overall. See the chart below and, for more details, www.cgdev.org. The United States scores well on trade and investment, and private giving by U.S. citizens is also strong, but with plenty of room for improvement on other dimensions, the United States ranked 12th.

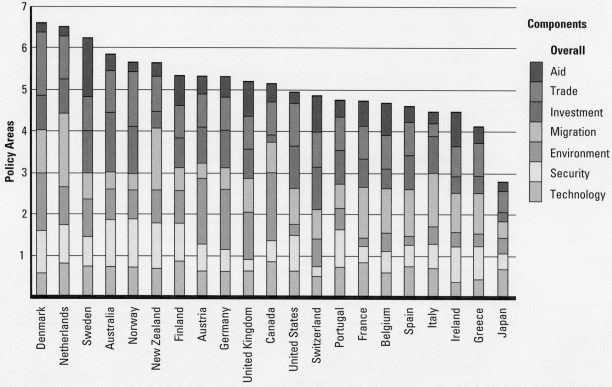

Source: Center for Global Development, http://www.cgdev.org/section/initiatives/_active/cdi (accessed 20 May, 2006).

Lower-cost capital may be available if the company can demonstrate that exports will be increased. Governments worldwide generally encourage exports, as they are viewed as positive for the economy. Therefore, some governments provide lower-cost capital if exports can be increased by doing so. One of the most common export incentives is export financing by a government agency that offers foreign buyers lower interest rates than they could get from other local capital markets. Sometimes the agency's loans are accompanied by aid grants, which need not be repaid.

Explain how money can be made—and lost—in the foreign exchange (FX) markets.

The foreign exchange (FX) markets are worldwide and collectively involve more money than any other market. On most days, you can trade money 24 hours somewhere in the world. As a result, there are ample opportunities for buying and selling foreign currency. Making or losing money in these markets depends on exchange rate movements.

Understand FX quotations, including cross rates.

FX information can be found in financial publications such as *The Wall Street Journal,* the *Financial Times,* and the financial section of major newspapers. *The Wall Street Journal* lists major currencies in terms of their trades with the US$. The spot rate (for delivery in two business days) is reported for all currencies. For the more heavily traded currencies, 30-, 60-, and 90-day forward rates are reported. Cross rates are exchange rates for trading directly between non-US$ currencies.

Describe currency exchange controls.

Many developing countries have instituted a system of currency exchange controls, which restrict the use of local and foreign currencies. Developing countries often have far less hard (convertible) currency than they need. They therefore ration the hard currency. Anyone wanting hard currency may have to apply to a government agency, specifying how much is wanted and the use to which it will be put.

Explain how financial forces such as tariffs, taxes, inflation, and the balance of payments affect international management.

Business managers must be prepared to react to financial forces that can affect their business. Tariffs are an added cost that, because they are changing, are not always predictable. Taxes also increase costs, but they tend to be more predictable in the short term. Inflation may impact where capital is sourced as well as the cost of doing business. The balance of payments may impact the ability to move funds. In general, the effects of these forces tend to increase costs or constrain the movement of funds.

central reserve asset (p. 305)

vehicle currency (p. 305)

intervention currency (p. 305)

spot rate (p. 306)

forward currency
    market (p. 306)

forward rate (p. 306)

trading at a premium (p. 307)

trading at a discount (p. 307)

cross rates (p. 307)

bid price (p. 307)

ask price (p. 307)

monetary policies (p. 308)

fiscal policies (p. 308)

law of one price (p. 308)

arbitrage (p. 308)

Fisher effect (p. 308)

international Fisher effect (p. 308)

purchasing power parity
    (PPP) (p. 308)

efficient market approach (p. 310)

random walk hypothesis (p. 311)

fundamental approach (p. 311)

technical analysis (p. 311)

Questions

1. In a U.S. financial paper, you see the quotation: "Norway (krone) U.S.$ equiv. .1601." What does that mean?

2. What is the difference between spot and forward currency rates? Why would someone be interested in buying a currency at the forward currency rate?

3. What is meant by saying that a currency is trading at a premium to the US$ in the forward market?

4. If you agree to pay a certain amount of foreign currency to someone in six months, who bears the currency fluctuation risk—you or the person you will pay? Explain.

5. What are currency exchange controls? Why are they imposed? What effect do they have in the country imposing them and elsewhere?

6. How might tariffs influence international business decisions?

7. How might knowledge of the Fisher effect aid an international manager?

8. How might the Big Mac index be useful for an international manager?

9. What are some ways in which inflation affects business decisions?

10. What is the importance of the balance of payments (BOP) to international managers?

Research Task

globalEDGE.msu.edu globalEDGE

Use the globalEDGE site (http://globalEDGE.msu.edu/) to complete the following exercises:

1. In general, your current position in a company based in the United States requires you to keep updated on trends in the *foreign exchange market*. As such, a recent capital project will require a significant greenfield investment in Japan. Download the most recent forecast that analyzes the U.S. dollar and Japanese yen and prepare a brief report. What particular trends must your company keep in mind while continuing with this investment project? Are there any dangers you should keep aware of in the near future?

2. As an entrepreneur, you are interested in expanding your business to either Sweden or Turkey. As part of your initial analysis, you would like to know how much minimum investment is needed to enter each of these markets. To have an appropriate estimate, you hire a consulting firm to perform an initial investment analysis. The consulting firm provides a short report concerning the level of minimum investment needed for each country. Taken from the report, the minimum investment amounts enclosed are: one hundred million Swedish krona and forty-five million Turkish lira. To make a clear comparison by using current exchange rates, you must convert each currency to U.S. dollars and suggest which country provides the better investment.

You are the chief executive officer of a multinational's subsidiary in a developing host country. The subsidiary has been in business for about eight years, making electric motors for the host country's domestic market, with mediocre financial results. Before you left the home country a month ago, you were told to make the subsidiary profitable or consider closing it.

After a month in the host country, you have discovered that it is running a worsening balance-of-payments (BOP) deficit and that the government officials are very concerned about the situation. They are considering various measures to stanch or reverse the deficit flow.

What measures might they adopt? Given that you would prefer to keep the subsidiary open, since it employs locals and contributes to the country's economy in other ways also, can you think of some ways your company might profit from or at least minimize the damage of these potential measures?

12

Labor Forces

Oternachi Financial Center, Tokyo, Japan

Globalization is not only striving to grow revenues by selling goods and services in global markets. It also means globalizing every activity of the company. . . . Globalization especially means finding and attracting the unlimited pool of intellectual capital—the very best people—from all around the globe.

—*General Electric, "Key Growth Initiatives"*

Differences in Labor Conditions: Examples of Japan and China

As is discussed in this chapter, there are many differences across regions and nations of the world regarding such human resource issues as the role of women in the work force, the presence of immigrant, child, or forced labor, and the extent of new labor moving from rural to urban areas. While it is not possible to discuss all of the different variations in labor conditions based on cultural or geographic factors, it will be illustrative to begin the chapter's discussion by considering two specific examples: Japan and China.

JAPAN

Japan's "jobs-for-life" culture is disappearing. The prestigious Toyota Motor Corporation has begun hiring experienced automotive designers on a contract basis. These new employees, who may be of any age or nationality, are being hired on the basis of experience, and they will be offered merit-based rather than seniority-based pay increases. In taking these steps, Toyota has made it easier for other companies to follow suit: Honda and Fujitsu are among the companies that have already done so. But changing practices regarding human resource management is typically a challenge and often is accompanied by a host of associated problems.

In the past decade, Japan has lost more than a million full-time jobs; at the same time, it has been creating part-time and temporary ones. Companies also are outsourcing services they once did in-house, such as accounting, information technology, marketing, personnel management, procurement, and training. Even many manufacturing operations have been moved to other nations where labor is cheaper and more abundant, such as China.

Japan's declining birthrate and growing number of elderly persons are creating what its government calls a "crisis" in the labor force. This could be good news for the people who are losing their jobs due to the end of the jobs-for-life culture; indeed, a labor shortage could result in new job opportunities for them.

However, the government is worried about meeting future pension liabilities. On the basis of current projections, Japan will have only two workers to pay for each pensioner by 2020, about half the number it had in 2005.

CHINA

China's shift toward a market economy has been dramatic. Since 1978, the proportion of the national economy attributable to state-owned enterprises has declined from 80 percent to approximately 15 percent.

China's shift from a rural to an urban economy has been equally dramatic. At least 300 million people have moved from villages to cities since the late 1970s, and up to 500 million more are expected to move by 2020.

In response to these trends, the need for skilled human resources in China has skyrocketed. Correspondingly, the number of students graduating from China's colleges has more than doubled since 2002. Yet, despite this surge in college-educated graduates, multinational companies say that the shortage of talented people is the biggest constraint on growth in China. This problem may largely be the result of an inability of traditional Chinese institutions to adequately adapt to the rapidly changing commercial and industrial context. For example, under the communist system, college "job allocation offices" placed students in lifetime jobs with the state and graduates had few employment options besides these

CONCEPT PREVIEWS

After reading this chapter, you should be able to:

identify forces beyond management control that affect the quantity and quality of labor in a nation

explain the reasons people leave their home countries to work abroad

discuss the reasons that some countries have guest workers

explain factors associated with employment policies, including social roles, gender, race, and minorities

discuss differences in labor unions from country to country

state-determined ones. In the more market-driven economy of contemporary China, the offices for aligning graduates with guaranteed jobs with state enterprises have disappeared, yet few employment agencies have been created to take their place. Currently, newly formed college "student employment centers" are attempting to meet new market needs, but they are understaffed and the learning curve is steep.

Many employers, particularly foreign companies operating in China, claim that Chinese schools—which emphasize memorization and minimize creativity—are not adequately preparing graduates for business careers. In many cases, classes are taught by professors with little real-world experience relevant to a market economy. As a spokesperson for L'Oreal, the multinational cosmetics and beauty supplies company, said, "Because of the characteristics of the China market, the best results are with the people we grow from the beginning. We form them in line with our culture."

In many cases, older workers from the United States are filling China's demand for experienced employees in manufacturing, education, and service industries. Of senior management expatriates working in China, 31.4 percent came from Hong Kong, 23.8 percent moved from the United States, 23.3 percent were European, and 21.4 percent came from other Asian countries. ■

Source: Leslie Chang, "China's Grads Find Jobs Scarce," *The Wall Street Journal,* June 22, 2004, p. A17; "Japan's Worry about Work," *The Economist,* January 26, 1999, pp. 35–36; "Spurring Performance in China's State-Owned Enterprises," www.forbes.com/business/2004/11/04/cx_1104mckinseychina6.html (July 28, 2006); Victor Mallet, "A Vast Human Tide Floods to the Cities," *Financial Times,* December 16, 2003, p. 5; Matt Forney, "Tug-of-War over Trade," *Time,* December 22, 2003, p. 43; James T. Areddy, "Older Workers from U.S. Take Jobs in China," *The Wall Street Journal,* June 2, 2004, p. B6; and Jihann Moreno, "Compensation Trends in Greater China," Hewitt Associates, www.hewittassociates.com/Intl/AP/en-CN/KnowledgeCenter/ArticlesReports/compensation_trends.aspx (July 28, 2006).

The quality, quantity, and composition of the available labor force within a nation are of great importance to an employer, especially since the employer must be efficient, competitive, and profitable.

labor quality

The skills, education, and attitudes of available employees

labor quantity

The number of available employees with the skills required to meet an employer's business needs

Labor quality refers to the attitudes, education, and skills of available employees. **Labor quantity** refers to the number of available employees with the skills required to meet an employer's business needs. Circumstances can arise in which there are too many available workers; this can be good or bad for the business.

If there are more qualified people than a company can economically employ, its bargaining position is strengthened and it can choose the best employees at relatively low wages. On the other hand, high unemployment can cause social and political unrest, which are usually not conducive to profitable business.

Many of the labor conditions in an area are determined by social, cultural, religious, attitudinal, and other forces discussed throughout this text. Other determinants of labor conditions are political and legal forces, and in this chapter we expand on some of those introduced in Chapters 9 and 10. In particular, we will look at labor, the reasons for its availability or scarcity, the types of labor likely to be available or scarce under different circumstances, and employer-employee relationships. We will see how these relationships are affected by government and by employee organizations such as labor unions.

Worldwide Labor Conditions and Trends

The quantity and quality of labor varies across nations and regions of the world and also over time. A brief review of demographic data provides a starting point for examining labor conditions. This section also examines other international labor trends, including the aging of populations, increasing migration from rural to urban areas, unemployment, immigration, participation by children in the labor force, and forced labor.

OVERALL SIZE AND SECTOR OF THE WORK FORCE

Let us begin by looking at the overall situation in the world, in terms of some very macro demographic data. In 2006, the world had 6.5 billion inhabitants, 46 percent of whom were under the age of 25 and 27 percent under the age of 15.[1] Due to high birthrates and a decline in the rate of infant mortality, populations in the developing nations tend to be growing as well as becoming younger. Approximately 43 percent of the world's 15- to 24-year-olds, a key source of new workers during the next decade, live in just two developing countries: India and China.[2]

In contrast, populations in many developed countries are projected to decline in the coming years, due to factors such as low birthrates and low levels of immigration. For example, between 2006 and 2050, Japan's population is projected to decline from 127.5 million to 99.9 million, Russia's from 142.9 million to 110.8 million, and Germany's from 82.4 million to 73.6 million. Countries that have admitted large numbers of immigrants, such as the United States, the United Kingdom, Canada, and Australia, are projected to have continued population growth due to the often-younger age and higher birthrates of the immigrant populations. For example, between 2006 and 2050, the United States is projected to grow from 298.4 million to 420.1 million, and Canada from 33.1 million to 41.4 million.

In which sectors of the economy is the work force working? On a worldwide basis, the proportion of jobs in the service sector has been increasing in recent decades, while the proportion employed in agriculture has been shrinking. Over the past decade, only the regions of the Middle East and North Africa have not seen an increase in the proportion of service sector jobs.[3] As shown in Figure 12.1, services are now the largest sector for labor force employment in most of the nations of the world, exceeding the proportion employed in either agriculture or industry.

AGING OF POPULATIONS

The rapid increase in the proportion of the world's population that is age 65 or older has received much attention in recent years. As shown in Figure 12.2, 7.4 percent of the world's population was 65 or older in 2006, versus 6.6 percent only a decade earlier. The proportion of those 65 or older is projected to increase to 8.4 percent of the world's population in 2015 and 16.4 percent by 2050.[4]

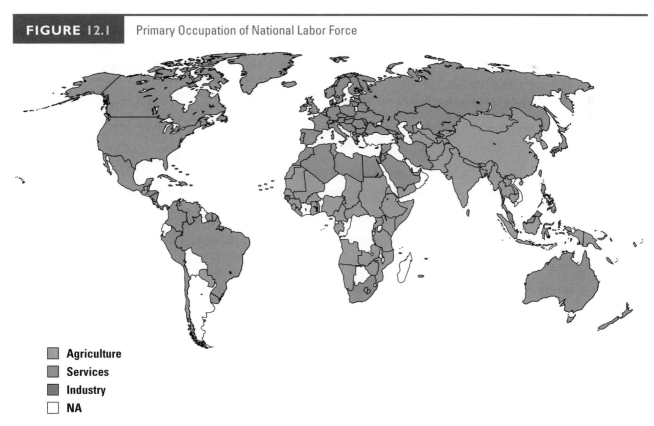

FIGURE 12.1 Primary Occupation of National Labor Force

- Agriculture
- Services
- Industry
- NA

Source: https://www.cia.gov/cia/publications/factbook/fields/2048.html (July 25, 2006).

mini **MNE**

>>Small Businesses and Jobs

Only 1 percent of the 23 million businesses in the EU have more than 250 employees, and only 7 percent have more than 9. Small businesses are particularly important in such nations as Italy, the Czech Republic, and Hungary, where companies with fewer than 20 employees account for over 90 percent of all employment. As a result, the European Commission has been directed to take several steps to mobilize and assist small businesses in job creation.

One step is the creation of the European Investment Fund to finance or guarantee job-creating projects. Another step is encouraging member-countries to simplify administrative formalities. They are also being encouraged to expand national or regional policies of support to small business. European tax systems have traditionally penalized small businesses, and the European Commission has issued a legally binding recommendation to EU member-countries to end this tax discrimination.

In Latin America, millions of women have turned to self-employment to support themselves and their families. They work as vendors, seamstresses, food makers, microscale manufacturers, and service providers and frequently expand to hire employees, subcontract, and grow to larger businesses. The Inter-American Development Bank's Microenterprise Division gives them access to credit on fair market terms and advice on managing their businesses and marketing their products. Loans can be in small amounts—as little as $50—to serve the needs of even the smallest-scale microentrepreneurs. Similar programs have been launched in sub-Saharan Africa and other less developed regions, generally with impressive results. (See Chapter 11 for more discussion of micro-lending.)

Men are not discriminated against and can get small business loans, but lenders say women are a better investment. For one thing, women are more likely than men to pay back their loans on time and in full. They also have a solid track record of using their loans to expand their businesses, boost profits, and hire new workers.

The United States Peace Corps is seeking people to help countries around the world in small business development. They want people with education or experience in all fields of business, including finance, marketing, accounting, international trade, management, retail operations, credit programs, information systems, hotel management, tourism, agribusiness, and cost analysis.

The Peace Corps has people in Africa, Latin America, Central Europe, and the former Soviet republics. Some of the countries that are hosting Peace Corps workers in small business are in Africa (Togo, Tonga, and Zimbabwe), in Latin America (Chile, Nicaragua, and Uruguay), and in Central or Eastern Europe (Czech Republic, Poland, and Slovak Republic). To discuss Peace Corps jobs, phone 1-800-424-8580 from anywhere in the United States or go to its Web site at www.peacecorps.gov.

Source: "About the Peace Corps," www.peacecorps.gov/index.cfm?shell=learn (July 27, 2006); *OECD Factbook*, http://titania.sourceoecd.org/vl-3065972/cl=20/nw=1/rpsv/factbook/data/02-04-03-t01.xls (July 27, 2006); "For Women: Big Gains from Micro-Business," *IDB Erta*, Inter-American Development Bank, 1994; and "EU Regulations: A Raw Deal for Small Businesses?" *EIU Views Wire*, March 16, 2006.

Not all nations or regions are experiencing the same extent of aging of their populations. This trend is more pronounced for the developed countries, which grew from 10 percent of the population being 65 or older in 1996 to 11.5 percent in 2006 and is projected to rise to 25.4 percent by 2050. An aging population in most of the developed countries will have important implications for labor force size and skill, for policies regarding immigration (for example, as a means of maintaining the size of the work force and population), for economic growth, and for a range of political issues related to pension plans, health care, and other key social, economic, and political factors in those nations. For example, the European Commission predicts that Europe's share of world output could decline from its current 18 percent to 10 percent by 2050, and Japan's from 8 to 4 percent, unless major policy changes are undertaken. In contrast, a more youthful United States could expand its world output share from 23 to 26 percent during the same time.

FIGURE 12.2

Percentage of
Population Age 65 or
Over

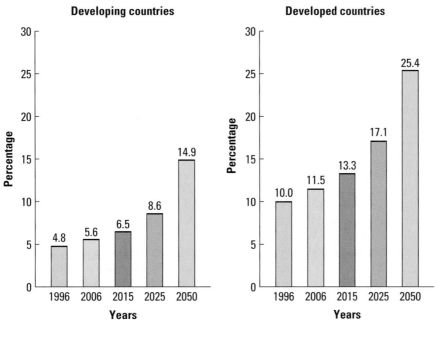

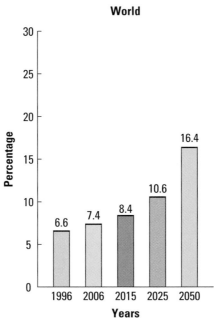

Source: U.S. Census Bureau, International, "Midyear Population, by Age and Sex," www.census.gov/cgi-bin/ipc/idbagg
(July 27, 2006).

In comparison with developed countries, the developing countries will have only about one-half the proportion of people age 65 and older, at least through 2025. India, a large developing country that had approximately one-sixth of the world's population of 20- to 64-year-olds in 2006, is projected to experience an even slower aging of its population. Due to India's large proportion of young people, its proportion of people age 65 or older is projected to rise from 4.9 percent of the nation's population in 2006 to 5.9 percent in 2015 and 14.6 percent in 2050. A much larger proportion of Indians will be of traditional working age (20 to 64) than will be the case for most of the rest of the world, especially the developed countries. That may have important implications for international companies (ICs), such as those considering where to locate production as well as those seeking markets for products that target working-age adults.

RURAL TO URBAN SHIFT

The population and labor force worldwide have been shifting dramatically from rural to urban during the past century. As shown in Figure 12.3, less than 29 percent of the world's population lived in urban areas in 1950. By 2007, over half of the population will be urban, and this proportion is projected to increase to 61 percent by the year 2030. Although the level of urbanization is higher in developed countries, the rate of urbanization was four times faster in developing countries from 1975 to 2005 as these nations experienced rapid increases in population as well as increasing economic development.

As populations migrate from rural areas to urban areas, particularly within developing nations, they also move from agriculturally based employment to employment in industry and service sectors. Often, this influx of labor from rural areas creates a pool of low-cost—but low-skilled—workers. While labor trainers for ICs in developing nations have found that the people learn industrial skills rapidly, a more difficult challenge is teaching new workers who come from farms and villages how to adjust socially and psychologically to work life in industry or service sectors. Some of these workers must be taught not only job skills but also the concept of time. They are not accustomed to reporting to work at the same time and place each workday, for example, or to meeting production schedules. They must be introduced to factory teamwork and to an industrial hierarchy. Frequently, the company must compromise and not attempt to change customary farm and village practices too quickly and completely.

A Spanish company opened a factory in Guatemala, hired local people, and tried to operate as if it were in Europe. The Spanish management installed work hours and production routines and schedules that had worked efficiently in Spain. But in Guatemala, in its early stage of economic development, the procedures were nearly disastrous.

The people refused to work and became hostile. Guatemalan troops were needed to protect the factory. Management at last considered local needs and compromised, and mutually satisfactory solutions were found.

The solutions included four-hour breaks between two daily work periods. During the breaks, the male employees took care of their farms and gardens and the female employees attended to household needs and cared for their children. As another part of the solution, the employees were willing to work on Saturdays to make up production lost during the breaks.

FIGURE 12.3

Increasing
Urbanization of the
World's Population

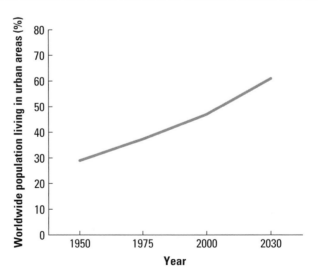

Source: *World Urbanization Prospects: The 2003 Revision* (New York: United Nations, 2003), pp. 3–4.

The first thought that typically comes to mind when you hear "international careers" is jobs in the corporate world, working for a Fortune 500 firm that services international markets and has a global reputation. This is not the only track to an international career. Many outstanding international career opportunities for people with desirable interpersonal and language skills are not in mainstream business but may require basic business expertise. Explore these options to become a part of the global work force:

- Travel, tourism, and hospitality (a major international industry found in virtually every country of the world).

- Engineering (all types).

- Health professions and health care management.

- Information technology and computer science (experiencing major worldwide growth).

- Translation and language teaching abroad.

- Environmental and natural resource management.

- International chambers of commerce.

- Foreign trade divisions of state offices of economic development.

- The U.S. government:

  U.S. Counselor Service

Foreign Service—U.S. State Department

Central Intelligence Agency and the National Security Agency

Agency for International Development (AID)

Export-Import Bank

International Trade Commission

U.S. Information Agency

Peace Corps

- International education exchange (teaching abroad).

- Volunteer and social service agencies.

- Arts and architecture.

The skills and experiences offered by any of these career options are highly sought after and readily transferable between the public and the private sectors.

World Wide Resources:

www.global.ucsb.edu/students/career_faq.html

www.state.gov/m/dghr/flo/rsrcs/pubs/12545.htm

www.transitionsabroad.com/listings/work/careers/keywebsitesprofessionspecific.shtml

Through compromise and patience, European managers, operating in a preindustrial setting, were able to achieve satisfactory production. They studied, negotiated, and adapted to local needs. The alternatives were low production and perhaps even a destroyed factory.

UNEMPLOYMENT

As we discussed in Chapter 2, trade liberalization is a key driver for development of nations and economies. However, at the same time, trade liberalization often has short- to medium-term implications for labor. This is especially the case in terms of creating "winners" and "losers" from the effects of trade and investment, both within and across nations. The individuals and groups who tend to be most susceptible to negative impacts from internationalization, due to their ability to cope quickly and effectively with trade-related reforms, include the poor, the elderly, women, and workers with low levels of skills. Compounding this issue is the fact that most developing countries lack well-developed programs—such as retraining programs, unemployment benefits, pension programs (especially ones that are portable between employers)—for dealing effectively with such a situation.[5]

Worldwide, there are more than 2.8 billion people classified as working, although 1.4 billion of these do not earn enough to enable themselves and their families to rise above the $2-per-person per-day poverty level. The overall level of unemployment is 192 million people, which is the highest volume ever. The highest level of unemployment is in the Middle East and North Africa, with 13.2 percent, followed by sub-Saharan Africa and Central and Eastern Europe and the Commonwealth of Independent States, both with 9.7 percent. Latin America and the Caribbean have a 7.7 percent rate of unemployment, and the developed economies are at 6.7 percent. Southeast Asia and the Pacific with 6.1 percent, South Asia with 4.7 percent, and East Asia with 3.8 percent had the lowest levels of unemployment.[6]

Over 88 million of the unemployed, 45 percent of the total, were youths between the ages of 15 and 24. Many of the youths who did have jobs were employed in positions that were only temporary or involuntarily part-time, with few benefits and limited potential for advancement. Unemployment also remains higher for women than for men in most countries, although that gap has been narrowing in the past decade. For example, in the OECD nations, the unemployment rate for men declined from 7.1 percent in 1994 to 6.6 percent in 2004. The unemployment rate for women in these countries declined from 8.2 percent to 7.4 percent over the same period of time.[7]

IMMIGRANT LABOR

labor mobility

The movement of people from country to country or area to area to get jobs

Although classical economists assumed that labor was immobile, we now know that **labor mobility** does exist. For example, at least 60 million people left Europe to work and live overseas between 1850 and 1970. During part of that time, between the end of World War II and the mid-1970s, some 30 million workers from southern Europe and North Africa flowed into eight northern European countries where they were needed because of the economic boom there. When possible, people move to secure better economic situations, regardless of their socioeconomic level, and immigration is at least partly the result of the relative supply of and demand for labor as well as regulations influencing those factors.

Figure 12.4 shows immigration into Organization for Economic Cooperation and Development (OECD) countries. This immigration is divided into two categories, *foreign-born* and *foreign*. The foreign-born population comprises those immigrants whose move is permanent and may include taking citizenship. The foreign population consists of those who are guest workers, transient and impermanent in their residence in the country.

The International Labor Organization estimates that there are 86 million migrant workers worldwide, with 34 million of them in developing nations.[8] However, international migrants increasingly are concentrated in developed countries, particularly the United States, Europe, and Australia.[9] Migrant labor ranges from highly skilled jobs such as in information technology or medicine to lower-skilled jobs in agriculture, cleaning, and domestic service. Many migrants are involved in "3-D" jobs—dirty, dangerous, and degrading—that a nation's own workers reject or for which there are not enough available workers.

FIGURE 12.4 Foreign and Foreign-Born Populations in Selected OECD Countries

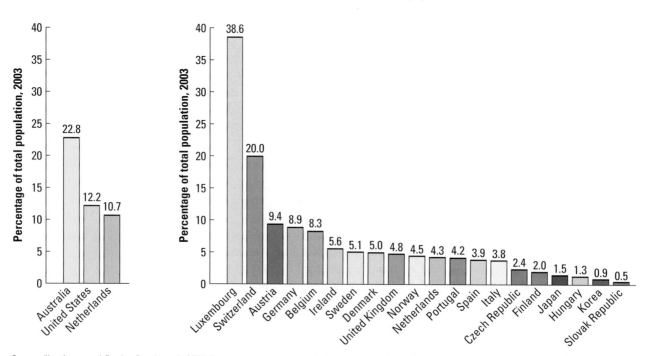

a) Foreign-born population, 2003

(b) Foreign population, 2003

Source: "Immigrant and Foreign Population," *OECD Factbook 2006—Economic, Environmental and Social Statistics*, http://puck.sourceoecd.org/vl=1424480/cl=13/nw=1/rpsv/factbook/data/01-03-01-t01.xls (July 28, 2006). Based on Population and migration-elderly population – ageing societies, *OCED FFactbook 2006: Economic, Environmental and Social Statistics*, ©**OECD** 2006. Used by permission.

The movement of large numbers of immigrants, often unskilled laborers, within and particularly between nations has become an increasingly salient issue in terms of human resource management as well as macro policy setting and political debate. The extent of this problem is illustrated by Malaysia's decision in July 2002 to deport illegal immigrants, an action that resulted in a significantly reduced work force nationally, as only 750,000 of the country's 2 million immigrant workers are legally registered.[10] Significant illegal immigrant populations also exist in other nations.[11] Estimates indicate that 10 to 15 percent of all migration is "irregular"—involving entry or work without authorization from the host countries.[12] High levels of exploitation, forced labor, and human rights abuses are associated with irregular migration.

Even legal immigration is an issue in many nations and regions. For example, several EU countries responded to fears of an unmanageable influx of workers from the EU's most recently admitted Eastern European member-states by erecting various restrictions to employment and social security programs. George Schöpflin, politics professor at London University's School of Slavonic and East European Studies, says: "Restrictions contradict the ideals of unity. But there are deep cultural fears of being overwhelmed by immigrants from the east."[13] In contrast, high levels of immigration have helped to promote economic growth in nations such as Spain, contributing to housing demand, growth in the construction sector, and expansion in other areas of the economy. About one-third of immigrants to the EU go to Spain, where the country's immigrant community has reached 9 percent of the population, a fourfold increase since 2000.[14]

Although the United States has only about 5 percent of the world's population, it has 20 percent of the world's migrants.[15] According to the U.S. Census Bureau, in 2004, 12 percent of the people residing in the United States were foreign-born, up from 5 percent in 1970, and 42 percent of the increase in the U.S. population between 2000 and 2005 came from immigration. Nearly half of the immigrants who have entered the United States since 2000 are in the country illegally.[16] About 58 percent of the new jobs created since 1995 have been filled with foreign-born workers, including over 85 percent of new positions for mechanics and construction workers and over 60 percent of service positions.[17] Overall, over 23 percent of the U.S. population either is foreign-born or has one or both parents who were foreign-born. Immigrants come to the United States from all over the world, with the largest number of foreign-born coming from Latin America (53 percent), Asia (25 percent), and Europe (14 percent).[18]

The International Labour Organization (ILO) estimates that migrant workers send home $250 billion per year.[19] This amount exceeds all official governmental assistance worldwide for development and is a major influence on economic development in many developing nations. Migrant workers also enhance home country development by transferring skills and technology when workers return to their home nations.

CHILD LABOR

According to the ILO, 218 million (one in seven) of the world's children age 5 to 17 work in streets, factories, mines, and rock quarries or as maids in homes.[20] Often they work and live in dangerous or filthy conditions for miserable wages or no compensation at all. Although most working children—122 million—are in Asia, the highest proportion is found in Africa, where 26 percent of

Thousands of immigrants and supporters rallied and marched in downtown Boston in March 2006 to protest restrictive new immigration policies being debated in Congress and to call for fair immigration reform.

child labor

The labor of children below 16 years of age who are forced to work in production and usually are given little or no formal education

all children work. **Child labor** also exists in developed countries, although the proportion is lower than is frequently found in developing nations. Overall, nearly 70 percent of child labor is in agriculture.

Sumptuous, high-pile, hand-knotted carpets produced in Nepal by children account for a significant portion of that country's export income. Nepal is one of the world's poorest countries, and it, along with other countries where child labor is prevalent, resents criticism from sources such as the ILO, which Nepal feels is dominated by the rich countries. Nepal and similar countries are suspicious of campaigns such as those by the ILO and others to eradicate countries' child labor and improve the lot of their work forces. They consider these to be masked attempts to wipe out one of the few advantages they enjoy in the world economy: low wages. They point out also that in the poorest countries, most children have no other opportunities. School exists for only the wealthy, a tiny portion of the overall population. The owner of a Nepalese carpet factory says, "If a child is not employed, it will beg or lie in the street, or use drugs."

Both the World Bank and UNICEF have made comments that are at least partly supportive of this point of view. The World Bank says that children's work can be in their own interests and that a family's survival may depend on it. UNICEF advocates banning only work that can harm children's development. It goes on to observe that forcing children out of factories and into schools may actually hurt them; unless their families are compensated for the lost income, such a policy can worsen their destitution.

Himnat Yenealem, a 13-year-old Ethiopian girl, works as a maid washing clothes, scrubbing floors, and roasting coffee beans for her employer, in exchange for shelter, food, and clothing. Her parents died of AIDS-related illnesses when she was 9, leaving her homeless. "I was in a bad dilemma, so I said 'yes' to working. I felt too scared. But at least this way, I wouldn't be homeless and I could try to upgrade myself," she explained. The woman she works for has been "moderate with me and never beat me for mistakes. She even let me go to school part time. I feel so happy about that, and now I work for her even harder."[21] In Ethiopia, only 38 percent of children attend school, and only 4 percent attend school without also working or housekeeping.

Governments of poor countries, once reluctant to even admit child labor problems, now are in a few cases trying to solve them. For example, in rural Brazil, families that promise to send their children to school can borrow a goat for breeding and keep the offspring. Police in Thailand have raided brothels holding slave child prostitutes. The Pakistani government is responding to parents' demands for better schools. In many cases, these government efforts are joined by, or even result from, initiatives from international companies.

Ikea, the giant Swedish home furnishings retailer, sources its carpets in the Indian carpet belt in the state of Uttar Pradesh. About 500,000 people work in carpet weaving there, including about 40,000 children. Apologists for child labor have claimed that children were better suited than adults for carpet weaving, due to their dexterity, and that children would be worse off if they were not employed in this business. However, Fida Hussain, who heads Deluxe Carpets in Badohi, India, disagrees with these assertions, saying, "Weaving carpets requires strength and, at every stage of production, adults are better at it." Further, "Children are put to work because their parents are in debt. It has nothing to do with how well they work." Seeking to minimize child labor and the damaging negative publicity that can accompany it, Ikea has begun a child labor initiative to source only from companies that do not use child labor. This effort includes a program to promote financial independence among poorer women in the carpet belt, giving them an opportunity to improve their work performance while simultaneously escaping the viselike grip of loan sharks and the resulting pressure to have their children take up employment. "Now that we are financially independent, we can take our children and put them in school," said one woman in the village of Suiyawan. Over 21,000 children have subsequently become literate, and several thousand women have gained financial independence.[22]

Are these efforts by governments, businesses, and nongovernmental agencies having an effect? The ILO's report *The End of Child Labour—Within Reach* claims that the number of child laborers declined by 11 percent (28 million children) between 2002 and 2006. An even sharper decline has occurred in the employment of children for hazardous work, where there has been a reported 33 percent reduction in the number of children employed.[23] Juan Somavia, the ILO's director-general, said, "We have witnessed a sea change in the awareness of child labor across the world and a broad consensus has emerged on the urgency of eradicating this scourge."[24]

However, the picture may not be as rosy as the ILO maintains. Its report is based on survey data from only 17 countries, including Brazil and India. However, nations such as Indonesia and China, which have large populations and a history of child labor, were not included in the surveys. Nor is Myanmar, a country with a weak record on many aspects of human rights, including child labor. While reducing child labor, particularly in its most hazardous forms, is a worthy goal, the attainment of this goal will require continued effort worldwide by governments, businesses, nongovernmental organizations, consumers, and the general public.

FORCED LABOR

Forced labor, which is most common in South and East Asia, northern and western Africa, and parts of Latin America, may affect as many as 27 million people today. Women, children, and low-income men are typical victims of forced labor. For example, the army in Myanmar (formerly Burma) has been reported to have forcibly recruited farmers, their wives, and children to work as porters, laborers, and human mine detectors.[25] Some forms of prison labor are also considered forced labor.[26]

BRAIN DRAIN

Record numbers of immigrants are moving to many OECD countries in search of jobs. The latest edition of the OECD's annual *Trends in International Migration* notes that even economic downturns in some OECD countries in the first part of the 21st century have not affected the upward trend in international migration that began in the mid-1990s.[27] There has been a significant increase in labor-related migration of both temporary and permanent workers and across all employment categories—skilled workers, seasonal employees, trainees, working holiday makers, staff transfers within multinational companies, and cross-border workers.

When skilled workers migrate from developing economies, a phenomenon known as **brain drain,** they generally do so for professional opportunities and economic reasons. Brain drain has become a serious problem for developing countries, especially when emigration involves the loss of such skilled professionals as scientists, IT specialists, engineers, teachers, and health care professionals. The World Bank says that the countries that are most impacted by brain drain are small, poor nations in Africa, Central America, and the Caribbean. For example, 90 percent of doctors trained in Kenya's public hospitals subsequently emigrate, leaving many areas of the country without adequate medical care.[28] Figure 12.5 shows 10 countries that have from 30 to 84 percent of their college-educated citizens living in other nations, suggesting how much these countries are being damaged by the loss of their most skilled workers.

Traditionally, a major destination for these skilled workers has been the United States, due to such factors as the existence of top-quality universities, dynamic companies, an open, merit-based economic system, the social environment, and the standard of living. Because of the salary and research opportunities available, the United States continues to attract scientists and engineers from other countries, and these immigrants have become an essential element for the health of the U.S. economy. For example, almost 25 percent of college-educated workers in the United States are foreign-born, as are over 50 percent of workers with doctorates in engineering. Roughly 53 percent of foreign students remain in the United States after receiving doctorates in science. Figure 12.6 shows the country of birth for foreign-born individuals in the United States who have a doctoral degree in science or engineering. Over one-third of these people are from the developing countries of China and India.

brain drain
The loss by a country of its most intelligent and best-educated people

FIGURE 12.5

Brain Drain: Countries
with the Highest
Percentage of Their
College-Educated
Citizens Living in
Other Countries

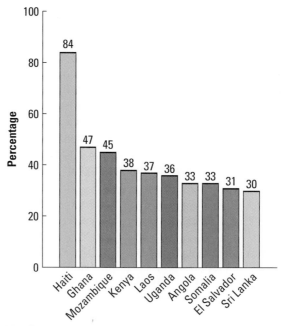

Note: Chart includes only those nations with populations of at least
5 million people.

Source: *International Migration, Remittances and the Brain Drain* (Washington, DC: World Bank, 2005). Reprinted by permission of The World Bank via The Copyright Clearance Center.

FIGURE 12.6

Foreign-Born
Individuals with
Science or
Engineering
Doctorate Degree,
Living in the U.S., by
Nation of Birth, 2003

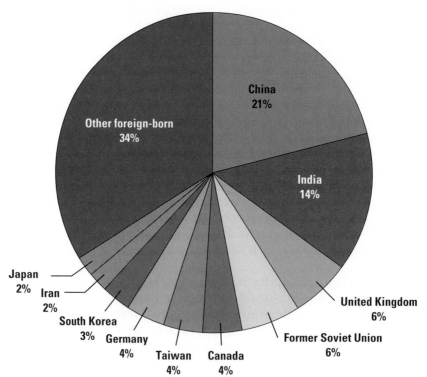

Source: *Science and Engineering Indicators 2006,* National Science Foundation, Division of Science Resources Statistics, www.nsf.gov/statistics/seind06/c3/fig03-39.htm (July 29, 2006).

Seeing the benefits that the United States has received from attracting these skilled foreign workers, countries such as the United Kingdom, Canada, and Australia have reformed their immigration policies to improve their ability to attract the best minds from abroad. The result of this competition is the creation of even more opportunities for skilled workers to migrate, threatening to exacerbate the brain drain problem in developing countries. For example, the UN expected 100,000 high-tech professionals per year to leave India for positions abroad.[29]

Government authorities who are concerned with the loss of skilled workers have come to realize that there must be changes in order to avoid being sucked into a downward cycle of underdevelopment. A high level of emigration of skilled workers is symptomatic of deep economic, political, and social problems in a country. There must be faster creation of new, well-paying jobs, not only to stop the costly loss of human capital but also to avoid serious political repercussions. The pressure of the unemployed educated is also forcing officials in many areas to soften the terms for foreign investment as an option for creating incentives for these skilled people to stay in their home country.

Reverse Brain Drain   Recently, American educators and businesspeople have become concerned about a *reverse brain drain,* a trend related to the growth of outsourcing and a willingness of the federal government to allow "controversial" scientists to move to other countries.[30] The growth of outsourcing in developing economies such as India is beginning to pull Indian talent back home. As one recent returnee said, "We give up the swimming pool in favor of a maid." American firms are contributing aggressively to this aspect of reverse brain drain as they outsource knowledge work—engineering, software, product design, and development—to such countries as China, India, and Russia. Intel chairman Craig Barrett has warned that Russia, China, and India already have as many as 250 million to 500 million knowledge workers—the kind of highly educated, technologically skilled employees who can write computer code, design sophisticated products, and manage high-end production processes.

Some of the scientists involved in controversial science, such as stem cell research, which is limited in the United States by the federal government, are moving to environments where such cutting-edge research is supported.

In some developing countries whose scientists and engineers have gone to industrialized nations, organizations sponsored by local industry and occasionally by governments have reverse-brain-drain programs. For example, the National Science and Technology Development Agency of Thailand sponsors a Reverse Brain Drain Association.[31]

GUEST WORKERS

Countries that receive many refugees or have high birthrates may have too many people for the available jobs, but there are also countries that have too few people. France, Germany, the Scandinavian countries, and Switzerland, all of which have low birthrates, fall into the latter category. And to those countries have come the so-called **guest workers** to perform certain types of jobs, usually in service, factory, or construction work. Most of the guest workers in these countries are from such places as Turkey, Eastern Europe, and North Africa. See the Worldview on the next page for a discussion of guest workers in Japan.

Guest workers provide the labor that host countries need, which is desirable as long as the economies are growing. But when the economies slow, fewer workers are needed and problems appear. Unemployment increases among citizens, who then want the jobs held by guest workers. To appease their citizens, some countries refuse to renew guest workers' permits. In other countries, where work is seasonal, guest workers are deported at the end of the season instead of being permitted to stay and take other work.

guest workers
People who go to a foreign country legally to perform certain types of jobs

Considerations in Employment Policies

Companies considering doing business in international markets must consider a range of issues related to the employment policies to use. Some of these issues, such as social status, sexism, racism, the existence of minorities within traditional societies, and overall labor situations commonly encountered in developing nations, are discussed in this section.

Guest Workers in Japan?

Although Japan is facing a shortage of labor in many sectors, a situation exacerbated by the rapid aging of its population, the country is famous for its resistance to immigration. To help address this problem, Japan established an elaborate system in the 1990s to create more temporary openings for foreigners of Japanese descent. Brazil, with the largest population of people of Japanese descent outside Japan, subsequently has been the source of over 300,000 persons. The highly restrictive Japanese system also allows entry by other qualified persons, including those qualifying under training-with-employment schemes established primarily for people from less developed countries in the region, but work visas are offered in only 17 fields of employment. For example, Vietnam has approximately 3,000 workers legally in Japan under training-employment programs.

Beyond those restricted categories, Japan does not have guest workers in the European sense, where they are legal. Yet there are thousands of other foreign workers in Japan, coming mostly from such nations as Vietnam, the Philippines, Bangladesh, and Pakistan. These workers commonly enter Japan with tourist or entertainment visas, as students, or as trainee-probationers, often on false passports, and then they find jobs and stay. In 2006, then Prime Minister Junichiro Koizumi said there were 250,000 illegal migrant workers in Japan.

The law only prohibits these migrant laborers from working in Japan; it does not prohibit employers from hiring them. So clandestine workers in Japan essentially have no legal rights. They cannot force employers to pay fair wages or appeal to the police for help.

A Japan Labor Ministry survey showed that on average these illegal workers earn less than half the wages of their Japanese coworkers. Firms save even more on labor costs because illegal workers do not receive the insurance or other benefits usually demanded by Japanese employees. These non-Japanese laborers often work 60 to 70 hours a week in small factories, the fast-food industry, or construction.

Japan's contractors and smaller manufacturers have begun to depend on cheap foreign labor to offset rising costs and competition from lower-cost nations such as China. Even at much higher legal wages and benefits, there is a severe shortage of Japanese laborers who are willing to perform the dangerous or dirty work done by the illegal workers.

The situation is particularly dangerous for young women employed in the bars and massage parlors of Japan's ubiquitous "entertainment industry." As frequently happens, young women come to Japan expecting to work as waitresses or hotel clerks, but exploitative business owners take their passports away and force them to work as prostitutes.

Japan historically has relied heavily on foreign workers to fill labor shortages, but it is far from a melting pot. Thousands of Koreans and Chinese were forcibly recruited during World War II to work in factories and mines. Most of the more than 600,000 people of Korean and Chinese ancestry who remain in Japan are virtually indistinguishable from their Japanese neighbors. Over 75 percent were born in Japan and speak Japanese fluently. Nevertheless, they are still classified as "resident aliens," must carry alien registration cards, and are regarded as "other" by many Japanese.

Source: Charles Barneholtz, "Guests, but Not So Welcome," www.westernreview.com/barney3.htm (July 28, 2006); "Migration News: Japan, Korea," http://migration.ucdavis.edu/mn/more.php?id=3191_0_3_0 (July 28, 2006); Wolfgang Herbert, *Foreign Workers and Law Enforcement in Japan* (New York: Columbia University Press, 1997); "Assessment for Koreans in Japan," www.humansecuritygateway.info/data/item819082824/view (July 28, 2006); and "Guest Workers Urged to Learn New Language," www.vneconomy.com.vn/eng/index.php?param=article&catid=09&id=74ff2a118356a5 (July 28, 2006).

SOCIAL STATUS

Chapter 6 discussed the importance of culture to international business. Culture is especially important with respect to the labor force, since culture so dominates human behavior and attitudes. Understanding social status is necessary to understanding cultures because in some cultures, social divisions are more extreme than in others. The Worldview on page 337 provides a brief overview of social status in three nations: the United Kingdom, India, and Japan.

SEXISM

Acceptability of women as full participants in the work force ranges from a trend toward improvement in the United States and Western Europe to almost no acceptability in some other countries. In many countries, laws, customs, and attitudes continue to act as barriers to women in business. Sexism, the denial of equal participation in a society for women, developed as an inherent part of many cultures, based as they are on patriarchal values. Greater awareness of the importance of providing equal opportunity for both genders and changing attitudes toward the roles of women in society in general and business in particular have made it possible for women to succeed in business in many parts of the world. Culture and tradition, though, continue to make full and equal participation difficult for women.

WORLD view

Social Status in the United Kingdom, India, and Japan

United Kingdom

The class system in the United Kingdom may be eroding, but people there are still classified by the accents they acquire at home and school. When Margaret Thatcher was elected prime minister, commentators saw fit to point out that she was "only" the daughter of a small-store owner even though her accent was "upper class," apparently acquired at Oxford University. Although class differences do not cause riots in the United Kingdom, as caste differences have in India, a foreign employer should nevertheless be conscious of the possibilities for friction arising from lack of knowledge of those differences and their potential impacts.

India

There are societies in which people's social status is established by the *caste* into which they are born. India presents an extreme example of the caste system. Intercaste battles that cause fatalities and home burnings still occur occasionally between upper-caste Hindus and the untouchables, whom Mahatma Gandhi called *Harijans*, the children of God. An employer must tread carefully when both upper-caste Hindus and Harijans are in the employee pool.

Caste remains pervasive in India, a populous country of growing importance in the world. Any businessperson venturing to India must understand some facts about caste. At the top is the *Brahmin* (priest, teacher), followed by the *Kshatriya* (variously landholder, warrior, or ruler). At the third level is the *Bania* (businessman), which is a step above the *Shudra* (laborer). The top three are considered upper caste and include 15 percent of India's population and have ruled the country for 3,000 years. Another 50 percent of the population belongs to the laboring, or Shudra, caste. Roughly 20 percent are casteless or untouchables considered beyond the pale of Hindu society. The remaining 15 percent belong to other religions—11 percent are Muslim, and the others are Buddhists, Christians, Parsis, and Sikhs.

Caste rules are rigid, and those who deviate from them are shunned. Caste divides Indian society into groups whose members do not intermarry and usually will not eat with each other.

Change is occurring, though. The young, including the children of the Brahmins and Kshatriya, no longer view civil service as the career of choice. Many want to get an MBA and go into business; money, rather than power, is what motivates many young people. Another change is the conversion of Hindus to other religions to escape their low caste or untouchable status.

Japan

In Japan, there remains a caste holdover from the 17th century, when the feudal Togugawa regime imposed a rigid social pecking order on the country. The warrior-administrator samurai were at the top. Below them were farmers and artisans, then merchants, and, at the very bottom, those with occupations considered dirty and distasteful, such as slaughterers, butchers, and tanners.

As in India, where discrimination against untouchables is illegal, all natives of Japan who are of the Japanese race are legally equal. However, the descendants of the lowest Japanese class remain trapped in their ghettos, working in small family firms that produce knitted garments, bamboo wares, fur and leather goods, shoes, and sandals. They call themselves *burakumin* (ghetto people) and claim they number about 3 million people living in some 6,000 ghettos. Their average income remains below that of other Japanese.

The word *burakumin* is almost never aired in the Japanese media, and foreign books that touch on the problem have all references to it deleted when they are translated into Japanese. One woman, Sue Sumii, although she was not a burakumin, lived near one of their ghettos and recorded and decried its residents' plight in speeches, articles, and a series of stories. Sumii made links between the Japanese imperial family's wealth and burakumin wretchedness and between the shared religious roots of emperor worship and scorn for the burakumin.

Women encounter major problems in making or retaining progress, as sexism is widespread throughout the world. It is often difficult for women to do business in Saudi Arabia and other Middle Eastern countries. For example, the law and customs in Saudi Arabia have prevented the commingling of men and women in the workplace, and women have been prohibited from driving vehicles. Reports of sexism, particularly versus migrant workers, are rampant.[32] Yet, even in Saudi Arabia, the role of women is changing. For example, programs have recently been set up to encourage women to start businesses, the range of sectors in which women can work has been expanded, and women managers can have males as their subordinates.[33]

Worldwide, 59 percent of all businesses include women in senior management positions, although women fill less than 19 percent of all senior management jobs. Women are senior managers in 70 percent of New Zealand businesses, although only one-third of all senior management positions in New Zealand are held by women. Only 22 percent of senior managers in Australia are female. Only 29 percent of companies in Japan have filled senior management slots with women, and women constitute only 8 percent of senior managers. In Russia,

FIGURE 12.7 Female Illiteracy

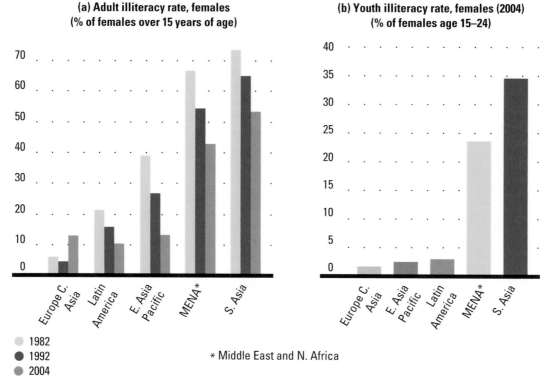

(a) Adult illiteracy rate, females
(% of females over 15 years of age)

(b) Youth illiteracy rate, females (2004)
(% of females age 15–24)

● 1982
● 1992   * Middle East and N. Africa
● 2004

Source: *World Development Indicators,* World Bank (2006). Copyright © 2006 by World Bank. Reproduced with permission of World Bank in the format textbook via Copyright Clearance Center.

89 percent of the companies have staffed senior management positions with women, and 42 percent of their management positions are filled by women.[34]

Women's Education   Studies show a persistent correlation between the length of women's schooling and birthrates, child survival, family health, and a nation's overall prosperity. As Figure 12.7 indicates, women's education is making marked improvements, with the rate of illiteracy declining significantly across all regions during the past two decades. An increasing number of countries are realizing the importance of educating females. For example, the Egyptian government is integrating a successful concept of girl-friendly community schools into the formal education system. These schools use female teachers, active learning, and child-centered class management. In one region of China, villages and households that send girls to school are given priority for loans or development funds. A promising initiative in Tanzania aims to find solutions to obstacles to the social and academic development of girls by encouraging girls to speak out about their problems.[35] In the United States, for the first time, the group of women between the ages of 25 and 35 has more formal education than does its male counterpart. About half the students in American business schools are now women.

Problems Persist   Even in countries where women have made some strides, their progress is not necessarily secure. When the fundamentalist Islamic government took control from the shah in Iran in 1979, it separated the sexes, ordering women to return to their strict traditional dress and roles. In recent years, women have regained some opportunities. Iran is a society with firm gender roles, as are Afghanistan, Iraq, and many other collectivist societies with high "power distance" (see Chapter 6, "Sociocultural Forces"). Even in the United States today, women have made great advancements yet continue to face discrimination, especially in advancing into the higher levels of business management.

Another measure of the prevalence of women in positions of authority is the proportion of their membership in national parliaments. Figure 12.8 shows the percentages of seats held

FIGURE 12.8 Women in Parliament, Selected Nations, 2006

Seats held as % of total, *

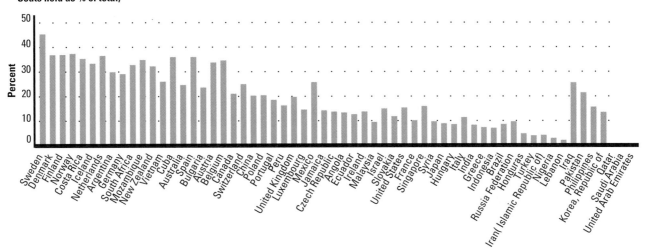

* Lower or single house.

Source: UN Statistics Division, "Seats Held by Women in National Parliament, Percentage," http://mdgs.un.org/unsd/mdg/SeriesDetail.aspx?srid=557 (July 30, 2006).

for various nations, with Sweden having the highest at 45.3 percent and Qatar, Saudi Arabia, and the United Arab Emirates having the lowest, with zero percent. Note that the proportion of women in parliament lags their proportion in the society as a whole for each one of these countries.

Another persistent gender-related problem in the labor markets is the issue of maternity and ensuing family responsibilities. Although in the United States there is much talk of "family-friendly" business practices, as Table 12.1 indicates, the maternity leave arrangements in the United States are not comparable to those of EU countries. The challenges for women who choose to be mothers and have professional careers just begin at childbirth. There is no public day care and only the best employers make such support available. Depending on location, private day care standards vary greatly.

Throughout most of the world, women on average still earn only a fraction of the level of pay that men earn for comparable positions, as shown in Table 12.2 for the OECD nations. However, as this table shows, the gap between women and men has been shrinking in most of the OECD countries.

RACISM

Unfortunately, examples of racial conflicts and discrimination are found worldwide. There are black-versus-white conflicts in the United States, South Africa, Great Britain, and elsewhere, and Arab-, Indian-, or Pakistani-versus-black conflicts in Africa. Racial friction exists related to the guest workers in parts of Europe. There has been bloody conflict in Sri Lanka between Tamils and Sinhalese. The list goes on: Bosnia, Kosovo, Zimbabwe, Rwanda, Burundi, the Sudan.

If we think of racism as a form of extended and institutionalized prejudice, globalization, as it increases individual contacts among quite different people, may work against racism. This hope may not be shared by some, who see the process of globalization as a source of increased racism. The reasoning for hope is that successful international managers develop a global mind-set,[36] made up of cognitive complexity and a cosmopolitan attitude that, in its openness to the world and valuing of difference, leaves no room for racism.

The United Nations–sponsored World Conference on Racial Discrimination, Xenophobia, and Related Intolerance, held in South Africa, has initiated efforts to establish nation-level bodies to address these particular issues: trafficking in women and children, migration

TABLE 12.1   Maternity Leave Legislation

Country	Maternity Leave			Parental Leave		
	Length (weeks)	Payment (% earnings)	Continuation of Payment by Employer	Length (months)	Maximum Child Age (years)	Payment
Austria	16	100	Low-wage workers	3–24	2	410 euros/month
Netherlands	16	100	No	6	8	Unpaid
Spain	16	100	No	—	3	Unpaid
Luxembourg	16	—	No	6	5	1,487 euros/month
Germany	14	100	No	—	3	306 euros/month
Greece	14	100	No	3.5	3.5	Unpaid
Italy	18	80	No	10	3	30% earnings
France	16–26	84	Yes	—	3	461 euros/month
United Kingdom	14	90	No	3.25	5	Unpaid
Portugal	12.5	100	No	6	3	Unpaid
Denmark	18	67	Yes	2–12	8	920 euros/month
Finland	17.5	66	Yes	6.5	3	10 euros/day
Belgium	15	82 first month, 75 rest	No	3	4	505 euros/month
Ireland	14	70	No	3.5	5	Unpaid
Sweden	12	80	—	18	8	80% earnings
United States	12	Unpaid	No	—	—	—

Source: Ghazala Azmat, Mara Güell, and Alan Manning, "Gender Gaps in OECD Countries," www.oecd.org (2004).

and discrimination, gender and racial discrimination, racism against indigenous peoples, and protection of minority rights. See the United Nations Personal Pledge against Racism in Figure 12.9.

MINORITIES IN TRADITIONAL SOCIETIES

traditional societies
Tribal peoples before they turn to organized agriculture or industry; traditional customs may linger after the economy changes

minorities
A relatively smaller number of people identified by race, religion, or national origin who live among a larger majority

Traditional societies present opportunities as well as problems for employers. In some societies, merchants, businesspeople, and bankers are looked down on and people prefer political, religious, military, professional, or agricultural careers. In such societies, outsiders may dominate commercial and banking activities. Some examples are the Indians and Pakistanis in East Africa, the Chinese in Southeast Asia, and the Greeks in Turkey.

An advantage for a foreign employer moving into these societies is that such **minorities** may be immediately available, bringing financial and managerial skills to the employer. They speak the local language and usually one or more others, and they are less nationalistic than the majority. A disadvantage is that such people are often unpopular with the majority local population. Foreign employers can easily become too dependent on minority employees, thus becoming isolated and insulated from the world of the majority. Discrimination against such minorities has often occurred. In Uganda, for example, the government seized the property, shops, and land of people of Indian and Pakistani heritage, drove them out, and turned the seized assets over to native Ugandan citizens. In Zimbabwe, the government seized the land and assets of whites and gave these assets to black Zimbabweans, most of whom were supporters of President Mugabe's ruling party.

TABLE 12.2	Ratio of Wages, Women versus Men, Selected OECD Countries	
Country	**1990–1993**	**1999–2001**
Australia	0.80	0.84
Austria	0.68	0.80
Belgium	0.75	0.88
Canada	0.69	0.74
Denmark	0.83	0.86
Finland	0.75	0.82
France	0.75	0.88
Hungary	0.81	0.79
Iceland	0.87	0.84
Ireland	0.80	0.80
Italy	0.83	0.85
Japan	0.56	0.64
Netherlands	0.72	0.79
Norway	0.85	0.86
Poland	0.82	0.85
Spain	0.72	0.86
Sweden	0.78	0.83
Switzerland	0.69	0.78
United States	0.73	0.78
United Kingdom	0.69	0.75
West Germany	0.74	0.81

Source: Nicole M. Fortin, "Gender Role Attitudes and the Labour Market Outcomes of Women across OECD Countries," www.econ.ubc .ca/nfortin/genderole.ppt (July 30, 2006).

LABOR IN DEVELOPING NATIONS

The labor situation in many developing economies faces several formidable challenges. First are the effects of poverty, which, as we have seen, impact the quality of the labor force. Low education levels, which are found in many developing nations, especially among females, are a critical handicap. In addition, with the growth of globalization, businesses in many developing nations face global-level competition. Increasingly, there is less tolerance in the globalizing marketplace for local inefficiencies. As if these developments were not enough in the way of challenge, the devastations of HIV/AIDS, exacerbated by local poverty, low levels of education, and social unrest, have created labor shortages that many developing nations will face for the foreseeable future. In these economies, up-skilling, or training the local work force to minimally acceptable standards, is a primary employer challenge.

In developing nations where there is a high level of education, outsourcing of production, IT support, and, increasingly, service functions such as customer service help lines and marketing lead follow-ups have been the recent trend. This has become a political issue in the United States, because it represents jobs transferred from the U.S. economy to a developing economy such as India. But from the developing country's point of view, it may be seen as one of the benefits of globalization.

Employer-Employee Relationships

The relationship between employers and employees varies in countries around the world. In some countries, employers must deal with strong labor unions. In others, employers must deal with governments representing employees. In any case, a company seeking to employ people must be aware of the local employment context.

FIGURE 12.9

UN Pledge against
Racism

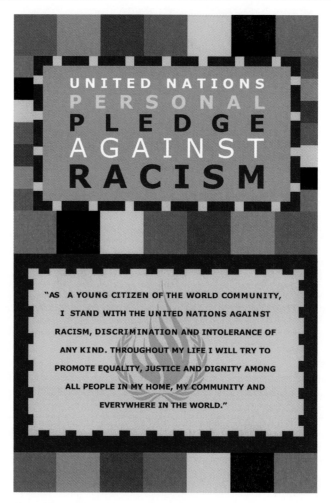

Source: Photo courtesy of UN, www.UN.org/WCAR (2006).

IMPORTANCE OF PROPER PREPARATION WHEN ENTERING A MARKET

labor market

The pool of available potential employees with the necessary skills within commuting distance from an employer

When a foreign company arrives in a **labor market,** it must take what it finds. Of course, a prudent company will study the labor market when considering whether to invest in a country. A company does not even have to travel to a prospective host country to gain information about its labor force. In addition to *Foreign Labor Trends* released by the Bureau of International Labor Affairs of the U.S. Department of Labor, two good information sources are the *Handbook of Labor Statistics* (available from the Bureau of Labor Statistics of the U.S. Department of Labor in Washington, D.C.) and the *Yearbook of Labor Statistics* (published by the United Nations' International Labor Office in Geneva, Switzerland). These sources give information for most countries of the world on several subjects, including the number of labor strikes, or work stoppages, per year. The number of workers who went on strike is indicated, as is the number of working days lost. Last, but perhaps most informative, the days lost per thousand employees in nonagricultural industries for each country is reported. The countries about which those labor figures are reported vary greatly in size, culture, labor laws, and militancy of labor unions. Thus, the days lost per thousand is the only direct comparison among them. Figure 12.10 shows the average number of working days lost through labor disputes per 1,000 employees for selected OECD nations across the most recent decade. These statistics are all raw numbers, and potential employers should investigate more deeply when considering a labor market.

Here are some other questions that employers should look into: (1) Was the period abnormal for any of the countries? (2) Were the strikes peaceful, or were they accompanied by violence, destruction, or death? (3) Were the strikes industrywide, or were they only against

FIGURE 12.10   Country Strike Rates, Selected OECD Nations

Working days lost per 1,000 employees, annual average 1995–2004

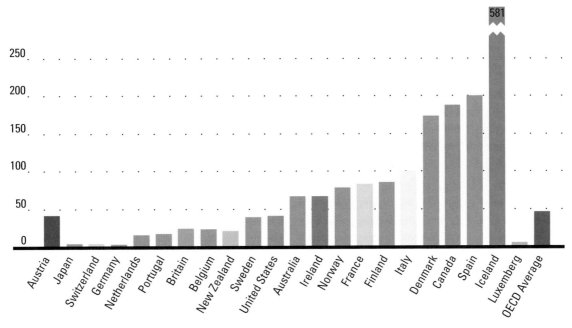

Source: Rachel Beardsmore, "International Comparisons of Labour Disputes in 2004," in Office for National Statistics (U.K.), *Labor Market Trends,* April 2006, p. 119, http://www.statistics.gov.uk/articles/labour_market_trends/Int_labourdisputes.pdf (November 13, 2006). © Crown Copyright. Reproduced under the terms of the Click-Use License.

selected employers? (4) Were the strikes wildcat (unannounced), or was there usually warning that they were coming? and (5) Do the unions and the workers abide by labor agreements, and if not, what can the employer do?

Companies planning to invest in traditional-society developing countries will examine the cultural, religious, tribal, and other factors discussed elsewhere in this text. Of course, religious, racial, and linguistic schisms are not confined to developing countries.

LABOR UNIONS: EUROPE, UNITED STATES, AND JAPAN

Labor unions vary significantly from country to country. Labor unions tend to be more effective in developed countries, but even comparing Europe, the United States, and Japan, it is apparent that labor unions serve different purposes and influence employee matters differently.

European labor unions are usually identified with political parties and socialist ideology. A sense of worker identity is common in these unions, probably because European labor gained freedom from feudalism as well as various rights and powers through collective action.

In the United States, by contrast, laborers already possessed many civil rights, including the vote, by the time unions became important. As a result, unionism in the United States often has been viewed as more pragmatic than political and more concerned with the immediate needs of workers.

Labor legislation in the United States has mostly confined itself to the framework of **collective bargaining.** Collective bargaining is the process in which a union represents the interests of everyone in a bargaining unit (which sometimes includes both union members and nonmembers) in negotiations with management. In Europe, government's role is more active, with wages and working conditions frequently legislated. Many Latin American governments are very active in employer-employee relationships, frequently because the unions are weak and the union leaders are inexperienced or uneducated.

labor unions
Organizations of workers

collective bargaining
The process in which a union represents the interests of a bargaining unit (which sometimes includes both union members and nonmembers) in negotiations with management

In Germany and France, the influences of law and government administrative actions on work conditions are extensive and evident. Labor negotiations are conducted on national or regional levels, and in France, government representatives take part in the negotiations.

Japanese unions are enterprise-based rather than industrywide and, as a result, tend to identify strongly with the interests of the company. For example, if unions are convinced a high wage increase would hurt the company's competitiveness, they tend to not ask for much of a pay raise.

Labor Union Membership Trends   For the past four decades there has been a steady decline in union membership internationally. The reasons for this trend are several:

- Employers have made efforts to keep their businesses union-free, including putting employees on business boards and instituting profit-sharing plans. This co-option approach has had its desired effect in many cases.

- More women and teenagers have joined the work force, and since theirs are usually secondary incomes, they accept lower wages and have little loyalty toward organized labor.

- The unions have been successful. Their results have led to wage increases, which have led to higher costs and lower competitiveness of their employers, which have led to layoffs, downsizing, and movement of jobs to lower-cost locations. So in this sense, unions have been the victims of their own success.

- As developed countries transition to a knowledge economy, the industrial jobs that have formed the core of union membership are declining.

MULTINATIONAL LABOR ACTIVITIES

The internationalization of business has been under way for many years, and international companies have expanded rapidly since the 1950s. National unions have begun to perceive opportunities for companies to escape the organizing reach of unions through the relatively simple step of international outsourcing, transferring production to another country. Unions see such steps as dangerous. To combat those dangers, national unions have begun to (1) collect and disseminate information about companies, (2) consult with unions in other countries, (3) coordinate with those unions' policies and tactics in dealing with some companies, and (4) encourage international companies' codes of conduct. Such multinational labor activity is likely to increase, although unions are divided by ideological differences and are frequently strongly nationalistic. Vastly more effort and money have been spent on lobbying for protection of national industries than on cooperating with unions in other countries.

An important first arena in which successful multinational unionism may develop is the European Union. The EU member-countries are steadily eliminating or harmonizing their tariffs, taxes, monetary systems, laws, and much more. As further progress is made in this harmonization process, the resulting atmosphere may be more hospitable for the cooperation of national unions.

Also working in this area is the European Trade Union Confederation (ETUC), an umbrella organization representing 81 national union federations, representing 60 million members in 36 nations.[37] Some ETUC member-unions are doing very well on their own, cooperating across borders in pursuit of a common goal.

The U.S. union federation, the AFL-CIO, cooperates with labor organizations worldwide, including ETUC, the International Confederation of Free Trade Unions (ICFTU), the Asia Pacific Regional Organization (APROICFTU), and the Latin America Regional Organization (ORIT-ICFTU).

Union Network International was formed in 2000 to promote global union efforts in response to the increasing level of globalization of industries and employers. Based in Switzerland, it includes 900 unions with over 15 million members in over 140 nations.

International Labor Organization   The International Labor Organization (ILO) is a specialized agency of the UN whose purpose is to promote social justice and internationally recognized human and labor rights worldwide. The ILO was founded in 1919 and is the only surviving major creation of the Treaty of Versailles, which founded the League of Nations. It became the first specialized agency of the UN in 1946. Today, the ILO formulates international labor standards in the form of treaties and recommendations setting minimum standards for basic labor rights: freedom of association, the right to organize, collective bargaining, abolition of forced labor, equality of opportunity and treatment, and other standards regulating working conditions. More information can be obtained at the ILO's Web site, www.ilo.org.

Trade Union Advisory Committee to the OECD   As discussed in Chapter 4, the Organization for Economic Cooperation and Development (OECD) is an international organization designed to assist with economic development issues in its member-nations. The Trade Union Advisory Committee (TUAC) is an international trade union organization with consultative status with the OECD and its various committees. TUAC's role is to ensure that labor issues are considered in global markets. TUAC represents the views of the trade union movement as it regularly consults with the various OECD committees. More information about TUAC can be found at the organization's Web site, www.tuac.org.

Would Harmonized Labor Standards Boost Trade and Income?   Labor unions, human rights activists, and some developed country governments argue that access to their markets should be dependent on improved labor standards in developing countries and that trade sanctions should be imposed for violation of those standards (the so-called social clause). Other governments in both developed and developing countries see the social clause as protectionism. Yet even in trade agreements, governments argue for strict labor standards. NAFTA, which was negotiated among the United States, Canada, and Mexico, includes major sections involving labor matters.

According to the International Monetary Fund (IMF), the economic arguments for harmonizing labor standards are weak. In fact, well-intentioned attempts to impose higher labor standards on developing countries may actually be detrimental to workers, especially if they are enforced through trade sanctions. Low labor standards are not the primary source of developing countries' comparative advantage, while most labor standards—such as minimum wages—are not attainable in many poor countries.

Higher labor standards, the IMF points out, are primarily a consequence rather than a cause of economic growth, and the surest way to improve labor standards in poor countries is through economic growth, which international trade facilitates. Accordingly, pursuing trade and labor market policies conducive to high growth rates will be far more effective in raising labor incomes than will be mandating levels of wages and benefits or imposing trade sanctions for perceived violations.

Summary

Identify forces beyond management control that affect the quantity and quality of labor in a nation.

Labor quality and labor quantity are forces beyond a company's control. A finite number of employees are available in any labor pool with the skills required to meet an employer's needs. Populations are aging and are projected to decline in many developed countries in coming years. Labor is shifting significantly from rural to urban locations, especially in developing nations. Unemployment remains a problem in many regions and particularly among youths between the ages of 15 and 24. Large numbers of immigrant laborers, often unskilled, are moving within and particularly between nations. Although progress is being made, an estimated one in seven children between the ages of 5 and 17 is a laborer and most of these child laborers are in the developing countries.

Explain the reasons people leave their home countries to work abroad.

In many parts of the world, wars, revolutions, racial and ethnic battles, and political repression cause people to flee. Others go to other countries in hopes of better jobs and pay.

Discuss the reasons that some countries have guest workers.

Guest workers move to a host country to perform specific types of jobs, usually in service, factory, or construction work. But when a country's economy slows, its native workers may want the jobs held by guest workers. Racial friction has developed in some countries because of guest workers.

Explain factors associated with employment policies, including social roles, gender, race, and minorities.

ICs typically must adjust their labor practices to succeed in international markets, due to a range of factors influencing employment policies and practices. Even where laws have changed to prohibit the practice, cultural, historical and other factors cause social status to be a relevant consideration regarding employment practices. Although women are making progress toward equality in many nations, sexism remains a problem throughout the world. Women continue to have higher levels of illiteracy and lower levels of wages than their male counterparts in virtually all regions of the world, and they are underrepresented in business and political positions of authority. Racism also remains an issue worldwide.

Discuss differences in labor unions from country to country.

Historically, labor unions have tended to be more political in Europe and more pragmatic in the United States. In response to globalization of businesses, many unions have begun to establish international collaboration in an effort to extend their influence.

Key Words

labor quality (p. 324)
labor quantity (p. 324)
labor mobility (p. 330)
child labor (p. 332)

brain drain (p. 333)
guest workers (p. 335)
traditional societies (p. 340)
minorities (p. 340)

labor market (p. 342)
labor unions (p. 343)
collective bargaining (p. 343)

Questions

1. a. How could an excess of qualified employees be beneficial for an employer?
   b. How could it be detrimental?

2. Why is the average age of the population increasing in some nations, particularly the developed countries? What are some of the implications of this trend, especially for international companies?

3. Classical economists assumed the labor factor of production to be immobile. Is this assumption correct in the modern world? Explain.

4. Analyze arguments made by representatives of Nepal and other poor countries in justifying the child labor they utilize.

5. What is brain drain, and why does it occur? What actions might countries take in order to reduce or even reverse brain drain?

6. What trends are evident in the way women are treated relative to men in terms of education, employment, and positions of authority? How and why do these trends vary across countries and regions of the world?

7. In several Southeast Asian and South Pacific countries, the Chinese minority is prominent in banking, finance, and business. What are the dangers for a foreign employer staffing the local company primarily with such a minority?

8. What is a major difference between unions in Europe, the United States, and Japan?

9. What are the prospects for effective multinational union collaboration? Discuss.

Research Task

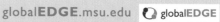
globalEDGE.msu.edu   globalEDGE

Use the globalEDGE site (http://globalEDGE.msu.edu/) to complete the following exercises:

1. The participation of women in the labor force varies from one country to another. After finding a report on *International Labor Comparisons*, find information concerning labor force participation rates by gender for France, Germany, Japan, Sweden, and the United States. For the last year in which data were available for these five countries, develop a ranking based on the level of participation of women in the workforce. Which country had the highest level? Which had the lowest?

2. According to this textbook, a nation's immigration policy is a good reference point for examining labor mobility. Using CIA's *World Factbook* Web site, identify five countries with the highest net immigration rate in Europe.

Your company, an international company based in the United States, has decided to expand aggressively in Asia. It plans to outsource many of its raw materials, to subcontract, and to manufacture and market throughout Asia, from Japan in the north through New Zealand in the south.

You were appointed to organize and direct this major new effort and to determine where to locate the regional headquarters for the Asian division. After considerable study, you selected the island nation of Luau.

Luau's advantages are several. It is about equidistant between New Zealand and Japan. It was a British colony, so the main language is English. It has a relatively efficient telecommunications system, good ports, and good air service to all the major Asian destinations in which you are interested and to the United States.

Not least important, the Luau government is delighted to have your company locate and invest there. It has made very attractive tax concessions to the company and to its personnel who will move there.

The company moves in, leases one large building, and puts out invitations to bid on the construction of a larger building, which will be its permanent headquarters. Now, as you begin to work more with the private banking and businesspeople of Luau and less with government officials, you begin to be more aware of a Luau characteristic that you had not thought much about previously. Almost all the middle- and upper-management personnel in the business and finance sector are of Chinese extraction. The native population of Luau, which constitutes the great majority, is Micronesian.

On inquiring why the Chinese are dominant in banking and business while the Micronesians stay in farming, fishing, government work, and manual labor, you are told that this is the way it developed historically. The Chinese enjoy and are good at banking and business, while the native Luauans do not like those activities and have stayed with their traditional occupations. The two groups buy and sell from and to each other, but there are almost no social relations and very little business or professional overlap between the groups. Occasionally, some of the Micronesians study abroad, and some work abroad for periods; when they return, they frequently go to work in a bank or business or take a government position.

You must staff your headquarters with middle- and lower-management people and with clerical help. You find that the only applicants for the jobs are Chinese, and you select the best available. They are quite satisfactory, and the operation gets off to a good start.

Then, as the months pass, you notice a gradual change of attitude toward you and the company among government officials and among the people in general. They have become less friendly, more evasive, and less cooperative. You ask your Chinese staff about it, but they have noticed nothing unusual.

What could be happening? Why might the Chinese staff not notice it? What might you do to improve government and public relations?

International Business 國際商務 Gli Affari Internazionali Los negoc

Affaires Internationales عربية

ócios Internacionais Παγοσμιο Business Los negocios internacionales

عربية عربية

Negócios Internacionais Gli Affari Inter

Affaires Internationales

gócios Internacionais Los negocios internacionales Παγοσμ

ionales Geschäft International Business

gócios Internacionais Gli Affari Internazionali 國際商務

Παγοσμιο Business Los negocios internacionales

section four

The Organizational Environment

In the preceding three sections, the primary focus has been on the broad environmental context in which international businesses compete. Section One introduced you to issues regarding the nature of international business, including international business, trade, and investment. Section Two presented the framework of international organizations and the monetary system in which international business functions. Section Three discussed forces that affect international business and with which management must cope.

In Section Four, our attention shifts away from the external environment and focuses instead on the business itself, including actions that managers can take to help their companies compete more effectively as international businesses. In identifying potential management responses and solutions to problems caused or magnified by the foreign and international environments, this book is intended to be only an introduction to international business. Deeper discussions into specific areas can be found in textbooks specializing in those areas.

Chapter 13 deals with the concept of international competitive strategy and how companies use strategic planning to address international business opportunities and challenges. Chapter 14 looks at organizational design and the different ways in which international companies can be structured. Chapter 15 deals with assessing and analyzing international markets. Chapter 16 explores ways in which a company can enter international markets. Chapter 17 deals with practices and procedures for exporting and importing. Chapter 18 explores international marketing and ways in which it differs from domestic marketing. Chapter 19 deals with operations management in international companies, including management of international supply chains. Chapter 20 presents material on managing human resources in international businesses, particularly nonexecutive, technical, or sales employees. Chapter 21 covers financial management issues that arise in conjunction with international business activities.

International Competitive Strategy

What business strategy is all about— what distinguishes it from all other kinds of business planning—is, in a word, competitive advantage. Without competitors there would be no need for strategy, for the sole purpose of strategic planning is to enable the company to gain, as effectively as possible, a sustainable edge over its competitors.

— *Kenichi Ohmae, McKinsey & Company consultant*

Thinking Strategically about the Future in an Uncertain World

What would happen if the prices of oil or copper were to skyrocket (as they did during much of 2005 and 2006) or suddenly crash? What are the chances of a host government nationalizing an industry, such as Bolivia did in its oil and natural gas sector in May 2006? What are the implications of increasing urbanization and industrialization in emerging markets, such as India, China, or Brazil? These are examples of scenarios—stories about possible futures—that the global energy company Royal Dutch Shell employs in its strategic planning process. The objective of this process is to force executives to question their assumptions about the environments in which the company operates and successfully incorporate the uncertainty and potential changes that might profoundly impact their strategic and operational performance around the world.

Back in the 1970s, Shell used scenario planning as a fundamental tool for thinking strategically about the future, working on how to handle uncertainty in the company's long-range planning. The strategic planning group adapted techniques developed by the Rand Corporation for the U.S. Department of Defense. They developed scenarios in order to improve the quality of decisions that had huge financial implications for Shell, expensive undertakings such as whether to build a new offshore oil rig or begin exploring for oil in new areas.

Recently, companies like Shell have begun modifying their approach to using scenarios in their strategic planning efforts. Formerly, the planners made the scenarios and presented them to the line managers—a kind of "show and tell." There was no involvement of the managers. Now there is an emphasis in the company on getting managers to bring scenarios into their decision processes because Shell's top management is convinced that scenario building is an important management tool.

The objective of scenario planning is to envision possible futures in a more realistic light, plan for uncertainties and discontinuous events, and develop strategies to help a company cope with these potential future states. Scenario planning helps to emphasize that the business environment is uncertain and might evolve in totally different ways, thus helping to challenge traditional perspectives regarding the organization and its environment. This provides a useful context for developing long-term strategic plans, as well as shorter-term contingency plans, which are appropriate for risky and uncertain operating situations. Scenario planning gives close attention to external and internal factors that may normally not be considered relevant but that have influence on the future.

Scenarios are plausible and challenging stories, but they are not forecasts; that is, they do not extrapolate from past data to make predictions. In fact, they are a means to force managers to realize that their assumptions based on past experience no longer apply. Also, if managers have thought out the possible outcomes, they should be quicker to react when one of those outcomes occurs. As Shell's former planning head expresses it, "They can remember the future."[a]

Managers typically work in teams of six to eight people to build scenarios. They first agree about the

CONCEPT PREVIEWS

After reading this chapter, you should be able to:

explain international strategy, competencies, and international competitive advantage

describe the steps in the global strategic planning process

explain the purpose of mission statements, vision statements, values statements, objectives, quantified goals, and strategies

describe the methods of and new directions in strategic planning

explain home replication, multidomestic, regional, global, and transnational strategies and when to use them

describe the sources of competitive information

discuss the importance of industrial espionage

Gli Affari Internazionali
cionales
onales Geschäft Παγοσμιο Business
Negócios Internacionais Los Negócios Internacionais
internacionales Affaires Internationales 國際商務 Παγοσμιο Business

decision that must be made and then gather information by reading, observing, and talking with knowledgeable people. Next, the team works to identify the driving (environmental) forces and the "critical uncertainties" (the unpredictables) and prioritizes them. Three or four scenarios are commonly prepared, based on issues critical to the success of the decision. Each should depict a credible future and not be written to show the best-case, worst-case, and most likely situations. The team then identifies the implications of the scenarios and the leading indicators management must follow.

A member of a consulting firm that trains managers to use scenarios writes:

Using scenarios is rehearsing the future, and by recognizing the warning signs and the drama unfolding, one can avoid surprises, adapt, and act effectively. Decisions which have been pretested against a range of what fate may offer are more likely to stand the test of time, produce robust and resilient strategies, and create distinct competitive advantage. Ultimately, the end result of

scenario planning is not a more accurate picture of tomorrow, but better decisions today.[b]

The uncertainty of the world seems to have increased rather dramatically in recent years, especially in the aftermath of events such as the "9/11" tragedy in the United States, instability in global oil markets, or the tsunami that struck Asia in 2004. As a result, it is likely that international companies and their managers will demonstrate an increased interest in scenario planning as an essential part of their strategic planning activities. ∎

[a]"A Glimpse of Possible Futures," *Financial Times,* August 25, 1997, p. 8.

[b]"Using Scenarios," *GBN Scenario Planning,* www.gbn.org/usingScen .html (March 20, 1998).

Source: A. J. Vogl, "Big Thinking," *Across the Board* 41, no. 1 (January–February 2004), pp. 27–33; Julie Verity, "Scenario Planning as a Strategy Technique," *European Business Journal* 15, no. 4, pp. 185–95; "20:20 Vision," *Global Scenarios,* www.shell.com/b/b2_03.html (March 15, 1998); and Hugh Courtney, "Decision-Driven Scenarios for Assessing Four Levels of Uncertainty," *Strategy and Leadership* 31, no. 1, pp. 14–22.

In the preceding three sections of this book, the primary focus has been on the broad environmental context in which international businesses compete. This discussion has included the theoretical framework for international trade and investment, the international monetary and other organizations that influence international business, and the financial, economic, physical, social, political, legal, and other institutions found in various nations. Our attention now shifts away from the external environment, and we focus instead on the business itself, including the actions managers can take to help their companies compete more effectively as international businesses. In this chapter, we will discuss the concept of international strategy and how companies use strategic planning and the analysis of competitive forces to improve their global competitiveness.

The Competitive Challenge Facing Managers of International Businesses

In Chapter 2, we discussed some of the important reasons that motivate companies to pursue international business opportunities, including the potential to increase profits and sales through access to new markets; to protect existing markets, profits, and sales; and to help satisfy management's overall desire for growth. However, in order to succeed in today's global marketplace, a company must be able to quickly identify and exploit opportunities wherever they occur, domestically or internationally. To do this effectively, managers must fully understand why, how, and where they intend to do business, now and over time. This requires that managers have a clear understanding of the company's mission, a vision for how they intend to achieve that mission, and an understanding of how they plan to compete with other companies. To meet these challenges, managers must understand the company's strengths and weaknesses and be able to compare them accurately to those of their worldwide competitors. Strategic planning provides valuable tools that help managers address these global challenges.

What Is International Strategy, and Why Is It Important?

International strategy is concerned with the way firms make fundamental choices about developing and deploying scarce resources internationally.[1] International strategy involves decisions that deal with all the various functions and activities of a company and the interactions among them, not merely a single area such as marketing or production. To be effective, a company's international strategy needs to be consistent among the various functions, products, and regional units of the company (internal consistency) as well as with the demands of the international competitive environment (external consistency).

The goal of international strategy is to achieve and maintain a unique and valuable competitive position both within a nation and globally, a position that has been termed **competitive advantage.** This suggests that the international company must either perform activities different from those of its competitors or perform the same activities in different ways. To create a competitive advantage that is sustainable over time, the international company should try to develop skills, or competencies, that (1) create value for customers and for which customers are willing to pay, (2) are rare, since competencies shared among many competitors cannot be a basis for competitive advantage, (3) are difficult to imitate or substitute for, and (4) are organized in a way that allows the company to exploit fully the competitive potential of these valuable, rare, and difficult-to-imitate competencies.[2]

> *Wal-Mart has become a strong competitor in the international retailing industry because it has been able to develop more effective processes for performing critical activities, such as the logistics of tying point-of-purchase data to the company's inventory management and purchasing activities. Competitors have had continued difficulties matching Wal-Mart's competencies, enabling Wal-Mart to consistently earn a return on sales that is twice the average of its industry. As a result, Wal-Mart has been able to exploit these competencies internationally by entering markets such as Canada, Mexico and other Latin American countries, Europe, and Asia, as we see in the minicase at the end of this chapter.*

Managers of international companies that are attempting to develop a competitive advantage face a formidable challenge since resources—time, talent, and money—are always scarce. There are many alternative ways to use these scarce resources (for example, which nations to enter, which technologies to invest in, and which products or services to develop and offer to customers), and these alternatives are not equally attractive. A company's managers are forced to make choices regarding what to do and what *not* to do, now and over time. Different companies make different choices, and those choices have implications for each company's ability to meet the needs of customers and create a defensible competitive position internationally. Without adequate planning, managers are more likely to make decisions that do not make good sense competitively, and the company's international competitiveness may be harmed.

Global Strategic Planning

WHY PLAN GLOBALLY?

Companies are confronting a set of political, economic, social, technological, legal, and environmental forces that are increasingly complex, global, and subject to rapid change. In response, many international firms have found it necessary to institute formal global strategic planning to provide a means for top management to identify opportunities and threats from all over the world, formulate strategies to handle them, and stipulate how to finance and manage the strategies' implementation. Strategic plans help to ensure that decision makers have a common understanding of the business, the strategy, the assumptions behind the strategy, the external business environment pressures, and their own direction, as well as of promoting consistency of action among the firm's managers worldwide. Strategic plans also encourage the participants to consider the ramifications of their actions in the other geographic and functional areas of the firm. These plans provide a thorough, systematic foundation for raising key questions about what a business should become and making decisions regarding what resources and

international strategy
The way firms make choices about acquiring and using scarce resources in order to achieve their international objectives

competitive advantage
The ability of a company to have higher rates of profits than its competitors

competencies the company should develop, when and how to develop them, and how to use those competencies to achieve competitive advantage. This is intended to help the organization to respond more effectively to challenges than can its competitors. Strategic planning is also intended to help increase the likelihood of strategic innovations, promoting the development, capture, and application of these new ideas in order to promote success in a challenging competitive environment. McKinsey's 2006 Global Survey revealed that 85 percent of respondents perceived their company's business environment to be "more competitive" or "much more competitive" than it was five years earlier, with the intensity of competition increasing for both small and large companies and across all industries.[3] Despite complaints about the challenges of effectively implementing planning efforts, especially within large and international companies, Bain & Company's Management Tools & Trends survey reported that strategic planning continues to be the most commonly used management tool among global executives.[4]

GLOBAL STRATEGIC PLANNING PROCESS

Global strategic planning is a primary function of a company's managers, and the ultimate manager of strategic planning and strategy making is the firm's chief executive officer. The process of strategic planning provides a formal structure in which managers (1) analyze the company's external environments, (2) analyze the company's internal environment, (3) define the company's business and mission, (4) set corporate objectives, (5) quantify goals, (6) formulate strategies, and (7) make tactical plans. For ease of understanding, we present this as a linear process, but in actuality there is considerable flexibility in the order in which firms take up these items. In company planning meetings that one of the authors attended, the procedure was iterative; that is, during the analysis of the environments, committee members could skip to a later step in the planning process to discuss the impact of a new development on a present corporate objective. They then often moved backward in the process to discuss the availability of the firm's assets to take advantage of the environmental change. If they concluded that the company had such a capability, the committee would try to formulate a new strategy. If a viable strategy was developed, the members would then establish the corporate objective that the strategy was designed to attain.

Global and Domestic Planning Processes Similar

You will note that the global planning process, illustrated in Figure 13.1, has the same basic format as the planning process for a purely domestic firm. As you know by now, most activities of the two kinds of operations are similar. It is the variations in values of uncontrollable forces that make the activities in a worldwide corporation more complex than they are in a purely domestic firm.

Analyze Domestic, International, and Foreign Environments

Because a firm has little opportunity to control these forces, its managers must know not only what the present values of the forces are but also where the forces appear to be headed. An environmental

---

FIGURE 13.1 The Global Strategic Planning Process

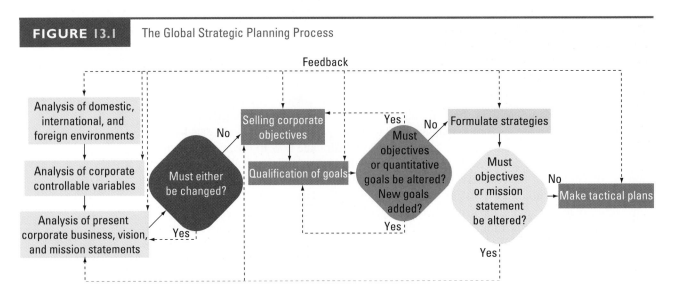

scanning process similar to the market screening process described in Chapter 15 can be used for continuous gathering of information. Yet recognition of the nature and implications of the current and future domestic, international, and foreign environments is an essential input into the global strategic planning process, as indicated by the following assessment by General Electric:

"Future economic growth will be uneven. To succeed, companies must navigate major global trends that will have significant impact on valuation. These include:

- An increasingly interdependent global economy wracked by excess manufacturing capacity and the resulting price pressure. This is why unemployment remains stubborn and margin growth is tough to achieve. Winning companies will invest in innovation and build new revenue streams from their current capabilities.

- A new economic order of global competitiveness and growth. Competition from places like China and India has evolved beyond low-cost manufacturing labor to include highly competitive engineering graduates who earn less than production workers in the developed world. Winning companies must think globally, but understand local consequences. Only competitive companies can serve investors, employees and stakeholders during this dramatic phase of globalization.

- A move to consolidate distribution channels, which creates value for consumers but makes it difficult for manufacturers to maintain margins. Winning companies will have strong direct sales forces, low costs and value propositions that tie their own profitability to their customers'.

- An opportunity to build growth platforms based on unstoppable demographics. Winning companies will sustain long-term growth by betting on high-growth markets to which they can bring unique technical and management capabilities.

- A more volatile and uncertain world. The underlying insecurity created by 9/11 and the stock market bubbles will not end soon. Winning companies will keep the confidence of customers, investors and employees by maintaining financial and cultural strength."[5]

Analyze Corporate Controllable Variables An analysis of the forces controlled by the firm will also include a situational analysis and a forecast. The managers of the various functional areas will either personally submit reports on their units or provide input to the planning staff (if there is one), who will in turn prepare a report for the strategy planning committee.

Often management will analyze the firm's activities from the time raw materials enter the plant until the end product reaches the final user, what is often called a *value chain analysis*. As part of this process, management must address three key questions about the business: (1) Who are the company's target customers? (2) What value does the company want to deliver to these customers? And (3) how will this customer value be created? The value chain analysis itself focuses primarily on the third question, and it refers to the set of value-creating activities that the company is involved with, from sources for basic raw materials or components to the ultimate delivery of the final product or service to the final customer. A simplified value chain is shown in Figure 13.2. The goal of this analysis is to enable management to determine the set of activities that will comprise the company's value chain, including which activities the company will do itself and which will be outsourced. Management must also consider where to locate various value chain activities (for example, should assembly be done in the company's home nation, located in a

Today's clothing sale prices appeal to customers but may pose challenges for businesses. To succeed in today's competitive global environment, companies need to navigate several major global trends, including an increasingly interdependent global economy wracked by excess manufacturing capacity and the resulting price pressure.

FIGURE 13.2

The Value Chain

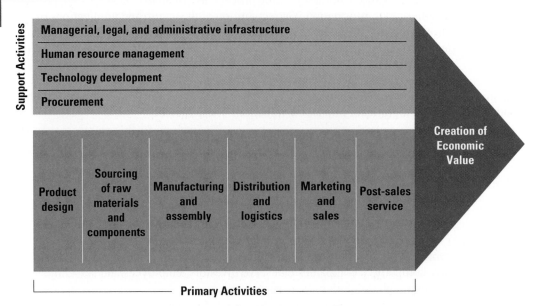

Source: Adapted from M. E. Porter, *Competitive Advantage* (New York: Free Press, 1985).

lower-cost location abroad, or located close to a customer abroad?). It is also necessary for management to examine the linkages among the activities in the value chain (for example, between sales and product development, in order to ensure that customer needs are effectively communicated and incorporated in new products). Linkages must be examined not merely across activities within the company but also in terms of managing relationships with external entities such as suppliers, alliance partners, distributors, or customers within and across nations. The desired outcome of this analysis is the identification and establishment of a superior set of well-integrated value chain activities and linkages, a system that will permit the organization to more effectively and efficiently develop, produce, market, and sell the company's products and services to the target customers, thereby creating the basis for global competitive advantage.

Knowledge as a Controllable Corporate Resource In today's highly competitive, rapidly changing, and knowledge-intensive economy, companies have the potential to achieve competitive advantages through leveraging their organizational knowledge across national boundaries. This organizational knowledge base includes the capabilities of employees (individually and in teams) as well as the knowledge that gets built into the overall organization through its various structures, systems, and organizational routines. As a valuable, scarce, and often unique organizational resource, knowledge is increasingly recognized by management as the basis for competitive advantage. As a result, managers are undertaking efforts to identify and evaluate the pool of knowledge that is contained within their companies on a global basis, including assessments of which knowledge and associated competencies will be the foundation for the company's future success. To help accelerate the acquisition, development, and exploitation of competitively valuable knowledge, managers are developing sets of techniques and practices to facilitate the flow of knowledge into and within their companies, to build knowledge databases, to transfer best practices within and across their international network of operations, and otherwise to create the foundation for a knowledge-based competitive advantage.

To effectively manage knowledge, companies must encourage individuals to work together on projects or somehow share their ideas. Much valuable knowledge is tacit, which means that it is known well by the individual but is difficult to express verbally or to document in text or figures. As a result, systems are needed in order to convey this tacit knowledge to others, possibly by converting it into explicit, codified knowledge and then making this knowledge accessible quickly and effectively to other employees who need it. In addition, to effectively design and deliver products that meet customers' needs, it is often necessary to also gain access to valuable knowledge of suppliers, customers, and other partner organizations. In some cases, it is even necessary to establish company facilities in other locations in order to gain access to this knowledge. For example, both Nokia and Ericsson established offices in the Silicon Valley in order to tap into the latest thinking of suppliers and customers located in that region and then transfer this knowledge back to headquarters in Europe. Companies face an ongoing challenge of creating mechanisms that will systematically and routinely identify opportunities for developing and transferring knowledge and for ensuring that subsidiaries are willing and able both to share what they know and to absorb knowledge from other units of the company. They also must ensure that this proprietary knowledge is managed in a way that will protect it from diffusion to competitors, in order to help the company maintain its competitiveness over time.

> *Sharp Electronics of Japan announced that it would begin production of system liquid crystal displays (LCDs) and build a plant for end-to-end manufacturing of large LCD televisions. Both production initiatives would be based in Japan, due to the need for close linkages between R&D and manufacturing personnel in order for Sharp to maintain competitiveness in production technology. Moving these operations to lower-cost locations abroad could have constrained the flow of ideas between Sharp's operating units, thereby hindering production improvements and the potential for fresh R&D initiatives. To limit leakage of proprietary production technology to competitors, Sharp patents many of its innovative product and production technologies. While patent applications can ensure rights to the patent holder, they also reveal technological details to the public, and proving patent violations can be expensive and time-consuming. Therefore, Sharp also identifies critical technologies that it strategically decides not to patent, choosing to instead keep these technologies completely in-house, concealed from other companies. In this way, Sharp attempts to create a barrier against competitors who try to lever off of Sharp's innovations.[6]*

The importance of knowledge and its management is recognized by international companies such as DuPont, which states, "Knowledge intensity is a DuPont term meaning getting paid for what the company knows rather than simply for what it makes. Knowledge intensity is the opposite of capital intensity. It's creating value from two centuries of experience, know-how and brand equity."[7]

> *In order to receive a $900 million contract to provide high-tech electricity-generating turbines to China, General Electric was forced to agree to share its sophisticated technology— which GE had spent over $500 million developing—with two Chinese companies that wanted to manufacture the equipment themselves eventually. Wanting to compete in advanced manufacturing sectors in the future, China pushes foreign companies to give access to their crown jewels in technology in exchange for access to the huge Chinese market. In the case of GE's turbine contract, Chinese officials wanted to get not only the drawings for the turbine but also the modeling and mathematics underlying the shape of the blades, how blades were cooled during rotation, and the chemistry associated with the blades and with the thermal protective coating on them. Said Delbert Williamson, who was GE's president of global sales, "It was a difficult negotiation. They're interested in having total access to technology and we're interested in protecting the technology that we made significant financial investment in."[8]*

After the analysis of corporate controllable variables, the planning committee must answer questions such as the following: What are our strengths and weaknesses? What are our human and financial resources? Where are we with respect to our present objectives? Have we uncovered any facts that require us to delete goals, alter them, or add new ones? After completing this internal audit, the committee is ready to examine the company's mission, vision, and values statements.

Define the Corporate Mission, Vision, and Values Statements
These broad statements communicate to the corporation's stakeholders (employees, stockholders, governments, partners, suppliers, and customers) what the company is, where it is going, and the values that will guide the behavior of the organization's members. Some firms combine two or all three of these into a single statement, whereas others have separate statements. The **mission statement** defines the purpose for a company's existence, including its business,

mission statement
A broad statement that defines the organization's purpose and scope

objectives, and approach for reaching those objectives. A **vision statement** is a description of the company's desired future position, of what it hopes to accomplish if it can acquire the necessary competencies and successfully implement its strategy. In contrast, a **values statement** is intended to be a clear, concise description of the fundamental values, beliefs, and priorities of the organization's members, reflecting how they want to behave with each other and with the company's customers, suppliers, and other members of the global community. A Booz Allen Hamilton/Aspen Institute survey of corporations in 30 countries revealed that 89 percent of these organizations had explicit, written statements of corporate values and that greater success in linking a corporation's values to its operations was related to superior financial results.[9] Over time, the planning committee must evaluate these statements against the changing realities uncovered in the external and internal analyses and then alter them when necessary.

Some Examples Johnson & Johnson has a mission statement that says:

Our Mission is to pursue the growth of Johnson & Johnson based on providing scientifically sound, high quality products and services that help heal, cure disease, and improve the quality of life for people everywhere.[10]

Unilever states the following about its mission:

Unilever's mission is to add vitality to life. We meet the everyday needs for nutrition, hygiene, and personal care with brands that help people feel good, look good, and get more out of life.[11]

Amazon.com states the following:

We seek to be Earth's most customer-centric company, where customers can find and discover anything they might want to buy online, and endeavor to offer customers the lowest possible prices.[12]

DuPont states the following in defining the vision of the company and its mission:

We, the people of DuPont, dedicate ourselves daily to the work of improving life on our planet. We have the curiosity to go farther . . . the imagination to think bigger . . . the determination to try harder . . . and the conscience to care more. Our solutions will be bold. We will answer the fundamental needs of the people we live with to ensure harmony, health and prosperity in the world. Our methods will be our obsession. Our singular focus will be to serve humanity with the power of all the sciences available to us. Our tools are our minds. We will encourage unconventional ideas, be daring in our thinking, and courageous in our actions. By sharing our knowledge and learning from each other and the markets we serve, we will solve problems in surprising and magnificent ways. Our success will be ensured. We will be demanding of ourselves and work relentlessly to complete our tasks. Our achievements will create superior profit for our shareholders and ourselves. Our principles are sacred. We will respect nature and living things, work safely, be gracious to one another and our partners, and each day we will leave for home with consciences clear and spirits soaring.[13]

Sumitomo Corporation of Japan states its nine basic values as being:

(1) Integrity and sound management: To comply with laws and regulations, while maintaining the highest ethical standards, (2) Integrated Corporate Strength: To create no boundaries within the organization; always to act with a company-wide perspective, (3) Vision: To create a clear vision of the future, and to communicate to share it within the organization, (4) Change and Innovation: To accept and integrate diversity in values and behavior, and to embrace change as an opportunity for action, (5) Commitment: To initiate, own, and achieve organizational objectives, (6) Enthusiasm: To act with enthusiasm and confidence, and to motivate to others through such action, (7) Speed: To make quick decisions and act promptly, (8) Human Development: To fully support the development of others' potential, and (9) Professionalism: To achieve and maintain high levels of expertise and skills.[14]

After defining any or all of the three statements, management must then set corporate objectives.

Katherine McCormick

Katherine McCormick is director of international marketing for Trans-Union, working at World Headquarters in Chicago, Illinois, where she leads international marketing projects in Canada, Mexico, Dominican Republic, Guatemala, Honduras, Nicaragua, Costa Rica, Chile, Trinidad and Tobago, Italy, Thailand, India, China (mainland and Hong Kong SAR), and South Africa. Katherine has traveled professionally in over 24 countries. TransUnion is a global intelligence leader, providing technology and analytical tools to help businesses around the world make better business decisions at every stage of the customer life cycle, including acquisition, customer management, and collections, and throughout the entire residential loan process. As director of international marketing, Katherine serves as the marketing generalist for associates leading international marketing projects, providing guidance for marketing efforts as well as strategic direction. In providing this direction, she continually works to enhance brand awareness through positioning, product performance and development, public relations, and promotional activities (e.g., trade shows). Katherine also oversees international communications and brand audits and executes brand architecture decisions within and across markets in the form of joint ventures and cobrand programs to ensure the success of current and future international acquisitions.

Katherine's advice on how to get a job in international business:

- "Don't look for a job in international business right from the get-go; first find a company that has business overseas and try to get a job working with them in your area of expertise. As soon as you can, let them know your interests in international business and try to network internally to introduce yourself to the international leaders. A couple years later, when you have gained experience with the company and have had exposure to the international business unit, you can try to make a move."

- "If international business is your true passion, pursue it wholeheartedly. Don't give up. Network as much as you can and travel internationally as much as you can."

Katherine's advice on succeeding in international business:

- "The ability to develop relationships and relate to people of different backgrounds and cultures is critical. I cannot stress that enough. You must be able to demonstrate a knowledge and understanding of the country you are working with. I find that patience, flexibility and creativity are a must for international business workers. You can't have a U.S. mindset and be successful!"

- "Job-related skills depend on the industry you are in, but what I look for when hiring someone is that they have traveled extensively and have had exposure to different cultures. You need to demonstrate an intimate understanding of the differences that exist in U.S. business vs. business in other countries."

Katherine's most memorable international business experience:

- "TransUnion was a sponsor at a conference two years ago in China. We hosted an event with music, cocktails and food right on the Great Wall of China as the sun was setting. I had one of those 'I get paid to do this!' moments where I was in awe of how truly blessed I am to do what I do."

World Wide Resource:

www.transunion.com/business

Set Corporate Objectives Objectives direct the firm's course of action, maintain it within the boundaries of the stated mission, and ensure its continuing existence. McDonald's states that its vision is "to be the world's best quick service restaurant experience. Being the best means providing outstanding quality, service, cleanliness, and value, so that we make every customer in every restaurant smile." To achieve this vision, the company focuses on three worldwide objectives: (1) to be the best employer for its people in each community around the world, (2) to deliver operational excellence to its customers in each of its restaurants, and (3) to achieve enduring profitable growth by expanding the brand and leveraging the strengths of the McDonald's system through innovation and technology.[15]

Intel's mission is to "delight our customers, employees, and shareholders by relentlessly delivering the platform and technology advancements that become essential to the way we work and live." Its objectives are stated as (1) extend leadership in silicon and platform manufacturing, (2) deliver architectural innovation for market-driving platforms, and (3) drive worldwide growth.[16]

How does Intel know whether it achieves these objectives? How will the company assess whether it has successfully delivered "architectural innovation for market-driving platforms," for example?

Quantify the Objectives In order to enhance a company's ability to develop and implement an effective strategy, one that will enable the company's objectives to be attained, it is important that efforts be made to quantify these objectives.

> *At BP, the U.K.-based energy multinational, strategic objectives are established through a process directed by headquarters. Implementation of these objectives is decentralized to the business units. Performance contracts are set in place for the executive management from each of the company's business units and strategic performance units, holding these managers accountable for that area of the business. The performance contracts include financial and operating performance objectives, as well as nonfinancial elements such as safety and environmental performance. The company states that it attempts to establish objectives that "(1) are challenging but achievable, (2) enable us to be responsive to change, (3) are clear and unambiguous to all, both within and outside the company, (4) provide indicative ranges of performance against which we can measure progress in a balanced way, (5) can be agreed [to] and accepted by all whose performance is measured against them, (6) encompass both clear financial or operational benefits, as well as clear social and environmental objectives, and (7) are intended to deliver value to the company's shareholders but with due care to all our stakeholders' interests."[17]*

Of course, strategic planning for international operations typically involves a range of qualitative as well as quantitative factors, which complicates efforts to quantify objectives. However, when objectives can be quantified in a relevant manner, they should be. For example, the stated objectives of 3M, a $21 billion diversified technology company with worldwide operations, included (1) growth in earnings per share of more than 10 percent a year on average, (2) growth in economic profit exceeding growth in earnings per share and return on invested capital among the highest among industrial companies, (3) at least 30 percent of sales from products introduced during the past four years, and (4) 8 percent productivity improvement per year, measured in terms of sales per employee in local currencies.[18] Similar quantification of objectives is evident for Goodyear Tire and Rubber Co., the world's largest tire company with manufacturing in 29 nations and sales and marketing operations in virtually every nation, which announced the following:

> *Goodyear's objectives for the 2006–2008 time period include:*
>
> 1. *To build on recent performance improvements by further reducing costs by $750 million to $1 billion. About one-third of the cost is expected to come from business process improvements and product reformulations.*
>
> 2. *Reduce the company's global manufacturing footprint, with anticipated savings of $100 million to $150 million per year. The target is to reduce the company's manufacturing capacity by 15 million to 20 million tires, or approximately 8 percent to 12 percent of its capacity.*
>
> 3. *Exploit its new purchasing office in China to increase the company's low-cost sourcing of tires, raw materials, indirect materials, and capital equipment, with targeted savings of $150 million to $200 million.*
>
> 4. *Simplifying the way the company processes transactions and the way it is organized, reducing costs by $150 million to $200 million from reducing selling, administrative, and general expenses.*
>
> 5. *Reduce working capital requirements, freeing cash to meet financial obligations and invest in improving performance.[19]*

These examples illustrate that despite the strong preference of most top managers for verifiable objectives, they frequently do have nonquantifiable or directional goals. One of PepsiCo's objectives, for example, is to accelerate profitable growth. Although this goal is not quantified, it does set the direction for managers and requires that they formulate more specific strategies to attain it. Incidentally, objectives do tend to be more quantified as they progress down the organization to the operational level, because, for the most part, strategies at one level become the objectives for the succeeding level. Up to this point, only *what, how much,* and *when* have been stipulated. *How* these objectives are to be achieved will be determined in the formulation of strategies.

Formulate the Competitive Strategies Generally, participants in the strategic planning process will formulate alternative **competitive strategies,** and corresponding plans of action, that seem plausible considering the directions the external environmental forces are taking and the company's strengths, weaknesses, opportunities, and threats (something that endangers the business, such as a merger of two competitors, the bankruptcy of a major customer, or a new product that appears to make the company's product obsolete).

competitive strategies
Action plans to enable organizations to reach their objectives

Suppose (1) their analysis of the external environment convinces them that the Japanese government is making it easier for foreign firms to enter the market and (2) the competitor analysis reveals that a Japanese competitor is preparing to enter the United States (or wherever the home market is). Should the firm adopt a defensive strategy of defending the home market by lowering its price there, or should it attack the competitor in its home market by establishing a subsidiary in Japan? Management may decide to pursue either strategy or both, depending on its interpretation of the situation.

When developing and assessing strategic alternatives, it is important to remember that companies competing in international markets confront two opposing forces: reduction of costs and adaptation to local markets. In order to be competitive, firms must do what they can to lower costs per unit so that customers will not perceive their products or services as being too expensive. This often results in pressure for some of the company's facilities to be located in places where costs are low, as well as for developing products that are highly standardized across multiple nations.

However, in addition to responding to pressures to reduce costs, managers also must attempt to respond to local pressures to modify their products to meet the demands of the local markets in which they do business. This modification requires that the company differentiate its strategy and product offerings from nation to nation, reflecting differences in distribution channels, governmental regulations, cultural preferences, and similar factors. However, modifying products and services for the specific requirements of local markets can involve additional expenses, which can cause the company's costs to rise.

As a consequence of these two opposing pressures, companies basically have five different strategies that they can use for competing internationally: home replication, multidomestic, regional, global, and transnational. As suggested in Figure 13.3, the strategy that would be most appropriate for the company, overall and for various activities in the value chain, depends on the amount of pressure the company faces in terms of adapting to local markets and achieving cost reductions. Each of these strategies has its own set of advantages and disadvantages, as summarized below.

Home Replication Strategy* According to this typology, companies pursuing a home replication strategy typically centralize product development functions in their home country. After they develop differentiated products in the home market, these innovations are then transferred to foreign markets in order to capture additional value. To be successful, the company has to possess a valuable distinctive competency that local competitors lack in the foreign markets. The company's home country headquarters usually maintains tight control over marketing and product strategy, and the primary responsibility of local subsidiaries is to leverage home country capabilities. The extent of local customization of product offerings or marketing strategy tends to be limited. However, competitive advantage depends on the effective management of the international product life cycle that was discussed in Chapter 3. As a result, once local demand and circumstances justify such an investment, the company will tend to establish manufacturing and marketing functions in each major country in which it does business. This strategy can be appropriate if the company faces relatively weak pressures for local responsiveness and cost reductions. When there are strong pressures for local responsiveness, however, companies pursuing a home replication strategy will be at a disadvantage compared to competitors that emphasize customization of the product offering and market strategy for local conditions. Companies pursuing a home replication strategy may also face high operating costs, due to duplication of manufacturing facilities across the markets they serve.

---

*Although a home replication strategy is sometimes called an "international strategy," to avoid the potential for confusion between this specific use of "international strategy" and the more general term *international strategy,* we will use only the term *home replication strategy* for this strategic framework.

FIGURE 13.3

Cost and Adaptation
Pressures and Their
Implications for
International
Strategies

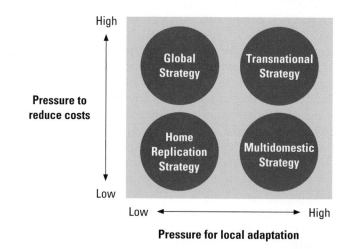

Examples of firms pursuing home replication strategies include Microsoft and McDonald's. For example, Microsoft has traditionally developed the core architecture for the company's computer operating system and application software products at its headquarters in Washington state. Subsidiaries in other nations have engaged in relatively limited product customization, primarily to address such basic differences as alphabet or language.

Multidomestic Strategy A multidomestic strategy tends to be used when there is strong pressure for the company to adapt its products or services for local markets. Under these circumstances, decision making tends to be more decentralized in order to allow the company to modify its products and to respond quickly to changes in local competition and demand. Subsidiaries are expected to develop and exploit local market opportunities, which means that knowledge and competencies are expected to be developed at the subsidiary level. By tailoring its products for specific markets, the company may be able to charge higher prices. However, local adaptation of products usually will increase the company's cost structure. In order to effectively adapt products, the company will have to invest in additional capabilities and knowledge in terms of local culture, language, customer demographics, human resource practices, government regulations, distribution systems, and so forth. Adapting products too much to local tastes may also take away the distinctiveness of a company's products. For example, KFC's chicken outlets in China are highly popular because they are perceived to reflect American values and standards, something that might be lost if the company tried to adapt the stores and products to be more like other Chinese food outlets. The extent of local adaptation may also change over time, as when customer demands start to converge due to the emergence of global telecommunications, media, and travel, as well as reduced differences in income between nations. The cost and complexity of coordinating a range of different strategies and product offerings across national and regional markets can also be substantial.

> Schneider Electric, a large French electrical products company with operations in 130 countries, attempts to serve international customers through a strategy that adapts products to the standards and practices of each country. Local operations have a high level of autonomy and are strongly rooted in their host nations. The organizational structure is designed to react quickly and effectively to local market conditions, facilitating customized innovations for local customers' needs. As an example, Schneider is trying to exploit its localization strategy to dominate several sectors of the marketplace in China. Chief Operating Officer Jean-Pascal Tricoire said, "China is a core country for us and is as important as the United States and Europe," likely to become the third-largest market for Schneider after the United States and France. Schneider's business in China is expected to maintain an average annual growth rate of at least 20 percent through 2009, and localization is a primary strategy to achieve this growth rate. Schneider Electric China has about half of the corporation's employees and is expected to expand the Chinese workforce from 4,000 to 7,000 by 2007. The

Regional Strategies for Competing Globally

Many researchers in the field of international business have argued that the emergence of broad economic liberalization, declining transportation costs, advances in telecommunications and computer technology, and other factors have produced a "borderless" world. In such a world, it has been argued that a global strategy is an appropriate or even necessary approach for multinational companies to adopt in order to achieve success.

Multinationals do represent a major force driving economic globalization, with the 500 largest multinational enterprises being responsible for about half of world trade and over 90 percent of the global stock of foreign direct investment. Yet investigations of large multinationals in manufacturing and service sectors reveal that most of these companies generate the majority of their revenues within a single region rather than having broad and deep penetration of international markets as a whole. For the large majority of these firms, an average of about 80 percent of their worldwide revenues are generated within their home region of the three largest economic regions of North America, the European Union, and Asia. These data suggest that, at least for most companies and industries, the world marketplace is triad-based rather than global in nature.

Some researchers have suggested that this triad-based competitive situation, sometimes termed *semiglobalization,* may merely reflect a stage in the evolution of international companies. From this perspective, increased globalization of sales and other value chain activities may be expected to occur over time as companies accumulate sufficient international experience and are thus able to successfully more fully extend their reach globally. Experimentation and innovation with business models may be necessary in order to accomplish this. There may also be a "threshold of internationalization" beyond which a multinational's performance may decline, at least until the competencies necessary for more globally dispersed operations are able to be developed and managed successfully. In fact, some research which has found that multinationals' revenues tend to

be concentrated in a single nation also suggests that broader assessment of value chain activities than merely sales—including sourcing of labor, capital, production, and knowledge—might produce a less region-centric interpretation of multinationals' strategies.

Nevertheless, one result of this recent research on the region-based nature of multinational sales is the potential value to be derived from thinking of international strategy within the context of a region-by-region perspective, rather than merely a nation-by-nation versus a global basis. In part, this argument emphasizes the continued heterogeneity that companies may encounter in the world's marketplaces, such as differences in local cultures, discriminatory treatment from national or regional governments or other governing bodies, and complexities of dealing with multiple institutions in the host markets. To the extent that a multinational's market position varies substantially across regions, strategies may also need to vary by region in order to accommodate the differing competitive circumstances that confront an international company. Yet, even when considering the appropriate strategy to use within each region, it may be useful to consider the relative extent of pressure for local adaptation versus pressure to reduce costs, as discussed in this section, "Formulate the Competitive Strategies."

Source: Alan M. Rugman and Alain Verbeke, "A Perspective on Regional and Global Strategies of Multinational Enterprises," *Journal of International Business Studies* 35, no. 1 (2004), pp. 3–18; J. Michael Geringer, Paul W. Beamish, and Richard C. DaCosta, "Diversification Strategy and Internationalization: Implications for MNE Performance," *Strategic Management Review* 10, no. 2 (1989), pp. 109–19; Lei Li, "Is Regional Strategy More Effective than Global Strategy in the U.S. Service Industries," *Management International Review* 45, special issue (2005), pp. 37–57; Pankaj Ghemawat, "Semiglobalization and International Business Strategy," *Journal of International Business Studies* 34, no. 2 (2003), pp. 138–52; Eden Yin and Chong Ju Choi, "The Globalization Myth: The Case of China," *Management International Review* 45, pp. 103–20; Allen J. Morrison, David A. Ricks, and Kendall Roth, "Globalization versus Regionalization: Which Way for the Multinational?" *Organizational Dynamics* 19, no. 3 (1991), pp. 17–29; and Pankaj Ghemawat, "Regional Strategies for Global Leadership," *Harvard Business Review*, December 2005, pp. 98–108.

company's Chinese research and development center will triple to 300 employees. Already accounting for 70 percent of production in the Asia Pacific region, Schneider will also add more production capability in China and diversify its operations into components and parts.[20]

Global Strategy   A global strategy tends to be used when a company faces strong pressures for reducing costs and limited pressure to adapt products for local markets. Strategy and decision making are typically centralized at headquarters, and the company tends to offer standardized products and services. Overseas offices are expected to adopt the most efficient strategies found within the entire corporation. Value chain activities are often located in only one or a few areas, to assist the company in achieving cost reductions due to economies of scale. International subsidiaries are expected to transmit information to headquarters and to submit to centralized controls imposed by headquarters. There tends to be strong emphasis on close coordination and integration of activities across products and markets, as well as the development of efficient logistics and distribution capabilities. These strategies are common in industries such as semiconductors (e.g., Intel) or large commercial aircraft (e.g., Boeing). However, global strategies may also confront challenges such as limited ability to adjust quickly and effectively to changes in customer needs across national or regional markets, increased transportation and tariff costs for exporting products from centralized production sites, and the risks of locating activities in a centralized location (which can, for example, cause the firm to confront risks from political changes or trade conflicts, exchange rate fluctuations, and similar factors).

> *Vodafone Group PLC of Britain, the world's largest cell phone operator, discovered that too much emphasis on implementing a global strategy could be a problem. In 2002, the company acquired control of the third-largest Japanese cell phone operator, J-Phone Co., a fast-growing company with an image for being on the cutting edge of cellular technology. The company was subsequently rebranded under the Vodafone name, and Vodafone heavily promoted its image as a global brand and company. Said Arun Sarin, Vodafone's CEO, "We acquired a lot of companies to become what we are today. Now we have to make this series of companies work as one operating company." Being a service provider in 28 nations allows Vodafone to specify technical requirements to handset manufacturers and to achieve powerful economies of scale in sourcing. The company is trying to achieve a standard Vodafone "look and feel" for all of its cellular phones, in order to enhance the company's branding and pricing power. Sarin said, "Branding is a very big issue for us. When you think about fast food, you think of McDonald's. When you think about a soft drink, you think of Coke. What we would like is when people think mobile products and services, they go to Vodafone."*
>
> *Yet, after its acquisition, Vodafone's Japanese operations suffered and the company lost market share to market leaders NTT DoCoMo Inc. and KDDI Corporation. In a nation where consumers love the latest technological gadgets, Vodafone's phones were viewed as dull and unoriginal. New subscriptions were declining, year after year, and annual revenues fell. The problem? How to implement a global strategy while simultaneously meeting the demands of the local market. Vodafone failed to provide Japanese consumers with technologically sophisticated, feature-packed phones, instead offering a narrow, run-of-the-mill product line. "They just discontinued popular phones and popular services. They were looking at the global market instead of looking at what Japanese users wanted," said Hayato Yoshida, a salesperson at a Tokyo mobile phone retailer. Vodafone was also late in introducing the newest cellular services being offered by competitors. For example, Vodafone's emphasis on global services resulted in a delay in its Japanese launch of 3G phones: preferring to offer phones that functioned both within and outside Japan led to longer development times and delayed product introduction by more than a year after DoCoMo introduced its own 3G service. Kazuyo Katsuma, a telecom analyst with J.P. Morgan, said, "The biggest reason they are struggling is a mismatch of their strategy and the Japanese environment." Rather than achieving success through mere global scale and standardization, Sarin commented, "It is . . . becoming increasingly clear that the greatest benefits come from strong local and regional scale." In 2006, Vodafone conceded defeat and sold its Japanese operations, booking an $8.6 billion charge for losses associated with Japanese investment."[21]*

Transnational Strategy A transnational strategy tends to be used when a company simultaneously confronts pressures for cost effectiveness and local adaptation and when there is a potential for competitive advantage from simultaneously responding to these two divergent forces. The location of a company's assets and capabilities will be based on where it would be most beneficial for each specific activity, neither highly centralized as with a global strategy nor widely dispersed as with a multidomestic strategy. International subsidiaries are expected to contribute actively to the development of the company's capabilities, as well as developing and sharing knowledge with company operations worldwide. Typically, more "upstream" value chain activities, such as product development, raw materials sourcing, and manufacturing, will be more centralized, while the more "downstream" activities, such as marketing, sales, and service, will be more decentralized, located closer to the customer. Of course, achieving an optimal balance in locating activities is a challenge for management, as is maintaining this balance over time as the company faces changes in competition, customer needs, regulations, and other factors. Management must ensure that the comparative advantages of the locations of the company's various value chain activities are captured and internalized, rather than wasted due to limitations of the organization's people, structures, and coordination and control systems. The complexity associated with the strategic decisions, as well as the supporting structures and systems of the organization, will be much greater with a transnational strategy. Caterpillar, for example, has tried to manufacture many of the standardized components of its products in a few locations worldwide. At the same time, the company has set up assembly operations in each major market, sometimes accompanied by specialized local production capability, thereby promoting its ability to tailor products to local needs.

When considering the four types of strategies discussed above, it is also important to remember that management must consider the corporate culture when choosing among strategic alternatives. If the company decides to put into effect a quality control system that includes quality circles and heretofore has had little employee participation in decision making, the strategy will have to include the cost of and time for training the employees to accept this cultural change.

Standardization and Planning   While the preceding discussion addressed basic strategic alternatives at a business or corporate level, it should be remembered that not all activities of an organization confront the same mix of globalization and localization pressures (also see the Worldview box on page 363, "Regional Strategies for Competing Globally"). For example, historically, more aspects of research and development and manufacturing have been standardized and coordinated worldwide by companies than has been the case for other value chain activities such as marketing. Many top executives believe marketing strategies are best determined locally because of differences among the various foreign environments. Yet there remains a desire within many international companies to achieve benefits from standardizing various elements of marketing strategies as well as the total product itself, which leads to their inclusion in the global strategic planning process. Of course, the standardization of elements of a firm's marketing strategy can also be the *result* of strategic planning as the company's managers search for ways to lower costs and present a uniform company image as a global producer of quality products. In making such strategic plans, however, it is essential that companies look beyond what makes sense under current circumstances and also consider how the situation may change in the future and the implications of these changes. This helps to explain companies' increasing use of scenarios in the planning process.

Scenarios   As discussed in the introductory example of this chapter, because of the rapidity of changes in the uncontrollable variables, many managers have become dissatisfied with planning for a single set of events and have turned to **scenarios,** which are multiple, plausible stories for probable futures. Scenario analysis allows management to assess the implications for the company of various economic conditions and operating strategies. Managers can brainstorm various "what-if" scenarios, raising and challenging their assumptions and projected outcomes before committing to a specific course of action. Often, the what-if questions reveal weaknesses in present strategies. Some of the common kinds of subjects for scenarios are large and sudden changes in sales (up or down), sudden increases in the prices of raw materials, sudden tax increases, and a change in the political party in power. Frequently, scenarios are used as a learning tool for preparing standby or contingency plans, enhancing the company's ability to perform within uncertain international markets. (See the Worldview box on page 366, "Scenarios: Improving Strategic Planning by Telling Stories.")

scenarios
Multiple, plausible stories about the future

Contingency Plans   Many companies prepare **contingency plans** for worst- and best-case scenarios and for critical events as well. Every operator of a nuclear plant has contingency plans, as do most producers of petroleum and hazardous chemicals since such ecological disasters as the *Valdez* oil spill and the tragic Bhopal gas leak occurred. Because of the important impact on profits of changes in the prices of jet fuel, contingency planning is a common strategic activity for domestic and international airlines. The deadly terrorist attack on the World Trade Center in New York on September 11, 2001, an event that also severely impacted operations of numerous companies, reminded many organizations of the importance of developing contingency plans to ensure the effective continuation of their operations in the event that their headquarters or other key locations are attacked or otherwise incapacitated for a period of time.

contingency plans
Plans for the best- or worst-case scenarios or for critical events that could have a severe impact on the firm

Scenarios: Improving Strategic Planning by Telling Stories

A key role of strategic planning is to describe and effectively communicate a future that is attractive enough to help create, and to capture, the competitive advantages that arise from preparing for this future and helping to make it happen. In essence, a key element in strategic planning is telling stories, creating scenarios regarding the future. A popular and increasingly utilized strategic planning tool, scenarios are carefully developed stories that integrate a variety of ideas about the future, including key certainties and uncertainties, and present these ideas in a useful and comprehensible manner. Scenarios should be developed in a manner that is consistent with and helps to clarify the priorities of the company, and these stories are then tied into strategic and operational decisions that a company must make today and over time.

Although the origins of scenario planning are unclear, the multinational company Royal Dutch/Shell is widely recognized as a pioneer in popularizing the technique. Shell made scenario planning a staple of its strategic planning efforts 30 years ago, when it was confronted with a severe and unexpected global oil shortage. In dealing with such uncertainty and change, traditional strategic planning approaches based on extrapolation of historical conditions are of limited value. Managers find it difficult to break away from their existing view of the world, one that results from a lifetime of training and experience. Through presenting other ways of seeing the world, scenarios allow managers to envision alternatives that might lie outside their traditional frame of reference. Such an approach is particularly useful for international companies that face high levels of change and uncertainty regarding political, technological, competitive, and other forces because it allows management to anticipate and prepare for opportunities and threats that cannot be fully predicted or controlled. Examples of scenarios created by Shell to assist in anticipating and responding to such uncertainty can be viewed at www.shell.com/home/Framework?siteId=royal-en&FC2=&FC3=/royal-en/html/iwgen/our_strategy/scenarios/introduction_to_global_scenarios/intro_jvdv_scenarios_28022005.html.

Because of the problems inherent in the list of objectives that had characterized 3M's strategic planning efforts, the company adopted a scenario-based approach that it termed "planning by narrative." First, the strategic planner sets the stage as any storyteller does. This includes an analysis of the current situation, including uncontrollable environmental forces and corporate controllable variables. Then the narrator discusses the dramatic conflict. What are the obstacles to success? Once the obstacles are presented, the plan must show how the firm can conquer them and triumph. The audience is made aware of the writers' thought processes in arriving at their conclusions, and the assumptions are brought out in the open, enabling executives to evaluate the plan and then ask perceptive, incisive questions and offer valuable advice. One 3M manager stated, "If you just read bullet points, you may not get it, but if you read a narrative plan, you will. If there's a flaw in the logic, it glares out at you. With bullets, you don't know if

the insight is really there or if the planner has merely given you a shopping list." 3M management believes that narrative plans can motivate and mobilize an entire organization.

In his classic book, *The Art of the Long View,* Peter Schwartz identifies the following seven steps to successful scenario planning:

1. Determine the area, scope, and timing of the decisions with greatest relevance to or impact on your organization.

2. Research existing conditions and trends in a wide variety of areas (including those areas you might not typically consider).

3. Examine the drivers or key factors that will likely determine the outcome of the stories you are beginning to build.

4. Construct multiple stories of what could happen next.

5. Play out what the impact of each of these possible futures might be for your business or organization.

6. Examine your answers and look for those actions or decisions you'd make that were common to all two or three of the stories you built.

7. Monitor what does develop so as to trigger your early response system.

De Kluyver and Pearce identify four qualities that should be embodied in the final set of scenarios:

1. Relevance to the users (e.g., executives or middle management).

2. Internal consistency.

3. Descriptiveness regarding futures that are generically different, rather than merely being variations on a single theme.

4. Able to be acted upon in an environment that will exist for a period of time, and thus give the organization a chance to benefit from its preparations and resulting actions, rather than for a future that will be very short-lived.

The primary value of scenario planning efforts is not so much the strategic plans that are created but, instead, the transformation in strategic thinking that results from this activity.

Source: "Planning for What's Next," *Growth Strategies,* August 2002, pp. 3–4; Anthony Lavia, "Strategic Planning in Times of Turmoil," *Business Communications Review,* March 2004, pp. 56–59; Ian Wylie, "There Is No Alternative to . . . ," *Fast Company,* July 2002, p. 106, http://pf.fastcompany.com/magazine/60/tina.html (October 16, 2004); Peter Schwartz, *The Art of the Long View—Planning for the Future in an Uncertain World* (New York: Doubleday, 1996); Shell, "Introduction to Shell Global Scenarios to 2025 by Jeroen van der Veer, Chief Executive," www.shell.com/home/Framework?siteId=royal-en&FC2=&FC3=/royal-en/html/iwgen/our_strategy/scenarios/introduction_to_global_scenarios/intro_jvdv_scenarios_28022005.html (June 28, 2006); Don Sull, "Good Things Come to Those Who Actively Wait," *Financial Times,* February 6, 2006, p. 8; Cornelis A. de Kluyver and John A. Pearce II, *Strategy: A View from the Top* (Upper Saddle River, NJ: Pearson Prentice Hall, 2006), p. 39; and Gordon Shaw, Robert Brown, and Philip Bromiley, "Strategic Stories: How 3M Is Rewriting Business Planning," *Harvard Business Review,* May–June 1998, pp. 41–50.

Prepare Tactical Plans Because strategic plans are fairly broad, tactical (also called *operational*) plans are a requisite for spelling out in detail how the objectives will be reached. In other words, very specific, short-term means for achieving the goals are the objective of tactical planning. For instance, if the British subsidiary of an American producer of prepared foods has as a quantitative goal a 20 percent increase in sales, its strategy might be to sell 30 percent more to institutional users. The tactical plan could include such points as hiring three new specialized sales representatives, attending four trade shows, and advertising in two industry periodicals every other month next year. This is the kind of specificity found in the tactical plan.

STRATEGIC PLAN FEATURES AND IMPLEMENTATION FACILITATORS

Sales Forecasts and Budgets
Two prominent features of the strategic plan are *sales forecasts* and *budgets*. The sales forecast not only provides management with an estimate of the revenue to be received and the units to be sold but also serves as the basis for planning in the other functional areas. Without this information, management cannot formulate the production, financial, and procurement plans. Budgets, like sales forecasts, are both a planning and a control technique. During planning, they coordinate all the functions within the firm and provide management with a detailed statement of future operating results.

Plan Implementation Facilitators
Once the plan has been prepared, it must be implemented. Two of the most important plan implementation facilitators that management employs are policies and procedures.

Policies Policies are broad guidelines issued by upper management for the purpose of assisting lower-level managers in handling recurring problems. Because policies are broad, they permit discretionary action and interpretation. The object of a policy is to economize managerial time and promote consistency among the various operating units. For example, if a company's distribution policy states that sales will be made through wholesalers, marketing managers throughout the world would know that they should normally use wholesalers and avoid selling directly to retailers. Similarly, publicity regarding the widespread occurrence of bribery in various international markets has prompted numerous companies to issue policy statements condemning this practice. Managers have thus been put on notice by these statements that they are not to offer bribes.

Procedures Procedures prescribe how certain activities will be carried out, thereby ensuring uniform action on the part of all corporate members. For instance, most international corporate headquarters issue procedures for their subsidiaries to follow in preparing annual reports and budgets. This assures corporate management that whether the budgets originate in Thailand, Brazil, or the United States, they will be prepared using the same format, which facilitates comparison.

Performance Measures
A key part of strategic planning is measuring performance in order to assess whether the strategy and its implementation are proceeding successfully or whether modifications may need to be made. Companies need to consider at least three types of measures when assessing strategic performance: (1) measures of the company's success in obtaining and applying the required resources, such as financial, technological, and human resources; (2) measures of the effectiveness of the company's personnel, within and across the firm's international network of operations, in performing their assigned jobs; and (3) measures of the company's progress toward achieving its mission, vision, and objectives and doing so in a manner consistent with the company's stated values.[22] A range of concepts and tools, including the balanced scorecard and triple-bottom-line accounting, have been promoted as alternatives for helping to measure strategic performance. For example, the balanced scorecard approach is based on an integration of strategic planning with a company's

budgeting processes, and short-term results from the balanced scorecard can serve as a means of monitoring progress in achieving strategic objectives.[23]

KINDS OF STRATEGIC PLANS

Time Horizon
Although strategic plans may be classified as short-, medium-, or long-term, there is little agreement about the length of these periods. For some businesses, long-range planning may be for a five-year period. For others, this would be the length of a medium-term plan; their long range might cover 15 years or more. Short-range plans are usually for one to three years; however, even long-term plans are subject to review annually or more frequently if a situation requires it. Furthermore, the time horizon will vary according to the age of the firm and the stability of its market. A new venture is extremely difficult to plan for more than three years in advance, but a five- or six-year horizon may be sufficient for a mature company in a steady market.

Level in the Organization
Each organizational level of the company will have its level of plan. For example, if there are four organizational levels, as shown in Figure 13.4, there will be four levels of plans, each of which will generally be more specific than the plan that is at the level above. In addition, the functional areas at each level will have their own plans and sometimes will be subject to the same hierarchy, depending mainly on how the company is organized.

METHODS OF PLANNING

top-down planning
Planning process that begins at the highest level in the organization and continues downward

Top-Down Planning
In **top-down planning,** corporate headquarters develops and provides guidelines that include the definition of the business, the mission statement, company objectives, financial assumptions, the content of the plan, and special issues. If there is an international division, its management may be told that this division is expected to contribute $75 million in profits, for example. The division, in turn, would break this total down among

---

FIGURE 13.4

3M Strategic
Planning Cycle

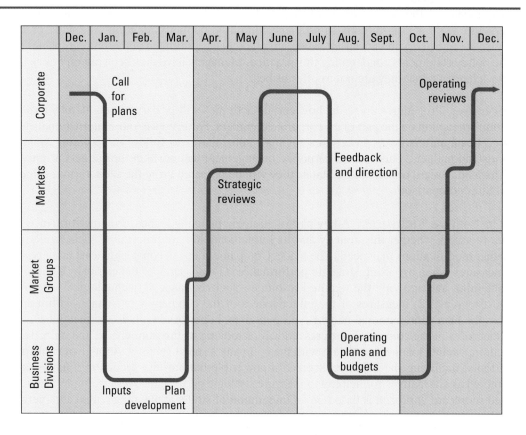

the affiliates under its control. The managing director in Germany would be informed that the German operation is expected to contribute $5 million; Brazil, $800,000; and so on. An advantage of top-down planning is that the home office, with its global perspective, should be able to formulate plans that ensure the optimal corporatewide use of the firm's scarce resources. This approach may also promote creativity, since a corporatewide perspective on market opportunities may yield insights that are not readily observable lower in the organization, such as by managers within individual national markets.

Disadvantages of top-down planning are that it restricts initiative at the lower levels and shows some insensitivity to local conditions, particularly within ethnocentric management teams. Furthermore, especially in an international company, there are so many interrelationships that consultation is necessary. Can top management, for example, decide on rationalization of manufacturing without obtaining the opinions of the local units as to its feasibility?

Bottom-Up Planning **Bottom-up planning** operates in the opposite manner. The lowest operating levels inform top management about what they expect to do, and the total becomes the firm's goals. The advantage of bottom-up planning is that the people responsible for attaining the goals are formulating them. Who knows better than the subsidiaries' directors what and how much the subsidiaries can sell? Because the subsidiaries' directors set the goals with no coercion from top management, they feel obligated to make their word good. Their hands-on perspective may allow them to recognize potentially innovative opportunities to create and leverage value, thus serving as a basis for improved performance or even strategic experimentation. However, bottom-up planning has a disadvantage: Since each affiliate is free to some extent to pursue the goals it wishes to pursue, there is no guarantee that the sum total of all the affiliates' goals will coincide with those of headquarters. When discrepancies occur, extra time must be taken at headquarters to eliminate them. Japanese companies, particularly larger firms, almost invariably use bottom-up planning because they strive for a consensus at every level.

bottom-up planning
Planning process that begins at the lowest level in the organization and continues upward

Iterative Planning It appears that **iterative planning** (see Figure 13.4) is becoming more popular, especially in global companies that seek to have a single global plan while operating in many diverse foreign environments. Iterative planning combines aspects of both top-down and bottom-up planning. An example of iterative planning is the approach used in 3M.

iterative planning
Repetition of the bottom-up or top-down planning process until all differences are reconciled

In 2005, 3M generated over 60 percent of its $21.2 billion in sales from outside the United States, where it has operations in over 60 nations and sales in over 200. Strategic planning plays a key role in the company's resource allocation decisions and global expansion. Figure 13.4 illustrates how 3M's iterative planning process functions. Planning starts with the operating managers of the company's six operating business segments, who analyze strengths and weaknesses and external forces, such as new technology and government regulatory changes; perform a competitor analysis; and determine the company resources they will need to achieve their objectives. Their plans then go to the Market Group, in which from three to five business divisions are typically located. They are reviewed by the Market Group management and consolidated for presentation to the strategic planning committee, consisting of the 12 vice presidents at headquarters who represent the Markets into which the Market Groups are divided. The plans are reviewed, and the results of this review are discussed with the Market Group management. Any differences between Market and Market Group managements are reconciled.

Two months later (July), the corporate headquarters' management committee, to which the strategic planning committee vice presidents belong, reviews the plans and votes on spending priorities. Feedback and direction are given to the business divisions, which then prepare operating plans and budgets by December and submit them to headquarters. They are finalized with corporate worldwide plans.

A few days before the December operating reviews, the management committee holds brainstorming sessions to discuss trends and developments over the coming 15 years. The general manager of each business division presents the best picture possible for that industry for the period. The outcome of this meeting is a broad guide for strategic planning. Although operating managers do the planning, the director and staff of a planning services and development unit provide an analysis of 3M's 20 principal competitors worldwide and any other information the divisions require. They also try to identify opportunities and new products.

As an indication of the vitality of the organization, 3M's chairman and CEO stated, "Our objective is to double the number of qualified new 3M product ideas and triple the value of products that win in the marketplace. We're already seeing good results. . . . Our new product pipeline holds the potential to generate more than $5 billion of annual sales."[24]

NEW DIRECTIONS IN PLANNING

Strategic planning, particularly in its more traditional, bureaucratic form that typified the 1960s and 1970s and still is practiced in too many companies today, has been described as a calendar-driven ritual, not an exploration of the company's potential. This traditional strategic planning approach commonly consisted of a company's CEO and the head of planning getting together to devise a corporate plan, which would then be handed to the operating people for execution. Too frequently, companies' annual strategic planning processes have become ritualistic and devoid of discovery, with the planners working "from today forward, not from the future back, implicitly assuming, whatever the evidence to the contrary, that the future will be more or less like the present."[25] Tending to generate projections based on historical conditions and performance, this traditional planning approach tended to fall victim to collective—and frequently outdated—mind-sets about the competitive environment. Not surprisingly, the resulting strategic planning documents often failed to be implemented successfully.

Increasingly, the old process is being replaced by a *strategic management* approach, which combines strategic thinking, strategic planning, and strategic implementation and which is increasingly recognized as a fundamental task of line management rather than merely specialized planners in staff positions. Although still susceptible to problems such as groupthink, this more contemporary approach attempts to incorporate changes in three areas: (1) who does the planning, (2) how it is done, and (3) the contents of the plan.

Who Does Strategic Planning?
By the mid-1970s, strategic planners had become influential executives, especially in many large U.S. corporations. They were accustomed to writing a blueprint for each subsidiary, which they would then present to the management of each operating unit. The planners' power grew and the operating managers' influence waned, and of course there was hostility between the two groups.

By the 1980s, detailed long-range planning was no longer practical for most international companies, due to world uncertainty, and stronger international competition made a practical knowledge of the company and the industry an essential input to strategic planning. This brought senior operating managers into the planning process, enabling companies to change the role and reduce the size of their planning staffs.

> *General Electric's widely renowned central planning department was dismantled under former chairman Jack Welch. The company's business unit heads have now been made responsible for planning. As a result, they meet with GE's chairman and CEO, Jeffrey Immelt, and his top management team to tell them what their plans are, the new products they are investigating, and what their competition is doing. These meetings are conducted not merely during the annual strategic planning process but on an ongoing basis at other times of the year, as appropriate. The Corporate Executive Council, a group of top GE executives, also meets four times a year to study each business and where it is headed. No one in the company has the formal title of strategic planner.*

Although CEOs report that they would like to spend about one-third of their workday on strategy, strategic planning is no longer something that only the company's most senior executives do.[26] Top management, at the urging of strategy consultants, is assigning strategic planning to teams of line and staff managers from different businesses and functional areas, much as it has done with process-improvement task forces and quality circles. Frequently these teams include a range of ages—from junior staff members who have shown the ability to think creatively to experienced veterans near retirement age who will "tell it like it is." Another difference between the new and the old approaches: Formerly, planning was a company activity done in seclusion. Now, consultants say it should include interaction with such parties as important customers, distributors, suppliers, and alliance partners, in order to gain firsthand experience with the firm's markets. Other important stakeholders such as governments or stakeholder activists are also relevant influences, if not necessarily direct participants, in this strategic planning process. Incorporating these diverse perspectives can help a company to identify creative and effective ways to address the challenge of increasingly uncertain and changing international competitive environments. A.G. Lafley, the CEO of Procter & Gamble, commented, "Like it or not, we are in a global economy and a global political world. Honest to god, the responsibility is huge."[27] As a result, engaging in broad "dialogue among stakeholders" is not a choice, but a requirement, for an international company and its executives.

"We have lots of information technology. We just don't have any information."

How Strategic Planning Is Done By the 1980s, firms were using computer models and sophisticated forecasting methods to help produce the voluminous plans we just mentioned. Those plans were not only huge but also very detailed. As a Texas Instruments executive put it, "The company let its management system, which can track the eye of every sparrow, creep into the planning process, so we were making more and more detailed plans. It became a morale problem because managers knew they couldn't project numbers out five years to two decimal points."[28]

The heavy emphasis on these methods tended to result in a concentration on factors that could be quantified easily. However, the less quantifiable factors relating to sociopolitical developments around the world were becoming increasingly important. Also, the rapid rise in the levels of uncertainty made it clear to top managers that there was no point in using advanced techniques to make detailed five-year forecasts when various international crises were exposing the nonsense of many previous forecasts. Before 1973, for example, there had been great discussion about whether the price of crude oil would ever go above $2 per barrel.

Because of these problems, many firms have moved toward less structured formats and much shorter documents. General Electric's former chairman, Jack Welch, said, "A strategy can be summarized in a page or two."[29]

The top management of companies generally accepts the fact that "a good strategic planning process must allow ideas to surface from anywhere and at any times."[30] As indicated in Figure 13.1, objectives and strategies are intertwined, as are tactics and strategy. If the planning team is unable to come up with suitable tactics to implement a strategy, the strategy must be altered. In a similar fashion, if strategies cannot be formulated to enable the firm to reach the objective, the objective must be changed.[31]

Contents of the Plan The contents of the plan are also different. Many top managers say they are much more concerned now with focusing on issues, strategies, and implementation and with incorporating creative, forward-looking ideas that are essential to competitive success within a changing and uncertain international environment. The planning director of Royal Dutch/Shell, the British-Dutch energy transnational, said:

> The Shell approach has swung increasingly away from a mechanistic methodology and centrally set forecasts toward a more conceptual or qualitative analysis of the forces and pressures impinging on the industry. What Shell planners try to do is identify the key elements pertaining to a particular area of decision making—the different competitive, political, economic, social, and technical forces that are likely to have the greatest influence on the overall situation. In a global organization, the higher level of management is likely to be the most interested in global scenarios—looking at worldwide developments—while the focus becomes narrower as one proceeds into the more specialized functions, divisions, and business sectors of individual companies.[32]

In the contemporary global competitive environment, where firms often must place bigger bets on new technologies and other competitive capabilities, companies cannot afford to devote large amounts of money in one direction only to discover years later that this was the wrong direction for investing. "Bets on aircraft engine technology must be made up to 10 years before they result in a sale. Investments in regional jet engine technology that GE began making in the 1980s paid off last year (2002) in the winning bid to supply the engine for China's new regional jet, the ARJ-21."[33] Clearly, as indicated in this comment from Jeffrey Immelt, chairman and CEO of General Electric, competition in today's global competitive environment requires an approach to strategic planning that effectively incorporates a long-term perspective to strategic decision making and resource allocation decisions.

SUMMARY OF THE INTERNATIONAL PLANNING PROCESS

Perhaps a good way to summarize the new direction in planning is to quote Frederick W. Gluck, a principal architect of the strategic management practice in the multinational management consulting firm McKinsey & Co. Gluck said that if major corporations are to develop the flexibility to compete, they must make the following major changes in the way they plan:

1. Top management must assume a more explicit strategic decision-making role, dedicating a large amount of time to deciding how things ought to be instead of listening to analyses of how they are.

2. The nature of planning must undergo a fundamental change from an exercise in forecasting to an exercise in creativity.

3. Planning processes and tools that assume a future much like the past must be replaced by a mind-set that is obsessed with being first to recognize change and turn it into a competitive advantage.

4. The role of the planner must change from being a purveyor of incrementalism to being a crusader for action and an alter ego to line management.

5. Strategic planning must be restored to the core of line management responsibilities.[34]

Analysis of the Competitive Forces

The success of strategic management and the strategic planning process depends in large part upon the quality of information that goes into the process, as well as the interpretation of this information. Decisions are only as good as the information that goes into them, and "the biggest single problem in international planning is the lack of efficient and good competitive information." This is the conclusion of *Business International*'s study of 90 worldwide companies. The study also found that many companies have no organized approach to global competitive assessment; whatever is done is diffused among the various parts of the company. Yet competitor intelligence techniques are increasingly being viewed as a weapon for outmaneuvering competitors and increasing revenues, and there is growing use of organized competitor assessment and competitor intelligence systems, especially for larger companies and those that are competing internationally.

IS COMPETITOR ASSESSMENT NEW?

Sales and marketing managers have always needed information about their competitors' products, prices, channels of distribution, and promotional strategies to plan their own marketing strategies. Sales representatives are expected to submit information on competitors' activities in their territories as part of their regular reports to headquarters. It also has been common practice to talk to competitors' customers and distributors, test competitors' products, and stop at competitors' exhibits at trade shows. Larger firms maintain company libraries whose librarians regularly scan publications and report their findings to the functional area they believe would have an interest in the information. At times, companies have even resorted to **industrial espionage** in order to obtain information about their competitors.

industrial espionage

Act of spying on a competitor to learn secrets about its strategy and operations

Two representatives from a Taiwanese firm that wanted to steal information about an anti-cancer drug from Bristol-Myers Squibb were trapped in an FBI sting operation. The Taiwanese representatives thought they were dealing with a Bristol-Myers scientist who was going to provide the technical data they were seeking, in return for $200,000 cash, a $1,000 monthly retainer, and a share of future profits. When the agreement was reached, the FBI, which had been filming the operation, moved in for the arrest.[35]

Inasmuch as gathering information about the competition has been going on for so long, what is different about present-day **competitor analysis**? Essentially, the difference lies in top management's recognition that (1) increased competition has created a need for a broader and more in-depth knowledge of competitors' activities and (2) the firm should have a **competitor intelligence system (CIS)** (sometimes called a *business intelligence system*) for gathering, analyzing, and disseminating information to everyone in the firm who needs it. A competent competitor intelligence department should be able to obtain at least 80 percent of the information the company wants, using publicly available sources.[36] This is because most corporations fail to identify their most essential information and commonly disclose it willingly to anybody who asks for it. Moreover, many firms hire consultants or firms specializing in competitor analysis to provide information, and others send employees to seminars to learn how to do it themselves. Some even employ former CIA agents or investigators to handle data gathering and analysis.

"Overzealous" subcontractors working for Procter & Gamble phoned the hair care division of P&G's archrival Unilever. Falsely claiming that they were students, these subcontractors asked for sensitive information, which Unilever provided. In addition, Unilever employees frequently threw out sensitive documents, without first shredding them. The P&G subcontractors trespassed onto Unilever's property and retrieved some of these sensitive documents from the dumpster. (If they had waited until the dumpster was moved to the street, their actions would not have been trespassing and removal of the papers would have been legal.) These actions by the subcontractors, which effectively generated competitively valuable information albeit by crossing legal and ethical boundaries, were discovered by P&G's CEO and voluntarily reported to Unilever.[37]

Effective use of competitor intelligence systems can result in the legal and ethical acquisition of competitively valuable information that can provide a company with a range of benefits, such as the ability to (1) improve bidding success by better understanding competitors' costs, markups, and contractual priorities; (2) identify key customers for competitors, in order to better target marketing and sales efforts; (3) identify plant or other facility expansion plans of competitors, or changes in strategic priorities or investments among businesses or product lines; and (4) improve understanding of competitors' product formulations, production volumes, and supply chains.

SOURCES OF INFORMATION

There are five primary sources of information about the strengths, weaknesses, and threats of a firm's competitors: (1) within the firm, (2) published material, including computer databases, (3) suppliers/customers, (4) competitors' employees, and (5) direct observation or analysis of physical evidence of competitors' activities. These sources are all used in the United States and other industrialized countries, but they can be especially helpful in developing nations, which usually have a paucity of published information.

Within the Firm
As was mentioned previously, a firm's sales representatives are the best source of information about competitors. Librarians, when firms have them, can also provide input to the CIS. Another source is the technical and R&D people, who, while attending professional meetings or reading their professional journals, frequently learn of developments before they become general knowledge. Incidentally, government intelligence agencies from all countries subscribe to and analyze other nations' technical journals.

Published Material
In addition to technical journals, other types of published material provide valuable information. Databases such as *ABI Inform, Dialog, Dow Jones News/Retrieval, Lexis-Nexis,* and *NewsNet* enable analysts to obtain basic intelligence about sales, revenues,

competitor analysis
Process in which principal competitors are identified and their objectives, strengths, weaknesses, and product lines are assessed

competitor intelligence system (CIS)
Procedure for gathering, analyzing, and disseminating information about a firm's competitors

profits, markets, and other data needed to prepare detailed profiles of competitors. These services also enable users to create clipping folders based on search words such as the names of competitors, major customers, and suppliers, or words describing a product's technology.

The amount of useful information on the Internet, including general and specialist search sites, online versions of journals and other publications, and various monitoring services, continues to grow.* Company Web sites can be an important source of basic information about a company, including information about products, services, pricing, locations, financial performance, strategy, and key executives. Monitoring services can be hired, for a fee, to track a company or industry that you are interested in, notifying you whenever news appears on the Internet or in other locations. England's Economist Intelligence Unit and the United States' Predicast publish useful industry reports, and under the Freedom of Information Act, American firms and their foreign competitors can get information about companies from public documents. Public data sources such as building permits, environmental reports, and SEC reports can contain a wealth of competitively valuable information. Aerial photographs of competitors' facilities are often available from the U.S. Environmental Protection Agency (EPA) or the U.S. Geological Survey if the company is near a waterway or has done an environmental impact study. The photos may reveal an expansion or the layout of the competitor's production facilities. Be careful not to take unauthorized aerial photographs—this is trespassing and is illegal.

Suppliers/Customers Companies frequently tell their customers in advance about new products to keep them from buying elsewhere, but often the customer passes this information on to competitors. A company's purchasing agent can ask its suppliers how much they are producing or what they are planning to produce in the way of new products. Because buyers know how much their company buys, any added capacity or new products may be intended for sale to the firm's competitors. They can also allege that they are considering giving a supplier new business if the sales representative can prove the firm has the capacity to handle it. Salespeople often are so eager for the new business that they divulge the firm's total capacity and the competitor's purchases to prove they can handle the order.

Competitors' Employees Competitors' employees, actual or past, can provide information. Experienced human relations people pay special attention to job applicants, especially recent graduates, who indicate they have worked as interns or in summer jobs with competitors. They sometimes reveal proprietary information unknowingly. Companies also hire people away from competitors, and unscrupulous ones even advertise and hold interviews for jobs they don't have to get information from competitors' employees.

Direct Observation or Analysis of Physical Evidence Companies sometimes have their technical people join a competitor's plant tour to get details of the production processes. A crayon company sent employees to tour a competitor's plants under assumed names. Posing as potential customers, they easily gained access and obtained valuable information about the competitor's processes; admittedly, this was unethical, although standing outside a plant to count employees and learn the number of shifts a competitor is working is not considered unethical.

We have already mentioned the common practice of reverse engineering, which is an example of analyzing physical evidence, but intelligence analysts even buy competitors' garbage. It is illegal to enter a competitor's premises to collect it, but it is permissible to obtain refuse from a trash hauler once the material has left the competitor's premises. Another interesting analysis was done by a Japanese company, which sent employees to measure the thickness of rust on train tracks leaving an American competitor's plant. They used the results to calculate the plant's output.

*Presumably, you have seen the many endnotes in this text citing Internet sources and have looked at the Internet site directory we have provided on the McGraw-Hill/Irwin Web site (www.mhhe.com/ball11e) that is solely for sources of business information.

We have pointed out when an act is legal or illegal, and we have also commented on whether, in our opinion, it was ethical. Certainly, businesspeople have a responsibility to use all ethical means to gather information about their competitors.

USING COMPETITOR ASSESSMENT TO LOOK FORWARD, NOT BACK

Most companies have traditionally focused their competitor assessment activities to compile competitor profiles, newsletters, or other deliverables that are intended to reveal what actions a competitor has recently taken. Yet the strategic advantage of this sort of information can be limited. Instead, executives need to ensure that their competitor assessment efforts are focused on delivering predictive and actionable information, allowing them to anticipate threats and opportunities and to avoid "surprises." The competitor assessment activities should enhance information sharing and strategic decision making across the levels of the organization, and promote the use of competitor intelligence practices within a range of functional areas. Especially when tied into strategic planning techniques such as scenario analysis, the organization can anticipate and prepare for potential competitor moves, as well as develop intelligence indicators that can be scanned in order to quickly alert the company's managers when a significant competitive change is taking place. As a result of such efforts, executives may be able to improve the level of competitive awareness in their companies and enhance prospects for developing strategies for preemptively launching or defending products, or otherwise positioning themselves for advantage over competitors.[38]

BENCHMARKING

This is an increasingly popular way for firms to measure themselves against world leaders. Whereas competitor analysis will help a firm to spot differences between its performance in the market and that of its competitors, it does not provide a deep understanding of the processes that cause these differences. **Benchmarking,** in contrast, improves a company's performance through the identification and application of best practices within and across the company's various operations and sales activities.

benchmarking
A technique for measuring a firm's performance against the performance of others that may be in the same or a completely different industry

Benchmarking involves several stages:

1. Management examines its firm for the aspects of the business—the products, services, or processes—that need improving and the appropriate metrics to use in assessing performance on these aspects.

2. It then looks for companies that are world leaders in performing similar processes.

3. The firm's representatives visit those companies, talk with managers and workers, and determine the best operating practices that enable those companies to perform so well. Because the people who are going to use the newly acquired knowledge are line personnel, they, not staff people, should make these visits.

4. The company then conducts appropriate analyses to identify ways to not merely imitate but also innovatively tailor the best practices and incorporate them into their own activities, and it implements these practices in a manner that can meet the company's performance goals and is acceptable to the organization's members.

The problem, of course, is identifying which company to use as a benchmark. Some firms have been successful in choosing companies in their own industries, but often the ideal benchmark is in a related or perhaps even a completely different industry. Managers have a choice of using one or more of the four basic types of benchmarking:

1. *Internal:* comparing one operation in the firm with another. Because it is in-house, internal benchmarking is relatively easy to implement. It produces about a 10 percent improvement in productivity and can facilitate the creation of a network through which innovative ideas and information can be exchanged.

WORLD view

Using Industrial Espionage to Assess Competitors

Shekhar Verma, an Indian software engineer who had been fired from Bombay-based Geometric Software Solutions Ltd. (GSSL), claimed that he had the source code for Solidworks Plus' 3-D computer-aided design package. GSSL provides offshore outsourcing services in the area of information technology for clients in the United States and elsewhere, and the company had been debugging this software package for Solidworks. Verma had offered to sell the source code to a number of Solidworks' competitors, and Nenette Day had responded with interest to Verma's offer. She arranged to meet him in the Ashoka hotel in New Delhi. After confirming that he actually possessed Solidworks' source code, Day agreed to pay Verma $200,000 for the information. After she left the room, agents from India's Central Bureau of Intelligence (CBI) rushed in and arrested him. They did not arrest Day, because she was actually an agent from the FBI's Boston Cybercrime Unit, working undercover with the CBI on this case. Verma's arrest resulted in the first prosecutorial filing in India regarding outsourcing-related theft of intellectual property.

The theft of trade secrets, particularly involving competitors, is a chronic concern for businesses of all types. For years, companies have been acquiring information about each other by hiring competitors' employees, talking to competitors' customers, and so forth. Recently, however, intensified competition has motivated firms to become more sophisticated in this endeavor, even to the point of committing illegal acts. Mitsubishi was indicted on charges of stealing industrial secrets from Celanese, and Hitachi pleaded guilty to conspiring to transport stolen IBM technical documents to Japan. In another instance, a Russian spy was able to get samples of vital metal alloys by posing as a visitor and picking up metal shavings on crepe rubber soles on his walk through the plant. Businesspeople traveling abroad routinely report incidents of briefcases and laptop computers being tampered with or of hotel rooms being searched while they are away. Richard Isaacs, senior vice president of a company specializing in protecting intellectual assets, reported, "We had a client trying to do business in France, a country that believes it has an obligation to support local industry. Our client assumed that the way his French competitors always fractionally underbid him was a case of bad luck. Being less trusting, we had him hand-carry his next bid in a locked briefcase that was rigged to detect being opened. His proposal, a bogus one, was purloined and returned while he was at dinner, the detection system revealed. The next morning he went to his office, removed a diskette that was taped to his body, and printed out the real bid, which he then hand-delivered. A competitor later told him, 'I see you're learning.' "

These are not isolated incidents. A survey of Fortune 1000 companies by the American Society for Industrial Security claims that intellectual property losses from foreign and domestic espionage may total more than $300 billion. Major companies reported more than 1,100 documented and 500 suspected incidents of economic espionage. The Computer Security Institute's (CSI's) annual survey revealed that 64 percent of the 538 participating companies and large institutions acknowledged that they had suffered financial losses during the prior year due to breaches of their computer systems, most occurring over the Internet. Key targets for espionage included research and development, customer lists, and financial data. Perhaps not surprisingly, high-tech firms, especially in Silicon Valley, were the most common targets.

Economic espionage, which can damage competitive advantage, erode market share, reduce sales, and damage investor confidence, is expected to intensify as the race to control scarce resources and global markets increases. The rise of the knowledge-based economy has caused information to become a more important and valuable portion of many corporations' assets, and information is portable and increasingly compressible. "Basically, someone can put an entire file cabinet onto something they can slip into their pocket and walk out with" or transmit via e-mail, said Mark Radcliffe, an attorney with the technology-focused law firm Gray Gary. Today's offices have a range of technological options for storing vast amounts of data, including thumb-size USB memory sticks, portable hard drives, external CD burners, personal digital assistants, portable MP3 players, digital memory pens, and digital cameras.

Given this situation, protecting valuable intellectual assets against economic espionage has proved to be an increasing challenge. Companies are becoming more physically distributed, and their management and administration more dispersed. They increasingly rely on distributed, computer-based information systems, which can result in more potential sites from which competitors can collect valuable information. Although few companies have anybody assigned specifically to deal with espionage directed against them, almost all large companies and many smaller ones have competitive intelligence departments, often with substantial levels of funding. A Chinese spy manual noted that 80 percent of the desired military intelligence was available through public sources. A similar figure might be applicable to corporate spying, especially with the growing number of company Web sites holding increasingly detailed information about organizational structures, products, employees, facilities, contact information, and other potentially valuable data.

"Intellectual property has become one of the major targets of the illicit gaining of information," says Michael Marks, a director of Spymaster Communications and Surveillance Systems of the

2. *Competitive:* comparing the firm's operation with that of a direct competitor. Obviously, this is the most difficult kind of benchmarking to do. Productivity improves about 20 percent.

3. *Functional:* comparing the firm's functions with similar functions at firms in one's broadly defined industry—American Airlines' comparing its freight handling procedure

United Kingdom. "The terrible thing today is that if you gain access to a company's computer, you can get access to all of its inner secrets. In the past, you gained information piecemeal from people and departments; now it's centralized on computers and the amount of corporate internal fraud is quite astounding." Perhaps surprisingly, leading-edge technologies are not the only ones being targeted. In less economically developed nations, there is often a preference for older, "off-the-shelf" hardware and software that costs less, is easier to purchase or produce, and can be readily applied within their economic context. It appears that mid-level companies might be targeted even more than large companies for industrial espionage activities, particularly since they have more competitors to engage in espionage and they often have inadequate controls on proprietary information.

Governments and corporations have made attempts to respond to the growing challenges of economic espionage. The U.S. government passed the Economic Espionage Act in 1996, which made it a federal crime to provide American businesses' trade secrets to a foreign entity. The law does not apply to non-U.S. citizens who commit such acts outside American borders, however. In 2001, the Group of Eight leading industrial nations agreed to collaborate more closely to fight international computer-based crime (dubbed "cyber crime") and to possibly develop common law enforcement standards. The European Union proposed a cyber crime framework that would call for mandatory jail sentences for cyber crimes that cause significant damage to a business, but this framework would have limited enforceability if the crime was committed by someone in a country outside the EU. In 2004, Japan enacted legislation that made it a crime to leak corporate trade secrets. Yoshinori Komiya, director of the intellectual property office in the Ministry of Economy, Trade and Industry, said, "The flow of technology out of Japan is leading to a decline in competitiveness and employment. We believe that there is some technology that should be transferred, but what is happening now is that technology that top management does not want transferred is getting passed on." Elsewhere in Asia, notoriously high levels of counterfeiting and piracy indicate the widespread extent of industrial espionage, and the vast proportion of countries lack strong legislative frameworks to deal effectively with the issue. An executive from Sony stated, "We would certainly welcome a comprehensive regulatory system to protect intellectual property in countries such as China and South Korea." Clearly, much opportunity remains for governments to effectively attack the problem.

Corporations have attempted to introduce improved security systems to counter the threat of industrial espionage, causing the worldwide corporate market for monitoring and filtering products to grow to nearly $1 billion. One thing that companies can do is focus their efforts on identifying the aspects of their business that are most critical to protect from espionage. Each industry is unique and the bases for competitive advantage vary across companies. That means each company has to analyze its own strategy, operations, and capabilities and identify what provides it with a competitive advantage, things that it does not want competitors or other organizations to know. In many cases, key activities or knowledge can be isolated, and the company can focus on effectively managing the type and number of employees that might have access to them. In the West, it is common to restrict knowledge of sensitive projects to a small group of people, but in places such as Japan a large group of people usually has access to all of the information, even on very important projects. Some companies refrain from filing patents on manufacturing processes, fearing that difficulties in determining whether such processes are being copied makes it difficult to protect these valuable trade secrets. Sometimes operational security requirements will require the development and management of highly elaborate systems to control information. Yet managing the risk may also include a range of simpler actions. For example, Samsung banned the use of camera phones in some of its facilities in order to keep spies from taking pictures of new product models and transmitting them to competitors or others.

Despite these efforts, the FBI says that foreign spies have increased their attacks on American industry. After the cold war ended, most nations shifted the bulk of their spying to economic espionage. The *Annual Report to Congress on Foreign Economic Collection and Industrial Espionage* estimated that industrial espionage and the loss of proprietary information costs U.S. companies over $300 billion a year, or more than a General Electric or Wal-Mart corporation annually. The FBI told Congress that at least 23 countries were actively involved in industrial espionage against the United States and that FBI agents were involved in 800 separate investigations into economic spying by foreign countries. The major offending nations include China, Japan, Israel, France, Germany, Russia, South Korea, Taiwan, and India. The FBI confirmed that economic spying by countries considered friends as well as by adversaries is increasing. Yet it does not take James Bond–type technologies and procedures for these spies to be effective. The U.S. Office of Counterintelligence reports that the methods most widely used for acquiring sensitive information or technologies include e-mail, phone, and fax.

Source: Jim Joyce, "The Reality of Espionage," *Communications News*, May 2006, p. 38; Jeffrey Benner, "Nailing the Company Spies," *Wired News*, March 1, 2001, www.wired.com/news/print/0,1294,41968,00.html (September 1, 2002); William A. Wallace, "Industrial Espionage Experts," www.newhaven.edu/california/CJ625/p6.html (September 1, 2002); National Counterintelligence Center, *Annual Report to Congress on Foreign Economic Collection and Industrial Espionage 2000* (Washington, DC: National Counterintelligence Center, 2000), www.ncix.gov/nacic/reports/fy00.htm (September 1, 2002); "FBI Warns Companies to Beware of Espionage," *International Herald Tribune*, January 13, 1998, p. 3; Michael Barrier, "Protecting Trade Secrets," *HR Magazine*, May 2004, pp. 52–57; Mei Fong, "The Enemy Within," *Far Eastern Economic Review*, April 22, 2004, pp. 34–36; Richard Isaacs, "A Field Day for Spies: While a Deal Advances," *Mergers and Acquisitions*, January 2004, pp. 30–35; Michiyo Nakamoto, "Japan Goes after Industrial Spies," *Financial Times*, February 9, 2004, p. 8; and Michael Fitzgerald, "At Risk Offshore: U.S. Companies Outsourcing Their Software Development Offshore Can Get Stung by Industrial Espionage and Poor Intellectual Property Safeguards," *CIO*, November 15, 2003, p. 1.

with that of Federal Express, for example. Functional benchmarking is easier to research and implement than competitive benchmarking. It frequently can improve productivity, with improvements of 35 percent or more having been reported by numerous companies and studies.

4. *Generic:* comparing operations in totally unrelated industries. When Xerox decided to improve its order-filling process, it went to L.L.Bean, a mail-order house famous for filling orders quickly and correctly. Although the industries and the kinds of products were very different, Xerox saw that both firms handled a wide variety of shapes and sizes that made it necessary to pack them by hand. By learning from Bean, Xerox reduced its warehousing costs 10 percent.

When Nissan's Infiniti division wanted to change the negative view many people have of service in the car industry, it went to famous service companies for its role models. McDonald's taught the Infiniti team the value of a clean, attractive facility and teamwork. Nordstrom, the department-store chain, taught Infiniti the importance of rewarding employees for providing outstanding service. When China Air wanted to enhance its competitiveness in the international air travel industry, it conducted a benchmark quality comparison relative to key competitors, including British Airways, Singapore Airlines, and Virgin Airlines, across a range of service dimensions in economy, business, and first-class air travel.[39]

Although sometimes a visit to another firm will provide an idea that can be used without change, generally some adaptation will be needed. The basic purpose of benchmarking is to make managers and workers less parochial by exposing them to different ways of doing things so as to encourage creativity, promote organizational learning, enhance cost and performance, and build competitive advantage.

Summary

Explain international strategy, competencies, and international competitive advantage.

International strategy is concerned with the way in which firms make fundamental choices about developing and deploying scarce resources internationally. The goal of international strategy is to create a competitive advantage that is sustainable over time. To do this, the international company should try to develop skills, or competencies, that are valuable, rare, and difficult to imitate and that the organization is able to exploit fully.

Describe the steps in the global strategic planning process.

Global strategic planning provides a formal structure in which managers (1) analyze the company's external environment, (2) analyze the company's internal environment, (3) define the company's business and mission, (4) set corporate objectives, (5) quantify goals, (6) formulate strategies, and (7) make tactical plans.

Explain the purpose of mission statements, vision statements, values statements, objectives, quantified goals, and strategies.

Statements of the corporate mission, vision, and values communicate to the firm's stakeholders what the company is and where it is going, as well as the values to be upheld among the organization's members in their behaviors. A firm's objectives direct its course of action, and its strategies enable management to reach its objectives.

Describe the methods of and new directions in strategic planning.

Strategic planning is traditionally done either in a top-down, bottom-up, or iterative process. Operating managers, rather than dedicated staff planners, now have assumed a primary role in planning. Firms use less structured formats and much shorter documents. Managers are more concerned with issues, strategies, and implementation.

Explain home replication, multidomestic, regional, global, and transnational strategies and when to use them.

When developing and assessing strategic alternatives, companies competing in international markets confront two opposing forces: reduction of costs and adaptation to local markets. As a result, companies basically have five different strategies that they can use for competing internationally: home replication, multidomestic, global, transnational, and regional. (Regional strategies are included because, as some researchers have argued, considering them is of value since few firms are truly global in their scope and operations.) The most appropriate strategy, overall and for various activities in the value chain, depends on the amount of pressure the company faces in terms of adapting to local markets and achieving cost reductions. Each of these five strategies has its own set of advantages and disadvantages.

Describe the sources of competitive information.

Sources of competitive information are within the firm, published material, suppliers/customers, competitors' employees, and direct observation or analysis of physical evidence.

Discuss the importance of industrial espionage.

Industrial espionage is costing domestic and international companies billions of dollars annually in lost sales and may even put a company's long-term competitiveness and survival at risk. The threat of espionage is increasing, particularly as information and knowledge increasingly represent the foundation for companies' competitiveness.

international strategy (p. 353)

competitive advantage (p. 353)

mission statement (p. 357)

vision statement (p. 358)

values statement (p. 358)

competitive strategies (p. 361)

scenarios (p. 365)

contingency plans (p. 365)

top-down planning (p. 368)

bottom-up planning (p. 369)

iterative planning (p. 369)

industrial espionage (p. 372)

competitor analysis (p. 373)

competitor intelligence system (CIS) (p. 373)

benchmarking (p. 375)

1. What is international strategy, and why is it important?

2. What is the difference between strategic planning conducted in domestic companies and that conducted in international companies?

3. Suppose the competitor analysis reveals that the American subsidiary of your firm's German competitor is about to broaden its product mix in the American market by introducing a new line against which your company has not previously had to compete in the home market. The environmental analysis shows that recent weakness in the dollar-euro exchange rate is expected to continue, making American exports relatively less expensive in Germany. Do you recommend a defensive strategy, or do you attack your competitor in its home market? How will you implement your strategy?

4. You are the CEO of the Jones Petrochemical Company and have just finished studying next year's plans of your foreign subsidiaries. You are pleased that the European plan is so optimistic because that subsidiary contributes heavily to your company's income. But OPEC is meeting next month. Should you ask your planning committee, which meets tomorrow, to construct some scenarios? If so, about what?

5. Your firm has used bottom-up planning for years, but the subsidiaries' plans differ with respect to approaches to goals and assumptions—even the time frames are different. How can you, the CEO, get them to agree on these points and still get their individual input?

6. What are the main strengths and weaknesses of each of the competitive strategies: home replication, multidomestic, regional, global, and transnational? Under what circumstances might each strategy be more or less appropriate?

7. What strategic issues arise as a firm considers an international transfer of skills and products resulting from its distinctive competencies in its home country?

8. What is scenario analysis? Why would scenario analysis be of value to an international company? What might limit the usefulness of such an approach?

9. What are some information sources used in competitor analysis? What ethical issues might be involved in using these various sources?

Use the globalEDGE site (http://globalEDGE.msu.edu/) to complete the following exercises:

1. Your company has developed a new product that is expected to achieve high penetration rates in any country where it is introduced regardless of average income. Considering the costs of the product launch, the management team has decided to initially introduce the product only in countries that have a sizable population base. Using the *World Population Data Sheet*, published by the Population Reference Bureau, you are asked to prepare a preliminary assessment of the top ten countries by population. Since growth opportunities are another major concern, the average population growth rate for each country should be listed for management's consideration.

2. You are working for a company that is planning to invest in a foreign country. Management has requested a report regarding the attractiveness of alternative countries based on the potential return of foreign direct investment (FDI). Accordingly, the ranking of the top 25 countries in terms of FDI attractiveness is a crucial ingredient for your report. A colleague mentioned a potentially useful tool called the "FDI Confidence Index" which is updated periodically. Find this index and provide additional information regarding how the index is constructed.

Minicase 13.1   Wal-Mart Takes On the World

Founded in the U.S. state of Arkansas by Sam Walton in 1962, Wal-Mart has developed into the largest retailer in the world and the largest company on the Fortune 500 list, with sales of $312.4 billion in fiscal 2006. Embodying high levels of service, strong inventory management, and purchasing economies, Wal-Mart overpowered competitors and became the dominant firm in the U.S. retail industry. After rapid expansion during the 1980s and 1990s, Wal-Mart faces limits to growth in its home market and has been forced to look internationally for opportunities.

Many skeptics claimed that Wal-Mart's business practices and culture could not be transferred internationally. Yet, in its first decade of operations outside the United States, the company's globalization efforts progressed at a rapid pace. As of 2006, over 40 percent of Wal-Mart's stores were located outside the United States. Its more than 2,700 international retail units employ over 450,000 associates in 13 international markets. In fiscal 2007, Wal-Mart planned to open at least 220 additional international units. Wal-Mart's sales from international operations are expected to reach $78 billion in 2007, a level that is expected to increase substantially over the next decade. If the international business were an independent chain, it would be the fourth-largest retailer in the world, behind Wal-Mart's U.S. operations, Home Depot, and Carrefour.

Globalizing Wal-Mart: Where and How to Begin?

When Wal-Mart began to expand internationally, it had to decide which countries to target. Although the European retail market was large, to succeed there Wal-Mart would have had to take market share from established competitors. Instead, Wal-Mart deliberately selected emerging markets as its starting point for international expansion. In Latin America, it targeted nations with large, growing populations—Mexico, Argentina, and Brazil—and in Asia it aimed at China. Because the company lacked the organizational, managerial, and financial resources to simultaneously pursue all of these markets, Wal-Mart pursued a very deliberate entry strategy for the emerging markets, focusing first on the Americas rather than the more culturally and geographically distant Asian marketplace.

For its first international store, opened in 1991 in Mexico City, the company used a 50-50 joint venture. This entry mode helped Wal-Mart manage the substantial differences in culture and income between the United States and Mexico. Its Mexican partner, the retail conglomerate, Cifra, provided expertise in operating in the Mexican market and a base for learning about retailing in that country. When it entered Brazil in 1996, Wal-Mart was able to leverage its learning from the Mexican experience to take a majority position in a 60-40 venture with a local retailer, Lojas Americana. When the company subsequently entered Argentina, it did so on a wholly owned basis. After gaining experience with partners, in 1997 Wal-Mart expanded further in Mexico by acquiring a controlling interest in Cifra, which it renamed in 2000 to Wal-Mart de México S. A. de C. V. By 2006, Wal-Mart operated 808 units in Mexico in 30 states, achieving annual sales of $15.8 billion and employing over 130,000. It accounts for over half of all supermarket sales in Mexico.

Still, learning the dos and don'ts was a difficult process. "It wasn't such a good idea to stick so closely to the domestic Wal-Mart blueprint in Argentina, or in some of the other international markets we've entered, for that matter," said the president of Wal-Mart International. "In Mexico City we sold tennis balls that wouldn't bounce right in the high altitude. We built large parking lots at some of our Mexican stores, only to realize that many of our customers there rode the bus to the store, then trudged across those large parking lots with bags full of merchandise. We responded by creating bus shuttles to drop customers off at the door. These were all mistakes that were easy to address, but we're now working smarter internationally to avoid cultural and regional problems on the front end."[a] Wal-Mart's initial entry into Brazil used greenfield store sites and emphasized aggressive pricing to build market share, but the French retailer Carrefour and other Brazilian competitors retaliated, launching a costly price war. Wal-Mart's strength in international sourcing was initially of limited assistance in Brazil, since the leading sales category—food— was primarily sourced locally, where Carrefour and others already had strong relationships with local suppliers. Over time, Wal-Mart changed its competitive emphasis to customer service and a broader merchandise mix than smaller local companies could match. The company also pursued acquisitions to supplement internal growth, buying 118 Bompreço stores in 2004 and 140 Sonae stores in 2005. By 2006, Wal-Mart was the third-largest retailer in Brazil, operating 293 stores and employing 50,000 associates.

The Challenge of China

The lure of China, the world's most populous nation, proved too great to ignore. Wal-Mart was one of the first international retailers in China when it set up operations in 1996. Before Wal-Mart's arrival, state-owned retailers typically offered a limited range of products, often of low quality, and most stores were poorly lit, dirty, and disorganized.

Concerned about their potential impact on local firms, Beijing restricted the operations of foreign retailers. These restrictions included requirements for government-backed partners and limitations on the number and location of stores. Initially, Wal-Mart's partner was Charoen Pokphand, a Thai conglomerate with massive investments in China and a strong track record with joint ventures. This venture was terminated after 18 months, due to differences regarding control. A new venture was subsequently formed with two politically connected partners, Shenzhen Economic Development Zone and Shenzhen International Trust and Investment Corporation, and Wal-Mart was able to negotiate a controlling stake in the venture. The first Chinese Wal-Mart store was in Shenzhen, a rapidly growing city bordering Hong Kong. The company chose to concentrate its initial activities in Shenzhen while it learned about Chinese retailing.

Wal-Mart had many well-publicized miscues while learning how to do business in China. For example, some household items found at American Wal-Marts are not found in the Chinese stores. "Their shopping list isn't as extensive as ours. If you ask the majority of people here what a paper towel is, they either don't know or they think it's some kind of luxury item," said the president of Wal-Mart China.[b] The company eliminated matching kitchen towels and window curtains, since the wide variety of Chinese window sizes caused people to make their own curtains. Consumers purchased four times the number of small appliances than projected, but Wal-Mart no longer tries to sell extension ladders or a year's supply of soy sauce or shampoo to Chinese customers, who typically live in cramped apartments with limited storage space. Yet, although "people say the Chinese don't like sweets, we sure sell a lot of M&Ms," said Joe Hatfield, president of Wal-Mart's Asian retailing operations.[c]

Operationally, the scarcity of highly modernized suppliers in China frustrated Wal-Mart's initial attempts to achieve high levels of efficiency. Bar coding was not standardized in China, and retailers had to either recode goods themselves or distribute labels to suppliers, procedures that increased costs and hindered efficiency. Pressured to appease the government's desire for local sourcing of products, while maintaining the aura of being an American shopping experience, Wal-Mart's solution was to source about 85 percent of the Chinese stores' purchases from local manufacturers but heavily weight purchasing toward locally produced American brands (such as products from Procter & Gamble's factories in China). Wal-Mart also mass-markets Chinese products that were previously available only in isolated parts of the country, such as coconut juice from Guangdong province, hams and mushrooms from rural Yunnan, and oats from Fujian province. "What this place is going to look like 10 to 20 years from now—and what the consumer will be ready to buy—is hard to even think about. There are 800 million farmers out there who've probably never even tasted a Coke," said Hatfield.

Wal-Mart also learned the importance of building relationships with agencies from the central and local governments and with local communities. Bureaucratic red tape, graft, and lengthy delays in the approval process proved to be aggravating. The company learned to curry favor through actions such as inviting Chinese officials to visit Wal-Mart's headquarters in the United States, assisting local charities, and even building a school for the local community. Wal-Mart expected its small-town folksiness to be a strong asset in China. "Price has been an issue, but there's always somebody who can undersell you. A young person who's smiling and saying, 'Can I help you?' is a big part of the equation. Most places in this country you don't get that," said the president of Wal-Mart International.[d] "Over the last two years, Wal-Mart has learned a tremendous amount about serving our Chinese customers, and our excitement about expanding in the market and in Asia has never been stronger."[e]

Wal-Mart was only the 20th-largest retailer in China at the end of 2005, with sales less than half those of industry leader Carrefour of France. Wal-Mart's 59 stores in China, employing over 30,000 associates, represented a small fraction of its worldwide retailing operations. Yet, Wal-Mart estimated that its operations in China could be nearly as large as in the U.S. within 20 years and the lessons Wal-Mart has learned have positioned the company to exploit future market-opening initiatives in China. It purchases nearly $20 billion worth of local merchandise annually, making it China's sixth-largest export market if it were a company. Wal-Mart's objective is to use its existing stores and growing supplier network as a basis for the creation of a nationwide chain. Wal-Mart's head of Asian operations stated, "We are not just going to march out all over China." The focus was instead on expanding slowly, trying to make friends and gain respect as it does so. In March 2006, the company announced that it would hire about 150,000 workers in China during the next five years as part of its planned expansion strategy.

A major change in Wal-Mart's China growth strategy occured in October 2006. It was announced that the company had outbid competitors Carrefour, the United Kingdom's Tesco, and Lianhua of China to acquire Trust-Mart, a chain of over 100 supercenters located in 20 cities across China. This acquisition, for approximately $1 billion, would immediately give Wal-Mart the largest network of food and department stores in China, with combined sales of over $3 billion for 2006.

A Different Approach for Entering Canada and Europe

After focusing initial international expansion efforts on large developing nations, Wal-Mart began to pursue the Canadian and European markets. Strong, entrenched competitors in these mature, developed country markets hindered Wal-Mart's prospects for obtaining critical mass solely through internal growth. Rather than first developing its retail operations from scratch, as in Latin America and Asia, Wal-Mart entered via acquisitions.

The company entered Canada by acquiring 122 Woolco stores in 1994. Wal-Mart quickly restructured the money-losing Canadian operations, applying many of the practices that had been successful in the United States. Transition teams were brought in from the United States to help with the transformation, and within two years the Canadian operations were profitable. Its 278 stores, employing 70,000 associates, now account for more than 35 percent of the Canadian discount- and department-store retail market. Wal-Mart's "Buy Canadian" program, launched in 1994, has resulted in more than 80 percent of the company's merchandise being purchased from suppliers that operate in Canada.

In Europe, Wal-Mart entered Germany by acquiring the profitable 21-unit Wertkauf hypermarket chain in 1998 and 74 Interspar stores in 1999. The company entered the United Kingdom in 1999 through the acquisition of the 229-store ASDA Group. These acquisitions allowed Wal-Mart to build market share quickly within the highly advanced and competitive European retail market. From this base, additional growth is anticipated through the opening of new stores, supplemented with further acquisitions. By 2006, the company had 88 Supercenters in Germany. It is the second-largest supermarket chain in the United Kingdom, with 321 stores and 140,000 associates, but has been losing ground to industry leader Tesco Plc.

Although successful in rapidly building European market share, Wal-Mart still encountered difficulties. Acquiring two German companies within a year proved too much for the company to handle with its limited European infrastructure. Efforts to centralize purchasing and leverage Wal-Mart's famous competencies in information systems and inventory management were stymied by problems with suppliers that were not familiar with such practices.

The introduction of Wal-Mart's "always low prices" approach met resistance from competitors and regulators. Indeed, the company was ordered by Germany's Cartel Office to raise prices, charging that Wal-Mart had helped to spark a price war by illegally selling some items below cost. Wal-Mart also challenged existing retail practices regarding hours of operation. Laws required shops to close by 8 P.M. on weekdays and 4 P.M. on Saturdays and to remain closed on Sundays. However, Wal-Mart stores began to open by 7 A.M., two hours earlier than most competitors, and the company has lobbied for additional reforms to allow later closing times. These changes have sparked vehement opposition from smaller competitors and employees' unions.

As it struggled to build a strong competitive base, Wal-Mart Germany lost between $120 million and $200 million in 1999, and the losses continued each year following. Lacking the scale of operations to create competitive advantage, and facing strong competition in a mature marketplace, in July 2006 Wal-Mart announced that it was selling its German operations to a competitor, Metro. Earlier that year, Wal-Mart had also announced that it was selling its Korean operations to competitor Shinsegae after Wal-Mart failed to achieve successful scale and performance in that Asian market.

A Base for Continued Globalization Efforts

Wal-Mart's path to internationalization has been littered with challenges. The company has persevered and seems to have learned from its mistakes, however, and it seems well positioned for continued growth. In 2005, the company acquired one-third of Central American Retail Holding Co. which has 363 stores in Guatemala, Honduras, El Salvador, Nicaragua, and Costa Rico, and it increased its share to 51 percent in 2006 and changed the name to Wal-Mart Central America. There are still many potential markets for a Wal-Mart store, and the company is committed to exploiting these opportunities, whether they are at home or abroad. International is Wal-Mart's fastest-growing division, and the company announced that it was exploring growth opportunities in Russia and India, indicating that these countries might soon be part of the company's international market coverage.

India: Anticipating the Opening Up of a Billion-Person Market

Wal-Mart is currently positioning for entry into India, which has the largest population of any nation the company is not currently in. Although it is the world's eighth-largest retail market at $250 billion, the inefficiency of the Indian retail sector is well known. Over 95 percent of retail sales are made through tea stands, newspaper stalls, and mom-and-pop stores. Strict government barriers have prevented foreign-owned retail businesses, although that situation might change soon. "Many smart people—much smarter than I— believe that India could be the next China," said John Menzer, the former head of Wal-Mart's international operations and current vice chair of the company's U.S. stores. "So, certainly, as a retailer it's a place where we'd like to be."[f]

However, exploiting the potential of India could be a major challenge, particularly given the country's notoriously frustrating bureaucracy and poor infrastructure. Wal-Mart will have to learn to manage highly protectionist and anticapitalist political parties, a bad road system, frequent power outages, and lack of adequate distribution and cold-storage systems, among other concerns. The diversity of the country could also prove problematic, with 18 official languages and widely varying regional consumer cultures. Savvy new Indian chains, such as Provogue and Shoppers' Stop, are starting to emerge, and nationalistic sentiments may produce much consternation for expansion efforts of foreign companies such as Wal-Mart.

In preparation for an eventual opening of the market, Wal-Mart has been building a foundation by establishing relationships with Indian suppliers, distributors, and consumers. The company has been conducting market studies, hiring a team of local managers, and building relationships with Indian politicians and bureaucrats. In 2005, Wal-Mart purchased $1.5 billion in Indian products for export and sale in its stores abroad. "What we found in China as we get stores on the ground and get more mass, we get to know a lot more of the suppliers. And when we know the suppliers, it gives us the opportunity to learn the product of the suppliers and actually export them," said Mr. Menzer.[g] Clearly, Wal-Mart will need to understand the political and market dynamics and exploit the lessons it has learned from entering other emerging markets in order to achieve success when the Indian market finally opens up.

Discussion Questions

1. Why has Wal-Mart viewed international expansion as a critical part of its strategy?

2. What did Wal-Mart do to enable the company to achieve success in Canada and Latin America? Why did Wal-Mart fail to achieve similar success in Europe?

3. What should Wal-Mart do—or not do—to help ensure that the company achieves success in China and India?

[a]"ASDA Purchase Leads Way for Wal-Mart's International Expansion," *Wal-Mart Annual Report 2000,* p. 10.

[b]James Cox, "Great Wal-Mart of China Red-Letter Day as East Meets West in the Aisles," *USA Today,* September 11, 1996, p. B1.

[c]Tyler Marshall, "Selling Eel and Chicken Feet—Plus M&Ms and Sony TVs," *Los Angeles Times,* November 25, 2003, p. A15.

[d]Cox, "Great Wal-Mart of China Red-Letter Day."

[e]"Wal-Mart China Expansion to Accelerate," www.Walmartstores.com/newsstand/archive/prn_980605_chinaexpan.shtml (June 5, 1999).

[f]Eric Bellman and Kris Hudson, "Wal-Mart Stakes India Claim," *The Wall Street Journal,* January 18, 2006, p. A9.

[g]Ibid.

Source: "International Operations," www.walmartfacts.com/newsdesk/wal-mark-fact-sheets.aspx#a1826 (June 28, 2006); Peter Wonacott, "Wal-Mart Finds Market Footing in China," *The Wall Street Journal,* July 17, 2000, p. A31; "Big Chains Set for Post-WTO Scrap," *South China Morning Post,* November 3, 2000, p. 5; Glenn Hall, "Wal-Mart Germany Told to Raise Prices: Choking Small Retailers," *National Post,* September 9, 2000, p. D3; Wal-Mart, "Timeline," http://walmartstores.com/GlobalWMStoresWeb/navigate.do?catg=6 (June 28, 2006); Mike Troy, "In South America, Ahold's Loss Is Wal-Mart's Gain," *DSN Retailing Today,* March 22, 2004, pp. 1–2; and "Wal-Mart to Become Biggest Big-Box in China," http://money.cnn.com/2006/10/16/news/international/walmart_hypermarkets.reut/index.htm?postversion=2006101706 (October 17, 2006).

14 Organizational Design and Control

We are in the midst of a major transition from organization and management practices that began around the turn of the 20th century. Our cloudy crystal ball won't allow us to see which organization structure or model will dominate the 21st century. Since we're no longer in an age of mass production and standardization, there won't likely be just one type. Rather, we'll see our top organizations grow and shed a variety of structures and models to suit their changing circumstances.

—Jim Clemmer, in "High Performance Organization Structures and Characteristics"

Kraft Foods—Reorganizing to Become a "Best of Global and Best of Local" Company

Kraft Foods announced a complex reorganization of its worldwide operations in 2004, with a goal of transforming the company into an integrated, global company. With over $34 billion in sales and 94,000 employees worldwide, Kraft is the largest branded-food and -beverage company headquartered in North America and the second largest in the world, behind Nestlé. Kraft's mission is "to be widely recognized as the undisputed leader of the global food industry." The company's products—including such brands as Kraft cheese, Maxwell House coffee, Nabisco cookies and crackers, Philadephia cream cheese, Jello desserts, Oscar Mayer meats, and Post cereals—are sold in over 155 nations.

Kraft's reorganization was triggered in part by slowing growth in several product categories, especially within developed country markets, which caused a decline in earnings in recent years. Many of the company's performance difficulties were attributed to problems with its prior organizational structure. To address this situation, under its new structure, Kraft is creating a matrix organization that includes:

1. A new global marketing and category development group to accelerate growth and global expansion through developing global category strategies, new product platforms, and marketing excellence.

2. Two geographic-based commercial units, for the regions of North America and International. These units will be responsible for driving strong results, country by country, through local consumer and customer knowledge, local sales and marketing execution, and responsibility for profits and losses.

3. Key functions, including technology and quality, supply chains, finance, human resources, law, information systems, corporate and governmental affairs, and strategy and business development, will be managed on a global basis in order to achieve greater economies of scale, better lever technologies and best practices internationally, and drive brands and ideas around the world faster.

4. The activities of the preceding three groups will be coordinated with the company's five global product sectors—snacks and cereals, cheese and food service, beverages, convenient meals, and grocery.

Kraft's CEO said, "The most important opportunities and pressing challenges that we face today and going forward demand that we become a more unified, global company. But in becoming more global, we must keep and strengthen the local expertise that has built our success. By moving quickly to create Kraft's new global 'One Company' structure, we can immediately begin to capture the 'best of global and best of local' and act with greater focus and speed than ever before." In terms of enhanced organizational effectiveness, Kraft's leadership anticipated that this outcome would be achieved through accelerated innovation, improved application of category/functional expertise, strong local execution, improved management

CONCEPT PREVIEWS

After reading this chapter, you should be able to:

explain why the design of organizational structure is important to international companies

discuss the organizational dimensions that must be considered when selecting organizational structures

discuss the various organizational forms available for structuring international companies

explain the concept of the virtual corporation

explain why decisions are made where they are among parent and subsidiary units of an international company (IC)

discuss how an IC can maintain control of a joint venture or of a company in which the IC owns less than 50 percent of the voting stock

list the types of information an IC needs to have reported to it by its units around the world

Gli Affari Internazionali

nales Geschäft Παγοσμιο Business

Negócios Internacionais   Los Negócios Internacionais

ternacionales   Affaires Internationales 国際商務 Παγοσμιο Business

development, and faster decision making. Enhanced efficiency would be facilitated by elimination of functional duplication and facility consolidation. The new organizational structure resembles that of other major consumer products companies, such as Gillette and Procter & Gamble.

A particular objective of the reorganization was to produce a more integrated and balanced global business by accelerating Kraft's growth outside its home market of the United States and generating a higher proportion of international sales, consistent with the performance of key rivals such as Nestlé and Unilever. The maturing North American region generated a 1 percent decline in profits in 2005, versus a more than 20 percent profit growth in international markets. Overall, Kraft's international sales grew from less than a quarter of total company revenues in the early 1990s to over 31 percent in 2005. Kraft's executive vice president commented, "This new structure will help us accelerate our growth and move faster as a company in our decision-making process. All of it is designed to help us deliver realistic, sustainable growth for our shareholders."

Within Kraft's international segment, developed country markets accounted for over 60 percent of sales in 2005. Approximately 60 percent of these revenues were concentrated in just four nations: Germany, France, Italy, and the United Kingdom. As with other developed countries, these markets were confronting problems of slowing population growth, increasingly value-conscious consumers, high trade concentration, and the growing role of discount retailers and private-label products. In developed countries, the company anticipated that its reorganization would promote growth by leveraging its leading share positions in core categories, while building superior brand value and accelerating innovation.

Another important objective of Kraft's new organizational structure was to enhance growth prospects within developing country markets. Revenues from developing markets had increased from $1 billion in 1992 to $2 billion in 2000 and $4 billion in 2005. These markets represented only about 12 percent of overall revenues, and the company envisioned substantial future growth from these areas. In the developing markets, Kraft planned to expand its core categories into large countries with the greatest growth potential. The four top developing countries that Kraft planned to focus on—Mexico, Brazil, Russia, and China—had a combined population of nearly 2 billion but represented less than $1.5 billion of Kraft's annual sales in 2005.

Under the new structure, Kraft's strategy for developing country markets is based on four main components: (1) Introduce additional snack, beverage, and cheese categories in developing markets where it already has a presence, (2) introduce additional brands across key price segments within the categories where it already has a presence, (3) enter developing markets where it does not yet have a presence, and (4) pursue tactical fill-in acquisitions, especially in snacks and beverages. Strategic and operational improvements from the new matrix structure were expected to enhance the implementation of these initiatives and Kraft's position in the global food and beverage industry. ■

Source: "Company Structure Encourages Best of Global, Best of Local," www.kraft.com/profile/company_structure.html (June 20, 2006); Neil Buckley, "Kraft Works to Become a More Global Business," *Financial Times,* January 9, 2004, p. 20; "Kraft Foods Announces New Global Organizational Structure," January 8, 2004, www.industrypages.com/artman/publish/Industry News 3702.stm (July 24, 2004); "Strategies for Growth," http://164.109.46.215/investors/strategies.html (July 24, 2004); "Visuals from Presentation by Roger Deromedi, CEO, Kraft Foods, to Investment Community, January 27, 2004," http://media.corporate-ir.net/media_files/nys/kft/presentations/kft_o40127b2326.pdf (July 24, 2004); Business Wire, "Kraft Foods Inc. Reports 2005 Results and Issues 2006 Outlook; Announces Expanded Restructuring Program as Part of Sustainable Growth Plan," January 30, 2006, p. 1.

organizational structure

The way that an organization formally arranges its domestic and international units and activities, and the relationships among these various organizational components

Organizations exist for the purpose of enabling a group of people to effectively coordinate their collective activities and accomplish objectives.[1] **Organizational structure** refers to the way that an organization formally arranges its various domestic and international units and activities and the relationships among these organizational components. A company's structure helps to determine where formal power and authority will be located within the organization, and this structure is what is typically presented in a company's organization chart.

Creating and evolving the structure of an international organization over time are fundamental tasks of senior management. Few executives except those in the senior levels of the organization are capable of establishing or changing the overall structure of an international company, because people at an organization's lower levels lack the broad perspective necessary for making the various trade-offs that will influence the organization as a whole. Nevertheless, all of the company's managers have to perform their job responsibilities within the context created by this structure. Further, most managers need to be able to effectively structure the various activities that are within their area of responsibility and to do so in a manner that is consistent with the company's overall structure. As a result, developing an understanding of the different ways in which international companies can be structured and the relative strengths and weaknesses of each of the various structural alternatives is an essential skill for managers.

In this chapter, we will discuss the different organizational forms an international company can take and key strategic issues that managers must address in choosing among these various organizational designs. Included in the discussion will be the identification of concerns that managers have regarding their ability to control the international activities of their companies.

What Is Organizational Design, and Why Is It Important for International Companies?

Organizational design is a process that deals with how an international business should be organized in order to ensure that its worldwide business activities are able to be integrated in an efficient and effective manner. As suggested in Figure 14.1, in designing an international organization, it is essential that the structures and systems being implemented are not merely consistent with each other but also consistent with the environmental context in which the organization is operating and the strategy the company is using for competing in this international environment. The size of the organization and the complexity of its business operations must also be considered in the design of a company.

The structure of an international company must be able to evolve over time, in order to enable the organization to respond to change and to efficiently and effectively reconfigure the way in which its competencies and resources are integrated within and across various units of the enterprise. This is a major challenge for the management of international companies, especially as these companies' activities are increasingly dispersed across the globe as well as subject to rapid and ongoing environmental and strategic change. Failure to successfully deal with this challenge threatens the organization's performance and, indeed, its long-term survival.

The international company's strategic planning process itself, because it encompasses an analysis of the firm's external environments as well as its strengths and weaknesses within these environments, often discloses a need to alter the organization. Changes in an international company's strategy may require changes in the organization, but the reverse is also true. For instance, a new CEO may join the firm, or the company may acquire a company in another nation or in another area of business activity. Strategic planning and organizing are so closely related that usually the structure of the organization is treated by management as an integral part of the strategic planning process.

ORGANIZATIONAL DESIGN CONCERNS

Two of the concerns that management faces in designing the organizational structure for an IC are (1) finding the most effective way to departmentalize to take advantage of the efficiencies gained from the specialization of labor and (2) coordinating the activities of those

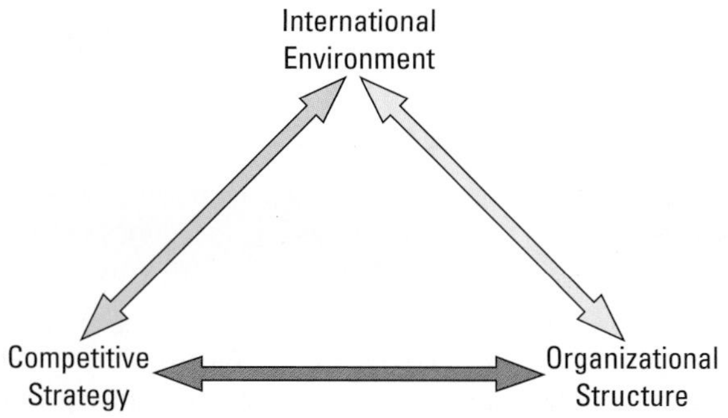

FIGURE 14.1

The Relationship among International Environment, Competitive Strategy, and Organizational Structure

International Environment

Competitive Strategy

Organizational Structure

departments to enable the firm to meet its overall objectives. As all managers know, these two concerns run counter to each other; that is, the gain from increased specialization of labor may at times be nullified by the increased cost of coordination. It is the search for an optimum balance between them that often leads to a reorganization of the international company's structure.

As suggested in the introductory case on Kraft Foods, there are four primary dimensions that need to be considered when designing the structure of an international company:

1. *Product and technical expertise* regarding the different businesses that the company participates in.

2. *Geographic expertise* regarding the countries and regions in which the company operates.

3. *Customer expertise* regarding the similarity of client groups, industries, market segments, or population groups that transcend the boundaries of individual countries or regions.

4. *Functional expertise* regarding the various value chain activities that the company is involved with.

International companies can and do vary with respect to the way in which these four dimensions are structured and integrated. No single structure is best for all companies and contexts. Rather, managers have to consider the nature of their company's international operating environment and strategy—both currently and how they are expected to change in the future—when deciding when and how to modify the company's organizational structure. In the sections below, we discuss the most common types of organizational designs for international companies. In reality, due to the complex nature of their operating environments and nuances of their historical origins and evolution, the structure of many international companies deviates to some extent from these basic organizational designs. Nevertheless, understanding attributes associated with these basic designs can assist managers of international companies in selecting an organizational structure appropriate for their current and anticipated future circumstances.

EVOLUTION OF THE INTERNATIONAL COMPANY

international division

A division in the organization that is at the same level as the domestic division and is responsible for all non-home country activities

As discussed in Chapters 2, 3, and 16, companies have often entered foreign markets first by exporting and then, as sales increased, by forming overseas sales companies and eventually setting up manufacturing facilities. As the firm's foreign involvement changed, its organization frequently changed as well. It might first have had *no one* responsible for international business; the firm's marketing department might have filled the export orders. Next, an export department might have been created, possibly in the marketing department; and when the company began to invest in various overseas locations, it could have formed an **international division** to take charge of all overseas involvement. Larger firms, such as Ford, IBM, and Goodyear, commonly organized their international divisions on a regional or geographic basis (Figure 14.2). Today, we still see companies—both those that are relatively modest in size and those that are some of the largest in the world—that are organized into a primary domestic division, supplemented by an international division to serve the rest of the world.

| **FIGURE 14.2** | International Division |

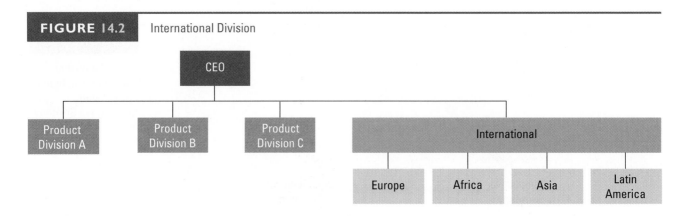

Michelle Teteak

Michelle Teteak is senior vice president–multinational consultant for the Northern Trust Company and works at corporate headquarters in Chicago, Illinois. Michelle works with multinational organizations on global pension plan management strategies for client companies with employees located worldwide, most notably in the United States, Canada, the United Kingdom, Netherlands, Germany, Ireland, Luxembourg, Switzerland, Belgium, Australia, Sweden, Norway, Japan, and Mexico. With the downturn in the equity markets a few years ago, pension plans worldwide came to be in underfunded positions. Subsidiaries looked to their corporate headquarters to make up the funding shortfalls. Many multinationals were surprised by the funding requirements they faced. Corporate management's desire to avoid future surprises, combined with growth in global pension plans because of an increasingly global workforce and more stringent regulatory reporting on worldwide pension plans, is driving multinational organizations to effect new forms of global pension management. Northern Trust offers three main services to multinationals that enable them to better govern their foreign pension plans: (1) consolidated headquarter reporting, (2) global custody, and (3) cross-border pension pooling. Michelle leads the business development process for each of these services and works to strategize the best solution for each multinational client and its employees on the basis of its profile.

Michelle's advice on how to get a job in international business:

- "Take advantage of networking opportunities offered to you by your parents, teachers, counselors, managers, mentors, etc."
- "Take advantage of foreign semester study programs through your schools."
- "Position yourself with a global company and express your interest in an international assignment."
- "Be patient—often you are most valuable to your company as an international representative after you have earned broad experience at the home office."

- "Show dedication and hard work in everything you do—show you can be trusted."
- "Embrace a mentoring relationship (not necessarily your manager). These informal relationships can prove to be very helpful. Seek a mentor if one is not occurring naturally."
- "Consider the timing of the international portion of your career. Often these are not life-long assignments. Balance the timing so that you have enough experience to be valuable, yet do not find yourself away from home too much during periods that might require more personal commitment, such as trying to start and raise a family or caring for an elder."

Michelle's advice on the skills required to succeed in international business:

- *Solid writing, communication, and presentation skills:* It is especially important to be concise and direct (yet thorough) with your written and spoken words when dealing with multiple countries to avoid any misunderstandings.
- *Solid understanding of your product/service:* Many questions are asked in international business, and people will see right through you if you do not have a firm command of your material.
- *Ability to understand what is important to different cultures* and then adjust your interaction accordingly.
- *Tolerance for different cultures* and different ways of doing things.
- *Responsiveness:* Often very little differs between you and the global competition—the degree of your responsiveness with clients and prospects can truly set you apart.
- *Tenaciousness, patience, and flexibility:* Global projects can take a while to implement—you need to stick with the opportunities to the end. You also need to be available for business interaction well outside of "normal" working hours and often in the middle of the night, if necessary, to accommodate varying time zones.

"International travel sounds glamorous; however, this is not always the case. It is great when you can build in a few extra days to explore new countries. Realistically, business demands are such that more often than not, you are in and out of locations and may not see more than the airport and office buildings. If you are able to handle the logistical challenges, an international career can be very exciting and assisting a company with global growth can be very rewarding."

World Wide Resource:

www.ntrs.com

Met-Pro Corporation, a New York Stock Exchange–listed company involved in the manufacture of a range of pollution control and fluid handling equipment, achieved sales of $85.1 million in the 2006 fiscal year. The company is organized into eight product divisions that provide sales and service for the company's "home market" of the United States and Canada. All sales and service activities involving other nations and regions of the world are handled by a separate International Division.[2]

Wal-Mart Stores, Inc., the world's largest retailer, with over $312 billion in sales in fiscal 2006, is organized into three business segments: Wal-Mart Stores, Sam's Club, and International. These segments account for 67.2, 12.7, and 20.1 percent of the company's overall sales, respectively. The International segment is responsible for operating several different types of retail stores and restaurants, including discount stores, supercenters, and Sam's Clubs, in 13 countries and Puerto Rico.[3]

As their overseas operations increased in importance and scope, most managements, with some exceptions, felt the need to eliminate international divisions and establish worldwide organizations based on *product, region, function,* or *customer classes.* At secondary, tertiary, and still lower levels, these four dimensions—plus (1) process, (2) national subsidiary, and (3) international or domestic—provide the basis for subdivisions. As a result, as they grow over time, most international companies move away from the use of international divisions and instead implement one of the global structures that we present in the following sections of this chapter. The initial choice of organizational structure after discarding the international division is usually one based on either global product or global geographic factors. These alternative paths for the design and evolution of the international company are presented in the international stages model of organizational structures, which was originally developed by John Stopford and Louis Wells and is shown in Figure 14.3.[4]

Managements that changed to these types of organizations felt they would (1) be more capable of developing competitive strategies to confront the increasing global competition, (2) obtain lower production costs by promoting worldwide product standardization and manufacturing rationalization, and (3) enhance technology transfer and the allocation of company resources.

Global Corporate Form—Product   Frequently, this structure represents a return to pre-export department times in that the domestic product division has been given responsibility for global line and staff operations. In the present-day global form, product divisions are responsible for the worldwide operations such as marketing and production of products under their control. Each division generally has regional experts, so while this organizational form avoids the duplication of product experts common in a company with an international division, it creates a duplication of area experts. Occasionally, to avoid placing regional specialists in each product division, management will have a group of managerial specialists in an international division who advise the product divisions but have no authority over them (see Figure 14.4). For

---

FIGURE 14.3

The International Structural Stages Model

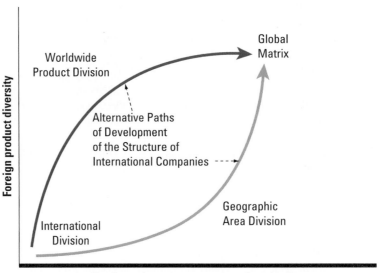

Source: Based on John M. Stopford and Louis T. Wells, *Strategy and Structure of the Multinational Enterprise* (New York: Basic Books, 1970).

FIGURE 14.4   Global Corporate Form—Product

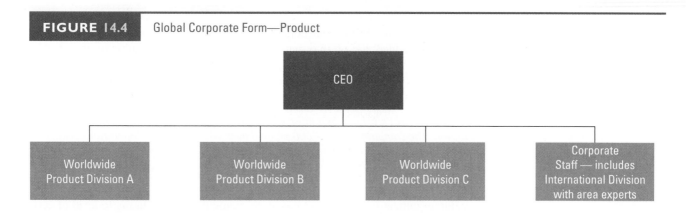

FIGURE 14.4   Global Corporate Form—Product

example, all of General Electric's businesses are managed through a global line-of-business structure, and investment opportunities are identified and assessed on a global basis by managers within each of these business areas.

> *Deutsche Post World Net, a global logistics services provider, has approximately 500,000 employees in over 220 countries and territories and 2005 revenues of over €44.5 billion. Based in Germany, the company is structured into five divisions: Mail (including Deutsche Post), Express (including DHL), Logistics (including the DHL Business division), Financial Services (including Postbank), and Services (established at the beginning of 2006).[5]*
>
> *After the merger of Exxon and Mobil, the energy company restructured its operations worldwide. To improve the capital productivity of the combined organizations, ExxonMobil moved from a multifunctional, geographically based regional organization to an organization based on global businesses to facilitate identification and sharing of technology and best practices worldwide. Under the new structure, each global business is responsible for running its operations on a worldwide basis.[6]*

Global Corporate Form—Geographic Regions

Firms in which geographic regions are the primary basis for division put the responsibility for all activities under area managers who report directly to the chief executive officer. This kind of organization simplifies the task of directing worldwide operations, because every country in the world is clearly under the control of someone who is in contact with headquarters (see Figure 14.5).

Of course, this organizational type is used for both multinational (multidomestic) and global companies. Global companies that use it consider the division in which the home country is located as just another division for purposes of resource allocation and a source of management personnel. Some U.S. global companies have created a North American division that includes Canada, Mexico, and Central American countries in addition to the United States, possibly in part to emphasize that the home country is given no preference.

The regionalized organization appears to be popular with companies that manufacture products with a rather low, or at least stable, technological content that require strong marketing ability. It is also favored by firms with diverse products, each having different product

FIGURE 14.5   Global Corporate Form—Geographic Regions

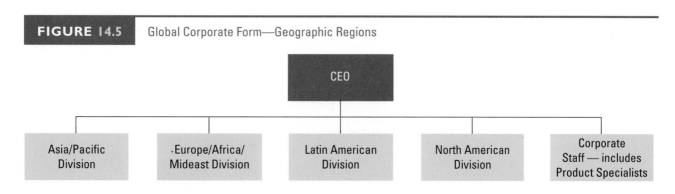

requirements, competitive environments, and political risks. Many producers of consumer products, such as prepared foods, pharmaceuticals, and household products, employ this type of organization. The disadvantage of an organization divided into geographic regions is that each region must have its own product and functional specialists, so although the duplication of area specialists found in product divisions is eliminated, duplication of product and functional specialists is necessary.

> *Mittal Steel is the world's largest and most global steel company, with 2005 revenues of over $28 billion. The company has 224,000 people, over 30 steel-making operations scattered across 16 nations, and customers in over 150 countries. The company's global operations are organized within three geographic regions: (1) the Americas, (2) Europe, and (3) Asia and Africa.[7]*

An interesting organizational structure based on regional factors relating to level of economic development rather than geography was introduced by Kimberly-Clark:

> *Kimberly-Clark Corporation is one of the world's largest producers of health and hygiene products, with sales in over 150 countries and manufacturing in 37. The company reorganized its main business operations into a developing and emerging markets business unit in addition to a developed market business unit. This change replaces its previous structure based on geographic regions. Three global businesses—Personal Care, Consumer Tissue, and Business-to-Business—continue to exist. The logic for moving to a developed/developing market structure was that countries in regions such as Western Europe and North America face a different set of competitive pressures from those faced by emerging countries in Asia, Latin America, and elsewhere. For example, the company's Kleenex tissues and Huggies disposable diapers are much more extensively used in developed country markets than in the developing countries. "We are facing many of the same issues in developing markets: How do you drive innovation at an affordable cost? Combining the emerging markets into one division will give that part of the company a louder voice," said Thomas J. Falk, Kimberly-Clark's CEO. "These changes will increase our speed in pursuing growth opportunities around the world, improve our execution of global strategies, and enable more consistent brand positioning and deployment of other best practices," Falk said.[8]*

Production coordination across regions presents difficult problems, as does global product planning. To alleviate these problems, managements often place specialized product managers on the headquarters staff. Although these managers have no line authority, they do provide input to corporate decisions concerning products.

Global Corporate Form—Function

Few firms are organized by function at the top level. Those that are obviously believe worldwide functional expertise is more significant to the firm than is product or area knowledge. In this type of organization, those reporting to the CEO might be the senior executives responsible for each functional area (marketing, production, finance, and so on), as in Figure 14.6. The commonality among the users of the functional form is a narrow and highly integrated product mix, such as that of aircraft manufacturers or oil refining companies.

FIGURE 14.6   Global Corporate Form—Function

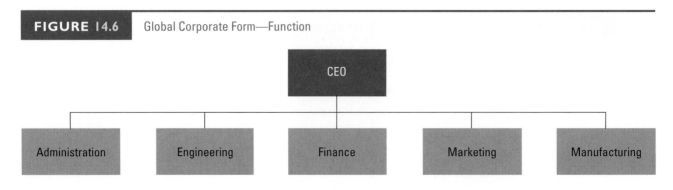

Genentech, the San Francisco, California, company that was the first to bring a biotechnology drug to market, achieved revenues of $6.6 billion in 2005, including over $870 million from foreign markets. The company is organized into four functional areas: research, product development, product operations, and commercial operations.[9]

Hybrid Forms   In a **hybrid organization,** a mixture of the organizational forms is used at the top level and may or may not be present at the lower levels. Figure 14.7 illustrates a simple hybrid form. Such combinations are often the result of a regionally organized company having introduced a new and different product line that management believes can best be handled by a worldwide product division. An acquired company with distinct products and a functioning marketing network may be incorporated as a product division even though the rest of the firm is organized on a regional basis. Later, after corporate management becomes familiar with the operation, it may be regionalized.

hybrid organization
Structure organized by more than one dimension at the top level

> *Unilever, the global consumer products company, had 2005 revenues of almost $47 billion and over 550,000 employees. To speed up decision making and execution within the fast-paced consumer products sector, Unilever has adopted a hybrid structure that includes three regions (Europe, Americas, and Asia Africa), two product segments (Foods and Home and Personal Care), and five functions (finance, human resources, IT, communications, and legal).*[10]

A mixed structure may also result from the firm's selling to a sizable, homogeneous class of customers. Special divisions for handling sales to the military or to original equipment manufacturers, for example, are often established at the same level as regional or product divisions.

Matrix Organizations   The **matrix organization** has evolved from management's attempt to mesh product, regional, and functional expertise while still maintaining clear lines of authority. It is called a matrix because an organization based on one or possibly two dimensions is superimposed on an organization based on another dimension. In an organization of two dimensions, such as area and product, both the area managers and the product managers will be at the same level, and their responsibilities will overlap. An individual manager—say, a marketing manager in Germany—will have a multiple reporting relationship, being responsible to the area manager and in some instances to an international or worldwide marketing manager at headquarters. Figure 14.8 illustrates an extremely simple matrix organization based on two organizational dimensions. Note that the country managers are responsible to both the area managers and the product line managers.

matrix organization
An organizational structure composed of one or more superimposed organizational structures in an attempt to mesh product, regional, functional, and other expertise

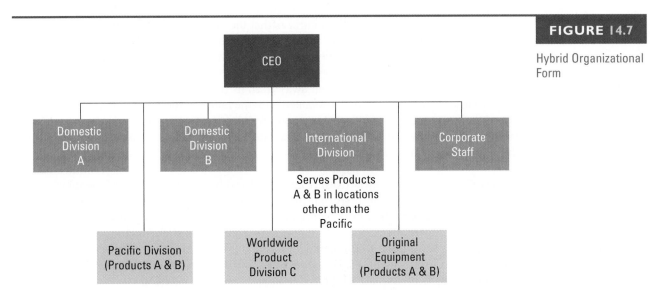

FIGURE 14.7

Hybrid Organizational Form

FIGURE 14.8

Regional–Product
Matrix

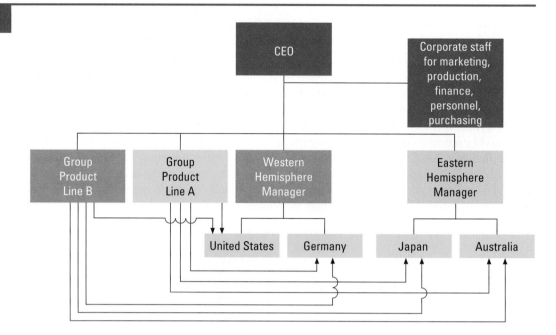

Nokia, the Finnish multinational that is the world's largest maker of cellular phones, established a matrix based on four business groups (mobile phones, multimedia, networks, and enterprise solutions) and two functionally based areas (customer and market operations, and technology platforms).[11]

BP, the British multinational with primary operations in oil, gas, and petrochemicals, is organized in a matrix based on 3 businesses (exploration and production; gas, power and renewables; and refining and marketing), 4 regions (Europe; the Americas; Africa, Middle East, Russia, and the Caspian; and Asia, the Indian Subcontinent, and Australasia), and 10 functions (diversity and inclusion; global property management and services; health, safety, security, and the environment; human resources management; marketing; planning; procurement; technology; finance and tax; and accounts).[12]

Michelin, the French manufacturer of tires, has a complex five-way matrix structure based on 9 product lines, a technology center, 5 geographic zones (Europe, North America, South America, Africa and Middle East, and Asia-Pacific), 10 group services, and distribution networks.[13]

Problems with the Matrix   Although at one time it seemed that the matrix organizational form would enable firms to have the advantages of the product, regional, and functional forms, the disadvantages of the matrix form have kept most worldwide companies from adopting it. One problem with the matrix is that the two or three managers (if it is a three-dimensional matrix) must agree on a decision. This can lead to less-than-optimum compromises, delayed responses, and power politics in which more attention is paid to the process than to the problem. When the managers cannot agree, the problem goes higher in the organization and takes top management away from its duties.

Because of these difficulties associated with the matrix structure, many firms have maintained their original organizations based on product, function, region, or international divisions and have built into the structure accountability for the other organizational dimensions; this is called by some a **matrix overlay.**

matrix overlay
An organization in which top-level divisions are required to heed input from a staff composed of experts of another organizational dimension in an attempt to avoid the double-reporting difficulty of a matrix organization but still mesh two or more dimensions

Matrix Overlay   The matrix overlay attempts to address the problems of the matrix structure by requiring accountability of all functions in the organization while avoiding the burdensome management stresses of a pure matrix structure. We have already mentioned how a firm organized by product may have regional specialists in a staff function with the requirement that they have input to product decisions. They may even be organized in an international division, as was mentioned previously. Conversely, a regional organization would have product managers on its staff who provide input to regional decisions.

Strategic Business Units   **Strategic business units (SBUs),** a concept that General Electric is credited with originating, are an organizational form in which product divisions have been defined as though they were distinct, independent businesses. An SBU is defined as a self-contained business entity with a clearly defined market, specific competitors, the ability to carry out its business mission, and a size appropriate for control by a single manager. Most SBUs are based on product lines, such as Caterpillar's 22 autonomous profit center business units.[14] If a product must be modified to suit different markets, a worldwide SBU may be divided into a few product/market SBUs serving various markets or groups of countries. Shell Chemical Company's SBUs, which it calls product business units (PBUs), are global.[15] BP's business units, which it calls strategic performance units (SPUs), are also global.[16]

strategic business unit (SBU)
Business entity with a clearly defined market, specific competitors, the ability to carry out its business mission, and a size appropriate for control by a single manager

CHANGES IN ORGANIZATIONAL FORMS

The rapidly changing business environment caused by increased global competition, customer preference for custom-made rather than mass-produced products, and faster technological change is pressuring companies to step up their search for organizational forms that will enable them to act more quickly, reduce costs, and improve the quality of product offerings. Not only are they mixing older, established forms; they are also changing to different forms, many of which are modified versions of long-established forms with new names.

What is new is the acceptance by many companies of the need for frequent reorganization. Present in these reorganizations, called *reengineering* by many, are a significant reduction in the levels of middle management, restructuring of work processes to reduce the fragmenting of the process across functional departments, improvement in the speed and quality of strategy execution, empowerment of employees, and the use of computers for instant communication and swift transmittal of information. CEOs are striving to make their organizations lean, flat, fast to respond, and innovative.

> *Vodafone, an international telecommunications services company based in the United Kingdom, reorganized itself in mid-2006 into three business groups: European operations; emerging markets and other affiliates; and new services and technologies. The objective of the structural change was "to focus the business according to different market and customer requirements. There are three key principles to the new structure: (1) to drive operational benefits and cost reduction from local and regional scale in more mature markets, (2) to drive profitable growth from the company's emerging market portfolio, and (3) to position the company to capture new revenue streams by extending its reach into converged and IP (internet protocol) services."[17]*
>
> *Coca-Cola, the world's largest beverage company, announced the creation of the new position of president, Coca-Cola International, in early 2006. This position includes responsibility for all operations outside North America. Chairman and Chief Executive Officer Neville Isdell said, "As we focus even more intently on execution, it is appropriate that our international operations—which accounted last year for more than 70 percent of our total volume and close to 80 percent of our total operating income—be put under the leadership of a dedicated, full-time executive with extensive operational expertise."[18]*

CURRENT ORGANIZATIONAL TRENDS

Two organizational forms are now receiving the attention of many CEOs: the virtual corporation and the horizontal corporation.

Virtual Corporation   A **virtual corporation,** also called a *network corporation,* is an organization that coordinates economic activity to deliver value to customers using resources outside the traditional boundaries of the organization. In other words, it relies to a great extent on third parties to conduct its business. Outsourcing once was used for downsizing and cost reduction, but now companies are using it to obtain specialized expertise that they don't have but need in order to serve new markets or adopt new technology.

The evolution of the technology infrastructure has made possible changes in the work force and working methods, such as teleworking, home offices, and flexible working practices. All these factors have contributed to the increase in virtual corporations. Global networking on the

virtual corporation
An organization that coordinates economic activity to deliver value to customers using resources outside the traditional boundaries of the organization

Accenture's "Virtual" Global Structure

Accenture Ltd. delivers a range of consulting, outsourcing, and technology services to clients around the world, harnessing its more than 129,000 employees to generate revenues of over $15 billion in 2005. Its clients include 87 of the companies listed on the Fortune Global 100 and almost two-thirds of the Fortune Global 500 largest international companies. Yet, according to the company's senior management, Accenture has neither an operational headquarters facility nor any formal branch facilities. Instead, the company's approach to organizing its global operations might be termed *virtual*.

Prior to 2000, Accenture had been the consulting arm of the now-defunct Arthur Andersen accounting company. During that time, the consulting operations had been managed for decades by the Swiss-based Andersen Worldwide. After consulting was split off from Andersen's accounting operations and subsequently became a separate organization under the name Accenture, the partners could not agree on a location for the new, Bermuda-incorporated company's headquarters. Since they typically spent a major portion of their time on the road, Accenture's executives decided to live where each of them wanted and forgo an organization built around a central headquarters. As a result, the chief financial officer lives in California's Silicon Valley, the chief technology officer lives in Germany, and many of the company's globally diverse work force of consultants are traveling nearly nonstop to client sites worldwide. Even the company's Boston-based CEO, Bill Green, doesn't have a permanent desk or office location.

Coordinating this geographically dispersed work force is facilitated by technology. Employees log on to Accenture's intranet daily, either from home, from a hotel or airport, or from a temporary cubicle in one of the company's 110 leased locations around the world. Employees identify where they are working that day, access files and e-mails, download or share documents, and conduct a myriad of other tasks. Phone calls are patched through to wherever the employee is located, and clients often do not realize that they are speaking to a consultant or executive who might be nations or continents away. Team meetings are often conducted by teleconference, although scheduling such meetings can be problematic due to the different time zones of the participants. A "magic hour" for scheduling global teleconferences is 1 p.m. London time, which is midnight in Australia, 9 p.m. in Beijing, and 5 a.m. in California. This time "isn't too grim" for anyone, comments Adrian Lajtha, who as the head of Accenture's financial services group spends about 85 percent of his time traveling.

Every six weeks or so, the 23 members of the company's executive leadership team meet face-to-face for several days, with the location for the meetings rotating among different cities worldwide. Says Mr. Green, "We land somewhere, meet clients in the area, meet employees, then get together as a team to make decisions—and head out again." Says Mr. Lajtha, "Anyone who says managing this way is easy is lying."

Source: "Have Advice, Will Travel," *The Wall Street Journal*, June 5, 2006, pp. B1, B3; Accenture, Ltd., "Company Description," www.accenture.com/Global/About_Accenture/Company_Overview/CompanyDescription.htm (June 20, 2006); Yongsun Paik and David Y. Choi, "The Shortcomings of a Standardized Global Knowledge Management System: The Case Study of Accenture," *Academy of Management Executive* 19, no. 2 (2005), pp. 81–84; and Glenn Simpson, "The Economy: Consultants Accenture, Monday Take Steps That May Reduce Taxes," *The Wall Street Journal*, eastern ed., July 3, 2002, p. A2.

Internet has made worldwide outsourcing possible for firms of all sizes. Dell Computer is a well-known example of a company that has used tight integration with its global network of suppliers in order to assemble and deliver semicustomized computers to its international customers within days of receiving an order, and without carrying large volumes of expensive inventory that is prone to losing value through technological obsolescence. The nearby Worldview box, "Accenture's 'Virtual' Global Structure," discusses one company that has developed a virtual alternative to more traditional organizational structures.

Although the name is new, the virtual corporation concept has existed for decades. It has been extremely common for a group of construction firms, each with a special area of expertise, to form a consortium to bid on a contract for constructing a road or an airfield, for example. After finishing the job, the consortium would disband. Other examples of network organizations are the various clothing and athletic shoe marketers such as DKNY, Nike, and Reebok. The latter firms are also called *modular corporations*.

The virtual corporation concept has several potential benefits. In particular, it permits greater flexibility than is associated with more typical corporate structures, and rather than building competence from the ground up and incurring high start-up costs that could limit future production decisions, virtual corporations form a network of dynamic relationships that allow them to take advantage of the competencies of other organizations and respond rapidly to changing circumstances. However, this form of organization can have disadvantages, including the potential to reduce management's control over the corporation's activities (it is vulnerable to the opportunistic actions of partners, including cost increases, unintended "borrowing" of technical and other knowledge, and potential departure from the relationship at inappropriate times). From the standpoint of employees, this form of organization may replace the security of long-term employment and the promise of ever-increasing salaries with the insecurity of the market—a global market.

Horizontal Corporation   Another organizational form, the **horizontal corporation,** has been adopted by some large technology-oriented global firms in highly competitive industries such as electronics and computers. Firms such as 3M, General Electric, and DuPont have chosen this organizational form to give themselves the flexibility to respond quickly to advances in technology and be product innovators. In many companies *teams* are drawn from different departments to solve a problem or deliver a product.

This organization has been characterized as "antiorganization" because its designers are seeking to remove the constraints imposed by the conventional organizational structures. In a horizontal corporation, employees worldwide create, build, and market the company's products through a carefully cultivated system of interrelationships. Marketers in Great Britain speak directly to production people in Brazil without having to go through the home office in Germany, for example.

Proponents of the horizontal organization claim lateral relationships incite innovation and new product development. They also state that this approach to organizing helps to place more decision-making responsibility in the hands of middle managers and other skilled professionals, who do not have to clear each detail and event with higher-ups. The objective is to substitute cooperation and coordination, which are in the interest of everyone, for strict control and supervision. Pursued effectively, this approach can help to develop international communities of skilled workers that create and exploit valuable intangible assets.[19]

CORPORATE SURVIVAL IN THE 21ST CENTURY

Managers in many international companies can expect to make greater use of the *dynamic network structure* that breaks down the major functions of the firm into smaller companies coordinated by a small-size headquarters organization. Business functions such as marketing and accounting may be provided by separate organizations—some of them owned partially or fully by the international company, some of them not—that are connected by computers to a central office. To attain the optimum level of vertical integration, a firm must focus on its core business. Anything not essential to the business can often be done cheaper, faster, and better by outside suppliers.[20]

As companies engage in the global battles of the 21st century, we must remember that organizations, like people, have life cycles. In their youth, they're small and fast-growing, but as they age, they often become big, complex, and out of touch with their markets. The firms of tomorrow must learn how to be both large and entrepreneurial. As one CEO put it, "Small is not better; focused is better."

Control

Every successful company uses controls to put its plans into effect, evaluate their effectiveness, make desirable corrections, and evaluate and reward or correct executive performance. The challenges associated with achieving effective control are more complicated for an international company than for a one-country operation. In earlier chapters, we discussed several of the complicating causes. They include different languages, cultures, and attitudes; different taxes and accounting methods; different currencies, labor costs, and market sizes; different degrees of political stability and security for personnel and

How to Become More Globally Competitive

A recent survey suggests that over 75 percent of new research and development sites planned for the 2006–2009 period will be established in China and India.

A recent survey of senior executives revealed that the primary strategy adopted by respondents to become more competitive globally was to concentrate on core businesses. Other structural changes adopted by about 70 percent of the companies included flattening the organization by removing layers of management, merging with other companies to form new structures, decentralizing business units, and forming new global business units.

Dow Chemical Company, which has operations in over 175 countries, is an example of a firm that has made changes to become more globally competitive. Dow changed its organizational structure from a geographic matrix to one of global business processes and 16 global business units that have individual global profit-and-loss responsibility. Management layers in the organization were reduced from 10 to 12 down to 4 to 6. Said Dow's CEO, "Dow is now making two to three times the earnings it used to make at an equivalent position in the global chemical market cycle, and we are earning the cost of capital at the trough of the cycle, something we have never done before."

Ninety percent of the executives responding to one survey stated that the strategies that have been effective in increasing their firms' global competitiveness are (1) placing profit-and-loss responsibility at lower levels in the firm, (2) reducing operating expenses, and (3) forming strategic alliances with customers, suppliers, and competitors.

Another noteworthy result was that those respondents who had adopted value chain strategies judged the following strategies to be most effective in increasing a firm's global competitiveness:

1. Planning jointly with suppliers and customers.

2. Maintaining less inventory.

3. Managing production on a global basis.

Another survey revealed that innovation is becoming increasingly global, and over 75 percent of new research and development sites planned for the 2006–2009 period will be established in China and India. Yet most executives reported that their companies were struggling to establish the organization structures and systems that were required in order to manage and integrate global innovation activities. Respondents projected that they could achieve a 37 percent improvement in time to market and a 24 percent reduction in costs if they had an innovation network that was efficiently organized and integrated with their worldwide operations. Achieving that would be enhanced if companies would (1) centralize decision making on research and development project portfolios to take advantage of the power of the company's international network, (2) standardize organizational structure, systems, and processes throughout the global innovation network, so that time was not lost in trying to understand how other sites operated, and (3) develop a diverse set of global managers and then allow them to make necessary adjustments for national and cultural circumstances that might affect the efficiency of operations.

Other surveys suggest widespread dissatisfaction among executives regarding their companies' ability to respond to change, especially with regard to information technology structures and systems. Concerns included the adequacy of access to relevant, real-time business information; difficulty in adapting and modifying key business processes and more rapidly delivering applications for competitive advantage; and the overall ability of the company's information technology infrastructure to keep up with the increasing pace of change and be able to promote the creation of business value.

Source: Booz Allen Hamilton, "The Growth of Global Innovation Networks Creates New Management Challenges," www.boozallen.com/home/services/services_article/3220998?tid=934306&1pid=660624 (June 21, 2006); Tim Stevens, "Winning the World Over," *Industry Week Online*, November 15, 1999, www.industryweek.com/CurrentArticles/asp/articles.asp?Article10=~656 (November 28, 1999); "New Study Finds Executives Dissatisfied with Their Companies' Ability to Sense and Respond to Business Change; Despite Current Challenges in Keeping Pace, IT Viewed as More Important Than Ever," www.webmethods.com/meta/default/folder/0000005139?pressReleaseDetails%5Fparam0=6879 (June 21, 2006); and "IP Adoption Is Key Competitive Advantage to Global Survey of Senior Executives," www.att.com/news/2005/10/17-1 (June 21, 2006).

property; and many more. For these reasons, international companies need controls even more than do domestic ones.

subsidiaries
Companies controlled by other companies through ownership of enough voting stock to elect board-of-directors majorities

SUBSIDIARIES

The words **subsidiaries** and **affiliates** sometimes are used interchangeably, and we shall examine first the control of those in which the parent has 100 percent ownership. This avoids for now the additional complications of joint ventures or subsidiaries in which the parent has less than 100 percent ownership. We shall deal with those later in the chapter.

SUBSIDIARIES 100 PERCENT OWNED: WHERE ARE DECISIONS MADE?

affiliates
A term sometimes used interchangeably with *subsidiaries,* but more forms exist than just stock ownership

There are three possibilities. Theoretically, all decisions could be made either at the international company (IC) headquarters or at the subsidiary level. As common sense would indicate, they are not; instead, some decisions are made at headquarters, some are made at subsidiaries, and—the third possibility—some are made cooperatively. Many variables determine which decision is made where. Some of the more significant variables are (1) product and equipment, (2) the competence of subsidiary management and reliance on that management by the IC headquarters, (3) the size of the IC and how long it has been one, (4) the detriment of a subsidiary for the benefit of the enterprise, and (5) subsidiary frustration. We discuss each of these variables in the sections that follow.

Product and Equipment

As to decision location, questions of standardization of product and equipment and second markets can be important for international companies. In Chapter 18, we will discuss how large global manufacturers of consumer products, such as Procter & Gamble (P&G) and Colgate, are developing standardized products from the outset for global or at least regional markets. In these situations, the affiliates have to follow company policy. Of course, in the case of P&G, representatives of the affiliates have an opportunity to take part in the product design, contrary to the way new products were typically introduced before the globalization strategy became so popular. Then, as we discussed in Chapter 3 on the international product life cycle, new products often have been introduced first in the home market. After the production process has been stabilized, the specifications are sent to the affiliates (second markets) for local production, where adaptations can be made if the local managements deem them necessary for their markets.

In a firm without a global product policy, the preference of the operations management people in the home office has always been to standardize the product or at least the production process in as many overseas plants as possible, as we will explain in Chapter 19. If, however, any subsidiary can demonstrate that the profit potential is greater for a product tailored for its own market than what the company would realize from global standardization, the subsidiary ordinarily is allowed to proceed. Of course, the decision in such a case is cooperative in that the parent has the power to veto or override its subsidiary's decision.

Competence of Subsidiary Management and Headquarters' Reliance on It

Reliance on subsidiary management can depend on how well the executives know one another and how well they know company policies, on whether headquarters management feels that it understands host country conditions, on the distances between the home country and the host countries, and on how big and old the parent company is.

Moving Executives Around   Many ICs have a policy of transferring promising management personnel between parent headquarters and subsidiaries and among subsidiaries. Thus, the manager learns firsthand the policies of headquarters and the problems of putting those policies into effect at subsidiary levels.

A result of such transfers, which is difficult to measure but nevertheless important, is a network of intra-IC personal relationships. This tends to increase the confidence of executives in one another and to make communication among executives easier and less subject to error. Another development is that some ICs have moved their regional executives into headquarters to improve communications and reduce cost.

Understanding Host Country Conditions   One element in the degree of headquarters' reliance on subsidiary management is the familiarity of headquarters with conditions in the subsidiary's host country. The less familiar or the more different conditions in the host country are perceived to be, the more likely headquarters is to rely on subsidiary management.

How Far Away Is the Host Country?   Another element in the degree of headquarters' reliance on subsidiary management is the distance of the host country from home headquarters. Thus, an American parent is likely to place more reliance on the management of an

Indonesian subsidiary than on the management of a Canadian subsidiary. This occurs for two reasons: American management typically perceives management conditions in Canada to be more easily understood than conditions in Indonesia, and Indonesia is much farther from the United States than Canada is, not merely geographically but also in terms of culture, politics, and other variables.

Size and Age of the IC

As a rule, a large company can afford to hire more specialists, experts, and experienced executives than can a smaller one. The longer a company has been an IC, the more likely it is to have a number of experienced executives who know company policies and have worked at headquarters and in the field. Successful experience builds confidence. In most ICs, the top positions are at headquarters, and the ablest and most persistent executives will typically get positions there eventually. Thus, over time, the headquarters of a successful company is run by experienced executives who are confident of their knowledge of the business in the home and host countries and in combinations thereof.

It follows that in larger, older organizations, more decisions are made at headquarters and fewer are delegated to subsidiaries. Smaller companies, in business for shorter periods of time, tend to be able to afford fewer internationally experienced executives and will not have had time to develop them internally. Smaller, newer companies often have no choice but to delegate decisions to subsidiary managements. However, with the increasing pace of change and intensity of competition in many markets of the world, as well as continued differences across many markets, even large and experienced companies are finding the need to delegate at least some decision making authority to subsidiary managements in order to effectively sense pressures for adaptation, to serve as tools for developing and communicating innovation, and to promote effective execution of strategy.

Benefiting the Enterprise to the Detriment of a Subsidiary

An IC has opportunities to source raw materials and components, locate factories, allocate orders, and govern intrafirm pricing that are not available to a non-IC. Such activities may be beneficial to the enterprise yet may result in **subsidiary detriment.**

subsidiary detriment
Situation in which a small loss for a subsidiary results in a greater gain for the total IC

Moving Production Factors

For any number of reasons, an IC may decide to move factors of production from one country to another or to expand in one country in preference to another. In addition to the cost, availability, or skill levels of labor, other possible reasons include such factors as taxation, market, currency, and political stability issues.

The subsidiary from which factors are being taken would be unenthusiastic about giving up control over existing activities. Its management would be slow, at best, to cut the company's capacity or to downsize or eliminate local operations. Headquarters would typically have to make such decisions.

Which Subsidiary Gets the Order?

Similarly, if an order—say, from an Argentine customer—could be filled from a subsidiary in France or another in South Africa or a third in Brazil, parent headquarters might decide which subsidiary gets the business. Among the considerations in the decision would be transportation costs, production costs, comparative tariff rates, customers' currency restrictions, comparative order backlogs, governmental pressures, and taxes. Having such a decision made by IC headquarters avoids price competition among members of the same IC group.

Multicountry Production

Frequently, the size of the market in a single country is too small to permit economies of scale in manufacturing an entire industrial product or offering a full range of services for that one market. An example is Ford's production of a light vehicle for the Asian market. In that situation, Ford negotiated with several countries to the end that one country would make one component of the vehicle for all the countries involved. Thus, one country makes the engine, a second country has the body-stamping plant, a third makes the transmission, and so forth. In this fashion, each operation achieves the efficiency and cost savings of economies of scale. Of course, this kind of multinational production demands a high degree of IC headquarters' control and coordination.

Which Subsidiary Books the Profit?   In certain circumstances, an IC may have a choice of two or more countries in which to declare profits. Such circumstances may arise where two or more units of the IC cooperate in supplying components or services under a contract with a customer unrelated to any part of the IC. Under these conditions, there may be opportunities to allocate higher prices to one unit or subsidiary and lower prices to another within the global price to the customer.

If the host country of one of the subsidiaries has lower taxes than the other host countries, it would be natural to try to maximize profits in the lower-tax country and minimize them in the higher-tax country. Other differences between host countries could dictate the allocation of profit to or from the subsidiaries located there. Such differences could include currency controls, labor relations, political climate, and social unrest. It is sensible to direct or allocate as much profit as reasonably possible to subsidiaries in countries with the fewest currency controls, the best labor relations and political climate, and the least social unrest, for example.

The intrafirm transaction may also give a company choices regarding profit location. Pricing between members of the same enterprise is referred to as *transfer pricing,* and while IC headquarters could permit undirected, arm's-length negotiations between itself and its subsidiaries, this might not yield the most advantageous results for the enterprise as a whole.

Price and profit allocation decisions like these are usually best made at parent company headquarters, which is supposed to maintain the overall view, looking out for the best interests of the enterprise. Naturally, subsidiary management does not gladly make decisions to accept lower profits, largely because its evaluation may suffer as a result of the apparent reduction in performance at the subsidiary level.

The following two tables illustrate how the total IC enterprise may profit even though one subsidiary makes less. Assume a cooperative contract by which two subsidiaries are selling products and services to an outside customer for a price of $100 million. The host country of IC Alpha levies company income taxes at the rate of 50 percent, whereas IC Beta's host country taxes its income at 20 percent. The customer is in a third country, has agreed to pay $100 million, and is indifferent to how Alpha and Beta share the money. The first table below shows the enterprise's after-tax income if Alpha is paid $60 million and Beta is paid $40 million. Thus, after tax, the enterprise realizes $62 million.

	Receives ($ millions)	Tax ($ millions)	After Tax ($ millions)
Alpha	$60	$30	$30
Beta	40	8	32
			$62

The second table shows the after-tax income if Alpha is paid $40 million and Beta is paid $60 million. Thus, after taxes, the enterprise realizes $68 million.

	Receives ($ millions)	Tax ($ millions)	After Tax ($ millions)
Alpha	$40	$20	$20
Beta	60	12	48
			$68

These simple examples illustrate that the IC would be $6 million better off if it could shift $20 million of the payment from Alpha to Beta, while the customer is no worse off, as it pays $100 million in either case. Alpha, having received $20 million less in payment, is $10 million worse off after taxes, but Beta is $16 million better off and the enterprise is $6 million ahead on the same contract. Given the number of countries and tax laws in the world, there are countless combinations for how such savings can be accomplished. Financial management awareness and control are the keys.

We do not mean to leave the impression that the host and home governments are unaware of or indifferent to transfer pricing and profit allocating by ICs operating within their borders. The companies must expect questioning by host and home governments and must be prepared to demonstrate that prices or allocations are reasonable. This may be done by showing that other companies charge comparable prices for the same or similar items or, if there are no similar items, by showing that costs plus profit have been used reasonably to arrive at the price. As to allocation of profits, the IC in our example would try to prove that the volume or importance of the work done by Beta or the responsibilities assumed by Beta, such as financing, after-sales service, or warranty obligations, justify the higher amount being paid to Beta. Of course, the questioning in this instance would come from the host government of Alpha if it got wind of the possibility of more taxable income for Beta and less for itself.[21]

> *Several large U.S. companies are being investigated by the U.S. Treasury Department and the Internal Revenue Service because of the approaches that they have used for allocating intellectual property and other assets to their subsidiaries in low-tax Ireland. It has been suggested that the approaches used by these companies to value assets across subsidiaries and to allocate revenues and profits has cost the American government billions of dollars in taxes and other fees. Microsoft's Round Island One (RIO) subsidiary in Ireland, for example, controls over $16 billion in assets. Most of RIO's assets are associated with copyrighted software code. This code is asserted to have originated in Microsoft's U.S. operations but subsequently been transferred to RIO at submarket rates. As a result, RIO controls the rights for licensing Microsoft software in Europe, the Middle East, and Africa, and the earnings from this licensing activity are credited to the Irish operations. RIO is the most profitable company in Ireland, and it pays no U.S. taxes. Through earning its income in foreign countries that tax at lower rates, such as Ireland, Microsoft's effective worldwide tax rate declined in one year from 33 percent to only 26 percent.[22]*

Subsidiary Frustration

An extremely important consideration for parent company management is that the management of its subsidiaries be motivated and loyal. If all the big decisions are made, or are perceived to be made, at the IC headquarters, the managers of subsidiaries can lose incentive and prestige or face with their employees and the community. They may grow hostile and disloyal.

Therefore, even though there may be reasons for headquarters to make decisions, it should delegate as many as is reasonably possible. Management of each subsidiary should be kept thoroughly informed and be consulted seriously about decisions, negotiations, and developments in its geographic area. The trend for many ICs of shifting power away from subsidiaries toward the parent has caused predictable frustration to subsidiary management, sometimes followed by resignations. Some companies reporting this development were IBM, Nestlé, European International, and CS First Boston.

JOINT VENTURES AND SUBSIDIARIES LESS THAN 100 PERCENT OWNED

A *joint venture* may be, as defined in Chapter 16, a corporate entity between an IC and local owners or a corporate entity between two or more companies that are foreign to the area where the joint venture is located, or it may involve one company working on a project of limited duration (constructing a dam, for example) in cooperation with one or more other companies. The other companies may be subsidiaries or affiliates, but they may also be entirely independent entities.

All the reasons for making decisions at IC headquarters, at subsidiary headquarters, or cooperatively apply equally in joint venture situations. However, headquarters will almost never have as much freedom of action and flexibility in a joint venture as it has with subsidiaries that are 100 percent owned.

Loss of Freedom and Flexibility

The reasons for that loss of freedom and flexibility are easy to see. If shareholders outside the IC own control of the affiliate, they can block efforts of IC headquarters to move production factors away, fill an export order from another affiliate or subsidiary, and so forth. Even if outside shareholders are a minority and cannot directly control the affiliate, they can bring legal or political pressures on the IC to prevent it from diminishing the affiliate's profitability for the enterprise's benefit. Likewise, the local partner in a joint venture is highly unlikely to agree with measures that penalize the joint venture for the IC's benefit.

Control Can Be Had
With less than 50 percent of the voting stock and even with no voting stock, an IC can have control. Some methods of maintaining control are:

- A management contract.
- Control of the finances.
- Control of the technology.
- Putting people from the IC in important executive positions.

As might be expected, ICs have encountered resistance to putting IC personnel in the important executive positions from their joint venture partners or from host governments. The natural desire of these partners and governments is that their own nationals have at least equality in the important positions and that they get training and experience in the technology and management.

REPORTING

For controls to be effective, all operating units of an IC must provide headquarters with timely, accurate, and complete reports. There are many uses for the information reported. Among the types of reporting required are (1) financial, (2) technological, (3) market opportunity, and (4) political and economic.

Financial
A surplus of funds in one subsidiary should perhaps be retained there for investment or contingencies. On the other hand, such a surplus might be more useful at the parent company, in which case payment of a dividend is indicated. Or perhaps another subsidiary or affiliate needs capital, and the surplus could be lent or invested there. Obviously, parent headquarters must know the existence and size of a surplus to determine its best use.

Technological
New technology should be reported. New technology is constantly being developed in different countries, and the subsidiary or affiliated company operating in such a country is likely to learn about it before IC headquarters hundreds or thousands of miles away does. If headquarters finds the new technology potentially valuable, it can gain competitive advantage by being the first to contact the developer for a license to use it.

Market Opportunities
The affiliates in various countries may spot new or growing markets for some product of the enterprise. This could be profitable all around, as the IC sells more of the product while the affiliate earns sales commissions. Of course, if the new market is sufficiently large, the affiliate may begin to assemble or produce the product under license from the parent company or from another affiliate.

Other market-related information that should be reported to IC headquarters includes competitors' activities, price developments, and new products of potential interest to the IC group. Also of importance is information on the subsidiary's market share and whether it is growing or shrinking, together with explanations.

Political and Economic
Not surprisingly, reports on political and economic conditions have multiplied mightily in number and importance over the past 20 or so years as revolutions—some bloody—have toppled and changed governments. Democracies have replaced dictatorships, one dictator has replaced another, countries have broken apart or reunited—changes have been occurring on almost every continent.

"DE-JOBBING"

The conditions that created jobs 200 years ago—mass production and large organizations—are disappearing. Technology enables companies to automate production lines where many job holders used to do repetitive tasks. Instead of long production runs where the same thing has to be done again and again, firms are increasingly customizing production. Big firms, where most of the good jobs used to be, are unbundling activities and farming them out to little firms. New computer and communication technologies are **de-jobbing** the workplace, changing from the traditional, fixed-jobs approach to one in which teams perform tasks. And the composition of these teams changes as the tasks evolve.

de-jobbing
Replacing fixed jobs with tasks performed by evolving teams

Today's organization is rapidly being transformed from a structure built out of jobs into a field of work needing to be done. A fast-moving organization, such as Intel, will hire a person to be part of a specific project. As the project changes over time, the person's responsibilities and tasks change with it. Then the person is assigned to another project, probably before the first is finished, and then maybe to a third. As projects evolve and change, the person will work with several team leaders, keeping different schedules, being in various places, and performing a number of different tasks.

hierarchy
A body of persons organized or classified according to rank or authority

Hierarchy Implodes   Under these conditions, **hierarchy** cannot be maintained; people no longer take their cues from a job description or a supervisor's instructions. Signals come from the changing demands of the project. Workers focus their efforts and collective resources on work that needs doing, changing as that changes.

Traits of Companies with De-Jobbed Workers   Companies with de-jobbed workers share four traits:

- They encourage employees to make the kinds of operating decisions that used to be reserved for managers.

- They give employees the information they need to make such decisions.

- They give employees lots of training to create the kind of understanding of business and financial issues that used to concern only an owner or executive.

- They give employees a stake in the fruits of their labor—a share of the profits.[23]

MANAGING IN A WORLD OUT OF CONTROL

The Internet may be the closest thing to a working anarchy the world has ever seen. Nobody owns it, nobody runs it, and most of its half-billion or so citizens get along by dint of online etiquette, not rules and regulations. The Internet was built up without any central control because the U.S. Defense Department wanted to ensure that the Net could survive a nuclear attack. The Net has proved to be a paragon of hothouse expansion and constant evolution. Though it may be messier and less efficient than a similar system designed and run by an agency or company, this organically grown network is also more adaptable and less susceptible to a systemwide crash.

The consequence for management in a world out of control, such as the Internet, is a recipe developed at MIT for devising a system of distributed control: (1) Do simple things first, (2) learn to do them flawlessly, (3) add new layers of activity over the results of the simple task, (4) don't change the simple things, (5) make the new layer work as flawlessly as the simple one, and (6) repeat ad infinitum. Many organizations would benefit by adopting organizing principles as deceptively simple as these.

Increasingly, the most successful companies, like the machines and programs so many of them now make, and the networks on which they all will rely will advance only by evolving and adapting in this organic, bottom-up way. Successful leaders will have to relinquish control. They will have to honor error because a breakthrough may at first be indistinguishable from a mistake. They must constantly seek disequilibrium.

Control: Yes and No

We have spoken of control within the IC family of parent, subsidiaries, affiliates, and joint ventures. This deals with where decisions are made on a variety of subjects under different circumstances.

Timely and accurate reporting to the parent is necessary for success of the IC family. The trend in this area of control is toward centralized decision making, with more being done by the parent.

The other control of which we have spoken involves the design, production, and order-filling functions of companies. Here, the explosion of software, computer networks, and information technology, including the Internet, has tended to decentralize and de-job organizations. More and more, workers do evolving tasks with changing teams of other workers. Hierarchies dissolve and successful leaders relinquish control as workers are trained and encouraged to cope with evolving tasks and rewarded for coping well.

Summary

Explain why the design of organizational structure is important to international companies.

The structure of an international organization involves how its domestic and international units and activities are arranged and where formal power and authority will be located inside the company. It helps determine how efficiently and effectively the organization will be able to integrate and leverage its competencies and resources within and across various units of the enterprise, and thus contribute to successful implementation of the company's strategy.

Discuss the organizational dimensions that must be considered when selecting organizational structures.

The organizational structure selected for a company must be consistent with the organization's capabilities and resources, as well as with the environmental context in which the organization operates and with its strategy. In selecting an organizational structure, managers of an international company must consider the requirements for expertise in terms of product and technology, geography, customer, and function.

Discuss the various organizational forms available for structuring international companies.

Companies may (1) have an international division, (2) be organized by product, function, or region, or (3) have a mixture of them (hybrid form). To attain a balance between product and regional expertise, some managements have tried a matrix form of organization. Its disadvantages, however, have caused many managements to put a matrix overlay over a traditional product, regional, or functional form instead of using the matrix.

Explain the concept of the virtual corporation.

A virtual corporation enables companies to come together quickly to take advantage of a specific marketing opportunity. Because each member concentrates on what it does best, a virtual corporation can have capabilities superior to those of any member. Once the opportunity ends, the virtual corporation normally will disband.

Explain why decisions are made where they are among parent and subsidiary units of an international company (IC).

Several considerations govern where decisions are made in an IC family of organizations. They include the desirability of standardizing products as opposed to differentiating them for different markets, the competence of organization managements, the size and age of the IC, the benefit of one part of the family to the detriment of another, and building confidence or avoiding frustration of management.

Discuss how an IC can maintain control of a joint venture or of a company in which the IC owns less than 50 percent of the voting stock.

Control can be maintained over a joint venture or a company in which the IC owns less than 50 percent of the voting stock by several devices, including a management contract, control of the finances, control of the technology, and putting people from the IC in key executive positions.

List the types of information an IC needs to have reported to it by its units around the world.

Subsidiaries should report to the IC information about financial conditions, technological developments, market opportunities and developments, and economic and political conditions.

Key Words

organizational structure (p. 386)
international division (p. 388)
hybrid organization (p. 393)
matrix organization (p. 393)
matrix overlay (p. 394)

strategic business unit (SBU) (p. 395)
virtual corporation (p. 395)
horizontal corporation (p. 397)
subsidiaries (p. 398)

affiliates (p. 399)
subsidiary detriment (p. 400)
de-jobbing (p. 404)
hierarchy (p. 404)

Questions

1. Why is organizational structure an important issue for international companies?

2. What are the main strengths and weaknesses of the use of an international division as part of a company's organizational structure? Under what circumstances might such a structure be an appropriate choice for a company?

3. Compare and contrast geographic and product structures for international companies.

4. Your matrix organization isn't working; decisions are taking too long, and it seems to you that instead of best solutions, you're getting compromises. What can you, the CEO, do?

5. You are the CEO of Mancon Incorporated, and you have just acquired Pozoli, the Italian small-appliance maker (electric shavers, small household and personal care appliances). It has been in business 30 years and has manufacturing plants in Italy, Mexico, Ireland, and Spain. Its output is sold in more than 100 markets worldwide, including the United States. Your company is now organized into two product groups—shaving and personal care—along with an international division at the top level. How are you going to include Pozoli in your organization? Explain your rationale.

6. It is obvious that in formulating new strategies, management may uncover a need to change its organization. Can you describe some situations where the reverse may be true?

7. In determining whether decisions will be made by the parent company or by its subsidiaries, what are the considerations when equipment and products are standardized worldwide rather than tailored to individual national circumstances and markets?

8. a. In an IC, what are some decisions that could result in detriment for a subsidiary but greater benefit for the enterprise?

   b. In such circumstances, where will the decision be made—at IC headquarters or at the affected subsidiary?

9. What measures can be utilized to control subsidiaries that are less than 100 percent owned by the firm or joint venture partners in which the firm has no ownership?

10. Some companies use standardized organizational controls across their entire organization, in that the same control systems are used for each unit or operation worldwide. For example, companies such as Starbucks, Kentucky Fried Chicken, or McDonald's apply the same rigid quality controls throughout all aspects of their organizations, even as they expand internationally. Why would a company such as these impose rigorous corporate quality standards, regardless of the country in which it operates? What modifications in these quality standards, if any, should the company permit because of differences across nations or regions of the world? Why is the company allowing these modifications to occur?

11. Explain the argument that the world is de-jobbing.

Research Task

globalEDGE.msu.edu

Use the globalEDGE™ site (http://globalEDGE.msu.edu) to complete the following exercises:

1. *Fortune* magazine conducts an annual survey and publishes the rankings of the "Global Most Admired Companies." Locate the most recent publicly available ranking, follow the link to the best and worst companies, and focus on the nine factors highlighted by *Fortune* magazine. On the basis of these data, prepare an executive summary of the strategic and organizational success factors of a company of your choice.

2. Your firm seeks to maximize the infrastructure of the most globalized countries so that its products and services are more accessible worldwide. A coworker recently informed you that an A. T. Kearney report on globalization may assist in better assessing which countries may be optimal to begin worldwide operations. Locate the report, and identify the five most globalized countries. What are the measures used in the report to determine each country's level of globalization?

Electrex, Inc., manufactures electronic and electrical connectors used on such diverse products as computers, home appliances, telecommunications, and the air bag and antiskid systems of automobiles. The company has been in business since 1965. The table below provides the important financial information for the last five years.

For some time, Electrex had been exporting to Asia, where its major markets are Australia, Singapore, Malaysia, Thailand, South Korea, China, and Taiwan. When its foreign sales were confined to exports, the company functioned well with an export department whose manager reported to the company's marketing manager. In 2005, however, another American firm tried to enter the Taiwan market, and there were rumors that a Taiwanese firm from a related industry was searching for a licensor in the United States to supply it with manufacturing technology. As a result, Electrex decided to set up its first foreign plant in Taiwan. When it did, it hired financial and marketing people with Asian experience and established an international division at headquarters to oversee the Taiwan operation. The president felt that the situation would be repeated in China, Singapore, and perhaps other nations. These were all good export markets at the time, but it was reasonable to suppose that some competitor would soon set up manufacturing facilities in one or more of them, which could dramatically impact the potential for exporting to these markets. Having a small international division with some Asian expertise that is responsible for monitoring these markets would help the firm avoid being surprised by a competitor's move.

After the Taiwan Electrex plant was in production, more firms in that nation were willing to do business with the company than had been the case when it had served the market through exports. In fact, the major portion of the 2006 sales increase was due to improved sales to Taiwan. However, the new customers also brought the company into a new, higher level of competition than it had known before. Other Taiwanese competitors were bringing out new products at a considerably faster rate than Electrex was. The president wondered if horizontal linkages across functions, such as the linkages automakers have used to reduce their design time, might help his firm. Also, on his trips to Taiwan, the marketing people told him things about the market and the competitors that were not being sent to the Electrex home office.

It was obvious to the president that overseas production and growth in overseas sales demanded a reorganization of the firm. Even though the company had only one plant overseas, in Taiwan, the president was confident that other plants would soon be needed. How should the company be organized to handle the new foreign production facilities? How can Electrex reduce the time needed to bring new designs to market?

Electrex Five-Year Financial Highlight Summary ($ millions)

	2006	2005	2004	2003	2002
Net sales	$353.0	$298.2	$271.9	$257.4	$231.1
Gross profit	134.1	116.3	110.3	106.7	94.9
Selling, general, and administrative expense	70.5	61.2	55.8	51.8	45.1
Income from operations	63.6	55.1	54.5	54.9	49.8
Income taxes	23.9	20.9	20.9	21.8	20.9
Effective tax rate (%)	37.6	37.9	38.3	39.7	42.0
Net income	39.7	34.2	33.6	33.1	28.9

Competition within the International Company Minicase 14.2

Worldwide (W) is an IC with subsidiary manufacturing plants in several countries around the world. W has just won a very large contract to supply locomotives to Paraguay, which is modernizing its entire railway system with financing from the World Bank.

W's home country is the United States, and W can manufacture parts of or the complete locomotives in its U.S. plants. W subsidiary companies in Spain, Argentina, and Australia can also manufacture parts of the complete locomotives. The managers of all those subsidiaries know about the big new contract, and each is eager to get the work involved in performing it.

A meeting of the subsidiary chief executive officers (CEOs) is called at W's headquarters in New York to discuss which plant or plants will get the work. The manager of the American locomotive division is also at the meeting, and she makes a strong case that her plant needs the work. It has laid off 3,000 workers, and this big job would permit it to recall them. In addition, the American factory has all the latest technology, some of which has not been shared with the subsidiaries.

Each CEO argues that there is unemployment in his or her host country and that, as a responsible citizen, he or she must hire more local people. Doing so, moreover, would reduce hostility in the host country and give the subsidiary defenses against political attacks on foreign-owned companies. One subsidiary CEO suggests that each subsidiary and the American division enter competitive bids and let Paraguayan Railways make the decision.

You are the CEO of W and have the responsibility for allocating parts of or all the work to one or more of the plants. List and explain the considerations that will govern your decisions.

15

Assessing and Analyzing Markets

Think locally, offer value, and be patient. That last one is key: You can make an elephant dance. But it takes time to learn the right tune.

—*Om Malik on marketing to India,* Business 2.0, *July 2004*

Marketing Research

Clotaire Rapaille is a charlatan—or possibly an adviser your company simply cannot do without. Originally a psychologist treating autistic children in Europe, Rapaille now operates from a mansion in upstate New York, where top management seeks his advice on "the code" that will allow them access to the Indian, French, or Norwegian psyche. And from there, this insight should help them understand the motivations that will draw these people to buy their products.

Rapaille's earlier insights came when comparing French and American attitudes toward cheese. For the French, he says, cheese is alive, and the French would not put cheese in the refrigerator any more than one would put one's cat in the fridge. Both are "alive." But for Americans, Rapailles's insight is that cheese is "dead," so Americans seal it in a plastic "casket" and put it in a refrigerator, which is really a "morgue." Americans are more concerned about safety than taste: The French reverse these preferences. So more French than American consumers die from eating cheese: But the Americans eat a relatively sterile and tasteless product, while the French enjoy a variety of cheeses that Americans cannot fathom.

Rapaille was also influential in the development of Chrysler's PT Cruiser, the retro car that has enjoyed great success. Chrysler does acknowledge that he was involved but downplays his role in its development. Rapaille has in total 50 of the Fortune 100 firms as clients. He claims that teams under his direction have "broken the code" for "anti-Americanism," "China," "seduction," the "teen Internet," and more. A recent excursion to India led him to pronounce that the caste system was simply a "practical" way of signaling to all their places in society. "It's not a problem, it's a solution," he summarizes.

Rapaille displays a certain confidence bordering on arrogance, and he follows a research method that is unusual, to say the least. Rather than relying on focus groups or surveys, he "breaks the code" of certain countries in roughly three-hour sessions. In these sessions, paid respondents first discuss the topic of interest; then they are asked to tap into their emotional reactions; and finally Rapaille explores, as he puts it, their "reptilian brain." It is the last that he finds useful. "Never believe what people say," Rapaille says. "I want to understand why people do what they do." Ultimately, he has respondents on the floor in the fetal position, reliving childhood memories. From this process, he says, he discovers cultural archetypes, which are long-lasting, although opinions may change more readily. Former clients have scoffed at him, using "the cheese is dead" as a constant mantra, mocking his methods. Yet many of the same clients come back to him, as P&G has come back 35 times.

As managers, we may (or may not) hire Clotaire Rapaille or his company. But international managers must search constantly for methods, both new and old, that will allow them to analyze foreign markets and to understand these markets. It is to this topic that we now turn. ∎

Source: Danielle Sacks, "Crack This Code," *Fast Company,* April 2006, pp. 97–101: www.pbs.org/wgbh/pages/frontline/shows/persuaders/interviews/rapaille.html (October 3, 2006); www.archetypediscoveries.com (October 4, 2006); "Pushing Your Buy Button: Neuroscience Meets Marketing," *Forbes,* 2003, www.archetypediscoveriesworldwide.com/6.pdf.; and "The Last Word: Clotaire Rapaille," *Newsweek,* international ed., www.msnbc.msn.com/id/4710897 (October 4, 2006).

CONCEPT PREVIEWS

After reading this chapter, you should be able to:

discuss environmental analysis and two types of market screening

explain market indicators and market factors

describe some statistical techniques for estimating market demand and grouping similar markets

discuss the value to businesspeople of trade missions and trade fairs

discuss some of the problems market researchers encounter in foreign markets

explain the difference between country screening and segment screening

identify the sources of information for the screening process

discuss the utility of the Internet as a source of market research data

As described above, Clotaire Rapaille's seeming skill at reducing complex motivations to understandable "sound bites" may or may not ring hollow, but we can appreciate our need as managers to understand complex foreign markets.

While noting our fascination with Rapaille's methods, many international managers might prefer a more systematic approach as outlined in this chapter. In the following pages we describe in some detail a market screening process.

The first step in the market screening process is determining the basic need potential. We shall describe this process fully in the next section. **Market screening** is a modified version of environmental scanning in which the firm identifies markets by using the environmental forces to eliminate the less desirable markets.

Environmental scanning, from which market screening is derived, is a procedure in which a firm scans the world for changes in the environmental forces that might affect it.[1] For some time, environmental scanning has been used by managers during the planning process to provide information about world threats and opportunities. Those who do environmental scanning professionally may belong to such organizations as the Society of Competitive Intelligence Professionals (www.scip.org). In addition, environmental scanning services are available from a number of private firms. Examples of such service providers include Smith Brandon International (www.smithbrandon.com) and Stratfor, Inc. (www.stratfor.com).

Market screening assists two different kinds of firms. One is selling exclusively in the domestic market but believes it might increase sales by expanding into overseas markets. The other is already a multinational, but wants to avoid missing potential new markets. In both situations, managers require an ordered, relatively fast method of analyzing and assessing the nearly 200 countries (and multiple market segments within countries) to pinpoint the most suitable prospects.

Market Screening

Market screening is a method of market analysis and assessment that permits management to identify a small number of desirable markets by eliminating those judged to be less attractive. This is accomplished by subjecting the markets to a series of screenings based on the environmental forces examined in Section Three. Although these forces may be placed in any order, the arrangement suggested in Figure 15.1 is designed to progress from the least

market screening
A version of environmental scanning in which the firm identifies desirable markets by using the environmental forces to eliminate the less desirable markets

environmental scanning
A procedure in which a firm scans the world for changes in the environmental forces that might affect it

---

FIGURE 15.1

Selection of Foreign Markets

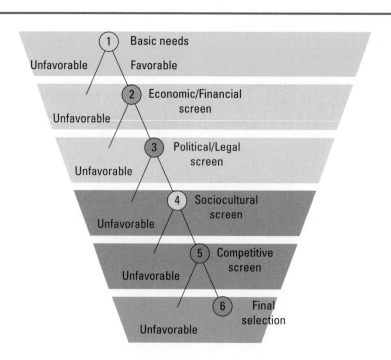

to the most difficult analysis based on the accessibility and subjectivity of the data. In this way, the smallest number of candidates is left for the final, most difficult screening.

TWO TYPES OF SCREENING

In this chapter we will look at two types of market screening procedures. The first, which could be called **country screening,** takes countries as the relevant unit of analysis. The second, which we might call **segment screening,** is based on a subnational analysis of groups of consumers.

country screening
Using countries as the basis for market selection

segment screening
Using market segments as the basis for market selection

INITIAL SCREENING

Basic Need Potential
An initial screening based on the basic need potential is a logical first step, because if the need is lacking, no reasonable expenditure of effort and money will enable the firm to market its goods or services. For example, the basic need potential of certain goods is dependent on various physical forces, such as climate, topography, and natural resources. If the firm produces air conditioners, the analyst will look for countries with warm climates. Manufacturers of large farm tractors might not consider Switzerland a likely prospect because of its mountainous terrain, and only areas known to possess gold deposits are probable markets for gold-dredging equipment.

Generally, producers of specialized industrial materials or equipment experience little difficulty in assessing their basic need potential. A builder of cement kilns, for example, can obtain the names and addresses of cement plants worldwide through the Web site of the Portland Cement Association, near Chicago. A list of firms in an industry, often on a worldwide basis, is available either from the industry association or from specialized trade journals. What about less specialized products that are widely consumed? For example, it is problematic to establish a basic need for chocolate and harder still to do so for MP3 players, consumer robots, or movies on DVD. In this case we are moving from needs to wants.

Foreign Trade
Analysts who want to know where American competitors are exporting their products can go to the Web site of the International Trade Administration (ITA), www.ita.doc.gov. The U.S. Department of Commerce also has the report *U.S. Exports of Merchandise* on the National Trade Data Bank (NTDB), which is available online for a subscription fee. This report's information is especially useful, as it includes both units and dollar values, permitting the analyst to calculate the average price of the unit exported. Commerce compiles and releases foreign trade statistics on a monthly and cumulative basis in its report *U.S. International Trade in Goods and Services,* commonly referred to as the FT900. Recently the FT900 showed, for instance, that U.S. income from royalties and licensing increased each year from 2004-2006. It is published as a press release.

For help in their search for markets, analysts can obtain from the nearest Department of Commerce office numerous studies prepared by U.S. embassies. *Annual Worldwide Industry Reviews* and *International Market Research Reports* indicate major markets for many products.

The *Country Market Surveys* indicate products for which there is a good, established market in a given country. We shall discuss these publications in greater detail in Chapter 18. Other countries publish similar data. For example, the data office of the European Community, Eurostat, publishes an annual, *External Trade,* and JETRO, the Japanese External Trade Organization, publishes a wide assortment of trade and industry data, many of which are put on its Internet site.

Imports Don't Completely Measure Market Potential   Even when a basic need is clearly indicated, experienced researchers will still investigate the trade flows to have an idea of the magnitude of present sales. Management is aware, of course, that imports alone seldom measure the full market potential. Myriad reasons are responsible, among which are poor marketing, lack of foreign exchange, and high prices (duties and markups). Nor can imports give much indication of the potential demand for a really new product.

Moreover, import data indicate only that a market has been buying certain products from abroad and are no guarantee that it will continue to do so. A competitor may decide to produce locally, which in many markets will cause imports to cease. Change in a country's political structure also may stop imports, as we saw in the case of Iran after the revolution there, where orders worth billions of dollars were suddenly canceled. Nevertheless, import data do enable the firm to know how much is currently being purchased and provide managers with a conservative estimate of the immediate market potential at the going price. If local production is being considered and calculations show that goods produced in the country could be sold at a lower price, the firm can reasonably expect to sell more than the quantity being imported.

SECOND SCREENING—FINANCIAL AND ECONOMIC FORCES

After the initial screening, the analyst will have a much smaller list of prospects. This list may be further reduced by a second screening based on the financial and economic forces. Trends in inflation, exchange, and interest rates are among the major financial points of concern. The analyst should consider other financial factors, such as credit availability, paying habits of customers, and rates of return on similar investments. It should be noted that this screening is not a complete financial analysis. That will come later if the market analysis and assessment disclose that a country has sufficient potential for capital investment.

Economic data may be employed in a number of ways, but two measures of market demand based on them are especially useful. These are *market indicators* and *market factors*. Other methods for estimating demand that depend on economic data are *trend analysis* and *cluster analysis*.

market indicators
Economic data used to measure relative market strengths of countries or geographic areas

Market Indicators
Market indicators are economic data that serve as yardsticks for measuring the relative market strengths of various geographic areas.

As an example, we developed an index of e-commerce potential for Latin America so that the countries in the region could be compared. The results appear in Table 15.1. In this methodology, we assembled data on 20 Latin American countries and then ranked the countries against each other. We wanted to include indicators of the strength and growth rate of the overall economy, as well as factors related more specifically to e-commerce or to communications that would aid the growth of e-commerce. We developed three indexes. Each indicator is given equal weight in each index.

Market size = size of urban population + electricity consumption

Market growth rate = average growth rate in commercial energy use + real growth rate in GDP

E-commerce readiness = mobile phones per 1,000 + number of PCs per 1,000 + Internet hosts per million people

The rankings on these three indexes were then utilized to form a composite ranking. We called this composite ranking "e-commerce potential." As you can see in Table 15.1, utilizing our methodology the countries with the most e-commerce potential appear to be Chile, Costa Rica, Jamaica, and Brazil, while Paraguay, Nicaragua, and Haiti appear to have the least potential.

market factors
Economic data that correlate highly with market demand for a product

Market Factors
Market factors are similar to market indicators except that they tend to correlate highly with the market demand for a given product. If the analyst of a foreign market has no factor for that market, he or she may be able to use one from the domestic market to get an approximation. Moreover, an analyst who works for a multinational firm may be able to obtain market factors developed by comparable subsidiaries. To be able to transfer these relationships to the country under study, the analyst must assume that the underlying conditions affecting demand are similar in the market.

estimation by analogy
Process of using a market factor that is successful in one market to estimate demand in a similar market

We can illustrate this process, which is called **estimation by analogy,** by using the following example: If a supplier of laptops knows that one-fifth of all laptops are replaced every year in the United Kingdom, he or she might use the same relationship to estimate demand for replacement computers in a new overseas market. If there are 3 million existing laptops in the new market, the analyst might forecast that 3 million $\times$ 0.20, or 600,000, replacement laptops will be sold annually. The constant in the country under study may be somewhat different (it usually is), but with this approach, the estimates will be in the right ballpark. Many

Countries	Market Size	Market Growth Rate	E-Commerce Readiness	Overall E-Commerce Potential
South America				
Argentina	4	17	3	6
Bolivia	17	5	15	15
Brazil	5	12	3	4
Chile	1	5	1	1
Colombia	11	7	9	9
Ecuador	14	1	9	6
Paraguay	12	16	15	17
Peru	12	3	15	11
Uruguay	7	20	9	12
Venezuela	2	19	7	9
Caribbean				
Dominican Republic	10	9	9	9
Haiti	20	18	20	19
Jamaica	3	14	2	3
Central America				
Costa Rica	6	2	3	2
El Salvador	15	13	9	12
Guatemala	17	11	9	12
Honduras	15	4	19	15
Mexico	6	15	3	6
Nicaragua	17	10	15	17
Panama	5	6	7	4

Source: Michael S. Minor and Alexandra Brandt, "A Possible Index of E-Commerce Potential for Latin America," working paper, January 8, 2002, updated June 2006 by Adeseguno Oyedele. Reprinted with permission of the authors.

such factors exist, and generally research personnel, either at the home office or in foreign subsidiaries, are familiar with them.

Trend Analysis   When the historical growth rates of either the pertinent economic variables or the imports of a product are known, future growth can be forecast by means of **trend analysis.** A time series may be constructed in a manner similar to the way a regression model is made, or the arithmetic mean of past growth rates may be applied to historical data. Caution is advised when using the second method because if the average annual growth rate is applied mechanically, in just a few years the dependent variable may reach an incredible size. For example, a 5 percent growth rate compounded annually will result in a doubling of the original value in only 15 years. Because trend analysis is based on the assumption that past conditions affecting the dependent variable will remain constant, analysts will generally modify the outcome to take into account any changes that can be foreseen. Often there are obvious constraints that will limit growth. One of these constraints is the near certainty that competitors will enter the market if large increases in demand continue for very long.

trend analysis
Statistical technique by which successive observations of a variable at regular time intervals are analyzed to establish regular patterns that are used for establishing future values

Cluster Analysis and Other Techniques   As multinationals extend their presence to more markets, managers are searching for ways to group countries and geographic regions by common characteristics. **Cluster analysis** divides objects (market areas, individuals, customers, and other variables) into groups so that the variables within each group are similar. For example, all the people sitting at a table in a restaurant are a "cluster." Marketers, for example, use cluster analysis to identify a group of markets where a single promotional approach

cluster analysis
Statistical technique that divides objects into groups so that the objects within each group are similar

In any building process, the right tools are necessary to get the job completed. Listed below are a number of solid analytical tools and skills that can be applied to analyzing global markets. If you understand how to use them and apply them appropriately, you will typically generate higher-quality analytical results and then be able to make better decisions. (To find out more about any of these tools, try an Internet search or check out one of the Web sites listed below.)

- Pareto Principle (80/20 rule)
- Project management process
- Market development planning
- Feasibility study
- Boston Consulting Group Matrix
- SWOT analysis
- Porter's Five Forces Model
- PEST and PESTELI analysis
- PRO's & CON's weighted analysis
- SOSTAC Planning Model
- P&L account planning, accounting, and reporting
- ROI analysis
- Business plan–marketing plan writing
- Strategies and tactics of sales

High-quality secondary market data and economic statistics about global markets are becoming readily available with just a few keystrokes and will support your market understanding for better application of these tools. When it comes to using the results these tools will generate, here are two concepts to always keep in mind:

- *The First Law of Cybernetics states,* "The unit within the system with the most behavioral responses available to it controls the system."

- *P. T. Barnum said,* "If you can't put your idea on the back of your business card, you don't have a clear idea."

Make sure that you have enough analytical data to make a solid recommendation, and then you own the recommendation. When you present your recommendations, you will look professional if you do so in a clear, succinct, and understandable way.

World Wide Resources:

www.internationalbusinessstrategies.com

http://dir.yahoo.com/Business_and_Economy/Trade/Statistics

http://unstats.un.org/unsd/default.htm

http://unstats.un.org/unsd/methods/inter-natlinks/refs3.htm

www.marketresearch.com

www.imriresearch.com

can be employed; attorneys can use it to group nations according to similarities in certain types of laws; and so forth. In other words, cluster analysis is used to classify a "mountain" of information into meaningful "piles."

Periodic Updating   If the estimates are altered appreciably in the periodic updatings that all long-term forecasts undergo, managers may change the extent of the firm's involvement to be in line with the new estimates. Fortunately, the alternative forms of participation in a market permit the firm to become progressively more involved, with corresponding increases in investment. Most companies can enter a market in stages, perhaps in this sequence: exporting, establishment of a foreign sales company, local assembly, and, finally, local manufacturing.

Even when the decision is whether to produce overseas, management may plan to assemble a combination of imported and domestically produced parts initially and then progressively to manufacture more components locally as demand rises. Automobile manufacturers have begun a number of foreign operations employing this strategy.

THIRD SCREENING—POLITICAL AND LEGAL FORCES

The elements of the political and legal forces that can eliminate a market from further consideration (or make it more attractive) are numerous.

Entry Barriers   Import restrictions can be positive or negative, depending on whether managers are considering exporting (can the firm's products enter the country?) or setting up a foreign plant (will competitive imports be kept out?). If an objective is 100 percent ownership, will the nation's laws permit it, or is some local participation required? Will the government accept a minority local ownership, or must a minimum of 51 percent of the subsidiary be in the hands of nationals? Are there laws that reserve certain industries for either the government or its citizens?[2] Is the host government demanding that the foreign owner turn over technology to its proposed affiliate that it wishes to keep at the home plant? Perhaps the host government has local content restrictions that the prospective investor considers excessive. There may be a government-owned company that would compete with the proposed plant. Depending on the circumstances and how strongly management wishes to enter the market, any one of these conditions may be sufficient cause to eliminate a nation from further consideration.

Profit Remittance Barriers   When there are no objectionable requisites for entry, a nation may still be excluded if there are what management believes to be undue restrictions on the repatriation of earnings. Limits linked to the amount of foreign investment or other criteria may be set, or the nation may have a history of inability to provide foreign exchange for profit remittances.

Policy Stability   Another factor of importance to management in studying the possibilities of investing in a country is the stability of government policy. Is there continuity in policy when a new leader takes office, for example? What is the political climate? Is the government stable, or is there infighting among government leaders? How about the public? Is there visible unrest? Do the armed forces have a history of intervention when there are public disturbances? Business can adapt to the form of government and thrive as long as the conditions are stable. But instability creates uncertainty, and this complicates planning. An often-heard complaint is, "They've changed the rules again."

It is important to make a distinction between *political stability* and *policy stability.* Rulers may come and go, but if the policies that affect businesses don't change very much, these political changes really may not be important. In fact, if one measures political stability in terms of changes in leadership at the top, the United States is politically unstable compared to many countries!

Sources of analysis on political and policy stability are numerous. Some, such as Stratfor, have already been mentioned. In addition, Business Environment Risk Intelligence S.A. (www.beri.com) and Political Risk Services (www.prsgroup.com) publish rankings comparing countries on the issue of political risk. You may also want to review the discussion of country risk assessment in Chapter 9.

FOURTH SCREENING—SOCIOCULTURAL FORCES

A screening of the remaining candidates on the basis of sociocultural factors is arduous. First, sociocultural factors are fairly subjective. Second, data are difficult to assemble, particularly from a distance. The analyst, unless he or she is a specialist in the country, must rely on the opinions of others. It is possible to hire consultants, who typically are "old hands" with experience in the country or region. Others may have a particular methodology, such as Clotaire Rapaille mentioned at the beginning of the chapter. Also, professional organizations and universities frequently hold seminars to explain the sociocultural aspects of doing business in a particular area or country.

Reading *Overseas Business Reports* (U.S. Department of Commerce), international business publications *(Business International, Financial Times, The Economist),* and specialized books will augment the analyst's sociocultural knowledge. The use of a checklist of the principal sociocultural components, as explained in Chapter 6, will serve as a reminder of the many factors the analyst must consider in this screening.

Although there are many difficulties, it is possible that recent immigrants or students from foreign countries may be used to shed light on potential sociocultural issues.

One of the authors took a visiting speaker who was originally from Japan to visit a local firm. This business, which manufactured dessert items such as individual cherry pies, wanted to break into the Japanese market but had not been successful. The Japanese speaker tasted the product and told them firmly that their cherry pie was too sweet for Japanese palates. We found that this company had never actually asked a Japanese person for a reaction to its products! Although the firm needed to confirm this single opinion by using other methods, the taster nonetheless offered insight into an issue about which the firm was unaware.

A danger, of course, is that immigrants and students have been affected by their residence abroad. Therefore, they are not necessarily reliable indicators of the reaction your product might receive from an audience "back home."

After the fourth screening, the analyst should have a list of countries for which an industry demand appears to exist. However, what management really wants to know is which of these markets seem to be the best prospects for the *firm's* products. A fifth screening based on the competitive forces will help provide this information.

FIFTH SCREENING—COMPETITIVE FORCES

In this screening, the analyst examines markets on the basis of such elements of the competitive forces as:

1. The number, size, and financial strength of the competitors.

2. Their market shares.

3. Their marketing strategies.

4. The apparent effectiveness of their promotional programs.

5. The quality levels of their product lines.

6. The source of their products—imported or locally produced.

7. Their pricing policies.

8. The levels of their after-sales service.

9. Their distribution channels.

10. Their coverage of the market. (Could market segmentation produce niches that are currently poorly served?)

Concerning item 10, it may be important to examine regional or ethnic subcultures in a particular foreign market. These subcultures may be natural or at least identifiable segments for which specific marketing programs may be successful. This is analogous to the fact that there are sufficient Hispanic, Chinese, and other subcultures in the United States to merit the importation of Chinese and Latin American products into the United States.

Perhaps other countries have significant immigrant or subcultural populations whose needs you already understand and can serve. As an example, Japan has a small but growing population of immigrants from Latin America whose parents emigrated from Japan to Latin America in earlier times. These returnees tend to preserve their Latin heritage in Japan and might provide a market niche for firms whose strength is marketing to Latin Americans rather than to the Japanese.

Countries in which management believes strong competitors make a profitable operation difficult to attain are eliminated unless management (1) is following a strategy of being present wherever its global competitors are or (2) believes entering a competitor's home market will distract the competitor's attention from its home market, a reason for foreign investment we discussed in Chapter 3.

FINAL SELECTION OF NEW MARKETS

While much can be accomplished through analysis, there is no substitute for personal visits to markets that appear to have the best potential. An executive of the firm should visit those countries that still appear to be good prospects. Before leaving, this person should review the data from the various screenings along with any new information that the researcher can supply.

On the basis of this review and experience in making similar domestic decisions, the executive should prepare a list of points on which information must be obtained on arrival. Management will want the facts uncovered by the desk study (the five screenings) to be corroborated and will expect a firsthand report on the market, including information on competitive activity and an appraisal of the suitability of the firm's present marketing mix and the availability of support services (warehousing, media agencies, credit, and so forth).

Field Trip   The field trip should not be hurried; as much time should be allotted to this part of the study as would be spent on a similar domestic field trip. The point is to try to develop a "feel" for what is going on, and this can't be accomplished quickly. For example, while Japanese youths model themselves after American basketball stars by wearing Nike sneakers, it appears that they change into off-brand sneakers when they actually play basketball. As another example, it seems to be relatively common for men to shop in grocery stores in Chile, as compared to elsewhere in Latin America. And there is not much tradition in East Asia of men taking on the "do-it-yourself" projects for which Home Depot and similar brands are famous. This type of insight is not likely to develop without actual visits to the market.

Government-Sponsored Trade Missions and Trade Fairs   When government trade specialists perceive an overseas market opportunity for an industry, they may organize a **trade mission.** The purpose is to send a group of executives from firms in the industry to a country or group of countries to learn firsthand about the market, meet important customers face-to-face, and make contacts with people interested in representing their products. Because of discounted airfares, hotels, and so forth, the cost to the firm may be less than it would pay if it went on its own.

> **trade mission**
> A group of businesspeople and/or government officials (state or federal) that visits a market in search of business opportunities
>
> **trade fair**
> A large exhibition, generally held at the same place and same time periodically, at which companies maintain booths to promote the sale of their products

Moreover, the impact of a group visit is greater than that of an individual visit. Before the mission's arrival, consulate or embassy officials will have publicized the visit and made contact with local companies they believe are interested. For example, in 2002 the prime minister of Canada led a group of Canadian businesses on a trade mission to Germany and Russia, resulting in agreements representing $584 million in business for Canadian firms.[3] State governments, trade associations, chambers of commerce, and other export-oriented organizations also organize trade missions.

Probably every nation in the world holds a **trade fair** periodically. Usually each nation has a specifically marked area (Chinese pavilion, Argentine pavilion, etc.) at the fairgrounds where its exhibitors have their own booths staffed by company sales representatives. Trade fairs are open to the public, but during certain hours (generally mornings), entrance is limited to businesspeople interested in doing business with the exhibitors.

While most fairs in developing countries are general, with displays of many kinds of products, those in Europe are specialized. A famous example is the annual CeBIT computer and telecommunications trade fair—the largest computer-related trade fair in the world—held annually in Hannover, Germany. Over 450,000 people made the trip to this show in 2006 alone to see exhibits from 6,167 exhibitors.[4]

Besides making contact with prospective buyers and agents (direct sales are often concluded), most exhibitors use these fairs to learn more about the market and gather competitive intelligence. They not only receive feedback from visitors to their exhibits but also have the opportunity to observe their competitors in action.

Visitors explore the exhibits at the CeBIT Technology Fair in Hannover, Germany. Besides making sales contacts, most exhibitors use these fairs to learn more about the market and gather competitive intelligence. They not only receive feedback from visitors to their exhibits but also have the opportunity to observe their competitors in action.

Sometimes Local Research Is Required   For many situations, the manager's field report will be the final input to the information on which the decision is based. Occasionally, however, the proposed human and financial resource commitments are so great that management will insist on gathering data in the potential market rather than depending solely on the desk and field reports.[5] This would undoubtedly be the position of a consumer products manufacturer that envisions entering a large competitive market of an industrialized country. It might also be the recommendation of the manager making the field trip if he or she discovered that market conditions were substantially different from those to which the firm was accustomed. Often, in face-to-face interviews, information is revealed that would never be written. In these situations, research in the local market not only will supply information on market definition and projection but also will assist in the formulation of an effective marketing mix.

Research in the Local Market
When a firm's research personnel have had no experience in the country, management should probably hire a local research group to do the work. Generally, home country research techniques may be used, though they may need to be adapted to local conditions. It is imperative, therefore, that the person in charge of the project have experience either in that country or in one that is culturally similar and preferably in the same geographic area.

If secondary data are unavailable, the researchers must collect primary data, and here they face other complications caused by *cultural problems* and *technical difficulties.*

Cultural Problems If the researchers are from one culture and are working in another, they may encounter some cultural problems. When they are not proficient in the local language or dialect, the research instrument or the respondents' answers must be translated. As we learned in the chapter on sociocultural forces, a number of languages may be spoken in a country, and even in countries where only one language is used, a word's meaning may change from one region to another.

Other cultural problems plague researchers as they try to collect data. Low levels of literacy may make the use of mail questionnaires virtually impossible. If a husband is interviewed in a market where the wife usually makes the buying decisions, the data obtained from him are worthless. Nor is it always clear who should be interviewed. Respondents sometimes refuse to answer questions because of their general distrust of strangers. In other instances, the custom of politeness toward everyone will cause respondents to give answers calculated to please the interviewer; this is known as *social desirability bias.*

Often, people have practical reasons for not wanting to be interviewed. In some countries, income taxes are based on the apparent worth of individuals as measured by their tangible assets. In such countries, when asked if there is a stereo or TV in the household, the respondent may suspect the interviewer of being a tax assessor and refuse to answer. To overcome such a problem, experienced researchers often hire college students as interviewers because their manner of speech and their dress correctly identify them as what they are.

Technical Difficulties As if the cultural problems were not enough, researchers may also encounter technical difficulties. First, up-to-date maps are often unavailable. The streets chosen to be sampled may have three or four different names along their length, and the houses may not be numbered. In Japan, it is said, only cab drivers can find street addresses. Telephone surveys can be a formidable undertaking, because in some markets only the wealthy have telephones. Although China is the largest mobile phone market in the world, over three-fourths of the nation's cell phone users are in just three cities—Beijing, Shanghai, and Guangzhou.[6]

Mail surveys can be troublesome too, as mail deliveries within a city may take weeks or are sometimes not made at all. For instance, the postal service in Italy has been so slow (two weeks for a letter to go from Rome to Milan) that Italian firms have used private couriers to go to Switzerland to dispatch their foreign mail. The response to a mail survey is often low if the respondent must go to the post office to mail a letter. To increase returns, firms often offer such premiums as lottery tickets or product samples to persons who complete a mail questionnaire.

In some nations, researchers may have to obtain government permission to conduct interviews and, in some cases, submit questionnaires for prior approval. Some countries prohibit certain kinds of questions. For example, you cannot ask Egyptians about the ownership of consumer durables, and in Saudi Arabia you are not permitted to ask questions about nationality.[7]

>>Some Tips on Market Research

Wonder how to begin to get that elusive "feel" for a country from survey data? As we mentioned, one way is to do it yourself via surveys and personal visits. Two other methods involve the use of an outside firm. Under one scenario, you can hire an outside firm to do customized research for your firm's needs. The second involves using surveys that are administered only partially, or not at all, with your specific firm in mind.

CUSTOMIZED RESEARCH

Many firms that can do multicountry surveys on behalf of clients belong to ESOMAR (www.esomar.nl), the European Society of Opinion and Marketing Research. Originally member-firms were European, but there are now 4,000 members in over 100 countries.

Consumer products firms often utilize ethnographic research techniques, sometimes referred to as "corporate anthropology," to develop detailed understanding. A number of firms specialize in this type of research. These firms do extensive "on-the-ground" research, watching consumers actually use products, rather than relying on surveys or focus groups. An example of these specialist firms is Point Forward (www.pointforward.com). In one project the firm helped Lipton examine Japanese tea drinking, leading to new offerings designed to appeal to younger Japanese, who aren't drinking tea at the rate of their elders. Another firm is Envirosell (www.envirosell.com), which specializes in research on shopping.

GENERAL SURVEYS

General surveys are not done with a specific firm in mind. There are three types of general survey. The first is the *omnibus survey*. Omnibus surveys are regularly scheduled surveys conducted by research agencies with questions from different clients (that is, they are wholly or partially "syndicated"). Since several firms contribute questions, the cost is spread across several users and the surveys are relatively fast. However, these surveys can ask only a limited number of questions that are directly relevant to a particular client, and the sample may not be representative of a particular firm's potential target market. As an indication, the ESOMAR directory lists 12 firms in Argentina and 23 firms in Japan that do omnibus surveys.

One example of a firm involved in administering omnibus surveys is A. C. Nielsen (www.acnielsen.com). Although we may know Nielsen best from the "Nielsen ratings," its TV-watching media measurement service, the firm offers services in over 100 countries. Nielsen does an omnibus survey in China, among other countries. Another familiar firm—the Gallup Organization (www.gallup.com)—is involved in this type of research in a variety of countries.

In the second type of noncustomized general survey, market research firms do surveys of their own devising whose results they then market to a variety of firms. An example is the recent Asian Pacific Consumer Confidence Poll in 13 Asian Pacific markets, a Nielsen survey. Nielsen can even track TV-watching habits in China and India. Another firm that does industry-level surveys spanning a number of countries for general sale is Frost & Sullivan (www.frost.com). Frost & Sullivan recently published a report on the world voice-over Internet protocol (VOIP) market.

NONPROFIT SURVEYS

The third type of survey is administered by a government or nongovernment agency, generally not for profit. The Eurobarometer surveys (http://europa.eu.int/comm/public_opinion) are administered several times a year to thousands of respondents in European countries, under the auspices of the European Commission. Recent reports of Eurobarometer results with implications for consumer behavior include reports on attitudes toward vacations, food product safety, the young, and the family. Although these surveys are not specifically directed toward consumption issues, they are free and may be useful. Since 1995 a similar survey, called a *barómetro,* has been conducted in Latin America (www.latinobarometro.org).

THE INTERNET

The number of firms that do surveys on or about the Internet is increasing. Nielsen has a subsidiary devoted to research in Internet marketing called Nielsen NetRatings (www.nielsen-netratings.com). Another such firm is Forrester Research (www.forrester.com). In a recent report, Forrester forecast that European online trade, which represented less than 1 percent of total business trade in 2001, would skyrocket to 22 percent of trade by 2006. In the future, the technology of Internet surveys may offer any firm the opportunity to do its own surveys anywhere in the world. At the present, however, the penetration of the Internet is limited to well-to-do persons in some countries. It is not currently possible to rely on the Internet to provide access to members of all target markets.

Research as Practiced The existence of hindrances to marketing research does not mean it is not carried out in foreign markets. As you might surmise from the discussion of the availability of secondary data, marketing research is highly developed in many areas where markets are large and incorrect decisions are costly. Problems like the ones we have mentioned are prevalent in the developing nations, but they are well known to those who live there. It does not take long for the newcomer to become aware of them either, because long-time residents are quick to point them out.

Analysts tend to do less research and use simpler techniques in these nations because often the firm is in a seller's market, which means everything produced can be sold with a minimum of effort. Moreover, competition is frequently less intense in developing nations because (1) there are fewer competitors and (2) managements are struggling with problems other than marketing, which keep them from devoting more time to marketing issues. Even in Mexico, an important market for American firms, marketing research is less popular.[8] Although the situation is changing, the most common technique continues to be a combination of trend analysis and the querying of knowledgeable persons such as salespeople, channel members, and customers. Researchers then adjust the findings on the basis of subjective considerations.

Segment Screening

As was mentioned earlier, when a company intends to do business in several countries, managers can choose two broad market screening approaches: country segments or market segments. In the first approach, Brazil may be viewed as a target market segment. Using the second approach, while Brazil is the physical location of a large group of consumers, the important variables for segmentation are commonalities in needs and wants among consumers *across nationalities*. These consumers may reside in different countries and speak different languages, but they have similar desires for a product or service. From this perspective, age, income, and psychographics (lifestyles) are the essential means of identifying market segments. The relevant marketing question is not where consumers reside but whether they share similar wants and needs. The targeted consumers may be global teens, middle-class executives, or young families with small children: Each of these segments may share wants and needs across borders. An example comes from "phone surfers"—young Japanese who actively use their mobile phones to surf the Internet. The small phone screen and tiny keys may be a big turnoff for older computer users in the West who have frequent access to desktop or laptop PCs. But youngsters in the West have grown up with television games, Game Boys, and iPod nanos, and they readily adapt to the small screens and tiny buttons that are a part of using cell phones as an Internet device.

Because we usually organize the world mentally in terms of countries, we naturally tend to want to analyze markets as country segments. It is much more difficult to think of ourselves as market segments that extend across borders. Also, as was mentioned in the discussion of sociocultural differences, these data can be difficult to secure. Nonetheless, it is important to do this because this approach is the logical outgrowth of the marketing concept.

And the fact that certain types of data are difficult to gather doesn't mean that the data can be ignored. There is an old saying about research: "If you can count it, that ain't it." In our context, the easy-to-generate data are not necessarily the important data.

Among the criteria for these segments are that they should be:

1. *Definable:* We should be able to identify and measure segments. The more we rely not on socioeconomic indicators but on lifestyle differences, the more difficult this becomes, but the more accurate the resulting analysis is likely to be.

2. *Large:* Segments should be large enough to be worth the effort needed to serve a segment. Of course, as we get closer to flexible manufacturing, the need to find large segments is beginning to recede. Further, the segments should have the potential for growth in the future.

3. *Accessible:* If we literally cannot reach our target segment for either promotional or distribution purposes, we will be unsuccessful.

4. *Actionable:* If we cannot bring components of marketing programs (the 4 Ps of product, promotion, place, and price) to bear, we may not be successful. For example, in Mexico, the price of tortillas was formerly controlled by the government. Therefore, competition on the price variable was impossible. Foreigners could not penetrate the Mexican market for the standard tortilla by offering a lower price.

5. *Capturable:* Although we would love to discover market segments whose needs are completely unmet, in many cases these market segments are already being served. Nonetheless, we may still be able to compete. Where segments are completely "captured" by the competition, however, our task is much more difficult.[9]

TWO SCREENING METHODS, RECONSIDERED

In the final analysis, our view of the rest of the world is organized along national lines. However, it may be useful to attempt to leave that viewpoint behind when examining international markets.

With the increasing recognition of the existence of subcultures *within* nations and similarities between subcultures *across* nations, the international businessperson may wish to expand his or her horizon beyond the conventional view of the nation as the relevant "unit of analysis."

The next chapter takes up a series of related questions. Are our needs and desires becoming more and more alike, or are the differences in consumption preferences between us more relevant than the similarities?

Summary

Discuss environmental analysis and two types of market screening.

A complete market analysis and assessment as described in this chapter would be made by a firm that either is contemplating entering the foreign market for the first time or is already a multinational but wants to monitor world markets systematically to avoid overlooking marketing opportunities and threats. Many of the data requirements for a foreign decision are the same as those for a similar domestic decision, though it is likely that additional information about some of the international and foreign environmental forces will be needed. Essentially, the screening process consists of examining the various forces in succession and eliminating countries at each step. The sequence of screening based on (1) basic need potential, (2) financial and economic forces, (3) political and legal forces, (4) sociocultural forces, (5) competitive forces, and (6) personal visits is ordered so as to have a successively smaller number of prospects to consider at each of the succeedingly more difficult and expensive stages.

Explain market indicators and market factors.

Market indicators are economic data used to measure relative market strengths of countries or geographic areas. Market factors are economic data that correlate highly with the market demand for a product.

Describe some statistical techniques for estimating market demand and grouping similar markets.

Some statistical techniques for estimating market demand and grouping similar markets are trend analysis and cluster analysis.

Discuss the value to businesspeople of trade missions and trade fairs.

Trade missions and trade fairs enable businesspeople to visit a market inexpensively, make sales, obtain overseas representation, and observe competitors' activities.

Discuss some of the problems market researchers encounter in foreign markets.

Cultural problems, such as a low level of literacy and distrust of strangers, complicate the data-gathering process, as do technical difficulties, such as a lack of maps, telephone directories, and adequate mail service. These hindrances to marketing research do not prevent the work from being done. There is a tendency in some markets, however, to do less research and use simpler techniques.

Explain the difference between country screening and segment screening.

If we utilize country screening, we assume that countries are homogeneous units (that is, "everyone living in Mexico or Chad is essentially the same"). In segment screening, we focus our attention not on the nation as a homogeneous unit but on groups of people with similar wants and desires (market segments) across as well as within countries.

Identify the sources of information for the screening process.

The sources of information for the screening process are the environmental forces.

Discuss the utility of the Internet as a source of market research data.

Both the mini-MNE box and the Worldview box in this chapter offer insights into how the Internet is used—or may be used—to generate information. In some countries, however, the Internet is used only by relatively well-to-do and well-educated persons. What are the implications for our ability to do market research directly with potential consumers on the Internet?

Key Words

market screening (p.410)

environmental scanning (p. 410)

country screening (p. 411)

segment screening (p. 411)

market indicators (p. 412)

market factors (p. 412)

estimation by analogy (p. 412)

trend analysis (p. 413)

cluster analysis (p. 413)

trade mission (p. 417)

trade fair (p. 417)

Questions

1. Select a country and a product that you believe your firm can market there. Make a list of the sources of information you will use for each screening.

2. What is the basis for the order of screenings presented in the text?

3. A firm's export manager finds, by examining the UN's *International Trade Statistics Yearbook,* that the company's competitors are exporting. Is there a way the manager can learn to which countries the U.S. competitors are exporting?

4. Do a country's imports completely measure the market potential for a product? Why or why not?

5. What are some barriers related to the political and legal forces that may eliminate a country from further consideration?

6. Why should a firm's management consider going on a trade mission or exhibiting in a trade fair?

7. What are the two principal kinds of complications that researchers face when they collect primary data in a foreign market? Give examples.

8. What do the market size index and the market growth rate index tell you?

9. Consider the market segment screening method. Take a lifestyle segment—say, people who like do-it-yourself home decorating. How would the segment screening method suggest that you go about identifying potential foreign markets?

10. You are a consultant to the developers of the Spider-man computer game. You will tell the CEO where the likely overseas markets are. What do you do?

11. Assume that your academic unit (probably a college of business) wants to open a campus in a foreign country and that the dean has asked you to prepare a list of possible countries. How would you go about fulfilling the dean's requirement?

Use the globalEDGE™ site (http://globalEDGE.msu.edu) to complete the following exercises:

1. *Market Potential Indicators (MPI)* is an indexing study conducted by the Michigan State University Center for International Business Education and Research (MSU-CIBER) to compare emerging markets on a variety of dimensions. Provide a description of the indicators used for this index. Which of the indicators would have greater importance for a company that markets MP3 players? Considering the MPI rankings, which developing countries would you advise this company to enter first with such a product?

2. The National Retail Federation's *Stores* magazine lists the top 250 global retailers ranked by annual sales. This ranking provides economic, demographic, and industry insights on the global marketplace. Locate the ranking and provide a list of the top 10 companies for the latest year available. What is the percentage of Japanese companies on this list of global retailers?

The Sugar Daddy Chocolate Company   Minicase 15.1

Jack Carlson started the Sugar Daddy Chocolate Company five years ago and is now selling about $1 million annually. Carlson would like to expand sales, but the U.S. market is very competitive. He has a friend with a small business who is now making 20 percent of his sales overseas. He wonders if any chocolates are exported.

To find out, he calls a friend of his who is a professor of international business at the university and tells him that he wants to find out if chocolate is being exported. He asks the professor to research the following questions:

1. Is chocolate being exported?

2. Which are the six largest importing nations?

3. Which of these are growing markets?

4. Carlson's export competition would probably come from which countries?

16

Entry Modes

Our development strategy adapts to different markets addressing local needs and requirements. We currently use three business strategies: joint ventures, licenses, and company-owned stores.

—Starbucks Corporation

EBay: An Early Entrant in International Markets

EBay, the online auction house, has been profitable since it started in 1995. In 2004 eBay sold more than $44.3 billion worth of products, which generated over $4.5 billion in revenues and over $340 million in pro forma net income for itself. It has profited from a network effect. Networks are like a snowball rolling, gathering size as they go. The more sellers eBay attracts, the more buyers turn to it, and that in turn draws more sellers. So eBay has grown by nearly 80 percent per year over the last five years.

EBay's business model has also succeeded abroad, where it already generates approximately half of all its revenues and which is predicted to produce an increasing proportion of eBay's revenues. The company has predicted that its operations in Europe alone could end up matching the size of its U.S. business, and more than half of its revenue will soon come from Web sites in 28 countries outside the United States. It aggressively buys firms abroad. An example is its 2004 acquisition of mobile.de, an online German site dedicated to buying and selling automobiles, and its 2005 acquisition of Skype, which provides Internet-based voice and video connections for users worldwide.

EBay has certainly profited from its early mover position, and no rival has been able to mount more than a feeble challenge. (Ask whether anyone in your class knows who the number-two company is in the online auction market.)

Early entrants, however, are by no means guaranteed success. As an example, first movers into China have often not succeeded. Often, early entrants may score some initial successes in a few affluent cities but be unable to repeat that success on a countrywide basis. For example, Procter & Gamble scored early successes with shampoo, but its multiple brands confused customers and local rivals undercut its prices, so its 50 percent market share in 1998 dropped to 30 percent in 2002.

Similarly, a recent book details the $418 million lost by a fund set up to invest hundreds of millions of dollars in China. At least in part, this misadventure was the result of having to deal with joint venture partners (of which more later). ■

Source: "A Survey of E-Commerce," *The Economist,* May 15, 2004, p. 12; "A Survey of Business in China," *The Economist,* March 20, 2004, p. 9; "Doing Business in China: The Perils of Pat," *The Economist,* April 24, 2004, p. 85; EBay Inc., "About the Company," http://pages.ebay.com/aboutebay/thecompany/companyoverview.html (August 3, 2006); and EBay Inc., *Annual Report 2005,* http://investor.ebay.com (August 3, 2006).

CONCEPT PREVIEWS

After reading this chapter, you should be able to:

explain the international market entry methods

discuss the debate on whether being a market pioneer or a fast follower is most useful

identify two different forms of piracy and discuss which might be helpful and harmful to firms doing international business

discuss the channel members available to companies that export indirectly or directly or manufacture overseas

In the opening example we saw that eBay, a market pioneer, has done very well as it expanded internationally but that several early entrants into China have done poorly. Not all pioneers capitalize on their potential advantages, yet some evidence does suggest that pioneers gain and maintain a competitive edge in new markets. For instance, researchers have found that surviving pioneers hold a significantly larger average market share when their industries reach maturity than do firms that were either fast followers or late entrants in the product category.

On the other hand, pioneers can certainly fail. One recent study, which took failed pioneers into account and averaged their performances with those of the more successful survivors, found that, overall, pioneers did not perform as well over the long haul as followers. Of course, what measures are used can be important here: Volume and market share are not the only dimensions by which success can be measured.

The truth is that there really is little evidence one way or the other concerning the effect of the *timing* of a firm's entry into a new market on its ultimate profitability in that market or the value generated for shareholders.

In many cases a firm entering into international markets becomes a follower by default, because a quicker competitor simply beats it by entering into the market first. But even when a company has the capability of being the first mover, there are possible advantages to letting others go first and shoulder the initial risks while the follower observes the pioneers' shortcomings and mistakes.

A pioneering firm stands the best chance for long-term success in market-share leadership and profitability when (1) the pioneering firm is insulated from the entry of competitors (high entry barriers), at least for a while, by strong patent protection, proprietary technology (such as a unique production process), or substantial investment requirements; or (2) the firm has sufficient size, resources, and competencies to take full advantage of its pioneering position and preserve it in the face of later competitive entries. Indeed, some recent evidence suggests that organizational competencies such as R&D and marketing skills not only affect a firm's success as a pioneer but also influence the company's decision about whether to be a pioneer in the first place. Firms that lack the competencies necessary to sustain a first-mover advantage may be more likely to wait for another company to take the lead and then enter the market later.

On the other hand, a follower will most likely succeed when there are few legal, technological, cultural, or financial barriers to inhibit entry (low entry barriers) and when it has sufficient resources or competencies to overwhelm the pioneer's early advantage. The most successful fast followers tend to have the resources to enter the new market on a larger scale than the pioneer. Thus, they can quickly reduce their unit costs and offer lower prices than incumbent competitors.[1]

Thus, the evidence is not clear on whether we should be first—or nearly first—into a foreign market. Even after that decision, we have other decisions to make regarding which entry mode we should use in entering the market first (or not). (See Table 16.1.)

Entering Foreign Markets

As you learned in Chapter 1, we can use a variety of names to identify large firms that operate on a multicountry scale: *global, multidomestic,* and *international* firms or companies, *multinational enterprise (MNE)* or *multinational company (MNC), international company (IC), transnational,* and even *multicultural multinational.* Long before companies become any of these, however, they are usually smaller companies with only domestic experience. In this chapter we examine the very start, that is, the entry into international operations. We first examine nonequity modes of market entry, followed by equity-based modes. We then will complete the chapter by discussing international channels of distribution and the different members involved in these channels.

NONEQUITY MODES OF ENTRY

Most firms begin their involvement in overseas business by exporting—that is, selling some of their regular production overseas. This method requires little investment and is relatively free of risks. It is an excellent means of getting a feel for international business without

TABLE 16.1	Modes of Market Entry

Nonequity-Based Modes of Entry
Export
  Indirect
  Direct
Subcontracting
Countertrade (discussed in Chapter 21)
Licensing
Franchising
Contract manufacturing
Management contract
Contract manufacturing

Equity-Based Modes of Entry
Wholly owned subsidiary
Joint venture
Strategic alliance (may also be nonequity)
Merger and acquisition (M&A)

committing a great amount of human or financial resources. If management does decide to export, it can choose between *direct* and *indirect* exporting. We can also consider the use of nonequity options such as turnkey projects, licensing, franchising, management contracts, and contract manufacturing.

Indirect Exporting
Indirect exporting is simpler than direct exporting because it requires neither special expertise nor large cash outlays. Exporters based in the home country do the work. Exporters available are called a number of different things, including (1) *manufacturers' export agents,* who sell for the manufacturer, (2) *export commission agents,* who buy for their overseas customers, (3) *export merchants,* who purchase and sell for their own accounts, and (4) *international firms,* which use the goods overseas (mining, construction, and petroleum companies are examples).

Indirect exporters, however, pay a price for such service: (1) They pay a commission to the first three kinds of exporters; (2) foreign business can be lost if exporters decide to change their sources of supply; and (3) firms gain little experience from these transactions. This is why many companies that begin in this manner generally change to direct exporting.

indirect exporting
The exporting of goods and services through various types of home-based exporters

Direct Exporting
To engage in **direct exporting,** the export business is handled by someone within the firm. The simplest arrangement is to give someone, often the sales manager, the responsibility for developing the export business. Domestic employees may handle the billing, credit, and shipping initially, and if the business expands, a separate export department may be set up. A firm that has been exporting to wholesale importers in an area and serving them with visits from either home office personnel or foreign-based sales representatives frequently finds that sales have grown to a point that will support a complete marketing organization.

Management may then decide to set up a **sales company** in the area. The sales company imports in its own name from the parent and invoices in local currency. It may employ the same channels of distribution, though the new organization may permit the use of a more profitable arrangement. This type of organization can grow quite large, often invoicing several millions of dollars annually. Before building a plant in Mexico, for many years Eastman Kodak imported and resold cameras and photographic supplies while doing a large business in local film developing. Many firms that began with local repair facilities later expanded to produce simple components. Gradually, they produced more of the product locally until, after a period of time, they were manufacturing all the components in the country.

direct exporting
The exporting of goods and services by the firm that produces them

sales company
A business established for the purpose of marketing goods and services, not producing them

The Internet has made direct exporting much easier. For the beginning exporter, the possibility of making availability of your product or service known abroad is much increased. And although it is likely that a substantial international presence on the Internet will require a significant investment, the cost of trial is now very low.

Turnkey Projects

A *turnkey project* is an export of technology, management expertise, and in some cases capital equipment. The contractor agrees to design and erect a plant, supply the process technology, provide the necessary suppliers of raw materials and other production inputs, and then train the operating personnel. After a trial run, the facility is turned over to the purchaser.

The exporter of a turnkey project may be a contractor that specializes in designing and erecting plants in a particular industry, such as petroleum refining or steel production. It may also be a company in the industry that wishes to earn money from its expertise by delivering a plant ready to run rather than merely selling its technology. Another kind of supplier of a turnkey project is the producer of a factory.

> One of the authors used to sell Goodyear latex to a U.S. manufacturer of paint driers. The manufacturer found it could lock in contracts to supply its products overseas by selling investors in developing countries a complete paint factory. It designed the plant, hired a contractor to erect it, trained the people to operate it, and provided ongoing technical assistance after the factory was delivered to the owners. The company also acted as a distributor for American producers of other inputs and manufacturers of paint-making machinery.

Licensing

licensing

A contractual arrangement in which one firm grants access to its patents, trade secrets, or technology to another for a fee

Frequently, worldwide companies are called on to furnish technical assistance to firms that have sufficient capital and management strength. By means of a **licensing** agreement, one firm (the licensor) will grant to another firm (the licensee) the right to use any kind of expertise, such as manufacturing processes (patented or unpatented), marketing procedures, and trademarks for one or more of the licensor's products.

The licensee generally pays a fixed sum when signing the licensing agreement and then pays a royalty of 2 to 5 percent of sales over the life of the contract (five to seven years with an option for renewal is one common way to structure such agreements). The exact amount of the royalty will depend on the amount of assistance given and the relative bargaining power of the two parties. In 2005, the total paid to American firms in royalties and license fees amounted to $57.4 billion, versus only $24.5 billion that U.S. firms paid out to foreign licensors.

>>Where Will Your Cargo End Up?

A new naval patrol ship drops anchor in front of cargo vessel in the bay of Jakarta, Indonesia, in August 2004. Thailand will join three other Southeast Asian navies in patrolling the vital Strait of Malacca shipping lane to combat piracy and terrorism, Indonesia's military chief said.

The 2003 release of the movie *Pirates of the Caribbean* pushed actor Johnny Depp's career into the stratosphere, and the arrival of the second installment in 2006 continued this ascent. Swashbuckling is back on the big screen.

But pirates are not just movie characters. The beginning exporter may find that real piracy is a threat to precious cargo. The danger of being a sailor is increasing because of piracy. The number of sailors killed on the high seas in early 2004 was nearly double the number for the same period in 2003.

Over 2,000 sailors were taken hostage in the 10 years from 1992 to 2002. Pirates today can be anyone from highly trained guerrillas to rogue military units (such as in Indonesia) to international criminal gangs or cartels. Pirates might belong to international terrorist organizations (particularly Abu Sayaf out of the Philippines, which has strong links to al Qaeda as well as Asian crime syndicates and the heroin trade), or they might simply be local down-and-out fishermen who see a rich prize steaming by and can't resist trying to capture it (poverty has driven many to piracy in the Caribbean, Nigeria, Bangladesh, and elsewhere). The main areas pirates seem to operate in are west of Indonesian waters to as far east as Taiwan and the Philippines (favoring the vital shipping lanes through the Malacca Strait and the dangerous waters of the South China Sea), as well as off the coast of Brazil,

off the Somali coast of East Africa, and off West Africa. The vital Malacca Strait, in particular, is plagued by pirates, as $500 billion in goods passes through the strait annually, sometimes as many as 600 ships a day. The Strait, which in some places is less than a mile wide, is a target-rich environment for pirates and one that is not particularly well policed, although Indonesia, Malaysia, and Singapore signed an agreement in 2004 to coordinate patrols there.

Most ships are relatively defenseless: Crews are small and seldom carry weapons. They rely instead on antipiracy devices, such as carpet tacks spread on decks, fire hoses, deck patrols, dummies set at the railings at night, brilliant deck lights, and new satellite tracking devices that can help the International Maritime Bureau and local navies locate hijacked ships. But it is nearly impossible to keep determined pirates off a ship, and it is best for a crew not to resist (as in many cases pirates do not kidnap or kill). Some shipping companies that have the resources have employed more high-tech and expensive measures, such as wiring decks to administer lethal electric charges, closed-circuit TV cameras to detect someone slipping aboard a ship, and, particularly in the case of cruise ships, armed mercenaries (some cruise lines are known to use Nepalese Gurkhas).

Nor is piracy just financially motivated. According to Jonathan Pearce, "There is increasingly an *ideological slant* to modern piracy. In Indonesia, it appears that Islamic militants, like terrorists the world over, are mixing their religious fervour with the juicy temptations of crime. I am frankly surprised that there has not been more written on how easy it would be for a terrorist group to get hold of even a small-sized motor boat, fill it chockfull of explosives, sail it up the Thames, the Rhine or any other major river you can think of, and blow it up."

Source: Jonathan Pearce, "Modern Piracy on the High Seas," February 18, 2004, www.samizdata.net/blog/archives/005583.htm (July 28, 2004); "Pirates Attack LPG Tanker off Indonesia," *The Business Times*, July 28, 2004, http://business-times.asia1.com.sg/sub/shippingtimes/story/0,4574,123788,00.html (July 29, 2004); and "Review of Dangerous Waters," www.self-help-hub.com/Dangerous_Waters_Modern_Piracy_and_Terror_on_the_High_Seas_04 52284139.html (July 29, 2004).

In the past, licensing was not a primary source of income for international firms. This changed in recent years, however, especially in the United States, because (1) the courts began upholding patent infringement claims more than they used to, (2) patent holders became more vigilant in suing violators, and (3) the federal government pressed foreign governments to enforce their patent laws.

This forced foreign companies to obtain licenses instead of making illegal copies. Texas Instruments (TI), for example, sued nine Japanese electronics manufacturers for using its

A woman sits beside her stall with Pierre Cardin shirts on a Hanoi street in June 2004. The shirts are made under French designer Pierre Cardin's firm license by a local garment factory. Each shirt sells for around 10 US dollars.

patented processes without paying licensing fees. The defendants have paid the company over $1 billion since 1986. Although the company does not publish its royalty receipts in its income statements, to give you an idea of the magnitude of the earnings from royalties associated with its 6,000 patents, TI announced 10-year agreements with both Hyundai Electronics and Samsung Electronics. Each of these agreements was projected to yield royalty payments of more than $1 billion to Texas Instruments.[2]

Technology is not the only thing that is licensed. In the fashion industry, a number of designers license the use of their names. Pierre Cardin, one of the largest such licensors, reported over 900 licenses in over 170 countries for everything from a broad range of clothing to such items as skis, frying pans, sardines, floor tiles, and silk cigarettes. These licenses have earned the company approximately $75 million annually. As Mr. Cardin himself commented, "If someone asked me to do toilet paper, I'd do it. Why not?"[3]

Are you giving Coca-Cola free advertising on your t-shirt? The company's manager for merchandise licensing expects the company to make millions from an agreement with the founder of Gloria Vanderbilt. He says the firm agreed to the arrangement because "clothes enhance our image. The money is not important."

Another industry, magazine publishing, is licensing overseas editions. For example, you can buy *Cosmopolitan* in over 100 countries, and it is printed in 32 different languages.[4] *Playboy* is available in 20 different international editions, in addition to the U.S. version.[5]

Despite the opportunity to obtain a sizable income from licensing, many firms, especially those that produce high-tech products, will not grant licenses. They fear that a licensee will become a competitor upon expiration of the agreement or that it will aggressively seek to market the products outside its territory. At one time, licensors routinely inserted a clause in the licensing agreement that prohibited exports, but most governments will not accept such a prohibition.

franchising

A form of licensing in which one firm contracts with another to operate a certain type of business under an established name according to specific rules

Franchising

Firms have also gone overseas with a different kind of licensing—**franchising.** Franchising permits the franchisee to sell products or services under a highly publicized brand name and a well-proven set of procedures with a carefully developed and controlled marketing strategy. Of some 500 U.S. franchisers with approximately 50,000 outlets worldwide, fast-food operations (such as McDonald's, Kentucky Fried Chicken, Subway, and Tastee-Freeze) are the most numerous—McDonald's alone has approximately 30,000 restaurants in 120 countries outside the United States. Other types of franchisers are hotels (Hilton), business services (Muzak, The UPS Store), fitness (Curves, Jazzercise), home maintenance (Service-Master, Nationwide Exterminating), and automotive products (Midas).

management contract

An arrangement by which one firm provides management in all or specific areas to another firm

Management Contract

The **management contract** is an arrangement under which a company provides managerial know-how in some or all functional areas to another party for a fee that typically ranges from 2 to 5 percent of sales. International companies make such contracts with (1) firms in which they have no ownership (examples: Hilton Hotel provides management for nonowned overseas hotels that use the Hilton name, and Delta provides management assistance to foreign airlines), (2) joint venture partners, and (3) wholly owned subsidiaries. The last arrangement is made solely for the purpose of allowing the parent to siphon off some of the subsidiary's profits. This becomes extremely important when, as in many foreign exchange–poor nations, the parent firm is limited in the amount of profits it can repatriate. Moreover, because the fee is an expense, the subsidiary receives a tax benefit.

contract manufacturing

An arrangement in which one firm contracts with another to produce products to its specifications but assumes responsibility for marketing

Contract Manufacturing

International firms employ **contract manufacturing** in two ways. One way is as a means of entering a foreign market without investing in plant facilities. The firm contracts with a local manufacturer to produce products for it according to its specifications. The firm's sales organization markets the products under its own brand.

When Gates Rubber licensed its V belt technology to General Tire's Chilean plant, it drew up a novel licensing agreement that included contract manufacturing. General Tire was obliged to produce part of its output with the Gates label. Gates executives knew that in Chile, once General Tire began production, the government would stop the importation of all V belts, including theirs. Gates would gain in a number of ways: (1) It would earn a royalty on all belts made in Chile, (2) it would have belts made in Chile to Gates' specifications without making any investment in production facilities, and (3) competition from a dozen importers would be eliminated. There would be only one local competitor, General Tire. General Tire gained because it increased its product mix and offered another product to its present channels of distribution.

The second way is to subcontract assembly work or the production of parts to independent companies overseas. Although the international firm has no equity in the subcontractor, this practice does resemble foreign direct investment. When the international firm is the largest or only customer of the subcontractors, it has in effect created in another country a new company that generates employment and foreign exchange for the host nation. Frequently, the international firm will lend capital to the foreign contractor in the same way that a global or multinational firm will lend funds to its subsidiary. Because of these similarities, this practice is sometimes called *foreign direct investment without investment.*

EQUITY-BASED MODES OF ENTRY

When management does decide to make a foreign direct investment, it usually has several alternatives available, though not all of them may be feasible in a particular country. They are:

1. Wholly owned subsidiary

2. Joint venture

3. Strategic alliances

Wholly Owned Subsidiary

A company that wishes to own a foreign subsidiary outright may (1) start from the ground up by building a new plant (greenfield investment), (2) acquire a going concern, or (3) purchase its distributor, thus obtaining a distribution network familiar with its products. In this last case, of course, production facilities will typically have to be built.

Historically, firms making a foreign direct investment generally have preferred wholly owned subsidiaries, but they have not had a marked preference for any of the three means of obtaining them. However, this has not been the case for foreign investors in the United States, who have demonstrated a general preference for acquiring going concerns for the instant access to the market they provide. Moreover, they also have one less competitor after the purchase. Figure 16.1 shows the level of investments into the United States by foreign investors that was used for acquiring American firms versus creating new businesses. In 2005, 91 percent of the $86.8 billion that was invested was used for acquiring companies, versus only $7.6 billion that was spent to create new businesses. The average size of an acquisition in recent years has been about nine times that of an investment to create a new firm.

Of course, international companies do not use merger and acquisition (M&A) only to enter the United States. As Table 16.2 shows, cross-border M&As are a prominent characteristic of foreign direct investment across almost all nations of the world. In 2004, of total foreign direct investments of $648 billion, nearly 59 percent ($381 billion) was spent worldwide on cross-border M&As. The proportion of FDI that was accounted for by M&As is even higher in the developed countries. In 2004, over 83 percent ($316 billion) of the $380 billion in FDI inflows was associated with cross-border M&As.

Sometimes it is not possible to have a wholly owned foreign subsidiary. The host government may not permit it, the firm may lack either capital or expertise to undertake the investment alone, or there may be tax and other advantages that favor another form of investment, such as a joint venture.

Joint Venture

A **joint venture** may be (1) a corporate entity formed by an international company and local owners, (2) a corporate entity formed by two international companies for the purpose of doing business in a third market, (3) a corporate entity formed by a government

joint venture
A cooperative effort among two or more organizations that share a common interest in a business enterprise or undertaking

FIGURE 16.1

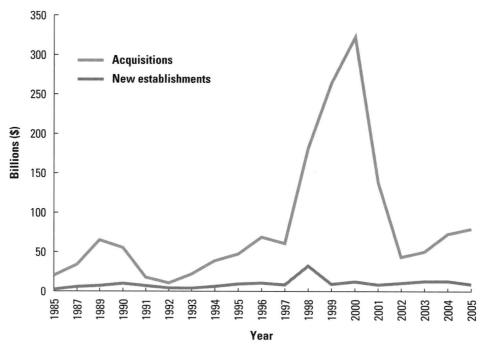

Sources: *Survey of Current Business,* June, various years, http://www.bea.gov/bea/pubs.htm (August 3, 2006).

agency (usually in the country of investment) and an international firm, or (4) a cooperative undertaking between two or more firms of a limited-duration project. Large construction jobs such as a dam or an airport are frequently handled by this last form.

> *Several years ago, Ford and Volkswagen formed a novel joint venture in which their operations in Argentina and Brazil were merged into a holding company, Autolatina, in an effort to eliminate the losses suffered by both. The joint venture, owned 51 percent by Volkswagen and 49 percent by Ford, assembled products based on VW and Ford designs, but both companies marketed the vehicles through their own distribution channels. Although sales subsequently reached $7.58 billion, the companies decided to terminate the operation. One industry expert says that Ford wanted to leave because Autolatina did not fit its new global strategy of having global vehicles. In a news release, the companies said the termination of the joint venture reflected "the necessity of the companies to make better use of the force and resources of their worldwide organizations."[6]*

Sometimes, forming a joint venture can allow the partners to avoid making expensive and time-consuming investments of their own, while simultaneously helping to avoid a dangerous competition with another company.

> *When the CEO of General Mills decided to enter the European market, where a very tough rival, Kellogg, was entrenched, he knew it would be very expensive to set up manufacturing facilities and a huge marketing force. However, he knew that another food giant, Nestlé, the world's largest food company, had a famous name in Europe, a number of manufacturing plants, and a strong distribution system. It also lacked strong cereal brand names, something that General Mills, the number-two American cereal company, had. Just two weeks after the initial discussions, General Mills and Nestlé formed a joint venture: Cereal Partners Worldwide. General Mills provided the cereal technology, brand names, and cereal marketing expertise. Nestlé supplied its name, distribution channels, and production capacity. Cereal Partners Worldwide distributes cereals everywhere in the world except the United States and Canada. Within two years, the new company had already passed Quaker Oats, the longtime number two in Europe after Kellogg, and the company's profit margins have been increasing steadily. According to General Mills's vice chairman, building factories and distribution channels from scratch would have taken years: "We felt a sense of urgency." General Mills and PepsiCo won approval from the European Union to merge their European snack food businesses into what became the largest company in the European snack market.[7]*

| TABLE 16.2 | Cross-Border Mergers and Acquisitions for Selected Countries and Regions, 1990–2005 (in billions of U.S. dollars) |

	1990	1995	1996	1997	1998	1999	2000	2001	2002	2003	2004	2005
World												
Sales	151	187	227	305	532	766	1144	594	370	297	381	716
Purchases	151	187	227	305	532	766	1144	594	370	297	381	716
Developed countries												
Sales	134	164	1886	232	443	680	1056	496	308	244	316	598
Purchases	143	173	197	269	509	701	1088	534	341	257	340	626
Developing countries												
Sales	16	17	36	67	83	74	71	86	45	40	55	101
Purchases	7	13	30	35	22	63	49	56	28	31	40	83
United States												
Sales	55	53	68	82	210	252	324	185	73	70	82	106
Purchases	28	57	61	81	137	120	159	96	78	82	110	148
Canada												
Sales	6	12	11	9	16	24	77	42	16	5	20	27
Purchases	3	13	9	19	36	19	40	39	13	16	34	23
European Union												
Sales	62	75	82	115	188	357	587	213	194	126	179	429
Purchases	87	81	97	142	284	517	802	327	214	121	165	387
United Kingdom												
Sales	29	36	31	40	91	133	180	69	53	31	58	172
Purchases	26	30	36	58	95	214	382	112	69	57	47	91
France												
Sales	8	8	14	18	17	24	35	14	30	18	20	32
Purchases	22	9	15	21	31	89	159	59	34	9	15	46
Germany												
Sales	6	8	12	12	19	40	247	49	47	25	36	63
Purchases	7	19	18	13	67	86	59	57	45	20	19	42
Latin America & Caribbean												
Sales	10	9	21	41	64	42	45	36	22	12	25	31
Purchases	2	4	8	11	13	45	19	27	12	11	16	14
South, East, & South-East Asia												
Sales	4	6	10	19	16	28	21	33	17	20	24	45
Purchases	3	7	18	18	6	11	21	25	11	17	19	35
Africa												
Sales	1	1	2	4	3	3	3	16	5	6	5	11
Purchases	0	1	2	3	3	6	7	3	2	1	3	16

Note: *Sales* refers to the dollar volume of sales of companies from the specified nation to companies headquartered in other nations. *Purchases* refers to the dollar volume of purchases of foreign companies by companies headquartered in the specified nation.

Source: Various country fact sheets; *World Investment Report 2003*, United Nations Conference on Trade and Development (New York: United Nations, 2003); and *World Investment Report 2006*, United Nations Conference on Trade and Development (New York: United Nations, 2006).

When the government of a host country requires that companies have some local participation, foreign firms must engage in joint ventures with local owners to do business in that country. In some situations, however, a foreign firm will seek local partners even when there is no local requirement to do so.

Virgin, 7-Eleven, MTV, and others are all MVNOs. A Mobile Virtual Network Operator is a mobile phone operator that does not own its own network. Instead, MVNOs have arrangements with traditional mobile operators to buy minutes of use (MOU) for sale to their own customers. So Virgin Mobile USA actually uses the Sprint network: Sprint has the equipment, and Virgin adds cachet and the ability to target the youth market. America Movil of Mexico targets the Hispanic community in the United States. Big media brands such as Disney are also interested in the possibility of being MVNOs, since the ability to watch television is the next frontier in mobile phones.[8]

Strong Nationalism   Strong nationalistic sentiment may cause the foreign firm to try to lose its identity by joining with local investors. Care must be taken with this strategy, however. Although a large number of people in many developing countries dislike multinationals for "exploiting" them, they still believe, often with good reason, that the products of the foreign companies are superior to those of purely national firms. One solution to this ambivalence has been to form a joint venture in which the local partners are highly visible, give it an indigenous name, and then advertise that a foreign firm (actually the partner) is supplying the technology. Even wholly owned subsidiaries have followed this strategy.

Expertise, Tax, and Other Benefits   Other factors that influence companies to enter joint ventures are the ability to acquire expertise that is lacking, the special tax benefits some governments extend to companies with local partners, and the need for additional capital and experienced personnel.

Merck, one of the world's largest makers of ethical drugs, spent $313 million to acquire 50.5 percent of Banyu Pharmaceutical in Japan. Management had been dissatisfied with the performance of Merck's Japanese subsidiary in the world's second-largest ethical drug market. With this acquisition, the 600-person sales force of Merck-Japan was augmented by Banyu's 350 sales representatives. Merck's chairman said, "To bring new products effectively to market in Japan required a larger and more effective marketing organization. With a controlling interest in Banyu, I would hope for a better penetration of the Japanese market." Merck subsequently purchased the remainder of Banyu and made it a wholly owned company, increasing its ability to control and integrate its operations worldwide.

Some firms, as a matter of policy, enter joint ventures to reduce investment risk. Their strategy is to enter into a joint venture with either native partners or another worldwide company. Still others, such as Ford and Volkswagen, have joined together to achieve economies of scale. Incidentally, any division of ownership in a joint venture is possible unless there are specific legal requirements.

Disadvantages of Joint Ventures   Although a joint venture arrangement offers the advantage of a smaller commitment of financial and managerial resources and thus less risk, there are some disadvantages for the foreign firm. One, obviously, is that profits must be shared. Furthermore, if the law allows the foreign investor to have no more than 49 percent participation, it may not have control. If the stock markets in these countries are small or nonexistent, it is generally impossible to distribute the shares widely enough to permit the foreign firm with its 49 percent to be the largest stockholder.

Lack of control over the joint venture is the reason why many companies resist making such arrangements. They feel that they must have tight control of their foreign subsidiaries to obtain an efficient allocation of investments and production and to maintain a coordinated marketing plan worldwide. For example, local partners might wish to export to markets that the global company serves from its own plants, or they might want to make the complete product locally when the global company's strategy is to produce only certain components there and import the rest from other subsidiaries.

In the recent past, numerous governments of developing nations passed laws requiring local majority ownership for the purpose of giving control of firms within their borders to their own citizens. Despite these laws, control with a minority ownership may still be feasible.

Control with Minority Ownership   There have been occasions when the foreign partner has ensured its control by taking 49 percent of the shares and giving 2 percent or more to its local law firm or another trusted national. Another method is to take in a local majority

partner, such as a government agency, an insurance company, or a financial institution, that is content to invest merely for a return while leaving the venture's management to the foreign partner (this is called a "sleeping" partner).[9] If neither arrangement can be made, the foreign company may still control the joint venture, at least in the areas of major concern, by means of non-ownership-based control mechanisms such as a *management contract.*

Control of Joint Ventures through Management Contracts   Management contracts, which were discussed earlier in this chapter under nonequity-based modes of entry, can enable the global partner to control many aspects of a joint venture even when holding only a minority position. If it supplies key personnel, such as the production and technical managers, the global company can be assured of the product quality with which its name may be associated. It may also be able to earn additional income by selling the joint venture inputs manufactured in the home plant. This is possible because the larger global company is more vertically integrated. A local paint factory, for example, might have to import certain semi-processed pigments and driers that the foreign partner produces in its home country for domestic operations. If these can be purchased elsewhere at a lower price, the local majority could insist on other sources of supply.

This rarely happens, because the production and technical managers can argue that only inputs from their employer will produce a satisfactory product. They are the experts, and they generally have the final word.

Strategic Alliances

strategic alliances
Partnerships between competitors, customers, or suppliers that may take one or more of various forms, both equity and non equity

Faced with expanding global competition, the growing cost of research, product development, and marketing, and the need to move faster in carrying out their global strategies, many firms are forming **strategic alliances** with customers, suppliers, and competitors. In fact, consultants Ernst & Young in a 12-country study found that 65 percent of non-U.S. and 75 percent of U.S. companies are engaged in some form of strategic alliance.[10] The aim of these companies is to achieve faster market entry and start-up; gain access to new products, technologies, and markets; and share costs, resources, and risks. Alliances include various types of partnerships and may or may not include equity. Companies wanting to share technology may cross-license their technology (each will license its technology to the other). If their aim is to pool research and design resources, they may form an R&D partnership.

> *Intel, Motorola, and Advanced Micro Devices, three of the most prominent names in the computer chip industry, announced the formation of a not-for-profit company named EUV (Extreme Ultraviolet). Valued at $250 million, the project was the largest American commercial research partnership ever formed up to that time between industry and government. The three government laboratories will get the rights to use the resulting technologies as they wish, and the computer chip companies will have the right to use them to create faster chips. In 2005, EUV Technology's LPR1016 Reflectometer was awarded R&D Magazine's "R&D 100 Award" and heralded by the magazine's editors as "one of the 100 most technologically significant products introduced into the marketplace over the past year."[11]*
>
> *Nokia, Ericsson, and Motorola (which at the time jointly accounted for over 75 percent of the world's mobile phone sales) formed a joint venture with Psion (then a major manufacturer of handheld computers). An objective of the venture was to license Psion's software and develop it into an operating system for the next generation of "smart" mobile phones that could link to the Internet and perform many of the functions of a palm-top computer. Motorola subsequently left the alliance, but Japan's Panasonic, Germany's Siemens, Korea's Samsung, and the Swedish-Japanese Sony Ericsson joint venture subsequently joined as equity partners in this alliance. The alliance is intended to enhance the competitiveness of the partners' future lines of wireless phones and other handheld devices as well as reduce their potential dependence on Microsoft and its Windows CE operating software.[12]*

Alliances May Be Joint Ventures   Other companies carry the cooperation further by forming joint ventures in manufacturing and marketing.

> *Nissan of Japan was a struggling automaker in the 1990s, with $20 billion in debt and declining market share. Renault of France decided to form an alliance with Nissan rather than merge the companies. Renault sent Carlos Ghosn to become CEO and president of Nissan. Ghosn's team developed and implemented an aggressive turnaround plan, one that has*

provided benefits for both partners. They have leveraged their size and competencies to enter new markets more rapidly and with lower costs, since they do not need to build new plants. For example, Renault has used Nissan's assembly plants in Mexico, and Nissan uses Renault's Brazilian plant and distribution network. The alliance has increased sales, profitability, and market capitalization for both of the partners. In 2006, these two partners began discussing the possibility of an alliance with another ailing automaker, General Motors of the United States.

Trading versus Pooling Alliances A useful distinction can be made between pooling and trading alliances. *Pooling alliances* are driven by similarity and integration, while *trading alliances* are driven by the logic of contributing dissimilar resources. These two types are typically different in their goals (common vs. compatible goals), optimal structures (many vs. few partners), and managerial challenges (low vs. high coordination needs).[13]

Alliances versus Mergers and Acquisitions Generally mergers and acquisitions are not considered alliances. However, both may be ways for firms to get their hands on new technology, by either acquiring or working with smaller, innovative firms.

The merger between Canadian brewer Molson and U.S. brewer Coors was analyzed as a union of two "struggling" mid-size beer companies. Sandoz, a Swiss pharmaceutical manufacturer, acquired Gerber for $3.7 billion in order to double the size of its food products division. Two years later, because of the increased global competition and the mounting cost of technology, Sandoz and Ciba Geigy, another Swiss drug company, merged to form Novartis, which then became the second-largest pharmaceutical firm in the world.

Future of Alliances Many alliances fail or are taken over by one of the partners. The existence of two or more partners, which are often competitors as well as partners and typically have differences in strategies, operating practices, and organizational cultures, often causes alliances to be difficult to manage, particularly in rapidly changing international competitive environments.[14] Alliances can also allow a partner to acquire the firm's technological or other competencies, and thereby raise important competitive concerns. The management consulting firm McKinsey & Co. surveyed 150 companies whose alliances with Japanese partners had been terminated. It found that three-quarters of the alliances had been taken over by Japanese partners.

Despite the challenges involved with forming and managing alliances successfully, there is no question that some alliances have accomplished what they set out to accomplish. CFM International, the alliance between General Electric and France's Snecma Moteurs, has been producing jet engines for more than two decades. Airbus Industrie, an alliance among British, French, German, and Spanish aircraft manufacturers, is now the world's largest commercial aircraft producer. It seems that alliances in their various forms will continue to be used as important strategic and tactical weapons, particularly given the financial, technological, political, and other challenges facing companies involved in increasingly competitive international marketplaces.

Channels of Distribution

Another entry mode decision to be made concerns channels of distribution. The channel system through which a product and its title pass from the producer to the user involves both controllable and uncontrollable variables. We shall discuss the uncontrollable aspects in this section, where we examine all the uncontrollable forces, and then return to them in Chapter 17, when we will consider them as controllable variables in the marketing mix.

How can a channel of distribution be both controllable and uncontrollable? It is controllable to the extent that the channel captain* is free to choose from the available channel members those that will enable the firm to reach its target market, perform the functions it requires at a reasonable cost, and permit it the amount of control it desires. If the company considers that the established channels are inadequate, it may assemble a different network.

---

*The *channel captain* is the dominant and controlling member of a channel of distribution.

For example, Coca-Cola became dissatisfied with its penetration in China and India of only large urban areas. It launched efforts to penetrate tiny villages. This required it to send dealers into farm villages to reach the tiniest retailers, including betel-nut vendors and repair shops, which sell small quantities of the diminutive (6.5-ounce, 200-milliliter) contoured glass bottles per year.[15]

International Channel-of-Distribution Members

The selection of channel-of-distribution members to link the producer with the foreign user depends, first of all, on the method of entry into the market. As was discussed earlier in this chapter, to supply a foreign market, a firm must either export to a foreign country or manufacture in it. If the decision is to export, the firm may do so *directly* or *indirectly*. Figure 16.2 shows that management has considerable latitude in forming the channels.

INDIRECT EXPORTING

For indirect exporting, a number of U.S.-based exporters (A) sell for the manufacturer, (B) buy for their overseas customers, (C) buy and sell for their own account, or (D) purchase on behalf of foreign middlemen or users. Although each type of exporter usually operates in the manner explained below, any given company may actually perform one or more of these functions.

A. Exporters That Sell for the Manufacturer

1. *Manufacturers' export agents* act as the international representatives for various noncompeting domestic manufacturers. They usually direct promotion, consummate sales, invoice, ship, and handle the financing. They commonly are paid a commission for carrying out these functions in the name of the manufacturer.

2. *Export management companies (EMCs)* act as the export department for several noncompeting manufacturers. They also transact business in the name of the manufacturer and handle the routine details of shipping and promotion. When the EMC works on a commission basis, the manufacturer invoices the customer directly and carries any financing required by the foreign buyer. However, most EMCs work on a buy-and-sell arrangement under which they pay the manufacturer, resell the product abroad, and invoice the customer directly. Depending on the arrangement, the EMC may act in the name of the firm it represents or in its own name.

3. *International trading companies* are similar to EMCs in that they also act as agents for some companies and as merchant wholesalers for others. This, however, is only part of their activities. They frequently export as well as import, own their own transportation facilities, and provide financing. W. R. Grace was at one time a major trading company that operated on the Pacific coast of South America. It owned sugar mills, large import houses, various manufacturing plants, a steamship company, and an airline. Although a number of European and American international trading companies have been in operation for centuries, certainly the most diversified and the largest are the Japanese **sogo shosha** (general trading companies).

   a. *Sogo shosha:* The general trading companies were originally established by the *zaibatsu*—centralized, family-dominated economic groups, such as Mitsui, Mitsubishi, and Sumitomo—to be the heart of their commercial operations. The general trading companies obtained export markets, raw materials, and technical assistance for other companies of the zaibatsu and also imported goods for resale. Included in the zaibatsu were not only banks and general trading companies but also transportation, insurance, and real estate companies and various manufacturing firms. Although the zaibatsu were forced to dissolve after World War II, the companies that had been their major components survived. Although unified ownership and management ceased after World War II, cross-shareholdings and collaborative relationships resulted in the close coordination of many business activities among the affiliated companies. In recent years, the level of cross-shareholdings and coordination has evidenced some decline, a development promoted by liberalization of

sogo shosha
The largest of the Japanese general trading companies

FIGURE 16.2

International
Channels of
Distribution

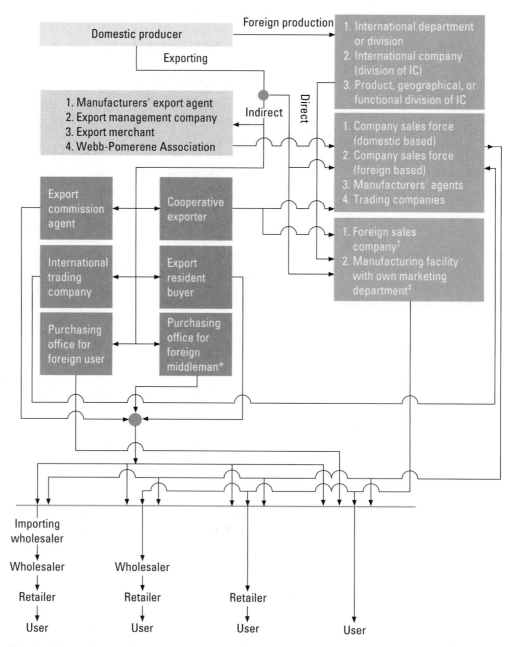

*There should be no direct connection between this category and the user. For simplification, a separate line to eliminate the user is not shown.

†Can be wholly owned or a joint venture. The foreign sales company may sell imports as well as local production from the licensee, contract manufacturer, or joint venture.

‡Can be wholly owned, a joint venture, or a licensee.

Source: From *World Development Report 1999/2000* by World Bank. Copyright by World Bank. Reproduced with permission of World Bank in the format textbook via Copyright Clearance Center.

financial markets, pressures for improved performance and corporate governance, and other factors.

In the 1980s, Japan had several thousand general trading companies. There are 20 general trading companies with more than 2,000 Japanese and overseas business locations. Their combined sales amount to over $1 trillion annually.[16] Mitsui & Co., for example, had sales of over $10.5 billion in 2006 and employed 6,089 employees in 172 offices worldwide.[17] Although Mitsui & Co. is huge, it is only one company in the Mitsui Group, which consists of several hundred companies encompassing a wide range of businesses, including steelmaking, shipbuilding, banking, insurance, paper, electronics, petroleum, warehousing, tourism, and nuclear energy. The Mitsui Group is not a legal entity but exists as an informal organization of major enterprises that have related interests and related financial structures. They cooperate in promoting the economic interests of group members. To ensure cooperation, the top executives of the major components of the former Mitsui zaibatsu meet for a weekly luncheon.

b. *Korean general trading companies:* Similar in scope to the Japanese sogo shosha, the Korean general trading companies are owned by the huge Korean diversified conglomerates called *chaebol.* They are responsible for a major part of Korea's exports and are also that country's principal importers of key raw materials.

c. *Export trading companies:* Impressed by the success of the Japanese, Taiwanese, and Korean general trading companies, the Reagan administration obtained passage of the Export Trading Company Act. This measure provided the mechanism for creating a new indirect export channel, the **export trading company (ETC).** For the first time in U.S. history, businesses were permitted to join together to export goods and services or offer export facilitating services without fear of violating antitrust legislation. Bank holding companies were also permitted to participate in ETCs. This has not only increased the ability of trading companies to finance export transactions but also given them access to the banks' extensive international information systems. Furthermore, because ETCs can import as well as export, they can engage in countertrade by selling their customers' products in other markets. Concerns raised within the World Trade Organization regarding the ETC Act led to a revocation in 2002 of many of the aspects of this act. Any potential exporter may apply to the Department of Commerce for a *certificate of review,* a legal document that provides immunity from state and federal antitrust prosecution and significant protection from certain private antitrust lawsuits. The certificate allows firms and associations to engage in joint price setting and joint bidding and gives them the freedom to divide export markets among companies and jointly own warranty, service, and training centers in various overseas markets. Note that the benefits of the ETC Act are available to *all exporters,* not just export trading companies. The Commerce Department has issued over 100 certificates covering 4,400 companies. Most companies that have received certificates are export intermediaries for two or more firms from the same industry, although now the majority of the certificates are being issued to groups of companies. For example, the National Tooling and Machining Association is a national trade association with 3,150 members. The American Film Marketing Association (170 members) is another example.

export trading company (ETC)
A firm established principally to export domestic goods and services and to help unrelated companies export their products

B. Exporters That Buy for Their Overseas Customers

1. *Export commission agents* represent overseas purchasers, such as import firms and large industrial users. They are paid a commission by the purchaser for acting as resident buyers in industrialized nations.

C. Exporters That Buy and Sell for Their Own Account

1. *Export merchants* purchase products directly from the manufacturer and then sell, invoice, and ship them in their own names so that foreign customers have no direct dealings with the manufacturer, as they do in the case of an export agent. If export merchants have an exclusive right to sell the manufacturer's products in an overseas territory, they are generally called *export distributors.* Some EMCs may actually be export distributors for a number of their clients.

2. Sometimes called *piggyback exporters,* **cooperative exporters** are established international manufacturers that sell the products of other companies in foreign markets along with their own. Carriers (exporters) may purchase and resell in their own name, or they may work on a commission basis. Carriers, like EMCs, serve as the export departments for the firms they represent. Large companies, such as General Electric and Borg-Warner, have been acting as piggyback exporters for years.

cooperative exporters
Established international manufacturers that export other manufacturers' goods as well as their own

3. *Webb-Pomerene Associations* are organizations of competing firms that have joined together for the sole purpose of export trade. At this time, there are fewer than 25 such associations. The Motion Picture Association (MPA), which is the legacy of a Webb-Pomerene Association, is the primary organization combating movie piracy around the world.

D. Exporters That Purchase for Foreign Users and Middlemen

1. Large foreign users, such as mining, petroleum, and international construction companies, buy for their own use overseas. The purchasing departments of all the worldwide companies are continually buying for their foreign affiliates, and both foreign governments and foreign firms maintain purchasing offices in industrialized countries.

2. *Export resident buyers* perform essentially the same functions as export commission agents. However, they are generally more closely associated with a foreign firm. They may be appointed as the official buying representatives and paid a retainer, or they may even be employees. This is in contrast to the export commission agent, who usually represents a number of overseas buyers and works on a transaction-by-transaction basis.

DIRECT EXPORTING

If the firm chooses to do its own exporting, it has four basic types of overseas middlemen from which to choose: (a) manufacturers' agents, (b) distributors, (c) retailers, and (d) trading companies. These may be serviced by sales personnel who either travel to the market or are based in it. If the sales volume is sufficient, a foreign sales company may be established to take the place of the wholesale importer. The manufacturing affiliates of most worldwide companies also import from home country plants or from other subsidiaries products that they themselves do not produce.

manufacturers' agents
Independent sales representatives of various noncompeting suppliers

a. **Manufacturers' agents** are residents of the country or region in which they are conducting business for the firm. They represent various noncompeting foreign suppliers, and they take orders in those firms' names. Manufacturers' agents usually work on a commission basis, pay their own expenses, and do not assume any financial responsibility. They often stock the products of some of their suppliers, thus combining the functions of agent and wholesale distributor.

distributors
Independent importers that buy for their own account for resale

b. **Distributors,** or *wholesale importers,* are independent merchants that buy for their own account. They import and stock for resale. Distributors are usually specialists in a particular field, such as farm equipment or pharmaceuticals. They may be given exclusive representation and, in return, agree not to handle competing brands. Distributors may buy through manufacturers' agents when the exporter employs them, or they may send their orders directly to the exporting firm. Instead of hiring manufacturers' agents, exporters may employ their own salespeople to cover the territory and assist the distributors. For years, worldwide companies such as Caterpillar and Goodyear have utilized field representatives in export territories.

c. *Retailers,* especially of consumer products, are frequently direct importers. Contact on behalf of the exporter is maintained either by a manufacturers' agent or by the exporter's sales representative based in the territory or traveling from the home office.

trading companies
Firms that develop international trade and serve as intermediaries between foreign buyers and domestic sellers and vice versa

d. **Trading companies** are relatively unknown in the United States but are extremely important importers in other parts of the world. In a number of African nations, trading companies not only are the principal importers of goods ranging from consumer products to capital equipment but also export such raw materials as ore, palm oil, and coffee. In addition, they operate department stores, grocery stores, and agencies for automobiles and farm machinery. Although many trading companies are large, they are in no way comparable in either size or diversification (products and functions performed) to the sogo shosha. Trading companies in Brazil, Korea, Taiwan, and Malaysia are a recent development. They are of little use to exporters to those countries inasmuch as their primary function is to promote their own country's exports. On the other hand, the English *importer/factor,* which

Piracy as Product Diffusion

Ash, Pikachu, and Misty (background) in 4Kids Entertainment's animated adventure "Pokemon3," distributed by Warner Bros. Pictures.

Although we earlier discussed the threats to shipping from pirates, piracy can also contribute to the global spread of a product—sort of market entry by accident.

Japanese *anime* has global sales of $80 billion, 10 times what it was a decade ago. Japanese Prime Minister Junichiro Koizumi has called it the "savior of Japanese culture." Disney has purchased the American right to a number of anime films. The Cartoon Network shows several anime series as part of its Adult Swim programming. TOKOPOP will publish 400 volumes of translated Japanese comics for U.S. consumption.

Two decades ago there was no U.S. market for Japanese anime. The change occurred not through a concerted push from Japanese media companies but in response to American fans who pulled anime in.

Although Japanese anime was exported to the West in the early 1960s, some saw it as inappropriate for American children and by the late 1960s it was available only in Japanese overseas communities. The advent of the video tape recorder allowed dubbing and sharing, and soon anime fans were contacting both Japanese and G.I.s stationed in Japan for tapes. Fan clubs emerged as essentially lending libraries and dubbing centers. In the late 1980s and 1990s amateurs began dubbing these tapes

into English: This "fansubbing" spread. In the early 1990s large-scale anime conventions brought artists and distributors from Japan, who were astonished to see this thriving content they had never marketed. They returned to Japan ready to service this market commercially. The fan clubs continued their operations, but stopped fansubbing and distributing titles as they became commercially available.

This "piracy" is now supported by the commercial industry, which in fact sponsors events where fan-made *manga*,* highly derivative of the commercial product, is sold. The media companies use these events to publicize their own releases, spot new talent, and monitor shifts in audience tastes.

The idea that some piracy actually helps to diffuse new products is not limited to Japanese anime. It has also been tested for software.

Careful analysis actually found that software piracy is not necessarily harmful to a software firm seeking to launch a new product, since it establishes initial adopters (pirates) and speeds up software diffusion: These initial adopters then influence others to buy the product. Generally speaking, however, as the product diffuses in the market, the level of protection against piracy should be increased.

*Anime in Japan refers to an animated film, and manga is a printed cartoon.

Source: Henry Jenkins, "When Piracy Becomes Promotion," *MIT Technology Review,* August 10, 2004; Ernan Haruvy, Vijay Mahajan, and Ashutosh Prasad, "The Effect of Piracy on the Market Penetration of Subscription Software," *Journal of Business* 77 (April 2004), pp. S81–S108; and Ashutosh Prasad and Vijay Mahajan, "How Many Pirates Should a Software Firm Tolerate? An Analysis of Piracy Protection on the Diffusion of Software," *International Journal of Research in Marketing* 20, no. 4 (2003), pp. 337–53.

performs some of the functions of a trading company, is of value to exporters. It will, on behalf of foreign manufacturers, warehouse goods, price them for the local market, deliver anywhere in the country, and factor (buy the seller's accounts receivable). The exporter must still develop the sales, however. Another form of trading company is owned by the state. State trading companies handle exports and imports in North Korea and Cuba, and in noncommunist nations where an industry is a government monopoly, such as petroleum in Mexico, exporters or their agents must deal with these government-owned entities.

Wholesale Institutions   In developed nations, the marketer will be able to select wholesalers that take title to the goods (merchant wholesalers, rack jobbers, drop shippers, cash-and-carry wholesalers, truck jobbers) and those that do not (agents, brokers). However, just as in the United States, as retailers have become larger, they have sought to bypass wholesalers and purchase directly from local manufacturers and foreign suppliers.

Diversity of Wholesaling Structures   Generally, wholesaling and retailing structures vary with the stage of economic development. In developing countries that depend on imports to supply the market, the importing wholesalers are large and few in number and the channels are long. Historically, many of the importers were trading companies formed by international companies to import the machinery and supplies required by their local operation and to export raw materials for use in the home country plants. To obtain distributor prices, they were required by their suppliers to sell to other customers as well. Some of these operations became extremely diversified, owning automobile and industrial machinery agencies, grocery stores, and department stores. They literally could and did supply a complete city and an industry with all of its requirements.

As colonies became nations, the new governments began applying pressure to convert these trading companies to local ownership. Furthermore, these countries were industrializing, which meant more goods were being produced locally and fewer goods were being imported. Many of the local manufacturers were able to take control of the channels from the import jobber. To obtain more extensive market coverage, they canceled the importing wholesaler's exclusivity and gave their product lines to new wholesalers, many of which were formed by ex-employees of the importer. As economic development continued, markets broadened, permitting greater specialization by more and smaller wholesalers.

We began the chapter with a discussion of whether being first in the market meant profitability, and discovered that the answer is, "It depends." Whether one is first, an early follower, or a late entrant, there are still chances for success.

Summary

Explain the international market entry methods.

Methods of entering foreign markets can be assessed as nonequity- or equity-based. Nonequity-based modes of entry include indirect or direct exporting, turnkey projects, licensing, franchising, management contracts, and contract manufacturing. Equity-based modes of market entry include wholly owned subsidiaries, joint ventures, and strategic alliances.

Discuss the debate on whether being a market pioneer or a fast follower is most useful.

A firm can succeed from any position, as the examples illustrate. In general, however, a follower is more likely to succeed if it has lots of resources. Smaller, less-well-financed followers are less likely to be successful.

Identify two different forms of piracy and discuss which might be helpful and harmful to firms doing international business.

Piracy on the high seas is clearly harmful to the exporter and the importer, as well as to members of the ship crews. On the other hand, piracy as a form of distribution may or may not be harmful to the parties involved.

Discuss the channel members available to companies that export indirectly or directly or manufacture overseas.

Channel members are available to those who (1) indirectly export or are exporters that sell for manufacturers, (2) buy for their overseas customers, or (3) purchase for foreign users or middlemen. Direct exporters use manufacturers' agents, distributors, retailers, and trading companies. Firms that manufacture overseas generally have the same kinds of channel members as they have in their domestic market, although their manner of operation may be different from what they are accustomed to.

Key Words

indirect exporting (p. 427)

direct exporting (p. 427)

sales company (p. 427)

licensing (p. 428)

franchising (p. 430)

management contract (p. 430)

contract manufacturing (p. 430)

joint venture (p. 431)

strategic alliances (p. 435)

sogo shosha (p. 437)

export trading company (ETC) (p. 439)

cooperative exporters (p. 439)

manufacturers' agents (p. 440)

distributors (p. 440)

trading companies (p. 440)

1. What are the methods by which a firm can enter foreign markets?

2. What two forms of piracy are discussed in the chapter? Which one is never beneficial to an exporter? Which one might be beneficial?

3. What is the difference, if any, between a joint venture and a strategic alliance?

4. Under what conditions might a company prefer a joint venture to a wholly owned subsidiary when making a foreign investment?

5. Why would the foreign partner in a joint venture wish to have a management contract with the local partner?

6. Why would a global firm or multinational require that a wholly owned foreign subsidiary sign a management contract when it already owns the subsidiary?

7. What is indirect exporting, and how does it differ from direct exporting? What are the main types of indirect exporting, and what are the primary strengths and weaknesses of each type?

8. How do sogo shosha differ from their American counterparts?

9. What entry mode do fashion designers such as Pierre Cardin, and some high-tech firms like Texas Instruments, share in common?

---

globalEDGE globalEDGE.msu.edu

Use the globalEDGE™ site (http://globalEDGE.msu.edu) to complete the following exercises:

1. Your firm is a small international business (IB) consulting services provider that has thus far only had clients based in the United States. However, a recent internal initiative is encouraging the internationalization of your firm. Each IB consultant will be traveling for 50 to 75 percent of all work assignments. In developing your strategic plan for the next five years, you want to analyze future travel patterns. For this analysis, you wish to identify the 25 largest passenger airports in the world. A friend mentions to you that a Web site called *Geohive* lists this information. Find the list, and identify which countries are represented in this list. Do you see any patterns?

2. Your firm is a large conglomerate, involved in every business sector, that until now has focused exclusively on the domestic market of the United States. However, given a recent economic boom internationally, your firm has decided to assess which countries might be suitable for exporting its many products and services. Your manager recently stated that the five countries you must focus on for this preliminary analysis are Brazil, China, Russia, South Africa, and the United Arab Emirates. A colleague has indicated that a database of *Country Market Analysis* reports prepared by the WTO International Trade Centre might assist you. Assess the national import profile of each country, and include the following in your report for all five countries: (1) the highest-ranking identifiable category of products or services and (2) the top two countries from which these products or services are currently imported.

Method of Entry—The McGrew Company Minicase 16.1

The McGrew Company, a manufacturer of peanut combines, has for years sold a substantial number of machines in Brazil. However, a Brazilian firm has begun to manufacture them, and McGrew's local distributor has told Jim Allen, the president, that if McGrew expects to maintain its share of the market, it will also have to manufacture locally. Allen is in a quandary. The market is too good to lose, but McGrew has had no experience with foreign manufacturing operations. Because Brazilian sales and repairs have been handled by the distributor, no one in McGrew has had any firsthand experience in that country.

Allen has made some rough calculations that indicate the firm can make money by manufacturing in Brazil, but the firm's lack of marketing expertise in the country troubles him. He calls in Joan Beal, the export manager, and asks her to prepare a list of all the options open to McGrew, with their advantages and disadvantages. Allen also asks Beal to indicate her preference.

1. Assume you are Joan Beal. Prepare a list of all the options, and give the advantages and disadvantages of each.

2. Which of the options would you recommend?

3. Assuming that the president's calculations are correct and that a factory to produce locally the number of machines that McGrew now exports to Brazil will offer a satisfactory return on investment, what special information about Brazil will you want to gather?

17

Export and Import Practices

Containers in the shipping yard at the Port of Hamburg, Germany

The fact that trade protection hurts the economy of the country that imposes it is one of the oldest but still most startling insights economics has to offer. The idea dates back to the origin of economic science itself. Adam Smith's *The Wealth of Nations,* which gave birth to economics, already contained the argument for free trade: by specializing in production instead of producing everything, each nation would profit from free trade.

Jagdish Bagwati, professor, Columbia University,
The Concise Encyclopedia of Economics

How a Box Transformed the World

Fifty years ago, on April 26, a war-surplus oil tanker, the *Ideal-X*, left port in Newark, New Jersey, with a steel frame welded to its deck. The frame held aluminum containers that were off-loaded five days later in Houston, onto trucks. That was the beginning of a revolution in shipping that has made our world smaller. Containerization drastically reduced shipping costs and allowed manufacturers to leave the waterfronts and move, literally, offshore, to take advantage of cheap labor to produce goods that previously could not be exported profitably.

Malcolm McLean, a North Carolina farm boy turned trucker, had hauled cotton bales to Hoboken, where he had to sit around a whole day for his shipment to be unloaded. He waited, and he watched the process. It was slow, hard labor and gave rise to pilferage, as well. His idea was to detach the truck bodies and ship them on boats made to hold them.

No one understood how the box would change everything having to do with export and import, ships and ports, goods traded, trade routes, and labor unions. Marc Levinson, author of *The Box: How the Shipping Container Made the World Smaller and the World Economy Bigger*, calls containerization a monument to the most powerful law in economics, the law of unintended consequences. ∎

Source: Wally Bock, "A Man Who Changed the World," *Monday Memo*, June 11, 2001, www.mondaymemo.net/010611feature.htm (August 1, 2006); Marc Levinson, *The Box: How the Shipping Container Made the World Smaller and the World Economy Bigger* (Princeton University Press, 2006); Marc Levinson, "Unforeseen Consequence: How a Box Transformed the World," *Financial Times*, April 25, 2006, p. 17.

CONCEPT PREVIEWS

After reading this chapter, you should be able to:

explain why firms export and the three challenge areas of exporting

identify the sources of export counseling and support

discuss the meaning of the various terms of sale

identify some sources of export financing

describe the activities of a foreign freight forwarder

outline the export documents required

identify import sources

explain the Harmonized Tariff Schedule of the United States (HTSUSA)

Export—Why and Why Not?

With the added, complex dimensions of doing business overseas, why do companies become involved in exporting instead of staying in the home country? There are a number of reasons, all of which are linked to the business goal to increase profits and sales or to protect them from being eroded. Here are the most common reasons companies export:

- To serve markets where the firm has no or limited production facilities. Many large multinationals, like DuPont, supply some of their foreign markets by exporting because no firm, no matter how large, can afford to manufacture a complete product line in every country where its goods are sold. Markets without local factories are supplied through exports from the home country or from a foreign affiliate. In markets of sufficient size to justify the production of some but not all of the product mix, the affiliate will supplement local production with imports. A car plant in a developing nation may produce the least expensive cars and import luxury models. Also, the more vertically integrated plants may export semifinished products that are inputs for the less integrated subsidiaries.

- To satisfy a host government's requirement that the local subsidiary have exports. Governments of developing nations often require that the local affiliate export, and some require that it earn sufficient foreign exchange to cover the cost of its imports. This is why Ford located a radio plant in Brazil that exports to Ford's European assembly plants.[1]

- To remain price-competitive in the home market. Many firms import labor-intensive components produced in their foreign affiliates, or export components for assembly in countries where labor is less expensive and import the finished product.

- To test foreign markets and foreign competition inexpensively. This is a common strategy for firms that want to test a product's acceptance before investing in local production facilities. Exports may also enable firms to test market strategies and make adjustments with reduced risk in a smaller market. If the strategy or product fails, the firm can withdraw without having a costly and sometimes damaging failure to the entire firm. There is, however, a downside to this strategy: Whatever the firm does in the foreign market may be seen by a competitor. This is especially true for large, global firms such as Unilever and Procter & Gamble (P&G). Former P&G CEO Edwin Artzt changed the company's strategy for introducing new products. Rather than postpone a global launch until the firm accumulated marketing experience in a country, P&G began to introduce products on a worldwide basis early in their development to avoid giving competitors time to react in other markets.

- To meet actual or prospective customer requests for the firm to export. This type of accidental exporting is fairly common. A foreign buyer often will search for something it cannot find locally by consulting the Internet or the *Thomas Register,* a publication listing American producers for hundreds of products.

- To offset cyclical sales in the domestic market.

- To achieve additional sales, which allow the firm to use excess production capacity to lower per-unit fixed costs.

- To extend a product's life cycle by exporting to currently unserved markets where the product will be at the introduction stage of the life cycle.

- To respond strategically to foreign competitors that are in the firm's home market by entering their home market.

- To achieve the success the firm's management has seen others achieve by exporting.

- To improve the efficiency of manufacturing equipment, which usually works better at or near full capacity.

The 12 Most Common Mistakes Made by New Exporters

1. **Failure to obtain qualified export counseling and to develop a master international strategy and marketing plan before starting an export business.** To be successful, a firm must first figure out what its goals and objectives are and develop a plan for how they will be achieved. Unless the firm is fortunate enough to possess a staff with considerable export expertise, taking this crucial first step may require qualified outside guidance.

2. **Insufficient commitment by top management to overcome the initial difficulties and financial requirements of exporting.** Establishing a firm in foreign markets usually takes more time than doing so in domestic ones. Although the early delays and costs involved in exporting may seem difficult to justify compared to the situation in established domestic markets, the exporter should take a long-term view of this process and carefully monitor international marketing efforts through these early difficulties. If a good foundation is laid for export business, the benefits derived should eventually outweigh the investment.

3. **Insufficient care in selecting overseas sales representatives and distributors.** The selection of each foreign distributor is crucial. The complexity introduced by overseas communication and transportation requires that international distributors act with greater independence than do their domestic counterparts. Since a new exporter's history, trademarks, and reputation may be unknown in the foreign market, foreign customers may buy on the strength of a distributor's reputation. A firm should therefore conduct a personal evaluation of the personnel handling its account, the distributor's facilities, and the management methods employed.

4. **Chasing orders from around the world instead of establishing a basis for profitable operations and orderly growth.** If exporters expect distributors to promote their accounts actively, the distributors must be trained and assisted and their performance must be monitored continually. This may require a company executive located in the distributor's geographic region. New exporters may want to concentrate their efforts in one or two geographic areas until they have sufficient business to support a company representative. Then, while this initial core area is expanded, the exporter can move into the next targeted geographic area.

5. **Neglecting export business when the home market booms.** Often companies turn to exporting when business falls off in their home market. When domestic business starts to boom again, they neglect their export trade. Such neglect can harm the profits and motivation of a company's overseas representatives, strangle its own export trade, and leave the firm without recourse when domestic business falls off again.

6. **Failure to treat international distributors and customers on an equal basis with their domestic counterparts.** Often, companies carry out institutional advertising campaigns, special discount offers, sales incentive programs, special credit term programs, warranty offers, and so forth, in the home market but fail to make similar assistance available to their international distributors and customers. This is a mistake that can destroy the vitality of overseas marketing efforts.

7. **Assuming that a given market technique and product will automatically be successful in all countries.** What works in one market may not work in others. Each market has to be treated separately until the company has sufficient knowledge about its export markets to generalize about them.

8. **Unwillingness to modify products to meet regulations or cultural preferences of other countries.** Local safety codes and import restrictions cannot be ignored, nor can cultural preferences. If necessary modifications are not made at the factory, the distributor must make them, often at greater cost and perhaps not as well.

9. **Failure to provide service, sales, and warranty information in locally understood languages.** Although many people may speak English, assume that they will want to read instructions and product information in their own language. This holds for customers and distributors.

10. **Failure to consider the use of an export management company.** If a firm decides it cannot afford its own export department, it should consider the possibility of using an export management company (EMC).

11. **Failure to consider licensing or joint venture agreements.** Import restrictions in some countries, insufficient personnel or financial resources, or an overly limited product line can cause many companies to dismiss international marketing as unfeasible. Yet many products that compete on a national basis in a home market can be marketed successfully in many markets of the world through licensing or joint venture arrangements.

12. **Failure to provide readily available servicing for the product.** A product without the necessary service support can acquire a bad reputation in a short period, potentially preventing further sales.

Source: Adapted from *Small Business Success, Vol. 1, Pacific Bell Directory,* in cooperation with the U.S. Small Business Administration, 2006.

The two major reasons U.S. firms give for not exporting are their preoccupation with the vast American market and a reluctance to become involved in a new, unknown, and therefore risky operation. When managers of nonexporting firms are probed further on why they are not active in international markets, they generally mention the following three areas in which they lack knowledge: locating foreign markets, payment and financing procedures, and export procedures.

Considerable assistance is available from the federal and state departments of commerce, banks, the Small Business Administration, small business development centers, and private consultants, to mention a few sources. Too few managers are taking advantage of this assistance. Below we examine each of the areas that hinder managers in developing exporting capability: locating foreign markets, payment and financing procedures, and export procedures.

Locating Foreign Markets and Developing a Plan

The first step in locating foreign markets is to determine whether a market exists for the firm's products. The initial screening step described in Chapter 16 indicated a procedure to follow that will pose no problem for an experienced market analyst who is well acquainted with the available sources of information and assistance. However, newcomers to exporting, especially smaller firms, may still be at a loss as to how to begin their foreign market research. For them, a number of helpful export assistance programs are available. Once the potential exporter has established that there may be a market for the firm's products, it's time to draft the export marketing plan.

SOURCES OF EXPORT INFORMATION, COUNSELING, AND SUPPORT

Export.gov is the U.S. government's trade portal, established by the Department of Commerce. It brings together resources on exporting from a number of government agencies, including the U.S. International Trade Administration, U.S. Commercial Service, Department of Commerce, Export-Import Bank, Agency for International Development, Small Business Administration, Department of State, and Overseas Private Investment Corporation. See www.export.gov/exportcounseling.html. A good place to start is at the Trade Information Center, the first stop for information about all federal export assistance programs as well as country and regional market information. Support is available by phone or e-mail. The Trade Information Center Web site is www.ita.doc.gov/td/tic. There you will find links to government export programs, trade promotion events, and trade lead information.

For firms that already are exporting, the International Trade Administration (ITA) offers a wide range of export promotion activities that include export counseling, analysis of foreign markets, assessment of industry competitiveness, and development of market opportunities and sales representation through export promotion events. Three departments in ITA work together to provide these services:

1. *Market Access and Compliance (MAC):* MAC specialists seek to open foreign markets to American products by developing strategies to overcome obstacles faced by U.S. businesses in foreign countries and regions. They also monitor foreign country compliance with trade agreements.

2. *Trade Development:* This department promotes the trade interests of American industries and offers information on markets and trade practices worldwide. Its industry desk officers work by sector with industry representatives and associations to identify trade opportunities by product or service, industry sector, and market. They also develop export marketing plans and programs. Trade Development experts also conduct executive trade missions, trade fairs, and marketing seminars.

3. *U.S. Commercial Service (USCS):* The USCS has commercial officers working in 107 U.S. domestic locations and 150 countries who can provide background information on foreign companies and assist in finding foreign representatives, conducting market research, and identifying trade and investment opportunities for American firms. The district offices also conduct export workshops and keep businesspeople

With the growing volume of shipments between countries daily, there is demand for people to work in entry-level positions in import–export management. Managing the movement of products into and out of countries is a fundamental task in international trade, and job opportunities exist in every type of business dealing with foreign customers or suppliers and ranging in size from small businesses to Fortune 500 companies. To succeed in import–export management, you will need to know about the fundamentals of business, customer service, international business considerations, purchasing, marketing, fundamental import–export operations, documentation for licenses, bills of lading, insurance, domestic and foreign country customs laws, and international trade regulations for the countries in which the importer–exporter is dealing. Language skills are valuable. Entry-level salaries are in the range of $31,000 to $42,000, midlevel salaries are between $46,000 and $64,000, and salaries for top-level import–export managers range from $69,000 to more than $96,000, based on experience. Here are places where import–export management jobs can be found:

- Import–export houses
- International trading companies
- Manufacturers of all sizes that trade internationally
- Wholesalers importing or exporting products
- Retail chains (positions at the corporate level)

- Purchasing departments for international companies
- Customhouse brokers
- Freight forwarders
- Supply chain management organizations
- Airlines and ocean shipping firms

To advance your career and move into higher levels of import–export management, you may want to earn the U.S. Customs broker's license.

World Fact: According to the U.S. Census Bureau, the following 10 countries are the United States' largest trading partners (listed in rank order of largest to smallest in terms of import and export dollars): (1) Canada, (2) Mexico, (3) Japan, (4) China, (5) Germany, (6) United Kingdom, (7) France, (8) Republic of Korea (South Korea), (9) Taiwan, and (10) Singapore.

World Wide Resources:

www.export911.com

www.fibre2fashion.com/texterms/exim/exim_terms1.htm

importexportcoach.com

www.ita.doc.gov/

www.exporthotline.com

informed about domestic and overseas trade events that offer potential for promoting American products.

The Office of International Trade of the Small Business Administration (SBA) offers assistance through SBA district offices to current and potential small business exporters through two programs that are provided in field offices around the country, Business Development and Financial Assistance. The Office of International Trade also works through the SCORE program, in which experienced executives offer free one-on-one counseling to small firms; Small Business Development Centers (SBDCs), located in many universities and colleges, which give export counseling, especially to inexperienced newcomers; Centers for International Business and Research (CIBERs), located in 30 U.S. universities, which also assist firms with exporting; and U.S. Export Assistance Centers, which are one-stop offices ready to help small and medium-size businesses with local export assistance.

The Department of Commerce Export Assistance Program (EAP) helps potential exporters narrow down their potential markets. It has offices in over 100 U.S. cities and 80 foreign cities. After learning about the company and its products, the EAP international trade specialist might advise the potential exporter to consult the National Trade Data Bank (NTDB), a service that selects the most recent trade promotions, "how to" publications, and international trade and economic data from 15 federal agencies and puts them on one CD-ROM that is updated monthly. The NTDB provides a comprehensive guide for new exporters and a source of specific product and regional information for experienced exporters searching for new markets. It also contains the Foreign Traders Index, a list of foreign importers that includes descriptions of each and the products it wishes to import. From this list, the exporter can prepare a list of those interested in its products for contact. An individual can subscribe to the NTDB as part of the trade and economic information available at the Commerce Web site, www.stat-usa.gov.

The U.S. Embassy in Kenya. When a firm is exploring exporting options, one source of information regarding potential business partners and market opportunities might be the Gold Key Service offered by many U.S. Embassies.

The trade specialist might also suggest using the Trade Opportunities Program (TOP), which provides current sales leads from overseas firms that want to buy from or represent American firms. These leads are accessible through STAT-USA free of charge at a Federal Depositary Library and as a component of the subscription service through STAT-USA. TOP leads are also published weekly in leading commercial newspapers. Another possibility is advertising in *Commercial News,* a catalog-magazine published bimonthly to promote American products and services in overseas markets.[2]

Once the existence of a potential market is established, the firm must choose between exporting indirectly through U.S.-based exporters and exporting directly using its own staff. If it opts for indirect exporting as a way to test the market, the trade specialist can provide assistance. If the firm prefers to set up its own export operation, it must then obtain overseas distribution. The exporter may use the Export.gov portal to find agents, distributors, or joint venture partners.[3] Credit reporting agencies, such as Dun & Bradstreet, the Finance, Credit, and International Business Association (FCIB), and the exporter's bank will supply credit information.

If the firm wants to make a foreign trip, Commerce offers the *Gold Key Matching Service* through many U.S. embassies. This is tailored for managers of American companies who are coming to visit the country and includes orientation briefings, market research, introductions to potential partners, and assistance in developing a marketing strategy for the particular country. The U.S. Commercial Office makes the arrangements. The Foreign Agricultural Service of the U.S. Department of Agriculture offers similar services to potential exporters of agricultural products.

The Department of Commerce also organizes trade events known as "Show and Sells" that are helpful in both locating foreign representatives and making sales. There are four kinds:

1. *U.S. pavilions:* Commerce selects about 100 global trade fairs every year for which it recruits American companies to participate at a U.S. pavilion. Preference is given to fairs in markets suitable for firms that are ready to export. Exhibitors receive extensive support from Commerce in management and overseas promotional campaigns to attract business audiences.

2. *Trade missions:* These focus on an industry sector. Participants are given detailed marketing information, advanced publicity, logistical support, and prearranged appointments with potential buyers and government officials. Generally, a mission consists of 5 to 12 business executives.

3. *Product literature center:* Commerce trade development specialists represent U.S. companies at various international trade shows, where they distribute literature. They then tell the companies who the interested visitors were so that the companies can follow up.

4. *Reverse trade missions:* The U.S. Trade Development Agency may fund visits to the United States by representatives of foreign governments so that they can meet with American industry and government representatives. The foreign officials represent purchasing authorities interested in buying U.S. equipment for specific projects.

The Long and the Short of Exporting

DuPont has been able to remain a competitor in the tough chemical export market because exports have been a part of its strategic thinking since it first exported to Spain in 1805. It paid increasingly serious attention to exports in 1978, when the dollar fell sharply, making U.S. exports cheaper for foreigners to buy. There were other strategic reasons to increase the focus on exports at DuPont: "We recognized that our business was changing from national to regional or global, so you didn't have a lot of options," says P. J. Roessel, DuPont's director of international planning. "If you didn't participate in those foreign markets, your competitors would gradually get stronger and come and eat your lunch in the U.S."

DuPont's marketing strategy is to promote the sale of U.S. exports by its 165 overseas manufacturing subsidiaries. "We have plotted back for 25 years and have found that as we have invested and built abroad, exports have gone up in complete tandem," says Roessel. "Such subsidiaries are able to 'pull' products from the parent company to achieve real market synergy." A Japanese DuPont subsidiary, for example, makes engineering plastics for autos and has developed markets for polyester and acetyl products made by DuPont in the United

States. In 2005, DuPont's exports from the United States amounted to $6.575 billion, making the company one of the largest U.S. exporters. It now has operational locations in 70 countries.

On the other hand, the Canadian firm Crosskeys Systems Corporation had no exports in 1992, its first year of operation, and no plans for exporting. However, the management of the information technology company changed its plans in 1995 when it realized it had earned 65 percent of its revenues from a single U.S.-based customer. In 1997, only five years after it began operations, the firm's export revenues reached C$17.3 million and then almost doubled to C$32.2 million. In just six years, sales revenues grew from C$87,000 to C$36.7 million, 420 times the first year's revenues. Because of its success, Crosskeys was an attractive target, and was taken over by the British company Orchestream, which was then, in turn, bought by the Texas-based Metasolv.

Source: "DuPont at a Glance," *About DuPont*, www.dupont.com/corp/gbl-company/overview.html (July 27, 2006); "Crosskeys Systems Corporation," *Best Practices and Exporting Successes*, Industry Canada, October 15, 2003, http://strategis.ic.gc.ca/epic/internet/intawv-uamo.nsf/en/qv01666e.html (July 31, 2004); *Dupont 2005 Data Book*, www.dupont.com/corp/news/publications/dupfinancial/databk.pdf (July 25, 2006); and "Dupont Worldwide," www1.dupont.com/NASApp/dupontglobal/corp/index.jsp?page=/content/US/en_US/overview/worldwide/index.html (July 28, 2006).

In addition to the federal government, other sources of assistance available to the exporter include state governments, all of which have export development programs and many of which have export financing programs. In the private sector, the World Trade Centers Association, a membership organization of nearly 300 centers worldwide, provides networking opportunities and an online trading system.

EXPORT MARKETING PLAN

As soon as possible, the firm needs to draft its export marketing plan. An experienced firm will already have a plan in operation, but newcomers may need to wait until they have accumulated at least some information from foreign market research. Essentially, the export marketing plan is the same as the domestic marketing plan. It should be specific about the markets to be developed, the marketing strategy for serving them, and the tactics required to carry out the strategy. Sales forecasts and budgets, pricing policies, product characteristics, promotional plans, and details on arrangements with foreign representatives are required. In other words, the export marketing plan spells out what must be done and when, who should do it, and what the costs are. An outline for an export marketing plan appears in the appendix at the end of this chapter. In Chapter 18 we focus on the marketing mix, but two aspects of the mix require some explanation here: export pricing and sales agreements for foreign representatives.

One pricing area of concern for many firms beginning to export is the need to quote **terms of sale** that differ from those used in domestic markets. For foreign transactions, the exporter needs to be familiar with **INCOTERMS,** 13 trade terms that describe the responsibilities of the buyer and seller in international trade.[4] They were created by the International Chamber of Commerce and are revised every 10 years. For example, for domestic sales, the company may be quoting a price **FOB (free on board)** factory, which

terms of sale
Conditions of a sale that stipulate the point at which all costs and risks are borne by the buyer

INCOTERMS
Universal trade terminology developed by the International Chamber of Commerce

FOB (free on board)
Pricing policy in which risks pass from seller to buyer at the factory door; U.S. equivalent of Ex-Works

Ex-Works
INCOTERM equivalent of FOB

means all costs and risks from that point on are borne by the buyer. The INCOTERM equivalent is **Ex-Works.** Foreign customers, however, will expect one of the following terms of sale:

1. *FAS (free alongside ship, port of call):* The seller pays all the transportation and delivery expense up to the ship's side and clears the goods for export.

2. *CIF (cost, insurance, freight, foreign port):* The price includes the cost of the goods, insurance, and all transportation and miscellaneous charges to the named port of final destination.

3. *CFR (cost and freight, foreign port):* CFR is similar to CIF except that the buyer purchases the insurance, either because it can be obtained at a lower cost or because the buyer's government, to save foreign exchange, insists on use of a local insurance company.

4. *DAF (delivered at frontier):* The term *DAF* is often used by exporters to Canada and Mexico. The price covers all costs up to the border, where the shipment is delivered to the buyer's representative. The buyer's responsibility is to arrange for receiving the goods after they are cleared for export, carry them across the border, clear them for importation, and make delivery to the buyer.

CIF and CFR terms of sale are more convenient for foreign buyers because to establish their cost, they merely have to add the import duties, landing charges, and freight from the port of arrival to their warehouse. New exporters need to remember the miscellaneous costs—wharf storage and handling charges, freight forwarder's charges, and consular fees—incurred in making a CIF shipment. Note that the domestic marketing and general administrative costs included in the domestic selling price are frequently greater than the actual cost of making a CIF export sale.

The preferred pricing method is the use of the *factory door cost* (production cost without domestic marketing and general administrative costs), to which are added the direct cost of making the export sale, a percentage of the general administrative overhead, and a profit margin. This percentage can be derived from managers' estimates of the part of their total time spent on export matters. The minimum FOB, or Ex-Works, price is the sum of these costs plus the required profit margin. If research in a market has shown either that there is little competition or that competitive prices are higher, then of course the exporter is free to match the competition in that market (price skim) or set a low price to gain market share (penetration pricing). The course of action taken will depend on the firm's sales objectives, just as in the domestic market.

The other area of major difference in exporting is the sales agreement. It should specify as simply as possible the duties of the representative and the firm. Most of what is contained in the contract for a domestic representative can be used in export also, but special attention must be paid to two points, the designation of the responsibilities for patent and trademark registration and the designation of the country and state or province whose laws will govern any contractual dispute. To be absolutely safe, the firm should register all patents and trademarks. Policing them may be left to the local representative; however, the firm should have the help of an experienced international attorney when drawing up an agreement. Exporters from any country are likely to prefer to stipulate the laws of their home country. Many nations, especially those of Latin America, follow the Calvo Doctrine, which holds that cases should be tried under local and not foreign law.

Payment and Financing Procedures

The second major hurdle for new exporters is to build an understanding of the payment and financing procedures involved in export sales. We'll review the process of export payment and the terms used, approaches to export financing, and other government incentives that have been established to support exporters in the finance area.

David Kratka, president of MMO Music Group, a small producer of sing-along tapes for karaoke machines in Elmsford, New York, didn't have to search for foreign business; foreign customers came to him. Although this seems like an enviable situation, in reality, Kratka figures the company probably lost foreign sales in the 1980s because he was too busy attending to the domestic market. He didn't have time to answer faxes and telephone calls from Asia and Europe. A year after Kratka finally decided he could no longer handle the foreign inquiries alone, he hired an international sales director. By mid-1995 foreign sales were about 15 percent of the firm's total $8 million sales. This was up from 5 percent before the director was hired.

MMO Music is still in business (as Pocket Songs), and the company's founder, Irv Kratka, was acknowledged as the "father of karaoke" in 1995. Of course, the cassette tapes have given way to the CD and CD + G (lyrics on a screen) format.

Other companies find it easier and more economical to get exporting help from an outsider. A consulting firm, Global Resource Associates, taught exporting techniques to CoBatCo, a waffle-griddle maker in Illinois with 21 employees. Exports amounted to 13 percent of total sales in only three years.

Other small-firm managers without the time or international expertise to handle foreign sales turn to export management companies (EMCs) that typically handle everything from sales and distribution to credit and shipping, charging a fee of 10 to 15 percent of the shipment's value. The advantage of this approach is that experts handle the export function. The disadvantage is that the control of the company's export business lies in the hands of outsiders.

Source: "The History of Karaoke," www.pocketsongs.com/MainPages/karaokehistory.asp (July 29, 2006); "About Pocket Songs: The Karaoke Music Super Store," www.pocketsongs.com/MainPages/about.asp (July 29, 2006); and Global Resource Associates, www.fastrack-global.com (July 29, 2006).

EXPORT PAYMENT TERMS

Payment terms, as every marketer knows, are often a decisive factor in obtaining an order. As a sales official of an international grain exporter put it, "If you give credit to a guy who is broke, he'll pay any price for your product." This is somewhat exaggerated, but customers will often pay higher prices when terms are more lenient, especially in countries where capital is scarce and interest rates are high. Among the payment terms offered by exporters to foreign buyers are cash in advance, open account, consignment, letters of credit, and documentary drafts. We'll look at each of these in turn.

When the credit standing of the buyer is not known or is uncertain, *cash in advance* is desirable. However, very few buyers will accept these terms, because part of their working capital will be tied up until the merchandise has been received and sold. Furthermore, they have no guarantee that they will receive what they ordered. As a result, few customers will pay cash in advance unless the order is for a custom-made product.

When a sale is made on *open account,* the seller assumes all of the risk, and therefore such terms should be offered only to reliable customers. The exporter's capital is tied up until payment has been received. However, exporters that insist on less risky payment terms, such as a letter of credit, may find that they are losing business to competitors who do sell on open account. Well-known global firms such as Mercedes Benz do not accept the extra cost of obtaining letters of credit and give their business to suppliers that will offer them open account terms. To establish the buyer's credit, exporters can get credit reports and credit information on foreign firms from several agencies such as Dun & Bradstreet, Owens Online, and Asian CIS.

Consignment means that goods are shipped to the buyer and payment is not made until they have been sold. All of the risk is assumed by the seller, so such terms should not be offered without making the same extensive investigation of the buyer and country as that recommended for open account terms. Multinationals frequently sell goods to their subsidiaries on this basis.

Only cash in advance offers more protection to the seller than does an export **letter of credit (L/C).** This document is issued by the buyer's bank, which promises to pay the seller

letter of credit (L/C)
Document issued by the buyer's bank in which the bank promises to pay the seller a specified amount under specified conditions

confirmed L/C
A confirmation made by a correspondent bank in the seller's country by which it agrees to honor the issuing bank's letter of credit

irrevocable L/C
A stipulation that a letter of credit cannot be canceled

a specified amount when the bank has received certain documents stipulated in the letter of credit by a specified time. Generally, the seller will request that the letter of credit be *confirmed* and *irrevocable.* In a **confirmed L/C,** a correspondent bank in the seller's country confirms that it will honor the issuing bank's letter of credit. With an **irrevocable L/C,** once the seller has accepted the credit, the customer cannot alter or cancel it without the seller's consent. Figure 17.1 is an example of a bank's confirmation of an irrevocable letter of credit. If the letter of credit is *not* confirmed, the correspondent bank (Merchants National Bank of Mobile) has no obligation to pay the seller (Smith & Co.) when it receives the documents listed in the letter of credit. Only the issuing bank (Banco Americano in Bogotá) is responsible. If the seller (Smith & Co.) wishes to be able to collect from an American bank, it will insist that the credit be confirmed by such a bank. This confirmation is generally done by the correspondent bank, as it is in Figure 17.1. When the Merchants National Bank of Mobile confirms the credit, it undertakes an obligation to pay Smith & Co. if all the documents listed in the letter are presented on or before the stipulated date. Note that nothing is mentioned

---

FIGURE 17.1

Letter of Credit

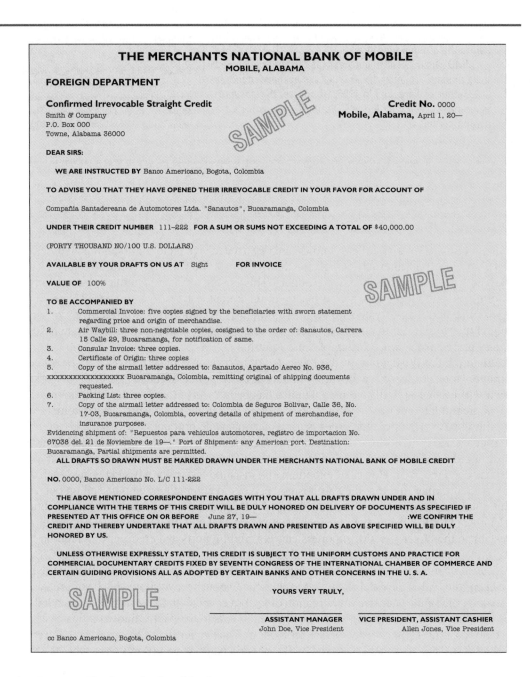

---

about the goods themselves; the buyer has stipulated only that an **air waybill** issued by the carrier be presented as proof that shipment has been made. Even if bank officials know that the plane had crashed after the takeoff, they would still pay Smith & Co. Banks are concerned with documents, not merchandise.

Before opening a letter of credit, a buyer frequently requests a **pro forma invoice.** This is the exporter's formal quotation containing a description of the merchandise, price, delivery time, proposed method of shipment, ports of exit and entry, and terms of sale. It is more than a quotation, however. Generally, the bank will use it when opening a letter of credit, and in countries requiring import licenses or permits to purchase foreign exchange, government officials will insist on receiving copies.

Figure 17.2 illustrates the routes taken by the merchandise, letter of credit, and documents in a letter-of-credit transaction between a U.S. seller and a German buyer. When the German buyer accepts the terms of sale that provide for a confirmed and irrevocable letter of credit, she goes to her bank to arrange for opening the required letter. The buyer will furnish the bank with the information contained in the pro forma invoice, specify the documents that the exporter must present to obtain payment, and set the expiration date for the credit.

The German bank then instructs its correspondent bank in the United States to confirm the credit and inform the seller that it has been established. The seller prepares the merchandise for shipment and notifies the freight forwarder, which books space on a ship, prepares the export documents, and arranges to have the merchandise delivered to the port. The documents, together with a sight or time draft drawn by the seller, are presented to the U.S. bank, which pays the seller and forwards the documents for collection to the German bank. To obtain the documents that give title to the shipment, the buyer in Germany must either pay the *sight draft* or accept a *time draft.* Having done so, the buyer receives the documents, which are then given to the customhouse broker. The customhouse broker acts as the buyer's agent in receiving the goods from the steamship line and clearing them through German customs.

If the exporter believes the political and commercial risks are not sufficient to require a letter of credit, the exporter may agree to payment on a *documentary draft basis,* which is

air waybill
A bill of lading issued by an air carrier

pro forma invoice
Exporter's formal quotation containing a description of the merchandise, price, delivery time, method of shipping, terms of sale, and points of exit and entry

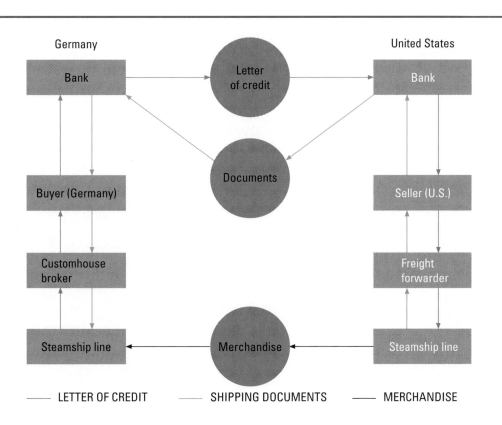

FIGURE 17.2

Letter of Credit Transaction

—— LETTER OF CREDIT   —— SHIPPING DOCUMENTS   —— MERCHANDISE

FIGURE 17.3

Sight Draft

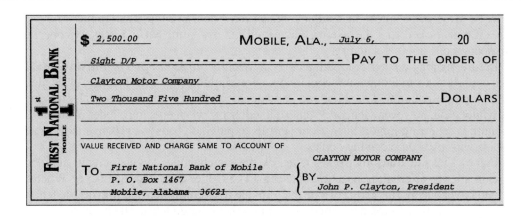

export draft

An unconditional order drawn by the seller that instructs the buyer to pay the draft's amount on presentation **(sight draft)** or at an agreed future date **(time draft)** and that must be paid before the buyer receives shipping documents

less costly to the buyer. An **export draft,** shown in Figure 17.3, is an unconditional order drawn by the seller on the buyer instructing the buyer to pay the amount of the order on presentation **(sight draft)** or at an agreed future date **(time draft).** Generally, the seller will ask its bank to send the draft and documents to a bank in the buyer's country, which will proceed with the collection as described in the letter-of-credit transaction.

Although documentary draft and letter-of-credit terms are similar, there is one important difference. A confirmed letter of credit guarantees payment to the seller if the seller conforms to its requirements. There is no guarantee with a documentary draft. An unscrupulous buyer can refuse to pay the draft when presented and then attempt to bargain with the seller for a lower price. The seller must then acquiesce, try to find another buyer, pay a large freight bill to bring back the goods, or abandon them. If the seller chooses the last alternative, customs will auction off the goods, and chances are that the original buyer will be able to acquire them at a bargain price. The seller would receive nothing.

Figure 17.4 illustrates that the risks and costs vary inversely among the various export payment terms.

EXPORT FINANCING

Although exporters would prefer to sell on the almost riskless letter-of-credit terms, increased foreign competition and the universally tight money situation are forcing them to offer credit. To do so, they must be familiar with the available sources and kinds of export financing, both private and public.

Private Source   Commercial banks have always been a source of export financing through loans for working capital and the discounting of time drafts. A bank may discount an export time draft, pay the seller and keep it until maturity or, if it is the bank on which the

FIGURE 17.4

Payment Risk/Cost Trade-Off

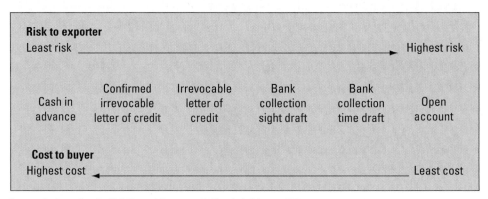

Source: *Business America* (U.S. Dept. of Commerce Publication), February 1995.

>>Dump the L/Cs; Pay with Plastic!

The safe and laborious way to guarantee both payment and shipment of an export or import order has been with letter-of-credit (L/C) payment terms. But there has always been a risk that conversion rate changes would result in a loss. For some situations, credit cards provide a good alternative. For example, the president of a small manufacturing company said that if his company hadn't accepted payment by credit card, it couldn't have done business in 95 countries. He's also pleased that with the immediate completion of the sale, credit card companies guarantee that payment is made directly to the seller's bank account within 72 hours at the daily U.S. dollar rate, avoiding transaction losses on the foreign exchange conversion and increasing cash flow.

For information on using credit cards to accept payments, see sites such as www.usa.visa.com/business. Come to think of it, maybe PayPal will become an alternative. With over 105 million accounts in 55 markets, PayPal is becoming a third alternative. See Paypal's site (https://www.paypal.com/cgl-bin/webscr?cmd=xpt/merchant/Index-outside) or that of Moneybookers (www.moneybookers.com/app), which is especially friendly to international transactions.

Source: www. paypal.com (July 31, 2006).

draft is drawn, "accept" it. By accepting a time draft, a bank assumes the responsibility for making payment at maturity of the draft. The accepting bank may or may not purchase (at a discount) the draft. If it does not, the exporter can sell a **banker's acceptance** readily in the open market.

In recent years, two new types of financing have been developed, factoring and forfaiting. **Factoring** permits the exporter to be more competitive by selling on open account rather than by means of the more costly letter-of-credit method. This financing technique is the sale of export accounts receivable to a third party, which assumes the credit risk. Factoring is essentially discounting without recourse. A factor may be a factoring house or a special department in a commercial bank. Under the export factoring arrangement, the seller passes its order to the factor for approval of the credit risk. Once the order has been approved, the exporter has complete protection against bad debts and political risk. The customer pays the factor, which in effect acts as the exporter's credit and collection department. The period of settlement generally does not exceed 180 days.

Forfaiting is the purchase of obligations that arise from the sale of goods and services that fall due at some date beyond the 90 to 180 days that is customary for factoring. These receivables are usually in the form of trade drafts or promissory notes with maturities ranging from six months to five years. Because forfaited debt is sold without recourse, it is nearly always accompanied by bank security in the form of a guarantee or *aval*. Whereas the guarantee is a separate document, the aval is a promise to pay that is written directly in the document. The forfaiter purchases the bill and discounts it for the entire credit period. Thus, the exporter, through forfaiting, has converted its credit-based sale into a cash transaction. Although banks have traditionally concentrated on short-term financing, they have become involved in medium- and even long-term financing because numerous government and government-assisted organizations are offering export credit guarantees and insurance against commercial and political risks.

Public Source
The U.S. Export-Import Bank (**Ex-Im Bank**) is the principal government agency responsible for aiding the financing of American exports, through a variety of loan, guarantee, and insurance programs. Ex-Im Bank's programs are available to any American export firm regardless of size. The bank provides two types of loans, direct loans to foreign buyers of American exports and intermediary loans to responsible parties, such as a foreign government lending agency that relends to foreign buyers of capital goods and related services. An example of the latter is a maintenance contract for a jet passenger plane. Both programs cover up to 85 percent of the value of the exported goods and services, with repayment terms of one year or more.

banker's acceptance
A time draft with maturity of less than 270 days that has been accepted by the bank on which the draft was drawn, thus becoming the accepting bank's obligation; may be bought and sold at a discount in the financial markets like other commercial paper

factoring
Discounting without recourse an account receivable

forfaiting
Purchasing without recourse an account receivable whose credit terms are longer than the 90 to 180 days usual in factoring; unlike factoring, political and transfer risks are borne by the forfaiter

Ex-Im Bank
Principal government agency that aids American exporters by means of loans, guarantees, and insurance programs

Ex-Im Bank's *Working Capital Guarantee* helps small businesses obtain working capital to cover their export sales. It guarantees working capital loans extended by banks to eligible exporters with exportable inventory or export receivables as collateral. The guarantee provides repayment protection for private sector loans to buyers of U.S. capital equipment and related services.

Ex-Im Bank also offers *export credit insurance*. An exporter may reduce financing risks by purchasing insurance to protect against the political and commercial risks of a foreign buyer's defaulting on payment. The coverage may be comprehensive or be limited to political risk only. Since its inception in 1934, Ex-Im Bank has supported more than $400 billion in American exports, mostly to developing markets.[5]

Other Public Incentives Other government incentives for trade, although not strictly a part of export financing, are so closely related to it that we mention them here. These are the Overseas Private Investment Corporation and the foreign trade zone.[6]

Overseas Private Investment Corporation (OPIC)
Government corporation that offers American investors in developing countries insurance against expropriation, currency inconvertibility, and damages from wars and revolutions

The **Overseas Private Investment Corporation (OPIC)** is a government corporation formed to stimulate private investment in developing countries. It offers investors insurance against expropriation, currency inconvertibility, and damages from wars or revolutions. OPIC also offers specialized insurance for American service contractors and exporters operating in foreign countries. Exports of capital equipment and semiprocessed raw materials generally follow these investments.

Foreign trade zones (FTZs) are duty-free areas designed to facilitate trade by reducing the effect of customs restrictions. These areas may be free ports, transit zones, free perimeters, export processing zones, or free trade zones. In each instance, a specific and limited area is involved, into which imported goods may be brought without the payment of import duties. There are hundreds of these areas in more than 28 countries. Of the five types, the free trade zone is the most common.

foreign trade zone (FTZ)
Duty-free area designed to facilitate trade by reducing the effect of customs restrictions

free trade zone
An area designated by the government as outside its customs territory

The **free trade zone** is an enclosed area considered to be outside the customs territory of the country in which it is located. Goods of foreign origin may be brought into the zone for eventual transshipment, reexportation, or importation into the country. While the goods are in the zone, no import duties need be paid. Examples range from the Zhuhai Free Trade Zone, near Macao in China, to Chabahar in Iran. In the United States, free trade zones have been growing in popularity, and 230 of these zones, with over 400 subzones, are now in operation.[7] Many are situated at seaports, but some are located at inland distribution points. Goods brought into the FTZ may be stored, inspected, repackaged, or combined with American components. Because of differences in the import tariff schedule, the finished product often incurs lower duty than would the disassembled parts. Bicycles have been assembled in the Kansas City FTZ for that reason. Importers of machinery and automobiles improve their cash flow by storing spare parts in an FTZ, because duty is not paid until they are withdrawn.

customs drawbacks
Rebates on customs duties

In addition to their advantages to importers, FTZs can also benefit exporters. By using FTZs, exporters may be eligible for accelerated export status in regard to excise tax rebates and **customs drawbacks.** These customs duty rebates are available for items such as tires, trucks, and tobacco products. The federal government collects the tax when the item is manufactured; when it is exported, the tax is rebated. The processing time for tax rebates can be initiated by putting the goods into FTZs because a product is considered exported as soon as it enters the FTZ. Although U.S. Customs has had the duty-drawback program in place for 200 years, many firms do not claim the money they're owed. As a result, each year up to $2 billion in customs duty refunds goes unclaimed.[8] FTZs offer another benefit to exporters: When manufacturing or assembly is done in FTZs using imported components, no duties need ever be paid when the finished product is exported.

Export Procedures

When those new to exporting are concerned about the complexity of export procedures, they are generally referring to documentation. Instead of dealing with the two documents used in domestic shipments, the freight bill and the bill of lading, export novices are suddenly confronted with five

TABLE 17.1   Official Procedures for Exporting and Importing

Region or Economy	Documents for Export (number)	Time for Export (days)	Cost to Export (US$ per container)	Documents for Import (number)	Time for Import (days)	Cost to Import (US$ per Container)
East Asia & Pacific	6.9	23.9	884.8	9.3	25.9	1,037.1
Europe & Central Asia	7.4	29.2	1,450.2	10.0	37.1	1,589.3
Latin America & Caribbean	7.3	22.2	1,067.5	9.5	27.9	1,225.5
Middle East & North Africa	7.1	27.1	923.9	10.3	35.4	1,182.8
OECD	4.8	10.5	811.0	5.9	12.2	882.6
South Asia	8.1	34.4	1,236.0	12.5	41.5	1,494.9
Sub-Saharan Africa	8.2	40.0	1,561.1	12.2	51.5	1,946.9

Source: World Bank, International Finance Corporation, http://www.doingbusiness.org/ExploreTopics/TradingAcrossBorders (Sept. 29, 2005).

to six times as many documents, depending on the country. Table 17.1 summarizes documentation requirements for major groups. Additional data on specific countries are available at the World Bank's Doing Business site, www.doingbusiness.org/ExploreTopics/TradingAcrossBorders.

"Exports move on a sea of documents" is a popular saying in the industry, and it seems an accurate description. Many firms give at least part of this work to a *foreign freight forwarder,* who acts as an agent for the exporter. Foreign freight forwarders prepare documents, book space with a carrier, and in general act as the firm's export traffic department. If asked, they will offer advice about markets, import and export regulations, the best mode of transport, and export packing. They also will supply cargo insurance. After shipment, they forward documents to the importer or to the paying bank, according to the exporter's requirements. We look now at the two basic elements of exporting, the paperwork and the actual transportation of goods. Then, in the next section, we look at import procedures, often the mirror image of export procedures.

EXPORT DOCUMENTS

Correct documentation is vital to the success of any export shipment. Interestingly enough, error rates reported for export and import documentation hover around 50 percent. Think of the impact of that—goods waiting in a container, on a dock, or in a warehouse, tying up working capital. We'll review the two sets of documents required to ship and collect goods.

"Any fruits or vegetables?"

Source: © The New Yorker Collection 1998 Mick Stevens from cartoonbank.com. All Rights Reserved.

Shipping Documents Shipping documents are prepared by exporters or their freight forwarders so that the shipment can pass through U.S. Customs, be loaded on the carrier, and be sent to its destination. They include the domestic bill of lading, the export packing list, the shipper's export declaration, the export licenses, the export bill of lading, and the insurance certificate. The first two documents are nearly the same as those used in domestic traffic, so we'll focus here on the other four.

The **shipper's export declaration (SED)** is required by the Department of Commerce to control exports and supply export statistics. An SED contains:

1. Names and addresses of the shipper and consignee.

2. U.S. port of exit and foreign port of unloading.

3. Description and value of the goods.

4. Export license number and bill-of-lading number.

5. Name of the carrier transporting the merchandise.

Shippers or their agents (foreign freight forwarders) deliver the SED to the carrier, which turns it in to U.S. Customs with the carrier's manifest (list of the vessel's cargo) before the carrier leaves the United States. An **automated export system (AES)** with electronic filing was introduced in 2004. The goals of this paperless reporting are to speed up export processing and reduce the 50 percent error rate on the forms.

An *export license* from the U.S. federal government is required for all exported goods except those going to U.S. possessions or, with a few exceptions, to Canada. These licenses are either validated or general. A **validated export license** is required for strategic materials and all shipments to unfriendly countries. This is a special authorization for a specific shipment and is issued by the Department of Commerce Office of Export Administration. It is required for scarce materials, strategic goods, and technology. The Department of State issues the validated license for war materials. A **general export license** is used for all products that do not require the validated license.

An **export bill of lading (B/L)** serves three purposes: It functions as a contract for carriage between the shipper and the carrier, a receipt from the carrier for the goods shipped, and a certificate of ownership. B/Ls are either *straight* or *to order*. A straight bill of lading is nonnegotiable. Only the person stipulated in it may obtain the merchandise on arrival. An order bill of lading, however, is negotiable. It can be endorsed like a check or left blank. With an order B/L, the holder is the owner of the merchandise.

The *insurance certificate* is evidence that the shipment is insured against loss or damage while in transit. Unlike domestic carriers, oceangoing steamship companies assume no responsibility for the merchandise they carry unless the loss is caused by their negligence. Marine insurance may be arranged by either the exporter or the importer, depending on the terms of sale. The laws of some countries may require that the importer buy such insurance, thus protecting the local insurance industry and saving foreign exchange. If the exporter has sold on sight draft terms, the firm carries the risk while the goods are in transit. In this case, the exporter should buy contingent interest insurance to protect it in the event that the shipment is lost or damaged and collection from the buyer is not successful. We believe that the exporter selling on CFR terms (the buyer purchases the insurance) should also buy contingent interest insurance to protect itself in case the buyer's insurance does not cover all risks.

There are three kinds of marine insurance policies: basic named perils, broad named perils, and all risks. *Basic named perils* include perils of the sea, fires, jettisons, explosions, and hurricanes. *Broad named perils* include theft, pilferage, nondelivery, breakage, and leakage in addition to the basic perils. *All risks* covers all physical loss or damage from any external cause and is more expensive than the other policies. War risks are covered under a separate contract. Premiums depend on a number of factors, such as the goods insured, the destination, the age of the ship, whether the goods are stowed on deck or under deck, the volume of business, how the goods are packed, and the number of claims the shipper has filed. Brokers will sometimes admit that in the long run it is preferable not to file numerous small claims, even if justified, because the higher premiums charged for future shipments will be greater than the money recovered.

Collection Documents   The seller is required to provide the buyer with collection documents to receive payment. These documents vary among countries and customers, but some of the most common are invoices, both commercial and consular, certificates of origin, and inspection certificates.

Export invoices are similar to domestic invoices. The commercial invoice includes additional information, such as the origin of the goods, export packing marks, and a clause stating that the goods will not be transshipped to another country. Invoices for letter-of-credit sales name the bank and the credit numbers. Some importing countries require that the commercial invoice be in their language and be visaed or endorsed by their local consul. The *consular invoice* is a special form purchased from the consul, prepared in the language of the country, and then visaed by the consul. Along with the export invoice, many governments require a *certificate of origin,* which is usually issued by the local chamber of commerce and visaed by the consul.

An *inspection certificate* is required frequently by buyers of grain, foodstuffs, and live animals. In the United States, inspection certificates are issued by the Department of Agriculture. Purchasers of machinery or products containing a specified combination of ingredients may insist that an American engineering firm or laboratory inspect the merchandise and certify that it is exactly as ordered. The EU requires the **CE (Conformite Europeene) mark** on about half of the exports it receives from the United States. This mark indicates that the merchandise conforms to European health, safety, and environmental requirements.[9] The certification process has been streamlined, and most merchandisers can self-certify that their merchandise conforms to EU regulations. Inspection by authorized testing houses is required of hazardous goods.

CE (Conformite Europeene) mark EU mark that indicates that the merchandise conforms to European health, safety and environmental requirements

EXPORT SHIPMENTS

Most newcomers to exporting are so focused on making their sale and handling the documentation that they fail to be concerned about the actual physical movement of their goods. Innovations in material-handling techniques can help exporters reduce costs and perhaps reach markets they previously could not serve. Containerization, LASH, RO-RO, size, and air freight all offer increasingly cheaper, faster, and safer transportation solutions, shrinking our globe.

One means of drastically reducing both theft and handling costs is to use containers. *Containers* are large boxes—8 feet by 8 feet by 10, 20, or 40 feet—that the seller fills with the shipment in the firm's warehouse. Their origins are interesting, as explained in the chapter's opening section. Once packed, the containers are then sealed; they are opened when the goods arrive at their final destination. Containers are transported by truck or rail from the warehouse to shipside for loading. From the port of entry, railroads or trucks deliver them, often unopened even for customs inspection, to the buyer's warehouse. In most countries, customs officials go to the warehouse to examine the shipment. This integrated process reduces handling time and the risk of damage and theft because the buyer's own employees unload the containers.

If the importer or exporter has a warehouse on a river too shallow for ocean vessels, the firm can save time and expense by loading containers on barges. *LASH* (lighter aboard ship) vessels provide direct access to ocean freight service for exporters and importers located on shallow inland waterways. Sixty-foot-long barges ("lighters") are towed to inland locations, loaded, and towed back to deep water, where they are loaded aboard anchored LASH ships.

Another innovation in cargo handling is *RO-RO* (roll on–roll off) ships. Loaded trailers and any equipment on wheels can be driven onto these specially designed vessels. RO-RO service has brought the benefits of containerization to ports that have been unable to invest in the expensive lifting equipment required for containers.

Ship size continues to expand. Until recently, the standard largest size was "Panamax," which fit through the Panama Canal's locks with only feet to spare. "Post-Panamax" ("Suezmax," "capesize") ships are too big for the canal—nearly 44 feet too wide and over 200 feet longer than the canal can accept. Some 160 of these ships will be put in operation over the next few years, many to carry Chinese exports. So Panama must build a third set of even larger locks.

Air freight has had a profound effect on international business because it permits shipments that once required 30 days to arrive in 1 day. Huge freight planes carry payloads of 200,000 pounds, most of which goes either in containers or on pallets. Airlines guarantee overnight delivery from New York to many European airports and claim that their planes can be loaded or unloaded in 45 minutes.

Newcomers to exporting might assume that ocean freight is a better choice than air freight because ocean freight is so much cheaper. Comparison of total costs of each mode may suggest otherwise. Total cost components that may be lower for air freight include insurance rates, because of much less chance of damage during shipment; packing costs, because

Shoes for People with Two Left Feet

For days, cargo thieves were watching construction crews enlarging one of Los Angeles's large container terminals. Toward the end of the work, the crews began moving the fences out to the expanded perimeter. When they ran out of heavy-security fence, they used lightweight fencing temporarily. This was the chance the thieves had been waiting for. That night, they cut the fence and drove a tractor-trailer truck up to a line of containers. After breaking into a number of them, they found one full of sports shoes that retailed for $150 a pair. They connected it to their tractor-trailer and escaped in the darkness.

But it was the importer who had the last laugh. A week later, the police found the abandoned container with its cargo intact. The thieves didn't know that the importer routinely shipped all its left shoes in one container and its right shoes in another. They had stolen a container with left shoes. Instead of buying expensive global positioning devices, the importer used cheap, low-tech methods. Ship all left shoes.

Source: "Sneaking Up on Security," www.internationalbusiness.com/feb/log297.htm (February 20, 1998).

---

the shipment does not need the heavier, more costly export packing, which is usually done by an outside firm; customs duties, when calculated on gross weights; replacement costs for damaged goods, again because of the reduced damage risk; and inventory costs, because the rapid delivery by air freight often eliminates the need for expensive warehouses. For example, Mercedes-Benz includes in the price of its luxury sports car Brabus SLR McLaren air freight from Bottrop, Germany, to anywhere in the world. Another cost saving is that machinery shipped by air does not require a heavy coat of grease to protect it from the elements, as does machinery sent by ship. Table 17.2 provides a sample comparison of the cost elements of ocean and air freight.

Even when the total shipping costs are higher for air freight, shipping by air may still be advantageous for several reasons:

1. *Total cost may decrease.* Getting the product to the buyer more quickly results in a more satisfied customer and faster payment, which speeds up the return on investment and improves cash flow. The firm's capital is released more quickly and can be invested

TABLE 17.2 | Sea-Air Total Cost Comparison, Shipment of Spare Parts

	Ocean Freight (with warehousing)	Air Freight (no warehousing)
Warehouse administrative costs	$ 1,020	—
Warehouse rent	1,680	—
Inventory costs		
Taxes and insurance	756	$ 396
Inventory financing	288	192
Inventory obsolescence	1,800	0
Seller's warehouse and handling costs	1,810	1,140
Transportation	420	2,400
Packaging and handling	300	120
Cargo insurance	72	36
Customs duties	132	127
Total	$8,278	$4,411

in other profit-making ventures or used to repay borrowed capital, thus reducing interest payments. Production equipment may be assembled and sent by air so that it goes into production sooner, without the transit and setup delays associated with ocean shipments, a strong sales argument. These production and opportunity costs, although difficult to calculate, are part of the total cost.

2. *Either the firm or the product may be air-dependent.* Perishable food products being shipped to Europe, Japan, and the Middle East are in this category, as are live animals (newly hatched poultry and prize bulls) and fresh flowers. Without air freight, firms exporting such products would be out of business.

3. *The market may be perishable.* For goods with short life cycles, such as high-fashion products, delivery speed matters. When a fashion fad dies, its market goes with it.

4. *Competitive position may be strengthened.* The sales argument that spare parts and factory technical personnel are available within a few hours is a strong one for an exporting firm competing with overseas manufacturers.

Importing

In one sense, importers are the reverse of exporters: They sell domestically and buy in foreign markets. However, many of their concerns are similar. As in the case of exporters, there are small firms whose only business is to import, and there are global corporations for which importing components and raw materials valued at millions of dollars is just one of their functions. We will examine sources for imports, the role of customhouse brokers, and the payment of import duties here.

SOURCES FOR IMPORTS

Before importing, a firm may have difficulty determining whether the desired items exist and, if so, where to find them. How does the prospective importer identify import sources? There are a number of ways. First, similar imported products may already be in the market. By simple close examination, you can learn where they are made and often by whom. U.S. law requires that the country of origin be clearly marked on each product or on its container if product marking is not feasible (individual cigarettes, for example). The consul or embassy of the country of origin can help with names of manufacturers. One of the principal duties of all foreign government representatives is to promote exports, and they do this through newsletters, trade shows, industry shows, and collaborative events with their home country chamber of commerce group and other organizations, such as, for Japan, the Japan External Trade Organization (JETRO), which has a number of offices outside Japan. The process is the same if the product is not being imported. You simply have less information with which to begin.

Other sources of information are electronic bulletin boards such as those of the World Trade Centers. Accidental importing also occurs with some frequency. When you visit a foreign country, look for products that may have a market at home. Finding one could put you into a new business, one that makes foreign travel tax-deductible.

Now we turn to some of the technical aspects of importing, customhouse brokers and import duties.

CUSTOMHOUSE BROKERS

In every nation, there are **customhouse brokers,** whose functions parallel those of foreign freight forwarders but are on the import side of the transaction. As the agent for the importer, the customhouse broker brings the imported goods through customs, which requires that they know well the many import regulations and an extensive, complex tariff schedule. If a customs official places the import in a category requiring higher import duties than the importer had planned on, the importing firm may not be able to compete. To levy customs, evaluators everywhere generally use units shipped for products that carry specific duties and the invoice

customhouse brokers
Independent businesses that handle import shipments for compensation

price for ad valorem duties. There are some exceptions. The practice of U.S. Customs is to use the transaction price, which appears on the commercial invoice accompanying the shipment, plus any other charges not included in the transaction price. These may be royalty or license fees, packing, or any assists. *Assist* is the U.S. Customs term applied to any item that the buyer provides free or at reduced cost for use in the production or sale of merchandise for export to the United States. Examples are molds and dies sent overseas to produce a specific product, a common practice of importers who want the goods produced using their design, and components and parts that the buyer provides for incorporation in the finished article.

Customhouse brokers also provide other services, such as arranging transportation for the goods after they have left customs if the exporter has not arranged for it. They also keep track of which imports are subject to import quotas and how much of the quota has been filled at the time of the import. No matter which port the goods arrive at, U.S. Customs knows immediately the quantity that has been imported. Merchandise subject to import quotas can be on the dock of an American port awaiting clearance through customs, but if the quota fills anywhere during the wait, those goods cannot be imported for the rest of the fiscal year. The would-be importer can put them in a **bonded warehouse** or a foreign trade zone, where merchandise can be stored without paying duty, and wait for the rest of the year; abandon them; or send them to another country. Importers of high-fashion clothing have lost millions of dollars when quotas became filled and they had a shipment that had not yet cleared. They could not sell the clothing until the following year, by which time it was out of fashion.

Customs has moved to the **Automated Commercial System (ACS)** to track, control, and process all commercial goods imported into the United States. ACS reduces the paperwork, cuts costs, and facilitates merchandise processing. Importers that use the system to file import documents can also pay the customs fees and import duties electronically all in one transaction. Like AES, ACS interfaces with other government agencies to transfer data electronically on import transactions for faster cargo release. An Automated Manifest System also speeds the flow of cargo and entry processing, with the result that cargo remains on the dock for less time before its release to the importers.[10]

IMPORT DUTIES

Every importer should know how U.S. Customs calculates import duties and the importance of the product classification system, the **Harmonized Tariff Schedule of the United States (HTSUSA),** the American version of the global tariff code, the Harmonized System. The Harmonized System is a classification system for the over 200,000 commodities traded internationally, and it includes interpretive notes that help determine the classifications.

In HTSUSA each product has its own unique number. Figure 17.5 shows a page from the HTSUSA. All member-countries use the same system, and so it is possible to describe the product in any language by using the first six digits. The other four digits are for use just in the United States. The HTSUSA also shows the *reporting units,* which U.S. Customs uses in its paperwork. The last three columns have to do with the rate of duty.

Rates of duty are broken down into three levels for each item—general, special, and a third-rate level for countries not considered friends of the United States. HTSUSA is accessible on the Internet.[11]

New importers would do well to follow this advice: Disclose fully to the U.S. Customs Service all foreign and financial arrangements before passing the goods through U.S. Customs. The penalties for fraud are high. Get the advice of a customhouse broker *before* making the transaction. Frequently, a simple change in the product description can result in a much lower import duty. For example, jeans carry higher duties if the label is outside the back pocket instead of under the belt. If the words on the label are stylized, the duties are higher as well. Any clothing that is ornamented has higher duty. One importer brings in plain sports shirts and then sews on an animal figure after the products are in the United States. One last word of advice: Calculate carefully the landed price in advance. If you are unsure of the import category, ask U.S. Customs to determine the category in advance and to put it in writing, just like advanced rulings from the Internal Revenue Service. At the time of importation, customs inspectors must respect this determination.

bonded warehouse
An area authorized by customs authorities for storage of goods on which payment of import duties is deferred until the goods are removed

Automated Commercial System (ACS)
Electronic tracking system used by U.S. Customs to track, control, and process all commercial goods imported into the United States

Harmonized Tariff Schedule of the United States (HTSUSA)
American version of the Harmonized System used worldwide to classify imported products

FIGURE 17.5

Page from the
HTSUSA

HARMONIZED TARIFF SCHEDULE of the UNITED STATES (1995)
Annotated for Statistical Reporting Purposes

XVI
84–62

Heading/ Subheading	Stat. Suf- fix	Article Description	Units of Quantity	Rates of Duty		
				General	1 Special	2
8461		Machine tools for planing, shaping, slotting, broaching, gear cutting, gear grinding or gear finishing, sawing, cutting-off and other machine tools working by removing metal, sintered metal carbides or cerments, not elsewhere specified or included:				
8461.10		Planing machines:				
8461.10.40		Numerically controlled	....	4.4%	Free (A,CA,E,IL,J, MX)	30%
	20	Used or rebuilt	No.			
	60	Other	No.			
8461.10.80		Other	....	4.4%	Free (A,CA,E,IL,J, MX)	30%
	20	Used or rebuilt	No.			
	40	Other, valued under $3,025 each ...	No.			
	80	Other	No.			
8461.20		Shaping or slotting machines:				
8461.20.40	00	Numerically controlled	No....	4.4%	Free (A,CA,E,IL,J, MX)	30%
8461.20.80		Other	....	4.4%	Free (A,CA,E,IL,J, MX)	30%
	30	Used or rebuilt	No.			
	70	Other, valued under $3,025 each ...	No.			
	90	Other	No.			
8461.30		Broaching machines:				
8461.30.40		Numerically controlled	....	4.4%	Free (A,CA,E,IL,J, MX)	30%
	20	Used or rebuilt	No.			
	60	Other	No.			
8461.30.80		Other	....	4.4%	Free (A,CA,E,IL,J, MX)	30%
	20	Used or rebuilt	No.			
	40	Other, valued under $3,025 each ...	No.			
	80	Other	No.			
8461.40		Gear cutting, gear grinding or gear finishing machines:				
8461.40.10		Gear cutting machines	....	5.8%	Free (A,CA,E,IL,J, MX)	40%
	10	Used or rebuilt	No.			
		Other:				
	20	For bevel gears	No.			
		Other:				
	30	Gear hobbers	No.			
	40	Gear shapers	No.			
	60	Other	No.			
8461.40.50		Gear grinding or finishing machines	....	4.4%	Free (A,CA,E,IL,J, MX)	30%
	20	Used or rebuilt	No.			
	40	Other, valued under $3,025 each ..	No.			
		Other:				
	50	For bevel gears	No.			
	70	Other	No.			
8461.50		Sawing or cutting-off machines:				
8461.50.40		Numerically controlled	....	4.4%	Free (A,CA,E,IL,J, MX)	30%
	10	Used or rebuilt	No.			
	50	Other	No.			
8461.50.80		Other	....	4.4%	Free (A,CA,E,IL,J, MX)	30%
	10	Used or rebuilt	No.			
	20	Other, valued under $3,025 each ..	No.			
	90	Other	No.			
8461.90		Other:				
8461.90.40		Numerically controlled	....	4.4%	Free (A,CA,E,IL,J, MX)	30%
	10	Used or rebuilt	No.			
	40	Other	No.			
8461.90.80		Other	....	4.4%	Free (A,CA,E,IL,J, MX)	30%
	10	Used or rebuilt	No.			
	20	Other, valued under $3,025 each ..	No.			
	80	Other	No.			

Source: Harmonized Tariff Schedule of the United States (Washington, DC: U.S. Government Printing Office, 1995), p. 84-62.

Summary

Explain why firms export and the three challenge areas of exporting.

Smaller firms, like larger ones, export to increase sales. Some begin to export accidentally, while others seek out foreign customers. Large multinationals export to serve markets where they have no manufacturing plants or where the local plant does not produce all of the product mix. Some host governments require an affiliate to export, and many firms export to remain competitive in the home market. Exporting is also an inexpensive way to test foreign markets. A product's life can be extended by exporting the product to markets where it is at the introduction stage of the product life cycle. The three challenge areas of exporting are (1) locating foreign markets, (2) payment and financing procedures, and (3) export procedures.

Identify the sources of export counseling and support.

The Trade Information Center, Small Business Administration, Small Business Development Centers, Department of Agriculture, state offices for export assistance, and World Trade Centers Association are some sources of export counseling. The Department of Commerce, the federal department in charge of export assistance, offers many programs covering all aspects of exporting. Commerce also assists in locating foreign representatives and making sales through trade fairs, matchmaker programs, and catalog and video shows.

Discuss the meaning of the various terms of sale.

Various terms of sale are possible in exporting. *FAS* (free alongside ship) means the seller pays all transportation expenses to the ship's side and is required to clear the goods for export. *CIF* (cost, insurance, and freight) means the seller quotes a price that includes cost of goods, insurance, and transportation to a specified destination. *CFR* (cost and freight) is like CIF except that the buyer pays the insurance costs. *DAF* (delivered at frontier) means that the seller's obligations are met when the goods have arrived at the border and been cleared for export. The buyer's responsibility is to arrange for its forwarder to pick up the goods after they are cleared for export, clear them for importation, and make delivery.

Identify some sources of export financing.

Some sources of export financing are commercial banks, factors, forfaiting, the Export-Import Bank (Ex-Im Bank), and the Small Business Administration.

Describe the activities of a foreign freight forwarder.

Foreign freight forwarders act as agents for exporters. They prepare documents, book space on carriers, and function as a firm's export traffic department.

Outline the export documents required.

Correct documentation is vital to the success of any export shipment. Shipping documents include export packing lists, export licenses, export bills of lading, shipper's export declaration, and insurance certificates. Collection documents include commercial invoices, consular invoices, certificates of origin, and inspection certificates.

Identify import sources.

Prospective importers can identify sources in a number of ways. They can examine the product label to see where the product is made and then contact the nearest embassy of that country to request the name of the manufacturer. Foreign chambers of commerce and trade organizations provide information on their countries' exporters. Electronic bulletin boards and data banks are also useful.

Explain the Harmonized Tariff Schedule of the United States (HTSUSA).

The HTSUSA is the American version of the Harmonized System used worldwide to classify imported products. A sample page from the HTSUSA is shown in Figure 17.5, and the listings can be viewed online at www.usitc.gov/tata/hts/index.htm.

Key Words

terms of sale (p. 451)

INCOTERMS (p. 451)

FOB (p. 452)

Ex-Works (p. 452)

letter of credit (L/C) (p. 453)

confirmed L/C (p. 454)

irrevocable L/C (p. 454)

air waybill (p. 455)

pro forma invoice (p. 455)

export, sight, and time drafts (p. 456)

banker's acceptance (p. 457)

factoring (p. 457)

forfaiting (p. 457)

Ex-Im Bank (p. 458)

Overseas Private Investment Corporation (OPIC) (p. 458)

foreign trade zone (FTZ) (p. 458)

free trade zone (p. 458)

customs drawbacks (p. 458)

shipper's export declaration (SED) (p. 460)

Questions

1. What are the common terms of sale quoted by exporters? For each, explain to what point the seller must pay transportation and delivery costs. Where does the responsibility for loss or damage pass to the buyer?

2. a. Explain the various export payment terms that are available.

   b. Which two offer the most protection to the seller?

3. What is the procedure for a letter-of-credit transaction?

4. The manager of the international department of the Cape Cod Five Bank learns on the way to work that the ship on which a local exporter shipped some goods to Spain has sunk. She has received all the documents required in the letter of credit and is ready to pay the exporter for the shipment. In view of the news about the ship, the manager now knows that the foreign customer will never receive the goods. Should the manager pay the exporter, or should she withhold payment and notify the overseas customer?

5. What is a foreign trade zone? Check with a customhouse broker or a U.S. Customs official or do some online research to determine the advantages of a foreign trade zone over a bonded warehouse.

6. What are the purposes of an export bill of lading?

7. An importer brings plain sports shirts to this country because the import duty is lower than it is for shirts with adornments. The importer then sews on a figure of a fox in this country. Should the importer do this operation in a foreign trade zone?

8. How would you find sources for a product that you want to import?

9. What does a customhouse broker do?

10. What does a freight forwarder do?

Research Task

globalEDGE globalEDGE.msu.edu

Use the globalEDGE site (http://globalEDGE.msu.edu) to complete the following exercises:

1. Your company is planning to expand its operations to Morocco. Considering each country has its own import and export regulations, prepare a report for top management of your company on Morocco's foreign trade barriers, listing current regulations and limitations on trade for both imports and exports in Morocco.

2. You own a company that specializes in fishery products. Until now, your firm has been selling to European markets (e.g., Germany, France, and the United Kingdom). Based on your experience with these companies, you are confident in your ability to engage in international business transactions appropriately. Therefore, you are convinced that it is time to expand into Asian markets. Nevertheless, the size of investment is significant, and you must have a clear picture of the current agricultural import regulations and standards for Asian countries. Using reports created by the U.S. Foreign Agriculture Service, find information on major agricultural import regulations and standards for Malaysia and Thailand.

State Manufacturing Company, a producer of farm equipment, had just received an inquiry from a large distributor in Italy. The quantity on which the distributor wanted a price was sufficiently large that Jim Mason, the sales manager, felt he had to respond. He knew the inquiry was genuine, because he had called two of the companies that the distributor said he represented, and both had assured him that the Italian firm was a serious one. It paid its bills regularly with no problems. Both companies were selling to the firm on open account terms.

Mason's problem was that he had never quoted on a sale for export before. His first impulse was to take the regular FOB factory price and add the cost of the extra-heavy export packing plus the inland freight cost to the nearest U.S. port. This price should enable the company to make money if he quoted the price FAS port of exit.

However, the terms of sale were bothering him. The traffic manager had called a foreign freight forwarder to learn about the frequency of sailings to Italy, and during the conversation she had suggested to the traffic manager that she might be able to help Mason. When Mason called her, he learned that because of competition, many firms like State Manufacturing were quoting CIF foreign port as a convenience to the importer. She asked him what payment terms he would quote, and he replied that his credit manager had suggested an irrevocable, confirmed letter of credit to be sure of receiving payment for the sale. He admitted that the distributor, however, had asked for payment against a 90-day time draft.

The foreign freight forwarder urged Mason to consider quoting CIF port of entry in Italy with payment as requested by the distributor to be more competitive. She informed him that he could get insurance to protect the company against commercial risk. To help him calculate a CIF price, she offered to give him the various charges if he would tell her the weight and value of his shipment FOB factory. He replied that the total price was $21,500 and that the gross weight, including the container, was 3,629 kilos.

Two hours later, she called to give him the following charges:

1. Containerization $ 200.00
2. Inland freight less handling   798.00
3. Forwarding and documentation   90.00
4. Ocean freight   2,633.00
5. Commercial risk insurance   105.00
6. Marine insurance (total of items
   $1-5 \times 1.1 = \$27,858.60$ at 60¢/$100)*   167.15

During that time, Mason had been thinking about the competition. Could he lower the FOB price for an export sale? He looked at the cost figures. Sales expense amounted to 20 percent of the sales price. Couldn't this be deducted on a foreign order? Research and development amounted to 10 percent. Should this be charged? Advertising and promotional expense amounted to another 10 percent. What about that? Because this was an unsolicited inquiry, there was no selling expense for this sale except for his and the secretary's time. Mason felt that it wasn't worth calculating this time.

If you were Jim Mason, how would you calculate the CIF port of entry price?

*Total coverage of marine insurance is commonly calculated on the basis of the total price plus 10 percent.

1. Who issued the letter of credit (shown on page 469)?
2. Is it irrevocable?
3. Has it been confirmed?
4. If so, by whom?
5. Who is the buyer?
6. Who is the seller?
7. What kind of draft is to be presented?
8. What documents are required?
9. What are the terms of sale?
10. When does the letter of credit expire?
11. Where does the seller go for payment?
12. Who pays the freight?
13. Who pays the marine insurance?
14. Must the steamship company attest that the merchandise has been loaded on ship?
15. What is the reason for your answer to question 14?

MORGAN GUARANTY TRUST COMPANY
OF NEW YORK
INTERNATIONAL BANKING DIVISION
23 WALL STREET, NEW YORK, N.Y. 10015   March 5, 20___

Smith Tool Co. Inc.
29 Bleecker Street
New York, N.Y. 10012

> On all communications please refer to
>
> **NUMBER IC — 152647**

Dear Sirs:
We are instructed to advise you of the establishment by
. Bank of South America, Puerto Cabello, Venezuela . . . .
of their IRREVOCABLE Credit No. 19845 . . . .
in your favor, for the account of John Doe, Puerto Cabello, Venezuela . . . .
for U. S. $3,000.00 (THREE THOUSAND U. S. DOLLARS) . . . .
available upon presentation to us of your drafts at sight on us, accompanied by:
Commercial Invoice in triplicate, describing the merchandise as indicated below

Consular Invoice in triplicate, all signed and stamped by the Consul of Venezuela

Negotiable Insurance Policy and/or Underwriter's Certificate, endorsed in blank, covering
marine and war risks

Full set of straight ocean steamer Bills of Lading, showing consignment to the Bank of
South America, Puerto Cabello, stamped by Venezuelan Consul and marked "Freight Prepaid",

evidencing shipment of UNA MAQUINA DE SELLAR LATAS, C.I.F. Puerto Cabello, from United
States Port to Puerto Cabello, Venezuela

Except as otherwise expressly stated herein, this credit is subject to the Uniform Customs and Practice
for Documentary Credits (1974 revision), International Chamber of Commerce Publication No. 290.

The above bank engages with you that all drafts drawn under and in compliance with
the terms of this advice will be duly honored if presented to our Commercial Credits
Department, 15 Broad Street, New York, N. Y. 10015, on or before March 31, 20* on which
date this credit expires.

We confirm the foregoing and undertake that all drafts drawn and presented in
accordance with its terms will be duly honored.
Yours very truly,

Authorized Signature
Immediately upon receipt, please examine this instrument and if its terms are not clear to
you or if you need any assistance in respect to your availment of it, we would welcome your
communicating with us. Documents should be presented promptly and not later than 3 P.M.

Appendix: Sample Outline for the Export Business Plan

I. Purpose—Why has the plan been written?

II. Table of contents—Include a list of any appendixes.

III. Executive summary—This is short and concise (not over two pages) and covers the principal points of the report. It is prepared after the plan has been written.

IV. Introduction—Explains why the firm will export.

V. Situation analysis.

    A. Description of the firm and products to be exported.

    B. Company resources to be used for the export business.

    C. Competitive situation in the industry.

        1. Product comparisons.

        2. Market coverage.

        3. Market share.

D. Export organization—personnel and structure.

VI. Export marketing plan.

   A. Long- and short-term goals.

      1. Total sales in units.

      2. Total sales in dollars.

      3. Sales by product lines.

      4. Market share.

      5. Profit and loss forecasts.

   B. Characteristics of ideal target markets.

      1. GNP/capita.

      2. GNP/capita growth rate.

      3. Size of target market.

   C. Identify, assess, and select target markets.

      1. Market contact programs.

         (a) U.S. Department of Commerce.

         (b) World Trade Centers.

         (c) Chamber of Commerce.

         (d) Company's bank.

         (e) State's export assistance program.

         (f) Small Business Administration.

         (g) Small Business Development Center in local university.

         (h) Export hotline directory.

      2. Market screening.

         (a) First screening—basic need potential.

         (b) Second screening—financial and economic forces.

            (1) GNP/capita growth rate.

            (2) Size of target market.

            (3) Growth rate of target market.

            (4) Exchange rate trends.

            (5) Trends in inflation and interest rates.

         (c) Third screening—political and legal forces.

            (1) Import restrictions.

            (2) Product standards.

            (3) Price controls.

            (4) Government and public attitude toward buying American products.

         (d) Fourth screening—sociocultural forces.

            (1) Attitudes and beliefs.

            (2) Education.

            (3) Material culture.

            (4) Languages.

         (e) Fifth screening—competitive forces.

            (1) Size, number, and financial strength of competitors.

            (2) Competitors' market shares.

            (3) Effectiveness of competitors' marketing mixes.

            (4) Levels of after-sales service.

            (5) Competitors' market coverage— Can market segmentation produce niches that are now poorly attended?

         (f) Field trips to best prospects.

            (1) Department of Commerce trade mission.

            (2) Trade missions organized by state or trade association.

   D. Export marketing strategies.

      1. Product lines to export.

      2. Export pricing methods.

      3. Channels of distribution.

         (a) Direct exporting.

         (b) Indirect exporting.

      4. Promotion methods.

      5. After-sales and warranty policies.

      6. Buyer financing methods.

      7. Methods for ongoing competitor analysis.

      8. Sales forecast.

VII. Export financial plan.

    A. Pro forma profit and loss statement.

    B. Pro forma cash flow analysis.

    C. Break-even analysis.

VIII. Export performance evaluation.

    A. Frequency.

        1. Markets.

        2. Product lines.

        3. Export personnel.

    B. Variables to be measured.

        1. Sales by units and dollar volume in each market.

        2. Sales growth rates in each market.

        3. Product line profitability.

        4. Market share.

        5. Competitors' efforts in each market.

        6. Actual results compared to budgeted results.

18 Marketing Internationally

Procter & Gamble European headquarters in Geneva, Switzerland

A global company should always go about its business in a way that's responsive to the major differences from one country to another, in terms of, for example, how retailing or distribution or payment systems work. But the core product or service should remain unchanged, ... since that is what is "globalized."

—Theodore Levitt, author of the landmark Harvard Business Review *piece on standardization, "The Globalization of Markets"*

But when it comes to questions of taste and, especially, aesthetic preference, consumers do not like averages.... The lure of a universal product is a false allure.

—Kenichi Ohmae

Procter & Gamble's Path to Globalization

Procter & Gamble's global marketing efforts have brought results—Ariel, Tide, Pert, Pantene, and the Gillette-owned brands accessed by its 2005 acquisition. Today some of the 210-plus P&G brands are major brands everywhere around the world, and 21 of them are in the top-ranked billion-dollar sales category. In addition, 53 percent of P&G sales were outside the United States in 2005. China is the second-largest market by sales volume, and 4 percent of the 2006 sales originated in the Northeast Asia group. These results are remarkable given that P&G faces more pressures in many foreign markets than it does in its U.S. markets. For example, in the European markets, because the EU makes shipping across borders quite easy, competition in the household products sector is stiff. In France, P&G competes against Swedish, Danish, and Italian firms in many of its product categories. There are also unanticipated issues possibly related to nationalism that P&G repeatedly is required to address in foreign markets. In China in October 2006, P&G stopped selling its skin care products and began a massive refund effort when China's General Administration of Quality Supervision, Inspection and Quarantine said it had found trace levels of the metals chromium and neodymium in P&G products. In such situations, localization is mandated.

P&G's strategy for its international markets has evolved in an interesting way. In the 1940s, P&G's approach was to export its core products from the United States, build foreign demand, and then establish local sales companies and possibly production facilities. None of those products was launched with global distribution in mind. P&G's philosophy was to employ overseas the same policies and procedures that had worked for it in the United States. As a result, 15 years were needed for P&G to get Pampers into 70 countries. However, in the early 1990s, Edwin Artzt, then P&G's CEO, changed the firm's marketing strategy. Instead of waiting to introduce a new product worldwide until after it had accumulated marketing experience, the company would introduce products on a worldwide scale early in their development. The aim of this approach was to avoid giving competitors time to react in all other markets. As Artzt put it, "If P&G were introducing Pampers today, it would plan to get the product into world markets in five years or less." Today the present P&G CEO, A. G. Lafley, has commented that P&G can manage a worldwide rollout in less than 18 months.

At times in the past, the company has used a regional rather than a global approach, changing many of its products to suit the regional markets. Camay's smell, Crest's flavor, and Head & Shoulders' formula are some examples of products that varied from one region to another, as did the company's marketing strategy. Occasionally, P&G has recycled ad campaigns from the United States to other markets. For example, when the firm introduced Orange Crush in Peru, it used a TV spot showing a small boy who promised to save his soccer-playing brother's Orange Crush but then succumbed to temptation and drank it himself. This spot was credited with an important role in a 60 percent sales increase.

Now P&G has organized into three global business units, Beauty and Health, Household Care, and Gillette. Using this simple structure, it sells products in over 180 countries, primarily through mass merchandisers, grocery stores, membership club stores, and drugstores. P&G's global marketing officer, James Stengel, is

CONCEPT PREVIEWS

After reading this chapter, you should be able to:

explain why there are differences between domestic and international marketing

discuss why international marketing managers may wish to standardize the marketing mix

explain why it is often impossible to standardize the marketing mix worldwide

discuss the importance of distinguishing among the total product, the physical product, and the brand name

explain why consumer products generally require greater modification for international sales than do industrial products or services

discuss the product strategies that can be formed from three product alternatives and three kinds of promotional messages

explain "glocal" advertising strategies

discuss some of the effects the Internet may have on international marketing

discuss the distribution strategies of international marketers

Gli Affari Internazionali

onales Geschäft Παγοσμιο Business

Negócios Internacionais   Los Negócios Internacionais

internacionales   Affaires Internationales   国際商務   Παγοσμιο Business

473

reluctant to apply the phrase "think global, act local" as P&G's marketing mantra today, because he is convinced that the relationships and interaction are more sophisticated than that. "I think P&G may be ahead in thinking through what the right balance is on global and local. My buzz word is that we must win with local consumers, day in day out. It's as simple and as difficult as that." To do so demands localization, woven seamlessly into the product mix. For example, each national or regional market has its own Internet presence. You can begin exploring P&G's global operations and markets at www.pg.com/company/who_we_are/globalops.jhtml. ■

Source: Procter & Gamble, *2006 Annual Report*, www.pg.com (October 6, 2006); "Survey: Creative Business: The World's Biggest Marketing Job: P&G," *Financial Times*, April 23, 2002; "P&G Suspends Skincare Sales in China," *Financial Times*, September 22, 2006, www.FT.com (October 7, 2006).

The opening vignette illustrates how P&G has changed its marketing strategy from using the same procedures and policies overseas that have proved successful in the United States to making global plans, adjusting them for regions, and then adapting products to satisfy local demands.

Whether a policy or technique is first designed for global use and then adapted for local market differences or, as in the case of the Orange Crush advertisement, the idea comes from the home country and then is used overseas, marketers must know where to look for possible differences between marketing domestically and marketing internationally. Sometimes the differences are great; at other times there may be few or even no differences.

Whether the differences between international and domestic marketing are great or small, marketers everywhere must know their markets, develop products or services to satisfy their customers' needs, price the products or services so that they are readily acceptable in the market, make them available to buyers, and inform potential customers, persuading them to buy.

Added Complexities of International Marketing

Although the basic functions of domestic and international marketing are the same, the international markets served often differ widely because of the great variations in the uncontrollable environmental forces—sociocultural, resource and environmental, economic and socioeconomic, legal, financial, and labor—that we examined in Section Three. Moreover, even the forces we think of as controllable vary across markets within wide limits. For example, distribution channels to which the marketer is accustomed may be unavailable. This is the case in Japan and in China. Certain aspects of the product may need to be different, for a number of reasons that range from taste and aesthetic preferences to voltage patterns and altitude issues. Then, too, the promotional mixes often must be dissimilar. Finally, distinct cost structures of specific markets may require that different prices be set.

The international marketing manager's task is complex. She or he frequently must plan and control a variety of marketing strategies, rather than a single unified and standardized one, and then coordinate and integrate those strategies into a single marketing program. Even marketing managers of global firms, such as P&G's global marketing officer, James Stengel, who may want to use a single worldwide strategy realize that doing so is impossible. They must know enough about the uncontrollable variables to be able to make quick and decisive implementation changes when necessary. P&G's recent issues in China with alleged skin care product contamination are a case in point.

Both global and multinational marketing managers, much like their domestic counterparts, have the same general challenges. They must develop marketing strategies by assessing the firm's potential foreign markets and analyzing the many alternative marketing mixes. Their aim here is to select target markets that the firm can serve at a profit and then to formulate combinations of tactics for product, price, promotion, and distribution channels that will best serve those markets. In Chapter 15, we examined the market assessment and selection process in the international domain; in this chapter, we shall study the formulation of the marketing mix for the international environment.

The Marketing Mix (What to Sell and How to Sell It)

The *marketing mix* is a set of strategy decisions made in the areas of product, promotion, pricing, and distribution in order to satisfy the needs and desires of customers in a target market. The number of variable factors included in these four marketing areas is large, making possible hundreds of combinations. Often a company's domestic operation has already established a successful marketing mix, and the temptation to follow the same strategies and tactics overseas is strong. Yet, as we have seen, important differences between the domestic and foreign environments are likely to make a wholesale transfer of the mix—its standardization—impossible, however desirable such a transfer may be from a business viewpoint. The question that the international marketing manager must resolve for each market is, "Can we standardize worldwide, should we make some changes, or should we formulate a completely different marketing mix?"

STANDARDIZE, ADAPT, OR FORMULATE ANEW?

Often top management would prefer to standardize the marketing mix globally; that is, the strategic decision makers would prefer to use the same marketing mix in all of the firm's markets because standardization can produce significant cost savings. If the product sold in the domestic market can be exported, regardless of where the product is made, there can be longer production runs, which lower manufacturing costs. In addition to these economies of scale, the longer experience curve, or learning curve, can create economies as well: The more experience we have doing something, the better we get at that activity, usually. Both of these economies, scale and experience, apply to marketing. A standardized approach can result in significant savings.

When advertising campaigns, promotional materials (catalogs, point-of-purchase displays), and sales training programs can be standardized, the expensive creative work and artwork need be done only once. A standardized corporate visual identity (CVI) (firm name, slogan, and graphics) can help project a consistent image for a multinational with publics dispersed across geographic locales.[1] Standardized pricing strategies for firms that serve markets from several different subsidiaries prevent the embarrassment of having an important customer receive two unequal price quotations for the same product. In summary, in addition to the cost benefits from standardization of the marketing mix, control and coordination are easier, and time spent preparing the marketing plan is reduced significantly.

In spite of the advantages of standardization, almost all firms find that this chapter's opening quote by Kenichi Ohmae is accurate for them: Standardization is seldom as easy as it seems. Many firms find it necessary to modify the present marketing mix or develop a new one. The extent of the changes depends on the type of product, the environmental forces, and the degree of market penetration desired. Further, given that the very concept of standardization is in a state of tension with the marketing principle, which centers on the needs of the buyer, not the seller, we probably should not be too disappointed that the economies that would come with complete standardization are almost never available to the seller, especially the seller in consumer goods.

Even Coca-Cola, the firm often portrayed as the exemplar of the standardized product, has found that its increasingly standardized strategy had run its course. According to Coca-Cola's former chair Douglas Daft: "As the [20th] century was drawing to a close, the world had changed course, and we had not. The world was demanding greater flexibility, responsiveness and local sensitivity, while we were further consolidating decision making and standardizing our practices. . . . The next big evolutionary step of 'going global' now has to be 'going local.' "[2] The tuition for Coke's learning was its loss of international market share to its competition, both global and local.

PRODUCT STRATEGIES

The product is the central focus of the marketing mix. If it fails to satisfy the needs of consumers, no amount of promotion, price cutting, or distribution will persuade people to buy. Consumers will not repurchase a detergent if the clothes do not come out as clean as commercials say they will. They will not be deceived by advertisements announcing friendly service when their own experience demonstrates otherwise.

In formulating product strategies, international marketing managers must remember that the product is more than a physical object. The **total product,** which is what the customer buys, includes the physical product, brand name, accessories, after-sales service, warranty, instructions for use, company image, and package (see Figure 18.1). That the total product is what the customer purchases may present the company with product adaptation opportunities that are less expensive and easier than would be the case if every adaptation had to alter the product's physical characteristics. Different package sizes and promotional messages, for example, can create a new total product for a distinct market. The relative ease of creating a new total product without changing the manufacturing process explains why there is more physical product standardization internationally than one might expect. Remember that a product can be localized by adaptation of the package, brand name, accessories, after-sales service, warranty, instructions for use, and company image.

Consider two products that Cadbury-Schweppes, the British-based food and soft-drink multinational, produces: tonic water and chocolate. Tonic water is a global product physically, but as a total product it is multidomestic because people in different markets buy it for different reasons. The French drink it straight, while the English mix it with alcohol. Chocolate is neither a global physical product nor a global total product; it is eaten as a snack in some areas, put in sandwiches in others, and eaten as a dessert elsewhere. Because of strong local preferences, it also varies greatly in taste, going from its pure, bitter taste to a quite sweet taste or a taste with some heat, depending on what is added to it. Nestlé instant coffee is produced in 200 different blends globally, all of which are sold under the brand name Nescafé, so there is brand-name globalization and physical product localization.[3]

Type of Product   The amount of change to be made in a product is affected by whether it is a consumer or industrial product or service and by the foreign environmental forces. Generally, consumer products require greater adaptation than do industrial products. If the consumer products are stylish or the result of a fad, they are especially likely to require changes. These product types form a continuum ranging from insensitive to the foreign environment to highly sensitive, as shown in Figure 18.2.

Industrial Products   As Figure 18.2 suggests, many industrial products can be sold unchanged worldwide. Chips, for example, are used wherever computers are manufactured. If product changes are required, they may be cosmetic, such as converting gauges to read from

---

FIGURE 18.1

Components of the Total Product

Total product

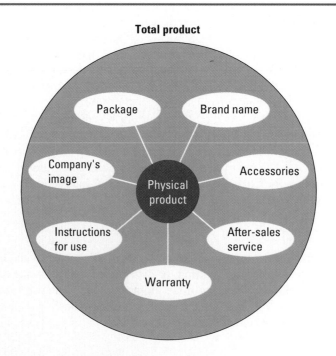

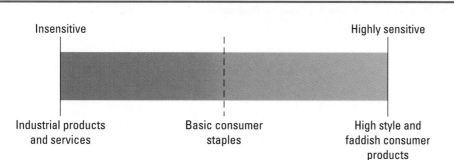

FIGURE 18.2

Continuum of
Sensitivity to the
Foreign Environment

Insensitive ──────────────────────────── Highly sensitive

Industrial products and services ── Basic consumer staples ── High style and faddish consumer products

the metric system to the U.S. or British Imperial system of feet and inches or printing instructions in another language. Note that the U.S. adherence to the feet and inches measurement system (the U.S. system) may limit export possibilities, since the majority of countries follow the metric system and want their machinery and parts to be on the metric scale. The United States, Liberia, and Burma are the three nations that have not switched to the metric system, also known as the *SI* or *International System of Units*.

When product adaptations are necessary, they may be relatively simple ones, such as lengthening pedals and changing seat positions to compensate for consumer preferences among markets. However, somewhat more drastic modifications in the physical product may be necessary. In developing countries, there is a tendency to both overload equipment and overlook its maintenance. To overcome these market differences, manufacturers such as Caterpillar and Allis-Chalmers established thorough training programs as a part of the total product purchase wherever their products are sold. The other alternative is to modify the equipment, perhaps using a simpler bearing system that requires little maintenance.

Occasionally adaptations are necessary to meet local legal requirements, such as those that govern noise, safety, or exhaust emissions. To avoid the need to change the product, some manufacturers design it to meet the most stringent laws even though it will be overdesigned for the rest of its markets. In some instances, governments have passed strict laws with the intent of protecting a local manufacturer from import competition. When this occurs, the company may prefer to design the product for the country with the next most stringent laws and stay out of the first market. Of course, this is what the government had in mind when it passed the law. However, a word of caution based on one of the author's experiences: The company in this situation would be advised to test the local manufacturer's product before giving up on the market. On occasion, the local product also has failed to meet the specifications. When confronted with this evidence, the government has had to change its laws.

Consumer Products Although consumer products generally require greater modification to meet local market requirements than do industrial products, some of them can be sold unchanged to certain market segments that have similar characteristics across countries. Consumer products of this kind include a number of luxury items, such as automobiles, sports equipment, and perfumes. Every country in the world contains a market segment that is more similar to the same segment in other countries with respect to economic status, buyer behavior, tastes, and preferences than it is to the rest of the segments in the same country. This market segment includes the cosmopolitan consumers: foreign-educated and well-traveled citizens and expatriates. Many products and services foreign to local tastes and preferences have been successfully introduced in a number of countries by first being marketed to these similar groups. Gradually, members of other market segments have purchased these products and services until consumption has become widespread.

While "jet-setters" may share much in common across countries, marketers tend to find greater dissimilarities in social and cultural values as they go down the economic strata in each country. It follows from this that, in general, the deeper the desired immediate market penetration is, the greater must be the product modification. Remember that this observation does not suggest that for deeper market penetration, the physical product has to be changed. Perhaps a modification of one of the other elements of the total product is sufficient—a different

On Global Marketing

Employees stand behind the counter of the first McDonald's fast-food restaurant in New Delhi, India. The store features Maharaja Macs and Vegetable Burgers with Cheese on its menu.

"The globalization of markets is at hand. With that, the multinational commercial world nears its end and so does the multinational corporation. Different cultural preferences, national tastes and standards, and business institutions are vestiges of the past." So said the marketing scholar Theodore Levitt, a Harvard Business School professor emeritus in 1983. Levitt cited such examples as Coca-Cola, Pepsi-Cola, McDonald's, and Revlon. Though he sensed that the world markets were changing, his conclusion was too simple.

Coca-Cola's own advertising director replied, "What looks good as a generalization sometimes doesn't follow. The world is certainly becoming more globalized, but the global village is certainly not here, nor will it ever be." At PepsiCo, overseas offices choose and reedit commercials made in the United States. Local operations also produce local products. An example is the soft drink Shani, a currant-and-blackberry soda popular in the Mideast during Ramadan, the Muslim holy month. As for McDonald's, it sells beer in Germany, the McAloo Tikki in India, pot pies in Australia, and noodles in the Philippines. "We rely on the people native to the country to develop marketing programs," says the marketing vice president.

In a 20-year retrospective on Levitt's article, Sir Martin Sorrell, chief executive of the WPP Group, noted that Levitt's perspective had ignored the power of the customer. "The customer is in control," he said. "There will continue to be substantial and enduring differences around the world in what and how consumers consume." In fact, Sorrell expressed the opinion that firms' marketing focus would become even more localized over the coming years. To sum up, the success of global marketing depends on the kind of product and on knowing when product or promotional adaptations are beneficial.

Source: Theodore Levitt, "The Globalization of Markets," *Harvard Business Review*, May–June 1983, pp. 92, 96; "Ad Fad," *The Wall Street Journal*, May 12, 1988, pp. 1, 17; WWP, http://ww2.wpp.com (October 8, 2006); and Garry Emmons, "Globalization Revisited," www.alumni.hbs.edu/bulletin/2003/september/globalization.html (June 20, 2004).

---

size or color of the package, a change in the brand name, or a new positioning, if the product is consumed differently. Different emphasis in after-sales service is also important.

An example illustrates the repositioning and repackaging possibilities. Mars, one of the largest privately owned and family operated companies, faced a drop in Bahrain's imports of candy when it was ready to launch M&Ms. Fortunately, its marketing research discovered that Bahrainis consider the peanut to be a health food, so Mars repositioned its peanut M&Ms as a health food. The company also was able to turn the hot Gulf climate to its advantage by emphasizing the packaging through its traditional slogan, "M&Ms melt in your mouth, not in your hand." As you will see later in this chapter, Mars followed promotional strategy number 2, same product–different message, although even part of the message (the slogan) remained the same.

Services   The marketing of services, like the marketing of industrial products, is generally less complex globally than is the marketing of consumer products. The consulting firm Accenture has 110 offices in 48 countries offering the same kinds of business expertise as the firm provides in the United States.[4] However, laws and customs sometimes do mandate that providers alter their services. For example, Manpower cannot operate in some markets because in those countries, private employment agencies are against the law. Accounting laws vary substantially among nations, but the large accounting firms operate globally, making local adaptations where necessary. Ernst & Young has 114,000 professionals in 140 countries.[5] VISA, MasterCard, and American Express are examples of successful companies in the global credit card industry. They had combined billings of $1.7 trillion in 1996; nine years later, Visa alone had card sales volume of just over $4 trillion.[6]

Foreign Environmental Forces   In Section Three we examined the foreign environmental forces extensively, so here we will limit our discussion to a few concrete examples of how some of these forces might affect product offerings.

Sociocultural Forces   Dissimilar cultural patterns often require changes, either in the physical product or in aspects of the total product, in food and other consumer goods. The worldwide variation in consumer preferences for clothes washing is a challenge for appliance makers. The French want top-loading washing machines, and the British want front-loaders; the Germans insist on high-speed machines that remove most of the moisture in the spin-dry cycle, but the Italians prefer slower spin speeds because they let the sun do the drying. Hence, Whirlpool must produce a variety of models, although after buying the Philips appliance business in 1991 and Maytag in early 2006, it has taken huge steps toward integrating a collection of independent national companies into regional manufacturing facilities and product platforms, on the model of integration in the Whirlpool European organization that shares a few common platforms. When Whirlpool's European integration began in 1994, its CEO at the time argued that the national differences are exaggerated: "This business is the same all over the world. There is great opportunity to leverage that sameness."[7] After a painful restructuring in which Whirlpool closed a surplus Spanish plant, laid off 2,000 workers, centralized inventory control, and reduced its 36 European warehouses to 8, both European sales and operating margins improved. In fact, Whirlpool has created a "world washer," called Duet in the United States and Dreamspace in Europe, combining the U.S. preference for large-load capacity, the European preference for front-loading machines,[8] and sensor technology that selects wash time and water consumption.

While some international firms, such as Campbell's, have been extremely successful in employing the same brand name, label, and colors worldwide, other firms learn they must change names, labels, or colors because of cultural differences. Gold appears frequently on packages in Latin America because Latin Americans view it as a symbol of quality and prestige. Procter & Gamble found that a gold package has value in Europe, too, after it launched its silver-boxed Crest Tartar Control Formula in the United Kingdom, which was followed two months later by Colgate's equivalent in a gold box. P&G officials agreed that Colgate's choice of gold was better than their silver. They explained that silver was how the product was packaged in the United States.[9] The meaning that colors have for people in different cultures is also a marketing consideration. For example, in the Netherlands blue is considered warm and feminine, but the Swedes consider it masculine and cold.

Even if the colors can remain the same, instructions on labels must be translated into the language of the market. Firms selling in areas where two or more languages are spoken, such as Canada, Switzerland, Belgium, and the United States, may need to use multilingual labels. Where instructions are not required, as in the case of some consumer or industrial products whose use is well known, there is an advantage to printing the label in the language of the country best known for the product. A French label on a perfume helps strengthen the product's image in the United States.

A perfectly good brand name may have to be scrapped because of its unfavorable connotations in another language. An American product failed to survive in Sweden because its name translated to "enema." In Latin America, a product had to be taken off the market when the manufacturer found that the name meant "jackass oil." Of course, this problem occurs in both directions, as a Belgian brewery found when it tried to introduce its Delerium Tremens lager to the U.S. market. American authorities told the company the name was an incitement to drinking.[10] Sometimes a firm will not use a perfectly good name because the firm makes assumptions about the impact of the name on foreign locals and doesn't test

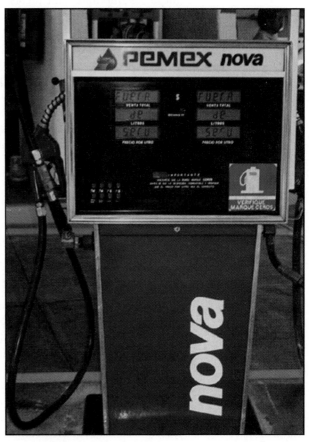

Pemex gasoline doesn't go.

Will "Smart Mobs" Dictate Consumer Trends?

Product preferences and social trends wash across countries and continents. Evidence is clear that the speed of diffusion of these trends is increasing. And the mechanisms for even faster diffusion are already with us—technologies such as myspace, wikis, instant messaging, and cell phones. At least one thinker has dubbed what happens when technology connects people together as "smart mobs." In 2001, Philippine president Joseph Estrada was ousted after a wave of popular protests. Although this was not the first time a leader was toppled by protesters, this incident is noteworthy because the protests were organized by wireless communication—a smart mob.

Just as protesters can be assembled quickly by wireless communication, partygoers can stay in touch by phone and move from one party to another in coordinated (but largely leaderless) movements. Howard Rheingold, who may have coined the "smart mobs" term, noticed flocks of Japanese teenagers converging on public places, coordinated by text messages. Some smart mobs have even become institutionalized—for example, the

Aula community in Helsinki and cyberspace is composed of Finns who use mobile media to socialize and collaborate in geographic and virtual places simultaneously. In the United States the Dodgeball service lets you contact it from a location, say, a bar, and identifies which of your friends is in the area. The practice of "bluejacking"—sending messages to other Bluetooth-enabled phones in an area—is also growing.

From a marketing standpoint, the word-of-mouth marketing capability these innovations represent is desirable. The combination of mobile communications and the Internet provides a good environment for word-of-mouth transmission of product news.

Source: Malcolm Gladwell, *The Tipping Point: How Little Things Can Make a Big Difference* (Boston: Little, Brown, 2000); Sean Carton, "It's Not about the Technology," www.clickz.com/tech/lead-edge/print.php/1443551 (August 12, 2002); Dan Gilmore, "Finland's Smart Mobs," www.siliconvalley.com/mld/siliconvalley/business/columnists/dangillmor/ejourna l/3772371.htm (September 17, 2002); Howard Rheingold, *Smart Mobs: The Next Social Revolution* (Cambridge, MA: Perseus, 2002); various postings from www.aula.cc.; and Eric Bender, "Social Lives of a Cell Phone," *MIT Technology Review*, July 12, 2004.

---

these assumptions with locals. This is what happened with the Nova. As the story goes, Chevrolet couldn't sell Novas in (the storyteller picks a Spanish-speaking country) because Nova means *no va* ("doesn't go") in Spanish. But the two words are pronounced very differently—*Nova* has the accent on the first syllable, whereas the accent for *no va* falls on the *va*. Therefore, to someone speaking Spanish, the words have very different meanings. Native Spanish-speaking people would be likely to connect *nova* with "star," which is probably what General Motors had in mind. You may be surprised to learn that Pemex, the government-owned petroleum monopoly in Mexico, once called its regular gasoline *Nova*.

An important difference in social forces to which American marketers are not accustomed is people's preference in other nations for making daily visits to small neighborhood specialty shops and large, open markets where they can socialize while shopping. More frequent buying involves smaller packages, which is important to a shopper who has no automobile in which to carry purchases. However, this custom is changing in Europe, where consumers are demanding the kinds of assortments that only a large store can offer. Shopping frequency is also slowing as European women are finding that they have less free time than previously. The solution has been the huge combination supermarket–discount house (*hypermarché* in France) with ample parking, located in the suburbs. A similar situation has been occurring in Mexico, especially since NAFTA ended many of the country's import restrictions.

There is a parallel here to the situation that began in the 1940s in the United States. The same conditions of rising incomes, a growing middle class, and a large number of working wives have combined to put a premium on the shopper's time, and just as occurred in the United States, mass merchandising and catalog and Internet shopping have moved in to fill this need.

Legal Forces   Legal forces can be a formidable constraint in the design of product strategies because if the firm fails to adhere to a country's laws governing the product, it will be unable to do business in that country. Laws concerning pollution, consumer protection, and operator safety are being enacted rapidly in many parts of the world and limit the marketer's freedom to standardize the product mix internationally. For example, American machinery manufacturers exporting to Sweden have found that Swedish operator safety requirements are stricter than those required by the Occupational Safety and Health Act (OSHA), so if they wish to market in Sweden, they must produce a special model. Of course, product standards set ostensibly to protect a nation's citizens can be effective in protecting indigenous industry from foreign competitors.

Laws prohibiting certain classes of imports are common in developing nations, as potential exporters learn when they research the world for markets. Products considered luxuries, as well as products already being manufactured, are among the first to be excluded from importation, but such laws also affect local production.

Foods and pharmaceuticals are especially influenced by laws concerning purity and labeling. Food products sold in Canada, whether imported or produced locally, are subject to strict rules that require both English and French on the labels as well as metric and inch/pound units. The law even dictates the space permitted between the number and the unit—"16 oz." is correct, but "16oz." is not. The Venezuelan government has decreed that the manufacturer or the importer must affix to the package the maximum retail price at which many products can be sold. Because of Saudi Arabians' concern about avoiding food containing pork, the label of any product containing animal fat or meat that is sold in Saudi Arabia must identify the kind of animal used or state that no swine products were used.

Legal forces also may prevent a worldwide firm from employing its brand name in all its overseas markets. Managements accustomed to the American law, which establishes the right to a brand name by priority in use, are surprised to learn that in code law countries, a brand belongs to the person registering it first. Thus, the marketer may go into foreign markets expecting to use the company's long-established brand name only to find that someone else owns it. The name may have been registered by someone who is employing it legitimately for his or her own products, or it may have been pirated, that is, registered by someone who hopes to profit by selling the name back to the originating firm.

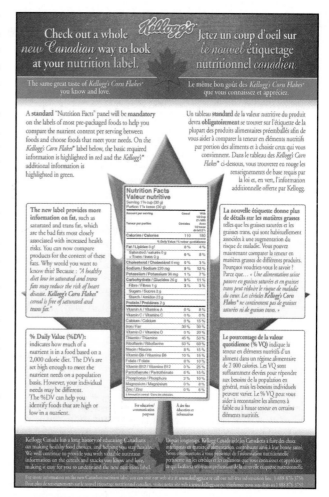

Firms planning to market their products in Canada must adhere to that country's strict labeling regulations, requiring labels to include both English and French as well as metric and inch/pound units.

To avoid this predicament, the firm must register its brand names in every country where it wants to use them or where it might use them in the future. And this must be done rapidly. The Paris Convention grants a firm that has registered a name in one country only six months' priority to register it elsewhere. To be certain that it has enough names for new products, Unilever, the English-Dutch manufacturer of personal care products, has over 100,000 trademarks registered throughout the world, most of which are not in use but are kept in reserve.

The use of domain names on the Internet shows that these problems have not decreased. A study found that American Express, for example, had registered the domain name "americanexpress" in 19 countries, while in 11 others the name was registered to someone other than American Express. In a more extreme example, CBS found that it had 4 registrations but others had 46. When kanji characters became an option for registering Japanese domain names, tiny Web Japan Co. got a head start by registering some 100 domain names, including those of major corporations.[11]

Economic Forces   The disparity in income throughout the world is an obstacle to worldwide product standardization. Some products are priced too high for some consumers in developing nations, and so the firm must adjust to the consumers' ability to pay. Such adjustments may include simplification or repackaging. Procter & Gamble sells shampoo for individual use in India, in addition to the regular bottle quantity. Many of the DVD players sold in India are \$45 do-it-yourself assembly kits.[12] In addition, many consumers throughout the world buy cell phone air time by purchasing prepaid cards worth only a few dollars or even by renting cell phones by the call from intermediaries. As C. K. Prahalad points out in his *The Fortune at the Bottom of the Pyramid*, the 5 billion people in poverty in developing nations have \$14 trillion in purchasing power.[13]

In some cases the foreign subsidiary cannot afford to produce as complete a product mix as does the parent. Most automobile manufacturers assemble the less expensive and higher-volume line locally and broaden the local product mix by importing, when permitted, the luxury cars. International firms practice this marketing technique whenever possible because a captive foreign sales organization is available to promote the sales of the home organization's exports and because the revenue derived helps pay the subsidiary's overhead. Yet GM has been successful with its Buick in China by introducing the Buick as a premium brand and then moving to mid-range and economy vehicles. Despite a late start in the market (1994), GM ranks second only to Volkswagen, which has been there for two decades. Sales for GM in China rose over 50 percent between 2003 and 2004 and hit a record in 2005. Thanks to Buick, GM has 11.2 percent of the market in China.[14]

Physical Forces   Physical forces, such as climate and terrain, also militate against international product standardization. Manufacturers of clothes washers have found success in India by "hardening" their machines against heat, dirt, and power outages. The heat and high humidity in many parts of the tropics require that electrical equipment be built with extra-heavy insulation. Consumer goods that are affected by moisture must be specially packaged to resist its penetration. Thus, pills are wrapped individually in foil and baked goods are packaged in tin boxes to prevent their degradation by moisture.

High altitudes frequently require product alteration. Food manufacturers have found that they must change their cooking instructions for people who live at high altitudes because at such altitudes cooking takes longer. The thinner atmosphere requires that producers of cake mixes include less yeast as well. Gasoline and diesel motors generate less power at high altitudes, so the manufacturer must often supply a larger engine.

Mountainous terrain implies high-cost highways, and so in the poorer countries, roads may require heavy-duty capabilities. Trucks traveling poorer-quality roads need tires with thicker treads and heavy-duty suspensions. Because of the rough ride, packaging must be stronger than that used in the United States. From these examples, we can appreciate that even though an unchanged product may be culturally and economically acceptable in a market, the effect of the physical forces alone may be strong enough to require some product modification.

Environmental forces may play a major part in foreign product strategies. Their influence is pervasive in the design of the entire marketing mix. A useful guide for the marketing mix preparation is a matrix in which the marketing mix variables are tabulated against the environmental forces. Such a guide is at the end of this chapter.

PROMOTIONAL STRATEGIES

promotion
Any form of communication between a firm and its publics

Promotion, one of the basic elements of the marketing mix, is communication that secures understanding between a firm and its publics to bring about a favorable buying action and achieve long-lasting confidence in the firm and the product or service it provides. Note that this definition employs the plural *publics*, because the seller's promotional efforts must be directed to more than just the ultimate consumers, including retailers and other members of the distribution channel.

Promotion both influences and is influenced by the other marketing mix variables. Nine distinct promotion strategies are possible, by combining the three alternatives of (1) marketing the same physical product everywhere, (2) adapting the physical product for foreign markets, and (3) designing a different physical product with (*a*) the same, (*b*) adapted, or (*c*) different messages.[15] We examine below the six strategies most commonly used:

1. *Same product–same message:* When marketers find that target markets vary little with respect to product use and consumer attitudes, they can offer the same product and use the same promotional appeals in all markets. Avon, Maidenform, and A.T. Cross follow this strategy.

2. *Same product–different message:* The same product may satisfy a different need or be used differently elsewhere. This means the product may be left unchanged but a different message is required. Honda's early "You meet the nicest people on a Honda" campaign appealed to Americans who used their motorcycles as pleasure vehicles, but in Brazil Honda stressed the use of motorcycles as basic transportation. Honda has captured about 90 percent of the Brazilian motorcycle market.

3. *Product adaptation–same message:* In cases where the product serves the same function but must be adapted to different conditions, the same message is employed with a changed product. In Japan, Lever Brothers puts Lux soap in fancy boxes because much of it is sold as gifts.

4. *Product adaptation–message adaptation:* In some cases, both the product and the promotional message must be modified for foreign markets. In Latin America, Tang is especially sweetened, premixed, and ready to drink in pouches. Unlike Americans, Latin Americans do not drink it for breakfast. There it is promoted as a drink for mealtimes and for throughout the day but not for breakfast.

5. *Different product–same message:* In many markets the potential customers cannot afford the product as manufactured for developed markets. To overcome this obstacle, companies frequently produce a very distinct product for these markets. Substituting a low-cost plastic squeeze bottle for an aerosol can and a manually operated washing machine for an automated one are two examples. The promotional message, however, can be very similar to what is used in the developed markets if the product performs the same functions.

6. *Different product for the same use–different message:* Frequently, the different product requires a different message as well. Welding torches rather than automatic welding machines would be sold on the basis of low acquisition cost rather than high output per hour. The governments of developing countries faced with high unemployment would be persuaded by a message emphasizing the job-creating possibilities of labor-intensive processes rather than the labor saving of highly automated machinery.

The tools for communicating these messages—the promotional mix—are advertising, personal selling, sales promotion, public relations, and publicity. No one of these tools is inherently superior to the others, though circumstances in a given situation may dictate that one of them be emphasized more than the others. Just as in the case of the product strategies, the composition of the promotional mix will depend on the type of product, the environmental forces, and the amount of market penetration desired.

Advertising   Among all the promotional mix elements, **advertising** may be the one with the greatest similarities worldwide. This is the case because much advertising is based on American practices. U.S. ad agencies have followed their corporate customers into the global realm through wholly owned subsidiaries, joint ventures, and working agreements with local agencies. The decision to go global, as Apple has with the iPod, or to go either local or regional, as Intel, P&G, and McDonald's all have, is not an easy one. One commentator observes that the trend is toward localization, at least for a while.[16]

> **advertising**
> Paid, nonpersonal presentation of ideas, goods, or services by an identified sponsor

Cultural dimensions play a major role in these decisions. Here is a summary of their influence, adapted from work by the scholar and researcher Lars Perner:[17]

Directness vs. indirectness: U.S. advertising tends to be direct. What are the product benefits? Such bluntness may be considered too pushy for Japanese consumers, where such directness is read as arrogance. How could the seller presume to know what the consumer would like?

Comparison: Comparative advertising is banned in most countries and would probably be counterproductive in Asia, seen as an insulting instance of confrontation and bragging, even if it were allowed. In the United States, comparison advertising has proved effective (although its implementation is tricky).

Humor: Although humor is a relatively universal phenomenon, what is considered funny differs greatly across cultures, so pretesting is essential.

Gender roles: A study found that women in U.S. advertising tended to be shown in more traditional roles than in Europe or Australia. Some countries are more traditional than the United States. A Japanese ad describing a camera as "so simple that even a woman can use it" was not found to be insulting.

Explicitness: Europeans tend to tolerate more explicit advertisements, often with sexual overtones, than do Americans.

Sophistication: Europeans, particularly the French, demand considerably more sophistication than Americans, who may react more favorably to emotional appeals.

Popular vs. traditional culture: U.S. ads tend to employ contemporary, popular culture, often including current music, while those in more traditional cultures tend to refer more to classical culture.

Information content vs. fluff: American ads often contain puffery, which was found to be ineffective in Eastern European countries because it resembled communist propaganda. The Eastern European consumers instead want facts.

Global and Regional Brands   Manufacturers are increasingly using global or regional brands for a number of reasons:

1. Cost is most often cited. By producing one TV commercial for use across a region, a firm can save up to 50 percent of the production cost.

2. There is a better chance of obtaining one regional source to do high-quality work than of finding sources in various countries that will work to the same high standard.

3. Some marketing managers believe their companies must have a single image throughout a region.

4. Companies are establishing regionalized organizations where many functions, such as marketing, are centralized.

5. Global and regional satellite and cable television is widely available.

Economies of scale are one reason some firms emphasize the regional or global standardization of advertising. Coca-Cola, for example, once estimated that it saved over $8 million annually in the cost of thinking up new imagery by repeating the same theme everywhere.

The head of a consulting firm specializing in brands and corporate identity has a different idea. He says, "There are too many businesses out there doing the same thing. Global branding is a way of saying your company makes a difference, which moves you up the pecking order."[18] Look at the value placed on the world's most valuable brands (Table 18.1).

Global or National   The debate continues among international marketers about using global, regional, or national brands. Companies that acquired successful regional or national brands on purchasing the original owner have been extremely cautious about converting them to their global brands. Nestlé is an example of a large global firm that uses both. Nestlé tries to achieve consumer familiarity and marketing efficiency by using two brands on a single product, a local brand that may be familiar and appeal only to a small group of consumers and a corporate strategic brand such as Nestlé or Nescafé. In some markets, in Asian ones, for example, product quality across many categories is suggested by a shared brand. This developed from the *keiretsu* structure as evidenced by Mitsubishi, C. Itoh, and Mitsui.

Private Brands   Private brands have become serious competitors for manufacturers' brands and are responsible for a shift in power from manufacturers to retailers. Private labels have flooded Japan's large supermarket chains, capturing one-third of the British and Swiss food markets and one-fifth of the French and German markets. The trend toward private labels also has caught on in Spain and the Netherlands. The Swedish food group Axfood AB notes that it profits twice from private-label manufacturing: first when it sells the product (such as ketchup) at a lower price to its stores, and then when the profit margin is higher when selling to the ultimate consumer.[19]

TABLE 18.1	Comparing Global Brand Values, 2004–2006	
Rank 2006 (2004)	**Brand**	**Value ($ millions)**
1 (1)	Coca-Cola, U.S	$67,000
2 (2)	Microsoft, U.S.	56,926
3 (3)	IBM, U.S.	56,201
4 (4)	GE, U.S.	48,907
5 (5)	Intel, U.S.	32,319
6 (6)	Nokia, Finland	30,131
7 (9)	Toyota, Japan	27,941
8 (7)	Disney, U.S.	27,848
9 (8)	McDonald's, U.S.	27,501
10 (11)	Mercedes-Benz, Germany	21,795
11 (12)	Citibank, U.S.	21,458
12 (10)	Marlboro, U.S.	21,350
13 (13)	Hewlett-Packard, U.S.	20,458
14 (14)	American Express, U.S.	19,641
15 (16)	BMW, Germany	19,617
16 (15)	Gillette, U.S.	19,579
17 (18)	Louis Vuitton, France	17,606
18 (17)	Cisco, U.S.	17,532
19 (19)	Honda, Japan	17,049
20 (20)	Samsung, Korea	16,169

Source: "The Top 100 Brands 2006," *BusinessWeek Online*, www.bwnt.com/brand/2006 (October 10, 2006).

Availability of Media   Satellite TV broadcasters make possible numerous programming networks to provide service to millions of households in dozens of countries and in many languages. International print media include local, national, and regional editions. *The European*, a daily newspaper; the international edition of *The Herald Tribune;* the Asian and European editions of *The Wall Street Journal;* and the international editions of the *Manchester Guardian* and *The Financial Times* are some of the newspapers with wide circulation. Advertisers can also go to other media to reach their markets. Cinema advertising is heavily used in many parts of the world (including Norway, Austria, the United Kingdom, and Brazil), as are billboards. In a number of developing countries, automobiles equipped with loudspeakers circulate through the cities announcing products, and street signs are furnished by advertisers whose messages hang on them. Homeowners can get a free coat of paint by permitting advertisers to put ads on their walls. Busses and trains carry advertisements. Where mail delivery is reliable, direct mail is a powerful medium, as are trade fairs. Probably one of the most ingenious campaigns ever was that of a tea company that gave away thousands of printed prayers with a tea commercial on the other side to pilgrims bound for Mecca.

The point is that media of some kind are available in every market, and the local managers and ad agencies are familiar with the advantages of each kind. Media selection is extremely difficult for international advertising managers who try to standardize their media mix from the home office. The variation in media availability is a strong reason for leaving this part of the advertising program to the local organization.

Internet Advertising   We mentioned the importance of the Internet as a market research tool in Chapter 15, and it is important as an advertising medium as well. Among the appealing factors of online advertising in the international sphere are the following:

1. The Internet provides an affluent, reachable audience. A high number of users in a wide variety of countries read English or other common languages well. Native-language sites are strongly preferred, though.

2. Unlike TV or newspaper ads, Internet communications are two-way. They are cheap. And they are possibly less regulated than other advertising forms. In Europe, where direct advertising of prescription drug products is banned, Internet sites are a way to provide potential consumers with product information. The disclaimer that the information is for U.S. audiences only may be ignored.

3. The possibility exists of involving customers in determining which messages and information they receive. For this reason, there is some possibility that company Web offerings will be tailor-made by the user. This customization increases the application of the marketing concept.

4. Although the Internet doesn't reach all possible groups, for some groups it may be among the best media choices. For teenagers in particular, Internet advertising can be important because teenagers spend less time watching TV than any other demographic group, preferring to spend time on the Internet or to play computer games.

Type of Product   Buyers of industrial goods and luxury products usually act on the same motives the world over; thus, these products lend themselves to a standardized approach. Such standardization enables manufacturers of capital goods, such as General Electric and Caterpillar, to prepare international campaigns that require very little modification in their various markets. Certain consumer goods markets are similar, too. Another set of characteristics also permits firms to use the same appeals and sales arguments worldwide: when the product is low-priced, is consumed in the same way, and is bought for the same reasons. Examples of such products are gasoline, soft drinks, detergents, cosmetics, and airline services. Firms such as Exxon (Esso), Coca-Cola, Apple and Avon have used the international approach successfully. Generally, the changes they have made are a translation into the local language and the use of indigenous models.

Foreign Environmental Forces   Like variations in media availability, foreign environmental forces act as deterrents to the international standardization of advertising, and as you would expect, among the most influential of these forces are the *sociocultural* forces, which we examined in Chapter 6.

A basic cultural decision for the marketer is whether to position the product as foreign or local. Which way to go seems to depend on the country, the product type, and the target market. In Germany, for example, consumers are not at all impressed by the carmaker that announces it has American know-how. At the same time, such purely American products as bourbon, fast-food restaurants, and blue jeans have made tremendous inroads there and in the rest of Europe.

Similarly, in Japan and elsewhere in Asia, the national identity of some consumer products enhances their image. The rage among Chinese teenagers is anything from Korea. The influence of American-style fast-food restaurants on Japanese youth was emphasized in a survey taken by the Japanese Ministry of Agriculture, which found that more than 50 percent of the country's teenagers would rather eat Western foods than the traditional dishes. U.S.-based fast-food restaurants such as McDonald's (Japan's largest restaurant business), KFC (the third largest), Dairy Queen, and Mister Donut account for half the total restaurant business. And KFC is zeroing in on an even larger Asian market—it had well over 2,000 restaurants in China at the beginning of 2006 and is expanding by over 200 units a year.[20] An indication of the significance of national identity is the Japanese *anime*-style cartoons that dominate the time slots in the after-school and Saturday morning American TV schedules.[21]

The experience of suppliers to the youth market indicates that this, too, is an international market segment, much like the market for luxury goods. A former director of MTV Europe observed that "18-year-olds in Paris have more in common with 18-year-olds in New York than with their own parents. They buy the same products, go to the same movies, listen to the same music, sip the same colas. Global advertising merely works on that premise." This similarity suggests that marketers can formulate global advertising campaigns for these consumers that will require little more than a translation into the local language, unless the product strategy goes with a foreign identity. That decision should be made with local input.

Because communication, the reason for advertising, is impossible if the language is not understood, translations must be made into the language of the consumers. Unfortunately for the advertiser, almost every language varies from one country to another. The same word may be perfectly apt in one country while connoting something completely different in another. To avoid connotation errors in translation, the experienced advertising manager will use a back translation and plenty of illustrations with short copy.

Because a nation's laws generally reflect public opinion, the cultural forces tend to be closely allied to the legal forces, which exert a strong and pervasive influence on advertising. We have seen how laws affect media availability; they also restrict the kinds of products that can be advertised and the copy employed in the advertisements.

American firms accustomed to using comparative advertising at home are surprised to find that legal restrictions on this technique exist in some markets. Since the early 1990s PepsiCo has used comparative advertising to knock Coca-Cola, and wherever possible, Coke has used the courts to stop the ads. PepsiCo launched a series of TV commercials, the Pepsi Challenge campaign, in 1995 to test the comparative advertising laws of 30 countries. The ads presented the competitor's product in a way that is specifically prohibited in some countries as unfair advertising. The marketing head of PepsiCo said that the company "intended to push the envelope on comparison advertising in markets around the world."[22] Because of the grueling legal battle between PepsiCo and Coca-Cola over the Pepsi Challenge campaign, as well as other conflicts over comparative advertising, laws in various Latin American countries were found to be inadequate. To avoid the passage of more laws, members of the advertising industry have established self-regulatory bodies in a number of these nations to settle disputes out of court.[23] In Europe, the EU Commission authorized comparative advertising subject to restrictions because some member countries permitted it while others did not. Germany's comparative advertising law is so strict that Goodyear couldn't use its multinational tire campaign stating that nylon tire cord is stronger than steel.

Advertisers in the Islamic countries face limitations, although these vary widely across the Middle East. A recent study shows that women appear about as often in Lebanese and Egyptian TV ads as in U.S. ads, although only half as often in Saudi ads. The women were just as likely to be dressed "immodestly" in Lebanese as in U.S. ads, although less often in Egyptian and never in Saudi ads.[24] In Japan, images of Western women in suggestive poses were acceptable, while similar images of Japanese women were not.

Are these teens in Japan or the United States? Japan. But, like teens in the United States, they wear Levi's and carry American skateboards.

Globalization versus Localization   With so many obstacles to international standardization, what should be the approach of the international advertising manager? The opinion of some experts is that good brands and good product ideas can cross international borders but each may have to be adjusted for the local market. Let's examine this situation more closely.

A global product and a global brand, such as Apple's iPod or the Big Mac, reaches many markets unchanged or virtually unchanged. An ability to standardize both the product and the brand can lead to valuable cost savings.[25] Such products tend to be innovations. A global product with a local brand is often the result of mergers. Germany's Henkel, owner of Right Guard, Dial Soap, and other consumer products, has kept local packaging and standardized the physical product, its soap powder. Such a combination of localization of the product packaging and standardization of the contents makes manufacturing efficiencies possible. The final option, a local product with a local brand, is the most localized approach and is appropriate when, for perhaps cultural reasons, the product that sells well in one country will not transfer to another, or does so for quite a different set of purposes. Dish soaps that are adjusted for the hardness of local water and sell under local names is an example. P&G's Fairy Liquid, a dishwashing soap that is a leading brand in the United Kingdom, similar to Joy in the U.S. market, is one example of localization of the product on both brand and content. Remember, too, that, as the director of multinational accounts at McCann-Erickson claims, social classes across different countries have shared sensibilities: "A male middle executive in Italy has more in common with a male middle executive in the U.K. than with a farmer in Italy. It is those shared sensibilities that make global branding possible."[26] That is, if the marketer can identify those segments and reach them.

Such global branding approaches look for similarities across segments and countries to capitalize on them by providing promotional themes with worldwide appeal. A second approach believes that even though human nature is the same everywhere, it is also true that a Spaniard will remain a Spaniard and a Belgian a Belgian. Thus, it is preferable to develop separate appeals to take advantage of the differences among customers in different cultures and countries.

Neither Purely Global nor Purely Local   You probably have already gathered from this discussion that for most firms neither a purely global nor a purely local campaign is the best way to handle international advertising. In fact, companies at either end of the global-local spectrum, with purely global campaigns or only local campaigns, tend to be moving toward the middle, with a "glocal" approach. Advertisers have followed glocalization to reduce costs. It allows them to develop a common strategy for large regions.[27] Coca-Cola says simply, "Think globally, but act locally."

Gillette's Panregional Approach   Gillette has its advertising organized in the following regional and cultural clusters: pan-Latin America, pan-Middle East, pan-Africa, and pan-Atlantic. The company believes it can identify the same needs and buying motives among consumers in regions or countries linked by culture, consumers' habits, and level of market development for their products. Gillette might use the same European-style advertising for Australia and South Africa, but in Asia it would link developing economies such as the Philippines, Indonesia, Thailand, and Malaysia. It will market the Asian tigers—Singapore, Hong Kong, and Taiwan—together but will handle Japan, China, and India separately. In the summer of 2005, Gillette introduced a modified version of its Mach 3 Turbo in India using a local marketing agency. The agency parked modified trucks with shaving booths, sound systems, and female marketers outside call centers and shopping malls. Trial led many of the consumers to switch immediately to the Gillette razor, giving up the traditional double-edged razor that is still common in India.[28] With its regional-where-possible approach to marketing, Gillette is moving toward a global marketing strategy in the markets where such an approach might be appropriate, while allowing for regional and national differences.[29]

programmed-management approach
A middle-ground advertising strategy between globally standardized and entirely local programs

Programmed-Management Approach   The **programmed-management approach** is another middle-ground advertising strategy in which the home office and the foreign subsidiaries agree on marketing objectives, after which each subsidiary puts together a tentative advertising campaign. This is submitted to the home office for review and suggestions. The campaign is then market-tested locally, and the results are submitted to the home office, which reviews them and offers comments. The subsidiary then submits a complete campaign to the home office for review. When the home office is satisfied, the budget is approved and the subsidiary begins implementing the campaign. The result may be a highly standardized campaign for all markets or one that has been individualized to the extent necessary to cope with local market conditions. The programmed-management approach gives the home office a chance to standardize those parts of the campaign that can be standardized but still permits flexibility in responding to different marketing conditions.

Personal Selling   Along with advertising, personal selling constitutes a principal component of the promotional mix. The importance of this promotional tool compared to advertising depends to a great extent on the relative costs, the funds available, media availability, and the type of product sold.

Manufacturers of industrial products rely more on personal selling than on advertising to communicate with their overseas markets. However, producers of consumer products may also emphasize personal selling overseas, especially in the developing countries, because this may be more effective in the local environment.

Personal Selling and the Internet   Evidence suggests that the Internet, when used to build trust (through consumer orientation, competence, dependability, candor, and likability[30]), can be an effective tool in personal selling. It may be enhanced by face-to-face communication as well. There are evolving approaches to trust building in a virtual environment that seem to be working, such as the eBay community and other sales and social sites.

International Standardization   By and large, the organization of an overseas sales force, sales presentation, and training methods are very similar to those employed in the home country, whenever possible. Avon was following the same plan of person-to-person selling in its major markets when, without notice, China outlawed door-to-door selling in 1998. The Chinese government claimed to be concerned about consumer safety and fraudulent pyramid schemes.[31] The success of Amway in China, whose personal selling may have come close to proselytizing, may also have been a concern. Avon had begun in China in 1990 with a $40 million manufacturing base in Guangzhou, which started manufacturing in 1998. To comply with Chinese law, Avon China shifted to a retail model and in 2006 provided products through a network of 6,000 beauty boutiques and 1,000 beauty counters. In mid-2006, China approved Avon for person-to-person selling in China. It will resume the successful model, running the personal selling out of its 7,000 retail sites. Meanwhile, during the same period in Venezuela and Russia, Avon was extremely successful with the same personal selling approach it uses in the United States. It has also been successful in Mexico, but when it entered the Mexican market, local experts predicted that its plan would fail because the Mexican middle-class woman is not home during the day. She is socializing. The wall around the house would keep the Avon lady from reaching the front door, and when she rang the bell, the maid would not let her in. Other American firms had used this approach and had failed for these reasons. However, Avon made small but important changes. It mounted a massive advertising campaign to educate Mexicans as to what they could expect from the visits, which used the standardized U.S. advertising, adding some education about the selling approach. In addition, Avon recruited educated, middle-class women as representatives and trained them well. They were encouraged to visit their friends, too. In both China and Mexico, changing the essentially American plan as necessary for legal reasons and cultural differences supported Avon's successful entry.

Other firms also follow their home country approach. Missionary salespeople from pharmaceutical manufacturers such as Pfizer and Upjohn introduce their products to physicians, just as they do in the United States. Salespeople calling on channel members perform the same tasks of informing middlemen, setting up point-of-purchase displays, and fighting for shelf space as do their American counterparts.

In international business, the saying "Nothing happens till somebody sells something" holds critical meaning considering the significant investments of money, time, and human capital required to establish a base of sales in a foreign market. Marketing creates and drives sales in foreign as well as domestic markets. The principles of marketing apply to all markets globally, but the overriding international business concept of "think globally, act locally" requires marketing flexibility to be able to make strategic and tactical marketing decisions based on a keen understanding of local consumers and market conditions.

Here are a few tips from the U.S. Department of Labor:

Marketing career and job description: There will be special prospects in international marketing because international marketing employees are faced with a vast array of social, economic, and political conditions combined with added responsibilities due to decentralized decision making and the increased distance between offices and central offices. International planning and managerial jobs typically are offered to those who have obtained some experience in international marketing at the company's central offices. Beginning positions in international marketing at a company's central offices can include a vast array of different responsibilities, but for those with a master's degree they normally include research, planning, and coordination efforts.

International marketing career opportunities: Although a few American firms such as Colgate-Palmolive, CPC International, Eli Lilly, Gillette, and Nestlé hire for international marketing positions, most companies choose people who have shown their worth working in domestic operations. Since so many international jobs are awarded to personnel within the firm, the best way to obtain such a job is probably by beginning in a domestic sales job for an international company.

Career training and qualifications: It is helpful to be fluent in related foreign languages as well as have lived in one or more of the countries the company trades with. Potential workers should have a solid and broad foundation in marketing, based particularly on sales management and market research. The majority of firms hiring for international marketing positions will hire those with bachelor degrees or MBAs, preferring MBAs of course.

World Wide Resources:

International Marketing:
www.careers-in-marketing.com

International Market Development:
www.mba.com/mba/AssessCareersAndTheMBA/MBA
CareerOpportunities/ADayintheLifeProfiles/Marketing
DayinLifeProfiles_related/MeganOsorioInternational
MarketDevelopmentManager.htm

International Product Management:
www.mba.com/mba/AssessCareersAndTheMBA/MBA
CareerOpportunities/ADayintheLifeProfiles/Marketing
DayinLifeProfiles_related/CristinaBarbuProductManager
.htm

International Brand Management:
www.mba.com/mba/AssessCareersAndTheMBA/MBA
CareerOpportunities/ADayintheLifeProfiles/Marketing
DayinLifeProfiles_related/NicolasAmayaAssociate
BrandManager.htm

International Advertising:
http://marketing.monster.com/articles/advertisingabroad

International Public Relations:
http://marketing.monster.com/articles/prcareersabroad

International Sports Marketing:
http://marketing.monster.com/articles/sportsabroad

International Market Research:
http://text.tns-global.com/index.htm
www.marketresearchworld.net
www.fita.org/trade_info.html

Source: Bureau of Labor Statistics, U.S. Department of Labor.

Recruitment   Recruiting salespeople in foreign countries is at times more difficult than recruiting them at home because sales managers may have to cope with the stigma attached to selling that exists in some areas. There is also the need to hire salespeople who are culturally acceptable to customers and channel members. This can be difficult and costly in an already small market that is further subdivided into several distinct cultures with different customs and languages.

sales promotion

Any of various selling aids, including displays, premiums, contests, and gifts

Sales Promotion   **Sales promotion** provides the selling aids for the marketing function and includes activities such as the preparation of point-of-purchase displays, contests, premiums, trade show exhibits, money-off offers, and coupons.

The international standardization of the sales promotion function is not difficult, because experience has shown that what is successful in the United States generally proves effective overseas, although often at a diminished rate. Couponing is a good example. A Nielsen report surveyed consumers on cost-saving measures that would move them to increased coupon use. In the United States 46 percent of consumers stated that they would increase coupon use, while the global average was 19 percent.[32] One major difference on coupon use among markets is the method of distribution. In the United States, the freestanding insert is most frequently used, while in Europe coupons are distributed in stores, usually on the package itself. In some European countries couponing is illegal. This is because price discrimination among consumers is illegal. In other countries, the selling price of specific goods is set within a narrow range.

When marketers are considering transferring sales promotion techniques to other markets, they must consider some cultural constraints.

Sociocultural and Economic Constraints   Cultural and economic constraints influence sales promotions. For example, a premium used as a sales aid for the product must be meaningful to the purchaser. A kitchen gadget might be valued by an American but will not be particularly attractive to a Latin American of similar economic status with two maids. Putting a prize inside the package is no guarantee that it will be there when the purchaser takes the package home. While living in Mexico, one of this book's authors bought a product for the plastic toy it contained. When he opened the package at home, there was no toy. Examining the package closely, he found that a small slit had been made in the top. Where labor costs and store revenues are low, the income from the sale of these premiums is an extra profit for the retailer.

Contests, raffles, and games have been extremely successful in countries where people love to play the odds. If Latin Americans or the Irish will buy a lottery ticket week after week, hoping to win the grand prize playing against odds of 500,000 to 1, why shouldn't they participate in a contest that costs them nothing to enter? Point-of-purchase displays are well accepted by retailers, though many establishments are so small that there is simply no place to put all the displays that are offered to them. Sales promotion may not be as sophisticated overseas as it is in the United States, and our experience indicates that even American subsidiaries do not make sufficient use of the ideas coming from headquarters. The marketing manager who prepares a well-planned program after studying the constraints of the local markets can expect excellent results from the time and money invested.

Public Relations   **Public relations** is the firm's communications and relationships with its various publics, including the governments where it operates, or as one writer has put it, "Public relations is the marketing of the firm." Although American internationals have had organized public relations programs for many years in the United States, they have paid much less attention to this important function elsewhere. Informing the local public of what they are doing has been overlooked by some U.S. corporations. For example, the Ford Foundation, a philanthropy begun in 1936 by Edsel Ford and two Ford Motor Company executives, has an international graduate fellowships program (IFP) to provide $280 million in graduate fellowships for students from Africa, the Middle East, Asia, Latin America, and Russia between 2000 and 2012.[33] Yet this information is not referenced by the overseas Ford Motor Company sites.

Nationalism and antimultinational feeling in many countries have made it imperative that companies with international operations improve their communications to their nonbusiness publics with more effective public relations programs. International pharmaceutical manufacturers are viewed with suspicion by the public in developing nations because, although their products may alleviate suffering, they do so at a profit, made from the poor. To improve their images, major pharmaceuticals have begun programs related to disease globally. Their AIDS campaigns in Africa have received much public attention. One of the most vexing problems for firms is how to deal with critics of their operations and motives. Some try to defuse criticism by holding regularly scheduled meetings at which topics of interest are debated. Others prefer to meet with critics privately, though they may find themselves caught in a never-ending relationship in which the critics continually escalate their demands.

A strategy that has been employed successfully by some firms is to address the issue without dealing directly with the critics. Instead, the firms work with international or governmental agencies. For example, in China recently a number of foreign firms that have achieved success—among them Toshiba, Philips, and Canon—have found themselves under

public relations
Various methods of communicating with the firm's publics to secure a favorable impression

fire by the Chinese media. Scott Kronick of Ogilvy Public Relations Worldwide recommended that if the coverage was too unbalanced, firms should complain to the Propaganda Department. Although the department is not actually part of the government, it is a committee of the Central Committee of the Communist Party of China, whose chairperson is an alternate member of the Politburo.[34]

Another alternative is to do nothing. If the criticism receives no publicity, it may die from lack of interest. Yet sometimes a libeled company chooses to defend its reputation in court. McDonald's was the victim in London when Helen Steel and Dave Morris distributed leaflets accusing the company of starving the Third World, exploiting children in its advertising, and destroying the Central American rain forests. It was also cruel to animals, they alleged, because at times chickens were still conscious when their throats were cut. McDonald's sued Steel and Morris in 1994. It became the longest libel trial in history, ending two and a half years later. McDonald's was awarded $98,000 in damages in a case it had spent $16 million to pursue. Despite the award, which McDonald's has never collected, there is now a major anti-McDonald's Web site (www.McSpotlight.org) dedicated to protests against McDonald's, and October 16 has become established as Worldwide Anti-McDonald's Day.[35]

PRICING STRATEGIES

Pricing, the third element of the marketing mix, is an important and complex consideration in formulating the marketing strategy. Pricing decisions affect other corporate functions, directly determine the firm's gross revenue, and are a major determinant of profits. Most pricing research has been done on North Americans, and this raises serious problems for its generalizability.[36] Americans like sales, for example, while consumers in countries where goods are more scarce may attribute sales to low quality rather than to a desire to gain market share. There is some evidence that perceived price-quality relationships are quite high in Britain and Japan. Thus, discount stores have had difficulty in both these markets. In developing countries, there is less trust of outsiders in the market. Cultural differences may influence the effort a buyer puts into evaluating deals in these markets, where buy decisions rest on relationships. That consumers in some economies are usually paid weekly rather than biweekly or monthly may influence the effectiveness of framing attempts as well. "A dollar a day" is a much bigger chunk from a weekly than a monthly paycheck.

Pricing, a Controllable Variable   Effective price setting consists of more than mechanically adding a standard markup to a cost. To obtain the maximum benefits from pricing, management must regard pricing in the same manner as it does other controllable variables. Pricing is one element of the marketing mix that can be varied to achieve the marketing objectives of the firm.

For instance, if the marketer wishes to position a product as a high-quality item, setting a relatively high price will reinforce promotion that emphasizes quality. However, combining a low price with a promotional emphasis on quality could result in a contradiction that would adversely affect credibility with the consumer. Pricing can also be a determinant in the choice of middlemen, because if the firm requires a wholesaler to take title to, stock, promote, and deliver the merchandise, it must give the wholesaler a much larger trade discount than would be demanded by a broker, whose services are much more limited.

These examples illustrate one of the reasons for the complexity of price setting: the interaction of pricing with the other elements of the marketing mix. In addition, two other sets of forces influence this variable: the interaction between marketing and the other functional areas of the firm and environmental forces.

Interaction between Marketing and the Other Functional Areas   To illustrate this point, consider the following:

1. The finance people want prices that are both profitable and conducive to steady cash flow.

2. Production supervisors want prices that create large sales volumes, which permit long production runs with their associated lower cost benefits.

3. The legal department worries about possible antitrust violations when different prices are set according to type of customer. It also worries about global trademark protection and intellectual property issues.

4. The tax people are concerned with the effects of prices on tax loads.

5. The domestic sales manager wants export prices to be high enough to avoid having to compete with company products that are purchased for export and then diverted to the domestic market (one aspect of parallel importing).

The marketer must address all these concerns and also consider the impact of the legal and other environmental forces that we examined in Section Three. Table 18.2 at the end of this chapter examines this aspect of pricing in greater detail.

Standardizing Prices

Companies that pursue a policy of unified, global corporate pricing know that pricing is acted on by the same forces that militate against the international standardization of the other marketing mix components. Pricing for the overseas markets is more complex because managements must be concerned with two kinds of pricing: **foreign national pricing,** which is domestic pricing in another country, and **international pricing** for exports.

foreign national pricing
Local pricing in another country

international pricing
Setting prices of goods for export for both unrelated and related firms

Foreign National Pricing   Some foreign governments fix prices on just about everything, while others are concerned only with pricing on essential goods. In nations with laws on unfair competition, the minimum sales price may be controlled rather than the maximum. The German law is so comprehensive that under certain conditions even premiums and cents-off coupons may be prohibited because they violate the minimum price requirements.

Prices can vary because of cost differentials on opposite sides of a border. One government may levy higher import duties on imported raw materials or may subsidize public utilities, while another may not. Differences in labor legislation cause labor costs to vary. Competition among local suppliers may be intense in one market, permitting the affiliate to buy inputs at better prices than those paid by an affiliate in another market.

Competition on the selling side may be diverse also. Frequently, an affiliate in one market will face heavy local competition and be limited in the price it can charge, while in a neighboring market a lack of competitors will allow another affiliate to charge a higher price. As regional economic groupings reduce trade barriers among members, such opportunities are becoming fewer because firms must meet regional as well as local competition.

International Pricing   International pricing involves the setting of prices for goods produced in one country and sold in another. The pricing of exports to unrelated customers falls in this category and has been addressed in Chapter 17. A special kind of exporting, *intracorporate sales*, is common among large companies as they attempt to require that subsidiaries specialize in the manufacture of some products and import others. Their imports may consist of components that are assembled into the end product, such as computer chips made in one country that are mounted on boards built in another, or they may be finished products imported to complement the product mix of an affiliate. In either case, judgment is needed in setting a **transfer price.**

It is possible for the firm as a whole to gain while both the buying and the selling subsidiaries "lose," that is, receive prices that are lower than would be obtained through an outside transaction. The tendency is for transfer prices to be set at headquarters so that the company may obtain a profit from *both* the seller and the buyer or locate its profit in lower-tax environments. The selling affiliate would like to charge other subsidiaries the same price it charges all customers, but when combined with transportation costs and import duties, such a price may make it impossible for the importing subsidiary to compete in its market. If headquarters dictates that a lower-than-market transfer price be charged, the seller will be

transfer price
Intracorporate price, or the price of a good or service sold by one affiliate to another, the home office to an affiliate, or vice versa

unhappy because its profit-and-loss statement suffers. This can be problematic for managers whose promotion bonuses depend on the bottom line. Figure 18.3 shows how firms can protect profits from taxation with transfer pricing.

Increasingly the Internet is redefining pricing options. It is a tremendous tool for comparing prices—already sites can scan hundreds of outlets for prices on certain goods—and so national boundaries may mean less and less. In a sense, world prices for consumers may be on the way to being achieved. The effect extends to business-to-business pricing as well.

DISTRIBUTION STRATEGIES

The development of distribution strategies is difficult in the home country and even more so internationally, where marketing managers must concern themselves with two functions rather than one: getting the products *to* foreign markets (exporting) and distributing the products *within* each foreign market.

Interdependence of Distribution Decisions
Distribution decisions are often interdependent with the other marketing mix variables. For example, if the product requires considerable after-sales servicing, the firm will want to sell through dealers with the facilities, personnel, and capital to purchase spare parts and train service people. Channel decisions are critical because they are long-term decisions; once established, they are far less easy to change than those made for price, product, and promotion. Coca-Cola recently made a major decision to change its channel system in China; at great cost it moved from using a traditional channel, where competing interests of the channel members were slowing up their connection to the market, to building relationships with its small retail sellers.[37]

Standardizing Distribution
Although management would prefer to standardize distribution patterns internationally, there are two fundamental constraints on doing so: the variation in the availability of channel members among the firm's markets and the environmental forces present in these different markets. International managers have found flexibility around an overall policy to be effective. The subsidiaries implement the distribution policy and design channel strategies to meet local conditions.

Availability of Channel Members As a starting point in their channel design, local managers have the successful distribution system used in the domestic operation. Headquarters' support for a policy of employing the same channels worldwide will be especially strong when the entire marketing mix has been built around a particular channel type, such as direct sales force or franchised operators. McDonald's is an example of a firm that relies primarily on franchise operators at home and abroad.

FIGURE 18.3

Hiding Profits with Transfer Pricing

GREAT BRITAIN	JAMAICA	UNITED STATES
An item costs $100 to produce. It is sold to a Jamaican subsidiary for $100.	The Jamaican subsidiary resells the item for $200 to a U.S. subsidiary.	The American subsidiary sells the item at cost for $200. No profit earned. No tax paid.
Tax rate: 52% Tax paid: $0	Tax rate: 5% Tax paid: $5	Tax rate: 34% Tax paid: $0

Foreign Environmental Forces Environmental differences among markets add to the difficulty in standardizing distribution channels. Basic geographic differences matter greatly in distribution, as explained in Chapter 7. Just think about Switzerland's challenges. Changes caused by the cultural forces generally occur over time, but those caused by the legal forces can be radical and quick. To illustrate, hypermarkets are changing distribution patterns everywhere, including Europe. The EU's Royer Law gives local urban commissions, often dominated by small merchants, the power to refuse construction permits for supermarkets and hypermarkets.

Japan's Large Scale Retailers Law, very similar to the Royer Law, had also slowed the opening of large retailers. However, the Japanese government scrapped the law completely in 1997. The Japanese have adopted Internet shopping, and one result is that retail stores now seem almost superfluous. When Sony launched its electronic pet *Aibo* (Japanese for "companion") in 1999, it sold out of stock in 20 minutes on SonyStyle.com; no units were shipped to stores. Sony later opened physical SonyStyle stores in addition to its existing Sony outlets.[38]

Another restriction of distribution has been tried in the EU. Manufacturers have attempted to prevent distributors from selling across national borders, but the EU Commission has prohibited them from doing so by invoking EU antitrust laws. Exclusive distributorships have been permitted, but every time the manufacturer has included a clause prohibiting the distributor from exporting to another EU country, the clause has been stricken from the contract. In effect, a firm that has two factories in the EU with different costs, and thus distinct prices, is practically powerless to prevent products from the lower-cost affiliate from competing with higher-cost products from the other affiliate.

Economic differences also make international standardization difficult, although marketers can adapt to economic changes. In Japan, women no longer have time to shop and prepare the traditional Japanese foods. They fill their needs by purchasing more convenience foods advertised on TV with home delivery or by going to the more than 50 chains of convenience stores. The largest, 7-Eleven, has about 11,000 stores, many of which are run by former small shopkeepers.

Can retailing be globalized? Retailers such as France's Carrefour, with stores in France, Spain, Brazil, Argentina, and the United States, think it can. So do Safeway, Gucci, Cartier, Benetton, and Toys 'R' Us, which have made aggressive penetration in Canada, Europe, Hong Kong, and Singapore. Kaufhof, the German retailing giant, has 100 shoe stores located in Austria, France, Switzerland, and Germany and is also the leading mail-order shoe retailer in Europe. Wal-Mart, now with operations in 14 countries, is learning that global retailing takes localization.

Disintermediation

The term *disintermediation* refers to the unraveling of traditional distribution structures and is most often the result of being able to combine the Internet with fast delivery services such as FedEx and UPS. Increasingly, these tools are shaking up traditional distribution channels and making possible rapid service with or without a distribution structure. Our increasing ability to ship products quickly may mean that the lack of dedicated channels makes less difference over time.

CHANNEL SELECTION

Direct or Indirect Marketing

The first decision that management must make is whether to use middlemen, because there is frequently the option of marketing directly to the final user. Sales to original equipment manufacturers (OEMs)* and governments are usually made directly, as are the sales of high-priced industrial products such as turbines and locomotives, because the firm is dealing with relatively few customers and transactions but with large dollar value. Even in these cases, export sales may be made by local

---

*Original equipment manufacturers buy components that are incorporated into the products they produce (for example, spark plugs to an automobile manufacturer).

agents if management believes this is politically expedient or if the country's laws demand it. Other types of industrial products and consumer goods are marketed indirectly. The channel members are selected on the basis of their market coverage, cost, and susceptibility to company control. They must also be able to perform the functions required by management.

Factors Influencing Channel Selection
The factors that influence the selection of market channels may be classified as the characteristics of the market, the product, the company, and the middlemen.

Market Characteristics
The obvious place to start in channel selection is at the target markets. Which among the alternatives offers the best coverage? The firm may require multiple channels for multiple target markets. Large retailers, governments, and OEMs may be handled by the company's sales force or manufacturers' agents, while smaller retailers are supplied through wholesalers.

Product Characteristics A low-cost product sold in small quantities per transaction generally requires long channels, but if the goods are perishable, short channels are preferable. If the product is highly technical, it may be impossible to obtain knowledgeable middlemen, so the manufacturer is forced either to sell directly through company-owned distributors or to train independent middlemen. Caterpillar has enjoyed tremendous success by choosing the second alternative.

Company Characteristics A firm that has adequate financial and managerial resources is in a good position to employ its own sales force or agents. A financially weak company must use middlemen that take title to and pay for the goods. If management is inexperienced in selling to certain markets, it needs to employ middlemen who have that experience.

Middlemen's Characteristics Most industrial equipment, large household appliances, and automobiles require considerable after-sales servicing, and much of the firm's success in marketing depends on being able to deliver it. If the firm is not prepared to provide this service, it cannot use agents. The same is true for warehousing and promotion to the final user. If the firm is unable to perform these functions or perceives a cost advantage in not performing them, it must select middlemen that will service, warehouse, and promote its products. It may be that no channel members are available to reach the firm's target markets and perform the desired functions. If there are none, management must decide to refrain from entering the market, select other target markets, or create a new channel. For example, if a frozen-food processor finds that cold-storage facilities are nonexistent, it can either abandon the market or persuade middlemen to acquire the facilities. In a number of overseas markets, firms have purchased the necessary equipment such as warehouse freezers, refrigerated trucks, and so on, and rented, leased, or sold them on easy terms to distributors and retailers. To develop its distribution channel members in Brazil, an Italian cheese producer there supplied cold-storage equipment and set up gathering facilities for the dairy farmers. The company provided veterinarians and dairy experts to teach the dairy farmers how to maintain their herds and increase output. Nestlé has similar programs in its developing country markets.

FOREIGN ENVIRONMENTAL FORCES AND THE MARKETING MIX MATRIX

The matrix[39] in Table 18.2 summarizes many of the constraints on the internationalization of the marketing mix that have been discussed in this chapter and in Section Three. Table 18.2 can serve as a reminder of the many factors marketing managers should consider when contemplating the standardization of marketing mix elements.

Factors Limiting Standardization	Product	Price	Distribution	Personal Selling	Promotion
1. Physical forces	1. Climatic conditions—special packaging, extra insulation, mildew protection, extra cooling capacity, special lubricants, dust protection, special instructions 2. Difficult terrain—stronger parts, larger engines, stronger packing	1. Special product requirements add to costs 2. Difficult terrain—extra transportation costs, higher sales expense (car maintenance, longer travel time, more per diem expense)	1. Difficult terrain—less customer mobility, requiring more outlets, each with more stock 2. Varying climatic conditions—more stock needed when distinct products required for different climates	1. Buyers widely dispersed or concentrated—affects territory and sales force size 2. Difficult terrain—high travel expense, longer travel time, fewer daily sales calls 3. Separate cultures created by physical barriers—salespeople from each culture may be needed	1. Cultural pockets created by barriers—separate ads for languages, dialects, words, customs 2. Different climates—distinct advertising themes
2. Sociocultural forces	1. Consumer attitudes toward product 2. Colors of product and package—varying significance 3. Languages—labels, instructions 4. Religion—consumption patterns 5. Attitudes toward time—differences in acceptance of time-saving products 6. Attitudes toward change—acceptance of new products 7. Educational levels—ability to comprehend instructions, ability to use product 8. Tastes and customs—product use and consumption 9. Different buying habits—package size 10. Who is decision maker? 11. Rural-urban population mix	1. Cultural objections to product—lower prices to penetrate market 2. Lower educational level, lower income—lower prices for mass market 3. Attitudes toward bargaining—affects list prices 4. Customers' attitude toward price	1. More and perhaps specialized outlets to market to various subcultures 2. Buyers accustomed to bargaining—requires small retailers 3. Attitudes toward change—varying acceptance of new kinds of outlets 4. Different buying habits—different types of outlets	1. Separate cultures—separate salespeople 2. Varying attitudes toward work, time, achievement, and wealth among cultures—difficult to motivate and control sales force 3. Different buying behavior—different kinds of sales forces 4. Cultural stigma attached to selling?	1. Language, different or same but with words having different connotations—advertisements, labels, instructions 2. Literacy, low—simple labels, instructions, ads with plenty of graphics 3. Symbolism—responses differ 4. Colors—significances differ 5. Attitudes toward advertising 6. Buying influence—gender, committee, family 7. Cultural pockets—different promotions 8. Religion—taboos and restrictions vary 9. Attitudes toward foreign products and firms
3. Legal-political forces	1. Some products prohibited 2. Certain features required or prohibited 3. Label and packaging requirements	1. Varying retail price maintenance laws 2. Government-controlled prices or markups 3. Antitrust laws 4. Import duties 5. Tax laws	1. Some kinds of channel members outlawed 2. Markups government-controlled 3. Retail price maintenance 4. Turnover taxes	1. Laws governing discharge of salespeople 2. Laws requiring compensation on discharging salespeople	1. Use of languages 2. Legal limits to expenditures 3. Taxes on advertising 4. Prohibition of promotion for some products 5. Special legal requirements for some products (cigarettes, pharmaceuticals)

(Continued)

Factors Limiting Standardization	Product	Price	Distribution	Personal Selling	Promotion
3. Legal-political forces (continued)	4. Varying product standards 5. Varying patent, copyright, and trademark laws 6. Varying import duties 7. Varying import restrictions 8. Local production required of all or part of product 9. Requirements to use local inputs that are different from home country inputs 10. Cultural stigma attached to brand name or artwork?	6. Transfer pricing controls	5. Only government-owned channels permitted for some products 6. Restrictions on channel members—number, lines handled, licenses for each line 7. Laws on canceling contracts of channel members	3. Laws requiring profit sharing, overtime, working conditions 4. Restrictions on channel members	6. Media availability 7. Trademark laws 8. Taxes that discriminate against some kinds of promotion 9. Controls on language or claims used in ads for some products
4. Economic forces	1. Purchasing power—package size, product sophistication, quality level 2. Wages—varying requirements for labor-saving products 3. Condition of infrastructure—heavier products, hand- instead of power-operated 4. Market size—varying width of product mix	1. Different prices 2. Price elasticity of demand	1. Availability of outlets 2. Size of inventory 3. Size of outlets 4. Dispersion of outlets 5. Extent of self-service 6. Types of outlets 7. Length of channels	1. Sales force expense 2. Availability of employees in labor market	1. Media availability 2. Funds available 3. Emphasis on saving time 4. Experience with products 5. TV, radio ownership 6. Print media readership 7. Quality of media 8. Excessive costs to reach certain market segments
5. Competitive forces	1. Rate of new product introduction 2. Rate of product improvement 3. Quality levels 4. Package size 5. Strength in market	1. Competitors' prices 2. Number of competitors 3. Importance of price in competitors' marketing mix	1. Competitors' control of channel members 2. Competitors' margins to channel members 3. Competitors' choice of channel members	1. Competitors' sales force—number and ability 2. Competitors' emphasis on personal selling in promotional mix 3. Competitors' rates and methods of compensation	1. Competitors' promotional expenditures 2. Competitors' promotional mix 3. Competitors' choice of media
6. Distributive forces	1. Product servicing requirements 2. Package size 3. Branding—dealers' brands	1. Margins required by channel members 2. Special payments required—stocking, promotional	1. Availability of channel members 2. Number of company distribution centers 3. Market coverage by channel members 4. Demands of channel members	1. Size of sales force 2. Kind and quality of sales force	1. Kinds of promotion 2. Amounts of promotion

Explain why there are differences between domestic and international marketing.

Whether a policy or a technique is designed for global use or is first used in the home market and then used overseas, marketers must know where to look for possible differences between marketing domestically and marketing internationally. Sometimes there are great differences; sometimes there are none. Although the basic functions of marketing are the same for all markets, international markets can differ greatly because of the variations in the uncontrollable environmental forces. The marketing manager must decide if the marketing program can be standardized worldwide, if some changes must be made, or if a completely different marketing mix must be prepared.

Explain why international marketing managers may wish to standardize the marketing mix.

International marketing managers prefer to standardize the marketing mix regionally or worldwide because there can be considerable cost savings from marketing the same product and using the same promotional material and the same advertising. A standardized marketing mix is easier to control, and less time is spent preparing the marketing plan.

Explain why it is often impossible to standardize the marketing mix worldwide.

A manager may not be able to standardize the marketing mix worldwide because of differences in the environmental forces. The amount of change depends considerably on the product type and the degree of market penetration desired by the manager.

Discuss the importance of distinguishing among the total product, the physical product, and the brand name.

Much of the confusion about whether a global firm can have global products arises because the discussants do not differentiate between physical and total products. A total product is easier than a physical product to standardize. A brand name or a product concept may be standardized even though the physical product varies among markets. Also, a firm may have to use a different brand name in a market because its

present one has a bad connotation or because it may already be copyrighted by someone else.

Explain why consumer products generally require greater modification for international sales than do industrial products or services.

Industrial products and services generally can be marketed globally with less change than can consumer products because they are less sensitive to the foreign environment, as Figure 18.2 indicates.

Discuss the product strategies that can be formed from three product alternatives and three kinds of promotional messages.

Six commonly used promotional strategies can be formulated by combining the three alternatives of marketing the same product everywhere, adapting it, or designing a new product with the same, adapted, or different message.

Explain "glocal" advertising strategies.

International advertising agencies will design an international program for an advertiser and then make local adjustments that local managers deem necessary. The programmed-management approach is an advertising strategy for combining inputs from global advertising advocates of the home office with the opinions of local managers.

Discuss some of the effects the Internet may have on international marketing.

Among those mentioned are (1) making more pricing data available worldwide, (2) potentially making traditional channel structures less important, and (3) making the offering much more personalized and therefore more in line with the marketing concept.

Discuss the distribution strategies of international marketers.

Although an international firm might prefer to standardize its distribution patterns internationally, the facts that the same kinds of channel members are not available everywhere and that environmental forces vary among markets make standardization difficult or impossible at times.

total product (p. 476)
promotion (p. 482)
advertising (p. 483)

programmed-management approach (p. 488)
sales promotion (p. 490)
public relations (p. 491)

foreign national pricing (p. 493)
international pricing (p. 493)
transfer price (p. 493)

Questions

1. "Consumers are not standardized globally; therefore, with global brands, you either get lowest common denominator advertising or you get advertising that's right somewhere but wrong elsewhere." This is an actual statement by a CEO of an international advertising agency. What's your opinion?

2. What future do you see for global advertising?

3. Are there any advantages to standardizing the marketing mix worldwide?

4. Why are manufacturers increasing their use of global and regional brands?

5. What is the basis for Gillette's taking its panregional approach?

6. What is a generality about similarities of social and cultural values in a country?

7. Why is food retailing changing in Europe and Japan?

8. In a question for an earlier chapter, we asked you to assume the role of consultant to the developers of the Spiderman computer game. From the standardization/adaptation perspective, what changes, if any, would you make to your game to appeal to various foreign markets?

9. On the basis of the discussion in the personal selling section about problems with Internet communication, which of the following two firms is more likely to be successful? Firm A expects to use the Internet as a tool to continue the relationships with its foreign customers that were first set up in person. Firm B expects to use the Internet to make a first sale to overseas buyers. The firm's salespeople will then make personal selling trips to those firms that have already proved they are worth a visit because they have made a first purchase over the Internet.

10. Does the Venezuelan (and Colombian) system of requiring that every product be marked with a maximum price—*precio valido al publico,* or pvp— operate to the benefit of manufacturers? Of retailers? Of end users? Why or why not?

Research Task

Use the globalEDGE™ site (http://globalEDGE.msu.edu) to complete the following exercises:

1. Locate and retrieve the most current ranking of *global brands*. Identify the criteria that are utilized in these rankings. Which country has considerable representation in the top 100 global brands list? Prepare a short report identifying the countries and industries that possess global brands and the potential reasons for success. Are there any specific industries in which countries represented on the list may have a specialization?

2. Thorough planning is essential to export success. In this respect, pricing for specific markets is one of the critical components for successfully planning a multinational export initiative. One aspect of determining the proper price of your firm's market offerings in a given market is determining the cost of living in each general location. According to a colleague, a simple way to do this is by locating a report on this subject by the human resource consulting firm Mercer. Considering that your company emphasizes a strategy based on price competitiveness, prepare an executive summary of how to perform an initial pricing analysis for international markets. In addition, which 10 cities worldwide have the highest cost of living?

Minicase 18.1 U.S. Pharmaceutical of Korea*

U.S. Pharmaceutical of Korea (USPK) was formed in 1969. Its one manufacturing plant is located just outside Seoul, the capital. Although the company distributes its products throughout South Korea, 40 percent of its total sales of $5 million were made in the capital last year.

There are no governmental restrictions on whom the company can sell to. The only requirement is that the wholesaler, retailer, or end user have a business license and a taxation number. Of the 400 wholesalers in the country, 130 are customers of USPK, accounting for 46 percent of the company's total sales. The company also sells directly to 2,100 of the country's 10,000 retailers; these account for 45 percent of total sales. The remaining sales are made directly to high-volume end users, such as hospitals and clinics.

Tom Sloane, marketing manager of USPK, would prefer to make about 90 percent of the company's sales directly to retailers and the remaining 10 percent directly to high-volume users. He believes, however, that this strategy is not possible because there are so many small retailers. Not only is the sales volume per retailer small, but there is also a risk involved in extending the retailers credit. USPK tends to deal directly with large urban retailers and leaves most of the nonurban retailers to the wholesalers.

However, the use of wholesalers bothers Sloane for two reasons: (1) He has to give them larger discounts than he gives retailers that buy directly from the firm, and (2) because of the intense competition (300 pharmaceutical manufacturers in Korea), his wholesalers frequently demand larger discounts as the price for remaining loyal to USPK.

This intense competition affects another aspect of USPK's operations—collecting receivables. USPK has found that many wholesalers collect quickly from retailers but delay paying USPK. Instead, they invest in ventures that offer high short-term returns. For example, lending to individuals can bring them interest rates of up to 3 percent a month. The company's receivables, meanwhile, range from 75 to 130 days. Wholesalers are also the cause of another problem. Many are understaffed and have to rely on "drug peddlers" for sales. The drug peddlers (there are perhaps 4,000 just in Seoul) make most of their money either by cutting the wholesalers' margins (selling at lower-than-recommended prices) or by bartering USPK's products for other pharmaceuticals. They do this by finding retail outlets where products are sold for less than the printed price. They exchange USPK's products at a discount for other drugs, which they sell to other retail outlets at a profit. As a result, USPK's products end up on retailers' shelves at prices lower than those that the company and its reputable wholesalers are selling them for.

The pharmaceutical industry has made some progress in persuading wholesalers and retailers to adhere to company price lists, but nonadherence is still a serious problem. One issue that manufacturers have not been able to resolve yet is the manner in which demands from hospitals and physicians for gifts should be handled.

Sloane believes the industry can do much to solve these problems, although intense competition has thus far kept the pharmaceutical manufacturers from joining together to map out a solution.

1. What should Tom Sloane and U.S. Pharmaceutical of Korea do to improve collections from wholesalers?

2. How would you handle the distribution problem?

3. Can anything be done through firms in the industry to improve the situation?

4. How would you handle the demands for gifts?

*Based on an actual situation in Korea.

An Ethical Situation* Minicase 18.2

The Swiss pharmaceutical global corporation Hoffman-La Roche has made a major breakthrough in the relief of a serious disabling disease that affects 3 percent of the world's population. Its new product Tigason is the first product that effectively controls severe cases of psoriasis and dyskeratoses, skin disorders that cause severe flaking of the skin. Sufferers from these diseases frequently retreat from society because of fear of rejection, thus losing their families and jobs. Tigason does not cure the diseases, but it causes the symptoms to disappear.

There is one potential problem. Because of the risk of damage to unborn babies, women should not take the drug for one year before conception or during pregnancy. Hoffman-La Roche is well aware of the potential for harm to the company if the product is misused. It has seen the problems of another Swiss firm, Nestlé. After much discussion, the company has decided the product is too important to keep off the market. It is, after all, the product that gives the greatest relief to sufferers.

The marketing department is asked to formulate a strategy for disseminating product information and controlling Tigason's use.

As the marketing manager, what do you recommend?

*This is an actual situation.

19 Global Operations and Supply Chain Management

Creating overseas production sites merely in order to meet local consumption looks an increasingly fragile basis for foreign investment. A much better one is the ability to make the best use of a company's competitive advantages by locating production wherever it is most efficient. Today's multinationals create widespread networks of research, component production, assembly, and distribution.

—*Martin Wolf, global business analyst*

Zara: Transforming the International Fashion Industry through Innovative Supply Chain Management

After World War II, the leading designers of women's fashions typically looked to Paris and other European fashion centers for insight into what clothing to offer to the markets. Upscale fashion houses like Chanel, Armani, and Gucci displayed their clothing lines twice a year in glamorous fashion shows, which provided the foundation for upscale boutiques to make their merchandise purchase decisions. These designs, which often cost thousands of dollars, were affordable only by the very rich. As a result, the designs were subsequently copied by mall retailers and sold to the masses at lower prices, helping to ensure that consumer trends moved in sync with the fashion industry. The limited parameters of what designs were being produced helped to simplify planning and allowed clothing companies to survive even when they took six to nine months to bring a product from design to market.

That business model is disappearing rapidly. The international women's fashion industry is currently undergoing a major transformation, toward what has been termed "fast fashion"—involving up-to-the-minute fashion, low prices, and a clear market focus. Helping to lead this revolution is a Spanish company called Zara. One of the world's most rapidly expanding retailers, with a chain of nearly 1,000 clothing stores located in leading cities across 62 countries, Zara's annual sales exceed $4.5 billion. The company is known for its fashionable and affordable clothing, offered in stores that project a modern, clean, and stylish image. Zara's competitive advantage, however, comes from its world-class supply chain management skills and its ability to reengineer the clothing supply chain.

The company's strategy of speed and flexibility has enabled Zara to shorten the fashion cycle almost to the point where it no longer exists. Store managers and roving observers use handheld devices to collect and send information regarding which designs are being well received by the buying public, which ones are not, and what will be the next hot trend. At headquarters, this information is used by its staff of over 200 in-house designers to help stay on top of fashion trends. Zara's information systems also enable the company to better manage inventory, the primary cost of goods sold for clothing manufacturers and retailers. The textile manufacturers used by the company are mostly located close to Zara's headquarters, rather than lower-cost sources in the Far East that can lengthen the cycle time to market. In those cases where it does buy fabric from more distant mills, Zara buys cloth only in four colors, enabling it to postpone dyeing and printing until the last possible moment.

Zara uses information technology and advanced supply chain management techniques to maintain tight control and integration of the various elements of the entire process, from textile mill to retail store. As a result, Zara has reduced the cycle time from initial garment design to appearance on hangers in the company's retail stores to as little as 14 days—versus a cycle time

CONCEPT PREVIEWS

After reading this chapter, you should be able to:

understand the concept of supply chain management

recognize the relationship between design and supply chain management

describe the five global sourcing arrangements

appreciate the importance of the added costs of global sourcing

understand the increasing role of electronic purchasing for global sourcing

understand the just-in-time (JIT) production system and potential problems with its implementation

understand synchronous manufacturing and mass customization

comprehend the concept of Six Sigma systems and their application

explain the potential of global standardization of production processes and procedures, and identify impediments to standardization efforts

know the two general classes of activities, productive and supportive, that must be performed in all manufacturing systems

Gli Affari Internazionali
acionales
ionales Geschäft Παγοσμιο Business
Negócios Internacionais Los Negócios Internacionais
internacionales Affaires Internationales 国際商務 Παγοσμιο Business

of 3 to 15 months for most of its rivals' products. Rapid turnaround times also mean the company can keep its best-selling designs well stocked, limit excess inventory of designs that do not resonate with the consumer, and add looks that were not initially in its collections. "If I tried to source my collections in Asia, I would not be able to get them quickly enough to our stores. By manufacturing close to home, I can scrap collections when they are not selling. And without this rapid response, I would not be able to extract a good relation between quality, price and fashion, which is what our customers have come to expect," said Jose Maria Castellano, the CEO of Inditex and architect of Zara's fast-fashion business model.

As a result of these innovations, Zara can design merchandise inspired by and similar in style to what appears in fashion shows of the world's most prestigious fashion brands in Paris and Milan—and can have the merchandise on sale throughout the Zara chain long before the original designer's products have reached the market. A consequence, ironically, is that consumers may perceive the original product to be a copy, rather than Zara's offerings.

The company's business strategy also focuses on continual renewal of clothing lines. It ruthlessly removes its product lines, even ones that have been selling well, every three weeks or so. This approach enables Zara to have a near-continuous stream of new merchandise, always offer fresh styles, and help its customers to never feel out of fashion. Producing a range of 11,000 different items per year, Zara's culture of reacting very quickly to new fashion trends means that each time a customer walks into a Zara store, she can get the feel of entering a new place, one with fresh styles on display. Customers have thus come to know Zara as a chain offering a steady stream of new, "gotta-have-it" merchandise, and the limited availability of its merchandise promotes impulse purchases—a "grab it while you can" mentality among shoppers. To enhance its legitimacy in the fashion world and promote the style of its offerings, Zara uses top fashion models in image ad campaigns that are placed in leading fashion magazines such as *Vogue*.

Even high-end shoppers who have traditionally been loyal to designer labels have begun to mix high fashion with the fast-fashion products pioneered by companies such as Zara. Cost, quality, and design have become lower priorities than an ability to deliver a constant stream of fashionable new merchandise. Attracted by the rapid introduction of new styles and the excitement of buying 10 inexpensive knockoff designs for less than the price of a single "authentic" jacket, even many wealthy customers have become loyal to Zara's fast-fashion approach. For example, a long pink boucle jacket similar to a current offering from the

Chanel collection cost $129 at Zara, versus an original (albeit one with additional pearl buttons and a skirt) that was priced at $7,326. "Once it was embarrassing to be seen entering these stores. But now, not at all," proclaimed Franca Sozzani, the editor-in-chief of *Vogue Italia.*

Zara's revolutionary approach to the fashion industry means that it dictates industry standards on such dimensions as time to market, order fulfillment, costs, and customer satisfaction, as well as the ability to manage the linkages between these factors. The result is that high-end designers and fashion houses are being pressured to change their own operations and improve their ability to compete on speed. "What luxury brands can learn from these companies is their short time to market and constantly new merchandise. Even in the luxury business, customers want new merchandise all the time," explained Fabio Gnocchi, director of worldwide operations for the Italian fashion house Etro SpA. Building strong relationships with suppliers and improving capabilities in supply chain management seem to be requirements for other retailers hoping to respond to the fast-fashion model.

Propelled by the company's outstanding operational capabilities and execution in supply chain management, the Zara label has not only become the strongest Spanish consumer brand. It has also become a label with impressive international pull within the fashion industry and a major factor in transforming the industry globally. Fast fashion already makes up more than 12 percent of the market in the United Kingdom and 18 percent in Spain, and the U.S. fast-fashion segment is expected to increase dramatically from the 1 percent it had in 2005. Daniel Piette, fashion director for the upscale fashion house Louis Vuitton, described Zara as "possibly the most innovative and devastating retailer in the world." As Zara shows, effective supply chain management can indeed result in international competitive advantage. ■

Source: Leslie Crawford, "Inditex Sizes Up Europe in Expansion Drive," *Financial Times,* February 1, 2005, p. 18; "Zara," www.inditex.com/en/who_we_are/concepts/zara (July 17, 2006); Grupo Inditex,*2005 Annual Report,* www.inditex.com/en/shareholders_and_investors/investor_relations/annual_reports (July 17, 2006); Sarah Raper Larenaudie, "Inside the H&M Fashion Machine," *Time,* Spring 2004, pp. 48–50; "Branding Espana to the Rest of the World," *Brand Strategy,* March 2004, p. 12; Cecilie Rohwedder, "Style and Substance: Making Fashion Faster; As Knockoffs Beat Originals to Market, Designers Speed the Trip from Sketch to Store," *The Wall Street Journal,* February 24, 2004, p. B1; Teri Agins, "Pick-and-Mix Shoppers Force Fashion Industry to Abandon Old Models," *The Asian Wall Street Journal,* September 10–12, 2004, pp. A1, A10; Leonie Barrie, "Making a Mark: Some of the Issues to Watch in 2004: Fast Fashion Continues to Speed Up," *Just-Style,* January 2004, pp. 17–19; and Stephen Tierney, "New Research Proves Link between Supply Line and Bottom Line," *Frontline Solutions,* October 2003, p. 31.

As firms continue to enter global markets, global competition increases. This forces management of both international and domestic companies to search for ways to lower costs while improving their products or services in order to remain competitive. Sometimes the desired results are obtained through improvements within existing operations, such as the Six Sigma programs discussed later in this chapter. Other times, improved competitiveness is pursued by having the company open new—or transfer existing—operations abroad or find alternative outside sources for the labor, raw materials, or other inputs that it is currently sourcing from other organizations. A third option involves **outsourcing,** that is, hiring others to perform some of the noncore activities and decision making in a company's value chain, instead of continuing to do them in-house. Commonly, outsourcing firms provide key components of data processing, logistics, payroll, and accounting, although any activity in the value chain can be outsourced. It is common that managements will pursue some combination of these different options in their efforts to enhance their companies' international competitiveness. The efforts to improve the efficiency and effectiveness of a firm's international operations are often referred to as **supply chain management.** In this chapter, we will discuss the topic of global supply chain management and critical issues in the management of global operations, including global sourcing, manufacturing systems, productivity and performance of international manufacturing operations, and issues associated with the global standardization versus localization of international operations.

outsourcing
Hiring others to perform some of the noncore activities and decision making in a company's value chain, rather than having the company and its employees continue to perform those activities

Managing Global Supply Chains

Supply chain management has become an increasingly popular and strategically important topic in international business in recent years. *Supply chain* refers to the activities that are involved in producing a company's products and services and how these activities are linked together. The concept of supply chain management involves the applications of a total systems approach to managing the overall flow of materials, information, finances, and services within and among companies in the value chain—from raw materials and components suppliers through manufacturing facilities and warehouses and on to the ultimate customer.[1] Supply chains are an integral part of global quality and cost management initiatives, since a typical company's supply chain costs can represent over 50 percent of assets and over 80 percent of revenues.[2] Figure 19.1 illustrates a global supply chain for an American laptop computer company. This example broadly illustrates the activities and linkages involved in transforming initial designs into finished goods and support services delivered to the consumer, including product design, suppliers that provide the various inputs, assembly and testing activities, warehousing and distribution of finished goods, and the sales and technical support operations.

Because inventory is carried at each stage in the supply chain, and because inventory ties up money, it has been argued that the ultimate goal of effective supply chain management

supply chain management
The process of coordinating and integrating the flow of materials, information, finances, and services within and among companies in the value chain from suppliers to the ultimate consumer

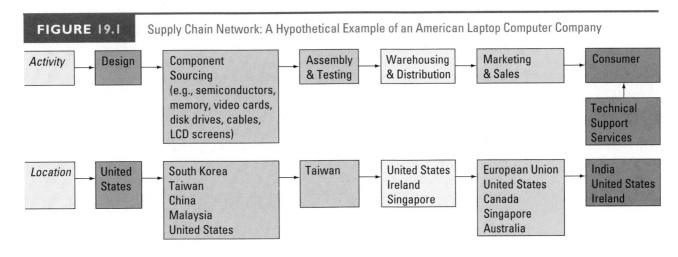

| **FIGURE 19.1** | Supply Chain Network: A Hypothetical Example of an American Laptop Computer Company |

Activity → Design → Component Sourcing (e.g., semiconductors, memory, video cards, disk drives, cables, LCD screens) → Assembly & Testing → Warehousing & Distribution → Marketing & Sales → Consumer ← Technical Support Services

Location → United States → South Korea / Taiwan / China / Malaysia / United States → Taiwan → United States / Ireland / Singapore → European Union / United States / Canada / Singapore / Australia → India / United States / Ireland

systems is to reduce inventory, consistent with the prerequisites that the company's products be available when needed and at the desired level of quality and quantity. For that reason, it is critical that the operations at each stage in the supply chain are synchronized in order to minimize the size of these buffer inventories. Shorter, less predictable product life cycles, as well as the impact of unplanned economic, political, and social events, have placed further emphasis on the achievement of effective supply chain performance.[3] New technologies, including Web-enabled tools for supply chain planning, execution, and optimization, have enhanced the availability of data and integration with suppliers and customers, helping to enhance the international competitiveness of companies that have adopted and mastered these technologies.

As highlighted in the Wal-Mart minicase at the end of Chapter 13 or the Zara example at the beginning of this chapter, global supply chain management has been receiving increasing attention because many companies have achieved significant international competitive advantage as a result of the manner in which they have configured and managed their global supply chain activities. Some organizations, such as the computer and information technology company Dell, have reconfigured their international supply chains to substantially reduce or eliminate activities such as finished goods warehousing and retail stores, thus reducing costs and increasing effectiveness.[4] Other companies, such as the Hong Kong export trading company Li and Fung, have transformed their operations to enter into new, value-adding activities in an industry's value chain.[5] Effective supply chain management can also enhance a company's ability to manage regulatory, social, and other environmental pressures, both nationally and globally.

> *In the* McDonald's Worldwide Corporate Responsibility Report, *the company states, "Supporting responsible actions in our supply chain helps to advance important social, economic, and environmental goals and will ensure the continued supply of high-quality ingredients we need in the future. That's why social responsibility is one of our key strategic supply chain priorities." McDonald's manages performance of its global chain of suppliers in such areas as food quality and safety, rain forest protection, fisheries sustainability, reducing impacts of packaging, promoting antibiotic effectiveness, biotechnology awareness, and animal welfare.*[6]

Design of Products and Services

An important factor in the structure and management of a company's global supply chain is the issue of design. The design of a company's products and services has a fundamental relationship with the type of inputs that the company will require, including labor, materials, information, and financing. As we discussed in Chapter 13, an important consideration in design is the extent to which the international company's products and services will be standardized across nations or regions or adapted to meet the different needs of various markets. The decision on standardization versus localization of designs is impacted by a range of competitive, cultural, regulatory, and other factors and is an important strategic consideration for a company.

> *The multinational automaker Ford set up a pioneering assembly plant in Camacari, Brazil, that includes in-house suppliers, just-in-time parts delivery, and a "just in sequence" flexible assembly line that can produce a range of different models. However, Ford's performance in Latin America suffered due to attempts to sell "tropicalized" versions of autos designed for the United States and Europe that had only minor adaptations for the local market, such as reinforced suspensions to better handle rugged roads. In response, Ford of Brazil developed a small team of local engineers, dubbed the "Amazon group," to design a vehicle more specifically oriented toward consumer needs in Latin America. The final product, an affordable light sport-utility vehicle called the Ecosport that was well suited to the more rugged Latin American operating context, achieved such success with consumers that Ford captured 80 percent of the SUV market in Brazil. Export demand has also been brisk from nations such as Argentina, Chile, Venezuela, and Mexico. "Local design has been the key to success," said David Breedlove, Ford's product development director for South America. "We used to copy U.S. models and then we recognized the need to focus on the South American market."*[7]

A traditional approach to product design has been termed the "over-the-wall" approach. This involves a sequential approach to design: an initial step in which the designers prepare the product's design, followed by sending the newly created design to the company's manufacturing engineers, who must then address the production-related problems that often result from their exclusion from the initial design activity. Of course, decisions on product and service design are seldom made in isolation, because of the problems that can arise from such an orientation.

An alternative approach to design is to promote cross-functional participation in the design stage, thereby helping to identify and avoid many of the potential sourcing, manufacturing, and other difficulties that can be associated with a particular design. Many companies also involve key customers in the design activities, to ensure that designs are consistent with the customers' needs. Using this type of concurrent engineering approach allows the proposed designs to be subjected to earlier assessments on cost, quality, and manufacturability dimensions, thereby enhancing the efficiency and effectiveness of subsequent manufacturing and supply chain management activities. Indeed, design decisions must often be integrated with assessment of the various supply chain considerations, such as whether and where the company can obtain the inputs needed for the company's operations, whether the firm will source locally or from foreign locations, and whether the company has the capability to produce and deliver the product or service in a competitively viable manner.

> *Nokia, the worldwide leader in wireless handsets and a leading competitor in wireless networks, has initiated a program called "Design for Environment" (DfE) as part of the company's global environmental strategy. The goal of Nokia's DfE initiative is to design products (including packaging) that have improved environmental performance, while simultaneously meeting cost, performance, quality, and other requirements. In part, the DfE program is intended to help Nokia to conform to new environmental legislation being introduced by the European Union and legislative bodies in other parts of the world, such as the United States, China, Japan, and Korea. But these efforts also reflect Nokia's attempt to be an industry leader in environmental performance and to better meet the evolving environmental needs of wireless operators and users worldwide. The DfE program ensures that Nokia's designers integrate environmental considerations associated with raw material supply, supplier activities, assembly and testing operations, product use, and end-of-life practices (i.e., reuse, recovery, recycling, and disposal) in all of their product design activities.*[8]

Sourcing Globally

REASONS FOR SOURCING GLOBALLY

Although the primary reason for sourcing globally is to obtain lower prices, there are other reasons. Perhaps certain products the company requires are not available locally and must be imported. Another possibility is that the firm's foreign competitors are using components of better quality or design than those available in the home country. To be competitive, the company may have to source these components or production machinery in foreign countries. The term **offshoring** is commonly used for a company's relocating of activities to foreign locations.

offshoring
Relocating some or all of a business's activities or processes to a foreign location

When deciding to source internationally, companies can either set up their own facilities or outsource the production to other companies. Outsourcing has become an increasingly common option for companies, as they try to focus scarce resources on their core competencies and leverage the skills of other companies to reduce costs and capital investments, improve flexibility and speed of response, enhance quality, or provide other strategic benefits. The activities can be outsourced either to another company in the same country or to a company in another country (the latter would constitute "offshore outsourcing").

Global access to vendors, falling costs of interactions, and improved information technologies and communication links are providing companies with unprecedented choices regarding how to structure their businesses. Any part of the value chain can be outsourced, including product design, raw material or component supply, manufacturing or assembly, logistics, distribution, marketing, sales, service, human resources, or other activities. Done properly, including a strong link to strategy, outsourcing can deliver dramatic increases in value for companies and their customers.

Outsourcing decisions, including the decision to use global sources of supply, are extensions of the make-or-buy decisions of earlier eras. The pros and cons of these decisions usually include comparisons of costs as well as managerial control of confidential product design specifications, delivered quantity, quality, design, and delivery time and method. Other considerations include the manufacturing expertise required to make the raw material or components and the added cost of not being able to take advantage of the scale or larger volumes a vendor may have. In global purchasing, these issues are exacerbated by such factors as distance, different languages of buyers and sellers, and different national laws and regulations. Over time, many organizations have developed the ability to manage these obstacles fully or in part, thus enabling global outsourcing to become a viable option for an increasing number of firms. When possible, it is better for companies to initially outsource simple activities and gradually outsource more complex activities as both the outsourcer and the service provider gain experience.

The lure of global sourcing is the existence of suppliers with improved competitiveness in terms of cost, quality, timeliness, and other relevant dimensions. For example, certain nations may provide access to lower-cost or better-quality minerals or other important raw materials or components compared to what might be available domestically (such as bauxite in Jamaica or dynamic random-access memory chips in South Korea). In addition, the existence of industrially less developed countries with inexpensive and abundant unskilled labor may provide an attractive source of supply for labor-intensive products with low skill requirements. This helps explain why many relatively standardized and labor-intensive operations (such as the assembly of athletic shoes or men's dress shirts) have moved away from the more industrialized countries, where labor is more expensive. The international product life cycle theory, which was discussed in Chapter 3, helps to explain this migration of operations from the developed to the less developed nations of the world. As these emerging economies develop industrially, and some have developed rather rapidly, they have typically moved forward on the product and process continuum from high-labor-content products made with light, unsophisticated process equipment, such as sewing machines, to more sophisticated processes and more complex, lower-labor-content machinery, or even to skill-intensive engineering and design services.

The rate at which developing nations shift to more sophisticated processes is often more rapid than the initial emergence of these processes in a developed country. In part, this may be a result of an emerging nation's ability to transfer technology and processes previously invented and commercialized in the more developed nations, thus avoiding the cost and time of inventing these technologies on its own. There can be important implications for nations that may be losing jobs as a result of the migration of developing nations into more sophisticated, higher-value sectors. Many times, a worker put out of a high-labor-content job in a more industrially developed nation may lack the ability or training to move up the ladder to a more sophisticated job. Governments, concerned with the potential loss of jobs, may attempt to take actions to prevent or delay movement of the work to the developing country.

The ability to effectively and efficiently use global sources has been enhanced by the plummeting cost of communications, widespread use of standardized interfaces such as World Wide Web browsers, and the increasing pace at which companies are automating and digitizing data. As more of a company's operational activities are automated, it becomes easier and more economical to outsource these activities. Increasing numbers of companies have begun to compete for outsourcing business, and customers have become more accustomed to using these services.

GLOBAL SOURCING ARRANGEMENTS

As was suggested in Chapter 16, any of the following arrangements can provide a firm with foreign products:

1. *Wholly owned subsidiary:* May be established in a country with low-cost labor to supply components to the home country plant, or the subsidiary may produce a product that either is not made in the home country or is of higher quality.

In international business, just-in-time manufacturing and lean manufacturing are increasingly important strategic concerns that can critically impact the bottom line of any organization operating globally. Third-party logistics suppliers are growing in importance because they are assuming responsibility for the logistics of supply chain management of many world-class corporations. Demand is increasing for professionals trained in purchasing, inventory control, warehouse management, and inbound/outbound distribution management worldwide. Managing global operations is an emerging field, and here are a number of career opportunities, with salary information, for you to consider:

Entry Level

- Buyer/planner
- Inventory analyst
- Transportation coordinator
- Import/export clerk
- Quality assurance technician
- Salary range: mid $20s–mid $30s

Mid-level Management

- Purchasing manager
- Logistics manager

- Inventory control manager
- Director of quality assurance
- Manager of quality compliance
- International transportation manager
- Salary range: mid $40s–mid $50s+

Senior Level Management

- Director of supply chain management
- Director of import-export management
- Vice president–logistics
- Vice president–production and inventory control
- Salary range: $70,000+

World Wide Resources:

www.supplychainmanagement101.com

www.logisticsmgmt.com

www.glscs.com

2. *Overseas joint venture:* Established where labor costs are lower, or quality higher, than in the home country to supply components to the home country.

3. *In-bond plant contractor:* Home country plant sends components to be machined and assembled or only assembled by an independent contractor in an in-bond plant.

4. *Overseas independent contractor:* Common in the clothing industry, in which firms with no production facilities, such as DKNY, Nike, and Liz Claiborne, contract with foreign manufacturers to make clothing to their specifications with their labels.

5. *Independent overseas manufacturer.*

IMPORTANCE OF GLOBAL SOURCING

A strong relationship exists between global sourcing and ownership of the foreign sources. *Intrafirm trade,* which includes trade between a parent company and its foreign affiliates, accounts for 30 to 40 percent of exports of goods and 35 to 45 percent of imports in the case of the United States.[9]

In U.S. industry, the proportion of purchased materials in the overall cost of goods sold has been rising for several decades, from an average of 40 percent in 1945 to 50 percent in 1960 and 55 to 79 percent today.[10] There are several reasons for this phenomenon, including greater complexity of products and increasing pressure for firms to focus on their core business and outsource other activities in which they lack strong competitive ability.

In addition, competitive pressures and an emphasis on reduced concept-to-market cycle times in many product and service sectors have resulted in a rapid increase in the number of new products that are made available to the market. It has been estimated that at least 50 percent of products currently on the market were not available five years ago. This development has created additional pressure to locate suppliers worldwide that can provide inputs at competitive prices and quality and with quick responsiveness to market changes.

FINDING GLOBAL SOURCES

The import sources discussed in Chapter 17 are the ones a professional purchasing agent would contact to learn about independent foreign sources. Foreign consulates and embassies are especially useful in furnishing the names of national firms searching for foreign customers. Many countries have programs to promote their industries that are similar to those of the U.S. Department of Commerce. As part of their sales promotional programs, local branches of foreign banks will generally assist in locating sources in their home countries when requested. Some even have newsletters with offers from firms in the home country to sell as well as buy.

THE INCREASING USE OF ELECTRONIC PURCHASING FOR GLOBAL SOURCING

Simply entering "exporter" and the name of the product in a search engine will bring up the Web sites of dozens of exporters around the world that have online catalogs and information on how to order their products. There are also buyers, some of them from large companies, looking for products. In recent years, many firms have set up electronic procurement (e-procurement) exchanges, individually or in conjunction with other firms, to identify potential suppliers or customers and facilitate efficient and dynamic interactions among these prospective buyers and suppliers.

> *BAE Systems, the Boeing Company, Lockheed Martin Corporation, Rolls-Royce, and Raytheon have a combined annual procurement budget of over $80 billion, more than 37,000 suppliers, and hundreds of airline and government customers. Those five companies formed Exostar.com, a global, Web-based business-to-business (B2B) electronic marketplace for the aerospace and defense industry, with the goal of helping member companies to simplify and standardize procurement processes, streamline supply chains, reduce costs, improve productivity, and reach new markets.*
>
> *John Rose, chief executive of Rolls-Royce, stated, "Exostar will allow us to reduce material and procurement costs, shorten lead times, and reduce our inventory. It will also enable us to collaborate more effectively with partners on designs for future projects. Exostar will allow design teams to hold shared, secure information, which can receive input from around the world. This will allow us to bring ideas to life in the marketplace more quickly, enabling a rapid response to customer requirements." By 2006, Exostar connected over 300 procurement systems, located in 20 different nations, and had over 16,000 registered trading partners.[11]*

Other ambitious B2B e-procurement projects have been announced in automobile manufacturing (e.g., Covisint.com, an integrated auto parts supplier exchange developed by Ford, DaimlerChrysler, and General Motors), chemicals (e.g., ChemConnect.com), steel (e.g., e-steel.com), insurance, petroleum, hospital supplies, electric utilities, and a wide range of other industries. Wal-Mart conducts all of its business with suppliers via a proprietary B2B network.

In many companies, the purchasing function has been neglected for many years, often being viewed as a prime candidate for outsourcing to other firms. However, purchasing is increasingly being considered a strategic function, a trend encouraged by rapid developments in e-procurement. While direct production–oriented goods have been the focus of management attention for many years, the purchasing of goods and services that are not part of finished goods—termed *indirect procurement*—is also critical. Including such items as maintenance, repair, operating supplies, office equipment, and other services and supplies, indirect procurement can account for as much as 70 percent of the total purchasing expenditures in a company. Although many organizations have continued to rely on traditional paper-based processes for indirect procurement despite their cost and inefficiency, new technologies are quickly encouraging change in this approach, even for small and mid-size companies.

Options for Global Electronic Procurement
Among the most basic transactions that can occur over electronic purchasing exchanges are catalog purchases. Suppliers will provide a catalog of the products available, and buyers can access, review, and place orders for desired items at a listed price. The supplier can keep the catalog updated in real time, adjusting prices according to inventory levels and the need to move particular products. Electronic

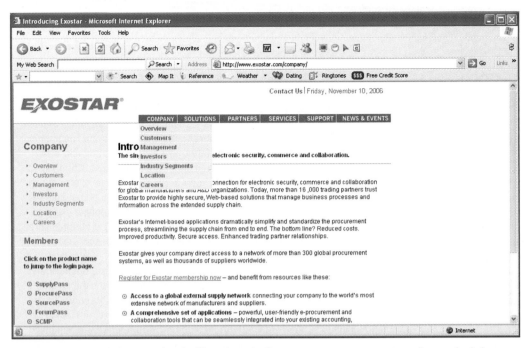

Web sites like Exostar help companies simplify and standardize procurement processes, streamline supply chains, reduce costs, improve productivity, and reach new markets.

Source: Exostar. Used by Permission.

exchanges can also permit buyers and suppliers to interact through a standard bid/quote system in which buyers can post their purchasing needs online for all prospective suppliers to view and the suppliers can then submit private quotes to the buyer. The buyer can then select among the submitted quotations on the basis of price, delivery times, or other factors. Industry-sponsored exchanges can also facilitate obtaining letters of credit, contracting for logistics and distribution, and monitoring daily prices and order flows, among other services.

Benefits of Global Electronic Procurement Systems

The benefits of electronic purchasing initiatives can be quite substantial. For example, Oracle Corporation announced that it would save $2 billion annually from companywide e-business initiatives that have allowed the company to streamline operations, cut costs, and improve productivity in supply chain management and customer response.[12] Research found that suppliers cut invoice and ordering errors by an average of 69 percent when using an e-marketplace, enhancing efficiency and reducing costs.[13]

> *Owens Corning established a goal of eliminating 80 percent of the company's paper invoices, meaning that all centralized purchasing would be done electronically (the remaining 20 percent of purchasing is decentralized). The company had four main goals when it launched its e-procurement initiative: hard-dollar cost reductions, supply chain visibility, business process integration, and a common, standardized process for all suppliers. Another major benefit of e-procurement has been a decreased need to rework invoices that are received either in incorrect formats or with incorrect information, cutting the number of reworked invoices by 70 percent. Jim Hawkins, e-sourcing project team leader, said the response by the company's suppliers has been mixed. "We've had suppliers who have jumped on . . . others really struggle or are not comfortable with the idea." While he says the transition to the company's new e-procurement system has been much easier for smaller and less technically advanced suppliers, "E does not necessarily stand for easy. Moving to electronic interchange is never as easy as you think it will be at first."[14]*

Smaller companies are also using the Internet to purchase raw materials as well as to sell their products to customers, often on a worldwide basis. Developments such as e-procurement exchanges have opened the door for many smaller suppliers, which now have to spend very little to get into the market, lowering barriers to entry to domestic and international market opportunities. As asserted by Amanda Mesler, managing director of KPMG Consulting in

>>Cognizant Technology Solutions: Sourcing Low-Cost Talent Internationally to Achieve Global Competitive Advantage

India has become a global center for high-technology businesses in recent years, with an estimated 800,000 information technology (IT) workers by 2006. The IT services sector has been supported by the Indian government for decades, a position enhanced by strong educational systems established by the British during colonial times. "The difference between India's universities and a school like Harvard is that an Indian university is harder to get into," said Mukesh Mehta, vice president of corporate systems for Metropolitan Life Insurance Company, which outsources IT services to an Indian supplier. Companies such as Microsoft, Oracle, and Sun have established research and development (R&D) facilities in Bangalore, Mumbai, and other Indian cities in an effort to utilize inexpensive and well-trained Indian engineers instead of expensive talent in the United States. IDC, a market research firm, estimated that by 2007, 23 percent of all IT work done for U.S.-based companies will be offshore, up from 5 percent in 2003.

One company seeking to exploit this opportunity is Cognizant Technology Solutions of Teaneck, New Jersey. With an electrical engineering degree from Cambridge and an MBA from Harvard Business School, the company's chairman and CEO, Kumar Mahadeva, was well prepared to build a technology-based business. Observing the thriving software industry that was emerging in India in the early 1990s, Mahadeva recognized an opportunity. He realized that he could achieve a strong cost advantage over other U.S. companies by employing talented entry-level programmers in India for $6,000 to $9,000 per year, compared to an average salary in the United States of about $50,000. He founded Cognizant in 1994 as a division of Dun & Bradstreet Corporation, initially focusing on large-scale full life-cycle software projects.

Providing software development and maintenance services, Cognizant competes on the basis of price, speed, and agility. The centerpiece of the company's operations is an innovative "offshore-onshore" business model. Under this model, about 30 percent of the company's more than 28,000 computer science and engineering professionals work at customer sites in the United States or other Western nations, and the remainder work at one of its 28 development centers, primarily located in India. Cognizant's hourly billable rates of $24 were substantially below comparable rates from domestic American providers, which charged upward of $70 per hour.

Once a contract has been signed, a global "virtual project team" is set up. A small portion of the team is located at the client's site, mainly Indian nationals who come for a couple of years to handle project management activities and manage client relationships on a daily basis. The remainder of the team is located in India, where software development, coding, maintenance, and other activities are completed on an around-the-clock, seven-days-a-week basis. This approach allows Cognizant's project managers to interact intensely with its clients during working hours in the West, intimately understanding the clients' strategies and needs, while prototype development, coding, and system upgrading activities are conducted overnight in a "chasing the sun" model of customer support.

To facilitate effective management of the offshore and on-site components of the multinational team, the company has set up a satellite- and fiber-optic-cable–based voice/data communications infrastructure, including e-mail and videoconferencing capabilities. To minimize misunderstandings and other problems as thoughts are translated from one culture to another, Cognizant's recruitment efforts target English-speaking students from computer science, engineering, and information technology programs at leading Indian universities. The company also provides extensive project management training programs. In addition, the company has a proprietary Project Management Tool that allows project managers to monitor the workflow of individual team members and track the status of components and various development activities.

Despite a fiercely competitive marketplace, Cognizant has achieved sustained success with its innovative business model. The company went public in 1998 on the Nasdaq, and by 2006 it had nearly 200 clients, primarily in health care, financial services, and manufacturing/ retail/logistics, including a number of prominent domestic and international companies such as Nielsen Media Research, the Body Shop, GM, Sears, Levis, United Healthcare, and Northwest Airlines. Included each year from 2002 to 2006 on *BusinessWeek*'s listing of the top 100 "hot growth" companies, Cognizant has quickly soared to a market valuation of approximately $9 billion, revenues of $1 billion, and a rate of growth that is more rapid than the industry as a whole.

Source: Interviews with executives at Cognizant Technology Solutions; Cognizant Technology Solutions, *2005 Annual Report*, www.cognizant.com/html/content/casestudies/annualreport/AnnualReport05.pdf (July 17, 2006); Alex Salkever, "Recognizing Cognizant as a High-Tech Bargain," *BusinessWeek*, March 28, 2000, www.businessweek.com/bwdaily/dnflash/mar2000/sw00328.htm (September 25, 2004); Cognizant Technology Solutions, www.cognizant.com (July 17, 2006); and Larry Greenemeier, "Offshore Outsourcing Grows to Global Proportions," *Information Week*, February 11, 2002, www.informationweek.com/story/IWK20020207S0011 (September 25, 2004).

Houston, Texas, "The promise of an exchange is that it allows them [smaller companies] to leverage their size further and get into more markets, especially globally and internationally, than they ever have before."[15]

Overall, emerging industry-based B2B exchanges can help optimize the supply chain across an entire network of organizations, not merely within a single company. These exchanges can create value by aggregating the purchasing power of buyers, improving process efficiency, integrating supply chains, enhancing content dissemination, and improving overall market efficiency within and across nations.

PROBLEMS WITH GLOBAL SOURCING

Although global sourcing is a standard procedure for half the U.S. firms with sales over $10 million, it does have some disadvantages.[16] Inasmuch as lower price is the primary reason companies make foreign purchases, they may be surprised that what initially appeared to be a lower price is not really lower once all the costs connected to the purchase are considered.

> *In their rush to source from China, many companies are blindly walking into a strategic trap. The trap is thinking sourcing from China will result in lower product costs, when, in reality, the supply chain dynamics will drive up overall costs and reduce profitability—thereby creating an opening for a competitor.[17]*

For purchases of capital goods, such as manufacturing equipment, many U.S. buying organizations now use "life cycle costing" to analyze purchasing decisions through the life of the purchased item, including trade-in or future estimated salvage value. Even on components, firms increasingly are including full costing, including the use of activity-based costing systems, to ensure that all the costs associated with foreign sourcing (e.g., transportation, insurance, increased inventory levels to insulate against delays in delivery) are fully recognized when they make purchasing decisions.[18] It is essential that global sourcing decisions be closely linked to the organization's strategy and that explicit objectives for suppliers (such as delivery times and cost objectives) be defined and incorporated in contracts, ideally with incentives for meeting or exceeding them. Cross-company teams should also be developed in order to enhance the likelihood that best practices can be effectively shared between the organization and its suppliers, in order to avoid supply problems.

Added Costs   The buyer must understand the terms of sale discussed in Chapter 17 because international freight, insurance, and packing can add as much as 10 to 12 percent to the quoted price, depending on the sales term used. The following is a list of the costs of importing, with an estimate of the percentage of the quoted price that each cost adds:

1. International freight, insurance, and packing (10–12%).

2. Import duties (0–50%).

3. Customhouse broker's fees (3–5%).

4. Transit or pipeline inventory (5–15%).

5. Cost of letter of credit (1%).

6. International travel and communication costs (2–8%).

7. Company import specialists (5%).

8. Reworking of products out of specification (0–15%).

Explanation of Added Costs   To be certain of the cost of freight, insurance, and packing, the prospective importer should request a quotation with sales terms of CIF port of entry and stipulate that the merchandise be packed for export unless all shipments will be sent by air freight. As discussed in Chapter 17, import duties can be extremely high if the exporting country is in column 2 of the Harmonized Tariff Schedule for the United States (HTSUSA). Unless the goods enter duty-free, the duty must be added as part of the landed cost. To estimate the import duty, the importer should ask the customhouse broker for assistance. Brokers have experience in customs classification and usually can get nonbinding opinions from the customs inspectors with whom they work. If the product will be imported regularly, the importer should ask U.S. Customs to provide a binding tariff classification. This will be made in writing and must be honored by customs officials.

Costs for inventory in the pipeline will vary according to the exporter's delivery promise. If it can ship from stock and air freight is a viable means, the importer may be able to work with only two weeks' inventory. If, however, the exporter must produce to fill the order and ship by ocean freight, it may need two months' inventory. Carrying costs include the opportunity cost of capital, the cost of storage facilities, insurance, pilferage, depreciation, taxes, and handling.

If there is considerable import activity, the importer may want to set up an import group of employees to be in charge of the operation. One other item that requires explanation is the rework expense and scrap charges. Sometimes a foreign exporter will submit a sample of the article it is quoting that is perfect in every respect, yet the actual shipment may include various pieces out of specification. If the importer has not made arrangements in the purchasing contract for rebates or replacement, the costs can escalate severely.

Other Disadvantages

One disadvantage an importer should not have to face is an increase in price because the home currency has lost value as a result of exchange rate fluctuation. For example, if an American importer requires that the exporter quote dollar prices, the importer has no exchange rate risk. However, if the firm has a large volume of imports and the dollar is unstable, management may want a quotation in foreign currency. In that case, the chief financial officer of the importing company probably will protect the company from exchange rate risk by using one of the hedging techniques discussed in Chapter 21. Hedging has been used for many years by companies that operate internationally, particularly if their raw materials include one or more of the commodities traded on established commodities markets. In most cases, such hedging has been done not for speculative reasons but as a means of protecting the company from the risk of rapid price fluctuations.

The emergence of e-procurement has also been accompanied by problems. E-procurement and electronic commerce as a whole cannot be isolated from the company's overall business system. Many early efforts at developing e-procurement systems have been made in isolation and have subsequently failed to deliver on their potential. Successful electronic commerce initiatives include connections to traditional systems for fulfilling procurement and other value chain activities, as well as considerations on how to manage the transition to new, electronic approaches. The traditional functions of purchasing—supplier determination, analysis, and selection—still have to be accomplished before the actual purchasing via e-procurement. In most instances, a company may be able to use the Internet for quicker data acquisition about possible suppliers and generally from a much broader information base than was previously available in a timely manner. Ensuring that a supplier is selected that can meet all the company's conditions for its raw material in terms of quality, delivery, price, and so forth, remains a challenge, particularly in a broadscale e-procurement network involving suppliers with which the company is not familiar. Suppliers located in emerging nations may also encounter difficulty in accessing and supporting sophisticated IT infrastructures, which can impact e-procurement performance.

Security also is often a significant concern for e-procurement. For B2B electronic commerce to achieve its full potential, access to the company's internal systems from outside is critical. Companies are wary of opening up the details of their business—including pricing, inventory, or design specifications—to competitors, as well as risking the loss of brand equity and margins. In addition, exposing internal business systems to access via the Internet can expose the firm to a wide range of potential security issues, such as unauthorized entry ("hacking") and fraudulent orders. Although extensive research and development efforts have been undertaken in encryption technology and other technology and processes to ensure integrity, much progress still remains to be achieved before these systems can be considered fully secure. Different country standards are also of concern in attempting to implement international e-procurement systems. Governmental concerns with potential anticompetitive effects of collaboration among competitors may also cause problems for industrywide B2B exchanges.

Manufacturing Systems

Inasmuch as international firms maintain manufacturing facilities in countries at various levels of development—facilities utilizing factors of production that vary considerably in cost and quality from one country to another—it is understandable that manufacturing systems will also vary considerably even within the same company. Therefore, a single company may have a combination of plants that range from those with the most advanced production technology, such as plants in Japan and the United States, to those with the less advanced technology of most developing nations.* The manufacturing systems in place within and across a company's international operations can have important implications for the way in which the company's global supply chain is set up and managed.

ADVANCED PRODUCTION TECHNIQUES TO ENHANCE QUALITY AND LOWER COSTS

Growing international competition requires increasing efforts from companies to achieve efficiency and effectiveness in their international production activities. As a result, companies all over the world have pursued ways to improve their competitiveness, putting into place advanced production systems such as just-in-time supply chains or highly synchronized manufacturing systems. Others have installed computer integrated manufacturing (CIM), utilizing computers and robots to further improve productivity and quality. Although these innovations can be a major challenge to implement successfully, their impact on international companies' competitiveness can be impressive.

> *What did Japan have to do to achieve international competitiveness after its manufacturing infrastructure was destroyed in World War II? Japanese manufacturers realized that because of the limited size of the country's economy, they would have to export to grow. They were also aware that because of the country's lack of natural resources, they would have to earn foreign exchange from exports to pay for the importation of energy sources such as petroleum and coal, as well as raw materials. In order to meet the requirements of export markets, Japanese companies would have to provide high-quality products at low prices. But during the initial postwar years, "Made in Japan" meant poor quality and shoddy manufacture to the rest of the world. In the 1950s, the Japanese brought in various American experts on manufacturing and quality improvement techniques, such as Juran, Feigenbaum, and Deming.[19] W. Edwards Deming, a statistician who had taught thousands of American industrial engineers how to use statistics in manufacturing during the war, helped teach Japanese manufacturers that statistics can be used to analyze what the system is doing and get it under control to produce quality products while simultaneously controlling costs.[20]*

As illustrated in the above example, when examining the components of their costs, Japanese managers realized what all firms know: Inventory costs are a major factor. Getting rid of inventory can lower labor cost by 40 percent, for example. To operate without inventory, however, Japanese manufacturers had to meet certain requirements:

1. Components, whether purchased from outside suppliers or made in the same plant, had to be defect-free, or the production line would be shut down while the workers in all successive operations waited for usable inputs.

2. Parts and components had to be delivered to each point in the production process at the time they were needed, hence the name **just-in-time (JIT)**. Henry Ford incorporated elements of JIT in his moving assembly lines in the early 1900s.

   just-in-time (JIT)
   A balanced system in which there is little or no delay time and idle in-process and finished goods inventory

3. Customers everywhere want delivery when they make the purchase, and so sellers maintain inventories of finished products. Sales often are made because one firm can supply the product from stock but a competitor cannot. How long do you want to wait for delivery of your car after you buy it? Eliminating inventories of finished goods while still responding quickly to customers' orders required the manufacturers to set up flexible production units, which necessitated rapid setup times.

*There are always exceptions to this generalization.

4. It was also necessary to reduce process time. One way to do this is to lower the time needed to transport work in progress from one operation to the next. American and European preoccupation with economic order lots resulted in their grouping machines by function (all drill presses together, punch presses together, and so forth), but transporting the machines' output to the next functional area takes time and costs money. Japanese firms grouped machines according to the workflow of a single product (a separate production line for each product), which virtually eliminated transport cost. Also, because parts were arriving immediately from one operation to the next, when the output of the preceding operation was defective, that operation could be stopped until the cause was rectified. Since each succeeding operation acted as quality inspection, this also lowered production costs because fewer defective parts were produced.

5. Flexible manufacturing allows product changes to be made rapidly, but each change in the production line still costs money. Therefore, the manufacturers simplified product lines and designed the products to use as many of the same parts as possible. This also contributed to the company suppliers' acceptance of the JIT concept because they received fewer but larger orders, which permitted longer, less costly (fewer production changeovers) production runs.

6. For just-in-time to be successful, manufacturers had to have the cooperation of their suppliers. They could not follow the common American practice of having numerous vendors, which buyers often play against one another to get the best price. Japanese firms used fewer vendors and sought to establish close relationships with them, including calling them in during the design of the product.

7. To lower costs, improve quality, and lower production times, Japanese managements required that product designers, production managers, purchasing people, and marketers work as a team.

8. Getting these people together enabled suppliers to suggest using the lower-cost standard parts they regularly produce, manufacturing to indicate when a design change could simplify the production process, and marketing to contribute the customer's viewpoint, *all before the first product was produced*.[21]

Reducing costs has been critical in recent years as companies, especially those from developed countries, face increasing competitive threats from lower-cost nations such as India and China. The competitive challenges posed by these nations have been viewed as a major cause of the "hollowing out" of the industrial sector in nations such as Japan, the United States, and Germany as manufacturing and assembly activities have been relocated to lower-cost locations, such as China, Mexico, or Eastern Europe.

total quality management (TQM)
System in which the entire organization is managed so that it excels on all dimensions of product and services that are important to the customer

quality circle (quality control circle)
Small work group that meets periodically to discuss ways to improve its functional areas and the quality of the product

Improve Quality   To improve quality, everyone in the organization—from top management to workers—has to be committed to quality. **Total quality management (TQM),** a companywide management approach to ensure quality throughout the organization, was invented in the Bell Laboratories in the 1920s. Teams are necessary in the implementation of TQM, and one useful kind of team is the **quality circle,** an idea of Ishikawa, a Japanese quality expert.[22] Look at how the president of Komatsu, Caterpillar's Japanese competitor, describes the use of quality circles in his company.

The objective of the quality circle is to take part of the responsibility for the quality goal of each section: "Quality circle members are aware of the extent to which their achievement of their objectives will contribute to the results of their department, and also to the business of the company as a whole."

A small group of employees, led by a foreman who has previously received quality control education, independently undertakes quality control activities. The circle's activities are divided among subdivisions of the circle led by a person junior to the foreman. Here is an example that illustrates that quality circles are used in all functional areas, not just in manufacturing.

One day, telephone operators received complaints from outside callers regarding delays in answering telephones, so they surveyed company employees, who confirmed that the com-

Chasing the Sun

"Big Ben strikes 5, and a team of engineers in London saves the latest files on a major design project and heads home to their flats. At about that time, a second team is pouring its first cups of coffee in rainy Seattle, eight time zones behind, and setting to work where the Brits left off. At the end of their eight-hour day, the Americans flip the proverbial baton over the Great Wall to a Beijing team, who will later complete the 24-hour cycle by giving way to the London team arriving for breakfast."

Sound far-fetched or futuristic? Think again, because this type of activity is occurring in a growing number of multinational corporations. Driven by increasing global competition and pressure to reduce concept-to-market cycle time, many international competitors—particularly in high-technology sectors such as information technology—have been forced to fundamentally rethink the way they structure their operations. The result is an approach termed *global, concurrent engineering*, or "chasing the sun" in more common terms.

Facilitated by rapid advances in computing and telecommunications technology and infrastructure, companies such as Hewlett-Packard (H-P), Boeing, and Cognizant Technology Solutions (discussed in the mini MNE box in this chapter) are trying to gain an advantage over their competitors by developing systems that permit around-the-clock development of new products. As stated by Mark Canepa, who is responsible for workstation systems strategy at H-P, "There's enormous pressure to make better and better products, faster than the competition, and time to market is the biggest differentiator." In rolling out its latest major initiative, the Open Enterprise Computing program, H-P is using a "virtual" team of specialists from around the world who are linked with each other—and with an array of international customers and partners—regardless of location and time.

Leveraging 24-hour global computer networks, project-focused Web sites, and teams of engineers and other technical personnel located at various offices around the globe, companies such as H-P are attempting to enable around-the-clock communication among clients and coworkers and thereby facilitate continuous real-time engineering enhancements, updating of blueprints, and related project management activities. In essence, they are attempting to revolutionize the way business is conducted. The benefits can be particularly valuable if around-the-clock systems are implemented during or before the detailed design phase of an international project, which tends to result in a significant improvement in the quality of designs through multiple reviews by different, geographically dispersed teams.

Implemented properly, these new approaches can yield valuable cross-fertilization of ideas to stimulate productivity and innovation among international teams, produce staggering reductions in lead time for new projects, and deliver a flood of new and enhanced products and services to the market ahead of competitors. The result: a powerful advantage in the demanding global competitive marketplace.

Source: Ray Bert, "Around the World in 24 Hours," *ASEE Prism*, American Society of Engineering Education, March 2000, www.asee.org/prism/march/html/feature2.html (September 25, 2004); Rossmore Group, "Chasing the Sun," www.rossmore.co.uk/pdfs-downloads/contact3.pdf (July 17, 2006); David Evans, "Chasing the Sun," *Computer Weekly*, April 27, 1995, p. 33; and James Ott, "Cargo 'Mods'; Boeing Applies Production Expertise to Its 747-400SF Conversion Program," *Aviation Week & Space Technology*, April 5, 2004, p. 56.

---

plaints were valid. They then studied the average time they were taking to answer a call and found that it was 7.4 seconds. They called the telephone company, which informed them that its standard was three seconds. The quality circle then discussed how to reach the three-second standard.[23]

Problems with Implementing the JIT System   Many manufacturers in the United States and elsewhere rushed to Japan to study the just-in-time "miracle" and mistakenly copied only one part of it: the narrow focus on scheduling goods inventories, called by some "little JIT." They failed to realize that what is important is "big JIT," a *total system* covering the management of people, materials, and relations with suppliers (also called *lean production*).[24] Moreover, many did not understand that JIT includes TQM, of which continuous improvement is an integral part.

Another difficulty was the difference in attitudes (a cultural force) between Japanese and Western managers. American managers and unions still valued highly the specialization of worker functions based on **Taylor's scientific management system.** This system contradicts the principles of quality circles: (1) participative decision making and (2) problem-solving capabilities of workers. Americans, pressured for quick results, were disappointed when quality circles did not offer immediate solutions for improvement. The practice of not guaranteeing long-term employment also made it more difficult to attain company loyalty for JIT. A further problem in implementing JIT systems was failure to train and integrate suppliers into the system.

Taylor's scientific management system
System based on scientific measurements that prescribes a division of work whereby planning is done by managers and plan execution is left to supervisors and workers

In trying to transform their supply chains, operations management experts also realized that there could be problems with JIT itself:

1. JIT is restricted to operations that produce the same parts repeatedly because it is a *balanced* system; that is, all operations are designed to produce the same quantity of parts. Yet repetitive operations may appear only in parts of the manufacturing process. It is far less useful for job shops (firms or departments within larger firms that specialize in producing small numbers of custom-designed products)* in which there is no dominant flow of production through the processes.

2. Because JIT is a balanced system, if one operation stops, the entire production line stops—there is no inventory to keep succeeding operations working.

3. Achieving a balanced system is difficult because production capacities differ among the various classes of machines. It may require five lathes to keep one punch press busy, for example, and it takes dozens of tire-building machines to use the output of just one calender, a huge machine (similar in size to a newspaper printing press) that rubberizes the fabric used in making tires. This problem is less severe for large production units, of course.

4. JIT makes no allowances for contingencies, and so every piece must be defect-free when it is received and delivery promises must be kept. **Preventive (planned) maintenance** is crucial. A sudden machine breakdown will stop the entire production process.

> *Toyota found out how vulnerable its just-in-time system is to the failure of just one supplier to deliver a part at the planned time. A fire at one of its keiretsu members, the exclusive producer of its brake parts, shut down all of the company's auto plants in Japan, causing it to lose a week's production. Not only did the fire paralyze Toyota's manufacturing activities; it caused hundreds of other Toyota suppliers to stop the production of its parts. After the fire, Toyota's chairman acknowledged that the just-in-time inventory system needed improvement. His company had to give orders to more than one supplier to prevent further crippling stoppages caused by a lack of parts. The single supplier concept, of course, has been a key component of its kereitsu network.[25]*

5. Much trial and error are required to put the system into effect.[26]

Synchronous Manufacturing

Synchronous Manufacturing The problems with JIT, especially the long time required for its installation in a manufacturing system, caused some firms to realize that something else was needed to assist them in gaining market share. Many turned to **synchronous manufacturing,** also called the *theory of constraints (TOC),* a scheduling and manufacturing control system that seeks to locate and then eliminate or minimize any constraints to greater production output, such as machines, people, tools, and facilities. The system's output is determined by and limited to the output of the slowest operation (**bottleneck**) that is working at full capacity.

A computer program developed by Dr. Goldtratt, the originator of TOC, schedules work, taking into consideration bottleneck and nonbottleneck operations. This makes scheduling much faster because production schedules and simulation can be done on a computer instead of having to arrive at schedules by trial and error, as is necessary with JIT. Also, once a bottleneck is discovered, the operations manager can concentrate on increasing the production rate of that process. After resolving that, the manager can repeat the process on the next-slowest operation.[27]

Instead of attempting to achieve a balanced system like JIT, in which the capacities of all operations are equal, synchronous manufacturing aims to balance the *product flow* through the system, which leaves output levels of the various operations *unbalanced.* For example, with the bottleneck operation producing at full capacity, perhaps only 60 percent capacity is needed at another operation. Because there is no reason for this operation to produce over 60 percent of its capacity, it is stopped at that point; anything more would be unwanted

---

preventive (planned) maintenance
Maintenance done according to plan, not when machines break down

synchronous manufacturing
An entire manufacturing system with unbalanced operations that emphasizes total system performance

bottleneck
Operation in a manufacturing system whose output sets the limit for the entire system's output

---

*Job shop also refers to a production system in which departments are organized around specific operations (grinding, drilling, and so forth).

inventory. Inasmuch as work is assigned to each operation rather than to the entire system, as in JIT, there is no need for more work in process than that which is actually being worked on. Inventory may also be placed near the bottleneck to avoid any shutdown in this crucial operation, and sometimes, unlike the case with JIT, there may even be a quality control inspector to check the bottleneck operation's input.

As we mentioned previously, management's attention is focused on the bottleneck rather than on the other operations, because a production increase at the bottleneck means an increase for the entire production system; an increase in a nonbottleneck operation adds to only that machine's idle time.

Note another important difference between JIT and synchronous manufacturing: A defective part or component at any point in the production process can shut down a JIT system. But because a synchronous manufacturing system has excess capacity in all operations except at the bottleneck, any defective part produced before the bottleneck can be remade, and thus the entire system is not stopped.

Incidentally, as firms adopt new manufacturing techniques such as synchronous manufacturing, they find that traditional accounting methods are inadequate to measure the costs of overhead. Managers are turning to *activity-based costing* to allocate the overhead burden according to its components, which vary among products.

Mass Customization **Mass customization** refers to a company's use of flexible, usually computer-aided, manufacturing systems to produce and deliver customized products and services for different customers worldwide. These systems typically combine the low unit costs and rapid production speeds associated with mass-production processes with the flexibility of customization for the demands of individual customers. As an approach to manufacturing, mass customization has been around since at least World War II, when Toyota began using it. Mass customization is now applied to varying degree by a range of companies in such fields as computers (Dell), greeting cards (Hallmark), clothing (L.L.Bean), footwear (adidas), diamond rings (adiamondisforever.com), and cars (Land-Rover).

There are four basic approaches to mass customization: (1) collaborative—a company helps customers choose the required product features; (2) adaptive—the company offers a

mass customization
The use of flexible, usually computer-aided, manufacturing systems to produce and deliver customized products and services for different customers worldwide

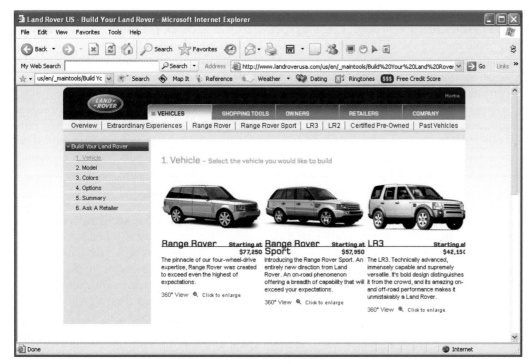

Through the use of computer-aided manufacturing systems, Land-Rover is able to produce and deliver customized cars for different customers worldwide.

Source: Land Rover US

standard product that users can modify themselves; (3) cosmetic—only the product's presentation is customized, such as packaging or color; and (4) transparent—customers are provided with individualized product or service offerings without their knowing it, such as Web site interfaces).[28]

Mass customization is usually appropriate in situations where there is the potential for delaying the task of differentiating the product for a particular customer until the last possible point in the supply network. This typically requires that the company reconceptualize the design of its product as well as the design and integration of the processes used for producing and delivering the product to customers. In practice, this means reconceptualizing and often reconfiguring the company's entire supply chain. But the benefits of such a comprehensive approach to operations are that the company will be able to function at maximum efficiency and to rapidly respond to customers' needs, while maintaining a minimum level of inventory.

Six Sigma
Business management process for reducing defects and eliminating variation

Six Sigma   **Six Sigma** is a business management process that combines rigorous analytical tools with a well-defined infrastructure and leadership from the top in order to solve problems and optimize processes. It concentrates on eliminating variation and reducing defects from work processes, and as defects go down, so do costs and cycle time, while customer satisfaction goes up.

Six Sigma literally means a maximum of 3.4 defects per million occurrences, versus the Two or Three Sigma level (more than 300,000 unsatisfactory experiences per million customer contacts) at which most businesses operate. It has been estimated that up to one-third of the work done in the United States consists of redoing what was already done previously and that the cost of poor quality consumes 20 to 40 percent of the total effort.[29] Six Sigma attempts to overcome this problem.

The Six Sigma approach includes five steps: define, measure, analyze, improve, and control. It begins by defining the process, asking who the customers are and what their problems are. Key characteristics important to the customer are identified, along with the processes that support these characteristics. Next, Six Sigma focuses on measuring the process, including categorizing key characteristics, verifying measurement systems, and collecting data. The third step is analysis, converting raw data into information that provides insight into the process and identifies the fundamental and most important causes of defects or problems. Six Sigma then focuses on improving the process, including developing solutions to the problem, implementing the changes, and assessing whether additional changes are required. Finally, the process is put under control to monitor and sustain performance over time. In essence, Six Sigma is a method for creating a closed-loop system for making continuous improvements in business processes.

In selecting projects for Six Sigma, there should be a clear link with business priorities, as reflected in the organization's strategic and annual operating plans. A project should represent a breakthrough in terms of significant improvements in both process and bottom-line results, with clear, quantitative measures of success. Projects should also be able to be completed within about three to six months (or be divided into subprojects of such duration), in order to maintain progress and company interest in the project.[30]

The CEO is often the driving force for implementing Six Sigma. The *champion,* who is responsible for the project's success, provides the necessary resources and breaks down organizational barriers. A major portion of a champion's bonus is typically tied to his or her success in achieving Six Sigma goals, helping ensure that the projects will have a substantial impact on the business. Project leaders are called "Black Belts" (BBs), typically individuals with a history of accomplishment and significant experience. Project team members are called "Green Belts" (GBs), and they do not spend all their time on Six Sigma projects. Both BBs and GBs tend to be change agents, and they should be open to generating and rigorously evaluating new ideas. Master Black Belts (MBBs), who are resources for project teams, are typically experienced BBs who have worked on many projects, have knowledge of advanced tools, have received business and leadership training, and have teaching experience. The primary responsibility of MBBs is training and mentoring new BBs.[31]

A Quality Online survey found that the biggest advantage of Six Sigma among organizations using the methodology was increased cost savings (45 percent of respondents), followed by an increase in customer satisfaction (20 percent), reduction of defects (15 percent), increased company growth (10 percent), and increased quality (5 percent). As one respondent said, "It is hard to pinpoint any single advantage of Six Sigma for a company. Engaging in Six Sigma increases customer satisfaction, lowers overall cost, and decreases defects, which is a competitive advantage for any company."[32]

Credited with originally creating Six Sigma, since 1987 Motorola's Six Sigma initiatives have generated documented savings in the company of over $16 billion as well as reducing the cost of poor quality by over 84 percent per unit and increasing employee productivity by 12 percent per year.[33]

The Six Sigma methodology involves reevaluation of the value-adding status of many elements of an organization (some being modified, others being discontinued). As a result, moving from Two Sigma to Six Sigma thinking often requires that companies rethink the way they do things and that they adapt their culture, sometimes dramatically. In challenging the existing way of doing things, Six Sigma may yield conflict with the organization's system of values and ethics.

Successful culture change requires a concerted, long-term effort, particularly if the organization is multinational, with subsidiaries and offices around the world. The way organizations change is influenced by organizational and national culture, which impact such things as how companies ascribe status, recognize performance, structure reporting lines, and communicate internally. This means that culture and cultural change must be actively managed from the outset. Increased acceptance may require that the organization (1) demonstrate the need for Six Sigma, (2) shape the vision of a Six Sigma culture and associated behaviors, (3) identify and properly manage organizational resistance to Six Sigma (including technical, political, and organizational sources), and (4) change the systems and structures of the organization (including hiring, development, performance assessment, and rewards for organizational personnel).[34] It is also essential to maintain the involvement and commitment of functional groups that provide the resources, data, and expertise necessary for successful implementation of Six Sigma change initiatives, including finance, information technology, human resources, engineering, R&D, and purchasing.

Logistics

Logistics refers to managerial functions associated with the movement of materials such as raw materials, work in progress, or finished goods. The effectiveness of supply chain management efforts is strongly influenced by how a company manages the interface of logistics with sourcing and manufacturing, as well as with other activities such as design, engineering, and marketing.[35] Given the strong emphasis on minimization of inventory and handling in supply chains, especially under just-in-time systems, the way a product (or the components and materials that will go into a product) is designed can significantly influence the cost of delivering the product. For example, packaging and transportation requirements for a product can significantly influence logistics costs, and these factors should be addressed during design as well as in other steps in the value chain.

Many companies have chosen to outsource their logistics needs to outside specialists, particularly for managing international logistics activities. Companies such as Federal Express, DHL, and UPS have developed expertise in handling and tracking materials within and across nations, including sophisticated computer technology and systems for tracking shipments. For example, Federal Express's Web site (www.fedex.com) allows a company to arrange pickups and then monitor the status of each item being transported, including information on the time the shipment was picked up, when and where it has been transferred within FedEx's network, and delivery location, time, and recipient. Many of these logistics companies have developed systems whereby their customers' in-house information systems are integrated with the logistics company's shipping and tracking systems. It is also common

Johnson Controls: Exploiting Design and Manufacturing Excellence for Global Advantage

Johnson Controls (JCI) was founded in 1885 to market its founder's invention, the electric room thermostat. By 2006, JCI had 136,000 employees in 1,000 locations worldwide and was generating annual revenues of nearly $28 billion, 60 percent from international markets. Its primary business is automotive parts and systems, although it has substantial activities in the building controls business as well.

In the early 1980s, JCI was known for heating controls and plastic containers, not automotive products. Until about 1985 auto manufacturers made car seats in their own factories. Then JCI and another company, Lear, conceived the idea of supplying those essential parts of a car's interior. Now JCI estimates that nearly 90 percent of the seating in American-made cars is outsourced, while in Europe the comparable proportion is 75 percent. According to JCI, demand from automakers to have only a single supplier of seating systems is expected to continue to grow "due to opportunities system integration creates for cost reduction, parts consolidation, weight reduction, quality and safety improvements, enhanced functionality, and vehicle differentiation."

Initially, JCI's auto seating business was focused on production of car seat frames, making them vulnerable to lower-priced competition. Over the past 15 years, JCI has focused on developing a broad range of assembly, integration, and R&D skills that help set it apart from competitors worldwide. JCI now designs and assembles not only seats but entire vehicle cockpits, and it conducts more customer research on interiors than any automaker.

Because of its unique capabilities, JCI has continual contact with an automaker's entire design and engineering team, beginning early and continuing throughout the vehicle planning process. As a result, JCI obtains proprietary information that yields deep insight into the automaker's needs and activities. JCI is now striving to increase its engineers' input to the design and engineering work so that it can use the results in the seats of other car manufacturers. "Three years ago, 80 percent of our development work was done on behalf of individual customers and only 20 percent was our own proprietary designs," said JCI's president. "Today the proportion is about 60:40 and our goal is to turn this to 20:80." Overall, these are capabilities that traditional parts suppliers cannot match, making JCI a supplier of choice in markets around the world, reducing bidding volatility and allowing it to plan with greater certainty. As Bill Fluharty, vice president of Industrial Design in JCI's Automotive Group, stated, "Tier One suppliers in the automotive industry earn their success primarily through being highly efficient manufacturers, producing parts and components that meet customer specifications. Intuitively, such a situation would suggest a limited role for design. But at Johnson Controls, that's not the case. Our industrial design team has established itself as a highly integrated and valued part of the organization. We have a 20-year track record of accomplishment, and we feel we're a significant influence on the success of our company."

As JCI's customers move overseas, they expect JCI to supply them from local facilities. In response, JCI is "growing globally by expanding regional capabilities as well as making the investments to follow [its] customers as they expand their global presence." Although most of JCI's 260 plants are in the United States and Europe, it has also established facilities in Eastern

---

for logistics companies to offer a broad range of services beyond shipping, including warehousing, distribution management, and customs and brokerage services.

Standardization and the Management of Global Operations

standards

Documented agreements containing technical specifications or other precise criteria that will be used consistently as guidelines, rules, or definitions of the characteristics of a product, process, or service

Standards are documented agreements containing technical specifications or other precise criteria that will be used consistently as guidelines, rules, or definitions of the characteristics of a product, process, or service. Standards help ensure that materials, products, processes, and services are appropriate for their purpose. Credit cards and phone cards are produced to an accepted standard, including an optimal thickness of 0.76 mm, so that these cards can be used worldwide. The same symbols for automobile controls are displayed in cars throughout the world, no matter where the vehicles are produced.

In most countries standards have been developed across product lines and for various functions. In the United States, for example, the standards developed by the American Society for the Testing of Materials (ASTM) and other organizations are used in lieu of specific detailed requirements to ensure an expected level of use and quality. In Europe, the most used standard for quality is ISO 9000. This is a set of five universal standards for a quality assurance system that has been agreed to by the International Organization for Standards (ISO), a federation of standards bodies from approximately 100 countries. The intention is that ISO 9000 standards will be applicable worldwide, avoiding technical barriers to trade attributable to the existence of nonharmonized standards between countries and thus facilitating international exchange of

Europe, India, China, Mexico, and other locations around the world in order to meet customer needs. Many are satellite plants located close to big car factories, to which seats are delivered straight to the assembly line as needed. JCI serves every major automaker, and it delivered interior components for over 35 million 2006 model-year vehicles. To manage the complexity of a global production system, JCI is creating a standardized business operating system and a single, global infrastructure, helping to eliminate variation and inefficiencies across factories.

JCI has also implemented an Internet-based database that employees worldwide can use to post and retrieve factory-tested best practices and ideas for improving performance in such areas as quality, cost, timelines, productivity, and morale of employees. Global engineering teams in JCI's technology centers in Germany, France, Japan, and the United States can collaborate in real time. A private Web site allows JCI's suppliers to provide real-time status updates, provide quotations, submit cost reduction ideas, and generate progress reports. It also helps JCI's program managers to quickly identify problems. Customers can have real-time access to key information about product launches and enhanced communication with members of product development teams. As the company states, "There are not significant differences between JCI and its competitors in the types of machinery we use, or the infrastructure investments we make, yet we have been able to separate ourselves from the competition. Our advantage, and growth, comes from our ability to continually add value. We've been successful at doing this because of the quality of our management and employees, and their commitment and ability to think of innovative solutions for customers."

Another strategy of JCI's has been to expand its role from supplying seating to supplying nonseating parts of car interiors, including doors, instrument panels, electronics, storage, roof interiors, and trim. This move to supply a "total interior" service to automakers has been successful, and today JCI is the world's largest independent supplier of automotive interior systems. As JCI's CEO said, "A key growth driver continues to be our ability to find new ways to serve customers. In our interiors business that means supplying larger modules and creating distinctive consumer features that help us garner a greater share of the vehicle interior." In pursuit of its goal, JCI has introduced Six Sigma principles throughout its facilities worldwide, including training over 2,000 people in its techniques, to facilitate the discovery of new ways of enhancing product quality and service delivery. The thousands of projects completed as part of the company's Six Sigma program have produced substantial savings in costs as well as improved performance quality. For example, the program reduced electrical installation defect rates in the United Kingdom from 21 to 3 percent by improving electrical drawings. In Germany, it reduced errors on incoming vendor invoices by 80 percent, eliminating costly reworking. In Japan, it increased productivity on a just-in-time seat production line by 70 to 75 percent. In the United States, it eliminated unnecessary tooling changes caused by incorrect or incomplete engineering drawings of automotive interiors, saving over $2 million per year for JCI and $3.5 million per year for its customers. The program is being extended beyond JCI to also include suppliers, in an effort to further enhance supply chain effectiveness for itself and its customers.

Source: Adrian Slywotzky and Richard Wise, "Three Keys to Groundbreaking Growth: A Demand Innovation Strategy, Nurturing Practices, and a Chief Growth Officer," *Strategy & Leadership* 31, no. 5 (2003), pp. 12–19; Johnson Controls, *Annual Report 2005*, www.johnsoncontrols.com/annualreports/2005/JC_05report_spreads.pdf (July 18, 2006); Adrian Slywotsky, "Go Ahead, Take a Risk," *The Wall Street Journal*, June 22, 2004, p. B2; Bill Fluharty, "A Place at the Table: Taking Design from Service to Corporate Function," *Design Management Review*, Spring 2004, pp. 17–22; Jyoti Thottam, "What Can America Make?" *Time*, January 12, 2004, p. B1; and Gary S. Vasilash, "Creating the Inviting Interior," *Automotive Design and Production*, January 2004, pp. 34–35.

goods and services. If a product or service is purchased from a company that is registered to the appropriate ISO 9000 standard, the buyer will have important assurances that the quality of what was received will be what was expected. Indeed, registered companies have reported dramatic reductions in customer complaints as well as reduced operating costs and increased demand for their products and services. The United States has adopted the ISO 9000 series verbatim as the ANSI/AQC900 series.

The most comprehensive of the standards is ISO 9001. It applies to industries involved in the design, development, manufacturing, installation, and servicing of products and services. The standards apply uniformly to companies, regardless of their size or industry. In general, companies that want to do business in Europe must have ISO 9000 registration, and many companies also require registration by their suppliers to provide further assurance of compliance. There is also an ISO 14000 series that provides a similar framework for quality assurance in the area of environmental management.

Although it has been widely adopted as a standard for quality, not all quality "experts" agree that ISO 9000 is superior to other alternatives: "The focus of the standards is to establish quality management procedures, through detailed documentation, work instructions, and record keeping. These procedures . . . say nothing about the actual quality of the product—they deal entirely with standards to be followed." Phil Crosby, a noted quality expert and the author of several practitioner quality books, states, "It is a delusion that sound management can be replaced by an information format. It is like putting a Bible in every hotel room with the thought that occupants will act according to its contents."[36]

The advantages of synchronous manufacturing and TQM are compelling reasons why numerous global and multinational corporations are installing them worldwide. Certainly, customers everywhere want quality products at low prices. Firms from industrialized nations commonly copy home country manufacturing systems when setting up and operating in their subsidiaries in other industrialized nations.

> *Intel, the worldwide leader in supplying semiconductor memory products and related computer components, introduced an approach called "Copy Exactly" for achieving standardization in its factories. "Copy Exactly solves the problem of getting production facilities up to speed quickly by duplicating everything from the development plant to the volume-manufacturing plant." Managers from high-volume facilities participate in the development plant as new process technology is created. "Everything at the development plant—the process flow, equipment set, suppliers, plumbing, manufacturing clean room, and training methodologies—is selected to meet high-volume needs, recorded, and then copied exactly to the high-volume plant. Time after time, factory yields start at higher levels, and even improve when multiple factories come online using Copy Exactly."[37]*

In addition to those just mentioned, there are other important, although perhaps less obvious, reasons for global standardization. The following sections discuss some of these reasons.

ORGANIZATION AND STAFFING

Some of the reasons for the global standardization of a firm's manufacturing systems are the effects on organization and staffing.

Simpler and Less Costly When Standardized
The standardization of production processes and procedures simplifies the manufacturing organization at headquarters because their replication enables the work to be accomplished with a smaller staff of support personnel. Fewer labor hours in plant design are involved because each new plant is essentially a scaled-up or scaled-down version of an existing one. The permanent group of experts that international companies maintain to give technical assistance to overseas plants can be smaller. Extra technicians accustomed to working with the same machinery can be borrowed from the domestic operation as needed.

Worldwide uniformity or standardization in manufacturing methods also increases headquarters' effectiveness in keeping the production specifications current. Every firm has hundreds of specifications, and those specifications are constantly being changed because of new raw materials or manufacturing procedures. If all plants, domestic and foreign, possess the same equipment, notice of a change can be given with one indiscriminate notification (e.g., a mailing); there is no need for highly paid engineers to check each affiliate's list of equipment to see which ones are affected. Companies whose manufacturing processes are not unified have found that maintaining a current separate set of specifications for each of 15 or 20 affiliates is both more costly (larger staff) and more error-prone.

An Intel employee checks wafers processing in a vertical diffusion furnace, one of the many tools through which wafers must pass as they go through the hundreds of steps that make up the manufacturing process. Intel, the worldwide leader in supplying semiconductor memory products and related computer components, uses a "Copy Exactly" strategy, which solves the problem of getting production facilities up to speed quickly by duplicating production facilities.

Logistics of Supply
As we discussed at the beginning of this chapter on the value of a supply chain management orientation, management has become increasingly aware that greater profits may be obtained by organizing all of its companies' production facilities into one logistical supply system that includes all the activities required to move raw materials, parts, and finished inventory from vendors, between enterprise facilities, and to customers. The standardization of processes and machinery provides a reasonable guarantee that parts manufactured in the firm's various plants will be interchangeable. This assurance of interchangeability enables management to divide the production of components among a number of subsidiaries to achieve greater economies of scale and take advantage of the lower production costs in some countries.

Rationalization   **Manufacturing rationalization,** as this production strategy is called, involves a change from a subsidiary's manufacturing only for its own national market to its producing a limited number of components for use by all subsidiaries.

> *SKF, a major bearing manufacturer with headquarters in Sweden, was able to reduce the number of types of ball bearings produced in five major overseas subsidiaries years ago from 50,000 to 20,000. Of the 20,000 remaining types, 7,000 have been rationalized among the five plants, and the other 13,000 are produced solely by one or another subsidiary for its local customers.*[38]

For manufacturing rationalization to be possible, the product mix must first be rationalized; that is, the firm must elect to produce products that are identical worldwide or region-wide. Once this has been done, each subsidiary can be assigned to produce certain components for other foreign plants, thus attaining a higher volume with a lower production cost than would be possible if it manufactured the complete product for its national market only. Obviously, this strategy is not viable when consumers' tastes and preferences differ markedly among markets. For less differentiated products, however, manufacturing rationalization permits economies of scale in production and engineering that would otherwise be impossible.

Purchasing   When foreign subsidiaries are unable to purchase raw materials and machinery locally, they generally look for assistance from the purchasing department at headquarters. Because unified processes require the same materials everywhere, buyers can handle foreign requirements by simply increasing their regular orders to their usual suppliers and passing on the volume discounts to the subsidiaries. However, when special materials are required, purchasing agents must search out new vendors and place smaller orders, often at higher prices.

CONTROL

All the advantages of global standardization cited thus far also pertain to the other functions of management. Three aspects of control—quality, production, and maintenance—merit additional discussion.

Quality Control   When production equipment is similar, home office control of quality in foreign affiliates is less difficult because management can expect all plants to adhere to the same standard. The home office can compare the periodic reports that all affiliates submit and quickly spot deviations from the norm that require remedial action, such as a large number of product rejects. Separate standards for each plant because of equipment differences are unnecessary.

Production and Maintenance Control   A single standard also lessens the task of maintenance and production control. The same machinery should produce at the same rate of output and have the same frequency of maintenance no matter where it is located. In practice, deviations will occur because of the human and physical factors (dust, humidity, temperature), but at least similar machinery permits the home office to establish standards by which to determine the effectiveness of local managements. Furthermore, the maintenance experience of other production units in regard to the frequency of overhauls and the stock of spare parts needed will help plants avoid costly, unforeseen stoppages from sudden breakdowns.

PLANNING

When a new plant can be built that is a duplicate of others already functioning, the planning and design will be both simpler and quicker because they are essentially a repetition of work already done:

1. Design engineers need only copy the drawings and lists of materials that they have in their files.

2. Vendors will be requested to furnish equipment that they have supplied previously.

(margin note)
manufacturing rationalization
Division of production among a number of production units, thus enabling each to produce only a limited number of components for all of a firm's assembly plants

3. The technical department can send the current manufacturing specifications without alteration.

4. Labor trainers experienced in the operation of the machinery can be sent to the new location without undergoing special training on new equipment.

5. Reasonably accurate forecasts of plant erection time and output can be based on experience with existing facilities.

In other words, the duplication of existing plants greatly reduces the engineering time required in planning and designing the new facilities and eliminates many of the start-up difficulties inherent in any new operation. To be sure, a newly designed plant causes problems when it is erected domestically, but those problems tend to be greater when the plant is located in a different environment at a great distance from headquarters. Just how important the savings from plant duplication are was emphasized in a study of the chemical and refining industries that indicated that the cost of technology transfer was lowered by 34 and 19 percent for the second and third start-ups, respectively.[39]

Since the case for global standardization of production is so strong, why do differences among plants in the same company persist?

Impediments to Standardization of Global Operations

Generally, it is easier for international corporations to standardize the concepts of total quality management and synchronous manufacturing in their overseas affiliates than it is to standardize the actual manufacturing facilities. Units of an international multiplant operation differ in size, machinery, and procedures because of the intervention of the foreign environmental forces, especially the economic, cultural, and political forces.

ENVIRONMENTAL FORCES

Let us examine the impact of the three kinds of forces just mentioned.

Economic Forces   The most important element of the economic forces that impedes production standardization is the wide range of market sizes, discussed in Chapter 18.

> *A number of studies confirmed by personal experience have shown that the foremost criterion for plant design is the output desired. Once this is known, the engineering department of a multiplant operation will check to see whether a factory already has been built with a capacity similar to the output specified. If so, this facility will serve as a design standard for the new plant, though modifications may be made to eliminate any problems encountered in the original design. Many large multiplant firms actually have standard designs for large, medium, and small production outputs.*

To cope with the great variety of production requirements, the designer generally has the option of selecting either a *capital-intensive process* incorporating automated, high-semimanual-output machinery or a *labor-intensive process* employing more people and general-purpose equipment with lower productive capacity. The automated machinery is severely limited in flexibility (variety of products and range of sizes), but once set up, it will turn out in a few days what may be a year's supply for some markets.[40] For many processes, this problem may be resolved by installing one machine of the type used by the hundreds in the larger home plant. However, sometimes this option is not available; some processes use only one or two large machines, even in manufacturing facilities with large output, as we mentioned in the discussion of standardized manufacturing. Until recently, when the option was not available, plant designers had to choose between the high-output specialized machinery and the lower-output general-purpose machines mentioned earlier. The major differences are that general-purpose machines require skills that are built into a special-purpose machine. The general-purpose machine usually produces a product of lower quality and higher per-unit costs than does the special-purpose machine.

Nestlé: Standardizing Processes and Systems to Exploit Global Opportunity

Nestlé is the world's largest food and beverage company, with over 500 factories around the world and over 250,000 employees. In 2005, it achieved sales of $75 billion from its portfolio of well-known brands, such as Nescafé, Taster's Choice, Arrowhead, Perrier, Carnation, Libby's, Dreyer's, PowerBar, Stouffer's, Lean Cuisine, Kit Cat, Butterfinger, Purina, and Friskies.

At the end of the 1990s, Nestlé's CEO, Peter Brabeck, confronted a difficult challenge. Although present around the world, Nestlé had traditionally operated as "a collection of independent fiefdoms," rather than as an integrated global company. As a result, although his company was achieving excellent growth, the high overhead expenses from inefficiency and duplication of efforts caused Nestlé's profit to be below the industry's average. The company's primary coffee brand, Nescafé, had over 200 formulations to suit various local tastes. Nestlé's vast, inefficient global supply chain, compounded by wasteful purchasing practices and inefficient operational and marketing efforts, was constraining performance. In the area of enterprise planning systems, Nestlé had 14 different SAP systems operating in various countries, each with different ways of formatting data and handling forms. Information technology costs were spiraling out of control. Trying to control the thousands of supply chains, dozens of demand forecasting methods, and the diverse array of methods for invoicing customers and collecting receivable was proving to be increasingly difficult.

To address this problem, Brabeck launched the Global Business Excellence (GLOBE) program in 2000, the most ambitious business process reengineering program Nestlé had ever attempted. GLOBE would develop a single, standardized system that would enable managers worldwide to forecast demand, purchase supplies, collect receivables, and promote and sell the company's 127,000 different sizes and types of products. Projected to cost approximately $2.5 billion, the GLOBE project had 3 main objectives:

- *Best practices:* GLOBE would compile a set of best practices from throughout the scattered Nestlé operations and make these business processes available to managers across all nations, products, and functions. By creating a common business process architecture, Nestlé would have a common, transparent way for addressing activities such as sales forecasting, production planning, purchasing, and customer service.

- *Data standardization:* To create a standardized set of Nestlé data, GLOBE would establish common coding for items such as raw and packaging materials, finished goods, vendors, and customers. By consolidating this information, Nestlé's managers could readily obtain a global picture of how much product the company purchased, globally, from each supplier; how much the company sold, on a product-by-product basis, to key international customers such as Wal-Mart or Carrefour; and how many units of products such as Butterfingers or Kit Kat chocolate bars had been sold through different channels, such as supermarkets or vending machines.

- *Common information systems:* To support the first two objectives, a common global information system was required. Developing this system would involve reducing the company's data centers from about 100 to only 4, standardizing computer hardware and software, and establishing global agreements with key suppliers such as SAP, Microsoft, and Dell.

Brabeck hoped that GLOBE would enable Nestlé to use information as a competitive advantage through facilitating better decision making, better management of complexity, improved speed and flexibility, and improved focus on customers. Benefits would include an improved ability to regroup elements of Nestlé's business, respond faster to global business trends, drive down operational business costs, enhance insight into customers, ensure product safety and traceability, and exploit economies of scale to further enhance the company's global competitiveness. Nestlé predicted that it could reduce the number of suppliers from 600,000 to 167,000 and simultaneously reduce costs by $750 million a year.

Implementation of the GLOBE initiative would take many years to complete, and it encountered a number of problems. Nestlé had a long-established culture of decentralization and relative autonomy at the country level. Country managers resisted the GLOBE effort, fearing that it would hurt their bottom-line performance and reduce their authority. Managers were trying to compete within a mosaic of divergent local and national markets, each with different requirements for logistics, sales, and customer service. These managers rebelled against the concept of imposing standardized methods for supply chain or customer relationship management. However, if it was mandated that a method would be standardized, then each of the managers tended to lobby for his or her own country's practice to be selected as the global template, arguing that the particular way in his or her country was "best." Trying to address these complaints and complete a radical transformation of Nestlé, and to do so within an initially projected time frame of about three and a half years, appeared foolhardy to many in the company.

Nestlé's leadership did not waver in its resolve. Ronald Hafner, the global relationship partner for Nestlé from Pricewaterhouse Coopers, said the company's executives "laid down the law: standardize everything. The plan did not allow for any deviation." A team was formed to oversee the process, beginning with efforts to obtain and screen a set of prospective best practices from throughout Nestlé's global operations, and then convert these into a standardized set of processes and information systems to apply universally. This process took over a year. The company then selected a handful of nations to serve as the initial test markets for the standardization process, with rollout expanding over time as system integrity was proved. "The biggest challenge is in the mind," said Martial Rolland, managing director of Nestlé India. "Yes, it's an equipment change. But, ultimately, it's a mind change."

Eventually the templates were developed and installed, and the implementation continued despite opposition. By June 2006, GLOBE had been rolled out to over 90,000 users, 300 factories, 350 distribution centers, and 250 sales offices. Nestlé projected that 80 percent of the company would be operating under GLOBE systems by the end of 2006. GLOBE has provided the foundation for Nestlé to operate as a truly global company. The company's leaders hope that this project will give Nestlé a sustainable advantage over its global competitors, which have not yet undertaken such a phenomenal change of systems and mind-set.

Source: Nestlé "GLOBE," www.ir.nestle.com/Nestle_Overview/Operational_Performance/Globe/GLOBE.htm (July 18, 2006); "Nestlé at a Glance," www.nestle.com/NR/rdonlyres/74F5A6ED-C072-4CD2-B701-C1AE3C5E482C/0/carte_GB.pdf (July 18, 2006); Chris Johnson, "GLOBE: Unlocking Our Potential," www.ir.nestle.com/NR/rdonlyres/3D107E55-7B6C-4E4C-9E92-2414E602F136/0/GLOBEMrChrisJohnson.pdf (July 18, 2006); Tom Steinert-Threlkeld, "Nestlé, Pieces It Together," *Baseline*, January 2006, pp. 36–52; Larry Barrett, "Roadblock: Regional Managers," *Baseline*, January 2006, p. 50; and Nestlé 2005 Financial Statements, www.investis.com/reports/ZMgj68xYd5Ot82w/report.php?type=0 (July 18, 2006).

A third alternative is available: computer-integrated manufacturing (CIM), which many international firms are using. However, its cost and high technological content generally limit its application to the industrialized nations and the more advanced developing nations. CIM systems enable a machine to make one part as easily as another in random order on an instruction from a bar code reader of the kind used in supermarkets. This reduces to one the economic batch quantity—the minimum number of a part that can be made economically by a factory—and it facilitates the potential for mass customization that we discussed earlier in this chapter. There is a limit, nevertheless, to the variety of shapes, sizes, and materials that can be accommodated.

Another economic factor that influences the designer's selection of processes is the *cost of production.* Automation tends to increase the productivity per worker because it requires less labor and results in higher output per machine. But if the desired output requires that the machines be operated only a fraction of the time, the high capital costs of automated equipment may result in excessive production costs even though labor costs are low. In situations where production costs favor semimanual equipment, the designer may be compelled to install high-capacity machines instead because of a lack of floor space. Generally, the space occupied by a few high-capacity machines is less than that required for the greater number of semimanual machines needed to produce the same output. However, because the correct type and quality of process materials are indispensable for specialized machinery, the engineers cannot recommend this equipment if such materials are unobtainable either from local sources or through importation. Occasionally, management will bypass this obstacle by means of **backward vertical integration;** that is, manufacturing capacity to produce essential inputs will be included in the plant design even though it would be preferable from an economic standpoint to purchase those materials from outside vendors. For example, a textile factory might include a facility for producing nylon fibers.

backward vertical integration

Arrangement in which facilities are established to manufacture inputs used in the production of a firm's final products

The economic forces we have described are fundamental considerations in plant design, yet elements of the cultural and political forces may be sufficiently significant to override decisions based on purely economic reasoning.

Cultural Forces   When a factory is to be built in an industrialized nation that has a sizable market and high labor costs, capital-intensive processes will undoubtedly be employed. However, such processes may also be employed in developing countries, which commonly lack skilled workers despite their abundant supply of labor. This situation favors the use of specialized machines because although a few highly skilled persons are needed for maintenance and setup, the job of *attending* these machines (starting, feeding stock) can be performed by unskilled workers after a short training period. In contrast, general-purpose machinery requires many more skilled operators.

These operators could be trained in technical schools, but the low prestige of such employment, a cultural characteristic, affects both the demand for and the supply of vocational education. Students do not demand it, and the traditional elitist attitude of the educational administrators in many developing nations causes resources to be directed to professional education instead of to the trades where they are needed.

Firms that attempt to reduce their requirements for skilled workers by installing automatic machinery are of course left vulnerable to another cultural characteristic of the developing countries: absenteeism. If the setup and maintenance crews fail to report to work, the entire production line may be shut down. Some managers resolve this problem by training a few extra people as backups. Having extra personnel is viewed as production insurance necessary to keep the plant in operation. This extra expense may be far less than the expense of handling the greater number of labor-management problems resulting from a larger work force in a nonautomated factory with a similar capacity.

These economic and cultural variables, important as they are, are not the only considerations of management; the requirements of the host government must be met if the proposed plant is to become a reality.

Political Forces When planning a new manufacturing facility in a developing country, management is frequently confronted by an intriguing paradox. Although the country desperately needs new job creation, which favors labor-intensive processes, government officials often insist on the most modern equipment. Local pride may be the cause, or it may be that these officials, wishing to see the new firm export, believe that only a factory with advanced technology can compete in world markets. They not only may be reluctant to take chances on "inferior" or untried alternatives but also may feel that low-productivity technology will keep the country dependent on the industrialized countries. In some developing countries, this fear has been formalized by laws prohibiting the importation of used machinery.

> *Global automakers have announced investments of over $10 billion in factories in China. However, most of the large automakers' plants are not designed to exploit China's large pool of low-cost labor. Rather, the plants are about as capital-intensive as American auto plants. Part of the reason for this is the Chinese government's desire to lure the latest technology, a goal it has promoted by a range of incentives. Acceding to these demands of the government can also be simpler for the automakers. As Mustafa Mharatem, the senior economist at General Motors, states, "Because of the way information travels these days, people in developing countries aren't any longer willing to buy cars that are one or two generations old. And if you're going to do the current-generation car, then keeping the process as similar as processes around the world makes sense."[41]*

SOME DESIGN SOLUTIONS

More often than not, after consideration of the environmental variables, the resultant plant design will be a hybrid or one using intermediate technology.

Hybrid Design Commonly, in designing plants for developing countries, engineers will use a hybrid of capital-intensive processes when they are considered essential to ensure product quality and labor-intensive processes to take advantage of the abundance of unskilled labor. For example, they may stipulate machine welding rather than hand welding but then use semimanual equipment for the painting, packaging, and materials handling.

Intermediate Technology In recent years, the press of a growing population and the rise in capital costs have forced the governments of developing nations to search for something less than highly automated processes. They are becoming convinced that there should be something midway between the capital- and labor-intensive processes that will create more jobs, require less capital, but still produce the desired product quality. Governments are urging investors to consider an **intermediate technology,** which, unfortunately, is not readily available in the industrialized nations. This means that international companies cannot transfer the technology with which they are familiar but must develop new and different manufacturing methods. It is also possible that the savings in reduced capital costs of the intermediate technology may be nullified by higher start-up costs and the greater expense of its transfer.

intermediate technology
Production methods between capital- and labor-intensive methods

Local Manufacturing System

BASIS FOR ORGANIZATION

Except for plants in large industrialized nations, the local manufacturing organization is commonly a scaled-down version of that found in the parent company. If the firm is organized by product companies or divisions (tires, industrial products, chemicals) in its home nation, the subsidiary will be divided into product departments. Manufacturing firms that use process organizations (departmentalized according to production processes) in the domestic operation will set up a similar structure in their foreign affiliates. In a paper-box factory, separate departments will cut the logs, produce the paper, and assemble the boxes. The only noticeable difference between the foreign and domestic operations is that in the foreign plant all these processes are more likely to be at one location because of the smaller size of each department.

HORIZONTAL AND VERTICAL INTEGRATION

The local manufacturing organization is rarely integrated either vertically or horizontally to the extent the parent is. Some vertical integration is traditional, as in the case of the paper-box factory, and some will occur if it is necessary to ensure a supply of raw materials. In this situation, the subsidiary might be more vertically integrated than the parent, which depends on outside sources for many of its inputs. However, the additional investment is a deterrent to vertical integration, as are the extra profits gained by supplying inputs to these captive customers from the home plants. Some countries prohibit vertical integration for certain industries. In Mexico, for example, severe restrictions on private investment (Mexican or foreign) in the petroleum and petrochemical industry still exist and keep producers of products that use petrochemicals from achieving backward vertical integration. In contrast, some countries require a percentage of local content in finished products. When the subsidiary cannot meet the requirement by local sourcing, it may be forced to produce components that its parent does not.

Horizontal integration is much less prevalent in foreign subsidiaries, although restaurant chains, banks, food-processing plants, and other industries characterized by small production units will, of course, integrate horizontally in the manner of the domestic company. Overseas affiliates themselves become conglomerates when the parent acquires a multinational.

DESIGN OF THE MANUFACTURING SYSTEM

A *manufacturing system* is essentially a functionally related group of activities for creating value. The design of a manufacturing system influences the flow and efficiency of activities in a plant. Although the manufacturing system as described below is basically one for producing tangible goods, nearly everything that is said applies equally to the production of services. Factors involved in the efficient operation of a manufacturing system include:

1. Plant location

2. Plant layout

3. Materials handling

4. Human element

Plant Location   Plant location is significant because of its effect on both production and distribution costs, which are frequently in conflict. The gain in government incentives and in the lower land and labor costs obtained by locating away from major cities may be offset by the increased expense of warehousing and transportation to serve those markets. Management will, after ascertaining that adequate labor, raw materials, water, and power are available, seek the least-cost location, or the one for which the sum of production and transfer costs is minimized. Management's first choice may then be modified by market requirements, the influence of competitors' locations, employee preference (climate, recreational facilities), and conditions imposed by the local authorities.

> *Sony shifted production of camcorders destined for the U.S. market from China to Japan. Although manufacturing costs may be higher than in China, the company justified its decision to produce these high-value-added products in Japan, stating, "By making the camcorders in Japan we can cut our lead times to half of what they are when they are made in Shanghai."*[42]

Governments that are anxious to limit the congestion of large urban areas may either prohibit firms from locating in the major cities or offer them important financial inducement to locate elsewhere.

Firms that have come to a country to take advantage of low labor costs and export their production have a limited selection of plant locations. They must locate in *export processing zones,* as we discussed in Chapter 2, such as Mexico's in-bond manufacturing zones. Similar zones exist in South Korea, Taiwan, Singapore, and some 50 other nations.

Plant Layout   Modern practice dictates that the arrangement of machinery, personnel, and service facilities should be made before the erection of the building. In this way, the building is accommodated to the layout that is judged most capable of obtaining a smoothly functioning production system.

The designer must attempt to obtain the maximum utility from costly building space while providing room for the future expansion of each department. Space can become critical very quickly if forecasts, especially for new products, prove to have been unduly pessimistic. Managements of plants located in developing countries may attempt to stint on space for employees' facilities, reasoning that the workers' standard of living in these countries is lower and that they will accept less just to have employment. Often, however, foreign labor laws are more demanding than those of the home country.

Materials Handling   Considerable savings in production costs can be achieved by a careful planning of materials handling, which, as you have seen, is a major consideration in synchronous manufacturing. Operations managers often failed to appreciate that inefficient handling of materials could cause excessive inventories of partly finished parts to accumulate at some workstations while at others expensive machinery was idle for lack of work (bottleneck). This concerned marketers too, because poor materials handling can result in late deliveries and damaged goods, which in turn lead to order cancellation and a loss of customers. Therefore, marketers must also be included in the total quality control approach that we discussed earlier in this chapter.

Human Element   The effectiveness of the manufacturing system depends on people, who are in turn affected by the system. Productivity suffers when there is extreme heat or cold, excessive noise, or faulty illumination. Colors also influence human behavior—pale colors are restful and unobtrusive, whereas bright colors attract attention. Plant designers take advantage of this fact by painting the walls of the working areas pale blue and green but marking exits with bright yellow and painting safety equipment red. This practice is accepted nearly everywhere, although, as we indicated in Chapter 6 in the discussion of cultural forces, color connotations vary among cultures.

For safety and ease of operation, controls of imported machinery must frequently be altered to accommodate smaller workers. Extra lifting devices, unnecessary in the home country, may be required. Where illiteracy is a problem, safety signs must include pictures. For example, a picture of a burning cigarette with a red line through it may substitute for a "no smoking" sign. Plants in multilingual nations and plants that employ large numbers of foreign workers require warnings in more than one language.

Because of the prohibitive cost of automobiles in many developing nations, employees ride bicycles to work, and so bicycle stands must be provided in parking lots. Special dietary kitchens are necessary when workers from more than one culture work together. These and other special conditions caused by environmental differences must be reckoned with in the design of the manufacturing system.

OPERATION OF THE MANUFACTURING SYSTEM

Once the manufacturing system has been put into operation, two general classes of activities, *productive* and *supportive,* must be performed.

Manufacturing Activities   After the initial trial period, during which workers become familiar with the manufacturing processes, management will expect the system to produce at a rate sufficient to satisfy market demand. It is the function of the line organization—from operations manager to first-level supervisor—to work with labor, raw materials, and machinery to produce on time the required amount of product with the desired quality at the budgeted cost.

Although competitors such as Apple, Gateway, and IBM have closed or relocated their computer manufacturing operations to lower-cost locations such as Asia, Dell has expanded its European manufacturing facilities, which are based in Ireland. Dell's survival is due to managerial systems dedicated to sustained operational improvements that help compensate for higher European labor rates. Nicky Hartery, who runs the 3,000-employee plant, says, "We're at all times looking for better, faster ways of doing things. Our staff are aligned not just to making PCs, which I would call sustaining engineering, but there's a development engineering function—developing better tools, better techniques, improved tools, improved techniques—so that our throughput is significantly better and the quality of what we do is significantly better." A team of 50 to 80 people works full-time on identifying ways of improving processes and the plant's continuous-improvement culture has resulted in productivity gains of 3 to 4 percent per quarter. The plant's lean production approach, based on JIT procedures and strong supply chain management practices, allows it to carry only two hours of inventory, while its suppliers' inventory has simultaneously declined by 40 percent in the past year. Most components come directly from delivery truck to assembly line. "We don't just work on productivity within the four walls of the factory," said Hartery. "I don't think we'd survive doing that. We have to make sure it is the right model, end to end, from our vendor base, our sub-tier vendor base, all the way to our customer." Rather than depending on expensive high-technology equipment, he argues, the plant's performance is the result of superior application of human intelligence.[43]

Obstacles to Meeting Manufacturing Standards

Management must be prepared to deal with any obstacle to meeting the manufacturing standards. Among these obstacles are (1) low output, (2) inferior quality, and (3) excessive manufacturing costs.

Low Output   Any number of factors may be responsible for the system's failure to meet the design standards for output, and these factors can be the source of managerial uncertainty.

1. Raw materials suppliers may fail to meet delivery dates or may furnish material out of specification. This is a common occurrence in the sellers' markets of developing countries, but it is also occasionally a problem in the industrialized countries. The purchasing department must attempt to educate the vendor about the importance of delivery dates and specifications, although the effectiveness of this strategy is limited when, as is often the case in developing nations, there is only one supplier. Increasing the price paid and sending technicians to assist the vendor generally improve this situation.

2. Poor coordination of production scheduling slows the delivery of finished products when, for example, completely assembled automobiles wait for bumpers. Scheduling personnel may require additional training or closer supervision. Often, scheduling personnel—or any production workers, for that matter—are unaware of the importance of their jobs because they have not been shown "the big picture." Firms find that teaching employees why they do what they do, as well as how, pays off in creating a better attitude, which results in higher productivity. This has become crucial as firms strive for participative management, which is essential to synchronous manufacturing.

Cultural forces of attitude toward authority and the great difference between educational levels, common in many countries, establish a gulf between managers and workers. In fact, this is one of the reasons Japanese affiliates have had trouble introducing their production methods in the United States, where distances between managers and workers are much smaller than they are in most developing nations. Getting the participative management necessary for JIT and synchronous manufacturing will necessitate workers making sizable cultural changes, which in our opinion will require many years to attain.

Another cultural problem is the desire to please everyone and the aversion to long-range planning. You have seen the importance of planning for the success of JIT, and you also learned that firm production schedules at least a month long may be necessary. The desire to please everyone, which is prevalent in some cultures, tends to cause neglect of the schedule while production stops to attend the latest request from a customer. Moreover, because the markets are smaller in developing countries than they are in industrialized nations, product variations will have to be pared even more and production systems will have to be even more flexible, if possible.

3. *Absenteeism,* always a problem for production managers everywhere in meeting production standards, becomes even more significant in a bottleneck operation of a synchronous manufacturing system. Imagine the problems that occur when an entire department is idled because workers are at home helping the extended family with the harvest. When poor transportation systems make getting to work difficult, companies frequently provide transportation. To counteract absences due to illness and injury, they subsidize workers' lunches—prepared by trained nutritionists—and provide special shoes and protective clothing. Of course, management has the problem of educating workers not to remove the restraining apparel that they have never used before.

Low morale conducive to high absenteeism will result if foreign managers trying to introduce the participative management necessary for synchronous manufacturing fail to assume the role of *patron* that most workers in developing countries expect. When employees have personal problems, they assume that the boss, not the personnel office, will find a solution. Personal debts, marital problems, and difficulties with the police are all part of manager-employee relations.

All too often, expatriate managers accept high absenteeism and low productivity as the norm instead of attempting to correct them. Yet those who apply all the corrective means used at home, making adjustments for the foreign environment when necessary, do achieve notable success. One corrective measure, the discharge of unsatisfactory workers, is frequently impossible to apply because of legal constraints, but a consistent, energetic program of employee training, good union and labor relations, and the use of such morale builders as employee recognition, company reunions, sponsorship of team sports, and even suggestion boxes with rewards can be as successful in a foreign location as in the domestic operation.

Inferior Product Quality   Good quality is relative. What passes for good quality in the industrialized nations may actually be poor quality where a lack of maintenance and operating skills requires looser bearing fits and strong but more unwieldy parts. If the product or service satisfies the purpose for which it is purchased, the buyer considers it to be of good quality.

Product quality standards are not set arbitrarily. It is the responsibility of the marketers, after studying their target market, to choose the price-quality combination they believe is most apt to satisfy that market. On the basis of this information, the quality standards for incoming materials, in-process items, and finished products should be established.

When the headquarters of global corporations insist that all foreign subsidiaries maintain the high-quality standards of the domestic plants, a number of problems can occur. Production may have to accept inputs of poorer quality when there is no alternative source of supply and then rework them. As we have pointed out, quality tolerances are especially tight for automated machinery. Finished-product standards set by a home office concerned about maintaining its global reputation can cause a product to be too costly for the local market. Many international companies resolve this problem by permitting the subsidiary to manufacture products of lower quality under different brand names. If they want the local plant to be a part of a worldwide logistics system, they may require a special quality to be produced for export. In some areas, "export quality" still denotes a superior product. Quality control, by the way, is not left exclusively in the hands of the subsidiary. Nearly all worldwide corporations require that their foreign plants submit samples of the finished product for testing on a regular basis.

Excessive Manufacturing Costs   Any manufacturing cost that exceeds the budgeted cost is excessive and naturally is of concern to the marketing and financial manager as well as to production personnel. Low output for any of the reasons we have discussed may be the cause, but the fault may also lie with the assumptions underlying the budget. Overoptimistic sales forecasts, the failure of suppliers to meet delivery dates, the failure of the government to issue import permits for essential raw materials in time, and unforeseen water or power failure are a few of the reasons output may be lower than expected.

Managers have always tried to limit inventories of raw materials, spare parts for plant machinery, and finished products, and those managers with synchronous manufacturing systems have a goal of almost complete elimination. But when there is uncertainty of supply, as in most developing nations, stocks of these items can quickly get out of control. Production tends to overstock inputs to avoid the expense of changing production schedules when a given raw material has been exhausted. Maintenance personnel lay in an excessive stock of spare parts because they worry about not having something when they need it. Marketers, fearful of the frequent delays in manufacturing, overreact by building up finished goods inventories to avoid lost sales. When sales decrease, manufacturing may continue to produce finished products rather than lay off workers because the labor laws in many countries, unlike American labor laws, make employee layoffs both difficult and costly. In countries where skilled workers are in short supply, management does not dare to lay them off even if the law permits because these people will obtain employment elsewhere. The only alternative in the short run is to keep the factory running.

Finance, the one headquarters department that would ordinarily act to limit inventory building, will not move aggressively to stop this practice in countries afflicted with hyperinflation. It knows that under this condition, sizable profits can be made by being short in cash and long in inventory.

Supportive Activities

Every manufacturing system requires staff units to provide the *supportive activities* essential to its operation. Two of these, quality control and inventory control, were examined in the previous section. Let us look now at the purchasing, maintenance, and technical functions.

Purchasing   Manufacturing depends on the purchasing department to procure the raw materials, component parts, supplies, and machinery it requires to produce the finished product. The inability to obtain these materials when needed can result in costly shutdowns and lost sales. If the buyers agree to prices higher than what competitors are paying, the firm must either sell the finished product at higher prices or price competitively and earn less profit. The quality of the finished product may suffer if the quality of the purchased materials is inadequate.

For many years, some have referred to purchasing as the "management of outside manufacturing," and this was never more true than it is today with the globalization of industry. If the purchasing function is to fit in with the rest of the global operations of a firm, it must increasingly behave in the manner of a manager of manufacturing and as a key component in achieving integrated global supply chain management. In the past, the purchasing function often was responsible only for buying the cheapest possible inputs. However, as discussed in this chapter, there are many other considerations besides cost that need to be managed by the purchasing function.

Even in the industrialized countries before JIT was introduced, purchasing agents rarely could satisfy all of their companies' needs by waiting for the suppliers' representatives to come to them. They had to seek out and develop suppliers by visiting their plants and arranging for their companies' production and technical personnel to discuss material problems with the vendors' counterparts. In the developing countries, where many suppliers do not retain a sales force because they can sell everything they produce, supplier development assumes greater importance. The ability to locate vendors can easily compensate for a lack of other skills that management would require of a buyer at home.

When the firm depends heavily on imported materials, the prime criterion for hiring will be the purchasing agents' knowledge of import procedures and their connections with key government officials. The purchasing agents must constantly monitor government actions that can affect the availability of foreign exchange. They will often buy as much as possible of regularly consumed materials because they know they can always sell the excess to others, possibly at a profit.

Whether to fill the critical position of purchasing agent with a local citizen or with someone from the home office is often the subject of considerable debate at headquarters. A native has the advantage of being better acquainted with the local supply sources and government officials, but he or she might suffer from such cultural disadvantages as a tendency to favor members of the extended family or to accept as a normal business practice the giving (scarce supply) or receiving (plentiful supply) of bribes. An employee from the home office, in contrast, will be experienced in company purchasing procedures and should be free of these cultural disadvantages. Managers are not so naive as to believe that belonging to a certain culture guarantees that an individual will or will not engage in unethical activities. However, the tendency to commit these acts may be greater when there are no cultural constraints.

Maintenance   A second function supporting manufacturing is the maintenance of buildings and equipment. The goal of maintenance management is to ensure an acceptable level of production, and the costs of achieving this can be substantial. One European paper company estimated, for example, that maintenance costs averaged about 30 percent of the total fixed costs of its operations in China. Several possibilities are available for accomplishing this task. As was noted several times in this chapter, JIT has caused other parts of the manufacturing function to assume greater importance, and maintenance of plant production capacity is one of these parts. Before JIT, inventory was the solution to many managerial problems by hiding the causes and effects of these problems. The removal by JIT systems of inventory as a buffer has forced industry to give greater consideration to these problem areas, one of which is the maintenance of anticipated processing capacity. This may entail the prevention of unscheduled work stoppages caused by equipment failure.

There are two primary alternatives for dealing with maintenance problems. The first option is planned maintenance or preventive maintenance. The objective here is to prevent failure before it occurs, because failure is more expensive to repair and is disruptive to production schedules. The second alternative is breakdown maintenance. That is, when a machine or another element in the production process fails, it will be repaired. Although we have all heard the saying "If it works, don't fix it," this is seldom the best maintenance alternative. There are indeed situations when companies let a process go until failure—such as lightbulbs, which we do not usually replace until they fail. However, in production activities it is often appropriate to have a redundant or backup system.

In general, companies are concerned with maintenance because unanticipated system failure and downtime are a drain on scarce productive capacity. In a global context, there may be difficulty in obtaining imported spare parts and machinery, threatening the continued productive ability of a firm. As a result, the machine shops of many maintenance departments may actually manufacture some of these items in order to keep machines operating.

It is common practice in industrialized countries to establish preventive maintenance programs in which machinery is shut down according to plan and worn parts are replaced. Such programs are especially important for a synchronous manufacturing system, as you learned earlier in this chapter. With advance notice of a shutdown, the manufacturing department can schedule around the machine, or by working the machine overtime the department can temporarily build up inventories, permitting the manufacturing process to continue during its overhaul. In other words, the company is able to maintain an acceptable level of output to service the anticipated demands of customers.

This concept is not widely accepted in developing countries, where firms seem to take a fatalistic attitude toward equipment: "If it breaks down, we'll repair it." This may be attributable to the concept that preventive maintenance in most instances requires a greater degree of skill and knowledge than does breakdown maintenance.

Furthermore, in a seller's market, maintenance personnel are pressured by production and marketing managers to keep machinery running. This short-term view allows no time for scheduled shutdowns. Subsidiaries that do practice preventive maintenance with overhaul periods based on headquarters' standards frequently find these standards inadequate because of local operating conditions (humidity, dust, and temperature) and the manner in which the operators handle the machinery. When the amount of spare parts ordered with the machinery is based on domestic experience, it is often insufficient because of differing local conditions in other nations, including the skill and training of the local machine operators and maintenance workers.

In one sense, proper maintenance is more critical than 100 percent attendance of workers. The absence of one worker from a group of six interchangeable workers usually will not halt manufacturing, but if a key machine for which there is no substitute suddenly breaks down, the entire plant can be idled.

Technical Function   The function of the technical department is to provide operations management with manufacturing specifications. Usually, technical personnel are also responsible for checking the quality of inputs and the finished product. The task of the technical department in a foreign subsidiary is not simply one of maintaining a file of specifications sent by the home office, because difficulty in obtaining the same kinds and quality of raw materials as those used by the home plants may require substitutions that necessitate the complete rewriting of specifications.

The affiliate's technical manager is a key figure in the maintenance of product quality and thus is extremely influential in selecting sources of supply. Global and multidomestic companies go to great lengths in persuading host governments and joint venture partners of the need to place one of their people in this position. In this way, they are certain to keep the affiliate as a captive customer purchasing all the inputs that the more highly integrated parent manufactures.

Summary

Understand the concept of supply chain management.

Supply chain management is the process of coordinating and integrating the flow of materials, information, finances, and services within and among companies in the value chain, from suppliers to the ultimate consumer. Supply chain management is integral to the achievement of cost and quality objectives in companies and to international competitiveness.

Recognize the relationship between design and supply chain management.

The design of a company's products and services has a fundamental relationship with the types of inputs the company will require, including labor, materials, information, and financing. Concurrent engineering approaches to design allow proposed designs to be subjected to earlier assessments on cost, quality, and manufacturability dimensions, enhancing the efficiency and effectiveness of subsequent supply chain management activities.

Describe the five global sourcing arrangements.

A firm may establish a wholly owned subsidiary in a low-labor-cost country to supply components to the home country plant or to supply a product not produced in the home country. An overseas joint venture may be established in a country where labor costs are lower to supply components to the home country. The firm may send components to be machined and assembled by an independent contractor in an in-bond plant. The firm may contract with an independent contractor overseas to manufacture products to its specifications. The firm may buy from an independent overseas manufacturer.

Appreciate the importance of the added costs of global sourcing.

International freight, insurance, and packing may add 10 to 12 percent to the quoted price, depending on the sales term used. Import duties, customhouse broker's fees, cost of letter of credit, cost of inventory in the pipeline, and international travel are some of the other added costs.

Understand the increasing role of electronic purchasing for global sourcing.

The establishment of electronic purchasing systems on a company or industry basis can influence the number and type of suppliers available internationally to firms. Although there are a number of challenges to their use, electronic purchasing systems can produce significant reductions in the costs of inputs, both direct and indirect products and services. These systems can also permit the optimization of supply chains across networks of organizations, not merely within a single company.

Understand the the just-in-time (JIT) production system and potential problems with its implementation.

JIT requires coordinated management of materials, people, and suppliers. JIT's goal is to eliminate inventories, reduce process and setup times, and use participative management to ensure worker input and loyalty to the firm. JIT includes total quality management (TQM), of which continuous improvement is an integral part. JIT is restricted to repetitive operations. It is a balanced system, and so if one operation stops, the whole production line stops. But it is difficult to achieve a balanced system. In addition, JIT makes no allowances for contingencies. A sudden breakdown will stop the entire production system. Finally, putting JIT into effect is a slow process.

Understand synchronous manufacturing and mass customization.

The goal of synchronous manufacturing is unbalanced manufacturing scheduling rather than the balanced scheduling of

JIT; attention is focused on the bottleneck of the manufacturing system, and scheduling for the entire operation is controlled by the output of the bottleneck operation. Mass customization involves the use of flexible, usually computer-aided manufacturing, systems to produce and deliver customized products and services for different customers worldwide.

Comprehend the concept of Six Sigma systems and their application.

Six Sigma is a business management process that concentrates on eliminating variation and reducing defects from work processes. The five steps of the Six Sigma approach—define, measure, analyze, improve, and control—represent a method for creating a closed-loop system for making continuous improvements in business processes. The Six Sigma methodology often requires that companies rethink the way they do things and that they adapt their culture, sometimes dramatically. Successful culture change requires a concerted, long-term effort, particularly if the organization is multinational, with subsidiaries and offices around the world.

Explain the potential of global standardization of production processes and procedures, and identify impediments to standardization efforts.

Standards help to ensure that materials, products, processes, and services are appropriate for their purpose, helping companies to meet market and competitive demands. Standardization of activities helps to simplify organization and control at headquarters because replication enables the work to be accomplished with a smaller staff of support personnel and internal best practices can more readily be applied across a company's international operations. However, differences in the foreign environmental forces, especially the economic, cultural, and political forces, cause units of an international multiplant operation to differ in size, machinery, and procedures, complicating efforts to achieve standardization of processes and procedures.

Know the two general classes of activities, productive and supportive, that must be performed in all manufacturing systems.

A manufacturing system is essentially a functionally related group of activities for creating value. After the system is operable, two general classes of activities, productive and supportive, must be performed. Productive activities are all those functions that are part of the manufacturing process. Among the important supportive activities are purchasing, maintenance, and the technical function.

Key Words

outsourcing (p. 505)

supply chain management (p. 505)

offshoring (p. 507)

just-in-time (JIT) (p. 515)

total quality management (TQM) (p. 516)

quality circle (quality control circle) (p. 516)

Taylor's scientific management system (p. 517)

preventive (planned) maintenance (p. 518)

synchronous manufacturing (p. 518)

bottleneck (p. 518)

mass customization (p. 519)

Six Sigma (p. 520)

standards (p. 522)

manufacturing rationalization (p. 525)

backward vertical integration (p. 528)

intermediate technology (p. 529)

Questions

1. What recent developments have caused supply chain management to become increasingly important to international companies?

2. What are the main differences between sequential and concurrent approaches to the design of products and services?

3. Why would a company choose to source raw materials, components, or other products or services from a foreign supplier? What are the strengths and weaknesses of using foreign suppliers?

4. What are the trade-offs for a firm that uses a just-in-time production system?

5. Why does the cost of raw materials represent about 55 to 79 percent of the cost of goods sold in U.S. industry, and why has this proportion been increasing over time?

6. Who is responsible for inventory? Where does the cost of carrying inventory show up, on the balance sheet or the income statement?

7. What are the costs of carrying inventory? Is the Japanese version of the cost of carrying inventory in agreement with your calculation? (*Hint:* Start your carrying cost calculation with the opportunity cost of invested capital.)

8. What advantages does synchronous manufacturing have over JIT?

9. What difficulties do you see for global firms when they implement synchronous manufacturing in their plants located in developing countries? Are there any advantages that are more valuable to them than to plants in industrialized nations?

10. What is mass customization? What is necessary in order for a company to effectively implement a mass-customization approach to serving its customers?

11. What is the benefit to a buyer company and to a vendor company of standards such as ISO 9000?

12. What is the connection between manufacturers' insistence on receiving components with zero defects from outside suppliers and JIT?

13. What are the advantages to a worldwide firm of global standardization of its production facilities?

14. What is Six Sigma? Why are companies increasingly using Six Sigma processes in their operations? What concerns might there be regarding the implementation of Six Sigma within an international company? How might a company go about addressing these concerns?

15. Discuss the influence of the uncontrollable environmental forces in global standardization of a firm's production facilities.

16. Who should be in charge of the purchasing function of an overseas affiliate, a local person or someone from the home office? Why?

17. What is the importance of preventive maintenance? Why might it be difficult to establish a preventive program in an overseas plant? Do you know of any situations for which breakdown maintenance is a viable alternative?

Research Task

globalEDGE.msu.edu globalEDGE

Use the globalEDGE site (http://globalEDGE.msu.edu) to complete the following exercises:

1. The travel of products by large transport containers has become a primary method by which goods are transported worldwide. Since your firm is involved in the U.S. supply chain industry, a report is needed concerning the 10 largest container ports outside the United States. Using a Web site called *Geohive* as your resource to provide such a list, analyze the relative volume passing through each of the 10 largest ports in your report. What is the relative difference between the container ports ranking first and tenth in your report?

2. Struggling to remain competitive in the medical devices industry, your firm has decided to begin sourcing components internationally. Though your firm's current operations are only in the United States and the Netherlands, you must assess the relative costs for manufacturing medical devices in a variety of cities worldwide. Your manager, previously a consultant with KPMG, indicates that the *Competitive Alternatives* surveys published annually by KPMG may assist you. Develop two brief reports to answer the following questions: (a) Which three cities in the survey have the lowest and highest manufacturing costs for your firm's specific industry? (b) Do you think that changing your firm's sourcing strategy will resolve the current problems?

Minicase 19.1 Penwick–El Pais

Maquinas para el Hogar Penwick is a manufacturing subsidiary of Penwick Home Appliances in Boston. It is located in El Pais, a nation with 25 million inhabitants whose GNP per capita is $1,980. The country's annual inflation rate is about 30 percent, but the local company makes a good profit, in part because it keeps large stocks of components and raw materials purchased as much as 12 months before they are needed for production. The finished products are sold at prices set as if the raw materials and components had been purchased recently; hence the high profits. Penwick's competitors use the same strategy.

Penwick–El Pais has three competitors, none of which produces as complete a product mix or as many variations in each of the product lines of refrigerators, kitchen stoves, and washing machines as does the local Penwick plant. José Garcia, the local marketing manager, is proud that Penwick–El Pais makes as many kinds of products and variations of products as the much larger home plant, and he has told the managing director of the local company that it is the wide product mix that maintains Penwick–El Pais's number-one position in sales. Manuel Cardenas, the local operations manager, and Garcia frequently have heated discussions because

538   **Section 4**   The Organizational Environment

Cardenas wants to make fewer product variations. Garcia accuses him of wanting to make black stoves like Henry Ford made black cars, but Cardenas claims he could double his output if he could make fewer kinds of products with fewer variations. Cardenas knows the value of long manufacturing runs and tries to get them. Garcia retorts that if Cardenas would pay attention to what he wants instead of making what Cardenas wants to make, he could sell more.

This is a sore spot with Cardenas because he tries hard to produce a new product according to Garcia's written request. If Garcia's memo says he wants a new-size refrigerator in three colors to be available with or without beverage coolers or ice cube makers, these are the models Cardenas asks the product design department to design and make production specifications for. Garcia at one time or another has asked to attend meetings with Cardenas and his staff, but Cardenas considers this a waste of time. After all, he doesn't waste the design department's time by asking to attend their meetings; why should a salesperson attend his meetings? He has enough problems with the high prices for parts that the purchasing department people give him. When he complains, they tell him that everything he orders is special manufacture for the vendors. Cardenas says that's their problem; this is what the design department specifies, and this is what he has to use to build the product.

Cardenas has more pressing problems. Headquarters has adopted a new manufacturing system, synchronous manufacturing, and now wants him to do the same. In fact, he had to send his assistant manager to Boston for a month's training. Now she and the design manager, who also went, are back, and they have brought one of the home office experts with them. They're all going to have a long meeting with him this afternoon. Cardenas has read about synchronous manufacturing in technical journals and feels it does seem to have some advantages. But all of them have been in highly industrialized nations, and there are a lot of cultural and economic differences between El Pais and those countries.

You might role-play this case. Imagine you are a member of the three-person group that has come from Boston. Even though you know the local plant has orders to convert to synchronous manufacturing, you still have to win over the local personnel.

1. What will you say?

2. Can you think of any advantages that might be even more important for the local plant than they are for the larger home plant?

3. What problems do you foresee in putting synchronous manufacturing in place?

20

Human Resource Management*

Paradoxically, in spite of the opportunities for [human resource management, or HR] to contribute to globalization in added-value ways, the HR function is not perceived in many companies as a full partner in the globalization process. Sometimes it is viewed as an obstacle, slowing down the process through bureaucratic central procedures. The ethnocentric and parochial HR systems and policies inherited from the past, focused on the parent company and projected onto the rest of the world, are all too often a barrier to the implementation of effective global organizational processes.

—*Paul Evans, Vladimir Pucik, and Jean-Louis Barsoux,* The Global Challenge, *2002*

*An earlier version of this chapter was prepared with the assistance of Jere Ramsey of California Polytechnic State University.

Becoming an Expatriate, or Expat, as They Are Sometimes Called

You are happy and proud; you can hardly wait to get back to your office to phone your family with the news. Your boss has called you in and said, "We have a problem in Asia that we need you to solve." You are doing well with the company in the home, domestic market, but now the company has discovered markets away from home, and you have not seen anything away from home since you and your college friend backpacked in the Argentine mountains to Bariloche. You have read about dining at Singapore's Raffles Hotel with the ghost of Somerset Maugham, exploring Bangkok's temples, and enjoying the helicopter and Rolls-Royce service and harbor views of Hong Kong's Peninsula Hotel.

You are about to become an **expatriate**. Your family will love it, and the foreign experience will be your passport to your company's top executive positions. Your career will be made. Right?

Maybe. You must be very careful. For too many employees who take foreign assignments, it is out of sight, out of mind, and you may find yourself well out of the loop. On the other hand, however, these assignments can be passports to the top if you take the right steps before you make the move.

If at all possible, arrange to have someone fairly high in the company hierarchy be your mentor, ideally a person who has also served in an expatriate role so that there can be a base of international experience that you can draw from. That home country mentor should keep you advised of changes and developments in the company back at home and should keep your name in consideration and not forgotten while you are on your assignment abroad. You might also consider finding a mentor in the host country, who can assist you in understanding the local culture, introduce you to valuable business contacts, and help you in interpreting situations that you encounter while in your position abroad.

Before you take the job, you should insist that your bosses tell you exactly what the company expects you to accomplish. Are you to get a plant up and running, install systems or practices that are currently in use in the home country, arrange customer financing, negotiate investment, or perhaps groom a host country replacement? Will this be an extended on-site assignment, such as two to four years in length, or will it merely involve one or several short-term assignments that are primarily intended to work on a specific problem or transfer specific knowledge?

Of course, there is the chance that despite all your efforts and precautions, your company will forget or not value you. Realizing this possibility, you should have been profiting from your foreign assignment by doing your job well; learning new markets; gaining proficiency in the language, which will permit you to better understand the culture; and networking. The networking can be done by being active in such things as local chambers of commerce, social clubs, and sports clubs.

All this will make you valuable to other companies and make them aware of you. In essence, you have received a million dollars' worth of training paid for by your company, and you and other companies can utilize it. After all, this is an important source of third country national executives. ■

CONCEPT PREVIEWS

After reading this chapter, you should be able to:

discuss the importance of creating a company "global mind-set"

explain the relationship between competitive strategies (international, multidomestic, regional, and transnational) and international human resource management approaches (ethnocentric, polycentric, regiocentric, and global)

compare home country, host country, and third country nationals as IC executives

explain the difficulties of finding qualified executives for international companies (ICs) and the importance of foreign language knowledge

explain what an expatriate is and some of the challenges and opportunities of an expat position

discuss the increasing importance of accommodating the trailing spouse of an expatriate executive

identify some of the complications of compensation packages for expatriate executives

expatriate

A person living outside his or her country of citizenship

The effectiveness of every organization depends to a great extent on the nature of its work force and how well its human resources are utilized. Their effective use depends on management's policies and practices. Management of a company's human resources is a shared responsibility. The day-to-day supervision of people on the job is the duty of the operating managers, who must integrate the human, financial, and physical resources into an efficient production system. However, the formulation of policies and procedures for (1) estimation of work force needs, (2) recruitment and selection, (3) training and development, (4) motivation, (5) compensation, (6) discipline, and (7) employment termination is generally the responsibility of personnel managers working in cooperation with executives from marketing, production, and finance as well as the firm's lawyers.

Finding the right people to manage an organization can be difficult under any circumstances, but it is especially difficult to find good managers of overseas operations. Such positions require more and different skills than do purely domestic executive jobs. The right persons need to be bicultural, with knowledge of the business practices in the home country plus an understanding of business practices and customs in the host country. And to fully understand a culture, any culture, it is usually necessary to speak the language of its people. Only with a good grasp of the language can one understand the subtleties and humor and know what is really going on in the host country. Although difficult to locate, such managers do exist, and they may be found in (1) the home country, (2) the host country, or (3) a third country.

> *Siemens, the German engineering and electronics conglomerate, generates almost 80 percent of its sales outside its home country, up from 45 percent in 1990. As a result, 60 percent of its employees are located outside Germany. Heinrich von Pierer, Siemens' CEO and president, says, "We need employees and managers who are close to our customers and understand their needs." Siemens relies on local managers to oversee its far-flung network of operations. In Italy, most of the managers are Italian, while in the United States, most of the managers are American. In China, he has directed his 200 managers, who are mainly expatriates from the West, to develop Chinese managers to succeed them in their posts within the next five years. Yet, despite the localization of managerial talent, the company remains German at its core. "English increasingly is becoming our company's common language, but the rules and culture in Germany are still a bit different." As a result, he emphasizes his desire to have more young foreign managers spend time working in Germany, so that they can function better within the company's culture.*

global mind-set

A mind-set that combines an openness to and an awareness of diversity across markets and cultures with a propensity and ability to synthesize across this diversity

Research by Vijay Govindarajan and Anil Gupta indicates that many CEOs feel that developing a company **global mind-set** is a "prerequisite for global industry dominance."[1] Govindarajan and Gupta identify four possible mind-sets, determined by individuals' or organizations' level of knowledge differentiation and their skill in knowledge integration. They define a global mind-set as "one that combines an openness to and awareness of diversity across cultures and markets with a propensity and ability to synthesize across this diversity." Percy Barnevik, who served as the leader for the merger of Swedish Asea with Swiss Brown Boveri to create the global engineering and manufacturing giant ABB, aptly observed, "Global managers have exceptionally open minds. They respect how different countries do things, and they have the imagination to appreciate why they do them that way. But they are also incisive, they push the limits of the culture. Global managers don't passively accept it when someone says, 'You can't do that in Italy or Spain because of the unions,' or 'You can't do that in Japan because of the Ministry of Finance.' They sort through the debris of cultural excuses and find opportunities to innovate."[2]

The International Human Resource Management Approach

Chapter 13 explained that two competing forces, the pressure to achieve global integration and reduce costs and the pressure to respond to local differentiation, determine which of four alternative competitive strategies (home replication, multidomestic, global, or transnational) a company should adopt. A company's competitive strategy should, in turn, drive the organization's approach to international human resource management (IHRM).

Heenan and Perlmutter developed a model that considers these four competitive strategies to determine whether the organization's approach to IHRM should be **ethnocentric, polycentric, regiocentric,** or **geocentric.**[3] Further, along with this decision, the employees used in the organization may be classified into one of three categories: (1) **home country nationals** or **parent country nationals (PCNs),** (2) **host country nationals (HCNs),** and (3) **third country nationals (TCNs).** These relationships are illustrated in Table 20.1.

Recruitment and Selection of Employees

The recruitment and selection of employees, frequently referred to as *staffing*, should be determined in a manner consistent with one of the four IHRM approaches the organization is pursuing, as discussed below.[4]

ETHNOCENTRIC STAFFING POLICY

Companies with a primarily international strategic orientation (characterized by low pressures for cost reduction and low pressures for local responsiveness) may adopt an ethnocentric staffing policy. In this approach, most decisions are made at headquarters, using the home country's frame of reference. ICs utilize citizens of their own countries, or PCNs, in key foreign management and technical positions.

At first, PCNs are usually not knowledgeable about the host country culture and language. Many such expatriates have adapted, learned the language, and become thoroughly accepted in the host country, although it is also common that such managers encounter difficulty overcoming the biases of their own cultural experience and being able to understand and perform effectively within the new operating context.

Labor negotiators and other specialists may be sent to troubleshoot such problems as product warranty, international contracts, taxes, accounting, and reporting. Teams may be sent from the home country to assist with new plant start-up, and they would probably stay until subsidiary personnel were trained to run and maintain the new facilities.

An advantage to using home country citizens abroad is to broaden their experience in preparation for becoming high-level managers at headquarters. Firms earning a large percentage of their profits from international sources require top executives who have a worldwide perspective, both business and political. It is difficult to impossible to acquire that sort of perspective without living and working abroad for a substantial period of time.

If new technology for the subsidiary is involved, the parent company will probably station at least one of its technologically qualified experts at the subsidiary until its local personnel learn the technology. In this way, the home office can be confident that someone is immediately available to explain headquarters' policies and procedures, see that they are observed, and interpret what is happening locally for the IC's management. Positions that an IC must take or demands that it must make are sometimes not popular with a host government. It can seem unpatriotic for a host country national to do such things, whereas the host government can understand, and sometimes accept, such positions or demands from a foreigner.

> *One of the authors remembers the relief expressed by the Argentinean executives of an Argentine subsidiary of an American IC because an American manager was present to press the Argentine government for what seemed to be unusually extensive payment guarantees. The contract was for a product that, while partly manufactured and assembled in Argentina, was mostly manufactured in the United States and imported into Argentina. The Argentinean executives feared that the very specific and high-level payment guarantees would antagonize government officials. The subsidiary was an Argentine company, subject to that country's laws and dependent in part on business from government departments and government-owned companies. Its managers were residents and would stay in Argentina, while the American was there only until the signing of this contract and the guarantees. After he flew away, the local people could blame him and the American parent IC, thus deflecting anger and resentment from themselves.*

<hr>

ethnocentric
As used here, related to hiring and promoting employees on the basis of the parent company's home country frame of reference

polycentric
As used here, related to hiring and promoting employees on the basis of the specific local context in which the subsidiary operates

regiocentric
As used here, related to hiring and promoting employees on the basis of the specific regional context in which the subsidiary operates

geocentric
As used here, related to hiring and promoting employees on the basis of ability and experience without considering race or citizenship

home country national
Same as parent country national

parent country national (PCNs)
Employee who is a citizen of the nation in which the parent company is headquartered; also called *home country national*

host country national (HCN)
Employee who is a citizen of the nation in which the subsidiary is operating, which is different from the parent company's home nation

TABLE 20.1

Strategic Approach, Organizational Concerns, and the International Human Resource Management Approach to Be Used

Aspects of the Enterprise	Orientation			
	Ethnocentric	**Polycentric**	**Regiocentric**	**Geocentric**
Primary strategic orientation/stage	Home Replication	Multidomestic	Regional	Transnational
Perpetuation (recruiting, staffing, development)	People of home country developed for key positions everywhere in the world	People of local nationality developed for key positions in their own country	Regional people developed for key positions anywhere in the region	Best people everywhere in the world developed for key positions every where in the world
Complexity of the organization	Complex in home country, simple in subsidiaries	Varied and independent	Highly interdependent on a regional basis	"Global web," complex, independent, worldwide alliances/network
Authority, decision making	High in headquarters	Relatively low in headquarters	High regional headquarters and/or high collaboration among subsidiaries	Collaboration of headquarters and subsidiaries around the world
Evaluation and control	Home standards applied to people and performance	Determined locally	Determined regionally	Globally integrated
Rewards	High in headquarters, low in subsidiaries	Wide variations, can be high or low rewards for subsidiary performance	Rewards for contribution to regional objectives	Rewards to international and local executives for reaching local and worldwide objectives based on global company goals
Communication, information flow	High volume of orders, commands, advice to subsidiaries	Little to and from headquarters, little among subsidiaries	Little to and from corporate headquarters, but may be high to and from regional headquarters and among countries	Horizontal, network relations
Geographic identification	Nationality of owner	Nationality of host country	Regional company	Truly global company, but identifying with national interests ("glocal")

Source: Adapted from David A. Heenan and Howard V. Perlmutter, *Multinational Organization Development* (Boston: Addison-Wesley, 1979).

Executives with the Right Stuff Are in Big Demand

Demand for executives with the "right stuff" is the case everywhere, but it is particularly true in developing economies. One can look at China and Latin America for examples of what is meant by this.

Kodak's Chinese operation brought in Western managers who were excellent with the technical aspects of their jobs. Nevertheless, they failed miserably because they did not understand the culture of the country.

In an attempt to solve the problem, Kodak and other foreign companies recruit Chinese-speaking staff from Asian and other countries. But there are still cultural considerations, says Kay Kutt, managing director of Cendant Intercultural Assignment Services, Asia-Pacific division. "It's almost worse than sending a Westerner, to send someone who has the Chinese language but not Chinese values," as she puts it. Local hires are less costly than expatriates and they often have better understanding of the Chinese market and customers. Having a boss who is a local can be motivating to ambitious junior employees, and can enhance communication and morale. As Wal-Mart China executive Du Limin says about the response of her Chinese employees, "They take me as their big sister and they confide their family issues with me. That is impossible if you're an expatriate." Yet finding an adequate number and quality of local talent in China can be difficult for international companies. "Companies want to localize but the majority of people who are local mainland Chinese don't have experience

with global principles," said Joy Chen, a principal at the executive search firm Heidrick & Struggles.

Hundreds of non–Latin American businesses trying to operate in that region have openings for bilingual executives. "Our objective is to find the best talent that we can for any position that is open . . . and knowing a second language does create an advantage," said Mark Bailey, director of staffing at General Mills. But merely being fluent in the language does not mean that prospective employees have the skills required for a particular position. These companies are looking for people who can operate in a dual mode, combining U.S. efficiency and business culture with the Latin way of doing things, which is more personal and requires knowledge of Spanish or Portuguese.

An example of cultural contrast is given by Ignacio Kleinman of I-Network.com. An American might try to close a deal over the phone, but the Latin style is to take a plane ride to the customer's country, have lunch, and talk about soccer and the family. "Afterward, that Latin customer is going to feel closer to you," Kleinman says. "If there is no personal chemistry, there is likely to be no business."

Source: Julian Teixeira, "More Companies Recruit Bilingual Employees," www.shrm.org/ema/EMT/articles/2004/Fall04teixeira.asp (July 25, 2006); Cui Rong, "More Firms in China Think Globally, Hire Locally," *The Wall Street Journal*, February 27, 2006, p. 29; "Leaders of the Right Stuff in Big Demand," *Financial Times*, June 7, 2000, p. 12; Jiang Yan, "Thirst for Talent," *China Business Weekly*, September 12–18, 2005, p. 4; "Latino Talent Pinch Hobbling U.S. Firms' Expansion Plans," *Los Angeles Times*, June 25, 2000, pp. C1, 5; and Amy Yee, "China's War for Talent Hots Up," *Financial Times*, February 16, 2006, p. 8.

POLYCENTRIC STAFFING POLICY

When the company's primary strategic orientation is multidomestic, with low pressures for cost reduction and high pressures for local responsiveness, a polycentric approach may be used, involving human resource policies that are created at the local level for the specific context in which the local operations operate. Companies primarily hire HCNs for subsidiaries and PCNs for headquarters' positions; movement from the local subsidiaries to headquarters' positions is uncommon.

When HCNs are employed at the subsidiary level, there is no problem of their being unfamiliar with local customs, culture, and language. Furthermore, the first costs of employing them are generally lower (compared to the costs of employing home country nationals and paying to move them and their families to the host country), although considerable training costs are sometimes necessary. If there is a strong feeling of nationalism in the host country, having nationals as managers can make the subsidiary seem less foreign. As Fujio Mitarai, chairman and CEO of Canon, said, "If you look at capital investment strategy, marketing, research and development, those types of activities are international. But if you talk about people, humans, it is quite local in nature."[5]

The government development plans and laws of some countries demand that employment in all sectors and at all levels reflect the racial composition of the society. In other words, more skilled and managerial slots must be given to the local people. If foreign-owned

third country national (TCN)

Employee who is a citizen of neither the parent company nation nor the host country

firms in Indonesia fail to hire enough *pribumi* (indigenous Indonesians), those firms are likely to encounter difficulties with reentry permits for foreign employees as well as with other government licenses and permits that they need. Bribery requests have been known to increase until more pribumi were hired and promoted. Malaysia threatens to revoke the operating licenses of foreign-owned firms that fail to have a satisfactory number of *bumiputra* (indigenous Malays) in sufficiently elevated jobs.

A disadvantage of hiring local managers is that they are often unfamiliar with the home country of the IC and with its corporate culture, policies, and practices. As Liu Zhengrong, head of human resources for the German chemical group Lanxess, said of hiring local managers, "You lose something in terms of communication with the headquarters, but you get more hints about the local marketplace."[6] Differences in attitudes and values, as discussed in Chapter 6, can cause these locally hired managers to act in ways that surprise or displease headquarters. Also, local managers may create their own upward immobility if, because of strong cultural or family ties, they are reluctant to accept promotions that would require them to leave the country to work at parent headquarters or at another subsidiary.

Foreign-owned companies that hire and train local, host country people frequently experience a common, and disruptive, IHRM problem. The best of these people may be pirated away by local firms or other IC subsidiaries, as local executive recruiters are constantly on the lookout to make raids and entice the most talented employees to leave the original IC and join another firm that is seeking to overcome its own shortage of skilled personnel.

Finally, there can be a conflict of loyalty between the host country and the employer. For example, the host country national may give preference to a local supplier even though imported products may be less expensive or of better quality. Local managers may oppose headquarters' requests to set low transfer prices in order to lower taxes payable to the host government.

REGIOCENTRIC STAFFING POLICY

Companies with a regional strategic approach (with slightly higher pressures for cost reduction and slightly lower pressures for local responsiveness than the multidomestic strategy) can employ a regiocentric staffing approach. In this approach, regional employees are selected for key positions in the region, employing a variety of HCNs and TCNs.

The disadvantages often encountered when using employees from the home or host country can sometimes be avoided by sending third country nationals (TCNs) to fill management posts. A Chilean going to Argentina would have little cultural or language difficulty, but IC headquarters should be careful not to rely too heavily on similarities in language as a guide to similarities in other aspects of cultures. Mexicans, for example, would have to make considerable adjustments if they were transferred to Argentina, and they would find a move to Spain even more difficult. This is because the Mexican culture, in general, is far less European than that of either Argentina or Chile. Although the latter two cultures are certainly not identical, they do have many similarities. A fair generalization is that after an executive has adapted once to a new culture and language, a second or succeeding adaptation is easier.

An employer should not count on cost savings in using third country nationals. Although they may come from countries where salary scales are lower, in such countries as Brazil and most of the nations of northwestern Europe, salaries may be higher than American companies are paying at comparable position levels. Furthermore, many multinationals give international status* to both home country nationals and third country nationals, who then receive the same perquisites and compensation packages for the same job.

---

*International status is discussed later in this chapter.

Companies with a transnational strategic orientation, driven simultaneously by high pressures for cost reduction and high pressures for local responsiveness, follow a geocentric staffing policy. These organizations select the best person for each job without considering national origin and can therefore capitalize on the advantages of each staffing policy. With a geocentric staffing policy, HRM strategy tends to be consistent across all subsidiaries, borrowing best practices from wherever they may be found across the company's worldwide network of operations rather than showing preference only to the practices used at headquarters within a local context.

Training and Development

Training and development involve efforts to facilitate the acquisition of job-related knowledge, behavior, and skills. The training and development of managers and other key IC employees vary somewhat, depending on whether the candidate is from the home country, the host country, or a third country.

HOME OR PARENT COUNTRY NATIONAL

Relatively few recent college graduates are hired for the express purpose of being sent overseas. Usually they spend a number of years in the domestic (parent) company, and they may get into the company's international operations by design and persistence, by luck, or by a combination of those elements. They may first be assigned to the international division at the firm's headquarters, where they handle problems submitted by foreign affiliates and meet visiting overseas personnel.

If the company feels that it probably will send PCNs abroad, it will frequently encourage them to study the language and culture of the country to which they are going. Such employees will probably be sent on short trips abroad to handle special assignments and to be exposed to foreign surroundings. Newly hired PCNs with prior overseas experience may undergo similar but shorter training periods.

Axcelis Technologies, Inc., a manufacturer of semiconductor-processing equipment based in Beverly, Massachusetts, decided to outsource some of its engineering jobs to India. Cultural differences between India and the United States were a concern for Axcelis' management: India is a "high context" society that relies heavily on moral codes and relationships, while the United States is a "low context" nation that depends on legal codes and is very direct. Worrying that some of its American workers might resent or otherwise not be able to work effectively with their new Indian co-workers, the company trained 60 employees about Indian cultural practices. The training included such topics as how to shake hands and why Indian workers might not make eye contact during meetings, as well as role-playing of Indian-U.S. interactions. Randy Longo, human resources director at Axcelis, said, "At first, I was skeptical and wondered what I'd get out of the class. But it was enlightening for me. Not everyone operates like we do in America."[7]

It is increasingly possible for American ICs to supplement their in-house training for overseas work with courses in American business schools. In recognition of the growing importance of international business, those schools are expanding the number and scope of international business courses they offer. In addition, a number of university-level business schools are now operating in other countries.

Visitors from the United States tour an outsourcing firm in Bangalore, India, in March 2004. Relatively few recent college graduates are hired for the express purpose of being sent overseas. When a company feels managers are ready for an overseas assignment, it may send them on short trips abroad to handle special assignments and to be exposed to foreign surroundings.

A large problem that has plagued employers is caused by the families of executives transferred overseas. Even

Are Women Appropriate for International Assignments?

Although women make up about 47 percent of the work force in the United States, they represent only a relatively small fraction of the population of expatriates. Why this difference, especially with the pressing need for finding and developing competent global leaders? Adler examined three myths about women in international management:

Myth 1: Women do not want to be international managers.

Myth 2: Companies refuse to send women abroad.

Myth 3: Foreigners' prejudice against women renders them ineffective.

When Adler tested these myths empirically, neither the first nor the third was supported, but only the second one. Adler's research suggested that 70 percent of her sample of international companies were hesitant to select women for expatriate assignments. Why? Among the reasons expressed were that women in dual-career relationships would experience problems with international assignments, that gender-based prejudice would limit women's performance in many challenging countries or cultures, that women might feel lonely and isolated in an international assignment or be subjected to sexual harassment, or that the men making selection decisions regarding international assignments were themselves biased by traditional views and stereotypes regarding the appropriateness of assigning women to expatriate positions.

Is this hesitancy by companies regarding selecting women for international assignments justified? Research has shown that women are just as eager to go abroad as are men, sometimes more so. Additional research has shown that gender is unrelated to the performance ratings of expatriates, with the adjustment of expatriates to the host country context, or with the intention of expatriates to leave their ICs. Recent studies have even suggested that the skills and identity typically associated with women (e.g., attentiveness to personal aspects of business and skill in building interpersonal relationships) may actually give women an edge over men for some expatriate assignments. In addition, rather than cultural attributes serving as a barrier to the effectiveness of

women expats (e.g., a women-unfriendly environment in some host country cultures), as has sometimes been argued in explaining why women could not or should not be assigned to international positions, these structural aspects may serve as an advantage for women in international roles. For example, Taylor and Napier reported on the success of female expatriates in Japan in achieving improved cross-cultural adjustment and work success due to their having higher visibility and memorability as a result of their gender and their status as foreigners. Indeed, women may be able to divert attention from gender by demonstrating individualized sources of legitimacy and power, such as functional expertise and experience, and thereby enhance their effectiveness in international assignments.

So are ICs listening and selecting more women for expatriate assignments? In 1994, the GMAC Global Relocation Services annual Global Relocation Trends Survey showed that only 8 to 10 percent of expatriates were women. Ten years later, the proportion had risen to 18 percent. By 2005, it was up another 5 percent, to 23 percent of all international assignees. Expectations are that this proportion will continue to increase in coming years, particularly as more women are moving into management positions. Apparently, myths about the appropriateness of women candidates for international assignments are beginning to be shattered, and ICs are taking advantage of this pool of talented employees for promoting the organizations' international success.

Source: Jan Selmer, "Adjustment of Western European vs. North American Expatriate Managers in China," *Personnel Review* 30, no. 1–2 (2001), pp. 6–21; Paula M. Caligiuri and Rosalie L. Tung, "Male and Female Expatriates Success in Masculine and Feminine Countries," *International Journal of Human Resource Management* 10, no. 5 (1999), pp. 763–82; Mary G. Tye and Peter Y. Chen, "Selection of Expatriates: Decision-Making Models Used by HR Professionals," *Human Resource Planning* 28, no. 4 (2005), pp. 15–20; Nancy J. Adler, "Women Do Not Want International Careers: And Other Myths about International Management," *Organizational Dynamics* 13, no. 2 (1984), pp. 66–80; "Expatriate Workforce Demographics," *HR Magazine* 51, no. 5 (May 2006), p. 16; Sully Taylor and Nancy Napier, "Working in Japan: Lessons from Women Expatriates," *Sloan Management Review* 37, no. 3 (1996), pp. 76–84; and Paula M. Caligiuri and Wayne Cascio, "Can We Send Her There? Maximizing the Success of Western Women on Global Assignments," *Journal of World Business* 33 (1998), pp. 394–417.

though the employee may adapt to and enjoy the foreign experience, the family may not, and an unhappy family may sour the employee on the job or even split up the marriage. In such cases, the company may have to ship the family back home at great expense—seldom less than $25,000. Consequently, many companies try to assess whether the executive's family can adapt to the foreign ambience before assigning the executive abroad. This is part of the subject of expatriates that is dealt with later in this chapter.

HOST COUNTRY NATIONAL

The same general criteria for selecting home country employees apply to host country nationals. Usually, however, the training and development activities undertaken for HCNs will differ from those used for home country nationals in that host country nationals are more likely to lack knowledge of advanced business techniques, particularly those that are specific to business applications and operations of the IC, and knowledge of the company as a whole.

HCNs Hired in the Home Country

Many multinationals try to solve the business technique problem by hiring host country students on their graduation from home country business schools. After being hired, these new employees are usually sent to IC headquarters to receive indoctrination in the firm's policies and procedures as well as on-the-job training in a specific function, such as finance, marketing, or production.

HCNs Hired in the Host Country

Because the number of host country citizens graduating from home country universities is limited, multinationals must also recruit locally for their management positions. To impart knowledge of business techniques, the company may do one or more things. It may set up in-house training programs in the host country subsidiary, or it may utilize business courses in the host country's universities. The IC may also send new employees to home country business schools or to parent company training programs. In addition, employees who show promise will be sent repeatedly to the parent company headquarters, divisions, and other subsidiaries to observe the various enterprise operations and meet the other executives with whom they will be communicating during their careers. Such visits are also learning experiences for the home office and the other subsidiaries.

> *Craig Barrett, Chairman of the semiconductor giant Intel, views the current international business environment as undergoing "probably the biggest change in the history of mankind," the opening of China, as well as Brazil, Russia and India, to the global economy. This is creating major new markets, as well as potential competitors, for his company, and one of Intel's responses is to aggressively recruit the best talent he can find, especially in host countries. More than a third of Intel's employees are now outside the United States. "We are going to go after the best international resources wherever they are. There are great engineers in China and they also happen to cost less than in the United States. China happens to be our fastest growing marketplace and having your presence there is important."[8]*

THIRD COUNTRY NATIONAL

Hiring personnel who are citizens of neither the home country nor the host country is often advantageous. TCNs may accept lower wages and benefits than will employees from the home country, and they may come from a culture similar to that of the host country. In addition, they may have worked for another unit of the IC and thus be familiar with the company's policies, procedures, and people. This can simplify the training and development requirements for such recruits.

The use of TCNs has become particularly prevalent in the developing countries because of shortages of literate, not to mention skilled, locals. It can be an advantage to get someone already residing in the country who has the necessary work permits and knowledge of the local languages and customs.

> *Jianjiang Group, the largest hotel operator in China and also government owned, found its Shanghai home base being attacked by numerous international hotel chains. To compete it had to do something to enhance its performance on service and branding—two dimensions that have largely been lacking among Chinese firms. As a result, rather than looking for a manager in China as the company had traditionally done, it instead hired a headhunting firm specifically to recruit a Westerner from an established hotel chain. Christopher Bachran, with over 30 years of hotel industry experience including nearly 20 years in Southeast Asia, was ultimately persuaded to join Jianjiang. Part of the deal he negotiated, though, was authorization to bring in 4 to 6 senior managers from outside China, in areas such as operations, food-and-beverage operations, sales, marketing, human resources, and engineering services.[9]*

Host Country Attitudes

If the host government emphasizes employment of its own citizens, third country nationals will be no more welcome than will home country people. Actually, third country nationals could face an additional obstacle in obtaining necessary work permits. For example, the host government can understand that the German parent company of a subsidiary would want some German executives to look after its interest in the host country. It may be harder to convince the government that a third country native is any better for the parent than a local executive would be.

Generalizations about TCNs Are Difficult

We must be careful with generalizations about third country personnel, partly because people achieve that status in different ways. They may be foreigners hired in the home country and sent to a host country subsidiary either because they have had previous experience there or because that country's culture is similar to their own. Third country nationals may have originally been home country personnel who were sent abroad and became dissatisfied with the job but not with the host country. After leaving the firm that sent them abroad, they take positions with subsidiaries of multinationals from different home countries. Another way in which third country nationals can be created is by promotion within an IC. For instance, if a Spanish executive of the Spanish subsidiary of an Italian multinational is promoted to be general manager of the Italian firm's Colombian subsidiary, the Spanish executive is then a third country national.

As multinationals increasingly take the *geocentric* view toward promoting (according to ability and not nationality), we are certain to see greater use of TCNs. This development will be accelerated as more and more executives of all nationalities gain experience outside their native lands. Another, and growing, source for third country nationals is the heterogeneous body of international agencies. As indicated in Chapter 4, these agencies deal with virtually every field of human endeavor, and all member-countries send their nationals as representatives to the headquarters and branch office cities all over the world. Many of those people become available to, or can be hired away by, international companies.

Expatriates

In Chapters 1 and 2, we discussed the fact that many of the world's leading international companies obtain 50 percent or more of both their revenues and their profits abroad, and that international markets are becoming increasingly important to success for even small and medium-size companies. To exploit these international opportunities, staffing of positions in international operations is an important strategic issue. Although many of the employees may be hired in the host country (called *inpatriates*), ICs have continued to send employees on foreign assignments. Some of the international positions, especially those that deal with addressing a specific technical problem or transferring specialized knowledge, will be staffed with home or third country employees who are on short-term assignments (called *flexpatriates*). Yet companies will continue to staff many key positions with expatriates, employees who are relocated to the host country from the home country or a third country, with the assignment lasting for an extended period of time (two to four years is a common length of time for an expatriate assignment). In fact, about 80 percent of medium- and large-size companies have employees working abroad, and 44 percent of responding companies in a recent survey said that they were increasing the use of expats.[10] The average age of expats is getting somewhat younger as well, with 54 percent now being between 20 and 39 years, versus 41 percent in 1994.[11]

Why use expatriates rather than just hire local employees? Expatriates can bring technical or managerial skills that are scarce in the host country; they can help transfer or install companywide systems or cultures; they may provide a trusted connection for facilitating oversight or control over foreign operations; or the international assignment may enable the expat to develop the skills and experiences that will allow a subsequent promotion into leadership positions of greater scope and responsibility within the IC.

The costs of using expatriates are substantial, estimated at about $50 billion annually for U.S. companies, so the performance of expatriates is an important issue for ICs.[12] Yet various studies report that failure rates for expatriate assignments—including failing to achieve performance targets for an international assignment or prematurely returning from the assignment—range from 25 to 45 percent.[13] Furthermore, approximately 20 percent of expatriates leave their companies within six months of their return from abroad, hindering the IC's ability to retain and leverage the skills and experience that the expatriate has gained from the international assignment. A major cause of expatriate performance problems is culture shock, which is discussed in the nearby Worldview entitled "Culture Shock."

To enhance expatriate performance, ICs should consider the support that they provide to the employee predeparture, while away on assignment, and upon repatriation.[14] Preassignment, the focus of support efforts should be on ensuring that the expatriate has the skills needed for successful performance in the foreign assignment, including language and cultural training, career counseling, and any needed technical or other skill development. Support during assignment includes the use of mentors (both home and host country), career counseling, and communication strategies to ensure that the expatriate remains connected to the IC's strategy, people, policies, and culture. Repatriation support, including management of the relocation to the home or other nation and reintegration into the company, is discussed later in this section. Organizational support has been shown to be a predictor of the success of expatriates' adjustment to their international postings.[15]

THE EXPATRIATE'S FAMILY

It has been suggested that as many as 9 out of 10 expatriates' failures are family-related, and 81 percent of the employees who declined relocations in 2005 cited family concerns as the basis for their decision. In contrast to immigrants, who typically commit themselves to becoming part of their new country of residence, expats usually are only living temporarily in the new nation, so they often fail to adopt the host country's culture and seldom attempt to gain citizenship in that nation. Many expatriates and their family members also experience culture shock, which can significantly impact the quality of the international experience. The cultural adaptation pressures may be particularly great for the accompanying spouses, especially since they often are unable to work in the host country and may experience more challenges with regard to their personal identity. Spouses also typically need to interact more extensively with the local host community than do their expatriate partners, for such things as shopping, schools, and the management of domestic help, and related issues exacerbate adjustment pressures.[16] The stress an overseas move places on spouses and children will ultimately affect employees no matter how dedicated they may be to the company. Unhappy spouses are the biggest reason for employees to ask to go home early, and relocation expenses for high-level executives can run into the hundreds of thousands of dollars. Even worse, the company is losing a "million-dollar corporate-training investment" in the executive. On the other hand, expatriates tend to have better satisfaction and performance when their spouses and other family members are able to adjust well to the new host country context.[17]

A family purchases train tickets in London. It has been suggested that as many as 9 out of 10 expatriates' failures are family-related.

Trailing Spouses in Two-Career Families   The number of two-career families is growing, and that can complicate matters when one spouse is offered a juicy job abroad. The implications of the international assignment for the employee's partner and the partner's career prospects is a major factor impacting expatriate adjustment and performance.[18] It is reported that 20 to 25 percent of the spouses of expatriates are unable to obtain employment in the host country, even though 60 percent of them were employed before their spouse's international assignment began.[19] In efforts to ease the problem, some companies are starting programs that

Culture Shock

Culture shock refers to the anxiety people experience when they move from a culture that they are familiar with to one that is entirely different. Because familiar signs and symbols are no longer present in the new culture, a person experiencing culture shock tends to feel lack of direction, or inadequacy from not knowing what to do or how things are done in the new culture. Physical and emotional discomfort and feelings of disorientation and confusion are a common experience for people who go to other nations to work, live, or study. Many expatriates and members of their families are affected by culture shock, sometimes to a very great degree.

Researchers have identified three different dimensions associated with cross-cultural adjustment. The first is associated with the work context, such as the extent of job clarity, inherent conflict in the person's role, and amount of discretion associated with completing the job tasks. Adjustment to the general environment, the second dimension, is associated with reacting to differences in housing, food, education, health, safety, and transportation. The third dimension, interaction with local nationals, involves adjusting to differences in behavioral norms, ways of dealing with conflict, communication patterns, and other relationship issues that can produce anger or frustration. An expatriate can experience some degree of culture shock associated with any or all of these three dimensions.

Phases of culture shock

Culture shock often consists of distinct phases, although not everyone progresses through all of the phases. These phases include:

- *The honeymoon phase:* This phase begins when one first encounters the new culture. During this phase, differences between the familiar and the new culture are seen in a positive way, things seem fascinating and wonderful (e.g., the new foods, pace of life, habits of the people). New experiences tend to be filtered through the lens of one's home culture, often relying on stereotypes to interpret the host culture.

- *The distress phase:* This phase, which can occur within a few days, weeks, or months of arrival, involves increasing annoyance with the minor, and sometimes great, differences between the old and new cultures. Common feelings include impatience, anger, sadness, and discontent during the process of transitioning between one's traditional old ways and the ways of the new country. Some people never break out of this phase, and in severe cases it can trigger an expatriate or family member to return home prematurely from an overseas assignment. Some people will reject the new culture and only remember the good things of their home culture. Much of their time may be spent speaking their own language, watching videos or television shows from their home country, eating traditional foods from home, and socializing only with other expatriates from the home country (often spending much of this time complaining about the host culture).

- *The acceptance phase:* For those who survive the second phase, or skip it completely, the next phase will involve becoming accustomed to the differences associated with the

new culture, without reacting positively or negatively to the differences. As you gain some understanding of the new culture, some degree of pleasure may be felt about the culture, as well as some sense of psychological balance. You are more comfortable with the host country's language and customs, although there still may be difficulties, and you can begin to compare and evaluate the old ways versus the new ones.

- *The integration phase:* In this phase, you realize that the new culture has both bad and good things to offer, and you have a more substantive sense of belonging. Your focus returns to the basic concerns of everyday living and working and to establishing goals for living.

- *Reverse culture shock:* Once a person has grown accustomed to a new culture, returning to one's home culture can produce the same experiences as described in the preceding phases. Having become accustomed to things as they are in the host culture, you may find that you no longer feel fully at ease in your home culture. Things may have changed during your time abroad, and probably you yourself have changed in many ways. As a result, it often takes a while to successfully reacclimate.

Coping with culture shock

A number of suggestions have been made regarding how to deal effectively with culture shock. Some of the more common are:

- Prepare before departure, through such things as reading about the country and its culture, so that the new place and its people will seem more familiar once you arrive and you will be better prepared to deal with differences that you encounter.

- Be open-minded about the culture that you are visiting, and try to maintain a healthy, accepting attitude toward the new culture and the experiences you are having.

- Develop patience, avoid trying too hard, and practice relaxation and stress reduction techniques, such as exercise, meditation, and a healthy sense of humor.

- Maintain contact with the new culture, including learning the language and getting involved with social activities.

- Find cultural guides or mentors who can help you to learn and understand the new culture.

- Be attentive to relationships with your family and friends and at work to reinforce your support network during stressful periods.

Although adjusting to a new culture can be a frustrating and difficult process, it can also be a vibrant, renewing time of life, stimulating you to reconsider many aspects of your life and beliefs and allowing you to grow as a person.

Source: Lalervo Oberg, "Culture Shock and the Problem of Adjustment to New Cultural Environments," www.worldwide.edu/travel_planner/culture_shock.html (July 23, 2006); Duncan Mason, "Culture Shock: A Fish Out of Water," http://international.ouc.bc.ca/cultureshock/printext.htm (July 23, 2006); Margaret A. Shaffer, David A. Harrison, and K. Matthew Gilley, "Dimensions, Determinants, and Differences in the Expatriate Adjustment Process," *Journal of International Business Studies* 30, no. 3 (1999), pp. 557–81; and "Culture Shock," http://edweb.sdsu.edu/people/CGuanipa/cultshok.htm (July 23, 2006).

give trailing spouses more help in adjusting. Such help may take the form of assisting with job hunting in the host country, writing CVs, providing language and cultural training, identifying career opportunities, or giving tips on local interview techniques. If all else fails, some companies even hire a trailing spouse themselves. An added complication is that in many countries, the employee's spouse does not have the legal right to work, as work permits for foreigners may be difficult or nearly impossible to acquire.

Expatriate Children May Suffer the Most   Children are an important but often overlooked consideration when planning for an international move, parti-cularly since 45 percent of expats have children between the ages of 5 and 12.[20] Although an overseas stint may be seen as critical for career advancement of a parent, it can wreak havoc upon children's lives. Children are seldom involved in the initial decision making process associated with a move abroad. This can result in the children's experiencing many feelings, such as insecurity, frustration and powerlessness, from being uprooted from friends and many of the sources of their own identity. A move does not merely involve changing schools; there are also new systems, new learning styles, new language, and so forth, that the child must contend with. Sometimes these children are referred to as *third culture kids* (or *TCKs*) because they often speak several different languages, hold passports from more than one country, and have difficulty explaining where they are from (where "home" is). As a consequence of these challenges, companies are increasing their focus on easing the disruptions faced by children. For example, the Bennett Group, a Cendant Corporation unit in Chicago, gets the children of a family about to be transferred to a foreign city in touch with expatriate children who have already settled successfully into that city. There is even a Web site, www.Ori-and-Ricki.net, specifically designed for expatriate children.

LANGUAGE TRAINING

Foreign language skill has been shown to be a critical factor influencing effective adjustment of expatriates and their family members within the host country, and American companies are taking more seriously the language abilities of their employees. But neither they nor most Australian, British, Canadian, and New Zealand firms appear to be sufficiently serious about ensuring language fluency, since few ICs ensure that adequate time and resources are devoted to language training prior to or during international assignments. The English speakers appear to be stuck in a **language trap.**

The English language has become the *lingua franca* of the world; in effect, it is everybody's second language. In China alone, up to one-fifth of the population is learning English. This does not mean that English has taken over life in other parts of the world. For example, according to the EU, only 47 percent of Western Europeans (including the British and Irish) speak English well enough to carry on a conversation. If you want to sell shampoo or cell phones, you have to do it in Danish, Finnish, French, German, Greek, Italian, Portuguese, Spanish, Swedish, or whatever the local language or dialect may be. Even the British and U.S. media companies that stand to benefit most from the spread of English have been hedging their bets; CNN broadcasts in Spanish, and the *Financial Times* has launched a daily German-language edition.

When you are trying to sell to potential customers, it is much better to speak their language. As English speakers try to sell abroad, it is far more likely that their customers will speak English than that the English speakers will be able to speak the customers' language. Customers can then hide behind their language during negotiations.

If your career involves international business—and few can avoid at least some exposure to it—it is likely to suffer to at least some extent if you speak English only. A survey carried out on behalf of the Community of European Management highlighted the value recruiters place on multilingual ability. A large majority responded that English alone is not sufficient.[21] Chinese language skills will become more and more useful and sought after. China is the world's most populous country, and there are very large numbers of Chinese—often businesspeople—living outside China. In coming decades, perhaps Chinese will become the new "hot" language to know.

language trap
A situation in which a person doing international business can speak only his or her home language

BUILDING YOUR GLOBAL RÉSUMÉ — Speak a Foreign Language

The quickest way to identify yourself as a prospective international business professional is to speak a foreign language. As an American, speaking a foreign language puts you into an extremely small group of people who are bilingual, and being bilingual is a critical asset of the international business professional. U.S. Department of Education data show that:

- Less than 1 percent of American high school students study globally important languages such as Arabic, Chinese, Japanese, Farsi, Korean, Russian, or Urdu.

- More than 200 million Chinese are studying English, but only approximately 24,000 Americans study Chinese.

You don't need to speak like a native, but to at least be able to be conversant or conversational is typically looked upon favorably and seen as a sign of commitment by your foreign counterparts. Even though English is considered the "language of business," the ability to speak a foreign language gives you an advantage in dealing internationally and professionally—it puts you in the "priority group" on the international career track.

World Fact: There are approximately 6,800 languages spoken in the world, and with dialects, this number could exceed 10,000. Mandarin Chinese is spoken by the most people (836+ million), followed by Hindi (333+ million), Spanish (332+ million), and English (322+ million).

Culture Cue: In Japan and Pacific Rim countries, your business card is a critical and mandatory business tool. Treat it seriously. The information it typically contains should be accurately translated into the language of the country you are visiting, because your foreign counterparts will most likely be able to read both sides.

World Wide Resources:

www.solvit.org.uk

www.foreignword.com

REPATRIATION—THE SHOCK OF RETURNING HOME

There is often reverse culture shock when an expatriate returns to the home company and country. The expatriate will have gained new skills and knowledge, and the company's attitudes and people will have changed. Expatriates who have become accustomed to high levels of autonomy while abroad often struggle with the more restrictive work context when they return home, as well as experiencing the common frustration of failing to be promoted or have their job expectations fulfilled after repatriation.

That is why planning for an expat's return should start well before the overseas assignment even begins. The person and the employer should discuss up front how the assignment will fit the employee's long-range career goals and how the company will handle the return. When expats come back, companies have to understand that they are going to be different and harness their new knowledge.[22] Nevertheless, only 49 percent of ICs have repatriation programs, and 68 percent of expatriates report that they do not have any guaranteed position in their IC after the end of their international assignment.[23] "We are seeing rapid globalization, and it's going to become a real problem to find people who are willing and qualified to go overseas if everyone hears about people who were not satisfied" after they are repatriated, said Lisa Johnson, the director of consulting services for Cendant Mobility.[24]

Above, we spoke of the pain that is often suffered by an expat family's children; returning home can prove even more traumatic. That is especially true for those who have spent their formative years abroad. Repatriation counseling is available, which includes distinct children's programs and begins months before the family heads home.[25]

EXPATRIATE SERVICES

Although most U.S. expatriates currently continue health coverage with their company's domestic plans, we can expect that to change in the near future as expatriate health care programs are being created to assist companies and expatriates with claims administration, language translations, currency conversions, and service standardization.[26] Banks are also developing expatriate services, allowing expatriates to sign up for services online and providing 24-hour assistance to their customers, regardless of where in the world the expatriate is working.[27] Specialized companies are being developed to provide expatriate tax services.[28]

In recognition of expatriate family issues, some companies have begun to prepare and assist these families. Assistance may take the form of realistic job previews for expatriates (and sometimes for their family members), training in the culture and language of the host country, assistance in finding suitable schools or medical specialists, or even arranging for long-distance care for elderly relatives or parents while the family is living abroad. House-hunting help may be given, and the new transplants should be taken on grocery and hardware shopping trips with locals and expats who have been in the host country for a while. Locals can teach you the social norms and where to shop and not to shop. Expats can teach you where to get things only expats want. Web sites that focus on expatriate issues and can assist you in preparing for, adjusting to, or returning from an expatriate assignment include www.ExpatExpert.com and www.branchor.com.

> *An example of the types of organizations that can assist expatriates and their companies is a unit of Prudential Financial, called Prudential Relocation, which has 36 years of experience in relocation services. The unit promotes itself as being "a full-service global mobility management firm dedicated to supporting the recruitment, retention, and relocation of your most important asset: your human capital. We provide comprehensive, integrated domestic and international relocation services." The unit has 1,300 employees, fluent in 35 languages, who are focused on relocation issues across 82 nations.*[29]

Compensation

Establishing a compensation plan that is equitable and consistent and yet does not over-compensate the overseas executive is a challenging, complex task, especially since a "one-size-fits-all" approach does not match up well with the reality of diverse company and country assignments. Rebecca Powers of Mercer Human Resource Consulting said, "More companies are now sending employees on expatriate assignments, so there is a greater need to keep pace with the cost of living changes. Employers need to be proactive in managing their expatriate programs to ensure they receive a proper return on their investment and employees are compensated fairly."[30] If ICs are not able to compensate in a manner that is perceived to be fair and attractive, it will become ever more difficult to attract the quantity and quality of potential expatriates needed to satisfy the company's international requirements.

The method favored by the majority of American ICs has been to pay a base salary equal to that paid to a domestic counterpart and then, in the belief that no one should be worse off for accepting foreign employment, to add a variety of allowances and bonuses. Table 20.2 provides an example of some of the compensation costs for sending an American manager on a two-year assignment to Russia. Many international assignments will entail significantly higher levels of additional costs, when compared to those in the home country, than suggested by this example.

SALARIES

The practice of paying home country nationals the same salaries as their domestic counterparts permits worldwide consistency for this part of the compensation package. Because of the increasing use of third country nationals, those personnel are generally treated in the same way.

Some firms take the equal-pay-for-equal-work concept one step further and pay the same base salaries to host country nationals. In countries that legislate yearly bonuses and family allowances for their citizens, a local

© 1997 Roger Beale. Used by permission.

TABLE 20.2   Total Compensation Costs for Sending an Expatriate American Manager to Russia

The following compensation costs are illustrative of those an IC might encounter annually when sending an American manager and his or her family (spouse, two children) to Russia for a two-year assignment.

Compensation Component	Annual Cost (US$)
Base salary	$150,000
Incentive plan	15,000
Location differential (hardship premium)	5,000
Housing allowance	75,200
Cost-of-living allowance	6,200
Automobile allowance	36,500
Home leave	10,000
Educational assistance	24,000
Relocation/repatriation expenses	22,000
Total compensation before tax	**$343,900**
Tax assistance	51,200
Total compensation expense	**$395,100**
Other Expenses	
Preparation services (passports, visas, language training, etc.)	2,800
Settling-in services	3,600
Emergency leave	6,000
Total annual cost for expatriate	**$407,500**

Source: "U.S. Firms Extend Global Reach," *Workforce Management*, December 2004, p. 142.

national may receive what appears to be a higher salary than is paid the expatriate, although companies usually make extra payments to prevent expatriates from falling behind in this regard. In the United Kingdom, it is the practice to pay executives relatively lower salaries and to provide them with expensive perquisites, such as chauffeured automobiles, housing, and club memberships. A number of American companies follow British practices in compensating their executives working in Britain.

ALLOWANCES

allowances

Employee compensation payments added to base salaries because of higher expenses encountered when living abroad

Allowances are payments made to compensate expatriates for the extra costs they must incur to live as well abroad as they did in the home country. The most common allowances are for housing, cost of living, tax differentials, education, and moving.

Housing Allowances   Housing allowances are designed to permit executives to live in houses as good as those they had at home. A common rule of thumb is for the firm to pay all of the rent that is in excess of 15 percent of the executive's salary.

Cost-of-Living Allowances   Cost-of-living allowances are based on differences in the prices paid for food, utilities, transportation, entertainment, clothing, personal services, and medical expenses overseas compared to the prices paid for these items in the headquarters' city. Many ICs use the U.S. Department of State index, which is based on the cost of these items in Washington, D.C., but have found it is not altogether satisfactory. For one thing, critics claim this index is not adjusted often enough to account for either the rapid inflation in some countries or the changes in relative currency values.

TABLE 20.3	Ranking of 50 Cities from Most to Least Expensive, 2006		

Rank	City	Rank	City
1	Tokyo, Japan	26	Abidjan, Ivory Coast
2	Osaka, Japan	27	Warsaw, Poland
3	London, U.K.	28	Prague, Czech Republic
4	Moscow, Russia	29	Taipei, Taiwan
5	Seoul, South Korea	30	Shanghai, China
6	Geneva, Switzerland	31	Bratislava, Slovak Republic
7	Zürich, Switzerland	32	Düsseldorf, Germany
8	Copenhagen, Denmark	33	Luxembourg
9	Hong Kong	34	Singapore
10	Oslo, Norway	34	Frankfurt, Germany
11	Milan, Italy	36	Dakar, Senegal
12	Paris, France	37	Munich, Germany
13	New York City, USA	38	Berlin, Germany
13	Dublin, Ireland	39	Tel Aviv, Israel
15	St. Petersburg, Russia	40	Glasgow, U.K.
16	Vienna, Austria	41	Athens, Greece
17	Rome, Italy	41	Brussels, Belgium
18	Stockholm, Sweden	43	Barcelona, Spain
19	Beijing, China	44	Los Angeles, USA
20	Sydney, Australia	45	White Plains, USA
20	Helsinki, Finland	46	Madrid, Spain
22	Istanbul, Turkey	47	Birmingham, U.K.
22	Douala, Cameroon	48	Zagreb, Croatia
24	Amsterdam, Netherlands	49	Hamburg, Germany
24	Budapest, Hungary	50	Hanoi, Vietnam
		50	San Francisco, USA

Source: Used with permission Mercer Human Resource Counsulting, 2006 Cost-of-Living Survey, www.mercerhr.com/pressrelease/details.jhtml/dynamic/idContent/1142150 (July 23, 2006).

Another objection is that the index does not include many cities in which the firm operates. As a result, many companies take their own surveys or use data from the United Nations, the World Bank, the International Monetary Fund, or private consulting firms. Figures and comparisons on costs of living, prices, and wages can also be found in private publications. Table 20.3 provides a ranking of 50 cities, from most to least expensive as of 2006.

Allowances for Tax Differentials   ICs pay tax differentials when the host country taxes are higher than the taxes that the expatriates would pay on the same compensation and consumption at home. The objective is to ensure that expatriates will not have less after-tax take-home pay in the host country than they would at home. This can create a considerable extra financial burden on an American parent company because, among other things, the U.S. Internal Revenue Code treats tax allowances as additional taxable income. There are other tax disincentives for Americans to work abroad.*

*For more on this subject and other effects of U.S. laws on American ICs, see the taxation section in Chapter 11.

Education Allowances

Expatriates are naturally concerned that their children receive educations at least equal to those they would get in their home countries, and many want their children taught in their native language. Primary and secondary schools with teachers from most industrialized home countries are available in many cities around the world, but these are private schools and therefore charge tuition. ICs either pay the tuition or, if there are enough expatriate children, operate their own schools. For decades, petroleum companies in the Middle East and Venezuela have maintained schools for their employees' children.

Moving and Orientation Allowances

Companies generally pay the total costs of transferring their employees overseas. These costs include transporting the family, moving household effects, and maintaining the family in a hotel on a full expense account until the household effects arrive. Some firms find it less expensive to send the household effects by air rather than by ship because the reduction in hotel expenses more than compensates for the higher cost of air freight. It has also been found that moving into a house sooner raises the employee's morale.

Companies may also pay for some orientation of the employees and their families. Companies frequently pay for language instruction, and some will provide the family with guidance on the intricacies of everyday living, such as shopping, hiring domestic help, and sending children to school.

BONUSES

bonuses

Expatriate employee compensation payments in addition to base salaries and allowances because of hardship, inconvenience, or danger

Bonuses (or *premiums*), unlike allowances, are paid by firms in recognition that expatriates and their families undergo some hardships and inconveniences and make sacrifices while living abroad. Bonuses include overseas premiums, contract termination payments, and home leave reimbursement.

Overseas Premiums

Overseas premiums are additional payments to expatriates and are generally established as a percentage of the base salary. They typically range from 10 to 25 percent. If the living conditions are extremely disagreeable, the company may pay larger premiums for hardship posts. The U.S. Department of State maintains a list of hardship differential pay premiums that is often used as a reference by ICs and expats. Table 20.4 shows the hardship differentials for selected cities as of 2006.

Contract Termination Payments

These payments are made as inducements for employees to stay on their jobs and work out the periods of their overseas contracts. The payments are made at the end of the contract periods only if the employees have worked out their contracts. Such bonuses are used in the construction and petroleum industries and by other firms that have contracts requiring work abroad for a specific period of time or for a specific project. They may also be used if the foreign post is a hardship or not a particularly desirable one.

Home Leave[31]

ICs that post home country—and sometimes third country—nationals in foreign countries make it a practice to pay for periodic trips back to the home country by such employees and their families. The reasons for this are twofold. One, companies do not want employees and their families to lose touch with the home country and its culture. Two, companies want to have employees spend at least a few days at company headquarters to renew relationships with headquarters' personnel and catch up with new company policies and practices.

Some firms grant three-month home leaves after an employee has been abroad about three years, but it is a more common practice to give two to four weeks' leave each year. All

City and Country	Differential Pay Premium, %
Kabul, Afghanistan	25
Bahrain	10
Sarajevo, Bosnia-Herzegovina	15
Sao Paulo, Brazil	10
Sofia, Bulgaria	20
Beijing, China	15
Bogota, Columbia	5
Cairo, Egypt	15
Athens, Greece	5
Calcutta, India	25
Jakarta, Indonesia	25
Baghdad, Iraq	25
Tel Aviv, Israel	10
Seoul, Korea	5
Mexico City, Mexico	15
Lagos, Nigeria	25
Warsaw, Poland	5
Riyadh, Saudi Arabia	20
Johannesburg, South Africa	5
Columbo, Sri Lanka	20
Bangkok, Thailand	10
Istanbul, Turkey	10
Kiev, Ukraine	20
Caracas, Venezuela	15

Source: U.S. Department of State, "Hardship Differential and Danger Pay," January 2006, www.state.gov/m/a/als/qtrpt/60845.htm (July 23, 2006).

transportation costs are paid to and from the executive's hometown, and all expenses are paid during the executive's stay at company headquarters.

COMPENSATION PACKAGES CAN BE COMPLICATED

One might think from the discussion to this point that **compensation packages,** while costly—the extras frequently total 50 percent or more of the base salary—are fairly straightforward in their calculation. Nothing could be further from the truth.

What Percentage? All allowances and a percentage of the base salary are usually paid in the host country currency. What should this percentage be? In practice, it varies from 65 to 75 percent, with the remainder being banked wherever the employee wishes. One reason for such practices is to decrease the local portion of the salary, thereby lowering host country income taxes and giving the appearance to government authorities and local employees that there is less difference between the salaries of local and foreign employees than is actually the case. Another reason is that expatriate employees have various expenses that must be paid in home country currency. Such expenses may include professional society memberships, purchases during home leave, payments on outstanding debts in the employee's home country (e.g., mortgage, school loans), and tuition and other costs for children in home country universities.

compensation packages
For expatriate employees, packages that can incorporate many types of payments or reimbursements and must take into consideration exchange rates and inflation

What Exchange Rate?   Inasmuch as most of the expatriate's compensation is usually denominated in the host country currency but established in terms of the home country currency to achieve comparable compensation throughout the enterprise, a currency exchange rate must be chosen. In countries whose currencies are freely convertible into other currencies, this presents no serious problem, although the experienced expatriate will argue that an exchange rate covers only international transactions and may not represent a true purchasing power parity between the local and home country currencies. For instance, such items as bread and milk are rarely traded internationally, and living costs and inflation rates may be much higher in the host country than in the home country. International companies attempt to compensate for such differences in the cost-of-living allowances.

More difficult problems must be solved in countries that have exchange controls and nonconvertible currencies. Without exception, those currencies are overvalued at the official rate, and if the firm uses that rate, its expatriate employees are certain to be shortchanged. Reference may be made to the free market rate for the host country currency in free currency markets in, for example, the United States or Switzerland or to the black market rate in the host country, but these do not give the final answers. In the end, all companies must pay their expatriate employees enough to enable them to live as well as others who have similar positions in other firms, regardless of how the amount is calculated.

A common compensation component at many American companies is a stock plan that gives employees opportunities to acquire the company's stock on favorable terms. Such programs are designed to increase loyalty and productivity, but they sometimes run into problems outside the United States.

Share ownership is unknown or restricted in numerous countries. PepsiCo's vice president of compensation and benefits says, "We had to develop a customized approach in every country we operate in." DuPont discovered it could not give stock options in 25 of 53 nations, primarily because those countries' laws ban or limit ownership of foreign shares.

COMPENSATION OF THIRD COUNTRY NATIONALS

Although some companies have different compensation plans for third country nationals, there is a trend toward treating them the same as home country expatriates. In either event, there are areas in which problems can arise. One of these areas is the calculation of income tax differentials when an American expatriate is compared with an expatriate from another country, a situation exacerbated by tax changes passed by the U.S. Congress in 2006.[32] This results from the unique American government practice of taxing U.S. citizens even though they live and work abroad and treating tax differential payments made to those citizens as additional taxable income. No other major country taxes its nationals in those ways.

Another possible problem area is the home leave bonus. The two purposes of home leave are to prevent expatriates from losing touch with their native cultures and to have them visit IC headquarters. A third country national must visit two countries instead of only one to achieve both purposes, and the additional costs can be substantial. Compare the cost of sending an Australian employee home from Mexico with that required to send an American from Mexico to Dallas.

Regardless of problems, the use of third country nationals is growing in popularity. As businesses race to enlarge their ranks of qualified international managers, third country nationals are in greater demand. They often win jobs because they speak several languages and know an industry or country well.

As the number of third country nationals employed as executives by ICs continues to grow, the possible combinations of nationalities and host countries are virtually limitless, further complicating compensation efforts.

INTERNATIONAL STATUS

In all of this discussion, we have been describing compensation for expatriates who have been granted **international status.** Merely being from another country does not automatically qualify an employee for all the benefits we have mentioned. A subsidiary may hire home country nationals or third country nationals and pay them the same as it pays host country employees. However, managements have found that although an American, for example, may agree initially to take a job and be paid on the local scale, sooner or later bad feeling and friction will develop as that person sees fellow Americans enjoying international status perquisites to which he or she is not entitled.

international status
Entitles the expatriate employee to all the allowances and bonuses applicable to the place of residence and employment

Sometimes firms promote host country employees to international status even without transferring them abroad. This is a means of rewarding valuable people and preventing them from leaving the company for better jobs elsewhere.

Thus, international status means being paid some or all of the allowances and bonuses we have discussed, and there can be other sorts of payments as individual circumstances and people's imaginations combine to create them. Compensation packages for expatriates and other international executives are sufficiently important and complicated to have become a specialization in the personnel management field; at one firm, the title is "international employee benefits consultant." Help is also available from outside the IC. From time to time, the large consulting firms publish pamphlets advising about the transfer of executives to specific countries.

PERKS

Perks originated in the perquisites of the medieval lords of the manor, whose workers paid parts of their profits or produce to the lords to be allowed to continue working. Today, perks are symbols of rank in the corporate hierarchy and are used to compensate executives while minimizing taxes. Among the most common perks are:

Cars, which may include chauffeurs, especially for executives higher up the organization ladder.

Private pension plan.

Retirement payment.

Life insurance.

Health insurance.

Emergency evacuation services (for medical or other reasons).

Kidnapping insurance.

Company house or apartment.

Directorship of a foreign subsidiary.

Seminar holiday travel.

Club memberships.

Hidden slush fund (such funds may be illegal, but some corporations are said to have them).

WHAT'S IMPORTANT TO YOU?

While working abroad as an executive of an American multinational, one of the authors had a colleague who was an American expatriate married to a French woman. They had raised a family in several countries where they had been assigned by the company. Together with some other cosmopolites, they devised a table of items deemed important to at least one of them in choosing a city for the location of a company facility that employs foreigners.

The list included the usual items, such as cost of living, safety of personnel, medical facilities, housing, and schools. It also included such other items as availability of good wine at reasonable prices, quality of theater and whether it was live or cinema, number and type of one-star or better *(Michelin Guide)** restaurants, type and accessibility of sports facilities for both participants and viewers, and shopping facilities for fashionable clothes.

The table of items was circulated informally throughout the firm's many locations, and many cities in its network were graded as to each item on a 1-to-10 scale. When the New York headquarters saw the table, there was much mirth and merriment; suggestions—perhaps not all of them serious—were made as to additional items about which they would like information when they visited the cities.

However, the mirth and merriment subsided as more and more executives being assigned or reassigned abroad used the table to demand better compensation packages. Some even refused transfers because of the ratings given a city.

Also important to employees may be the number of vacation days they are likely to get from country to country. As to vacation days, Europeans are well ahead of Americans and Japanese. The minimum number of legally mandated paid days of vacation for full-time workers who have worked for at least one year in a company is 10 in Japan, while in France and Sweden it is five weeks, in Germany, the Netherlands, and Ireland it is four weeks, and in Spain it is 30 days. The U.S. has no national requirement, but the average ranges from 8 days at small private companies to 10 days at medium and large-size companies.[33]

Also of importance in decisions on where to locate a business operation are considerations such as cost of living, business environment, and office rents. Table 20.3 shows cost-of-living comparisons for a number of the world's cities. The survey compares the prices of goods and services typically consumed by the families of executives being sent abroad. You will note that although Tokyo, Osaka, and London are the most expensive, many of the cities ranked in the top 50 are located in emerging countries.

Despite labor market problems and less attractive market opportunities, the quality of the business environment in West European and North American countries remains higher than that in most emerging markets because those countries possess sophisticated institutions, such as advanced financial sectors, reliable legal systems, and political stability, that companies value.

There are numerous sources of information available about living, managing, and working abroad. One is Meridian Resources Associates, which offers a range of Web-based and other resources to prepare managers for successful performance in international contexts. For example, Meridian's highly acclaimed Web-based "GlobeSmart" program is a Web tool providing business managers with quick and easy access to extensive knowledge on over 50 topics in order to help the trainee conduct business effectively with people from 40 countries around the world. Other titles available from Meridian include "Managing in China," "Working with China," "Working with Japan," "Globally Speaking," "Working with Americans," "Living in Asia," "Assignment USA," and "Information on Consulting and Training Services." Meridian can be contacted by phone at 1-800-626-2047 or 1-415-321-7900 or at www.meridianglobal.com.

---

*The *Michelin Guide* rates restaurants and hotels in France and neighboring countries.

Discuss the importance of creating a company "global mind-set."

Successful managers in international companies must demonstrate a combination of high knowledge differentiation and high knowledge integration.

Explain the relationship between competitive strategies (home replication, multidomestic, regional, and transnational) and international human resource management approaches (ethnocentric, polycentric, regiocentric, and global).

Recognize that competitive strategy should be a primary determinant of the IHRM policies that an IC will use.

Compare home country, host country, and third country nationals as IC executives.

Sources of IC executives may be the home country, host countries, or third countries, and their differing culture, language, ability, and experience can strengthen IC management.

Explain the difficulties of finding qualified executives for international companies (ICs) and the importance of foreign language knowledge.

Knowledge of a people's language is essential to understand its culture and to know what's going on, as every effective manager must.

Explain what an expatriate is and some of the challenges and opportunities of an expat position.

Expatriate positions allow employees to work in foreign locations, which can provide the foundation for learning and growth, both personally and professionally, and a basis for movement upward in an organization's hierarchy. Expats can also find themselves "out of sight, out of mind," with unclear performance objectives and bases for performance evaluation. The families of many expatriates find the adjustment to a foreign posting difficult to manage successfully.

Explain the increasing importance of accommodating the trailing spouse of an expatriate executive.

The growing prevalence of two-career families is complicating problems of accommodating the spouse of an executive who is being transferred to another country.

Identify some of the complications of compensation packages for expatriate executives.

Expatriate manager compensation packages can be extremely complicated. Among other sources of complications are fluctuating currency exchange rates and differing inflation rates. Basic elements of those packages are salaries, allowances, and bonuses.

Key Words

expatriate (p. 542)

global mind-set (p.542)

ethnocentric (p. 543)

polycentric (p. 543)

regiocentric (p. 543)

geocentric (p. 543)

home country national (p. 543)

parent country national (PCN) (p. 543)

host country national (HCN) (p. 543)

third country national (TCN) (p. 545)

language trap (p. 553)

allowances (p. 556)

bonuses (p. 558)

compensation packages (p. 559)

international status (p. 561)

Questions

1. Why should the international human resource management approaches used by an international company be closely linked to the competitive strategy the company is using?

2. Compare and contrast ethnocentric, polycentric, regiocentric, and geocentric staffing policies.

3. In staffing a multinational organization for service outside the IC home country, what are some advantages and disadvantages of hiring home country personnel?

4. Why has there been an increasing use of third country nationals in the foreign operations of ICs?

5. Why are problems involving the trailing spouses of expatriate executives so common? What are some companies doing to solve those problems?

6. What is the English language trap?

7. Why are expatriate employees frequently paid more than their colleagues at equivalent job levels in the home office?

8. Why are compensation packages for expatriates more complicated than those for domestic employees?

9. What are some of the quality-of-life issues executives should consider before taking their families into an expatriate experience?

10. Suppose you are the CEO of an American multinational. On your staff and in the U.S. operating divisions of your company are several bright, able, dedicated female executives. They are also ambitious, and in your company, international experience is a must before an executive can hope to get into top management. An opening comes up for the position of executive vice president in the company's Mexican subsidiary. One of the women on your staff applies for the position, and she is well qualified for the job, better than anyone else in the company. Would you give her the position? What are the arguments pro and con?

11. Using the company example in question 10, suppose another position becomes available, this one as treasurer of the Japanese subsidiary. The chief financial officer of the company's California division applies for this job. She has performed to everyone's satisfaction, and she seems thoroughly qualified to become the treasurer in Japan. In addition, she speaks and writes Japanese. She is the daughter of a Japanese mother and an American father, and they encouraged her to become fluent in both English and Japanese. Would you give her the job? Why or why not?

Research Task

globalEDGE.msu.edu globalEDGE

Use the globalEDGE site (http://globalEDGE.msu.edu/) to complete the following exercises:

1. Mercer HR Consulting measures the overall *Quality of Living* for many cities worldwide. Locate the report and find the cities ranking highest and lowest. Also, provide a brief explanation on what measures are included in determining a city's quality of living and how multinational corporations can use this information.

2. The text discusses the importance of establishing a good compensation plan for foreign employment. Using the *Quarterly Reports for Living Costs Abroad*, published by the U.S. Department of State, provide a report comparing the cities of Melbourne and Lima.

Minicase 20.1 Casey Miller: Should She Accept an International Assignment?

Casey Miller, a 37-year-old manager with Techtonics International, had just returned to her office early on a Thursday afternoon. During a lunchtime meeting in the company's executive lunchroom, her boss had just offered her a chance to move to Shanghai, China, where she would be in charge of establishing the company's new office for the East Asia region. As she sat at her desk looking out over the Los Angeles skyline, she was filled with a mix of excitement and trepidation. Should she accept the position she was offered? Or should she pass on this opportunity and wait for something else in the future? What factors should she consider in making this important decision?

Casey had joined Techtonics shortly after completing her bachelor's degree in business, starting as an assistant sales manager. Since then, she had been promoted several times and was now the vice president in charge of North American operations for one of Techtonics's main business areas, overseeing a work force of more than 2,100 people and sales in excess of $500 million. Identified as one of the "rising stars" in Techtonics, and mentored by one of the senior vice presidents of the company, she seemed to have no limits to her career path.

Casey had always dreamed of living and working abroad. As a student, she studied abroad for a semester in Spain and spent a month afterward traveling around Europe with several friends. After graduation, she worked on a six-month internship with AIESEC, working for a small exporting company based in Poland. Since joining Techtonics, her international experience had primarily consisted of business trips to Canada or Mexico, attending several conferences and visiting a few selected client companies in Europe and Asia, and going on two extended vacations: one to Thailand and another to the Caribbean. When her boss mentioned the possibility of going to China, she could barely contain her enthusiasm!

However, Casey also began to think about her family and how an international assignment might impact them. Her husband,

Jerry, was an accountant in the Los Angeles office of a large accounting firm. Although he had a successful career, she thought that he might be open to a change. She also had two children: Jerry, Jr., who was 8, and Susan, who was 12. How would they respond to moving to a new country? Would now be a good time for such a move, or would it be better to wait for a few years?

And what if she was to accept the offer to go to China? What issues would she need to discuss with the company regarding the implications of a move to China? Her boss said that he would like to have Casey's decision within about a week and that she would need to move to Shanghai within four to six months if she accepted the job.

As she watched the traffic begin to jam up on the freeway outside her office building, Casey thought about reaching for her cell phone and calling her good friend for advice on how to deal with the job opportunity that she had been offered.

If you were a good friend of Casey Miller, what recommendation would you give regarding whether she should accept the international assignment that has been offered to her and what issues she should focus on in making such a decision?

21

Financial Management and Accounting

Quick decisions are unsafe decisions.

—Sophocles, 496–406 BC

Arrange whatever pieces come your way.

—Virginia Woolf

Chinese IPOs Abandon New York

Just after his appointment as chairman of the U.S. Securities and Exchange Commission, Christopher Cox told a room filled with Chinese financial regulators and politicians in Beijing that their country's capitalism was in danger of meeting the same end as did the Qing dynasty. It was a bloody end that closed China's imperial age in 1911.

We have all learned to be polite to our hosts, a lesson easily forgotten when you are annoyed. The SEC chairman was annoyed with China's approach to its financial markets, as are many internationally focused financiers in the United States. And he let his annoyance show, another cultural gaffe. China has chosen to stay away from, or protect its capital markets and companies from, foreign influence. That means less business for the U.S. exchanges and banks—a lot less business, so it appears.

The China Construction Bank went to the Hong Kong market in late 2005 with an initial public offering (IPO) of $9.2 billion, the largest single offering in five years. This looks like the beginning of a trend. According to the consulting company McKinsey, the next entries into the top 100 global company lists will come from Asian emerging markets. That Asian stock exchanges could dwarf New York is a reasonable concern for Christopher Cox. In the last year alone, Chinese companies have raised more than US$14 billion through IPOs based in Hong Kong. That is larger than the total amount Chinese companies have raised in New York in the past 10 years, $12 billion.

Investment bankers explain China's preference for Hong Kong as a desire to avoid the high-cost U.S. burdens of regulation and compliance, most of which they attribute to the Sarbanes-Oxley Act, the demanding corporate reporting legislation the United States introduced in the wake of a series of financial scandals. These rules are blamed because they add costs and legal risks. The *Financial Times* reports that an Asian finance director "estimates the extra cost of employing lawyers and accountants to comply with the legislation at tens of millions of dollars a year."* In addition, the Sarbanes-Oxley rules put quoted companies at additional risk of costly, time-consuming class action suits. One of the reasons Asian companies liked to list in the United States was the prestige that came with doing so, and another was the available liquidity. But with the China Construction bank listing, it looks as if there's enough liquidity in Hong Kong to support major offerings. That offering drew in US$80 billion of demand from investors across the globe.

In markets that restrict foreign ownership of investments, such as India and Taiwan, companies have issued global depository receipts, which are traded on global markets but held by local banks, and thus, legally, they are traded as domestic shares.

The paradox, that increasing globalization of capital flows is marginalizing New York's financial market, may lead these very markets to more international involvement through mergers and acquisitions of the markets themselves.

In Chapters 5 and 11, we spoke of some of the major financial forces international managers face in their daily operations. Now we look at how managers deal with these forces. We begin with the major financial management issue, how the company's capital is structured, and then move to cash management strategies, including multilateral netting and strategies created by

CONCEPT PREVIEWS

After reading this chapter, you should be able to:

explain capital structure choices and their potential impact on the MNC

describe the process of multilateral netting and what its contribution is to cash flow management

describe the importance of leading and lagging in cash flow management

categorize foreign exchange risks into transaction exposure, translation exposure, and economic exposure

describe the basic idea of a swap transaction and its various applications

explain a currency swap contract and its usefulness to the financial manager

recognize the usefulness and dangers of using derivatives

explain the role of and approaches to sales without money

identify the major challenges faced in international accounting

describe the international accounting standards' convergence process and its importance

currency fluctuations. Other financial management issues that have direct impact on the financial management of the firm are taxation and transfer pricing. Because accounting practices and standards change across national borders, we conclude with a look at some of these differences and the move toward convergence of standards in international accounting. In our discussion, when we describe specific practices, we will do so using the U.S. MNC for the sake of simplicity, remembering that MNCs can be any nationality. ■

*Francesco Guerrera and Andrei Postelnicu, "A Not So Foreign Exchange: China Shuns the West as a Location for Its Big Corporate Share Offers," *Financial Times*, November 18, 2005, p. 13.

Capital Structure of the Firm

We have seen that firms are becoming increasingly international in their markets and their sourcing in order to exploit attractive opportunities. Such an opportunity is also available for the capital structure of the firm, and, increasingly, chief financial officers (CFO) have been tapping international financial markets, both public and private. In fact, the private equity market has been growing by leaps and bounds.[1] Because financial markets are not globally integrated, varying opportunities arise among them with varying costs. So if a CFO can raise capital in a foreign market at a lower cost than that in the home market, such an opportunity may be attractive as a way to increase shareholder value.

The firm raises capital through its retained earnings and then, externally, through either equity, the issuing of shares, or debt (leveraging). Many firms choose to issue stocks in foreign markets, in part to tap into a broader investor pool, which can raise the stock price and reduce the cost of capital. This also may have a significant marketing advantage, raising the profile of the brand name abroad. Foreign companies that have issued shares in the United States include Unilever, Fuji Film, Canadian Pacific, KLM, Sony, Toyota, and Cemex. Sometimes, foreign shares are directly traded in the American stock markets, but many times, they are traded in the form of **American depository receipts (ADRs),** the U.S. version of the global depository receipts mentioned above. These receipts represent shares that are held by the custodian, usually an American bank, in the stock's home market. They are denominated in dollars and traded on the U.S. exchange, eliminating the need to have a broker in the country of issue and the issue of currency exchange. Because there is concern about foreigners having control of domestic assets, in some countries there may be restrictions on foreign ownership of equity. These restrictions are more prevalent in developing countries. For example, in India, Mexico, and Indonesia, foreign ownership in specific sectors is limited to 49 percent. Some sectors in developed nations are also protected from foreign ownership, often through an approval process. Such is the case in the United States and in the United Kingdom. For example, in the United States in 2006, Dubai Ports World, a major United Arab Emirates–based shipping and cargo firm, withdrew its $6.8 billion acquisition bid for the British Peninsular & Oriental Steam Navigation Co. of London. The British firm had been running portions of six major U.S. ports, and the security concerns in the United States became a public issue. Rather than face almost certain rejection at the government approval stage, Dubai Ports withdrew its bid for the U.S. portion of the British business. Another example is U.S. airlines, which must be directed and operationally controlled by a U.S. citizen.[2]

Debt markets are the other source of capital for the firm, and increasingly the tendency is to tap local markets first. That may mean that a foreign subsidiary of the Japanese firm Toyota would look first to its foreign market in the United States for funds to use in the U.S. operations. In this area, multinational corporations (MNCs) have an advantage over purely domestic companies because, in addition to obtaining funds at the corporate level, they can explore borrowing in their domestic and international debt markets, increasing the opportunities to reduce the cost of capital. They also have access to **offshore financial centers,** locations that specialize in financing by nonresidents, where the taxation levels are low and the banking regulations are slim. Switzerland, the Cayman Islands, Hong Kong, and the Bahamas are examples of offshore financial centers.

Debt financing is thought to be less expensive than is equity financing, since the interest paid on the debt is usually tax-deductible, while dividends paid out to investors are not. Yet the choice of debt or equity financing is also influenced by local practice.

American depository receipts (ADRs)

Foreign shares held by a custodian, usually a U.S. bank, in the issuer's home market and traded in dollars on the U.S. exchange

offshore financial center

Location that specializes in financing nonresidents, with low taxes and few banking regulations

FIGURE 21.1

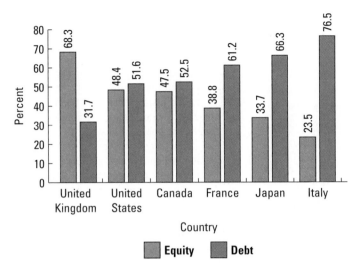

Source: Adapted from S. Besley and E. Brigham, *Essentials of Managerial Finance*
(Mason, OH: Thompson South-Western, 2005), chap. 9.

Companies in the United States, the United Kingdom, and Canada tend to rely on equity more heavily than do companies in many other countries. Figure 21.1 illustrates the different equity and debt capital structures of firms in selected countries. In both Japan and Germany, banks traditionally play a more central role than do the stock markets in the financing picture. In Japan, we find the interlocking relationships of the *keiretsu,* where related companies in a larger family, such as Mitsubishi, Sumitomo, and C. Itoh, are connected with interlocking ownership of stocks and bonds, with the company bank at their center. Essentially, this structure eliminates the stakeholder conflicts between bondholders and stockholders, an appropriate characteristic for a national culture where harmony is an important cultural value.

In addition to differing tax treatments and local practices, other country-level policies may influence the firm's capital sturcture. Exchange controls may limit dividend payments to foreign equity holders, and national policies designed to encourage local reinvestment may control the remission of dividends.

Decsions a financial manager would make in the process of raising capital are:

1. In what currency should the capital be raised, considering an estimate of its long-term strength or weakness?

2. How should the capital raised be structured between equity and debt?[3]

3. What are the sources of capital available? Should money be borrowed from a commercial bank by an ordinary loan, a bank as part of a swap, another company as part of a swap, another part of the MNC, or a public offering in one of the world's capital markets, for example, in the New York or Eurobond market?

4. If the decision is made to use one of the world's capital markets, management must then decide in which of those markets it can achieve its objectives at the lowest cost. The MNC can shop among the national markets in such diverse centers as New York, London, Paris, Zurich, Bahrain, Singapore, Tokyo, and the Cayman Islands.

5. Are there other sources of money available? For example, if the company is in a joint venture operation, the joint venture partner may be a source of money. Or perhaps there is private capital available. This source of funds is rapidly internationalizing. Or if the move is into a country or area that wants the MNC's technology or management knowledge, or the jobs that will be created, the government may be a source of low-cost funds. Under such circumstances, the company may also be able to negotiate tax reductions or holidays.

>>Microloans: Debt That Is Almost Always Paid in Full

With the help of PADME, an ACCION partner in the West African country of Benin, Fatouma Dijbril Issifou was able to obtain a loan and make more profit selling vegetables. She is now able to save money to fulfill her dreams and comfortably provide for her family.

You might think it would be utter folly to lend money to a developing country. What about a loan to a new small business or entrepreneur such as a vegetable stand or a tailor in a developing country?

Worldwide, development organizations are finding that some of the world's poorest entrepreneurs repay their debts at rates approaching 100 percent. To encourage grassroots private business in Latin America, Asia, and Africa, these organizations are expanding programs that already lend thousands of small entrepreneurs amounts ranging from $50 to several hundred dollars. Tiny businesses in developing countries commonly repay these "microloans" faithfully because of community pressure and the security of a favorable credit rating. Microloans rescue them from the clutches of loan sharks and let them borrow again in hard times. The money helps them start or expand their businesses—selling vegetables, sewing, repairing shoes, making furniture, and the like—and boosts their local economies.

The micro-credit concept was developed by Professor Muhammad Yunus, a U.S. trained PhD economist, through the Grameen Bank in Bangladesh, which he established to administer his program, and ACCION, a U.S. micro-credit organization. Dr. Yunus was awarded the Nobel Peace Prize in 2006.

The microloan repayment performance shines when compared with that of some sovereign nations. It also looks mighty good compared with a default rate of 5.4 percent among U.S. recipients of federally guaranteed student loans. ACCION reports a repayment rate over the life of its program of 97 percent.

ACCION International spokesperson Gabriela Romanow cites the case of Aaron Aguilar, an unemployed factory worker in Monterrey, Mexico, who borrowed $100 to buy clay and glazes for making figurines with his wife in their backyard. In six years, the couple took out and repaid five loans and built their business to 18 full-time employees.

Sometimes borrowers have to struggle against setbacks that might seem weird in a developed nation. One group of women in Cameroon received $100 from Trickle Up, another microloan agency, to start a rabbit-breeding business, but the rabbit ate her offspring, recalls Mildred Leet, Trickle Up's cofounder. Undaunted, the women switched to chickens and made enough money selling eggs to branch out into tomatoes and tailoring, ultimately opening two shops.

AVERAGE LOAN: LATIN AMERICA—$634; AFRICA—$594; UNITED STATES—$3,647

Fatouma Dijbril Issifou, a client of ACCION partner PADME in Parakou, Benin, sold vegetables as a child, along with her mother, in Benin, West Africa. Fatouma inherited the stall and was ready to live the subsistence life that had passed on to her. She knew, though, that if she could expand her business, her children could go to school. She learned about PADME from a friend. PADME saw Fatouma's drive and approved her for a loan of $130. She used it to buy bulk vegetables at lower costs. A second loan for $260 allowed for inventory expansion. She reports earnings of about $2 on a bushel of carrots and a little more for a kilo of potatoes.

This may not seem like much, but for Fatouma, the loans made a huge difference. Before the loans, she was able to save just $13 a year to invest in her tiny stand, and she struggled to support her three children. Today, two of them are in school, and the youngest is eager to follow in their footsteps. "The loans have helped me a lot," she says. "I can buy medicine and there is enough food for the children. Now, I don't worry anymore."

Critics point out, though, that one microloan is not going to pull a budding entrepreneur out of poverty, let alone a whole country. As ACCION's examples show, a series of loans is probably necessary, combined with training and support. When Tufts University received an endowment to set up a microloan program, specialists were ready to warn Tufts of the ethical aspects of microloans: Its program needs to be much more than banking.

Source: www.ACCION.org (July 8, 2006); Rashmi Dyal-Chand, "The Pitfalls of Microlending," *Boston Globe*, November 13, 2005, www.boston.com/news/globe/editorial_opinion/oped/articles/2005/11/13/the_pitfalls_of_microlending (July 7, 2006).

6. How much money does the company need and for how long? For instance, if the company is moving into a new market or product, there will probably be a period during product introduction or plant construction when the new venture will need more capital than it can generate.

Cash Flow Management

The management of cash flows is an important part of international financial management that differs from the management of cash and cash flows in a purely domestic firm, although there are some basic commonalities. For example, all firms would want to source funds in low-cost markets and place excess funds where they would get the best return. The global cash management picture is more complex than that of a domestic firm due to the number of national locations in which the firm has subsidiaries. For an MNC, operating in 25 local currencies is not uncommon. Two common cash flow management techniques used are multilateral netting and leading and lagging.

MULTILATERAL NETTING

In addition to the currencies, the types of cash flows associated with subsidiaries can vary as well, including loans from the parent to the subsidiary and increased investment in the form of equity capital. The flows from the subsidiary back to the parent might include cash from sales, dividends, royalties, and fees. One common strategy for cash management is **multilateral netting.** Multilateral netting is a centralized approach in which subsidiaries transfer their net cash flows within the company to a cash center that disperses cash to net receivers.

multilateral netting
Strategy in which subsidiaries transfer net intracompany cash flows through a centralized clearing center

Why should companies consider this centralized process? First of all, the transfer of funds has a cost attached to it, called the *transaction cost,* and the funds while in transit are not working for the company. By reducing the transfer transactions, the costs are reduced and there are fewer foreign exchange transactions, as well. They too, have a cost. Netting would require each subsidiary with a net payable position to transfer its funds to a central account once a month, where the central account manager would then transfer funds to the net receivers. Compare the two approaches in Figure 21.2. Without netting, reconciling the positions would require eight transactions and $1.2 million in transit. With netting, there are four transactions, and 600,000 in transit. Plus, the foreign exchange transaction costs are reduced.

LEADING AND LAGGING

Sometimes, especially in developing economies, the government might prohibit currency conversion or the repatriation of profits or royalties. This could be caused by low foreign reserves and evidenced by a worsening trade account balance. Such host government actions leave the MNC unable to move cash assets out of the country, not a good position to be in when the reason for making the foreign investment in the first place is to provide returns to the shareholders.

FIGURE 21.2   Advantages of Multilateral Netting

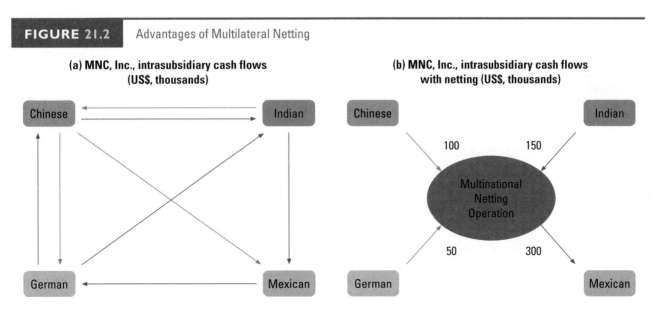

(a) MNC, Inc., intrasubsidiary cash flows (US$, thousands)

(b) MNC, Inc., intrasubsidiary cash flows with netting (US$, thousands)

>>An Integrated Approach to Risk

MNEs set up centralized finance departments in the 1970s, and they have tended to look at risks in isolation. They have hedged foreign exchange and developed an interest rate strategy, for example, but they have looked at these risks separately. The next step will be to pull all the risk analysis together and centralize it. That might mean looking at commodity trends, currencies, and interest rates, as well as pension commitments, from a central, companywide perspective. Smaller companies will have an easier time of doing this, since one of the barriers to such integration is internal territoriality and company politics. For example, shifting the analysis of commodity price increase risk in an MNC from the procurement department to the corporate finance department or treasury would be a formidable challenge, as would moving the pension analysis out of the human resource department.

Source: Gillian Tett, "The Corporate View: Treasury: Living in a Time of Great Challenge," *Financial Times*, May 31, 2006, p. 5.

blocked funds

Funds whose conversion from a host currency or repatriation is not allowed by a host government

There are several ways to address the issue of **blocked funds.** One useful technique is **leading and lagging,** which involves the timing of payments. A lead approach is to collect receivables early when the foreign currency is expected to weaken and fund payables early when the foreign currency is expected to strengthen. A lag approach is to collect receivables late when the currency is expected to strengthen and fund payables late when the currency is expected to weaken. Leading and lagging can be coordinated among MNC subsidiaries to reposition funds and help to compensate for blocked funds or funds about to be blocked.

leading and lagging

Timing payments early (lead) or late (lag), depending on anticipated currency movements, so that they have the most favorable impact for company

In addition to leading and lagging, another way to deal with blocked funds includes using the blocked funds to purchase goods on the local market and then export them. Such exports might include air travel on a domestic carrier of the government blocking funds for the MNC worldwide, paying for such travel in local, blocked currency and having business meetings in the country where the funds are blocked, so that these funds are expended for corporate purposes.

Foreign Exchange Risk Management

When operating across different currencies, MNC managers regularly encounter currency exchange rate movements. These unanticipated shifts present risks to the international business because they represent unplanned-for changes in the value of assets and liabilities. These significant risks are usually categorized into three types: transaction exposure, translation exposure, and economic exposure. These exposures result in positions that are either uncovered or covered, that is, hedged.

TRANSACTION EXPOSURE

transaction exposure

Change in the value of a financial position created by foreign currency changes between the establishment and the settlement of a contract

Transaction exposure occurs when the firm has transactions denominated in a foreign currency. The exposure is due to currency exchange rate fluctuations between the time the commitment is made and the time it is payable. For example, an order for German diesel truck engines is placed by a Massachusetts company, for payment in 180 days in euros, €150,000 (US$189,000 at the then-prevailing exchange rate of $1.26 per euro). If the euro strengthens against the dollar to $1.38 when the company converts its dollars to euro, the engines' price in dollar terms would increase by $18,000 to US$207,000. In this case, there would be a cash flow effect for the importer but no effect for the exporter. Had the exporter quoted the engines' price in U.S. dollars, the situation would have been reversed.

The key issue with a transaction exposure is that the business has made a contract to pay or accept payment in another currency. An initial observation is that the company could avoid this exposure by refusing to enter into such contracts. Yet the desire to conduct business across currency borders suggests a willingness to accept this risk. One party will always have to, and doing so might be a part of the contract negotiation strategy. There are other approaches to dealing with eliminating the risk of a transaction exposure, or **hedging,** at the operations level. Remember the discussion of leading and lagging? Let's look at an example.

The U.S. company Nucor is exporting to Spain a €20 million boutique steel order, made from recycled steel, payable in euros. Nucor has accepted the foreign exchange risk as a part of its marketing strategy. It may also have factored a currency shift expectation into its euro pricing.

Here are the foreign exchange and interest data:

EU interest rate:	2.75
U.S. interest rate:	5.00
Spot rate	$1.2553
Forward rate	$1.28 (one year forward)

Nucor would like to lag its receivable, since the market indicates that the dollar may well weaken further against the euro. That suggests that Nucor will be able to buy more dollars for its receivable in the future. And the Spanish customer may well want to lag the payment as well if there is no incentive for early payment. If the customer is Euro-based, the currency's strengthening against the dollar will have no appreciable effect on its cash flows.

In another way to hedge on transaction exposure through company actions, many multinationals follow a centralized practice similar to multilateral netting: *exposure netting.* The firm will run a centralized clearing account that matches and nets out foreign exchange exposures across currencies or across currency families. Working with currency families recognizes that some currencies tend to move in lockstep with one another.

There are also ways to hedge foreign currency exposure by engaging in contracts known as *hedges* and *swaps.* A **forward market hedge** involves a quite simple transaction: The company sells forward its foreign currency receivables for its home currency, matching the time forward to the due date of the receivables. When the Spanish company pays, Nucor will deliver the amount to its bank, the partner in the forward market hedge contract. Nucor will not have been exposed to currency risk in the Spanish sale. Because the forward market hedge is a way to cover the complete exposure in a given transaction, it is the most widely used approach. Yet because the forward market hedge assumes all of the foreign exchange risk, it eliminates the chance of gaining from a currency move in the company's favor.

An approach to hedging an exposure but not losing the opportunity to gain from a currency appreciation is a *foreign currency option.* With a **currency option hedge,** you purchase an option to buy or sell a specific amount of currency at a specific time, but the option can be exercised or not. These hedges are *calls*—or contracts with an option to buy—for foreign currency payables and *puts*—or contracts to sell—for foreign currency receivables. Since these are options, if the market works against you, you can exercise the contract. If the market works for you, you don't need to exercise the option.

The money markets also afford an opportunity to hedge a foreign transaction. In a **money market hedge,** Nucor would borrow euros in the European money market in the amount of the receivables from the Spanish sale. The basic idea here is to match the balance sheet asset with a liability in the same currency. Here's how the money market hedge works: Nucor borrows $20 million for a period that matches the receivable's due date. Then Nucor converts the euros to dollars at the spot rate and then invests them. The euros that are received from the Spanish company will be used to close out the euro loan. Then the invested dollars plus their interest provide Nucor the dollar amount for the Spanish sale.

Swap contracts are also used to hedge foreign currency exposure. This is an agreement to exchange currencies at specified rates and on a specified date or sequence of dates. Swaps are quite flexible and may be undertaken for long periods, much longer than in the forward market. So if Nucor had a series of sales in the EU over the next 10 years, all denominated in euro, it could enter into a series of swaps so that the exchange rate or series of exchange rates would be known in advance. We discuss swaps in greater detail below.

hedging
A process to reduce or eliminate financial risk

forward market hedge
Foreign currency contract sold or bought forward in order to protect against foreign currency movement

currency option hedge
An option to buy or sell a specific amount of foreign currency at a specific time in order to protect against foreign currency risk

money market hedge
A method to hedge foreign currency exposure by borrowing and lending in the domestic and foreign money markets

swap contract
A spot sale/purchase of an asset against a future purchase/sale of an equal amount in order to hedge a financial position

TRANSLATION EXPOSURE

translation exposure
Potential change in the value of a company's financial position due to exposure created during the consolidation process

Translation exposure occurs when subsidiary financial statements are consolidated at the corporate level for the companywide financial reports. Since the foreign subsidiaries operate in nondollar currencies, there is a need to translate subsidiary financial reports to the parent company's currency during the corporate consolidation process. Exchange rate movements can have substantial impact on the value of these financial statements, which may affect per-share earnings and stock price. Take a U.S. company that has subsidiaries in Brazil, Japan, Spain, and the United Kingdom. The subsidiary financial reports will be prepared in their own currency, so amounts in four currencies will be translated. Any changes in the exchange rates will affect the dollar values. Such changes, either gains or losses, are not reflected in cash flow; they are paper or unrealized changes.

current rate method
An approach in foreign currency translation in which current assets and liabilities are valued at current spot rates and noncurrent assets and liabilities are translated at their historic exchange rates

The issue related to translation exposure is what currency exchange rate to use for the translation. There are two basic approaches, the current rate method and the temporal method. By the **current rate method,** assets and liabilities are translated at the rate in effect the day the balance sheet is produced. By the **temporal method,** monetary items such as cash, receivables, and payables are translated at the current exchange rate. Fixed assets and long-term liabilities are translated at the rates in effect the date they were acquired or incurred. In the United States, Financial Accounting Standards Board (FASB) Statement 52 establishes when use of each method is appropriate, depending on the functional currency of the subsidiary. Approaches to translation exposure differ by country.

temporal method
An approach in foreign currency translation in which monetary accounts are valued at the spot rate and accounts carried at historical cost are translated at their historic exchange rates

Many organizations do not hedge translation exposure because hedging a translation exposure can actually increase transaction exposure. If the translation exposure is hedged through a matching foreign exchange liability, such as a debt, then that debt is an exposure at the transaction level. Transaction exposure is fundamental to a corporation's value. Hedging of translation exposure is discussed below in our focus on swaps.

ECONOMIC EXPOSURE

economic exposure
The potential for the value of future cash flows to be affected by unanticipated exchange rate movements

Economic exposure occurs at the operations level and results from exchange rate changes on projected cash flows. Unlike transaction exposure, which addresses the individual transaction, economic exposure is firmwide and long-term. For example, when the dollar strengthens, as it did in the 1990s, U.S. export prices increased in terms of other currencies, and so sales plummeted. U.S. exported goods became less price-competitive in foreign markets. Yet when the dollar weakens, as it did in mid-2006, U.S. export prices become more attractive in foreign markets. These changes are examples of the possible effects of economic exposure. Economic exposure can affect both the dollar value of the company's foreign assets and liabilities and the company's cash flow, because it has an impact on foreign sales. Asset exposure includes the fixed assets as well as the financial assets. The exposure of cash flow to currency fluctuation is known as *operating exposure.* Operating exposure is difficult to measure. It involves both the cash flows and the larger commercial context, the competitive conditions connected to obtaining inputs and selling. For example, if a foreign supply becomes more costly in home currency terms because of a home currency weakening, the added cost might be covered through pricing or through switching the supply source. The company may be able to pass the cost increase on to the buyer or to switch into a lower-cost market for the supply. Such options contribute to the reduction of exposure and actually involve the company's competitive position and the structure of the market.[4] The management of economic exposure draws on the hedging and swap contracts we have discussed as ways to manage transaction exposure, on flexibility in sourcing, and on a portfolio approach to foreign market involvement.

Swaps and Derivatives

We mentioned swaps above as a way to protect against transaction risks. They are actually more likely to be used against translation risks and are most likely to be used to raise or transfer capital. In this section, we examine their wide range of uses separately and address the dangers of derivatives.

U.S. Law Has Unintended Consequences for Overseas Funding

The U.S. American Jobs Creation Act of 2004 was an attempt by Congress to encourage U.S. MNCs to bring home their foreign cash holdings by cutting the tax paid on repatriated cash. In fact, under this repatriation provision, the corporation is allowed a deduction equal to 85 percent of the repatriated cash amount. Bank of America calculates that this is an effective tax rate of 5.25 percent on repatriated dividends instead of the usual 35 percent rate. Such an opportunity encourages managers to consider repatriation of earnings in low-tax countries and not keep earnings for reinvestment. Instead, managers look to the local debt markets for loans to cover working capital and investment needs. Thus, this opportunity created by the U.S. American Job Creation Act has motivated managers to examine their sources of funds and how they finance their subsidiaries. In the process, many companies realized that they had unused debt capacity in certain subsidiaries that offered the opportunity to raise funds locally. Most MNCs have funded from the center out and down, through equity and debt, but now capital markets in developing countries look more attractive in terms of raising capital locally, especially for local bond issues, according to Michael Corbat, head of Citigroup's global corporate bank. Foreign debt is attractive, too, because it is a way to hedge the foreign exchange risk connected to a subsidiary's earnings. Citigroup, General Electric, and auto manuffacturers have been at the forefront of these developing bond markets.

Such transfer of financial risk to the subsidiary comes at a good time, too, when several developing nations have threatened more restrictive repatriation rules or outright nationalization. Sourcing funds locally has many advantages—it offers a currency foreign exchange risk hedge at no cost, it helps to maintain good political relations with host country financiers and politicians, and because locals are involved, it may even offer protection against nationalization. For U.S. MNCs, all this began with an effort by the U.S. government to bring cash home to stimulate job growth.

Source: *CapitalEyes*, Bank of America e-newsletter, July 2005, www.bofabusinesscapital.com/resources/capeyes/a07-05-291.html?bucket=5 (accessed July 3, 2006); David Wighton, "New Trend: Subsidiary Financing: Financial Risk Takes a Local Approach," *Financial Times*, June 28, 2006, p. 3.

SWAPS

We look now at four types of swaps—spot and forward market swaps, parallel loans, bank swaps, and currency swaps—that are useful as hedges against foreign currency risk exposure. Interest rate swaps are also available on the market.

Spot and forward market swaps is a two-step hedging transaction that involves matching an exposure with a forward transaction. Suppose an American parent company wants to lend euros to its Italian subsidiary and avoid currency exchange risk. First, the parent company will buy euros in the spot market and lend them to the subsidiary. Then, at about the same time, the parent will buy the same amount of U.S. dollars to be paid for in euros for forward delivery at the due date of the loan. The short euro position is covered with the euros repaid by the subsidiary, and the parent receives the dollars. The cost will depend on the discount rate in the forward market compared to the spot market rate.

> **spot and forward market swaps**
> Use of the spot and forward markets to hedge foreign currency exposure

Parallel loans avoid the foreign market. They involve matching loans across currencies. Continuing with our example of the American parent and its Italian subsidiary, let's add an Italian parent company and its American subsidiary. Assume that each parent wants to lend to its subsidiary in the subsidiary's currency. The Italian parent lends the agreed amount in euros to the Italian subsidiary of the American parent. At the same time and with the same loan maturity, the American parent lends the same amount (at the spot EU-US$ rate) in U.S. dollars to the American subsidiary of the Italian parent. Each loan is made and repaid in one currency, thus avoiding foreign exchange risk.

> **parallel loans**
> Matched loans across currencies that are made to cover risk

Parallel loan swaps can be adapted to many circumstances and can involve more than two countries or companies. If a subsidiary in a blocked-currency country has a surplus of that currency in its local operation, perhaps the local subsidiary of another IC needs capital.[5] The other MNC would like to provide that capital but does not want to convert more of its hard currency into a soft currency. The subsidiary of the first MNC lends its surplus currency to the subsidiary of the second MNC. The parent company of the second MNC lends the parent company of the first MNC an equivalent amount in some other currency that it can use.

Interest may or may not be charged on swaps, usually depending on whether interest rates in the two countries are similar or are widely different. If the gap is large, the borrower getting the higher-cost currency might pay an equivalently higher rate of interest on repayment.

"We need two hundred million bucks by Friday—any ideas?"

Source: Cartoon Features Syndicate

bank swap
Swap made between banks to acquire temporary foreign currencies

currency swap
An exchange of debt service of a loan or bond in one currency for the debt service of a loan or bond in another currency

interest rate swap
An exchange of interest rate flows in order to manage interest rate exposure

derivative
A contract whose value is tied to the performance of a financial instrument or commodity

You may have observed that we have not mentioned banks in our discussion of swaps. These company-to-company loans are competition for commercial banks, but some banks will facilitate negotiations or act as a broker between clients in arranging swaps. Investment banks and other money brokers sometimes facilitate or even instigate swaps as a service to clients.

Banks swaps also exist. They may be between banks (commercial or central) of two or more countries for the purpose of acquiring temporarily needed foreign exchange or may be with MNCs. A typical use of a bank swap is to finance the expansion of an MNC subsidiary in a developing country whose currency is soft and nonconvertible or blocked. The mechanics are simple. Assume that a Swiss MNC wishes to expand a subsidiary's plant in Indonesia and, in doing so, to minimize foreign exchange risks and avoid exchanging any more hard convertible Swiss francs (CHFs) for soft Indonesian rupiahs (IDRs). The Swiss parent company may deal either with a commercial bank in Indonesia or with the Indonesian central bank. The Swiss MNC deposits CHFs in a Swiss bank to the credit of the Indonesian bank. In turn, the Indonesian bank lends IDRs to the Indonesian subsidiary. At an agreed future date, the Indonesian bank repays the CHFs and the subsidiary repays the IDRs. In this example, the Indonesian rupiahs are lent and repaid in Indonesia and the Swiss francs are lent and repaid in Switzerland, which eliminates the need to use the foreign exchange markets. Thus, exchange market costs are avoided, and both parties obtain a foreign currency for which they have a use.

Currency swaps help companies raise money in an environment in which they are not well known and must therefore pay a higher interest rate than would be available to a local or better-known borrower. For example, a medium-size American company may have need of Swiss francs, but even though it is a sound credit risk, it may be relatively unknown in Switzerland. If it can find, or if a bank or broker can pair it with, a Swiss company that wants U.S. dollars, the swap would work as follows: The American company would borrow U.S. dollars in the United States, where it is well known and can get a low interest rate; the Swiss company would borrow Swiss francs in Switzerland for the same reason. They would then swap the currencies and service each other's loans; that is, the Swiss company would repay the US$ loan, while the American company would repay the CHF loan.

Interest rate swaps have grown on the currency swap model, and they arbitrage the fixed and floating rate markets. Two parties, usually a foreign bank and a U.S. company unknown in the foreign market, exchange interest rates on borrowing made in the foreign market, fixed for floating and floating for fixed. Interest rate swaps allow a company to alter its interest rate exposure.

HEDGES AND SWAPS AS "DERIVATIVES"

Currency value changes are one of the risks against which international business managers use hedges and swaps. These vehicles are sometimes referred to as **derivatives,** contracts whose value changes over time based on the performance of an underlying commodity or financial instrument. The term *derivative* covers standardized, exchange-traded futures and options contracts as well as over-the-counter swaps, options, and other customized instruments.[6] These contracts can be seen to shift risk from a party that does not want to bear it to one that does, hoping for a large reward. However, if used unwisely for speculation, derivatives contracts can be as dangerous as the risks against which they are supposed to protect. Investor Warren Buffett called them "financial weapons of mass destruction."[7] One of the most notorious derivatives disasters occurred in the early 1990s when Nick Leeson, a manager in the futures trading market at Barings Bank, the oldest investment bank in the United Kingdom, made unauthorized speculative trades in his employer's account.

Leeson's trades were initially profitable, so the question of their authorization did not arise, interestingly enough. When his trading resulted in losses, he used the banks' error account to

In the 2005 AACSB international publication *Why Management Education Matters,* the authors defended the economic value of the MBA degree and stated that the average compensation for MBAs had increased from $56,000 to $387,600 over the 10-year period from 1992 to 2002. Though this included bonuses and other compensation, holding an MBA has significant economic value when compared to the $43,000 average salary for those holding a nonmanagement college degree. And for international MBAs the nonsalary valued-added benefits of paid international travel and foreign experiences clearly enhance the attractiveness of this additional level of education. So where are the top MBA programs? Here are several to consider, listed in rank order by two publications:

U.S. News & World Report

1. Thunderbird American Graduate School
2. University of South Carolina (Moore)
3. University of Pennsylvania (Wharton)
4. New York University (Stern)
5. Columbia University

Business Week

1. INSEAD (Paris)
2. Queen's University (Ontario)
3. IMD (Switzerland)
4. London Business School

5. University of Toronto
6. Western Ontario University
7. Rotterdam School of Management
8. IESE (Barcelona)
9. HEC (Paris)
10. York University (Toronto)

World Fact: The average American works 46.2 weeks per year, but the French average 40 weeks per year. In many European countries the practice is to take the entire month of July or August off for holiday in addition to other government or local culturally designated holidays.

Culture Cue: In many parts of the world, but primarily in Latin America and Asia, Americans are viewed as working too much and criticized for not spending enough time with family and friends and having little respect for elders.

World Wide Resources:

www.careerdynamo.com

www.princetonreview.com/mba/research/articles/find/internationalDifferences.asp

www.bschool.com/best_b-schools.html

hide them. By the end of 1992, the account's losses were over £2 million, which ballooned to £208 million by the end of 1994. In early January, the day before the Kobe earthquake, Leeson placed a short straddle (a type of short selling) for derivatives in the Singapore and Tokyo stock exchanges, betting that the markets would not move overnight. The Kobe earthquake, on January 17, 1995, sent Asian markets into chaos, and Leeson's investments along with them. Each attempt he made to recover his losses was a riskier bet, and his losses mounted, reaching $1.4 billion, twice the trading capital of Barings. The bank collapsed.

Derivatives are not exactly new—Japanese rice traders, for example, used futures in the 17th century. But derivatives have become much more sophisticated and widely used in recent years. Examples of the vast number of potential applications are derivatives that can be written so that they will pay out if temperatures rise above a certain figure, which could be a boon for an electric utility in the summer, or if snowfall during the winter is lower than expected, which could help a ski resort. The gross market value of global OTC derivative contracts has soared. The combined financial markets and OTC derivatives total for 2004 recorded by the Bank for International Settlements was $273 trillion. The total market for OTC derivatives recorded by the Bank for International Settlements in the fourth quarter of 2005 was $344 trillion.

Credit default swaps (CDSs), an exotic derivative less than a decade ago, have become one of the key building blocks of the bond and loan markets. CDSs appeal to bankers because they can reduce their exposure to a particular client without the client becoming aware that the loan has in effect been sold. Admitting that a loan has been syndicated to other institutions can be damaging to the client relationship. Banks are the main buyers of CDS cover, while insurers are the main sellers. As the market has developed, CDSs have become tradable securities in their own right.[8]

A logical question at this point might be, "Are derivatives safe?" The short answer is that they are risk-management tools. Used properly, they can be remarkably effective; firms and institutions of all sorts use them to take or limit risks in ways that were not possible until recently. Risk management is a tricky, three-stage process, conceptually simple but in implementation quite complex:

- Identify where the risks lie.

- Design an appropriate strategy for managing them.

- Select the right tools to execute the strategy.

The implementation of their risk strategy may become too complex for many managers. Just as it is uneconomical and dangerous for the executives of most firms to identify and solve all their legal problems, it may be that many firms need outsiders' help in devising and executing risk-management strategies. As long as the firms' managers keep control of basic decisions, it may be best to leave the execution of hedging strategy and the final choice of instruments to outside experts.

NETWORKING TO FIND PARTNERS

How do financial managers learn about potential partners for swaps, parallel loans, and other derivatives? In many cases, their international banks are the answer. In an increasing number of instances, they are finding partners at risk-management meetings such as the Risk Management Conference. These conferences are sponsored by publications such as the *Financial Times, Euromoney,* the *Asian Wall Street Journal,* and *Business International* and by international financial houses. At such meetings, financial executives meet their counterparts from other MNCs as well as people representing banks, other financial organizations, and international agencies such as the World Bank and regional development banks. Increasingly, such networking provides the partners they need to protect their organizations and/or profit using derivatives contracts.

Our discussion so far has assumed that money is playing a role in the exchange. There are situations in which countries do not have the foreign currency to pay for imports. In such cases, sales without money are an option.

Sales without Money

A number of countries desire goods and products for which they do not have the convertible currency to pay. That has not prevented efforts by many suppliers to sell to them anyway. Such countries are usually less developed and poor. There are two main approaches to non-monetary trade, countertrade and industrial cooperation.

COUNTERTRADE

countertrade
The trade of goods or services for other goods or services

Countertrade is the trade of goods and services for other goods and services. In the international environment, it often involves the substitution of developing country goods for foreign exchange so that purchases from the developed country can be completed. Countertrade usually involves two basic contracts, one for the purchase of developed country products or services and one for the purchase of developing country products. Six modifications of countertrade are counterpurchase, compensation, barter, switch, offset, and clearing account arrangements. These contracts may be relatively simple, involving only two countries or companies, or quite complex, calling for a number of countries, companies, currencies, and contracts.

counterpurchase
Countertrade in which the goods supplied do not rely on the goods imported

In **counterpurchase,** the goods supplied by the developing country do not rely on the goods or products imported from the developed country. An example of counterpurchase is PepsiCo's arrangement with Russia, to which PepsiCo sells the concentrate for Pepsi-Cola, which is then bottled and sold in that country. In exchange, in lieu of money, PepsiCo has exclusive rights to export Russian vodka for sale in the West. In 1990, the two parties renewed and expanded their agreement, increasing the amounts of Pepsi-Cola and vodka to be sold and adding a new element to account for an excess of Pepsi-Cola demand in Russia over the demand for Russian vodka in the West. PepsiCo has also committed itself to buying at least 10 Russian-built freighters and tankers. PepsiCo intends to lease them on the world market through a Norwegian partner.

In **compensation** transactions, the developing country makes payment in products produced by use of developed country equipment. These products are shipped to the developed country in payment for the equipment. Dresser Industries has a compensation agreement with Poland for tractors. Poland is paying with tractors and other machines that Dresser then markets.

Barter is an ancient form of commerce and the simplest sort of countertrade. The developing country sends products to the developed country that are equal in value to the products delivered by the developed country to the developing country.

Counterpurchase agreements helped PepsiCo enter the Eastern European market. As a result, the company continues to grow and expand its operations in that region. For example, this PepsiCo truck is one of a fleet of 70 vehicles based in Warsaw, Poland.

Switch trading developed to deal with the problem of there being no market in the developed country for the developing country's goods. When a third party is brought in to dispose of these products, we have switch trading.

Offset occurs when the importing nation requires that a portion of the materials, components, or subassemblies of a product be procured in its local market. The exporter may set up a parts manufacturing and assembly facility in the importing country.

Clearing account arrangements are used to facilitate the exchange of products over a specified time period. When the period ends, any balance outstanding must be cleared by the purchase of additional goods or settled by a cash payment. The bank or broker acts as an intermediary to facilitate settlement of the clearing accounts by finding markets for counter-purchased goods or by converting goods or cash payments into products desired by the country with a surplus.

Frequently, countertrade agreements and their executions are not reported publicly. Indeed, the parties often prefer privacy and confidentiality for competitive reasons and to avoid setting precedents for future deals. Therefore, estimates of the extent of countertrade vary widely. The U.S. Commerce Department and the United Nations estimate that between 10 and 20 percent of world trade is now subject to some form of countertrade and that the proportion is growing.[9] In addition to countertrade, industrial cooperation is another approach to trade without—or with less—money.

INDUSTRIAL COOPERATION

Industrial cooperation, which developing countries favor, requires long-term relationships, with part or all of the production being done in the developing country. A portion of the products are sold in the developing country or in other developing countries. We have identified five methods used in industrial cooperation:

1. *Joint venture:* Two or more companies or state agencies combine assets to form a new and distinct economic entity, and they share management, profits, and losses.

2. *Coproduction and specialization:* The factory in the developing country produces certain agreed-on components of a product, while a company in the developed country produces the other components. The product is then assembled at both locations for their respective markets.

3. *Subcontracting:* The developing country factory manufactures a product according to specifications of the developed country company and delivers the product to the developed country company, which then markets it.

4. *Licensing:* The developing country and developed country parties enter into a license agreement whereby the developing country enterprise uses developed country technology to manufacture a product. The developed country company is paid a license royalty fee in money or in product. The developing country usually prefers to pay in product.

compensation
Countertrade in which the developing country makes payment in products produced by use of developed country equipment.

barter
A direct exchange of goods or services for goods or services without the use of money

switch trading
The use of a third party to market products received in countertrade

offset
Trade arrangement that requires that a portion of the inputs be supplied by the receiving country

clearing account arrangement
A process to settle a trading account within a specified time

industrial cooperation
An exporter's commitment to a longer-term relationship than that in a simple export sale, in which some of the production occurs in the receiving country

5. *Turnkey plants:* The developed country party is responsible for building the entire plant, starting it, training developing country personnel, and turning over the keys to the developing country party. The developing country will pay in products of the new plant.

Two threads run through countertrade and industrial cooperation. The first is that the developing country does not have enough hard, convertible currency to buy what it wants from the developed country. That leads to the second thread, which is the effort of the developing country to substitute goods for currency.

Taxation and Transfer Pricing

income tax
Direct tax levied on earnings

value-added tax (VAT)
Indirect tax collected from the parties as they add value to the product

withholding tax
Indirect tax paid by the payor, usually on passive income

branch
Legal extension of the parent company

subsidiary
Separate legal entity owned by the parent company

transfer price
The cost of intracompany sales of goods or services

In Chapter 11, we discussed taxation as a financial force and outlined three major types of taxation that governments around the world use—income tax, value-added tax, and withholding tax. **Income tax** is a direct tax levied on earnings. **Value-added tax (VAT)** is an indirect tax, in that the tax authority collects it from the person or firm that adds value during the production and marketing process, not from the owner of the item taxed. The ultimate user of the product pays the full amount of tax that is rebated to the others in the value chain. Thus, the government is collecting the tax on the value added in the process. The **withholding tax** is also an indirect tax, in that it is paid not by the person whose labor generates the income but by the business that makes the payment for the labor. Usually the withholding tax is levied on passive income such as royalties, dividends, and interest. Governments follow two approaches to the jurisdiction of their taxes, either worldwide or territorial. A worldwide approach is to tax residents of the country on their worldwide income. The United States follows a policy of worldwide taxation, and it can be argued convincingly that, despite tax treaties, such taxation put U.S. firms operating foreign subsidiaries at a disadvantage compared with their foreign domestic competitors.[10] A territorial taxation policy taxes income earned within the nation's borders. There are tax credits, based on treaties that reduce or eliminate double taxation for U.S. residents and companies, as long as the foreign tax liability is less than the U.S. equivalent would be.

How the foreign operations of a company are organized is key to its U.S. tax liability on foreign earnings. If the operation is a **branch,** that is, an extension of the parent company, not a separate legal entity incorporated in the foreign country, its losses may be deducted by the parent company from its U.S. taxable income. If the foreign entity is a **subsidiary,** that is, a separate legal entity incorporated in the foreign country, its ownership by the MNC may be minority, that is, between 10 and 50 percent. Such minority company income, both active and passive, is taxed only when it is remitted to the parent company. If the foreign subsidiary is actually controlled by the parent company, with more than 50 percent ownership, it is known as a *controlled foreign corporation (CFC)* and its active income is taxed in the United States when that income is remitted to the parent company but its passive income (royalties, licensing fees, dividends, service fees) is taxed as it occurs. When deciding where to locate and how to structure a foreign operation, MNC managers would want to review the tax rates of possible locations and also consider what legal form their operations should take. Often, start-ups have several years of losses, so establishment of a branch rather than a subsidiary might generate valuable losses, from a tax point of view, for the parent company.

Transfer pricing is another way for MNCs to reduce their tax liability. The **transfer price** is the bookkeeping cost of goods transferred from one unit of a business (subsidiary or division) to another in another country or tax jurisdiction. For example, a high transfer price on goods coming to the parent from a foreign subsidiary will move profits from the parent to the subsidiary side of the MNC. This result may be used to shift the impact of tax rates from the parent company's home country to that of the subsidiary. This sort of move makes sense if the tax rate in the home country is higher than that in the subsidiary's country. Conversely, the tax impact could be shifted to the home country from the subsidiary. One caveat is that the transfer price can never be lower than the cost of the transferred product's inputs. If this were to happen, the MNC would be open to charges of dumping. Transfer pricing has many uses because it allows an MNC to adjust the amount of profit its individual businesses are showing.

International Accounting

The purpose of accounting in all countries is to provide managers with financial data for use in their decision making and to provide external constituencies (investors, governments, lenders, suppliers, etc.) the quantitative information they seek to inform their decisions. Also, it provides data governments need to levy taxes. The idea of what constitutes useful data, separate from their reliability, varies from country to country. For example, in Germany, the primary users of financial information historically have been creditors, so accounting focuses on the balance sheet, which contains information about the company's assets. By contrast, in the United States, investors are major users of financial information, and they look to the income statement as a sign of the company's future.[11] An international company has to address transactions in foreign currencies, a situation that has an obvious impact on the practice of accounting. But the differences do not end there. Different needs of varying constituencies in different countries have led to large variations in financial statements across the globe. That is to say, culture plays a significant role in the practice of accounting. Sidney Gray has applied Geert Hofstede's work on cultural dimensions, explained in Chapter 6, to the practice of accounting. In this section, we examine both transactions in foreign currencies and the role of culture in accounting, and then we go on to look at possible convergence among these various approaches.

ACCOUNTING AND FOREIGN CURRENCY

There are two points at which operating in a foreign currency raises issues from an accounting perspective: when transactions are made in foreign currencies and when branches and subsidiaries operate in foreign currencies and their results need to be made a part of the parent company's financial reports. We look first at transactions and then at translation and consolidation, the two processes involved in merging subsidiary financial results with those of the parent company.

When the U.S.-based company has foreign currency–based transactions such as sales, purchases, and loans (made and taken), they need to be recorded as revenues, expenses, assets, or liabilities. Suppose the transaction is a purchase of Swiss watches in Geneva for 25,000 Swiss francs (CHFs). How is this handled when the company books are prepared in U.S. dollars? The transaction is entered in dollars at the exchange rate at purchase. Let's say it's $1.224/CHF. The purchase entry would be $30,600. Accounts payable would also be $30,600, and the exchange rate notation "CHF 25,000 @ $1.224" would be made. Now, if the payment is immediate or stipulated in US$, that would be fine. But if the transaction is stipulated in CHF and if there is a time lag and the exchange rate moves, the underlying dollar value of the purchase would change. Let's say the exchange rate moves to $1.26/CHF at the 60-day point, when the payable is due. Now the U.S. company has to pay $31,500. The $900 difference constitutes a foreign exchange loss. In this case, the journal entries would remain the same, and the loss (or gain) would be recorded in the income statement. This process is described by FASB 52, which requires that companies record foreign currency–based transactions at the spot rate at the time of the transaction. Any gains or losses from changes in exchange rates for items carried as payables or receivables are posted in the income statement.

Now to our second concern about foreign currencies in accounting operations. When a U.S. MNC's foreign subsidiary reports results, these results need to be translated into the parent company's operating currency, dollars, and made to conform to U.S. GAAP. Then these various results are aggregated into one financial report. This process is called **consolidation**. The two basic approaches to translation, the current rate method and the temporal method, were described above in our discussion of foreign currency translation risk. The objective of these two methods is to accurately reflect business results.

Choice of translation method depends on the **functional currency** of the foreign operation. The functional currency is the primary currency of the operation, the currency in which cash flows, pricing, expenses, and financing are denominated. If the functional currency is the local one, the current rate method must be used. If the functional currency is that of the parent company, the temporal method must be used. The current rate method translates assets at the spot rate on the day the balance sheet is prepared. The income statement is translated at an average exchange rate for the reporting period. Owner's equity is translated at the rates in

consolidation
The process of translating subsidiary results and aggregating them into one financial report

functional currency
The primary currency of a business

effect when the stock was issued and when retained earnings were posted. With the temporal method, monetary assets are translated at the spot rate. Fixed assets are translated at their acquisition exchange rates. The income statement items are translated at the average rate for the period, except that cost of goods sold and depreciation are translated at their historic rates.

In inflationary economies, you can imagine that translation presents special problems. If the local currency is the functional currency, fixed assets could disappear if the current rate method were used for translation. This phenomenon has been called the "disappearing plant." To address the translation issues presented by inflationary economies, FASB 52 mandates that the translation be performed as if the functional currency were the reporting currency, using the temporal method. That way, fixed assets and other large, important accounts will not lose value compared to their book value.

ACCOUNTING AND CULTURE

We know that accounting follows different patterns in different parts of the world. Gray suggests that differences in accounting measurement and disclosure practices, that is, how companies value assets and what information companies provide, are influenced by culture. His study classified countries on two dimensions, secrecy-transparency and optimism-conservatism. Figure 21.3 summarizes this classification.[12]

The dimension of secrecy-transparency measures the degree to which companies disclose information to the public. As Figure 21.3 suggests, Germany, Japan, and Switzerland tend to value secrecy or privacy over transparency. In the United Kingdom and the United States, there is more disclosure and less privacy. The dimension of optimism-conservatism measures the degree to which a company is cautious in its valuing of assets and measuring of income. Accounting reports in countries with more conservative asset-valuing approaches tend to understate assets and income, while those in countries whose asset-valuing approach is more optimistic tend toward overstatement. In France, Germany, and Japan, public companies' capital structure tends to depend more on debt rather than equity, with banks being a major source of the debt. Banks are concerned with liquidity. A conservative statement of profits may reduce tax exposure and dividend payouts, contributing to cash reserves that can be

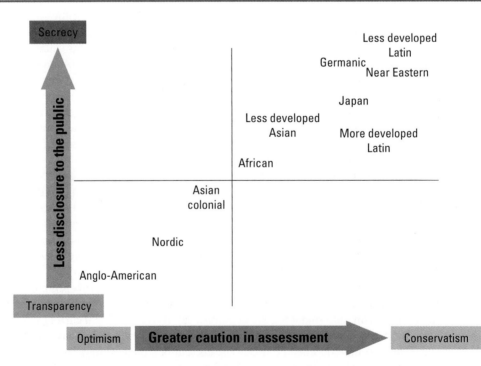

FIGURE 21.3

Cultural Differences in Measurement and Disclosure for Accounting Systems

Source: Adapted from Lee Radebaugh and Sidney J. Gray, *Accounting and Multinational Enterprises*, 5th Edition (New York: John Wiley & Sons, 2002).

tapped for debt service. On the optimism measure, U.S. and, in a more restrained way, U.K. companies want to show impressive earnings that will attract investors.

Until 2005, there were considerable differences in reporting standards across selected countries. With the income statement, called the *profit and loss account (P&L)* in the United Kingdom, the basic understanding of what constituted income varied considerably. For example, how to measure inventory differed, as did the treatment of goodwill and depreciation methods for property and equipment. In Germany, income was declared only when a contract was completed, while in the United Kingdom and Japan, a percentage completion method was used, as in the United States.

CONVERGENCE OF ACCOUNTING STANDARDS

Largely due to globalization and MNCs' desires to list stock in foreign markets to tap into their potential as a source of shareholders, a process known as *cross-listing,* there is a growing movement toward convergence of accounting standards. Such harmonization requires long and careful negotiation. The body that establishes accounting standards in the United States is a private organization, the Financial Accounting Standards Board (FASB). The more international body is the International Accounting Standards Board (IASB), whose predecessor organization was founded in 1973 by a multilateral effort among accounting bodies in Australia, Canada, France, Germany, Japan, Mexico, the Netherlands, the United Kingdom, Ireland, and the United States. In 2002, both FASB and IASB agreed in principle on harmonization of standards and convergence. The FASB's standards are the U.S. Generally Accepted Accounting Principles (U.S.GAAP), while the IASB's standards are the International Financial Reporting Standards (IFRS). Significant progress has been made on this commitment by a negotiating group, with a target date of 2009. With so many important and heavily detailed aspects of specific standards to be reconciled, the progress toward convergence is impressive.

In the meantime, the EU Parliament and the Council of Europe decided to require IASB standards for financial reporting as of June 15, 2005, for public businesses unless they have a small business exemption, and as of December 15, 2005, for small businesses. Australia and New Zealand have joined the EU in this step forward. The transition seems to have gone smoothly. Presently there are over 75 countries that require public companies to list using IFRS. That represents a broad-based negotiation process by many countries in the world and creates pressure for FASB to converge. The Security and Exchange Commission has indicated that when it is satisfied that IASB standards are reliable, it will follow them. So there is an increasing tilt toward IASB. Deloitte and Touche partner D. J. Gannon has called the U.S. acceptance of IFRS "inevitable."[13] The U.S. market is the only major market that follows U.S. GAAP at this point.[14] With convergence, financial markets around the world will become more integrated because the statements will be comparable.

In 2002, the U.S. Congress passed the Sarbanes-Oxley Act, largely as a result of a series of corporate scandals in which accounting practices were at the center. Sarbanes-Oxley also provides motivation for the private FASB to harmonize with IASB. It allocated the Security and Exchange Commission responsibility for recognizing the standard setter.[15] Table 21.1 summarizes the progress IFRS has made in its move toward becoming the world standard.

TRIPLE-BOTTOM-LINE ACCOUNTING

Increasingly, companies have made efforts to report on their environmental, social, and financial results. Such a reporting framework has been termed **triple bottom line (3BL),** a term credited to John Elkington in his 1997 book, *Cannibals with Forks: The Triple Bottom Line of 21st Century Business.*[16] The book's argument is that capitalism can become civilized; capitalists can be taught to eat with forks, due to consumer pressure and other social forces. Corporate capitalism can become sustainable capitalism. Elkington argues that there are seven drivers of this transformation: markets, values, transparency, life-cycle technology, partnerships, time, and corporate governance. This approach supports sustainability, which we discussed in Chapter 7, and corporate social reform (CSR). As we have seen in our earlier discussion of sustainability, it is a systems concept that has three major aspects: the

triple bottom line (3BL)

A results or impact report on the environmental, social, and financial impacts of the business

Required IFRS	Europe/Central Asia		Americas	Asia-Pacific	Africa/Middle East
	Armenia	Latvia	Bahamas	Australia	Egypt
	Austria	Lithuania	Barbados	Brunei	Jordan
	Bangladesh	Luxembourg	Costa Rica	Nepal	Kenya
	Belgium	Macedonia	Dominican Republic	Singapore	Kuwait
	Bulgaria	Malta	Ecuador	Taiwan	Malawi
	Croatia	Netherlands	Guyana		Mauritius
	Cyprus	Norway	Haiti		Oman
	Czech Republic	Poland	Honduras		Tunesia
	Denmark	Portugal	Jamaica		
	Estonia	Romania	Panama		
	Finland	Russia	Papua New Guinea		
	France	Slovakia	Peru		
	Georgia	Slovenia	Trinidad & Tobago		
	Germany	Spain			
	Greece	Sweden			
	Hungary	Switzerland			
	Ireland	Tajikistan			
	Italy	Ukraine			
	Kyrgystan	United Kingdom			
Converging with IFRS	Moldova		Argentina	New Zealand	Iran
	Uzbekistan		Brazil	China/Hong Kong	Israel
			Canada	India	Pakistan
			Cayman Islands	Indonesia	South Africa
			Chile	Japan	Zimbabwe
			Guatemala	Malaysia	
			Mexico	Philippines	
			United States	South Korea	
			Uruguay	Thailand	
			Venezuela		

environmental or ecological, the social, and the economic. Presently we measure at the economic level, and where required by government or social pressure, we measure at the environmental level, as with emission controls and hazardous waste, and at the social level, as with the Equal Employment Opportunity Commission's enforcement of the federal civil rights laws. Yet even in the environmental and social areas, we tend to know more about the problems—what is reported in the media—than about the company-level thinking on these important issues. Companies should measure and make public the environmental and social effects of their decisions. That is, in summary, the major argument for 3BL.

The major argument against 3BL is neither a substantive disagreement with the desirability of ecologically responsible business practices that support sustainability nor a disagreement with the idea of business being socially responsible; rather, it is the claim that measurement will not get us closer to the desired state. Wayne Norman and Chris MacDonald argue that social performance and environmental impact cannot be objectively measured in ways that are comparable to our economic measurements of a firm's activities.[17] They point out that the rhetoric may be appealing but no widely implementable framework exists for measuring a company's performance in environmental and social areas, although there are high levels of consulting in these areas. In fact, they suggest that a focus on the measurement of these activities may well detract from efforts to figure out ways to combine sustainability and social responsibility with positive economic results, which is a more difficult challenge. There is a parallel with codes of ethics: What matters is what a

Sarbanes-Oxley Not a Good Export

Harvey Pitt, former chairman of the SEC (2001–2003), has lashed out at the U.S. Congress for its required export of a hastily written and poorly conceptualized law, the Sarbanes-Oxley Act (SOX), enacted in the wake of the corporate scandals of 2001. Its "one size-fits-all" approach to regulation stifles innovation, creativity, risk taking, and competitiveness. Worse, Pitt says, "Congress's exportation of SOX's standards has created huge difficulties for multinational companies and produced scorn for U.S. standards." He suggests that the scorn is justified, that there are better standards out there. What he characterizes as "American geocentrism" has resulted in the loss of foreign listings on U.S. exchanges and the movement of IPOs to non-U.S. sites.

Faced with evidence that they are increasingly irrelevant in the global economy, U.S. stock exchanges have been out on the market, trying to buy foreign exchanges. This means that the SOX requirements, in addition to applying to any company with a U.S. listing, will apply to companies listed on U.S.-owned foreign exchanges. For example, if Euronext, a European stock exchange with subsidiaries in Belgium, France, Netherlands, Portugal and the United Kingdom, is U.S.-owned, SOX will impose U.S. regulatory standards across all these subsidiary exchanges. Harvey Pitt argues that this would not be a step in the right direction.

Source: Harvey Pitt, "Sarbanes-Oxley Is an Unhealthy Export," *Financial Times*, June 21, 2006, p. 15.

company actually does, not whether a code of ethics is hanging on the wall of every office. The poster is rhetoric. Posting it is not ethical action. Decisions in the field that have to do with implementation are what matter, as well as how the organization's members understand the company's values and what those values say about their duties to stakeholders.

International Finance Center

The increasing complexity of global financing, combined with increasing global competition, has encouraged MNCs to pay more attention to financial management, as mentioned earlier in "An Integrated Approach to Risk." International financial management has become increasingly different from domestic financial management, and in several MNCs the centralized finance operation has become a profit center and is no longer merely a service. Some of the new developments are (1) floating exchange rates, whose fluctuations are sometimes volatile, (2) growth in the number of capital and foreign exchange markets where an MNC can shop for lower interest costs and better currency rates, (3) different and changing inflation rates from country to country, (4) advances in electronic cash management systems, (5) realization by financial managers that through innovative management of temporarily idle cash balances of the MNC units, they can increase yields and the enterprise's profit, and (6) the explosive growth of the use of derivatives to protect against commodity, currency, interest rate, and other risks. As a result, many MNCs have established international finance centers. Such operations can balance and hedge currency exposures, tap capital markets, manage inflation rate risk, manage cash management technological innovation, manage derivatives use, handle internal and external invoicing, help a weak-currency affiliate, and strengthen affiliate evaluation and reporting systems.

Summary

Explain capital structure choices and their potential impact on the MNC.

The firm raises capital through its retained earnings, and then, externally, through either equity, the issuing of shares, or debt (leveraging). Firms may choose to issue stocks in foreign markets, in part to tap into a broader investor pool, which can raise the stock price and reduce the cost of capital. Such local issues also may have a significant marketing advantage. Debt markets

are the other source of capital for the firm, and increasingly the tendency is to tap local markets first. Offshore financial centers, where taxation is low and banking regulations are slim, are also a source of debt financing. Debt financing is thought to be less expensive that equity financing, but local practices and taxation are some of the factors that are considered in making decisions about the capital structure of the firm.

Describe the process of multilateral netting and what its contribution is to cash flow management.

Multilateral netting is a centralized approach through which subsidiaries transfer their net cash flows within the company to a cash center that disperses cash to net receivers. It leads to cost savings.

Describe the importance of leading and lagging in cash flow management.

Leading and lagging involve the timing of payments. A lead approach is to collect receivables early when the foreign currency is expected to weaken, and fund payables early when the foreign currency is expected to strengthen. A lag approach is to collect receivables late when the currency is expected to strengthen, and fund payables late when the currency is expected to weaken. It is a helpful technique when there are expectations that host governments may block fund transfers.

Categorize foreign exchange risks into transaction exposure, translation exposure, and economic exposure.

Transaction exposure occurs when the firm has transactions denominated in a foreign currency. The exposure is due to currency exchange rate fluctuations between the time the commitment is made and when it is payable.

Translation exposure occurs when subsidiary financial statements are consolidated at the corporate level for the companywide financial reports. Since the foreign subsidiaries operate in nondollar currencies, there is a need to translate subsidiary financial reports to the parent company's currency during the corporate consolidation process.

Economic exposure is at the operations level and results from exchange rate changes on projected cash flows. Unlike transaction exposure, which addresses the individual transaction, economic exposure is firmwide and long-term.

Describe the basic idea of a swap transaction and its various applications.

Swaps invlove matching an exposure with a forward transaction. Spot swaps are at the spot exchange rate at a stipulated time in the future, and forward market swaps are at a forward market rate. Many financial instruments may be matched in these swaps, including parallel loans, bank swaps, and currency swaps.

Explain a currency swap contract and its usefulness to the financial manager.

A currency swap is used to raise money in an environment in which the company raising the funds is not well known. The company finds a local partner, and then each company borrows in its home market at preferred rates. They then swap the loans. This is done to reduce interest rate costs.

Recognize the usefulness and dangers of using derivatives.

Derivatives are contracts whose value changes over time based on the performance of an underlying commodity or financial instrument. The term *derivative* covers standardized, exchange-traded futures and options contracts as well as over-the-counter swaps, options, and other customized instruments.[18] These contracts can be seen to shift risk from a party that does not want to bear it to one that does, hoping for a large reward. Used unwisely for speculation, derivatives contracts can be as dangerous as the risks against which they are supposed to protect.

Explain the role of and approaches to sales without money.

Non-monetary trade may be a way for countries that don't have hard currency to import goods. There are two main approaches to non-monetary trade, countertrade and industrial cooperation. Countertrade usually involves two basic contracts, one for the purchase of developed country products or services and one for the purchase of developing country products. Industrial cooperation involves long-term relationships, including local production, with part or all of the output sold in the host country.

Identify the major challenges faced in international accounting.

International accounting has to address transactions in foreign currencies, In addition, different needs by varying constituencies in different countries have led to large variations in financial statements across the globe. These cultural differences also have to be bridged in international accounting.

Describe the international accounting standards' convergence process and its importance.

The body that establishes accounting standards in the U.S. is the private organization, the Financial Accounting Standards Board (FASB). The more international body is the International Accounting Standards Board (IASB). The FASB's standards are the U.S. Generally Accepted Accounting Principles (U.S. GAAP), while the IASB's standards are the International Financial Reporting Standards (IFRS). Significant progress has been made towards convergence by a negotiating group, with a target date of 2009. Convergence is important for further integration of global markets.

Key Words

American depository receipt (ADR) (p. 568)

offshore financial center (p. 568)

multilateral netting (p. 571)

blocked funds (p. 572)

leading and lagging (p. 572

transaction exposure (p. 572)

hedging (p. 573)

forward market hedge (p. 573)

currency option hedge (p. 573)

money market hedge (p. 573)

swap contract (p. 573)

translation exposure (p. 574)

current rate method (p. 574)

temporal method (p. 574)

economic exposure (p. 574)

spot and forward market swaps (p. 575)

parallel loans (p. 575)

Questions

1. You are establishing your first overseas subsidiary. As you consider how to capitalize your business, what are your concerns about using the local and home country debt and equity markets?

2. A local exporter has signed a sales contract that specifies payment of $3 million in Saudi riyals in six months. Discuss the hedge options you would advise the exporter to consider.

3. Why would an MNC set up a centralized cash management operation?

4. What are the dangers associated with derivatives contracts?

5. What are the differences between transaction and translation exposure? Can you hedge for both simultaneously?

6. You want to sell into a high-inflation economy that has a strong agricultural sector. What types of countertrade arrangements might you explore?

7. The cultural analysis of accounting Gray presents suggests that transparency is the result of a cultural characteristic of some countries and secrecy of others. Could the same attributes be explained by the hypothesis that transparent cultures are less trusting and need the transparency to satisfy their cultural distrust? What do you think?

8. How might Sarbanes-Oxley influence the progress of the convergence of international accounting standards?

9. How might triple-bottom-line accounting improve the social and environmental behavior of companies?

10. What is your assessment of the movement pushing for 3BL? Explain your thinking.

Research Task

globalEDGE   globalEDGE.msu.edu

Use the globalEDGE site (http://globalEDGE.msu.edu/) to complete the following exercises:

1. The globalEDGE site offers a Country Comparison tool through its Country Insights section that allows for comparing countries based on statistical indicators. Utilize this tool to identify in which of the following countries the accounting historic cost principle cannot provide accurate results: Argentina, Bulgaria, Ecuador, Indonesia, Latvia, Malaysia, Mexico, Romania, Russia, and Senegal. Utilize the "rank countries"

tool to identify other countries in which the historic cost principle would not provide valid results.

2. Deloitte Touche Tohmatsu hosts an *International Accounting Standards* (IAS) Web page that provides information and guidelines regarding accounting guidelines approved by IASC. Locate the Web site, go to the section on standards, and prepare a short description of the international accounting standards for recording inventory levels.

Dealing with Transaction Risk in a Yuan Contract   Minicase 21.1

You are the finance manager of an American multinational that has sold US$6 million of your high-tech product to a Chinese importer. Because of stiff competition for the contract against other American and European companies, you agreed that the negotiators could accept payment in yuan. This concession may have won your company the contract.

The sales contract calls for the Chinese importer to make three equal payments at 6, 12 and 18 months from the date of delivery. Your plan is to translate the yuan to dollars on their receipt; your company has no operations in China and no need for the currency. How could you cover your transaction exposure?

In 1984, Guy Laliberté left his home in Canada to make his way across Europe as a circus performer. There he and other artists performed in the street. The troupe was called Cirque du Soleil—"circus of the sun." It started with a simple dream: a group of young artists getting together to entertain audiences, see the world, and have fun doing it.[1] Laliberté and company quickly found that their entertainment form without words—stilt-walking, juggling, music, and fire breathing—transcended all barriers of language and culture. Though he understood that an entertainer could bring the exotic to every corner of the world, Laliberté did not envision the scope to which his Cirque du Soleil would succeed. Today Cirque performs nine permanent shows, such as *Algeria,* which is touring Japan, and *Mystere, O,* and *ZUMANITY,* all with permanent homes at the MGM Mirage resorts in Las Vegas. In 20 years of live performances, 44 million people have seen a Cirque show.[2] Despite a long-term decline in the circus industry, Cirque has increased revenue 22-fold over the last 10 years.[3]

Cirque du Soleil is a family of more than 600 individuals from 40 different countries. Each of Cirque's 3,000 employees is encouraged to make contributions to the group. This input has resulted in rich, deep performances and expansion into alternative media outlets such as music, books, television, Web sites, and merchandising. The company's diversity ensures that every show reflects many different cultural influences. Many different markets will have an exotic experience at a Cirque show, regardless of which show is playing where. Cirque does target specific markets with products designed to engage a particular audience. Yet Cirque has little need to adapt its product to new markets; the product is already a blend of global influences. The result is a presentation of acrobatic arts and traditional, live circus with an almost indescribable freshness and beauty.

Cirque du Soleil's commitment to excellence and innovation transcends cultural differences and the limits of many modern media. Its intense popularity has made Cirque both the global standard of live entertainment and the place for talented individuals from around the world to perfect their talents. The extent of the diversity, however, does pose a host of unique challenges. Every employee must be well versed in various forms and styles. To foster cultural enrichment, Cirque purchases and shares a large collection of art with employees and gives them tickets to different events and shows.

The performers work in the most grueling and intimate situations, with their lives depending on one another. The astounding spectacles they create on stage result from hours of planning, practice, and painstaking attention to detail among artists from diverse cultures who speak 25 different languages. Sensitivity, compromise, and hunger for new experiences are prerequisites for success at Cirque. The organization has learned the art of sensitivity and compromise in its recruiting. Cirque du Soleil has had a presence in the Olympics for a decade. It works closely with coaches and teams to help athletes consider a career with Cirque *after* their competitive years are over, rather than luring talent away from countries that have made huge investments in athletes. This practice has given Cirque a huge advantage in the athletic community, a source of great talent from all over the world.

Guy Laliberté has not forgotten his own humble beginnings as a Canadian street performer. Now that Cirque du Soleil has achieved an international presence and incredible success—the group expects to be doing $1 billion in annual gross revenue by 2007—it has chosen to help at-risk youth, especially street kids. Cirque allocates 1 percent of its revenues to outreach programs targeting youth in difficulty, regardless of location in the world.[4] Guy understands that to be successful in a world market, one must be a committed and sensitive neighbor. Cirque's headquarters in Montreal is the center of an urban revitalization project sponsored by Cirque. Community participation and outreach bring the company international goodwill and help Cirque du Soleil transcend many of the difficulties global brands often face when spanning cultures.

Questions for Discussion

1. Why is Cirque du Soleil successful throughout the world? How does the product transcend culture differences between countries?

2. How have the five major drivers of globalization influenced Cirque du Soleil?

3. Why is it important for Cirque du Soleil to be a good corporate citizen? How does the organization strive to fulfill this role?

Sources

1. "Founder's Message," www.cirquedusoleil.com.

2. Mario D'Amico, and Vincent Gagné, "Big Top Television," *Marketing* 109, no. 26 (August 9–August 16, 2004), p. 20.

3. Chan Kim and Renee Mauborgne, "Blue Ocean Strategy," *Harvard Business Review,* October 2004, p. 77.

4. "Social Action," www.cirquedusoleil.com.

In April 2006 when President Hu Jintao of China visited the United States on a four-day business mission, his first stop was Seattle, home to Microsoft, Boeing, and Starbucks. Although these firms rolled out the red carpet for Jintao, his trip was not without controversy. From Capitol Hill to the floor of U.S. factories, many are charging that when it comes to trade, China isn't playing fair.

With 1.3 billion people, China has the largest population in the world. Its economy is exploding with 10 percent economic growth annually. Oil consumption in China is surging, helping to drive up the price on the world market. China now produces more steel than the United States, Japan, and Europe combined, in mills subsidized by interest-free loans, an undervalued currency, and export tax breaks.[1]

As China's economy has grown, so have Western concerns about its undervalued currency; rampant piracy of movies, music, and software; and generous subsidies to attract businesses. U.S. politicians argue that as a result of such practices, Chinese firms are producing goods much cheaper than American companies are, a situation contributing to a $200 million trade imbalance. Chinese officials spurn these accusations, arguing that banks are chasing firms in China to lend them money.[2]

Evidence points to the contrary. Zachary Mottl owns a manufacturing business in Chicago. His revenues have declined 50 percent in the last six years. Competing with the Chinese on price has hurt profits. A bracket Mottl's company makes, for example, sells for $1.10, while the price in China is 41 cents—a price the Chicago firm simply cannot meet. Many experts believe that a significant revaluation of its currency by China would have some impact on the large price discrepancy between China and the United States.

Another contentious issue is piracy. Problems with piracy in China still remain severe and widespread, according to a senior U.S. commerce official.[3] Though laws against piracy exist, China has not been able to enforce them at the local level. As a result, the United States is raising red flags over illegal Chinese copies of software, music, and movies. For instance, 90 percent of the DVDs in China are thought to be illegal; the piracy is costing U.S. producers $2 billion a year. According to Dan Glickman, president of the Motion Picture Association of America, some films are on the street in China at the same time as, or in some cases before, their worldwide release.

Asia expert Derek Mitchell says that going after China on economic grounds is risky, because the country is so important to the U.S. economy. China has long provided the inexpensive labor to produce much of the world's goods. Now it offers foreign sellers the world's largest consumer market. China is a big buyer of all things American. From Wal-Mart to GM to Reebok, U.S. firms have a strong presence there. American exports to China have grown 160 percent in five years.

China is playing another vital role in the U.S. economy as an increasing number of Chinese-branded products make their way to stores abroad. In the past decade, a number of prominent Chinese brands have emerged in China. Many Chinese manufacturers are looking to take their brands global after successfully marketing to more than 1 billion domestic consumers.[4] If they can expand these products to foreign markets, Chinese companies could end up producing the world's most popular brands. Chinese firms have been manufacturing products for well-known firms like Sony and Xerox, but now the Chinese firms are taking their manufacturing expertise and selling products with their own brand names.

Many Chinese brands have arrived in America. Leading Chinese appliance manufacturer Haier has accelerated its push into U.S. markets. Haier already has products in the top 10 U.S. retail chains and more than 240 subsidiaries worldwide, with manufacturing facilities in the United States.[5] Lenovo, the number-one selling PC in China, is also known throughout Asia. In 2006, Lenovo took its first steps toward making a name for itself in the United States when it unveiled a series of notebooks and desktops under the Lenovo brand.[6] Television manufacturer SVA is another Chinese brand looking for American customers with its competitively priced flat-screen TVs at Target and Office Depot. Tsingtao is the number-two Asian beer in the United States, after Japan's Sapporo.[7] Finally, Chinese automobile manufacturer Chery may be heading to America. Chery's best-selling export is a four-door compact priced between $7,000 and $8,000. In 2008 the company hopes to compete globally and export 300,000 to 400,000 cars.[8] Chinese brands are proving they can compete globally.

Questions for Discussion

1. Is China cheating when it comes to international trade? How big a problem is piracy?

2. How dependent is the U.S. economy on China? How far should the United States push China on matters such as currency, piracy, and subsidies?

3. What impact could Chinese brands have on international trade? Do you think brands from China will become as popular as brands from Japan?

Sources

1. Pete Engardio and Catherine Yang, "The Runaway Giant," *BusinessWeek,* April 24, 2006, p. 30.

2. Andrew Browne, "Rapid Economic Growth at Home Adds to Heat on Hu to Adjust Yuan," *The Wall Street Journal,* April 20, 2006, p. A1.

3. Andrew Yeh, "China's Piracy Problems Remain Severe," *FT.com,* September 14, 2005, p. 1.

4. Gordon Orr, "Building Chinese Brands beyond China," *FT.com,* August 25, 2005, p. 1.

5. Laura Heller, "Manufacturers Long for Brand Equity," *Retailing Today,* August 7, 2006, pp. 1–2.

6. Edward F. Moltzen, "Lenovo Takes Off," *CRN,* February 27, 2006, p. 14.

7. Leslie P. Norton, "Let's Lift a Glass to Tsingtao," *Baron's,* June 12, 2006, p. M6.

8. Gordon Fairclough, "China Auto Exports May Roil Rivals," *The Wall Street Journal,* February 16, 2006, p. A2.

 # Chapter 3 Video Case Wal-Mart in China

Chinese cities have been making the dramatic leap from communism to capitalism in the past few decades. A striking example is Shanghai, where one can ride on the world's fastest train and stay in the world's tallest hotel. The "dragonhead" of an industrial boom in the Yangtze River delta, Shanghai transformed its Pudong section in less than 15 years from an economically stagnant semi-rural area to a futuristic financial capital.[1] The state-owned industries that have dominated the city's economy since 1949 are giving way to private enterprises, both local and foreign-owned.

Among the new businesses Shanghai's Pudong area boasts is a Wal-Mart Supercenter, one of 15 stores the retailer opened in China in 2005. Locating in large urban centers, Wal-Mart has enticed throngs of Chinese consumers with its large, clean stores, wide selection, helpful employees, and low, low prices.

Wal-Mart has been operating stores in China since the early 1990s. Its efforts to establish outlets in China were slowed by government regulations that limited foreign retail companies to operating in only a few large cities and required them to offer at least 35 percent of each store to local business partners.[2] In December 2004, the government in Beijing started to allow foreign retailers to invest independently in any Chinese city. Wal-Mart has not rushed to take advantage of the changes in laws governing foreign direct investment, however, and has continued to develop stores with joint venture partners.[3] By mid-2006, Wal-Mart operated 56 stores in China that employed 30,000 people, and it planned to open 20 more stores by year-end and add 150,000 employees over the next five years.

Opening stores in China poses several challenges. In many Chinese cities, the best real estate is controlled by the local government, which may give preference to state-owned retailers. Each supercenter requires hiring and training 500 employees. Wal-Mart has been pressured by the All-China Federation of Trade Unions (ACFTU), a powerful organization closely tied to the Chinese government that wants to establish unions in foreign companies in China. Wal-Mart, which has no unionized stores in the United States, has said that it would work with ACFTU to start grass-roots unions in each of its stores throughout China.[4]

The biggest challenge, according to Wal-Mart's Asia CEO Joe Hatfield, is finding qualified managers.[5] Like most multinational firms today, Wal-Mart looks for local talent to fill management positions. In the mid-1990s, almost all foreign firms' management positions in China were filled by foreigners; now one consulting firm in Beijing says that Chinese workers hold about 70 percent of foreign companies' top positions. Executives at foreign companies in China find that local employees cost less to employ than managers from Western countries and that they have a better understanding of the Chinese market.[6]

In China Wal-Mart has replicated its corporate culture, with its Five Commitments of Merchandising, red shirts for employees, and store pep rallies and cheering. It *has* altered the store offerings to cater to Chinese consumers, who mostly walk to stores and buy small quantities of food every day or two. While offering a broad mixture of food and general merchandise as usual, supercenters in China devote a large portion of floor space to food, especially perishable products. Shoppers can select from a vast array of produce and live grass fish, turtles, lobsters, and bullfrogs. The favorite item in most supercenters is the freshly prepared lunch of two meats, two vegetables, rice, and a cup of hot soup—all for less than $1.[7]

The stores carry many U.S. brands, such as Crest toothpaste, Clairol shampoo, Oreos, and Gatorade, but almost all the merchandise is made in China. China-based suppliers each year provide $18 billion of merchandise, mostly toys, footwear, Christmas decorations, and sporting equipment. Wal-Mart accounts for 3 percent of China's total exports; if it were a country, it would be China's sixth-largest export market.[8]

Wal-Mart executives have long seen China, with its population of 1.3 billion, as the best prospect for long-term global growth. One executive said China is the one place in the world where Wal-Mart could replicate the success it has achieved in the United States.[9] Wal-Mart operates more than 2,000 stores outside the United States, and international sales amount to 20 percent of the company's overall sales of $285 billion from roughly 5,700 stores. While the company's China stores now amount to less than 2 percent of its international sales, analysts have predicted that Wal-Mart could gain $20 billion in sales a year by gaining just 3 percent of the Chinese retail market.[10] It faces competition in China from French retailer Carrefour SA, which operates 61 hypermarkets and eight supermarkets there. China's largest foreign retailer, Carrefour arrived in China a year later than Wal-Mart but expanded more quickly, often avoiding central government restrictions by making alliances with local governments. Carrefour executives view local retailers as having the advantage in a large economy like China's, but they say they will match Wal-Mart's expansion in China store for store.[11]

Questions for Discussion

1. What were some of the reasons behind Wal-Mart's entry into the Chinese retail market?

2. What advantages has Wal-Mart gained by forming joint partnerships with Chinese developers?

3. Why do you think Wal-Mart sees China as its best bet for repeating the success it has achieved in America?

Sources

1. "Dragonhead Dreams," *The Economist,* January 7, 2006, p. 56.

2. Clay Chandler, "The Great Wal-Mart of China," *Fortune,* July 25, 2005, p. 104.

3. Mike Troy, "Can Presence in China Really Double by 2006?" *DSN Retailing Today,* August 8, 2005, p. 22.

4. Mei Fong, "Wal-Mart Meets with Officials from China Union," *The Wall Street Journal,* August 10, 2006, p. A2.

5. Chandler, "The Great wal-Mart."

6. "Firms in China Think Globally, Hire Locally," *The Wall Street Journal,* February 27, 2006, p. B1.

7. Chandler, "The Great wal-Mart."

8. Ibid.

9. Ibid.

10. "Wal-Mart Stores Inc.: Retailer Plans to Nearly Double Stores in China by End of 2006," *The Wall Street Journal,* July 26, 2005, p. D7.

11. Chandler, "The Great wal-Mart."

 # Chapter 4 Video Case U.S. Farmers and CAFTA

In the summer of 2005, Congress passed the Central America Free Trade Agreement (CAFTA), one of the most controversial trade pacts in U.S. history.[1] The agreement to open trade between the United States and Costa Rica, the Dominican Republic, El Salvador, Guatemala, Honduras, and Nicaragua continues to be a hot topic in rural America. Proponents of CAFTA argue that the pact will benefit U.S. consumers and businesses as well as improve economic conditions in Central America; critics claim the agreement will result in losses of jobs and production in America.[2]

What farmers think of CAFTA depends on what they produce. Duane Alberts, a fifth-generation corn and dairy farmer in southeastern Minnesota, runs a high-tech operation. He thinks that America produces the best agricultural products in the world and they should be exported as much as possible. That's why he is a strong supporter of liberalizing trade with the Dominican Republic and the five Central American nations. According to Alberts, CAFTA creates the opportunity to have another 44 million consumers of American-produced agricultural goods, whether pork, beef, corn, or others.

Hog farmers, for example, could have a much larger market. Before CAFTA, pork entering Central American countries was subject to import duties as high as 47 percent. Hence, not much pork was exported to the region. Larry Liepold, president of the Minnesota Pork Producers Association, believes that under CAFTA farmers will export a lot more pork. He points out how the pork industry has benefited in the past from other free trade agreements. After the North American Free Trade Agreement (NAFTA) was passed, the number of pigs exported to Mexico rose greatly. The pork industry also benefited from free trade agreements involving Korea, Taiwan, and Australia—a prime example, Leopold says, that free trade agreements are working.

Most American agricultural groups endorsed CAFTA, with the belief that it will allow farmers to sell more of their products outside the United States. One group of farmers, however, has been very vocal in its opposition to CAFTA. Sugar producers are not directly subsidized by the U.S. government as are farmers of most other commodities. Instead, the government sharply limits the import of sugar, which means American farmers don't face competition from abroad and thus can charge higher prices. Some sugar producers think that if import limits are lifted, countries will be able to dump sugar on the American market at far below cost. Sugar beet farmer Mark Olson notes that every other country subsidizes the production of sugar. When a country produces more than it needs, the excess supply gets dumped on the world market below production cost. Olson believes that as efficient as American sugar production is, it can't compete with foreign governments.

Sugar producers see CAFTA as the end of the U.S. sugar industry, which employs 140,000 people. Ninety percent of the sugar processed in America is done in farmer-owned co-ops like the Southern Minnesota Beet Sugar Cooperative. Co-op president John Richmond thinks CAFTA will result in less sugar production and less profit and will eventually cause U.S. producers to discontinue production. The Bush administration maintains that sugar farmers are exaggerating the impact of CAFTA, which would allow less than 2 percent more sugar from Central America into the United States.

Free trade advocates like Russell Roberts of George Mason University say it's time to stop protecting the sugar industry. He thinks the price of sugar in the United States is about double what it would be in a free market. This cost translates into higher profits for sugar farmers and higher prices for U.S. consumers for many products that contain sugar—such as ketchup and many others. The sugar industry put up a valiant fight. Sugar accounts for just 1 percent of all agricultural goods, but the industry is a large donor to political campaigns and has many allies in Washington, such as Republican Gil Gutknecht from Minnesota. He is not convinced that CAFTA will lead to greater exports, and he says that NAFTA did not help most American farmers.

The Bush administration defends NAFTA, saying it led to 30 percent economic growth in the United States, Canada, and Mexico. The verdict on CAFTA is still out, but as the agreement is coming to fruition, investment is picking up in the Central America region. The largest announcement has come from the International Textile Group's Core Denim Business, which plans to build a $100 million mill in Nicaragua employing about 750 workers.[3] As more nations implement the agreement—all but Costa Rica are expected to do so with certainty—export-oriented businesses and infrastructure projects are expected to benefit immediately.[4]

Questions for Discussion

1. What is the purpose of CAFTA?

2. What are the arguments in favor of CAFTA? What are the arguments against CAFTA?

3. Do you think history suggests that CAFTA will be successful? Explain your answer.

Sources

1. Lara L. Sowinski, "What Can DR-CAFTA Do for You?" *World Trade,* March 2006, pp. 68–69.

2. Glenn Hubbard, "CAFTA: A Win-Win Case," *BusinessWeek,* July 4, 2005, p. 102.

3. Kathleen DesMarteau, "CAFTA-DR Investment Increases," *Apparel,* June 2006, p. 33.

4. "Honduras Economy: Growth Remains Robust," *EIU ViewsWire,* July 19, 2006.

 Chapter 5 Video Case International Monetary Fund: Economic Aid in South Korea and Uganda

The International Monetary Fund (IMF) was established in 1944 in the midst of World War II, in an atmosphere of intense protectionism and nationalism. Since then, it has grown into a major international coalition of 184 members, including all of the world's major industrial countries, and become a leading force in the global economic system.

The IMF describes its main goals as providing stability in the international financial system and contributing in the fight against poverty worldwide. The international group uses a three-pronged strategy to promote global financial stability. It lends money to nations in financial crisis, it examines member-countries' economies and the general world economic outlook,

Video Case

and it helps financially troubled members set up sound fiscal practices.

The IMF is probably most well known as a lender to countries in financial crisis. When Asian financial markets collapsed in the late 1990s, South Korea borrowed $21 billion from the IMF to keep its banks from failing. Korean companies had borrowed excessive amounts of money, much of it in dollars rather than Korean won. When the value of the won fell on foreign exchange markets, Korean companies had to earn more profits to service their debt and many went bankrupt. Large South Korean corporations had borrowed huge amounts of money from banks and other institutions that they themselves controlled; when the companies encountered financial problems, so did the banks.

To obtain IMF loans, a country must agree to policies designed to stabilize the crisis, often by controlling inflation and currency exchange rates. Governments also must address underlying problems in their financial structure, budgets, banking practices, or corporate policies. In South Korea's case, the IMF required that the country restructure its banking and other corporate sectors.

The IMF's role in reducing world poverty is illustrated in Uganda, where since 1989 it has provided expertise and funds to combat economic decline from decades of political instability and ineffective financial policies. To qualify for a new IMF program, Uganda had to devise a plan to reduce poverty and spur economic growth. With the World Bank, the IMF helped the nation obtain $1 billion in debt relief, savings Uganda has put into education and health care. IMF officials say that such debt reduction initiatives, for which 26 countries qualified in mid-2003, work because a nation's government has ownership of the program.

Each IMF member contributes funds and holds voting power according to a quota based on the size of its economy compared to the world economy. Critics have argued that the major industrial nations, such as the United States, Germany, and Japan, dominate policy. IMF officials counter that because decisions require a 70 or 85 percent majority, a coalition of developing nations could veto a decision since together they comprise 37 percent of the total voting power. Officials also point out that members with the largest quotas do not always share the same opinion.

Another criticism is that the prospect of IMF intervention leads to the problem of "moral hazard," a situation in which people make reckless decisions because they know they will be rescued if things go wrong. Critics claim that because both parties think little risk is involved, governments borrow more than they can afford from foreign investors who otherwise would not make such questionable loans. IMF officials say that a country would never risk a debilitating financial crisis simply to get bailed out by the IMF, and they explain that investors assuming too much risk have indeed lost money, for example, in Russia in 1998, when the IMF did not lend money to cover the country's debt load. Because countries are required to repay IMF loans, officials explain, there is no such thing as an IMF bailout.

Questions for Discussion

1. Evaluate the IMF's quota system, which determines the contributions and voting share of members. Is it equitable? Is there a better way to determine members' financial responsibility or decision-making power?

2. What safeguards does the IMF have in place so that it does not encourage moral hazard?

3. Horst Kohler, the IMF's managing director, says that reducing poverty in low-income countries is as important as maintaining financial stability. Do you think this goal is appropriate for an international organization? Why or why not?

Chapter 6 Video Case The Peace Corps

Since 1960, Americans by the thousands have answered the call to service and have given more than two years of their lives as Peace Corps volunteers. Far from home and its comforts, they have lived and worked under unfamiliar and often extreme conditions, in countries such as Belize, Armenia, Ghana, Poland, China, Latvia, and Malawi, to name only a few. They have dug ditches, taught high school chemistry, set up computer centers, educated people about AIDS, counseled teens, and conducted a myriad of other activities.

The Peace Corps' overall goal is improving the development of infrastructure in impoverished areas of the world. In working toward that goal, the nonprofit organization must recognize cultural differences on a scale beyond what many global business organizations must do in their operations. In each unique location and for each project, the Peace Corps not only factors in cultural differences but makes bridging these differences its mission.

The Peace Corps traces its roots and mission to 1960, when John F. Kennedy, then a U.S. senator, challenged college students to serve their country by living and working in developing countries. In 1961 Congress authorized the Peace Corps as a federal agency with the purpose of promoting world peace and friendship by the United States. The organization was established to target three international needs: (1) to help interested countries meet their needs for trained workers; (2) to promote a better understanding of Americans; and (3) to promote a better understanding of other peoples on the part of Americans. Since the first group of volunteers—5,000 of them—the Peace Corps has placed more than 170,000 Americans in 136 host countries.

The talented volunteers provide skills in fields ranging from information technology to agriculture to medicine within communities that desperately need those skills. To facilitate the Peace Corps' mission, the workers must take a crash course on local culture to ensure sensitivity to the differences between American culture and that of the host country. Communication is a vital ingredient. Speaking a foreign language is not a necessity for volunteers, but most of them become at least passably fluent in the local tongue. Perhaps more significant than spoken language is mastering unspoken language and adopting local customs and mores so that a Peace Corps volunteer becomes part of the community. To blend in and fit comfortably, the Americans must make most of the concessions in cultural relationships; they are the ones who are serving, after all. Indeed, the volunteers ask a great deal of a community simply by bringing unfamiliar technology and methodology to a place with its own traditions.

Some of the most sensitive cultural differences are religious. While the Peace Corps is a secular organization—one not based on religious belief—many of its volunteers are motivated by personal religious convictions to provide service to others. Religion often plays an important role in how the group achieves its mission. Peace Corps volunteers are taught to be sensitive to the religions of the local communities where they serve, so that they may practice their own beliefs as much as possible without unintentionally challenging the local people's beliefs.

Information technology is a significant novelty that the Peace Corps brings to impoverished communities. In many locations, the volunteers are the first to expose a community to the Internet. Volunteers apply the methods of instant communication and on-demand access to obtain information in areas like ecology, agriculture, and meteorology. With this wealth of information and well-placed volunteers, the Peace Corps can fill a community's educational gaps caused by poverty or the loss of skilled, local members to more profitable, urban markets.

Peace Corps volunteers become like family to the communities they serve, even though they often are of a different race or economic background. Strong ties result from long, painstaking study of the culture and a patient program of personal compromise and diplomacy that earns the community's respect. Successes in the areas of medicine, agriculture, and business development play an important role in the Peace Corps mission, of course, but such successes could not be achieved without the personal relationship between the volunteers and those they serve.

While Peace Corps members volunteer their time and expertise, they receive benefits other than pay. The organization provides transportation costs, complete medical and dental care, and a living allowance that enables them to live in a manner similar to the local people. After completing their 27 months of service, volunteers receive about $6,000 to use as they prefer—to travel, continue their education, make a move, or obtain housing.

Questions for Discussion

1. Why is religion one of the most important and sensitive cultural factors for Peace Corps volunteers?

2. How does the Peace Corps use technology in its international mission? Which cultural aspects of technology must it consider?

3. What language issues present challenges for Peace Corps volunteers? How does the organization meet those challenges?

 ## Chapter 7 Video Case Clearing the Air

The argument surrounding global warming has centered on how best to reduce emissions of carbon dioxide and other greenhouse gases that are causing the world's climate to change. While a solution is sought, the costs are already being felt by businesses and cities around the world. Consider the following:

• Because icy roads are melting, Canadian diamond

miners must airlift equipment rather than trucking it in, at a large increase in cost.

• Oil companies must build stronger rigs and cities stronger seawalls because of the severity of storms and rising seas.

• Since the rainy season is now too short for rice and the dry season too hot for potatoes, agriculture is threatened in Mali, Africa.

- Later winters in British Columbia have let beetles spread, killing 22 million acres of pine forests.

- Villages in Alaska may be forced to relocate because of the loss of permafrost and protective sea ice.

- A surge in parasites associated with higher water temperature is threatening the Yukon River fishing industry.[1]

Now the global-warming debate is heating up in cities across the United States. Instead of waiting for federal mandates, several of the nation's municipalities are taking their own measures to curb greenhouse gases. Seattle is a good example. As the cruise ship *Diamond Princess* arrives at the port of Seattle, it discharges exhaust from its huge diesel engine. Under an agreement with the city, the engine is shut down while the ship docks. As the ship loads and unloads passengers, power is supplied from an electrical connection on shore. This method keeps nearly 200 tons of sulfur dioxide emissions from entering Seattle air over the summer.

Most ships keep the diesel engine running while in port. But Seattle mayor Greg Nickels has a plan for Seattle to meet the terms of the Kyoto Agreement, which calls for the United States to reduce greenhouse gas emissions 7 percent below 1990 levels by the year 2012. President George W. Bush pulled the United States out of the treaty in 2001, saying the science about global warming was unclear: "The Kyoto Protocol was fatally flawed in fundamental ways. No one can say with any certainty what constitutes a dangerous level of warming, and therefore, what level must be avoided."

Mayor Nickels disagrees that global warming isn't a proven problem. He cites an unusually warm winter in the Pacific Northwest that closed ski resorts and threatened the city's water supply. He thinks that mild winter, along with hurricanes in Florida, heavy rains and mudslides in Southern California, and the heat wave in Europe, constitutes a clear trend. When the Kyoto Protocol took effect in 141 countries in 2005, but not in the United States, Nickels put forth the U.S. Mayors' Climate Protection Agreement at a U.S. Conference of Mayors meeting. The initiative would reduce dependence on fossil fuels by promoting wind and solar energy and more efficient vehicles and biofuels. In unanimous support, 168 mayors in 37 states—both blue and red—committed their cities to the Kyoto Agreement. By April 2006, 218 mayors in 39 states representing nearly 44 million Americans have signed on.[2] The cities constitute a diverse group ranging from liberal to conservative, Vermont to California. The common denominator is concern for what global warming is doing to these cities.

The concern is not unfounded. In the Pacific Northwest, National Park Service geologist John Riedel says global warming could create a water shortage. He says carbon dioxide in the atmosphere is higher than at any time since records have been kept. The average temperature in

the Northwest has risen almost 2 degrees in the last century. About 40 percent of the ice cover in the mountains, where most of the region gets its water supply, has been lost over the last 150 years. Riedel thinks global warming is without a doubt the cause. To try to solve this problem, Seattle is offering developers incentives to build energy-efficient buildings. The city has also converted many of its vehicles to biodiesel fuel.

President Bush has maintained throughout his presidency that actions to reduce greenhouse gases are too costly. He thinks abiding by the Kyoto Treaty would harm the economy and cost Americans 5 million jobs. The mayors argue there are business opportunities in reducing greenhouse emissions. For instance, John Plaza founded Seattle Biofuels to manufacture biodiesel fuel, which is a low-polluting fuel made from soybean oil. The company is profitable, with revenues between $8 million and $10 million. Companies such as Aventive, a producer and marketer of ethanol, and VeraSun, the second-largest ethanol producer in the United States behind Archer Daniels Midland, have successfully gone public and have brought in more than $800 million in their initial offerings.[3]

The new technology has problems, such as the cost of converting to the new fuels. Even the mayors who support curbing emissions are concerned whether a city-by-city approach will work. Even though Seattle has reduced its own emissions by 60 percent since 1990, greenhouse gases from all sources in the Puget Sound area are expected to increase 20 percent above the 1990 level within a few years. In Portland, Oregon, greenhouse emissions have fallen 13 percent on a per capita basis; with population growth, however, the total emissions in the region have barely dropped below 1990 levels. There are limits to what a city can do by itself. Mayor Nickels remains optimistic that cities will eventually make it impossible for the federal government to say no. In the meantime, President Bush is advocating that industries take voluntary steps to reduce emissions.

Questions for Discussion

1. Do you think it is critical for the United States to develop a strategy to halt the trend toward global warming? Why or why not?

2. At which level should greenhouse emissions be attacked—city, state, or federal? Do you support the Kyoto Treaty, or do you agree with the Bush administration's stance?

3. What are some of the environmental and economic consequences of failing to reverse the trend toward global warming? What can we learn from cities such as Seattle and Portland?

Sources

1. John Carey, "Business on a Warmer Planet," *BusinessWeek,* July 17, 2006, p. 26.

2. Margot Roosevelt, "Saving One City at a Time," *Time,* April 3, 2006, p. 48.

3. Joseph Chang, "Biofuels Cash In on Field of Dreams," *Chemical Market Reporter,* July 17–July 23, 2006, p. 14.

Chapter 8 Video Case Three Billion New Capitalists

If you want to see where the world's economy is heading, look to the East. That's the message in *Three Billion New Capitalists: The Great Shift of Wealth and Power,* by Clyde Prestowitz, an expert on Asia who began his career as a trade negotiator in the Reagan administration. Prestowitz believes that India and China are on a course to become global leaders and that, without taking dramatic steps, the United States will fall behind.[1] The factory workers in China and the outsourced jobs in India that we hear about signal the beginning of a shift in economic power, a shift that Westerners will need to accept.

Prestowitz maintains that America is seeing the middle of a two-part revolution. First are the 3 billion people from China, India, and the former Soviet bloc entering the global economy at the same time. These 3 billion people represent a population at least as large as that of the United States, and larger than that of Japan or of any country in Europe. This population is highly skilled and can perform any type of work "every bit as good" as can workers in the United States, Japan, or any of the other developed countries, and it can do so for 10 cents, maybe 25 to 30 cents, on the dollar. By "every bit as good," Prestowitz means as good as or better than the output of top U.S. doctors, professors, business leaders, entrepreneurs, and so on. Educated in our best universities, trained in our best hospitals, or with start-up experience in the Silicon Valley, these individuals are returning home to China and India, where there are great opportunities waiting for them.

China leads the pack as a center for global outsourcing, thanks to its large population of nearly 1.5 billion people. Within the last decade, outsourcing has begun to move into service areas, such as human resources, call centers, and finance and accounting functions.[2] India alone had revenues of $22 million last year from answering customer phone calls, managing computer networks, and writing software for firms all over the world; Russia has followed India's lead into the software industry.[3]

The second revolution, according to Prestowitz, is that the Internet and transportation companies like Federal Express have eliminated time and distance. Any task done on the Internet is only seconds away from anyplace in the world. Even manufacturing firms with products to deliver can reach virtually anywhere in the world in 36 hours. Effectively, people throughout the world are sitting together at the same table.

In order to compete in this connected environment, the United States must be more competitive. First, better education and more training for workers are required. But training and education will not be enough, and a new approach to international economics is needed. The U.S. semiconductor industry offers a good example. Prestowitz argues that the United States is the best place in the world to make these products, yet two-thirds of the plants being built today are in Asia. The economic development leaders of many Asian countries use tax incentives and capital to make it very lucrative for U.S. firms to manufacture semiconductors in their countries. The decision to locate a plant in Asia has little to do with market forces or free trade. Yet neither Democratic nor Republican administrations in the United States have responded to what Prestowitz thinks is, in effect, bribery.

Some argue that concerns about China and India are similar to the fear America had about Japan 15 to 20 years ago. Many believed that Japan was becoming a world power and that, without a national competitive industrial policy, America would be left behind. Of course, this scenario never really materialized, and the U.S. economy has done fairly well in the last two decades. But, Prestowitz thinks, the current challenge is different from the one posed by Japan in the 1980s. In response to Japan, the U.S. government established an organization to promote development of the U.S. semiconductor equipment industry. Agreements were negotiated with Japan to stop the dumping of chips on U.S. markets and to open Japanese markets to more foreign products. Success in the 1990s is due at least in part to these government actions. What is occurring now in China and India is quite similar to the situation with Japan in the 1980s, but the population is much larger, more countries are involved, and China is a much tougher player than Japan.

Some analysts maintain that the U.S. economy continues to grow faster than the economies of Japan or Europe. Prestowitz is concerned that this growth is fueled by debt. The United States has moved from being the world's largest net creditor to the largest net debtor, with a $3 trillion debt, growing at $700 million annually. The country is using 80 percent of its global savings, and if it reaches 100 percent, the economic outlook isn't good. Paul Volcker, former undersecretary of the U.S. Department of the Treasury and chairman of the Federal Reserve, has warned of a major financial crisis in the next five years; he puts the probability at 75 percent.

While the emergence of China and India poses serious competition for the United States, these countries face major challenges themselves. The United States has stable institutions, the best graduate schools, the best infrastructure, and an entrepreneurial culture that encourages innovation. India and China, on the other hand, face obstacles of energy availability, energy cost, water availability, and pollution.[4] As these nations become large energy users, with no other source of oil, they will be more dependent on the Middle East than is the United States. The aging population is becoming an issue in China, especially given its policy of one child per family, and pension and health care issues will be difficult to address. India has favorable demographics, with half the population under the age of 25. For India, already the fourth-largest economy in the world, a competitive business environment, a thriving service sector, and an increase in foreign investment point to a bright future.[5]

Prestowitz maintains that the United States should want both India and China to succeed, since a failed China and India would not help the United States. He calls for a complementary economic relationship that lets all parties succeed. What is needed is a strategy enabling the United States to take the steps necessary to compete and meet the challenges that lie ahead.

Questions for Discussion

1. What economic and socioeconomic factors explain the optimistic economic outlook for China and India?

2. What role does the cost of labor play in the rise of China and India? How can U.S. firms compete in this environment?

3. Should the U.S. government take actions in response to incentives used by Asian countries to attract American firms? If so, what actions would you suggest?

Sources

1. Hardy Green, "Paperback Picnic," *BusinessWeek,* June 26, 2006, p. 108.

2. "The Global Outsourcing 100," *Fortune,* April 3, 2006, pp. A1–A8.

3. Andy Reinhardt, Manjeet Kripalani, Geri Smith, and Jason Bush, "Angling to Be the Next Bangalore," *BusinessWeek,* January 30, 2006, p. 62.

4. Colum Murphy, "Interview," *Far Eastern Economic Review,* April 2006, pp. 58–59.

5. Joseph Luna, "A Matter of Time: India's Emerging Economic Prowess," *Harvard International Review,* Winter 2006, pp. 36–39.

 # Chapter 9 Video Case Controversy over U.S. Port Security

In early 2006, it came to the attention of Congress and the American people that a company from the United Arab Emirates would soon manage six major U.S. ports, including New York–New Jersey. When Dubai Ports World (DPW) arranged in November 2005 to buy British-based Peninsula & Oriental Steam Navigation Co. (P&O) for $6.9 billion, the management of the six U.S. ports was part of the deal.

In the huge controversy that ensued, opponents claimed an Arab company presented too many possible security risks to have authority over U.S. trade entry points vulnerable to terrorism. Less than five years after 9/11, fearing more terrorist attacks, many Americans were baffled and angered at the idea of an Arab-based company in charge of U.S. ports. Congress considered passing special legislation to prevent an Arab-owned company from operating U.S. port terminals. Even

Republican members did not align with President George W. Bush, a supporter of free trade who backed the deal and threatened to veto any congressional action to stop it. The controversy ended when DPW, in order to "preserve its strong relationship with the United States," announced it would find an American company to take over management of the six ports.

The port controversy showed that Americans and their leaders lacked knowledge of U.S. port management and security. Dubai Ports World would not have been the first foreign operator of a U.S. port—far from it. More than 60 percent of the container terminals at the country's 10 busiest ports are managed to some degree by foreign operators, some of which are controlled by foreign governments.[1] The DPW deal erupted into a public controversy for political reasons. A Miami firm, Continental Stevedoring & Terminals, Inc., had been wrestling with the British-owned P&O over divisions of port operations in Miami. When the DPW purchase of P&O was announced, this gave Continental a chance to take its turf battle from the courts to the political arena, where fear of terrorism was a top issue. Continental used a Washington lobbyist to build congressional opposition to the deal on the grounds of national security.[2]

Port security is a vital matter, with 90 percent of the world's cargo shipped by container and 46 percent of all U.S. imports arriving by oceangoing cargo containers.[3] Terminal operators, however, do not inspect containers unloaded at ports. Most port authorities act as landlords who lease waterfronts to ocean carriers and stevedoring firms.[4] Federal agencies, including U.S. Customs and Border Protection, part of the Department of Homeland Security, are responsible for U.S. port security.

Federal agents inspect about 5.5 percent of the 9 million containers entering the United States each year. After the DPW furor, some members of Congress proposed that all containers be scanned. Nearly everyone in the maritime industry agrees that even if federal agencies had the resources, inspecting all containers is not the answer to security concerns. It would take weeks to move cargo containers through a port if each had to be opened and inspected. Such delays would kill just-in-time manufacturing—since many U.S. companies now keep only a day's supply of parts—and cause slowdowns and shutdowns. Instead of supporting impractical screening requirements, some industry analysts recommend steps such as a national portwide identification system for cargo containers, background checks on all port employees, and certification programs ensuring that foreign firms have security standards in place to prevent the inclusion of contraband in cargo containers.[5]

The maritime industry has argued for years that U.S. harbors need more federal funding, not only to enhance security but also to manage growing trade. The American Association of Port Authorities has said that the United States needs to invest more than $17 billion to upgrade and modernize port facilities to handle the growth in trade and $3 billion to meet proposed federal requirements for cargo screening.[6]

In May 2006 Congress passed the Security and Accountability for Every (SAFE) Port Act, which authorized $5.5 billion for port security and required that the government finish installing radiation screening equipment at major U.S. ports by the end of 2007. The bill allows the United States to deny entry to cargo from countries that refuse to cooperate with increased security checks abroad.[7] Some observers expect Congress to enact a law requiring that foreign companies file information about proposed acquisitions in the United States, particularly those giving control over infrastructure, and granting itself the power to approve or disapprove foreign acquisitions that might affect national security.[8]

Questions for Discussion

1. What political forces are illustrated in the DPW port controversy?

2. Should Congress have the power to restrict foreign investment and ownership in the United States? Why or why not?

3. Why was the prospect of U.S. ports being controlled by a Dubai-owned company so alarming to Americans, when other foreign companies already managed U.S. ports? Should any foreign-owned companies be allowed to manage U.S. infrastructure?

Sources

1. James Aaron Cooke, "The DP World Controversy Could Help Our Seaports," *Logistics Management,* April 2006, p. 80.

2. Neil Shister, "Dubai Ports Controversy Misses the Big Picture," *World Trade,* April 2006, p. 6.

3. Jeffrey L. Holmes, "The Container Security Initiative," *Fleet Equipment,* August 2004, p. 15.

4. Cooke, "The DP world Controversy."

5. Robert J. Verdisco and Morrison G. Cain, "Safe Ports, Secure Economy," *Retail Merchandiser,* February 2002, p. 9.

6. Cooke, "The DP world Controversy."

7. R. G. Edmonson, "House Passes Safe Ports Bill," *Journal of Commerce,* May 4, 2006, p. 1.

8. "Stricter Exon-Florio Process Expected after Ports Flap," *Mergers and Acquisitions,* April 2006, p. 12.

 ## Chapter 10 Video Case The Challenge of Illegal Immigration

Every day, border patrol guards along the Rio Grande seize illegal immigrants sneaking into the United States. Many get through, knowing where they can cross the border from Mexico. It is along the Mexican border that issues of immigration are keenly understood and that anxiety and disagreement abound over what to do about undocumented workers, a majority of whom are Hispanic. According to Diana Palacious, city manager of Crystal City, Texas, "The face of this country is changing, and some people want to find any way possible to keep that from happening." Crystal City is a town of migrant workers in which Latinos make up the majority of the population and now hold political offices. The immigration debate in Crystal City is passionate nonetheless. Residents think some illegal immigrants come to work the system, while others like Judge Joe Luna say they come out of necessity and should be paid a fair wage.

The Latino town of Maywood, California, took the debate to a new level. City leaders vowed to defy any crackdown on illegal immigrants. Mayor Felipe Aguirre made it clear that the city of Maywood would not have its police officers act as immigration agents. "We would not have the city employees ask anybody who comes into city hall whether they have legal documents or not," Aguirre said.

The impact of illegal immigration, once felt most severely in Texas, California, and Arizona, is now felt far and wide in the United States. Besides those three states, Florida, New York, Illinois, New Jersey, and North Carolina account for two-thirds of the undocumented population. In a growing number of cities across the country, illegal workers are lining up on street corners for jobs. An estimated 12 million illegal immigrants live in the United States, and the federal government and many corporations are being pressured to reduce the number of illegals.[1]

For years federal agents conducted job site raids and arrested undocumented workers; employers were generally fined. Then the Department of Homeland Security, in its efforts to curb illegal immigration, began using laws traditionally directed against drug smugglers and organized crime. In one case, immigration and custom agents arrested dozens of illegals in raids of more than 40 plants nationwide owned by the global firm IFCO Systems, supplier of shipping containers and pallets to large retailers. The investigation mainly targeted seven current and former executives thought to have directly aided in the employment and harboring of illegal aliens. Advocates of tougher enforcement say this approach is long overdue.

Some are taking matters into their own hand. Four current and former workers at carpet maker Mohawk Industries in the town of Calhoun, Georgia, brought a class action against the company; their suit claims Mohawk conspired to depress their wages by hiring illegal immigrants.[2] The U.S. Supreme Court chose to hear the case; observers noted that a rejection of Mohawk's defense would imply that companies hiring illegals would basically have to become the border patrol.

Politicians, both Republicans and Democrats, are responding to public concern about the huge numbers of illegal immigrants living in the United States. In late 2005 the U.S. House of Representatives passed legislation making it a felony for businesses to hire illegal workers. Companies that incorrectly fill out certain paperwork on employees could be fined $25,000. "It doesn't take too many of those (fines) to drive a small business out of business," says John Gay of the National Restaurant Association.[3] The U.S. Senate favored a guest-worker program that would allow foreigners to take jobs Americans do not fill. Polls show that most Americans want to curb illegal immigration but also support some form of the temporary guest-worker program supported by President George W. Bush and approved by the U.S. Senate.[4] Illegals would have to pay back taxes and go to the end of the citizenship line. Despite these requirements, restrictionists called the Senate bill "amnesty."[5] A compromise between the two houses is likely to require that companies confirm the legal status of all current and prospective employees. Angelo Amador, the immigration policy director for the U.S. Chamber of Commerce, calls that plan a bureaucratic nightmare that would cost employers at least $12 billion in compliance.[6]

Immigration is a huge issue for many U.S. businesses, which rely on foreign workers for their labor needs. In March 2006 Bill Gates told congressional leaders that immigration is Microsoft's number-one issue in Washington. "If we hope to maintain our economic and intellectual leadership in the United States, we must renew this commitment [to immigration]," he said in a letter to lawmakers. "Unless there is reform, American competitiveness will suffer as other countries benefit from the international talent that U.S. employers cannot hire or retain."[7]

While America's illegal immigrants have become the target of mostly negative national attention, the buying power of 12 million consumers has attracted the interest of U.S. companies. Immigrants, documented or not, are seen by many as a potential source of growth, with more than 700,000 new consumers added to the economy each year.[8] In the spring of 2006, more than 1 million immigrants in cities from Los Angeles to New York stayed away from work and school and took to the streets to protest calls for sealing borders and to demonstrate the extent of their economic power. This sea of humanity vowed to push for immigration reform so that they can continue to call America home.

Questions for Discussion

1. What are the pros and cons of illegal immigrants' obtaining jobs in America?

2. What legal forces are most relevant to illegal immigration? Why is it difficult to enforce U.S. immigration laws?

3. Is it realistic to think that the vast numbers of illegal immigrants can be returned to their native lands? If not, what impact might the presence of so many illegals have on the legal environment?

Sources

1. Richard S. Dunham, "Immigration Reform: Why Business Could Get Burned," *BusinessWeek,* April 10, 2006, p. 41.

2. Brian Grow, "A Body Blow to Illegal Labor?" *BusinessWeek,* March 27, 2006, p. 86.

3. Dunham, "Immigration Reform."

4. "Illegal Immigration: Better Nothing at All than Congress's Draconian Bill," *Financial Times,* July 19, 2006, p. 18.

5. "An Immigration Compromise?" *The Wall Street Journal,* August 7, 2006, p. A12.

6. Dunham, "Immigration Reform."

7. Ibid.

8. Brian Grow, Adrienne Carter, Roger O. Crockett, and Geri Smith, "Embracing Illegals," *BusinessWeek,* July 18, 2005, p. 56.

Chapter 11 Video Case China: Changing the Yuan/Dollar

On July 21, 2005, after months of political pressure from the United States, the Chinese government revalued the yuan by raising it 2.1 percent higher against the U.S. dollar.[1] For over a decade the yuan had been pegged—or fixed—to the U.S. dollar at a rate of 8.28 yuan for every dollar. Critics of China's currency policy, including U.S. Treasury secretary John Snow, maintained that the yuan was undervalued, a situation that allowed Chinese exporters to undercut competitors worldwide. Talk on Capital Hill centered on the United States' large trade deficit with China and possible trade sanctions. How much effect China's revaluation will have on the global economy is uncertain.

The revaluation of the yuan may take the United States a step toward getting what it wants, though a small one, says Nariman Behravesh, chief economist at the economic forecasting firm Global Insight. The meager 2.1 percent increase amounts to little or nothing, and much depends on what China does next. If the Chinese continue raising the value of the yuan through a series of steps, Behravesh believes this could make a difference. Peter Morici, business professor at the University of Maryland and former chief economist at the International Trade Commission, agrees that the revaluation is a very small step toward the goal of the United States. By some estimates, the yuan is undervalued by as much as 40 percent, he says. With a 2 percent increase, Chinese exporters can make up the price changes by slightly improving their productivity. Even if the yuan is allowed to float consistently, it will take a long time to reduce China's comparative advantage in manufacturing labor costs.[2]

Slightly increasing the yuan's value when it is so undervalued is part of China's development strategy to increase exports, since the undervaluation provides a large subsidy to exporters. To maintain this favorable situation, China has to purchase dollars in amounts equal to about one-third the value of its exports. This purchase translates into a 33 percent subsidy on Chinese exports. In other words, China has an export-driven industrial policy.

The revaluation may or may not have a heavy impact on China's imports, depending on the extent of the revaluation. While Behravesh agrees the 2 percent will do little in terms of raising the price of imports, further changes in the value of the yuan will reduce the competitiveness of Chinese exports and increase the competitiveness of U.S. exports. The initial 2 percent, however, is simply nowhere close to making a difference.

According to Morici, the slight revaluation is much more a political move on China's part than an economic one. President George W. Bush and Secretary Snow have been very accommodating to the Chinese, pressuring them only to the extent that there was congressional pressure to do so. The revaluation enables Snow to say he delivered something, though it isn't much. Behravesh agrees that politics played an important role, but adds that China also revalued the yuan for other reasons. China has been receiving large sums of speculative money to finance investments. Raising the exchange rate even a small amount reduces the inflow of money as China looks to cool down its economy.

Will a revalued yuan allow Chinese workers to earn more and producers to see a better payday? Assuming the yuan continues to increase, Behravesh thinks the purchasing power of the average Chinese worker will rise, as will the standard of living. If the yuan stays as it is, the slight change will have little impact. The current policy of maintaining an undervalued yuan keeps prices low, but it also keeps individuals poor and profits thin. Unless the Chinese government does more to alter its policy on its currency, Behravesh expects leaders to come under continual pressure to increase the value of the yuan. Nonetheless, at the one-year anniversary of the yuan's revaluation, a similar move had not occurred.[3]

Chapter 12 Video Case Outsourcing

What seems to many like a smart business strategy has become the central focus in the debate about ethics in corporate America. *Outsourcing,* in its simplest form, is using an outside vendor to do work that is normally performed in-house.[1] Now the term generally refers to sending jobs outside the United States to foreign workers to realize cost savings. Offshore outsourcing began with manufacturing jobs leaving the United States in the late 1970s. In the late 1980s and early 1990s, software development was being outsourced to other countries; since the late1990s, with Internet bandwidth more affordable to transmit graphs, images, audio, and video, U.S. companies are outsourcing information technology (IT) services, such as tax return processing and financial and insurance services.

Today outsourcing is a strategy so widespread that almost any company of any size engages in the practice to take advantage of cheaper labor and production overseas. Outsourcing manufacturing jobs to China is so prevalent that many believe it is a major cause of the United States' $200 billion trade deficit with that country.[2] More than 70 percent of the Fortune 2000 companies say outsourcing is an important part of their overall growth strategy; India remains the leading offshore destination.[3]

Moving jobs offshore has taken center stage in the controversy surrounding American job loss. Proponents of outsourcing argue that it saves money and makes U.S. firms more competitive. In most cases the objective of outsourcing is a 20 percent savings in cost.[4] The city of Chicago, for instance, saved approximately $10 million over a three-year period by outsourcing its information technology systems, and the time it took to deliver services to citizens was reduced by 35 percent.[5]

Countless firms have reaped the cost-saving benefit of outsourcing, but many people in the United States decry the loss of jobs for Americans. The Manufacturers Alliance, a business and public policy research group, says that from 1999 to 2002, U.S. manufacturing plants declined by 20,000, while U.S. companies opened 246 facilities in foreign countries. Now thousands of white-collar jobs are moving overseas each year. One research firm estimates that at least 3.3 million jobs in service industries, accounting for $136 billion in wages, will leave the United States by 2015 for countries where workers earn less.[6]

Some point out that savings accrued through outsourcing allows firms to create new, higher-paying jobs domestically. By the year 2008, according to a recent study, 317,367 jobs will be created in the United States across many industries, a result of companies in several sectors saving $20.9 billion by outsourcing just their computer operations. This prospect is little consolation for the 276,954 workers who hold the computer-related jobs this same study predicts will be moving offshore by 2010.

Herein lies the crux of the debate over outsourcing. Is it good business that benefits everyone, or is it an insensitive and unethical practice that is consuming the livelihood of American workers? According to Jack Welch, the renowned former CFO of General Electric, if a firm cannot remain competitive, it can't pay the employees. Outsourcing is necessary for U.S. firms to compete globally. Others argue that Welch is missing the bigger picture. In the long run, businesses that say no to outsourcing and keep jobs in the United States will foster greater trust and goodwill among workers, unions, and consumers.

Some industry watchers contend that for American workers to survive outsourcing, they must learn new skills, which will also enhance the competitiveness of U.S. firms in the global marketplace. Companies are often reluctant to train older workers in new skills, and workers who are left without jobs often don't have the means to learn these skills on their own.[7] For workers whose jobs are eliminated because of outsourcing, training programs are essential to provide skills needed for the new jobs being created. When North Carolina started losing numerous jobs overseas, the state revamped its education system with the goal of creating a globally competitive workforce. Besides making the curriculum more rigorous from preschool through eighth grade, North Carolina plans to redesign high schools to give every student the chance to earn two years of college by the time they graduate, as well as to create new, small career-themed schools that emphasize engineering, science, or business.[8] If there is one point of agreement in the debate about outsourcing, it is that the best jobs will go to those with the greatest skills.

Questions for Discussion

1. Does outsourcing violate the trust between management and labor?

2. What are the arguments in support of outsourcing? The arguments against?

3. Where do you stand on the debate? Is it ethical or unethical? Support your stance.

Sources

1. Sunita S. Ahlawat and Sucheta Ahlawat, "Competing in the Global Economy: Implications for Business Education," *Journal of the American Academy of Business,* March 2006, pp. 101–5.

2. "Learning to Live with Offshoring," *BusinessWeek,* January 30, 2006, p. 122.

3. Stephanie Overby, "2006 Global Outsourcing Guide," *CIO,* July 15, 2006, p. 1.

4. George C. Elliott, "International Outsourcing: Values vs. Economics," *Quality Progress,* August 2006, pp. 20–25.

5. "The Global Outsourcing 100," *Fortune,* April 3, 2006, pp. A1–A8.

6. Ahlawat and Ahlawat, "Competing."

7. Catherine L. Mann, "How to Ease the Pain of Globalization," *CIO,* February 1, 2006, p. 1.

8. Barbara Kantrowitz, "The Future Is in Their Hands," *Newsweek,* June 12, 2006, p. 46.

Chapter 13 Video Case GM Global Research Network

With only about 12 percent of the world's population of 6 billion owning cars or trucks, the auto industry today is a growth industry with lots of room for expansion. There is potential for global annual sales of 65 to 70 million vehicles for 2010, with much of the expansion in China, India, Russia, and Brazil.[1] GM plans to take advantage of this potential with a strategy of alliance and technology networks. The auto giant is laying the groundwork for a new generation of cars and trucks with a new business model that partners with other auto companies and uses an extensive network of the world's brightest researchers and engineers.

GM is the world's largest automaker, with manufacturing operations in 32 countries and sales in 200 countries. Its approach to globalization has included forming an alliance network that includes General Motors, Opel/Vauxhall/Holden, Saab, Fiat Auto, Isuzu, Subaru, and Suzuki. Together, these companies sell more than 13 million vehicles a year.[2] Alliances with some of these companies, which produce cars that are smaller and lower-priced than the usual entry-level vehicles in the United States, will allow GM to build a presence in Asian markets more quickly.

Global competition has forced auto companies to increase their focus on innovation. Years before the design of a vehicle begins, research and development specialists are at work seeking the next level of innovation. Emission and safety regulations, along with competition from Europe and Asia, prompted GM to redirect its technology priorities. GM has changed its business model to reflect the technology revolution and the expanding technical leverage capabilities around the world, according to Alan Taub, executive director of GM Global Research and Development. Relying on technology requires a network of research minds not only in the United States but throughout the world. GM has recruited engineers and scientists from North and South America, Europe, the Middle East, China, Taiwan, India, and Korea.

"It became very clear to me that a research model based on bringing the best minds to Michigan just isn't going to work any more," says Larry Burns, head of GM's research and development since 1998. "There's too much talent all over the world."[3] Today, for every two researchers and engineers working inside GM labs, there is one external partner. The change requires a work force that is global, mobile, and comfortable working with many different cultures.

GM has formed research partnerships with other manufacturers, suppliers, universities, and governmental agencies. Research projects include internal combustion engine development, fuel cell technology, advanced chassis systems, electronics and communications systems, and many others.[4] The GM research model is evident at the GM Sweden Science Office at Saab headquarters in Trollhattan, Sweden. This new venture is developing centers of expertise and coordinating GM research and development activities. A $26 million agreement with the Swedish government supports automotive research in Sweden and extends for at least three years. GM hopes to build up its Saab division and to support efforts elsewhere by using Saab's core expertise—innovation of interiors, safety, and turbo engines. The Sweden Science Office is part of a strategy to leverage the company's global engineering resources, relationships, skills, and knowledge to increase the quality of research.

GM uses a two-pronged approach to technology research. In its innovation program, engineers can approach R&D management and be funded to take an idea from the drawing board to production. An example is improving driver interfaces. GM engineers are working on devices that let drivers watch the road while using navigation systems, climate control, mobile phones, or sound systems.[5] The second part is the company's strategic technologies program, which calls for a panel of GM experts to determine the 10 areas fundamental to the future of the company and of the entire auto industry.

Three areas key to GM's future research are powertrain control, electronic control and software, and hydrogen and fuel cells. The fuel cell and hydrogen technologies, R&D chief Burns says, provide an opportunity to relieve our 98 percent dependence on petroleum as an energy source for vehicles.[6] He envisions that a fuel cell engine, with one-tenth of the moving parts of an internal combustion engine, will provide enormous design opportunities. Combined with research on advanced materials, fuel cell development could make the car of the future safer, friendlier to the environment, and more affordable—an advantage in reaching new global markets.

Questions for Discussion

1. How is technology influencing strategy at GM? What factors should managers at GM consider when developing an international strategy?

2. Does GM have a competitive advantage? If so, what is it? If not, what does the firm need to do to establish one?

3. How can GM's global research network assist in the global strategic planning process?

Sources

1. Larry J. Howell and Jamie C. Hsu, "Globalization within the Auto Industry," *Research Technology Management,* July–August 2002, pp. 43–49.

2. Ibid.

3. "Interview—Larry Burns: Global Search," *The Engineer,* September 19, 2005, p. 30.

4. Howell and Hsu, "Globalization."

5. "Interview."

6. Ibid.

 # Chapter 14 Video Case   DHL Global Delivery Service

The express delivery business has become a multibillion-dollar industry. Companies such as UPS, FedEx, DHL, TNT, and the United States Postal Service (USPS) have developed vast transportation and service networks to deliver millions of packages daily around the world, many overnight. FedEx, for instance, processes 1.4 million items on a typical night through its Memphis hub, where they are scanned, routed, sorted, and shipped to arrive at their destination by the next morning. UPS processes 1 million packages each day through its world port in Louisville, Kentucky; it delivers 230 packages every second during the holidays. Growing worldwide demand for express delivery has led to intense competition and has forced firms to improve efficiency and performance. Through mergers and acquisitions, new technology, and improved service, firms continue to battle for a share of this lucrative market. A case in point is DHL.

DHL was founded in San Francisco in 1969 by Adrian Dalsey, Larry Hillblom, and Robert Lynn; the initials of the last names formed the company name.[1] Major competitors include FedEx, UPS, and the U.S. Postal Service. Today, DHL is an $18.6 billion company, making it the market leader in international express delivery. DHL did not gain this position overnight; for years it expanded throughout the world until it developed a complete global network, refined to the point where it could serve customers worldwide, including Fortune 500 companies. As a result, DHL is the largest express carrier in both Europe and Asia, with a 40 percent share of each market.[2]

While DHL is a hugely successful company, it is dominated in the U.S. market by FedEx and UPS, which together have a 78 percent share of the domestic market, compared to DHL's 7 percent share.[3] By acquiring Airborne Express in 2003, DHL bolstered its express shipping infrastructure on the domestic level. The integration of the two companies was difficult, since each had different business models, different customers, and different geographic considerations.[4] By taking the best of both companies and making them work together, the new DHL is the number-one international delivery service. The company carries more than 1 billion shipments a year in more than 200 countries and territories worldwide. Serving more than 4.2 million customers, DHL generates revenues in excess of $50 billion a year.

To meet customer expectations of speed and reliability, DHL must maintain efficient operations at each point of the sorting and delivery process. The delivery process originates with the customer, who contacts DHL and advises that a package is ready and indicates where it is going. A courier picks up the package within 15 minutes of the time requested, whether prescheduled for large customers or ad hoc for small customers. Scanning activities, including the names of the sender and the receiver, weight, contents, and address for delivery, are performed at the customer's site. The package is then transported to a service center for shipment. Bar codes allow both DHL and the customer to track the package while en route. Known as "track and trace," the system has the fundamental purpose of giving customers peace of mind. While tracking was historically done through the DHL customer service department, customers now can have shipping-process equipment in their offices or can track packages on the Internet.

Packages are shipped from the local service office to the hub for sorting. Once sorted, packages are shipped to a regional sorting facility. Sometimes the sorting facility is a gateway where all international shipments must go to clear customs before leaving the United States. DHL employs a regional hub system. The U.S. hub is located in Cincinnati, while gateways are located in Miami, New York (JFK), Dallas, Los Angeles, and San Francisco. All packages are fed through the hub system. A package shipped from Orlando to Miami, for instance, would first go to Cincinnati and then to Miami. Hubs primarily service gateways, and a gateway is usually a port that services local pickup and delivery centers as well as exports to foreign destinations. For instance, the Miami gateway also services all of Latin America.

Gateways generally operate from Tuesday through Saturday. A morning shift handles planes coming in from hubs such as Cincinnati. An evening shift is mainly an outbound operation, sending packages that have arrived during the day from service centers out to the hubs. Couriers pick up from and deliver directly to the customer. International delivery requires some extra steps to clear packages through customs, which is located on site at the gateways.

DHL continues to expand its distribution facilities and build on Airborne's domestic network. With more than 700 daily flights in the United States, DHL hopes to challenge market leaders FedEx and UPS through its service to customers—better, quicker, and to more parts of the world. Express delivery groups such as these are taking an increasing role in the global economy as companies seek greater speed and reliability in their supply chains.[5]

Questions for Discussion

1. How do express delivery companies help customers improve efficiency? What types of organizational designs are most effective in this environment?

2. Why is it important for DHL to achieve superior performance? How does the company improve efficiency?

3. What role do express delivery companies play in the global economy? What techniques discussed in this chapter could DHL use to establish controls?

Sources

1. http://en.wikipedia.org/wiki/DHL.

2. Mark Ritson, "DHL Is Struggling to Deliver in the U.S.," *Marketing,* April 5, 2006, p. 21.

3. Jack Ewing, Dean Foust, and Michael Eidam, "DHL's American Adventure," *BusinessWeek,* November 29, 2004, p. 126.

4. Rick Whiting, "Best of Two Worlds," *InformationWeek,* June 26, 2006, pp. 48–49.

5. Andrew Ward, "FedEx Delivers Strong Results on Solid Growth," *Financial Times,* June 22, 2006, p. 27.

 # Chapter 17 Video Case   Cretors & Co.

Chicago-based Cretors & Co. is the world's oldest and largest manufacturer of machines for popping and flavoring popcorn. Other products include machines for roasting and flavoring nuts, spinning cotton candy, and making other concession items. In business since 1885, Cretors began exporting its machines as early as 1897 and now ships equipment throughout the world. Exports were about 36 percent of its sales in 2002.

This small, family-run business, valued at around $10 million, dominates the world market for commercial machines for movie theaters. While Canada, Mexico, and Western European countries are its largest international customers, Cretors sells throughout Europe, North and South America, and Asia. The firm sells internationally through distributors, who often learn of Cretors' products through trade shows, word of mouth, and its Internet Web site and then contact the company and request to sell its equipment. Personal relationships with distributors are essential elements in building an export business, says Charlie Cretors, the great-grandson of the company's founder and its current CEO. Distributors link Cretors to customers not only for initial sales but also for after-sales service and support.

Flexibility has enabled Cretors to meet several challenges of international sales. Its various financing methods include open accounts (for smaller orders and established customers) and deposits or full payment (for large or unique orders and new customers). The company modifies machines for specific markets to meet different voltage, safety, and operating requirements. Cretors works with customers to reduce their costs. The manufacturer has altered equipment so that its resulting classification minimizes import duties. When shipping, Cretors packs its machines into containers and adds other suppliers' products that a distributor might want from the United States. This practice of combining shipments fosters goodwill for Cretors and strengthens its international partnerships.

Questions for Discussion

1. Exporters face the problem of locating foreign markets. How does Cretors deal with this problem?

2. What are the benefits of using distributors to sell in foreign countries? What are the possible drawbacks? Why might foreign distributors see Cretors as a desirable business partner?

3. How does Cretors meet the challenges of financing international sales?

 Chapter 18 Video Case Domino's Pizza in Mexico

Domino's Pizza learned the hard way that moving into foreign markets without local input can be challenging. According to Tim McIntyre, vice president of communications for Domino's, the firm expected foreign cultures to adapt to Domino's offerings. After a few years, millions of dollars, and several attempts to penetrate foreign markets, the pizza company executives realized they would be more successful if Domino's abandoned its one-size-fits-all approach and adapted to the cultures of foreign countries. Patrick Doyle, executive president of Domino's international division, explains: "Local operators can act quickly to make changes in promotional and pricing strategies. If we were trying to do all of that from here in Ann Arbor, we would have a big struggle."[1]

One example of the problems Domino's encountered took place when it attempted to use its U.S. slogan "One Call Does It All" in England. What the firm failed to realize was that a call in England meant a personal visit. Customers couldn't understand why Domino's was celebrating the fact that all you had to do was come to the store and pick up your pizza.

Domino's venture outside the United States began in 1983 in Winnipeg, Canada. Since Domino's made the decision to focus more on local markets, overseas business has steadily increased. By 1995, Domino's had 1,000 stores outside the United States, 1,500 by 1997, and 3,000 in 2006. Today, Domino's has a presence in more than 50 markets and plans to go into more countries in the future. Domino's goal in all markets is to be the leader in the *delivery* pizza business. According to Michael Lawton, vice president of international operations, Domino's has succeeded in every market it has entered.

Domino's operates consistently throughout the world. Storefronts are similar at all Domino's outlets worldwide. The internal operation of the stores is also very similar. This has led to some interesting situations. In 1985, Domino's discovered there was no Japanese word for pepperoni, the most popular topping in the world. Japanese consumers thought it was some kind of small pepper and returned pizzas when they discovered it was a meat product. Today, it is the number-one topping in Japan, and the Japanese word for pepperoni is *pepperoni.*

Domino's has made several additions to its standard menu to adapt to local preferences. Examples include squid in Japan, tuna and sweet corn in England, lamb and pickled ginger in India, and barbecued chicken in the Bahamas, to name a few. Adjustments have also been made to accommodate different cultures. In India, pepperoni was replaced with spicy chicken in respect to the Hindu reverence for cows. Site selection in the Philippines is based on *feng shui,* the belief that prosperity is a function of building design and the arrangement of equipment inside. Special street maps were created in the United Arab Emirates because streets have three different names used interchangeably.

Mexico is the largest international market for Domino's, whose presence there is greater than that of McDonald's and Burger King combined.[2] Since entering the Mexican market in 1990, Domino's has grown to more than 500 stores. This growth can be attributed to several factors. The North American Free Trade Agreement (NAFTA), signed in 1993 and put into effect the following year, opened the door for restaurant investment; Mexico's trade with the United States and Canada has tripled since NAFTA was implemented.[3] Alberto Torrado, an innovative franchisee, has encouraged Domino's growth by bringing a new understanding of food and franchising to Mexico. When he started, there were no Domino's franchises. Torrado had to educate people about the franchise concept, the types of support Domino's provides, and the royalties it requires. This was no easy task. But by nurturing stores and providing training and services such as accounting and marketing support, Torrado helped Domino's grow into a powerhouse in Mexico.

Domino's has repositioned since it first entered Mexico at the high end of the market, targeting upper-middle-class consumers. Domino's pizzas were expensive, and that strategy was effective until the Mexican economy collapsed. Domino's shifted its target market by lowering prices and advertising that pizza is a great meal for the entire family. The company became much more profitable with this approach, another factor contributing to Domino's rise to being the number-one restaurant chain in Mexico.

Questions for Discussion

1. What problems did Domino's encounter when trying to standardize its product throughout the world? Why was local input beneficial?

2. How did the pizza giant adapt to different markets and cultures?

3. What factors have contributed to Domino's success in Mexico?

Sources

1. Amy Garber, "Operators across Globe Hungry for Slice of Domino's Pie," *Nation's Restaurant News,* January 19, 2004, p. 4.

2. Julia Boorstin, "Delivering at Domino's Pizza," *Fortune,* February 7, 2005, p. 28.

3. Ron Ruggless, "Crossing the Border," *Nation's Restaurant News,* December 8, 2003, p. 29.

 Chapter 19 Video Case — Starbucks: Building Relationships with Coffee Growers

Starbucks, the world's largest supplier of premium coffee, works hard to guarantee a steady supply of quality coffee beans. An international giant, the company has nearly 6,000 outlets in 30 countries and sales of over $3.5 billion. Starbucks relies on the coffee bean for its success and faces the challenge of maintaining quality standards during a time of expansion and a global coffee crisis.

Coffee is produced in 70 tropical nations, and the quality varies tremendously. Starbucks buys a grade of coffee that is grown at high altitudes and that possesses a density or compaction of flavors as a result. For five years the supply of this specialty coffee exceeded demand and prices dropped below production costs for many growers. The situation drove many growers out of business. Those who remained were forced to cut back on crop maintenance, which resulted in lower quality. To continue to expand globally, Starbucks must ensure a steady supply of specialty coffee in the years ahead. When the supply of quality beans drops, Starbucks and other buyers must spend more time searching for specialty coffee.

One strategy Starbucks is using to face this challenge is to build long-term relationships with suppliers.

The company purchases beans primarily from smaller farmers, invests in their operations, and teaches them how to produce specialty coffee. The firm also pays more for coffee—often above market price—which helps suppliers survive during a period of price volatility. In an effort to stabilize prices, Starbucks offers long-term contracts at set prices. Growers are assured future sales at established prices, and Starbucks is guaranteed a predictable supply of quality coffee. Another benefit to both parties is that farmers can use the profit to invest in their business and ensure supply in the years to come. Starbucks' risk is reduced as the company continues to grow and needs more beans.

Starbucks also has established other relationships as part of its global efforts. It partnered with two nonprofit organizations, Ecological Enterprise Ventures and Conservation International, to offer affordable credit to Latin American coffee growers. The credit works like bridge loans to ecologically friendly farmers in need of money to hold them over until the crop is harvested and to pay pickers. The loans help farmers survive so that they can be a constant source of coffee in the future. Starbucks also has partnered with Conservation International to encourage environmentally friendly growing practices. In Mexico, for example, trees had been cut down so that coffee trees could be planted in the sun. Trees are no longer cut down, and the result is the popular Shade Grown Mexico, a smooth, mellow coffee grown in shade.

Starbucks has also begun selling Fair Trade Coffee in its stores. Many workers in the coffee industry face terrible working conditions, and many growers are paid such low prices that they face poverty or debt. To be Fair Trade–certified, coffee producers must belong to democratically run cooperatives or associations and must implement crop management and environmental protection plans. Producers are guaranteed a fair price, long-term relationships with importers, and credit.

Questions for Discussion

1. Why is it important for Starbucks to guarantee a steady supply of coffee beans? How does the available supply of specialty coffee influence Starbucks' global expansion efforts?

2. Why are relationships with suppliers critical to Starbucks' success? What strategies are used by Starbucks to develop long-term relationships with suppliers?

3. How does Starbucks benefit from its relationships with Ecological Enterprise Ventures and Conservation International? Do you agree with Starbucks' decision to sell Fair Trade Coffee? Explain.

 ## Chapter 20 Video Case — Johnson & Johnson: Creating a Global Learning Organization

Headquartered on a small campus in New Jersey, Johnson & Johnson (J&J) is one of the most globalized companies in the world. The organization is made up of over 230 companies operating primarily in the health care and personal care industries. Johnson & Johnson has manufacturing facilities in more than 60 countries and sells products in virtually every country in the world. Known for its customer-based values, the highly decentralized organization faces a major challenge managing many diverse companies.

The foundation of the Johnson & Johnson culture for all its companies is its Credo, a set of value statements that provides guidelines for employees. For nearly 70 years, the Credo has created the cultural ties that bind the organization, although—by design—the (J&J) family of companies is anything but tied together. Johnson & Johnson began to decentralize long before decentralization became fashionable in corporate America. Each of its companies is encouraged to act independently, deciding whom to hire and what products to produce. Decentralization has become so ingrained in the organization that each business is able to operate as a separate entity, which is part of Johnson & Johnson's strength: It is a very large organization with the flexibility of a smaller one.

The organization gains competitive advantage by letting the diverse companies create their own identities and pursue their own markets. In this environment, knowledge management injects life into the organization and translates into profits. Every year each company invests millions of dollars in education and training for its work force, consistent with the Credo values. With the core competencies of most jobs today changing rapidly, organizations like Johnson & Johnson face the challenge of reacting quickly to meet the learning needs of employees. Traditional methodologies limit a company's ability to react quickly and efficiently.

To maintain a decentralized structure, provide development for all employees, and deliver knowledge and skills rapidly, Johnson & Johnson created eUniversity in 2002. It's an electronic platform that offers a searchable resource for learning and development opportunities for J&J employees around the world.[1] With so many companies and more than 100,000 employees spread across the globe, eUniversity consolidates disparate learning technologies into a single system and allows J&J to control quality and costs.[2] It connects learning units as opposed to simply implementing a new technology.

The principle of eUniversity is to tap into the independence of each Johnson & Johnson group and capture the diversity of thought. This complex principle requires making use of both Web-based education and the classroom. The time together is spent in application and real-life problem solving instead of simply learning basic concepts. More than 75 Johnson & Johnson companies have offered training programs to other J&J companies through eUniversity. This cross-fertilization of knowledge has given employees not only an opportunity to learn but also a career competitive advantage. Participation has grown, and now a new user registers every 1.3 minutes; over three years, J&J employees completed 900,000 courses.[3]

Johnson & Johnson has realized several benefits from eUniversity. First, employees have learned much more from peers in similar situations than management thought they would. Second, smaller companies have gained access to the best learning experiences of the other companies, which was not possible before. Third, Johnson & Johnson has leveraged vendor-produced content across its courses and saved costs. Classroom training for sales representatives has been reduced by 30 to 40 percent, travel costs have dropped 20 percent, and the number of actual selling days for qualified sales reps has increased.[4]

Questions for Discussion

1. Why is eUniversity a valuable human resource tool for the Johnson & Johnson organization?

2. How does eUniversity manage to operate effectively in a decentralized environment?

3. What are the benefits of eUniversity to individual employees and to the organization?

Sources

1. www.jnj.com.

2. Kee Meng Yeo, "Johnson & Johnson: A New Paradigm for Learning Systems Management," *Chief Learning Officer Magazine,* March 2006, www.CLOmedia.com/content/anmviewer.as?a=1282&print=yes.

3. Ibid.

4. Ibid.

Endnotes

Negócios Internacionais · Internationales Geschäft · 国際商務 · Παγοσμιο Business · Los negocios internacionales Παγοσμιο · Gli Affari Internazionali

CHAPTER 1

1. For example, see Cornelis A. de Kluyver and John A. Pearce, II, *Strategy: A View from the Top*, 2nd ed. (Upper Saddle River, NJ: Pearson Prentice Hall, 2006), p. 38; InvestorDictionary.com, "Multinational Corporation: What's the Definition?" http://investordictionary.com/definition/multinational+corporation.aspx (July 6, 2006); and "Multinational Corporation," http://en.wikipedia.org/wiki/Multinational_corporation (July 6, 2006).

2. UNCTAD, "Transnational Corporations Statistics," www.unctad.org/templates/Page.asp?intItemID=3159&lang=1 (July 6, 2006).

3. Anne-Wil Harzing, "An Empirical Analysis and Extension of the Bartlett and Goshal Typology of Multinational Corporations," *Journal of International Business Studies,* First Quarter 2000, pp. 101–19; and C. A. Bartlett and S. Goshal, *Managing across Borders: The Transnational Solution* (Boston: Harvard Business School Press, 1989).

4. "The Black Death," www.insecta-inspecta.com/fleas/bdeath/bdeath.html (July 2, 2006); and Robbie Robertson, "Globalization Is Not Made in the West," www.globalpolicy.org/globaliz/define/2005/0413notmadeinthewest.htm (July 5, 2006).

5. "A Quick Guide to the World History of Globalization," www.sas.upenn.edu/~dludden/global1.htm (July 2, 2006); "Dutch East India Company," http://en.wikipedia.org/wiki/Dutch_East_India_Company#History (July 3, 2006); BBC News, "Globalization: What on Earth Is It About?" http://news.bbc.co.uk/1/hi/special_report/1999/02/99/e-cyclopedia/711906.stm (July 2, 2006); and "The Growth of Global Industry," *The Wheel Extended,* no. 4 (1989), p. 11.

6. "Multinationals Come into Their Own," *Financial Times,* December 6, 2000, p. 16.

7. Bayer, "History," www.bayer.com/bayer-group/history/page701.htm (July 3, 2006).

8. Alfred D. Chandler, Jr., and Bruce Mazlish (eds.), *Leviathans: Multinational Corporations and the New Global History* (New York: Cambridge University Press, 2005), pp. 66, 88–89.

9. Fred W. Riggs, "Globalization Is a Fuzzy Term but It May Convey Special Meanings," *The Theme of the IPSA World Congress 2000,* July 1999, www2.hawaii.edu/~fredr/ipsaglo.htm (July 29, 2000); and "Globalization," http://en.wikipedia.org/wiki/Globalization (July 2, 2006).

10. Theodore Levitt, "The Globalization of Markets," Harvard Business Review 61, no. 3 (May–June 1983), pp. 92–93.

11. Daniel Yergin, "The Word of the Week," *Daily Davos Home Views,* February 3, 1999, www.dailydavos.com/nw-srv/printed/special/davos/vw; and Daniel Yergin, "The Word of the Week," *Newsweek.com,* www.daily-davos.com/nw-srv/printed/special/davos/vw/vw0199tu_1.htm.

12. www.globality.org.uk (July 3, 2006).

13. "Running a Global Company Well Poses Major Operational Challenges," http://knowledge.wharton.upenn.edu (July 4, 2006), p. 2.

14. World Trade Organization, *International Trade Statistics 2005,* (Geneva: World Trade Organization, 2005).

15. "Foreign Direct Investment Flows," UNCTAD GlobStat database, http://globstat.unctad.org/html/index.html (July 4, 2006); "Foreign Affiliates in Host Economies," UNCTAD GlobStat database, http://globstat.unctad.org/html/index.html (July 4, 2006); "International Trade in Merchandise and Services," UNCTAD GlobStat database, http://globstat.unctad.org/html/index.html (July 4, 2006); World Trade Organization, *International Trade Statistics 2005;* and UNCTAD, *World Investment Report 2005* (New York:.United Nations, 2005).

16. UNCTAD, *World Investment Report 1997* (New York: United Nations, 1997), p. XV.

CHAPTER 2

1. The International Monetary Fund's Programme on Transnational Corporations uses the stock of foreign direct investment as a measure of the productive capacity of international corporations in foreign countries.

2. T. Callen and W. J. McKibben, "Policies and Prospects in Japan and the Implications for the Asia-Pacific Region," IMF Working Paper WP/01/131, International Monetary Fund, September 2001, p. 13.

3. Internet URLs are as follows:
   a. Office of Trade and Economic Analysis, www.ita.doc.gov/td/industry/otea.
   b. *U.S. Foreign Trade Highlights,* www.ita.doc.gov/industry/otea/usfth.
   c. *U.S. Commodity Trade with Top 80 Trading Partners,* www.ita.doc.gov/td/industry/otea/usfth/top80cty/top80cty.html.
   d. *U.S. Industry and Trade Outlook 2002,* www.ita.doc.gov/td/industry/otea/outlook/index.html.

4. Bureau of Economic Analysis, "U.S. International Investment Position, 2005," June 29, 2006, www.bea.gov/bea/newsrelarchive/2006/intinv05.htm (July 15, 2006).

5. Russell B. Scholl, "The International Investment Position of the United States at Year-End 1999," *Survey of Current Business,* July 2000, pp. 46–56, www.bea.doc.gov/bea/pubs.htm; and Bureau of Economic Analysis, "U.S. International Investment Position, 2005."

6. Japan External Trade Organization, "Foreign Direct Investment in Japan Rises over 60% in April–September 2003 ," January 15, 2004, www.jetro.go.jp/en/market/trend/topic/2004_01_fdi.html (July 15, 2006);*Outward Direct Investment by Country and Region* (Tokyo: Ministry of Finance, June 1, 2000), www.mof.go.jp/english/fdi/e1c008h2.htm (November 13, 2000); and JETRO, *White Paper on Foreign Direct Investment 2000,* www.jetro.go.jp/it/e/pub/whitepaper/invest2002.pdf (August 24, 2002).

7. "Technical Notes," *World Development Report 2001* (Washington, DC: World Bank, 2001), p. 231.

8. Ibid., p. 232.

9. "Economic Performance," *Human Development Report 2005,* pp. 266–69, www.sd.undp.org/HDR/HDR05e.pdf (July 11, 2006).

10. "Incentives and State Aids Granted to the Enterprises in Turkey," www.turkisheconomy.org.uk/investment/incentives.htm (July 11, 2006).

11. "International Performance Outshines Domestic Results," *Business International,* September 29, 1986, p. 305.

12. "The 100 Largest U.S. Multinationals," *Forbes,* July 18, 1994, pp. 276–79.

13. Jon E. Hilsenrath, "U.S. Multinationals Reap Overseas Bounty," *The Wall Street Journal,* April 4, 2005, p. A2.

14. William C. Gruben and Sherry L. Kiser, "NAFTA and Maquiladoras: Is the Growth Connected?" www.maquilaportal.com/public/navegar/nav48.htm (June 30, 2002).

15. "Maquila Overview," www.maquilaportal.com/Visitors_Site/nav21.htm (July 12, 2006).

16. Takashi Kozu, Ko Nakayama, Aiko Mineshima, and Yumi Saita, "Changes in Japan's Export and Import Structures," *Bank of Japan Monthly Bulletin,* May 2002.

17. "U.S. Companies See 1992 as a Opportunity," *San Jose Mercury News,* March 26, 1989, p. 1.

CHAPTER 3

1. Government administrators involved in project evaluation are increasingly applying socioeconomic rather than purely financial criteria. For example, social rates of discount and opportunity costs are considered rather than the pure costs of borrowing money. Although marketing managers do not have to be development economists any more than they need to be specialists in marketing research, they should have knowledge of the basic concepts.

2. "Fortress of Mercantilism," *Insight,* July 18, 1988, pp. 15–17.

3. Brian Bremner, "Don't Let 'Mr. Dollar' Get Away with It; Japan's Zembei Mizoguchi Is Driving Down the Yen; He Ought to Be Stopped," *BusinessWeek,* March 22, 2004, p. 76; and Sebastian Moffett and Jason Sapsford, "As the Yen Surges, Tokyo Remains on the Sidelines," *The Wall Street Journal,* November 26, 2004, p. A2.

4. David Ricardo, "The Principles of Political Economy and Taxation," in *International Trade Theory: Hume to Ohlin,* ed. William R. Allen (New York: Random House, 1965), pp. 62–67.

5. The idea that only hours of labor determine production costs is known as the *labor theory of value.* In fairness to Ricardo, we must admit that he included the cost of capital as "embodied labor" in his labor costs. Actually, the theory of comparative advantage can be explained by the cost of all factors of production.

6. Eli F. Heckscher, "The Effect of Foreign Trade on the Distribution of Income," *Economisk Tidskrift* 21 (1919), pp. 497–512; and Bertil Ohlin, *Interregional and International Trade* (Cambridge, MA: Harvard University Press, 1933).

7. The economist Bela Belassa, in his *Stages Approach to Comparative Advantage,* published by the World Bank in 1977, found in a study of 26 developed and developing nations that "the intercountry differences in the structure of exports are in a large part explained by differences in physical and human capital endowments."

8. J. Sachs and H. Shatz, "Trade and Jobs in U.S. Manufacturing," cited in *The Economist,* October 1, 1994, p. 19.

9. Dennis R. Appleyard, Alfred J. Field, Jr., and Steven L. Cobb, *International Economics,* 5th ed. (Burr Ridge, IL: McGraw-Hill Irwin, 2006), pp. 151–55, provide a substantial review of different explanations for the Leontief paradox, including citations to a number of empirical studies that have tested these alternative explanations.

10. Appleyard, Field, and Cobb, *International Economics,* pp. 174–77.

11. R. Vernon, "International Investment and International Trade in the Product Cycle," *Quarterly Journal of Economics* 80 (1966), pp. 190–207.

12. Many new products come not from the manufacturer's laboratories but from its suppliers of machinery and raw materials.

13. Belassa, *Stages Approach to Comparative Advantage,* pp. 26–27.

14. Akira Takeishi and Takahiro Fujimoto, "Modularization in the Auto Industry: Interlinked Multiple Hierarchies of Product, Production, and Supplier Systems," Working Paper 01-02, Institute of Innovation Research, Hitotsubashi University, Tokyo, February 2001; Larry Weiss, "Automakers Test Labor-Cutting Strategy in Brazil," *Labor Report on the Americas,* March–April 1999, www.labournet.de/branchen/auto/vw/modular.html (July 7, 2006); Ronaldo Couto Parente, *Strategic Modularization in the Brazilian Automotive Industry: An Empirical Analysis of Its Antecedents and Performance Implications,* Ph.D. thesis, Temple University, Philadelphia, August 2003, http://baru.ibict.br/tede-ibict/tde_arquivos/1/TDE-2004-11-08T12:48:34Z-48/Publico/RonaldoParente.pdf (July 7, 2006); and Gregory L. White, "Chrysler Makes Manufacturing Inroads at Plant in Brazil," *The Wall Street Journal,* August 13, 1998.

15. Richard B. Chase, F. Robert Jacobs, and Nicholas J. Aquilano, *Operations Management for Competitive Advantage,* 11th ed. (Burr Ridge, IL: McGraw-Hill Irwin, 2005).

16. Paul R. Krugman, "Increasing Returns, Monopolistic Competition and International Trade," *Journal of International Economics* 9, no. 4 (1979), pp. 469–79; and Paul R. Krugman, "Scale Economies, Product Differentiation and the Pattern of Trade," *American Economic Review* 70, no. 4 (1980), pp. 950–59.

17. Gerard Tellis and Peter Golder, "First to Market, First to Fail? Real Causes of Enduring Marketing Leadership," S*loan Management Review* 37, no. 2, cited in "Why First May Not Last," *The Economist,* March 16, 1996, p. 65.

18. Alfred Marshall, *Principles of Economics,* 8th ed. (London: Macmillan, 1920).

19. Michael E. Porter, *The Competitive Advantage of Nations* (New York: Free Press, 1990).

20. For example, see Christophe Lecuyer, *Making Silicon Valley: Innovation and the Growth of High Tech, 1930–1970,* (Cambridge, MA: MIT Press, 2005).

21. John H. Dunning, "The Competitive Advantage of Countries and the Activities of Transnational Corporations," *Transnational Corporations,* February 1992, pp. 135–68.

22. John H. Dunning, *The Globalization of Business* (London: Routledge, 1993), p. 106.

23. "Footwear Industry Tells Congress 'Shoe Gap' Threatens U.S. Defense," *The Wall Street Journal,* August 24, 1984, p. 21; and Thomas A. Pugel, *International Economics,* 13th ed. (New York: McGraw-Hill Irwin, 2007), pp. 197–98.

24. See Hossein Askari, John Forrer, Jiawen Yang, and Tarek Hachem, "Measuring Vulnerability to U.S. Foreign Economic Sanctions," *Business Economics* 40, no. 2 (April 2005), pp. 41–55.

25. Lance Davis and Stanley Engerman, "History Lessons: Sanctions: Neither War nor Peace," *Journal of Economic Perspectives* 17, no. 2 (Spring 2003), p. 187.

26. Gary C. Hufbauer, "Economic Sanctions: America's Folly," in *Economic Casualties: How U.S. Foreign Policy Undermines Trade, Growth, and Liberty,* ed. S. Singleton and D. T. Griswold (Washington, DC: Cato Institute, 1999), pp. 91–99; and Askari et al, "Measuring Vulnerability."

27. Hendrik Van den Berg, *International Economics* (New York: McGraw-Hill Irwin, 2004), p. 240.

28. Larry Elliott, "Two Countries, One Booming, One Struggling: Which One Followed the Free-Trade Route?: A Look at Vietnam and Mexico Exposes the Myth of Market Liberalisation," *The Guardian,* December 12, 2005, p. 23.

29. Dexter Robers and Paul Magnusson, "China's Trade Boss: Vice-Premier Wu Li Has an Iron Will; She'll Need It When She Comes to Washington to Lead Talks," *BusinessWeek,* April 12, 2004, p. 16; Chris Cziborr, "Chipmakers Watch as U.S., China Fight over Chip Tax," *Orange County Business Journal,* March 29–April 4, 2004, p. 6; Dai Yan, "Agreement Ends First Complaint at WTO," *China Daily,* July 15, 2004, p. 2; and Office of the Foreign Trade Representative, *2004 National Trade Estimate Report on Foreign Trade Barriers* (Washington, DC: United States Trade Representative, 2004), p. 60.

30. "How to Lower Price of Ethanol; Kill the Tariff, Help Consumers," *Rocky Mountain News,* May 14, 2006, p. 5E; Alan Beattie, "Brake on Biofuels as Obstacles Clog the Road," *Financial Times,* May 9, 2006, p. 6; and "Holman W. Jenkins, Jr., "What's Wrong with Free Trade in Biofuels," *The Wall Street Journal,* February 22, 2006, p. A15.

31. "Brie and Hormones," *The Economist,* January 7, 1989, pp. 21–22; "Europe's Burden," *The Economist,* May 22, 1999, p. 84; and Office of the Foreign Trade Representative, *2006 National Trade Estimate Report on Foreign Trade Barriers,* March 2006, www.ustr.gov/Document_Library/Reports_Publications/2006/2006_NTE_Report/Section_Index.html (July 9, 2006), p.242.

32. Andrew Bounds, "Sino-EU Trade Relations Wane over Footwear Tariffs Dispute," *Financial Times,* July 5, 2006, p. 4; David Rennie, "Mandelson Child Shoe Levy 'Will Hit the Poor," *The Daily Telegraph,* July 5, 2006, p. 2; Tobias Buck, "How EU Textile Quotas Became a Chinese Puzzle," *Financial Times,* August 24, 2005, p. 2; Alexandra Harney, "Limits

Force Chinese Clothing Makers to Tighten Their Belts," *Financial Times,* August 24, 2005, p. 2; and "EU to Decide Shoe Dumping Action," http://news.bbc.co.uk/2/hi/business/4789346.stm (July 8, 2006).

33. Hugo Gurdon, "The U.S. Should Unsign Kyoto," *The Wall Street Journal Europe,* October 11, 2002, p. A6: and Alistair Ulph and Laura Valentini, "Is Environmental Dumping Greater When Plants Are Footloose?" *Scandinavian Journal of Economics* 103, no. 4 (December 2001), p. 673.

34. Robert Anderson, "Slovakia's 'Soviet' Skills Set to Create Car World-Beater," *Financial Times,* April 20, 2006, p. 4; John Gapper, "It Is Time for the Big Three to Shut Up," *Financial Times,* October 20, 2005, p. 19; "The New Rules of Trade," National Review, April 18, 1994, pp. 40–44; and Marc Champion and Adam Z. Horvath, "EU Expansion Fuels Debate on Taxes," *The Wall Street Journal,* May 3, 2004, p. A18.

35. "Agriculture: Support Estimates, 2004," *OECD in Figures—2005 Edition* (Paris: OECD, 2005), http://dx.doi.org/10.1787/758034618756 (July 31, 2006).

36. Paul Wolfowitz, "Doha's Last Chance," *The Wall Street Journal,* July 1, 2006, p. A10; Scott Miller, "France Digs In for Subsidy Fight," *The Wall Street Journal Europe,* May 16, 2006, p. 1; Juliane von Reppert-Bismarck, "EU to Take Up Disclosing Who Gets Farm Aid; Publishing Subsidy Lists Could Fuel Global Pressure to End Agricultural Support," *The Wall Street Journal,* November 7, 2005, p. A18; and "Agriculture: Support Estimates, 2004," *OECD in Figures—2005 Edition* (Paris: OECD, 2005).

37. "The Fruits of Free Trade: Protection's Price," *2002 Annual Report—Federal Reserve Bank of Dallas,* Federal Reserve Bank of Dallas, www.dallasfed.org/fed/annual/2002/ar02f.html (June 30, 2004).

38. "Non-Tariff Barriers: A Rising Trend in World Trade," *World Economic Situation and Prospects 2006* (New York: United Nations, 2006).

39. Council of the European Union, "Council Regulation (EC) No 1964/2006 of 29 November 2005 on the Tariff Rates for bananas," http://europa.eu.int/eur-ex/lex/LexUriServ/site/en/oj/2005/l_316/l/31620051202en00010002.pdf (July 9, 2006); and Scott Miller, "Trading Partners Meet New EU," *The Wall Street Journal,* May 4, 2004, p. A17.

40. "A Summary of the Final Act of the Uruguay Round," www.fas.usda.gov/itp/policy/gatt/sum_fact.html#cAgreement (December 18, 2000).

41. World Trade Organization, *Annual Report 2003* (Lausanne, Switzerland: WTO, 2003); OECD, *Farm Household Income, Issues and Policy Responses* (Paris: OECD, 2003).

42. *Report on United States Barriers to Trade and Investment* (Brussels: European Commission, December 2003).

43. Office of the Foreign Trade Representative, *2006 National Trade Estimate Report on Foreign Trade Barriers.*

44. Ibid.

45. Ibid.

46. G. Thomas Sims, "Uncommon Market: Corn Flakes Class Shows the Glitches in European Union," *The Wall Street Journal,* November 1, 2005, p. A1.

47. Office of the Foreign Trade Representative, *2006 National Trade Estimate Report on Foreign Trade Barriers,* pp. 238–41; Doris de Guzman, "EU Biotech Labeling Laws Frustrate Ag Industry," *Chemical Market Reporter,* July 14, 2003, p. 14; and "Moment of Truth over GM as U.S. Files WTO Complaint," Friends of the Earth, Belgium, May 13, 2003, www.foeeurope.org/press/2003/AW_13_May_moment.htm (April 15, 2004).

48. The OECD publishes *Costs and Benefits of Protection,* which evaluates a wide range of studies on import restrictions of manufactured goods in OECD countries. Patrick A. Messerlin, *Measuring the Costs of Protection in Europe: European Commercial Policy in the 2000s* (Washington, DC: International Institute for Economics, 2001), examined costs in 22 highly protected industries in the EU. The 2002 annual report of the Federal Reserve Bank of Dallas, www.dallasfed.org/fed/annual/2002/ar02f.html (July 9, 2006), provides a listing of the jobs saved and total costs of protecting these jobs for 20 selected industries.

49. World Trade Organization, *Annual Report 2003.*

50. Kofi A. Annan, "Help the Third World Help Itself," *The Wall Street Journal,* November 29, 1999, p. A19. Copyright 1999 by Dow Jones & Co. Inc. Reproduced with permission of Dow Jones & Co. Inc. in the format textbook via Copyright Clearance Center.

51. Charles Kindleberger, *American Business Abroad* (New Haven, CT: Yale University Press, 1969), pp. 43–44.

52. See, for example, J. H. Dunning, *Multinational Enterprises and the Global Economy* (Addison-Wesley, 1992); and F. T. Knickerbocker, *Oligopolistic Reaction and Multinational Enterprise* (Boston: Harvard Business School, 1973).

53. Stephen Hymer, *The International Operations of International Firms: A Study in Direct Investment* (Cambridge, MA: MIT Press, 1976).

54. Ricard Caves, "International Corporations: The Industrial Economics of Foreign Investment," *Economica,* February 1971, pp. 5–6.

55. R. Z. Aliber, "A Theory of Direct Investment," *The International Corporation* (Cambridge, MA: MIT Press, 1970), pp. 17–34.

56. A. Rugman, *International Diversification and the Multinational Enterprise* (Lexington, MA: Lexington Books, 1979).

57. F. T. Knickerbocker, *Oligopolistic Reaction and Multinational Enterprise.*

58. E. M. Graham, "Transatlantic Investments by Multinational Firms: A Rivalistic Phenomenon," *Journal of Post-Keynesian Economics, Fall* 1978, pp. 82–99.

59. P. Buckley and M. Casson, *The Future of Multinational Enterprise* (New York: Macmillan, 1976).

60. John H. Dunning, *International Production and the Multinational Enterprise* (London: George Allen & Unwin, 1981), pp. 109–10.

CHAPTER 4

1. Martin Wolfe, "Why Washington and Beijing Need Strong Global Institutions," *Financial Times,* April 19, 2006, p. 13.

2. See www.un.org/partners/business/other/pages/factsheets/fs3.htm (accessed May 19, 2006).

3. United Nations, www.un.org.

4. See www.global-challenges.org/000why-and-how.html (accessed May 20, 2006).

5. Michael D. Kennedy, "The Cultural Politics of Energy Security," University of Michigan, September 23, 2005; www.witbd.org/articles/nato.html (accessed May 11, 2006).

6. See NATO treaty, Article 5, www.nato.int.

7. "NATO, Russia Agree to Partnership," *The Wall Street Journal,* May 15, 2002, p. A14.

8. See www.aseansec.org/64.htm (accessed May 19, 2006).

9. See www.wto.org/english/news_e/pres 98_e/pr88_e.htm (accessed May 12, 2006).

10. See www.wto.org/English/thewto_e/whatis_e/tif_e/fact4_e.htm (accessed May 11, 2006).

11. "GATT Comes Right," *The Economist,* December 18, 1993, pp. 13–14.

12. See www.wto.org (accessed May 12, 2006).

13. Elizabeth Becker, "Delegates from Poorer Nations Walk Out of World Trade Talks," *New York Times,* September 15, 2003, p. 1.

14. Scott Miller, "French Resistance to Trade Accord Has Cultural Roots," *The Wall Street Journal,* May 16, 2006, p. 1.

15. The Australian government issues helpful WTO Doha bulletins that are posted at www.dfat.gov.au/trade/negotiations/wto_bulletin (accessed May 12, 2006).

16. See http://trade.businessroundtable.org/trade_2006/wto/success.html (accessed May 12, 2006).

17. Jagdish Bhagwati, "How to Resolve the Deadlock Holding Back World Trade Talks," *Financial Times,* November 15, 2005, p. 15.

18. Guy de Jonquières, "WTO Urged to Act on Regional Pacts," *Financial Times,* February 6, 1997, p. 10.

19. "EU Slips Up over Banana Imports," *Financial Times,* July 18, 2000, p. 7.

20. Perez Alfonze, "The Organization of Petroleum Exporting Countries," *Monthly Bulletin* (Caracas), no. 2 (1966).

21. *International Petroleum Encyclopedia* (Tulsa, OK: Pennwell Publishing, 1979), pp. 194–95, table 6.

22. Luis Vallenilla, *Oil: The Making of a New Economic Order* (New York: McGraw-Hill, 1975).

23. James Cook, "Comeuppance," *Forbes,* May 9, 1983, pp. 55–56.

24. "The Impact of Lower Oil Prices," *IMF World Economic Outlook,* May 1994, pp. 20–21.

25. The G8 Research Centre at the University of Toronto, an independent education and research body, is accessible at www.g7.utoronto.ca.

26. UNDP, *Human Development Report 2005*, www.undp.org

27. To view a short film that summarizes the criticism of a 2005 G8 meeting, see www.camcorderguerillas.net/FILMS/G8.

28. Ambassador Rob Portman was the U.S. trade representative as of April 2005. He was appointed by President Bush to be director of the Office of Management and Budget (OMB) in April 2006. Susan Schwab was nominated as U.S. trade representative. She had been deputy trade representative. See www.ustr .gov/Document_Library/Press_Releases/2006/ March/Joint_Statement_from_the_Meeting_ of_the_NAFTA_Free_Trade_Commission.html.

29. See www.ustr.gov, under "trade facts."

30. See the Canadian Broadcasting Corporation's summary at www.cbc.ca/news/ background/softwood_lumber.

31. See www.cocef.org and www.nadb.org.

32. See www.era.anthropology.ac.uk/ Era_Resources/Era_Peasants/theory12.htm.

33. "The Paper Chase," *The Economist,* March 16, 2006. See www.economist.com/displaystory.cfm?story_id=5636381 (accessed May 18, 2006).

34. "The Diminishing of Brazil," The Economist, May 11, 2006. See www.economist.com/ displaystory.cfm?story_id=6919442 (accessed May 18, 2006).

35. See www.export.gov/fta/complete/CAFTA (accessed May 18, 2006).

36. "Venezuela Quits Andean Trade Block," BBC News, April 20, 2006, http://news.bbc .co.uk/1/hi/business/4925056.stm (accessed May 23, 2006).

37. See www.oas.org/main/main.asp?s Lang=E&sLink=http://www.oas.org/36ag/english (accessed May 18, 2006).

38. Derek Urwin, *The Community of Europe: A History of European Integration since 1945* (New York: Longman, 1991), p. 8.

39. World Trade Organization, www.wto.org/ English/news_e/pres05_e/pr401_e.htm, (accessed May 13, 2006).

40. See the EU Web site for further information on accession: http://ec.europa.eu/comm/ enlargement/towards_EU_membership/index_en.htm (accessed May 13, 2006).

41. *The Wall Street Journal,* June 23, 2004, p. C16.

42. "Charlemagne," *The Economist,* May 11, 2006. See www.economist.com (accessed May 19, 2006).

43. See http://europa.eu/abc/history/index_en .htm (accessed May 13, 2006).

44. BBC News report, May 11, 2006, http://news.bbc.co.uk/1/hi/world/europe/476-2495.stm (accessed May 13, 2006).

45. See http://europa.eu/abc/panorama/ howorganised (accessed May 15, 2006).

46. This is as of the end of 2004 and will change when new countries join the EU. See www.consilium.europa.eu/cms3_fo/showPage .asp?id=242&lang=EN&mode=g (accessed May 14, 2006).

47. "Bringing New Practices to Europe's Top Table," *Financial Times,* July 3, 2002, p. 9.

48. See http://ec.europa.eu/budget/budget_ glance/where_from_en.htm (accessed May 14, 2006).

49. Wendell H. McCulloch, Jr., "United States of Europe?" *Backgrounder,* Heritage Foundation, no. 706, May 5, 1989.

50. Simon Wilson, "The Shocking Fraud at the Heart of the EU," *Money Week,* November 18, 2005, www.moneyweek.com/file/ 4567/eu-fraud-2411.html/ (accessed May 20, 2006).

51. Raphael Minder, "Turnout Low among New Member States," *Financial Times,* June14, 2004, p. 2.

52. "Increasingly, Rules of Global Economy Are Set in Brussels," *The Wall Street Journal,* April 23, 2002, p. A1.

53. See http://europa.eu.int/scadplus/leg/en/ lvb/l21210.htm (accessed May 17, 2006).

54. See http://mkaccdb.eu.int/cgi-bin/stb/mk-stb.pl (accessed May 17, 2006).

55. See http://ec.europa.eu/comm/external_ relations/japan/intro/eco_trade_relat.htm (accessed May 17, 2006).

56. See http://ec.europa.eu/comm/trade/ issues/bilateral/countries/usa/index_en.htm (accessed August 20, 2006).

CHAPTER 5

1. Financial Action Task Force, "Annual and Overall Review of Noncooperative Countries or Territories, 2005." See www.fatf-gafi.org/ document/4/0,2340,en_32250379_32236992_33 916420_1_1_1,00.html (accessed June 1, 2006).

2. Patrick M. Jost and Harjit Singh Sandhu, "The Hawala Alternative Remittance System and Its Role in Money Laundering," Interpol, 2000. See www.interpol.int/Public/Financial-Crime/MoneyLaundering/hawala/default.asp? (accessed June 1, 2006).

3. Cheol S. Eun and Bruce G. Resnick, *International Financial Management* (Burr Ridge, IL: McGraw-Hill Irwin), p. 25.

4. Charles N. Henning, William Pigott, and Robert Haney Scott, *International Financial Management* (New York: McGraw-Hill, 1978), p. 149.

5. Albert C. Whitaker, *Foreign Exchange,* 2nd ed. (New York: Appleton-Century-Crofts, 1933), p. 157.

6. Davie Hume, *Of the Jealousy of Trade,* 1758, http://cepa.newschool.edu/het/profiles/ hume.htm (accessed May 26, 2006).

7. Paul Krugman, "The Gold Bug Variations," November 1996, www.pkarchive.org/cranks/ goldbug.html (accessed May 26, 2006).

8. Ibid.

9. Jacques Rueff, *La réforme du système monétaire international* (Paris: Plon, 1973).

10. Quoted by Gareth Smyth, "Iranians' Scramble to Buy Gold Highlights Tensions," *Financial Times,* April 20, 2006, p. 6.

11. A. Acheson et al., *Bretton Woods Revisited* (Toronto: University of Toronto Press, 1972).

12. IMF, "Articles of Agreement,". www.imf.org/external/pubs/ft/aa/aa01.htm (accessed May 26, 2006).

13. *Federal Reserve Bulletin,* September 1969 and January 1974.

14. *Federal Reserve Bulletin*, December 1971 and January 1974.

15. The Triffin paradox was pointed out by Yale economist Robert Triffin.

16. "The IMF at a Glance: Factsheet," April 2006. See www.imf.org/external/np/exr/facts/ glance.htm (accessed May 30, 2006).

17. IMF, April 2006. See www.imf.org/external/np/exr/facts/finfac.htm (accessed May 25, 2006).

18. As of April 2006. See www.imf.org/external/np/exr/facts/quotas.htm (accessedMay 26, 2006).

19. Chris Giles and Krishna Guha, "Shake-up Agreed on IMF World Trade Role," *Financial Times,* April 24, 2006, p. 1.

20. Jeffrey Sachs, "How the Fund Can Regain Global Legitimacy," *Financial Times,* April 20, 2006, p. 13.

21. Andrew Balls, "IMF Dilemma as New Loans Start to Decline," *Financial Times,* December 28, 2005, p. 4.

22. The World Bank Group, www.worldbank.org.

23. See www.bis.org (accessed May 27, 2006).

24. www.imf.org. These are 2005 data.

25. Bank for International Settlements, "Central Bank Survey of Foreign Exchange and Derivatives Market Activity in 2004," March 17, 2005, http://www.bis.org/press/p050316.htm? (accessed May 28, 2006).

26. "World Market," *Financial Times,* June 1, 2002, p. 26.

27. Federal Reserve Bank of New York, "Foreign Exchange Rates." See www.ny.frb.org/ markets/fxrates/historical/fx.cfm (accessed May 28, 2006).

28. Herbert Stein, "Balance of Payments," in *The Concise Encyclopedia of Economics,* David R. Hendersen, ed., 1993, www.econlib .org/library/Enc/BalanceofPayments.html (accessed May 29, 2006).

29. Ibid.

30. Bureau of Economic Analysis, U.S. Department of Commerce, U.S. International Transactions, Fourth Quarter and Year 2005, March 14, 2006. See http://www.bea.gov/bea/ newsrel/transnewsrelease.htm (accessed May 3, 2006).

31. Stein, "Balance of Payments."

32. Ibid.

33. Ibid.

34. "Some Facts about the SDR," *IMF Survey,* April 1, 1996.

35. IMF, "Articles of Agreement."

CHAPTER 6

1. "How to Win Friends and Influence Clients," *The European,* January 21–27, 1994, p. 11.

2. I. Brady and B. Isaac, *A Reader in Cultural Change,* vol. 1 (Cambridge, MA: Schenkman Publishing, 1975), p. x.

3. Hy Mariampolski, *Ethnography for Marketers: A Guide to Consumer Immersion* (Thousand Oaks, CA: Sage Publications), p. 123.

4. "Cultural Traits," *Future Culture,* www.wepworld.com/future/tcoc.htm (January 2, 1998).

5. Vern Terpstra and Kenneth David, *The Cultural Environment of International Business* (Cincinnati: South-Western, 1985), p. 7.

6. E. T. Hall, *Beyond Culture* (Garden City, NY: Doubleday, 1977), p. 54.

7. "Make It Simple," *BusinessWeek,* September 9, 1996, pp. 96–104; "P&G Viewed China as a National Market and Is Conquering It," *The Wall Street Journal,* September 12, 1995, p. A1; "P&G Rewrites the Marketing Rules," *Fortune,* November 6, 1989, pp. 34–46; and "After Early Stumbles, P&G Is Making Inroads Overseas," *The Wall Street Journal,* February 6, 1989, p. B1.

8. "P&G's Joy Makes an Unlikely Splash in Japan," *The Wall Street Journal,* December12, 1997, p. B1.

9. Yung-Cheng Shen and Ting-Chen Chen, "When East Meets West: The Effect of Cultural Tone Congruity in Ad Music and Message on Consumer Ad Memory and Attitudes," *International Journal of Advertising* 25, no. 1 (2006), pp. 51–70.

10. One of the writers installed new production equipment in a Spanish factory to replace old but still serviceable machinery. Before leaving for a week's work in Madrid, he tested the equipment, trained some workers to use it, and advised the supervisor that it was ready. On his return, he was surprised to find that the new equipment was not being used. The supervisor explained that the old machinery was working well and he didn't want to "disrupt production." Actually, the new equipment was easier to use and would greatly increase output. Realizing that drastic action was called for, the writer grabbed a sledgehammer and made a token effort to destroy the old equipment. Only then did the supervisor get the message. The action was unorthodox, but it did bring immediate results.

11. "Mouse Trap," *The Wall Street Journal,* March 10, 1994, p. A12.

12. This classification depends in part on M. J. Herskovits, *Man and His Works* (New York: Alfred A. Knopf, 1952), p. 634. It was embellished by anthropologists at the University of South Alabama.

13. "Nike Recalls Shoes Bearing Logo That Muslims Found Offensive," *The Oregonian,* June 25, 1997, p. A18: Marc Champion, "Muslim Outrage Mounts over Cartoons in EU," *The Wall Street Journal,* February 3, 2006, p. A6.

14. Minda Zetlin, "Feng Shui: Smart Business or Superstition?" *Management Review,* August 1995, pp. 26–27.

15. Anita Snow, "Ad Featuring 'Che' Guevara Sparks Furor," *The Monitor,* August10, 2000, p. 8a.

16. Herskovits, *Man and His Works,* p. 414.

17. "The Middle East Mirage," *International Management,* April 1989, p. 21.

18. Sanjyot P. Dunung, *Doing Business in Asia: The Complete Guide* (New York: Lexington Books, 1995).

19. "Middle East Mirage," p. 23.

20. "Revolution in Mexico City: The One-Hour Lunch," *International Herald Tribune,* October 20, 1999, p. 14.

21. "Boom Times Erode Spain's Siesta Time," *The Oregonian,* December 26, 1999, p. A24.

22. Thomas E. Maher and Yim Yu Wong, "The Impact of Cultural Differences on the Growing Tensions between Japan and the United States," *SAM Advanced Management Journal,* Winter 1994, p. 45.

23. "German View: You Americans Work Too Hard—and for What?" *The Wall Street Journal,* July 14, 1994, p. B1.

24. "Average Annual Hours in Manufacturing, 12 Countries, 1950–1996," *Foreign Labor Statistics,* http://stats.bls.gov/news.release/ prod4.t06.htm (January 7, 1998); "Working Hours per Full Working Week," *Japan 1997* (Tokyo: Keizai Koho Center, 1997), p. 97; and "Hours of Actual Work per Month, 1983–2001," Japan Ministry of Labor, http://jin.jcic.or.jp/ stat/stats/09LAB41.html (August 9, 2002).

25. It is difficult to translate adequately the connotations of the two words. No one proudly says he is an *obrero* even if he earns more than an *empleado* who is a file clerk.

26. "How the Japanese Are Changing," *Fortune,* Pacific Rim, 1990, pp. 15–22.

27. Samia Nakhoul, "Born to Be Untouchable," *Financial Times,* July 22–23, 2000, pp. i, iii.

28. Pravin K. Shah, "Religions of India," *Jain BBS Email Bulletin,* August 1994, http://Sun-SITE.sut.ac.jp.pub/academic/rel . . . dia/jain/ world_religions (June 6, 1997); and "History and Practices," *Sikhism in Brief,* www.sikhs. org/summary.htm (March 16, 2001).

29. "Taoism and the Taoist Arts," www .taoistsarts.net (August 15, 2002).

30. "Children of the Islamic Revolution: A Survey of Iran," *The Economist,* January 18, 1997, pp. 1–15.

31. "The Internet Economy Indicators," www.internetindicators.com/keyfindings.html (August 15, 2002).

32. Joseph Coleman, "Liquor Stores Phasing Out Beer Vending Machines," *The McAllen Monitor,* June 2, 2000, p. 6A.

33. "English Is Still on the March," *The Economist,* February 24, 2001, pp. 50–51.

34. Judy Dempsey, "Brussels Faces a Real Tongue Twister," *Financial Times,* January27/28, 2002, p. 2.

35. "Why Speaking English Is No Longer Enough," *International Management,* November 1986, p. 42.

36. An incident happened to one of the writers, newly arrived in Brazil, that went all over the country. The ad manager, a Brazilian, brought him a campaign emphasizing that car

owners should maintain 24 pounds per square inch in their tires to get maximum wear. To get the point across, life-size figures of a tire company salesman were made up, with the name of the company and a large "24" printed across his chest. Dealers were to set them up on a "D day." The writer, proud of the unusually good coordination of the campaign, began receiving calls from competitors. The message was that 24 in Brazilian Portuguese refers to gay men.

37. "French Watchdogs Seek to Limit English Web Sites," *The Mexico City News,* January 8, 1997, p. 32; and "French Lobby Loses Case," *Financial Times,* June 10, 1997, p. 2.

38. "Multilingual Website Widens the Way to a New Online World," *Financial Times,* February 7, 2001, p. 1.

39. "McDonald's: Burger and Fries a la Francaise," *The Economist,* April 17, 2004, pp. 60, 61.

40. "A Little Bad English Goes a Long Way in Japan's Boutiques," *The Wall Street Journal,* May 5, 1993, p. A1.

41. Among several sources are Nancy Armstrong and Melissa Wagner, *Field Guide to Gestures: How to Identify and Interpret Virtually Every Gesture Known to Man* (Quirk Books, 2003).

42. Gillian Tett, "Mori Gaffe May Hit Ruling Party's Poll Hopes," *Financial Times,* June 9, 2000, p. 16.

43. E. T. Hall, *The Hidden Dimension* (Garden City, NY: Doubleday, 1969), pp. 134–35.

44. Terri Morrison and Wayne A. Conaway, "Global Business Basics: The Problem of Proxemics," www.getcustoms.com/2004GTC/Articles/iw0100.html (July 26, 2004); "The Body Language of Proxemics," http://members.aol.com/Katydidit/bodylang.htm (July 19, 2006).

45. "A Global Guide to Gift Giving," *Los Angeles Times,* December 1, 1993, p. D4: Roger Axtell, *Do's and Taboos around the World* (New York: Wiley, 1990), pp. 113–47; and country-by-country gift-giving advice at www.giftelan.com/international_gift_giving.htm (July 26, 2004).

46. Neil H. Jacoby, Peter Nehemkis, and Richard Eells, *Bribery and Extortion in World Business* (New York: Macmillan, 1977), pp. 174–75.

47. "TI's Vision, Mission, Values Approach and Strategy," www.transparency.org/about_ti/mission.html#mission (July 26, 2004).

48. Herskovits, *Man and His Works,* p. 303.

49. Geert Hofstede, "Cultural Dimensions in Management and Planning," *Asia Pacific Journal of Management,* January 1984, p. 83; communication with Hofstede, October 27, 2004.

50. Hofstede, "Cultural Dimensions," p. 83.

51. Lisa Hoecklin, *Managing Cultural Differences* (Workingham, England: Addison-Wesley, 1995), pp. 28–30.

52. Ibid., p. 31.

53. Rose Knotts and Sheryann Tomlin, "A Comparison of TQM Practices in U.S. and Mexican Companies," *Production and Inventory Management Journal,* First Quarter 1994, p. 54.

54. Hoecklin, *Managing Cultural Differences,* pp. 31–32.

55. Hofstede, "Cultural Dimensions," pp. 81 and 84.

CHAPTER 7

1. M. E. Porter, *The Competitive Advantage of Nations* (New York: Free Press, 1990).

2. U.S. Department of State, Bureau of European and Eurasian Affairs, "Background Note on Austria," February 2006, www.state.gov/r/pa/ei/bgn/3165.htm, (accessed June 6, 2006).

3. *CIA Factbook,* June 1, 2006, www.cia.gov/cia/publications/factbook/geos/us.html (accessed June 6, 2006).

4. U.S. Department of Agriculture, Economic Research Service. See a.gov/Briefing/FruitandTreeNuts/Trade.htm (accessed June 6, 2006).

5. Federal Research Division, Library of Congress, "Afghanistan," Country Studies/Area Handbook Series, http://countrystudies.us/afghanistan/32.htm (accessed June 6, 2006).

6. World Facts, "Facts about Afghanistan," http://worldfacts.us/Afghanistan.htm (accessed June 6, 2006).

7. "Spain's Regions," *The Economist,* November 16, 1996, pp. 55–56.

8. BBC, "ETA Permanent Ceasefire Begins," March 24, 2006, http://news.bbc.co.uk/2/hi/europe/4839554.stm (accessed June 6, 2006).

9. Encyclopaedia Britannica, "Canadian Shield," www.britannica.com/eb/article-43264 (accessed June6, 2006).

10. United Nations, "The World Population Prospects, the 2004 Revision," February 24, 2005, www.un.org/esa/population/publications/WPP2004/wpp2004.htm (accessed July 6, 2006).

11. EUR Activ, EU News and Policy Positions, "EU Action Plan Seeks to Shift Freight to Rivers," January 18, 2006, updated May 29, 2006, www.euractiv.com/en/transport/eu-action-plan-seeks-shift-freight-rivers/article-151643 (accessed June 6, 2006).

12. BBC News Online, "Three Gorges Dam Wall Completed," May 20, 2006, http://news.bbc.co.uk/2/hi/asia-pacific/5000092.stm (accessed June 6, 2006).

13. International Rivers Network is an organization whose goal is to foster environmentally responsible river use. It is usually opposed to major dams because of the environmental degradation and violation of human rights these massive projects often involve. See www.irn.org.

14. One of the writers, representing a Chilean subsidiary of an American multinational, called on a large government-owned mine in Bolivia to sell Chilean-made products. The purchasing agent asked how anyone could expect her, a Bolivian, to buy goods made in Chile. Although appreciating that the parent company was American, she said, "The products are still made in Chile."

15. Rhoads Murphey, *The Scope of Geography,* 2nd ed. (Skokie, IL: Rand McNally, 1973), pp. 188–89.

16. Jared Diamond, *Guns, Germs, and Steel: The Fates of Human Societies* (New York: W.W. Norton 1997).

17. Andrew M. Karmack, *The Tropics and Economic Development* (Washington, DC: World Bank, 1976), p. 5.

18. There are many current ideas about the banning of DDT that do not take into account the science or actual history of DDT. Dr. Alan Lymbery, a parisotologist at Murdoch University, Australia, summarizes the current situation well. "The manufacture and use of DDT was banned in the US in 1972, on the advice of the US Environmental Protection Agency. The use of DDT has since been banned in most other developed nations, but it is not banned for public health use in most areas of the world where malaria is endemic. Indeed, DDT was recently exempted from a proposed worldwide ban on organophosphate chemicals.

"DDT usage for malaria control involves spraying the walls and backs of furniture, so as to kill and repel adult mosquitoes that may carry the malaria parasite. Other chemicals are available for this purpose, but DDT is cheap and persistent and is often a very effective indoor insecticide which is still used in many parts of the world.

"DDT is not used for outdoor mosquito control, partly because scientific studies have demonstrated toxicity to wildlife, but mainly because its persistence in the environment rapidly leads to the development of resistance to the insecticide in mosquito populations. There are now much more effective and acceptable insecticides, such as Bacillus thuringiensis, to kill larval mosquitoes outdoors. . . . Malaria is a major, ongoing disease problem in much of the developing world. Increases in the incidence of the disease have occurred for complex reasons. Reduced insecticide usage is one, but others include the resistance to treatment in both the parasite and the mosquito vectors, changes in land use that have provided new mosquito habitat, and the movement of people into new, high-risk areas.

"Most nations where malaria is a problem, and most health professionals working in the field of malaria control, support the targeted use of DDT, as part of the tool kit for malaria control. Most also agree that more cost-effective, less environmentally persistent alternatives are needed. There are some effective alternative chemicals for the control of adult mosquitoes, but preventing their further development is lack of investment by industry, because malaria is largely a disease of the poor." Feb. 2, 2004, *The Australian.* Quoted by Professor Ken Miles MBBS, FRCR, MSc (Nuclear Medicine), MD.

19. Joseph Kahn, "A Sea of Sand Is Threatening China's Heart," *New York Times,* June 8, 2006, p. 1.

20. Kenneth Deffeyes, *Hubbert's Peak: The Impending World Oil Shortage* (Princeton, NJ: Princeton University Press, 2001), p. 146.

21. "Third 'Major' Oil Discovery Is Made at El Nar in Sudan," *The Wall Street Journal,* January 21, 1997, p. B5; "Treasure under the Sea," *Financial Times,* May 1, 1997, p. 11; and "Pulling Oil from Davy Jones' Locker," *BusinessWeek,* October 30, 1995, pp. 74–76.

22. Association for the Study of Peak Oil and Gas, www.peakoil.net (accessed June 7, 2006).

23. Energy Information Administration, "Annual Energy Outlook 2005," www.eia.doe.gov/oiaf/aeo (accessed June 7, 2006).

24. Adam Porter, "'Peak Oil' Enters Mainstream Debate," *BBC News: UK edition,* June 10, 2005, http://news.bbc.co.uk/1/hi/business/4077802.stm co.uk/1/hi/sci/tech/3623549.stm (accessed June 6, 2006).

25. Canadian Association of Petroleum Producers, "Oil Sands Resources, Production and Projects," May 2006, www.capp.ca/default .asp?V_DOC_ID=1162 (accessed June 7, 2006).

26. Russell Gold, "As Prices Surge, Oil Giants Turn Sludge into Gold," *The Wall Street Journal,* March 27, 2006, p. 1.

27. Office of Deputy Assistant Secretary for Petroleum Reserves and Office of Naval Petroleum and Oil Shale Reserves, *Strategic Significance of America's Oil Shale Resource,* Vol. II: *Oil Shale Resources, Technology and Economics* (Washington, DC: U.S. Department of Energy, March 2004).

28. Greenpeace Australia Pacific, www.greenpeace.org.au/climate/causes/criminals/shaleoil/overview.html (accessed June 7, 2006).

29. Sasol, "Sasol Oil-from-Coal Process," www.sasol.com/sasol_internet/downloads/CTL_Brochure_1125921891488.pdf (accessed August 24, 2006).

30. On April 25, 1986, the world's worst nuclear power accident so far occurred at Chernobyl in Ukraine. The Chernobyl nuclear power plant, 80 miles north of Kiev, had four reactors, and while testing reactor number 4, personnel disregarded safety procedures. At 1:23 a.m. the chain reaction in the reactor became out of control, creating explosions and a fireball that blew off the reactor's heavy steel and concrete lid. See www.chernobyl.co.uk (accessed June 7, 2006).

31. Tim Flannery, "Nuclear: Back on the Horizon," *The Melbourne Age,* September 26, 2005 (accessed June 8, 2006).

32. Jeffrey Ball, "With a Big Nuclear Push, France Transforms Its Energy Equation," *The Wall Street Journal,* March 28, 2006, p. 1.

33. U.S. Energy Information Administration, "International Energy Outlook 2005," June 2005,. www.eia.doe.gov/oiaf/ieo/coal.html (accessed June 11, 2006).

34. U.S. Energy Information Administration, "International Energy Outlook 2004,", www.eia.doe.gov (accessed July 2, 2004).

35. Simon Romro, "Will Coal Be the Fuel of the 21st Century?" *New York Times,* May 31, 2006, www.iht.com/articles/2006/05/29/business/coal .php (accessed through ITH site June 8, 2006).

36. Keith Bradsher and David Barboza, "Clouds from Chinese Coal Cast a Long Shadow," *New York Times,* June 11, 2006, p. 1.

37. International Energy Agency, "Natural Gas," *Key World Energy Statistics 2005,* www.iea.org (accessed June 8, 2006).

38. American Wind Energy Association, "Global Wind Energy Market Report,", www.awea.org (accessed June 9, 2006).

39. American Wind Energy Association, "Record Year for Wind Energy," February 17, 2006, www.awea.org (accessed June 8, 2006).

40. Canadian Renewable Fuels Association, "Fuel Change," September 22, 2005, www .greenfuels.org/fuelchange/index.htm (accessed June 13, 2006).

41. www.fuelcells.org (accessed June 9, 2006).

42. Phillip Sutton, "Sustainability, What Does It Mean?" Green Innovations homepage, August 28, 2000, www.green-innovations.asn .au/sustblty.htm (accessed June 10, 2006).

43. Ibid.

44. Paul Hawken, *The Ecology of Commerce,* (New York: HarperCollins, 1994), p. 139.

45. Brundtland Commission, *Our Common Future: From One Earth to One World,* World Commission on Environment and Development (Oxford: Oxford University Press, 1987).

46. Economics Network, UK Higher Education Academy, "Development Survey on Definitions: Sustainable," www.economicsnetwork .ac.uk (accessed June 10, 2006).

47. Dino Mahtani, "Nigerian Oil Industry Helpless as Militants Declare War on Obasanjo," *Financial Times,* February 21, 2006.

48. Francesco Guerrera and Richard Waters, "IBM Chief Wants End to Colonial Companies," *Financial Times,* June 12, 2006, p. 1; Samuel Palmisano, "Multinationals Have Been Superseded," *Financial Times,* June 12, 2006, p. 15.

49. R. Edward Freeman, *Strategic Management: A Stakeholder Approach* (Boston: Pitman, 1984).

50. R. Edward Freeman, Andrew C. Wicks, and Bidhan Pamar, "'Stakeholder Theory' and the Corporate Objective Revisited," *Organizational Science* 15, no. 3 (May–June 2004), pp. 364–69.

51. F. R. Kluckhohn and F. L. Strodtbeck *Variations in Value Orientations* (Evanston, IL: Row Petersen, 1961).

52. "Sustainable Development Society Hosts Patagonia CEO Michael Crooke," *The Harbus Online,* Harvard Business School, May 10, 2004, www.harbus.org/news/2002/03/11News/Sustainable.Development.Society.Hosts.Patagonia.Ceo.Michael.Crooke-207418.shtml (accessed July 4, 2004).

53. Y. Chouinard, *Patagonia: The Next Hundred Years* (1995), p. 8, www.svn.org/initiativesfall2002/PDF_PatagoniaNext100Yrs.pdf (accessed September 17, 2004).

CHAPTER 8

1. Many of these factors also affect domestic firms, but multinational firms are generally more vulnerable and usually must act more quickly.

2. If management is interested in a country as a possible site for investment, it will require the same detailed information as it does for an area where the firm is already doing business.

3. *International Bibliography, Information, Documentation (IBID),* an excellent bibliography, is published quarterly by UNIPUB. It includes abstracts of publications and studies containing economic and demographic data.

4. "Country Classification," http://web .worldbank.org/WBSITE/EXTERNAL/DATASTA-TISTICS/0,,contentMDK:20420458~menuPK:64133156~pagePK:64133150~piPK:64133175~theSitePK:239419,00.html (October 7, 2006).

5. *2006 World Development Indicators,* table 1.6, http://devdata.worldbank.org (October 7, 2006). GNI is explained in *World Development Indicators 2001* (Washington, DC: World Bank, 2002), p. 15.

6. Friedrich Schneider and Dominik Enste, *Hiding in the Shadows: The Growth of the Underground Economy* (Washington, DC: International Monetary Fund, 2002), table 2, www.imf.org/external/pubs/ft/issues/ issues30/index.htm (June 30, 2004); and Friedrich Schneider and Robert Klinglmair, "Shadow Economies around the World: What do We Know?" March 2004, http://papers.ssrn .com/so13/papers.cfm?abstract_id=518526 (October 8, 2006).

7. World Bank, "Structure of Consumption in PPP Terms," *2000 World Development Indicators* (Washington, DC: World Bank, 2000), p. 224.

8. Joseph Khan, "Youth and His Hopes Die in Front of China Train," *San Antonio Express-News,* August 1, 2004, p. 21A.

9. "The Swoosh Index for Emerging Markets," *BusinessWeek,* May 5, 1997, p. 8; "Pangs of Conscience," *BusinessWeek,* July 29, 1996, pp. 46–47; "Nike, Inc.," *The Wall Street Journal,* September 23, 1997, p. B12; "Where Asia Goes from Here," *Fortune,* November 24, 1997, p. 104; and Matthew Forney, "How Nike Figured Out China," *Time Online Edition,* November 2004, www. time.com/time/globalbusiness/article/0,9171, 1101041025-725113,00.html (November 10, 2004).

10. "Debt Sustainability," *World Development Indicators 1997,* p. 225.

11. International Telecommunication Union, www.itu.int/ITU-D/icteye/Indicators/Indicators.aspx# (October 6, 2006).

12. *Human Development Report 2005* (New York: United Nations Development Program, 2005), pp. 232–34.

13. "Strictly Speaking, Wal-Mart May Need Lessons in French," *The Wall Street Journal,* April 13, 1994, p. B7; and "Wal-Mart Again Runs into Language-Law Trouble," *The Wall Street Journal,* June 24, 1994, p. A4.

CHAPTER 9

1. Ian Brownlie, *Principles of Public International Law* (Oxford, England: Oxford University Press, 1966), pp. 435–36.

2. "Why Planned Economies Fail," *The Economist,* June 25, 1988, p. 67. See also "Wounded Pride: Why Communism Fell," *The Economist,* May 25, 1991, pp. 98–99.

3. Jack Lowenstein, "Ready to Join the Big League?" *Euromoney,* October 1990, pp. 66–73.

4. Robert Graham, "Rightwing Coalition Confident of French Poll Win," *Financial Times,* June 8–9, 2002, p. 2.

5. *The Right Guide,* 4th ed. (Ann Arbor, MI: Economics America, 2000); and *The Left Guide,* 3rd ed. (Ann Arbor, MI: Economics America, 2001).

6. Richard L. Holman, "EC Widens Business Control," *The Wall Street Journal,* July 25, 1991, p. A10.

7. "Thatcher's Sales," *BusinessWeek,* December 10, 1990, p. 26.

8. Jill Leovy, "Lockheed Looks to Expand Its Airport Business," *Los Angeles Times,* May 31, 1994, pp. D1, 6.

9. Hilary Clarke, "Europe Flies Its Airport Revolution to the World," *The European,* May 22–28, 1997, p. 15.

10. Martin Dickson, "America's Sale of the Century," *Financial Times,* June 1, 1992, p. 12.

11. Roger Matthews, "Mozambique Brings In the British," *Financial Times,* June 17, 1997, p. 9.

12. Kathy Chen, "Cracking Open the Door," *The Asian Wall Street Journal,* April 14, 1997, p. 5.

13. "Privatization in Practice: Fourth Pan African Investment Summit," *Financial Times,* October 16, 2000, p. 14.

14. Gerhard Pohl, Robert Anderson, Stijn Claessens, and Simeon Djankov, "Privatisation and Restructuring in Central and Eastern Europe," World Bank Technical Paper No. 386 (Washington, DC: World Bank, June 1997); and Kevin Done, "Europe's Privatisation Fast Track," *Financial Times,* July 4, 1997, p. 10.

15. Gekko, "Random Walk: Wall Street," *National Review,* June 27, 1994, p. 26.

16. Virginia Marsh and Shawn Dorman, "Church Groups Catch the Privatization Spirit," *Financial Times,* January 8–9, 2000, p. 3.

17. "Water Industry: Frozen Taps," *The Economist,* May 31, 2003, p. 56. © 2003 The Economist Newspaper Group, Inc. Reprinted with permission. Further reproduction prohibited. Also, Colin Robinson, "Reviving the Scottish Water Industry," www.policyinstitute.info/AllPDFs/Robinson-Mar05.pdf (August 1, 2006).

18. John Lancaster, "U.S. Arms Sales in Gulf Risk Being Eroded by China and Others," *International Herald Tribune,* July 17, 1997, p. 6.

19. James Phillips and James H. Anderson, "International Terrorism: Containing and Defeating Terrorist Threats," *Issues 2000,* Heritage Foundation, Washington, DC, August 2000.

20. "The Price of Paying Ransoms," *The Economist,* September 2, 2000, p. 17.

21. Sarah Butcher, "No Hostages to Fortune," *Financial Times,* March 4, 2002, p. 10.

22. Butcher, "No Hostages to Fortune."

23. Sue Zesiger, "Freeze," *Fortune,* April 28, 1997, pp. 417–20.

24. Michael Bond, "Europe Alert over Threat of Nuclear Terrorism," *The European,* March 10–24, 1994, pp. 1, 2.

25. David Wessel, "Flow of Capital to Developing Nations Surges Even as Aid to Poorest Shrinks," *The Wall Street Journal,* March 24, 1997, p. A5.

26. www.duke/edu/~charvey/ Country_risk/pol .htm; and http://www.polrisk. com/products.htm. (July 21, 2002).

CHAPTER 10

1. "Shanghai Sees Law as Key to Being Commercial Hub," *Financial Times,* July 1, 2002, p. vi.

2. Mark A. Goldstein, "The UN Sales Convention," *Business America,* November 21, 1988, pp. 12–13.

3. A. H. Herman, "Growth in International Trade Law," *Financial Times,* March 30, 1989, p. 10.

4. Frances Williams, "GATT Joins Battle for Right to Protect," *Financial Times,* July 7, 1994, p. 7.

5. Jack Kemp, "Greenspan Is Right: Abolish Capital Gains Taxes," *The Wall Street Journal,* February 24, 1997, p. A22.

6. Madelaine Drohan, "The Fine Art of Avoiding Bewildering Italian Taxes," *The Globe and Mail,* September 28, 1996, p. D4.

7. Jonathan Schwarz, "Stimuli for Freer Trade," *Financial Times,* May 20, 1994, p. II.

8. "The Disappearing Taxpayer," *The Economist,* May 31, 1997, p. 15; and "Disappearing Taxes," *The Economist,* May 31, 1997, pp. 21–23.

9. "When We Wear the Black Hats," *The Wall Street Journal,* March 22, 1990, p. A16.

10. Richard L. Holman, "EC Antitrust Efforts Boosted," *The Wall Street Journal,* March 20, 1991, p. A17; and "EC Court Reinforces Commission's Antitrust Clout," *Eurecom,* April 1991, p. 1.

11. The Lex Column, *Financial Times* (London), June 16–17, 2001, p. 24.

12. Pierre Verkhhovsky and Clifford Chance, "Advising Japanese Clients on EU Competition Law" *International Journal of Competition Policy and Regulation,* www.global competitionreview.com/apar/jap_eu.cfm (July 30, 2004).

13. *The Economist,* June 9, 1979, pp. 91–92.

14. For example, see *Continental Ore Co. v. Union Carbide & Carbon Corp.,* 370 U.S. 690 (1962); *Timberline Lumber Co. v. Bank of America,* 549 F.2d 597 (9th Cir. 1976); and *United States v. Aluminum Co. of America,* 148 F.2d 416 (2d Cir. 1945).

15. "Brussels Clears AOL–Time Warner Merger," *Financial Times,* October 12, 2000, p. 24; and Mary Jacoby, "EU Hits Microsoft with $358.3 Million Penalty," *The Wall Street Journal* (July 13, 2006), p. A3.

16. John R. Wilke, "U.S. Court Rules Antitrust Laws Apply to Foreigners," *The Wall Street Journal,* March 19, 1997, p. B6.

17. "Japan's Fair Trade Commission, Pussycat," *The Economist,* October 23, 1993, pp. 85–86.

18. "Caught in a Web of Jurisdiction," *Financial Times,* May 15, 2002, p. 13.

19. "U.S. Endorses a Global Approach to Antitrust," *The Wall Street Journal,* September 15, 2000, p. A15; and "Call to Align Global Policy on Competition," *Financial Times,* September 15, 2000, p. 6.

20. "Plan for Global Insolvency Accord," *Financial Times,* October 26, 2000, p. 4.

21. Thomas G. Donlan, "Not So Free Trade: U.S. Preaches What It Doesn't Always Practice," *Barron's,* June 27, 1988, pp. 70–71.

22. Carolyn Lochhead, "Strict Liability Causing Firms to Give Up on Promising Ideas," *Washington Times,* August 22, 1988, p. B5.

23. Sandra N. Hurd and Frances E. Zollers, "Desperately Seeking Harmony: The European Community's Search for Uniformity in Product Liability Law," *American Business Law Journal* 30 (1992), pp. 35–68.

24. Ibid.

25. "Product Liability," *The Economist,* May 25, 1996, p. 67; and Katherine Dowling, "Wide-Ranging Suits against Manufacturers May Keep Lifesaving Medical Devices on the Shelf and out of Reach," *The Wall Street Journal,* August 19, 1997, p. A4.

26. Barbara Crutchfield George and Linda McCallister, "The Effect of Cultural Attitudes on Product Liability Laws," *Southwestern Association of Administrative Disciplines,* March 4, 1993; and Craig P. Wagnild, "Civil Law Discovery in Japan: A Comparison of Japanese and US Methods of Evidence Collection in Civil Litigation," Asia-Pacific Law and Policy Journal 3, no. 1 (Winter 2002), www.hawaii.edu/aplpj/pdfs/v3-01-Wagnild.pdf (July 20, 2006)..

27. Barbara Crutchfield George, "The U.S. Foreign Corrupt Practices Act: The Price Business Is Paying for the Unilateral Criminalization of Bribery," *International Journal of Management,* September 1987, pp. 391–402; and "Some Guidelines on Dealing with Graft," *Business International,* February 25, 1983, p. 62.

CHAPTER 11

1. Ronald McKinnon, "The Euro versus the Dollar," www.stanford.edu/~mckinnon/briefs/salvatoreJEPMKenen.pdf (accessed August 5, 2004).

2. Paul Solomon and the international economist Fred Bergson discussed the market psychology involved in the dollar's decline in a WGBH segment called "Dollar's Decline," on May 27, 2003. You can watch the video or read the interview at www.pbs.org/newshour/bb/economy/jan-june03/dollar_05-27.html (accessed June 23, 2006).

3. Bank for International Settlements, "Triennial Central Bank Survey of Foreign Exchange and Derivatives Market Activity, 2005," March 2005, www.bis.org/publ/rpfx05.htm (accessed June 21, 2006).

4. "U.S. Probes Whether Big Banks Stifle Rival in Currency Trading," *The Wall Street Journal,* May 15, 2002, p. A1.

5. Cheol S. Eun and Bruce G. Resnick, *International Financial Management,* 4th ed. (Burr Ridge, IL: McGraw Hill Irwin, 2007),

pp. 147–48. The technical explanations here are clearly described and well illustrated.

6. Ibid., p. 149.

7. Ibid., p. 151.

8. Cheol Eun and Sanjiv Sabherwal, "Forecasting Exchange Rates: *Do* the Banks Know Better?" *Global Finance Journal* (2002), pp. 195–215.

9. Richard Levich, "Evaluating the Performance of the Forecasters," in *The Management of Foreign Exchange Risk,* 2nd ed. (New York: Euromoney Publication), pp. 121–34.

10. Eun and Resnick, *International Financial Management,* p. 499.

11. *OECD Factbook 2006,* http://puck.sourceoecd.org/vl=14933899/cl=14/nw=1/rpsv/factbook/03-01-03.htm (accessed June 24, 2006).

CHAPTER 12

1. U.S. Census Bureau, International, "Midyear Population, by Age and Sex," www.census.gov/cgi-bin/ipc/idbagg (July 27, 2006).

2. Ibid.

3. *Global Employment Trends Brief* (Geneva: International Labour Office, January 2006).

4. U.S. Census Bureau, International, "Midyear Population, by Age and Sex."

5. UNCTAD, *Developing Countries in International Trade 2005* (New York: United Nations, 2005).

6. *Global Employment Trends Brief.*

7. "Standardised Unemployment Rates: Men," *OECD Factbook,* http://dx.doi.org/10.1787/814540438321 (July 27, 2006); and "Standardized Unemployement Rates: Women," *OECD Factbook,* http://dx.doi.org/10.1787/122757651858 (July 27, 2006).

8. *Facts on Labour Migration* (Geneva: International Labour Organization, 2006).

9. *Costs and Benefits of International Migration* (New York: Council on Foreign Relations, September 2005).

10. Mohamad Yusop bin Awang Damit, Tin Maung Maung Than, Anthony L Smith, Russell Heng et al., *Regional Outlook: Southeast Asia,* 2003–2004, p. 10.

11. For example, see *World Migration 2005: Costs and Benefits of International Migration* (New York: Council on Foreign Relations, September 2005), www.cfr.org/publication/8987/world_migration_2005.html (July 28, 2006).

12. *Facts on Labour Migration.*

13. Stefan Wagstyl, "Comment and Analysis," *Financial Times,* February 9, 2004, p. 11.

14. Leslie Crawford, "Immigrants Help Sustain Spain's Long Building Boom," *Financial Times,* April 19, 2006, p. 8.

15. *Costs and Benefits of International Migration.*

16. Steven A. Camarota, *Immigrants at Mid-Decade: A Snapshot of America's Foreign-Born Population in 2005* (Washington, DC: Center for Immigration Studies, December 2005), www.cis.org/articles/2005/back1405.html (July 29, 2006).

17. U.S. Census Bureau, "Percent of People Who Are Foreign Born: 2004," http://factfinder.census.gov/servlet/GRTTable?_bm=y&-_box_head_nbr=R0501&-ds_name=ACS_2004_EST_G00_&-mt_name=ACS_2004_EST_G00_R0501_US30&-format=US-30 (July 28, 2006).

18. The most recent immigration data from the U.S. Census Bureau can be accessed at www.census.gov/population.

19. *Facts on Labour Migration.*

20. *Facts on Child Labor—2006* (Geneva: International Labour Organization, 2006).

21. Emily Wax, "In Rural Ethiopia, Child Labor Can Mean Survival," *The Tribune* (San Luis Obispo, CA), January 4, 2006, p. A11; and "Brutal Ethiopian Nature and Politics Compound Child Labor Situation," *The Tribune* (San Luis Obispo, CA), January 4, 2006, p. A11.

22. Edward Luce, "Ikea's Grown-Up Plan to Tackle Child Labour," *Financial Times,* September 15, 2004, p. 7.

23. *The End of Child Labour—Within Reach* (Geneva: International Labour Organization, 2006), www.ilo.org/public/english/standards/relm/ilc/ilc95/pdf/rep-i-b.pdf (July 29, 2006).

24. Raphael Minder, "Child Labour on Decline, Says ILO," *Financial Times,* May 5, 2006, p. 7.

25. "Forced Labor," www.anti-slaverysociety.addr.com/forcedlabor.htm (July 28, 2006).

26. Matthias Busse and Sebastian Braun, *International Labor Review* 142, no. 1 (2003), p. 49.

27. OECD, "Trends in International Migration Reflect Increasing Labour-Related Immigration and Persistent Integration Problems," 2004, www.oecd.org. (August 2, 2004).

28. "Africa Economy: EU Foreign Ministers Bid to Stop Africa's Brain-Drain," *EIU ViewsWire* (New York), March 30, 2006.

29. *Science and Engineering Indicators 2002,* www.nsf.gov/sbe/srs/seind02/c3/fig03-21.htm (July 14, 2002, and August 12, 2002), and "UNDP Oldthink," *Foreign Policy,* October 2001, p. 15.

30. Alan M. Webber, "Reverse Brain Drain Threatens U.S. Economy," *USA Today,* February 23, 2004, www.USAtoday.com (February 24, 2004).

31. http://rbd.nstda.or.th/rbdweb/about_rbd/index.php (July 28, 2006).

32. "Exploitation and Abuse of Migrant Workers in Saudi Arabia," *Human Rights Watch,* http://hrw.org/mideast/saudi/labor/ (July 30, 2006).

33. Neil Heathcote, "Saudi Women Break into Business," *BBC News,* February 27, 2006, http://news.bbc.co.uk/1/hi/world/middle_east/4754430.stm (July 30, 2006).

34. Jillian Talbot, *Dominion Post,* February 25, 2004. p. C.1.

35. "Women and Girls: Education, Not Discrimination," *OECD Observer* (electronic edition), November 3, 2000.

36. N. Boyacigiller, S. Beechler, S. Taylor, and O. Levy, "The Crucial yet Illusive Global Mindset," in *The Blackwell Handbook of Global Management: A Guide to Managing Complexity,* ed. H. W. Lane, M. Maznevski, M. Mendenhall, and J. McNett (Oxford, UK, and Malden, MA: Blackwell, 2004).

37. European Trade Union Confederation, "Our Members," www.etuc.org/r/13 (July 28, 2006).

CHAPTER 13

1. For a discussion of strategy, see Michael E. Porter, "What Is Strategy?" *Harvard Business Review,* November–December 1996, pp. 61–78.

2. Jay B. Barney, "Looking Inside for Competitive Advantage," *Academy of Management Executive,* no. 9 (1995), pp. 49–61. Copyright 1995 by Academy of Management. Reproduced with permission of Academy of Management in the format textbook via Copyright Clearance Center.

3. "An Executive Take on the Top Business Trends: A McKinsey Global Survey," *The McKinsey Quarterly,* April 2006, www.mckinseyquarterly.com/article_print.aspx?L2=21&L3=114&ar=1754 (April 27, 2006).

4. Bain & Company, "About the Survey," www.bain.com/management_tools/about_overview.asp?groupCode=1 (June 12, 2006).

5. Jeffrey R. Immelt, chairman and CEO, GE, "Letter to Stakeholders," *General Electric 2003 Annual Report,* www.ge.com/ar2003/chairman/letter_1.jsp (August 3, 2004).

6. "Case Study: Keeping Proprietary Technology in Japan," 2003 JETRO White Paper on International Trade and Foreign Direct Investment (Tokyo: Japan External Trade Organization), p. 44; and Michiyo Nakamoto, "Japan Goes after Industrial Spies," *Financial Times,* February 9, 2004, p. 8.

7. DuPont, "Sustainable Growth," www2.dupont.com/Our_Company/en_US/glance/sus_growth/sus_growth.html (June 12, 2006).

8. Kathryn Kranhold, "China's Price for Market Entry: Give Us Your Technology, Too," *The Wall Street Journal,* February 26, 2004, pp. A1, A6.

9. Reggie Van Lee, Lisa Fabish, and Nancy McGaw, "The Value of Corporate Values," *Strategy + Business,* www.strategy-business.com/article/05206?gko=7869b-1876-9176155&tid=230&pg=all (June 12, 2006).

10. "J&J Mission," www.naukri.com/jg/johnson/global.htm (June 12, 2006).

11. Unilever, "Our Mission," www.unilever.co.za/company_mission.asp (June 12, 2006).

12. "General," *Amazon.com 2005 Annual Report,* http://library.corporate-ir.net/library/97/976/97664/items/193688/AMZN2005AnnualReport.pdf (June 12, 2006).

13. "Vision Statement," www1.dupont.com/NASApp/dupontglobal/corp/index.jsp?page=/content/US/en_US/overview/glance/vision/index.html (August 5, 2004).

14. Sumitomo Corporation, "SC Values," www.sumitomocorp.co.jp/english/company_e/scvalues/index.shtml (June 12, 2006).

15. "About McDonald's," www.mcdonalds.com/corporate/corp.html (September 15, 2002).

16. "Intel's Mission Statement, Values, and Objectives," www.intel.com/intel/company/corp1.htm (June 12, 2006).

17. BP, "Structure and Management: Overview," www.bp.com/sectiongenericarticle.do?categoryId=2010726&contentId=2015515 (August 5, 2004); and BP, "How We Run the Business: Our Objectives," www.bp.com/sectiongenericarticle.do?categoryId=26&contentId=2000563 (June 12, 2006).

18. "About 3M: Frequently Asked Questions," www.corporateir.net/ireye/ir_site.zhtml?ticker_MMM&script_1800 (December 12, 2000).

19. Goodyear Tire & Rubber, *2005 Annual Report,* p. 10, www.goodyear.com/investor/pdf/2005_annual_report.pdf (June 12, 2006).

20. Liu Baijia, "Schneider to Localize in China," *China Daily,* July 12, 2004, p. 10; and Schneider Electric, "Local Operations," www.schneiderelectric.com/wps/myportal/!ut/p/.cmd/cs/.ce/7_0_A/.s/7_0_PJ/_s.7_0_A/7_0_PJ?toservice=WIBPB_1042_CORP&wib-CountryDB=CORP&idContent=4d94ff2c0e40af49c1256e7f00468ff4&fromservice=AU-TON_0017_CORP (June 13, 2006).

21. Ginny Parker, "Going Global Can Hit Snags, Vodafone Finds," *The Wall Street Journal,* June 16, 2004, p. B1; David Pringle and Taska Manzaroli, "Vodafone Seeks to Buy Out Its Japanese Units," *The Wall Street Journal,* May 26, 2004, p. B2; Robert Budden and Tim Burt, "Brand Is a Big Issue; When People Think Mobile Products and Services, We Want Them to Go to Vodafone," *Financial Times,* December 22, 2003, p. 9; and "Vodafone's Global Ambitions Got Hung Up in Japan," *The Wall Street Journal,* March 18–19, 2006, p. 1.

22. Cornelis A. de Kluyver and John A. Pearce, II, *Strategy: A View from the Top,* 2nd

ed. (Upper Saddle River, NJ: Pearson Prentice Hall, 2006), p. 9.

23. Erik Berkman, "How to Use the Balanced Scorecard," *CIO Magazine,* May 15, 2002, www.cio.com/archive/051502/scorecard.html (June 13, 2006).

24. 3M, "To Our Shareholders," *3M Annual Report 2003,* p. 4.

25. Gary Hamel, "Strategy as Revolution," *Harvard Business Review,* July–August 1996, p. 70.

26. Eric D. Beinhocker and Sarah Kaplan, "Tired of Strategic Planning?" *The McKinsey Quarterly,* 2002 (special edition on risk and resilience), www.mckinseyquarterly.com/article_print.aspx?L2=21&L3=37&ar=1191 (April 13, 2006).

27. Alan Murray, "The CEO as Global Corporate Ambassador," *The Wall Street Journal,* March 20, 2006, p. 2.

28. "The New Breed of Strategic Planner," *BusinessWeek,* September 19, 1984, p. 64.

29. Ibid., p. 66.

30. Alfred Chan, "As in Chess, Strategic Planning Is a Good Move," *Enterprise 50,* http://biztimes.asial.com/bizcentre/Enterprise50/plan9701.html (March 19, 1998).

31. Andrew Campbell and Marcus Alexander, "What's Wrong with Strategy?" *Harvard Business Review,* November–December 1997, p. 46.

32. "Introduction to Shell Global Scenarios to 2025 by Jeroen van der Veer Chief Executive," www.shell.com/home/Framework?siteId=royal-en&FC2=/royal-en/html/iwgen/our_strategy/scenarios/introduction_to_global_scenarios/zzz_lhn.html&FC3=/royal-en/html/iwgen/our_strategy/scenarios/introduction_to_global_scenarios/intro_jvdv_scenarios_28022005.html (June 12, 2006); "20-20 Vision," Global Scenarios, www.shell.com/b/b2_03.html (March 15, 1998); and P. W. Beck, "Corporate Planning for an Uncertain Certain Future," *Long-Range Planning,* August 1982, p. 14.

33. Jeffrey R. Immelt, *General Electric 2003 Annual Report,* www.ge.com/ar2003/strategy/index_fla.jsp (August 3, 2004).

34. Frederick W. Gluck, "A Fresh Look at Strategic Management," *Journal of Business Strategy,* Fall 1985, p. 6.

35. "Corporate Spies Feel a Sting," *BusinessWeek,* July 14, 1997, pp. 75–77; and "For Pills, Not Projectiles," *The Economist,* July 12, 1997, p. 22.

36. Richard Isaacs, "A Field Day for Spies: While a Deal Advances," *Mergers and Acquisitions,* January 2004, pp. 30–35.

37. Ibid.

38. Bill Fiora, "Forward-Looking Intelligence," *Pharmaceutical Executive* 26, no. 2 (February 2006), pp. S22–26; and Outward Insights LLC, "Ostriches and Eagles: Competitive Intelligence Usage and Understanding in U.S. Companies," February 2005, www.outwardinsights.com (June 13, 2006).

39. A. M. Ahmed, M. Zairi, and K. S. Almarri, "SWOT Analysis for Air China Performance and Its Experience with Quality," *Benchmarking: An International Journal* 13, no. 1–2 (2006), pp. 160–173; and "What Ronald McDonald, Mickey Mouse Taught Nissan," *Business International,* February 22, 1993, pp. 57–58.

CHAPTER 14

1. Nitin Nohria, *Note on Organization Structure* (Boston: Harvard Business School, 1991).

2. Met-Pro Corporation, "International Division," www.met-pro.com/html/sales.htm (June 21, 2006); Met-Pro Corporation, "Form 10-K for Met Pro Corp," April 13, 2006, www.met-pro.com/html/news.htm (June 21, 2006); and Met-Pro Corporation, "Met-Pro Corporation Divisions and Subsidiaries," www.met-pro.com/html/subdiv.htm (June 21, 2006).

3. Wal-Mart Stores, Inc., *2006 Annual Report,* www.walmartfacts.com/docs/1779_2006annualreport_1547171566.pdf (June 21, 2006); and "International Overview," walmartstores.com/GlobalWMStoresWeb/navigate.do?catg=369 (June 21, 2006).

4. John M. Stopford and Louis T. Wells, *Strategy and Structure of the Multinational Enterprise* (New York: Basic Books, 1972).

5. Deutsche Post World Net, "The Group at a Glance," http://investors.dpwn.com/en/investoren/der_konzern_im_ueberblick/uebersichtsgrafik/index.htm (June 21, 2006); Deutsche Post World Net, *Annual Report 2005,* www3.financialreports.dpwn.com/2005/ar/en/servicepages/welcome?SESSID=8cf2ec8d7a14bedd6844b213736d6753e47a7d67 (June 21, 2006); and "Organization Chart," www.dpwn.de/dpwn?tab=1&skin=hi&check=yes&lang=de_EN&xmlFile=2002753 (June 21, 2006).

6. ExxonMobil, *2005 Annual Report,* http://exxonmobil.com/corporate/files/corporate/sar_2005.pdf (July 31, 2006); and "To Our Shareholders," *ExxonMobil 1999 Annual Report,* www.exxonmobil.com/shareholder_publications/c_annual_99/c_shareholder.html (December 12, 2000).

7. Mittal Steel, "Structure," www.mittal-steel.com/Company/Structure.htm (June 21, 2006); "Mittal Steel Company N.V.," http://finance.google.com/finance?q=mittal+steel&btnG=Search (June 21, 2006); and Mittal Steel, "Profile," www.mittalsteel.com/Company/Profile.htm (June 21, 2006).

8. Sarah Ellison, "Kimberly-Clark to Reorganize; High-Ranking Official to Retire," *The*

Wall Street Journal, January 20, 2004, p. A3; *Kimberly-Clark 10-K,* 2003, www.kimberly-clark.com (July 24, 2004); Kimberly-Clark, "Kimberly-Clark Announces Organizational and Senior Management Changes to Further Its Global Business Plan," http://investor.kimberly-clark.com/news/20040119-126799.cfm?t=n (June 20, 2006); and Kimberly-Clark, *2005 Annual Report,* www.rkonline.net/AR/KimberlyClark05/PDF/AR05.pdf (June 20, 2006).

9. Genentech, "Corporate Brochure," www.gene.com/gene/news/kits/corporate/pdf/corporate-brochure.pdf (June 21, 2006); and Genentech, Inc., *Form 10-K,* www.gene.com/gene/ir/downloadDoc.do?id=2801 (June 21, 2006).

10. Deborah Ball, "Unilever Shakes Up Its Management to Spur Growth," *The Wall Street Journal,* February 11, 2005, p. A2; Unilever, "Company Structure," www.unilever.com/ourcompany/aboutunilever/companystructure/default.asp (June 21, 2006); and Unilever, *2005 Annual Report,* www.unilever.com/Images/2005_Annual_Report_English%20amended_tcm13-35722.pdf (June 21, 2006).

11. Nokia Corporation, *Form 20-F,* www.nokia.com/NOKIA_COM_1/About_Nokia/Financials/nokia_form_20f_2005.pdf (June 21, 2006).

12. BP, "How BP Works," www.bp.com/sectiongenericarticle.do?categoryId=25&contentId=2014279 (June 21, 2006); and BP, "Organized for Growth," www.bp.com/genericarticle.do?categoryId=25&contentId=2006395 (June 21, 2006).

13. Michelin, "Organization," www.michelin.com/corporate/front/templates/affich.jsp?codeRubrique=11&lang=EN (June 21, 2006).

14. Caterpillar Inc., *2005 Annual Report,* www.cat.com/cda/files/329216/7/yecx0018_2005_annual_report.pdf (July 31, 2006).

15. Shell Chemicals, "Glossary & Trademarks," www.shellchemicals.com/glossary/1,1098,1159,00.html#P (June 21, 2006).

16. BP, "Organized for Growth."

17. Cassell Bryan-Low, "Vodafone Reorganizes, Names Morrow Head of Europe Group," *The Wall Street Journal,* April 7, 2006, p. B7; and Vodafone, "New Organisational Structure at Vodafone," April 6, 2006, www.vodafone.com/assets/files/en/vod1245gmprl.pdf (June 21, 2006).

18. Coca-Cola Company, "International Operations," January 17, 2006, www2.coca-cola.com/presscenter/nr_20060117_corporate_kent.html (June 21, 2006).

19. Lowell L. Bryan and Claudia Joyce, "The 21st-Century Organization," *The McKinsey Quarterly,* no. 3 (2005), www.mckinseyquarterly.com/article_print.aspx?L2=18&L3=30&ar=1628 (April 27, 2006).

20. Remo Häcki and Julian Lighton, "The Future of the Networked Company," *The McKinsey Quarterly,* no. 3 (2001), pp. 26–39.

21. Glenn R. Simpson, "Wearing of the Green: Irish Subsidiary Lets Microsoft Slash Taxes in U.S. and Europe; Tech and Drug Firms Move Key Intellectual Property to Low-Levy Island Haven; Center of Windows Licensing," *The Wall Street Journal,* November 7, 2005, p. A1.

22. "Microsoft Unit in Ireland Tops List; Top Profit Makers in Ireland Are Units of U.S. Companies," *The Wall Street Journal,* December 20, 2005, p. A1; "Plan Would End Use of Tax Havens for Patents," *The Wall Street Journal,* February 8, 2006, p. A1; Simpson, "Wearing of the Green"; Glenn R. Simpson, "U.S. Companies Might Overstate Irish Earnings for Tax Benefits," *The Wall Street Journal,* March 28, 2006, p. A6; and Jesse Drucker, "Symantec Is in $1 Billion IRS Dispute," *The Wall Street Journal,* June 20, 2006, p. A2.

23. William Bridges, "The End of the Job," *Fortune,* September 19, 1994, pp. 62–74. © 1994 Time Inc. Reprinted with permission.

CHAPTER 15

1. A good introduction to scanning the environment is Chun Wei Choo, "Environmental Scanning as Information Seeking and Organizational Knowing," *Prima Vera,* Working Paper Series 2002-01, http://primavera.fee.uva.nl/PDFdocs/2002-01.pdf (January 2002). Also see Ian Wylie, "There Is No Alternative to . . . ," *Fast Company,* www.fastcompany.com/online/60/tina.html (July 2002).

2. Virtually all governments have barriers to foreign direct investment and at the same time offer a variety of incentives to potential foreign investors. For example, Mexico currently restricts foreign investment in the petroleum industry. See, e.g.,UNCTAD, "Prospects for FDI Flows, Transnational Corporation Strategies and Promotion Policies: 2004–2007," www.unctad.org/sections/dite_dir/docs/survey_FDI.pdf (August 1, 2004).

3. "Team Canada 2002," www.tcm-mec.gc.ca/tc2002/menu-en.asp (August 1, 2004).

4. "CeBIT," www.cebit.de/homepage_e?x=1 (August 1, 2004); "Trade Show Statistics: Review 2006," www.cebit.de/7588?x=1 (October 5, 2006).

5. Secondary data and sometimes primary data will be gathered on a field trip, but the visitor rarely has the time or ability to conduct a complete field study.

6. Yuezhi Zhao, "The 'People's Phone' on Hold," *Foreign Policy,* July–August 2002, pp. 83–85.

7. "Third World Research Is Difficult, but It's Possible," *Marketing News,* August 26, 1997, p. 51.

8. For a sophisticated example in Mexico, see www.pearson-research.com/flash.shtml (August 1, 2004).

9. This approach was inspired by Masaaki Kotabe and Kristiaan Helsen, *Global Marketing Management* (New York: Wiley, 2003), p. 219.

CHAPTER 16

1. This discussion owes a great deal to Orville C. Walker, Jr., Harper W. Boyd, Jr., John Mullins, and Jean-Claude Larreche, *Marketing Strategy: A Decision-Focused Approach* (Burr Ridge, IL: Irwin/McGraw-Hill, 2003).

2. "Cross-License Agreement Expected to Bring More than $1 Billion to TI over Next 10 Years," press release, May 23, 1999, www.ti.com/corp/docs/press/company/1999/c99024.shtml (November 20, 2000).

3. Thayne Forbes, "Set the Right Royalty Rate," www.intangiblebusiness.com/Content/796 (August 3, 2006).

4. "Cosmopolitan," www.hearst.com/magazines/property/mag_prop_cosmo.html (August 3, 2006).

5. "Is *Playboy* Available outside North America?" www.playboy.com/worldofplayboy/faq/subscribing.html#4 (August 3, 2006).

6. "Bruised in Brazil: Ford Slips as Market Booms," *The Wall Street Journal,* December 13, 1996, p. A10; and "Ford and VW Split Up Venture in Latin America," *The Wall Street Journal,* December 2, 1994, p. A8.

7. Ian Friendly, "Cereal Partners Worldwide: A World of Opportunity," www.ir.nestle.com/NR/rdonlyres/4DC2CE3F-E882-4DE3-A023-987826A64416/0/cpw.pdf (August 2, 2006); and "Café au Lait, a Croissant—and Trix," *BusinessWeek,* August 24, 1992, p. 50.

8. "Mobile Telecoms: The Virtues of Being Virtual," *The Economist,* July 10, 2004, pp. 56–57; and "What Is an MVNO?" www.mobilein.com/what_is_a_mvno.htm (August 16, 2004).

9. Peter J. Buckley, Jeremy Clegg, and Hui Tan, "Knowledge Transfer to China: Policy Lessons from Foreign Affiliates," *Transnational Corporations* 13, no. 1 (April 2004), pp. 31–72.

10. Frank Tian Xie and Wesley J. Johnston, "Strategic Alliances: Incorporating the Impact of E-Business Technological Innovations," *Journal of Business and Industrial Marketing* 19, no. 3 (2004), pp. 208–22.

11. "About EUV Technology," http://euvl.com/about.php (August 3, 2006); and "Chip Makers Unite in Project to Raise Computer Power to New Levels," *International Herald Tribune,* September 12, 1997, p. 15.

12. Symbian, "Fast Facts," www.symbian.com/about/fastfacts/fastfacts.html (August 3, 2006); and "Symbian Cellphone Alliance Faces Growing Threat from Mi-

crosoft," *The Wall Street Journal,* November 6, 2000, pp. B1, B4.

13. Edward J. Zajac, "Creating an Academic Framework for Strategic Alliances," www.kellogg.northwestern.edu/kwo/sum02/indepth/theory.htm (August 8, 2004).

14. For discussion of challenges in managing international joint ventures and alliances, see Colette A. Frayne and J. Michael Geringer, "Challenges Facing General Managers of International Joint Ventures," in *Readings and Cases in International Human Resource Management,* 2nd ed., ed. M. Mendenhall and G. Oddou (Cincinnati, OH: South-Western, 1995), pp. 85–97; J. Michael Geringer and C. Patrick Woodcock, "Agency Costs and the Structure and Performance of International Joint Ventures," *Group Decision and Negotiation* 4, no. 5 (1995), pp. 453–67; and Colette A. Frayne and J. Michael Geringer, "Joint Venture General Managers: Key Issues in Research and Training," in *Research in Personnel and Human Resources Management,* ed. K. M. Rowland, B. Shaw, and P. Kirkbride (Greenwich, CT: JAI Press, 1993), supplement 3, pp. 301–21.

15. Leslie Chang, Chad Terhune, and Betsy McKay, "Coke's Big Gamble in Asia: Digging Deeper in China, India," *The Wall Street Journal,* August 11, 2004, pp. A1, A6.

16. "What Is Sogo Shosha?" www.fjt.co.jp/_jftc_sogo.htm (February 9, 1998).

17. Mitsui and Co., Ltd., "Corporate Info," www.mitsui.co.jp/en/company/index.html (August 3, 2006).

CHAPTER 17

1. Telephone conversation with Ford International representative.

2. *Commercial News USA,* U.S. Commercial Service, www.thinkglobal.us (July 29, 2006).

3. Export.gov, www.export.gov/partners.html#intlpartners (July 27, 2006).

4. "INCOTERMS 2000," www.iccwbo.org (July 30, 2006). These terms are copyrighted by the International Chamber of Commerce.

5. Export Import Bank, "Mission," www.exim.gov/about/mission.html (July 29, 2006).

6. A third support for exporters, the Foreign Sales Corporation (FSC), offered tax breaks for U.S.-owned foreign subsidiaries meeting specific criteria. This amounted to an export subsidy, claimed the EU. The claim was upheld by the WTO. Congress enacted legislation to end the FSC in May 2006.

7. Foreign Trade Corporation, "Foreign Trade Zone Resource Center," www.foreign-trade-zone.com/history.htm. (July 29, 2006).

8. See http://alliancechb.com (July 31, 2006).

9. Export.gov, Trade Information Center, "European CE Mark Requirements," http://web.

ita.doc.gov/ticwebsite/FAQs.nsf/6683DCE2E5871DF9852565BC00785DDF/ED3167DEE3B48B03852569B400586FFB?OpenDocument (July 31, 2006).

10. "Automated Commercial System," U.S. Customs and Border Protection, www.cbp.gov/xp/cgov/import/ operations_support/automated_systems/acs (August 2, 2006).

11. The HTSUSA is available at www.usitc.gov/tata/hts/index.htm l (August 3, 2006).

CHAPTER 18

1. T. C. Melewar and John Saunders, "International Corporate Visual Identity: Standardization or Localization?" *Journal of International Business Studies,* Third Quarter 1999, pp. 583–98; and Adesegun Oyedele, Osama J. Butt, and Michael S. Minor, "The Extent of Global Visual Identity as Expressed in Web Sites: An Empirical Assessment," working paper, 2004.

2. Douglas Daft, "Back to Classic Coke," *Financial Times,* March 27, 2000, p. 16.

3. "Multinational, Not Global," *The Economist,* December 24, 1988, p. 99; and "Nestlé Shows How to Gobble Markets," *Fortune,* January 16, 1989, p. 75.

4. "About Accenture," www.accenture.com (October 8, 2006).

5. "About Ernst & Young," www.ey.com/global/content.nsf/International/About_EY (October 10, 2006).

6. *2005 Annual Report,* www.visa.com (October 8, 2006).

7. "Call It Worldpool," *BusinessWeek,* November 29, 1994, pp. 98–99.

8. Peter Marsh, "The World's Wash Day," *Financial Times,* April 29, 2002, p. 6; http://duet.whirlpool.com (May 31, 2004); and "Whirlpool Corporation Announces Changes at Several Manufacturing Facilities in North America," October 3, 2006, www.whirlpool-corp.com (October 8, 2006).

9. "A Global Comeback," *Advertising Age,* August 20, 1987, p. 146.

10. "Belgium's Strong Drinks," *International Management,* June 1992, p. 65.

11. http://currents.net/newstoday/00/03/07/news4.html (December 1, 2000); and http://globalarchive.ft.com/globalarchive/article.html?id_001205001403 (December 5, 2000).

12. Om Malik, "The New Land of Opportunity," *Business 2.0,* July 2004, p. 78.

13. C. K. Prahalad, *The Fortune at the Bottom of the Pyramid: Eradicating Poverty through Profits* (Upper Saddle River, NJ: Wharton School Publishing, 2005).

14. GM Worldwide site, www.gm.com/company/corp_info/global_operations/asia_pacific/chin.html (October 10, 2006).

15. Warren J. Keegan, "Multinational Product Planning Strategic Alternatives," *Journal of Marketing,* January 1969, pp. 56–62, combines these strategies to formulate five product and promotional strategies.

16. Geoffrey Fowler, "Intel's Game: Play It Local but Make It Global," *The Wall Street Journal,* September 30, 2005.

17. Lars Perner, University of Southern California, www.ConsumerPsychologist.com (October 14, 2006).

18. "Shimmering Symbols of the Modern Age," *Financial Times,* October 17, 1997, p. 12.

19. "About Axfood: Strategic Matters," www.axfood.se/showdoc.asp?docId=3&channelId=103&folderid=22&objectname=Strategi&selectedchannelId=103&priority=2&startfolderid=22&setlanguageid=4 (August 2, 2004).

20. "KFC and McDonald's: A Model of Blended Culture," *China Daily,* June 1, 2004, www.chinadaily.com.cn/english/doc/2004-06/01/content_335488.htm (October 10, 2006); and Yum Brands, *Annual Report, 2006,* www.yum.com (October 10, 2006).

21. Douglas McCray, "Japan's Gross National Cool," *Foreign Policy,* May–June 2002, pp. 44–54.

22. "PepsiCo's New Campaign to Knock Rival Coca-Cola," *Financial Times,* January 19, 1995, p. 12.

23. "Mexico Unleashes Watchdog to Avoid Legal Ad Disputes," *Advertising Age,* September 18, 1995, p. 16.

24. Morris Kalliny, Grace Dagher, and Michael S. Minor, "The Impact of Cultural Differences and Religion on Television Advertising: A Content Analysis of the U.S. and the Arab World," presented at the American Marketing Association annual conference, August 2004.

25. "Brands That Stop at the Border," *Financial Times,* October 6, 2006, p. 10.

26. "Ad Agencies Take On the World," *International Management,* April 1994, pp. 50–52.

27. "World Brands," *Advertising Age,* February 2, 1992, p. 33.

28. Eric Pfanner, "On Advertising: A Race to Connect in India," *International Herald Tribune,* November 27, 2005, www.iht.com/articles/2005/11/27/business/ad28.php (October 12, 2006).

29. Advertising Age International, http://www.producto.com.ve/191/notas/ multinacionales.html (August 2, 2004).

30. Stephen X. Doyle and George Thomas Roth, "Selling and Sales Management in Action: The Use of Insight and Coaching to Improve Relationship Selling," *Journal of Personal Selling & Sales Management,* Winter 1992, p. 62.

31. Melissa Campanelli, "Avon's Calling in China," *DM News,* March 10, 2006. www.dm-news.com/cms/dm-news/international/36010.html (October 12, 2006).

32. "Our Social Lives and Personal Image the First to Suffer When the Going Gets Tough," ACNielsen, April 25, 2006, www2.acnielsen.com/news/20060425.shtml (October 13, 2006).

33. "Ford Foundation International Fellowships Program," www.fordfound.org (October 12, 2004).

34. "Agencies Responsible for Censorship in China," U.S. Congressional Executive Commission on China, www.cecc.gov/pages/virtualAcad/exp/expcensors.php (October 13, 2006).

35. "McDonald's Wins Its Libel Case against Two Activists in the UK," *The Wall Street Journal,* June 20, 1997, p. B2; and www. mcspotlight.org/case/index.html (May 31, 2004).

36. Lars Perner, "International Marketing," www.consumerpsychologist.com/international_continued.htm (October 14, 2006). These introductory observations draw closely on his work.

37. "Coke Ends Year on the Better Side of Earnings," *Financial Times,* December 31, 2005, www.ft.com (October 14, 2006).

38. Alexandra Nusbaum and Naoko Nakamae, "Store Wars in Cyberspace," *Financial Times,* February 8, 2000, p. 18; www.stonystyle.com (October 14, 2006).

39. The idea for this matrix, a checklist to help those working on the standardization of an element of the marketing mix to remember the impact of the uncontrollable forces, was developed by one of the authors who wishes, when he was an international marketing manager, that he had such a tool.

CHAPTER 19

1. Donald J. Bowersox, David J. Closs, and M. Bixby Cooper, *Supply Chain Logistics Management,* 2nd ed. (Burr Ridge, IL: McGraw-Hill Irwin, 2007), pp. 2–18.

2. Robert D'Avanzo, "The Reward of Supply-Chain Excellence," *Optimize,* December 2003, p. 68.

3. David Demers and Priya Sathyanarayanan, "Charting the Supply Chain DNA," *Supply Chain Management Review,* November–December 2003, pp. 48–58.

4. Joan Magretta, "The Power of Virtual Integration: An Interview with Dell Computer's Michael Dell," *Harvard Business Review,* March–April 1998, pp. 73–84.

5. Joan Magretta, "Fast, Global, and Entrepreneurial: Supply Chain Management, Hong Kong Style—An Interview with Victor Fung," *Harvard Business Review,* September–October 1998, pp. 3–14.

6. McDonald's Corporation, *McDonald's Worldwide Corporate Responsibility Report 2004,* www.mcdonalds.com/corp/values/socialrespons/sr_report.html (July 17, 2006), p. 12. Used with permission of McDonald's Corporation.

7. Geraldo Samor, "Ford Discovers Future Ideas in Brazilian Unit," *Pittsburgh Post-Gazette,* www.post-gazette.com/pg/06191/704782-185.stm (July 17, 2006); and Raymond Colitt, "Brazil Engineers Turnaround for Ford," *Financial Times,* September 28, 2004, p. 20.

8. Nokia, "Design for Environment," www.nokia.com/NOKIA_COM_1/About_Nokia/Environment/Publications/enviroinbrief.pdf (July 16, 2006).

9. William J. Zeile, "U.S. Affiliates of Foreign Companies: Operations in 2000," *Survey of Current Business,* August 2002, p. 161.

10. L. J. Krajewski and L. P. Ritzman, *Operations Management,* 5th ed. (Boston: Addison-Wesley, 1999), p. 456; J. Heizer and B. Render, *Principles of Operations Management,* 4th ed. (Upper Saddle River, NJ: Prentice Hall, 2001), p. 436, table 11.2; and Bowersox, Closs, and Bixby Cooper, *Supply Chain Logistics Management,* p. 81.

11. "The Founding Investors on Exostar," http://exostar.com/company/investors.asp (July 17, 2006); and "The Exostar Vision: Creating a Global Supply Network for the Aerospace and Defense Industry," http://exostar.com/company/overview/ (July 17, 2006).

12. Sam Jaffe, "Oracle: A B2B Rebirth That Few Foretold," *BusinessWeek,* April 6, 2000, www.businessweek.com (November 24, 2000).

13. Sam Fortescue, "Companies Warm to Doing Deals on e-Marketplaces," *Supply Management,* June 10, 2004, p. 10.

14. David Hannon, "Owens Corning Plans to Go 80% Paperless by End-2004," *Purchasing,* January 15, 2004, pp. 16–17.

15. Ibid.

16. Richard B. Chase, F. Robert Jacobs, and Nicholas J. Aquilano, *Operations Management for Competitive Advantage,* 11th ed. (Burr Ridge, IL: McGraw-Hill Irwin, 2006), chap. 10.

17. George Stalk, Jr., quoted in Paul B. Brown, "What's Offline," *New York Times,* June 10, 2006, p. B5.

18. Ronald C. Ritter and Robert A. Sternfels, "When Offshore Manufacturing Doesn't Make Sense," *The McKinsey Quarterly,* no. 4, 2004, www.mckinseyquarterly.com/article_print.aspx?L2=1&L3=106&ar=1510 (April 13, 2006).

19. J. M. Juran, "A History of Managing for Quality in the United States," *Quality Digest,* December 1995, pp. 34–45; and Lloyd Dobyns

and Clare Crawford-Mason, *Quality or Else* (Boston: Houghton Mifflin, 1991), p. 18.

20. Chase, Jacobs, and Aquilano, *Operations Management for Competitive Advantage,* pp. 320–21.

21. "Innovation," *BusinessWeek,* Special Issue, June 1989, p. 107.

22. Peter Kolesar, "Juran's Message to Japanese Executives in 1954: Some Lessons for Us in 2004," July 2004, www2.gsb.columbia.edu/divisions/dro/working_papers/2004/DRO2004-06.pdf (July 16, 2006).

23. "Motivation Systems for Small-Group Quality Control Activities," *Japan Economic Journal,* June 28, 1988, pp. 33–35.

24. Chase, Jacobs, and Aquilano, *Operations Management for Competitive Advantage,* chap. 12.

25. "Toyota to Recalibrate 'Just-in-Time,'" *International Herald Tribune,* February 8–9, 1997, p. 9; and "Brakes on a Toyota," *Financial Times,* February 7, 1997, p. 8.

26. Chase, Jacobs, and Aquilano, *Operations Management for Competitive Advantage,* chap. 12.

27. "Bottlenecks," http://members.aol.com/williamfla/bottle.htm (September 26, 2004); and Chase, Jacobs, and Aquilano, *Operations Management for Competitive Advantage,* chap. 18.

28. Bain and Company, "Mass Customization," www.bain.com/management_tools/tools_mass_customization.asp?groupCode=2 (July 17, 2006).

29. Joseph M. Juran and A. Blanton Godfrey, *Juran's Quality Handbook,* 5th ed. (New York: McGraw-Hill, 1999).

30. Ronald D. Snee, "Dealing with the Achilles' Heel of Six Sigma Initiatives," *Quality Progress* 34, no. 3 (March 2001), pp. 66–72.

31. James M. Lucas, "The Essential Six Sigma," *Quality Progress* 35, no. 1 (January 2002), pp. 27–31.

32. "Six Sigma Gets Its Day," *Quality* 41, no. 1 (January 2002), p. 48.

33. Dennis Sester, "Motorola: A Tradition of Quality," *Quality* 40, no. 10 (October 2001), pp. 30–34; and "Experience," www.motorola.com/content/0,,2403-5008,00.html (August 5, 2004).

34. George Eckes, "Making Six Sigma Last (and Work)," *Ivey Business Journal* 66, no. 3 (January–February 2002), pp. 77–81.

35. Chase, Jacobs, and Aquilano, *Operations Management for Competitive Advantage,* pp. 413–14.

36. Heizer and Render, *Principles of Operations Management,* p. 173.

37. Intel, "Copy Exactly, Factory Strategy," www.intel.com/pressroom/kits/manufacturing/copy_exactly_bkgrnd.htm (July 17, 2006).

38. Conversation with SKF executive.

39. D. J. Teece, "Technology Transfer by Multinational Firms," reprinted in M. Casson (ed.), *The International Library of Critical Writings in Economics I* (London, England: Edward Elgar, 1990), pp. 185–204.

40. A highly automated machine may make only one or two sizes or types of a product, whereas a general-purpose machine may be capable of producing not only all sizes of a product but other products as well. Its output, however, may be as little as 1 percent of that of a specialized machine.

41. David Wessel, "China Rewrites Rules for Building Wealth," *The Wall Street Journal,* January 29, 2004, p. A2.

42. Michiyo Nakamoto, "Sony Moves Camcorder Output," *Financial Times,* July 24, 2002, p. 19.

43. Dell, "Locations," www1.euro.dell.com/content/topics/topic.aspx/global/hybrid/careers/content/ebe52809-2b75-4be2-816a-489d9a58d7ef?c=ie&l=en&s=corp (July 18, 2006); and John Murray Brown, "How Dell Keeps Going in Europe," *Financial Times,* June 1, 2004, p. 6.

CHAPTER 20

1. Vijay Govindarajan and Anil Gupta, *The Quest for Global Dominance: Transforming Global Presence into Global Competitive Advantage* (San Francisco: Jossey-Bass, 2001), p. 106.

2. Ibid., p. 111.

3. David A. Heenan and Howard V. Perlmutter, *Multinational Organization Development* (Boston: Addison-Wesley, 1979).

4. Consistency between mind-set and IHRM practices was reported in Linda K. Stroh and Paula M. Caligiuri, "Strategic Human Resources: A New Source for Competitive Advantage in the Global Arena," *International Journal of Human Resource Management* 9, no. 1 (1998), pp. 1–17.

5. David Pilling and Francesco Guerrera, "We Are a Mixture: Western Style in Management but with an Eastern Touch," *Financial Times,* September 26, 2003, p. 13.

6. Geoff Dyer, "A Tale of Two Corporate Cultures," *Financial Times,* May 23, 2006, p. 8.

7. Pui-Wing Tam, "Cultural Training Smooths Outsourcing Issues," *The Wall Street Journal,* Midwestern Edition, May 25, 2004, p. A11. Copyright 2004 by Dow Jones & Co. Inc. Reproduced with permission of Dow Jones & Co. Inc. via Copyright Clearance Center.

8. Richard Waters and Tom Foremski, "Intel Insider Looks to Asia," *Financial Times,* September 22, 2003, p. 8.

9. Ben Dolven, "China Recruits Foreign Talent," *The Wall Street Journal,* Midwestern Edition, April 15, 2004, p. A13. Copyright 2004 by Dow Jones & Co. Inc. Reproduced with permission of Dow Jones & Co. Inc. via Copyright Clearance Center.

10. GMAC Global Relocation Services, *Global Relocation Trends 2003/2004 Survey Report,* www.gmacglobalrelocation.com/2003survey (July 24, 2006); and Mary G. Tye and Peter Y. Chen, "Selection of Expatriates: Decision-Making Models Used by HR Professionals," *Human Resource Planning* 28, no. 4 (2005), pp. 15–20.

11. "Expatriate Workforce Demographics," *HR Magazine* 51, no. 5 (May 2006), p. 16.

12. John C. Beck, "Globalization: Don't Go There . . . ," www.accenture.com/Global/Research_and_Insights/ (July 24, 2006).

13. Juan I. Sanchez, Paul E. Spector, and Cary L. Cooper, "Adapting to a Boundaryless World: A Developmental Expatriate Model," *Academy of Management Executive* 14, no. 2 (May 2000), pp. 96–106.

14. Deirdre McCaughey and Nealia S. Bruning, "Enhancing Opportunities for Expatriate Job Satisfaction: HR Strategies for Foreign Assignment Success," *Human Resource Planning* 28, no. 4 (2005), pp. 21–29.

15. Margaret A. Shaffer, David A. Harrison, and K. Matthew Gilley, "Dimensions, Determinants, and Differences in the Expatriate Adjustment Process," *Journal of International Business Studies* 30, no. 3 (1999), pp. 557–81.

16. Margaret A. Shaffer and David A. Harrison, "Forgotten Partners of International Assignments: Development and Test of a Model of Spouse Adjustment," *Journal of Applied Psychology* 86, no. 2 (2001), pp. 238–54.

17. Riki Takeuchi, Seokhwa Yun, and Paul E Tesluk, "An Examination of Crossover and Spillover Effects of Spousal and Expatriate Cross-Cultural Adjustment on Expatriate Outcomes," *Journal of Applied Psychology* 87, no. 4 (August 2002), p. 655.

18. GMAC Global Relocation Services, *Global Relocation Trends 2003/2004 Survey Report.*

19. Michael Harvey, "Dual-Career Expatriates: Expectations, Adjustment and Satisfaction with International Relocation," *Journal of International Business Studies* 28, no. 3 (1997), pp. 627–58; and Perri Capell, "What 'Trailing Spouses' Can Do," *The Wall Street Journal,* May 2, 2006, p. B6.

20. Expatica, "Helping Families Meet the Challenge of Moving Abroad," www.expatica.com/source/site_article.asp?subchannel_id=157&story_id=10453 (July 23, 2006); and Expatica, "How Children View Moving Abroad," www.consultus.net/pressroom/Cold_Feet_Expatriate.pdf (July 23, 2006).

21. Linda Anderson, "Language Skills Highly Ranked," *Financial Times,* April 23, 2001, p. 18.

22. Annette Haddad and Scott Doggett, "Road Home Hard after Working Overseas," *Los Angeles Times,* March 13, 2000, p. C2.

23. GMAC Global Relocation Services, *Global Relocation Trends 2003/2004 Survey Report*; and Kathryn Tyler, "Retaining Repatriates," *HR Magazine* 51, no. 3 (March 2006), pp. 97–102.

24. Tyler, "Retaining Repatriates."

25. Lublin, "To Smooth a Transfer Abroad, a New Focus on Kids," *The Wall Street Journal,* January 26, 1999, pp. B1, 14.

26. Joanne Wojcik and Sarah Veysey, "Expatriate Health Coverage Often Hard to Coordinate," *Crain Communications,* 2004, p. 10.

27. "The New Frontier of Banking," *Lafferty Publications Limited,* August 23, 2002, p. 10.

28. "Taxing Situations for Expatriates," *Crain Communications,* June 1, 2003, p. 100.

29. Prudential Financial, "About Us," www.prudential.com/HTMLEmbed/0,1469,int PageID%253D10006%2526blnPrinter-Friendly%253D0,00.html (July 22, 2006).

30. "Worldwide Cost of Living Survey 2006—City Rankings," www.mercerhr.com/pressrelease/details.jhtml/dynamic/idContent/1142150 (July 23, 2006).

31. Some writers regard paid home leave as an allowance, but our experience convinces us that it is a bonus, because ICs consistently give more frequent or longer home leaves to employees working in less desirable assignments.

32. Tom Herman, "Americans Working Overseas May See Big Jump in Tax Bill," *The Wall Street Journal,* May 20, 2006, p. B4.

33. "Vacation Time. How Much Is the Norm?" www.ilr.cornell.edu/library/research/QuestionOfTheMonth/archive/vacationtime.html (July 23, 2006).

CHAPTER 21

1. Peter Smith and James Politi, "Against the Flow: How 'Private Equity's Google' Is Profiting from Contrarianism," *Financial Times,* July 3, 2006, p. 1.

2. James Oberstar, House Transportation and Infrastructure Committee testimony before the U.S. Senate Committee on Commerce, Science and Transportation, May 9, 2006, www.house.gov/transportation_democrats/SenForeignOwnershipHearing (accessed July 15, 2006).

3. When equity securities (stock) are issued, part of the ownership is being sold. No money is being borrowed that must be repaid, as is the case when debt securities (bonds) are issued.

4. Cheol S. Eun and Bruce G. Resnick, *International Financial Management,* 4th ed. (Burr Ridge, IL: McGraw-Hill Irwin, 2007), pp. 228–34.

5. A blocked-currency situation arises either because there is no satisfactory market for the currency or because of a country's laws.

6. "Derivatives," *Financial Times Survey,* June 27, 1997, pp. i–viii.

7. "Risk: Living Dangerously," *The Economist,* January 22, 2004, www.economist.com/displaystory.cfm?story_id=2347805 (accessed July 6, 2006).

8. Charles Batchelor, "Credit Default Swaps Join Booming Derivatives Line-Up," *Financial Times,* February 11, 2004, p. 26.

9. Prema Nakra, "Countertrade and International Marketing: Take a Proactive Approach," December 27, 2005, www.i-b-t.net/anm/templates/trade_article.asp?articleid=206&zoneid=3 (accessed July 7, 2006).

10. Daniel Mitchell, "Job Creation and the Taxation of Foreign Earned Income," Executive Memorandum 911, The Heritage Foundation, 2004.

11. John Daniels, Lee Radebaugh, and Daniel Sullivan, *International Business: Environments and Operations,* 11th ed. (Upper Saddle River, NJ: Pearson, 2007), p. 639.

12. Sidney J. Gray, "Towards a Theory of Cultural Influence on the Development of Accounting Systems Internationally," *Abacus* 24, no. 1 (1998), pp. 1–15.

13. D. J. Gannon, "International Financial Reporting Standards: Of Growing Importance for U.S. Companies," Deloitte and Touche, 2003, www.iasplus.com/dttpubs/usifrs (accessed July 4, 2006).

14. "Use of IFRSs for Reporting by Domestic Companies," Deloitte, March 2006, www.iasplus.com/country/useias.htm#*? (accessed July 2, 2006).

15. "IFRS and US GAAP: A Pocket Comparison," Deloitte, 2005, www.deloitte.com/dtt/cda/doc/content/dtt_audit_2005ifrsusgaap_01_05_06.pdf (accessed July 2, 2006).

16. John Elkington, *Cannibals with Forks: The Triple Bottom Line of 21st Century Business,* (Gabriola Island, BC, Canada: New Society Publishers, 1997).

17. Wayne Norman and Chris MacDonald, "Getting to the Bottom of 'Triple Bottom Line,'" *Business Ethics Quarterly,* April 2004, www.businessethics.ca (accessed July 4, 2006).

18. "Derivatives," *Financial Times Survey,* June 27, 1997, pp. I–VIII.

Glossary

A

absolute advantage Theory that a nation has absolute advantage when it can produce a larger amount of a good or service for the same amount of inputs as can another country or when it can produce the same amount of a good or service using fewer inputs than could another country

ad valorem duty An import duty levied as a percentage of the invoice value of imported goods

advertising Paid, nonpersonal presentation of ideas, goods, or services by an identified sponsor

aesthetics A culture's sense of beauty and good taste

affiliates A term sometimes used interchangeably with subsidiaries, but more forms exist than just stock ownership

air waybill A bill of lading issued by an air carrier

allowances Employee compensation payments added to base salaries because of higher expenses encountered when living abroad

American depository receipts (ADRs) Foreign shares held by a custodian, usually a U.S. bank, in the issuer's home market and traded in dollars on the U.S. exchange

Andean Community (CAN) South American five-nation trading bloc

antitrust laws Laws to prevent price fixing, market sharing, and business monopolies

appropriate technology The technology (advanced, intermediate, or primitive) that most closely fits the society using it

arbitrage The process of buying and selling instantaneously to make profit with no risk

arbitration A process, agreed to by parties to a dispute in lieu of going to court, by which a neutral person or body makes a binding decision

Asian religions Primary ones: Hinduism, Buddhism, Jainism, and Sikhism (India); Confucianism and Taoism (China); and Shintoism (Japan)

ask price Sales price

Association of Southeast Asian Nations (ASEAN) Ten-member body formed to promote peace and cooperation in the Southeast Asian region

associations Social units based on age, gender, or common interest, not on kinship

Automated Commercial System (ACS) Electronic tracking system used by U.S. Customs to track, control, and process all commercial goods imported into the United States

automated export system (AES) U.S. Customs electronic filing system

B

backward vertical integration Arrangement in which facilities are established to manufacture inputs used in the production of a firm's final products

balance of payments (BOP) Record of a country's transactions with the rest of the world

banker's acceptance A time draft with maturity of less than 270 days that has been accepted by the bank on which the draft was drawn, thus becoming the accepting bank's obligation; may be bought and sold at a discount in the financial markets like other commercial paper

Bank for International Settlements Institution for central bankers; operates as their bank

bank swap Swap made between banks to acquire temporary foreign currencies

barter A direct exchange of goods or services for goods or services without the use of money

benchmarking A technique for measuring a firm's performance against the performance of others that may be in the same or a completely different industry

bid price Price offered to buy

biomass A category of fuels whose energy source is photosynthesis, through which plants transform the sun's energy into chemical energy; sources include corn, sugarcane, wheat

blocked funds Funds whose conversion from a host currency or repatriation is not allowed by a host government

bonded warehouse An area authorized by customs authorities for storage of goods on which payment of import duties is deferred until the goods are removed

bonuses Expatriate employee compensation payments in addition to base salaries and allowances because of hardship, inconvenience, or danger

boomerang effect Situation in which technology sold to companies in another nation is used to produce goods to compete with those of the seller of the technology.

bottleneck Operation in a manufacturing system whose output sets the limit for the entire system's output

bottom-up planning Planning process that begins at the lowest level in the organization and continues upward

brain drain The loss by a country of its most intelligent and best-educated people.

branch Legal extension of the parent company

Bretton Woods The New Hampshire town where treasury and central bank representatives met near the end of World War II; they established the IMF, the World Bank, and the gold exchange standard

bribes Gifts or payments to induce the receiver to do something illegal for the giver

C

Canadian Shield A massive area of bedrock covering one-half of Canada's landmass

capital account Record of the net changes in a nation's international financial assets and liabilities

capitalism An economic system in which the means of production and distribution are for the most part privately owned and operated for private profit

caste The group to which people belong in a system under which people's place or level in a multilevel society is established at birth as being the same level as that of their parents

caste system An aspect of Hinduism by which the entire society is divided into four groups (plus the outcasts) and each is assigned a certain class of work

CE (Conformite Europeene) mark EU mark that indicates that the merchandise conforms to European health, safety and environmental requirements

Central American Free Trade Agreement (CAFTA) FTA among the United States and several Central American nations

central reserve asset Asset, usually currency, held by a government's central bank

child labor The labor of children below 16 years of age who are forced to work in production and usually are given little or no formal education

clearing account arrangement A process to settle a trading account within a specified time

climate Meteorological conditions, including temperature, precipitation, and wind, that prevail in a region

cluster analysis Statistical technique that divides objects into groups so that the objects within each group are similar

collective bargaining The process in which a union represents the interests of a bargaining unit (which sometimes includes both union members and nonmembers) in negotiations with management

Collective Security Treaty Organization (CSTO) Security alliance of six members of the Commonwealth of Independent States (former Union of Soviet Socialist Republics)

Common Market Customs union that includes mobility of services, people, and capital within the union

communism Marx's theory of a classless society, developed by his successors into control of society by the Communist Party and the attempted worldwide spread of communism

comparative advantage Theory that a nation having absolute disadvantages in the production of two goods with respect to another nation has a comparative or relative advantage in the production of the good in which its absolute disadvantage is less

compensation Countertrade in which the developing country makes payment in products produced by use of developed country equipment.

compensation packages For expatriate employees, packages that can incorporate many types of payments or reimbursements and must take into consideration exchange rates and inflation

competition policy The European Union equivalent of antitrust laws

competitive advantage The ability of a company to have higher rates of profits than its competitors

competitive strategies Action plans to enable organizations to reach their objectives

competitor analysis Process in which principal competitors are identified and their objectives, strengths, weaknesses, and product lines are assessed

competitor intelligence system (CIS) Procedure for gathering, analyzing, and disseminating information about a firm's competitors

complete economic integration Integration on both economic and political levels

compound duty A combination of specific and ad valorem duties

confirmed L/C A confirmation made by a correspondent bank in the seller's country by which it agrees to honor the issuing bank's letter of credit

confiscation Government seizure of the property within its borders owned by foreigners without payment to them

Confucian work ethic Drive toward hard work and thrift; similar to Protestant work ethic

conservative A person, group, or party that wishes to minimize government activities and maximize private ownership and business

consolidation The process of translating subsidiary results and aggregating them into one financial report

contingency plans Plans for the best- or worst-case scenarios or for critical events that could have a severe impact on the firm

contract manufacturing An arrangement in which one firm contracts with another to produce products to its specifications but assumes responsibility for marketing

controllable forces Internal forces that management administers to adapt to changes in the uncontrollable forces

cooperative exporters Established international manufacturers that export other manufacturers' goods as well as their own

Council of the European Union Group that is the EU's primary policy-setting institution

counterpurchase Countertrade in which the goods supplied do not rely on the goods imported

countertrade The trade of goods or services for other goods or services

countervailing duties Additional import taxes levied on imports that have benefited from export subsidies

country risk assessment (CRA) An evaluation, conducted by a bank or business having an asset in or payable from a foreign country or considering a loan or an investment there, that assesses the country's economic situation and policies and its politics to determine how much risk exists of losing the asset or not being paid

country screening Using countries as the basis for market selection

cross investment Foreign direct investment by oligopolistic firms in each other's home countries as a defense measure

cross rates Currency exchange rates for trading directly between non-US$ currencies

culture Sum total of beliefs, rules, techniques, institutions, and artifacts that characterize human populations

currency devaluation The lowering of a currency's price in terms of other currencies

currency option hedge An option to buy or sell a specific amount of foreign currency at a specific time in order to protect against foreign currency risk

currency swap An exchange of debt service of a loan or bond in one currency for the debt service of a loan or bond in another currency

current account Record of a country's exports and imports in goods and services

current rate method An approach in foreign currency translation in which current assets and liabilities are valued at current spot rates and noncurrent assets and liabilities are translated at their historic exchange rates

customhouse brokers Independent businesses that handle import shipments for compensation

customs drawbacks Rebates on customs duties

Customs Union Collaboration that adds common external tariffs to an FTA

D

de-jobbing Replacing fixed jobs with tasks performed by evolving teams

demonstration effect Result of having seen others with desirable goods

derivative A contract whose value is tied to the performance of a financial instrument or commodity

developed A classification for all industrialized nations, which are the most technically developed

developing A classification for the world's lower-income nations, which are less technically developed

direct exporting The exporting of goods and services by the firm that produces them

direct investment The purchase of sufficient stock in a firm to obtain significant management control

direct investments Investments located in one country that are effectively controlled by residents of another country

discretionary income The amount of income left after paying taxes and making essential purchases

distributors Independent importers that buy for their own account for resale

Doha Development Agenda WTO extended conference on trade; also called *Doha Round*

domestic environment All the uncontrollable forces originating in the home country that surround and influence the firm's life and development

dumping Selling a product abroad for less than the cost of production, the price in the home market, or the price to third countries

dynamic capability Theory that for a firm to successfully invest overseas, it must have not only ownership of unique knowledge or resources but the ability to dynamically create and exploit these capabilities over time

E

eclectic theory of international production Theory that for a firm to invest overseas, it must have three kinds of advantages: ownership-specific, internalization, and location-specific

Economic and Social Council (ECOSOC) UN body concerned with economic and social issues such as trade, development, education, and human rights

economic exposure The potential for the value of future cash flows to be affected by unanticipated exchange rate movements

efficient market approach Assumption that current market prices fully reflect all available relevant information

environment All the forces surrounding and influencing the life and development of the firm

environmental scanning A procedure in which a firm scans the world for changes in the environmental forces that might affect it

environmental sustainability Economic state in which the demands placed upon the environment by people and commerce can be met without reducing the capacity of the environment to provide for future generations

estimation by analogy Process of using a market factor that is successful in one market to estimate demand in a similar market

ethnocentric As used here, related to hiring and promoting employees on the basis of the parent company's home country frame of reference

ethnocentricity Belief in the superiority of one's own ethnic group (see the *self-reference criterion* in Chapter 1)

Euro (€) Currency of the European Monetary Union

European Central Bank (ECB) Institution that sets and implements EU monetary policy

European Commission Institution that runs the EU's day-to-day operations

European Court of Justice (ECJ) Court that rules on issues related to EU policies

European Free Trade Agreement (EFTA) Four-nation non-EU FTA in Europe

European Monetary Union (EMU) Group that established use of euro (€) in the 12-country euro zone

European Parliament EU legislative body whose members are popularly elected from member-nations

European Union (EU) A body of 25 European countries dedicated to economic and political integration

exchange rate The price of one currency stated in terms of another currency

Ex-Im Bank Principal government agency that aids American exporters by means of loans, guarantees, and insurance programs

expatriate A person living outside his or her country of citizenship

export bill of lading (B/L) Contract of carriage between shipper and carrier: straight bill of lading is nonnegotiable; endorsed "to order" bill gives the holder claim on merchandise

export draft An unconditional order drawn by the seller that instructs the buyer to pay the draft's amount on presentation (sight draft) or at an agreed future date (time draft) and that must be paid before the buyer receives shipping documents

exporting The transportation of any domestic good or service to a destination outside a country or region; the opposite of importing, which is the transportation of any good or service into a country or region, from a foreign origination point

export processing zone A government-designated zone in which workers are permitted to import parts and materials without paying import duties, as long as these imported items are then exported once they have been processed or assembled

export trading company (ETC) A firm established principally to export domestic goods and services and to help unrelated companies export their products

expropriation Government seizure of the property within its borders owned by foreigners, followed by prompt, adequate, and effective compensation paid to the former owners

extended family Family that includes blood relatives and relatives by marriage

extortion Demand for payment to keep the receiver from causing harm to the payer

extraterritorial application of laws A country's attempt to apply its laws to foreigners or nonresidents and to acts and activities that take place outside its borders

Ex-Works INCOTERM equivalent of FOB

F

factor conditions Attributes that a country inherits, such as climate and natural resources, and those a country can mold, such as the labor force and infrastructure

factor endowment Heckscher-Ohlin theory that countries export products requiring large amounts of their abundant production factors and import products requiring large amounts of their scarce production factors

factoring Discounting without recourse an account receivable

fiscal policies Policies that address the collecting and spending of money by the government

Fisher effect The relationship between real and nominal interest rates: The real interest rate will be the nominal interest rate minus the expected rate of inflation

fixed currency exchange rates Rates that governments agree on and undertake to maintain

floating currency exchange rates Rates that are allowed to float against other currencies and are determined by market forces

FOB (free on board) Pricing policy in which risks pass from seller to buyer at the factory door; U.S. equivalent of Ex-Works

Foreign Corrupt Practices Act (FCPA) U.S. law against making payments to foreign government officials for special treatment

foreign direct investment Direct investments in equipment, structures, and organizations in a foreign country at a level that is sufficient to obtain significant management control; does not include mere foreign investment in stock markets

foreign environment All the uncontrollable forces originating outside the home country that surround and influence the firm

foreign national pricing Local pricing in another country

foreign sourcing The overseas procurement of raw materials, components, and products

foreign tax credits Allowances by which U.S. taxpayers who reside and pay income taxes in another country can credit those taxes against U.S. income tax

foreign trade zone (FTZ) Duty-free area designed to facilitate trade by reducing the effect of customs restrictions

forfaiting Purchasing without recourse an account receivable whose credit terms are longer than the 90 to 180 days usual in factoring; unlike factoring, political and transfer risks are borne by the forfaiter

forward currency market Trading market for currency contracts deliverable 30, 60, 90, or 180 days in the future

forward market hedge Foreign currency contract sold or bought forward in order to protect against foreign currency movement

forward rate The exchange rate between two currencies for delivery in the future, usually 30, 60, 90, or 180 days

franchising A form of licensing in which one firm contracts with another to operate a certain type of business under an established name according to specific rules

free trade area (FTA) Area in which tariffs among members have been eliminated, but members keep their external tariffs

free trade zone An area designated by the government as outside its customs territory

functional currency The primary currency of a business

fundamental approach Exchange rate prediction based on econometric models that attempt to capture the variables and their correct relationships

G

General Agreement on Tariffs and Trade (GATT) International agreement that functioned to encourage trade liberalization from 1947 to 1995

General Assembly Deliberative body of the UN made up of all member-nations, each with one vote regardless of size, wealth, or power

general export license Any export license covering export commodities for which a validated license is not required; no formal application is required

geocentric As used here, related to hiring and promoting employees on the basis of ability and experience without considering race or citizenship

global company (GC) An organization that attempts to standardize and integrate operations worldwide in all functional areas

global mind-set A mind-set that combines an openness to and an awareness of diversity across markets and cultures with a propensity and ability to synthesize across this diversity

gold standard The use of gold at an established number of units per currency

goods or merchandise account Record of tangible exports and imports

gross national income (GNI) The total value of all income generated by a nation's residents from international and domestic activity

Group of Eight (G8) Group of government leaders from industrialized nations that meets regularly to discuss issues of concern

guest workers People who go to a foreign country legally to perform certain types of jobs

H

Harmonized Tariff Schedule of the United States (HTSUSA) American version of the Harmonized System used worldwide to classify imported products

hedging A process to reduce or eliminate financial risk

hierarchy A body of persons organized or classified according to rank or authority

home country national Same as parent country national

horizontal corporation A form of organization characterized by lateral decision processes, horizontal networks, and a strong corporatewide business philosophy

host country national (HCN) Employee who is a citizen of the nation in which the subsidiary is operating, which is different from the parent company's home nation

human-needs approach View that defines economic development as a reduction of poverty and unemployment as well as an increase in income

hybrid organization Structure organized by more than one dimension at the top level

I

import substitution The local production of goods to replace imports

in-bond plants (maquiladoras) Production facilities in Mexico that temporarily import raw materials, components, or parts duty-free to be manufactured, processed, or assembled with less expensive local labor, after which the finished or semifinished product is exported

income distribution A measure of how a nation's income is apportioned among its people, commonly reported as the percentage of income received by population quintiles

income tax Direct tax levied on earnings

INCOTERMS Universal trade terminology developed by the International Chamber of Commerce

indirect exporting The exporting of goods and services through various types of home-based exporters

industrial cooperation An exporter's commitment to a longer-term relationship than that in a simple export sale, in which some of the production occurs in the receiving country

industrial espionage Act of spying on a competitor to learn secrets about its strategy and operations

inland waterways Waterways that provide access to interior regions

instability Characteristic of a government that cannot maintain itself in power or that makes sudden, unpredictable, or radical policy changes

intellectual property Patents, trademarks, trade names, copyrights, and trade secrets, all of which result from the exercise of someone's intellect

interest rate swap An exchange of interest rate flows in order to manage interest rate exposure

intermediate technology Production methods between capital- and labor-intensive methods

internalization theory An extension of the market imperfection theory: the concept that to obtain a higher return on its investment, a firm will transfer its superior knowledge to a foreign subsidiary rather than sell it in the open market

international company (IC) Either a global or a multidomestic company

International Court of Justice (ICJ) UN body that renders legal decisions involving disputes between national governments

international division A division in the organization that is at the same level as the domestic division and is responsible for all non-home country activities

international environment Interaction between domestic and foreign environmental forces or between sets of foreign environmental forces

international Fisher effect Concept that the interest rate differentials for any two currencies will reflect the expected change in their exchange rates

International Monetary Fund (IMF) Institution that coordinates multilateral monetary rules and their enforcement

international pricing Setting prices of goods for export for both unrelated and related firms

international product life cycle (IPLC) A theory explaining why a product that begins as a nation's export eventually becomes its import

international status Entitles the expatriate employee to all the allowances and bonuses applicable to the place of residence and employment

international strategy The way firms make choices about acquiring and using scarce resources in order to achieve their international objectives

intervention currency A currency used by a country to intervene in the foreign currency exchange markets, often to buy (strengthen) its own currency

irrevocable L/C A stipulation that a letter of credit cannot be canceled

iterative planning Repetition of the bottom-up or top-down planning process until all differences are reconciled

J

Jamaica Agreement The 1976 IMF agreement that allows flexible exchange rates among members

joint venture A cooperative effort among two or more organizations that share a common interest in a business enterprise or undertaking

just-in-time (JIT) A balanced system in which there is little or no delay time and idle in-process and finished goods inventory

K

Kyoto Protocol United Nations Framework Convention on Climate Change, which calls for nations to reduce global warming by reducing their emissions of the gasses that contribute to it

L

labor market The pool of available potential employees with the necessary skills within commuting distance from an employer

labor mobility The movement of people from country to country or area to area to get jobs

labor quality The skills, education, and attitudes of available employees

labor quantity The number of available employees with the skills required to meet an employer's business needs

labor unions Organizations of workers

language trap A situation in which a person doing international business can speak only his or her home language

law of one price Concept that in an efficient market, like products will have like prices

leading and lagging Timing payments early (lead) or late (lag), depending on anticipated currency movements, so that they have the most favorable impact for company

left wing A more extreme liberal position

letter of credit (L/C) Document issued by the buyer's bank in which the bank promises to pay the seller a specified amount under specified conditions

liberal In the contemporary United States, a person, group, or party that urges greater government involvement in business and other aspects of human activities

licensing A contractual arrangement in which one firm grants access to its patents, trade secrets, or technology to another for a fee

lingua franca A foreign language used to communicate among a nation's diverse cultures that have diverse languages

M

management contract An arrangement by which one firm provides management in all or specific areas to another firm

manufacturers' agents Independent sales representatives of various non-competing suppliers

manufacturing rationalization Division of production among a number of production units, thus enabling each to produce only a limited number of components for all of a firm's assembly plants

market factors Economic data that correlate highly with market demand for a product

market indicators Economic data used to measure relative market strengths of countries or geographic areas

market screening A version of environmental scanning in which the firm identifies desirable markets by using the environmental forces to eliminate the less desirable markets

mass customization The use of flexible, usually computer-aided, manufacturing systems to produce and deliver customized products and services for different customers worldwide

material culture All human-made objects; concerned with *how* people make things (technology) and *who* makes *what* and *why* (economics)

matrix organization An organizational structure composed of one or more superimposed organizational structures in an attempt to mesh product, regional, functional, and other expertise

matrix overlay An organization in which top-level divisions are required to heed input from a staff composed of experts of another organizational dimension in an attempt to avoid the double-reporting difficulty of a matrix organization but still mesh two or more dimensions

mercantilism An economic philosophy based on the belief that (1) a nation's wealth depends on accumulated treasure, usually gold, and (2) to increase wealth, government policies should promote exports and discourage imports

Mercosur (Mercosul) Economic free trade area in South America modeled on the EU

minorities A relatively smaller number of people identified by race, religion, or national origin who live among a larger majority

mission statement A broad statement that defines the organization's purpose and scope

monetary policies Government policies that control the amount of money in circulation and its growth rate

money market hedge A method to hedge foreign currency exposure by borrowing and lending in the domestic and foreign money markets

monopolistic advantage theory Theory that foreign direct investment is made by firms in oligopolistic industries possessing technical and other advantages over indigenous firms

most favored nation (MFN) clause Agreement that GATT member-nations would treat all members equally in trade matters

multidomestic company (MDC) An organization with multicountry affiliates, each of which formulates its own business strategy based on perceived market differences

multilateral netting Strategy in which subsidiaries transfer net intracompany cash flows through a centralized clearing center

N

national competitiveness A nation's relative ability to design, produce, distribute, or service products within an international trading context while earning increasing returns on its resources

national tax jurisdiction A tax system for expatriate citizens of a country whereby the country taxes them on the basis of nationality even though they live and work abroad

natural resources Anything supplied by nature on which people depend

newly industrialized economies (NIEs) The fast-growing upper-middle-income and high-income economies of South Korea, Taiwan, Hong Kong, and Singapore

newly industrializing countries (NICs) The four Asian tigers and the middle-income economies such as Brazil, Mexico, Malaysia, Chile, and Thailand

nonrevenue tax purposes Purposes such as redistributing income, discouraging consumption of products such as tobacco and alcohol, and encouraging purchase of domestic rather than imported products

nontariff barriers (NTBs) All forms of discrimination against imports other than import duties

North American Free Trade Agreement (NAFTA) Agreement creating a free trade area among Canada, Mexico, and the United States

North American Treaty Organization (NATO) Security alliance of 26 North American and European nations

O

official reserves account Record of the assets held by the government, gold, foreign currencies, and accounts in foreign banks; a balance of the country's foreign currency

offset Trade arrangement that requires that a portion of the inputs be supplied by the receiving country

offshore financial center Location that specializes in financing nonresidents, with low taxes and few banking regulations

offshoring Relocating some or all of a business's activities or processes to a foreign location

orderly marketing arrangements Formal agreements between exporting and importing countries that stipulate the import or export quotas each nation will have for a good

Organisation for Economic Cooperation and Development (OECD) Group of developed countries dedicated to promoting economic expansion in its member-nations

Organization of Petroleum Exporting Countries (OPEC) Cartel of 11 petroleum-exporting countries

organizational structure The way that an organization formally arranges its domestic and international units and activities, and the relationships among these various organizational components

outsourcing Hiring others to perform some of the noncore activities and decision making in a company's value chain, rather than having the company and its employees continue to perform those activities

Overseas Private Investment Corporation (OPIC) Government corporation that offers American investors in developing countries insurance against expropriation, currency inconvertibility, and damages from wars and revolutions

P

parallel loans Matched loans across currencies that are made to cover risk

parent country national (PCNs) Employee who is a citizen of the nation in which the parent company is headquartered; also called home country national

par value Stated value

passive processing The finishing or refining in Eastern European countries of semifinished goods from the West, which are then returned to the West after finishing; similar to Mexican maquiladora operations

polycentric As used here, related to hiring and promoting employees on the basis of the specific local context in which the subsidiary operates

population density A measure of the number of inhabitants per area unit (inhabitants per square kilometer or square mile)

population distribution A measure of how the inhabitants are distributed over a nation's area

portfolio investment The purchase of stocks and bonds to obtain a return on the funds invested

portfolio investments Long-term investments that do not give the investors control over the investment

preferential trading arrangement An agreement by a small group of nations to establish free trade among themselves while maintaining trade restrictions with all other nations

preventive (planned) maintenance Maintenance done according to plan, not when machines break down

private international law Laws governing transactions of individuals and companies that cross international borders

privatization The transfer of public sector assets to the private sector, the transfer of management of state activities through contracts and leases, and the contracting out of activities previously conducted by the state

product liability Standard that holds a company and its officers and directors liable and possibly subject to fines or imprisonment when their product causes death, injury, or damage

pro forma invoice Exporter's formal quotation containing a description of the merchandise, price, delivery time, method of shipping, terms of sale, and points of exit and entry

programmed-management approach A middle-ground advertising strategy between globally standardized and entirely local programs

promotion Any form of communication between a firm and its publics

promotional mix A blend of the promotional methods a firm uses to sell its products

Protestant work ethic Duty to glorify God by hard work and the practice of thrift

public international law Legal relations between governments

public relations Various methods of communicating with the firm's publics to secure a favorable impression

purchasing power parity (PPP) The number of units of a currency required to buy the same amounts of goods and services in the domestic market that one dollar would buy in the United States; the theory that predicts that currency exchange rates between two countries should equal the ratio of the price levels of their commodity baskets

Q

quality circle (quality control circle) Small work group that meets periodically to discuss ways to improve its functional areas and the quality of the product

questionable or dubious payments Bribes paid to government officials by companies seeking purchase contracts from those governments

quotas Numerical limits placed on specific classes of imports

R

random walk hypothesis Assumption that the unpredictability of factors suggests that the best predictor of tomorrow's prices is today's prices

regiocentric As used here, related to hiring and promoting employees on the basis of the specific regional context in which the subsidiary operates

Rhine waterway A system of rivers and canals that is the main transportation artery of Europe

right wing A more extreme conservative position

rural-to-urban shift The movement of a nation's population from rural areas to cities

S

sales company A business established for the purpose of marketing goods and services, not producing them

sales promotion Any of various selling aids, including displays, premiums, contests, and gifts

scenarios Multiple, plausible stories about the future

Secretariat The staff of the UN, headed by the secretary-general

Security Council Main policy-setting body of the UN, composed of 15 members including 5 permanent members

segment screening Using market segments as the basis for market selection

self-reference criterion Unconscious reference to one's own cultural values when judging behaviors of others in a new and different environment

services account Record of intangibles that are exchanged internationally

shale A fissile rock (capable of being split) composed of laminated layers of claylike, fine-grained sediment

shipper's export declaration (SED) U.S. Department of Commerce form used to control export shipments and record export statistics

short-term capital flows Changes in international assets and liabilities with an original maturity of one year or less

Six Sigma Business management process for reducing defects and eliminating variation

socialism Public, collective ownership of the basic means of production and distribution, operating for use rather than profit

sogo shosha The largest of the Japanese general trading companies

special drawing right (SDR) An international reserve asset established by the IMF; the unit of account for the IMF and other international organizations

specific duty A fixed sum levied on a physical unit of an imported good

spot and forward market swaps Use of the spot and forward markets to hedge foreign currency exposure

spot rate The exchange rate between two currencies for delivery within two business days

stability Characteristic of a government that maintains itself in power and whose fiscal, monetary, and political policies are predictable and not subject to sudden, radical changes

stakeholder theory An understanding of how business operates that takes into account all identifiable interest holders

standards Documented agreements containing technical specifications or other precise criteria that will be used consistently as guidelines, rules, or definitions of the characteristics of a product, process, or service

strategic alliances Partnerships between competitors, customers, or suppliers that may take one or more of various forms

strategic business unit (SBU) Business entity with a clearly defined market, specific competitors, the ability to carry out its business mission, and a size appropriate for control by a single manager

strict liability Standard that holds the designer/manufacturer liable for damages caused by a product without the need for a plaintiff to prove negligence in the product's design or manufacture

subsidiaries Companies controlled by other companies through ownership of enough voting stock to elect board-of-directors majorities

subsidiary Separate legal entity owned by the parent company

subsidiary detriment Situation in which a small loss for a subsidiary results in a greater gain for the total IC

subsidies Financial contributions, provided directly or indirectly by a government, which confer a benefit; include grants, preferential tax treatment, and government assumption of normal business expenses

supply chain management The process of coordinating and integrating the flow of materials, information, finances, and services within and among companies in the value chain from suppliers to the ultimate consumer

swap contract A spot sale/purchase of an asset against a future purchase/sale of an equal amount in order to hedge a financial position

switch trading The use of a third party to market products received in countertrade

synchronous manufacturing An entire manufacturing system with unbalanced operations that emphasizes total system performance

T

tariffs Taxes on imported goods for the purpose of raising their price to reduce competition for local producers or stimulate local production

tax treaties Treaties between countries that bind the governments to share information about taxpayers and cooperate in tax law enforcement; often called tax conventions

Taylor's scientific management system System based on scientific measurements that prescribes a division of work whereby planning is done by managers and plan execution is left to supervisors and workers

technical analysis An approach that analyzes data for trends and then projects these trends forward

technological dualism The side-by-side presence of technologically advanced and technologically primitive production systems

temporal method An approach in foreign currency translation in which monetary accounts are valued at the spot rate and accounts carried at historical cost are translated at their historic exchange rates

terms of sale Conditions of a sale that stipulate the point at which all costs and risks are borne by the buyer

territorial tax jurisdiction A tax system in which expatriate citizens who neither live nor work in the country— and therefore receive none of the services for which taxes pay—are exempt from the country's taxes

terrorism Unlawful acts of violence committed for a wide variety of reasons, including for ransom, to overthrow a government, to gain release of imprisoned colleagues, to exact revenge for real or imagined wrongs, and to punish nonbelievers of the terrorists' religion

third country national (TCN) Employee who is a citizen of neither the parent company nation nor the host country

top-down planning Planning process that begins at the highest level in the organization and continues downward

topography The surface features of a region

total product What the customer buys, including the physical product, brand name, accessories, after-sales service, warranty, instructions for use, company image, and package

total quality management (TQM) System in which the entire organization is managed so that it excels on all dimensions of product and services that are important to the customer

trade balance The balance on the merchandise account

trade fair A large exhibition, generally held at the same place and same time periodically, at which companies maintain booths to promote the sale of their products

trade mission A group of businesspeople and/or government officials (state or federal) that visits a market in search of business opportunities

trade-related intellectual property rights (TRIPS) the acronym TRIPS refers to the WTO agreement that protects copyrights, trademarks, trade secrets, and other intellectual property matters

trading at a discount Situation in which a currency's forward rate quotes are weaker than spot

trading at a premium Situation in which a currency's forward rate quotes are stronger than spot

trading companies Firms that develop international trade and serve as intermediaries between foreign buyers and domestic sellers and vice versa

traditional hostilities Long-standing enmities between tribes, races, religions, ideologies, or countries

traditional societies Tribal peoples before they turn to organized agriculture or industry; traditional customs may linger after the economy changes

transaction exposure Change in the value of a financial position created by foreign currency changes between the establishment and the settlement of a contract

transfer price Intracorporate price, or the price of a good or service sold by one affiliate to another, the home office to an affiliate, or vice versa

transfer price The cost of intracompany sales of goods or services

translation exposure Potential change in the value of a company's financial position due to exposure created during the consolidation process

treaties Agreements between countries, which may be bilateral (between two countries) or multilateral (involving more than two countries); also called conventions, covenants, compacts, or protocols

trend analysis Statistical technique by which successive observations of a variable at regular time intervals are analyzed to establish regular patterns that are used for establishing future values

Triffin paradox The concept that a national currency that is also a reserve currency will eventually run a deficit, which eventually inspires a lack of confidence in the reserve currency and leads to a financial crisis

triple bottom line (3BL) A results or impact report on the environmental, social, and financial impacts of the business

uncontrollable forces External forces over which management has no direct control, although it can exert an influence

underground economy The part of a nation's income that, because of unreporting or underreporting, is not measured by official statistics

unilateral transfer A transfer with no matched return flow, no reciprocity

United Nations (UN) International organization of 191 member-nations dedicated to the promotion of peace and global stability; has many functions related to business

unit labor costs Total direct labor costs divided by units produced

unspoken language Nonverbal communication, such as gestures and body language

Uruguay Round The last extended conference of GATT negotiations

validated export license A required document issued by the U.S. government authorizing the export of a strategic commodity or a shipment to an unfriendly country.

value-added tax (VAT) Indirect tax collected from the parties as they add value to the product

values statement A clear and concise description of the fundamental values, beliefs, and priorities of the organization's members.

variable levy An import duty set at the difference between world market prices and local government-supported prices

vehicle currency A currency used as a vehicle for international trade or investment

vertically integrated Descriptive term for a firm that produces inputs for its subsequent manufacturing processes

virtual corporation An organization that coordinates economic activity to deliver value to customers using resources outside the traditional boundaries of the organization

vision statement A description of the company's desired future position if it can acquire the necessary competencies and successfully implement its strategy

voluntary export restraints (VERs) Export quotas imposed by the exporting nation

withholding tax Indirect tax paid by the payor, usually on passive income

World Bank Institution that focuses on funding of development projects

World Trade Organization (WTO) A multinational body of 149 members that deals with rules of trade between nations

Photo Credits

Photo Credits Continued

Figure number	Credit	Page number
10-2	© Wolfgang Kaehler / Corbis	284
10-3	AP Wide World Photo	296
11-1	© Bridgeman Art Library, London / Superstock	302
11-2	Ryan McVay / Getty Images	305
11-3	Shawkat Khan / AFP / Getty Images	312
12-1	© Fujifotos / The Image Works	322
12-2	MedioImages / Getty Images	326
12-3	© Marilyn Humphries/ The Image Works	331
13-1	© Steve Chenn / Corbis	350
13-2	Tim Boyle / Getty Images	355
13-3	Courtesy of Katherine McCormick	359
14-1	eStock Photo	384
14-2	Courtesy of Michelle Teteak	389
14-3	© Royalty-Free / Corbis	398
15-1	Taxi / Getty Images	408
15-2	Getty Images	417
16-1	Getty Images	424
16-2	AP / Wide World Photo	429
16-3	Hoang Dinh Namal / AFP / Getty Images	430
16-4	Warner Bros. Pictures / Getty Images	441
17-1	The Image Works	444
17-2	AP / Wide World Photo	450
17-3	© Michael Newman / Photo Edit	466
18-1	AP Wide World	476
18-2	AFP / Douglas E. Curran / Getty Images	482
18-3	Victoria Ball	483
18-4	Kellogg Company	485
18-5	Catherine Karnow / Woodfin Camp	491
19-1	Photo courtesy of Inditex	502
19-4	Photo courtesy of Intel Corporation	524
20-1	Royalty Free / Getty Images	540
20-2	AP / Wide World Photo	547
20-3	The Image Bank / Getty Images	551
21-1	Antony Edwards / Getty Images	566
21-2	Rohanna Mertens for ACCION International	570
21-3	Pepsi-Cola Company	579

Name Index

Pearce, John A., II, 366, 609n, 618n
Pearce, Jonathan, 429
Perera, Wilfred, 238
Perlmutter, Howard V., 543, 544, 622n
Perner, Lars, 483, 621n
Pfanner, Eric, 621n
Phillips, James, 616n
Piette, Daniel, 504
Pigott, William, 612n
Pilling, David, 622n
Pitt, Harvey, 585
Platt, Nicholas, 4, 9
Pohl, Gerhard, 616n
Polaski, Sandra, 23
Politi, James, 623n
Porter, Adam, 615n
Porter, Michael E., 78, 79, 95, 192, 208, 209, 215, 356, 610n, 614n, 618n
Portman, Rob, 612n
Postelnicu, Andrei, 568
Pourian, Heydar, 141
Powers, Rebecca, 555
Prahalad, C. K., 482, 620n
Prasad, Ashutosh, 441
Pringle, David, 618n
Prosser, Ian, 9
Psacharopoulos, George, 244
Pucik, Vladimir, 540
Pugel, Thomas A., 610n

Q

Qaddafi, Muammar, 266

R

Radcliffe, Mark, 376
Radebaugh, Lee, 582, 623n
Radis, Michael, 266
Rajagopalan, S., 227
Rapaille, Clotaire, 409, 410, 415
Reagan, Ronald W., 24
Reid, T. R., 9
Render, B., 621n, 622n
Rennie, David, 610n
Reppert-Bismarck, Juliane von, 611n
Resnick, Bruce G., 612n, 617n, 623n
Resnick, David, 311
Restall, Hugo, 167
Rheingold, Howard, 480
Ricardo, David, 67–68, 69, 71, 79, 95, 97, 610n
Ricks, David A., 363
Riggs, Fred W., 609n
Riordan, Teresa, 285
Ritter, Ronald C., 621n
Ritzman, L. P., 621n
Robers, Dexter, 610n
Robertson, Robie, 609n
Robinson, Colin, 616n
Roessel, P. J., 451
Rohwedder, Cecilie, 504
Rolland, Martial, 527
Rolleri, Michael J., 71
Romanow, Gabriela, 570
Romro, Simon, 615n
Rose, John, 510
Roth, George Thomas, 621n
Roth, Kendall, 363
Roth, Philip, 8
Rueff, Jacques, 141, 612n

Rugman, Alan M., 363, 611n

S

Sabherwal, Sanjiv, 311, 617n
Sachs, Jeffrey D., 69, 143–144, 227, 610n, 613n
Sacks, Danielle, 409
Sadat, Anwar, 270
Saita, Yumi, 609n
Salazar, Emma Acosta, 145
Salazar, Ken, 82
Salkever, Alex, 512
Samor, Geraldo, 621n
Sanchez, Juan I., 622n
Sandhu, Harjit Singh, 612n
Santos, Jose, 11
Sapsford, Jason, 610n
Sarin, Arun, 364
Sathyanarayanan, Priya, 621n
Saunders, John, 620n
Schneider, Friedrich, 615n
Scholl, Russell B., 609n
Schopenhauer, Arthur, 138
Schöpflin, George, 331
Schroeder, Michael, 87
Schuman, Robert, 126
Schwab, Klaus, 13
Schwab, Susan, 612n
Schwartz, Peter, 366
Schwarz, Jonathan, 616n
Scott, Robert Haney, 612n
Seagal, Evan, 92
Seligman, Daniel, 23
Selmer, Jan, 548
Sester, Dennis, 622n
Shaffer, Margaret A., 552, 622n
Shah, Pravin K., 613n
Shapiro, Robert J., 23
Shatz, H., 69, 610n
Shaw, B., 620n
Shaw, Gordon, 366
Shen, Yung-Cheng, 613n
Shi Jiuyong, 278
Simpson, Glenn R., 395, 619n
Sims, G. Thomas, 611n
Slater, Joanna, 71
Sloan, Tim, 500–501
Slywotzky, Adrian, 523
Smith, Adam, 64, 65, 67, 69, 95, 97, 140
Smith, Peter, 623n
Smyth, Gareth, 612n
Snee, Ronald D., 622n
Snow, Anita, 613n
Solomon, Paul, 617n
Somavia, Juna, 333
Sophocles, 566
Sorrell, Martin, 478
Sozzani, Franca, 504
Spector, Paul E., 622n
Spinelli, Altiero, 126
Stalk, George, Jr., 621n
Steadman, Jon, 71
Steel, Helen, 492
Stein, Herbert, 152, 613n
Steiner, Brandon, 6
Steinert-Threkeld, Tom, 528
Stengel, James, 473–474
Sternfels, Robert A., 621n
Stevens, Tim, 398

Stiglitz, Joseph E., 102, 113
Stopford, John M., 390, 619n
Strodtbeck, F. L., 222, 615n
Stroh, Linda K., 622n
Sull, Don, 366
Sullivan, Daniel, 623n
Sullivan, William, 5
Sumii, Sue, 337
Summers, Lawrence, 303
Sutton, Philip, 218, 615n
Swann, Christopher, 303

T

Taddei, Tim, 230
Takeishi, Akira, 610n
Takeuchi, Riki, 622n
Talbot, Jillian, 618n
Tam, Pui-Cing, 622n
Tan, Hui, 620n
Taylor, Frederick W., 517
Taylor, Paul, 71
Taylor, S., 618n
Taylor, Sully, 548
Teece, D. J., 622n
Teixeira, Julian, 545
Tellis, Gerard, 610n
Terhune, Chad, 620n
Terpstra, Vern, 613n
Tesluk, Paul E., 622n
Teteak, Michelle, 389
Tett, Gillian, 572, 614n
Thatcher, Margaret, 260, 337
Thrush, Cody Abram, 296
Tierney, Stephen, 504
Tomlin, Sheryann, 614n
Tonelson, Alan, 22, 23
Tricoire, Jean-Pascal, 362
Triffin, Robert, 612n
Troy, Mike, 383
Truman, Harry, 112
Trumka, Richard, 21
Tung, Rosalie L., 548
Turek, Bogdan, 255
Turner, Shirley, 71
Tye, Mary G., 548, 622n
Tyler, Kathryn, 623n

U

Ulph, Alistair, 611n
Ulusoy, Ebru, 420
Urwin, Derek, 612n

V

Valentini, Laura, 611n
Vallenilla, Luis, 612n
Van den Berg, Hendrik, 610n
Van der Veer, Jeroen, 366
Van Lee, Reggie, 618n
Vasilash, Gary S., 523
Vaughn, Scott, 23
Verbeke, Alain, 363
Verkhovsky, Pierre, 616n
Verma, Shekhar, 376
Vernon, Raymond, 74, 610n
Verzity, Julie, 352
Veysey, Sarah, 623n
Vogl, A. J., 352
Von Pierer, Heinrich, 542–543

W

Wagner, Melissa, 614n
Wagnild, Craig P., 617n
Wagoner, G. Richard, Jr., 65
Wagstyl, Stefan, 617n
Walker, Orville C., Jr., 620n
Wallace, William A., 377
Wallström, Margot, 217
Walton, Sa, 380
Wang Shichun, 84
Waters, Richard, 615n, 622n
Wax, Emily, 617n
Webber, Alan M., 617n
Weinberg, Steven, 257
Weiss, Larry, 610n
Welch, Jack, 370, 371
Wells, Louis T., 390, 619n
Wessel, David, 616n, 622n
Wessels, Maja, 133
Whitaker, Albert C., 612n
White, Erin, 6n
White, Gregory L., 610n
Wicks, Andrew C., 615n
Wighton, David, 575
Wilke, John R., 616n
Williams, Frances, 616n
Williamson, Delbert, 357
Williamson, Peter, 11
Wilson, Simon, 612n
Wise, Richard, 523
Witoelar, Rachmat, 218
Wojcik, Joanne, 623n
Wolf, Hans, 207
Wolfe, Martin, 22, 23, 104, 502, 611n
Wolfensohn, James, 21, 23
Wolfowitz, Paul, 611n
Wonacott, Peter, 271, 383
Wong, Yim Yu, 613n
Woodcock, C. Patrick, 620n
Woolf, Virginia, 566
Wu Li, 610n
Wu Yi, 296
Wylie, Ian, 366

X

Xie, Frank Tian, 620n

Y

Yang, Jiawen, 610n
Yee, Amy, 545
Yemealem, Himmat, 332
Yergin, Daniel, 13, 609n
Yin, Eden, 363
Yoshida, Hayato, 364
Yuezhi Zhao, 619n
Yun, Seokhwa, 622n
Yunus, Muhammad, 570
Yusop bin Awang Damit, Mohamad, 617n

Z

Zairi, M., 619n
Zajac, Edward J., 620n
Zedillo, Ernesto, 23
Zeile, William J., 621n
Zesiger, Sue, 616n
Zetlin, Minda, 613n
Zollers, Frances E., 617n

Page numbers followed by n indicate notes.

International reserve asset, 153–154
International Seabed Authority, 216
  in Europe, 217
International status, 561
International strategy, 361n
International System of Units, 477
International technology life cycle, 76
International Telecommunications
  Union, 107–108, 238
International trade, 32
  in ancient world, 10
  balance of payments, 149–153,
    317–318
  and bodies of water, 202–207
  with Bretton Woods system, 143
  in changing world environment, 57
  commercial arbitration, 287
  direct government participation, 89
  direction of, 37–39, 69–79
  early modern era, 10
  and economic development, 42, 329
  effect of Smoot-Hawley Tariff, 87
  effects of topography, 195–197
  export processing zones, 54
  foreign direct investment amounts,
    31
  free trade argument, 21
  and GATT, 112–113
  geographic proximity, 194
  in globalization debate, 21–22
  with gold standard, 140–141
  Group of Eight, 119
  impact of European Union, 133–134
  impact of foreign direct investment,
    43
  importance for multinational
    corporations, 31
  increasing regionalization, 37–39
  information sources, 41, 411
  job creation from, 21
  and labor practices, 98–99
  and labor standards, 345
  leading to foreign direct
    investment, 47
  major trading partners, 39–41
  Massachusetts law, 279
  merchandise exports, 16–17
  nations most involved, 35–36
  in 19th Century, 12
  official procedures, 459–463
  and passive processing, 193
  preferential trading agreements,
    51–52
  regional trade agreements, 37
  service exports, 17
  by small and medium-size
    enterprises, 16, 33
  Trade Development Index, 42
  U.S. trading partners, 449
  of United States, 39–41
  volume of, 33–35
  and WTO, 110–116
  as zero-sum activity, 65
International Trade Administration, 33,
  411
  market access compliance special-
    ists, 448
  trade development unit, 448
  U.S. Commercial Service, 448
International Trade Association, 57
International Trade Center, 108
International Trade Commission, 83,
  85, 313
International Trade Organization, 112
International Trade Statistics, 28
International trade theory
  absolute advantage, 65–67
  and Chilean reforms, 64

comparative advantage, 67–69
competitive advantage, 78–79
differences in taste, 71–72
direction of trade, 72–73
economies of scale, 76–77
exchange rate influence, 72–73
experience curve, 76–77
factor endowment, 69–72
first-mover theory, 77
gains from trade/specialization,
  67
imperfect competition, 77
international product life cycle,
  74–75
law of comparative advantage, 64
Leontief paradox, 69–70
Linder theory, 73–74
mercantilism, 64–65
money and direction of, 72–73
national competitiveness, 78–79
production possibilities frontier,
  68–69
summary of, 79
technology life cycle, 76
terms of trade, 67
International Trade Update, 57
International trading companies
  definition, 437
  export trading companies, 439
  Japanese, 437–439
  Korean, 439
  United States, 439
  and WTO, 439
International Union of American
  Republics, 125
Internet, 13–15
  advertising on, 485–486
  aid to direct exporting, 428
  bloggers, 420
  for competitor analysis, 374
  cybercrime, 377
  data on suppliers, 514
  diffusion of social trends, 480
  domain names, 481
  for economic research, 249
  for electronic procurement,
    511–513
  English usage, 179
  hacking, 514
  for marketing research, 419
  for personal selling, 489
  and pricing options, 494
  sales processing systems, 16
Internships Abroad, 12
Interpol, 267–268
Intervention currency, 305
Intracorporate sales, 493
Intrafirm trade, 509
Inventory
  costs, 514
  just-in-time systems, 515
  overstated, 534
  in supply chain, 505–506
Investment; *see also* Capital raising
  and investing
  country risk assessment, 272
  cross investment, 94
  in human capital, 244
  international position of U.S., 49
  international theories of, 92–95
  portfolio investment, 41–42
  profit motive, 53
  restrictions in Mexico, 530
  restrictions on equity, 568
  tax incentives, 290
  and technology, 174
Investment risk reduction, 434
Iqtisad Iran, 141

Iran, 173
  demand for gold, 141
  status of women, 338
Iranian rial, 312
Iraq
  Persian Gulf War, 263–264
  reconstruction, 90
  sanctions against, 81
Irish Republican Army, 265
Irrevocable letter of credit, 454
Islam
  and advertising, 487
  description of, 172–173
  and piracy, 429
  and Sikhism, 172
  status of women, 337, 338
  Sunnis vs. Shiites, 173
Islamic fundamentalists, 265
ISO 9000 standards, 522–523
ISO 9001 standard, 423
ISO 14000 standards, 523
Israel, conflict with Arabs, 270
Italy
  compliance with tax laws, 289–290
  elderly population, 246
  terrorist activities in, 264
Iterative planning, 369–370

J

Jainism, 171
Jamaica Agreement, 146–148
Japan
  advanced production techniques,
    515–517
  anime films, 441
  Anti-Monopoly Law, 292
  automation, 175
  birthrate decline, 246
  caste system, 171
  comparative advantage, 75
  crisis in labor force, 323
  decline in output, 326
  dependence on raw materials, 55
  direction of trade, 38
  discrimination in, 171
  elderly population, 246
  English usage, 179
  exports, 37
  Fair Trade Commission, 293
  food regulations, 90
  foreign direct investment by, 43, 47
  foreign direct investment in U.S., 48
  foreign direct investment outflow, 44
  and French protectionism, 294
  general trading companies, 37
  gift giving, 181
  guest workers, 336
  immigrants, 416
  imports, 37
  industrial output, 303
  IMF quota, 143
  jobs-for-life culture, 323
  keiretsu, 484
  Kobe earthquake, 577
  labor conditions, 323
  labor unions, 343–344
  Large Scale Retailing Law, 495
  Ministry of Agriculture, 486
  Ministry of International Trade and
    Industry, 293
  negotiating ploys, 168
  number of trading companies,
    438–439
  phone surfers, 420
  politeness, 179
  population decline, 325
  Procter & Gamble in, 161–162
  product liability, 295

product liability laws, 295
protectionism in, 65
Shintoism, 172
SME exports to, 33
social status, 337
sogo shosha, 437–439
sugar industry protection, 85–86
terrorist attack, 268
Tokugawa regime, 337
Tokyo Disneyland, 162–163
trade secrets law, 377
trade with European Union, 133
value of farm subsidies, 84–85
voluntary export restraints, 89
women expatriates, 548
YouTube in, 420
zaibatsu, 292, 437
Japanese External Trade Organiza-
  tion, 411
Japanese Red Army, 265
Japanese yen, 148, 306, 307
Japan External Trade Organization,
  463
Japan Labor Ministry, 336
Jen, 172
Jihad, 173
Job allocation office, China, 322–324
Job creation, 71
  European Union, 326
Job losses
  de-jobbing, 403–404
  in Japan, 32
  in manufacturing, 508
  from NAFTA, 23
  to protectionism, 87
Job prestige, 169
Jobs, offshoring, 52
Jobs Abroad, 12
Jobs-for-life culture, 32
Job shops, 518
Joint venture, 579
  to acquire expertise, 434
  automobile industry, 432, 435–436
  cereal makers, 432
  control
    with management contracts,
      435
    with minority ownership,
      434–435
  definition, 402, 431
  disadvantages, 434
  for economies of scale, 434
  to enter foreign markets, 431–435
  failure to consider, 447
  formation of, 431–432
  global sourcing arrangement, 509
  local partnership, 433–434
  loss of freedom and flexibility,
    402–403
  management contract, 430
  in mobile phones, 433–434
  parent company control, 403
  pharmaceuticals, 434
  to reduce investment risk, 434
  reporting to parent company, 403
  as strategic alliances, 435–436
  and strong nationalism, 434
  tax benefits, 434
  from technology, 174
Jones Act of 1920, 90
Judges, 285
Jury system, 286
Just-in-time systems, 509
  as balanced systems, 518
  cooperation of suppliers, 516
  and cultural forces, 532–533
  definition, 515
  in local manufacturing, 532

innovation and, 215–216
nonfuel minerals, 215
ocean mining, 214
recoverable coal reserves, 213
of Switzerland, 191
wind power capacity, 213, 214
Navigation and Inland Waterway
Action and Development in
Europe, 204
Neighborhood markets, 480
Neo-mercantilism, 65
Nepalese Gurkhas, 429
Netherlands
foreign direct investment by U.S.
in, 47
foreign direct investment in U.S., 48
use of inland waterways, 204
Network corporation, 395
Networking, 578
New Guinean National Fisheries
Authority, 215
Newly industrialized economies, 231
Newly industrializing countries, 231
New markets
creation of, 49–53
selection of, 416–418
New product development, 517
NewsNet, 373
Newspaper advertising, 485
New York Department of Sanitation,
261
New Zealand farm subsidies, 85
Nigeria, population projections, 245
Nirvana, 169, 171
Nobel Peace Prize, 107
Nominal interest rate, 308
Nonconvertible currencies, 311
Nonequity modes of entering foreign
markets; *see* Foreign markets
Nonfuel minerals, 215
Nonprofit surveys, 419
Nonquantitative nontariff barriers,
89–91
Nonrenewable energy sources
coal, 212–213
natural gas, 213
nuclear power, 212
petroleum, 209–212
Nonrevenue tax purposes, 287
Nontariff barriers
nonquantitative
customs, 90
direct government
participation, 89
government procurement
policies, 90
standards, 90–91
quantitative
absolute quotas, 88
allocated quotas, 88–89
discriminatory quotas, 89
global quotas, 88
orderly marketing
arrangements, 89
quotas, 88–89
tariff-rate quotas, 89
voluntary export restraints, 89
North America
increase in trade by, 34
per capita ownership/consumption,
239
North American Commission for
Environmental Cooperation, 122
North American Development Bank,
122
North American Free Trade
Agreement, 13, 25, 33, 52, 194, 345
compared to European Union, 128

direction of trade, 37
disputes within, 121–122
economic growth from, 121
and electronics industry, 60
and environmental decline, 23
job losses from, 23
Labor Secretariat, 22
noneconomic concerns, 122
origin and operation of, 120–121
potential extension of, 122
statistics on, 121
and sugar subsidies, 87
and WTO, 115
North American Free Trade
Agreement Trade
Commission, 121
North Atlantic Treaty Organization,
268
map of, 110
origin and functions, 108
Norway
farm subsidies, 85
North Sea oil, 128
Nuclear power, 212
Nuclear terrorism, 267–268
Nuisance tariffs, 88

O

Occupational Safety and Health
Administration, 481
Ocean mining, 215
OECD; *see* Organization for Economic
Cooperation and Development
Office of Harmonization in the Interna-
tional Market, 284
Office of International Trade (SBA),
449
Office of Trade & Economic Analysis,
41
Office size, 180
Official prices, 88
Official reserves account, 152
Offset, 579
Offshore financial centers, 568
Offshoring
definition, 507
of jobs to India, 52, 70–71
Of The Jealousy of Trade (Hume),
140
Oil
from coal, 212
from natural gas, 212
reserves by country, 211
worldwide supply, 118
Oil-bearing shale, 211
Oil prices, 118
Oil sands, 211
Oligopolistic industries
competitor analysis by, 78–79
cross investment, 94
monopolistic advantage theory, 93
OLI model, 95
Omnibus surveys, 419
Open account, 457
Open Enterprise Computing program,
517
Operating exposure, 574
Operational plans, 367
Order bill of lading, 460
Order filling, 400
Orderly marketing arrangements, 89
Organizational design
and antiorganization, 397
based on economic development,
392
based on kinds of expertise, 390
case, 407
changes in forms, 394

current trends
horizontal corporation, 397
modular corporation, 396
virtual corporation, 395–397
defining, 387
departmentalizing, 387–388
dimensions of, 388
at Dow Chemical, 398
dynamic network structure, 397
evolution of international
companies, 388–395
evolving, 387
global business units, 473–474
for global competitiveness, 398
global corporate form
function-based, 392–393
product-based, 390–391
regional basis, 391–392
hybrid forms, 393
international divisions, 388–390
international structural stages
model, 390
Kraft Foods reorganization, 385–386
main concerns, 387–388
matrix organization, 393–394
matrix overlay, 394
network corporation, 395
product business units, 395
reengineering, 395
size and complexity of
organizations, 387
strategic business units, 395
and strategy changes, 387
survival into 21st century, 397
Organizational knowledge base, 356
Organizational level, 368
Organizational structure, 78–79
based on economic development,
392
concerns in designing, 387–388
creating, 386–387
definition, 386
evolving, 387
internal operating environment, 388
Organization for Economic
Cooperation and Development,
104, 119
Business and Industry Advisory
Committee, 117
Convention on Bribery, 298
country strike rates, 343
functions, 116–117
fundamental analysis, 311
GDP deflator, 315–316
immigrant categories, 330
income taxes, 288
male-female wage ratios, 341
maternity leave laws, 340
membership, 116–117
origin of, 117
tax treaties, 291
Trade Union Advisory Committee,
345
Trends in International Migration,
333
underground economy, 233
and unemployment, 113, 330
value of farm subsidies, 84–85
Organization of African Unity, 123
Organization of American States, 125
business education program, 12
Organization of Petroleum Exporting
Countries, 25, 104, 270
downstream markets, 55
economic strength, 118
exporting terrorism, 118
membership, 118
origin and history, 117–118

share of world oil supply, 118
Organizations
culture change, 521
effect of pricing strategies, 492–493
life cycles, 397
Original equipment manufacturers, 53,
495–496
Ottoman Empire, 10
Outlets to the sea, 206–207
Outsourcing, 71, 395
definition, 505
global sourcing, 507–508
logistics, 524
purchasing function, 510
union opposition to, 344
Overlapping demand, 73–74
Overseas Business Reports, 415
Overseas independent contractor, 509
Overseas joint venture, 509
Overseas premiums, 558
Overseas Private Investment
Corporation, 448, 458
Over-the-counter market, 307
Over-the-wall design approach, 507
Ownership-specific advantage, 94

P

Packaging, 479–480
Pakistan
population density, 246
population projections, 245
Palestine Liberation Organization, 270
Panama Canal, 461
Panamax-size ships, 461
Panregional advertising, 488
Paper script, 140
Papua New Guinea, 215
Parallel economy, 233
Parallel loans, 575
Parent country nationals; *see also*
Expatriate managers
advantages, 545–546
definition, 543
families of, 549
training for, 547–549
Paris Convention, 481
Paris Union, 283–284
Parity relationships, 308
Parliaments, women in, 338–339
Par value, 143
Passive processing, 193
Patent registration, 452
Patents, 283–284
new theory of, 285
United Nations attacks on, 284
Patent trolls, 284
Patent violations, 115–116
Patron, 533
Peace Corps, 326
Pegged currencies, 140
Pegged exchange rates, 146, 147
Penetration pricing, 452
Pension liabilities, Japan, 323
Pentagon attack, 265
Per capita income in Africa, 50
Performance measures, 367–368
Performance of contracts; *see*
Contracts
Periodic updating, 414
Perks, 561
Per se concept, 292
Persian Gulf War, 263–264
Personal selling
factors limiting standardization,
496–498
importance of, 489
on Internet, 489
missionary salespeople, 489

international, 74–75
  for supply chain management, 506
Product literature centers, 450
Product market imperfections, 93
Product mix rationalization, 525
Product preferences, 480
Product strategies
  consumer products, 477–478
  continuum of sensitivity to foreign
    environment, 477
  cultural differences, 479–480
  economic forces, 481–482
  factors limiting standardization,
    496–498
  foreign environmental forces,
    478–482
  and income disparities, 481–482
  industrial products, 476–477
  for international marketing,
    475–482
  legal forces, 480–481
  physical forces, 482
  physical product, 475
  repositioning, 478
  and services, 478
  sociocultural forces, 479–480
  total product, 476
  training programs, 477
Profit and loss account, 583
Profit remittance barriers, 415
Profits
  as investment motive, 53
  of joint ventures, 434
  of largest corporations, 32
  from new markets, 49–53
  of subsidiaries, 401–402
Pro forma invoice, 455
Programmed management approach
  to advertising, 488–489
Project leaders/teams, 520
Promotion
  definition, 482
  factors limiting standardization,
    496–498
  and marketing mix variables, 482
  standardization of, 475
Promotional mix, 247
Promotional strategies, 482–492
  advertising, 483–489
  commonly used, 482–483
  personal selling, 489–490
  public relations, 491–492
  sales promotion, 490–491
  tools for, 483
Promotion (jobs)
  bribery requests, 546
  geocentric view of promotion, 550
Promptness, 167
Property
  confiscation, 257
  expropriation, 256–257
Proprietary technology, 357
Protectionism, 55, 477; see also Trade
    restrictions
  arguments for and against, 80–92
  costs of, 91–92
  in France, 294
  in Japan, 65
  as legal force, 293–294
  in mercantilism, 65
  retaliatory trade war, 87
  rise of, 144
  for sugar industry, 85–86
Protestant work ethic, 169
Protocols, 280
Public Company Accounting
    Oversight Board, 299
Public international law, 280

Public relations
  definition, 491
  and nationalism, 491–492
Puffery, 484
Punitive damages, 295
Purchasing agents, 534–535
Purchasing function
  global standardization, 525
  indirect procurement, 510
  in local manufacturing, 534–535
  traditional, 514
Purchasing power parity, 148
  Atlas conversion factor, 234
  Big Mac index, 308–310
  consumption based on, 237
  and exchange rates, 308–310
  GNI based on, 234
  national comparisons, 235
Putonghua (Mandarin), 197
Puts, 573

Q

Quality
  improvement in Japan, 515–517
  improvement in U.S., 517–521
  inferior, 533
  in local manufacturing, 533
  technical function, 536
Quality circles, 516
Quality control, 525, 533
Quality Online survey, 521
Quantify from advanced production
    techniques, 515–521
Quantitative nontariff barriers, 88–89
Questionable or dubious payments,
    297
Questionable payments, 181–182
Quotas
  absolute, 88
  allocated, 88–89
  discriminatory, 89
  global, 88
  as legal force, 293–294
  and Multi-Fiber Agreement, 89
  orderly marketing arrangements, 89
  tariff-rate, 89
  voluntary export restraints, 89, 294

R

Racism
  and employment, 339–340
  minorities in traditional societies, 340
Raffles, 491
Random walk hypothesis, 310–311
Raw materials
  global sourcing, 508
  guaranteed supply of, 55–56
  suppliers of, 532
  in value chain, 355–356
Reagan administration, 439
Real GDP growth in Chile, 64
Real interest rate, 308, 316n
Recession, and consumer spending,
    303
Recruitment of salespeople, 490
Red tape, 258
Reengineering, 395
Regiocentric staffing policy, 543,
    546–547
Regional brands, 484
Regional currencies, 144
Regionalization of trade, 37–39
Regionalized organizations, 391–392
Regional strategies, 363
Regional trade agreements/groups
  African trade agreements, 123
  Andean Community, 125

Asia-Pacific Economic
    Cooperation, 125
Association of Southeast Asian
    Nations, 37
Central American Free Trade
    Agreement, 125
  currencies of, 144
  economic analysis of, 229
European Free Trade Agreement,
    122
European Union, 37
  major trading blocs, 120
Mercosur, 123–125
NAFTA, 37, 120–122
  share of world trade, 37
U.S.–Canada Free Trade
    Agreement, 37
  and WTO, 115
Registration, Evaluation, and
    Authorization of Chemicals
    (EU), 217
Regulations, 258
Related industries, 78
Religion
  animism, 173
  Asian, 169–172
  and business, 173
  and international law, 283
  Islam, 172–173
  Judeo-Christian tradition, 169
  and work ethic, 169
  world map, 170
Renewable energy sources, 213–214
Renmimbi, 312
Reorganization, 395
  at Kraft Foods, 385–386
Repackaging, 478
Repatriation, 554–555
Repatriation of earnings, 415, 575
Replacement number of children, 245
Reporting
  financial, 403
  market opportunities, 403
  political and economic, 403
  technological, 403
Reporting units, 464
Repositioning, 478
Research and development
  costs, 53
  partnership, 435
Reserve account, 153
Resident aliens, Japan, 336
Restructuring at Kraft Foods, 386
Retailers
  bypassing wholesalers, 441
  as importers, 440
Retailing
  cultural mistakes, 161–162
  globalization of, 495
  legal restrictions, 495
Retained earnings, 568
Retaliation
  for countervailing duties, 85
  for dumping, 83–84
  EU–U.S. dispute, 83
  for subsidies, 84–85
  tariffs as, 86–87
Retaliatory trade war, 87
Revenue from new markets, 52–53
Reverse brain drain, 335
Reverse culture shock, 552, 554
Reverse engineering, 374
Reverse imports, 37
Reverse trade missions, 450
Rework expense, 514
Rhine-Main-Danube Canal, 203–204
Rhine waterway, 203–204, 207
Right wing, 259

Riley Guide, 12
Risk, integrated approach to, 572
Risk/cost trade-off, 456
Risk diversification, 93
Risk Management Conference, 578
Risk management process, 578
Risk Ratings Review, 273, 274
Rivalry, 78–79
Roger and Me (Moore), 219
RO-RO ships, 461
Royal Spanish Academy, 179
Royer Law (EU), 495
Rule of law, 280
Rural-to-urban shift, 246–247
  in China, 323
  of labor force, 328–329
Russia
  expatriate costs, 556
  population decline, 325
Rwanda, 270

S

Sahara Desert, 195
Salaries, 555–556
Sales
  on international companies, 17
  intracorporate, 493
  at Kraft Foods, 386
  of largest companies, 19
  of largest corporations, 32
  and lower cost of goods sold, 53
  in new markets, 49–53
  protected by foreign markets, 53–54
  reason for exporting, 446
Sales agreement, 452
Sales company, 427
Sales forecasts, 367
Sales information, 447
Salespeople
  missionary, 489
  recruitment of, 490
Sales promotion
  definition, 490
  distribution methods, 491
  economic forces, 491
  sociocultural forces, 491
  standardization, 490–491
Sales representative, 447
Sales tax; see Value-added tax
Sales without money
  countertrade, 578–579
  industrial cooperation, 579–580
Samsura, 171
Sanctions, 81
Sarbanes-Oxley Act, 289–299, 567, 583
  foreign repercussions, 585
SARS epidemic, 10
Satellite television, 13
Saudi Arabia, 173
  food laws, 481
  Persian Gulf War, 263–264
  status of women, 337
Scale economies, 77
Scenario planning, 365, 366
  objective, 351
  at Royal Dutch/Shell, 351–352
Scenarios, 365
Scientific management, 517–518
Scientific tariff, 82–83
Scientists, foreign-born, 333
Scotland, privatization in, 263
Scrap charges, 514
Seattle antiglobalization protests,
    18, 21, 115
Secretariat of the United Nations,
    105, 107
Secretary General of the United
    Nations, 107

Value-added
    activities, 35
    goods, 192
    by Six Sigma program, 521
Value-added tax, 53, 131, 288–289, 314,
    580
Value chain
    activities, 363, 364
    analysis, 355–356
    outsourcing, 507–508
Value dimensions of culture, 184–187
Values
    in foreign environment, 24
    for sustainable business practices,
        222
Values orientation theory, 222
Values statements, 357–358
Vanadium, 215
Variable levy, 88
Vehicle currency, 305
Venezuela, 211
Vertical integration, 397, 530
Vertically integrated plants, 242, 446
Videoconferencing, 15
Vietnam, 336
Virtual corporation, 395–397
Virtual integration, 52
Virtual project teams, 512
Vision statements, 357–358
Volume of trade, 33–35
Voluntary export restraints, 89, 294

W

Wage rates
    male-female ratio, 341
    in Mexico, 54
    minimum wage, 69
    and unit labor costs, 238–241
Wall Street Journal, 71, 115, 141, 485
    exchange rate quotations, 305–307
War of the Pacific, 207
War on terrorism, 265
Warranty information, 447
Water's edge principle, 289
WealthBriefing, 313
Wealth of Nations (Smith), 64
Webb-Pomerene Associations, 440
What-if scenarios, 365
Wholesale importers, 440
Wholesale institutions
    bypassed by retailers, 441
    diversity of structures, 441–442

kinds of, 441
Wholly owned subsidiaries
    characteristics, 431
    global sourcing arrangements, 508
    management contract, 430
Why Education Matters, 577
Wind power, 213, 214
Wine making, 168
Withholding tax, 314–315, 580
Women
    education of, 338
    employment discrimination, 297
    illiteracy rates, 338
    international assignments for, 549
    in Iran, 338
    labor participation, 336–337
    in management, 337–338
    maternity leave laws, 339, 340
    in parliaments, 338–339
    ratio of wages to men, 339, 341
    self-employment, 326
    and sexism, 336–339
    unemployment among, 329–330
    in work force, 247
    workplace status, 183–184
Work
    attitudes toward, 168–169
    demonstration effect, 168
    job prestige, 169
    offshoring, 52
Work Abroad, 12
Workers; see also Job entries; Labor
        entries; Skilled workers
    and competitor analysis, 374
    de-jobbing, 404
    displaced by cheap labor, 82
    expatriate, 324
    immigrants, 330–331
    in maquiladoras, 54
    pirated by subsidiaries, 546
    specialization, 517
    unskilled, 331, 508
Work ethic, 169
Working capital guarantee, 458
World Bank, 25, 50, 52, 75, 139, 140,
    141, 578
    Atlas conversion factor, 234
    on bankruptcy, 283
    on brain drain, 333
    on child labor, 332
    climate studies, 208
    currency conversion, 234

and economic analysis, 230
economic data from, 228
economic development
    classification, 231
on energy use, 238
Enterprise Surveys, 276
establishment of, 144
income distribution data, 235
institutions of, 144–145
International Center for Settlement
    of Investment Disputes, 287
protests against, 21
report on sugar subsidies, 86
supporting banks, 145
and Three Gorges project, 206
World Development Indicators, 18,
    21, 136, 235, 237
World Conference on Racial Discrimi-
    nation, Xenophobia, and Related
    Intolerance, 339–340
World Court, 107
World Development Indicators, 18, 21,
    136, 235, 237
World Economic Forum, 13, 303
World environment, 57
World Fact Book (CIA), 147, 346
World Health Organization, 107
World Intellectual Property
    Organization, 284
World Intellectual Property
    Organization Arbitration and
    Mediation Center, 282
World Investment Report, 97
World Markets Research Centre,
    268, 269
World Meterological Organization,
    107
World Population Data Sheet, 379
World Trade, 57
World Trade Center attack, 265, 365
World Trade Centers Association,
    451, 463
World Trade Organization (WTO), 22,
    59, 104, 110–116
    and banana wars, 115
    challenges for, 115–116
    China's entry into, 55
    on counterfeit products, 283
    Country Market Analysis, 443
    creation of, 113
    decision making, 111
    and developing countries, 114–115

Doha Round, 85, 114–115, 143
on dumping, 84
early years of global cooperation,
    112
and economic analysis, 229, 230
and EU–U.S. trade dispute, 83
and Export Trading Company Act,
    439
and GATT, 112–113
Government Procurement
    Agreement, 90
health standards, 90–91
International Trade Statistics, 28
membership, 110–111
most favored nation clause, 112
and NAFTA disputes, 121–122
principles, 113–114
protests against, 115
and regional trade agreements, 115
Seattle protests, 18, 21
Trade Negotiation Committee, 111
trade-related intellectual property
    rights, 115–116
trade rules, 82
and trade wars, 115
U.S. complaint against China, 81
uneven benefits of globalization,
    113
and value-added tax, 289
World War I, end of gold standard,
    141
World War II, impact on Europe, 126
Worldwide Anti-McDonald's Day, 492
Worldwide tax policy, 580

Y

Yearbook of Labor Statistics, 342
Yoga, 171
Youth market, 183, 486–487
Youth unemployment, 329
YouTube, 420
Yugoslavia, ethnic cleansing, 267

Z

Zaibatsu, 292, 437
Zhuhai Free Trade Zone, 458
Zimbabwe
    instability in, 269–270
    land seizures, 340